Jos. E. Long

AT Г Frat

U of Md.

YEARBOOK

OF THE

UNITED STATES DEPARTMENT OF AGRICULTURE

—

1916

WASHINGTON
GOVERNMENT PRINTING OFFICE
1917

*   *   *   *   *

[AN ACT Providing for the public printing and binding and the distribution of public documents.]

*   *   *   *   *

Section 73, paragraph 2:

The Annual Report of the Secretary of Agriculture shall hereafter be submitted and printed in two parts, as follows: Part One, which shall contain purely business and executive matter which it is necessary for the Secretary to submit to the President and Congress; Part Two, which shall contain such reports from the different Bureaus and Divisions, and such papers prepared by their special agents, accompanied by suitable illustrations, as shall, in the opinion of the Secretary, be specially suited to interest and instruct the farmers of the country, and to include a general report of the operations of the Department for their information. There shall be printed of Part One, one thousand copies for the Senate, two thousand copies for the House, and three thousand copies for the Department of Agriculture; and of Part Two, one hundred and ten thousand copies for the use of the Senate, three hundred and sixty thousand copies for the use of the House of Representatives, and thirty thousand copies for the use of the Department of Agriculture, the illustrations for the same to be executed under the supervision of the Public Printer, in accordance with directions of the Joint Committee on Printing, said illustrations to be subject to the approval of the Secretary of Agriculture; and the title of each of the said parts shall be such as to show that such part is complete in itself.

ORGANIZATION OF U. S. DEPARTMENT OF AGRICULTURE.

Secretary of Agriculture, DAVID FRANKLIN HOUSTON.
Assistant Secretary of Agriculture, CARL VROOMAN.
Solicitor, FRANCIS G. CAFFEY.
Attorney in Charge of Forest Appeals, THOMAS G. SHEARMAN.
Chief Clerk, R. M. REESE.
Appointment Clerk, R. W. ROBERTS.
Expert on Exhibits, F. LAMSON-SCRIBNER.
Office of Information, G. W. WHARTON, *Chief.*
Weather Bureau, CHARLES F. MARVIN, *Chief.*
Bureau of Animal Industry, ALONZO D. MELVIN, *Chief.*
Bureau of Plant Industry, WM. A. TAYLOR, *Plant Physiologist and Pathologist and Chief.*
Forest Service, HENRY S. GRAVES, *Forester and Chief.*
Bureau of Entomology, L. O. HOWARD, *Entomologist and Chief.*
Bureau of Chemistry, CARL L. ALSBERG, *Chemist and Chief.*
Bureau of Soils, MILTON WHITNEY, *Soil Physicist and Chief.*
Bureau of Biological Survey, EDWARD W. NELSON, *Biologist and Chief.*
Division of Accounts, A. ZAPPONE, *Chief and Disbursing Clerk.*
Division of Publications, Jos. A. ARNOLD, *Editor and Chief.*
Bureau of Crop Estimates, LEON M. ESTABROOK, *Chief.*
States Relations Service, A. C. TRUE, *Director.*
Office of Public Roads and Rural Engineering, LOGAN WALLER PAGE, *Director.*
Office of Markets and Rural Organization, CHARLES J. BRAND, *Chief.*
Librarian, CLARIBEL R. BARNETT.
Insecticide and Fungicide Board, J. K. HAYWOOD, *Chairman.*
Federal Horticultural Board, C. L. MARLATT, *Chairman.*

3

CONTENTS.

6 *Contents.*

ILLUSTRATIONS.

COLORED PLATES.

HALFTONE PLATES.

TEXT FIGURES.

YEARBOOK OF THE
U.S. DEPARTMENT OF AGRICULTURE

REPORT OF THE SECRETARY OF AGRICULTURE.

WASHINGTON, D. C., November 15, 1916.

SIR: The half of agriculture embracing the marketing of farm products, rural finance, and rural organization has strikingly occupied attention during the last three and one-half years. Before 1913 little systematic thought had been devoted to it and there did not exist, either in the States or in the Nation, effective instrumentalities to furnish assistance and guidance to farmers in this field, nor had the laws necessary to remedy abuses and control unfavorable conditions been formulated or enacted. In view of the complexity and novelty of the problems, the accomplishments—legislative and administrative—have been notable and significant. This seems an opportune time to summarize them.

Early in 1913 a program for the ensuing four years was developed. This program in large measure has been executed. In the first place provision was made promptly for the creation of the Office of Markets and Rural Organization. Beginning with a modest sum, the appropriations for this office, including those for enforcing new laws to promote better marketing, have increased to $1,242,000. Quickly an effective organization was developed and to-day the Nation possesses in this department the largest and best trained and supported staff of experts dealing with the distribution of agricultural commodities and rural organization to be found anywhere in the world. It is engaged in investigating all the larger and more difficult problems confronting farmers in this new field.

The matter of establishing standards for staple agricultural products, of supervising the inspection of grains shipped in interstate and foreign commerce and the operations of cotton futures exchanges, of devising financial machinery suited to the needs of the rural population, of developing a better system of warehouses for agricultural products, and of Federal aid in highway construction, received careful attention. The result was the enactment of a number of highly important laws—the Cotton Futures Act, the United States Grain Standards Act, the United States Warehouse Act, the Federal Farm Loan Act, and the Federal Aid Road Act.

Under the Cotton Futures Act, which was enacted on August 18, 1914, and reenacted with amendments in the Agricultural Appropriation Act for the fiscal year 1917, standards for cotton have been established, the operations of the futures exchanges have been supervised, and cotton trading has been placed on a sounder basis.

The United States Grain Standards Act, which is included in the Agricultural Appropriation Act for the fiscal year 1917, will bring about uniformity in grading, enable the farmer to obtain a fairer price for his product and to improve its quality, and prevent or diminish materially the shipment of adulterated grain.

The United States Warehouse Act, also included in the Agricultural Appropriation Act for 1917, authorizes the Department of Agriculture to license bonded warehouses which handle certain agricultural products. It will make possible the issuance of reliable and easily negotiable warehouse receipts, promote the better storing of farm products, and encourage the standardizing of storages and of marketing processes.

The Federal Farm Loan Act was approved on July 17, 1916. It creates a banking system which will reach intimately into the rural districts, operate on terms suited to the farmer's needs under sympathetic management, intro-duce business methods into farm finance, bring order out of chaos, reduce the cost of handling farm loans, place upon the market mortgages which will be a safe investment for private funds, attract into agricultural operations a fair share of the capital of the Nation, and lead to a reduction of interest.

A provision in the Federal Reserve Act, which was ap-proved on December 23, 1913, authorized national banks to lend money on farm mortgages and recognized the peculiar needs of the farmer by giving his paper a maturity period of six months.

The Federal Aid Road Act, approved July 11, 1916, pro-vides for cooperation between the Federal Government and the States in the construction of rural post roads and of roads and trails within or partly within the National For-ests. This measure will conduce to the establishment of a more effective highway machinery in each State, strongly influence the development of good road building along right lines, stimulate larger production and better market-ing, promote a fuller and more attractive rural life, add greatly to the convenience and economic welfare of all the people, and strengthen the National foundations.

BUREAU OF MARKETS.

I have recommended in the estimates for the fiscal year 1918 that the name of the Office of Markets and Rural Or-ganization be changed to " Bureau of Markets." The im-portance of the work and the size of the organization fully justify this change, and there is widespread sentiment throughout the country in favor of it. It is in the interest of simplicity and convenience and will give the organization a title by which it is already generally known.

The work of the Office of Markets and Rural Organization has developed very rapidly, and some notable results have been secured. Definite assistance has been rendered to the fruit interests of the States of Oregon, Washington, Idaho, and Montana. An organization composed of cooperative associations, corporations operating for the producers, and individual growers was formed during the past year. The purpose of the organization is to secure broader distribution through the establishment of uniform grades and marketing methods. Through it the fruit industry of the Northwestern States should be placed upon a more efficient business basis. It comprises 65 per cent of the northwestern fruit industry, representing an investment of $150,000,000, and supporting approximately 20,000 growers. This is probably the most important single activity in forming cooperative organizations that has yet been undertaken by the department.

Well-tested systems of accounts and records for primary grain elevators, for live-stock shipping associations, and for cooperative stores have been issued. Systems for country creameries and cotton warehouses have been devised and are being tested under commercial conditions. Systems perfected by the department for farmers' cooperative elevators and for fruit and produce associations already are in extensive use. A plan for adapting farmers' grain-elevator companies to the patronage dividend basis has been worked out and published.

The issuance of monthly cold-storage reports on apples has been continued, and the work has been extended to include butter, eggs, and cheese. These reports show the cold-storage holdings throughout the country, and include a comparison of the holdings of the current year with those of the previous year. In cooperation with carriers, extensive investigations of the economic waste of foodstuffs in transit have been conducted. The object of these investigations is to secure better cooperation between shippers and carriers and greater efficiency in methods of handling, with a view to eliminate, or at least greatly to reduce, the present waste.

MARKETING LIVE STOCK AND MEATS.

A systematic survey of centralized live-stock markets, begun during 1915, has been extended to cover practically all the large stockyard centers. Arrangements have been made with 58 stockyard companies to secure monthly reports of live-stock receipts and shipments. A uniform system of market records has been adopted, at the instance of the department, by a number of the yards. Twenty-six companies are reporting stocker and feeder shipments separately, in accordance with a form prepared by the Office of Markets and Rural Organization.

An investigation of the organization and conduct of co-operative live-stock shipping associations, begun during 1915, has been completed and the results published. The directory of these associations now includes 485 organizations, aside from 440 other agricultural associations which ship live stock as a branch of their business. The farmers' cooperative packing-house movement was studied and a press bulletin on the subject was issued.

A conference relative to the marketing of live stock and meats was held at Chicago November 15 and 16, 1915, for the purpose of " ascertaining the essential facts pertaining to the industry with a view to bring about more stable marketing conditions, more efficient methods, closer cooperation, and a better understanding among all the interests connected with the industry." Representatives of all the National organizations and of other interests concerned with the live-stock and meat industry participated in the meeting. The proceedings were published as House Document No. 855, Sixty-fourth Congress, first session.

Methods and costs of marketing live stock and meats in the United States were investigated. Extensive schedules were sent to 10,500 correspondents of the Bureau of Crop Estimates. A summary and discussion of the returns, together with data on economic factors affecting the cost of marketing and distribution, has been published. A preliminary investigation of the sources, accuracy, and use of market reports on live stock and meats has been made. The results of this study also have been published and have been utilized in the development of plans for the organization of a demonstration market news service for live stock similar to that now conducted for perishable crops. An appropriation of $65,000 has been made available for the purpose. Other subjects which received attention are public abattoirs, transportation of live stock, organization and methods of the wholesale meat-packing industry, and local marketing of live stock and meats.

Surveys have been made of the marketing facilities for agricultural products in nine cities and advice has been given regarding the location, establishment, and management of municipal retail and wholesale public markets. Detailed studies also have been made of local conditions in other cities. The department now is prepared to furnish a model design for a public retail market, with the cost, fully equipped, estimated on the basis of square feet. Designs of model steel sheds for use on open farmers' markets also are available.

Investigations concerning methods of handling and grading perishable products and the practicability of the standardization of the products and their containers have progressed rapidly. Tentative grades for sweet potatoes of Arkansas and Bermuda onions of Texas have been worked out and adopted by the local growers' associations. Several standardization laws, Federal and State, have been enacted during the year. The most significant Federal legislation in this field is the United States Grain Standards Act. Congress also has established the 2, 4, and 12 quart sizes, with certain dimensions, as standards for Climax baskets for grapes and other fruits and vegetables, as well as the dry-measure one-half pint, pint, quart, or multiples of the quart as standards of capacity for baskets or other containers for small fruits, berries, and vegetables.

Preliminary plans have been formulated for the investigation of foreign markets for American farm products and for assistance in the development of the export trade under normal conditions. A representative of the department recently conducted investigations in Europe along this line. The work, in so far as possible, will be done in close cooperation with the Departments of State and Commerce.

A survey of State marketing activities has been made and the results published. Provision was made in the Appropriation Act for the fiscal year 1917 for cooperation with the several States in the employment of marketing agents. This provision should enable the department to bring about a close coordination of the marketing activities and policies of the various States with those of the department.

DEMONSTRATION MARKET NEWS SERVICE.

The value to producers of fruits and vegetables of the experimental market news service inaugurated in 1915 resulted in insistent demands for the extension of the work. During the past year telegraphic reports have been received from 33 important metropolitan markets and from officials of all railroads serving producing territory. The information thus secured has been furnished to growers, shippers, and distributors through 35 temporary offices in producing territories and 11 permanent offices in large cities. Statements from growers and shippers of tomatoes, strawberries, peaches, cantaloupes, watermelons, onions, grapes, apples, and potatoes indicate that the actual monetary saving due to a wider knowledge of market conditions has exceeded the cost of the service many fold.

The education of producers in the proper marketing of farm products, the avoidance of unnecessary losses due to diversions in transit, and the encouragement given to growers who desire to reach new consuming centers are some of the benefits resulting from this attempt to develop for the farmer a reliable business basis.

THE COTTON FUTURES ACT.

The work under the Cotton Futures Act, which was re-enacted with amendments at the last session of Congress, progressed satisfactorily. In addition to the Official Cotton Standards of the United States, which were promulgated on December 15, 1914, official cotton standards for tinges and stains were promulgated on January 28, 1916. Reproductions of these standards were furnished the future exchanges and spot markets which have adopted the official standards for white cotton.

While the compulsory use of the official standards extends only to contracts on future exchanges made subject to section 5 of the act, they were accepted and used voluntarily in all the more important spot markets and form the basis of their dealings. Demonstrations of the use of the standards have been conducted among farmers in many of the cotton-producing districts of the South, and arrangements have been made to provide 125 county agents in that region with reproductions of the standards. The interest in, and approval of, the Official Cotton Standards is not confined to this country. This is shown by the fact that the Rotterdam Cotton Exchange has adopted them.

As a result of the operation of the Cotton Futures Act, quotations for spots and futures have maintained a steady relation to each other. Future quotations now are better indications to the farmer of the value of his commodity than formerly. This uniformity has demonstrated the value of the future markets for legitimate hedging purposes. It is clear, therefore, that the general purposes of the act have been, and are being, accomplished.

GRAIN STANDARDS AND WAREHOUSE ACTS.

The Office of Markets and Rural Organization, in cooperation with the Bureau of Plant Industry, has been charged with the duty of administering the United States Grain Standards Act. Plans for its enforcement have been developed as rapidly as possible.

Official standards for shelled corn, effective December 1, 1916, were issued on September 1. These standards consist of 6 grades each for white corn, yellow corn, and mixed corn, and also a sample grade, making 19 grades in all. As the inspection requirements of the act are not operative as to any grain until standards for it have been established thereunder, the supervision of inspection and grading for the present will be confined to corn. Standards for wheat and oats are in process of determination. Studies for the purpose of securing the information necessary to establish standards for other grains, including the grain sorghums, are under way.

Tentative rules and regulations for the enforcement of the act were published and distributed on October 14, 1916, and all interested parties were given an opportunity to make suggestions concerning them. Public hearings were held in four of the large grain marketing and exporting centers and in Washington. The suggestions received by letter and at the hearings were fully considered in drafting the final form of the rules and regulations, which were promulgated on November 6, 1916, effective December 1, 1916.

Examinations have been held at various points to determine the competency of persons who have applied for licenses to inspect and grade shelled corn and to certificate the grade thereof. Licenses relating to other grains will not be issued until standards for them have been established.

In order that the work of licensed inspectors may be supervised properly, and appeals and disputes under the act dealt with promptly, it has seemed advisable for the present to divide the country into 32 districts. This number may be increased when standards for other grains have been established. The districting has been made with a view to place all sections of the country in convenient reach of a grain supervisor. In each district there will be an office of Federal grain supervision, usually in charge of a grain supervisor or a board of grain supervisors. The city in which the office is located has been designated in each case as the district head-quarters. The right to appeal or to refer a dispute in all cases must be exercised by sending the question for determination to the grain supervisor in charge of the particular district under whose jurisdiction it falls.

Grain producers and all branches of the grain trade have shown a commendable desire to cooperate with the department in bringing about the most beneficial operation of the law.

The administration of the United States Warehouse Act has been intrusted to the Office of Markets and Rural Organization. The rules and regulations for its enforcement are in course of preparation. A tentative draft will be published in the near future, and all interested parties will be given an opportunity to submit suggestions.

THE FOOD SUPPLY.

Interesting questions arise as to whether the domestic food supply of the Nation is keeping pace with the growth in population and as to what are the prospects for the future. The following table in this connection is illuminating:

Food supply of the United States.

Population: June 1, 1900_____ 75, 994, 575
June 1, 1910_____ 92, 174, 515
June 1, 1916_____ 101, 882, 479

Item.	Production.	
	Total.	Per capita.
Meats: Beef, veal, mutton, and pork (pounds):		
1899_____	18, 865, 000, 000	248. 2
1909_____	19, 712, 000, 000	213. 9
1915_____	22, 378, 000, 000	219. 6
Dairy products:		
Milk (gallons)—		
1899_____	7, 265, 804, 304	95. 6
1909_____	7, 466, 406, 384	81. 0
1915 (estimated [1])_____	7, 696, 844, 000	75. 5

[1] Based upon average annual increase, 1899 to 1909, as shown in census.

Food supply of the United States—Continued.

Item.	Production.	
	Total.	Per capita.
Dairy products—Continued.		
Butter and cheese (pounds)—		
1899	1,790,097,244	23.6
1909	1,942,378,069	21.1
1915 (no data available)		
Poultry products:		
Poultry raised (number)—		
1899		
1909	488,500,000	5.3
1915 (estimated)	555,500,000	5.5
Eggs (dozens)—		
1899	1,294,000,000	17.0
1909	1,591,000,000	17.3
1915 (estimated [1])	1,811,000,000	17.8
Fish (pounds):		
1900–1904	989,275,000	[2] 12.5
1908	1,046,541,000	[3] 11.6
1915 (no data available)		
Cereals: Corn, wheat, and rice (bushels):		
1899	3,333,868,710	43.9
1909	3,257,407,468	35.3
1915	4,094,986,999	40.2
Potatoes (bushels):		
1899	273,318,167	3.6
1909	389,194,965	4.2
1915	359,103,000	3.5
Sweet potatoes (bushels):		
1899	42,517,412	.56
1909	59,232,070	.64
1915	74,295,000	.73
Citrus fruits: Oranges, lemons, and grapefruit (boxes):		
1899	7,075,557	.093
1909	23,447,044	.254
1915 (estimated)	24,670,282	.272
Orchard fruits: Apples, peaches, and pears (bushels):		
1899	197,455,620	2.6
1909	190,433,327	2.1
1915	304,686,000	3.0
Small fruits (quarts):		
1899	463,218,612	6.1
1909	426,565,863	4.6
1915 (no data available)		
Sugar (pounds):		
1899	486,006,871	6.4
1909	1,688,300,143	18.3
1915	2,025,680,000	19.9

[1] Based upon average annual increase, 1899 to 1909, as shown in census.
[2] Based upon population June 1, 1902, 79,230,563.
[3] Based upon population June 1, 1909, 90,556,521.

These statistics cover the past 16 years. Within this period the population of the Nation has increased, in round numbers, 26,000,000, or 33 per cent. The articles dealt with cover the more important parts of the diet of the people. Meats and dairy products constitute 37 per cent of the average diet, fish 2 per cent, cereals 31 per cent, Irish and sweet potatoes 13 per cent, and other vegetables 8 per cent. It is notable that, notwithstanding the very rapid increase in population, the production per capita of the commodities indicated, with the exception of meats and dairy products, has remained approximately the same or has increased.

Similar statistics are not available for vegetables, other than Irish and sweet potatoes, but it is reasonable to assume that there has been at least a proportionate increase in production. The figures for Irish potatoes may be taken as a fair index of the normal increase of vegetable products. The potato acreage increased from 2,938,778 in 1899 to 3,668,855 in 1909, or 24.8 per cent, while the value of the product increased during the same period from approximately $98,400,000 to approximately $166,400,000, or 69.2 per cent. The value of all other vegetables increased during the 10-year period from $120,000,000 to $216,000,000 and the acreage by over 600,000. The statistics regarding canned vegetables are significant. In 1899, 19,300,000 cases of canned vegetables, valued at approximately $28,700,000, were packed in the United States. In 1909, 32,800,000 cases, having a value of approximately $51,600,000, were packed.

The area from which vegetables are drawn constantly is increasing, and improved canning, marketing, and transportation facilities have made it possible to supply our large markets with vegetables in greater variety throughout the year. It is a well-known fact that the consumption of fruits and vegetables has increased considerably in recent years and that they constitute a larger and more important part of the permanent diet of the people.

With all the agencies now available for improving agriculture there is ground for optimism as to the ability of the Nation not only to supply itself with food, but increasingly to meet the needs of the world.

INCREASING THE MEAT OUTPUT.

To increase the meat production of the United States has been one of the principal aims of the department in recent years. This can not be accomplished in a day, but requires steady constructive effort over a period of years. Whatever may have been the influence of the department's work, it is gratifying to note that the decline in beef production reached its lowest point in 1913, and that since that date there has been a material increase, while there has been a marked advance in the number of swine since the census year 1899. The number of sheep has continued to decline, but only to a slight extent. The number of animals slaughtered and the quantity of meat products prepared under Government inspection during the past fiscal year are the largest in the history of the service; yet this heavier slaughtering has been accompanied by an increase in the remaining stock of animals.

In December, 1913, a committee of experts was appointed to make a thorough survey of the meat situation. As a result of this study, the department recently issued a series of illuminating reports. They furnish information of value not only to the public but also to the department and suggest more definitely the lines of attack which the department should follow in its efforts to increase the meat supply.

The activities of the department have taken two principal directions—(1) checking and eliminating diseases and parasites and (2) increasing and improving stock raising by extending the industry where conditions are favorable and by pointing the way to better breeding and feeding.

COMBATING STOCK DISEASES.

The eradication of the southern cattle tick is proceeding more rapidly than ever before and is opening up for beef and dairy production a large territory. During the past fiscal year 31,358 square miles were released from quarantine and, in addition, 9,493 square miles were released on September 15, 1916. Within the past three years the quarantine has been removed from 106,810 square miles, making a total of 294,014 since the work was begun in 1906. This represents a territory greater than the combined areas of South Carolina, Georgia, Florida, Tennessee, Alabama, and Mississippi. More than 40 per cent of the original tick-infested territory has been cleared, and therefore the direct losses, originally estimated at $40,000,000 annually, are being greatly reduced.

The diseases known as sheep scabies and cattle scabies likewise are being eliminated rapidly from the Western States. During the fiscal year 1916, 43,243 square miles were released from quarantine for sheep scabies and 12,691 for cattle scabies. At present only 286,398 square miles remain under quarantine for sheep scabies and 3,817 for cattle scabies.

Hog cholera.—Hog cholera, always the cause of heavy losses throughout the country, is less prevalent this year than for many years. This is due, in marked degree, to the wise application of the protective serum devised by the department and to the demonstration work in certain selected counties. The beneficial results of the field demonstrations are shown by a comparison of statistics for the 14 experimental counties before the work was undertaken and after it had been in progress for a time. There was an increase in the number of hogs raised in these counties from 859,910 in 1912 to 1,334,644 in 1915, while during the same period there was a decrease in the number that died from 152,296 to 30,668. This is an increase of 474,734 in the number raised and a decrease of 121,628 in the number lost, or a total gain of 596,362 hogs. This demonstration shows what can be accomplished by the use of serum with sanitary measures, and undoubtedly has led to the extended use of such methods by farmers. The experimental plan would be impracticable and too expensive for the department to operate on a large scale, but the work will be continued in a modified form.

Contagious abortion.—Contagious abortion in recent years has reached such proportions as seriously to threaten the cattle-raising industry. It strikes at the source by curtailing the production of calves. It has been studied by the department, and vigorous efforts are being made to advise stock breeders as to its nature and means of prevention and eradication. The last Congress, upon the recommendation of the department, made a special appropriation of $50,000 for attacking the problem.

Foot-and-mouth disease.—I am glad to be able to report the complete suppression of foot-and-mouth disease during the year. The disease appeared near Niles, Mich., late in the summer of 1914 and reached 22 States and the District of Columbia. It extended entirely across the country, from Massachusetts on the east to Washington on the west, the region of greatest prevalence being from New York to Illinois.

After July 1, 1915, the disease occurred only in Illinois, Massachusetts, New York, Indiana, and Minnesota. Before the end of August it had been eradicated from the last three mentioned States. It recurred in Massachusetts in October, 1915, and was promptly suppressed. In Illinois the last herd of cattle affected by the natural spread of the disease was disposed of in February, 1916. The infection reappeared, however, early in May among some test animals on a previously infected farm. These animals had been placed there to determine, before the owner was allowed to restock his farm, whether the disinfection was effective. As the cleaning and disinfection of these premises had been done under very unfavorable weather conditions, the outbreak was not entirely unexpected. The diseased animals were slaughtered promptly and the premises again disinfected. There has been no recurrence of the disease anywhere in the United States. The last quarantine restrictions were removed June 5, 1916. Supervision by veterinary inspectors has been continued in the lately infected areas after removal of quarantine, as a precaution against any infection that may have remained.

This outbreak was the most serious invasion of this disease that has ever menaced the live-stock industry of the country. It was overcome only after a hard struggle in which the authorities of the various States affected cooperated cordially with the Federal Government. We are fortunate to have escaped with no greater losses. Other countries have been unable to eradicate the disease after it has gained a foothold and have to endure constant heavy losses. As a protection against future outbreaks of this or other diseases of a character to threaten seriously the live-stock industry, Congress has made a special appropriation of $1,250,000. It also has provided, upon the recommendation of the department, that breeding value, as well as meat or dairy value, may be taken into account in compensating owners for animals destroyed hereafter in the eradication work.

TUBERCULOSIS OF FARM ANIMALS.

Tuberculosis probably is the most common, destructive, and widely disseminated of the infectious diseases of domestic animals, especially of cattle and swine. Its seriousness is emphasized by the fact that it is transmitted to human beings. This may be prevented in reasonable measure by the pasteurization of milk and the inspection of meat. There remains, however, the problem of eliminating the disease from farm animals in order to prevent losses estimated at $25,000,000 a year in the United States. This is the greatest problem confronting the live-stock industry of the country. Its very magnitude discourages the undertaking of any general plan of eradication.

Despite all that has been done in the past 10 or 15 years, there is no indication that tuberculosis of cattle and hogs is on the decline in the United States. It has been reduced or partially checked here and there, and even eradicated from some herds; but generally it is as prevalent as ever. The disease can be prevented and some definite system of eradication should be inaugurated. Three undertakings seem practicable at this time.

Eradication from pure-bred herds.—The first is the eradication from pure-bred herds of cattle. It is not necessary to resort to compulsion. The department should be placed in position more fully to assist individuals who wish to undertake the complete eradication of the disease from their herds. It could apply the tuberculin test and, in case infected animals are discovered, advise and supervise their proper disposal or management. The ruthless slaughter of all tuberculin reactors is not necessary. Many of them may be safely retained under proper quarantine conditions and their offspring raised free from tuberculosis. This plan has the approval of the breed-record associations in general and of many individual breeders. Numbers of breeders have requested that their herds be tested. Compliance with these requests to the extent of the limited funds available has yielded very satisfactory results.

Eradication from hogs.—The second undertaking is the eradication of tuberculosis from hogs. The experts of the Bureau of Animal Industry believe that this would be relatively easy of accomplishment. Hogs do not convey the disease to one another to any appreciable extent. They contract it from cattle, chiefly in two ways—by being fed on nonpasteurized products from creameries and by following cattle of somewhat mature age in the feed lot and feeding upon the undigested grain. An educational campaign should be effective in removing these two sources of infection. It also may be desirable to have State laws requiring the pasteurization of skimmed milk and other products before they leave the creameries.

Eradication from restricted areas.—The third undertaking is complete eradication in restricted areas. The plan would be to select certain communities in which, after a thorough educational campaign had been made, the stock owners are willing to cooperate in eradicating the disease entirely from that territory. This would require the slaughter of infected animals and would necessitate reasonable indemnity for the animals slaughtered. The latter feature undoubtedly would require large expenditures.

The results accomplished in the District of Columbia afford an example of what can be done where systematic local eradication is undertaken. By means of repeated tuberculin testing, accompanied by the slaughter of the reacting animals, tuberculosis among cattle in the District has been reduced in a few years from nearly 19 per cent to slightly over 1 per cent. The joining of areas freed of tuberculosis in the manner proposed gradually should result in the elimination of the disease from groups of counties and from entire States.

Such an undertaking would be very similar to the plan of exterminating cattle ticks in the South. This work was begun systematically in 1906 in certain restricted areas on the border of the infested region. At first the opposition of the local people was almost unanimous. Even the fact that the tick is the carrier of splenetic fever was quite generally disbelieved. Persistent work in these few regions, however, eventually produced good results. Gradually the people were convinced that the tick is an evil; that its eradication would be advantageous; and that the cost would be small in comparison with the benefits. The tick-eradication movement is now going forward very rapidly. Furthermore, this activity was begun almost exclusively at department expense. Last year the department spent approximately $400,000 in tick eradication, while local agencies, including State and county governments, expended double that amount, or $800,000. This indicates what can be done when the people concerned appreciate the real significance and value of an undertaking.

Such a plan should succeed against tuberculosis. It is a large task. Its feasibility will have to be thoroughly established first, as was the case with tick eradication. In the beginning the methods for tick eradication were crude and cumbersome. Improvements were made, however, until the present efficient system was developed. These suggestions, if carried into effect, should assist in developing a comprehensive plan for dealing with the tuberculosis situation which will meet with approval and lead to ultimate success. The department has recommended in the estimates for the next fiscal year that an appropriation of $75,000 be made for the inauguration of the work.

DEVELOPMENT OF STOCK RAISING.

Experiments by the department, in cooperation with the State experiment stations, have shown conclusively that the South is well adapted to economical beef and pork production. It is beginning to take its place with other sections as a stock-raising territory. Numerous breeding herds are being established. The leading beef-cattle breeders' associations are featuring the southern trade, and two of them are holding sales in cooperation with the department. Cattle from southern herds have won the highest honors in northern show rings, and steers from southern feed lots, after being properly fattened, now command good prices in northern markets. This work is not for the benefit of one section alone; the entire country will profit from the extension of meat production into new territory.

A study of growing beef animals in the corn belt also was made, and records were obtained of the cost of raising calves from nearly 15,000 cows. The results show that calves, as a rule, can be raised at a profit, although the cost of production is higher than is usually thought.

The boys' and girls' pig and poultry clubs are valuable agencies for enlarging the meat output, as well as for training and developing the coming generation of farmers. The membership of both classes of clubs more than doubled during the year. The pig clubs now have more than 21,000 members and the poultry clubs 8,500.

National Forest ranges.—The investigations conducted at the instance of the committee appointed to study the meat situation indicate that there has been an increase of from 15 to 30 per cent in the carrying capacity of the National Forest ranges. This has been brought about by systematic regulation, better methods of handling stock, improving and increasing the number of watering places, opening up unused or inaccessible ranges, the building of drift fences, and the lessening of losses from poisonous plants. These ranges now are supporting over 1,750,000 cattle and 7,850,000 sheep, exclusive of calves and lambs. It is estimated that within the next 10 years their carrying capacity will be increased by an additional 15 per cent and that they will be capable of supporting fully 2,000,000 cattle and 9,000,000 sheep.

As previously pointed out, regulated grazing on the public lands outside the National Forests would permit a considerable addition to the country's meat supply. At present these lands, which include an area of over 250,000,000 acres, are not supporting the number of animals that formerly grazed upon them. By the application of a system of control and development similar to that used on the National Forests, it would be possible greatly to increase the number of meat-producing animals upon the public ranges.

Destruction of forage by rodents.—The grazing value of the western stock ranges is much reduced by the depredations of prairie dogs and ground squirrels. More than 22,000,000 acres in 12 States are infested with prairie dogs. These rodents often completely destroy the forage plants over considerable areas and cause enormous damage to grain and other crops. Ground squirrels occur in large numbers in 18 States. While they are less destructive to forage plants than prairie dogs, they consume large quantities of forage and grain. In North Dakota alone the annual loss to farmers from the destruction of grain by ground squirrels is estimated at over $3,000,000. The Bureau of Biological Survey has developed new methods of poisoning these pests at a cost of approximately 5 cents per acre. This is less than the grazing value of the land for a single year. The bureau practically has eradicated prairie dogs from more than 2,000,000 acres of public lands and ground squirrels from 500,000 acres. The complete elimination of them should enable the ranges and farms of the West to carry a million cattle and a million sheep more than at present.

Predatory animals.—The annual losses of live stock in the United States, mainly upon the public domain, from the depredations of such animals as wolves, coyotes, mountain lions, and bears, exceeds $12,000,000. Wolves and coyotes are subject to epidemics of rabies and, therefore, are peculiarly a menace to domestic animals and human beings. There was a serious outbreak of this disease among coyotes during the past year. It was prevalent in several States in the Northwest and was especially disturbing in Nevada.

Congress appropriated $200,000 for the destruction of predatory wild animals during the past year. The sum of $250,000 is available for this purpose during the fiscal year 1917. A force of hunters and trappers has been organized in the infested States, and 543 wolves, 19,170 coyotes, and many other predatory animals have been destroyed. As a single wolf has been known to kill more than $3,000 worth of stock in one year, the effect on the stock-raising industry

of the elimination of this number of destroyers is apparent.
A continuance of the campaign should eliminate a large part
of the losses from this source and also should check the
spread of rabies among wild animals.

THE SHEEP INDUSTRY.

Normally the United States imports from about two-
fifths to more than one-half of the wool required for domestic consumption. During the past three years importations have ranged from nearly 250 million to more than 500
million pounds each year, the average being over 300 million
pounds. The total consumption of lamb and mutton during the past 10 years has increased appreciably. In the
fiscal year 1907 more than 9½ million sheep and lambs were
slaughtered at plants subject to Federal inspection. The
number now averages about 13 million per annum.

In some sections of the United States there has been a
steady decline in sheep production since the earliest statistical reports. This has been true also in every other settled
country except Great Britain. The explanation undoubtedly is an economic one. In general, the primary purpose of
sheep growers has been to produce wool. This can not be
attained profitably on high-priced land. Naturally, therefore, with the increase in land values there is a rapid decline
in the number of sheep. In Great Britain meat has been the
principal product and wool the by-product, and the sheep
industry has flourished.

Waste land made productive.—If American farmers will
follow the British custom the industry can be put on a profitable and permanent basis. The greater number of sheep in
Great Britain are raised in the hills and on land comparable
to much of the " waste land " of American farms. The areas
in this country, especially in the East and in parts of the
South, now relatively little used, can profitably be devoted
to sheep production if the farmers will secure the proper
breed of sheep.

Sheep also can be made profitable on higher-priced land, as British experience shows. They compare favorably with other animals in economy of production. They require a minimum of expensive concentrated feeds. They exceed the other larger animals in the rate of maturity; lambs can be made ready for market at from four to six months. They make possible the economical and fuller use of labor. They are of assistance in keeping the farm free from weeds. The sheep farm is usually a weedless farm.

Extension of industry.—In the United States only one in seven farms of over 20 acres now supports sheep, with an average of one sheep of shearing age to 3 acres of land. The 300 million pounds of wool now imported annually could be secured from 50 million sheep, and this number could be added to our stock if a fourth of the remaining farms sustained one sheep for each 3 acres.

In 1914 the Animal Husbandry Division of the Bureau of Animal Industry and the Bureau of Crop Estimates canvassed crop reporters in 36 States in reference to sheep on farms. The replies indicated that the number could be increased 150 per cent without displacing other animals. It is to our settled areas, particularly in the Central, Southern, and Eastern States, that we must look for an increase in the number of sheep.

THE DAIRY INDUSTRY.

The profits of agriculture ultimately depend on the intelligent cultivation of the soil and the preservation of its fertility. Dairy farming is increasing in almost every section of the country, largely because it is the most economical form of agriculture so far as soil fertility is concerned. A ton of butter removes from the soil less than a dollar's worth of fertilizing elements. Dairying also is growing because dairy products are an important part of our food supply. Opportunities for dairying are found in every agricultural district. The different sections of the country have characteristic peculiarities, but all need milk and its products.

Cheese production.—In 1909 this country produced 1,622 million pounds of butter and 321 million pounds of cheese. In 1870 our cheese exports amounted to 57 million pounds. They steadily increased until 1881, when the total was 148 million pounds. After that date they decreased rapidly until in 1914 they had dropped to less than $2\frac{1}{2}$ million pounds. On the other hand, our imports of cheese amounted to $2\frac{1}{3}$ million pounds in 1870 and advanced slowly until 1900, when $13\frac{1}{2}$ million pounds were imported. From 1900 to 1914 the imports increased to 64 million pounds. Much of this cheese could and should be produced in the United States.

Most of the cheese in this country has been made in the territory around the Great Lakes, where climatic conditions are favorable to the handling of whole milk. All the valleys in the Rocky Mountain section and a large area on the Pacific coast offer splendid conditions for cheese production. So, also, does the mountain section of the South, including parts of West Virginia, Virginia, Tennessee, North Carolina, South Carolina, and Georgia. Three factories have been established in one of these States and have been very successful.

Cooperative associations. — Rigid selection, intelligent breeding, and skillful feeding are important factors in economical production. Cow-testing associations teach rigid selection and skillful feeding. Cooperative bull associations promote intelligent breeding. In cooperation with the various State agricultural colleges the department has greatly extended the work of these associations. For several years cooperative bull associations have been common in some parts of Europe. The first association of the kind in the United States was organized in Michigan in 1908. In this country their growth has not been rapid, but as a rule they have been successful. They provide for the joint ownership, use, and exchange of high-class, pure-bred bulls. If skillfully managed, these associations should become potent factors in the upbuilding of a more profitable dairy industry.

A large part of the work of the cow-testing associations and cooperative bull associations has been done in the North and West. In Wisconsin alone there are more than 50 cow-testing associations, while the cooperative bull associations have been especially successful in Massachusetts, northern Michigan, and North Dakota. The dairy industry in the Rocky Mountain and Pacific Coast States recently has made great progress, owing in part to the importation of carefully selected dairy cows and registered bulls from the East and Middle West. Its development in the South has been very marked during the past year. A beginning was made in the work of cow-testing associations and cooperative bull associations. Five of the agricultural colleges have organized creameries to encourage dairying and to provide a market for the increased production of milk and cream. These creameries furnish excellent facilities for teaching students improved methods of manufacturing and handling dairy products.

Community development in dairying.—Community development in dairying was undertaken by the department in a typical small creamery community in northern Iowa in 1910. The object of the experiment was to determine the practicability of employing skilled instructors to assist such communities in bringing the dairy business to a higher level. The work, which proved to be financially successful, was continued for five years, and similar work now is being carried on, with even greater success, in the vicinity of Grove City, Pa. If the 5,000 creameries in this country should adopt the community development plan, it doubtless would result in greatly enlarged profits for the patrons.

The creamery extension work has increased the efficiency of a large number of creameries. The department also has given assistance in building and equipping creameries, rear-

ranging the machinery, systematizing the methods of operation, eliminating losses, and improving the quality of the
products.

Research work.—The activities indicated are almost entirely of an educational nature. The department also is
conducting investigations relating to dairy problems on a
scale which is unequaled anywhere else in the world. Much
of this work, in its beginning, is of a highly technical nature,
but results are being accumulated which are of great practical value in the field demonstration work. Extensive study
of the types of bacteria in milk, their origin, and the channels through which they contaminate milk, has established
a reasonable basis for dairy sanitation. Perhaps the most
striking example of the application of the results of laboratory research to practice is the development of methods of
manufacture of some of the foreign cheeses which make up
the bulk of our cheese imports.

PRODUCTION OF FOOD CROPS.

The production of food crops adequate to meet the consuming needs of the country and the export demand. is a
matter of large importance to the American people. Our
potential agricultural resources in this respect are so varied
and ample that there can be no doubt of our ability abundantly to supply our domestic wants, when climatic conditions
are normal and the foreign demand is not excessive. One of
the greatest agricultural needs, therefore, is the stabilizing
of production.

Sharp fluctuation of yield and price from season to season
tends to stimulate speculative and superficial farming and
to discourage the systematic crop rotation and thorough cultural practice which are essential to an enduring and economically sound agriculture. It is obvious that, in large measure,
stabilization of production must be brought about through
the use of better adapted or improved crop varieties, more
systematic and rational crop rotations, and improved agri-

cultural practice generally, including, in many sections, larger attention to live-stock production.

The extent to which the productiveness of such a crop as corn can be improved through continued selection is illustrated strikingly by the results of work done by department specialists. For 14 seasons the yields of 10-acre fields of corn, planted on a 3,000-acre farm in Ohio with seed selected from the department cooperative improvement plots on the farm, have been contrasted with the farm yields of the same variety of corn less rigidly selected and grown under identical cultural conditions. During the first seven-year period the fields planted with department seed yielded 13.3 bushels per acre more than the farm fields, while for the second seven years the increase averaged 21.8 bushels per acre.

It should not be inferred that such increases in yield can be secured except through very efficient crop-improvement work; yet it is obvious that, as the principles of crop improvement are better understood and more generally applied, larger yields per acre should result. In addition, a great deal can be accomplished through increase of soil fertility and better cultural methods. Enough has been done in this direction by the State experiment stations and the department, and also by good farmers, to justify the expectation that considerably increased acre yields gradually will be brought about in a large part of the area adapted to the staple food crops.

EXTENSION OF AREAS OF PRODUCTION.

Very destructive climatic conditions never occur in this country with equal severity throughout all the staple-crop regions. It is highly desirable, therefore, further to broaden the areas for these staples as far as experience and sound economics may warrant. While progress in this direction necessarily is slow, it is gratifying to note that in recent years the production of corn in the Southern States has increased greatly. At the same time the frontier of commercial corn production has advanced steadily northward in the upper Mississippi Valley and Plains States.

Farther south and west, especially in western Kansas, Oklahoma, and the Panhandle of Texas, corn is being displaced to a considerable extent by the grain sorghums because they more regularly produce profitable crops. Approximately 4 million acres now are devoted to these crops. One of these sorghums has been changed by systematic breeding into a standard variety which produces a much larger yield of grain. Dwarf milo, a recent result of systematic breeding for low stature, has a higher grain-yielding power under adverse conditions than the tall variety. During the past four years it has become the leading variety grown in Oklahoma, Texas, and New Mexico. As the sorghum grains in large measure serve the same purposes as corn, the economic soundness to the Nation of their enlarged production is apparent.

In the Sacramento Valley of California, where this department has been investigating the possibility of rice culture, the acreage devoted to that crop has increased during the past five years from 1,400 to 67,000. The farm value of the current crop approximates $3,500,000. The increased production of wheat, oats, and other small grains in the Southeastern and South Central States, which was specially stimulated by the cotton-market crisis of 1914, tends to stabilize the food supply. In several States the acreage planted to these grains was enlarged by from 50 to 100 per cent.

Adaptation studies of the hard red winter wheats, which formerly were restricted to a limited part of the Central Plains region, have shown that they can be grown throughout a much larger area. During the past four years they have become established extensively in Montana and in the States of the Great Basin and the Pacific Northwest. In the States west of the Rocky Mountains they have largely replaced the soft wheats.

The area devoted to durum wheat has strikingly increased. This crop now is well established in western North Dakota, South Dakota, eastern Montana and Wyoming, and northeastern Colorado. As the durum varieties are more resistant to rust than other types and require less rainfall, their introduction by the department has proved to be of very great importance to the country. The durum production already has attained a magnitude of 40 million bushels in a single year.

Two new pure lines of Kherson oats have been developed in cooperation with the Iowa Agricultural Experiment Station and have been widely distributed in Iowa and adjoining corn-belt States. A large number of tests by farmers have shown a 10 per cent increase in yield over the varieties previously grown. Their adoption for the entire oat acreage of Iowa probably would result in an increase in production in that State alone of from 12 to 15 million bushels.

A systematic study of the soy bean, with a view to determine the relative adaptability of varieties to regions, the best methods of culture, harvesting, and threshing, and the uses to which it can be put, has been under way for several years. This study has thrown much light on its economic possibilities. It not only produces forage for live stock, but oil for various uses can be obtained from the seed, and meal, flour, and other food products can be made from the resulting cake. Through the efforts of the department, cotton-oil mills crushed during the past season over 100,000 bushels of southern-grown soy beans with satisfactory results from the oil standpoint, while soy-bean flour, or meal, and other food products made from the resulting cake, are being marketed by several manufacturers.

As the soy bean can be produced under widely varying climatic and soil conditions, it seems certain in the future to occupy a larger and more important place in our agriculture and in our food supply.

CALIFORNIA CITRUS INDUSTRY.

The citrus industry of California, although tracing its beginnings back to individual plantings by early settlers, owes its present magnitude and commercial importance in large measure to the introduction by this department many years ago of the Washington navel orange from Brazil. The present production of this variety in that State is estimated at approximately 27,000 carloads in a normal year, or about two-thirds of the total orange shipments of the State. It has, in fact, become the most important citrus-fruit variety in the world.

The results of several years of systematic study of citrus fruits in California show that important bud variations exist, even in standard varieties. This factor must be taken into account in their propagation in order to secure maximum productiveness and quality. In many of the best groves at least 10 per cent of the trees of the standard varieties are of inferior strains, which should be eliminated by top-working. The growers who have observed the experimental plots realize the importance of this work and already have undertaken the conversion of the undesirable trees by top-working on a rather large scale. This study will be extended to some of the deciduous-tree fruits.

As the economic soundness of commercial fruit orcharding to a considerable extent rests upon the maintenance of high average annual production, it is obvious that the results of this investigation are of fundamental importance to the fruit industry.

SUGAR-BEET INDUSTRY.

The production of beet sugar in the United States has increased during the past four years from less than 700,000 tons to approximately 900,000 tons. During the past year seven new localities for sugar-beet production have been developed. But for the existing shortage of sugar-beet seed a considerably larger increase of production would have been secured.

Stimulated by the inadequate supply of seed from European countries, American growers now are undertaking seriously the production of seed. Approximately 4,000 acres, which should produce about one-fourth of the present requirements, have been devoted to this purpose during the current year. A special appropriation made at the last session of Congress will enable the department to cooperate with the industry in solving some of the more technical problems involved. It is hoped that, as a result of this work, the industry may be freed from the menace of seed shortage which during the past two years seriously threatened its existence.

CONTROL OF PLANT DISEASES.

It is very clear that fuller knowledge of the distribution and the nature and methods of control of crop diseases is essential. In some seasons, when unusual climatic conditions prevail at critical periods, diseases greatly lessen or practically destroy particular crops throughout important producing districts. Progress has been made in determining their exact character and in developing methods of control, but the destructiveness of certain diseases under climatic conditions favorable to their spread necessitates still more energetic inquiry. It has been estimated that in years when cereal rusts are epidemic the losses from them alone amount at least to $180,000,000. No effective remedies have yet been found for these diseases. It seems probable, however, that through the development of suitable resistant varieties their eventual control in large part can be effected.

Distinct headway has been made in the study of diseases of fruits and vegetables. Many of them have proved amenable to spray control, especially when combined with rational field practice to prevent infection.

CITRUS CANKER.

Cooperative arrangements have been made with State officials of Florida, Texas, Louisiana, Mississippi, Alabama, Georgia, and South Carolina to insure the thorough inspection of nurseries and citrus groves for the purpose of promptly and completely eradicating citrus canker. This is an undertaking of great magnitude because of the extreme infectiousness of the disease and the wide area throughout which it has been disseminated. No final statement as to the outcome can be expected within a period of at least two years. The campaign, however, is progressing very satisfactorily in the commercially important orange and grapefruit regions of Florida. Supplemental protective measures, such as formalin treatments of infected soil and protective spraying of groves exposed to infection, are hastening the work of eradication materially. Even in the few places where citrus-canker outbreaks have occurred in commercial districts and in old trees, the disease can be eradicated promptly and effectively. Although thorough inspection of citrus plantings will be necessary, at least throughout the coming fiscal year, it is believed that Florida now is so nearly free of the disease as to render its eradication from that State practically certain. In Texas, Louisiana, Alabama, and Mississippi the work has been more difficult from the beginning because of the more scattered plantings and the relatively smaller interests involved. Furthermore, in all these States the unusually severe tropical storms of the present year have caused unexpectedly wide distribution of the disease in some areas. Even in these States, however, the progress of the work is encouraging, and if no further unusual drawbacks are encountered the disease will be effectively checked.

CONTROL OF INSECTS.

While all the State Experiment Stations support work in economic entomology, and while many other countries are

developing services in this direction, the Department of
Agriculture has by far the largest organization for the purpose of research on insect pests. It is virtually the leader
of the world in the warfare against injurious insects. It
has in its files biological notes on thousands of species and is
studying them from all points of view in its field laboratories. No less than 143 distinct projects are being investigated at the present time, involving possibly 500 of the
species of insects most injurious to crops, domestic animals,
stored foods, forest products, shade trees, and ornamental
plants. It is safe to say that some form of remedial treatment has been found for every markedly injurious insect in
the United States, but continued efforts are being made to
find something more effective or cheaper or simpler.

Many striking things have been accomplished. The pear
thrips, which at one time threatened the extinction of the
Pacific coast deciduous-fruit industry, is no longer feared.
Two serious pests of the clover-seed crop now can be handled
by slight variation of cropping methods. The bark-beetles
of our coniferous forests, which have imposed a loss comparable to that resulting from forest fires, can be controlled
at very little expense. Sprays and spraying machinery
have been developed which can be used successfully against
practically all leaf-feeding species. The fumigation of
nursery stock and of warehouses has been perfected. Such
injurious species as the onion thrips, the grape-berry moth,
the alfalfa weevil, the tobacco hornworm, and many others
of recent prominence, can be controlled. The spread of the
gipsy and brown-tail moths through our northern forests
and orchards has been prevented. These injurious insects
not only have been kept in a comparatively small territory,
but are being reduced in number year after year by active
scouting, spraying, banding, and egg destruction, and
through the aid of parasites brought from Europe and
Japan. Although the spread of the cotton boll weevil—

which represents probably the most difficult problem in insect control—has not been stopped, the investigations of the department's entomologists have shown the southern planter how to reduce greatly the potential damage and how to grow cotton in spite of the weevil.

An important development in this practical entomological work of recent years has been the establishment of a number of more or less temporary field laboratories, scattered over the country. Thus the expert workers are taken into the centers of activity of the injurious species. Great stress is being laid on what may be termed the cultural method of insect control. The intimate life round of the insect pest is studied in close connection with farming methods in order to ascertain whether by variation of cultural practice the insect damage can not be considerably reduced. Remedial work of this sort is extremely practical. Investigations have shown that in many instances partial or nearly complete control can be gained by some change in farm management. This naturally is the best remedy, except possibly in the case of introduced pests, where control can be secured by the employment of parasites or other natural enemies.

Technical methods of control, mechanical and chemical, including sprays and spraying machinery, fumigation for citrus orchards, nursery stock, mills and warehouses, or trapping methods and other means of mechanical destruction also have been studied and developed. In the large problems it frequently has happened that cultural, biological, and technical measures are used at the same time.

When the enormous annual losses from injurious insects are considered it is clear that the value of the department's work in applied entomology is very great.

PLANT QUARANTINES.

Important service is rendered to the farm and fruit interests of the country, under the Plant Quarantine Act, by preventing the introduction of new and dangerous insect pests and plant diseases. There are now in force nine foreign quarantines forbidding the entry, or permitting the entry only under restrictions, of various farm, orchard, and forest products which may harbor injurious insects or diseases. The more important quarantines relate to the Mediterranean fruit fly, perhaps the worst fruit pest of the tropical and subtropical countries; the pink bollworm, an insect which threatens to become the most serious enemy known to cotton; the potato wart, a disease which not only destroys the tuber but infects the soil; and the white-pine blister rust and the citrus canker, two diseases which became established in the United States prior to the passage of the act.

A number of domestic quarantines also have been promulgated. Under these quarantines many locally established plant diseases and insect pests, most of them of recent origin, are being so controlled, in cooperation with the States concerned, that their extermination ultimately can be effected or, at least, their spread can be checked. These quarantines relate principally to the gipsy and brown-tail moths in New England; the Mediterranean fruit fly and the pink bollworm in Hawaii; and diseases of sugar cane in Hawaii and Porto Rico.

In some instances plants and plant products are admitted only after certification by the proper official in the originating country and the issuance of permits by the department. They also are inspected by State or Federal experts before being released in this country. Such restrictions now apply to nursery stock of all kinds, fruits, certain plant seeds, and potatoes, and foreign lint cotton. The restrictions on cotton are designed to prevent the entry of the pink bollworm through cotton seeds which are found in all imported cotton. The cotton is subjected to fumigation in a vacuum, under supervision, by a new process devised by experts of the department.

The value of this service to the Nation is apparent. Undoubtedly many, if not all, of the plant diseases and pests mentioned now would have full lodgment or wider distribution in this country if the necessary action under the Plant Quarantine Act had not been taken to prevent their entry or to check their spread. It would be difficult to compute the resulting loss.

COOPERATIVE AGRICULTURAL EXTENSION WORK.

The second year's operation of the cooperative Agricultural Extension Act of May 8, 1914, has been attended with a steady development of the Nation-wide system of practical instruction in agriculture and home economics discussed in my last two reports. There has been a fuller coordination of the activities of the department with those of the agricultural colleges and more complete development of the relations between the extension forces in the States Relations Service and the scientific staffs in the various bureaus of the department, resulting in the better dissemination of approved scientific information.

POTASH FROM KELP.

In 1911 the Bureau of Soils was authorized by the Congress to make a survey of the Nation's resources in fertilizer materials, particularly in potash, for which this country was entirely dependent upon the German mines. As a result of this reconnoissance, it became evident that the largest and most immediately available source of potash in this country was the giant kelps of the Pacific coast. This conclusion was reached after detailed surveys had been made of the kelp groves of southern California, the Puget Sound region, and Alaska. The attention of the public was called to this source in the hope that private capital would undertake its development.

Germany in 1915 prohibited the exportation of all potash salts. This action greatly stimulated the attempts of American manufacturers to produce potash and resulted in the erection of eight large plants in southern California for the extraction of this material from kelp. These establishments were constructed at a cost ranging from $50,000 to $2,000,000 and are centered around two cities, Long Beach and San Diego, five at the former and three at the latter place. They are operating harvesting equipment having an aggregate daily capacity of 2,500 tons of raw kelp. On September 1, 1916, about 125,000 tons of raw kelp had been harvested and treated, yielding approximately 10 per cent of dry kelp.

Notwithstanding this comparatively rapid development in the kelp industry, the problem of extracting potash from kelp commercially has not been completely solved. It is essential that methods be devised for producing the numerous by-products which can be obtained from kelp. The plants now in operation, for the most part, are engaged only in the extraction of potash. Owing to the present abnormal prices for this material, they are devoting relatively little attention to the elaboration of processes for the recovery of by-products. If this situation continues, they probably will not be able to produce potash at a profit when conditions become normal. In the circumstances, it seems desirable for the department to demonstrate the commercial feasibility of producing potash and by-products from kelp with a view to put the industry on a sound economic basis. The Congress, upon the recommendation of the department, has made available $175,000 for the purpose. Plans have been formulated for erecting and operating, at some advantageous point on the coast of southern California, a plant with a daily capacity of not less than 200 tons of raw kelp, in order that the necessary experiments may be conducted.

It is hoped that these experiments will result in the establishment of a potash industry which will prove profitable and permanent and render this country independent of foreign sources in normal times. In any event, information will be obtained which should be very valuable if the present abnormal conditions persist or recur.

THE FOOD AND DRUGS ACT.

Early in 1913 it became apparent that the efficiency of the Bureau of Chemistry in administering the Food and Drugs Act was impaired seriously by lack of system. The laboratories, both in and out of Washington, were congested with samples collected by inspectors. The inspectors, who were responsible only to the chief inspector in Washington, worked independently of the chemists in the branch laboratories, with resulting loss of efficiency. There was great delay in analyzing samples and in detecting adulterations. It was apparent that the work of the inspectors and of the chemists should be coordinated and more closely supervised. To make the bureau an effective agency in preventing the shipment of adulterated and misbranded foods and drugs, complete reorganization was necessary.

ESTABLISHMENT OF DISTRICTS.

Accordingly, the field service of the bureau was set off from the central organization and divided into three districts, with headquarters at Washington, Chicago, and San Francisco. A single official, whose duty it is to coordinate the work of the inspectors and the laboratories, was placed in charge of each district. Several small branch laboratories were closed and the research work was concentrated in Washington. The reorganization has effected a material reduction in the cost of operation and has made possible the accomplishment of substantial results. It has enabled the bureau to concentrate the activities of its 46 inspectors against definite lines of food and drug products. The establishment of inspection districts, together with the creation in Washington of the Office of State Cooperative Food and Drug Control, has secured the active cooperation of State food and drug officials. This cooperation has been an important factor.

Instead of attempting to deal with food products indiscriminately, the Bureau of Chemistry during the past three years has given special attention to articles in common use, such as eggs, milk, beans, shellfish, citrus fruits, tomato products, canned foods, and cottonseed meal and other feed for animals. As a result of the activities of the bureau there has been a marked improvement in the quality of these products entering interstate commerce.

Concerted efforts of the inspectors have put an end to most of the interstate traffic in decomposed eggs. Campaigns have been conducted, in cooperation with the local authorities, to improve the milk supply of several localities. Efforts have been made to induce farmers to produce better milk and prosecutions have been instituted in many instances. As a result the milk supply of many cities and towns has been improved. Seizure proceedings have been instituted against a large number of shipments of canned beans containing substantial proportions of decomposed beans. With the assistance of the Public Health Service and the Bureau of Fisheries, sanitary surveys have been made of the oyster beds on the Atlantic coast. Sources of pollution and polluted areas were located and the information conveyed to oystermen. Seizures of shipments of polluted oysters were effected and a marked improvement in the oyster supply, from the standpoint of wholesomeness, has been noted.

Formerly it was the custom of many orange and grapefruit growers at times to pick the fruit from the trees while green or partly green in color and still unripe, and subject it to a sweating process so as to give it the characteristic yellow color of ripe fruit. The incentive to the grower was the higher price afforded by an early market. Green citrus fruit which has been colored so as to give it the appearance of ripe fruit is adulterated under the law. Several seizures have been made and the efforts of the department have resulted in a material decrease in the quantity of sweated immature fruit sent to market.

The inspection of canned tomatoes has been continued, and an improvement in the industry has been noted. Consideration also has been given to other canned foods, many of which have been found to be adulterated on account of imperfect methods of manufacture. A large number of shipments of cottonseed meal were found to have a protein content materially less than that declared upon the label, and appropriate action was taken.

SHERLEY AMENDMENT.

Special attention has been given during the last two years to the enforcement of the Sherley amendment. The amendment declares drugs to be misbranded if their labels contain false and fraudulent statements concerning their curative or therapeutic effects. A large number of criminal prosecutions have been successfully concluded and many cases are pending. A systematic plan has been developed for dealing with this problem, and already an improvement in the labeling of the medicinal preparations has resulted. Concerted efforts have been directed against spurious and adulterated drugs.

NUMBER OF CASES.

During the past three years the bureau has collected and analyzed at least 22,000 samples of domestic foods and drugs. It has afforded formal hearings to more than 9,000 manufacturers and shippers, and has sent to the Department of Justice, through the Solicitor, about 2,250 cases. Approximately 3,000 cases have been finally disposed of by the courts, the great majority having been uncontested and practically all those contested having been decided in favor of the Government. During the same period about 50,000 importations have been sampled, of which approximately 3,000 were refused entry, and 15,000 were admitted only after relabeling to conform to the provisions of the law.

RESEARCH AND EDUCATIONAL WORK.

During the past three years the research work of the Bureau of Chemistry, which previously had been confined largely to problems arising in connection with law enforcement, was extended to include work designed to prevent spoilage and waste, to increase production, and to develop new methods of utilizing products of the soil and sea. Investigations in the utilization and transportation of sea foods have resulted in a marked improvement in the canning of American sardines. Means also have been found to utilize the waste of this industry as an animal feed. Important improvements in the transportation of fresh shrimp and the shipment of fish under refrigeration have been made. Studies of the transportation and marketing of poultry and eggs have made possible the elimination of much waste due to decomposition resulting from faulty methods of packing and shipping. A process has been introduced for the manufacture of table salt which eliminates from it a poisonous ingredient formerly present in the salt obtained in certain sections. Important improvements also have been made in the processes involved in the manufacture of gelatin, sauerkraut, maple and sorghum sirups, cider, fruit juices and sirups, citric acid, lemon oil, jams, jellies, marmalade, preserves, corn meal, and stock feeds.

Much important work has been done in the application of the principles of physical chemistry to the study of a large series of food products. The work upon the chemistry of sugars is recognized universally as of fundamental importance. A study of the composition of vegetable proteins has been begun and already has yielded results which are certain to be of value in the feeding and fattening of farm animals.

STANDARDS FOR FOODS AND DRUGS.

Experience in connection with the administration of the Food and Drugs Act has strikingly emphasized the importance of enforceable standards for foods and drugs. Without them it is impossible to carry out completely the purposes of the act. In many instances protection of the consumer—the principal object of the law—can not fully be accomplished, nor can unfair practices on the part of unscrupulous manufacturers adequately be prevented. In some cases maintenance of prosecution is difficult and expensive, even when the articles involved clearly are adulterated or misbranded. To meet this situation, I have recommended in the estimates for the fiscal year 1918 that the Secretary of Agriculture be authorized to establish standards of strength, quality, or purity for articles of food and for those articles of drugs which are sold under or by a name not recognized in the United States Pharmacopœia or National Formulary. The suggestion provides that if any article fails to conform to the established standards it shall be deemed to be misbranded, unless it is labeled so as plainly and conspicuously to show how it differs from the standard.

The adoption of legally enforceable standards will benefit both the consumer and the honest manufacturer. They will give consumers exact information as to the quality of food and drug products and will enable manufacturers to produce articles which will meet the requirements of the act, putting competition on a fairer basis. They will be of great assistance to Federal and State officials in the enforcement of food and drug laws and will tend to promote uniformity among the various States.

INSPECTION OF ESTABLISHMENTS.

I have also recommended in the estimates that the department be given authority to inspect establishments producing foods or drugs intended for shipment in interstate or foreign commerce. No specific authority exists at the present time. While many manufacturers do not object to inspection of their factories, the lack of definite authority has caused considerable embarrassment in the enforcement of the Food and Drugs Act. There are many forms of adulteration which are exceedingly difficult to detect without inspection of the place of manufacture. This is particularly true of foods produced under insanitary conditions. In many instances it is impossible to determine from a chemical or bacteriological examination the conditions under which a particular food or drug was produced. It is unnecessary to emphasize the importance of sanitation in the preparation of food products. If the suggested authority be granted, the department should be able to improve the quality of food products, both by bringing to the attention of manufacturers any insanitary conditions that may be discovered and by securing evidence of production under insanitary conditions.

ROAD DEVELOPMENT.

The Office of Public Roads and Rural Engineering has extended its work of giving assistance in road and farm engineering problems to individuals or local communities in every State of the Union. There also has been placed upon it the burden of administering the Federal Aid Road Act. Immediately after the approval of the act plans were formulated for its administration. The appropriation of $5,000,000 for the fiscal year 1917, after deducting an amount sufficient for administrative expenses, was apportioned among the various States on the basis of three factors— population, area, and mileage of rural delivery and star routes—each factor having a weight of one-third. Rules and regulations were promulgated on September 1, 1916.

Thirty-two States have indicated their intention to assent to the provisions of the act—one through its legislature and the others through their governors. Before the department can undertake cooperation in any State, it is necessary to determine (1) whether the State has a legally constituted highway department within the meaning of the act and (2) whether the State has legally assented to the provisions of the act and is in a position to submit a program or scheme of work covering the five-year period and to meet the requirements of the act as to funds and maintenance of the roads constructed. This determination has been made in the case of nine States and, after certain details have been arranged, the department will be prepared to cooperate with all of them. Three States will await action by their legislatures before assenting to the provisions of the act. Tentative drafts of bills providing for State highway commissions have been prepared for two States which do not now have a highway agency within the meaning of the act. Eight States have submitted specific projects for consideration. In one of these States four projects have been approved tentatively and the necessary project agreements are in the course of execution.

The appropriation of $1,000,000 provided by section 8 of the act for the construction of roads and trails within or partly within the National Forests has been apportioned among the various States in which National Forests are located. Applications for the construction of roads in the Forests must be filed in the district office of the Forest Service for the district within which the proposed road is located. In States having highway departments the applications, before filing, must be referred to them for recommendation. Many applications have been submitted to the district offices and now are under consideration.

THE NATIONAL FOREST ENTERPRISE.

There have been many important developments—legislative and administrative—during the past year in connection with the National Forests. The value of the properties to the public and the use made of them increased steadily. Their returns to the Treasury last year, exceeding $2,800,000—an advance of more than $340,000 over the previous year—are only a partial indication of their service. The land classification work, having for its object the determination of the areas which permanently should be included in the Forests, progressed very rapidly. As a result there remained in public ownership at the close of the year 155,420,280 acres, several million acres having been restored to the public domain or opened to entry under the Forest Homestead law. There was a marked increase in the equipment of the Forests with roads, a matter of prime importance for the advancement of local community welfare and of no small importance for the economic development of the Forests themselves. An augmented volume of business, due to a larger number of timber purchasers, and a net addition of nearly three-fourths of a million to the number of stock grazed, together with a decided stimulus in prospecting and mining activities and in the use of the Forests for recreation and health, are further indications of broadening development.

PERMANENCE OF THE FORESTS.

Thus year by year the National Forest enterprise gains stability. In the long run the only means by which it can become stable is successful administration. Laws alone can not make it so. For a time the Forests were a great experiment. Whether the public benefits which their establishment had in view could be realized without accompanying intolerable drawbacks could be ascertained only through demonstration. An essentially constructive task was involved. The responsibility upon this department since it was placed in charge of the Forests has not been merely the routine discharge of definitely prescribed duties. It has been necessary to devise and apply methods for attaining broad general purposes embodied in laws by Congress. A vast land area was to be managed with a view to the most general, varied, and harmonious use. If these resources had not been made available to the public, a resistless demand for the abandonment of the project would have arisen. Through successful administration the permanence of the National Forests is becoming more and more assured. They are now a vital part of the economic life of the regions which use their resources. It is increasingly clear that National supervision and control of them is necessary and that they could not be abandoned without disastrous consequences to western industries and to local welfare.

ROAD DEVELOPMENT IN FORESTS.

In my reports of the last two years the need for more ample provision for road development in the National Forests was emphasized. Many of the Forests are located in the more remote portions of the western mountains. Roads are necessary for their protection, administration, and development. They are essential also for the upbuilding of the local communities. They are needed to open up agricultural regions which now are practically shut off from the market, to make possible the development of mines and to stimulate prospecting, to shorten the distances of travel between localities and through the States, to make accessible wood and timber required for local use and for the lumber industry, and to enable the public to visit and enjoy the Forests for recreation and health. At the last session of Congress this urgent need received recognition through the enactment of the Federal Aid Road Act. An appropriation of $10,000,000, to become available at the rate of $1,000,000 each year, was made. This legislation constitutes one of the most important and far-reaching steps in National Forest development which has been taken for a long time.

EASTERN FORESTS.

By making provision for the continued purchase of forest lands in the East, Congress once more has recognized the permanence of the National Forest policy. Three million dollars, expendable during the fiscal years 1917 and 1918, has been made available for this work. The purchase of lands in the Appalachian and White Mountains, with a view primarily to the control of stream flow affecting the navigability of rivers, began in 1911. Under the provisions of the Weeks Forestry Act there have been approved for purchase 1,396,367 acres, at an average cost of $5.22 per acre. The lands are in excellent condition and have been secured at very reasonable prices. These newly established Forests already are rendering important public service and are being used extensively. There is a marked demand for the timber upon them. The timber is cut in accordance with sound forestry practice. The White Mountain Forest in a short time should return to the Government as much as it costs to protect and administer it.

EXCHANGE OF LANDS.

Legislative advance also has been made in the approval by Congress of several important land exchanges. There are within the National Forests some private lands which are so intimately interlocked with Government lands as to embarrass protection and administration. At the last session of Congress authority was granted for the consolidation of Government holdings through exchange with private owners whose lands are within the boundaries of the Florida National Forest and within two of the Forests in the State of Oregon. These exchanges always are made on the basis of equal value and are greatly to the interest of the Government for the permanent development of the National property. The department for several years has been working with a number of the Western States to effect a consolidation, by exchange, of school lands scattered through the Forests. In South Dakota the exchange has been partially completed, while in Idaho and Montana all the details have been agreed upon. Congress appropriated special funds for this work in Montana and Washington. Further authority is required to clear away certain legal difficulties and to permit final action. It is hoped that the measure now before Congress to secure this end will be approved.

PROGRESS IN ADMINISTRATION.

The progress made last year, both in new legislation and in the actual work of administering the Forests, is simply a continuation of the advance which has characterized each successive recent year. The public investment in its Forest work has become greater through reforestation, extensive additions to the permanent improvements, betterment of forest and range conditions resulting from the application of sound methods of management, and, perhaps most important of all, great progress toward final determination of the areas to be permanently held by the Government. Boundary rectifications since March 4, 1913, have eliminated from the Forests a total of 11,028,114 acres. The permanent retention of these areas was found to be undesirable either because of their character or because the Government holdings were too scattered for economical and efficient management. In the same period more than 886,000 acres have been opened to settlement under the Forest Homestead Act.

UNWISE LEGISLATION.

Millions of dollars, appropriated by Congress for the improvement, development, and consolidation of the Forest holdings, have gone into the properties. Only on the assumption that the Forests are to be permanent would expenditures of this character be justifiable. Abandonment of the work after it has been carried to its present point would be a stultifying course. Nevertheless, repeated efforts in this direction still are made. Measures of various kinds, which, if adopted, seriously would injure or even render ineffective the whole National Forest enterprise, are urged. The proposal that the properties be turned over in their entirety to the several States has a waning support and no longer needs to be taken seriously. On the other hand, efforts frequently are made to secure the abolition of individual Forests. Proposals to do away with the Forests in

Alaska still find strong advocates. As pointed out in my last report, such action would be unwise and unfortunate. Action of this sort, however, can be met squarely on its merits, for the question of abolishing a National Forest raises a clear-cut issue which the public can not misunderstand.

A more serious danger to the National Forest system lies in the repeated efforts to open them to the action of some general land grant or to the laws applicable to the unreserved public domain. Each year there are introduced in Congress numerous proposals designed to open the Forests, or portions of them, to private acquisition or to disposition of one kind or another. One measure of this character passed both Houses of Congress during the last session and failed to become law only through the Presidential veto. It proposed to open the Forests to the acquisition of lands by any incorporated city or town for park and cemetery purposes and to counties for park purposes. Every public purpose of the proposed measure can be realized under existing law. So serious would be the effect of such a measure that, if enacted, undoubtedly it would be necessary within a few years actually to abandon a number of important Forests. In his veto message, after explaining that the measure was entirely unnecessary and would have unfortunate public consequences, the President said:

> But the most serious objection to the bill is that it subjects the National Forests to disposition under a general grant. At the very time while provision is being made for purchase by the Government of forested lands in the East for the protection of watersheds, it is proposed to permit similar lands in the West to be permanently alienated. I would respectfully urge that it is unwise to permit alienation of the National Forests under general legislation of this sort. If the process of piecemeal distribution is begun, independently of any oversight or control of the National Government, there is manifest danger that the Forests will be so disinte-

grated as to make their efficient administration impossible and the purposes for which they were established unattainable. Against such a process the National Forests should be carefully protected.

RECREATION USE OF THE FORESTS.

The use of the National Forests for recreation purposes continues to extend. This important aspect of forest utilization was discussed at length in my last report. It is not necessary again to enlarge upon it. As the upbuilding of the West goes on and cities and towns increase in number and size, provision for community needs along what may be called park lines increasingly will become a part of National Forest administration. Thousands of local recreation centers, public picnic and camping grounds, excursion points, and amusement resorts are being developed in places readily reached by large numbers of people, as well as at the innumerable lakes, mineral and hot springs, other marvels of nature, and spots of scenic beauty with which the mountains abound. Many of these places will attract visitors from distant parts of the country and will become widely known. Some of the areas, located near enough to cities and towns to be reached by considerable numbers of persons, serve already the purpose of municipal recreation grounds and public parks. To meet local needs along this line the department is cooperating with municipalities. It welcomes opportunities for cooperation in this direction, just as it does in the protection of Forest watersheds from which municipal water supplies are derived. These forms of public service can be rendered without difficulty in connection with the fulfillment of the general purposes of the Forests.

NATIONAL FORESTS AND NATIONAL PARKS.

The handling of the National Forest recreation resources inevitably raises the question of the relation of the National Forests and the National Parks. At present there is no clear distinction in the public mind between the two. Both

are administered for the benefit of the public along lines
which overlap. The Parks and Forests occur side by side
and have the same general physical characteristics—extensive areas of wild and rugged lands, for the most part timbered, with development conditioned upon road construction
and similar provisions for public use. They differ chiefly
in the fact that the attractions of the National Parks from
the recreational standpoint are more notable. Yet this is
not always true. Several of the Parks are inferior in their
natural features to portions of the Forests. The need of
drawing a clear distinction between National Parks and
National Forests and of a definite policy governing their
relation is increasingly evident. Parks are being advocated
where the land should stay in the Forests, while elsewhere
areas which should be made Parks continue to be administered as Forests—for example, the Grand Canyon of the
Colorado.

A National Park should be created only where there are
scenic features of such outstanding importance for beauty
or as natural marvels that they merit National recognition
and protection and, on this account, have a public value
transcending that of any material resources on the same
land—such areas, for example, as those now comprised in
the Yellowstone and Yosemite Parks and in the Grand
Canyon National Monument. The areas should be large
enough to justify administration separate from the Forests
and the boundaries drawn so as not to include timber, grazing, or other resources the economic use of which is essential
to the upbuilding and industrial welfare of the country. In
addition, when Parks are created from parts of the Forests,
the portions remaining as Forests should not be left in a
form difficult or impossible to administer.

CLEAR-CUT POLICY NECESSARY.

The importance of a clear-cut policy is evidenced by the
efforts frequently made to secure the creation of National

Parks out of areas containing great bodies of timber, extensive grazing lands, and other resources, the withdrawal of which from use would be uneconomic and prejudicial to the local and general public interest. In most cases the desire for a specific Park, where economic use of the resources also is essential, has led to the proposal for an administration of the area, after the creation of the Park, identical with the present Forest administration. Several such measures now are before Congress. Their enactment would result in a mere division of the public properties into Parks and Forests, having no distinction except in name; handled alike, but by duplicate organizations in different departments. Still more serious is the fact that the cutting up of the Forests would greatly cripple administration of the remaining lands. It would doubtless mean the abandonment of large areas which should remain under public ownership and control for timber production and watershed protection. It would greatly reduce efficiency in forest fire protection and in the handling of current business, increase the expense of protection and administration, and cause endless confusion to users, who in many cases would have to deal with two departments in developing resources when, for instance, logging and grazing units overlap.

The protection of the scenic features and the development of the recreational use of the lands is being taken care of in the National Forests. Some of the most unusual scenic areas in the Forests are best suited to a full Park administration. The bulk of the Forest areas, however, should continue in their present status, where they will be fully protected and developed for recreation purposes as a part of the Forest administration. The extensive road building, made possible by the $10,000,000 recently appropriated, will open them up rapidly.

An added cause of confusion is the fact that National Parks and National Forests are administered by two executive departments. While there is an effort to cooperate, nevertheless difficulties arise which could be wholly avoided if they were under one department. Unquestionably the administration of the Forests should remain in the Department of Agriculture, because of the close relationship of the work of the Forest Service to the activities of other bureaus of the same department, such as the Bureau of Plant Industry, Bureau of Animal Industry, Office of Public Roads and Rural Engineering, Bureau of Soils, Bureau of Biological Survey, and the Bureau of Entomology. Obviously, there are in the Forests many problems relating to live stock, plant growth, predatory animal and insect control, soil conditions, and road and trail work. These great bureaus are directly and intimately concerned with these problems. If the Forests were transferred to another department, that department either would have to duplicate these bureaus in part, or would have all the difficulties of cooperation with another department which seem to be inherent. Whether the National Park Service should be transferred to the Department of Agriculture is a matter for consideration. If the transfer should be made, it would be unnecessary and, in my judgment, unwise to consolidate the work of the two services. The Park Service should take its place in the organization of the department as an independent bureau, with its activities closely related to those of the Forest Service. Certainly, if the two services are to be administered by different departments, there should be the closest cooperation throughout. Such cooperation should include not only the question of the creation of new parks out of National Forests, but also fire protection on contiguous properties, game preservation, road building, and other activities.

Respectfully,

D. F. HOUSTON,
Secretary of Agriculture.

The PRESIDENT.

MEETING THE FARMER HALFWAY.

By CARL VROOMAN,
Assistant Secretary of Agriculture.

THE Federal Department of Agriculture is not a paternalistic agency, foisted by a benevolent despotism upon an apathetic people. It was created as the result of a widespread demand among the farmers themselves for governmental cooperation and aid. The United States Agricultural Society, one of the early farmers' organizations, was largely instrumental in securing the establishment of the Department in 1862. The Granger and Farmers' Alliance movements were the chief motive powers behind the legislation that in 1889 elevated it to the first rank as an executive department.

In the same way, nearly every step in the department's development during the past 50 years, instead of being taken by Federal authorities in aniticipation of a need, has been conceded as a tardy response to the insistent demands of the farming world. It is scarcely 3 years since the Federal Government first established an office for the fostering of rural organization, yet more than 60 years ago a speaker told the New Hampshire Board of Agriculture that "the only reason why the farmers of America are without power is because they have never learned to act in concert."

It is only 3 years also since the Federal Government took its first active steps toward fostering cooperation among farmers, yet in 1858 a farmers' convention at Centralia, Ill., took a stand in favor of wholesale buying and selling agencies for farmers. Moreover, it was at this historic convention and at later farmers' conventions that was generated the public sentiment in favor of railway regulation, which finally resulted in the creation of railroad or public-utility commissions in most of our States and of the Interstate Commerce Commission at Washington.

The farm-loan act, which was passed so recently that the regional banks are still in process of organization, is a belated reaction on the part of the Federal Government to a half century's demand on the part of practically every farm organization in the United States for financial legislation that would enable the farmer to get a more adequate supply of money, on longer time, on more liberal terms of payment, and at lower rates of interest.

Indeed, in spite of all that has been done for the farmer during the past 3 or 4 years, it can not be said even at present that the Federal Government has done more than meet the farmer halfway. It has been stated that the Department of Agriculture is an example of paternalistic state socialism. Nothing could be farther from the truth. In reality it is a notable example of self-help slowly achieved by the farmer working through his Government.

Until recently the Department of Agriculture devoted its appropriations and energies almost exclusively to problems of production, in spite of the fact that the equally important problems of distribution were constantly being called to the attention of the Government by the voice of the organized farmers of the country. The history of the scientific work of the department along the line of production for the past half century is a most interesting and illuminating chronicle of brilliant achievement. During that time a total of some $250,000,000 was expended, largely in research and experiment. The results of this research and experiment in the main have been a vast accumulation of facts about how to increase the productivity of nature and of human toil. The aggregate value of this work to the Nation is practically incalculable. It may safely be said, however, that *each year's* total of money put into the farmers' pockets through insect control and live-stock disease eradication, and the introduction of new crops and better farming methods, would easily liquidate the entire cost of the department since its creation.

Take the Bureau of Entomology alone. It has been conservatively estimated that the farmers of this country are better off by at least $100,000,000 each year than they would have been if this bureau had never been created. An example of this extraordinarily useful scientific work is the case of the Australian ladybird. Found by a scientific explorer of this bureau in the antipodes, and introduced into California, it saves the citrus-fruit growers of that State many millions of dollars *each year* through the practical eradication of the fluted scale, which until its natural enemy in the form of this little spotted beetle from the southern hemisphere was found, had threatened the utter destruction of the orange industry of that region.

Another noteworthy achievement of the department has been its fight against the southern cattle tick. In the Southern States the tick has been an almost universal scourge since there have been cattle there for it to feed upon. Only recently was this tick recognized as the sole agent in spreading Texas or splenetic fever, a disease that is deadly to imported cattle and destroys large numbers of native stock commonly supposed to be immune. The effect of this discovery was to stimulate a more determined attack upon the tick. In 1906 the Federal Government quarantined 728,561 square miles of tick-infested territory, and, having secured a small appropriation of $82,500 from Congress for this purpose, began the systematic eradication of the pest. Since then over 42 per cent of this territory—an area larger than the German Empire in Europe and more than four times as big as England, has been freed from this scourge. Last year was the most successful in the history of the campaign, nearly 50,000 square miles being freed. Appropriations for this work have been gradually increased, reaching $632,000 for 1917.

Of equal importance with the campaign for tick eradication is the fight that the department has been waging against hog cholera. This disease has been known in the United States since 1833, and there is to-day no part of the country altogether free from it. In the 20-year period from 1894 to 1913 it is estimated that the annual losses have ranged from a minimum of $27,000,000 to a maximum of $78,000,000. Ninety per cent of the hogs that die from disease are destroyed by cholera.

Although the study of hog cholera, which began in 1878, resulted in 1905 in the discovery by Dr. Dorsett, of the Bureau of Animal Industry, of a serum rendering hogs immune, it was not until 1914 that any considerable sum of money was placed in the department's hands for demonstrating to the farmers at large that they could protect their herds from the scourge. In February of that year Congress appropriated $500,000 for field work and for the inspection of establishments which were manufacturing the serum and shipping it in interstate commerce. As a result, the value of anti-hog-cholera serum is becoming much more generally recognized, and the character of the serum on the market is much improved. Last year enough serum was distributed for nearly 7,000,000 hogs—between one-eighth and one-ninth of all the swine in the country.

The Bureau of Plant Industry, at a cost of about $2,000, introduced into this country the sorghum plant, which is now yielding each year a $40,000,000 crop. Durum wheat, introduced at a cost of about $30,000, now produces an annual crop estimated to be worth from $40,000,000 to $50,000,000. Kafir corn, now worth to this country $15,000,000 a year; the navel orange, worth at least $10,000,000; and that old stand-by, Fultz wheat, the present annual value of which can not well be computed—all these, together with a number of other valuable crops, were introduced into this country at comparatively small expense by the Department of Agriculture.

Moreover, many improved farm methods have been introduced by the department. "Dry farming," for example, in spite of the fact that it has not realized the early expectations of its advocates, has opened up to agriculture vast areas of semiarid country which before were given over to the sagebrush and cactus, the rattlesnake, and the prairie-dog.

In a sense, the term "dry farming" is somewhat misleading. The Department of Agriculture is teaching farmers how successfully to conserve the moisture in the soil, and it has introduced various crops which do well with a minimum of moisture. Further than that it has been unable to go without having recourse to irrigation. The present position of the department with regard to dry farming is somewhat analogous to that of a member of the Illinois Legislature, who, on being asked by a committee of the Anti-Saloon League whether he was "wet" or "dry," replied that they could put him down as "moist." In other words, the best dry farming is in reality moist farming.

Another new method relates to the use of legumes for the maintenance of soil fertility. Legumes, it has been discovered, can be grown almost anywhere, provided soil acidity is corrected by lime and the soil is inoculated with the proper bacteria. George Washington imported various legumes from Europe year after year in a futile endeavor to grow them on his farms. He failed because at that time agricultural experts in this country knew nothing about the inoculation of the soil with the legume bacteria. Now every schoolboy knows how to go to an old alfalfa field, or to the roadside where sweet clover grows, and get enough bacteria-impregnated dirt to inoculate his field and make sure of a good stand of alfalfa.

But in spite of the fact that practically all the energies of the Department of Agriculture for nearly half a century were devoted to problems of production, strangely enough a large majority of the farmers of the country have never taken advantage of the new and more efficient farm methods taught. As a matter of fact, the average yields per acre in the United States to-day are very little more than they were 50 years ago, as shown in the following table:

Average yield per acre, United States, bushels by decade.

Crop.	1907–1916	1866–1875
Wheat	14.7	11.9
Corn	26.0	26.1
Oats	29.6	28.1

The slowness of this increase in production has been partly the farmers' fault and partly the fault of the department. The publicity work of the department long left much to be desired. Until recently many of our bulletins have been too technical and academic, rather than simple and practical. To men having a scientific education they were splendidly suggestive and helpful, but they were not so written that the average farmer could derive much benefit from them. Thus while each of the older bureaus of the department had many years of honest and invaluable research work to its credit, but comparatively little had been done, until during the past few years, toward putting the results of the work of the department's scientific men before the farmer properly condensed, correlated, and couched in terms easily understood.

Further, much of the information published on vitally important practical problems was scattered about in so many bulletins as to be entirely un-get-at-able by the average farmer. In order to secure the necessary information for a reorganization of his system of farming, he was required to read a score or so more or less technical bulletins, extract the practical instruction from them, and coordinate it for himself.

Moreover, what is good farm practice at the Arlington Experiment Station is not necessarily good farm practice throughout the country; indeed what is good farm practice at a State experiment station is not necessarily good farm practice even throughout that State. Heretofore the Federal department had not worked out and popularized among the farmers regional systems of scientific and successful farm practice for the great agricultural subdivisions of the Nation, nor had the State agricultural colleges been much more successful in working out and popularizing special systems adapted to the various localities in the several States.

This matter of adapting the teachings of the department and the colleges to local conditions is one of the most difficult problems that the apostles of the new agriculture have had to meet. The fact that this problem was not met and solved sooner is what has given rise to most of the prejudice felt by farmers throughout the country against scientific farming. Fortunately this problem is beginning to be more effectively handled by Federal and State agricultural agencies working through the county agent system which is rapidly spreading over the whole Nation.

While the demonstration method of promulgating new methods had been tested previously and successfully employed over a considerable area, it yet had had no Nationwide application, and was inadequately supported. However, the value of teaching by direct touch having been clearly proved, so commended itself to Congress that the agricultural extension act was passed in 1914. When this act is in full operation it should be possible, through Federal, State, and local funds, to place two county agents in each of the 2,850 rural counties of the Nation.

As a rule a county agent is a man who has been born and raised on a farm, has studied at an agricultural college, and has had experience with the practical application to actual farm conditions of scientific methods. He is a representative of the Federal Department of Agriculture and the State agricultural college. He studies local soil conditions, climatic conditions, marketing conditions, labor conditions, and credit conditions. Working in conjunction with the best farmers in his county and keeping in constant touch with the experts of the State agricultural college and of the Federal department, he gradually discovers how the teachings of the new agriculture can best be adapted to existing conditions on the individual farms of that county.

This county-agent movement is the greatest and most practical university extension movement ever inaugurated in any country. It is essentially nothing but learning democratized, learning brought out of the laboratory and the experiment field, out of the libraries and the bulletins, adapted to local conditions, and brought home to the farmer by the power of personal explanation and of actual demonstration.

I was told the other day by a banker from central New York that in two short years one of our county agents, located in his county, had done more for the farmers of that county than the entire Department of Agriculture and the State agricultural colleges had done for them during the 50 years preceding. This same wonder is being worked to-day in over 1,200 counties in this country—and the Smith-Lever bill is not yet 3 years old.

The county-agent force might well be compared to a system of irrigation ditches, tapping reservoirs of agricultural information which have been accumulating during a long half century in the Federal Department of Agriculture and in the State agricultural colleges. Through the county agents, at last this stored treasure is being carried directly to those who need it, working a miracle similar to that which makes the desert bloom.

Another instance of the very practical aid given by the county agent is the experience of an old Maine farmer who had lived to be 70 years old without ever having made more than a bare living on his hundred-acre farm. The land had been cropped to death. His sons, discouraged by the prospect, left home and went to work in the city. In due time one of these sons, having saved $2,000, came home and undertook to make the old place pay. He asked the county agent what he should do, and learned a new wrinkle about real farming.

The farm was worth on the market about $20 an acre. When the county agent told him that the first move was to spend $40 an acre for fertilizer it took his breath away, but he followed the county agent's advice on 17½ acres. From this small field that fall he sold $4,600 worth of potatoes. Deducting all expense, including that hitherto unheard-of fertilizer bill, the profit from his potatoes was $2,600. When he handed his father $1,300 as his half of the returns the old man said that he had never before seen that much money made from farming.

What that boy did any intelligent farmer in that section might do in a favorable year if he had as much cash to buy fertilizer with as that boy had. The new Federal farm-loan act will help our farmers to get the cash, and the new system of county agents that is being developed throughout the country will furnish practical and detailed instructions, so that henceforth a man need not live 70 years before he learns how to cash in his agricultural " chips " of land, labor, and experience.

Even more important than recent improvements in the department's methods of adapting agricultural information to local conditions, and of disseminating that information among the farmers, is the creation in 1913 of the Office of Markets and Rural Organization. The creation of this office was an innovation of epoch-making significance. Ever since the department was started the farmers of the country have been requesting the Government to help them solve their economic problems, have been urging the utter hopelessness of the attempt to build a successful agriculture upon the doctrine of increased production, without regard to the equally important problems of marketing and distribution. But owing to the mistaken theory that everybody is interested in increasing agricultural production, while nobody but the farmer is interested in making that production profitable, until recently no important attempt was made by Congress, by the agricultural colleges, or by the Federal Department of Agriculture to help the farmer solve his financial and economic problems. Indeed, the history of farm organizations in this country up to 1912 was the history of a long-drawn-out and unsuccessful effort on the part of the farmers to secure for themselves that governmental cooperation and help which governments were instituted among men to give to all citizens.

In the Middle West the dark seventies and eighties, which gave rise to the Granger movement, the Farmers' Alliance movement, and the Populist movement, were decades that tried men's souls. We who were boys on the plains in those days can well remember how grave were the problems that the farmers faced and how hopeless was the outlook for those who happened to be caught at an economic disadvantage. I remember reading when I was a small boy a little poem that greatly impressed me. It was entitled "The Mortgage." It was only a bit of fugitive verse, now long forgotten, but it expressed more poignantly than anything else I have ever read something that was then vital enough— the tragedy and pathos of the losing struggle which so many men and women were making out there in those days of high interest and cheap corn.

It used to seem to us that the blind forces of nature and the malevolent powers of human greed had conspired against us. Every few years the grasshoppers would sweep down in clouds and devour all our substance. Every now and then, too, there would come a drought that would ruin our crops. I have seen corn as beautiful as eye ever looked upon—green and fresh and high as a man's head—burned to a crisp within 48 hours by the hot winds from the southwest. Luckily, that happened only once in a while. But every year and all the time we had the mortgage hanging over us, embittering the very well-springs of life. It has been said—and I think with good reason—that more midland farmers' wives died of mortgage during those trying years than of tuberculosis and cancer together, and that more farmers' wives were sent to the madhouse by mortgage than by all other causes. The wrongs that drove the farmers to political revolt were real enough, and the agrarian legislation demanded and sneeringly stigmatized by its opponents as "hayseed socialism" was inspired by long decades of urgent need.

Of the early fruits of this movement the most significant were the so-called "granger laws," passed in several of the corn-belt States during the late sixties and early seventies. These laws in the main were short lived, but in the end they served to establish the principle of railroad regulation in State and Nation, and to bring about the creation of railroad and public-utility commissions in our various States and the powerful Interstate Commerce Commission at Washington. Unfortunately, however, no such concrete and beneficial effects on the farmers' other vital economic problems resulted from this movement.

It is true that some of the specific remedies demanded by the farmers were impractical, but these were mere details. Their basic demands were just. The evils they pointed out so insistently and at times so eloquently were real evils, and it is an amazing thing that during this long period our statesmen at Washington should have failed to grasp this fact and to devise some sound and effective substitutes for the unsatisfactory remedies suggested in all good faith by the organized farmers of the Nation.

During the past 4 years, for the first time in our history, Congress and the Department of Agriculture have persistently and intelligently conceived the economic phases of agriculture and have made a determined and consistent effort to find scientific and workable solutions for the farmer's most pressing financial and economic problems.

In addition to the creation of the Office of Markets and Rural Organization, a number of laws have been passed which are of immense economic importance to the farmer. Probably the most important one of these laws is that financial magna charta of the farmer, the farm-loan act. This is the first great financial measure ever passed by Congress primarily in the interest of the farmer. I have no doubt that in the future it will be strengthened by amendments with regard to some of its minor details, as was the Federal reserve bill, but in all fairness it must be recognized that this bill will do for the farmer very much what the Federal reserve act is doing for the business man. It will furnish the farmer with those fundamental necessities that he has been asking for, voting for, and praying for during the past half century:

First. More adequate credit facilities; or, in other words, capital in sufficient quantities and capital that is always available for the farmers' legitimate needs. Frequently in the past the time when the farmer needed money most was precisely the time when, because industrial and speculative centers were able to outbid him for it, it was most difficult or even impossible to secure it.

Second. Loans on longer time and easier terms of payment.

Third. Lower rates of interest.

These are the three most important financial needs of the farmer, and the present farm-loan act will supply these three primary financial necessities of rural life.

The United States grain-standards act of August 11, 1916, which seems destined to work a gradual reformation in our system of marketing grain, is another of these measures so pregnant of promise to the farmers. This act will stimulate the production of the best quality of grain. This will be an advantage not only to the farmer, but as well to the middle-man and to the consumer. No one will be interfered with save the man who wants to get a No. 1 grade of grain for a No. 4 price. The effect of this law on our foreign commerce in grain is certain in the long run to be very much to our advantage. It is a step in the direction of National efficiency and National economic preparedness.

Another of these measures is the bonded warehouse act of August 11, 1916, which was passed in response to a demand on the part of the farmers for a mechanism that would enable them to borrow money more easily and at a lower rate of interest on stored crops. In the past, when the bankers had plenty of money, those farmers with abundant credit usually could secure what money they needed at a reasonable rate of interest. The new method enables the farmer, no matter what his standing may be at his local bank, if he has a valuable crop, to store it and secure a bonded warehouse receipt, upon which he will be able to secure money at the lowest current rate of interest, either at the local bank or at any other bank that loans money on this kind of gilt-edged security. By eliminating the bankers' risk, and enlarging the field in which loans may be negotiated, interest rates to farmers are certain to be cut to the current standard figure.

The Federal aid road act of July 11, 1916, is the first comprehensive Federal good-roads law ever passed, and should also be cited in this connection. At last we are beginning to work out a National highway policy that coordinates the road work of the township, the county, the State, and the Nation into a single comprehensive National plan. As a result, a higher degree of efficiency henceforth will characterize our road work, and the farmer at last will get a dollar's worth of road for every dollar of taxes devoted to that end. This will be a new experience, for although we are spending in the United States anywhere from $200,-000,000 to $250,000,000 a year on roads, it is doubtful if we are getting more than from two-thirds to three-fourths of that amount in value. This is a matter of vital interest to every farmer, for the farmer pays no heavier tax than that of the effort expended by him while hauling his produce to markets over bad roads.

The cotton-futures act of August 11, 1916, is still another beneficent act in behalf of the farmer. Without going into details, it can be said that as a result of this law the Government is gradually eliminating the abuses which had crept into the cotton-future exchanges. The effect of this measure was immediate. The American cotton-future exchanges at once adopted the form of contract prescribed by the Secretary of Agriculture, and not only the exchanges, but the more important domestic spot markets, at once adopted the official cotton standards established. The net result has been that the prices of cotton which now are published every day throughout the country reflect the actual changes in the value of cotton rather than quotations of arbitrary fluctuations created by gamblers for their own benefit, as was too often the case in the past.

It is clear that as a result of this splendid program of constructive legislation a new agricultural epoch has begun. At last what for so long was merely the hope, the aspiration, the dream of the widely scattered, imperfectly organized tillers of our soil has become the avowed policy of the Federal Department of Agriculture, and has been written by Congress into the law of the land.

All the farmers' legitimate demands have not yet been granted. There is indeed still need for organized effort on their part, still need for educational campaigns in behalf of measures to meet those requirements of the farmer which still remain unsatisfied. But it is a great thing that the Federal Government at last is meeting the farmer at least halfway and has manifested not merely a willingness but a friendly desire to cooperate with him in the future in any constructive work that looks to the building up of our national prosperity on the basis of a permanently prosperous agriculture.

THE MEAT-INSPECTION SERVICE OF THE UNITED STATES DEPARTMENT OF AGRICULTURE.

By GEORGE DITEWIG,

Meat Inspection Division, Bureau of Animal Industry.

THE purpose of the meat-inspection service of the United States Department of Agriculture is to eliminate diseased or otherwise bad meat from the general food supply; to see that the preparation of the meats and products passed for human consumption is cleanly; to guard against the use of harmful dyes, preservatives, chemicals, or other deleterious ingredients; and to prevent the use of false or misleading names or statements on labels; in short, to protect the rights and health of the consumers of meat and meat food products to the fullest extent possible under the laws. The service is administered through the Bureau of Animal Industry of the department.

MEAT-INSPECTION LAWS AND REGULATIONS.

Federal inspection is maintained under the meat-inspection act of June 30, 1906, and supplementary legislation in the tariff act of October 3, 1913. Space will not permit giving an outline of the different provisions of the act of June 30, 1906; however, it is essential to an understanding of the scope of the service that the reader know that the food animals to which the law refers are cattle, sheep, swine, and goats, and that the slaughtering, packing, rendering, and meat-preparing establishments to which it applies are those which sell or ship their products in whole or in part in interstate or foreign commerce, and that it does not apply to those establishments the meats and products of which are neither sold nor shipped outside the confines of the State in which the plant is operated. Further, the act grants a qualified exemption from inspection to retail dealers supplying their customers, and also provides a similar exemption for the meat from farm-slaughtered animals. The tariff legislation referred to provides inspection for imported meats and products.

The meat-inspection regulations of the department for governing the service are clear and comprehensive and embody the recommendations of scientists and hygienists outside of the department as well as the judgment and experience of administrative officials and workers in the service as to what constitutes an efficient system of inspection and how best to attain the objects of the law. Copies of the regulations may be had free upon application to the Bureau of Animal Industry.

APPLYING FOR INSPECTION.

The proprietor or operator of an establishment of the kind which the law requires be operated under inspection must file an application and submit triplicate copies of plans and specifications of the plant. The plans are referred to the architect of the bureau to see whether the structure and arrangement conform to certain important requirements of the regulations. In addition, a qualified representative of the bureau is assigned to make a detailed inspection of the establishment to ascertain what sanitary additions or corrections must be made to place the plant in satisfactory condition, and to decide what facilities shall be provided to enable a ready and proper conduct of the inspection. Inspection is not inaugurated until a satisfactory compliance with the sanitary requirements is shown and proper facilities for the conduct of the inspection are provided.

GRANTING INSPECTION, OFFICIAL NUMBER.

Each establishment to which inspection is granted is given an official number. This number identifies the plant, and must appear in every instance as a part of the mark of inspection; that is, the mark or statement used on meats and products, or the containers thereof, to show that they have been inspected and passed under the Federal meat-inspection regulations. So long as the mark remains intact the number identifies the product wherever found. Further, with the granting of inspection and the assigning of an official number, a sufficient force of inspectors is detailed to the establishment to perform the inspections and enforce the regulations under the direction of an inspector in charge. For convenience the establishments which operate under Federal meat inspection are called " official establishments."

SANITATION.

The requirements as to sanitation in the establishments that operate under inspection occupy an important place in the meat-inspection regulations. Prior to 1906 the Secretary of Agriculture was without authority to fix and enforce such requirements, but when it was conferred by the meat-inspection act of that year the department proceeded to enforce sanitation in all establishments operated under Federal inspection. The first step taken was to require strict cleanliness as regards the rooms and equipment and in respect to the conduct of operations and the handling of products, and the second was to adopt rules governing plant and equipment construction.

The first part of the program, that is, strict cleanliness, was soon attained in the plants of good construction, and in as full a measure as could rightly be expected in those of the type of construction common to that period. As regards the second, it was apparent from the beginning that conformity with a certain type of construction must be had if good sanitary conditions were to be readily and surely maintained throughout the plants. Accordingly it was aimed to attain this quality in all plants by leading to the use of non-absorbent materials instead of the absorbent ones which had been so freely used in previous construction; to replace rough and pervious surfaces with smooth and impervious ones; to supplant artificial light with abundant natural light; to replace odor-laden air with fresh air wherever possible; to eliminate incomplete and defective systems of drainage and plumbing and to install such as are modern and effective; to require that sanitary and adequate dressing rooms, toilets, and lavatories be installed; to subject the water supply to the test of laboratory analysis to insure its purity; and to require a separation of the rooms and equipment used for edible products from those used for inedible materials. These improvements indicate the rules adopted by the department to mark the reform in plant and equipment construction. It is believed that the progress made has been excellent.

THE ANTE-MORTEM INSPECTION.

Under the Federal system not less than two examinations are made of the animals slaughtered in official establishments. The first is the ante-mortem inspection or examination of the live animal, the second the post-mortem inspection or examination of the carcass and the various organs and parts at the time of slaughter. The post-mortem is the more valuable of the two inspections, but both are necessary if it is to be determined with certainty in every instance that the flesh of the animal is sound, wholesome, and fit for human food.

The ante-mortem inspection is performed in the pens and alleys of the official establishments, except that at most of the large slaughtering centers it is found more convenient to conduct it in the public stockyards. The animals are carefully observed for evidence of disease or abnormal condition while at rest in the pens or as they move from the scales after weighing. If any of a lot show symptoms, then the entire lot is subjected to further and individual inspection. If the animals are swine and the symptoms indicate cholera, they are driven to a special pen for further examination and in certain cases to ascertain their temperatures and to make a record of the same. Other diseases or conditions in which the question of temperature is important are Texas fever, anthrax, blackleg, pneumonia, septicemia, and severe injuries. When a high temperature exists and there is doubt as to its cause, the affected animal is marked and may be held for observation and retaking of temperature.

FIG. 1.—" U. S. Suspect " tag. This kind of tag is affixed to the ear of live animals suspected of being diseased. Such animals are held for separate and special post-mortem examination.

When its appearance is such as to lead the inspector to suspect that an animal is affected with a disease or condition that may cause its condemnation in whole or in part on the post-mortem inspection, it is marked for identification by means of a serially numbered metal tag bearing the phrase " U. S. Suspect " affixed to the ear. Such an animal is termed a "suspect." A record of the tag number, the in-

FIG. I.—ANTE-MORTEM INSPECTION OF CATTLE.

All animals slaughtered at official establishments are first inspected alive. Those which are suspected of being diseased are marked for separate and special post-mortem examination.

FIG. 2.—ANTE-MORTEM INSPECTION OF SHEEP.

FIG. I.—CATTLE SLAUGHTER ROOM.

Abundant light, adequate ventilation, efficient drainage, metal and other impervious materials and smooth surfaces mark the construction of the sanitary slaughter room.

FIG. 2.—POST-MORTEM INSPECTION OF SWINE.

The first step in this inspection is to cut and examine for evidence of tuberculosis the lymph glands of the neck. The figure indicated by X is an inspector making this examination.

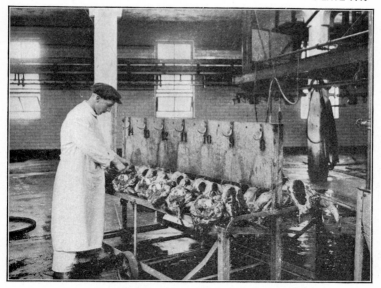

FIG. 1.—POST-MORTEM INSPECTION OF CATTLE HEADS.

The different pairs of lymph glands are cut and examined, particularly for tuberculosis, and the cheek muscles cut for detection of tapeworm cysts; the tongue and other parts also are carefully examined.

FIG. 2.—POST-MORTEM INSPECTION OF CATTLE.

As the several organs and parts are removed from the carcass they are placed before an inspector for complete and careful examination. The X indicates the veterinary inspector making this examination.

FIG. 1.—POST-MORTEM INSPECTION OF SWINE.

Immediately after their removal the organs are placed before the inspectors for examination

FIG. 2.—POST-MORTEM INSPECTION OF SHEEP.

The X indicates an inspector examining organs.

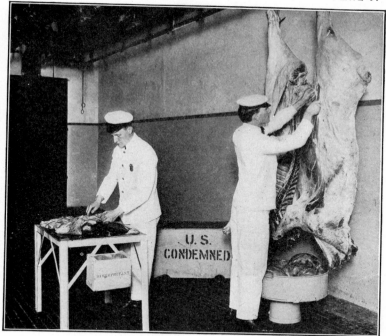

FIG. I.—POST-MORTEM INSPECTION OF CATTLE.
Illustrating the detail observed in the performance of the final post-mortem inspection.

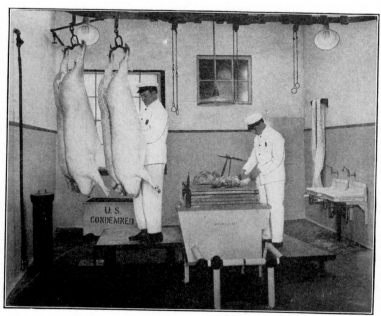

FIG. 2.—POST-MORTEM INSPECTION OF SWINE.
Illustrating the detail observed in the examination of retained swine.

FIG. I.—POST-MORTEM INSPECTION OF CATTLE.
If disease is present a detailed record is made of the conditions found.

FIG. 2.—POST-MORTEM INSPECTION OF SWINE.
After the head, organs, and other parts have been inspected and passed the carcass is carefully examined. The inspector performing this inspection is indicated by an X.

Fig. I.—Branding Hog and Cattle Carcasses.

The passed carcasses are marked with an abbreviation of the legend "U. S. Inspected
and Passed" and the official number of the establishment by means of an ink brand.
The ink used is composed of approved ingredients.

Fig. 2.—Sheep Chill Room.

"U. S. Inspected and Passed" mutton.

FIG. I.—MEAT-CURING CELLAR.

The curing of meats is supervised and the product inspected.

FIG. 2.—DRY SALT CURING CELLAR.

Government inspection and supervision of handling meats cured in dry salt.

spector's diagnosis, and of the animal's temperature, if that was ascertained, is made and sent to the inspector who is to conduct the post-mortem inspection. This information is given due weight by him in determining the final disposition of the animal. Suspects are kept apart and slaughtered separately from those which were passed on the ante-mortem inspection.

Animals which show symptoms of rabies, tetanus, milk fever, or railroad sickness, and hogs which are plainly sick with hog cholera, are condemned on the ante-mortem inspection. Such animals are marked by means of a serially numbered " U. S. Condemned " metal tag affixed to the ear. Animals so tagged may not be taken into the slaughter room, but must be destroyed and disposed of as required for condemned carcasses to prevent their use for food. Animals which are found dead or

Fig. 2.—" U. S. Condemned " tag. This tag is affixed to the ear of an animal condemned on the ante-mortem inspection.

in a dying condition on the premises of an establishment are condemned and disposed of in the same manner.

THE POST-MORTEM INSPECTION.

Each of the successive examinations, extending from the live animal to the finished meat food product, serves some particular purpose and has a relative value in a complete system of meat inspection. Omission of certain of the other examinations would result in some, though not vital, impairment of the service as a whole, but the post-mortem inspection is indispensable because its chief purpose is to detect disease and to eliminate the danger that threatens the consumer on this account. Further proof of its importance lies in the fact that aside from certain exceptional conditions it is not possible for even an expert to recognize or prove the presence of disease or the effects of disease by an examination of the meat alone after it has been cut from the carcass, but he can do so through a proper examination of the whole carcass together with the organs. Before entering upon a description of the post-mortem inspection procedures the meaning of the word " disease " as it is used in meat inspection should receive some explanation.

MEANING OF " DISEASE " IN MEAT.

The meaning of the term " disease " as used in meat inspection does not differ materially from the meaning given it in medical literature, and never in meat inspection is the seriousness of disease underestimated. There is, however, much popular misconception in regard to the nature of the different conditions to which the term is applied in discussing meat inspection. The common or popular error on this point arises from the broad assumption that every condition to which the term disease is applied is noxious and harmful to such a degree as to make unsafe or unfit for food all the flesh of an animal in which any of these conditions is found. The facts of pathology plainly refute such assumption. By using the microscope and laboratory tests and by applying the term in its most technical meanings, a pathologist could demonstrate disease or evidence of disease in any and every food animal that might be submitted for examination. But no pathologist would hold such demonstration to be proof that the flesh of every such animal is unsafe or unfit for human food.

The error in the popular conception might be more clearly shown by the use of a homely illustration or two: The peach or the pear with a small unsound spot, strictly speaking, is an unsound fruit, but with the spot cut away it may certainly be a sound and delicious article of food. So also with a bunch of grapes, some of which may be in bad condition while the others may be sweet and wholesome. Similarly, any one of certain diseases may exist in a circumscribed area or part of an animal. A clear illustration of this is the disease commonly called " lumpy jaw " of cattle. In many instances the tumor on the jaw attains a considerable size. Nevertheless, in very many such cases the disease is as distinctly localized as is the unsound spot on the pear, and aside from the affected part the flesh of the animal may be absolutely clean and wholesome. To carry the illustration further, in meat inspection tuberculosis is encountered far more frequently than is any other disease, and great care is exercised to detect its presence in even the minutest degree.

In a very considerable proportion of the cases found the lesions are confined to one or to a small number of the visceral lymphatic glands, or they may exist to a slight degree in an organ and in some of the lymph glands. An animal so affected is diseased, and yet in that form of the disease the lesions are so limited in number and so completely localized and hemmed in by encapsulating tissues, built up by the protective forces of the body, that the affected tissues are as distinct from the remainder of the animal economy as are the bad grapes from the good ones. With the bad ones removed the bunch becomes good food, and likewise the meat of this class of tuberculous animals must be regarded as sound and wholesome when the affected parts have been carefully removed.

The foregoing comparisons are used merely to illustrate the point that soundness and unsoundness may exist in the body at the same time in varying proportion, and that as a rule it is possible to separate and treat each portion according to its condition. In short, the point can be made clear by discarding the word "disease" for the moment and saying that the function of a scientific and rational meat inspection is to recognize and reject the meat or meat food product which is unsafe or unfit for human food, to pass that which is wholesome and fit, and, when doubt exists as to which of these conditions obtains, to resolve that doubt in favor of the consumer.

PROCEDURES.

The post-mortem inspection is made at the time of slaughter and includes a careful examination of the carcass and all its parts. Where the number of animals dressed per hour does not exceed a certain general limit, one inspector, constantly present, performs all the inspections. Where the number of inspections per hour exceeds certain general limits, the inspectors are increased accordingly and the work so arranged and coordinated that each inspector gives his entire attention to some particular part of it. Thus the work is in a sense specialized and the inspectors become specialists, with the result that a high individual and collective proficiency is attained and efficient inspection assured regardless of the rate of slaughter.

An important requirement in the conduct of this inspection is that the identity of the carcass and of each of its severed parts be carefully maintained until the inspection is completed, so that if there is disease in any one organ or part all the other parts and the carcass may be brought together for additional and final examination. Facilities for maintaining such identity are provided in the slaughter departments, and every inspector is supplied with serially numbered "U. S. Retained" tags, which he affixes to

the carcass and severed parts, and by means of which he retains them for the additional inspection. The different steps of the postmortem inspection are: Head inspection, viscera inspection, carcass inspection, final inspection, disposition, and marking.

FIG. 3.—"U. S. Retained" tag. This tag is affixed by the inspector to every carcass or product which he deems necessary to hold for further inspection.

HEAD INSPECTION.

In cattle heads the different pairs of lymphatic glands are cut into and examined, particularly for tuberculosis. The tongue is examined and, if necessary, is cut into. The presence in the flesh of cattle of a certain cyst capable of producing tapeworm in man can usually be determined by examining the inner and outer cheek muscles. Therefore, these muscles of cattle are laid open by deep slicing cuts for the detection of this cyst. A careful survey is made of the head as a whole for actinomycosis, deformities, etc. In the heads of swine certain lymphatic glands, which are favorite seats of tuberculosis, are incised in every instance and examined for evidence of that disease.

INSPECTION OF VISCERA.

As the several organs are removed from the carcass they are placed before the inspector, on a table, in pans or other suitable metal receptacles for examination. Facilities for promptly cleansing such equipment in the event of contamination through the contact of diseased viscera are at hand. The various organs and parts are carefully viewed and certain of them cut into while others are subjected to manual as well as visual examination. The entire procedure is methodical and designed to disclose disease or harmful condition if any exists in the parts under examination.

CARCASS INSPECTION.

This examination embraces a careful viewing of all surfaces and parts of the carcass, with particular attention given to the condition of the serous membranes of thoracic and abdominal cavities. Further, certain parts which more frequently than others are seats of disease are subjected to a manual as well as a visual examination.

The head, viscera, and carcass examinations together constitute the regular post-mortem inspection. The animals found to be free from disease or any doubtful condition are marked " Inspected and Passed," while those in which any disease or doubtful condition is found are retained for the final inspection.

THE FINAL POST-MORTEM INSPECTION.

The carcasses and parts retained on the regular inspection are sent to the final inspection room or place, where another inspector with special facilities at his command subjects them to a searching examination. This enables the inspectors engaged in the preliminary and regular inspections to continue their examinations of the animals which are before them without delay and without omission of any kind. The establishments in which slaughtering is done are required to provide these rooms or places for the final inspection and to equip them with all the facilities necessary for a ready, cleanly, sanitary, and efficient performance of the work.

Since the animals held for the final inspection are tagged or retained for cause, only veterinary inspectors who have become skilled through training and experience in the work are detailed to make such examinations and to determine the final dispositions. As indicating the detail observed in the conduct of this inspection, it need only be mentioned that a record is made, on appropriate forms, of the results of the examination of every animal showing disease in any degree. In this record the animal is identified by a tag or stamp number; the diagnosis and the nature, location, and extent of the lesions are indicated; and the disposition of the carcasses and the name of the inspector are shown. The final inspection reports for the last fiscal year preceding this writing alone contain a record covering approximately 3,500,000 retained animals.

As soon as the several examinations have been made and the dispositions determined, there remain two important acts, the performance of which completes the post-mortem inspection. They are the marking of each carcass to show plainly to every beholder the disposition made of it and to see that those carcasses and parts which are condemned are disposed of as required by the meat-inspection regulations to prevent the sale or use of the same as human food. Each of these procedures will be briefly described.

DISPOSITION OF CONDEMNED CARCASSES, MEATS, AND PRODUCTS.

The Federal meat-inspection regulations governing the disposal of condemned articles emphasizes three important requirements, strict observance of which is imposed upon every bureau employee whose duties relate in any way to their enforcement: First, that every condemned carcass, part of carcass, meat, or product be plainly marked to show that it is condemned, and that parts or products too small or which are of such nature that they can not be so marked be placed in appropriately marked containers; second, that all condemned articles shall remain in the custody of an inspector from the time they are condemned until properly disposed of, and that if the articles are not disposed of on the day they are condemned they shall be locked in the " U. S. Condemned " rooms or compartments, the locks of which are selected and supplied by the department and the keys of which remain in the custody of the inspector; and third, that the required destruction or denaturing of the condemned articles shall be done by the establishment in the presence of an inspector, who must render a report covering the transaction. The meat-inspection act specifically provides that the Secretary of Agriculture may withhold inspection from any establishment which fails to destroy for food purposes any condemned carcass or part thereof.

The customary method of treating condemned carcasses and parts is to convert them into grease and fertilizer by rendering them in a steam-pressure tank. The procedure as outlined and practiced under the Federal meat-inspection regulations is substantially as follows: The lower opening of the tank is securely sealed by an inspector with seals supplied by the department for the purpose; then the condemned articles and a sufficient quantity of denaturing material of a kind approved by the department is placed in the tank in the inspector's presence, after which the upper opening is also sealed, and it remains the duty of the inspector to see that a sufficient force of steam is turned into the tank and maintained a sufficient time effectually to destroy the contents for food purposes. The department seals on the tank may be broken only by an inspector. A small number of the establishments at which Federal meat inspection is maintained do not have steam-pressure tanks in which condemned meats may be denatured in the manner described. At these such meats and products are denatured by the addition of crude carbolic acid or other prescribed denaturing agent, or are destroyed by incineration.

THE PRODUCTS INSPECTION.

Because meat or other edible portion of an animal which was entirely sound and wholesome at the time of slaughter may become unsound or contaminated through improper care or handling, and because healthful products may be made unwholesome through adulteration or the addition of deleterious ingredients, and for the purpose of protecting the purchaser against false or misleading labels, a proper measure of control of the various operations of processing, preparing, and labeling meats and products becomes necessary. Such control is one of the functions of the Federal inspection. In other words, under the Federal system of the inspection extends from the live animal in the pen to the product in the labeled package. The bureau employees who conduct the products inspection are designated "lay inspectors" and are selected for their practical knowledge and experience in the handling and preparation of meats and meat food products; also for their skill in testing and passing on these articles as to soundness and fitness for food.

All the meats and products in official establishments, notwithstanding that they were previously inspected and passed, are reinspected as often as may be necessary to ascertain whether they remain sound and wholesome. The lay inspectors exercise a supervision over all such operations as the processing, curing, packing, marking, labeling, and shipping of meats and products. The materials added to products are examined to see that the regulations relating to prohibited ingredients are observed and that the requirements as to correctness of labeling are complied with. Samples of the different kinds of products are taken and referred to the meat-inspection laboratories for chemical or other technical examination. It

FIG. 4.—Facsimile of inspection brand. Brand used for marking carcasses, parts, and products to show that the same have been inspected and passed. The ciphers in the above imprint occupy the place reserved for the official number of the establishment.

is also the duty of the lay inspectors to see that the requirements of the regulations in regard to the cleanly and sanitary handling of products and as to the sanitary condition of the rooms and equipment are observed.

If upon reinspection of an article it is found to have become unfit for food from any cause, the original inspection mark or label thereon is removed or defaced and the article condemned.

THE INSPECTION MARKS, INSCRIPTIONS, ETC.

The mark of inspection is to identify the article and to show the condition of any particular carcass, meat, or product at the time the mark was applied. Under the Federal system, similar to that of the best European systems of meat inspection, three dispositions of a carcass are possible on the post-mortem inspection, depending on the conditions found. First, a carcass may be passed without restriction, meaning that when passed it was healthful, wholesome, and fit for

FIG. 1.—MANUFACTURE OF SAUSAGE.

All meats, spices, and casings used are inspected and the different steps of preparation supervised.

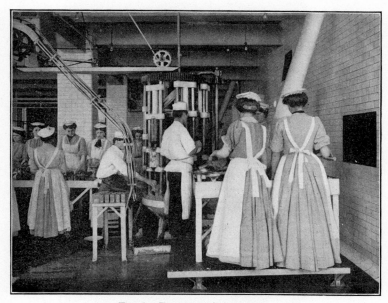

FIG. 2.—PRODUCTS INSPECTION.

Canning room scene. Filling and weighing cans.

FIG. 1.—PRODUCTS INSPECTION.
Inspection of smoked meats before they are wrapped and packed for shipment.

FIG. 2.—INSPECTING SMOKED HAMS.
The instrument in the inspector's hand is a steel "trier" used to test meats for soundness.

FIG. I.—PRODUCTS INSPECTION.

Inspection of fresh meats at car door. At official establishments inspection extends from the live animal to the meats and products as they are shipped from the plant.

FIG. 2.—SEALED RENDERING TANK.

The animals, meats, and products condemned under Federal inspection are rendered into grease and fertilizer. The Government seals on rendering tanks may be broken only in the presence of an inspector.

human food. Such a carcass is marked "U. S. Inspected and Passed," or an authorized abbreviation thereof. The official number of the establishment always appears as a part of such mark and serves to identify the carcass or part as having been inspected and passed at the establishment of that number. Second, a carcass or a part thereof may be condemned, meaning that it is unsafe or unfit for human food; therefore it must be destroyed or denatured to prevent its sale or use as human food. Such a carcass or part is marked "U. S. Condemned" and remains in the custody of an inspector until properly disposed of. Third, a carcass or a part thereof may be marked "Passed for Sterilization," meaning that it was passed on condition that it be rendered into lard or tallow, according to the species, or otherwise sterilized by methods approved by the Chief of the Bureau of Animal Industry. The explanation of this procedure is that the animal was affected with some condition

U. S. INSP'D AND CONDEMNED

Fig. 5.—"Condemned Brand." Used for marking condemned carcasses, parts, and products.

or disease in such a degree that it could not be passed unconditionally; nevertheless, all objectionable conditions and all doubt as to its safety and fitness for human food can be removed by subjecting it to a sterilizing process. This process is to meat somewhat as pasteurization is to milk. There is, however, on the side of sterilization the advantage of greater certainty in the attainment of its object because of the higher temperatures employed under this process.

The flesh of a carcass passed for sterilization, whether it be in the form of a cut, such as a ham, or a prepared product like canned meats, is marked "Prepared from Meat Passed for Sterilization." The container of such cut or product also bears this inscription.

Whenever it is possible to so apply it, the mark of inspection is stamped upon the carcass, cuts, and products themselves by means of a rubber or metal ink brand. In all cases the ink used is composed of approved ingredients. Occasionally burning brands are used for imprinting the mark on cured meats, such as hams, bacon, and similar articles. When it is not possible to affix the mark to the article itself, the required inscription is placed on the container of the article; in fact, all containers of inspected and passed meats and meat food products bear the inspection legend in the form of a printed label. The legend for all labels is "U. S. Inspected and Passed under act of Congress, June 30, 1906," or " U. S. Inspected and Passed by Department of Agriculture," or authorized abbreviation. The last quoted is the preferred form, and after July 15, 1917, will be the only one approved for labels printed after that date. Other marks of inspection, chiefly marks of convenience in the conduct of the inspection, are used, but those which have been described are the only ones in which the consumer is likely to feel concerned.

Consumers owe it to themselves to look for the mark of an efficient inspection, whether Federal, State, or municipal, on the meats and meat food products they buy, or on the containers of the same, but in doing so they should consider that the mark can not insure perishable foods against deterioration or other unfavorable change after they have been shipped from an establishment and beyond the jurisdiction of the inspection.

HONEST LABELS REQUIRED.

The legend "Inspected and Passed" means that the meat or product was sound, wholesome, and fit for human food when it was so marked; also that the packed article was correctly labeled. The meat-inspection act provides that when the inspected and passed meat or product is packed in any can, pot, tin, canvas, or other receptacle or covering, the establishment shall cause a label to be affixed to such container under the supervision of an inspector, stating that the contents thereof have been inspected and passed; the act also provides that no such meat or product shall be sold or offered for sale under any false or deceptive name. The regulations based on this provision of the law define at length what may or may not appear upon any label which is to be used in connection with meats and products. However, they all center to one purpose, namely, that the statements on the labels shall conform to the facts and correctly indicate the contents of the package. Copies of all labels intended for use in official establishments must first be submitted to the Washington office of the bureau for examination and approval.

INSPECTION OF IMPORTED MEATS AND MEAT FOOD PRODUCTS.

The regulations governing the admission of meat and meat food products from foreign countries require that every importation shall be accompanied by a certificate signed by an official of the national government of the country of origin, stating that the animals from which the meat or meat food product was derived received an ante-mortem and a post-mortem veterinary inspection, and that at the time of slaughter the meat and products were sound, healthful, wholesome, and otherwise fit for human food. Further, that they had not been treated with and contain no ingredient prohibited by the regulations of the United States Department of Agriculture. Meat or meat food product not accompanied by the required certificate is refused entry, and that from a country which does not maintain a system of meat inspection satisfactory to the Secretary of Agriculture is also refused.

Every consignment of imported meat or product is checked with the foreign inspection certificate upon arrival and is subjected to a thorough physical examination, and in most cases samples thereof undergo a laboratory examination. The meat or product is then admitted, refused entry, or condemned, according to the findings and the requirements of the regulations governing the inspection and handling of such imported articles.

The imported meat or product which is found to comply with the regulations and has been admitted into the United States is marked "U. S. Inspected and Passed," or an authorized abbreviation of the same, and with a letter or letters to denote the port at which inspection was made. When imported meats and products have been inspected and admitted the law directs that they shall be deemed and treated as domestic meats and products within the meaning of and subject to the provisions of the meat-inspection act.

PORK NOT MICROSCOPICALLY INSPECTED FOR TRICHINA.

Under the Federal meat inspection pork is not microscopically inspected for trichina. There is no practicable method of microscopic inspection which is even approximately effective for the prevention of trichinosis in persons who eat uncooked pork. Careful investigations in one of the European countries in which a highly developed system is in force have shown that nearly a third of all the cases of trichinosis, several thousand in number, which occurred during a period of 18 years were caused by pork which had been microscopically inspected and passed by the inspectors of that country as free from trichinæ. Evidence of this kind and various other considerations have led authorities to the conclusion that pork, even though it has been microscopically inspected, is not a safe article of food unless it has been properly cooked or otherwise treated to destroy any trichinæ which may be present.

In countries in which there is an established and widely prevalent custom of eating uncooked pork, microscopic inspection is perhaps justified as a means of reducing somewhat the danger of trichinosis, though, on the other hand, it tends to encourage the unhygienic custom of eating uncooked pork by creating a false sense of security in the minds of the public. Under the conditions which exist in the United States, microscopic inspection, in view of its great expense and the imperfect results, does not appear warranted. On the contrary, it is reasonably certain that if a comparatively small part of the huge sum that would be required annually for microscopic inspection were judiciously employed in extending the education of the public on the subject of trichinosis it would do more toward the prevention of the disease in this country than any system of microscopic inspection which could possibly be established.

In the United States most persons are careful to cook pork before eating it, and there is only a small fraction of the population, of foreign origin or under the influence of foreign food customs, who follow the dangerous practice of eating uncooked pork in one or more of its various forms of preparation, such as special kinds of sausage, hams, loin rolls, etc. Considerable quantities of products of the kind just mentioned are prepared in official establishments, and for the protection of the consumers, who may be either ignorant or careless of the dangers of raw pork, the Federal Government, as an alternative to the uncertain method of microscopic examination, requires that official establishments subject all articles consisting wholly or in part of pork, if of a kind customarily eaten without cooking, to certain prescribed processes which have been found to destroy trichinæ. It is important to note that these measures employed with reference to safeguarding pork products apply only to those which are of kinds customarily eaten without cooking, and do not apply to pork products, such as ordinary cured hams, bacon, and other products, which are customarily cooked before they are eaten, nor to fresh uncooked pork.

In view of the foregoing, it may be stated that the practice of thoroughly cooking pork offers the best safeguard against trichinosis, and in general it is the only preventive method which can be absolutely depended upon by the consumer. Therefore, the certain way of avoiding trichinosis is to eat no pork unless it has been properly cooked. Whoever fails to observe this precaution runs the risk of acquiring sooner or later a most painful and distressing disease which frequently terminates in death. Everyone should remember this simple rule of food hygiene: Cook pork well.

MEAT-INSPECTION LABORATORIES.

The regulations specify what may be added to meats for curing or other purposes. The use of substances which impair wholesomeness is prohibited and only harmless artificial coloring matters may be used, and when used their presence must be declared on the product or the label. As a rule ordinary examination will not discover the presence of prohibited materials; therefore, to insure adequate examination for ingredients not permitted, also to determine soundness by chemical or other test, district laboratories fully equipped to make chemical and other technical examinations are maintained. Samples of meats and meat food products and of the materials used in their preparation are sent to these laboratories for examination. The samples are collected by the inspectors unannounced and at sufficiently frequent intervals to detect improper practices should any such be attempted.

In addition to the central and district chemical laboratories, the meat-inspection service has the cooperation and service of the several other scientific laboratories of the Bureau of Animal Industry. Frequently inspectors submit samples of diseased or abnormal tissues for diagnosis. Such samples are referred to the Pathological Division, in the laboratories of which they are tested and examined. The chief laboratory of this division is in the city of Washington, with branch laboratories in two other cities for the convenience of the more distant field stations. The numerous parasites and parasitic conditions with which meat inspection is concerned are studied by the Zoological Division, while questions relating to the biochemic changes that occur in animal tissues are referred to the laboratories of the Biochemic Division for attention.

THE NEED OF STATE AND MUNICIPAL INSPECTION TO SUPPLEMENT FEDERAL MEAT INSPECTION.

The Federal system of meat inspection has been extended to all parts of the field authorized for it by law. It is estimated that about 60 per cent of the cattle, sheep, swine, and goats slaughtered in the United States and all imported meats are inspected under this system. This leaves approximately 40 per cent of the domestic meat supply outside of Federal control. Much of the latter, it is known, receives no adequate inspection.

Federal meat-inspection statistics show that certain percentages of the different species of animals slaughtered are affected with some disease or condition in such degree as to require their condemnation in whole or in part. Some of the establishments at which Federal inspection is maintained have endeavored to avoid the loss incident to condemnation by exercising great care in the purchase of animals, accepting only such as appear to be sound and healthy. This has the effect of reducing the losses at such establishments, but it also tends to divert the sale of the animals of doubtful soundness to establishments that operate without inspection. With our knowledge of the frequency of disease in food animals, the question of what becomes of the meats and products derived from the diseased and unfit animals slaughtered in the uninspected houses assumes greater hygienic importance than is usually accorded it. Dr. Charles Wardell Stiles, after having studied a large number of town and country slaughterhouses, said: "A well-regulated system of slaughterhouses is as necessary to public health as is a well-regulated system of schools to public education."

Many of the slaughterhouses which operate under no system of inspection have features that are not only objectionable but dangerous to health. Their construction is such as to make them incapable of being kept sanitary. Their water supply and drainage systems are inadequate and but little systematic attempt is made to keep them clean, and some are inexpressibly foul and filthy. Usually there is no protection of the meat against rats, flies, and other insects and vermin, and this condition is a dangerous source of contamination and infection. To remedy these conditions it has been proposed that municipalities provide central abattoirs at which all the slaughterers of a community may conduct their operations under sanitary conditions and an efficient system of inspection maintained. This proposal has very much to commend it; in fact, central municipal abattoirs have been established and operated with complete success in many of the cities of continental Europe, and several have been established in the United States.

PERSONNEL OF THE INSPECTION FORCE.

The personnel of the meat-inspection service is divided into two general classes—professional and nonprofessional. The professional is composed of veterinary inspectors, laboratory inspectors, an architect, and a sanitary engineer. The nonprofessional consists of employees designated lay inspectors.

The veterinarians must be graduates of accredited veterinary colleges and pass the civil-service examination for the position of veterinary inspector in the service. At each meat-inspection station an inspector is selected to take charge of the work and who reports directly to the Chief of the Bureau of Animal Industry. At stations where slaughtering is conducted only veterinary inspectors are placed in charge. The veterinary inspectors perform or supervise the regular ante-mortem and post-mortem inspections and perform all of the final post-mortem examinations. The laboratory inspectors are chemists and also must pass an examination in accordance with the civil-service requirements. They make the laboratory tests and inspections.

The lay inspectors are designated lay inspector, grade 2, and lay inspector, grade 1; they also are required to pass the civil-service examination. The lay inspectors, grade 2, are experienced and well informed in regard to packing-house operations; they supervise the curing, preparation, and marking of meats and products. They are trained in passing on meats and products as to soundness, and conduct the inspection and reinspection of meats and products. The lay inspectors, grade 1, are required to have at least 3 years' experience in handling food-producing animals before taking the civil-service examination. Their duties are to assist the veterinary inspectors in the ante-mortem and post-mortem inspections, and to perform other duties similar to those described for the lay inspectors, grade 2. After a certain period of service they are eligible for examination for promotion to the position of lay inspector, grade 2. It is the duty of every employee, whether veterinary inspector or lay inspector of either grade, to see that the sanitary regulations are observed in their respective departments.

Certain veterinary inspectors, selected for their experience and general qualifications, are known as traveling veterinary inspectors. They inspect the official stations and establishments in their respective territories and report to the chief of the bureau whether the regulations and instructions governing meat inspection are properly observed. Their visits are unannounced and their reports are valuable in the effort to secure a uniform inspection and the enforcement of the sanitary regulations.

The personnel at present consists in round numbers of 800 veterinary inspectors; 1,000 lay inspectors, grade 2; 700 lay inspectors, grade 1; and laboratory inspectors, administrative officers, and clerical forces to bring the total to about 2,650 persons.

STATISTICAL.

The following very brief statistical summary is by no means an adequate statement of all the work performed under the Federal meat-inspection system. It will suffice, however, to convey to the reader an idea of the magnitude of the service.

The number of establishments at which inspection is regularly maintained varies somewhat; however, for several years it has approximated 850, and includes practically every establishment of importance or large volume of operations in the United States. In the last five fiscal years preceding this writing the total of cattle, sheep, swine, and goats given both the ante-mortem and post-mortem inspections was in excess of an average of 58,500,000 per year. The average number of whole carcasses of such animals condemned during that period was more than 262,000 per year, while the number of parts of carcasses condemned per year was very much greater. The records of the inspection and reinspections of meats and products subsequent to the slaughter inspection show totals running into billions of pounds annually, while the amount condemned on reinspection on account of having become tainted, rancid, or otherwise unfit for human food has approximated 18,000,000 pounds per year.

For the fiscal year preceding this writing, the sum appropriated by Congress for meat inspection was $3,375,000, within which sum the service was maintained. In other words, the cost was less than 6 cents for each of the 58,500,-000 animals slaughtered. This charge covered the entire service from the first inspection of the live animal to the final examination of the meats in the finished products, when ready for delivery to dealers or consumers. In this connection it seems but right to add that there has been no sacrifice of efficiency and completeness to attain this low cost; on the contrary, it is the constant aim of the department to strengthen the service in these respects.

COLOR AS AN INDICATION OF THE PICKING MATURITY OF FRUITS AND VEGETABLES.

By L. C. CORBETT,

Horticulturist in Charge of Horticultural and Pomological Investigations, Bureau of Plant Industry.

FRUIT color is a factor intimately associated with fruit maturity. The small boy uninstructed in the arts is not attracted to the cherry tree until the fruits are colored, and he soon learns from experience to choose the fruits that are sweetest by his sense of color values associated with the perception of taste. While this is a simple illustration of the value of the color test for fruit maturity, it nevertheless illustrates the fact that unconsciously a value is placed on the color in fruits in order to arrive at an estimate of their palatability. This being the case, may there not be physiological activities or results directly associated with the life of the fruit which can in a measure be estimated by the color values in the fruit? That such is the fact is quite evident from the results observed in the behavior of various fruits which have been subjected to careful control conditions in repeated experimental tests conducted by the investigators of the United States Department of Agriculture.

A concrete and striking example of the value of fruit color as an index to fruit picking maturity is afforded in the results of the picking and storage investigations conducted to determine the factors contributing to the successful storage of the apple. Early in the work upon this subject, undertaken by Taylor and Powell, it became evident that some physiological activity of the fruit itself was intimately concerned with the phenomenon termed "scald" in the stored fruit. As the work progressed it became more and more evident that scalding could not be wholly attributed to storage-house conditions or management. It was possible with the perfection attained in refrigerating apparatus and in storage-house construction and insulation to maintain practically constant, uniform conditions in the houses. It was also possible to reproduce such conditions from year to year. Notwithstanding these facts, varying results as regards scald were obtained, not only from year to year, but in different lots of fruit in the same house. These results focused attention more clearly upon the fruit itself.

COMPARISON OF STAGES OF MATURITY.

Accordingly, a series of observations was conducted to ascertain the relation of early (immature), medium (mature), and late (overripe) picking to the behavior of the fruit in what had been determined to be the most nearly ideal storage temperature. As one of the important teachings of this investigation there appeared results such as are recorded in the color reproductions presented herewith. The immature fruit illustrated in Plate A, which is characteristic of early-picked fruits of the Rome Beauty apple in the Yakima Valley of Washington, is distinguished by more or less development of the red or overlay color, but the important point for consideration in connection with fruit at this stage of maturity is the composition of the ground color. A careful study of this specimen reveals the fact that much vivid leaf green is present in the skin of the apple. Fruit picked at this stage of development, when withdrawn after a storage period of six months at a constant temperature of 32° F., presented the appearance illustrated in Plate B. This shows an advanced stage of "scald," which when present to any appreciable extent decidedly affects the food value as well as the merchandising value of the fruit. It will be noted not only that the skin shows the characteristic browning of scald, but that the discoloration has extended far below the surface of the skin; in fact, the cells of the skin as well as many layers of cells in the flesh of the fruit have ceased to function, as is indicated by the browning of the walls.

The specimen shown in Plate C represents a fruit in which, before picking, there had been a slight increase in the development of the overlay color. The area covered was a little larger and the color more intense than in the apple shown in Plate A. The significant fact, however, is observed

R. C. STEADMAN. DEL.

A. HOEN & CO.

ROME BEAUTY APPLES OF NORTHWESTERN PRODUCTION PICKED TOO EARLY FOR HOLDING SATISFACTORILY AT NORMAL STORAGE TEMPERATURE OF 32° F. FOR A SIX-MONTHS' STORAGE PERIOD.

Fruits like the one in the upper figure, with a vivid leaf green area on the shaded side, are too immature for satisfactory storage, even though there is considerable color on the sunny side.

Cross section of a fruit at the same stage of maturity is shown in the lower illustration. The green color is apparent in the flesh.

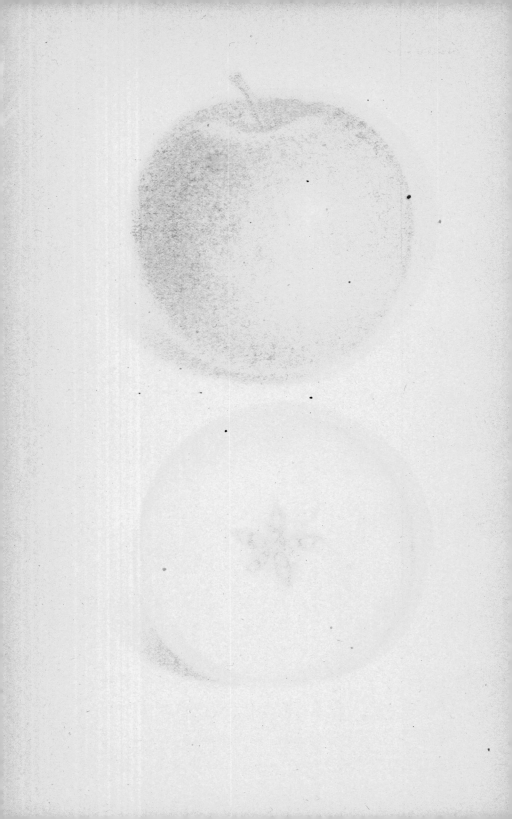

R.C.STEADMAN, DEL.   A.HOEN & CO

RESULTS OF HOLDING ROME BEAUTY APPLES, AT THE STAGE OF MATURITY
INDICATED IN PLATE A, AT 32° F. FOR SIX MONTHS.

External browning characteristic of fruits picked before the leaf green in the skin had
disappeared and held in storage six months is illustrated by the upper figure.

The cross section of the same fruit shows that several layers of cells immediately below the
skin, as well as the cells of the skin itself, have ceased to function and have become
discolored.

R. C. STEADMAN, DEL.

A HOEN & CO

ROME BEAUTY APPLES OF NORTHWESTERN PRODUCTION PICKED IN MORE
MATURE CONDITION THAN THOSE SHOWN IN PLATE A, BUT YET
TOO GREEN FOR SATISFACTORY BEHAVIOR IN STORAGE.

The coloring and the amount of leaf green in the skin of the fruit at the time of placing
it in storage is illustrated in the upper figure.

Cross section of the same fruit, showing that while the flesh carries less green a trace still
remains.

R.C.STEADMAN, DEL.   A.HOEN&CO.

CONDITION PRESENTED BY FRUITS OF THE SAME STAGE OF MATURITY AS
THOSE SHOWN IN PLATE C, AFTER BEING HELD SIX MONTHS IN
STORAGE AT A TEMPERATURE OF 32° F.

The surface of the apple carrying the leaf green, as shown in the upper figure, Plate C, has
assumed the characteristic baked-apple appearance of scalded fruit. The cells of the
discolored skin have ceased to function.

The cross section of the same fruit shows that the fruit was sufficiently mature at the
time of storage so that the discoloration has not penetrated deeper than the pigment cells.

R.C.STEADMAN, DEL.

A.HOEN & CO

ROME BEAUTY APPLES OF NORTHWESTERN PRODUCTION HARVESTED AFTER THE LEAF GREEN HAD DISAPPEARED AND THE TRUE YELLOW OF THE NORMAL GROUND COLOR FOR THE VARIETY WAS DISCERNIBLE.

Absence of leaf green, the presence of white, and light yellow in its place—true signs of picking maturity in this variety—are shown in the upper figure.

Cross section of the same fruit from which the green tint in the skin as well as in the flesh has disappeared.

R C STEADMAN DEL.

A HOEN & CO.

ROME BEAUTY APPLES OF THE SAME STAGE OF MATURITY AS THOSE SHOWN IN
PLATE E, AFTER HAVING BEEN HELD SIX MONTHS IN COLD STORAGE
AT A TEMPERATURE OF 32° F.

No loss of color or discoloration, but the deepening of the yellow in the ground color due
to progress of the ripening process, is shown in the upper figure.

The cross section of the fruit, shows no discoloration, but rather an increase in the yellow
tint in the flesh, characteristic of the maturing of the variety.

in the ground color. There is less intensity in the green pigment, and the leaf green, while still observable, is less intense, having in a measure been replaced by white, a phenomenon familiar to every close observer of changes in the color values of fruits as they ripen. The chlorophyll, or leaf green, has grown less vivid and has certainly decreased in amount. This fruit, while still too immature for best storage behavior, responds to a six months' period in storage in the manner shown in Plate D. This apple, while showing a considerable amount of scald, is by no means as badly affected as the fruit shown in Plate B. While the amount of skin discoloration shown in Plate D is considerably less than that shown in Plate B, and while this discoloration has not been communicated to the underlying flesh of the apple, so that for practical purposes the apple is sound and fit for eating or for culinary uses, yet its merchandising value has been greatly impaired because of the discoloration. The brown baked-apple appearance characteristic of scalded fruit is taken as an indication that the fruit has passed the limit of its commercial storage life. Any considerable amount of scald, therefore, rapidly depreciates the market value of the fruit affected and is a phenomenon to be overcome or avoided as far as practicable.

The extent to which scald can be overcome or avoided through picking by color, even in some of the varieties known to be unusually susceptible, is brought out in Plates E and F. The apple illustrated in Plate E brings out clearly the color values which the grower and picker must learn to recognize in order to be able to determine the stage of maturity to which the fruit must attain before it may be placed in cold storage at the temperatures recognized as satisfactory for the storage of apples and come out in a sound, attractive condition and possessing a high merchandising value.

A critical study of the color values of the apple shown in Plate E reveals the fact that there is only a trace of true leaf or chlorophyll green remaining in that part of the skin of the fruit least highly colored. This will invariably be found to be the side most shaded by the foliage of the tree and is therefore the least mature portion of the fruit. It is here that the skin pigments are least stable and most likely to be affected by the temperature. The leaf green, as has been noted, is small in amount, and its intensity is much less than in the fruits illustrated in Plates A and C. The ground color has been modified also, being, instead of greenish white, either white or yellowish white. Here we find the suggestion of the development of the true ground color of the fruit. The ground color or underlay in this variety is a shade of yellow, and as soon as there is a suggestion of the development of this characteristic color the fruit has reached a stage in its life when it can with safety be removed from the tree and placed under temperature conditions which slow down or inhibit the normal ripening processes to such an extent that instead of ripening to edible maturity in a period of a few weeks the ripening process is extended over a much greater period, which we term the normal storage period for the variety.

CONDITIONS DETERMINING THE STORAGE PERIOD.

The storage period of any variety of apple is long or short for that variety according to the degree of care exercised in picking it at the proper stage of maturity indicated by its growth and coloring and upon the treatment to which it is subsequently subjected. If it is harvested too green, even though the other factors contributing to successful handling and storage are carried out, the results shown in Plates B and D may be expected; but if, in addition to picking it too green, the fruit is allowed to stand in a warm packing room for several days previous to placing it in storage, the storage period will be shortened and the amount and seriousness of the scald augmented, provided the varieties to be stored behave normally in other respects in storage. The closer the condition of the fruit approaches that shown in Plate E the better it will carry in cold storage, assuming that it is carefully handled from the tree to the storage house, that it is not allowed to remain for more than a few hours at a high temperature after it is removed from the tree, and that whether placed in common or cold storage it is reduced to a temperature of 32° F. as soon as possible, the fewer hours the better, and then maintained without undue fluctuation at as nearly this temperature as is possible throughout the storage period.

Although the grower may observe and guard against all of the physical conditions which are known to affect the life of fruit in storage, such as careful handling, quick transfer from tree to storage room, and the maintenance of a suitable storage temperature, if the fruit itself has not reached a proper stage of maturity (Pl. E) the observance of these precautions will avail little. The physiological behavior of the fruit, even if stored under an ideal environment, will be that shown in Plate B if it is exceedingly immature, that shown in Plate D if it is approaching a satisfactory stage of maturity, and that shown in Plate F if it has reached a condition of maturity suitable for storage. Color, then, is the important factor by which the grower can determine the condition of ripeness of fruit for the best behavior in cold storage.

The illustrations here presented represent only one variety, and the color values shown are characteristic only of this variety. The general principle, however, holds for all varieties of apples and pears thus far subjected to cold-storage tests. In order to apply the lesson taught by the different stages of ripeness in the Rome Beauty apple here illustrated, it will be necessary merely to observe closely the true color values shown by each sort in the process of ripening and then to attempt to harvest the fruits at the time when these signs are most developed. In order to do this, the grower and picker must carefully train his sense of color values and observe closely the changes which take place in the make-up of the general color scheme of each variety. The points to be borne in mind are the decrease of the amount and intensity of leaf green in the skin of the fruit and the replacing of the green by white and gradually by yellow, if yellow is the normal ground color of the fruit, as is the case with the Rome Beauty apple.

The development to a slight extent of the normal ground color is desirable, but this process should not be allowed to go too far before it is checked by picking and placing the fruit in storage. This caution should be heeded, for it is found that overripe fruits are quite as unsatisfactory for long keeping in storage as are those picked too green. The ability to judge the stage of ripeness so as not to pick the fruit underripe or to allow it to remain on the tree until overripe is the end desired. Careful attention to the color scheme of varieties is one essential, and another is to evaluate color changes in the developing fruit so as to pick each individual fruit at a time when it will keep longest and hold its color best. A careful study of the plates here presented will serve as a foundation, but the picker must carry with him to the orchard an accurate mental picture based on close observation for each of the varieties in his collection. The more perfect the mastery of the color problem for each variety the greater will be the success with the variety in storage, other things being equal.

THE COLOR FACTOR IN TOMATOES.

As a further contribution to information concerning the relation of color to picking maturity in plant products other than apples, it is desirable to mention the relation which the color at picking time bears to the color and general character of the canned product, as well as catsup made from tomatoes. Tomatoes, like apples, present a wide diversity of colors, but since red is the desired color in canned tomatoes, catsups, and pulp, only those varieties possessing red or scarlet pigments will be considered.

The tomato during the process of ripening passes from the leaf-green color which characterizes it during the early period of its development to a whitish green before the normal fruit color begins to develop. The green tints give way to the white, and this in turn is replaced in the desirable canning sorts by red, which gains in intensity as the process of ripening progresses, until at full maturity the pigmentation is complete and permanent. When this stage has been reached there is no further increase in the intensity of the color, and when tomatoes which have reached this stage of ripeness are subjected to the temperatures required for proper sterilization in the operation of processing the canned product there is no loss in color and the product possesses the deep red so desirable in high-grade goods. At this stage of maturity the pulp can be concentrated by boiling to the consistency required for catsup without loss of color. If, on the other hand, the tomatoes are gathered before pigmentation is complete and are subjected to the processing required for canning or catsup making, the resulting product will not be of a deep red color, but will vary from a reddish straw color to light red, according to the degree of pigmentation attained by the fruits when harvested.

Before the passage of the food and drugs act, which requires that no food may be colored in a manner whereby inferiority is concealed, the question of the stage of maturity at which fruits or vegetables were picked or processed gave manufacturers little concern, for lack of coloring could be made up by sweating or by the use of dyes.

Now that such practices are discouraged by the regulations of the act, and the trade still requires high-colored and, fortunately, high-flavored products as well, the stage of maturity and the degree of pigmentation play an important part. Fortunately for the industry, nature has provided a method by which the demands of the trade can be met in a legitimate way; that way is via the ripe-fruit route.

Ripened tomatoes of desirable color will, when properly handled, produce a high-colored canned product or a high-colored catsup. Half-ripened red tomatoes will not produce a canned product or a catsup of a bright red color. The pigment in such fruits is not stable and fades slightly when the pulp is subjected to the temperatures required for sterilization or concentration. In the case of the tomato the heat of processing reduces the pigment and leaves a product varying from straw color through the shades of red, depending upon the stage of color development attained by the fruit when picked.

DISADVANTAGES OF HARVESTING IMMATURE PRODUCTS.

Immature apples when placed in storage develop various degrees of scald, depending upon the pigmentation or color development attained by the fruit up to the time of storage. As the apple matures it loses the leaf green which characterizes the young, immature fruit; this is replaced by white, and this in turn by the ground color and the normal pigmentation of the variety. Under common-storage or cold-storage conditions, immature fruits in which the chlorophyll, or leaf green, has not disappeared do not retain this color in storage, but assume the baked-apple appearance charac-

teristic of scalded fruit, the intensity or severity of the scalding depending upon the stage of maturity attained by the
fruit, as illustrated in Plates A, C, and E.

The practical result from placing immature apples in
storage is loss of color and that from processing immature
tomatoes is loss in color. In both cases deterioration is due
to unstable pigments in the product. The apples lose color
when fruits with imperfect pigmentation are subjected to
storage temperatures, whether or not the conditions to which
they are subjected are low enough to check normal ripening
processes. It would appear, on the other hand, that ripe
fruits have developed stable pigments which are not affected in the apple by cold-storage temperatures nor in the
tomato by the heat required for sterilization or concentration.

The practical lessons are: (1) Loss from scald will be
lessened by harvesting apples after the leaf green has disappeared and the normal ground color for the variety has
begun to develop; (2) high-colored and high-quality canned
tomatoes and high-colored and high-quality catsup can be
made only from ripe tomatoes of varieties possessing a red
pigment. The time for picking fruit for special purposes
must be determined by the behavior of the fruit. Put the
fruit to the test; it will give the answer.

FARMS, FORESTS, AND EROSION.

By Samuel T. Dana,
Assistant Chief of Forest Investigations, Forest Service.

INTRODUCTION.

"FARMS, forests, and erosion" may sound like a queer combination, but as a matter of fact the three are closely connected. Erosion is one of the most serious dangers that threaten our farms, and forests are one of the most effective means of preventing erosion. How true this is would be most startlingly demonstrated if all the forests of the country were to be wiped out overnight. Imagine how the water would pour off the mountains, cutting to pieces and washing away the land and destroying other property in its path.

The forest is, in fact, one of the best friends of the farmer in protecting his land from erosion and consequent damage. Just what this means, not only to the farmer, but to the Nation as a whole, becomes clearer when we remember that over half of the population of the country is rural; that there are more than 6,300,000 farms; that there are nearly 897,000,000 acres of farm land with a value of approximately $28,500,000,000; and that the annual production of farm crops is valued at some $5,500,000,000. Anything that exercises an important influence on interests of this magnitude is unquestionably deserving of the most careful consideration.

WHAT BECOMES OF THE RAINFALL.

IN THE FOREST.

When the Pilgrim fathers landed at Plymouth Rock in 1620 they found the new continent clothed with an almost unbroken expanse of virgin forest. Cool springs were abundant, streams ran clear, and excessive erosion had not left its mark upon the land. The geologic processes of land sculpture which have been going on since time immemorial were of course at work carving out the hills and valleys. Every year the soil on the steeper slopes was creeping a little farther on its way to the sea; every year there was some

107

change, however imperceptible, in the appearance of mother earth. At the same time another process was going on. Rocks were being decomposed and transformed into soil. This second process, though it, too, was slow, was in most places proceeding faster than the other. Soils were being formed more rapidly than they were removed, and the basis for the future farms of the country was gradually being built up. Such soil as was washed away consisted of the lighter particles, much of which, being deposited farther down in the more level portions of the streams, helped to build up the fertile alluvial plains. The entire action of nature was beneficial, rather than destructive.

Everyone who has been in a dense forest during a heavy storm knows how thoroughly it protects the soil and stores the water. The force of the rain is broken by the trees, the underbrush, and the litter on the ground, so that it does not beat upon the soil. Much of the precipitation reaches the earth by running down the twigs and branches. In a light shower nearly all of the rain may be intercepted by the leaves of the trees, so that one can stand in the forest without getting wet. Even in a heavy rain the water drips down so quietly as to have practically no beating effect upon the soil. There is no perceptible surface run-off until great quantities of rain have fallen. Instead, the water is soaked up by the organic matter, or humus, in the upper layers of the soil. This is really an enormous vegetable sponge capable of holding several times its own weight of water. As the rain falls it is absorbed by this sponge, then passed on to the reservoir of mineral soil beneath, and finally fed out gradually to the springs and streams. Then, too, surface run-off is checked by the mechanical obstruction offered by stumps, fallen twigs, branches, and even whole trees; and percolation of the water into the soil is made easier by the network of small roots and the channels left by the decay of large roots. Even when the rain is so heavy that the soil is unable to absorb all of the water at once, the excess flows off with no erosion. Streams coming from virgin forests are seldom muddy and are subject to comparatively small variations in flow.

IN THE OPEN.

The effect of heavy rains on the exposed soil of cleared fields is very different. There the rain beats upon the bare ground like millions of little hammers. The soil is compacted, its absorbing capacity is reduced, and first the finer and then the coarser, infertile particles are washed away. The water quickly gathers into little rivulets, then into streams, and finally into roaring torrents, all carrying with them ever-increasing quantities of soil and often stones and bowlders. Myriads of tiny channels appear as if by magic. These run together into small gullies, and the small gullies grow into large ones. The whole area is cut up by erosion and the eroded materials carried away to cause trouble at lower elevations.

It has sometimes been argued that because the erosion which takes place under natural conditions is beneficial, that which takes place after clearing is equally or even more so. This by no means follows, however. When erosion becomes excessive, not only is the soil at the upper elevations washed away more rapidly than it is formed, but the amount of sediment is so enormous that the streams can not handle it. The coarser, infertile materials, the proportion of which is greatly increased, are deposited on valuable farm lands along the middle courses of the streams, while the finer materials are carried farther down, where they help to fill up the navigable portions of the rivers.

When the early colonists cleared the first land for agriculture they paved the way for the excessive erosion which has since taken place. It was of course inevitable that over a large portion of the country forests should give way to farms. It was not inevitable, however, that this change should be accompanied by such disastrous consequences to the soil. Many causes have been responsible for the damage that has been wrought, but underlying them all is the prodigality and indifference to the future which is characteristic of people richly endowed with natural resources.

CAUSES OF EROSION.

CLEARING OF NONAGRICULTURAL LAND.

Injudicious clearing for cultivation of land on which a forest cover should always have been maintained has been one of the main causes of unnecessary erosion. Thousands of acres on slopes too steep for successful farming have been ruined in this way. Such land has been cheap and the settler frequently has been only too ready to cultivate it for a few years until it was worn out and then complacently move on to repeat the process elsewhere. Improper methods of agriculture have often hastened the devastation. Unfortunately, this has not been confined to the area itself. Once started, erosion has progressed in both directions, washing out and burying fertile lands below and eating back into forested lands above.

Complete clearing of lands that should have been only partially cleared has had the same result. Not infrequently it happens that part of an area can safely be cleared for farming if the rest of the area is left in forest. Failure to recognize this fact and to retain the forest where its protective influence is needed has been the direct cause of much unnecessary wasting of the soil.

FIRE.

Among the many evils chargeable to forest fires, their effect on the character of the run-off is by no means the least. Their tendency is in the same direction as clearing—to decrease the amount of water absorbed and consequently to increase surface run-off and soil washing.

From the standpoint of erosion every fire on hilly land is a menace—the steeper the slope the more serious the menace. Conflagrations which completely destroy the cover are, of course, most dangerous. Even light surface fires, however, are not to be disregarded. By destroying the humus and the carpet of weeds and other plants, these tend to harden the soil and to reduce materially its absorptive capacity. Repeated fires on the same area are particularly dangerous, since they gradually open up the stand, remove all trace of vegetable matter, and may cause the soil to harden and pack so as to be almost impervious. One or two specific examples may help to make clear the damage that may be done by even a single fire.

On the north side of the Soleduck Valley, in western Washington, some 12,000 acres were severely burned in 1907. All vegetable growth was destroyed and all soil cover removed. Very little vegetation started in the first four years following the fire, and during these years the slopes were subjected to considerable erosion. Soil and fragments of stone were carried in great quantities to the many gulches and water courses. In November, 1910, a combination of heavy snow, followed by a chinook wind and a warm rain, caused an enormous run-off of water, carrying with it great quantities of soil and rock. This shifting mass was so great that most of the creek channels, where they struck the flat, became choked with it and built up fan-shaped deltas, in some cases several acres being covered with débris from 1 to 6 feet deep. Even now erosion on these areas is considerable, although not nearly so great as during the first few years after the fire.

In the brush-covered foothills of southern California, near the town of Piru, is a small watershed of perhaps 1 square mile known as "Nigger Canyon." In October, 1912, approximately 100 acres of this were burned over and the cover completely destroyed. The following January a series of heavy rains caused unprecedented erosion on the area. Rocks from 2 to 2½ feet in diameter, so large that they could hardly be moved by a team, were brought down by the flood. A section of 1-inch iron pipe between 400 and 500 feet long was entirely washed out. Ten acres of orange orchard near the mouth of the canyon were covered with a deposit of gravel from 6 inches to 5 feet in depth, so that in many places the lower branches of the trees rested directly on the ground. Though the orchard was not destroyed it was so injured that it will be necessary to reset the buried area. Farther downstream, where the deposit was not so deep, the individual trees have been raised at considerable expense by means of a derrick. Near the first orchard the bed of the creek was so filled with débris that the orchard was in constant danger of being overflowed at high water, and it was necessary to construct a dike in order to confine the water to the main channel. Four acres of bottom land which had been cleared the year previous to the fire for planting to lemons were so covered with gravel and bowlders as to be completely ruined. Local residents state that while the precipitation that winter was heavy, they do not believe it was worse than in many other years. One owner expresses the opinion that there has been more damage from erosion in the 3 years since the fire than in the 22 years before.

DESTRUCTIVE LUMBERING.

All cutting, of course, changes to some extent the character and amount of the soil cover and therefore disturbs more or less the natural balance between rainfall and runoff. If the cutting is properly regulated, however, this effect may be so slight as to be practically negligible. It is nearly always possible to leave sufficient cover on the ground to prevent any ill effects from the opening up of the stand, and if fire is kept out this is soon supplemented by other vegetation which effectively protects the soil from erosion.

Unfortunately, past cuttings have not in all cases been properly regulated. Considerable unnecessary erosion may be laid to destructive lumbering carried on without regard to the future welfare of the forest itself or of the interests dependent on its protective cover. Clear cutting has been practiced on steep slopes where at least a part of the stand should have been left. Roads have been so located as to be subject to serious erosion. Deeply gouged skid trails, formed by dragging many logs down the same rut, have been left unprotected to wash out after every heavy rain. Worst of all, fires have been allowed to burn uncontrolled on the cutover areas. The dry mass of twigs, branches, and other inflammable material left after all lumbering operations adds to the fury of the flames and enables them to expose the bare soil to the mercy of the other elements.

One of the papers in the Yearbook of the Department of Agriculture for 1913 ("Economic Waste from Soil Erosion," by R. O. E. Davis) cites a specific example of the results of destructive lumbering. The owner was proceeding to remove all the timber possible from his tract with entire indifference as to the effect upon the soil of such a procedure. In one field where the entire forest cover had already been removed, great gullies had appeared and ruined the field for farming. One of the gullies extended for over half a mile to a creek bottom which had once been a fertile field, but was now covered in most places from 1 to 3 feet deep with sand which had been washed down from the cut-over area. When the lumberman was asked regarding his treatment of the land he replied that all he expected to get from it was the lumber; that he did not suppose he could sell it, because he "didn't think it worth anything as farm land, it washed

FIG. I.—THE RESULT OF CLEAR CUTTING AND FIRES.

This land is in the mountains, at too high an elevation for agriculture (over 10,000 feet), and should have been retained in forest.

FIG. 2.—ONCE A TROUT STREAM.

This stream formerly had a small but steady flow throughout the year and was named Trout Creek from the fish which made it their home. Cutting, overgrazing, and fires in the mountains at its headwaters have brought about steadily increasing washouts. So serious has been the damage to the railroad which originally ran along the bank that more than a million dollars would now be required to replace the track.

FIG. I.—HOW FARM LAND IS DESTROYED.

By being buried under a heavy deposit of sand and gravel brought down by a single flood from the cut-over and burned-over mountain watershed above, 11 acres out of the 45 acres of irrigated land on this farm were practically ruined. The irrigation works were also so damaged that no irrigation was possible the year following the flood.

FIG. 2.—A WASHED-OUT ROAD.

The washout occurred the next year after a severe fire in the mountains shown in the background. The gate, no longer used, shows where the road formerly ran—5 feet higher than its present location.

FIG. I.—FARMING NO LONGER POSSIBLE.

Land which formerly sold for $600 an acre has been rendered worthless by the deposit of sand, gravel, and bowlders brought down the year after a severe fire in the mountains shown in the background. Previous to the fire the stream bed had been an inconspicuous wash carrying only a small amount of water even in the rainy season.

FIG. 2.—A RESULT OF CARELESS FARMING.

The damage might have been prevented by proper terracing and cultivation. Even now reclamation of such land is both possible and profitable.

FIG. I.—FERTILE LAND RUINED BY EROSION.

If the soil-washing is not checked there is danger that the buildings in the background will eventually be undermined.

FIG. 2.—EROSION GAINING HEADWAY ON A STEEP SLOPE.

An effort is being made to check it by filling the gullies with brush.   Tree planting would also help.

FIG. I.—A RESERVOIR ENDANGERED.

Where vegetation is sparse erosion once started is very difficult to check. It is particularly serious in this case because the eroded area drains directly into a proposed reservoir site.

FIG. 2.—OVERGRAZING ANOTHER CAUSE OF SOIL WASHING.

The protective vegetation has been partly removed as a result of too heavy grazing by sheep. If grazing is not checked, the entire hillside may be destroyed.

FIG. I.—THE KIND OF LAND FOR A WOODLOT.

Timber growing pays better than farming on lands of this character.

FIG. 2.—A PROTECTED RIVER BANK.

During the Kansas River flood of 1903 the fringe of willows and cottonwoods protected this river bank from erosion, and the land back of it from burial under a mass of sand, gravel, and other infertile material.

so bad." His method of handling it was indeed ruining it
for either farm or forest, and in addition was contributing
to the ruin of fertile land below.

OVERGRAZING.

Although less spectacular than fire, overgrazing may be
equally serious in its effect on erosion. It is particularly
dangerous in those areas where precipitation is light and
where the vegetation even when ungrazed has a hard time
holding its own. The woodland areas in the Southwest are
typical examples. Here the natural balance between precipitation and run-off is so finely adjusted that very little
disturbance of the soil cover is required to upset it. Moreover, adverse climatic conditions make it very difficult for
vegetation to reestablish itself in such regions. Erosion
once started, therefore, is likely to be permanent.

The evil results of overgrazing are well illustrated in
central and southern Utah. Forest Service Bulletin 91 [1]
estimates that in the country surrounding the Manti National Forest, overgrazing, which occurred before this area
was included in the National Forests, has been responsible
through erosion and floods for a loss of $225,000. Among
the items of damage included are destruction of roads,
bridges, streets, and buildings; heavy depreciation of real-
estate values; ruin of crops; permanent injury to agricultural lands; filling up and destruction of reservoirs, canals,
and ditches; and even death.

Farther south, overgrazing on a single watershed has been
responsible for an annual loss of about $3,000 to the town
and farming community of Salina. Furthermore, the sand
and sediment carried by Salina Creek has filled up the main
channel of the Sevier River between Salina and Redmond
to such an extent that the river has submerged some 1,000
acres of valuable farming land worth about $100,000, and
has damaged other lands to the extent of about $50,000.

OTHER FACTORS.

In addition to the forest and other soil covers, the chief
factors having an influence on erosion are the amount and
character of the precipitation, the degree of slope, the geo-

---

[1] " Grazing and Floods : A Study of Conditions in the Manti National Forest,
Utah," by R. V. R. Reynolds.

logical formation, and the depth and composition of the soil. In general, anything that increases surface run-off increases erosion. Severe storms, steep slopes, and soils with relatively low water-absorbing capacity are, therefore, all dangerous because they tend to make it impossible for the soil to absorb the water as fast as it is supplied. This is the case with the torrential downpours of rain that occasionally occur in various parts of the country, and especially in the West. These are often known locally as " cloud-bursts," or, more expressively, as " gully-washers," particularly if damage results from them.

In July, 1915, for example, a cloud-burst in northern Washington did considerable damage in the rolling farming and grazing district known as " Happy Hill." Deep gullies were cut in the side hill at intervals of from 20 to 30 feet, crops were destroyed, live stock drowned, and several acres of fertile bottom land ruined by being buried under rocks and other débris. Altogether, the storm, which covered an area of only 2 or 3 square miles, was responsible for a damage of some $2,000. It should be noted, however, that one of the reasons why the unusually heavy precipitation was able to do so much damage in this case, as in many others, was the fact that the soil cover had already been broken by cultivation and overgrazing. It is a significant fact that " cloud-bursts " occur most frequently where the ground cover has been disturbed by fire or grazing, or in some other way. Equally severe downpours elsewhere are apt to excite little attention and to pass merely as heavy storms.

Under natural conditions the various forces are so adjusted that the damage from excessive erosion in most parts of the country is comparatively small. Some damage is, of course, inevitable, but such scars as are made are usually soon healed over by the growth of vegetation. As a rule it is only when the natural protective cover of forests, brush, grass, and other plants is disturbed that serious and long-continued erosion results.

KINDS OF EROSION.

SHEET EROSION.

Sheet erosion is marked by a more or less uniform washing away of the soil over the entire surface. It usually occurs on hillsides of only moderate slope and on the more cohesive soils. Every rain washes away some of the finer particles, but the progress of erosion is usually slow and the results not particularly conspicuous.

GULLY EROSION.

Gully erosion is much more noticeable than sheet erosion and usually progresses much more rapidly. In its early stages it is often characterized by the formation of numerous small, more or less parallel gullies, sometimes known as shoe-string gullies. Not infrequently gullies of this type are found on areas that have already suffered from sheet erosion. As they increase in size they vary in shape according to the character of the soil, from sharp-bottomed, V-shaped cuts with steep sides to broader depressions with more gently sloping, rounded sides.

Another type of gully has vertical, cliff-like sides which keep caving in as the water undermines them. Once started, it usually grows rapidly in length, breadth, and depth with every storm, until it has developed from a mere gash into a yawning chasm. It is the most striking form of gully erosion, the most rapidly progressive in its development, and the most difficult to check.

LANDSLIDES.

A landslide consists in the slipping down in a solid body of a considerable mass of the surface soil. Landslides usually occur where the soil rests on a smooth-faced, slippery substratum, or where the soil is of a " slick," micaceous character. They are caused by the soil becoming thoroughly saturated with water and then slipping off in a body from the underlying subsoil or rock. Railroad and highway cuts and the undermining of river banks often help to start them. Forest fires, by destroying the roots which pin the surface soil to the subsoil, are also a contributing cause. In November, 1910, for example, seven distinct slides took place on burned-over areas on the Rainier National Forest in western Washington. Some of these areas had been burned over only once, others repeatedly. The slides followed a series of warm, heavy rains which so saturated the soil that the decayed roots of the fire-killed trees and the short roots of the young, new growth were unable to hold it in place.

RIVER-BOTTOM EROSION.

Along river bottoms erosion is of still a different type. Here good valley land may be destroyed either by the wearing away of the river banks along the main channel or by the gouging out of new channels. Sometimes hundreds of acres of excellent agricultural land are so scoured out and stripped of their soil by a single flood as to be rendered valueless. The famous Kansas River flood of 1903, for example, completely destroyed 10,000 acres of excellent farming land and caused a total loss of at least $22,000,000. Such damage is indirectly due in large part to erosion farther up the stream and its tributaries. The eroded material brought down by the rivers is deposited in their lower portions, fills up the channels, and creates obstructions which cause the water to overflow in time of flood. Furthermore, the material brought down by the flood serves as a scouring agent which most effectively reinforces the work of the water. Prevention of erosion at the higher elevations is, therefore, an important step in checking erosion along river bottoms.

CUMULATIVE CHARACTER OF EROSION.

One of the worst features of erosion is its tendency to progress with ever-increasing rapidity. Once given a good start it will grow of itself. Where sheet erosion is taking place every bit of the surface soil washed away decreases by so much the water-absorbing capacity of that which remains, and hastens its removal down to the subsoil and often to the bare rock. Where gullies have been formed the runoff is concentrated in these and frequently scours them out with almost inconceivable force. Often, indeed, the undermining and caving in of the banks proceeds so rapidly during a heavy storm that it is dangerous to be too close an observer.

Moreover, the eroded material greatly increases the scouring power of the running water. The sediment of sand, gravel, and bowlders carried down the gullies and stream courses exercises a powerful influence in carving out their banks and tearing away formations which would not be affected by the water alone. This is especially true on steep slopes, since the transporting power of water varies as the sixth power of its velocity. In other words, when a current of 2 miles an hour can move only fragments of stone the size of a hen's egg, a torrent of 20 miles an hour can carry bowlders weighing nearly 100 tons. The tremendous scouring power which such a burden as this adds to the water and its effect in hastening the progress of erosion are obvious.

EFFECTS OF EROSION.

RUIN OF LAND.

Undoubtedly the most serious and far-reaching effect of erosion is the ruin of the land itself. Soil is, indeed, the most valuable natural resource possessed by any nation. It is the primary source from which we derive our food, our clothing, and our shelter—the basis, in fact, of civilization. Looked at from this standpoint it is as indispensable to existence as are air and water. Certainly its conservation is one of the most important steps for the welfare of the country.

Already some 4,000,000 acres of farm land have been ruined by erosion, and nearly twice as much more has been seriously damaged. In other words, erosion has rendered completely nonproductive an area capable of forming nearly 100,000 farms and of sustaining a population approximately equal to that of Arizona and New Mexico combined. Every year there is an unnecessary waste from erosion of more than 400,000,000 tons of soil material, an amount greater than that removed in digging the Panama Canal. Much of this comes from good farming land and all of it reduces by just so much the productive capacity of the country. In addition, thousands of acres of bottom land are ruined each year by being buried under infertile eroded materials brought down from the higher elevations.

Even a nation as rich in soil resources as the United States can not afford a loss of this magnitude. The day of reckoning will surely come when we shall pay the price for such prodigality. Continued waste of the soil can result only in failure to attain that development in production and population which our original endowment promised. So serious indeed is the situation that Dr. N. S. Shaler, formerly dean of the Lawrence Scientific School, was once moved to remark that if mankind can not devise and enforce ways of dealing with the earth which will preserve this source of life, " we must look forward to the time—remote it may be, yet clearly discernible—when our kind, having wasted its greatest inheritance, will fade from the earth because of the ruin it has accomplished."

LOSS OF FERTILITY.

Actual waste of the land is, however, by no means the only evil wrought by soil erosion. Loss of fertility must also be charged to its account. The finest particles of soil are naturally the first to be washed away, and the removal of these seriously impairs the physical and chemical quality of the soil. In the Piedmont section of North Carolina, for example, the plant food and humus contained in the 4,000,000 tons of soil washed away every year are valued at $2,000,000. A single week of heavy rain in August, 1908, is estimated to have impoverished the soils to the extent of more than $500,000. Figures are not available for the country as a whole; the loss certainly mounts high into the millions.

One of the most serious features of this loss is the fact that it is seldom fully appreciated, particularly when it is not accompanied by pronounced gullying. It is not at all an uncommon occurrence on certain soils for the top layers to be washed away so gradually and uniformly that the change is hardly perceptible. In such cases the farmer frequently does not realize that erosion is taking place. He attributes the decreasing fertility of the soil to the fact that it is getting " worn out," and eventually abandons the land without once suspecting that he himself is in any way responsible.

LOWERING OF THE WATER LEVEL.

Another important effect of erosion, too often overlooked, is its effect in lowering the level of the ground water. As gullies are deepened and stream channels lowered there is a constant tendency for the water in the upper layers of the soil to sink to the same level. Not infrequently this lowering of the ground water is sufficient to have an unfavorable influence on crop production, to make the use of the water for irrigation impracticable, and even to change the natural type of vegetation. A specific illustration of this which occurred in eastern Oregon may be cited.

A mountain meadow of some 200 acres was formerly well covered with an excellent growth of grass. The small stream which ran into it had no pronounced channel, but spread out so as to irrigate the entire area. Then came grazing, and then more grazing, until finally the sod began to be cut up and well-worn trails to be formed. Every spring, water would run down these trails until there was one deeper than the rest. This took the bulk of the flow and became the main drainage channel for the meadow. The channel was too small to accommodate all of the water, however, and the exposed soil soon began to erode. The banks at the lower end of the channel are now constantly caving in and being washed away, while at the same time the gully is growing deeper and deeper and working its way back toward the head of the meadow. As this development has taken place a striking change has occurred in the character of the vegetation. In the lower part of the area, where the lowering of the water level is most pronounced, the grass has entirely disappeared, and the land is now covered only with sagebrush and is worthless for grazing. Near the head of the meadow the grass still maintains its hold; but here also, unless the erosion is checked, the existing vegetation will be replaced in time by sagebrush and the value of the meadow entirely destroyed.

In addition to the loss of water through the deepening of drainage channels, the increased surface run-off which has accompanied erosion is a further cause of the lowering of the water level. This depletion of the water supply is of much more than local importance. In Bulletin 71 of the Bureau of Soils, for example, it is estimated that throughout an area of some 500,000 square miles in the eastern United States the natural level of the water in the ground has been lowered from 5 to 30 feet since the country was settled—the equivalent of 15 years' rainfall over the area depleted. Obviously such a drain on the water resources of the country, for the most part needless, can not be continued indefinitely.

DAMAGE TO IRRIGATION.

Erosion is also one of the most serious dangers that threaten irrigation. This is true for several reasons. The farmer on irrigated land is above all else dependent on a sufficient supply of stored water, which may come from either natural or artificial reservoirs or from both. Under normal conditions this storage is brought about primarily by the mantle of soil which clothes the mountains, protects the headwaters of the streams, and acts as a great natural reservoir. The effectiveness of this natural reservoir is decreased just in proportion as the soil is removed or its absorptive capacity diminished. Both of these effects are produced by erosion. The result is a greatly increased surface run-off after heavy rains, corresponding low-water stages during dry periods, and a marked decrease in the amount of water available for irrigation. Everyone who has seen how the water pours off a bare mountain side or a thoroughly compacted soil after a storm realizes how little of it nature is able to store for future use.

Furthermore, erosion has a secondary harmful effect in the filling up of artificial reservoirs with the soil brought down by the stream. Any increase in the amount of this sediment, therefore, means a corresponding decrease in the capacity of the reservoirs. In many cases dam sites at which storage reservoirs can be constructed at a reasonable cost are limited, and when this is true the silting up of the reservoirs means the eventual abandonment of the irrigated lands dependent upon them for water.

Water heavily laden with eroded material also decreases the efficiency and increases the cost of maintenance of other irrigation works, such as diversion dams, pipe lines, flumes, and canals. Sometimes it injures the crops to which it is applied, and not infrequently it seriously impairs or even completely ruins the land by burying it under a mass of sand, gravel, bowlders, and other coarse material.

An example of the damage that may be done to irrigated lands by erosion following even a small fire is afforded by a ranch in Cajon Canyon in southern California. Approximately 100 acres of comparatively low, brush-covered hills just above this ranch were burned over in the fall of 1914. The next spring all of the irrigating ditches lying immediately below the burned area were filled with sand and gravel, although no such trouble had been experienced previously. In some places the deposit of gravel was from 7 to 8 feet deep. In others, repeated filling up made it necessary to dig out the ditch three different times. Altogether some $800 was spent just for labor to repair the flumes which were burned out and to dig out the ditches. More serious than this, however, was the damage to the alfalfa crop. In the fall of 1914 one cutting of alfalfa on about 35 acres was lost, as a result of which it proved necessary to buy approximately $600 worth of stock feed during the winter. Worse still, the 1915 crop of alfalfa on 50 acres which had been seeded early in the spring was completely lost because the ditches could not be repaired soon enough to get water on the area in time to save the crop—a direct loss of perhaps $2,500.

In the spring of 1914 a little settlement on irrigated land in the foothills near Los Angeles suffered similar and heavier damage. The fall before, some 700 acres of the brush-covered watershed from which the settlement derives its water supply was completely burned over. Previous to the fire the stream draining this canyon had been hardly more than a serious wash, carrying so little water, even in the rainy season, that no one had thought of the possibility of its doing any damage. The next spring, however, a tremendous flood brought down hundreds of tons of eroded material. The inconspicuous wash widened until it carved out a stream-bed in places half a mile wide, in some spots gullied several feet deep, in others buried under from 8 to 10 feet of sand, gravel, and bowlders. Roads were washed out, irrigated orchards cut to pieces, and some land totally ruined. So serious was the damage that the county has spent several thousand dollars in correcting the stream channel and in constructing check dams in the canyon for the prevention of future floods. The total loss may be conservatively estimated at over $60,000—rather a heavy price to pay for a small fire.

LOSS OF WATER POWER.

In its relation to water power, erosion is of the utmost importance, because it interferes with the steady flow which is so essential to successful development. As in the case of irrigation, the capacity of the natural reservoir is depleted and artificial reservoirs are filled up. Many striking examples of this are afforded in the Southern Appalachians. In one reservoir which had a depth of 28 feet when the dam was first closed, an island had appeared in 2 years. Another pond about 4 miles long and 40 feet deep at the lower end had its upper part entirely filled in 4 years and near the dam was about three-fourths full. So serious is this effect that

in this region the attempt to use more than the unregulated
flow of the streams for water-power development has been
practically abandoned.[1]

Still another result of erosion in this connection is the
increase in the number and severity of floods. In a single
year the damage from floods to storage reservoirs, power
plants, and other property in the Southern Appalachians
amounted to $18,000,000.[1]

INTERFERENCE WITH NAVIGATION.

Erosion, because of its interference with navigation, has
been one of the factors responsible for our failure to develop
properly the inland waterways of the country. Increased
rapidity of run-off results in decreased low-water flow. At
the same time the sediment brought down by streams is deposited in their lower reaches. The action of both factors
tends in the same direction—to decrease the depth and hence
to impair the navigability of the stream. Many rivers formerly navigable have become so filled as to render them practically impassable by boats of even moderate size. Others
have to be constantly dredged in order to keep them open.

To take a single example: The Tennessee River has been
changed in comparatively recent years from a practically
clear to a sediment-bearing stream. A survey in 1896 of the
lower portion of the river, between Riverton, Ala., and Pa-
ducah, Ky., showed 49 bars through which it was calculated
that a channel could be opened by the removal of 650,000
cubic yards of sand and gravel. As the work developed it
proved necessary in some of the bars to remove several times
as much material as had been calculated, and others had to
be dredged several times. One, indeed, was opened five times
in 8 years. By 1908 several new bars had developed, 1,127,660
cubic yards had been dredged in 31 places, and the results
were stated to be fairly permanent in two-thirds of these.

GENERAL.

Altogether it has been estimated that erosion is responsible for an annual loss in this country of approximately
$100,000,000. To the farmer it means money out of his

[1] U. S. Geological Survey, Professional Paper 72, " Denudation and Erosion,"
by L. C. Glenn.

pocket from start to finish. It impairs the fertility and decreases the productivity of his land, and may even ruin it altogether; it renders irrigation more difficult and more costly; by reducing the possibilities of cheap water-power development it tends to keep up the price and check the more extended use of electricity; and by interfering with navigation it helps to prevent the development of a comprehensive system of cheap inland water transportation. But the farmer is not the only sufferer. The entire community is directly affected by the loss and is justified in taking heroic measures to remedy the evil.

PREVENTION OF EROSION.

CONTROL OF SURFACE RUN-OFF.

Since surface run-off is the primary cause of erosion, it is obvious that complete control of this would constitute a solution of the entire problem. In other words, if we cure the cause we shall also do away with the effects.

Some of the factors that influence surface run-off, and therefore erosion, are, of course, beyond our control. We can not alter the total amount or the distribution of the precipitation. Neither can we remake at will the geological formation, the general slope, or the depth and character of the soil. Some of these things, however, we can modify to a certain extent. By means of terraces we can break up the uniformity of the slope; by the addition of fertilizers and by proper methods of cultivation we can increase the absorptive capacity of the soil. Most important of all, we can, within the limits imposed by climate and soil, do almost what we will with the ground cover.

Prevention of erosion is, then, dependent primarily on the way in which we treat the protective cover of trees and other vegetation, and secondarily on the way in which we handle cleared lands. If the problem is to be solved we must cease to accelerate surface run-off by burning the forests and brush fields, overgrazing the range, clearing steep slopes for agriculture, and practicing antiquated methods of cultivation. On the contrary, the farmer, the forester, and the stockman must cooperate in seeing that the land is so used that surface run-off, particularly at the higher elevations, is reduced to a minimum. If this is done, erosion can be effectively controlled without interfering with the fullest use of our natural resources.

CLASSIFICATION OF LAND.

The first step toward controlling the run-off is to classify all land according to its liability to erosion and need of a protective cover. This might well be part of a broader classification aimed to devote all land to its highest use. Such a classification by competent authorities would perhaps accomplish more than any other one step not only in preventing erosion but in bringing about the fullest use of all our natural resources. Until Federal and State authorities take comprehensive action in this direction the individual will have to settle the question for himself as best he can with the knowledge at his disposal. So far as erosion alone is concerned, this should not be a very difficult matter.

FARM LAND.

How steep a slope can safely be cleared for farming depends largely on the character of the soil. It has often been said that no slope steeper than 15° should be cleared, and as a general guide this is probably as good as could be given. Yet slopes of less than 15° not infrequently show serious erosion under cultivation, while occasionally slopes of 20° and even more show none. The question, therefore, is one that must be settled separately for every locality, and even for every tract. As a rule, however, there is some cleared land in every vicinity which can be used as a guide. In case of doubt the safest course is to leave the land uncleared.

Some erosion must be expected on all slope land cleared for cultivation. On land really suitable for farming, however, this can be reduced sufficiently to prevent any marked deterioration. The general principle to be kept in mind is to prevent surface run-off just as far as possible. Water that is absorbed by the soil not only causes no erosion but increases the supply of ground water, diminishes drought, feeds the springs, and maintains a steady flow in the creeks and rivers.

One of the most effective methods for preventing erosion on cultivated land is terracing. Properly constructed terraces check the velocity of surface run-off and give the soil a chance to absorb far more water than would otherwise be possible. Their construction has been so frequently described in various agricultural publications that it need not be discussed here.[1] Their importance in any well-regulated scheme of farming should, however, be emphasized. There is scarcely a region in which they can not be used to advantage.

Numerous other measures can also be taken to convert surface into underground run-off. Deep plowing and fertilizing increase the absorptive capacity of the soil. On soils that become saturated quickly artificial drains help to carry off the surplus water. Contour plowing acts in the same general way as terracing. Winter cover crops and such crops as grapes and berries offer mechanical resistance to surface run-off and also bind the soil. Rotation of crops helps to retain the fertility and therefore the absorptive capacity of the soil. Occasional turning of the land into pasture for a few years is often beneficial. Properly located and constructed ditches help to carry away safely the excess run-off, and brush and stone dams serve to break its force. There is hardly a farm in the country where at least one, and usually several, of these measures should not be practiced.

FOREST LAND.

Forests, which are the highest type of vegetation, form the most effective cover for converting surface into subterranean run-off. They should therefore be retained on all areas which, if cleared, would either be in danger of erosion themselves or a menace to other areas. Paradoxical as it may sound, the crop production of the country would be greater if the forest cover were maintained where its protective influence is needed than would be the case if the entire area were cleared for farming.

MOUNTAIN FORESTS.—Water, like fire, is an unruly element which must be controlled at the outset if it is to be controlled at all. It is this fact that gives the mountain forests their peculiar importance. They catch the water at the begin-

---

[1] See, for example, Bureau of Plant Industry Circular 94; Department of Agriculture Bulletin 180; North Carolina Geological and Economic Soil Survey Bulletins 17 and 236; and South Carolina Agricultural Experiment Station Circular 20.

ning of its journey to the sea. They tackle the problem at its very source. Furtherfore, they afford protection where the precipitation is heaviest and the slopes steepest. For these reasons the great bulk of the land on the steeper slopes and at the higher elevations should be retained in forest, and the forest cover supplemented where necessary by small check dams and larger storage reservoirs. In no other way can the soil be kept on the mountain sides, surface run-off controlled, and the prosperity of the community safeguarded. In many regions farming, irrigation, municipal water supplies, water-power development, and navigation are all, in the last analysis, dependent upon the mountain forests.

Europe has already had its lesson. In the Apennines, near Florence, it is now possible to walk for miles on mountain slopes of bare rock where a century or so ago dense forests grew. France has spent millions of dollars in reforestation and engineering works in the Pyrenees and French Alps to control the torrents and the erosion which have resulted from forest destruction in the mountains.

In the United States marked progress is being made. Since 1891 the reservation under Federal ownership of forested public lands has been an established policy of the Government. One hundred and sixty-three million acres of National Forests, mainly in the mountains of the West, now protect both the forests and the various interests dependent on them. Another step in advance was taken in 1911, when Congress enacted legislation providing for the purchase of forest lands on the watersheds of navigable streams. Already some 400,000 acres of forest land have been acquired and some 900,000 acres more approved for purchase under this act. In addition, some 2,800,000 acres of mountain land are held as State forest reserves.

Much still remains to be done, however, before the mountain forests will exercise the influence of which they are capable in controlling surface run-off. Throughout the world, history has demonstrated unmistakably that unrestrained private ownership can not be relied upon to give such forests the protection that is necessary. They are a community asset, and community ownership or control is essential for their proper management. Until the Nation and the States realize this fact and act upon it, the problem of erosion, with all its attendant ills, will not have been solved.

WOODLOTS.—But the mountains are not the only place where a forest cover is necessary. Every farm has its patches which should be devoted to a woodlot—areas which are too rocky, poor-soiled, or steep to make cultivation practicable. Such areas if left barren are worse than useless because they form an actual menace to the rest of the farm. Woodlots on areas of this sort more than pay for themselves in the protection which they offer against rapid run-off and erosion. Not infrequently the very existence of a farm is dependent on the protection afforded by them. What timber they yield is clear gain.

Belts of timber may also be used advantageously to prevent erosion on long, moderately steep slopes. Unbroken slopes of this character which are otherwise suitable for farming often permit the run-off to gain such headway as to cause serious washing on their lower portions. Narrow belts of timber, which should, of course, be wider the steeper the slope, effectively check this tendency. The mechanical obstruction that they offer reduces the velocity of the water, which is then absorbed by the humus. A forest barrier is both more efficient and more profitable than any other.

RIVER BELTS.—Even along river bottoms the forest has its use. A fringe of trees along the main channel is of wonderful assistance in binding the banks and preventing the scouring out of adjacent lands. Although they have no effect on the height of flood waters, they offer a mechanical obstruction which checks the velocity of the water and causes the stream to deposit its load of sand, gravel, and other infertile débris. Instead of a raging torrent the flood is turned into a quiet overflow, carrying a burden of silt the deposit of which enriches the neighboring farm lands. Many examples of this were offered by the Kansas River flood of 1903. Farms where the river banks were protected by trees were in many cases actually benefited by the flood, while others without such protection were often completely destroyed. One farm protected in this way had some 200 acres enriched by a deposit of fine silt; another adjacent but unprotected farm had 16 acres gouged out to a depth of from 6 to 8 feet and 100 acres more ruined by being buried under from 1 to 3 feet of coarse sand. Every river which is in danger of floods, and therefore erosion, should have its banks protected by a belt of trees from a few to several hundred feet in width. For such a belt to be of the most benefit, however, the channel should be made as straight as possible and kept free from all obstructions, such as accumulations of logs and other débris. Nothing can prevent erosion on a stream so choked up that its channel is barely able to care for the normal flow.

FIRE PREVENTION.

From the standpoint of erosion it is fully as important to keep the forest floor in an absorptive condition as to maintain merely a stand of trees. Fires destroy both. They have no place in a well-managed forest, except occasionally as a help in securing natural reproduction, and then only under the direction of an expert. The prevention of uncontrolled fire is, indeed, an absolute necessity if the forest is to perform effectively one of its main functions.

Everyone recognizes a crown fire which destroys an entire forest as a disaster. But everyone is not yet educated to the realization that every surface fire, no matter how light, is a real menace. The mere fact that a fire is able to burn is sure proof that it is destroying organic material, and it is this organic material which makes the forest floor the great sponge that it is. Repeated fires will in time completely destroy this sponge. The change may be barely perceptible from year to year, but it is none the less sure. Every fire does its share toward removing the humus and making the forest less valuable for the storage of water and the prevention of erosion.

Adequate protection will not be secured, however, until the fire problem is attacked as systematically in the forest as it now is in the city. Laws to prevent the starting of forest fires, and a well-organized and well-equipped force to detect them as soon as possible and to extinguish them before they gain any considerable headway are essential in any protection system. To achieve such a result the efforts of forest owners, both public and private, must be supplemented by

FIG. I.—AN UNPROTECTED RIVER BANK.

During the Kansas River flood of 1903 this adjacent bank, which was unprotected by trees, was badly washed out and the farm land back of it seriously injured.

FIG. 2.—FARM LAND ALSO SUFFERS.

This steam thresher stood on land unprotected by a fringe of trees along the river. During the same flood it was buried in sand, a telephone line in the background was washed down, and the value of the entire farm greatly impaired.

FIG. I.—SOIL GONE; ONLY BARE ROCK LEFT.

The soil on this mountain slope has been washed out down to the bare rock as a result of the removal of the timber, followed by fires.

FIG. 2.—BOTTOM LAND BURIED UNDER SAND.

This fertile alluvial river bottom has been buried under a deposit of sand and other infertile material brought down as a result of erosion in the higher elevations at its headwaters.

FIG. I.—AN EXAMPLE OF THE CAVING GULLY.

This type of erosion often progresses very rapidly and is particularly difficult to stop.

FIG. 2.—BRUSH DAMS HELP TO CHECK EROSION.

An attempt was made to grow peaches on this area. Brush dams are now
being used to hold the soil preparatory to planting forest trees.

FIG. I.—THE CARRYING POWER OF WATER.

This huge bowlder, weighing some three tons, was washed down by a flood caused by rapid run-off from overgrazed lands on the upper part of the watershed. The carrying power of water varies as the sixth power of its velocity.

FIG. 2.—BOTTOM LAND STRIPPED OF ITS SOIL.

This alluvial bottom has been rendered worthless by the washing away of the soil. The small area in the center shows the soil level in the bottom, the best part of the whole farm, before the soil was removed.

the cooperation of the entire community. The public as a whole suffers from the evil and should cooperate in putting a stop to it.

GRAZING REGULATION.

The regulation of grazing, whether conducted on farm lands, on forest lands, or on intermediate lands devoted entirely to grazing, is important in preventing erosion. The most important precaution is to make sure that the grazing is not overdone. When carried to extremes it is a fruitful source of erosion because it reduces greatly the amount of surface vegetation, packs the soil, and forms well-worn trails in which the water readily collects. Such damage may be prevented by limitation of the number of stock grazed and by proper methods of handling.

One point to be borne in mind in determining whether an area should be used for grazing or forest production is the fact that a sod cover is not so efficient in decreasing the rapidity of surface run-off as a humus cover. A well-knit sod nearly always binds the underlying soil sufficiently to prevent erosion, but does not absorb water so readily. Consequently, certain areas that are not themselves in danger of erosion may be a more serious menace to farm lands below if devoted to grazing than if retained in forest.

On steep slopes where landslides are apt to occur, it may often be advisable to stop grazing during periods of very wet weather.

CONSERVATIVE LUMBERING.

The forest can be cut for its timber without serious danger of starting erosion, except on the highest, most exposed, and thinnest-soiled slopes. In such places the natural balance is very closely adjusted, and cutting should be prohibited entirely or limited to the removal of individual trees here and there. Areas of this sort should be set aside as " protection forests." These should be managed primarily with a view to retaining their protective value, and timber production should be treated as a purely secondary object.

Elsewhere ordinary lumbering operations may be carried on safely. Usually a sufficient cover of small trees, underbrush, and humus is left to protect the soil, and this is soon reinforced by new growth. Certain precautions must be observed, however. Such methods of logging should be adopted as will cause as few deeply gouged skid trails as possible. When soil and climatic conditions are such that these are liable to erode badly they should be filled up with brush and other slash left after logging. This will check the rapidity of the run-off and enable nature to repair the scar before serious damage results. Above all, the cut-over area should be protected from fire. Burning is permissible only as a silvicultural measure to assist natural reproduction, and then only under the direction of an expert. Uncontrolled fires following lumbering have caused far more damage than the cutting itself. They are a serious menace from every point of view and the greatest danger to be guarded against in connection with lumbering.

EDUCATION.

The most fundamental step that can be taken toward the prevention of erosion is education of the general public. The importance and extent of erosion, its causes, and methods of control should be made matters of common knowledge. In the last analysis an enlightened public sentiment is the only cure for a public evil.

Much can be done along this line in our educational institutions, especially in the common schools. Children in particular should have their interest actively aroused and their support enlisted. In one State "gully clubs" have been organized by the State forester. These are composed largely of school children who take an active part in the work of gully reclamation and particularly in finding and checking incipient gullies before it is too late. Why could not such organizations as boy scouts, girl scouts, and campfire girls be used in the same way? The normal child is never so happy as when doing something. Here is an outlet for his or her energies.

Much may be done also in the various agricultural organizations, such as the granges and farmers' institutes. County agents have an unequaled opportunity for effective educational work where it will do the most good. Legislatures can do their share by enacting adequate laws for the prevention of fire, the protection of mountain forests, and even of grazing and farm lands. It has been suggested that soil wash in cultivated or abandoned fields should be considered a public nuisance, and the holder of land on which it is permitted to occur held liable for resultant damages to neighboring lands and streams. This suggestion is based on the idea that the community has a right to take any action necessary to preserve its most valuable natural resource.

RECLAMATION OF ERODED LANDS.

NEED FOR PROMPT ACTION.

It should never be forgotten that to prevent an evil is infinitely better than to remedy it after it has once occurred. Nowhere is it more strictly true than in the case of erosion that "a stitch in time saves nine," and that "an ounce of prevention is worth a pound of cure." At the same time it is reassuring to know that erosion can be controlled if action is taken in time. If delayed too long, however, the process may have proceeded so far as to make control measures impossible except at a prohibitive cost. The golden rule in all reclamation work is to start early and stick to it; vigilance and persistence offer the only assurance of success.

The same measures which are effective in preventing erosion may also be used to control it after it has once started. Terracing, ditching, damming, deep plowing, contour plowing, fertilizing, straightening of stream channels, and forestation all have their place. Each case is a problem in itself, and the measures to be adopted depend on local conditions and the character of the erosion.

DAMS.

Small gullies may often be stopped by blocking them with cornstalks, straw, brush, logs, and similar material. These check the force of the water, and the gullies are gradually filled up with the sediment deposited. More pretentious dams may be made of earth, stones, or concrete. One device of this sort, known as a "christopher" or as the "Dickey system," consists of a dam beneath which is laid a sewer pipe with an upright arm. After every storm the basin behind the dam is filled with water to the height of this arm, which then carries the additional water off through the sewer. The sediment carried by the water is deposited in the basin until finally the gully is entirely filled. More effective drainage of the basin can be secured if it is also underlain by a tile drain connected with the sewer. The chief objection to dams in general is the danger of their being undermined by the water and washed out. This, of course, merely increases the evil, and is a danger that must be guarded against.

REVEGETATION.

Another method of reclaiming gullies is to cover their sides with vegetation. Herbs, shrubs, or trees, or sometimes a combination of all three, may be used for this purpose. Often it is wise to start the work with such plants as honeysuckle, Bermuda or other grass, Japan or native clover, or even sorghum or rye, and to follow these up later with trees. Black locust is a rapid-growing tree which is excellent for this purpose in places where the locust borer is not abundant. Willows, poplars, sycamore, yellow poplar, black walnut, shortleaf pine, white pine, and Norway pine may also be used to advantage in different parts of the country. The trees should usually be set fairly close together, say from 4 by 4 to 6 by 6 feet. The steeper the slope and the greater the danger of erosion, the closer should be the planting.

A combination of dams and revegetation may often prove advisable. This is especially true in particularly bad cases. Deep gullies with vertical sides are the most difficult to reclaim. Here the sides should first be flattened out by plowing back at their heads until uniform slopes of perhaps 15° have been established. Revegetation of these slopes should then be undertaken immediately. These measures should also be reinforced by dams if conditions are such that they will not be washed out.

On slopes where the soil is being washed away uniformly by sheet erosion it is usually possible to plant some cover crop. Best results are obtained by using a rotation of crops and by turning the land occasionally into pasture. Liberal fertilizing adds materially to the effectiveness of such measures.

Reforestation of denuded lands at the higher elevations will often serve to check erosion below. Along the main river bottoms the principal remedial measures to be used are straightening of the channels, removal of all obstructions, forestation of the banks, and in extreme cases the building of levees and revetment works.

FINANCIAL RESULTS.

That reclamation of eroded lands is not only practicable but often financially successful has been proved time and again. A badly eroded farm in Tennessee, for example, having a gully from 8 to 10 feet deep, was purchased for $53 an acre. The owner proceeded to reclaim the land at a cost of $10 an acre by filling the gully with débris and soil, adding manure, and planting rye. A few years later he refused an offer of $100 an acre for the farm.

Another owner reclaimed eroded land on his farm by plowing back the side walls of the gullies to a moderately gentle slope, planting them to peas, then to grass, pasturing the area for two years, and then repeating the rotation. Ten years later the reclaimed areas, which for 30 years previous had been practically worthless, were valued at $35 an acre. The owner estimates that even during the first year the returns were more than sufficient to pay for the labor expended in reclaiming them.

Still another owner reclaimed the gullies on his farm by planting them with black locust trees and sowing them to grass. Fifteen years later formerly worthless areas yielded good fence posts and excellent pasturage, and were then producing such crops as oats. During the same period the value of the entire farm had increased from $7.80 to $35 per acre.

CONCLUSION.

The problem of erosion and its control forms an integral part of any comprehensive plan for the development of our natural resources. If all land were put to its best use and so handled as to maintain its productivity the problem would be solved. This result can be attained, however, only by marked change in our present practice. A stop must be put to reckless destruction of the forest, to uncontrolled fires, to overgrazing, and to careless farming. For the sake of the farmer in particular and the public in general, steps should be taken to retain and restore the forest cover in the mountains, under public ownership or supervision. There should be brought home to the people as a whole the extent and seriousness of erosion and the necessity for its control by the community. When all these steps are taken, and not until then, will " farms, forests, and erosion " be a queer combination. When that day finally arrives we shall indeed have farms and forests, but no erosion.

THE PLANT-INTRODUCTION GARDENS OF THE DEPARTMENT OF AGRICULTURE.

By P. H. DORSETT,

Plant Introducer, Office of Foreign Seed and Plant Introduction, Bureau of Plant Industry.

FEW Americans, possibly not more than one in ten thousand, realize that plant introduction has given to the United States practically all of its commercial crops. Thousands of the new plant immigrants that enter the United States each year find their first home in the plant-introduction field stations, or gardens, of the Department of Agriculture. These are the " Ellis Island " of the plant immigrants, but they also are the workshops, field laboratories, and plant-propagation factories of the Office of Foreign Seed and Plant Introduction. They are situated at Miami and Brooksville, Fla., Chico, Cal., " Yarrow," near Rockville, Md., and Bellingham, Wash. Here the new plant arrivals are cared for and studied for the purpose of determining whether they are of economic importance, and those which promise to be of value are extensively propagated. From these stations the plants are distributed, upon orders from the Washington office, to specialists of the department and of the State experiment stations and to the thousands of private experimenters, special cooperators, and plant breeders throughout the country.

LOCATION OF THE GARDENS.

The almost complete freedom from frost and the general tropical character of the region in which the Miami station is located make it most advantageous for the propagation and preliminary testing of a wide range of new plant introductions from the tropical and subtropical regions of the world.

The Brooksville station, containing 35 acres in the hammock region of western Florida, was established after a careful search had been made for ideal conditions for the propa-

135

gation of plants coming from the moister but not tropical portions of China and Japan. The first Federal plantation of any considerable size of the Japanese timber bamboo is located at this garden. It is here that the propagation of the dasheen has been most successful and the chayote, a moisture-loving tropical vegetable, has grown luxuriantly.

The Chico Plant Introduction Field Station is located in one of the leading deciduous-fruit, nut, and citrus sections in northern California. The high summer temperature, abundance of water for irrigation, long growing season, and mild winters of this region make possible the propagation and testing of such widely different species of plants as alfalfa from the steppes of Siberia, hardy apples, pears, and cherries from Russia, chestnuts, jujubes, and persimmons from northern China, and citrus fruits from the Tropics.

The Yarrow garden was established primarily to meet the pressing demand for a place near Washington where newly introduced plants which the inspectors of the Federal Horticultural Board pass as apparently free from disease, but in regard to which there is a suspicion, may be cared for. Here they can be held or propagated and grown under observation for a season or until all possible danger of the development of disease is past and it is perfectly safe for the material to be distributed.

Extensive greenhouses, coldframes, and lath sheds have been provided at this garden, which admit of the propagation, care, and proper handling of the tropical and subtropical species in the rapidly growing stream of new plant immigrants. The hardy plant introductions are propagated, grown, and preliminarily tested in the nurseries and test orchards in the open.

The establishment of the Bellingham field station is the natural outcome of several years of experimentation carried on in various parts of the country to discover where flowering bulbs could be most successfully grown. It has been maintained for several years as a bulb garden, but is now being developed to include the propagation of a wide range of plants from western Europe, northern Japan, and the high mountain regions of western China.

PRECAUTIONS USED TO PREVENT THE INTRODUCTION OF INJURIOUS INSECTS AND DISEASES.

The thousands of new plant immigrants annually received in Washington in the form of seeds, plants, cuttings, etc., sent in by the agricultural explorers and correspondents of the office are unpacked and given an identification number in the specially equipped plant-inspection laboratory of the office in the presence of the inspectors of the Federal Horticultural Board, whose specific duties are to determine whether or not the material is in a condition to be distributed. If it is found to be affected with insect or other pests or with diseases, it is ordered into quarantine and the necessary treatment prescribed and administered. If found to be apparently free from insects and diseases, it is given a clean bill of health which permits it to be forwarded to the experimenters of the department for whom it was especially secured or to the plant-introduction gardens for propagation, cultivation, preliminary tests, and, later, if deemed advisable to be grown for distribution, to the special experimenters of the office.

The plant propagators at these gardens, who are personally responsible for the care and propagation of these new plant immigrants, have frequently to resort to every known practice of the craft to save an introduction arriving out of season or in a critical condition; and in some instances, when the plant introduced is unknown and no information regarding its identity can be secured, they must rely upon their own ingenuity in developing methods of handling such material in order to save what may eventually develop into an important new plant industry.

The necessary records of each new plant immigrant received at Washington include a Federal Horticultural Board inspection card, upon which is recorded the inspection and introduction number, the source and amount of material received, the dates of inspection, names of inspectors, and treatment prescribed; a plant-introduction card giving the plant-introduction and inspection numbers, by whom and from whence introduced, when received, its probable economic value, and such other available information as is considered important or of special interest; a plant-order card showing to whom the material was forwarded and the amount sent; and a shipping tag upon which is a certificate of inspection signed by the inspectors of the Federal Horticultural Board.

PRELIMINARY AND EXTENSIVE TESTS MADE.

The propagation houses, coldframes, lath sheds, greenhouses, and other equipment at the plant-introduction gardens of the department, together with trained superintendents, experienced plant propagators, and a corps of capable gardeners and laborers, afford excellent facilities for the propagation and preliminary testing of the thousands of new plants annually introduced by the Office of Foreign Seed and Plant Introduction.   They also make possible the efficient distribution of new plant material to specialists of this and other bureaus of the department, the State experiment stations, and to the thousands of private experimenters who, in occupying and developing the vast areas of agricultural lands of our country, are calling for something new to grow, either as an entirely new crop or to take the place of one that locally can no longer be grown commercially with profit.   Ornamental trees and flowering plants for yard and park planting are also very much in demand.

The new plants annually propagated at the department gardens, together with the test nurseries, test orchards, and permanent plantings, afford exceptional facilities for study to all who are interested in the development of a broader agriculture, and can avail themselves of the opportunity to visit these gardens and become personally familiar with the interesting new plant introductions.

It is at these plant-introduction field stations of the department that the agricultural experts determine which of the new plants show promise of being of economic value as direct producers and which are likely to prove valuable in plant breeding and selection experiments.

RECENT INTRODUCTIONS NOW BEING TESTED AT THE GARDENS.

Among the host of interesting new plant introductions which have been propagated at the various gardens, a few selected examples will give some idea of the range of species handled and the variety of the problems presented.

The jujube, *Ziziphus jujuba*, from China, is possibly as promising a plant commercially for California and the semi-arid South and Southwest as any of the other valuable crop and ornamental plants that have been introduced from the Far East.

The experimental tests made with this new alkali and drought resistant fruit at the Chico Plant Introduction Field Station, to determine the possible value of the strains and varieties that have been introduced from among the several hundred known to exist in China, have been very satisfactory. The fruit of the better varieties is fully as large as a large prune, and reddish or mahogany brown in color when ripe. While the jujube is a very good fresh fruit, it is undoubtedly of greatest value when processed with cane sugar or honey. Prepared jujubes are as delicate in flavor as many dates.

From the seed of the tung-oil tree (*Aleurites fordii*) an oil is made which the paint manufacturers of this country consider one of the best drying oils known to the trade. The importations of this oil are valued at from $2,000,000 to $3,000,000 per annum. Trees of this new plant immigrant distributed from the Chico garden in 1906–7 are doing well and bearing fruit in many places in the region extending from northern California to and throughout the Gulf States, but appear to be doing best in northwestern Florida and the southern parts of Georgia and Alabama.

The oil manufacturers are watching the experimental plantings of this tree with a great deal of interest.

The pistache tree (*Pistacia vera*), a promising introduction from central western Asia, presages another new industry for the United States. The small, green-fleshed nuts are most excellent to eat when roasted and salted, and are extensively used in the coloring and flavoring of ice cream and confections. The entire supply of these nuts at present comes from abroad. This country can, and surely should, grow what it needs. The trees do exceedingly well in the Sacramento and San Joaquin Valleys in California. A few of the grafted trees of some of the commercial varieties in the Chico test orchard are bearing a few nuts this season. Seedling trees near Fresno, Cal., have borne large crops of nuts for some years. Mr. Walter T. Swingle and several others who have studied the subject and are familiar with the conditions believe that in the not distant future pistache culture will be an established commercial industry of considerable importance in this country.

Budded and grafted plants of some of the best commercial varieties have been distributed to experimenters interested in testing out this introduction to determine the possibilities of its cultivation as a new plant industry.

The peculiar beauty of the Chinese pistache (*Pistacia chinensis*) and the great age to which it lives have suggested its trial as an avenue tree, and thousands of young trees have been distributed to parks throughout the country. A trial avenue a quarter of a mile long, planted at the Chico garden in 1910, already makes an excellent appearance.

The udo (*Aralia cordata*)[1] is a new salad plant from Japan that will probably succeed in practically every State in the Union. The crisp young shoots produced by this plant, when properly blanched, make a delicious salad or are excellent when cooked like asparagus. The culture and handling of udo is similar to that of asparagus. A few plants of udo should be in every home garden. It is believed that when the merits of this new introduction, both as a salad and vegetable, are better known, its cultivation will develop into an industry of considerable economic importance.

The Chinese varieties of persimmon (*Diospyros kaki*) vie with those of Japan in size, quality, beauty, and hardiness. Many varieties have been propagated at Chico and Yarrow, and the special Chinese stocks upon which they are grown in China have been used. The region in which the oriental persimmon can be successfully grown commercially includes California and the South, where the temperature does not fall much below zero. The culture of this excellent fruit is destined, sooner or later, to develop into an important industry. Dried persimmons form a staple food product of China and Japan.

The Chinese chestnut (*Castanea mollissima*) is an extremely interesting and possibly very valuable new plant introduction. This species, according to Mr. Frank N.

---

[1] Fairchild, David.   Experiments with Udo, the New Japanese Vegetable. U. S. Department of Agriculture Bul. 84, 1914.

Meyer, to whom belongs the credit of discovering that the chestnut bark disease (*Endothia parasitica*) is indigenous to China and Japan, is more or less resistant to this disease, which is threatening to destroy the American chestnut. A considerable quantity of nuts of this species sent by Mr. Meyer have been propagated and the trees distributed from our plant-introduction gardens to interested experimenters for growing and testing in disease-infested areas.

We have in Dr. W. Van Fleet's hybrid chinkapin-chestnut the result of a cross between *Castanea pumila* and *Castanea crenata*, an extremely promising new chestnut. A considerable number of the trees that are being grown experimentally appear to show rather marked resistance to the disease. Many of the plants have borne good crops of nuts within 18 months to 2 years from the planting of the seed. The trees will no doubt be small; the nuts, however, are of good size and of very good quality.

The Chinese dry-land elm (*Ulmus pumila*) is a promising new plant immigrant. This elm is found throughout northern China and Manchuria and is known to be very resistant to drought, neglect, and extremes of heat and cold. Seedling plants of this elm secured at Fengtai, near Peking, Chihli, China, in 1908, were grown and distributed from our Chico Plant Introduction Field Station. These early distributions proved sufficiently promising to justify its propagation in quantity for distribution throughout the United States. Our stock at the Chico garden being limited to a few small trees retained for permanent planting, it was necessary to resort to propagation by dormant hardwood cuttings. The tests with this elm at the Government Great Plains Field Station at Mandan, N. Dak., indicate that it is likely to be of very great value for windbreaks, shelter belts, and other plantings in the Great Plains region.

A promising small, early sweet cherry (*Prunus pseudocerasus* Lindley), introduced from Tanghsi, China, in 1906, was saved to the country by a chance graft. When this introduction was received at the Chico station, the gardener, after working practically all of the scions received upon nursery stock in the usual way, conceived the idea of running the few he had left into the small limbs of an old seedling cherry tree. The scions worked upon commercial stocks in the usual way all perished; two of those worked upon the old seedling tree survived, and in the following spring these grafts were in full flower before the buds of the seedling tree began to swell, and they ripened their fruit by the time the old tree was in flower, which was 10 days earlier than the earliest commercial cherries of that region. From the scions thus saved a large number of plants have been propagated and distributed throughout the country for experimental tests. At Yuba City and Vacaville, Cal., this introduction gives promise of being of considerable commercial importance as an early cherry for the eastern markets.

It is a curious fact that this Tanghsi cherry and not the Japanese flowering cherry is the true *Prunus pseudocerasus*, and its introduction puts in the hands of the American plant breeder a new oriental species of fruiting cherry which may prove valuable in the production of early strains of cherries.

The Davidiana peach (*Amygdalus davidiana*), a promising new stock for stone fruits other than the cherry, appears to be quite resistant to alkali and drought and well adapted to the deep alluvial soils of California. It is also succeeding at San Antonio and other places in Texas and has stood a temperature of —40° at the State Agricultural Experiment Station, Ames, Iowa, with little or no injury when 50 other varieties tested in comparison were either killed outright or seriously injured.

The fruit of this wild peach is small and inedible; however, the introduction may, on account of its extreme hardiness, prove valuable in hybridization experiments for the production of hardier types of commercial peaches.

Upward of 200 trees of this promising new plant immigrant have been planted in orchard form at the Chico station for the purpose of insuring a domestic seed supply.

The chayote (*Chayota edulis*), a little-known vegetable from tropical America, has been successfully grown in a limited way in California, Louisiana, and Florida, and can possibly be grown successfully in other parts of the country where the temperature does not fall much below freezing.

Many of those who have eaten the chayote consider it superior to our summer squash or vegetable marrow. The plant is a perennial vine that is comparatively easy to grow. The single-seeded, pear-shaped fruits, light green or creamy white in color, are produced in quantity in the fall and can be used then or stored and used as a fresh vegetable throughout the winter.

Bamboos are among the most useful and ornamental economic plants in the world. The first systematic planting of the timber and edible bamboos for experimental purposes in the United States on any considerable scale was made by the Government at the Plant Introduction Field Station at Brooksville, Fla., and at Avery Island, La., in cooperation with Mr. E. A. McIlhenny.

Canned and dried bamboo shoots are imported into the United States in considerable quantities for consumption by Chinese residents. The importation of bamboo canes for fishing rods and other purposes amounts to several millions of dollars annually. All of this material can and no doubt some day will be grown at home, for already most excellent shoots have been harvested from plantings in this country and poles of marketable size have been produced.

Flowering bulbs, which are imported into this country for forcing and ornamental planting at an expense to the people of the United States of at least $2,000,000 annually, have been grown at the Bellingham station with excellent success. Judging from the results of these experiments, there are many reasons to believe that the so-called " Dutch bulbs " can be successfully grown in commercial quantities in the Puget Sound region and probably in other sections of the United States. Tests so far made show that the home-grown bulbs are fully equal and in some respects superior to the imported stock.

In the spring of 1916 the flowers at Bellingham were unusually fine. The extensive masses of gorgeous colors made a scene of exceptional beauty. Fully 2,000,000 bulbs were in bloom, and in a single day upward of 2,000 people visited the garden and inspected and admired the flowers.

The avocado (*Persea americana*) as a salad fruit stands without a rival. It is also excellent served in the " half shell," with salt or with lemon and sugar. The tree is adapted for culture in southern Florida and southern California.

To assist in building up the avocado industry, which has recently awakened widespread interest in southern California and southern Florida, considerable areas of the Miami garden have been devoted to the preliminary testing of a large number of varieties, and some of the more important problems of the new industry are being worked out there.

The introduction of hardier types from Mexico and the hardier, hard-shelled varieties from the highlands of Guatemala, which ripen their fruit at a different season from the West Indian and South American varieties, it is believed, will result in an extension of the commercial culture of the avocado and secure a practically continuous crop of this most excellent fruit throughout the season.

The introduction of the East Indian mango (*Mangifera indica*) has been stimulated in Florida by the growing and fruiting of nearly 100 imported varieties at the Miami garden. The investigational work incident to the building up of the mango industry in this country has occupied a prominent place in the activities of this station, where most of the varieties now growing in Florida were propagated and where many of them have fruited.

While the foregoing brief descriptions indicate a few of the interesting new plant industries which are finding their beginnings in the Government plant-introduction field stations, even a bare list of the hundreds of species and varieties of plants which are now in process of propagation there would much exceed the limits of this article.

The work of the Office of Foreign Seed and Plant Introduction is to find, introduce, propagate, and distribute valuable new plants and also to assist in making possible the cultivation of some economic new plant immigrant upon every available acre of our agricultural lands. The field stations of the office are filled with the new beginnings of plant industries which later will add to the wealth and beauty of the country.

L. C. C. Krieger pinx.   A. HOEN & CO.

FRUITING BRANCH OF ONE OF THE LARGE-FRUITED VARIETIES OF THE
CHINESE JUJUBE GROWING AT THE CHICO PLANT INTRODUCTION
FIELD STATION   (*Natural Size.*)

FIG. I.—ONE OF THE PROPAGATING HOUSES AT THE YARROW FIELD
STATION.

This illustration shows a block of young broad-leaved evergreens, *Pittosporum floribundum*, from the Himalayas, large enough to be distributed to experimenters. The utmost care has to be exercised to keep these plants free from disease and insect pests.

FIG. 2.—LATH HOUSE AT THE MIAMI FIELD STATION FILLED WITH
TROPICAL AND SUBTROPICAL PLANTS.

The Miami garden has contributed largely to the agriculture of Florida through the study made there of new methods of propagating tropical plants, which heretofore were only grown from seeds.

FIG. 1.—A PORTION OF THE NURSERY PLANTINGS AT THE CHICO PLANT INTRODUCTION FIELD STATION.

Beyond the test nursery of citrus hybrids in the foreground are thousands of new plant introductions that are being grown for distribution during the season of 1916–17.

FIG. 2.—TEST ORCHARD AT THE PLANT INTRODUCTION FIELD STATION, CHICO, CAL.

Hundreds of varieties of new plants are here given a preliminary test, and it is here that many new plant immigrants fruit for the first time in the United States.

FIG. 2.—SEVERAL THOUSAND YOUNG TUNG-OIL TREES.

FIG. 1.—FRUITING BRANCHES OF ONE OF THE LARGE-FRUITED VARIETIES OF THE CHINESE JUJUBE S. P. I. 23455.

FIG. 1.—In the test orchard at the Chico Plant Introduction Garden this tree thrives remarkably well. The fruit is borne in quantity upon the deciduous leafy twigs, which resemble the compound leaves of leguminous trees, and not directly upon woody fruit spurs like those of most other northern fruits. FIG. 2.—A portion of a nursery block of young seedling tung-oil trees, Chico Plant Introduction Garden. From the nuts of this tree one of the best drying oils of commerce is obtained.

FIG. I.—CHINESE PISTACHE IN THE CHICO PLANT INTRODUCTION
GARDEN TEST ORCHARD.

This species is an excellent pollen bearer and is being experimented with as a stock for
the commercial pistache (*Pistacia vera*), a tree of which is to be seen at the right. It
is also a fine ornamental, shade, and avenue tree for California, parts of Arizona, New
Mexico, Texas, and the South.

FIG. 2.—LATH SHED AT THE CHICO FIELD STATION FILLED WITH UDO
SALAD PLANTS.

These were distributed during the season of 1911–12. The partial shade afforded by a
lath shed of this character makes it possible to grow many species of plants which otherwise could not be propagated where the sunlight is most intense.

FIG. I.—A BLOCK OF DR. VAN FLEET'S YOUNG HYBRID CHESTNUT
TREES AT THE CHICO PLANT INTRODUCTION FIELD STATION.

These were distributed during the season of 1915–16. They are hybrids between the
Japanese chestnut and the American chinquapin, and although smaller-growing trees
than the American chestnut, they produce good nuts and are more or less free from
the chestnut-bark disease.

FIG. 2.—DAVIDIANA PEACH SEEDLINGS IN MARYLAND.

This shows a portion of a nursery block of seedling stocks of a Chinese wild peach (*A myg-
dalus davidiana*) at the Yarrow Plant Introduction Field Station that were distributed
throughout the country to experimenters desiring to test a stock for various stone fruits
or to utilize it in plant-breeding experiments.

FIG. I.—CHAYOTE ARBOR AT BROOKSVILLE, FLA.

One of a number of experimental plantings at the Brooksville garden for the purpose of determining the desirability of this method of training the plants. The chayotes produced will be utilized in cooking and demonstration experiments and to direct public attention to the delicate character of this valuable vegetable for the South.

FIG. 2.—VIEW IN THE BROOKSVILLE PLANT INTRODUCTION FIELD STATION.

The road runs between a 3-acre planting of Japanese timber bamboo on the left, now 6 years old, and a nursery of young bamboo plants on the right, set out for the purpose of propagation. The small 3-room field laboratory on the right is equipped for preliminary field studies and has been used for microscopic investigations and cooking experiments in connection with the dasheen and chayote investigations.

JAPANESE TIMBER BAMBOO IN NORTHERN CALIFORNIA.

Portion of a 9-year-old planting of one of the large timber bamboos, *Phyllostachys bambusoides* (S. P. I. No. 12180), at the Chico Plant Introduction Field Station. Large, young, growing shoots in this planting have made a growth of 16 inches in 24 hours. This is about the usual rate of growth under normal conditions. Growths of 26 inches in 24 hours have been reported; such rapidity of growth, however, is under exceptionally favorable conditions.

Fig. 2.—An East Indian Grafted Mango in Fruit at Miami, Fla.

Fig. 1.—Budded Avocado Tree at the Miami Field Station.

Fig. 1.—Seedling avocado tree with large shoot growing from near the base, which came from a bud of a valuable and hardy variety worked into the stock 13 months previously. The bud sticks from one of which this bud was taken were secured in Antigua, Guatemala, at an altitude of 5,000 feet. The fruit was large, round, and hard shelled, with thick, firm flesh of excellent quality, pale yellow near the seed, changing to greenish yellow near the surface. Horticulturists in southern California and southern Florida are very much interested in the Guatemalan varieties of avocados, especially those coming from the higher elevations. Our growers need hardier types and varieties, and also those that will prolong the ripening season. Fig. 2.—The Sandersha mango from Bangalore, India, bears good, regular crops of large, kidney-shaped fruit, which, when well ripened, is of very good quality. This variety, while not of as high quality or as attractive as others that have fruited at the station and at other places in Florida, fruits with more regularity than many of these and is especially valuable for canning and preserving.

FIG. I.—VIEW OF A PORTION OF NARCISSUS PLANTINGS AT THE
BELLINGHAM GARDEN.

Madame Plemp in the foreground and Sir Watkin in the distance. This broad expanse
of yellow and green was wonderfully beautiful and inspiring.

FIG. 2.—AN APPROACH TO THE MIAMI PLANT INTRODUCTION FIELD
STATION.

On each side of the drive is a beautiful carissa hedge, *Carissa grandiflora*, an extremely
handsome shrub bearing sweet-scented, white flowers and edible fruits. This plant
is worthy of a place in the grounds of every home in southern Florida and southern
California. The large trees beyond the hedge on either side are different varieties
of the East Indian mango, a fruit which for quality, fragrance, and beauty has few
rivals.

A FEDERATED COOPERATIVE CHEESE MANUFAC-TURING AND MARKETING ASSOCIATION.

By HECTOR MACPHERSON, *Director Bureau of Organization and Markets, Oregon Agricultural College, and Field Agent, Office of Markets and Rural Organization*, and W. H. KERR, *Investigator in Market Business Practice, Office of Markets and Rural Organization.*

UNITY of purpose among its members, correct methods of conducting its business, and loyal support accorded its management are universally essential to the success of any cooperative enterprise. These fundamentals are exemplified in every well-known cooperative association. Each organization, however, has its own peculiar problems to face and has developed specific methods of meeting them, a study of which can not fail to be valuable to similar associations.

A survey of the cheese industry in Tillamook County, Oreg., discloses the importance of proper marketing methods in the stimulation of production and the beneficial effects of concentrated agricultural effort for a common purpose. The Tillamook County Creamery Association, among other things, has standardized the product of its member factories and eliminated unequal competition in matters of production and prices. Much of the success of the association, it seems safe to conclude, has been brought about through correct methods of business administration. A study of these methods should be valuable to other rural communities where less success has been attained in manufacturing and marketing cheese.

GENERAL AGRICULTURAL CONDITIONS.

Tillamook County lies near the northwest corner of the State of Oregon, between the Coast Range and the Pacific Ocean. The climate is mild, and abundant rains in winter, with cool, clear weather in summer, tend to produce abundant green feed and pasturage for stock almost the year around. This condition of climate is conducive to large yields of milk at low cost, with regard to both labor and purchased feeds. A small expenditure in buildings is sufficient to provide stables for the herds, so that the investment of the farmer is almost entirely of a type which will furnish earnings on the money invested. Land values, however, are sufficiently high to offset the saving in building prices as compared with the average dairying district.

A TYPICAL SMALL DAIRY FARM.

The following survey of a small dairy farm in the county is pertinent in so far as it is typical of the best farms of this character in Tillamook County.[1] The 53 acres of cleared river-bottom land in this farm were valued at $400 per acre in 1914, and $7,000 had been invested in improvements, including the house, barns, and all outbuildings. The total investment of $32,790 included, in addition, $2,390 worth of live stock, an automobile valued at $1,700, and $500 worth of machinery.

The farm supported, in 1914, 35 dairy cows valued at $60 each, 6 yearling heifers valued at $25 each, and a Jersey bull valued at $75. These cows were grade Holsteins, Jerseys, and Guernseys. No attempt had been made to grade the herd up to one breed. The proprietor owned a Holstein bull a few years ago, and had previously a Guernsey. Only the heifer calves from the best cows were kept, while all others were sold to local exporters when they were 2 or 3 weeks old. One horse was kept and used to haul the milk to the factory. There were 50 chickens on the place, the product of which was used mainly for home consumption, not more than $25 being realized from the trading of eggs at the store for groceries.

Since this is a dairy farm of the most highly specialized type, the income is derived almost entirely from milk disposed of through the cooperative cheese factory. In 1914, the milk sold produced 9,411.36 pounds of fat. The average price yielded was 38 cents a pound for butterfat, making a gross income from the dairy of $3,576.32.

The expenses for the year were $480 for wages; $100 for whole grain, bran, and ground barley, and $343.90 for taxes, making a total of $923.90. Subtracting this from the gross income, there remains $2,676.10 as interest on the investment and labor income for the owner. Charging 7 per cent on the total investment, or $2,295.30, there is left $380.80

---

[1] This survey was made in July, 1915, covering the year 1914.

as labor income. This comparison is hardly a fair one, however, since this farm represents a home value which it would cost the city dweller from $7,000 to $15,000 to duplicate.

It is not to be assumed, of course, that all farms, or even all river-bottom farms in Tillamook, are as productive as these 53 acres. In a few particulars, however, this farm is typical of the best lands of Tillamook County. In the first place, the cattle were pastured on the permanent pasture land of 33 acres, supplemented by the other 20 acres on the farm, which was pastured in early spring and in the fall after the hay had been cut. Another typical feature was the small quantity of grain and milled feed purchased. This particular farmer fed little or no grain to his cows, and yet an average of over $102 worth of butterfat was marketed from each cow during the year 1914. This return may be compared with that on another small farm where the average income from each of the 27 cows was $119.20 for the year 1914. This greater production was attained at an outlay of $296 for the purchase of 8 tons of clover hay and 8 tons of bran, making a cost for bran and clover of $10.96 a cow. Without taking into account the additional labor required, this would indicate a difference in net profit of $6.24 per cow, owing probably to the feed purchased.

The farm in this survey, however, with its small outlay for milled feed, represents the common practice of Tillamook dairymen more truly than does the farm upon which grain feeds and clover are used for 4 or 5 months of the year.

DEVELOPMENT OF THE INDUSTRY.

The first white settler reached Tillamook County on the first day of April, 1851. Three men made the trip from the Columbia in order to investigate the Indian tales of rich meadow land, splendidly watered, which was reported to lie back of the bay. From that date the county passed rapidly through the usual stages of the frontier settlement. Hunting, trapping, and fishing were good along the bays and numerous streams. But the rich prairie and bottom lands soon attracted the stockmen, whose herds usurped the dominion of the deer, the bear, and the mountain lion. As the settlement grew, the fertile soil and rich pastures bid for more complete utilization. Farms crowded out the range, making dairying a specialty.

Previous to 1893 dairying in Tillamook County was carried on in a primitive way common to communities in which dairying is conducted only as a side line. Cows were bred fresh in the spring and milked while the pasture was good, after which they were allowed to dry up until the following spring. Most of the butter was made in the homes of the farmers, packed in kegs, and shipped to commission men in neighboring coast cities.

Because of the varying quality of the butter produced under such conditions and the instability of the supply, returns usually were small in amount, while a period of from 6 months to a year sometimes elapsed between the date of shipping and the receipt of returns.

In 1890 the first serious attempt at scientific dairying was made in this locality, when certain of the methods employed in the production of butter in the Elgin district were followed. Three years later the first farmers' creamery in the county, the Tillamook Dairy Association, was established. The factory was completed in the spring of 1893 and was operated as a butter factory during its first season. Earlier in the same year a creamery was established in Tillamook County under private ownership, and the following spring it became the first cheese factory of Tillamook County.

From this beginning the movement spread until by 1899 there were 8 privately owned cheese factories in the county, producing a total of about 1,000,000 pounds of cheese a year, and four large creameries having an output of about 350,000 pounds of butter annually.

As cheese proved better adapted than butter to the uncertain transportation conditions of the locality, the number of cheese factories increased rapidly until in 1902 approximately 40 privately owned cheese factories were operating in the county, and half of these were very small plants handling the milk of from 1 to 3 farms.

COOPERATION IN MANUFACTURING CHEESE.

A new business type which was to bring far-reaching changes in the dairy industry of the county already had made its appearance by 1899, when the Tillamook Dairy Association was formed at Fairview. This factory was cooperative from the beginning, $1,000 being raised as capital, but this amount fell far short of meeting the needs of the association. Because of the limited number of farmers who could be induced to purchase stock in the new venture, the members then owning stock combined on a joint note and raised an additional $1,200, which represented the balance of the necessary capital. The factory first was employed in the manufacture of butter, but as prices were poor in this commodity, equipment was installed for the manufacture of cheese. This experiment proved quite as unsatisfactory and gave very little relief, and the factory reverted to the manufacture of butter.

Such conditions discouraged some of the members, who offered to pay their proportionate share of the losses and withdraw. Other members, however, were determined to make the creamery succeed and refused to relieve any member from his position in the society and his liability on the note, unless he should pay the whole $1,200. By this means the membership was held together. By the end of the second year the association had begun to succeed, and paid off its obligation without a levy on its members.

The success of this association led to the establishment of other local farmers' creameries. The cooperative movement has grown until now, out of a total of 23 factories in the county, but two are privately owned. A few farmers still are making their own cheese, but most of the small factories have ceased to operate and their place has been taken by larger and more economically managed plants, owned and controlled by the farmers in cooperation.

All of the factories, though for the most part cooperative, are corporations organized under the Oregon corporation law. The plan of organization is simple. A few of the most interested farmers make an inventory of the dairying assets of the neighborhood, taking into account the number of cows, the pasturage, and the crop conditions, from which a decision is reached whether the locality can support a cheese factory. If conditions are found favorable, a company is incorporated with sufficient capital to provide an adequate factory for taking care of the milk supply.

Cooperation between banks and farmers' companies in Tillamook County has been responsible, in a great measure, for the success of many of these creameries during the early stages of their existence, since funds have been provided at low rates of interest and for a long time.

PLAN OF OPERATION

The security offered in most cases took the form of a joint note of the members, but in some cases the note of the association, signed by the board of directors, was sufficient.

The management of these factories is vested in a board of from 3 to 5 directors. This board elects from its number a president, who is the legal head of the association. A secretary and a treasurer also are appointed by the board of directors. In the majority of Tillamook creameries these important officers may not be members of the board.

To meet the expenses of operation, a flat rate per pound is charged for manufacturing cheese. The standard price is 1¾ cents per pound. For the large factories this price is sufficient to meet all charges, including making, hauling, and inspection of cheese, entrance charges, insurance, the cost of marketing, and the annual addition to the sinking fund. In addition to meeting all these expenses the charge of 1¾ cents per pound provides for the accumulation of a considerable surplus in the case of large factories. Because in most cases these factories are not conducted as true cooperative associations, but are rather farmers' stock corporations, this surplus sometimes is distributed only to a small number of patrons who are stockholders. Associations which tend toward the stock-dividend policy have been known to pay as high as 100 per cent dividends upon their capital stock. This condition of affairs sometimes leads to discontent among the patrons who have not been able to share in the distribution of the surplus.

Where factories are conducted upon a strictly cooperative basis the policy is to pay a liberal rate of interest on capital invested, the remaining surplus being distributed to patrons in proportion to the milk they have supplied during the year. One such factory distributed a surplus by paying 10 per cent on capital stock and 2 cents on the hundred pounds of milk delivered at the factory.

The economic waste of conducting small factories for the manufacture of cheese is exemplified by comparing some of them with those of larger capacity. It has been found that whereas 1¾ cents per pound for making cheese is sufficient to produce a large surplus in factories with a heavy output, the same rate is not sufficient even to sustain the smaller factories, and for that reason these small factories are an expense rather than an advantage to the farmers patronizing them, providing there is a market for their product elsewhere at a lower cost.

CENTRALIZED MARKETING CONTROL.

The great influence of proper marketing methods on the success of cooperative manufacturing or marketing associations has been demonstrated fully in the experience of the Tillamook County cheese factories. Previous to the year 1904 the factories, on account of the lack of storage facilities, were compelled to ship their cheese, as fast as it was made, on consignment to jobbers and commission houses in the large centers of population on the Pacific coast. This necessity created a temporary congestion on the market in the cities receiving the bulk of the output during the period of high production, and especially was this true in Portland, Oreg. The depression in price which followed was maintained until the season of low production in the fall of the year, which also is the season of greatest consumption of cheese. The diminished supply and increasing demand generally brought about an immediate upward trend in prices which resulted in great profit to those dealers who had stored the cheese during the summer. Such a condition, resulting as it did in unsatisfactory prices to the producers, brought about a consolidation of the various factories of the county in an effort to market their output as a unit and to provide storage capacity so that the excess production of cheese during the summer could be held over at the point of production under the ownership of the association.

The efficiency of the cooperative plan of consolidated purchasing and marketing immediately began to have its effect upon privately owned factories, several of which went into bankruptcy or sold out to farmers' companies during the next two years. The added efficiency which secured higher prices under this plan of operation also brought greater returns to the farmers and stimulated the production of milk on all the farms previously supplying these factories. This gave a great impetus to the cooperative movement, so that by the spring of 1909 the cooperative selling agency was handling the output of 16 large factories and 3 private farm factories.

This cooperative plan of selling brought about the establishment of a central office supervised by a secretary-salesman who kept in touch with all the markets and arranged the sale of the entire output of the member factories. The increase in business transacted through this office also brought about the establishment of highly efficient accounting methods, which not only facilitated sales but also improved the quality of the output.

By having only one salesman to handle 90 per cent of the output of the county, the Tillamook factories have been able to get better prices for their cheese. The secretary-salesman knows that his prices must conform closely to the prices for eastern cheese. Hence, the price asked for Tillamook cheese is determined by eastern markets. To the price of New York or Wisconsin cheese is added the freight to the coast point, and from this rate the freight from Tillamook is usually deducted. Although this is the rule, the secretary-salesman explains that it is often broken. The whole cheese situation of the coast, with the supply on hand in the factories and their daily output, is taken into consideration. The secretary-salesman knows that eastern cheese is coming into his territory constantly, and that any attempt to raise the price unduly would stimulate such shipments and result in a hardship to his factories at a later date. By keeping in constant touch with the conditions in eastern markets, he is able to secure the highest possible average prices for cheese the year around.

Close acquaintance with jobbers and wholesalers throughout the Pacific coast has had its advantages. Bad debts have been reduced to the minimum. During the last 10 years the entire loss from this source will not amount to $500. As the sales have amounted to over $3,000,000 during that time, the losses from bad debts have amounted to only one-sixtieth of 1 per cent. The terms of sale stipulate cash within 30 days. The secretary-salesman has occasionally suspended business relations with a house which failed to make its payments promptly until it had complied with the terms of the contract.

The regularity with which the returns for cheese come in enables the factories to pay their patrons regularly. Punctual payment is no small factor in the success of the cooperative cheese factory, or, for that matter, in the success of any other farmers' marketing organization.

QUALITY STANDARDIZATION.

The gravest problem encountered in pooling the output of several factories was that of securing a uniform quality. Under the early operation of this plan, numerous complaints were received about the quality of the cheese. The cheese was shipped as it came from the different factories, and the cheese makers mixed their off-flavored and gassy cheese with their best product, bringing the whole output into disrepute. A meeting of the factories selling through one salesman was called, resulting in the organization of the Tillamook County Creamery Association, which began operations in 1909 with a membership of 9 of the largest factories. The object of this organization, according to its by-laws, was in part as follows: To bring the producers of the different creameries in Tillamook County together and maintain just and cordial relations among them, and by cooperation to advance their common interests; to foster and encourage domestic and foreign trade pertaining to the farming interests of Tillamook County and to acquire and disseminate valuable business information; and to adjust controversies between its members and generally to secure to its members the benefits of cooperation in the furtherance of their legitimate pursuits.

The most important action taken by the association was the placing of an inspector in the field to visit regularly each of the factories belonging to it. The duties of the inspector are to help improve the quality and increase the quantity of cheese obtained from the milk of the associated factories. Under his administration the factors responsible for poor cheese practically have been eliminated. Inefficient workmen have been removed, and the methods of making cheese in all of the factories have been standardized. Through the interchange of ideas among cheese makers, the good points responsible for high quality of output in one factory have been introduced in another, and improved methods, such as the use of a commercial starter and of acidity tests for whey, have brought about a much greater certainty as to the quality of the cheese.

While undoubtedly there is not nearly so much gassy cheese or high-acid cheese as there was formerly, there is still room for improvement in the quality, as the association has been working more for increased yield than for the highest quality. The increase in the average yield of cheese obtained per hundred pounds of milk is shown by an increase from 10.7 pounds in 1909 to 11.12 pounds in 1914.

The association now includes 18 factories, and the inspector visits each of these factories once a week. He tests one cheese out of each vat produced, and if the cheese is found to conform to a standard set by the Tillamook County Creamery Association the boxes required for the cheese inspected are stamped "Inspected by Tillamook County Creamery Association." If a vat of cheese for any reason falls below the required standard, the boxes are not stamped in this way and this cheese must be shipped in what are known as plain boxes. Indicative of the standard uniformly attained by the various cheese makers, it may be noted that the amount of cheese shipped in plain boxes is now less than 1 per cent of the total output. Plain-boxed cheese is usually consigned to be sold on commission for whatever it will bring, and under this plan of distribution its sale does not have any appreciable effect on the position of the better cheese on the market

BUSINESS PRACTICE.

The business practice followed in the Tillamook County Creamery Association concentrates the marketing and operating control in the hands of a secretary-salesman. The books of record necessary for tabulating and accounting for the operations in the several factories are kept under his direction in the central office. As the milk is received at the factories each morning, the cheese makers enter the milk receipts from each person on a tally sheet. At the beginning and the middle of the month composite tests are made of the milk supplied by each patron. At the end of the month the tally sheets are summarized in a monthly report showing the total amount of milk and the tests for each patron for the month. This monthly summary is sent to the secretary-salesman's office, where it is used as the

Comparative table of products handled by Tillamook County Creamery Association.

Factory No.—	Milk received.			Cheese produced.		
	1912	1913	1914	1912	1913	1914
	Pounds.	*Pounds.*	*Pounds.*	*Pounds.*	*Pounds.*	*Pounds.*
1	4,809,293	4,539,999	4,861,981	527,233	514,791	550,592
2	4,148,442	4,149,791	4,153,089	464,136	463,233	463,846
3	3,923,074	4,008,258	4,078,036	441,007	451,700	455,683
4	2,391,159	2,287,492	2,527,709	259,766	253,945	284,120
5	2,276,749	2,138,362	2,106,504	252,314	233,804	232,456
6	2,120,895	2,012,366	1,931,413	230,766	220,381	210,871
7	1,866,008	1,892,720	1,901,107	203,162	210,931	207,029
8	1,574,255	1,672,663	1,844,850	175,272	189,765	204,691
9	1,351,081	1,669,356	1,720,606	147,953	183,089	192,845
10	1,160,768	1,569,640	1,595,005	125,824	174,572	174,620
11	1,104,691	1,015,855	1,262,108	122,256	110,293	139,961
12	896,694	932,640	1,006,872	95,958	101,463	111,634
13	453,768	904,013	947,374	51,876	100,356	104,691
14	470,214	794,039	889,548	50,503	86,074	97,034
15	394,901	614,719	642,888	40,647	67,483	71,898
16	224,522	595,393	611,158	22,231	65,434	69,364
17	....	575,726	530,580	....	60,451	58,477
18	....	183,747	465,493	....	17,951	51,335
19	....	....	126,195	....	....	13,311
Total....	29,166,514	31,556,779	33,202,516	3,210,904	3,505,716	3,694,458

Factory No.—	Value of cheese.			Factory No.—	Value of cheese.		
	1912	1913	1914		1912	1913	1914
1	$86,480.88	$79,769.31	$84,799.84	12	$15,774.93	$15,457.76	$17,127.57
2	75,705.68	71,582.48	70,943.19	13	8,324.53	15,470.11	16,066.00
3	72,164.53	69,990.08	70,743.95	14	8,274.43	13,213.03	14,667.40
4	42,534.51	38,214.69	43,777.94	15	6,721.44	10,416.75	10,944.87
5	41,115.58	36,036.32	35,711.07	16	3,505.12	10,075.86	10,674.78
6	37,260.67	34,310.60	32,428.43	17	....	9,321.55	8,875.14
7	33,129.20	32,571.84	38,853.76	18	....	3,768.22	7,781.73
8	28,706.60	29,296.79	31,970.42	19	....	....	2,028.84
9	23,942.20	28,179.31	29,932.61				
10	20,801.26	26,974.72	26,585.03	Total....	524,618.61	541,748.46	568,395.53
11	20,177.05	17,099.04	21,481.96				

basis in making out the patron's monthly statement. In addition, each cheese maker is required to make out a weekly report to the secretary-salesman showing the total amount of milk received and the number of cheeses of the different kinds made for each day of the week. Supplementing these reports, the inspector is required to make out a report of the number of cheeses of each variety inspected and of the number of cases of each kind branded as "Inspected by Tillamook County Creamery Association." The inspector's reports are made out daily and cover the factories as inspected by him. By referring to the inspector's reports the secretary-salesman is enabled to keep an accurate account of the number of cheeses of each kind ready for market at all times. This process of accounting makes it possible to manufacture the different styles of cheese according to the market demand. In the relations of the central office with the different commission men who handle the output, the association is enabled to safeguard itself against bad accounts and to distribute its output in those markets where the highest level of prices obtains.

When the shipping season is at its height orders come in rapidly by telephone, telegraph, and mail, and it is not uncommon for sales to average over $3,000 a day during the months of May, June, and July.

Total products handled for the last seven years by the Tillamook County Creamery Association.

Year.	Milk.	Cheese.	Value.	Yield of cheese.[1]
	Pounds.	*Pounds.*		*Pounds.*
1908....	....	2,073,390	$259,355.29	....
1909....	23,416,524	2,506,612	386,135.81	10.70
1910....	23,639,664	2,541,057	400,044.84	10.75
1911....	24,131,802	2,619,229	358,206.29	10.85
1912....	29,139,514	3,211,004	524,718.61	11.02
1913....	31,566,888	3,505,516	541,748.46	11.10
1914....	33,202,516	3,694,458	568,395.53	11.12
Total.	....	20,151,266	3,038,604.83	....

[1] Per 100 pounds of milk.

The accounting records kept in the central office are arranged so as to account for the pounds of milk delivered by each patron. The value of this milk, figured either as to pounds or as to butterfat content, is credited to the patron's account, and at the end of the month a check for this amount, minus any deductions, is paid to the patron. All funds are disbursed by check, either over the signatures of the officers of the association or, in special cases, over the signature of the secretary-salesman. Supplementing this accounting system, the office operates a simple cost system, covering the manufacturing costs in the making of cheese.

Cost of manufacture and returns to farmers.

Factory No.—	Milk.	Yield of cheese per hundred-weight.	Cost per pound for making cheese.	Gross price of milk per hundred-weight.	Net returns to farmers.	
					From milk per hundred-weight.	From butter fat, per pound.
	Pounds.	*Pounds.*	*Cents.*			*Cents.*
1............	4,861,981	11.32	1.75	$1.744	$1.546	38.7
2............	4,153,089	11.17	1.75	1.708	1.513	37.8
3............	4,078,036	11.17	1.75	1.735	1.540	38.5
4............	2,527,709	11.24	1.75	1.732	1.535	38.4
5............	2,106,504	11.03	2	1.695	1.474	36.9
6............	1,931,413	10.92	2	1.679	1.461	36.5
7............	1,901,107	10.88	2	1.675	1.457	36.4
8............	1,844,850	11.09	2	1.733	1.511	37.8
9............	1,720,606	11.21	1.75	1.740	1.544	38.1
10............	1,595,005	10.95	1.75	1.667	1.475	36.9
11............	1,262,108	11.09	2	1.624	1.402	35.1
12............	1,006,872	11.08	2	1.701	1.479	37.0
13............	947,273	11.05	2.25	1.696	1.447	36.2
14............	889,548	10.91	2.25	1.649	1.403	35.1
15............	642,888	11.18	2.50	1.702	1.412	35.3
16............	611,158	11.35	2.25	1.747	1.492	37.3
17............	530,580	11.02	2.50	1.673	1.397	34.9
18............	465,493	11.03	2.50	1.672	1.396	34.9
19............	126,195	10.55	3	1.608	1.291	32.3
Total.....	33,202,516	11.12	....	1.712	....	....

The importance of an adequate cost system in both creameries and cheese factories can not be overestimated. Since these types of business, to a great extent, are factories wherein manufacturing costs are largely the basis of success or failure, great care should be taken that all the items which enter into the cost of making the finished article are taken into account.

SOME AMERICAN VEGETABLE FOOD OILS, THEIR SOURCES AND METHODS OF PRODUCTION.

By H. S. BAILEY,

Chemist in Charge, Oil, Fat, and Wax Laboratory, Bureau of Chemistry.

AS far back as we have any authentic records we find that the peoples of Asia Minor used the oil of the olive, and undoubtedly the original salad oil was that obtained from the fruit of the olive tree, which grows luxuriantly in all the Mediterranean countries. With the spread of civilization from its ancient home, the cultivation of olive trees and the utilization of their fruit extended as far as the west coast of Spain. The Phœnicians and early Romans carried this precious oil, which was not only concentrated food but fuel for their lamps as well, to distant countries, whose peoples doubtless quickly learned to prize it highly.

In comparatively recent years the demand for oils suitable for salad dressings and general food purposes has increased so rapidly that now, even in the Mediterranean countries, the total annual production of olive oil is only about one-half the consumption of all the vegetable food oils. Cottonseed, coconut, and peanut oils already are used extensively in the United States, corn oil is beginning to appear in the retail stores, and the sunflower oil of Russia, soy bean, poppyseed, sesame, and numerous other oils of Europe are now making, or sooner or later probably will make, their appearance among American edible oils. We are welcoming to our shores not only the peoples of the Old World, but with them their foods.

Edible oils are food in a form highly concentrated and usually readily assimilated. Pure oils and fats are practically free from water, an ingredient present to some extent in nearly every other food except sugars and thoroughly dried grains. Edible oils contain no indigestible substances, such as the crude fiber of vegetables and the cartilage and tendons of meats. Partly because they are obtained readily in this natural, concentrated condition and partly because of the wide distribution of oil-bearing materials, many of

159

these oils are among the cheapest of our food products. As compared with beef, for instance, at 25 cents a pound, cottonseed oil at 20 cents a quart will yield dollar for dollar more than five times the amount of body energy, although, of course, it has not the same tissue-building power.

Since the various vegetable food oils are similar in chemical composition and in digestibility, the question of their relative values for domestic use is one of preference rather than of absolute food value. Just which oil will be best suited to a particular individual often depends more upon the person to be nourished than upon the characteristics of the oil itself. It is a well-known fact that we are often more apt to digest without digestive disturbance a food which is palatable than one which is not; so in a final analysis the question of which oil is the best to use in the kitchen and upon the table resolves itself into the everyday question of what we like best and whether we can afford it. The Russian, accustomed to his sunflower oil, doubtless would think the bland, highly refined American cottonseed oil tasteless, while the Italian peasant, brought up on a low grade of olive oil, firmly believes that the better, sweeter grades he buys in America are adulterated or " diluted."

OLIVE OIL.

Olive oil is produced in Syria, Greece, Italy, southern France, and Spain, and in all the countries along the southern shore of the Mediterranean Sea, with the possible exception of Egypt. In the United States the olive now grows in California (where it was introduced by the early Mission fathers, who planted it wherever they established a mission) and to a less extent in Arizona.

While American olive oil is of high quality and commands a good price, especially in the West, the demand for pickled olives apparently is so great that it pays better to use most of the fruit in this way rather than to crush it for oil. The American olives are not nearly so rich in oil as those grown in Italy. In the " Mission " variety there is only about 20 per cent of oil and in the best " rubra " usually less than 30 per cent, while most of the varieties grown in southern Europe contain between 40 and 60 per cent of oil. By proper selection it will doubtless be possible to produce in the United States olives as rich as these if there is a sufficient demand for them, but at present the tendency seems to be toward the production of a large, firm fruit for pickling rather than of one with a high oil content.

For making the best grades of oil it is customary to gather the olives by hand just before they become fully ripe. The amount of oil present is said to increase gradually up to full maturity, but oil of a superior quality is obtained if the fruit is gathered before it begins to soften. In the manufacture of first-grade oil it is necessary in handling the fruit to guard against bruising, especially if the olives are to be held for even a short time before pressing.

Many producers of olive oil believe that in order to obtain the highest grades of oil the olives should be crushed without breaking the pits, which should be separated from the rest of the fruit before it is pressed. This is by no means always done, and there is reason to believe that it makes little difference whether or not the pits are removed.

The machinery employed for obtaining the oil from the fruit in different regions varies from the crude stone mortars and hand presses employed in Africa to the modern disintegrators and big hydraulic presses of the United States and parts of southern Europe. The process itself, however, is essentially the same to-day as it was a thousand years ago. In California the olives are crushed in immense flat pans by heavy wheels which roll around and around in these shallow bowls just as in the early days the old stones, turned by oxen yoked to the end of a pole, ground in their stone saucers the fruit for the Mission fathers.

The pulp as soon as crushed is put in heavy cloths or sacks and subjected to a gradually increasing pressure. The heavier the first pressing the lower will be the quality of the oil, but the greater the quantity. After this first oil, often called " Virgin " or " Sublime," has practically ceased to run from the press, the marc is wet down with cold water, or, in some instances, removed from the press and reground in a little water, then pressed again. The oil obtained in this second pressing is edible and appears on the market as second quality, or very often is found in the retail trade mixed with and sold as first-pressing oil. A third and sometimes a fourth grinding and pressing are given the pulp. These pressings are usually run hot, or at least hot water instead of cold is mixed each time with the marc. The quality of the oil from these hot pressings is comparatively low and the oil, unless chemically refined, is suitable only for making soap or for other tecnical uses. Abroad the final press cake, which usually contains from 10 to 20 per cent of oil, is extracted with carbon bisulphid or tetrachlorid, but apparently this method has not been found profitable in this country. The oil produced by the extraction process, freed as far as possible from the solvent, is a heavy, dark-green product known as sulphured oil or olive-oil foots and is used only for technical purposes.

The edible grades of oil as they come from the presses are run into tanks or cisterns and allowed to stand for a day or two. The oil gradually rises to the top, while the particles of pulp, water, and gelatinous material settle to the bottom. The clear oil is then dipped or siphoned off and sometimes washed with water to remove small quantities of foreign substances, which, if allowed to remain in the oil, would give it a cloudy appearance and cause it to become rancid in a short time. After standing at least a week in the finishing tank the oil is drawn off, usually through a filter, and is then ready for the table.

In order to procure for the market brands of oil which from year to year will-be as nearly uniform in flavor as possible, it has been the custom of the brokers and exporters of Italy to buy oils from various sources and then blend them. In this way certain cities which are centers for olive-oil exportation have become famous for their products. Originally the oils shipped from Lucca were blends of Italian oils of that immediate vicinity, but the demand for these oils has become so great that now many of the oils labeled Lucca are mixtures of Italian and non-Italian oils. While this type of misbranding of foreign oils is not easily prevented, the importation into the United States of olive oil adulterated with peanut, sesame, poppyseed, or cottonseed oil has practically ceased, now that all shipments are examined by the Department of Agriculture before their entry is permitted. During the last few years, however, a more insidious form of adulteration has been practiced to some extent by the foreign brokers, some of whom are mixing with highly flavored, dark-colored oils the bland, almost tasteless refined, or so-called rectified, olive oil. This oil is made from low-grade or rancid oil by treating it with a mineral acid, and possibly with other chemicals. The exact details of the process are a trade secret. So far as is known, the refining and blending of olive oils is not practiced in the United States, and the production of olive oil in this country meets only a small part of the demand for this, the oldest and most widely used of all the vegetable food oils.

COTTONSEED OIL.

Since so little of America is climatically suited to the cultivation of the olive, it is fortunate that we have another food oil which in nearly every respect satisfactorily takes its place—cottonseed oil.

Cottonseed oil is produced in Great Britain, Germany, France, Smyrna, India, China, and South America, but by far the larger portion is made in the United States. Several varieties of cotton seed are pressed in this country. These are generally grouped into two classes—the bald or black, the smooth, lint-free seeds of the Sea Island varieties, and the white or woolly, the seeds from the Upland and similar cottons which come from the gins with a fluffy white coat of lint on them. While there is a climatic and varietal difference in the chemical composition of the cotton seeds, all of them contain on an average about 20 per cent of oil.

The present annual production of cottonseed oil in this country is more than 3,000,000 barrels or 150,000,000 gallons. Of this we export in normal times about 700,000 barrels, chiefly to Mediterranean ports. Although we are by far the largest producers of this oil and export nearly a fourth of our crop, we also import from China and other countries some 10,000 barrels annually.

The machinery and processes used in the production of cottonseed oil in the United States are superior to those of any other country, and plants of American design and construction are in operation in Europe, Asia Minor, India, and China.

In the treatment required for the production of an edible oil there is one fundamental difference between cotton seed and the olive. The finest grades of olive oil are those expressed from the fruit with the least possible subsequent treatment, whereas before cottonseed oil is suitable for human food it must be refined, and in addition it is often bleached and deodorized.

In tracing the production of cottonseed oil from the raw seed to the finished edible product it will be followed through the crude-oil mill and then through the refinery. As is the case in any highly developed manufacturing process, there are many variations of the general methods used, and numerous so-called trade secrets are involved; yet the fundamental principles in all these processes are similar.

The cotton seed, as received at the crude-oil mill from the gins, is covered with short cotton fiber and is mixed with broken bolls, stones, nails, and similar trash, all of which must be removed before the seeds are ground. After being run through revolving screens which separate the larger pieces of trash, over shaking sieves and magnets, and through cyclone cleaners, to take out the sand, nails, and dust, the seeds are fed into the machines which remove the lint. These machines, known as delinters, consist of a series of fine-toothed buzz saws set close together on a rapidly revolving horizontal shaft. At the back of each machine is a long, cylindrical brush running so close to the saws that it catches the fiber that they have cut from the seeds and passes it on to the lint reel, which is set just behind it. Here the little, short cotton hairs which the gins failed to remove from the seed are compacted into a felt and rolled out like cotton batting, ready to go to the mattress maker or guncotton manufacturer.

As the seed comes from the last of a set of these linters it is nearly free from lint and ready for the hullers—mills which break the hard outer coat or hull and liberate the soft oil-containing meats. In order to separate the hulls and meats as thoroughly as possible, the material as it comes from the hullers is run over shaking screens. The hulls are passed through a second and sometimes a third huller, and then through additional separators until finally they come out practically free from any of the valuable oil-bearing interior portion. The meats when freed from the hulls are ground through a series of three or more heavy steel rolls and finally carried into the storage bins over the press room.

In the expressing of most of the edible oils frequently several grades are made by a re-pressing of the same batch of raw material. Cottonseed, however, at least in the United States, is pressed only once, and when hydraulic presses are used it is always heated or cooked before pressing. The cooking of the seed is the most important step in the making of the crude oil by the hydraulic or hot process. It requires experience and judgment on the part of the cooker to get the crushed meats in the proper condition to yield the maximum amount of the best possible grade of oil. The cooking is done in a shallow, steam-jacketed pan equipped with a mechanical stirrer, which, as it revolves, mixes the meats thoroughly and prevents uneven cooking. Inside, near the top of the pan, is a perforated steam pipe through which steam may be admitted to moisten the meats should they become too dry. In many mills a second pan, called a subheater, similar to the cooker, is installed just below it and used to hold the cooked batch until the presses are ready for it.

The type of press most commonly used in this country in the production of cottonseed oil is the steel box-frame hydraulic, which operates under a pressure of about 5,000 pounds per square inch. Such a press consists of a series of horizontal steel plates, about 14 inches wide by 34 inches long, set one above the other, about 5 inches apart, when the press is fully open. The plates are perforated or channeled and provided with closely fitting steel sides, so that the whole machine is really a series of steel boxes, without ends, piled one upon the other, the lowest box resting upon a hydraulic piston. Above the top frame is a heavy iron plate fastened to the piston cylinder by four vertical rods, which serve as guides for the sliding frames.

With the press fully open, that is, with the piston at its lowest point, a measured charge of cooked meal is dropped from the subheater, or holder, upon the strip of camel's hair or other press cloth in the cake-former. This cake-former is a steel block with a shallow groove, the size of a single press box in its upper surface. It is so constructed that after the meal has been run upon the press cloth and the two ends turned up over the charge, pressure can be applied from above or below, and the cake, now entirely covered with cloth except on its two long sides, can be subjected to a preliminary squeeze to compact it into shape. When the charge is in the cake-former pressure is applied for an instant and then released. A sheet of steel the width of the groove is slid underneath the cake, which is removed, cloth and all, from the former and pushed into the lowest frame of the press.

One after another all the boxes are thus charged until the press is filled; the compressed air is then turned on the hydraulic ram, forcing the frames upward, each against the one above it. The oil as it is squeezed through the cloths flows down over the sides of the press into a gallery around the bottom frame and out through troughs to the settling cistern. So perfectly has every detail of the construction and operation of these huge presses been worked out that they are often charged, pressed, and discharged ready for refilling in less than 20 minutes.

The dark-red crude oil, as it flows from the press, always contains some fine meal, which has been squeezed through the cloths. The larger particles of this meal collect in the oil troughs in the floor below the press, through which the oil flows to the settling tanks, and are shoveled out and repressed with the next batch of meats. To clarify the oil still further, before it is pumped or shipped to the refinery, it is held in settling tanks or cisterns until most of the finer particles have settled out.

In addition to the production of crude oil by the hydraulic process just described, an increasing amount is being made in mills equipped with a type of continuous-working press known as the expeller. Some of this oil is cold pressed, that is, the meats are not cooked before pressing, but in other plants the material fed into the expellers is treated in much the same manner as though it were intended for the hydraulic press. In the cold-press mills, after cleaning and delinting, the seed is merely ground, run through a tempering apparatus, where it is dried if too wet or blown with moist steam if too dry, and then fed into the expeller, hulls and all.

The expeller is built somewhat on the principle of the ordinary meat grinder, and is simply an interrupted screw revolving inside a slotted steel barrel. The ground seed enters through a hopper at one end of the barrel, is pressed along toward the other end, and finally discharged around a cone, which can be set in or out of the outlet orifice so as to give any desired pressure. The oil is squeezed from the seeds by the pressure of the screw, runs out through the small slits in the barrel, and after settling or, better, filtering through a filter press, is ready for shipment to the refinery.

The tempering of the seed, which is often necessary to make it press properly, is really a preheating process, and as the heat due to pressure and friction in the expellers is sufficient to make the oil and cake as they come from the press actually hot, the term "cold pressed" is not strictly applicable to oil obtained by the expeller process. Although this crude oil is very different from that obtained by the regular hot pressing, there is very little, if any, difference between the two oils after they have been refined.

As the yield of oil by either process is only about 45 gallons per ton, or less than 17 per cent of the weight of seed handled, and as a large part of the ground cake and hulls can be used as feed or fertilizer by the local farmers, the crude-oil mills often are located in the smaller towns throughout the cotton-growing sections. From these the oil is shipped in steel tank cars to more centrally situated refineries or to the packing houses and cooking-compound manufacturers of the North.

As previously stated, crude cottonseed oil is not suitable for human food, even when made from sound, sweet seed, for, although it has a pleasing nutty flavor, it contains coloring matter and other foreign substances such as the albuminous bodies and free fatty acids. The first step toward rancidity in an oil is, apparently, the formation of free fatty acids. The glycerids—chemical compounds of glycerin and fatty acids—begin to break up, and instead of the sweet neutral glycerids we have the acrid, free fatty acids and ordinary glycerin. Before the oil is marketable as a table oil, the acids must be neutralized and removed and the major portion of the coloring matter taken out. It is this process which is known as refining.

As the crude oil is received at the refinery it is run into storage tanks or pumped directly from the cars into the weighing tanks and then to the refining kettles—tall cylindrical sheet-iron tanks with conical bottoms and provided with a series of steam-heating coils extending part way up the sides. During the refining the oil is stirred either by some form of mechanical stirrer or by compressed air blown in through perforated pipes.

When a tank has been filled with crude oil to the extent, perhaps, of 100,000 pounds, the agitator is started and steam turned on to the heating coils until the desired temperature has been reached. This varies with different oils and in different plants, but is usually around 85° F. While the tank is being heated a sample of the oil is tested in the laboratory.

By the time the oil in the refining tank has been raised to the proper temperature the refiner knows from the laboratory report just how much caustic-soda solution to add to make a good refining. The lye solution is run rapidly into the oil and the agitation and heating continued until the dark-brown, almost black, particles of soap formed by the action of the lye on the free acids clot together into little spongy masses and begin to settle. The steam is turned off from the heating coils when the oil reaches about 120° F., the agitation is decreased, and finally stopped, and the tank allowed to stand several hours until the soap settles to the bottom, leaving the clear, golden-yellow oil above. This is siphoned off into a series of settling tanks, and after standing a while is transferred into a second and sometimes a third set of tanks. The oil at this stage is known as " summer yellow " and is used largely in making margarin and as a cooking oil. Before being placed on the market for table use the summer yellow oil as a rule is bleached and deodorized.

In addition to caustic soda or in place of it many other chemicals have been used in refining. A strong salt brine sometimes is added to produce a cleaner separation of the soap stock, and water glass, silicate of soda, and borax have been recommended, and, in the early days, bichromate of potash was tried.

Cottonseed oil, in common with most of the other edible vegetable oils, contains a large enough proportion of the so-called stearins, that is, glycerids of palmatic and similar fatty solids, so that in cold weather these separate out, giving to the oil a milky appearance which makes it undesirable for

SORTING OLIVES.

The olives are sorted by hand as they pass on moving belts in front of the girls, the imperfect and off-color fruit being culled out to be used for making oil.

FIG. 1.—OLD OLIVE MILL AND PRESS.

Goaded by a mission father, the oxen walked round and round, rolling the heavy stone wheel over the olives in the flat stone dish.   From time to time the pulp was scooped out into cloths and pressed in a stone saucer by means of the screw and lever.

FIG. 2.—GRINDING OLIVES.

Heavy rolls like great bull wheels running in a huge iron saucer grind the olives to a pulp, which is then elevated to the charging bins.

FIG. 1.—PRESSING OLIVES (BACK); STRIPPING THE CAKE (FRONT).

After pressing in the big hydraulic presses the cakes of olive pomace are wheeled to one side, the cloths stripped off and refilled with fresh pulp, and these new "cheeses" are then run back into the press.

FIG. 2.—DELINTER FOR CLEANING COTTON SEED.

In the delinters a gang of fine-toothed buzz saws cuts the lint from the cotton seeds and leaves the seed nearly bald ready for hulling.

FIG. 1.—PRESS ROOM.

From the steam-heated "cooker" the ground cotton seed is run into the "cake former" and the cakes, as fast as shaped, are transferred to the hydraulic presses, one cake to a shelf, 16 to a press.

FIG. 2.—OIL EXPELLER, PEANUT OIL MILL.

The peanuts flow continuously into this huge sausage-grinder sort of a machine and the oil in a bright yellow stream runs out below into the settling cisterns. The cake, in hot, fragrant ribbons, unwinds at the discharge end of the press into a conveyor.

use in cold climates. To produce an oil that will not "cloud up" and sometimes even solidify in winter, the summer yellow grade is "wintered," that is, held for a time in chill rooms or in tanks surrounded by cold brine until it becomes semisolid. This mushlike mass is then pressed, or run through centrifugals, to separate the solid stearin from the lower-melting oleins. The oil thus obtained is known as "winter yellow" and, if properly made, remains perfectly clear even in cold weather.

Housewives frequently show preference for particular colors in foods; thus, they demand greenish olive oil, golden-yellow butter, and light-yellow cottonseed oil. To meet the demand for a light-yellow oil and also to supply the lard-substitute maker with one from which he can produce a white cooking compound, the refined yellow oil must be decolorized. In this bleaching process the yellow oil is heated in tall steel tanks similar to those used in the refinery, and is thoroughly mixed with a small amount of fuller's earth, sometimes called clay by the refiner. This fuller's earth is mined in Florida and other sections of the United States, although until recently the best qualities were imported from England. Various kinds of charcoal and animal blacks are occasionally added to the fuller's earth in small quantities to assist in the decolorization. After the batch of oil and earth in the clay tanks has been thoroughly mixed and heated, it is pumped into filter presses. From these presses the oil runs bleached and clear, leaving behind in the cells of the press the decolorizing materials.

Deodorization is necessary in order to remove the undesirable flavors natural to the oil, or remaining as a result of the claying process, and to make it bland and nearly tasteless. At this point, anyone going through a refinery probably would find that the door to the next department bore the sign "Positively no admittance." Numerous processes for deodorizing oils have been patented and many unpatented processes also are in operation, the secrets of which are guarded as among the most valuable assets of the companies using them. Since there is scarcely any color, taste, or odor to the pure chemical glycerids which make up nearly 99 per cent of all the common food oils, practically all the color, odor, and characteristic flavors must be in the remaining 1 or 2 per cent. The flavor substances, as a rule, are much more volatile than the bulk of the oil, and can be removed by simply heating the oil in a very high vacuum. This process, unfortunately, is only applicable as yet to small-scale laboratory experiments, and in practice the deodorizing is effected by washing with steam or heated air. It is common knowledge that fats readily absorb strong odors from the atmosphere. The good housekeeper takes care that the onions and cooked cabbage are not shut up in her refrigerator with the butter and lard. The refiner also has learned that unless the odor-causing bodies are removed from contact with his oil as rapidly as they are liberated it is difficult to deodorize the oil properly. For this reason the deodorizing process is usually conducted under vacuum in large cylindrical tanks covered air-tight and having a big gooseneck outlet pipe at the top, which is connected to a vacuum exhaust system. The oil is heated by means of closed steam coils, and the odors are swept out with superheated steam or hot air, which is injected through perforated pipes or nozzles at the bottom of the tank and carried off by the vacuum pipe at the top.

From a cloudy, dark-red, sometimes strong, rancid-tasting, crude cottonseed oil there is thus produced by refining, bleaching, and deodorizing a clear, light-yellow, bland, almost tasteless, and odorless product, which for those who do not care for a marked characteristic flavor in their salad dressings or for the lard taste in their pastry is a very desirable food oil.

PEANUT OIL.

The peanut is now rapidly coming into prominence as one of the most satisfactory crops for those districts of the South in which the boll weevil is making the raising of cotton uncertain. The ravages of this pest, which has been gradually working northward and eastward through the Southern States, have decreased the production of cotton in some sections to such an extent that the local oil mills have been forced to ship their seed long distances or find some other material upon which to operate. The peanut not only supplies the crusher with a splendid raw material, but the hay and press cake make highly desirable cattle feeds.

It is not known whether the peanut, which is probably a native of Brazil, was used by the aborigines as a source of oil, but certainly in a comparatively short time after the early explorers carried this product of the Western World back to Europe its value as an oil material was realized. Peanut oil, or arachis oil as it is usually known abroad, may be expressed from any one of the many varieties of peanuts. That this oil is one of the most important of the world's food oils is shown by the fact that annually over 120,000 metric tons of peanuts in the shell, together with about 240,000 metric tons of shelled nuts, are crushed in Marseille alone, yielding 15,500,000 gallons of edible oil.

Abroad, peanut oil is made almost invariably from shelled nuts. Mills that buy the nuts in the shell first hull them by machinery designed particularly for that purpose. The foreign matter, such as sticks and stones, and a small quantity of unshelled peanuts are next removed by running the shelled stock over screens similar to the shakers used in the cotton-oil mills. The inner or red skins are then removed as completely as possible by an air blast or fan mill. When thoroughly cleaned the kernels are ground, usually by a system of corrugated rolls which do not crush them as fine as cotton seed is ground for the hydraulic presses. The material when ground is put into press cloths and pressed in a machine somewhat similar to the ordinary fruit or cider press used in this country. These presses have no protecting sides or boxes such as are commonly found in the American hydraulic press, and the pressure which is applied to the peanuts is much less than that used with cotton seed. When the press is full the pressure is applied and the material allowed to stand under pressure until a little over half the oil has been squeezed out. This gives what is known as cold-drawn oil, which is nearly colorless, has a pleasant, nutty taste, and needs no refining to make it suitable for salad or cooking purposes, provided, of course, the original peanut material was clean and free from rancid nuts.

After the first pressing the cakes are taken out of the cloths, reground, a small quantity of moisture added, and after being heated for a few minutes new cakes are formed and again pressed. The second oil thus obtained is inferior in quality to the oil of the first pressing and goes into a lower grade of edible oil. A third pressing and possibly in some mills a fourth, both of course after regrinding and heating, are sometimes made before the cake is exhausted.

In Europe the finest grades of peanut oil are used exclusively for edible purposes, and practically all that is produced in France is consumed there, only second-grade peanut oils being exported to the United States.

Of the five different varieties of peanuts grown in this country the Spanish is undoubtedly the best suited to oil production. It is adapted to a wide range of soil and climatic conditions, and contains an appreciably greater quantity of oil than do the Virginia Bunch, Virginia Runner, or African varieties.

The production of peanut oil on a large scale in this country is yet in its infancy, but the cottonseed-oil mills located in the peanut-growing territory and in charge of men thoroughly acquainted with oil machinery are rapidly taking up the pressing of peanuts.

While there are now perhaps 20 or 30 mills pressing peanuts, only a very few of these were built especially to handle this material. The others are cottonseed-oil mills, which have been remodeled to fit them for peanut-oil production. In some of these cottonseed-oil mills the unshelled peanuts, after being well cleaned to remove all the sticks, stems, stones, and adhering dirt, are run through disintegrators and then directly into expellers. In some only a part of the oil is expressed the first time and the cake returned for a second pressing, but more often only one pressing is made, which gives a lower grade of oil than would be obtained by a lighter partial crushing. In other mills cleaned shelled nuts are used, and when the stock is fresh and sound and not pressed too hard the first time the oil is of the highest quality obtainable.

The regular hydraulic presses also are being utilized for the production of peanut oil by those cottonseed-oil mills so equipped, and both shelled and unshelled nuts have been pressed, sometimes hot and sometimes without any cooking. This lack of uniformity in the American practice and the use of all sorts of stock from old, rancid, cull peanuts to prime fresh material have resulted in the production of oils of every quality, some of which require refining and bleaching the same as do cottonseed oils, while others are sweet and bright, ready for the table as soon as they have been filtered.

In even the best oil as it comes from the presses there is, of course, some insoluble matter, fine parts of the peanut, which must be filtered out to prevent a rapid spoiling of the oil. When good, sound stock is cold pressed and the oil well filtered, the peanut oil obtained, like that of the olive, is sweet and brilliant, ready for the housewife just as it comes from the mill, in fact, just as it existed in the peanuts themselves. Off-grade peanut oils, made either from spoiled nuts or from sound nuts improperly treated, can be refined and the disagreeable odor and flavor removed, but such oils are lacking in the characteristic sweet peanut taste of a virgin oil and are inferior for salad and general table purposes.

There is very little demand in the United States at the present time for a high-grade table peanut oil, but many who have tried the cold-pressed oil for salads consider it very satisfactory and think that practically the only difference between peanut oil and olive oil is one of flavor. Just as some people like grapefruit better than oranges, there are those who prefer an oil with a marked characteristic taste, such as olive oil, to a bland oil, such as refined cottonseed oil, and many who have become accustomed to peanut oil with its mild nutty flavor think it more palatable than any of the other vegetable food oils.

CORN OIL.

Within the last decade there has come into prominence in the United States another food oil which, like cottonseed oil, was originally a by-product. Corn oil, or, as it is sometimes called, maize oil, exists in the small germ portion of our common Indian corn. Although this germ itself is more than half oil, there is only from 3 to 6.5 per cent of oil present in the entire kernel. Were it not for the fact that in the preparation of cornstarch and brewer's grits, and sometimes in the making of corn meal and other corn products, the germ is more or less completely separated from the rest of the grain, corn oil doubtless would be a mere curiosity, as it would not pay to extract it.

Oils exposed to air and light, especially oils finely divided and mixed with the enzyms which occur to a greater or less extent in all oleaginous seeds, quickly become rancid and unfit for food. Because of this rapid deterioration in the oil portion of corn it has been found advisable to remove the germ from hominy and corn meal when these are to be kept for any length of time before being used. In the preparation of cornstarch, which is practically a pure carbohydrate, it is of special importance that all the corn germs be separated from the starchy portion of the grain.

In the degerminating of corn two distinctly different processes are now in use in the United States. In the older one, known as the wet process, the corn is soaked in dilute sulphurous acid for some time, and yields a germ in which the oil is already rancid when extracted. The corn oil made from these germs either has to be used for technical purposes or else refined to make it suitable for food. In the newer process, usually known as the dry process, no water is added to the grain, but the germs are removed by mechanical means. If the corn is sound the oil can be used for food purposes with little or no refining. Unfortunately the dry process yields only about one-fifth as much germ as the wet process, so that it has not entirely replaced the latter method, which is still generally used in the manufacture of starch and glucose. In making brewer's grits and corn meal a certain amount of germ may be left in the finished product, but it is essential that the corn itself should not be soaked, as this would spoil the finished product.

The wet process first came into use about 20 years ago, when it was discovered that the difference between the specific gravity of the corn germs and the rest of the kernel was such that the germs in certain strengths of starch water floated on top, while the major portion of the kernel settled to the bottom. In operating the wet process the shelled corn is first soaked for several days in large steep tanks in water containing a small amount of sulphur dioxid. The dilute acid added coagulates the glutinous material which otherwise would be difficult to remove later from the starch. During the steeping the corn swells and the germs become toughened, so that they are not readily broken up in the grinding process. The water and corn from the steep tanks are run together through attrition mills, which crack the grains and loosen the germs. The mixture, which, as it flows out of these grinders, is a sort of thin gruel, is fed into the germ separators—long rectangular steel tanks about 4 feet wide, with a semicircular bottom. These separators are filled with starch water of a specific gravity that will permit the germs to float and the grits to sink. As the gruel is fed in at one end of the separator it drops to the bottom and is gradually worked toward the other end of the tanks by a rapidly revolving beater. This beater removes the germs from the starchy portion of the grain, and as they rise to the top they are skimmed off by an endless belt which runs along just below the surface of the water. The starchy portion of the corn works along the bottom of the separator and is finally discharged through an automatic gate at the far end of the tank. The germs from the separator go next to a shaker screen of bolting cloth and are washed free from adhering starch particles by a spray of water. From this screen they are transferred to some form of moisture expeller which squeezes out the excess of water. They are then ready for the driers—long, nearly horizontal cylinders heated by steam or other means—which reduce the moisture content of the germs from 55 to not over 5 per cent. The dry germs are then put into bins and allowed to cool and cure for two or three hours, because if pressed immediately as they come from the kilns they are too brittle to give a satisfactory yield of oil.

The germs, after curing, are tough and leathery. They are then run through a series of flaking rolls which flatten them and break the oil cells, but do not grind the material into a flour which would be hard to hold in the oil presses. While hydraulic presses could be used, as in the cottonseed-oil mills, the general practice in the United States is to run the germs directly from the flaking rolls into expellers similar to those already described in connection with the production of cottonseed and peanut oils.

In the dry process the corn, instead of being soaked, is heated with live steam until it contains about 18 per cent of moisture. It is then put through a machine known as the automatic degerminator, which removes the bran from the whole corn, breaks the kernels, and partially separates the germs. From the degerminator the mixture of cracked corn and broken germs is passed through a series of screens and aspirators, where, by means of suction and sifting on wire screening, a further separation is made of the germ from the starchy portion of the corn kernel. The germ taken out by the aspirators is still partially mixed with grits and is again run through flaking rolls and aspirators, which suck out the lighter germ particles and leave the grits behind.

The pressing of the dry-process germs is similar in every way to that used in getting the oil out of the material obtained by the wet process. When the germ comes from the last aspirators it is tempered if necessary to insure the proper moisture content, being dried, if too wet, or moistened with live steam, if too dry, and is pressed in any suitable form of press.

Corn oil is not as yet a common household product, but it is now being placed upon the market in small retail packages for use as a table and cooking oil. For some time large quantities of the oil have been used for technical purposes, and since the methods for producing a sweet, attractive oil have been perfected, the manufacturers of edible fats are using increasing amounts of this product in making lard substitutes.

AGRICULTURE ON GOVERNMENT RECLAMATION PROJECTS.

By C. S. Scofield, *Agriculturist in Charge, Western Irrigation Agriculture,* and F. D. Farrell, *Agriculturist in Charge, Demonstrations on Reclamation Projects, Bureau of Plant Industry.*

FARMING UNDER IRRIGATION.

THE development of agriculture under irrigation involves conditions that are essentially different from those of ordinary farming. In general, the labor cost of crop production is somewhat greater, the necessary investment of capital is larger, and the requirements of social organization are more complex. These conditions require that irrigation farming shall yield larger returns than ordinary farming if it is to be successful. Of the three conditions mentioned the essential complexity of the social organization is the least understood by those who have to take part in it.

The development of an irrigation enterprise necessitates a period of pioneer existence. This period, unlike most of the pioneering with which many people are familiar, involves community problems which must be dealt with from the very beginning. On Government reclamation projects these problems are more conspicuous than elsewhere, chiefly because the colonists who occupy them have come together suddenly from widely different conditions of life and usually without previous experience to guide them.

The underlying purpose that has influenced legislative and administrative policies regarding Government reclamation has been to establish homes on the land rather than to provide the most efficient means for increased agricultural production. But successful home making is dependent upon a reasonable degree of material prosperity. Thus, the economic problems and possibilities of irrigation farming must be understood and realized if this great experiment in the reclamation of arid lands is to be made a success.

COURSE OF DEVELOPMENT.

Prior to the recent rapid expansion of irrigation development it was generally believed that the reclaimed lands could be utilized profitably for the production of such special crops as orchard fruits, truck crops, sugar beets, and alfalfa. Recent experience, however, has demonstrated that these crops can not be depended upon to meet the requirements of the situation. New projects do not show immediately the assortment or balance of industries that ultimately are to become established. There is instead a rather regular sequence of development, beginning with the production of alfalfa and small grains and gradually reaching a great diversity of crops and industries. Finally, out of this diversity a few major industries become permanent.

Almost invariably it is desirable to get the land seeded to alfalfa as soon as possible, not only because of the usefulness of the crop itself but also because its growth greatly increases the productivity of the soil. It is a common practice to seed wheat, oats, or barley as a nurse crop for the alfalfa. Moreover, many farmers plant small grains as a first-year crop because of the quick returns and as a method of preparing the new soils for the production of perennial crops. Hence, on the newly irrigated lands, alfalfa and small grains occupy a large proportion of the cultivated acreage. As the soils begin to respond to cultivation, sugar beets, potatoes, truck crops, orchard fruits, and, on the southwestern projects, cotton are added to the cropping system.

Thus the agriculture of these projects is gradually changing and developing toward a diversity which ultimately will include a number of different crops, with the chief emphasis placed on those which under local climatic and economic conditions prove to be most profitable. The rate and direction of this development vary, of course, on the different projects. If account is taken of the 24 Government reclamation projects now in operation, including at present about 19,000 farms with about 800,000 acres in production, the areas devoted to the more important crops are approximately as follows, in terms of the total irrigated acreage: Forage (chiefly alfalfa), 50 per cent; cereals (chiefly wheat, oats, barley, and corn), 25 per cent; fruit crops, 7 per cent; potatoes, 3 per cent; seeds (chiefly clover and alfalfa), sugar beets, and cotton, each 2 per cent; and truck crops, 1 per cent.

PROBLEMS OF CROP DISPOSAL.

The problems encountered in the production of crops are much less difficult than the problems of profitable disposal and utilization. The reclamation projects are all located in the sparsely settled Western States, far removed from the great consuming centers. Because of this fact the supply of crop products in these areas exceeds the local demand, and the problems of distant marketing must be worked out. Transportation costs from the reclamation projects to the great marketing centers are high. Furthermore, as the underlying purpose of Government reclamation is to provide homes for as many families as possible, the farm units on the reclamation projects are small. This results in a relatively small output per farm, and this in turn necessitates cooperation in marketing and in some of the enterprises of production. Groups of farmers must work together to attain those objects which the individual farmer is powerless to accomplish.

This does not mean that cooperation should be regarded as a panacea, but rather that the solution of certain specific problems of production and of marketing requires cooperation. In view of the fact that our farmers are still relatively inexperienced in matters of cooperation, there is need for a clear understanding of the purposes to be accomplished and for special attention to the methods of procedure.

To secure the necessary efficiency in meeting these problems of crop disposal requires that settlers on the reclamation projects endeavor as early as possible to develop definite agricultural industries for which the local conditions are favorable. It is the purpose of this paper to discuss briefly a number of the agricultural industries that have been or may become important on reclamation projects. This discussion may serve to show something of the present status of agriculture on these projects and to indicate what now appears to be the direction of progress.

THE SUGAR-BEET INDUSTRY.

The production of sugar beets has been one of the important industries on these irrigated lands. Where the climatic and soil conditions are favorable the crop has been fairly profitable, and while the returns are seldom very large they are reasonably certain. There is no serious marketing problem in this industry, because the beets are grown under contract at a price stipulated in advance of planting. The seed, and, if the farmer so desires, the necessary hand labor, are provided by the manufacturing company which purchases the beets. This company also provides field men to visit the farmer from time to time and advise with him as to the best cultural methods to use in producing the crop. These factors have been influential in maintaining and extending the irrigated area devoted to beets, in spite of the fact that the possible profit from beets appears to be less than from many other crops.

There are some undesirable features in the sugar-beet industry. The production of the crop requires much hand labor during two brief periods of the season—one in early summer, when the beets must be thinned and weeded, and one in the autumn, when the crop is harvested. In some places where the population is dense this labor may be locally available, but ordinarily it is necessary to import labor, and the people usually brought in and the circumstances under which they live are such that they constitute an undesirable social element. There is also a tendency in the sugar-beet industry toward the rental of land for beet production and toward continued cropping on the same land without a suitable crop rotation. Such intensive specialization does not make for the best development of an agricultural community. The production of sugar beets is possible only within reasonable distance of a sugar factory. These factories are large and expensive, so that unless a large acreage is available for beet production it is not feasible to construct a plant.

In respect to certain social and economic factors, the sugar-beet industry illustrates the essential points which need to be considered in the effective utilization of irrigated land. It is first of all a continuing or permanent industry. It is reasonably certain to yield a fair return on the labor and capital invested in production. The crop fits well into a rotation with alfalfa and the other common field crops. The advisory assistance of the field men employed by the sugar company is helpful, particularly to the inexperienced farmer. With an assured market for the crop, the farmer has every incentive to devote his bests efforts to increasing the efficiency of production, and the profits increase rapidly as the yields exceed the minimum which covers the cost of production.

In some of the points already enumerated the sugar-beet industry is essentially different from any other industry followed on irrigated land. While some of these practices are possible only with beet growing, others might be adapted, at least in part, to other industries with resulting advantage. While none of the sugar factories in this country is cooperative in the ordinary sense of that term, yet in another sense the cooperation between the manufacturer and the producer is very close and helpful. The widely prevalent custom of paying for the beets on a definitely adjusted scale of prices, so that the beets which are richer in sugar bring higher prices, is a stimulus to good farming, and the certainty of market and price, by eliminating one element of risk, also encourages the farmer to put forth his best efforts to secure high production.

POTATO PRODUCTION.

On several of the reclamation projects the soil and climatic conditions are favorable for the production of large crops of potatoes. A rotation in which this crop follows alfalfa not only makes for large yields of potatoes, but also leaves the land in good tilth for other crops. Yet potato production as an industry has not been important on many of the newer irrigated projects. This is due chiefly to the uncertainty of marketing. Were it possible to have for potatoes a market that is as definite and secure as that for sugar beets, the extent of the industry might now be much larger, even though the prices were to range below what is often received or ordinarily expected.

Where potato production is not well organized it has been the common experience that in only one year in three, or at

best one year in two, is the price such as to return a profit
to the grower. Sometimes there is no market or the prices
offered are so low that the crop is used for feed or allowed to
rot on the farm.

There are several obvious possibilities in the direction of
improving the marketing situation, particularly on the
northern projects. These possibilities may be achieved more
easily through community cooperation than by individual
action. There are two important demands for potatoes.
The larger, of course, is for food, but there is also an extensive market for seed for planting. In order to reach
either of these markets effectively it is of first importance
that a community go into the industry seriously, with the
purpose of continuing in it through years of poor prices as
well as through years of good prices. When a certain region
becomes known to the trade as a reliable source for potatoes
it soon comes to enjoy an advantage that is a great asset.
Buyers become accustomed to handling the crop and will
take it all up before going into newer regions to supply their
needs. The importance of community action in establishing
the potato industry can not be too strongly emphasized.
Without it the individual farmer on a reclamation project
can scarcely hope to find a profitable market.

The first step to be taken by a community is to limit the
number of varieties of potatoes that are to be grown and to
continue the production of the same varieties from year to
year. It is better to have only one variety, or at most two
varieties, in a community, because it is then possible to develop a discriminatory market, to establish a reputation,
and to ship in large lots of uniform character. Community
action in potato production also affords an opportunity for
the farmers to protect themselves against the introduction
of certain dangerous diseases that are carried with the seed.
It also makes possible the development of a system of certification of the product as being true to variety and free
from disease and thereby secures important market advantages.

SEED PRODUCTION.

The production of seed, particularly of forage crops,
has been developed on several reclamation projects and may
come to have a place among the important industries on

these projects. As the present time alfalfa seed is probably the most important of these crops. This country has not in recent years produced all the alfalfa seed needed, and large importations have been necessary. Speaking generally, the imported seed is less satisfactory than domestic seed, and since the outbreak of the European war these importations have been seriously interrupted. Notwithstanding these facts, which contribute to the ruling high prices of alfalfa seed, and the relative stability of the market for that commodity, serious difficulties are likely to be encountered in selling the crop. Similar difficulties are encountered in marketing the seeds of other plants. Seed crops are more susceptible to environmental conditions than most other crops. As a result, there are large variations from year to year in the available supplies and, consequently, in market prices. While these seeds are not so quickly perishable as are potatoes, the market demand and the prices fluctuate as widely. In view of these conditions the production of forage-crop seed should not be undertaken in a haphazard manner. A satisfactory industry can be developed only by intelligent and persistent attention to the business.

While community action may not be quite as essential in the seed industry as in potato production, it is, nevertheless, highly advantageous. By such action it is easier to develop reliable outlets for the seed and to establish a reputation which soon becomes an asset of material value. Seed-producing associations of farmers are useful not only as effective selling agencies, but they may provide for field inspection so as to insure the purity of the variety, and they may inspect, class, and certify the quality of the seed. These functions are of the utmost importance in meeting trade requirements and result in larger profits to the grower than can be expected where individuals act separately.

Because of the periodical fluctuation of yield and of market prices, the seed industry is uncertain and likely to be disappointing unless it is firmly established and continued from year to year. For the same reason it is inadvisable to devote a large proportion of the farm to the production of seed crops. The methods of production are often complicated and can be mastered only by constant attention to the business. The farmer who can irrigate his crops has a marked advantage in seed production over the farmer who can not, because of the critical water requirements of the seed crop. This feature, together with the relatively favorable climatic conditions that obtain in irrigated districts, gives advantages which should be made use of by irrigation farmers; but, on the other hand, these advantages do not justify exclusive specialization in the seed industry.

COTTON PRODUCTION.

The production of cotton is possible on only a few of the southwestern reclamation projects, and on these it has become important only recently. Interest in the possibility of utilizing these irrigated lands for cotton production has been stimulated by the decreased production in parts of the cotton belt, following the invasion of the boll weevil.

While much of the cotton so far produced on the irrigated lands has been of the ordinary short-staple varieties, it has become increasingly apparent that these must in time give place to varieties that yield the more valuable long staple, either of the American Upland or of the Egyptian type. It is economically unsound to devote high-priced irrigated land, having a long growing season, to the production of the cheaper types of cotton instead of the high-priced long-staple types, which have been found to yield equally well and for which there is a strong demand.

The production of cotton by irrigation enjoys certain important advantages which should be understood clearly and utilized more fully. Irrigation projects on which cotton production is possible are nearly all isolated from other cotton-producing regions. This isolation affords an opportunity to prevent the encroachment or invasion of certain insect pests, such as the boll weevil, and also, because of the definite limits of the community, it is easier to establish and maintain an industry based upon a single variety or type of cotton. The advantage to a community of isolation as an aid in preventing the invasion of noxious insects or plant diseases is so obvious as not to require discussion; but it may not be so generally appreciated that such isolation also favors the restriction of cotton production in a community to a single variety, or at least to a single type, and that such restriction is greatly to be desired.

SUCCESSFUL IRRIGATION DEVELOPMENT INVOLVES INTENSIVE FARMING, THICKLY SETTLED NEIGHBORHOODS, AND COMPLEX SOCIAL RELATIONS.

The underlying purpose of Government reclamation has been to provide homes on the land. (Photograph from the United States Reclamation Service.)

FIG. I.—IRRIGATING SUGAR BEETS.

Beet production is one of the most dependable industries for irrigated lands and is unique in that it has no marketing problems. (Photograph from the United States Reclamation Service.)

FIG. 2.—AN EXAMPLE OF INTENSIVE SPECIALIZATION IN FRUIT FARMING UNDER IRRIGATION.

A greater diversification of industries would be safer, though perhaps less spectacular. (Photograph from the United States Reclamation Service.)

FIG. I.—IN THE FIRST YEARS OF IRRIGATION FARMING AN EXCESS OF
ALFALFA HAY IS OFTEN PRODUCED.

This crop may be made more profitable if fed to live stock than if sold off the farm.

FIG. 2.—A SMALL FLOCK OF SHEEP CAN BE KEPT CHEAPLY AND BE
EXTREMELY USEFUL ON AN IRRIGATED FARM.

The sheep can utilize the aftermath on grain and hay fields and keep down the weeds
along fence rows and ditch banks.   (Photograph from the United States Reclamation
Service.)

FIG. 3.—THE FEEDING OF STEERS FROM THE SURROUNDING RANGES IS ONE
OF THE WAYS OF UTILIZING THE ALFALFA CROP TO ADVANTAGE.

The West must continue to produce increased quantities of meat, and irrigation farming
should stimulate rather than hinder progress in this direction.   (Photograph from the
United States Reclamation Service.)

Where only one kind of cotton is grown in a community it becomes possible to achieve results in production and in marketing that are quite out of the question where several different varieties or types are grown. This is more particularly true with long-staple cotton, where full market values can be secured only by maintaining the uniformity of the product from year to year. In order to maintain the uniformity of the product, it is necessary to make provision for a continuing supply of seed for planting which will reproduce the desired type of fiber and be free from the contamination which results from the accidental mixture of seed at the gin or cross-pollination between adjacent fields. Where several different kinds of cotton are grown in a community such contamination is very difficult to avoid. Furthermore, the conditions of cotton marketing are such that buyers and manufacturers are influenced in favor of localities from which they have learned to expect certain kinds of cotton to be produced regularly. On the other hand, they are likely to be apprehensive if they are offered several different kinds of cotton from the same region, for experience has shown that under such conditions intermixture and deterioration of the better sorts are inevitable, and that, too, without any compensatory improvement in the quality or uniformity of the poorer sorts.

In view of these facts it should be the aim of isolated cotton-growing communities to adopt some one variety of cotton to the exclusion of all others and then to take such steps as may be necessary to maintain the purity of all the seed used for planting. With a constant supply of pure planting seed it becomes a very simple matter to establish market grades or types of cotton that can be reproduced from year to year and find prompt sale at a premium over the mixed lots of the bulk of the cotton crop.

The cotton crop is one that responds to favorable conditions of growth with increased production, and it is possible on rich irrigated lands to produce crops large enough and valuable enough to find a place with other industries. Furthermore, cotton fits in well with a number of other irrigated crops. Cotton, following alfalfa, responds to the stimulus afforded by the preceding crop, and the early intertillage followed by the shading of the mature growth aids in the eradication of weeds. The soil is thus left clean and in good condition for other crops. The cotton seed is also a commodity of value and the by-products of its manufacture are important as a feed for live stock.

FRUIT PRODUCTION.

The production of orchard fruits has been one of the most conspicuous features of irrigation farming in this country. Some of the oldest and many of the best known irrigated sections owe their fame and prosperity to one or another of the fruit industries. In many of these sections the natural conditions are so favorable to the growth of the fruit that these industries may be expected to continue and even to be materially extended.

But not all of the irrigated lands of the West are suited to fruit production, and there have been serious disappointments in some new regions which have been exploited on the basis of orchard fruits. The causes for these disappointments have been too many and too complicated to be discussed here in detail. In general, they have been the high capitalization of the land and the difficulties of marketing. There have also been some production problems, but these have been less important. All these difficulties, combined with the widespread tendency of the farmers to rely on fruit production exclusively, have caused serious economic depressions in several of the more important fruit-growing sections.

Almost from the first the problems of fruit transportation and marketing have been acute. These problems have been dealt with largely through cooperation on the part of the growers, and sometimes with marked efficiency. Some of the most conspicuous instances of agricultural cooperation are to be found in this field. In fact, it is possible that much of the spirit of cooperation among irrigation farmers is due to the example of success in this direction achieved by fruit growers. This cooperation has brought into use high standards of fruit packing and has stimulated improved methods of production.

There is to be observed at present on irrigated lands a reaction from fruit production toward other industries. This readjustment is probably to be regarded merely as a phase of normal development. It is to be expected that fruit production will continue to be one of the important features of irrigation farming, though in many sections it will probably remain subsidiary to other industries.

PORK PRODUCTION.

One of the first crops of which there is a local oversupply on the reclamation projects is alfalfa. The acreage devoted to this crop, particularly during the early stages of the development of a project, is frequently greater than that devoted to all other crops combined and the yield is abundant. The cereal crops are also very important in the first years of irrigation farming. Under ordinary conditions neither alfalfa hay nor grain will bear the cost of transportation to the market centers. It therefore becomes necessary to convert these crops into some form of live-stock products which because of relatively high value per unit of weight will stand the transportation charges from the projects to places of manufacture or consumption.

The hog is one of the most efficient of farm animals in converting alfalfa and grain into a readily marketable product. The returns secured by pasturing hogs on irrigated alfalfa, supplemented with a light ration of grain, are frequently three to five times as great as could be obtained by selling the alfalfa as hay. If efficiently managed, hogs can be made to pay from 25 to 50 per cent more for grain than can be secured by the direct marketing of that crop. Furthermore, the amount of capital required to make a start in the swine industry is relatively small and the returns come quickly. The swine population of an irrigated farm can be made to increase from 500 to 1,000 per cent a year, and the animals are marketable before they are a year old. For these reasons the production of pork is one of the most promising industries for an irrigated farm. Much of the best progress made on several of the Government projects in recent years is directly attributable to the development of swine production. The abundance of cheap feeds, the favorable climatic conditions, and the advantages of isolation in the prevention and control of diseases all tend to reduce the cost of producing pork on these projects.

The successful establishment of the swine industry involves a number of factors to which careful attention must be given. These include matters of production and of marketing, and some of them are inseparably connected. Efficient production requires breeding for both quality and quantity, an intelligent understanding of the best methods of feeding, adequate housing facilities, and the control of diseases and pests affecting swine. Profitable marketing requires high quality, uniformity, an understanding of market requirements as to size and finish of the animals and as to time of delivery, and adequate arrangements for shipping and selling. In securing the necessary efficiency in these matters the individual farmer working alone is all but helpless. Some form of community action is imperative.

There is a great advantage in having only one breed in a community, as this facilitates improvements in breeding and marketing. Through an association the swine growers can be mutually helpful in working out problems of feeding and housing, as the interchange of ideas and experiences tends to eliminate mistakes and to popularize the best methods. Much can be done through community arrangements with respect to the utilization of the grain which is now shipped out in the fall by the farmers on or near the projects, while in the following spring the same kind of grain is shipped in, to be bought by swine growers at higher prices. This practice is obviously wasteful, and its elimination could be effected easily by concerted action.

The control of contagious diseases, particularly hog cholera, is impossible without community action. This fact is perhaps more conspicuous on the irrigated lands than elsewhere, because the germs of the disease may be carried in irrigation water and thus spread throughout the entire community; but, on the other hand, the isolation of the communities makes it comparatively easy to enforce the quarantine and sanitary regulations necessary to prevent or control the disease. In other words, the conditions on the projects, while especially requiring community action, also promote its effectiveness. The experience of the past two years in the control of hog cholera on certain of the reclamation projects has demonstrated fully that through community cooperation disease control is a purchasable service.

The size requirements of the swine industry on these projects should be understood clearly. Difficulty is commonly encountered in the early stages of the industry's development in making satisfactory shipping arrangements. When the total output of hogs is small, the railroads are unable to give as good service as when the output becomes sufficient to justify regular shipping schedules, live-stock trains, and other conveniences. Here, again, the importance of community action is obvious. If the community as a whole is actively interested in the establishment of the swine industry, satisfactory shipping arrangements can be made much more quickly than if the industry is forced to struggle along on a purely individual basis.

On the reclamation projects, where the farm unit is small, few farmers produce hogs in carload lots. Hence, the producer in marketing his output must sell to a local buyer or cooperate with his neighbors in shipping to market. Of the two, the latter is decidedly preferable and is properly a function of an association. Cooperative marketing already is being done with gratifying results on some of the projects. But the factors of successful cooperative marketing extend farther back than the mere act of collective shipping. The breeding and feeding practices need to be adjusted to the requirements of efficient marketing, so that animals of the desired size, finish, and number may be ready at the proper time. This, again, requires concerted action and community interest.

In the absence of real efficiency the swine growers are certain to suffer discouraging financial losses in periods of low prices for pork. Farmers should remember that productive efficiency, that is, low cost of production, is as much to be desired as high prices for the finished product. Fair prices, large consumption, and high efficiency are the things which promote the best development. With the proper consideration of these facts and with special attention to the community phases of pork production the farmers on the reclamation projects should be able to make swine production one of their most profitable industries.

DAIRYING.

It is not improbable that dairying has done more than any other live-stock industry to support irrigation agriculture in this country. This has been true not because the profits of dairy farming have been large, but rather because they have been comparatively certain. The dairy industry has saved the situation for hundreds of settlers when the expected returns from more spectacular industries have failed to materialize. The possibilities of dairying have not begun to be realized or even appreciated by the majority of irrigation farmers.

One of the chief favorable features of dairying is its continuity. It employs labor throughout the year and furnishes a steady cash income. The natural conditions on the reclamation projects are favorable to high production in dairying. All the necessary feeds can be grown cheaply and abundantly. This applies particularly to alfalfa hay, corn silage, and irrigated pastures. These, when properly combined, furnish practically all the feed required by dairy cows; and where concentrated feeds are abundant and cheap they, too, may be utilized profitably. A further advantage is the mild climate of most of the projects, which makes it unnecessary to provide expensive buildings.

The dairy industry combines well with pork production, the by-products of the dairy furnishing excellent feed for pigs. Sugar-beet production also fits in admirably with dairying, both in the employment of labor and in the utilization of manure. Perhaps no irrigated crop responds more markedly than sugar beets to the application of manure.

As the volume of the dairy products of the country increases and competition becomes more keen, there will be need for much higher dairy efficiency on the reclamation projects. While these areas have many natural advantages over the highly developed dairy districts in the Eastern and Central States, they are at some disadvantage in marketing and, at present, in the quality of dairy stock. Perhaps the greatest need of the dairy farmers on these projects is better cows. While the prices of dairy products remain fairly high, the availability of cheap feeds makes it possible for the settlers to make some profit from low-producing cows; but as production in the irrigated districts increases it will be necessary to cull out the less profitable individuals. As the local production expands, outside markets will have to be sought, and this will bring the irrigation farmers in direct competition with the more efficient dairymen of the older dairy regions. It is essential that the farmers on the reclamation projects foresee this development and prepare themselves for its requirements.

It is probable that the variations in individual efficiency are more marked in dairy cows than in any other domestic animals. These great variations are among the most conspicuous features of the dairy industry on the reclamation projects. Furthermore, the general level of productive efficiency is low. The average production per cow on these new irrigated lands could probably be increased 50 to 75 per cent through the introduction of better stock and the improvement of present herds through the use of good bulls and the general elimination of inferior cows. There is need also for improvement in methods of management.

Several of the reclamation projects, particularly those in the Northwest, are well situated for the production of cheese. The abundance of cold water, the cool summer climate, and the thickly settled neighborhoods are conditions which favor cheese making. The cheese industry within the past two years has experienced marked development on several of the northern projects, and there are indications of still further expansion.

The need for community action is perhaps even greater in the development of dairying than it is in pork production on these projects. Cooperation is needed in securing improved stock, in the local transportation of milk and cream, and often in manufacturing as well as in marketing; in fact, these functions can not be worked out satisfactorily without cooperation. The small farms, the newness of conditions, and the distances to market all result in a need for community interest. Necessity is developing a strong appreciation of these facts and the cooperative spirit on the reclamation projects is growing rapidly, among dairy farmers particularly.

THE SHEEP INDUSTRY.

The production of sheep has not been an important feature of irrigation farming. Feed crops grown on irrigated lands have been used extensively in finishing stock produced on the range and in wintering range ewes, but the breeding of sheep and year-long feeding on irrigated lands has not been extensive.

It is to be expected that finishing range sheep and wintering ewes will continue to be important on these lands, but the practice is not without its disadvantages. One drawback is the uncertainty of the market for the finished product. This, together with the high prices usually demanded for the feeder stock, makes winter feeding rather hazardous. Under favorable conditions, however, the farmer who feeds range sheep secures not only a direct profit from his feeding operations, but also a large quantity of manure, through the use of which his crop yields may be markedly increased.

The conditions on several of the reclamation projects are specially favorable for the production of sheep on the farms. Sheep not only furnish a profitable method of disposing of some of the leading crop products, but they are particularly useful in utilizing certain crop by-products and in eradicating weeds. The material left in the grain fields, beet tops, the aftermath in-hay fields, and the plant growth in fence rows and on ditch banks can be utilized profitably by sheep. A promising practice for many of the irrigated farms is to graze sheep on irrigated pastures. A pasture which will carry 2 cows to the acre will support 6 to 10 ewes and their lambs until the lambs are ready for market and still produce sufficient feed to carry the ewes through the season. By these means the irrigation farmer on many of the projects can keep from 20 to 100 breeding ewes with profit, the number depending on the size of his land holdings and the grouping of industries on his farm. Ordinarily there is much to be gained by developing pure-bred flocks as soon as practicable.

On certain of the projects which are adjacent to satisfactory grazing lands on the open range or in the National Forests a limited number of irrigation farmers can engage in sheep production on a larger scale. Small groups of farmers, each owning a few hundred sheep, can sometimes arrange to use the range cooperatively and to winter their flocks on individual farms. In this way the flocks may be carried through the summer at relatively low cost and be used profitably in the autumn and winter to consume forage and grain crops and by-products on the farm.

The problems of marketing the wool and mutton produced by the flocks, particularly the small ones, can be solved best by cooperation among the farmers. The same is true of many of the problems of efficient management. Such things as breeding, shearing, and dipping offer many opportunities for advantageous cooperation. Frequently much can be gained by cooperation between the small sheep growers and the large range sheep producers. The latter sometimes will contract for years in advance to purchase from the former all the pure-bred ram lambs produced on the small farms. Thus, a profitable market for half the offspring of the small flocks may be assured in advance, to the benefit of everybody concerned.

If good use is made of the opportunities for cooperation, both among the small farmers and between them and the extensive range sheepmen, there are but few projects where sheep production can not be made a lucrative part of the activities of the irrigated farm. Already there are some successful sheep-growing enterprises on the projects, but the full possibilities can not be realized until community attention is focused upon the industry.

BEEF PRODUCTION.

Like the sheep industry, beef production on the irrigated lands has been confined to the winter feeding and finishing of range stock. Aside from this, the development of an extensive beef-cattle industry on the reclamation projects depends primarily on the availability of cheap summer range. Doubtless there will be some instances of specialized beef production, based largely on the breeding of high-class pure-bred stock, in which the animals will be kept on the farms throughout the year. Except in such instances it is unlikely that the year-long feeding of beef cattle on these small farms will be found as profitable as the feeding of dairy cattle, hogs, and sheep.

Some of the projects are located near grazing areas which are not fully stocked or on which readjustments can be made which will provide range for stock owned by irrigation farmers. Where the grazing of these areas is properly controlled and efficiently managed, as in the National Forests, or where arrangements can be made to assure undisturbed occupation and use, there are opportunities for beef production. The proper utilization of such grazing areas would add materially to the crop-disposal possibilities of the adjacent irrigated lands.

Because of the small size of the beef herds which can be fed on these farms, successful summer grazing on the adjacent range lands requires some kind of cooperation. This may consist simply of hiring a herder who, for a fixed charge per head, will handle the stock during the grazing season; or more formal grazing associations may be organized. These associations are growing in number and efficiency on several of the projects and it seems likely that they will continue to increase. The activities of the grazing associations may include the hiring of a salaried herder; the furnishing of salt; systematic efforts to prevent the loss of stock from diseases, poisonous plants, and predatory animals; the furnishing of well-bred bulls; negotiations with the Forest Service and other agencies regarding the allotment and management of grazing areas; and provision for live-stock insurance. It is through increased cooperation, particularly in range utilization, that the beef industry on these projects is likely to reach its best development.

THE GROUPING OF INDUSTRIES.

In the preceding discussion of the different agricultural industries which rank as important on reclamation projects, only incidental reference has been made to their relations to each other either on the individual farm or in the community. These relations are matters of the greatest importance. There are very few situations where a farm or a community survives, still less achieves success and prosperity, through the exclusive development of a single industry. The requirements of crop rotation, the efficient use of labor, and the insurance of some source of income are the potent factors that make a diversification of industries imperative.

The number of industries which it is possible to carry on in any irrigated region is much larger than the number it is usually desirable to have. This enables the farmer to select from among the available industries a few which suit his fancy and appeal to his judgment.

Much of the possibility of success in farming depends upon the proper selection and grouping of major industries. This is a problem that usually can not be settled in advance of practical experience. It is not enough to decide merely to have a diversity of industries. Each should be considered not only as to its own possibilities under the natural conditions, but also in relation to the others with which it is to be associated. If possible, the selection should be such that each will be profitable in itself, but it is sometimes worth while to carry on one industry which yields little or no direct profit because of its indirect benefit to others in the group.

In new regions far from market the farmer should also be influenced in his selection of industries by the opinions or desires of his neighbors. It has been repeatedly pointed out that community cooperation is often essential to success in these irrigated districts, and such cooperation often may be extended to the selection of the kinds of crops or the kinds of live stock that ought to be used.

The important point that needs to be kept in mind is that the problem of the proper selection of industries merits serious consideration. A farmer should not embark upon an industry merely because it is momentarily attractive or because someone else has succeeded with it. He should canvass the whole situation thoroughly and test each industry from the following points of view:

(1) Is it adapted to local conditions of climate and soil and to the location of the project with respect to transportation and marketing?

(2) Can it be fitted in with the others that are being considered, so as to permit the effective distribution of labor throughout the year?

(3) Does it fit in with the others to occupy the available land and either benefit them or utilize to advantage their effects?

(4) Is it one that may be accepted generally in the community and thus permit such cooperation as is needful for success?

(5) Are the products subject to violent market fluctuations resulting from sudden scarcity or oversupply, so that special persistence is necessary to secure stabilization?

A careful consideration of these questions may determine the measure of success which will follow the farmer's selection of industries.

IMPORTANCE OF STABILIZING INDUSTRIES.

The proper establishment of any of these agricultural industries under the multiplicity of new and strange conditions may require years of time. The new settlers can not reasonably expect to develop in one or two years an efficiency or a reputation which will enable them to compete successfully with older communities. A period of pioneering is inevitable and readjustments are to be expected; but such readjustments should come about gradually and should be in the direction of constructive development.

Substantial prosperity requires that some of the industries in which the settlers engage be stabilized; that plans for their establishment be projected years in advance, just as the bona fide settler projects the plans for the establishment of his home. Periods of depression or adversity must be endured, and ideals of efficiency must be pursued constantly. Frequent and radical changes from one industry to another, stimulated among speculative settlers by market fluctuations, lead to inefficiency and failure. On the other hand, intelligent conservative practices, vigorously and constantly prosecuted, develop high industrial efficiency and thus promote general prosperity in these communities.

The agricultural commodities produced on reclamation projects must be shipped to distant markets. In order to sell to best advantage, these products must be well known in the market and come to be depended upon by the consuming public or the manufacturer. Much of the efficiency of marketing depends upon the establishment and maintenance of recognized grades or standards of the product. Such standards can be established and their recognition secured only by continued effort. These facts have an important bearing and should be considered seriously in connection with any proposal to establish a new industry on a reclamation project.

THE PLACE OF IRRIGATION FARMING IN WESTERN AGRICULTURE.

An unfortunate tendency that has been noticeable in the development of irrigation farming in the West has been to disregard its economic relation to the other agricultural enterprises of that region. The vast areas of land which surround the irrigated sections have long been important to the country as a whole because of their production of breadstuffs and meat. While the areas available for the production of wheat by dry farming and the range lands used for the support of live stock have been almost completely occupied by these industries, greatly increased production in both lines is still possible. These arid lands are certain to become increasingly important in meeting the requirements of the national food supply. Their possibilities have been by no means realized.

Grain production by dry farming and live-stock production on the ranges are subject to severe vicissitudes because of the periodical fluctuations in climatic conditions. The setbacks resulting from adverse seasons often cripple the farmers and stockmen to such an extent that they can not take advantage of the more favorable seasons that follow. The proper development of irrigation farming may be expected to aid in surmounting such difficulties, to the benefit of all concerned.

The irrigated lands that enjoy conditions favoring the high production of forage crops may properly become important as centers of stock feeding, not only in finishing stock but in wintering range stock and in carrying the animals through protracted periods of drought. Such enterprises not only furnish an economical means of utilizing the crops of the irrigated land, but also provide an outlet for some of the grain from adjacent dry farms.

The irrigation farmer who is confronted with the problem of marketing his crop products would do well to consider the possibilities that lie at hand in the way of cooperating with his neighbors on the dry farms and on the ranges. They, like himself, are subject to serious economic stresses. Some of these may be relieved through a better understanding of the situation and by making gradually such readjustments as are possible.

Irrigation farming has been the subject of extravagant exploitation, as well as the cause of severe disappointments. As a matter of fact, it ought to be regarded merely as one of the ways of making a home and a living and not primarily as a means of making money. Irrigated lands may be expected to support prosperous communities wherever industry and intelligence are devoted to the work. In some respects irrigation farming is probably less hazardous than some other agricultural enterprises, but success can be assured only by diligent and persistent endeavor.

THE DASHEEN; ITS USES AND CULTURE.

By ROBERT A. YOUNG,

Botanical Assistant, Office of Foreign Seed and Plant Introduction,
Bureau of Plant Industry.

INTRODUCTION.

ANYONE who has traveled much in the Tropics or the Orient, and especially one who has visited the Hawaiian Islands, can hardly have failed to make the acquaintance of the taro. Even those who have become well acquainted with it and learned really to like it, however, probably have not thought of the possibility of its successful introduction as a food crop into the United States. But such a thing has already come to pass, and a variety of the taro known as the Trinidad dasheen, from the island of Trinidad, West Indies, is now becoming established as a factor in the agriculture of the South.

There has been a growing need in the Southern States for more crops similar in character to the potato, to supplement the supply of that great staple food plant. The dasheen seems largely to meet this need. The comparative difficulty of growing more than one good crop of potatoes a year, the further difficulty of successful storage by small growers or dealers, and the fact that northern markets consume a large portion of the crop at good prices make the price of potatoes always high except in cities that are reached by water from the North when the supply is abundant there.

Dasheens for home use can be grown at small expense by most farmers in the South, and by many can be grown for local markets at prices no higher than for potatoes. Since the Trinidad dasheen contains about 50 per cent more protein and 50 per cent more starch and sugars than the potato, dasheens at equal prices would really be a cheaper food. This crop is adapted for cultivation in rich, moist, well-drained soils and matures in October and November. It requires at least seven months to reach full maturity.

Although the dasheen was introduced into the United States from the West Indies, it is believed to have come originally from China. This belief obtains partly because

199

the name dasheen appears to be a corruption of the French phrase " de la Chine," meaning " from China," and partly because other varieties, very closely allied to it, have been found in southern China.

DESCRIPTION OF THE DASHEEN.

The Trinidad dasheen[1] is an especially fine variety of a particular type of the taro. As will be seen from the leaves, it bears a strong resemblance to the ordinary elephant-ear plant. The two are closely related, though the elephant-ear " tuber " makes very poor eating in comparison with the dasheen.

Each hill of dasheens usually contains one or two large, central corms, besides a considerable number of lateral cormels, commonly called tubers. In rare cases there may be as many as three to five of the large corms in one hill. The corms of the Trinidad variety when grown in the right kind of soil are of at least as good quality as the tubers, and sometimes better. In texture and flavor the dasheen may be described as being between the chestnut and the potato.

ECONOMIC IMPORTANCE OF THE DASHEEN AND OTHER TAROS.

The taro, including the type recognized here as the dasheen, is one of the important food plants in most of the warm regions of the world. The culture of the crop is probably developed to a higher degree in the Hawaiian Islands than elsewhere. It is grown as an upland crop in certain parts of the islands, but much more extensively under irrigation. As an irrigated crop it is usually grown in patches from one-eighth to one-fourth acre in size, each plat being inclosed with dikes and being at a different level, so that the water runs from one to the other. The movement of the water is slow but continuous. The plants do not grow so tall as when grown in rich soil that is only moist. The season required for maturing a crop varies from 8 to 15 months, depending on the variety.

---

[1] Certain varieties of taros resemble the Trinidad dasheen, especially in the character of the tuberous part of the plant. These varieties constitute a distinct type of taro and are referred to here as dasheens. Where the dasheen is mentioned in this article the Trinidad variety is always to be understood.

P11820FS

FIG. I.—TARO FIELDS NEAR HONOLULU, WITH DIAMOND HEAD CRATER
IN THE BACKGROUND.

The dasheen is a fine-flavored variety of the taro, a root vegetable grown extensively in
Hawaii and widely in other warm regions of the world. Taro fields are flooded, while
the dasheen grows without irrigation in the Southern States.

P15814FS

FIG. 2.—DASHEEN PLANTS AT BROOKSVILLE, FLA.

Hills as they appear at the time of harvest, early in November, 7½ months after planting.
One of these hills produced 26 pounds of corms and tubers. A good average yield,
however, in rich soil is from 6 to 8 pounds per hill, or 360 to 475 bushels per acre.

P11916FS

FIG. 3.—A 4-ACRE FIELD OF THE TRINIDAD DASHEEN.

Plants as they appeared early in October at the United States Plant Introduction Field
Station, Brooksville, Fla. This field of dasheens is a little more than 6 months old.
The dasheen was first introduced into this country from the island of Trinidad, West
Indies, in 1905.

P19477FS

FIG. I.—A TYPICAL CORM OF THE TRINIDAD DASHEEN.

The cooked dasheen, in texture and flavor, is between the chestnut and the potato. The dasheen contains about half again as much protein and half again as much starch as the potato, and is consequently much drier. The corm here shown weighed 2½ pounds. The rings around the corm are the leaf scars, and the large light spots on the lower half are the scars formed by breaking off the side tubers. Some corms are more nearly spherical and others are more elongate, depending upon the soil and weather conditions and the length of the season.

P19312FS

FIG. 2.—TWENTY-THREE POUNDS OF DASHEENS, THE PRODUCT OF A SINGLE HILL.

In the center are five marketable corms, having a total weight of 11¾ pounds. Most hills, however, produce only one or two large corms each. At the left are eight first-grade tubers, which weighed 2½ pounds, making a total of 14¼ pounds of first-grade marketable dasheens. In the pile of tubers on the right some are of size and shape good enough to be classed as second-grade for market. The remainder are suitable for home table use, for seed, or for stock feed.

P11884FS

FIG. 1.—A HAWAIIAN POUNDING POI, NEAR LIHUE, ISLAND OF KAUAI, HAWAII.

Poi, the famous Hawaiian dish made from the taro, of which the dasheen is a selected variety, is an easily digested fermented food used often by Americans in Hawaii as a breakfast dish. It was formerly all made by this method, the taro being first cooked by steaming by means of heated stones in a pit.

P19787A-FS

FIG. 2.—A BED OF FORCED AND BLANCHED DASHEEN SHOOTS, FROM WHICH THE COVERING HAS JUST BEEN REMOVED.

In forcing and blanching dasheen shoots in the North, corms weighing 2 to 4 pounds are planted in a bed of moist, very sandy soil, with bottom heat, and the bed tightly inclosed above with boards or other material, to exclude light. The shoots are delicate in flavor and texture, the flavor suggesting that of mushrooms.

15860FS

FIG. I.—A CASSEROLE OF SLICED DASHEEN, BUTTERED, WHICH WILL BE READY FOR SCALLOPING AFTER THE ADDITION OF MILK.

Dasheen corms or tubers are pared raw and sliced with a fluted vegetable slicer. The cooking of this dish requires only a little more than half as long as scalloped potatoes. When well prepared it is one of the most satisfactory dishes made from the dasheen. Plain slices instead of latticework may be used.

P19422FS

FIG. 2.—STUFFED DASHEEN IN THE "HALF SHELL," FOR INDIVIDUAL SERVICE.

In preparing stuffed dasheens, the corm is cut from top to base and baked; the contents are then removed, seasoned, and returned to the half shells.

P19471FS

FIG. I.—DASHEEN CRISPS.

Raw dasheens are pared and sliced with a fluted slicer and fried slowly to a light brown in deep fat. For certain purposes this is one of the very best ways in which the dasheen can be prepared. They will often remain crisp for a week or more, if not exposed continuously to the air.

P15870FS

FIG. 2.—ROLLS MADE FROM WHEAT FLOUR IN COMBINATION WITH BOILED DASHEEN.

Bread made in this way is similar to that made with boiled potato in that it keeps moist longer than when flour alone is used. The bread is sometimes a little darker because of the dasheen, but the flavor is in no way impaired. One part of dasheen to two or three parts of flour gives excellent results.

P19478FS

FIG. I.—DASHEEN CORMELS OR "TUBERS."

Tubers of the grade here shown are referred to as first-grade tubers and are about two-thirds natural size. With many of smaller size or irregular shape, they grow clustered around one or more large corms. Under proper soil conditions they are of excellent quality and command a much better price than the smaller and irregularly shaped ones.

P15827FS

FIG. 2.—TWO BARRELS OF DASHEENS READY FOR COVERING AND SHIPPING.

They are usually covered with burlap. The holes near the top and similar ones near the bottom are for ventilation. The barrel at the right contains corms and that at the left selected tubers. When dasheens are well grown there is usually little difference in flavor and texture between the corms and tubers, though the corms are a little more mealy and many persons prefer them. The railroads have placed the dasheen on the same basis as the potato in freight classification, which makes it possible to ship dasheens in barrel lots to many northern points at a very moderate expense for transportation.

P8960FS

FIG. 3.—AN II-POUND HILL OF DASHEEN CORMS AND TUBERS, WITH SOIL AND ROOTS REMOVED, IN ACTUAL POSITION OF GROWTH.

The taro is eaten in Hawaii boiled or baked, like potatoes, or in the form of poi. It is as poi that it is eaten most largely. In making poi the taro is thoroughly cooked, by steaming or boiling, and peeled. With the addition of a little water it is then reduced, either by pounding with a stone pestle or pounder, the old method, or by grinding with a modern mill, to a sticky mass. The pounding process includes the wetting of the empty hand in a vessel of water, kept at the side, at each fall of the pounder and moistening the lower surface of the pestle as it is lifted for the next stroke. When the paste, or poi, has become perfectly smooth from the pounding, it is usually put into a covered receptacle for a day or so, in order to ferment. Poi made by the modern process is fermented in the same manner. The old method is still in use to a limited extent.

The taro is credited, wherever grown, with being more easily digested than most other starch foods, and poi is held to be the most easily digested form in which it can be prepared. Poi, however, is a dish that does not appeal strongly to most persons unaccustomed to it, and its use has not spread among other peoples. The expected increase in the use of the dasheen, and perhaps other taros, will be as a vegetable, or in the form of flour for use in combination with wheat or other flours in baking.

In many countries where the taro is cultivated, because of the inferiority of the varieties grown and the poor methods of cooking it, the vegetable is esteemed but little by Europeans and Americans. In parts of China, according to Mr. Frank N. Meyer, Agricultural Explorer for the Department of Agriculture, the taro is in the class of luxuries, and the very poor can rarely afford to eat it. In Japan, where it is classed among the so-called imos, it is said to be used by all classes of people, often being cooked with fish.

The taros and the yautias (another group of edible "aroids," as the plants of the arum family are called) are grown widely in tropical America and constitute a rather important part of the food supply of the native peoples. Dasheens, under the name "malanga," are brought from Cuba to Tampa, Fla., for the Latin-American people of that city.

For two centuries at least, from time to time, individuals have brought into the Carolinas and grown there on a small scale inferior varieties of the taro. Even now occasional patches of a rather strong flavored taro, known as the tanier, or tanya, are met with in the South Atlantic States.

A very inferior kind of taro, somewhat similar to the tanier just mentioned, is grown in the eastern Mediterranean region, especially in Egypt, where it is called " qolqas." It appears to be eaten only by the laboring classes. It has been imported into the United States, apparently for consumption by the oriental population in some of our eastern cities, but this market is now supplied by dasheens from the Southern States. Taros are also shipped to America from China and are sold in Chinese shops as " China potatoes."

INTRODUCTION OF THE DASHEEN.

Until the investigation of the aroid root crops was begun by the Department of Agriculture a few years ago, it does not appear that any serious attempts were ever made to grow them outside of tropical or subtropical regions except in Japan and China. As a preliminary part of this investigational work, there was assembled, first by Mr. O. W. Barrett, at the Porto Rico Agricultural Experiment Station, and later at Washington, D. C., the largest collection of varieties of these plants ever brought together. They were collected from every quarter of the globe where grown. From field tests made of these varieties in South Carolina and Florida it was found that the Trinidad dasheen, taking into account its adaptability to the climate and its food qualities, was especially well suited for culture and use in this country.

The propagation and testing work with the dasheen since 1911 has been carried on by the department principally at its Plant Introduction Field Station at Brooksville, Fla. A large number of people in the South, especially in the Southeast, are now growing the dasheen for home use, stock feed, and market.

USES OF THE DASHEEN.

It is not intended that the dasheen shall displace either the potato or the sweet potato in any market. A greater variety of starchy vegetables is needed, however, and the dasheen has been welcomed by many as an addition to the small list of those foods now in use in the United States. But for the present, at least, outside of the regions where grown it is not to be looked upon as a cheap food; the shipments are not yet large enough to bring the prices to the level which they may reach later. In the South, however, where the dasheen is grown it is expected that it will eventually come to be used extensively, partly as a matter of economy, and especially during the long season when potatoes have to be shipped from the North.

Most persons when eating the dasheen naturally think of comparing it with the potato. Many say they like it better; others equally well; and some not so well. However individual opinions may differ as to the relative merits of the two vegetables, a sufficiently large number of persons who have tried the dasheen have been so favorably impressed that there seems to be no question of its ultimate popularity as a table vegetable.

Dasheens, as well as other taros, are reputed to be more easily digested than many other starch foods. This ease of digestion has not been scientifically demonstrated, so far as is known, but the belief is current and doubtless has some basis in fact. The extremely small size of the taro starch grain, one of the smallest known in food plants, may possibly have some connection with its digestibility.

PREPARATION FOR THE TABLE.

Dasheens are suitable for use in the same manner and in quite as many ways as potatoes, with slight modifications, which are necessary in some cases on account of the differences in the texture of the two vegetables. Some housewives or cooks fail to get the best results, or fail completely, with dasheens at first, wholly from lack of care in following the directions for cooking and serving. It should be remembered that in order to give a new vegetable a fair trial every detail regarding its preparation for the table should be carefully followed. One common mistake is to bake or boil the dasheens too long; another is to cook them before the rest of the meal is prepared and so keep them standing for some time before they are served. Baked or boiled potatoes that are kept standing lose in palatability, and the dasheen loses quite as much if not served promptly. Dasheens do not require quite so long a time to cook as potatoes of the same size, and it is important to remember this, especially in boiling or baking them.

There is an almost endless variety of ways in which dasheens can be prepared for the table. A number of recipes have been worked out carefully and a few of these will be referred to here.

Baking is the most satisfactory method, in general, of cooking either large or small dasheens. Large ones (corms) are usually first parboiled for 10 to 20 minutes, in order to reduce the time necessary for baking and so avoid the possibility of charring the outside. A moderately hot oven is required. If the dasheens are well scrubbed, to remove the fibrous part of the skin, and the baking is properly done, a soft crust is formed, which is very delicious. Large dasheens may be served in the " half shell " if desired, the corms usually being cut in half before baking. They are made still more attractive by placing a lump of butter in a hole scooped out of the center of the cut surface. The halves of corms that are small enough can be served as individual portions and the larger ones used for several persons.

The interior of a well-grown dasheen is usually mealy when baked or boiled, though often more firm than a potato. It is sometimes of cream color, but more often it is grayish white or tinged with violet. The same seasoning is used as for potatoes, but on account of the comparative dryness of the dasheen more butter or gravy is generally needed. Too much importance can not be given to serving baked or boiled dasheens promptly after they are cooked.

Dasheens mashed like potatoes are likely to be too sticky to be attractive, but when put through a potato ricer after boiling or baking they make a most satisfactory dish. A ricer stronger than the ordinary ones on the market is desirable for the dasheen, because of its firm texture.

Scalloped dasheen made with either latticework or plain slices is a most satisfactory dish where a large company of persons is to be served and where the dish must of necessity stand for a time. The addition of a few slices of onion will bring out the dasheen flavor.

Stuffed dasheens, especially the large corms, are exceedingly attractive and when properly seasoned are as good as they look. The stuffed halves may be served one to a person or one for several persons, according to the size of the corm.

Dasheen crisps, made from raw dasheen with a fluted vegetable slicer and fried in deep fat, are declared by some epicures to be the most delicious of all dasheen dishes. The delicate nutty flavor of the dasheen is accentuated by this method of preparation. While these crisps are better when freshly made, they often keep their crispness for several days, depending on the amount of moisture in the air.

As a filling for fowl and other meats the dasheen can hardly be surpassed. Served au gratin, that is, cooked with grated cheese, it is equal to any similar dish. It makes a delicious salad and may be French fried or German fried, like potatoes. It can also be used boiled in making bread, as potatoes are used by many housewives, and with the same results.

DASHEEN FLOUR.

A very good flour has been made from dasheens. The corms and large tubers are pared and either sliced or shredded and then dried and ground in a flour mill. As the dasheen does not appear to contain gluten, the flour can not be used alone in baking, but must be used in combination with wheat or rye flour. Excellent bread, muffins, biscuits, crullers, griddlecakes, soups, and various other products are made by using dasheen flour in part. A proportion of one-fourth or one-third of dasheen flour is generally used.

DASHEEN SHOOTS.

A secondary use of the dasheen is the forcing of the large corms for their shoots.[1] These shoots are more tender than asparagus and have a delicate flavor not unlike that of mushrooms. They are forced in the dark in order to blanch them. The slight acridity which the blanched shoots contain is destroyed by the following methods of cooking:

(1) Cut the blanched shoots into 2-inch lengths, pour on an abundance of boiling water, add salt, and boil for 12 minutes; drain, pour on enough cold milk[2] so that the shoots will be completely covered

---

[1] A circular fully describing the forcing, blanching, and cooking of dasheen shoots will be sent without charge upon request to the U. S. Department of Agriculture, Washington, D. C.

[2] The change from hot water to cold milk or water when the shoots are nearly done is to keep them from becoming too soft.

when it boils, season with salt, and boil for 5 minutes; drain, season with butter, and serve on toast or plain. It is necessary to add a little butter [1] to the milk in boiling if skim milk is used. Cream sauce may be used in serving if desired.

(2) Instead of boiling in milk, after draining off the first water add a little piece of butter or bacon [1] and then cover the shoots with cold water, season with salt, and boil for 5 minutes. Drain and serve.

DASHEENS AS STOCK FEED.

Although extensive feeding experiments with the dasheen have not yet been made, as a stock feed it is probably equal in value to the potato, sweet potato, or cassava. For this purpose, however, as with potatoes and sweet potatoes, dasheens will, in general, be used only incidentally, as in cases of overproduction or of dasheens unsuited in size or quality for market. They seem, in the raw state, to be more palatable to stock than potatoes and, while doubtless less palatable than sweet potatoes, they contain a higher proportion of protein to starch and sugars than sweet potatoes. Both cattle and hogs eat them with relish after getting the taste, and pigs 8 months old have been fattened for the market in a month by turning them in the autumn into a patch of dasheens.

CULTURE OF THE DASHEEN.

PLANTING.

Dasheens are adapted for commercial culture only in the Southern States. They require a frostless season of at least seven months, with plenty of moisture, to fully mature a good crop. For a large crop of good quality the dasheen must be grown in a moist but well-drained rich sandy loam. The addition soon after planting of a fertilizer containing 8 to 12 per cent of potash, even in good soil, as a rule has a beneficial effect on the crop. A large proportion of either clay or muck in the soil produces strong-flavored or tough dasheens, which often are quite unfit for table use. However, those grown in muck soil yield heavily and are reported to be entirely satisfactory for stock feed.

Planting is done in February in southern Florida and as late as the early part of April in South Carolina. Whole

---

[1] The butter fat of the milk, or the bacon fat, appears to assist in destroying the acridity.

tubers are used and are planted singly, 2 to 3 inches deep. Tubers weighing 3 to 5 ounces each are better than smaller ones for planting, although the character of the soil and the amount of moisture present are much more important factors than the size of the tubers.

In rich soil about 12 square feet is allowed for each plant, the spacing being 4 by 3 or 3½ by 3½ feet. This permits horse cultivation with the ordinary farm implements.

Recently the dasheen has been found to be subject to the common root-knot[1] disease of the South, which attacks many cultivated plants and weeds. The effect of the disease is to reduce the yield of dasheens. The spread of root-knot in dasheen culture is largely controlled by reserving for seed the tubers from selected, healthy plants only and planting in land that is free from infection.

HARVESTING.

The digging of dasheens for home use can usually begin in the middle of September and the main crop be harvested at any time after the last of October. The digging can be done with a spade, or when the area is large enough to warrant it the plants can be turned over with a plow. When the dasheens are to be stored or shipped, the soil is shaken from the clumps as soon as possible after digging. The clumps are then left on the surface of the ground in the field for two to four days to dry. The tops and feeding roots are then broken from the corms and tubers.

In localities where autumn frosts are severe, harvesting should be done before they occur, as the corms and tubers are likely to be injured if exposed to frost after digging.

STORAGE.

When dasheens have dried sufficiently in the field and are stored, free from soil, in a covered but well-ventilated place, they usually keep well. It is better not to store them in large piles, but to spread them out so that the air can circulate rather freely among them. There are several rots[2] that are likely to attack dasheens in storage, or even while

---

[1] Byars, L. P. A nematode disease of the dasheen and its control by hot-water treatment. Phytopathology, vol. 7, No. 1, January, 1917.

[2] Harter, L. L. Storage-rots of economic aroids. Jour. Agric. Research, U. S. Dept. of Agriculture, vol. 6, No. 15, July 10, 1916, pp. 549–572.

on the ground, if the dasheens are left lying in the field too long after digging or otherwise are improperly handled in harvesting or storing.

The fibrous covering of dasheens in the field seems to enable them to withstand for a short time temperatures several degrees below freezing before digging, but a temperature in storage even as low as 41° F., if prolonged for several weeks, has been shown to be very injurious to them. The results of experiments indicate that where the storage temperature can be controlled, temperatures in the neighborhood of 50° F. are better than lower or much higher ones.

SHIPPING.

The dasheen is a good shipper, and as the railroads of the country have cooperated with the department so far as to place the new vegetable on the same footing as the potato in freight classification, shipment in barrel lots to most eastern and northern points is entirely practicable. The same protection against cold should be given dasheens in transit as is given potatoes.

The department is glad, so far as possible, to direct intending purchasers of dasheens to the most convenient commercial sources of supply.

CONCLUSION.

The dasheen is a recently introduced root crop, well adapted for culture in the Southern States. It is very similar to the potato in its food characteristics, but contains a higher percentage of nutritive material than that vegetable, owing to its lower water content. The flavor is delicately nutty. The crop matures in the autumn, when potatoes have to be shipped from the North, and is a good keeper. There seems to be no reason to doubt, therefore, that in time it will become firmly established in southern agriculture and be a welcome addition also to the limited list of starchy vegetables at present found on northern markets. Dasheens are easily shipped and the freight rates are no higher than for potatoes. The successful establishment of the dasheen industry means a new and valuable food crop for the Nation as a whole and at the same time an additional source of income for the South.

AN EXPERIMENT IN COMMUNITY DAIRYING.

By R. R. WELCH,

Dairy Division, Bureau of Animal Industry.

OUTLINE OF THE WORK.

COMMUNITY development in dairying was undertaken by the United States Department of Agriculture in the typical small-creamery community at Algona, Iowa, in September, 1910, to determine the practicability of employing a skilled instructor to assist in the development of successful dairy farming. Algona was chosen because it was a representative small-creamery community where little attention was given to real dairy farming and because of its stability, due to the fact that 65 per cent of the patrons lived on farms which they owned. Algona is in Kossuth County and has 3,500 inhabitants. The land in that region is naturally fertile. The farms vary in size from 20 to 200 acres, the average being about 160 acres. Most of the farmers were engaged in grain farming and stock raising, dairying being only a side line. When the experiment was started there were 44 farmers who, throughout the previous year, had regularly patronized the creamery, and 20 others who were patrons for only a short time in the summer.

Fifty of the herds contributing milk or cream to the creamery were divided as follows according to breed: Purebred Shorthorn 3, grade Shorthorn 33, purebred Red Polled 2, grade Red Polled 4, grade Guernsey 3, grade Jersey 2, purebred Holstein, Angus, and scrub, 1 each. The average number of cows in each herd was approximately 12. Forty pure-bred bulls were in service—3 Guernsey and 3 Jersey; the remainder were beef breeds.

The farmers in the community had grown and fed beef cattle for many years, and were not accustomed to feeding for milk production. Little clover hay was grown, and the feeds available were unsatisfactory for the production of milk. Timothy and bluegrass were in general use for summer pasture. Cows were put on pasture too early in the spring, and turned into the cornfields after the corn had been picked in the fall. On most farms they were allowed to remain in the fields of standing stalks until late in the winter. Only seven silos were found in the community, and little corn fodder was saved. Few farmers were interested in improving their cattle along dairy lines, and none kept dairy-production records.

THE FIELD MAN.

The Algona development project has been constantly in charge of a field man. He was furnished with a horse and buggy, which enabled him to make personal visits to all patrons of the creamery. His first work was to create an interest in dairying, and especially in better dairy methods. He assisted farmers in culling out the low producers from their herds, helped them select better bulls, drew plans for new dairy barns, assisted in remodeling old ones, helped lay concrete floors, and advised concerning the proper lighting and ventilation of dairy barns and the construction of silos. In all this work economy and efficiency received equal attention.

Under his direction the farmers began feeding for large and economical production, they kept individual production records, and many eliminated all animals that reacted to the tuberculin test. They reduced the expense of raising calves by shifting them earlier from whole milk to skim milk, used stanchions to save labor in feeding, and utilized suitable feeds to insure maximum growth. Through his influence the barns and yards were kept clean and sanitary, and the milk utensils were properly sterilized. Milking was done under sanitary conditions, the milk properly separated, and the cream immediately cooled and kept cool until delivered at the creamery.

These changes added little either to labor or expense, but practically did away with the delivery of sour cream at the creamery and resulted in better prices for butterfat. By constantly watching production costs and by working earnestly for cleaner dairy products and better prices, the farmers soon brought dairying in that community to a more profitable basis.

SPECIAL MEETINGS, PICNICS, AND CAMPS.

During the winter months special dairy meetings were held in the town or at a farm home. At each meeting a dairy problem was discussed and an effort made to get at the real facts. For instance, one meeting was designated as a " silo special." In this case invitations were sent to other creamery communities in the county. As a result, many silos were constructed in the community. Special meetings were also held for the study of dairy cattle, alfalfa, cow-testing associations, and various other dairy subjects. After each meeting the field men followed up the work by personal visits to the farms.

Farmers' picnics were held several times during the summer months, usually on some patron's farm where the best dairy methods could be observed. The farmers, their wives, and children went to the meeting in the forenoon and carried picnic dinners. During the forenoon the farmers inspected the buildings, live stock, and crops. In the afternoon, speakers from the State agricultural college and from the force of the State dairy and food commission were present. Local farmers also took part in the program and discussion, and the women and children assisted with music, readings, and recitations.

To interest the boys in dairying, and through them to influence their parents to adopt better methods, two encampments were held. Twenty-seven boys attended the first and a larger number the second. Tents were erected on a camping ground on the bank of a stream near one of the best-equipped dairy farms in that section. The boys prepared their meals, and did all other necessary work in connection with the maintenance of the camp. Baseball, swimming, and boating furnished amusement. At certain hours each day the boys visited the dairy farm and received instruction in the selection of dairy cattle; the feeding, care, and management of dairy stock; and the proper care of milk and cream. They studied the arrangement of the dairy barn, its light, ventilation, and sanitation, and noted the cleanliness of everything about the milk house. Opportunity was given to study the construction of the silo and to note the quality and condition of the silage. The boys learned to operate the Babcock tester and the cream separator. They saw the cows milked properly, and watched the weighing and recording of each cow's milk. The ideas of modern dairying acquired during the encampment were instrumental in influencing the boys' parents to make improvements in every line of dairy-farm management.

One winter a school of agriculture and domestic science was held in Algona, the instructors being furnished by the extension department of the Iowa State College of Agriculture. The course in agriculture included dairying, stock judging, and corn judging; and the course in domestic science consisted of lessons in cooking and sewing. From 4 to 5 o'clock each afternoon the schoolboys had work in judging corn and cattle, and the girls were instructed in cooking and sewing.

THE CREAMERY BUTTERMAKER.

The buttermaker of the Algona creamery worked in close cooperation with the field man, and assisted greatly along all lines of community development in dairying. His advice was especially helpful in dairy-herd improvement and in getting the farmers to adopt better methods of caring for milk and cream. He made many improvements in the creamery and greatly increased its efficiency. The average overrun for the year previous to the beginning of the study was 16.3 per cent, while that for 1915 was nearly 23 per cent. Better sanitary conditions on the farms and in the creamery improved the quality of the butter, and the better product brought better prices. A system of grading cream was established, and a premium paid for sweet cream. This gave the farmers more money with which to extend and improve their dairies. The modern methods established in the creamery attracted the attention of buttermakers in other creameries and influenced them to make many improvements. During the last year of the work a butter-scoring contest, open to all the buttermakers of the State, was held at Algona.

On January 10, 1914, the assistant State dairy and food commissioner of Iowa inspected and scored the Algona creamery for the purpose of determining whether the creamery should be granted the right to use the State butter trade-mark (fig. 6). To obtain this right a creamery must score 93 or better. The Algona creamery passed the test with a score of 99.

FIG. 1.—THE OLD CREAMERY AT ALGONA, IOWA, WHICH WAS USED FOR A FEW
YEARS AFTER THE EXPERIMENT IN COMMUNITY DEVELOPMENT BEGAN.

FIG. 2.—THE NEW MODERN SANITARY CREAMERY AT ALGONA, IOWA,
WHICH REPLACED THE CREAMERY ILLUSTRATED ABOVE.

FAR-REACHING EFFECTS OF THE WORK.

The development of the community experiment brought about the organization of a county buttermakers' association to encourage the extension of the work throughout the county and into other counties. A cow-testing association, organized in 1913, is assisting in determining which dairy animals should be disposed of, and is raising the average production and profit from year to year. A Holstein breeders' association was organized to promote the interests of that breed, and similar associations will be formed in the near future to look after the interests of other dairy breeds. The influence and support of the creamery board of directors was of much assistance. The members of the board were always prompt in making improvements in the creamery on the recommendation of the field man, and the board's influence was a potent factor in promoting better dairy methods throughout the community. A whitewash pump was provided, to be lent

Fig. 6.—Butter trade-mark.

to patrons. This encouraged the farmers to improve the appearance and cleanliness of the interior of their barns.

The local press gave much publicity to the dairy movement. One of the papers published a dairy column each week, using material written by the field man. A part of the column was devoted to local dairy-farm news, and occasionally the good results accomplished on some particular farm were emphasized. The papers also advertised dairy meetings and reported the work accomplished.

PROFITABLENESS OF THE WORK.

At the end of the five-year period a complete survey of the community was made to determine the results accomplished.

The following table shows net profits due to increased production per cow and to improvement in the quality of cream.

Sources of increased profits to creamery patrons.

	Increased net income from larger and more economical production of butterfat.	Increased net income due to better quality of butter manufactured.	Total net profit to patrons.
1911........	....	$2,060	$2,060
1912........	$2,694	2,309	5,003
1913........	3,965	2,422	6,387
1914........	6,435	2,641	9,076
1915........	6,956	2,687	9,643
Total..	20,050	12,119	32,169
Salary and expenses of field man for 5 years.....................................			11,196
Net profit above salary and expenses of field man.........................			20,973

During the 30-day period ended March 15, 1916, the cow-testing association records showed that there were 32 cows which gave more than 40 pounds of butterfat each, the highest being 71 pounds. The work of the cow-testing association, by eliminating low producers, added much to the value of every herd tested. The net financial gain through dairy-herd improvement due to selection, breeding, and feeding can not be closely estimated, but it is doubtless greater than the net gain from dairy products as itemized above.

As an example of the cash value of cow-testing records, the local auctioneer estimated that one farmer sold 19 head of dairy cattle at an average price from $10 to $12 a head more than he otherwise would have received.

CAUSES OF INCREASED PROFITS.

As the work progressed unprofitable cows were eliminated, better bulls were obtained, and up-to-date feeding methods were adopted. In order to reduce the cost of milk production much attention was given to the growing of such feeds as clover, alfalfa, and silage corn. During the five-year period the number of silos was increased from 7 to 44, or more than 600 per cent. Many herds that had been without shelter even in the coldest winter weather, and that had been compelled to gather a large part of their feed in the corn-fields, are now kept in comfortable barns and fed good rations, economically balanced. The water supply for dairy cows had previously been furnished in an open tank which in midwinter was often covered with several inches of ice, but now in cold winter weather tank heaters are in use on a large percentage of the farms.

In January, 1913, in competition with associations from 14 States, the Kossuth County Buttermakers' Association took the gold and silver medals for butter made from gathered cream, and during the same year the Algona butter-maker won several first prizes, among which was highest score at the National Dairy Show. This, in a way, illus-trates the improved dairy conditions on the farms. Before the development work began, 90 per cent of the cream was delivered in a sour condition, but during 1915, 89.4 per cent of all the cream received at the creamery was sweet, and the remainder, though sour, was of good quality. By following the advice of the field man, all improvements were made at little cost, and the net profits were very large in comparison to increased cost of production.

CONTINUANCE OF THE MOVEMENT.

Even without assistance, it seems certain that the Algona community will continue the development already started. Members of the cow-testing association and of the Holstein breeders' association are much interested in the continuation of the dairy movement. Since the beginning of this project the county-agent movement has met with great success in all parts of the country, and it is believed that community development in dairying can be carried on with advantage in close cooperation with, and perhaps under the direction of, county agricultural agents.

WHAT HAPPENED TO THE OLD CREAMERY.

The old creamery at Algona was on land owned by a rail-road, close to the stockyards, in an out-of-the-way place which was far from sanitary, and the machinery was in need of repair. Financial conditions were such that the old building had to be used until the development work improved the financial condition of the organization and permitted the construction of a new building. During this period every effort was made to keep the old building and equipment neat and clean. The results showed that much was accomplished in spite of adverse conditions.

The old creamery was discarded in 1914, and a modern brick-and-tile building was erected on the main street in the business section of the town. The general plan of this building was designed by the Dairy Division of the Bureau of Animal Industry and embodies the latest ideas on convenient and sanitary arrangement. Many creamery boards of directors from various parts of the State already have visited the creamery with the idea of incorporating the improvements in new creamery buildings soon to be erected in their own communities.

BETTER FARM HOMES.

As financial prosperity increased, living conditions among the farmers became more comfortable. When the work began, modern conveniences in farm homes were not common. At the end of the five-year period 18 patrons used furnace heat in their dwellings, 16 had gaslight in their homes, 4 had small electric-light plants, and 21 homes were equipped with baths and running water. The special dairy meetings, farmers' picnics, and boys' encampments developed a community spirit which greatly improved social conditions. The financial gain is the one most readily measured, but it is only a small part of the total results that came from this experiment in community development in dairying.

SUPPRESSION OF THE GIPSY AND BROWN-TAIL MOTHS AND ITS VALUE TO STATES NOT INFESTED.

By A. F. BURGESS,

In Charge of Gipsy Moth and Brown-tail Moth Investigations, Bureau of Entomology.

MANY years ago a circumstance occurred at Medford, Mass., which was destined to cause enormous expense and trouble in that community and throughout the neighboring States. About 1869, Prof. Leopold Trouvelot, a French naturalist who was a resident of Medford, introduced a few egg clusters of the gipsy moth for the purpose of conducting experiments on silk culture. During the course of the experiments some of the caterpillars escaped. Realizing that the insect was a serious pest in Europe, he made a careful search on the trees and in the woodland nearby for the purpose of destroying any that could be found. He also notified the Department of Agriculture at Washington. None of the insects which had escaped could be found, but as no injury resulted during the next few years, it was thought that the matter was not of great importance.

About 20 years later the neighborhood was invaded by swarms of caterpillars which were supposed by most of the residents to be a native species that had become unusually abundant. A study of the matter developed the fact that the insect which was defoliating the trees was the notorious gipsy moth of Europe and that it had become firmly established in the locality in which it had originally escaped and throughout the immediate surroundings. Its slow increase seemingly was remarkable, but this has been accounted for by the facts that the wood and brush land in the neighborhood was burned over every few years by forest fires, that insectivorous birds and other natural enemies were at that time abundant in the neighborhood, and that the destruction of a few caterpillars when the species was very rare would result in holding down the increase for a number of years.

The city of Medford and the State of Massachusetts soon interested themselves in a campaign to destroy this insect. It had become so abundant in many places during the early nineties that the trees in the residential sections were defoliated completely during early summer, and the caterpillars swarmed into houses, making themselves a general nuisance throughout the community. In some sections it was impossible to rent property on account of the abundance of the caterpillars, and real estate values declined rapidly. For 10 years a desperate battle was carried on by the State of Massachusetts to exterminate the insect, and during that period it was found to occur in greater or less numbers throughout 30 towns and cities, principally toward the north and west of Boston. This work reduced the infestations to such an extent that many citizens who, during the first part of the period, had been seriously annoyed by the pest, or had suffered severe loss from it, came to the conclusion that because it was seldom seen the work was unnecessary and no harm would result if measures for its control were discontinued.

In 1897 another foreign pest, namely, the brown-tail moth of Europe, was discovered in Somerville, Mass., and the effort to bring this insect under control added to the State's financial burdens. The caterpillars of this moth are provided with hairs which cause severe itching and urtication when coming in contact with the human skin, producing an eruption which is known by those who have experienced the trouble as the " brown-tail rash." Thus, while the gipsy-moth caterpillars were a nuisance on account of their large size and disagreeable appearance, the presence of caterpillars of the brown-tail moth in large numbers was actually unbearable on account of the poisoning which resulted to the residents.

Enough pressure was brought to bear, however, in the fall of 1899 to cause the discontinuance of State appropriations for the control of these insects. The residents soon found that this policy did not work as anticipated, for both insects increased at an alarming rate, and in the course of three or four years the infestation had become so bad that many citizens were forced to attempt control measures. The work which was done was not carried on in a systematic manner, and while a few exerted every effort to protect their property from the depredations of these insects and to keep their trees free from the caterpillars, many totally neglected to attend to the work, and the result was a general clamor for a systematic and thorough effort to abate the nuisance. During this period many acres of woodland became infested seriously and in the years which followed thousands of acres were defoliated during the early summer. Matters became so serious in 1905 that work was resumed by the Commonwealth of Massachusetts, but the law was framed in such a way that not only the State but the towns and cities and the owners of property were required to give financial support to the undertaking.

During the period when no work was being carried on by the State of Massachusetts the insects spread to Rhode Island, New Hampshire, and Maine, making the problem far more serious than before. In 1906 funds were appropriated by Congress to prevent the spread of these insects, and since that time Federal work for this purpose has been continued. It is true that both insects have spread over a much larger area since this work began, but that was to be expected, owing to the necessity of properly organizing the work and developing new and better methods for handling the problem on a scale unprecedented for insect control.

The gipsy moth and the brown-tail moth occur in greater or less numbers in all the New England States. The dispersion of the brown-tail moth covers a larger area than that of the gipsy moth, because both sexes of the brown-tail fly freely and, this being the case, it is very difficult to prevent their spread. These white moths are attracted to strong light, particularly electric arc lights, and about the 10th of July of each year they can usually be found in badly infested regions on poles, trees, or buildings near these lights. The extent to which they spread at this time depends largely on the temperature and the direction and velocity of the wind. These moths have been taken on the Nantucket Shoals lightship, which is 42 nautical miles from Nantucket, the nearest land, and as the infestation of that island by this insect is very slight it is probable that the moths came from a much greater distance. Frequent reports have been received from captains of sailing vessels that swarms of these moths have been encountered from 75 to 100 miles out at sea, although there is a possibility that there may have been a mistake in identifying the insect. These facts indicate that the possibility of rapid spread, so far as this insect is concerned, is very great, provided high temperature and favorable winds occur when the moths are flying. Fortunately, the prevailing winds in New England during early July are from a southerly or southwesterly direction, which tends to bring about a general spread of the insect toward the seacoast instead of inland.

The female moths deposit egg masses on the underside of the leaves of apple, pear, oak, cherry, rose, and numerous other trees and plants. The caterpillars hatch about the middle of August and feed for about a month. The eggs are usually laid on the leaves on the terminal twigs and the small caterpillars draw a number of these together to form a web, in which they remain during the winter. In the spring, as soon as the buds begin to expand, the caterpillars emerge from the webs and feed on the buds and developing leaves. They become full grown about the middle of June and spin cocoons either singly or in masses, from which the moths emerge during the first part of July. The large caterpillars, which are provided with many long hairs, are particularly poisonous.

The male and female gipsy moths differ in color, the former being chocolate brown, while the latter is light cream color, having wings marked with black. This insect is in the moth stage during early July, but, fortunately, the female moths are unable to fly on account of the size and weight of their bodies, so that their natural spread is not as rapid as is that of the brown-tail moth. Clusters containing 400 or more eggs are deposited by the females on trees or, in fact, on any material which furnishes a somewhat sheltered location. These clusters are about an inch long, oval in form, and are covered with yellowish hair from the body of the female. As the eggs do not hatch until the following spring, there is ample opportunity for the insect to be spread in the egg stage during the fall and winter if lumber, plant products, or other material upon which they are deposited is shipped to outside points. The caterpillars hatch late in April or early in May, depending on the season, and feed on the leaves which are beginning to expand. They continue to feed and develop until about the first of July, when pupation takes place, the moths emerging a week or more later.

During the first work which was done for the purpose of controlling the gipsy moth, a study was made of the manner in which this insect was spread. It was determined that while the female did not cause spread, since it was impossible for her to fly, egg clusters were frequently transported from place to place on shipments of lumber and other material, and that in cases where heavy infestations occurred the caterpillars might be carried a considerable distance on vehicles. It is a common habit of the larvæ, if they are disturbed, to spin silken threads which are attached to the trees and in this way lower themselves to the ground. Since the gipsy-moth campaign first began, an unprecedented development in means of rapid transportation has taken place. At first and for several years motor vehicles were practically unknown, but for the last few years the increase in this mode of transportation has been enormous. It has been found, however, as a result of much work and many experiments, that if the roadways are kept clear from heavy infestation the number of caterpillars distributed by motor vehicles is very small. A number of years ago the results of the scouting work, which consists of examining roadways, orchards, and wooded areas for infestation, indicated that many colonies were present the occurrence of which could not be explained by any known means of spread. Woodland infestations were found in places that were infrequently visited by men or animals. This led to a thorough study and a long series of experiments which proved conclusively that the small caterpillars, immediately after hatching, may be blown long distances by the wind. It has been proved that spread often occurs for a distance of from 12 to 20 miles in this way. These facts would seem to make the prevention of spread of the insect hopeless, if not impossible. But the same factors, namely, temperature and wind direction, which have brought about the greatest drift of infestation by the brown-tail moth toward the seacoast, are equally effective in connection with the spread of small gipsy-moth caterpillars. During the period when these minute larvæ can be blown by the wind it is necessary for the temperature to range from 60° F. upward, the higher temperature increasing the activity of the insect. This comparatively high temperature must be accompanied by strong winds if spread for any great distance is to result, and when the combination of high temperature and strong wind occurs in New England in the month of May the wind usually blows from the south or southwest. Variations in this general rule occur, depending on how far the locality is removed from the sea-

board, and these facts are taken into consideration in carrying on field work against this insect.

The task which has fallen to the Bureau of Entomology in
connection with gipsy-moth control has been to use every
effort possible to prevent the spread of the insect and to reduce the damage resulting therefrom. It has been necessary
to carry through many extensive experiments in order to
secure information for use in the field operations, and the
experimental work has formed the basis and groundwork for
the application of field methods. Prior to 1905 no effort was
made to introduce the parasites and natural enemies of the
gipsy moth or the brown-tail moth. A popular theory exists
that in its native home every insect is held within reasonable
bounds by parasites or natural enemies, and that each insect
has some one species of parasite or natural enemy which is
responsible for its control. When this natural check fails,
either on account of attack by its own enemies or for other
reasons, the original host will, for a time, become noxious.
The problem of utilizing the natural enemies of the gipsy
moth and the brown-tail moth appeared somewhat complicated, but the difficulties were not realized until after the
work was well under way. It soon became apparent that
neither of these pests was controlled by a single species of
parasite in its native home. Through the efforts of Dr. L. O.
Howard, Chief of the Bureau of Entomology, acting in cooperation with the State of Massachusetts and many foreign entomologists, as well as numerous agents employed by
the bureau, a large number, approximately 30 species, of
parasites and natural enemies of the gipsy moth and brown-
tail moth have been collected and shipped to the Gipsy Moth
Laboratory at Melrose Highlands, Mass. Shipments of this
sort have been received from most of the countries of Europe
and from Japan. The result has been that 7 or 8 species
have become established in the infested area and are helping
to solve the problem.

It has developed, however, that in Europe, at any rate,
the ravages of the gipsy moth are partially controlled by
several factors in addition to the work of the parasites.
A wilt disease which attacks the caterpillars and causes
heavy mortality among them is present not only there but

in this country, and is a powerful agent in curtailing the increase of the species. The character of the food plants is also of great importance. The tree growth of the infested region has been classified according to its adaptability as food for the gipsy moth. It has been found that practically all coniferous growth, if grown in solid stands, fails to support this insect; that ash is not subject to attack, and that maple and hickory are seldom injured to any great extent.

An effort is being made to encourage the growth in woodlands of the tree species just mentioned, and to discourage the growth and planting of oak, willow, and poplar, which are favored foods. Unfortunately the greater part of the infested area abounds in oak growth which, for the most part, is of poor quality and has a very low merchantable value. This fact discourages greatly the elimination of favored food plants in the infested area. Nevertheless some progress has been made in eliminating favored food plants in the heavily infested areas. Thinning work is being carried on by the Bureau of Entomology in the isolated colonies near the borders of infestation also, but in addition it has been necessary to treat the egg clusters found in these areas and to reduce the caterpillars by the application of sticky bands to the trees and by thorough spraying in order promptly to prevent further spread. The importation and colonization of natural enemies has served to reduce the infestation in the many localities in the worst infested sections. These factors are bringing about a gradual reduction in the main supply of the insect which, in case they were not employed, would serve as a stock for further distribution of the pest. Every effort is being made to prevent long-distance spread of both insects by carriage on products shipped to points outside the infested area. The territory infested is under quarantine by the Federal Horticultural Board and all products likely to carry the insect out of the infested area are inspected before they are allowed to be moved. The border territory is thoroughly inspected and the gross infestation in this region is being gradually reduced. It is inevitable that new colonies will be found from time to time outside the region now known to be infested, but substantial progress is being made in preventing any widespread dispersion of the insect.

Each State has its own organization which is attempting to reduce the infestation within its borders, and much effective work has been accomplished as a result. The work of the Bureau of Entomology is so ordered as to avoid duplication and prevent conflict with that carried on by the State authorities, and as these matters have been arranged in advance, little difficulty in this respect has been experienced.

The work which is being carried on in New England to prevent the spread of these insects is of the utmost importance to other States. It has been well said that " an ounce of prevention is worth a pound of cure," and this can be no better demonstrated than in the experience which Massachusetts has had with the gipsy moth. During the time when an attempt was made by the State to exterminate the insects in the nineties, the largest amount of money expended by the State in any one year was $200,000, and there is good reason to suppose that if this work had been continued the annual expenditure at the present time would have been materially decreased. The year after the work was resumed and thoroughly organized, an expenditure of nearly one-half million dollars was necessary, and the amount expended annually during most of the years since that time has been even greater. This was paid by State appropriation and by contributions required by law from infested towns and cities and from the owners of infested property. While recently the expenditure has been reduced somewhat, over a half million dollars is the yearly expenditure in Massachusetts at the present time, the money being raised by the same method.

The New England States are carrying the greater part of the burden of moth infestation because from them come mainly the funds for control work and they are suffering from the injury caused by the insects, but the money appropriated by the Federal Government, while assisting these States in some measure, is also providing insurance to the uninfested States, and that at a very low rate.

To illustrate the necessary expenditure by towns and cities in the infested area in order properly to control the gipsy moth, a few examples are cited. These are all taken from towns and cities in Massachusetts, where the infestation has been rather heavy during the last few years. The information in regard to population is based on the United

THE GIPSY MOTH (PORTHETRIA DISPAR).

Upper left, male moth with wings folded; just below this, female moth with wings spread; just below this, male moth with wings spread; lower left, female moth, enlarged; top center, male pupa at left, female pupa at right; center, larva; on branch, at top, newly formed pupa; on branch, just below this, larva ready to pupate; on branch, left side, pupæ; on branch, center, egg cluster; on branch, at bottom, female moth depositing egg cluster. All slightly reduced except figure at lower left. (From Howard and Fiske.)

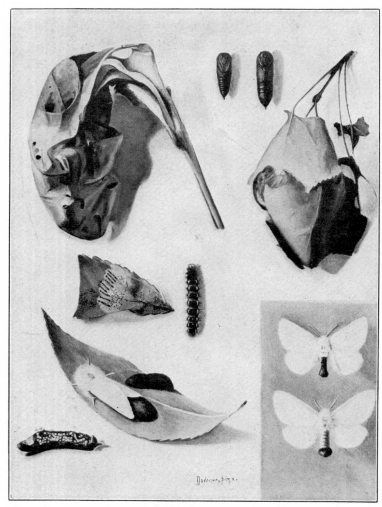

THE BROWN-TAIL MOTH (EUPROCTIS CHRYSORRHOEA).

Upper left, hibernating web; just below this, small larvæ feeding at left, larger larva at right; just below this, female moth depositing eggs at left, egg mass at right; lower left, egg mass with eggs exposed; top center, male pupa at left, female pupa at right; upper right, cocoon incased in leaves; lower right, male moth above, female moth below. All slightly reduced. (From Howard and Fiske.)

FIG. I.—WOODLAND COMPLETELY DEFOLIATED BY GIPSY-MOTH
CATERPILLARS.

FIG. 2.—APPLE ORCHARD COMPLETELY DEFOLIATED BY BROWN-TAIL
MOTH CATERPILLARS.

BROWN-TAIL MOTHS ON ELECTRIC ARC-LIGHT POLES.

FIG. I.—MIXED DECIDUOUS AND CONIFEROUS WOODLAND BEFORE
THINNING.

FIG. 2.—SAME WOODLAND AFTER FAVORED FOOD PLANTS HAD BEEN
REMOVED.

GIPSY-MOTH CATERPILLARS ON TREE TRUNK BENEATH STICKY BAND.

FIG. I.—MOTOR TRUCK SPRAYER IN OPERATION.

FIG. 2.—PAVING BLOCKS INFESTED WITH GIPSY-MOTH EGG CLUSTERS.

States census of 1910, while that on valuation is the record of the local authorities for the year 1915.

A town having an area of 16 square miles, a population of 559, and an assessed valuation of $465,513, is badly infested with the gipsy moth. In 1915 the expenditures made by the town, together with those made by property owners, amounted to $312.84, which was at the rate of 67 cents per $1,000 valuation, or 52 cents per capita. In addition to this expenditure, State aid to the amount of $1,322.80 was received.

A town having an area of 19 square miles, a population of 829, a valuation of $736,945, and about as heavily infested as the preceding, made similar expenditures of $968.31, which was at the rate of $1.31 per $1,000 valuation, or $1.17 per capita. In addition to this, State aid was received to the amount of $2,207.90.

In a third town, having an area of 7 square miles, a population of 7,090, and a valuation of $6,067,430, there was expended $3,898.83, which amounted to 64 cents per $1,000 valuation, or 55 cents per capita. In addition to this, $1,081.32 was received from the State. This town is a manufacturing community, rather thickly settled, with only a small area of woodland, and not as heavily infested as those previously mentioned.

A fourth town, containing 26 square miles, having a population of 6,681 and a valuation of $9,318,055, expended $4,447.14 on moth work, which was at the rate of 47 cents per $1,000 valuation, or 67 cents per capita. In addition to this, $407.08 was received from the State. This town is residential and has many large estates and some excellent farms, and was generally infested by the gipsy moth.

A city of 32 square miles, having a population of 145,986 and a valuation of $179,198,586, expended $17,190.77, which was at the rate of 9 cents per $1,000 valuation, or 12 cents per capita; $726.93 was received from the State. This city was not as badly infested by the gipsy moth as the towns which have been mentioned previously, but the brown-tail moth infestation was more severe.

For convenience in making comparisons, a summary of the foregoing information covering four towns and one city is given in the following table:

Expenditures for the control of the gipsy moth and brown-tail moth in certain towns and cities in Massachusetts.

Assessed valuation.	Area in square miles.	Population.	Town and owners' expenditures, 1915.			Additional State aid.
			Amount.	Per $1,000 valuation.	Per capita.	
$465,513	16	559	$312.84	$0.67	$0.52	$1,322.80
736,945	19	829	968.31	1.31	1.17	2,207.90
6,067,430	7	7,090	3,898.83	.64	.55	1,081.32
9,318,055	26	6,681	4,447.14	.47	.67	407.08
179,198,586	32	145,986	17,190.77	.09	.12	726.93

The foregoing figures indicate in a general way the expenditures that are likely to be necessary in towns and cities in uninfested States, in case the gipsy moth becomes established. It shows conclusively the amount of protection which other sections of the country are receiving as a result of the gipsy-moth work which is being done in New England. A large part of the funds expended by towns and cities has been used for the protection of shade and ornamental trees, it having been found impossible to carry on extensive work in woodlands, owing to the extreme cost of these operations.

The beauty and attractiveness of most cities and residential sections depend on the trees. These not only make the region attractive and a desirable place to live, but also add money value to the property. American cities are coming more and more to realize the importance and value of shade trees, and any step that can be taken for their protection or to prevent injury from insects is most desirable.

To prevent the introduction of serious pests into a region where they are unknown is far more important than to expend large sums of money in an attempt to bring about their control after they have been introduced and have successfully established themselves. This is precisely the work which is being attempted in New England on the gipsy-moth problem, and a record of expenditures from a few localities which may be considered as average samples indicates the benefit that other parts of the United States are deriving from this important work.

PROGRESS IN HANDLING THE WOOL CLIP: DEVELOPMENT IN THE WEST.

By F. R. MARSHALL,

Animal Husbandry Division, Bureau of Animal Industry.

THE sheep industry of the Western States the past two seasons·has been marked by high prices which have stimulated progress in breeding for both wool and mutton and by the introduction of more businesslike methods of handling the wool clip. For 30 years prior to the season of 1915 woolgrowers had not undertaken to grade their wools before shipment. During 1916, however, about 7,000,000 pounds of wool was graded and baled at the time of shearing. This amount included 81 clips, representing approximately 870,000 sheep. The work was done mainly in sheds constructed or remodeled in 1915 or 1916. Although these changes in methods of handling and selling wool have been confined to three far Western States, the innovations are applicable over the range-sheep territory.

Woolgrowers of Carbon and Sweetwater Counties, Wyo., have been particularly active. A new shearing shed modeled after the Australian plan, with a capacity for 3,000 sheep daily, was erected in 1915 in Sweetwater County. Another was remodeled to include the main features of Australian sheds. In 1916 two new sheds were erected in Carbon County and one in Sweetwater County and two others were re-modeled. Special facilities were provided in all of these sheds to permit systematic handling of fleeces. The clips were graded and shipped in bales, ready for final sale without the usual further handling undergone by most clips in the dealers' warehouses before sale to manufacturers is attempted. One clip had been graded and baled in Montana in 1914. Other clips were prepared in this way in that State and in Nevada in 1915 and 1916.

THE NEW SHEARING SHEDS.

Concerning the best methods and amount of labor which should be expended upon the fleeces in preparing them for shipment from the ranch, there has been discussion and uncertainty. The advantages of the new sheds, however, have been recognized by all sheepmen visiting them, and the only

227

hindrance to the erection of sheds in large numbers lies in their cost. This is especially a hindrance in cases, very common in the woolgrowing territory, in which the sheep owner is without assurance as to the length of time he can retain the range he is using.

The new sheds furnish more commodious pens for holding a supply of sheep ready for the shearers. They are elevated from 4 to 6 feet above the ground to allow discharging the shorn sheep back underneath the holding pen, thus removing the necessity of their crossing the board upon which the shearing is done. This results in fewer steps being taken by the shearers and less interference by sheep and shearers with the men or boys passing up and down the board in carrying the fleeces to the wool room. The arrangement to permit discharging the shorn sheep at the same side of the board as it entered is the first essential of a well-planned shed. It is secured by setting the shed on posts from 4 to 6 feet long. The sheep enter at an incline at one end of the holding pens.

After shearing, the sheep is put down the inclined chute as shown in figure 7 which leads to the ground below the holding pens. The pens from which the shearer catches his sheep are single, 8 feet by 5 feet 6 inches in size. This removes the opportunity for choice of sheep that exists when there are two shearers to a pen. The shafting that drives the shearing machines is arranged for attachment of gears each 5 feet 6 inches, thus requiring shearers to work at that distance from each other.

Double doors, each with double springs, render it easy for the shearer to get his sheep from the pen to the shearing floor. After shearing, the sheep are passed down the incline, the opening of which is in the same wall and at one side of the door to the pen. They then pass to the separate counting-out pens outside the shed, where each shearer's work can be examined and tallies correctly kept.

The holding pens, alley, and catch pens shown in the plan will hold at one time 30 sheep for each shearer. This allows the sheep to remain inside for a sufficient length of time to cause the amount of sweating that is needed to make the wool cut easily. This entire space is floored with 2 by 3 inch boards laid on edge, with $\frac{3}{8}$-inch space between, which insures complete cleanliness even for sheep that may lie down.

The space below the floor in the plan will hold 500 sheep and is used either to keep a supply of dry unshorn sheep or for sheltering newly shorn sheep during storms or cold weather. Dry shelter for the first night after shearing has

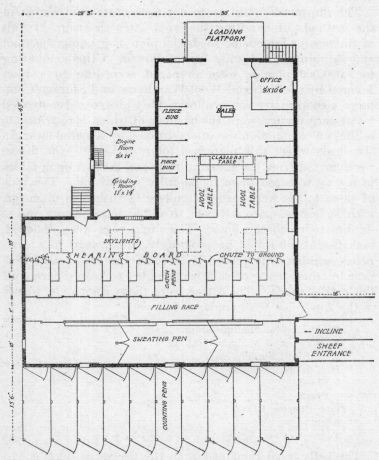

FIG. 7.—Floor plan of shearing shed. This plan includes the features of Australian sheds.

prevented many losses that otherwise would have occurred when shearing was done early in the season.

The arrangement of these sheds reduces the handling of the sheep to the minimum, thereby preventing injury and loss, particularly in ewes shorn before lambing. The improved working conditions render it more practicable to secure good shearing and humane treatment of the sheep by the shearers and penners.

PREPARING THE WOOL.

The improved facilities do not necessitate any change in the methods of handling the wool after shearing. In all of the new or remodeled sheds the plan of grading the wool and shipping in bales has been followed. Clips amounting to 5,000,000 pounds were prepared according to a plan favored by the National Wool Warehouse and Storage Company, a cooperative concern located in Chicago and controlled by western woolgrowers, the business of which is restricted to selling on commission the wools shipped by stockholders. In the sheds where this plan was followed in 1916 the fleeces were carried from the shearing floor and thrown upon tables in a way to cause them to lie fully spread out. The tops of these tables were made of rollers 1½ inches in diameter, with sufficient space between to allow loose, heavy pieces or dirt to reach the floor. The dung tags were removed, each fleece was rolled up separately, and passed to a competent grader, who placed it in some one of a set of bins near by, these being of sufficient number to keep separate all the grades made. The latter were those commonly in use in the American wool trade, as follows:

> Fine and Fine Medium Staple.
> Fine and Fine Medium Clothing.
> Half Blood Staple.
> Half Blood Clothing.
> ⅜ Blood.
> ¼ Blood.
> Low Quarter Blood.
> Braid.
> Tags.

The belly wool remained with the fleeces in these sheds. The bales were marked to show the grade, weight, and name or brand of the growers of the wool.

In four other sheds 118,800 sheep were shorn, yielding 983,700 pounds of wool. In these cases the plan of handling the wool was that followed in Australia and advocated by persons who have since formed an association incorporated as the "American Wool Improvement Association." According to this plan the belly wool was separated from the fleece by the shearer and all bellies from the same kind of sheep baled together. The fleeces were thrown spread out upon the wool tables, and before being rolled up were "skirted." This consisted in removing some of the wool from the edges of the fleece as it came to the table without the belly wool. In crossbred sheep and in some Merino sheep the britch or lower thigh wool is materially coarser than the body of the fleece, and when left in appears as a different quality and may serve to lower the value of the better wool. Skirting is practiced in Australia partly because of burrs in the lower parts of the fleece.

Instead of using the American system of grading in these sheds, the fleeces were classed according to the terms used in the Australian trade. These were: AA Combing, A Combing, AA Comeback, A Comeback, AA Halfbred, A Halfbred, AA 3/4 bred, A 3/4 bred, A Clothing, B Clothing, 1st pieces, 2d pieces, Bellies, Locks, Black, Stained pieces, and Tags. The finest wool was classed as combing or clothing, the other main classes ordinarily comprising fleeces from sheep carrying part of other than Merino blood. The 3/4-bred class corresponds to the American 1/4-blood. The 1st, 2d, and stained pieces were from the parts skirted off, and the locks largely from underneath the wool tables.

In both American and Australian practice a fleece is assigned to some one grade on the basis of what it is, regardless of the blood lines of the sheep producing it. The first-cross progeny of a Lincoln and a Merino might be supposed to produce a fleece which in fineness would be "half blood" or "half bred" in Australian terms. As a matter of fact not more than half the fleeces from sheep so bred will fall into either of those grades. The terms that have come into use in both countries stand for well-understood qualities, and the fact that they are really largely misnomers, if correspondence with the breeding of the sheep is considered, is of no practical importance. There seems to be no real advantage to be obtained from the introduction of a new set of terms in ranch grading of wools.

The AA and A divisions of each class were made on the basis of difference in shrinkage and character of wools of the same length and fineness. This subdivision is a logical one and is practicable with large clips or with good facilities for selling in small lots. Such facilities do not exist at present in United States wool markets. However, the cooperative warehouse company previously mentioned follows the plan of combining smaller lots of similar wools from a number of consigned clips, and after their sale makes the returns to each owner on the basis of the price for the combined lot. This practice also is followed by some concerns doing a part commission business, and in resale of mixed clips bought for speculation.

In neither set of sheds were fleeces tied before baling. When opened in the East the wools had lost nothing by baling and made a good appearance.

ADVANTAGES OF GRADING AT THE RANCH.

All of the woolgrowers who had their clips graded at home in 1915 did so again in 1916. Although some of them had in other years received reports of the warehouse grading of their clips, the lesson was by no means so valuable as that learned from seeing the work done at shearing time. Many growers realized for the first time the great amount of clothing wool they were producing and realized as well the variety of grades of wool that came from sheep supposedly of uniform character but in the breeding of which they had not adhered to a distinct standard of fleece in the selection of rams. The amount and value of wool from flocks bred on consistent systematic lines appeared in sharp contrast to the returns from the other and more numerous flocks representing no studied plan or system of breeding.

Those growers who are qualified to appraise their own wools fairly on the basis of examination and correct reading of market reports derive a selling advantage from grading at home. When the fleeces are sacked as they run the proportion of each grade of wool can be estimated only. No opportunity is offered to examine a pile of fleeces of one grade, and the attempt to place a fair value upon the clip results largely in guesswork. Too often the reported selling price of other wools of supposedly similar type is taken as a basis of determining value. The new plan makes it possible for the flockmaster who studies his wool to appraise his clip closely for guidance when considering offers received at home as against consignment for sale at eastern points.

FIG. I.—TYPE OF SHELTER FREQUENTLY USED FOR SHEARING SHEEP
ON WESTERN RANGES.

FIG. 2.—THE "PIONEER" AUSTRALIAN STYLE SHEARING SHED NEAR
BITTER CREEK, WYO.

FIG. 1.—SHEEP ENTERING SWEATING PENS OF A REMODELED SHEARING
SHED AT BITTER CREEK, WYO.

FIG. 2.—LOADING BALED WOOL AT THE "PIONEER" SHEARING SHED,
BITTER CREEK, WYO.

FIG. 1.—WOOL BUYERS INSPECTING CLIP OFFERED FOR SALE ON THE "SEALED BID" PLAN.

FIG. 2.—BALED WOOL AT WAMSUTTER, WYO., READY FOR LOADING ON CARS.

FIG. 1.

FIG. 2.

INTERIOR VIEWS OF EDUCATIONAL WOOL CAR RUN THROUGH WESTERN
STATES, 1916, BY THE BUREAU OF ANIMAL INDUSTRY IN COOPERATION
WITH AGRICULTURAL COLLEGES.

The new plan of preparing clips for market involves material expense, however, although this is in part offset by the lower freight rate on baled wools. Where the tags only are removed from the fleeces the rolling, grading, and baling require 5 more hands for a shed shearing 2,000 sheep daily than are needed for sacking the fleeces directly from the shearing board. Some sheep raisers assert that this expenditure is fully offset by the information gained as to the lines upon which their flocks should be bred and handled to secure wool of the maximum value.

SELLING RANCH-GRADED WOOL.

In 1915 a part of the home-graded wools was offered for sale at the sheds on the sealed-bid plan. Of the several buyers in attendance one or two represented eastern mills and the others represented concerns that buy wools for speculation. No sales resulted. Some entire clips of graded wools were sold privately at one price for the entire weight. The majority were consigned to eastern houses and sold at various times through the remainder of the year.

In 1916 the graded wools were mainly consigned to Chicago, Boston, and Philadelphia houses. Sales were made by the "interlotting" plan of combining lots of similar grade and value from various clips so as to make an offering of sufficient size to sell advantageously.

In neither season could it be said that a line was obtained upon the manufacturers' financial appreciation of the new system. To do this it would be necessary to sell publicly, in a single day and on an active market, fully similar wools prepared on the old and new lines.

Some manufacturers have expressed themselves as well pleased with the condition and preparation of the wools, but are very conservative in committing themselves as to any extra price. From the manufacturers' standpoint the new plan does not differ materially in effect from the old system under which he buys large lines graded from several clips in the dealer's warehouse. The selling agents reported strong objections to "overclassing," that is, the making of a larger number of grades than required by the principal commercial differences of the types of wool which the clip contains.

Aside from the material advantages of knowing the actual grading of his clip and seeing the work done, the wool-grower can expect added returns to equal or overbalance his extra expense only by securing wider competition for his clip. This can not reasonably be expected under the plan of selling the clip at home and as a whole. It can be secured by consignment to concerns receiving large amounts of wools similarly prepared. This allows them to interlot satisfactorily and insures mill buyers of a large and steady supply of such wools. Only by the more general use of such a system can growers secure wider competition for the purchase of their wools.

The consignment plan does not eliminate the middleman, but gets the wool from the range to the mill on the basis of commission charges rather than of intermediate speculation. Such commission selling houses need financial arrangements for making advances to consignors pending the sale of their clips. Mills can never absorb the country's clip in a few months. Commission agents, like dealers, must therefore offer their stocks as the market justifies, and consignors must trust the judgment of their agents in this regard.

Such selling arrangements might be established in cities in the producing States. Growers might be more willing to consign to home concerns, but considerable difficulty would arise in attempting to establish free and steady selling so far from the points of consumption. If growers do not care to deal with commission concerns at eastern points, or will not cooperate in the establishment and patronage of houses of their own, they can not expect wider competition for their wools.

No wool-handling warehouses as yet have taken advantage of the provisions of the new warehouse act. The negotiability of receipts issued by Government-licensed warehouses will facilitate the financing of such enterprises, and the fact of Government supervision may be expected to secure the confidence of prospective patrons.

ADAPTABILITY OF THE WYOMING PLAN TO OTHER STATES.

Improved methods of preparing wools for market have been adopted first in Wyoming, as a result of the progressiveness of the woolgrowers. In the particular counties prominent in the movement greater security as to tenure of range has resulted from cooperative lease and purchase of railroad lands unsuitable for settlement. The individual ownership of sheep is large. Thus it has been feasible to make a greater outlay in shed construction than is likely to be made in other sections. The essential features of these sheds, however, can be embodied in smaller structures, and where feed and water conditions permit, two or more owners might co-operate in the erection of a suitable shed and employment of necessary hands and graders.

The first season's operations present some difficulty in the training of boys to carry and roll the fleeces. An experienced man who understands this part of the work and who knows how to direct the labor available can have it working smoothly in a few days. Greater difficulty is likely to be experienced in securing competent graders. The men who do this work at the warehouses are competent for this work but need supervision. In the months in which the shearing is done it is generally possible to engage some of these men, but it is necessary to offer them the grading of a number of clips to compensate for the expense of travel and time lost in going from one shed to another or through the shearing being interfered with by bad weather. This consideration suggests the cooperation of a number of owners in the employment of graders and in the arrangement of shearing dates.

OTHER FORWARD STEPS.

During 1916 the counties of Otsego and Essex in New York State, through their farm bureaus, marketed their wools on the pooling basis. In Otsego County the plan had been introduced in 1915 and 20,000 pounds were handled that year. The sale was made at an advance of $4\frac{1}{2}$ cents per pound over the prices offered at the same time by the local dealers, who commonly buy at a uniform rate for resale to larger operators. In these cases no extra advantage in price was received by those who brought in the highest quality of wool. However, no really inferior wools were received. As larger quantities are received it will become practicable to do the grading needed to secure justice to all members.

In Louisiana 300,000 pounds of wool were pooled and sold in 1916 as a result of the efforts of the representative of the United States Office of Markets and Rural Organization and the extension service of the agricultural college.

During the first four months of 1916 the Animal Husbandry Division of the Bureau of Animal Industry cooperated with four western agricultural colleges in educational work concerning the growing and handling of wools. A car was fitted with material to explain the relation of shrink, grade, character, etc., to the value of wool. Fleeces of each of the common grades were shown, along with live sheep carrying the same grade of fleece. The exhibit attracted a great deal of attention and was visited by over 6,000 sheepmen and other interested persons in Wyoming, Utah, Montana, and Idaho.

BUSINESS ESSENTIALS FOR COOPERATIVE FRUIT AND VEGETABLE CANNERIES.

By W. H. KERR,

Investigator in Market Business Practice, Office of Markets and Rural Organization.

PRODUCERS in many sections of the United States have dreamed of wealth secured from a cooperative cannery which would make use of their surplus products unmarketable in the fresh state, and they have thrown away thousands of dollars in the organization and operation of plants which never should have been started. The canning of fruit and vegetables on a large scale is a manufacturing business that requires special skill and experience, and into which many elements enter that are not present in other types of cooperative enterprise in agriculture. Many canneries have been promoted for the purpose of selling machinery, creating salaried positions, or booming real estate, and still others for the purpose of unloading upon the farmers an enterprise which has been a failure as a private business. In most cases, cooperation in the canning of agricultural products on a commercial scale in the United States has been a failure. That cooperative canneries really handle a very small portion of the total business is shown by the fact that of approximately $158,000,000 worth of canned and dried fruits and vegetables marketed in 1914, they sold only $3,500,000 worth.

Nevertheless, a few successful cooperative fruit and vegetable canneries stand above the large number of failures as evidence that this business, if properly founded and conducted, can be made a success, and that it has a legitimate place in an efficient scheme of marketing perishable products. Practically all of the cooperative canneries in the United States are found in the Pacific Northwest and California, the annual business of these organizations ranging from as low as $50,000 to as high as $1,500,000 for a single cannery.[1]

---

[1] In cooperation with the Oregon Agricultural College, the Office of Markets and Rural Organization made a survey of the canning industry of the Pacific Northwest. In addition, the office investigated cooperative canning plants in California and other sections of the United States. From these studies the business essentials for success and the reasons for failure in the cooperative canning industry in the United States were ascertained.

NOT A BY-PRODUCTS BUSINESS.

It should be borne in mind that the canning business is by no means a by-product enterprise and that an institution built up primarily for the handling of culls and lower-grade fruit and vegetable products is not likely to be successful. Experience demonstrates that higher grades bring the better prices and are more profitable, and that large quantities of the first grades are essential in moving lower grades. Many canneries have failed because they were organized wholly to utilize that portion of the fruit crop that could not be sold on the market in its fresh state on account of its deteriorated condition or low grade. The use of such fruit results in an inferior quality of canned goods which is not readily salable and may be liable to seizure under the Federal and various State pure-food laws.

IMPORTANCE OF A SUITABLE LOCATION.

The places at which canneries can succeed are relatively few. Therefore, one of the first steps in considering the advisability of organizing a canning business should be a complete survey of the field to ascertain whether the conditions warrant the inauguration of the enterprise. A sufficient quantity of a suitable number of products is essential, for to be successful financially a cannery should be operated as continuously throughout the year as possible, thus avoiding loss in having idle machinery and in "steaming up" for a small pack. There are exceptions, however, as in the case of specialty canneries, where a single product, like beans, peas, corn, tomatoes, or certain other fruits and vegetables, is handled extensively. In such cases a large volume of business is done and the canneries are kept running at full capacity during the season in which the product is harvested. In the case of some fruit canneries, from one to two weeks may elapse between products, during which time high-salaried help and machinery are idle.

The most successful cooperative canneries now in operation put up or pack a wide variety of products over a long period, some starting with strawberries in May and continuing until December with late vegetables. By utilizing the various products as they mature, the operating period may be extended to about six and one-half months. While some products handled will barely pay the expense of canning and a fair return to the producer, it is economical to use them to keep the plant in operation throughout the season.

The cannery should be located as near as possible to the production center of the commodities which are to be used. This is essential, as in most cases the product must be delivered to the cannery with little delay after it is harvested. Canned goods, especially small fruits and vegetables, should be of superior quality, since inferior grades usually are a drug on the market. In addition to growing fruits and vegetables of superior quality, the quantity must be sufficient to allow such a volume of business that the overhead expenses will represent a small unit cost per case. Some canneries are successful when only 300,000 pounds of raw material are handled annually, but a cannery which puts up a variety of fruit and vegetable products usually can not receive a price that will allow a fair return to the grower if the output is less than this.

Since labor is an important item and in some instances is difficult to secure, it should have serious consideration at the outset. Canneries generally should be located near some center of population where it is possible to secure at a reasonable price the necessary pickers and cannery help to supplement those drawn from the community itself.

In many farmers' cooperative canneries the skilled help used in the manufacturing departments is made up of the sons and daughters of the farmer owners. Such a practice assists in the accumulation of "spending money" for the members of the farmer's family and gives to the cannery reliable and skilled help year after year. In some of the cannery sections berry-picking time is looked upon as vacation time, and many families in the Pacific Northwest and California look forward to it with delight. Families from the near-by cities, especially the women and children, move into the berry fields and spend from two to six weeks working as pickers. They derive a fair compensation and have an excellent outing. One cannery employs as many as 15,000 pickers in a season, and in these berry fields excellent accommodations and camping facilities are provided. The various forms of amusements, such as "merry-go-rounds" and "cane racks," which are located near the center of the fields, turn the evenings into a continual festival.

The sanitary conditions surrounding the cannery should be the best; the plant should be located so that there are good drainage and circulation of air, and no contaminating surroundings, such as slaughterhouses, garbage plants, and dumps. A plentiful supply of good water is necessary, and in order to be sure of the quality a chemical analysis should be made.

The roads should be good enough to provide transportation for products from the fields to the cannery with as little difficulty and jarring as possible. Spring wagons should be used for carrying highly perishable products, and the hauling should be done in the early morning or late evening in order to avoid the heat of the day.

Proximity to markets is frequently an important factor in deciding the location of a cannery, as freight charges play a large part in determining the final net price received by the cannery for its products. Wherever possible, a location should be chosen which affords ready access to local shipping facilities, bearing in mind always, however, the question of rates to marketing centers.

FINANCING CANNERY OPERATIONS.

Managers of several cooperative canneries give as their greatest handicap the lack of sufficient capital. Since the canning business is a manufacturing enterprise, it requires a much larger capital than the average cooperative undertaking. A few organizations have started with as little as $5,000 or $6,000 paid-in capital, when only few products were handled and business was being done on a small scale. To be successful, the association should have sufficient paid-in capital to make the plant and equipment practically free of debt at the time the first canning season opens.

Considerable money is necessary to meet operating expenses before the final returns from canned goods are received, which is often as long as 18 months, or more in some cases, after the raw material has been delivered. This delay necessitates a liberal fund for making advances to the grower at the time of the delivery of the raw material. Such advances range from 35 to 65 per cent of the estimated value of the produce. If the plant is free from debt, usually sufficient money can be secured from banks to finance the early season's operations, while during the latter part of the season additional money can be secured on warehouse receipts on the canned goods. Some of the larger canneries have as much as $200,000 worth of canned goods in their warehouses at one time, necessitating a proportionately large surplus fund and good credit to finance the business during the canning season. As an instance of good credit, a western farmers' cannery recently purchased a trainload of sugar for the year's operation, securing from one bank a loan of $85,000 to finance the deal. Such operations show clearly that farmers' organizations can secure credit and can be run on a strictly business basis if properly managed and supported.

Too often a member of a cooperative association feels that the organization is a thing apart from himself. Where possible, it is desirable that he be connected with the institution financially, either by membership fee or through the purchase of stock. The issuance of memberships under $25 should be discouraged. The member who has sufficient produce to make him interested in the cannery should be willing to invest at least $100 in a membership or take stock in the organization to this amount. If financially interested in the business, he can ill afford to allow the undertaking to fail.

PURCHASING THE PLANT AND EQUIPMENT.

In several instances farmers' organizations have purchased at a bargain the canning plant and equipment of private enterprises which have failed, and they have made a success of the business. On the other hand, a number of plants not suitable for farmers' canneries have been sold to cooperative companies, and time, money, and energy have been wasted in their operation. On this account the advice of some one well qualified to pass on the worth and suitability of the buildings and equipments should be secured when the purchase of an equipped plant is being considered.

When constructing a new plant provision should be made for adding to it from time to time. By using the unit plan of construction, additions can be made without necessitating an entire overhauling of the old unit, or the impairing of the operating efficiency. The cannery business has reached a stage which makes possible definite standards for plant efficiency.

Before constructing a cannery, plans should be secured from experienced engineers or cannery men. The floor plans and the machinery required will vary according to products handled. The mistake often is made of building a large plant and equipping it with unnecessary machinery. The best machines on the market should be purchased, but only as they are needed. Improvement is being made yearly in canning processes and machinery, and therefore advice from expert cannery men and processors should be secured before equipping the plant. The statements made by those desiring to sell machines or by others personally interested in promoting the enterprise should not be relied upon exclusively.

THE MANAGER.

Of all cooperative agricultural enterprises few require conservative, sound, keen business judgment to a greater extent than a cooperative cannery. Without a manager of the right kind, failure is almost inevitable. In many of the successful canneries the manager will be found to be some leader who is willing to make certain sacrifices, and to contribute his energy and ability to the organization at a comparatively small salary. The success of cooperative organizations often is due to the efforts of one individual, or a few individuals, who, being public spirited and having the interests of the community sufficiently at heart, contribute their efforts and make sacrifices, if necessary, for the purpose of advancing and improving the enterprise.

Dependence should not be placed wholly on local talent, however, in securing a manager. It probably will be necessary to pay an experienced man a salary which may seem high. If the association is not willing to pay for experience, the farmers frequently must gain this experience for themselves by several years of deficits, and frequently at a proportionately higher cost than that required in obtaining expert services. The danger in the learning-by-experience plan is that in the majority of cases, before the necessary knowledge is gained, the cannery has become but an unpleasant memory.

The manager should be familiar with manufacturing processes and organization and should have a knowledge of the methods of cost accounting as applied to a manufacturing business. He also should be an efficient salesman, as the sales end of the business is of great importance. Each year competition becomes keener, and ability in salesmanship becomes as necessary to success as quality of product. If the size of the organization warrants, it may be advisable to have a separate sales manager, who is familiar with the problems of the trade and is able economically and efficiently to market the output of the factory. The general manager also should be capable of handling men, and be one in whom the farmers will have confidence. As in any other cooperative enterprise, if there is not complete unity and confidence in the management a farmers' cannery lacks the necessary stability and cohesion for success.

In the small cannery, the general manager should be the processor also, while in the larger canneries the general manager should have a processor as his assistant. The mistake often is made of depending at first on local, inexperienced talent for processing. The processor should have had practical experience in the particular line of canning business in which he is to be engaged. Superficially considered, a good salary for a processor may seem an excessive expenditure, but the spoiling of the pack of one or two days because it is improperly put up would probably cover the cost of the best processor obtainable. Processing is an exacting business and not every one knows how properly to prepare the raw material for the can, or how to handle it after it is in the can, so that it will reach the consumer's table in proper condition.

SUPPORT REQUIRED OF THE GROWERS.

The nature of the farmer's business makes him an individualist, and the same difficulties are encountered in the operation of the cooperative cannery as in other lines of cooperative enterprise. The cooperative cannery must be conducted along sound business lines; sentiment and "gentlemen's agreements" have bankrupted many farmers' organizations. An equitable yet binding contract should be made between the grower and his organization. A regular supply of the right varieties and kinds of produce is necessary in order that a sufficient volume of business be had to operate the cannery. Therefore, the contract, if possible, should run for a period of years, and should specify the products and the varieties to be grown. In some of the successful canneries a few big growers have formed the nucleus of the enterprise, furnishing sufficient capital and produce to insure the necessary volume of business each year, regardless of the support given by the community generally.

Wherever the business is large enough to justify the expense, a field man should be secured to work among the farmer members, helping them to solve their difficulties, hearing their grievances, and explaining the principles and advantages of the association. Such work should include instruction as to varieties to be planted, care of the growing crops, and harvesting methods. Personal contact between the management and the grower members will help to keep the members loyal, since they will be in close touch with the business and, therefore, will take a keener interest in its affairs.

NEED OF A LIBERAL BUDGET.

Estimates for each year's expenditures should be made up in budget form as accurately and in as much detail as possible. The estimate of the amount of produce to be received and the possible returns from these goods in the canned state should be very conservative. Many failures have resulted because expenditures were made on an estimate which was far in excess of the actual business transacted.

For the first year's operation, the costs of putting up the different packs, the overhead expenses, etc., should be secured from similar canneries operating under like circumstances and should be used as a basis in making estimates. The season's run never can be foretold definitely, and it is not easy to retrench after the season has been well begun. The actual overhead expenses should be cut to the lowest possible point consistent with successful conduct. The overhead and direct expenses should be estimated in the budget and apportioned on a unit basis. During the operating season the budget should be checked up frequently and such changes made as are shown to be necessary.

Early in the season price quotations must be prepared, based on the unit-cost estimate. The latter, therefore, should be as accurate as possible. A large part of the output of most of the canneries is contracted for early in the season and sometimes long before any of the produce is delivered to the cannery. The basis of these contracts varies with different commodities and sections of the country. Peas, for example, may be paid for on the vine, by the pound or by the ton, either shelled or in the pod. Quotations at the cannery for different varieties of produce, therefore, are not comparable one section with another unless similar bases of payment are used. This explains in large measure the seemingly wide diversity in prices paid for like products in different localities.

METHODS OF KEEPING ACCOUNTS.

The cannery must maintain a modern system of cost records, so that all items of expense shall be charged properly to each case of finished goods. A separate account should be kept for each commodity packed in the different-sized cans, showing the various grades, and in the case of sirup goods the various degrees.

Accurate, itemized, direct-labor costs for work done on a piece basis should be kept. Most of the farmers' canneries pay for the preparing, stemming, and washing of raw material at so much per crate or box, and the filling of cans at so much per dozen. Much help is used which must be paid by the hour, such as machine operators, engineers, truckers, etc. Time records should be kept of this work and the cost of each activity properly apportioned to the day's pack.

The superintendent should make out daily reports showing the number of cans packed, quantities of fruits or vegetables used in the pack, material used, direct labor chargeable to the pack, and other operations. In the office a cost ledger and stock record can be used to assemble the different items and the cost of the finished goods, together with the number of cases carried to a finished-goods account for each commodity.

In addition to such a tabulated statement of the cost and quantity of each grade of commodity packed in the different-sized cans, a complete record of sales and sales costs should be kept up to date. There is thus available at all times a perpetual inventory of "spot stock" (canned goods) on hand, the cost of making and selling each kind of finished product, and the prices realized for each grade or class. Such information is imperative to the proper operation of a cannery.[1]

SIDE LINES.

Some canneries which handle large quantities of berries conduct a fresh-fruit shipping department in connection with their other business. When the fresh-goods market is profitable all berries of shipping quality are sold fresh. The sound fruit is sent to distant markets, ripe fruit to near-by markets, and fruit ready for immediate use goes into the cannery. At times when markets are not favorable all the fruit is canned and held until it can be sold at fair prices. Where the berries in the locality are of a superior quality, such an arrangement forms an ideal combination. One cooperative cannery association has shipped as many as 21 refrigerator cars of fresh red raspberries in one express train, at the same time operating two large canneries.

Several of the cooperative canneries in the Pacific Northwest also operate evaporators in which prunes, loganberries, apples, and a few raspberries are evaporated. Other canneries have vinegar plants, some of which have failed because of lack of knowledge or because of carelessness on the part of the managers. The use of green, dirty, or rotten stock, instead of carefully selected, high-quality, sound fruit is not uncommon, and in such cases good vinegar can not be manufactured. Many cider-vinegar plants have failed because of their inability to compete in the markets with grain-distilled vinegar. However, there is generally a good market in the surrounding territory for small quantities of a good grade of cider vinegar. Such enterprises as these, however, have started on a small scale and have been developed gradually, each advance being based on past experience.

---

[1] The Office of Markets and Rural Organization of the U. S. Department of Agriculture has a uniform system of accounts for fruit and vegetable canneries which is available on request from canneries or persons contemplating the organization of a cannery.

MEETING MARKET DEMANDS.

It is necessary for the manager to keep in close touch with market demands, marketing conditions, trade preferences, and improvements in the canning business in order that he may be able to market the products of the cannery to the best possible advantage. There are various preferences in the different canned-goods markets, which should be studied carefully before the markets are entered. The trade demands that certain products be put up in certain degrees of sirup, cans of various sizes, etc., and the successful cannery must conform to these demands.

The cost of produce, cans, packing, and freight is as great on a water-packed product as on the best sirup grade, the only additional cost of the latter being that of the sugar which enters into the process. Since goods of the higher grades usually bring far better average returns to the producer than those of the lower grades, farmers' canneries always should strive to increase their production of the best grades.

A few of the canneries successfully put up jellies, preserves, and high-grade products in glass. Others prepare berries for soda-fountain use by what is known as the cold-process method, and make sirups and other necessary fruit supplies for the fountain trade. Such business, if properly handled by an expert processor who can prepare the products in the best form possible, is a paying feature. In many cases fruit juices are placed in cans during the canning season and made up into jellies and jams, soda-fountain sirups, and similar products during the winter. This practice provides almost continuous employment for some of the skilled labor.

During the packing rigid inspection should be maintained in order that a product of uniform grade may be put up, and samples should be taken of each day's pack. Each shipment should be sampled before being sent out, and the sample tested in order to avoid any loss from inferior or spoiled goods which could not be detected from the outside, but which could be ascertained by opening the container. At all times the ultimate consumer should be kept in mind, as no cannery business can endure which does not please the final purchaser of its products.

The cannery must be in a position to furnish the trade regularly with the same products year after year. It is not possible to keep proper connections and retain the business which it has taken some time to build up if but a short supply is available one year and a comparatively large pack is put up the next. The best business that a cannery can cater to is that which will purchase certain quantities and kinds of different products year after year.

A large portion of the pack must be sold for future delivery, and, as jobbers insist that the goods be forthcoming, it is evident that great care must be exercised in estimating the pack in order to prevent an oversale. It is not unlikely that a number of cars will be sold as early as April for September or October delivery. Sales of mixed cars may be made, which it will take from June to November to get together if the order contains early products, such as strawberries, and fall products, such as squash or pears. Such sales necessitate large warehouse facilities.

FINDING A MARKET.

It is usual to market the products of the cannery through the regular organized and recognized trade channels for canned goods. The home trade or near-by trade should be canvassed thoroughly, as this business is much more profitable and satisfactory than that handled in more distant markets. Several canneries have attempted a special feature in marketing by putting up a miscellaneous assortment of canned goods to be sold directly to the consumer, but this has not met with any degree of success. In one State a large number of the cooperative canneries have formed an association and appointed a joint agent, who is a canned-goods broker, to handle their output. There is great need for greater cooperation among farmers' canneries in the standardization of packs, as well as in the formation of a uniform sales policy or central sales agency as far as the law permits.

The buyer or broker should be furnished with plenty of samples of everything packed and kept well acquainted with the varieties, grades, and quality of all products. Samples which are used for this purpose should be put up in the best possible form and should represent accurately the quality of the goods manufactured, both for the purpose of making sales and for the protection of the cannery in matters of rejections and adjustments.

Printed price catalogues should be prepared by the manager of the cannery and furnished to all jobbers, brokers, and others who are in the market for canned goods. All of the various factors entering into the determination of quotations should be considered very carefully—the actual cost of production, prevailing wholesale prices, condition of the market, probable output in other localities, and such other local factors as may be of influence. As conditions change throughout the season, quotations should be revised accordingly. The retail prices at which the goods probably will be sold also should be kept in mind in making quotations and fixing upon the grades which will be pushed. Specialization on the higher grades and higher-priced products will probably result in a greater return and larger profit to the cannery, since it is the general experience that high grades bring the best net returns to the producer.

By taking advantage of the experiences of others through many failures and by following closely the methods of successful organizations, farmers should succeed in the business of cooperative canning and find a ready market for their products.

THE EFFECT OF HOME DEMONSTRATION WORK ON THE COMMUNITY AND THE COUNTY IN THE SOUTH.

By BRADFORD KNAPP, *Chief*, and Miss MARY E. CRESWELL, *Assistant in Charge of Home Demonstration Work, Office of Extension Work in the South, States Relations Service.*

THE home demonstration work for women and girls, which is the complement of the farm demonstration work conducted by the men county agents, is now being carried on extensively throughout the South. This work began in 1910 with the girls' canning clubs, and led by gradual and logical steps into the present very broad and comprehensive work with both individuals and groups. In the fall of 1916 home demonstration work was in progress in 420 counties in the Southern States. The principal feature of the work is the lessons being taught by actual demonstrations in and around the home by the women and girls under the instruction of the women county agents.

One of the objects of the work is to develop a skill that shall result in economic independence of girls and women in the country. Their home has many functions not performed by the city home. It is a producing as well as a consuming center. Its contribution to the income of the farmer, especially in saving the waste and expense of conducting farming operations, often measures the difference between profitable farming and unprofitable farming. The skill and business ability of farm housewives and children are a notable contribution to the economic resources of the farm. In many cases incomes must be increased before standards of living can be raised or progressive community enterprises fostered. Proceeding upon this basis, the work in the South has added materially to the wealth, health, and happiness of country people.

HARRISON COUNTY, MISS.

Nine miles east of Wiggins, in Harrison County, Miss., the woman county agent has organized a home demonstration club. This club of country women, with the counsel and ad-

251

vice of the agent, decided to conduct their work by departments, such as canning, poultry, health, food, and home conveniences. Each department has a chairwoman, and the members are enrolled in the department in which they wish to work. Meetings are held semimonthly, each meeting being conducted by one department. Programs are so outlined that the topics will be beneficial and seasonable. For example, canning and preserving was taken up in summer; poultry raising was discussed actively during the fall and winter; while preparation of foods was studied in utilizing canning and poultry products. Home conveniences were so popular that they were made at all times of the year. The poultry department has its manager, who grades, tests, and ships the eggs brought in by club members each week and handles the business of selling and remitting to the members for the products sold. All of the work is carried out through practical demonstration in the homes. The success of the work under this plan of organization has proved so satisfactory that it has been extended to other communities and clubs in Harrison County.

These community clubs comprised both women and girls and have taken as one of their principal lines of work the equipment of home-science rooms in country schools. They have gone before the board of trustees and secured the building of additional rooms for the schoolhouses, while the equipment has been furnished by contributions from the skilled workmen of the community, both men and women, and by merchants of the towns. Thus these schools have been made real centers of community interest.

SAMPSON COUNTY, N. C.

A community in Sampson County, N. C., furnishes an excellent object lesson on the manner in which this work begins and progresses. In 1914 nine girls organized a canning club and were instructed by the home demonstration agent. A little later a women's club was organized among the mothers of the canning-club members to cooperate with them in canning for home and market. The success of this undertaking aroused a great deal of interest, and soon there was talk of a community organization. A picnic was held in the late summer, and a community club of both men and women was organized with a definite program along six lines, namely, social activity, education, agriculture, morality, sanitation, and home life. In these enterprises the community had the assistance of many public forces in the State interested in community development, such as the State extension service, through which the State department of agriculture, State agricultural college, and the United States Department of Agriculture were cooperating in the employment of county men and women agents, the State board of health, State department of education, farmers' unions, and other forces. The community organization made it easy to secure the services of these agencies. The State board of health made a complete survey of the sanitary conditions of the community. Diseases were eradicated in a number of cases, and sanitary conveniences were installed in every one of the 115 homes. During the school term following this service not a single case of contagious or preventable disease occurred. A special campaign was conducted against flies by screening homes and destroying breeding places.

In December this same community held a fair in Sampson County, the exhibits including farm and garden products, live stock, poultry, household products, and school work. During a "community service week" a sand and clay road was built from the village to the schoolhouse, which is the center of the community. Work in other sections of Sampson County has been taken up along the same lines, with the assistance of both the county agent and the home demonstration agent.

BRYAN COUNTY, OKLA.

In Bryan County, Okla., 65 women, under the guidance of the home demonstration agent, have entered the work in home dairying and poultry raising. They have purchased thermometers, square butter molds, and barrel churns, have made iceless refrigerators or cooling devices to keep butter and cream at the proper temperature, and in some instances have purchased separators. In every case the quality of the butter sold has been so improved under the instruction that a higher price has been obtained. Those who have been raising poultry have cooperated in the rearing of pure-bred fowls and in selling infertile eggs on the market. They have realized prices in advance of the ordinary market prices.

WALTON COUNTY, FLA.

Through the marketing of some samples of preserved figs from Florida, the State agent received a request to place an order for 5,000 jars of preserved figs uniformly packed and of high quality. The order was turned over to the canning-club girls of Walton County. The home demonstration agent of that county assisted in selecting the girls who had shown sufficient skill to undertake the work. Two girls in one community who had been at work for 3 years agreed to supply a thousand jars each. Another girl, assisted by her mother, undertook to produce another thousand, and two women of the neighborhood who had been working under the instruction of the home demonstration agent agreed to can the remaining 2,000 jars. Jars were purchased cooperatively, saving in cost and freight. To start the work the agent demonstrated the proper making and packing of these preserves at each of the homes selected. Each contributing member purchased a saccharimeter in order to produce sirup of uniform density, and painstaking care was exercised in gathering figs that were in good condition and in selecting those of uniform size. The result was a cooperative venture involving skill and organization in the community, and giving good returns to those engaged.

ETOWAH COUNTY, ALA.

Ruth Anderson, of Etowah County, Ala., in her second year of club work, had an excellent plat of one-tenth of an acre of beans and tomatoes. She is the second girl in a family of 11, and takes a great interest in her club work. The family home was small, dark, and crowded, and somewhat unattractive. One day a carpenter friend of her father saw her one-tenth acre and said he wished he had time to plant a garden. She told him she would furnish vegetables in exchange for some of his time. Thinking she was joking, he began to figure how many beans it would take to build a house, but Ruth told him about her canner, and he saw then that she was in earnest. After a while a bargain was made by which the carpenter agreed to begin work on the remodeling of the house if Ruth would furnish him with fresh and canned vegetables for the season. The other members of the family were soon interested in this undertaking and worked willingly to contribute their share to its success. When the house was partly finished Ruth won a canning-club prize given by a hardware merchant in Gadsden, the county seat. Silverware was offered her, but, intent upon completing the new house, she asked the merchant how much a front door of glass would cost, and learned that she could get the door, side lights, and windows for the price of the silverware. In this way Ruth brought light and joy to her family with her windows and door. To-day they live in a pretty bungalow that she helped to build with her gardening and canning work. At the age of 14, in the second year of her work, Ruth put up 700 cans of tomatoes and 750 cans of beans.

During the last 4 years the girls in the clubs in Etowah County put up 172,555 cans, the approximate value of which is $29,400. They have secured the cooperation of the Gadsden Chamber of Commerce and all the products not needed for home use have been marketed. The county has produced more than twice this amount of canned products as a direct result of the information disseminated through these girls. At the close of the summer season of 1916 every club girl in this county planted a winter garden, insuring a continuance of her earnings and contribution to the family diet during the winter.

HAMILTON COUNTY, TENN.

Hamilton County, Tenn., is the county in which Chattanooga is located. Chattanooga is a large manufacturing and railroad center. This county had a population of 89,267 in 1910. The last census shows that there are only 1,623 farms in the county, averaging 75 acres per farm, of which 41 acres per farm is classified as improved land. Values are somewhat above the average for the State. Only 47 per cent of the land of the county is in farms; 55 per cent of the land in farms is scheduled as improved land.

This county has had a woman engaged as home demonstration agent for the last four years. A prominent business man in Chattanooga, who has watched the progress of this work very closely since its beginning, states that before it was undertaken practically nothing had been done to arouse the interest of the young people in country life or home improvement. No community leadership existed, nor were there any organizations for girls and women in the rural districts. In April, 1912, an agent was employed. At first, interest was very slight. Practically no demand for the work came from rural people.

Canning clubs were organized at the four typical rural centers of the county. Very few seemed to be interested in completing the work the first year, but a canning demonstration at the University of Chattanooga at the close of the summer school did much to stimulate the interest in club work. A number of leading educators of the county and State gave talks at this time to the club members and teachers, indorsing the work and its objects. Six of the most skillful girls were taken to the State fair and entered a canning contest. They won distinction by packing and processing 80 three-pound cans of tomatoes in less than an hour. They also won a number of prizes.

In 1913 the county home demonstration agent was employed again and she was hired for the full 12 months. She devoted the summer to giving instruction and supervising demonstrations in gardening and canning carried on by the girls in practically every community in the county. Many varieties of fruits and vegetables besides tomatoes were put up. That year for the first time the parents began to appreciate the advantages, both educational and economic, of having their girls and boys trained in club work.

It was found that many rural housekeepers in the county used preservatives in canning. In fact, every case of glass jars sold by merchants in the county at that time generally had inclosed a package of " canning powders." The girls in the canning club were taught, in the presence of their mothers, to follow implicitly the instructions regarding sterilizing and processing and not to use preservatives. This was done as much for the mothers as for the girls. The re-

CANNING CLUB DAY AT THE UNIVERSITY OF CHATTANOOGA.

A helpful gathering in Hamilton County, Tenn.

Before improvement.

After improvement.

YELLOW CANNAS AND OTHER PLANTS USED BY CANNING CLUB GIRL TO
BEAUTIFY UNSIGHTLY FENCE.

FIG. I.—RUTH'S HOME BEFORE IMPROVEMENT.

FIG. 2.—RUTH'S HOME AFTER IMPROVEMENT.

sult proved to the mothers that chemical preservatives were not necessary for successful canning.

The social side of the club activities attracted much attention. Many of the girls had read of clubs but never thought they would be able to join. To the girls, vacation time had always been dreaded as a time full of work with no play and no companionship. The club meetings during vacation furnished a much-needed opportunity for social intercourse. In the beginning it was noticed that the few girls attending demonstrations for instruction brought their lunches and retired singly to eat them. Now, there is always a bountiful dinner spread, temptingly prepared and arranged, of which everyone is invited to partake. These all-day " picnics " or " canning parties " are very popular during the summer.

A little later poultry-club work was taken up. In this the girls were taught the proper feeding, raising, and handling of poultry, and the proper care and marketing of eggs.

In 1916 the entire county was organized, with an enrollment of over 200 girls in canning clubs and 280 members in the poultry clubs. The gardening season was a very disastrous one. The club girls, however, were among the few who were able to produce fresh vegetables, and they sold all they produced at advanced prices, on account of the condition of the market. While canning was done for home use very little commercial canning was carried on because of the price of fresh products. The reports of the girls show that they produced 104,639 pounds of tomatoes and canned 15,800 containers of fruits and vegetables. The total value of these products is estimated at $6,070.97.

All of these girls are regularly organized into clubs holding meetings at stated intervals throughout the year. In each of the rural schools of the county one teacher is in charge of the clubs and assists at meetings as local leader. In addition to canning they have carried on work in sewing, breadmaking, use of fireless cookers, and the like. The mothers of the girls have been active cooperators and assist in all of the meetings. In 1916 uniform caps and aprons for use in public demonstrations were made by 100 girls and uniform dresses by 15 advanced members.

In this work close cooperation has been received from many sources. During January, 1916, four short courses were held at the rural high schools of the county and the results of these short courses could be traced in remote districts. Another commendable instance of cooperation is that given by the summer school at the University of Chattanooga, where the Annual Canning Club Day is an established event, the last one having been attended by more than 200 girls. The program for this day includes reports from every club president in the county, singing club songs, and talks by some of the leading educators, and the girls give public demonstrations of their skill in the work. The day also has many social features.

The Chattanooga Clearing House Association, through the influence of prominent women of the city, presented an automobile for the use of the woman home demonstration agent in the county. Not only does this car solve the problem of transportation, thereby making for greater efficiency on the part of the agent, but it also enables the girls and women in various parts of the county to accompany the county agent to club meetings and other gatherings.

Through the girls' work just outlined the way was paved for the rapid development of demonstration work for women. The first approach to the work for women was made by visits to the homes for the instruction of the daughters. The first instruction to the women was mainly incidental to the girls' work, but much of this incidental work was of very great importance. The earliest demonstrations made by the women in their homes under the instructions of the home demonstration agent were in practical everyday cookery, stress being laid upon varied diet. The use of homemade fireless cookers was taught, and assistance was given in making simple sanitary improvements in the home and in selecting proper wearing apparel and household furnishings.

Ten rural women's clubs have been organized, each holding meetings every two weeks. Women who formerly seldom left their homes now attend these meetings regularly. A keener interest is manifested among them in the affairs of the home and community, and the pleasure and benefit derived from intercourse with others is evident. Six of these ten rural women's clubs are affiliated with a county organization, giving helpful intercourse between the women of the rural districts and the women of the city. The county agent meets regularly in turn with all these clubs. A uniform constitution and by-laws is used, but very little stress is laid on parliamentary law. The programs vary according to the plans and desires of the local members, but those sent out by the extension division of the University of Tennessee, representing that institution and the Department of Agriculture, are followed as closely as possible. The meetings are held in the country school buildings and at some of the homes. The materials for demonstrations usually are provided by the women themselves, who have an opportunity to express their preference as to the foods prepared. Lessons in serving and in the use of household conveniences are always in demand. A program which is always welcome includes the study of wearing apparel. To illustrate a lesson in wearing apparel the county agent borrows from some of the leading department stores of the city articles of wearing apparel for women, girls, and young children. By this means good taste, appropriateness, and the value of durability in the selection of garments are taught.

At some of the meetings members have been called upon to give demonstrations of the things they do best. There are 100 farm women members of the 10 clubs. Under the guidance of the county agent 35 of these women have made, in their own homes, all of the demonstrations outlined, including bread making, meat cookery, vegetable cookery, and canning, and have adopted these as a part of their daily and yearly tasks. The number of labor-saving and sanitary improvements in the home which have been made and installed include 40 fireless cookers, 4 iceless refrigerators, 150 fly traps, 40 homes screened against flies and mosquitoes, 15 porches screened, 15 more convenient ironing boards, 6 wheel trays for the saving of steps from the kitchen to the dining room, 3 homemade shower baths, 4 kitchen cabinets, 10 water systems, 3 dumb waiters, and a number of stools and other devices in the kitchen to enable the women to sit while they work. In addition to these homemade devices the following were purchased: Ten fireless cookers, 4 kitchen cabinets, 40 kerosene stoves, 25 gasoline irons, 15 canning outfits, 15 incubators, 10 brooders, and a number of home lighting devices.

Annually the East Tennessee Farmers' Conference is held at Knoxville at the College of Agriculture, which is very largely attended. In recent years it has had a woman's section. During the first year of the work for women in Hamilton County it was difficult to persuade any of the women and girls to attend this meeting. The last convention had a 50 per cent increase in the attendance of women, many of whom represented their clubs as delegates, while others provided their own expenses.

Perhaps one of the most commendable achievements is the operation of the market booth in the market house at Chattanooga. The influence of the county home demonstration agent materially aided in the establishment of the central market house by the city commissioners. On account of this fact and through the influence of many prominent women, the city commissioners gave a stall for the canning-club girls and their mothers. Recently a larger booth was provided, a canning outfit installed, and a gas stove fitted up for use in filling orders for baked fowl, jellies, fruit butters, etc. The club women of Chattanooga have given excellent cooperation in this venture. At present this exchange is running very smoothly, with a club girl in charge. Her percentage collected on sales in one week recently amounted to $18.40. The women are charged 15 per cent and the girls 10 per cent for the handling of their products. This percentage goes to those who spend their time in operating the booth. The sign above the stall is very attractive, and the girl in charge wears a simple white waist and the uniform cap and apron with the symbol of the club embroidered on it. Two girls are occupied in the work on Saturdays. Homemade articles of food are sold exclusively. These include bread, beaten biscuit, candy, cakes, and 4-H brand canned products. Before the establishment of this booth the disposal of canned goods was a problem. Now, no matter what the crop may be, the canned goods are sold locally at advanced prices. Many girls with unusual skill have customers who come in and purchase only articles made by these girls. During the holiday season holly wreaths and hand-crocheted articles are sold. Orders are also taken for handmade rugs, woven, braided, or crocheted.

The Girls' Canning Club Exchange has remarkable co-operation from other stall keepers in the market house, and the market master himself acts as sponsor for the club stall and renders every assistance in his power. The home demonstration agent visits the booth from time to time and gives suggestions and help in the successful management of the venture.

The effect of this work upon the women and girls of Hamilton County and upon the rural life itself is greater than this brief outline can indicate. The home demonstration work has become a permanent part of the educational activities of the county and has the cooperation of the city school system, county superintendent, rural-school teachers, federation of women's clubs, county and city public officials, and the men, women, and children who make up the farming population of the county.

ANSON COUNTY, N. C.

Anson County lies along the Yadkin River, on the southern boundary of North Carolina, in the Piedmont section, east and south of Charlotte. The last census showed that there were 3,332 farms, of which one-half were operated by white farmers. The average size of farms is 87 acres, of which 34.9 acres is improved land. Eighty-one per cent of the area of the county is in farms. The county may be considered one of the better counties of North Carolina. The percentage of farms operated by tenants is 63.6 per cent.

In 1913 a woman agent was employed for the first time, and a small canning club of 26 rural girls was organized. Fifteen of these girls are still at work as leaders in their communities. At four rural centers the girls gave " parties " to raise the money for the purchase of their canning-club outfits. The canning outfits purchased were used cooperatively either at the homes or at the schools. An excellent spirit of cooperation was manifested in the early stages of the work by such examples as follow: At one place one of the girls had no way of bringing her tomatoes to the place chosen for the canning demonstration. The other girls took turns in going after them, and one of the neighboring farmers did all of her plowing free of cost. On a number of occasions when club members were ill and unable to attend meetings the other members did the work for the disabled ones and canned their vegetables for them.

During the early history of the work it was difficult to get sufficient cans to supply the girls. The county superintendent of schoools worked actively with the home demonstration agent, and the second year the club members purchased all their cans cooperatively, resulting in an order for a carload containing 35,000 cans. In 1916 the business men entered into this cooperation and 70,000 cans were ordered for use in the county.

In 1916 in the girls' work there was an enrollment of 154 girls in the various clubs. Accurate reports were obtained from 130 of these, showing the production of 40,036 pounds of tomatoes, 31,794 pounds of beans, and 800 pounds of peppers. These girls put up 42,069 containers of products from their gardens and nearly 6,000 additional containers from the products of the farm and orchard, usually allowed to go to waste. They learned sewing and dressmaking by making their caps and aprons, and a few of them made uniform dresses.

The work has assisted in bringing about a spirit of mutual helpfulness that has had a good influence on the homes and the communities. It has broken down barriers existing between families because of differences in education, social standing, and wealth. It has caused the girls and mothers who have had better chances to reach out and help their less fortunate neighbors.

In the fall of 1915 a meeting was held on the front porch of one of the homes in Rocky River community. The home demonstration agent called the meeting by writing to her canning-club members, requesting them to ask their mothers and neighbors to come to the meeting and bring a few jars of products canned during the summer. There were 38 women present. The products brought furnished an introductory topic. The home demonstration agent talked to them about canning and preserving, and led from that to a talk about what might be done for the general improvement of their school building and grounds, and also regarding the development of pride of the people of their community.

Those present were urged to hold a general meeting for this purpose. They said that such a meeting had never been held in their school, and they were afraid that it would not amount to anything. However, two weeks later they held a meeting which resulted in the raising of $56. From this small beginning grew the movement which added a new room to the building, painted it inside and out, got additional funds for a library, and seeded the lawn in grass. Now they have an excellent two-teacher school. In the summer of 1916 they planted an acre in cotton and a border of flowers around the school building. They have a community club, holding regular meetings, and an excellent community fair.

Anson County now has 11 community clubs, in some of which both men and women are members. They have given special thought to the improvement of school buildings and grounds, better roads, campaigns against flies and other insects, study of foods, and social life for old and young. Such an organized community can better command the services of the county agent, the home demonstration agent, and the specialists of the extension division, as well as the officers of the State department of education and the Public Health Service.

In many of these clubs dairy work has been taken up, especially by getting the assistance of the dairy specialists from the extension division at Raleigh, who give illustrated lectures and special lessons in butter making, equipment used, etc. These lessons are given in the homes, resulting in great improvement in the home butter making. One woman reports that two years ago she used to send her butter to town in a tin bucket and received 15 cents per pound for it; now she sells all she can make for 30 cents per pound, put up in 1-pound prints.

Canning for market and home use appeals very strongly to these country women, and the proceeds of their sales have assisted them in the improvement of their homes. Poultry raising is also very popular, and there are 150 poultry-club members in the county. A recent report from four women shows that the income from poultry, eggs, and butter amounted in one year to $119, $160, $183, and $227, respectively.

The frequent holding of meetings and demonstrations in the homes has had a beneficial influence upon the home life itself. Better utensils for cooking have been purchased, and there has been a marked improvement in labor-saving devices and in the general quality of work done.

This county has one cooperative butter-selling association. During the winter turkeys and chickens are sold cooperatively at 2 cents per pound above the market price. Eggs are sold on the local market, because the price is excellent.

Such standards of quality and uniformity have been established in the home canning as to insure the sale of all the products put up by the women and girls.

This again is but a brief outline of some of the things accomplished in a single county. The people of Anson County are living under better conditions and the farm women realize the need and importance of more conveniences, especially labor-saving devices for the home. The skill and experience acquired by the women and girls have qualified them to earn more money on the farm and to contribute materially to the farm income. The relation of food to better health and more efficient work is more clearly understood. The sentiment for better education of the children has been greatly stimulated and better social conditions exist. The women feel that each contributes to the success and pleasure of the monthly meetings, annual picnics, and community fairs. The farm women of Anson County are developing into a community of interest and a high type of rural life.

DARLINGTON COUNTY, S. C.

Darlington County is located in the northeastern part of South Carolina. In 1910 it had a population of 36,027, and there were 4,207 farms in the county, according to the last census, 27.5 per cent of which are managed by the owners and 72 per cent by tenants. Among the white farmers about half are owners and half tenants. The large majority of the negro farmers are tenants. This is distinctly one of the better counties of the State, having a large production of very excellent cotton.

A home demonstration agent has been employed in the county for four years. As is usual in the counties of the

South, the work began with the girls in gardening and canning, gradually extending and broadening its influence and service to the mothers. Excellent results were obtained among the girls in gardening, canning, poultry work, and bread making. While the women were much interested, active demonstrations with them were not begun until the spring of 1915.

At present, however, 19 rural women's clubs hold regular meetings and have a total enrollment of 457 members, which is practically equal to one-half of the white owner farmers of the county. These women have carried out, under the instruction of the home demonstration agent, in their homes, during the past year, 190 demonstrations in bread making, 140 special demonstrations in meat cooking, 225 demonstrations in jelly making, 175 demonstrations in the cooking of vegetables, and 250 demonstrations in canning; 87 fireless cookers, 145 iceless refrigerators, and 160 flytraps have been made or installed; 70 houses have been screened against flies and mosquitoes, 11 wheel trays built, 12 convenient ironing boards constructed, and 3 waterworks systems installed. In addition to these things, the following have been purchased: Six barrel churns, 8 washing machines, 13 bread mixers, and 3 wheel trays.

Through the girls' work the interest in gardening in the county has increased rapidly. Winter gardens now contain cabbages, turnips, lettuce, onions, beets, carrots, kale, spinach, and collards. Formerly not only were winter gardens rarely to be found, but as a rule they contained only collards. During the winter of 1916–17, 101 winter-garden demonstrations were conducted by the girls and women under the advice of the home demonstration agent. Many hotbeds have been built at schoolhouses under the supervision of the agent. The plants from these are sold and the proceeds used in improving the schools, as by painting the schoolhouses, buying sanitary drinking fountains, building septic tanks, etc. A number of the women and girls are raising winter vegetables for sale in the near-by towns.

The raising of pure-bred poultry for market, better methods of cooking and serving food, home conveniences, school lunches, proper diet for the family, care of milk, making butter and cottage cheese, etc., have been lines that have attracted much attention and have increased the quantity and quality of these products used in the homes. The women also have been interested in the curing of hams and bacon for home use, and good methods have been introduced. In improvement of home grounds and the planting of flowers, trees, shrubs, and vines considerable work has been done.

Here again the social side of country life has been deeply touched, manifesting itself in many social gatherings and community fairs. In fact, Darlington County now enjoys one of the largest organizations for the work in any county in the South. Demonstration work has developed so rapidly and demands have been so insistent that, through the activities of the county people themselves, funds have been supplied for the employment of an assistant to the county home demonstration agent, both women being employed for 12 months in the year.

COMMENT.

It is difficult to present the results of a work which comes into such intimate contact with the home life. An attempt has been made to describe what is being done rather than to lay down any principles or policies to be pursued in the work. The activities described are typical of the home demonstration work now being conducted in the 15 Southern States, and is fairly comparable with that more recently started in the 33 Northern and Western States.

The State colleges of agriculture and the United States Department of Agriculture are cooperating in the work both in the North and in the South. Of the budget for home economics extension work for all of the 48 States for the fiscal year ending June 30, 1917, amounting to $778,177, $574,584 are being expended by the Southern States through the extension divisions of the colleges. In each of these States there are many commendable results of individual, community, and county effort, from which these few examples have been selected for presentation.

COOPERATIVE WORK FOR ERADICATING CITRUS CANKER.

By KARL F. KELLERMAN,

Associate Chief, Bureau of Plant Industry.

INTRODUCTION OF THE DISEASE.

FOR a little more than two years the Federal Government and the Gulf States have been engaged in a joint campaign for the purpose of eradicating from the United States the disease of citrus fruit and trees called citrus canker. This undertaking is unique in character in that it is the first instance of the use of Federal funds appropriated specifically for the eradication of a plant disease. It is of overwhelming importance to the citrus industry, because citrus canker has been recognized as the most contagious of all known plant diseases and the most destructive of commercial values.

The origin of the disease is obscure. It appears probable that it is native in Chosen (Korea) or in south China and that from China it has been carried to Japan during rather recent years, but there appears to be no doubt that it has been introduced into this country direct from Japan. The first observation regarding a plant disease which presumably was citrus canker is with reference to nursery stock introduced into Texas in 1911. It is not improbable that earlier shipments of nursery stock were infected, and it is certain that many later shipments of *Citrus trifoliata* orange seedlings from Japan, both into Texas and into other Gulf States, were infected.

DISEASE CHARACTERISTICS AND EARLY CONTROL EFFORTS.

Citrus canker is primarily a leaf-spot and fruit-spot, although it also affects twigs and even old bark and wood. In its early stages, however, it resembles the sour-scab of citrus trees, a troublesome but not an especially serious disease that is widely prevalent in the South. Until late in the year 1913 plant pathologists and nurserymen did not clearly distinguish between these two diseases, and, therefore, prior to its recognition and the determination of its serious character, the shipment of infected nursery stock was probably taking place throughout the southern areas where citrus culture was being extended.

267

During the seasons of 1913 and 1914 special efforts were made by State nursery inspectors, by nurserymen, and by citrus growers to check the spread of the disease by complete defoliation of infected stock followed by immediate and thorough spraying with strong Bordeaux mixture and by painting visible infections with Bordeaux paste. These treatments were ineffectual, however, and citrus growers in southeastern Florida became so concerned over the rapid and destructive spread of citrus canker and the failure of the methods usually employed for controlling plant diseases that they originated the plan of spraying infected trees with burning oil, thus completely destroying them. Eradication work of this character was undertaken immediately and financed almost entirely by private subscriptions, but the disease appeared to be gaining upon the forces attempting to control it. Recognizing that a severe epidemic menaced the citrus industry and that neither the citrus industry nor the States concerned were prepared to deal promptly and adequately with this emergency, on December 4, 1915, the Secretary of Agriculture suggested for consideration by the Congress the desirability of the immediate appropriation of sufficient funds to cooperate during the winter and spring with State officials, organizations of growers, and individuals to continue the eradication campaign under way in Florida and to organize similar inspection and eradication campaigns in the other States believed to harbor citrus canker.[1] As a further protection, under date of December 10, 1914, the Secretary of Agriculture promulgated a quarantine, effective January 1, 1915, that prevents the introduction into the United States from all foreign countries of citrus nursery stock, including buds, scions, and seeds.

An immediate and rapid inspection of the Gulf region by an agent of the Federal Horticultural Board of the Department of Agriculture, supplemented by reports from State officials, indicated the occurrence of infected citrus trees in more or less widely separated and sharply defined localities from southeastern Florida to southern Texas.

The cooperative work of inspecting citrus groves and nurseries and destroying infected trees was begun in Florida immediately upon the approval of the urgent deficiency act

---

[1] The urgent deficiency act approved Jan. 25, 1915, provided $35,000 for this purpose.

CITRUS-CANKER INFECTIONS ON THE LEAVES, YOUNG WOOD, AND FRUIT OF GRAPEFRUIT.

CITRUS-CANKER INFECTIONS OF THE LIGHT-BROWN, SPONGY, RAISED
CHARACTER FOUND CHIEFLY IN WARM MOIST WEATHER, SHOWING
THE MORE FLATTENED DARK SPOTS FREQUENTLY FOUND DURING
THE WINTER OR COOL, DRY WEATHER.

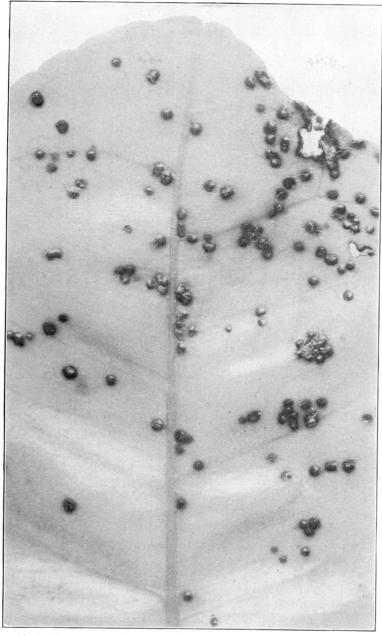

UPPER SURFACE OF PORTION OF GRAPEFRUIT LEAF ENLARGED 2½ DIAMETERS TO SHOW PROJECTING CHARACTER OF CITRUS-CANKER INFECTIONS.

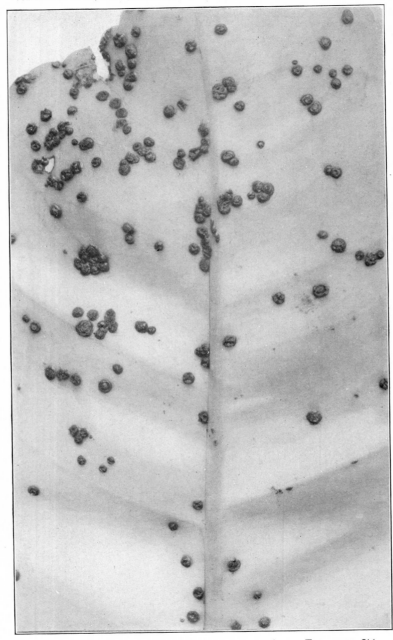

LOWER SURFACE OF PORTION OF GRAPEFRUIT LEAF ENLARGED 2½
DIAMETERS TO SHOW CHARACTER OF CITRUS-CANKER INFECTIONS.

of January 25, 1915, and shortly afterwards cooperative agreements for similar work were made with Alabama, Texas, Louisiana, and Mississippi.

Meantime the disease has been critically studied both in the laboratories of the Department of Agriculture and the State experiment stations, and its cause, though twice erroneously reported to be a fungus, has been definitely proved to be a bacillus new to science, which is apparently unable to infect plants other than the species of the genus Citrus or its close relatives. This new bacillus has been named *Pseudomonas citri.* The spots, or cankers, occurring on leaves, twigs, or fruit are not especially difficult to recognize. As shown in Plates LIX and LX, the cankers may vary from less than one-eighth to about one-fourth of an inch in diameter, and they may occur on green fruit (especially of lemon, grapefruit, and orange), on the bark (especially of young twigs), and upon leaves. By far the greater number of cases are found at first affecting only the leaves. The spots are reddish brown, raised slightly above the level of the healthy surface, and frequently are surrounded by a rather indistinct narrow yellowish zone. Leaves are especially characteristic, for, as shown in Plates LXI and LXII, the spots go clear through the leaf and are almost equally prominent on the upper and lower surfaces. They may be slightly mottled, and usually the older spots at least have broken through the thin outer layer or epidermis of the leaf. Before breaking through the leaf surface the cankers are smooth and almost waxy, but they afterwards have a corky appearance.

DRASTIC CONTROL MEASURES NECESSARY.

If spots or cankers fitting this description are found in any citrus grove, the owner of the property should at once take all possible precautions to avoid spreading the disease, lest it prove to be citrus canker. He should prohibit all visiting to that or adjacent groves, stop all cultivating or other work, and should send for a State specialist[1] to definitely determine the disease. If this is not possible, a few infected leaves may be picked off, wrapped in paper, sealed

---

[1] Aid may be requested from Wilmon Newell, Plant Commissioner, Gainesville, Fla.; G. C. Starcher, State Horticulturist, Auburn, Ala.; R. W. Harned, State Entomologist, Agricultural College, Miss.; E. Lee Worsham, State Entomologist, Atlanta, Ga.; J. B. Barrett, State Entomologist, Agricultural Experiment Station, Baton Rouge, La.; Ed. L. Ayers, Chief Nursery Inspector, Houston, Tex.

in a heavy envelope, and forwarded to State authorities or to the United States Department of Agriculture. After picking these infected leaves, the owner should thoroughly wash his hands in a disinfecting solution.

If a tree is found to be actually infected with citrus canker the wisest course to pursue is to burn it at once. Although this treatment is extremely severe, it is the only one which has been found practicable and effective in checking the spread of the disease. This method of eradication, first used in Florida in the autumn of 1914, has been adopted throughout the entire region where citrus canker has been found, and additional safeguards not at first recognized as necessary are now employed.

THOROUGH DISINFECTION PRACTICED.

Inspectors for citrus canker are required to wear suits similar to the overalls worn by thrashing crews or by garage mechanics, completely covering their usual clothes. Leggins and canvas hats are also required. These must be completely and thoroughly disinfected in a 1 to 1,000 solution of bichlorid of mercury before entering citrus properties and upon leaving citrus properties, and at the same time the inspectors must thoroughly disinfect their shoes, hands, and faces. The inspectors are instructed to avoid touching any citrus trees when inspecting them, though if it becomes necessary to move a limb in order to thoroughly inspect a tree, this can be done with especial precautions to avoid as far as possible the chances of spreading contagion from diseased spots as yet not visible to the naked eye. All apparatus taken into citrus groves, such as oil cans and special pumps for spraying oil or formalin, etc., must be thoroughly sprayed with disinfectants before being taken from the orchard. Upon finding infected trees, the ground under the tree should be sprayed thoroughly with a 5 per cent solution of formalin, and especially in properties where grove trees are of considerable size the spraying with a 1 per cent formalin solution of all apparently healthy trees adjacent to infected trees which are to be destroyed is advised.

These precautions are more extreme than have been found necessary in fighting any other plant disease, yet they are necessary on account of the extreme infectiousness or contagiousness of citrus canker; and partly because of this the success of the campaign for the eradication of citrus canker may be expected to establish a new era in preventive and control work in dealing with plant diseases.

THE SPREAD OF THE DISEASE.

There have been periods during which it has been impossible to continue work in all States because of occasional lack of funds.[1] As a whole, however, the campaign has been practically continuous up to the present time, and the distribution of the disease is not greatly different from what an experienced pathologist should have been able to predict from the circumstantial evidence more than a year ago. Knowing that infected nursery stock had been shipped into Texas in 1911, that suspected stock from Japan had at subsequent periods been shipped into other States, and that citrus stock exposed to infection in nurseries in each of the States concerned had been distributed, it is obvious that the disease must have been widely spread throughout the citrus-growing territory. As might have been expected, therefore, the more and more thorough inspections of the southern citrus territory showed that citrus canker was more widely distributed than the preliminary observations had indicated. Severe tropical storms during the two past seasons, in addition to the usual means of spreading the contagion, considerably increased the number of properties infected. Even at the worst, however, but a very small fraction of the citrus properties of the South have been infected, and those in California have escaped completely. Furthermore, the infected properties usually can be cleansed of the disease before many trees are lost.

The grapefruit, the orange, the lime, and the lemon are so readily infected with citrus canker that it does not appear probable that any method except that of complete destruction of all infected trees will serve to check the disease in any locality. With other varieties of citrus, and especially Satsuma oranges, it appears probable that the burning off of diseased leaves and branches, immediately followed by thorough spraying with strong disinfecting solutions, may arrest the spread of the disease, and careful

[1] Since the autumn of 1914 three Federal appropriations have been made for cooperative work for the eradication of citrus canker: $35,000 in the urgent deficiency act of Jan. 25, 1915; $300,000 in the urgent deficiency act of Feb. 28, 1916; and $250,000 in the agricultural appropriation act of Aug. 11, 1916. The State contributions, being often personal and local in their nature, are not in all cases completely recorded, but they are estimated to be $3,500 from Alabama, $300,000 from Florida, $2,000 from Georgia, $30,000 from Louisiana, and $11,000 from Texas; a grand total, from all sources, of $931,500.

and extensive tests of this modified plan are now under way. Even with Satsuma oranges it appears that the disease is almost uncontrollable if infected orange, grapefruit, or trifoliate orange plants are near by. Satsuma trees, on the other hand, frequently show the disease so slightly at first that the injuries are almost indistinguishable. Because of these facts, it is becoming obvious that in regions where citrus canker is appearing the attempt to grow these different varieties of citrus plants on the same property or even in the same general locality seriously jeopardizes the success of either variety.

ERADICATION CONTINGENT UPON CONTINUED EFFICIENT WORK.

The progress of the inspection and eradication work has been sufficiently encouraging during the past two seasons to give rise to the confident expectation of completely eradicating citrus canker from this country, provided effective work may be maintained constantly for a period of at least two or three years longer. All or practically all of the infected and suspected areas are known, and though it is impossible to find at once all dormant or undeveloped cases of canker, even in groves or nurseries where occasional diseased trees are found and burned, the number of infected trees appearing from month to month is decreasing, and the total number of infected trees during the past season was smaller than during the season before, especially in the commercially important orange and grapefruit regions.

The cost of conducting work of this character is very heavy; but, in view of the magnitude of the industry involved, the total sums expended to the present time represent but a small fraction of 1 per cent of the capitalized values that are threatened, and the continuation of the work appears to be both essential and well justified.

There remains always the hope that some less drastic method of combating citrus canker may be discovered, and therefore experiments are under way in different portions of the South carefully to test different methods of spraying and other treatments; it should at least be possible to develop spraying as an auxiliary method to a point where losses of trees from secondary infections may be negligible instead of forming as they now do a very considerable part of the loss caused by the spread of citrus canker.

THE PRACTICAL USE OF THE INSECT ENEMIES OF INJURIOUS INSECTS.

By L. O. HOWARD,

Entomologist and Chief, Bureau of Entomology.

INTRODUCTORY.

AMONG the many things which the Department of Agriculture has done for agriculture and horticulture in the United States, very few have been as spectacular and as immediately beneficial as the introduction of the Australian ladybird, or lady-beetle, from Australia in the eighties to destroy the white, fluted, or cottony-cushion scale, which at that time threatened the absolute extinction of the orange and lemon growing industry in California. The immediate and extraordinary success of this experiment attracted attention all over the civilized world, and, although it was followed by very many impractical and unsuccessful experiments of a similar nature, remains as the initial success in much beneficial work which since then has been carried on both in this country and in others.

The whole story of this work, and of later efforts of the same kind, has been told at length in Bulletin 91 of the Bureau of Entomology, published in 1911, but a competent résumé has never appeared in the Yearbook, and the retelling of it in more summary form will possibly prove of general interest.

THE AUSTRALIAN LADYBIRD AND THE FLUTED SCALE.

In the early seventies of the past century there appeared upon certain acacia trees at Menlo Park, Cal., a scale insect, which rapidly increased and spread from tree to tree, attacking apples, figs, quinces, pomegranates, roses, and many other trees and plants, but seeming to prefer orange and lemon trees. This insect, which came to be known as the white scale, or fluted scale, or the Icerya (from its scientific name), was an insignificant creature in itself, resembling a small bit of fluted white wax a little more than a fourth of

an inch in length. But when the scales had once taken possession of a tree they swarmed over it until the bark was
hidden; they sucked its sap through their minute beaks until
the plant became so feeble that the leaves and young fruit
dropped off, a black smut fungus crept over the young twigs,
and the weakened tree gradually died.

THREATENED EXTINCTION OF THE CALIFORNIA CITRUS INDUSTRY.

In this way orchard after orchard of oranges, worth a
thousand dollars or more an acre, was utterly destroyed, the
best fruit-growing sections of the State were invaded, and
ruin stared the fruit growers in the face. This spread was
rather gradual, extending through a series of years, and it
was not until 1886 that it was so serious as to attract national
attention.

In this year (1886) an investigation was begun by the
Department of Agriculture. Two agents of the Division of
Entomology, Messrs. D. W. Coquillett and Albert Koebele,
were sent to California to study the problem of remedies.
In the course of a year the complete life history of the insect
had been worked out and a number of washes had been discovered that, applied to the trees in the form of a spray,
would kill a large proportion of the pests at comparatively
slight expense (say from one-half to one-third of a cent per
gallon). It was soon found, however, that the average fruit
grower would not take the trouble to spray his trees, largely
from the fact that he had experimented for some years with
inferior washes and quack mixtures and from his lack of
success had become disgusted with the idea of using liquid
compounds; something easier, something more radical, was
necessary in his disheartened condition.

IMPORTATION OF THE AUSTRALIAN LADYBIRD AND ITS SPECTACU-
LAR SUCCESS.

Meantime, after much sifting of evidence and much correspondence with naturalists in many parts of the world, it
was decided by Prof. C. V. Riley, at that time Chief of the
Division of Entomology of the Department of Agriculture,
that the white scale was a native of Australia and had been
brought over to California accidentally upon Australian

plants. In the same way it was found to have reached South Africa and New Zealand, in both of which countries it had gradually increased and had become almost as great a pest as in California. In Australia, however, it did not seem to be abundant and was not known as a pest, which was assumed to be evidence of the fact that Australia was the native home of the species, and that there must exist there some natural check to its increase. It therefore became important to send a trained man to Australia to investigate this promising feature.

It happened at that time that the appropriation bill for the Department of Agriculture prohibited foreign travel, but it also happened that some appropriations had been made to the Department of State to provide for an exhibit from the United States which was to be held at an international exposition at Melbourne. So by arrangements with the Department of State and the United States commissioner to the Melbourne Exposition, Mr. Frank McCoppin of San Francisco, it was planned to send an expert assistant from the Division of Entomology to Australia to study the conditions of the fluted scale in regard to parasites and other natural enemies, his expenses being paid from exposition funds. Mr. Albert Koebele was chosen for this work. In order to justify this expenditure from exposition funds, the Department of Agriculture sent another agent, the late Prof. F. M. Webster, to prepare a report for the commission on the agricultural features of the international exposition.

Koebele proved to be an excellent choice. He was a skilled collector and the best man who could have been selected for this work. He at once found that Prof. Riley's supposition was correct—there existed in Australia small flies which laid their eggs in the fluted scales, and these eggs hatched into grubs which devoured the pests. He also found a remarkable little ladybird, a small, reddish-brown, convex beetle which breeds with marvelous rapidity and which, with voracious appetite and at the same time with discriminating taste, devours scale after scale, but eats fluted scales only and does not destroy other insects. This beneficial creature, now known as the Australian ladybird, or the Vedalia (fig. 8), was at once collected in large numbers, together with several other insects found doing the same work. Many hundreds of living specimens, with plenty of food, were packed in tin boxes and placed on ice in the ice box of the steamer at Sydney. They were carried carefully to California, where they were liberated upon orange trees already inclosed in gauze by Mr. Coquillett at Los Angeles.

The results more than justified the most sanguine expectations. The ladybirds reached Los Angeles alive, and, with appetites sharpened by the long ocean voyage, immediately fell upon the scales and devoured them one after another without rest. Their hunger temporarily satisfied, they began to lay eggs. These eggs hatched in a few days into active grublike creatures— the larvæ of the beetles — and these grubs proved as voracious as their parents; they devoured the scales right and left, and in less than a month transformed into beetles. And so the work of extermination went on. Each female

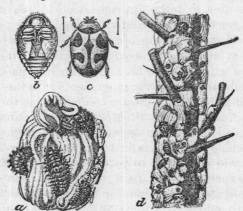

Fig. 8.—The Australian ladybird (*Novius cardinalis*), an imported enemy of the fluted scale: *a*, Ladybird larvæ feeding on adult female scale and its egg sac; *b*, pupa of ladybird; *c*, adult ladybird; *d*, orange twig, showing scales and ladybirds. *a–c*, Enlarged; *d*, natural size. (Marlatt.)

beetle laid on an average 300 eggs, and each of these eggs hatched into a hungry larva. Suppose that one-half of these larvæ produced female beetles, a simple calculation will show that in 5 months a single ladybird became the ancestor of 75 billions of other ladybirds, each capable of destroying very many scale insects.

Is it any wonder, then, that the fluted scale soon began to disappear? Is it any wonder that orchard after orchard was entirely freed from the pest, until in the course of less than 5 years hardly an Icerya was to be found in California? In fact, in less than a year from the time when the first of these hungry Australians was liberated from its box in Los Angeles the orange trees were once more in bloom and were resuming their old-time verdure. The Icerya had practically become a thing of the past.

The general effect of this extraordinary California success on the horticultural world at large was striking, but not wholly beneficial. Many enthusiasts, headed by certain Californians, concluded that it was no longer necessary to use insecticidal mixtures and that all that was necessary in order to eradicate any insect pest of horticulture or of agriculture was to send to Australia for its natural enemy. In fact, it is safe to say in a general way that, by blinding people to other and immediate measures of control, this success retarded the general warfare against injurious insects in the State of California.

The fact that the Vedalia preys only upon the fluted scale, and perhaps upon some very closely allied forms, was disregarded, and it was supposed by many fruit growers that it would destroy any scale insect. Therefore the people in Florida, whose orange groves were suffering from the long scale and the purple scale, sent to California for specimens of the Vedalia to rid their trees of these other scale pests. Their correspondents in California sent them specimens of the beetle in a box with a supply of the fluted scale for food. When they arrived in Florida the entire contents of the box were placed in an orange grove. The result was that the beneficial insects died and the fluted scale gained a foothold in Florida, a State in which it had never before been seen. It bred rapidly and spread to a considerable extent for some years and did an appreciable amount of damage before it was finally subdued.

On the other hand, the work of this predatory beetle in other parts of the world has been of the same successful character as that in California, wherever it has been introduced for the purpose of destroying the fluted scale or another species of the same genus. It was introduced into New Zealand, into South Africa, into Portugal, into the Hawaiian Islands, Italy, Syria, Egypt, and recently into the south of France, everywhere reducing the fluted scale from alarming numbers to practically none. In no case does it appear absolutely to have exterminated the fluted scale;

always a few are left, which sometimes multiply so as to necessitate a reintroduction of the Vedalia.

WHY THE AUSTRALIAN LADYBIRD WAS SUCCESSFUL.

It thus appears that in this ladybird beetle we have an almost perfect remedy against the fluted scale. There have been no failures in its introduction to any one of the different countries to which it has been carried. Its success has been more perfect than that of any other beneficial insect which has so far been tried in this international work, that which comes nearest to it being the introduction of the parasites of the cane leafhoppers into Hawaii, which will be referred to later. There are good reasons for this—rea-

sons which do not hold in the relations of many other beneficial insects to their hosts. In the first place, the Vedalia is active, crawls rapidly about in the larval state, and flies rapidly as an adult beetle, whereas the fluted scale is fixed to the plant, does not fly, and crawls very slowly when first hatched and later not at all. In the second place, the Vedalia is a rapid breeder and has at least two generations during the time in which a single generation of the scale insect is being developed. In the third place, it feeds upon the eggs of the scale insect;

Fig. 9.—The sugar-cane leaf-hopper (*Perkinsiella saccharicida*): Adult female. Much enlarged. (Kirkaldy.)

and in the fourth place, it seems to have no enemies of its own; and this is a very strange fact, since other ladybird beetles are destroyed by several species of parasites.

IMPORTATION OF BENEFICIAL PARASITIC INSECTS INTO HAWAII.

PARASITES OF THE SUGAR-CANE LEAFHOPPER.

We have just referred to the Hawaiian work in the introduction of parasites. About 1902 a leafhopper (fig. 9) was found upon the sugar cane in Hawaii. It appears to have been introduced with seed from Australia about 1898. It spread rapidly, and in 1903 damaged the crop to the extent of $3,000,000. An expert was sent that year to the United States to look for parasites. The next year this expert and another went to Australia, collected more than 100 species of parasites of leafhoppers, and, though failing with their first consignment, sent in cold storage, were successful with later shipments. The parasites reached Honolulu alive, were reared in confinement, and liberated in the cane fields. The year 1905 showed enormous loss from the leafhopper on many plantations. In 1906 certain of the parasites (see fig. 10) began to multiply very rapidly.

In 1907 one very large plantation, whose crop had dropped from 10,954 tons in 1904 to 1,620 tons in 1905 and to 826 tons

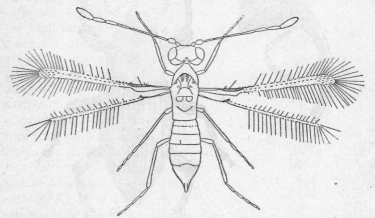

FIG. 10.—*Paranagrus optabilis,* a parasite of the sugar-cane leafhopper : Adult, highly magnified. (Perkins.)

in 1906, made the next year 11,630 tons, almost entirely as the result of the parasite introduction. In August, 1915, the writer visited Hawaii and found that the situation with regard to the sugar-cane leafhopper was almost perfect. The canes were not damaged in any respect so far as could be seen. The leafhoppers were still present, but in insignificant numbers. Where they had laid their eggs, these were almost invariably parasitized by one of the introduced parasites. There is, it is true, an occasional reappearance of the leafhoppers in numbers, following the destruction of the parasites by trash-burning, and, at the time of this visit, on one large plantation on the island of Hawaii 10,000 acres were so badly infested that a yield of only one-half a normal crop was expected. But such recrudescences as this are, and probably will be, fugitive.

A PARASITE OF THE SUGAR-CANE WEEVIL BORER.

Other results almost as valuable have been accomplished in Hawaii by the introduction of a fly which is a parasite of the sugar-cane weevil borer (fig. 11), an insect which tun-

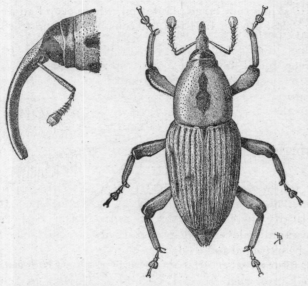

FIG. 11.—The sugar-cane weevil borer (*Rhabdocnemis obscurus*) : Adult weevil, from above; profile view of head and beak at left. Much enlarged. (Original.)

nels the canes and greatly reduces the crop. This parasitic fly was found in British New Guinea by Mr. F. Muir, an expert of the Sugar Planters' Association, and after much hardship and one failure it was successfully established in Hawaii with extraordinarily beneficial results.

This Hawaiian experience was described by Representative Mann in a speech made before Congress April 22, 1916, with the introductory remark, "I am going to narrate, very briefly, a fairy story"; but it was a true fairy story.

REASONS FOR THE SUCCESS OF THE HAWAIIAN WORK.

Here, again, there were good reasons for the striking success. The remote position of Hawaii and the simplicity of its native fauna—practically all of its pests having been introduced by commerce without their regular natural enemies and multiplying enormously on account of the very few native parasitic or predatory insects—account in part for the success, since in just the same way when natural enemies of imported pests are introduced they meet not only an absence of insects such as secondary parasites or native predatory species, but also find themselves in an equable climate permitting continuous breeding all the year round. As has been pointed out, the keen struggle for existence between the different native forms of insect life which is seen in continental lands is absent in these islands, and with introduced species the extreme simplicity of environment which they find is enormously favorable to their multiplication.

CONDITIONS UNDER WHICH THE PROBLEM IS SIMPLE AND EASY.

It follows, then, that with certain accidentally imported insects, nonfliers and attached to the same spot through practically their whole life, the introduction of active and more rapidly developing predators or parasites may reasonably be expected to be effective.

It follows, also, that injurious insects accidentally imported into such isolated islands as Hawaii in the north Tropics, which from their isolation have a very simple fauna, may be kept in check with some degree of certainty and with some degree of rapidity by the introduction, from their original home, of the parasites and natural enemies which there may have kept them in check.

WHY THE PROBLEM IS USUALLY COMPLEX AND DIFFICULT.

But with other kinds of injurious insects which have what is called a complete metamorphosis, and which may exist in the egg stage, in a crawling larval stage, in a quiescent pupal stage, and as a flying adult, and which in their native homes are parasitized by whole series of species of parasites, some attacking them in one stage and some in another, and still others in a third, it is not such a simple thing to introduce and acclimatize the parasites necessary to reconstitute the normal environment.

Moreover, in a great continental country like the United States, with its very old assemblage of insect forms of infinite variety, with its remarkable variations in climate, in altitude, in rainfall, we again have a much more complicated problem.

The original claim of the Californians, that you have only to send abroad for *the* parasite of any injurious insect to bring about its subjugation, is thus obviously erroneous. No trained entomologist would for a moment consider such a problem a simple one, except under conditions such as those described.

Hence it follows that with almost every accidentally introduced insect pest the problem of bringing in its natural enemies from its native home possesses very many factors which must be considered, and these factors differ with almost each kind of insect concerned. It is unwise and most unpromising to attempt heterogeneous and miscellaneous importations of parasites without careful study of the host insect on its home ground and in its natural environment throughout the whole range of its existence and a similar biological study of its parasites and natural enemies under such conditions.

IMPORTATION OF PARASITES OF THE GIPSY MOTH AND THE BROWN-TAIL MOTH.

Take the case of the gipsy moth and the brown-tail moth in New England, for example. Here we had two pests well known in Europe (the gipsy moth also being known in Japan) which had become accidentally established in New England and which multiplied and spread alarmingly. In their native homes entomologists had studied these insects in a way for many years. Many of their native parasites and other natural enemies had been recorded. It was well known that in ordinary years in their native homes 90 per cent of all that hatched were destroyed by these parasites and natural enemies. Hence, after the first effort to exterminate these insects before their spread had covered very many square miles had failed, owing to the stopping of appropriations by the State of Massachusetts, and the insects had again multiplied and spread over an area of nearly 4,000 square miles, it was considered to be a most promising operation to bring over from Europe and from Japan as many larvæ and pupæ of these insects as possible, with the certainty that a large percentage of them would contain parasites which, liberated upon American soil, would attack the gipsy-moth and brown-tail-moth larvæ and pupæ devastating the orchards and forests of New England. This was done, and by the wholesale, but with the distinct understanding that immediate beneficial results upon a noticeably gratifying scale could not be expected.

In varying numbers and with varying methods, the European and Japanese parasites of these two insects were imported every year from 1905 to 1913, further actual importation work being then interrupted by the great war. More than 30 species were imported during this time, and a number of the most important ones have been acclimatized and are rapidly spreading, and are at the present writing doing excellent work and in many localities destroying more than 50 per cent of the injurious insects. More than 18,000,000 individuals of the parasites have been colonized in parts of the infested area.

But this great experiment, extending over 11 years, has necessarily comprehended the methodical experimental study of all of the factors which affect the attempted acclimatization of species in a new environment, many of the characteristics of which are opposed to such naturalization. It has been, in the freely translated words of Dr. Paul Marchal, the eminent French biologist, " a gigantic biological analysis and synthesis bearing upon all the elements which constitute the harmonic groupings of plant-feeding insects, their predators, parasites, and hyperparasites—the taking apart piece by piece of the whole system, and its partial reconstruction in a new environment, forcing it to give the greatest possible stress to the elements most favorable to man and reducing to the minimum those which oppose their action."

DIFFICULTIES ENCOUNTERED IN THE WORK.

To indicate in a faint way some of the difficulties encountered and some of the fluctuations of hope and the contrary which came about from time to time, it will be only necessary to cite the experience with two of the imported species.

There exists in Japan an egg parasite of the gipsy moth, now known as the Schedius (fig. 12). The first specimens of this insect were reared from Japanese gipsy-moth eggs sent to this country in 1908, and others issued in April, 1909. They bred rapidly, laying their eggs in American gipsy-moth eggs (see fig. 13) brought into the laboratory,

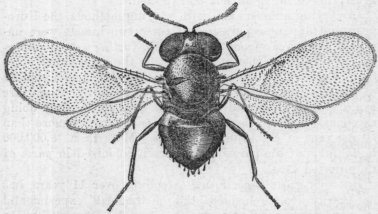

FIG. 12.—*Schedius kuvanae,* an egg parasite of the gipsy moth introduced from Japan : Adult female. Greatly enlarged. (Author's illustration.)

and on through the summer at the rate of one generation a month. By the first of the following year 1,000,000 individuals were present in the rearing cages in the field laboratory, and the following March the parasitized eggs were divided into 100 lots, each of which contained approximately 10,000 parasites, and were put out in colonies, while a large quantity of parasitized eggs remained and were placed in cold storage awaiting the appearance of fresh eggs of the gipsy moth in the latter part of the summer. This hope was vain, however, and when the eggs were taken from cold storage not a single living specimen remained. By the end of 1910 hopes of the survival of the species in the field were almost abandoned, but in spite of this the insect has finally accommodated itself to New England conditions and is breeding rapidly and spreading slowly from points where it succeeded in maintaining itself, and now exists by millions in regions infested with the gipsy moth.

Quite different was the experience with one of the European parasites, the *Parexorista cheloniae* (fig. 14), a species which exists also in America but which here does not seem to parasitize the brown-tail moth larva because it is apparently without defense against the poisonous barbed hairs of this caterpillar. On the other hand, in Europe this parasite is represented by a race, apparently identical with the American race, but which has become adapted to the brown-tail moth physiologically and there parasitizes it with impunity. Attempts were made, therefore, to introduce the European form. It was brought over and colonized by the thousands. In the following year numerous brown-tail moth caterpillars were found to have been parasitized by it, and great hopes were aroused. The year after, however, the condition of affairs was completely changed; the caterpillars were absolutely free from attack. Then the curious discovery

FIG. 13.—Egg masses of the gipsy moth. Enlarged. (Kirkland.)

was made that the imported European race and its first generation of descendants had hybridized with the American race and that the offspring had lost the immunization against the brown-tail moth poison. It therefore appeared that all efforts to acclimatize the European race would be useless, since, however great the number of individuals imported, the race would be absorbed by the American form. Possibly the American race may eventually acquire immunity, but, with the abundance of other food, this would be an enormously slow process.

GENERAL RESULTS ACHIEVED.

On the whole, the work has been very successful, and has helped in bringing about infinitely better conditions in New England so far as these pests are concerned, and, while it is practically certain that both gipsy moth and brown-tail moth will gradually spread westward, it is equally sure that the imported natural enemies will go with them, and that none of the long-continued disastrous outbreaks which we saw in Massachusetts in the years prior to 1905 will occur farther west.

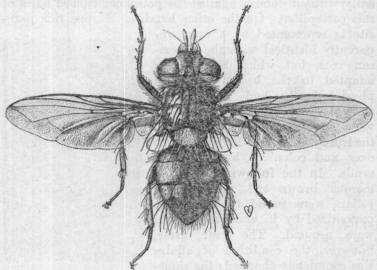

FIG. 14.—*Parexorista cheloniae*, a parasite of the brown-tail moth.   Greatly enlarged.   (Original.)

From all this it will appear that the practical handling of the natural enemies of injurious insects on the whole is by no means a simple rule-of-thumb operation. With a few species it can be done easily and with very perfect results; with other imported species it is a very complicated operation and will produce results which are palliative to a large degree, but by no means overwhelming in their effect.

INTRODUCTION OF THE PARASITE OF THE MULBERRY SCALE INTO ITALY.

Since the initial success with the Australian ladybird, literally hundreds of similar attempts have been made in different parts of the world. Some have met with a certain amount of success; others have been absolute failures. One of the most successful ones which may be mentioned incidentally is the importation from America and Japan into Italy of a minute parasite of the Diaspis scale insect which threatened the entire extinction of the mulberry trees and consequently of the silk industry in Italy. This little parasite (fig. 15), imported by Prof. Antonio Berlese, of Florence, and carefully reared and distributed, has brought about the approximate extinction of the scale insect throughout a large part of Italy. Here again, however, we had a fixed scale

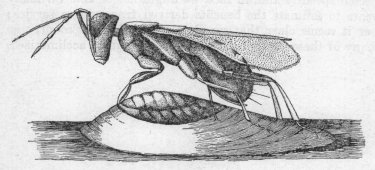

Fig. 15.—The parasite *Prospaltella berlesei* laying its eggs in a mulberry scale. Highly magnified. (Redrawn from Berlese.)

absolutely at the mercy of its imported natural enemy, which, at the same time, breeds naturally with greater rapidity than the scale insect.

OUTLOOK FOR THE BIOLOGICAL METHOD OF FIGHTING INSECTS.

There will be a very considerable development of this method of warfare against injurious insects in the future. It should be termed "the biological method of fighting insects," and, looking at the problem in a broad way, so far as this country is concerned, when we consider that more than one-half of our principal crop pests have been accidentally imported from other countries, there seems no reason why a systematic study of a very large number of parasitic and predatory insects native to the countries from which these pests were accidentally imported should not be made with a view of ultimate importation of all of them

into the United States. In fact, since there exist all over
the world beneficial insects, many of which can undoubtedly
be acclimatized here, and some of which will undoubtedly
prove of value to American agriculture, carefully planned
work should be begun looking to the ultimate increase of
our insect population by the addition of as many of these
beneficial forms as possible.

Of course this would mean a very great amount of careful
biological study in the countries of origin by men specially
trained in this sort of work, if results of value are to be
obtained. Strikingly beneficial results could not be expected speedily and, in fact, we might not be able for many
years to estimate the benefits derived from such a service;
but it seems clear that we should have in this country as
many of these surely beneficial forms as can be acclimatized.

STALLION LEGISLATION AND THE HORSE-BREEDING INDUSTRY.

By Charles C. Glenn,

Animal Husbandry Division, Bureau of Animal Industry.

PROGRESS in horse breeding has not kept pace with the progress made in many other agricultural lines. One of the principal causes of this condition has been the too general use of stallions lacking in quality and breeding and the failure on the part of owners of mares to appreciate fully the value of the sound, pure-bred sire of desirable conformation. The most successful horse breeders use such sires only, and they also give particular attention to the selection of mares, as unsound mares of poor conformation and breeding, as well as inferior stallions, are a hindrance to progress in horse breeding.

It is a deplorable fact that hundreds of farmers and mare owners have patronized the inferior stallion. They have failed to appreciate that a higher fee paid for the service of the sound, pure-bred stallion will be more than offset by the higher price received when the resulting colt is sold. Nor have they considered the fact that it costs as much to raise a mongrel as it does a high-grade or pure-bred.

Many States have aided the farmers by enacting legislation regulating the public service of stallions and jacks, with the prospect that there will be an ultimate improvement in the horses in the entire country. Farmers and mare owners can benefit themselves and add greatly to the efficiency of these laws by insisting on breeding their mares only to such stallions as will improve, rather than degrade, their stock.

REQUIREMENTS OF STALLION LEGISLATION.

In the State of Wisconsin a law regulating the public service of stallions and jacks became effective on January 1, 1906. Since that time 20 additional States have enacted legislation of a similar character. These States are: California, Colorado, Idaho, Illinois, Indiana, Iowa, Kansas, Michigan, Minnesota, Montana, Nebraska, New Jersey, New York, North Dakota, Oklahoma, Oregon, Pennsylvania, South Dakota, Utah, and Washington.

Wisconsin and a number of other States have amended their original laws, the object being to make them more effective and to give clearer classifications regarding licenses. Under the provisions of these laws certain standards and conditions must be met before a stallion or jack is permitted to stand for public service. These conditions vary somewhat. In some States certain diseases and unsoundnesses disqualify a stallion or jack for public service; in others, the stallion or jack is permitted to stand, but any unsoundness must be mentioned on the license certificate as well as on all posters, circulars, etc., used by the owner for advertising purposes.

The laws in most of the States require every stallion or jack claimed by the owner to be purebred to be registered in a studbook published by a society recognized by the State as authentic and reliable. Before a license is issued the certificate of registration and pedigree issued by one of these recognized societies, with an application for license and an affidavit certifying to the condition as regards soundness, must be presented to the State board or commission. All stallions and jacks for which such a certificate of registration from one of the recognized societies can not be produced are, if other conditions have been met, licensed as grade, crossbred, nonstandard-bred, mongrel, etc., and sound or unsound, according to the provisions of the law in the particular State.

Detailed information regarding these laws may be secured by addressing the officials in charge, whose names and addresses appear at the end of this article.

The figures shown in the several tables were compiled from reports furnished by the secretaries of the various stallion registration boards. These reports are not issued all at the same time of year, and the information given is taken from the last reports received.

Number of stallions, by breeds and classes, in 18 States.

State	Date	Belgian draft	Clydesdale	French draft	Percheron	Shire	Suffolk	Arabian	Cleveland Bay	French Coach	German Coach	Hackney	Morgan	Saddle	Standard-bred	Thoroughbred	Shetland pony	Welsh pony	Total pure-bred stallions	Grade stallions	Crossbred stallions	Mongrel stallions	Total stallions	Registered jacks	Unregistered jacks	Total jacks	Total stallions and jacks
California	July 31, 1915	104	18	35	336	50	2	3		7	27	3	3	9	109	11			712	272	2	350	1,336	114	181	295	1,631
Idaho	Nov. 15, 1915	50	11	18	204	53	2	2			4	3	2		27	1	1		357	432			789	4	50	54	843
Illinois	July 1, 1915	397	173	267	2,855	454	10	1	7	31	111	37	65	50	974	9	55	5	5,503	3,185	2		8,690				8,690
Indiana	Dec. 31, 1915	611	75	105	1,272	101	1	1	1	1	48	9	11	28	444	6	19		2,707	1,276	5	976	4,964	628	536	1,164	6,128
Iowa	...do...	944	332	516	3,185	523			6	18	54	18	55	34	624	6	53	5	6,367	2,686			9,053	233	589	822	9,875
Kansas	Oct. 1, 1915	201	38	294	2,038	88	2	6	6	18	37	9	25	28	416	6	53		3,224	1,360		1,151	5,735				5,735
Michigan	Sept. 1, 1915	196	69	36	664	46	2		3	1	12	7	8	2	172	8	10		1,213	398		275	1,886				1,886
Minnesota	Apr. 15, 1916	326	93	126	1,244	52	4		2	11	21	5	23	8	142	4		4	2,053	1,898			3,951				3,951
Montana	Dec. 31, 1915	75	24	51	488	61			6	8	6	4	4	8	39	3			767	423			1,190	9	2	11	1,201
Nebraska	July 1, 1914	339	82	270	1,586	273	12	1		6	31	3	4	6	233	14	1	1	2,852	2,213	1		5,065	96	1,061	1,157	6,222
New Jersey	1915	2	8		21						14	3	10	4	31				84	79			164	2	6	8	172
North Dakota	Dec. 31, 1915	207	117	84	1,037	161	6	2	2	3	14	3	3	4	84	3			1,602	608		757	2,967	14	58	72	3,039
Oregon	Nov. 1, 1915	92	52	21	312	55		3	1	3	31	2	10	10	72	5	3		670	284	2	232	1,188	24	100	124	1,312
Pennsylvania	Dec. 31, 1915	124	20	31	518	30			1	8	33	22	10		211	14	5		1,037	1,153			2,190	6	62	68	2,258
South Dakota	July 1, 1915	187	59	97	752	54	3			1	8	1	7	2	43	2	1		1,217	300		461	1,978	13	64	77	2,055
Utah	1915	31	14	9	104	23	3			4	2		3	3	17	9			219	63			282	7		7	289
Washington	July 1, 1914	100	13	31	318	94	3	3		6	16	3	3	3					584	534			1,118	18	83	101	1,219
Wisconsin	July 1, 1915	166	74	64	1,052	46	1	1		17	19	6	22	2	276	6	5	1	1,755	902	5	345	3,007	16	19	35	3,042
Total		4,152	1,272	2,055	17,986	2,164	61	7	19	142	477	134	249	167	3,914	87	158		32,923	18,066	17	4,547	55,553	1,184	2,811	3,995	59,548

The table on the preceding page shows the number of pure-bred stallions by breeds and the grades, crossbreds, and mongrels, as well as the registered and unregistered jacks, for those States from which these data were obtainable, the exceptions being Colorado, New York, and Oklahoma. No figures were received from Oklahoma, and those from Colorado give only the total number of licenses issued. Reference to these is made below. The law in New York became effective January 1, 1917. In some States a separate license is issued for nonstandard-bred stallions, and all these have been shown with the grades. This table shows the great popularity of the draft breeds, among which the Percheron

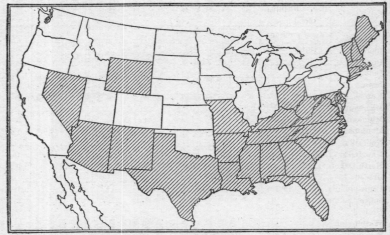

Fig. 16.—States in white have laws regulating the public service of stallions and jacks.

stands far in the lead, followed by the Belgian, Shire, French Draft, Clydesdale, and Suffolk in the order named. Of the light breeds the standard-bred stands practically alone.

In the two following tables, showing comparisons and percentages, only stallions have been considered. From the latest data received, 55,553 stallions are found to have been licensed for public service in all States having stallion license laws, excepting Colorado, New York, and Oklahoma. Of this number, 32,923, or 59 per cent, are pure-bred; 18,066, or 33 per cent, are grade; and 4,564, or 8 per cent, are crossbred and mongrel. Colorado reports only the total number of licenses issued, which was 1,430, jacks being included. Allowing a reasonable estimate for the number of jacks in this State, 56,000 stallions, in round numbers, are licensed for public service in all of these States, not including Oklahoma and New York. The distribution of the 55,553 stallions is given in the annexed table, with the percentage each class bears to the total number of stallions licensed.

Distribution of classes of stallions by States.

State.	Pure-bred.		Grade.		Crossbred and mongrel.		Total stallions.
	Number.	Per cent of total.	Number.	Per cent of total.	Number.	Per cent of total.	
California..........	712	53	272	21	352	26	1,336
Idaho..............	357	45	432	55	....	....	789
Illinois...........	5,503	63	3,185	37	2	....	8,690
Indiana...........	2,707	54	1,276	26	981	20	4,964
Iowa.............,	6,367	70	2,686	30	....	....	9,053
Kansas...........	3,224	56	1,360	24	1,151	20	5,735
Michigan..........	1,213	64	398	21	275	15	1,886
Minnesota.........	2,053	52	1,898	48	....	....	3,951
Montana...........	767	64	423	36	....	....	1,190
Nebraska..........	2,852	56	2,213	44	....	....	5,065
New Jersey........	84	51	79	49	1	....	164
North Dakota.....	1,602	54	608	20	757	26	2,967
Oregon............	670	56	284	24	234	20	1,188
Pennsylvania......	1,037	47	1,153	53	....	....	2,190
South Dakota.....	1,217	62	300	15	461	23	1,978
Utah..............	219	78	63	22	....	....	282
Washington.......	584	52	534	48	....	....	1,118
Wisconsin.........	1,755	58	902	30	350	12	3,007
Total........	32,923	59	18,066	33	4,564	8	55,553

ELIMINATION OF THE INFERIOR STALLION.

As has been indicated, prior to the enactment of these laws, stallions with every kind of breeding and affected with various diseases and unsoundnesses were standing for public service. The result was the production of a class of horses for which there was no demand.

It is well known that stallions of impure breeding lack the prepotency of the pure-bred and fail to stamp their offspring with breed characteristics and often even individual merit.

While it happens frequently that the size of the service fee, instead of the quality of the stallion, is the governing factor in deciding to what stallion a mare shall be bred, a lack of consideration, or knowledge, in the matters of soundness, breeding, and registration has been the cause for much of the patronage secured by the inferior stallion. Again, through misrepresentation on the part of some stallion owners many farmers have been deceived as to the true condition and breeding of a stallion. It is an almost invariable principle that like begets like, and breeders should not countenance the use of, nor support, sires lacking in those essentials necessary for the production of high-class horses.

It is not to be expected, however, that the unsound, inferior stallion will be eliminated quickly from breeding operations in this country. While it is generally agreed that their use should be stopped, the process of elimination must necessarily be gradual. There is, however, sufficient evidence that the demand for sound, pure-bred, registered sires is becoming more active. Among reasons for this may be mentioned the enactment of stallion legislation, which has caused all public service stallions to stand under their true colors as to breeding and soundness; the opportunity these laws give the farmer and mare owner to know exactly what a stallion is before either purchasing or breeding his mares; the publication of bulletins by the State agricultural colleges and experiment stations dealing with the problems of breeding, selection of sires, etc., and the assistance given by the officials in charge of the enforcement of the stallion license laws. Some of these State boards conduct bureaus of information, through which breeders may learn where desirable stallions of the various breeds may be safely purchased.

THE EFFECT OF STALLION LEGISLATION.

Perhaps the first and most important result of these laws is that they have made it possible for every farmer and mare owner to know exactly what a stallion is before breeding his mares, because stallion owners are compelled to represent their animals for just what they are.

They afford protection against false pedigrees and altered or forged certificates of registration, and benefit the owners of sound, pure-bred sires because they discourage the use of unsound, grade, and mongrel stallions.

The State authorities have found that hundreds of stallions that had been sold at high prices were either recorded in some unrecognized association or had been sold on altered certificates issued originally by reputable societies, the animals for which they had been issued having either died or been castrated, and thus there was created a practice of substitution that reached extensive proportions. These stallion laws now prevent a continuance of this practice when they are properly enforced.

The reports from the various State boards show that greater interest is being taken by farmers and mare owners in raising the standard of horses in their communities. A few instances will serve to show the beneficial effect resulting from this legislation.

In Idaho it has been found that many stallions brought into the State have been rejected and then shipped out to be sold elsewhere, that dealers are becoming more careful in their selection of stallions to be disposed of, and large numbers of breeders are buying pure-bred mares.

The report of the Illinois Stallion Registration Board for 1915 states that since the previous report 70 licensed stallions have been castrated and 146 sold to other States.

In Indiana the first year the law was in force 180 cases were found where certificates had been issued by societies not recognized by the law. Fortunately, however, in a number of instances the animals were found eligible to registration in recognized societies and pure-bred licenses eventually granted.

In 1909, prior to the enactment of the law, in the State of Kansas, over 2,000 grade and scrub stallions were advertised as pure-bred, while in 1915 not one such animal was so advertised.

In North Dakota the number of pure-bred stallions licensed has increased almost 50 per cent during the last 5 years, regardless of the fact that in the same period 242 stallions of pure breeding were refused licenses on account of unsoundness.

During the year 1915 in the State of Pennsylvania licenses were issued to 2,190 stallions, of which only 53 were reported as unsound.

In Wisconsin it is stated that horses are gradually improving in breeding, soundness, and quality. In 1906 the percentage of grade and scrub stallions licensed represented 60 per cent and the pure-breds 40 per cent, while in 1915 the grades and scrubs represented 42 per cent and the pure-breds had increased to 58 per cent.

A comparison with the year 1907, however, shows that from that time until 1915 the grades and scrubs have decreased from 65 per cent to 42 per cent, while the pure-breds have increased from 35 per cent to 58 per cent. These latter figures are considered more accurate in showing the results of the law, for the reason that all owners did not enroll their horses the first year.

Per cent of stallions in the several classes at dates of earliest and latest reports.

State and date.	Per cent pure-bred.	Per cent grade.	Per cent cross-bred and mongrel.	State and date.	Per cent pure-bred.	Per cent grade.	Per cent cross-bred and mongrel.
California:				New Jersey:			
July 30, 1912.....	42	18	40	Nov. 1, 1909.....	47	53	....
July 31, 1915.....	53	21	26	1915.....	51	49	....
Idaho:				North Dakota:			
Dec. 1, 1910......	40	60	....	Dec. 31, 1910......	43	57	....
Nov. 15, 1915....	45	55	....	1915.....	54	20	26
Illinois:				Oregon:			
Oct. 1, 1910......	55	45	....	May 20, 1912.....	58	25	17
July 1, 1915......	63	37	....	Nov. 1, 1915.....	56	24	20
Indiana:							
1914..............	53	27	20	Pennsylvania:			
1915	54	26	20	1908....	33	67	....
Iowa:				Dec. 31, 1915....	47	53	....
Jan. 1, 1913......	70	30	....	South Dakota:			
1915......	70	30	....	Sept. 1, 1910.....	52	16	32
Kansas:				July 1, 1915......	62	15	23
Oct. 1, 1910......	41	59	....	Utah:			
1915......	56	24	20	June 30, 1909.....	73	27	....
Minnesota:				1915.....	78	22	....
Apr. 1, 1908......	39	61	....	Washington:			
Apr. 15, 1916.....	52	48	....	July 1, 1912......	58	42	....
Montana:				1914......	52	48	....
Nov. 1, 1910......	61	39	....	Wisconsin:			
Dec. 31, 1915.....	64	36	....	Nov. 1, 1906.....	40	60	....
Nebraska:				July 1, 1915......	58	30	12
July 1, 1912......	49	51	....				
1914......	56	44	....				

The figures given in the table above show the percentage of increase or decrease in pure-breds and grades and mon-

FIG. I.—AN UNSOUND MONGREL STALLION.

One patronized because of the cheap service fee.   Now retired from service.

FIG. 2.—A GRADE TROTTING-BREED STALLION UNFIT FOR BREEDING
PURPOSES.

Courtesy of Wisconsin Experiment Station.

FIG. 1.—ANOTHER ILLUSTRATION OF AN UNSOUND GRADE STALLION.

Lack of patronage finally caused him to be retired from service. Courtesy of Wisconsin Experiment Station.

FIG. 2.—A GRADE PERCHERON STALLION THAT SERVED 80 MARES IN ONE SEASON.

His colts were raised at practically the same cost as pure-bred colts could have been reared. Courtesy of Wisconsin Experiment Station.

FIG. I.—GOOD TYPE OF TROTTING-BRED STALLION.

A sound horse and a safe sire for farmers desiring to breed horses of general purpose type.

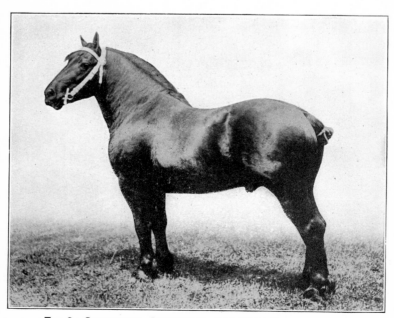

FIG. 2.—CHARACTER, SOUNDNESS, AND GOOD CONFORMATION.

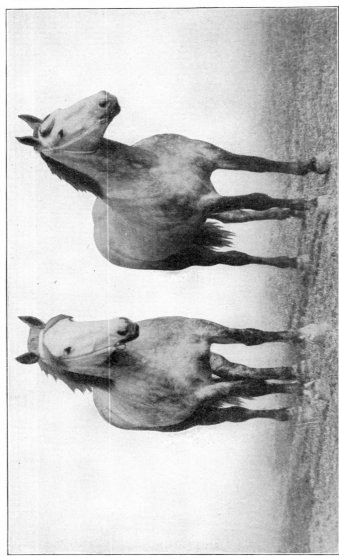

KEEP ONLY THE BEST MARES AND BREED THEM TO SOUND, PURE-BRED STALLIONS OF THE SAME BREED.

grels, the first report received from each State being compared with the last report received, with the exception of Iowa. The original law in this State became effective March 30, 1907, but as owners of grade stallions were not required to secure certificates of soundness until 1912 the figures for the latter year have been used for the purpose of comparison. In 1908 there were 4,491 pure-bred licenses issued. Therefore, the increase in the number of pure-breds in 1915 over 1908 is 42 per cent. In connection with this table it is explained that in some States the original laws did not provide for mongrel licenses, while the amended laws include this classification. It is proper, therefore, to assume that many stallions were licensed as grades under the original acts, although in reality nothing more than scrubs. Thus the percentage of grades and mongrels licensed in those States, as shown by the last reports, should be added together in order that a proper comparison may be made with the first reports, which did not call for mongrel licenses.

In Oregon, in 1915, while the figures show a slight decrease in the percentage of pure-breds and an increase in the percentage of grades and mongrels, the report shows 54 more pure-bred licenses issued than in 1914, and 22 less mongrels, there being a change of but one in the number of grades. This indicates that breeders are becoming better acquainted with the purpose of the law and that pure-bred stallions are taking their rightful place as the sires of Oregon's horses.

In Washington the number of pure-bred stallions licensed in 1914 increased 154, or 36 per cent, over the number in 1912, while the grades increased 227, or about 74 per cent. This seems to indicate that when the law became effective not all owners of grade stallions applied for licenses, and the further probability that leniency was shown in enforcing the law the first year.

However, the general increase in pure-breds and decrease in grades and mongrels is an indication that there is a gradual but continued improvement in the quality of stallions being used in these States. It indicates also that breeders are becoming more particular and better informed in the matters of soundness, breeding, and registration, and that owners of stallions who at first were, in some instances, inclined to oppose, are now aiding in the enforcement of the provisions of the laws.

It would be interesting to know just what is becoming of the unsound, grade, and mongrel stallions. It is indicated in the reports from the various States that as the patronage of these inferior sires decreases they are either castrated or shipped out, in most cases undoubtedly into States which have no law compelling them to stand under their true condition as to soundness and breeding, and where it is possible for them to continue their destructive influence upon the horse industry.

It is in these States that breeders should exercise the greatest caution before deciding to which stallion they will breed their mares. They should demand of the stallion owner that they be permitted to examine the certificate of registration and pedigree in order to learn whether the animal is properly registered in a reliable studbook, also whether the age, color, and description agree with the stallion whose service is being considered and whether the certificate has been altered or tampered with in any way. If the certificate has been changed or does not agree with the stallion, it is evident that something is wrong, and it will be much wiser to refuse the service of the stallion than to accept it, pay the fee, and run the risk of getting a nondescript foal, expensive to raise and for which there will be a poor market. It is imperative, therefore, that the breeders in these States should be protected. With no legislation governing the sale or public service of stallions, such States undoubtedly will receive unsound, grade, and nondescript horseflesh driven out of States that have properly and wisely safeguarded the interests of their horse breeders and farmers by enacting stallion legislation.

If a breeder is not familiar with pedigrees and registration societies, he should consult the State stallion registration board or his State agricultural college, giving all facts regarding the stallion whose service is being considered. In this way much information may be secured that will be of value in the future when the question of breeding comes up.

For the convenience and information of those interested, a list of the various State stallion registration boards or commissions follows, with the names and addresses of the officials in charge, to whom all inquiries regarding the various State laws should be addressed:

California, Charles W. Paine, secretary, Stallion Registration Board, Sacramento.

Colorado, E. McCrillis, secretary, State Board of Stock Inspection Commissioners, Denver.

Idaho, H. G. Bodle, State veterinarian, Live Stock Sanitary Board, Boise.

Illinois, B. M. Davison, secretary, Stallion Registration Board, Springfield.

Indiana, H. E. McCartney, secretary, Stallion Enrollment Board, La Fayette.

Iowa, A. R. Corey, secretary, Stallion Registration Division, Department of Agriculture, Des Moines.

Kansas, C. W. McCampbell, secretary, State Live Stock Registry Board, Manhattan.

Michigan, Judson Black, secretary, State Veterinary Board, Richmond.

Minnesota, J. S. Montgomery, assistant secretary, Stallion Registration Board, University Farm, St. Paul.

Montana, C. N. Arnett, secretary, Stallion Registration Board, Bozeman.

Nebraska, J. S. Anderson, secretary, Live Stock Sanitary Board, Lincoln.

New Jersey, F. C. Minkler, secretary, Live Stock Commission, New Brunswick.

New York, commissioner of agriculture, Albany.

North Dakota, E. J. Thompson, secretary, Stallion Registration Board, Agricultural College.

Oklahoma, W. L. Fowler, secretary, Oklahoma Live Stock Registry Board, Stillwater.

Oregon, Carl N. Kennedy, secretary, Stallion Registration Board, Corvallis.

Pennsylvania, Live Stock Sanitary Board, Harrisburg.

South Dakota, A. E. Beaumont, secretary, Live Stock Sanitary Board, Pierre.

Utah, W. E. Carroll, secretary, State Board of Horse Commissioners, Logan.

Washington, H. T. Graves, acting commissioner of agriculture, Olympia.

Wisconsin, A. S. Alexander, Department of Horse Breeding, University of Wisconsin, Madison.

A national association has been formed which is composed of representatives of the foregoing boards. The name of this organization is the National Association of Stallion Registration Boards, of which Prof. J. S. Montgomery is the secretary, with office at University Farm, St. Paul, Minn.

IMPORTANCE OF DEVELOPING OUR NATURAL RESOURCES OF POTASH.

By Frederick W. Brown,
*Assistant in Charge Investigation of Fertilizer Resources,
Bureau of Soils.*

GERMANY'S monopoly of the potash trade in time of peace and the abrupt cessation of all shipments with the beginning of hostilities in Europe emphasize the urgency of immediate development of American sources of one of the most valuable of chemical fertilizers. Within the last 70 years there has been a rapid development in the use of chemicals—nitrogen, phosphorus, and potassium—for inducing increased crop yields. Before the war there were 100 companies mining potash in Germany. More than 90 per cent of their enormous product was used for agricultural purposes. German producers of potash are combined in a syndicate under supervision of the Government. The Government fixes the minimum price for which it may be sold and limits the quantity that may be exported. In recent years the United States has taken one-fifth of the entire output of the German mines and one-half of all allowed to be exported. In 1913 this country bought about 1,000,000 tons, nearly all of which was used for fertilizer purposes. In common with the rest of the world, the United States has been dependent upon Germany; to what extent is shown by the fact that in December, 1913, muriate of potash sold here for $39 a ton and was quoted at $500 in December, 1915, with only small lots available.

Before the development of the German mines in the early seventies of the last century potash was derived largely from seaweed and by leaching wood ashes, and the supply, necessarily limited, was principally consumed in the arts. With the development of the German supply, however, the use of potash as a fertilizer ingredient has increased steadily.

There is no question of the general value of commercial fertilizers in farm practice. The farmer who wisely and systematically applies commercial fertilizer to his fields will raise larger and better crops than his neighbor who, with similar conditions of soil, climate, and rotations, and equal industry applied to cultivation, does not use fertilizers. This statement applies with the same force to the rich soils of the Mississippi Valley as to the soils of the eastern cotton States or of New England. Moreover, an analysis of the fertilizer investigations carried on by experiment stations in this country and abroad brings out the significant fact that, generally speaking, the use of a complete fertilizer—that is, one containing all three elements—gives larger returns than the use of one containing either one or two of the fertilizer ingredients.

An ample supply of potash has therefore in the last half century become an agricultural necessity. This is particularly true of certain large sections of this country where the soils are of such a character that profitable crops can be raised only when liberal applications of fertilizing ingredients are added, or where special crops are grown under a system of intensive agriculture. Throughout the cotton States, the tobacco-growing regions, the trucking sections of the Atlantic States, and in citrus-fruit and potato-growing regions the heavy application of commercial fertilizers, including potash, is now a recognized agricultural practice. With these conditions existing, it becomes evident that an adequate and reliable supply of potash has become necessary if American agriculture is to advance to meet the growing needs of increasing population.

Up to the stoppage of all shipments the German supply of potash has been adequate, but these mines are not inexhaustible, and a time will come when Germany will see the need of conserving her diminishing supply of this agricultural necessity for the use of her own farmers. When this time comes, either another source must have been found or American agriculture must suffer.

In recent years a number of possible sources of American potash have been brought to public attention. For convenience of treatment here they may be grouped into three classes—trade wastes, natural deposits, and kelp.

There are a number of industries in this country handling materials from which potash may be recovered as a by-product. Until recently little effort has been made to effect such recovery, and large amounts of potash have been allowed to escape into the air or to run off with waste waters.

CEMENT MANUFACTURE.

One of the more important sources of potash from such trade wastes occurs in connection with the cement industry. Throughout the country exist deposits of feldspar and other silicates containing potash. This potash, however, is in an insoluble form, and the containing rock must undergo treatment before the potash is liberated in a form to be taken up by the soil water and used by plants.

It seems unlikely that any process will be developed which will make it commercially profitable to treat the rock for the potash alone and discard the residue. The Bureau of Soils pointed out, however, some years ago, that the potash-containing silicates might be used in the cement industry and the potash saved as a by-product. It has been demonstrated in recent years that this procedure is entirely practicable through the installation of electrical precipitators in the flues of cement mills. One company has had this installation in operation for several years, and several other large mills are installing apparatus for the same purpose. In this process the combined insoluble potash contained in the clay used in cement manufacture is released and rendered soluble under the high temperature of the cement kiln and passes off with the dust in the stack, where it is caught and thrown down by electric precipitators. A large percentage of the potash contained in the raw mix is recovered in this way; and while the initial installation of the precipitators is somewhat expensive, the cost of operation is very small. If, therefore, the raw mix going into the cement kilns contains a sufficient percentage of potash, the process, even under normal conditions in the potash market, will pay an excellent return on the investment.

It may be of interest to state that the process was perfected with the object of abating the nuisance caused by the escape of fumes and dust from a cement mill and the consequent injury to citrus groves at Riverside, Cal. Cement mills so situated that the fumes and dust from their stacks constitute a nuisance to surrounding property may find it advisable to install the apparatus, even though the returns from the potash collected would not of themselves justify the expenditure.

Since 85,914,907 barrels of cement were produced in this country in 1915, this appears at present a very promising source of a domestic supply of potash.

BLAST FURNACES.

Similarly there is the possibility of a large supply of potash as a by-product of blast-furnace operations. Blast-furnace gas contains varying percentages of potash. In ordinary practice this gas is cleaned by passing it through dust catchers and washers and is then available for use in the stoves for heating the air used in the blast and under steam boilers. Recent practice has found a further use for the gas in operating gas engines, but for this purpose it must be further cleaned by passing it through secondary washers.

At present a small proportion of the potash which escapes from blast furnaces is collected in the stoves and boilers, but the greater part is lost in the wash waters or escapes from the flues. Moreover, the presence of potash fumes remaining in the gas as it comes from the primary washers is probably responsible for the condition so troublesome to furnace operators known as " smoky gas."

An experiment recently conducted by one of the largest steel mills of the country has shown that this necessary operation of cleaning the gas can be accomplished more satisfactorily and probably more economically by means of electrical precipitation than by the methods now used. In addition to furnishing a more effective cleaning of the gas, such an installation would recover practically all the potash.

This appears to be an important potential source of potash, as the aggregate amount now volatilized and lost in the blast furnaces of the country is very large. Efforts are now being made by the Bureau of Soils to determine this amount with some degree of accuracy.

WOOL WASTES.

Among the impurities contained in wool as it comes from the sheep, which must be removed before the wool can be used by the spinner, is a material called " suint." This really

FIG. I.—FRONT VIEW OF HARVESTER CUTTING KELP, SHOWING CONVEYER.

FIG. 2.—KELP HARVESTER, SHOWING GENERAL CONSTRUCTION.

FIG. 3.—BARGE OF HARVESTED KELP.

is the dried sweat of the sheep. It is soluble in water, and consists principally of potash salts. In addition to suint, crude wool also contains grease, and any process for recovering potash from wool must include the recovery of the grease also to be commercially profitable. Wool grease is used for dressing leather and for lubricating purposes, and is also the source of the very valuable lanolin compounds used in pharmaceutical preparations.

Probably the best method of wool scouring is called the "solvent process," and recovers the grease and suint separately. The wool is treated with a volatile solvent (gasoline, naphtha, or carbon disulphide) which removes the grease, and is then washed in warm water to extract the suint. The solution of wool grease then is distilled, in which operation the solvent passes off and is recovered for further use, and the grease is left as a residue. The solution of suint is evaporated and calcined for its potash.

In 1914 about 290,000,000 pounds of raw wool were produced in this country, and about 220,000,000 pounds were imported.

The potash content will average about $4\frac{1}{2}$ per cent of the weight of the crude wool, so that approximately 11,500 tons of potash might have been recovered from the wool scoured in the United States in that year. The Bureau of Soils is investigating the problem of extracting potash from wool in the hope of demonstrating its commercial feasibility.

WOOD WASTES.

The wood-using industries of the country produce a large amount of sawdust annually, and much of this is used as fuel in the furnaces of the plants. It is probable that much of the wood ashes so produced is now used for fertilizer purposes and to this extent serves as a source of potash. So much as is not so used should be, or should be leached for the recovery of potash salts. Wood ashes vary widely in their potash content, this variation being dependent on the species and on the part of the tree from which the wood is taken. It is impracticable, therefore, to estimate the amount of potash which might be derived from this source, but that it would come to several thousand tons is certain.

Many farmers use wood for fuel, and anyone so situated has at hand a source of potash which should be carefully saved. While the amount so secured by an individual necessarily will be small, in the aggregate a considerable saving would result. If home mixing of fertilizers is practiced, wood ashes should not be mixed with other ingredients, but should be applied to the soil separately, as the lime in the ashes has a tendency to liberate the nitrogen in certain other fertilizer constituents if mixed with them.

NATURAL DEPOSITS.

So far the extensive investigations of the Bureau of Soils and the Geological Survey have not disclosed any deposit of potash salts in this country comparable in extent or commercial importance with the German deposits. Such sources of potash salts as have come to light are confined to the desert basins of the West and are very small in extent. While some of these may become of local importance, the total potash which can reasonably be expected from them is too small to affect the situation beyond a limited area contiguous to the mines. It is, however, always possible that borings put down for water, oil, gas, or for any purpose may disclose the existence of such salts. This is true particularly in regions where rock-salt deposits are known to exist. It is highly desirable, therefore, that persons engaged in boring operations have this possibility always in mind and carefully examine all material brought up by the drill. The Bureau of Soils of the Department of Agriculture will analyze, free of charge, any samples of this kind which may be submitted.

NEBRASKA CARBONATE LAKES.

In western Nebraska there are a number of small lakes or ponds whose waters contain considerable quantities of potassium carbonate. These lakes are now being worked, and carbonate of potash containing about 28 per cent K_2O is being marketed. The public statement was recently made by the American representative of the German syndicate that these Nebraska lakes were furnishing about half the potash now being produced in the country.

In working these lakes, brine is pumped to the mill, where it is evaporated down to wet salts in vacuum pans. These wet salts are then passed through rotary driers, and are ready for shipment.

While the size of these lakes precludes the possibility of their ever furnishing a large supply of potash, it is to be hoped that the operators will succeed in perfecting their processes so as to be able to continue production upon a return to normal conditions.

ALUNITE.

In the south-central part of Utah, near Marysvale, there is a large deposit of the mineral alunite, an aluminum-potassium sulphate, from which potassium sulphate and alumina may be extracted after roasting at moderate temperatures. The technical difficulties of extraction are not serious, and in time alunite should become a valuable source of potash for the country. That the mines can be worked commercially for the potash alone is doubtful, however. The deposits occur in mountainous country, necessitating the construction of expensive tramways to bring the ore to the mill, and, once extracted, the potash salts must be carried east by rail, entailing heavy freight costs. Therefore a market must be found for the alumina as well as the potash.

Under the abnormal conditions brought about by the European war two companies have entered this field, and sulphate of potash from alunite actually has been shipped. It is doubtful if these companies could continue operating on their present systems under normal conditions and with potash selling at the figures quoted before the war. That many millions of tons of potash may be derived from this source, however, when the problems now confronting the operators have been solved, seems reasonably certain.

SEARLES LAKE.

A brine deposit in the Desert Basin area probably will prove of some importance as a commercial source of potash. This is the so-called Searles Lake, in California, a body of mud and crystalline salt, some 12 square miles in area and of undetermined depth. Beneath the surface are saline muds and sands saturated with brine which contains 7 per cent of potash. Recently it was announced that the persons claiming title to the property would proceed at once to exploit it commercially. So far, however, potash from this source has not been produced in any quantity. That Searles Lake brine ultimately will prove a valuable source of soluble potash seems highly probable. It has been estimated that it will furnish at least 4,000,000 tons of potassium chloride, and probably considerably more.

GREAT SALT LAKE.

The waters of Great Salt Lake and other natural brine bodies contain potash in small proportions. No method has been devised by which the potash may be recovered at a price which will permit competition with German salts. It is possible that such a method may be discovered, however, in which event a source of potash will be opened large enough to supply this country's needs for many years.

KELP.

Along the Pacific coast of North America, from Magdalena Bay, in Lower California, to the Shumagin Islands of the Alaskan Peninsula, are found beds of giant kelp of several species. These huge sea plants, sometimes growing to a length of 100 feet, contain a surprising amount of potash salts. Dried kelp of the most important species will run from 25 to 30 per cent of potassium chloride. At present these Pacific kelps appear to be one of the most hopeful sources of an adequate supply of potash for the country's needs. The realization of this hope is, however, like most new enterprises, beset with difficulties.

The beds are located close inshore, almost all of them being, in fact, within the 3-mile limit. The kelp is harvested by cutting the upright stem from 3 to 6 feet below the surface, which secures not only that portion but also the much larger portion which floats on the surface of the water. The wet kelp contains from 85 to 93 per cent of water. This must be removed. The plants are nonfibrous and of a gummy, gelatinous nature, making it difficult, if not impossible, to extract the water by pressure.

Several methods have been suggested for treating these kelps on a commercial scale with a view to their utilization for fertilizer purposes. The simplest is to dry and grind the material and market this ground product for direct application to the soil or for mixing in commercial fertilizers.

The drying can be accomplished in rotary driers such as are used for treating garbage and fish refuse, and the dried, ground kelp contains 25 per cent potassium chloride, 2 per cent nitrogen, and organic matter of value for improving the physical condition of many soils by the formation of humus. In addition, it possesses excellent mechanical properties for fertilizer-mixing purposes.

If the kelp grew on the eastern seaboard, close to the regions of large fertilizer demand, this method of treatment probably would be the most economical and satisfactory. Unfortunately, however, the kelp occurs on one side of the country and fertilizers are most extensively used on the other; and while the dried, ground kelp will have the benefit of water rates of transportation via the Panama Canal, about three-fourths of the material so transported consists of practically valueless matter, and the freight charges probably would prove too heavy an item to permit this method of utilization in the face of competition with German importations. Investigations are now being made in the hope of transplanting the Pacific kelps to the Atlantic coast. If this should be accomplished and the plants established in extensive beds, dried, ground kelp undoubtedly would become an important factor in the fertilizer situation.

Another process which is now being used is to burn the dried kelp and market the ash for its potash content. By this process the valuable nitrogen content is volatilized and lost, and a small part of the potash content is similarly destroyed. The heat produced in the combustion is also wasted. In addition, freight charges must be paid on worthless ash, and it is admitted by the companies now using the process that unless further economies are introduced the costs are too great for successful operation under normal conditions.

The process which seems most likely to succeed in commercial practice is to distill the dried kelp in retorts constructed on the general principle of the by-product coke oven. This results in a charred residue, containing all the potash salts, which may then be recovered by leaching and evaporation. In the process of distillation the nitrogen in the kelp is driven off and recovered in the form of ammonia; combustible gas is evolved in considerable quantities and is available for use as fuel in the retorts and under the evaporating vats, and charcoal and tarry products are recovered, which may be sold or used as fuel. Iodine and some other by-products also may be recovered.

It is probable that some such method of extraction which will conserve and use the heat units evolved in the reaction and save the by-products will prove necessary in the end to make the recovery of potash from kelp a profitable industry under normal conditions.

Since the beginning of the war and the stoppage of German potash shipments several large and responsible companies have erected plants on the southern California coast for the treatment of kelp. These companies are producing either dried, ground kelp, which at present prices for potash can be shipped East at a profit despite the long freight haul, or kelp ash, which results from burning the dried kelp. One of the companies is using a fermentation process and producing acetone for munition purposes, as well as high-grade potash salts.

However, with the development and demonstration of an economical method of extraction, an American potash industry should grow up on the Pacific coast which will furnish from these giant kelps a supply of high-grade potash salts adequate for all our needs. The Bureau of Soils is at present erecting an experimental plant at Summerland, Cal., to determine the best methods of extraction. Since most of the beds lie within the 3-mile limit, State legislation by the States of California, Oregon, and Washington, and Federal legislation as regards Alaska, is needed to provide protection against reckless and indiscriminate cutting and to furnish leasing regulations under which the private investor who desires to erect a plant for treating kelp may be assured of a supply of raw material free from encroachment by competitors. Efforts are now being made to secure action of this kind by the legislatures of the States interested and by the Federal Congress.

It will be seen from the foregoing that there are in this country a number of important sources of potash salts, and that, owing to the conditions brought on by the European war, these sources are in a way to be developed on a scale which offers hope that the American farmer and manufacturer may, in the not distant future, be made independent of foreign monopoly for supplies of potash.

COOPERATIVE BULL ASSOCIATIONS.

By JOEL G. WINKJER,
Dairy Division, Bureau of Animal Industry.

WHAT THE COOPERATIVE BULL ASSOCIATION IS.

COOPERATIVE bull associations are formed by farmers for the joint ownership, use, and exchange of high-class, pure-bred bulls. In addition they may encourage careful selections of cows and calves, introduce better methods of feeding, help their members market dairy stock and dairy products, intelligently fight contagious diseases of cattle, and in other ways assist in lifting the dairy business to a higher level. Incidentally, the educational value of such an organization is great.

CONSERVATIVE BUT STEADY GROWTH.

Cooperative bull associations have existed in Denmark since 1874, and in 1906 the number there had grown to 1,095, with a total membership of 26,200, owning 1,369 dairy bulls. In the United States the first cooperative bull association of which record exists was organized in 1908 by the Michigan Agricultural College. On July 1, 1916, there were 32 active bull associations in this country, with a total membership of 650, owning about 120 pure-bred bulls. The following tabulation shows the gradual but constant growth of bull associations in the United States up to the present.

Statement showing growth of cooperative bull associations in the United States to July 1, 1916.

State.	1908	1909	1910	1911	1912	1913	1914	1915[1]	1916
Michigan	1	4	7	6	10	15	15	14	14
Minnesota		1	1	1	1	2	2	2	3
North Dakota					1	2	1	1	1
Maryland					1	1	1	1	1
Vermont							1	1	1
Wisconsin							1	1	1
Connecticut								1	1
Maine								1	1
Oregon									1
Oklahoma									1
Iowa									1
South Carolina									3
Massachusetts									1
North Carolina									1
Illinois									1
Total	1	5	8	7	13	20	21	22	32

[1] In the 22 associations there were 540 members owning 3,600 cows and 90 bulls.

The history of the cooperative bull association shows that it is especially adapted to small herds where a valuable bull for each herd would constitute too large a percentage of the total investment. Thus the organization enables even the owners of small herds to unite in the purchase of one good bull and each to own a share in a registered sire of high quality. Though still in its infancy, the cooperative bull association movement promises eventually to become a very great factor in the improvement of our dairy cattle.

BETTER AND FEWER BULLS.

The typical cooperative bull association, as organized in this country, is composed of 15 to 30 farmers, and jointly owns 5 bulls, divides its territory into 5 " breeding blocks," and assigns 1 bull to each block. As many as 50 or 60 cows may belong to the farmers in each block, and the bull in the block should be kept on a farm conveniently situated. The blocks are numbered from 1 to 5, and to prevent inbreeding each bull is moved to the next block every 2 years. If all the bulls live, and if all are kept until each has made one complete circuit, no new bulls need be purchased for 10 years. In this way, by paying only a small part of the purchase price of one bull, each member of the association has the use of good pure-bred bulls for many years. Ordinarily the purchase price and the expense of supporting the bulls are distributed among the members of the association according to the number of cows owned by each.

A concrete example of a successful association is the Cooperative Holstein Bull Association at Roland, Iowa (fig. 17), which is composed of 16 farmers and is organized into 5 blocks. The farms are so situated that the bulls are at no great distance from the farm of any member. Before the association was formed each farmer had an average investment of $92 in a scrub bull. These bulls were disposed of when the association was formed and 5 pure-bred bulls were bought at $240 each, or an average of $75 for each member. A larger membership would reduce expenses still further. As in other associations, the Roland farmers united in the use of one breed and selected good bulls of that breed.

An advanced step which has not yet been taken by any association is the purchase of an exceptionally good bull to

mate with the best cows in the herds of every block. Such a
plan for improvement of the better cows of the herd is
applicable to pure-bred herds as well as grade herds.
For the pure-bred herd the cooperative bull association undoubtedly will do as much as for the grade herd, because it

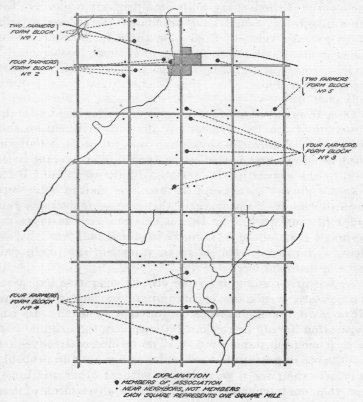

FIG. 17.—Map showing location of members of the Roland Cooperative Bull
Association.

enables the breeders of any class of stock to buy better bulls
than they otherwise could afford. In case the association is
large and composed of well-to-do breeders of pure-bred cattle, bulls of the highest class for use with all the cows are
within its reach financially.

LOW COST.

That the need of the introduction of pure-bred bulls is
urgent in many parts of the country is apparent from the

facts brought out by a study made by the Department of Agriculture of 8 districts in the States of Iowa, Minnesota, and Massachusetts, in which there were no associations. In this survey information was obtained regarding 1,219 farmers, owning 817 bulls, whose average value was $76. Had the owners of those cheap bulls been properly organized, the same investment would have purchased the necessary bulls of an average value of $283. On those farms nearly four times as many bulls were used as would have been required under proper organization. The farmers were therefore feeding four bulls when they should have been feeding only one.

Data from one of the first associations organized under the direction of the Department of Agriculture illustrate this very well. Before the association was formed the bulls in use had an average market value of $85. The average price paid by the association for registered bulls was $240. Price does not always correspond to value, yet, as the bulls were carefully selected, the price in this case is doubtless a fair index of true worth. In this association each farmer's investment for a share in a good registered bull was $10 less than his former investment in an animal of inferior breeding and doubtful merit.

Actual first-cost figures from other cooperative bull associations are even more encouraging. In fact, the figures given show the highest association cost reported. In one association having more than 100 members the original cost to each member was only $23. The members already have had the use of good pure-bred bulls for 4 years and probably will have their use 6 years longer without other additional cost than maintenance. At an average investment of less than $25 a member, another association with more than 50 members has had the use of good pure-bred bulls for more than 7 years, with prospects of being able to use them for 3 or 4 years more.

QUICK RETURNS ON INVESTMENT.

One hundred and fifty farmers in Maryland, Michigan, and Minnesota, when questioned regarding the value of cooperative bull associations, estimated that the use of sires belonging to the organization increased the value of the offspring in the first generation from 30 to 80 per cent, with an average of 65 per cent. Usually in business transactions in which there is a probability of great gain there is a possibility of heavy loss, but in the bull associations the chances of profit are good, with little probability of loss. It is true that some associations have disbanded, but no case in which any member has actually lost on his investment has been reported, even when the association continued in existence for only a short time. The investment is so small and the chance for herd improvement so great that the net returns greatly exceed the small original investment.

LINE BREEDING.

The association that is composed of five or six breeding blocks should keep and use all its good bulls as long as they are fit for service. Advancing the bull to the next block at the end of two years does not eliminate him, but makes it possible to avoid inbreeding. Line breeding, on the other hand, is a common and a very good practice, and the bull association offers exceptional opportunities for conducting that kind of breeding. In an association composed of breeders of pure-bred dairy cattle, carefully selected bulls produced in one block may be used in other blocks and the organization may thus continue indefinitely without purchasing bulls from outside sources, if such a plan seems most advisable. The same practice may be followed when a number of first-class registered cows are owned by members of any association. The cooperative bull association therefore offers an excellent opportunity for intelligent, long-continued line breeding. Skillful mating, when combined with careful selection of the best animals, makes very great improvement possible.

ELIMINATION OF THE SCRUB.

The value of the use of pure-bred sires and the need for elimination of the scrubs is shown in the accompanying illustrations. The cattle shown in Plate LXIX, figure 1, were owned by a farmer at the time he joined the association. He has better cattle now. Plate LXVIII shows pictures of scrub bulls. Every farmer will recognize the type, and certainly no farmer cares to breed his cows to such scrubs. A bull similar to the one shown in Plate LXIX, figure 1, was sold for $8 when a year old. The hide alone of a good yearling bull should easily bring half as much. The bull association eliminates the scrub bull and economically substitutes such bulls as the one shown in Plate LXX, figure 2.

COMMUNITY BREEDING ENCOURAGED.

Ten years ago a farmer in northern Wisconsin began to breed Guernseys in a Holstein district. Now he has a fine herd, and wonders why buyers never come his way. He is discovering that when buyers want Guernseys they naturally go to a Guernsey district. As a rule the breeders of pure-bred cattle already have learned this lesson. The principle is as true of grades as of registered stock, but many owners of grade cattle seem to have overlooked it. All dairy breeds are sometimes found in the same neighborhood, and even on the same farm several dairy breeds and all possible combinations of them are seen. Perhaps one year a Holstein bull is used, the next year a Jersey, and occasionally a bull of no particular breeding. In a grade herd recently studied there were Holsteins, Guernseys, Jerseys, and Shorthorns, and every possible cross and mixture of those breeds. The owner admits his cattle do not sell to advantage, and the reason is not hard to find. The bull association encourages the keeping of only one breed on the farms of its members, and the establishment of that breed in the community.

THE POWER OF HEREDITY.

In all bull-association work the power of heredity is recognized. This power is illustrated by the pictures of a high-class Guernsey bull, his dam, and his daughter. Since like tends to beget like in production as well as in appearance, there is little danger that the pure-bred bull whose ancestors for several generations were first-class individuals will inherit or transmit the qualities of some inferior remote ancestor. If he is well-formed, strong, and healthy he will almost certainly increase, in one generation, the income of the scrub or low-grade herd out of all proportion to his cost. In fact, the time may come when it will be possible to eliminate all bulls except those whose dams are in the advanced

TYPES OF SCRUB BULLS THAT FORTUNATELY ARE BECOMING LESS
COMMON.

FIG. I.—CATTLE OWNED BY A FARMER BEFORE JOINING A COOPERATIVE
BULL ASSOCIATION.

FIG. 2.—AN ASSOCIATION BULL.

FIG. I.—DAM OF BULL SHOWN IN FIGURE 2.
Year's record: 14,633 pounds of milk; 714 pounds of butterfat.

FIG. 2.—A WELL-BRED BULL.

FIG. 3.—DAUGHTER OF BULL SHOWN IN FIGURE 2.
Year's record: 18,458 pounds of milk; 906 pounds of butterfat.

A WELL-BRED BULL, HIS DAM, AND HIS DAUGHTER.

registry. If the best bulls in the world were used to their full capacity in pure-bred herds, and if only good pure-bred bulls were used in the ordinary dairy herds, the income from the dairy business could be vastly increased.

IMPROVEMENT DUE TO SIRE.

Few organizations have been in operation long enough for the producing daughters of an association bull to be compared with their dams. The following figures received from an association at New Windsor, Md., show the improvement due to the sire:

Average butterfat production of daughters of association bulls compared with that of their dams.

	Pounds.
Bull No. 1 (7 producing daughters):	
Dams	208. 3
Daughters	270. 5
Each daughter excelled her dam.	
Bull No. 2 (7 producing daughters):	
Dams	226. 4
Daughters	281. 6
Five of the daughters excelled their dams.	
Bull No. 3 (2 producing daughters):	
Dams	254. 0
Daughters	369. 5
Each daughter excelled her dam.	

At the price of 30 cents a pound for butterfat the 7 daughters of bull No. 1 will earn in 4 years' time $500 more than their dams. It is only when the lifetime-production records of all his daughters are computed and compared with those of their dams that the full value of the bull's services to one generation can be known. In addition to this, his influence on the herd will be noticeable for many generations. This illustrates the great value of a good bull. The damage done by an inferior bull may be equally great. No other argument should be necessary in urging that every association be particularly careful in selecting bulls.

Pure-bred bulls are not all equally valuable. The daughters of some are much inferior to their dams, while the daughters of others greatly excel their dams. The bull should always be superior to the best cows in the herd. Cows should be well bred and carefully selected, but association bulls should be even better bred than the cows and still more carefully selected. All bulls used should be from advanced-registry dams having a butterfat record of not less than 400 pounds and from high-producing ancestors.

NOT MONEY ALONE.

The educational value of a cooperative bull association doubtless exceeds the net cash returns, for, as a rule, all members of the association become greatly interested in the improvement of their dairy herds. They study live-stock pedigrees, individual conformation, and production records. They hold meetings at which dairy problems of all kinds are discussed. Even boys take an added interest in the farm, and especially in the dairy herd. At Esmond, N. Dak., the association held a cattle show in July, 1916. Cows, bulls, and young stock were exhibited. The show was held in connection with a three-day chautauqua, and it was estimated that 5,000 people visited the show and the chautauqua. Great interest centered about the boys' stock-judging contest, which was one of the features of the occasion. The educational value of such work can hardly be overestimated.

At Washington, Mich., the work of the bull association led to an annual five days' agricultural school in winter and an annual summer picnic. At the picnics small cash prizes are given for the best heifers exhibited. This association consists of 22 members who invested $25 each, for which they have already had the use of good pure-bred bulls for 6 years.

NO SERIOUS WEAKNESS.

There appears to be no fundamental weakness in cooperative bull associations. Instead of spreading abortion, tuberculosis, or other communicable disease, the results so far seem to indicate the reverse. For example, the Roland, Iowa, association will not allow any one of its members to get the benefits of the association until his herd has been tested for tuberculosis and all reactors eliminated. One farmer who did not dispose of the reactors after the tuberculin test was applied was refused the use of bulls until he complied with the rules of the association. The educational work of each association makes the members alert to prevent the introduction and spread of disease of any kind. The well-managed bull association requires that the cattle of each member shall be tested for tuberculosis and takes every known precaution to prevent the introduction of infectious abortion.

HOW TO ORGANIZE.

When a number of neighboring farmers, interested in the same breed, desire to organize a cooperative bull association, they should have a meeting, elect a temporary chairman and secretary, enter into a free and general discussion of the entire subject, and then decide upon the advisability of forming a permanent organization. A high point of efficiency is reached when there are five breeding blocks and approximately 60 cows in each block. Some successful organizations, however, have a smaller number of blocks and as few as 35 cows to the block. The greatest care should be taken in selecting bulls, as inferior bulls will completely defeat the purpose of the organization. Some farmer, centrally located, should be selected to take care of the bull, and each farmer should pay his share of the purchase price. In addition, each farmer pays his share of all other expenses, including the support of the bull; his share of these expenses should not exceed $10 to $15 annually.

It is greatly to the advantage of a cooperative association that it be incorporated. This facilitates the transaction of business, equitably distributes responsibility, and gives the organization greater prestige in the community. In order to avoid mistakes in organization and operation, including selection of bulls, the association should early communicate with the local county agricultural agent, the State agricultural college, or the Dairy Division of the United States Department of Agriculture.

FARM TENANTRY IN THE UNITED STATES.

By W. J. SPILLMAN and E. A. GOLDENWEISER.

Office of Farm Management.

THE problems relating to tenant farming have received comparatively little attention in this country until very recent years, because of the fact that desirable public lands were still available and the man who wanted to farm could acquire ownership for a nominal sum. Under such conditions no very large proportion of farmers were willing to become tenants. Even where tenant farming had become established the terms were generally very favorable to the tenant. In many regions where now the prevailing custom is for the tenant to give half the crop, the usual custom a generation ago was to give a third. But with the virtual exhaustion of the public domain, so far as highly desirable farm land is concerned, tenant farming began to increase and discussions of the problems connected with this type of farm operation appeared in the agricultural press in ever-increasing volume. That a certain percentage of tenant farms-should exist where public lands can no longer be had practically for the taking is natural and inevitable.

Tenantry is one of the normal steps by which young men with limited capital become farm owners. In general, every farm will change ownership at least once each generation, and a very great number do so several times during the average business life of the ordinary man. The percentage of changes in farm ownership that occur through inheritance is surprisingly small, as will be shown presently. An additional small percentage of farms are purchased with capital derived from other industries. The remaining farms must in some way be more or less completely recapitalized once each generation; that is, must be made to pay for themselves, either wholly or in part.

As a rough indication of the proportion of American farms which must thus be recapitalized once in a lifetime, or, in other words, must be made to pay for themselves either partly or wholly, the following data may be cited.

Studies made by Mr. H. H. Clark, of the Office of Farm
Management, in three townships in Sedgwick County,
Kans., show that 5.9 per cent of the present owners acquired
their farms through inheritance; 13.7 per cent are farming
land obtained under the homestead act; the remaining
80.4 per cent bought the farms they now own, three-fourths
of them on deferred payments averaging 44 per cent of the
total purchase price, the other fourth paying cash in full.
In most of these latter cases the purchase money was obtained from the sale of other farms. A few cases represent
capital taken from other industries. The conditions under
which approximately 60 per cent of these farms were purchased require that, in order that full ownership may be
acquired during the life of the present occupant, each of
the farms must provide not only a living for the family
upon it and interest on indebtedness, but an additional
income that will enable the average purchaser during his
occupancy to put aside 44 per cent of the purchase price.

Similar studies in five townships in a rich agricultural
county in Illinois gave the following results: 15.5 per cent
of the present farm owners obtained their farms by inheritance; 69 per cent of them bought on deferred payments,
the average mortgage given at the time of purchase representing 63 per cent of the purchase price; the remaining
15.5 per cent paid cash in full at the time of purchase. In
this case 69 per cent of the farms, in order that their present owners may during their occupancy obtain full title
free from debt, must produce a living for the farm family,
interest on the mortgage, and permit a saving of 63 per
cent of the total purchase price.

HOW RECAPITALIZATION IS EFFECTED.

In the studies above referred to the complete history of
each farm owner was obtained so far as possible. In the
great majority of cases these men began either as hired men
or worked on the home farm for several years after arriving
at maturity. In this way they obtained sufficient capital
to become tenants.[1] After a few years as tenants they were

---

[1] In the case of young men who stay on the home farm, the usual course is for the father,
when the son marries, to establish him in business as a tenant. It is understood that in this
discussion the stage of "hired man" includes young men who stay on the home farm some
years after reaching maturity.

able to save enough to make a first payment on a farm, giving a mortgage for the balance. In the majority of cases these mortgages are slowly canceled, leaving the farmer, at an advanced period of his life, a full owner.

Where this process of acquiring ownership proceeds in a normal manner, it is evident that a considerable proportion of the farmers operating at any particular time must be tenants; and the presence of tenant farming under such conditions represents a normal, healthful condition of agriculture. Not only that, but there will be a considerable proportion of mortgaged farms; and in so far as existing mortgages represent progress from tenantry to ownership, they indicate a healthful condition of agricultural affairs.

Figure 18 shows the percentage of mortgaged farms, with the average amount of the mortgage per farm, for each State in the Union. With some notable exceptions, the higher percentages of mortgaged farms are found in those sections of the country where agriculture is in a flourishing condition and where the gradual process of acquiring ownership is making normal progress. The scope of this article does not permit consideration of the exceptional cases to which reference has just been made.

TENANT FARMING A STEP TOWARD OWNERSHIP.

That in a general way tenant farming represents a step toward ownership is shown clearly in figure 19. This figure, based upon census statistics, shows that 76 per cent of farmers under 25 years of age are tenants. In the next age group, representing farmers from 25 to 34 years of age, the percentage of tenantry falls to 55. In the succeeding groups the percentage falls with each 10-year advance in age to 37, 27, 21, and 15. It may be assumed that these older men represent, in the main, those who have been unable to lay by enough to acquire ownership. But these figures indicate that by far the greater proportion of the young men who start out as tenants succeed in becoming owners. Figure 19 shows that aside from some of the Western States, where settlement is still in progress, and some of the Southern States, where the situation is complicated by the census classification of "croppers" as tenants, similar conditions prevail in all sections of the country.

Figure 20 shows that for the last two census periods there has been, in general, a decrease in the percentage of tenantry among farmers of advanced years. In the North, in the last

MORTGAGED FARMS
PER CENT OF ALL FARMS
1910

AVERAGE MORTGAGE PER FARM DOLLARS	STATE	PER CENT OF FARMS MORTGAGED PER CENT
4,048	IOWA	51.8
2,116	WISCONSIN	51.4
2,493	NORTH DAKOTA	50.9
1,826	NEW JERSEY	49.6
1,107	MICHIGAN	48.2
1,025	VERMONT	46.9
1,864	MINNESOTA	46.3
1,758	MISSOURI	46.3
2,326	KANSAS	44.8
1,556	NEW YORK	43.7
1,114	OKLAHOMA	43.5
1,309	CONNECTICUT	43.2
1,361	MASSACHUSETTS	40.9
2,802	CALIFORNIA	40.5
3,154	NEBRASKA	39.4
3,135	ILLINOIS	39.2
1,433	INDIANA	38.8
2,897	SOUTH DAKOTA	38.2
1,518	DELAWARE	37.2
1,457	MARYLAND	36.5
2,017	WASHINGTON	34.1
2,060	OREGON	33.7
1,715	UNITED STATES	33.6
1,917	IDAHO	33.4
1,584	TEXAS	33.3
586	MISSISSIPPI	32.9
1,368	PENNSYLVANIA	31.1
1,355	RHODE ISLAND	29.6
1,491	OHIO	28.9
538	ALABAMA	26.9
845	MAINE	26.6
2,508	COLORADO	26.4
842	NEW HAMPSHIRE	25.6
903	SOUTH CAROLINA	24.0
1,294	UTAH	22.9
540	ARKANSAS	21.4
2,692	MONTANA	21.1
2,749	WYOMING	19.7
906	KENTUCKY	19.6
794	GEORGIA	19.0
1,190	LOUISIANA	19.0
517	NORTH CAROLINA	18.5
2,805	DIST. OF COLUMBIA	18.4
727	TENNESSEE	16.9
4,738	NEVADA	16.7
887	VIRGINIA	16.0
652	FLORIDA	14.8
2,772	ARIZONA	12.9
710	WEST VIRGINIA	12.6
854	NEW MEXICO	5.4

FIG. 18.—Average mortgage per farm and percentage of farms mortgaged, by States. (Census of 1910.)

census period, there has been a decrease in percentage of tenantry for every age group except the first, the increase for the entire period being due to the number of young men under 25 years of age who have passed from the status of farm laborer to that of tenant. It is to be presumed that a large proportion of these will ultimately become owners. In

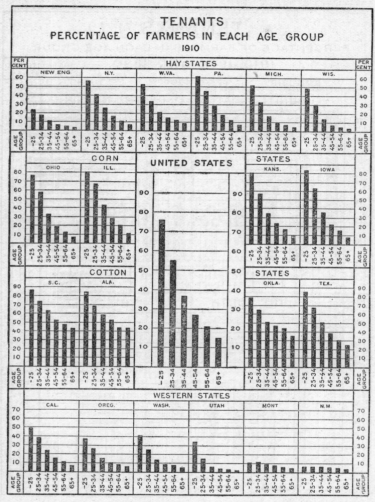

Fig. 19.—Percentage of tenants among farmers, by age groups, in the United States and in selected States. (Census of 1910.)

the South there has been a decrease of tenantry for the age groups over 45 years. In the case of men younger than this there has been an increase. In the West there was a marked decrease in the percentage of tenantry in every age group during the last census period. Taking the country as a whole, the only notable increase in tenantry for any age group was for the men under 25 years.

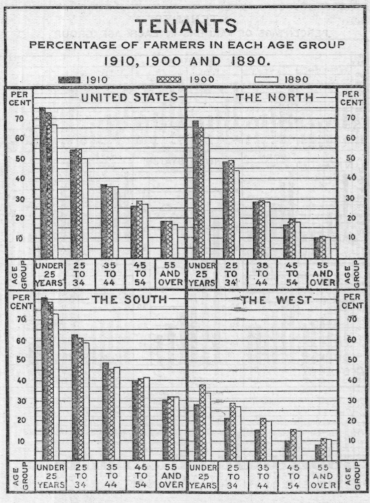

FIG. 20.—Percentage of tenants among farmers, by age groups, in the United States and in the three grand divisions for the last three census periods.

It seems to be fairly clear, therefore, that recent increase in tenant farming in this country in the main represents a healthful condition. Young men who formerly homesteaded land must now pursue a different course in acquiring a footing on the land. Increasing numbers of them are becoming tenants.

Figure 21 shows that during the period from 1890 to 1900 there was a more marked increase in the percentage of

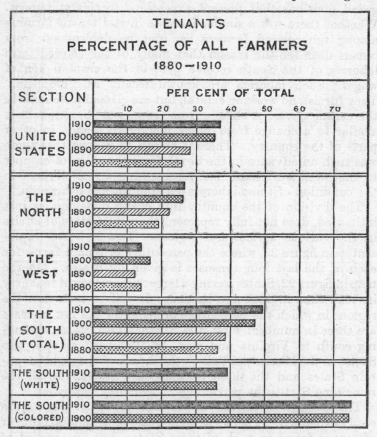

FIG. 21.—Percentage of tenant farmers in the United States and in the three grand divisions for the last four census periods, and of white and colored farmers in the South for the last two census periods.

tenantry than during any other recent census period, and this applies to all sections of the country. This was the period when the exhaustion of the public domain began to make itself felt and when a large number of men began to pursue the more normal course, outlined above, in becoming farm owners. This diagram also shows that during the last census period the only marked increase in the percentage of tenant farms in any of the grand divisions of the country was among the white farmers of the South, though, as will be seen later, there are localities in each of these grand divisions that present exceptions to this statement. Whether there was a similar increase in real tenant farming among the colored farmers can not be determined from census data for the reason that many of the colored farm laborers of the South receive part of the crop in lieu of wages. Such laborers are known locally as "croppers." They furnish no working capital, but are classed as tenants in the census data. A change from cropper to share tenant is similar to a change from hired laborer to tenant in other parts of the country. There is reason to believe that there was such an advance in the South from the stage of cropper to that of share tenant, this representing a real advance in the condition of these laborers—a step toward ownership.

The division of the country into grand divisions, as just intimated, does not fully represent the actual state of affairs in the various agricultural regions. This is better represented in figure 22, where the percentage of tenant farms for each of the last four censuses is given by States. On the map in figure 22, States having a larger percentage of tenantry in 1910 than in 1900 are shaded. It will be seen that the regions in which the percentage of tenantry did not increase are three in number: First, the Northeastern States, extending south to Virginia and west to Michigan; second, two States in the Mississippi Valley; third, four of the eight mountain States and the three Pacific Coast States. In all the remaining States the percentage of tenantry increased.

The conditions in the last-named group of States are easily explained. There was an increase in the actual number of tenant farms in each of these States, but on account of the settlement of new land and the breaking up of large tracts into small farms in some of them, the number of farms operated by owners increased at a much higher ratio, facts which are well brought out in figures 23 and 24. The percentage of tenant farms therefore decreased while the number increased, because the number of farms operated by owners increased even more rapidly. Thus in Colorado the number of farms operated by owners increased 97.6 per cent, while the number operated by tenants increased 50.3 per cent. Conditions were similar in each of the seven States in question.

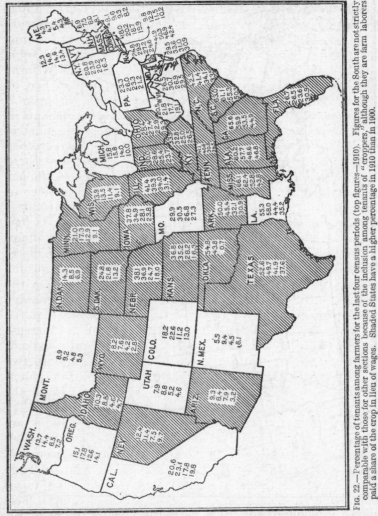

FIG. 22.—Percentage of tenants among farmers for the last four census periods (top figures—1910). Figures for the South are not strictly comparable with those for other sections because of the inclusion among tenants of "croppers," although they are farm laborers paid a share of the crop in lieu of wages. Shaded States have a higher percentage in 1910 than in 1900.

In the State of Missouri there was a slight decrease in the total number of farms, both those operated by owners and those operated by tenants, while in the State of Louisiana there was a slight decrease in the number of tenants

because of the conditions arising from the general spread of
the boll weevil over the cotton fields in that State during
the last census period.   Perhaps a similar change may be

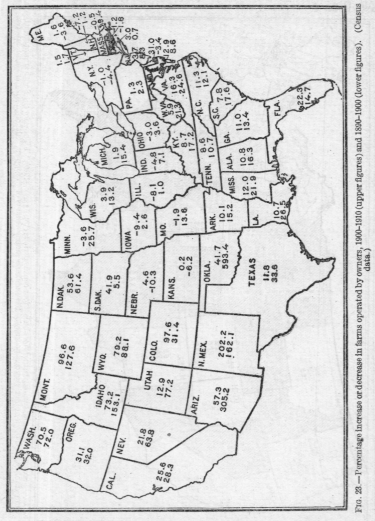

FIG. 23.—Percentage increase or decrease in farms operated by owners, 1900–1910 (upper figures) and 1890–1900 (lower figures).   (Census data.)

shown in some of the other cotton-producing States at the
next census, though this by no means necessarily follows.

As a partial explanation of the decrease in the percentage
of tenantry in the northeastern States, attention is called

to the facts shown in figure 25.   If a line be drawn separating
those States in the Northeast in which the average increase
in the price of farm land during the last census period was
less than 60 per cent from the States in which it was greater

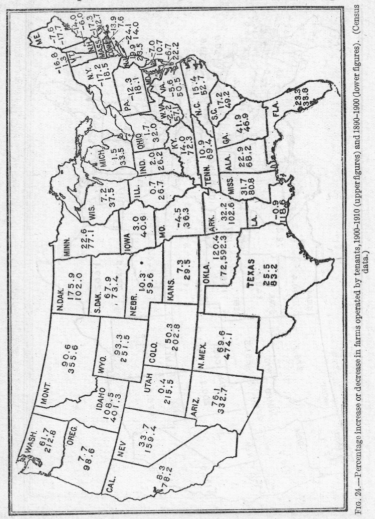

Fig. 24.—Percentage increase or decrease in farms operated by tenants, 1900–1910 (upper figures) and 1890–1900 (lower figures).   (Census data.)

than this, it will, with few exceptions, divide the States in
which the percentage of tenantry decreased from those in
which it increased, the percentage of tenantry having decreased where the price of land increased least.   The excep-

tions are Ohio, where the increase in the price of farm land was almost exactly 60 per cent, but where tenantry increased slightly, Virginia and West Virginia, in which States land increased more than 60 per cent in value, while ten-

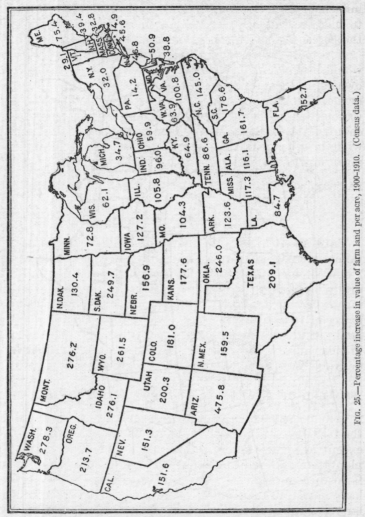

FIG. 25.—Percentage increase in value of farm land per acre, 1900–1910. (Census data.)

antry decreased, and Maine, where tenantry decreased, while the price of farm land increased 75 per cent. This increase in the price of farm land in the State of Maine is due to marked development of certain types of intensive farming, which of itself does not necessarily have any effect upon the percentage of tenantry. The general conclusion seems justified, therefore, that where land is increasing rapidly in value, unless other factors have a preponderating influence, there is a tendency for the percentage of tenantry to increase, while where land is increasing slowly in value the percentage of tenantry does not tend to increase.

It is not known what a normal percentage of tenantry would be under conditions where the major portion of farm owners pass through the various stages of hired man, tenant, owner with mortgage, and owner free from debt. There are reasons for assuming, however, that in some parts of the country the percentage of tenantry is below this normal, while in other parts it is above. Some of these reasons are given in what follows.

FACTORS THAT REDUCE THE NORMAL PERCENTAGE OF TENANTRY.

AVAILABILITY OF PUBLIC LANDS.

Until about 1890 public lands to be had almost for the taking were available to practically all who wanted them. Under such conditions the proportion of tenants would naturally be smaller than normal, because of the ease of acquiring ownership in land. Rather than suffer the inconveniences of tenant farming men would go west and homestead land. Statistics show that the percentage of tenant farming in this country was very low at the time when settlement of desirable new lands was in rapid progress. (See fig. 22.)

SMALLNESS OF FARMS AND LOW PRODUCTIVITY OF LANDS.

Tenant farming does not prevail generally in regions where the farms are very small or the productivity of the soil low, except in regions where the problem is complicated by the plantation system of farming. A large proportion of tenant farms become such because their owners have grown old and have no one to take charge of the farm. If the farm is not large enough or productive enough to make the income from the rent sufficient to support the farmer in retirement, the tendency for the aging owner to retain the operation of the farm is strong. This undoubtedly is one of the causes of the decrease in the percentage of tenantry in the northeastern States, for in these States farms are generally much below the average for the country in size. Another factor that probably has operated in this case is the fact that the type of farming undergoing most rapid development in the northeastern States, namely, vegetable growing, does not lend itself readily to a tenant system. Attention has already been called to the fact, illustrated in figure 25, that the price of farm land increased only slightly in this section of the country during the last census period. This fact, together with the smallness of the average farm, makes it possible, in many cases, for the farm laborer to omit the tenant stage in his progress toward ownership. It also makes it possible for men having a small capital saved in other industries to become owners. All these factors doubtless have operated in causing the decrease in the percentage of tenantry in the northeastern States.

FACTORS THAT INCREASE THE PERCENTAGE OF TENANTRY.

SIZE OF FARM AND PRODUCTIVENESS OF LAND.

Where a farm is large enough or productive enough to give a rental income sufficient for the support of a family, there is a strong tendency, as the farmer grows old, for him to turn the farm over to a tenant, unless he happens to have sons who can assume the management. The accompanying table gives some of the evidence on which this conclusion is based. The counties of four States—Pennsylvania, Ohio, Illinois, and South Carolina—are arranged in four groups of equal numbers, the first consisting of those counties having the largest average value of farm products per acre and the last of those counties having the smallest, the second and third groups being intermediate. The last column of the table shows the percentage of tenant farmers in each of the four groups. In every case it will be observed that the percentage of tenantry decreases as the average acre value of farm products decreases. In previous publications of the Office of Farm Management it has been shown that the percentage of tenantry decreases also as the size of the farm decreases for farms in the same geographic region. This comparison does not hold between distinct sections of the country. But in general the percentage of tenantry is higher on the large farms of the Middle West than on the small farms of the Northeast. The high percentage of tenantry in the cotton-growing States is due to other causes (partly to the inclusion of "croppers" with tenants).

Relation of value of farm products per acre to percentage of tenantry.

States and groups of counties.[1]	Average value of farm products, per acre.	Per cent tenants of all farmers.	States and groups of counties.[1]	Average value of farm products, per acre.	Per cent tenants of all farmers.
Pennsylvania:			Illinois:		
First group	$12.55	50.1	First group	14.71	31.9
Second group	9.98	45.5	Second group	8.17	22.7
Third group	8.03	38.9	Third group	6.29	18
Fourth group	5.77	29.6	Fourth group	4.79	14.4
Ohio:			South Carolina:		
First group	12.83	34.5	First group	13.18	69.3
Second group	10.39	33.3	Second group	10.14	67.4
Third group	8.51	26.8	Third group	8.05	66.1
Fourth group	5.47	18	Fourth group	5.58	43.1

[1] The counties in each State were arranged in descending order of value of farm products per acre, and then divided into four groups, each having an equal number of counties. The average value of products per acre and the average percentage of tenantry was calculated for each group.

INCREASE IN MARKET VALUE OF LAND.

Attention has already been called to the fact that tenantry is increasing in those sections of the country where the market value of land is increasing most rapidly, with certain notable exceptions, which have already been explained. Where the value of farm land is high a longer time is required for the tenant to accumulate the capital necessary for making a first payment on a farm than where it is low. Where the value of land is increasing there is a tendency to capitalize the annual rate of increase in the price at which the land is held. Where this condition exists it becomes exceedingly difficult for the man who buys a farm on deferred payments to succeed. He must not only make the farm produce a living for himself and family, but he must make it pay interest on a capitalization based partly on rental value and partly on annual increase in value, in addition to saving enough to cancel the mortgage. As this matter is somewhat difficult to make clear, it may be well to give an illustration.

In a farm-management survey in Ellis County, Tex., the average price at which the land was held was $139 per acre. The rental income from this land amounted to 3.7 per cent of this valuation. The current rate of interest on borrowed capital in this section averages about 8 per cent. But because of the very marked advantages in land ownership, those owning land are usually content to accept a smaller income on their capital. They are justified in this because of the great security of the investment and the numerous other advantages that arise from land ownership. If we assume that 5 per cent is a satisfactory income for real-estate investments in this region, while the rental income is only 3.7 per cent, then the price of the land includes capitalization of annual increase in value amounting to 1.3 per cent. That is, the farmer who buys this land at the average price of $139 per acre looks to rent for 3.7 per cent income on his investment and to annual increase in value for 1.3 per cent income. If we assume that the income on real estate should be 8 per cent, while the rental income is only 3.7 per cent, then there should be an annual increase in value of 4.3 per cent to justify the present market price. Taking the census valuations of farm land in Ellis County for 1880 and 1910, there has been during this 30-year period an actual annual increase of 5.9 per cent. It would appear, therefore, that the present price of the land does not fully capitalize the present annual rate of income. This is as it should be, for there is no prospect that this rate of increase can continue indefinitely. Now, the tenant who makes a first payment on a piece of land must make the farm earn enough in addition to his living to pay interest on the deferred payments, and where the price of land is higher than its true rental value the interest which he has to pay is greater than the rent which a tenant must pay. This fact deters tenants from attempting to become owners. Hence we find that, in general, in those sections of the country where the land is increasing rapidly in value the percentage of tenantry is considerably above the normal.

It should be stated here that where land is increasing rapidly in value, some men without sufficient capital to pay for an entire farm make a first payment with the object of holding the land a few years in order to get the benefit of increase in value and then sell. In so far as this practice prevails, it tends to decrease the percentage of tenantry; but the number who thus buy land speculatively is small in comparison with those who remain tenants because the rate of increase is capitalized in the price they are compelled to pay for a farm.

CAPITALIZATION OF THE ADVANTAGES OF LAND OWNERSHIP.

It has already been pointed out that the safety of investments in land and the other advantages that arise from land ownership lead men to purchase land at prices which make it necessary for them to accept a low rate of income on their investment. In other words, the price at which agricultural land is held, especially in those sections of the country where farming is most profitable, are greatly in excess of their actual rental value when capitalized at current rates of interest. For reasons given under the previous heading, this makes it difficult for a tenant to acquire ownership. because on his deferred payments he must pay a rate of interest considerably higher than the rate which land owners are willing to accept on their investment. The price he pays for land represents capitalization on the basis of a secure and otherwise preferred investment, while the rate which he must pay for money—that is, the rate of interest he must pay on his deferred payments—is the current rate for the use of borrowed capital.

ADVANTAGE OF TENANTRY FOR BEGINNERS WITH SMALL CAPITAL.

The scope of this paper does not permit a discussion of the desirability or undesirability of tenant farming from the standpoint of its effect upon citizenship or on the general welfare. It deals rather with the forces that control the percentage of tenantry in different regions and under different conditions. We shall now consider some of the factors that influence the individual.

HIGHER RATES OF INCOME ON WORKING CAPITAL THAN ON FIXED.

As has already been said, landowners are willing to accept a relatively low rate of income on their investment. But there is no reason for such low rate of income on the working capital used in farming. Farm-management surveys have shown a decided difference in the rates of income on these two classes of property. This is brought out in the following table:

Rate of interest on investment.

Received by—	Average.	Georgia.	Indiana.	Illinois.	Iowa.	Arizona.	Texas.
Owner operators...	6.5	8.0	4.7	5.5	4.7	8.6	5.9
Landlords.........	4.3	7.3	3.5	3.6	3.2	4.9	3.5

In the case of operators who own the land they farm the investment consists of land and of working capital, while the return received by landlords is almost entirely based on an investment in land. The rate of interest in the case of owners is determined by subtracting from the net income of the operator the estimated value of his own labor and dividing the balance by the total investment; in the case of landlords the net rent received is divided by the investment.

It appears from the table that the owner operators receive an average return of 6.5 per cent, while the landlords receive only 4.3 per cent. The difference in favor of the operators is found in every State included in the table and indicates that an investment in real estate alone brings a lower relative return than a mixed investment in land and working capital. This difference may represent in part the owner's returns for his personal managerial ability, but it is certain that a considerable portion of the difference is due to the fact that a secure and otherwise preferred investment in land commands a lower rate of interest than a less secure investment in working capital. Thus it is seen that for the man with small capital there is considerable advantage in farming on the tenant basis. For a man with a large amount to invest the situation is different, partly because his funds, if invested entirely in working capital, may necessitate a larger farm than he is capable of managing to advantage and partly because, if he has enough money to buy a good-sized farm that yields a good living, other considerations besides the rate of interest on the investment enter into the problem.

While the higher rate of income from working capital as compared with real estate results in higher returns on investment for tenants than for owners, the investment of owners is much larger, on the average, than that of tenants. Hence in the surveys made in the six States included in the above comparison the income received by tenants, above the wages of their labor, the use of the house, and the food and fuel supplied directly by the farm, was only $627, as compared with $1,430 for owners.

FARM INCOME OF OWNERS AND TENANTS WITH SIMILAR CAPITAL.

Closely related to the facts just stated is the additional fact that the net income of tenants with small capital is much greater than that of owners *with the same amount of capital.* This is shown in the accompanying table, which gives the farm incomes of owners and tenants in Gloucester County, N. J., grouped according to the capital of the farm operator and illustrating a condition that is found in practically all the Department's farm-management surveys.

Comparative incomes of owners and tenants with equal capital, Gloucester County, N. J.

Amount of capital.	Owners.			Tenants.		
	Number of farms.	Average size of farm.	Average farm income.	Number of farms.	Average size of farm.	Average farm income.
$1,000 and less	None.	....	....	11	42.9	$567
$1,001–$2,000.	None.	....	....	28	77.0	675
2,001– 3,000.	None.	....	....	25	113.2	897
3,001– 5,000.	24	40.1	$291	11	103.0	1,727
5,001– 7,000.	34	59.0	752	2	175.5	2,240
7,001– 9,000.	30	65.6	992	1	200.0	5,123
9,001–11,000.	22	79.4	1,340	None.	....	....
11,001–14,000.	31	105.7	1,689	None.	....	....
14,001–17,000.	12	101.2	2,711	None.	....	....
Over $17,000..	9	148.8	3,202	None.	....	....
All farms.....	162	77.2	1,269	78	91.5	976

It will be noticed that in the groups of farmers having less than $3,000 capital every farmer is a tenant. Even those with less than $1,000 capital are making incomes that permit a fair standard of living, while those with $2,000 to $3,000 capital have incomes that permit considerable saving, especially if the farmer and his family are frugal, because each of these farmers has, in addition to the income shown in the table, all that the farm furnishes toward the family living, including milk, butter, poultry, eggs, fruits, vegetables, and often fuel. In the next group, having from $3,000 to $5,000 capital, there are 35 farmers. Twenty-four of these are owners of farms averaging about 40 acres in size. The remaining 11 have remained tenants and are operating farms about two and a half times as large as owners with the same capital. Their average farm income is about six times as great as that of the corresponding owners. In the higher groups the number of tenants is so small that the averages do not mean much. It is significant, however, that the two tenants amongst the 36 farmers in the group having from $5,000 to $7,000 of capital make incomes about three times as large as do the owners. The one tenant in the next group makes about five times as much as the average of his 30 compeers. In the groups having more capital than this all the farmers are owners.

It may seem strange that where farmers can make so much more money as tenants than they can as owners there should be such a strong tendency toward ownership. The table shows that just as soon as the average income is sufficient to permit anything like a satisfactory standard of living the majority of tenants become owners, thus sacrificing perhaps two-thirds of their income. The amount they thus sacrifice shows what the average farmer considers the advantages of ownership to be worth. It is not necessary to discuss these advantages here; most of them are obvious.

There is, however, another reason why so few tenants with large capital are found. A large amount of capital, all invested as working capital, suffices for the operation of a very large business, exceeding, in fact, the managerial ability of many farmers. It is only within the limits of his managerial ability that it is wise for the farmer with considerable capital to remain a tenant rather than pass into the owner class.

There are two reasons for the greater incomes made by tenants as compared with owners having the same amount of capital. One is the higher rate of income on working capital as compared with fixed capital represented by real estate, already discussed. Another reason even more important is the fact that with a given amount of capital invested entirely as working capital, the operator can manage a very much larger area of land, and other things being approximately equal, the farmer's income is usually roughly proportional to the magnitude of the business he conducts. Note in the preceding table that in the group of farmers having from $3,000 to $5,000 capital, the size of the 11 farms operated by tenants is about two and a half times that of the 24 farms operated by owners. In the next two groups the tenant farms are about three times as large as the owner farms.

In this connection the average size of tenant farms as compared with owner farms is of interest. Data concerning this point are given in figure 26, which shows graphically both the area of improved land and the total farm area for the average farm operated by its owner and the average tenant farm in selected States. It will be seen that outside of the cotton-belt States, in nearly every case the average tenant farm is larger than the average owner farm. The exceptions are easily explained. They are Nebraska, Kansas, Colorado, Utah, and Missouri. In these States most of the tenant farms are in those sections of the State where the farms are relatively small. If the comparison could be made between the tenant farms in these States and the owner farms in the same localities, there is no question that the average tenant farm would be shown to be larger than the average owner farm. Where the conditions are such that the farm laborer can in a few years save enough money or establish sufficient credit to provide the necessary working capital for a farm of considerable size, the tenant usually selects a farm as large as he can manage with the working capital available. If he undertakes tenant farming on a smaller farm the results frequently are disastrous. Not only that, but the majority of farms offered to tenants average larger in size than those not thus made available, for the reason that the rental income from the large farm will best support the retired owner.

The conditions shown in the cotton States, among both white and colored farmers, involve considerations which it is not within the province of this paper to discuss. It is seen, however, that in all these States the average tenant farm is smaller than the average owner farm, and this is true whatever the race of the farmer. This is due in part to the inclusion of "croppers" with tenants in the census figures. As elsewhere explained, the cropper is a hired

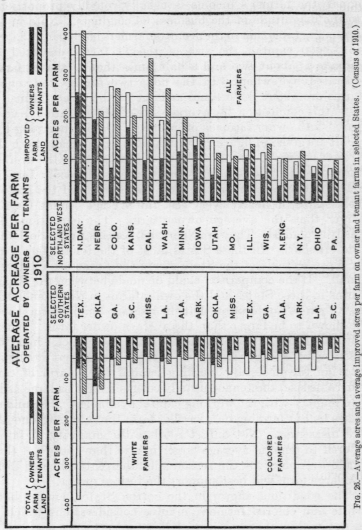

Fig. 26.—Average acres and average improved acres per farm on owner and tenant farms in selected States. (Census of 1910.)

laborer who receives a share of the crop in lieu of wages. The small average acreage tended by croppers makes tenant farms smaller in the cotton States than they would be if the term "tenant" were limited to classes comparable with tenants in other sections. Another reason why the average tenant farm of the cotton States is so small lies in the fact that the area of cotton a family can manage is limited by the amount that can be picked in season, and on good land this is a very small area.

PRINCIPAL DEFECTS OF THE AMERICAN SYSTEM OF TENANT FARMING.

The serious defect of our system of tenantry is the lack of suitable provisions for maintaining the fertility of the soil. There are two general causes for this condition. In the first place, tenant farming is more or less new in many localities, and the problem of arranging a lease contract that will provide against loss of fertility has not been generally solved, though it has been worked out in numerous individual instances and quite generally in some localities. In the second place, a striking feature of the system of tenant farming which prevails in this country is the short average length of tenure. The following table shows that for the United States as a whole, at the last census, one-third of the tenant farmers had been on their present farms less than 1 year; 17 per cent of them were in their second year on the same farm; about 30 per cent had been on the same farm for from 2 to 5 years, 12 per cent for from 5 to 10 years, and less than 8 per cent for more than 10 years. The longest average tenure is shown for colored tenants in the South; the next longest for tenants in the northern States. The shortest average tenure is shown for white tenants in the South. This is partly accounted for by the fact that tenantry amongst the white farmers in the South is increasing more rapidly than anywhere else in the country. One of the reasons for this increase is the gradual replacement of colored by white tenants in many sections.

Length of tenure on tenant farms in the United States.

[From census of 1910.]

Type of tenure and years on farm.	Tenants having been on same farm each specific number of years (per cent).				
	United States.	The North.	The West.	The South.	
				White.	Colored
All tenants:					
Less than 1 year	33.4	27.6	33.0	42.1	28.8
1 year but less than 2 years	17.1	17.8	18.5	18.0	15.0
2 years but less than 5 years	29.6	30.5	31.8	26.9	32.0
5 years but less than 10 years	12.0	14.7	11.0	8.4	13.7
10 years and over	7.9	9.4	5.7	4.6	10.5
Cash tenants:					
Less than 1 year	26.1	25.8	31.4	34.8	18.9
1 year but less than 2 years	16.0	17.4	18.3	17.6	13.1
2 years but less than 5 years	31.9	30.8	32.2	30.0	34.6
5 years but less than 10 years	15.0	15.6	11.7	11.0	18.1
10 years and over	11.0	10.4	6.4	6.6	15.3
Share tenants:					
Less than 1 year	37.3	28.6	34.7	44.6	36.2
1 year but less than 2 years	17.8	18.1	18.8	18.2	16.5
2 years but less than 5 years	28.4	30.3	31.2	25.8	30.1
5 years but less than 10 years	10.4	14.2	10.3	7.5	10.4
10 years and over	6.1	8.8	5.0	3.9	6.8
Average years on same farm:					
All tenants	3.0	3.4	2.6	2.2	3.6
Cash tenants	3.8	3.7	2.8	2.8	4.8
Share tenants	2.6	3.3	2.5	2.0	2.7

It will be noted that the average tenure among cash tenants is everywhere longer than it is among share tenants. For the United States as a whole the average length of time the average cash tenants have been on the farms they are now operating is 3.8 years, while for share tenants it is 2.6 years. The cash tenant makes, on the average, a larger income than the share tenant and is not so soon discouraged by the frequent reduction in yield caused by the methods ordinarily employed in tenant farming. This is true in spite of the fact that the average crop yields on share-tenant farms usually are larger than on cash-tenant farms, the difference being more than made up by the smaller amount of rent paid by cash tenants.

REASON FOR SHORT TENURES.

In sections where systems of farming prevail that rapidly burn the humus out of the soil and where in consequence crop yields have become low, the farm income of the average tenant farmer is low. This makes him dissatisfied with his condition, and he naturally hopes by changing from one farm to another to better himself. For similar reasons the landlord is inclined to change tenants, hoping by the change to secure a better tenant. These two facts taken together account in part for the very short tenures which are so prevalent in this country.

The remedy for this condition is not a simple one, nor is there any panacea for it. In general, however, the remedy involves a course of procedure that will result in better incomes for the tenant. This, of course, will mean also greater profits to the owners of the land. Except in dairy regions, where it is customary for the landlord to furnish half the productive live stock, tenant farms are, in general, not so well stocked as owner farms. This is partly due to the general lack of capital on the part of tenant farmers and partly to the lack of permanence of tenure; but it is also due in part to lack of information on the part of both landlord and tenant as to the conditions of leasing on live-stock farms that would make the agreement equitable to both parties concerned. In sections where tenant farming has long been established, more especially in those regions where live-stock farming prevails, this problem has largely been worked out in practice. But new farms are continually passing from owner operation to tenant operation, thus bringing about the relation of landlord and tenant between people who lack information on the subject of lease contracts.

THE LEASE CONTRACT.

It is therefore clear that the big problem to-day in connection with tenant farming in the United States is that of the details of the lease contract. The Office of Farm Management regards this as one of the outstanding problems in farm economics in this country and is devoting serious study to it. A study is being made of the details of agreements between landlord and tenant on farms of all sizes and types in all parts of the country where tenant farming is well developed. These studies have shown that a few fundamental principles govern in all such cases. The laborer is entitled to his wage; the owner of property is entitled to interest on his investment and to sufficient income to replace worn-out equipment. We have already seen that land, because of the unique stability of the investment, commands a low rate of income. On the other hand, working capital is entitled to a high rate of income—just how high it is not yet possible to say with any degree of certainty. It is believed, however, that these studies will ultimately reveal what is a fair and equitable division of the proceeds of the farm between labor, fixed capital, and working capital for all the more important types of farming and for farms of different sizes in all parts of the country.

It does not necessarily follow from what has been said above concerning short tenures in this country that lease contracts should cover long periods of years. The essential thing is that they should provide a system of farming that will build up the fertility of the land. This may be accomplished under lease contracts made for short periods. It has been found in the investigations of the Office of Farm Management that in some of the localities in which tenant farming has prevailed for a considerable period tenants contracting only from year to year remain on the farm longer on the average than those who contract for longer periods. Very long lease contracts are hardly practicable, except under conditions of permanent tenure. In this country, where so large a proportion of tenants merely represent a step in the progress toward ownership, the period of the lease must, and should, be shorter, on the average, than in countries where practically all the land is farmed by tenants.

SEWAGE DISPOSAL ON THE FARM.

By George M. Warren,

Hydraulic Engineer, Office of Public Roads and Rural Engineering.

POPULAR indifference to the effective disposal of sewage has existed so long and so universally that only within comparatively recent years has it been realized that this waste product of human life is poison and must be kept from the food and drink of man. From the specific germs or poisons that may be carried in sewage at any time there may result typhoid fever, tuberculosis, hookworm disease, cholera, dysentery, diarrhea, or other dangerous ailments, and it is not improbable that certain obscure maladies may be traced eventually to the poisonous effects of drainage from human waste. The poison is invisible to the naked eye and it may be carried by many agencies and by devious routes and be unsuspectingly received into the human body. Infection may come from the swirling dust of the railway roadbed, from personal or indirect contact with transitory or chronic carriers of disease, from green truck grown in gardens fertilized with night soil or sewage, from food prepared or touched by unclean hands or visited by flies and vermin, from milk handled by sickly and careless dairymen, or milk cans and utensils washed with polluted water from wells, springs, brooks, and lakes receiving the surface wash or the underground drainage from sewage-polluted soil, and from many other sources.

Typhoid fever is peculiarly a rural disease, and a few examples clearly indicating the responsibilities and the duties of people who live in the country are cited herewith. The accounts are condensed from reports by the Massachusetts State Board of Health and the health commissioner of Virginia.

In September and October, 1899, 63 cases of typhoid fever, resulting in 5 deaths, occurred at the Northampton (Mass.) insane hospital. This epidemic was conclusively traced to celery, which was eaten freely late in August and which was grown and banked in a plot that

347

had been fertilized in the late 'winter or early spring with the solid residue and scrapings from a sewage filter bed situated on the hospital grounds.

In November and December, 1900, 7 cases of typhoid fever at Waltham (Mass.) were, with little doubt, caused by infected milk from a farm where the sewage in a cesspool containing the discharges of a person sick with the disease in August was dipped out and spread upon the ground by the same man who afterward milked the cows.

In 1909, 60 persons spending Labor Day at a country hotel in Worcester County, Mass., were infected from the milk handled by a table maid who .was coming down with typhoid fever.

In 1915, typhoid fever in a home at Brookneal, Va., was caused by the accidental entry of sewage into a drilled well following the choking and flooding of the house sewer with rain water. Within 14 days 5 of the 8 children were stricken and the eldest, a girl of 20 years, died 3 weeks later.

Early in June, 1915, a case of typhoid fever developed in the upper one of about 25 humble mountain homes situated along a small brook in Washington County, Va. Probably few of the houses had privies, and water was obtained from several small springs close to the edge of the brook. On July 3, 15 cases of typhoid fever had developed in 8 different families down the ravine, and it is probable that the spread of the disease was due in large degree to the pollution of the springs from the lack of care in handling the discharges of patients higher up the run.

Not to dispose of sewage promptly invites nuisance, but not to dispose of sewage cleanly and completely invites disease. It is not enough that human filth is taken 50, 75, 100, or 150 feet away from a well or spring, or that it is taken merely to lower ground. Given loose or open subsoil, seamy ledge, or long-continued pollution of one plot of ground, the zone of contamination is likely to extend and readily may reach quite distant wells, especially at such times as well-waters are lowered by drought or heavy pumping. Whatever the system of sewage disposal, it should be entirely and widely separated from the water supply, and, if possible, the surface of the sewage in any privy, leaky vault, or cesspool should be lower than the lowest water in any near-by well. The practice of applying human excreta or sewage to land upon which are grown truck crops, especially celery, lettuce, radishes, cucumbers, tomatoes, melons, and other vegetables consumed raw by man, constitutes a serious menace to health and should be discontinued.

SEWAGE AND SEWERS DEFINED.

Under average conditions the daily waste of an adult human is about 1½ to 2 quarts of foul matter consisting largely of undigested or partially digested foods and saline excretions. With these wastes there may be mixed refuse liquids and many substances entering into the economy of the household, such as grease, milk, bits of food, fruits, vegetables, paper, rags, etc. This refuse product constitutes sewage and the underground pipe which conveys it is a sewer. Since sewers carry foul matter, they should be water-tight, and this feature of their construction distinguishes them from drains or removers of relatively pure surface or ground water.

NATURE OF SEWAGE.

Sewage, then, is water containing small amounts of mineral, vegetable, and animal matter, dissolved and undissolved. It contains enormous numbers and many species of very minute living organisms or bacteria and dead organic matter. For the most part, the living organisms are, so far as known, not only harmless, but are of the utmost importance in the processes of nature. They may be termed tiny scavengers which multiply with great rapidity, their useful work being the converting of dead organic wastes into liquids and gases, decomposing the dissolved organic matter, and oxidizing and nitrifying the organic residues.

HOW SEWAGE DECOMPOSES.

If a bottle of fresh sewage be kept in a warm room changes occur in the appearance and nature of the liquid. At first it is light in appearance and its odor is slight. It is well supplied with free oxygen, since this gas, dissolved from the atmosphere, is always found in natural waters. In a short time the solids in the sewage separate mechanically according to their relative weights, sediment collects at the bottom, and a greasy film covers the surface. Later, the solids tend to break apart, the sewage grows darker, and the odor becomes more offensive. There is an increase in the amount of ammonia and a decrease in free oxygen, and when the former is at its maximum and the latter is exhausted, the sewage is said to be stale.   Beyond this stage the process becomes a putrefying one.   Bacterial life probably secures minute quantities of oxygen from the breaking up of organic substances, and, as compounds containing nitrogen are decomposed, various foul-smelling gases are liberated.   Sewage in this condition is known as septic sewage.   Eventually the liquid in the bottle clears, its color fades appreciably, the odor disappears, and a dark-brown, insoluble, earth-like substance remains as a deposit.   Complete reduction of this deposit requires a long period of time, perhaps many years.   Within any ordinary limits there still remains more or less organic residue which rots very slowly, but which, if given sufficient time, may be reduced to mineral substances and so become suitable for plant food.

The changes above described are wholly natural and are analogous to what always takes place when animal or vegetable matter decays.   The process is affected vitally by environment.   For example, bacterial activities may be checked or destroyed by violent agitation, extremes of heat or cold, strong light, or chemicals.

PRACTICAL UTILITIES FOR VARIOUS CONDITIONS.

PIT PRIVY.

Upon thousands of small farms there is no privy whatever and excretions are deposited carelessly about the premises. Such practice should not be countenanced in any community. In order to suggest a fairly effective remedy for such conditions and to impress upon the mind fundamental and far-reaching principles, use will be made of a very familiar, though homely, illustration which is furnished by the house cat.   The cat instinctively selects warm, loose soil wherein to deposit and bury her excretions.   What of value can we gather from the example?

(1) The site selected is well drained.   Were it otherwise the soil would be cold and wet.

(2) The site is not shut in, but is open to the purifying influences of sunlight and air.

(3) The excretions are deposited in loose topsoil permeated with air and teeming with low forms of both plant and animal life.   These natural agencies disintegrate the waste organic matter and reduce it to inorganic substances beneficial to the soil and suitable for plant food.

(4) The excretions are covered promptly. Hence they are not visited by flies, are not likely to be washed over the surface by rains, and suggest nothing offensive to sight or other senses.

A privy which realizes some of the features and principles mentioned above is shown in figure 27. This is a portable affair not unlike the " sentry boxes " used upon con-

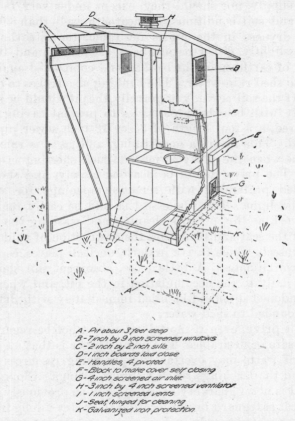

A - Pit about 3 feet deep
B - 7 inch by 9 inch screened windows
C - 2 inch by 2 inch sills
D - 1 inch boards laid close
E - Handles, 4, pivoted
F - Block to make cover self closing
G - 4 inch screened air inlet.
H - 3 inch by 4 inch screened ventilator
I - 1 inch screened vents
J - Seat, hinged for cleaning
K - Galvanized iron protection.

FIG. 27.—Portable pit privy, for use where land is abundant and cheap, but unless handled with judgment can not be regarded as safe.

struction work, and is suitable for localities where land is abundant and cheap. Its main purpose is to secure, at minimum cost and with least attention, a fixed place for the deposit of excretions where the filth can not be tracked by man, spread by animals, reached by flies, nor washed by rain. The privy is light and inexpensive and is placed over a hole or pit in the ground. When the pit becomes one-half or two-thirds full, the privy can be lifted readily by the handles and carried by two persons to a new location. The pits should be shallow, preferably not over 3 feet in depth, and never should be located on ground of which the surface or strata slope toward a well, spring, or other source of domestic water supply, nor should they, except under very favorable slope and soil conditions, be nearer a well than 300 feet. Since dryness in the pit is desirable, the site should be raised slightly, either naturally or artificially, and 10 or 12 inches of earth should be banked and compacted against all sides to shed rain water. The banking also serves to exclude flies. If the soil is sandy or gravelly, the pit should be sheeted roughly with boards or palisades to prevent caving; or, if preferred, a 3-foot length of 15 or 18 inch sewer pipe may be used. This makes a good lining, and, as it is raised and cleaned when the privy is moved, such sheeting is permanent. The privy should be boarded closely, and should be provided preferably with screened openings for ventilation and light. The whole seat should be easily removable or hinged, as this permits cleaning and washing the underside of the seat and facilitates the destruction of spiders and other insects which thrive in dark, unclean places, especially in warm climates. A little loose, absorbent soil should be added daily to the accumulation in the pit, and when a pit is abandoned it should be filled immediately with dry earth and mounded to shed water.

A pit privy, even if moved often, can not be regarded as either safe or desirable. The great danger is that accumulations of waste may overtax the purifying resources of the soil and the leachings reach wells or springs. Slope of the ground is not a guaranty of safety, but, as previously stated, the great safeguard lies in locating the privy a long distance from the water supply or having it actually lower than the water level of the latter.

SANITARY PRIVY.

The next step in the evolution of sewage disposal is the sanitary privy, which, as its name implies, is one productive of clean conditions and surroundings. Its construction must be such that it is practically impossible for filth or germs to be spread above ground, to escape by percolation underground, or to be accessible to flies, vermin, or rodents. Furthermore, it must be cared for in a cleanly manner, else it ceases to be sanitary. To secure these desirable ends, the sanitarians of many States and countries have devised numerous types of tight-receptacle privy. Considering the small cost and the proved value of some of these types, it is a sad commentary that so few are seen on American farms.

The receptacle or container for a sanitary privy may be small, such, for example, as a galvanized-iron pail, bucket, or garbage can, to be removed from time to time by hand; it may be large, as a barrel or a metal tank, either fixed or mounted for moving; or it may be a stationary metal or masonry tank or vault. The essential requirement in the receptacle is permanent water-tightness to prevent pollution of soils and wells. An exception to this rule is that class of privy in which the liquids drain through perforations in the bottom of the receptacle and are removed to a safe distance in a tight drain or sewer or are collected in a second water-tight container. Wooden pails or boxes, which warp and leak, never should be used. Where a vault is used, it should be shallow to facilitate emptying or cleaning. Moreover, if the receptacle should leak, it is better that the escape of liquid should be in the top soil, where bacterial life is most abundant. Sanitary privies are further classified, according to the method used in treating the excretions, as "dry earth," "chemical," or "liquefying."

DRY-EARTH PRIVY.

A simple out-door privy of the dry-earth type is shown in figure 28. It is 4 feet square, center to center of supporting posts, and no stock heavier than 2 by 4 inches is used in construction. The sills are secured to concrete, cedar, chestnut, osage orange, or other durable posts set about 3 feet in the ground. The boarding should be tight, so as to exclude flies and insects, and the windows and vents should be screened. Provision should be made also for the free play of air under and about the structure as shown in the drawing. The receptacle is a galvanized-iron garbage can costing about 75 cents. It fits very closely under the seat, held in position by two cleats nailed to the floor. Heavy brown-paper bags for lining the can may be had at slight cost. The use of these bags helps to keep the can clean and facilitates emptying it. Painting with black asphaltum serves a similar purpose and protects the can from rust. The can should be emptied frequently and the contents buried 1 to 2 feet below the ground surface at a point remote from wells or springs.

A - Removable container   D - Vent flue
B - Screened windows   E - Hinged seat
C - Screened vents   F - Concrete piers

Fig. 28.—Outdoor, dry-earth, removable-container privy. Durable construction, well ventilated, and screened. With proper care is sanitary and unobjectionable.

Wherever infectious intestinal disease exists, the contents of the can should be destroyed by burning or be made sterile by boiling or by complete incorporation with strong chemical reagents before it is buried. Even if disease is not manifest, burning or sterilizing of all waste of this description is a safe, sanitary precaution. It is human nature to take chances, however, and such practice is not common among any except sanitation enthusiasts.

Figure 29 shows an indoor dry-earth closet, with a brick vault, which was constructed in 1817 upon a farm at Westboro, Mass. This vault was built beneath the northeast rear

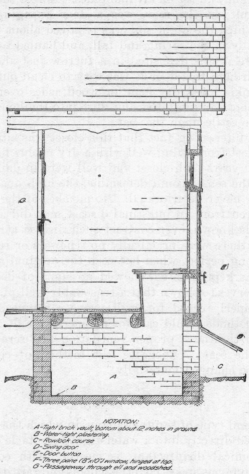

NOTATION:
A—Tight brick vault, bottom about 12 inches in ground
B—Water-tight plastering.
C—Rowlock course
D—Swing door
E—Door button
F—Three pane (8"x10") window, hinged at top.
G—Passageway through ell and woodshed.

FIG. 29.—Indoor dry-earth, tight masonry vault privy, constructed in 1817 and in use nearly 100 years. Note the water-tight and shallow vault and its convenience.

corner of a small raised ell which was partitioned so as to give a hired man's bedroom, a woodshed, a small tool room, and passageways to a rear outer door and to the closet. The vault was 6 feet long by 5 feet wide, and the bottom was 1 foot below the surface of the ground. The brickwork was laid in mortar, and that part below the ground surface was plastered on the inside. The outside of the vault was exposed to light and air on all four sides. Across the long side of the vault, in the rear, was a door swinging upward, through which the night soil was removed about twice each year, usually in the spring and fall, and hauled to a near-by field, where it was deposited in a furrow just ahead of the plow. Through this door it was easy to clean out the vault or to sprinkle loose, dry loam or wood ashes over fresh excreta without carrying dirt and dust into the house or causing dust to settle upon the seat.

It is an interesting fact that this closet was situated only about 30 feet from a dug well with a dry rubble lining. For almost 100 years both closet and well were in daily use, but as far as the senses could determine, the high quality of the well water never deteriorated. No member of the household ever suffered from an intestinal disease, nor did any visitor, so far as is known, ever contract such disease at this home. Although there were practically no renewals or repairs during this long period, when last seen the original seat, which always was kept painted, showed no signs of decay. This example serves to shown that a reasonably well planned utility, if properly cared for, will prove a sound investment. Modern methods would call for a concrete vault of guaranteed water-tightness, proper ventilation and screening, and hinging the seat. Otherwise, the method of construction need not be changed materially.

CHEMICAL CLOSET.

The second type of sanitary privy, in which the excretions are received directly into a water-tight receptacle containing liquid chemical disinfectant, is meeting with considerable favor upon farms and in country schools and railroad stations. Such privies are known by various trade names. One is a chemical tank closet in which the container or receptacle is large and irremovable. A simple type of chemical closet is shown in figure 30, with the essential features indicated in the notations. These closets, with vent pipe and appurtenances ready for setting up, retail for from $18.50 upward. Commercial disinfectants cost from \$1.50 to \$2 per gallon. Such closets are compact, simple, of good appearance, and easy to install or move. But their efficiency depends largely on the manner of installation and handling. To insure complete

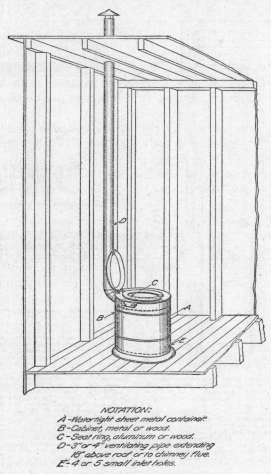

NOTATION:
A -Watertight sheet metal container.
B -Cabinet, metal or wood.
C -Seat ring, aluminum or wood.
D -3" or 4" ventilating pipe extending
      18" above roof or to chimney flue.
E -4 or 5 small inlet holes.

FIG. 30.—Chemical closet.

sterilization, the chemical must be strongly disinfectant and must permeate every particle of the waste matter. Strong draft through the vent pipe and prevention of low temperatures in the container also are very essential.

LIQUEFYING CLOSET.

The third type of sanitary privy, known as the liquefying or septic closet, makes use of bacterial action as an aid to disposal. The excretions are deposited in a tight receptacle

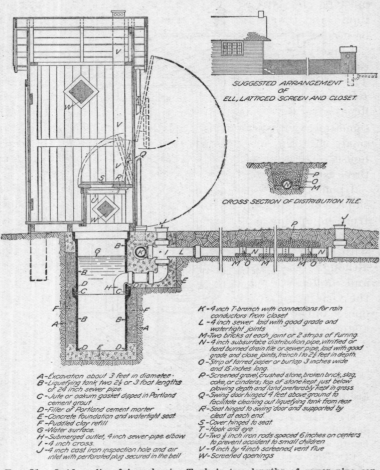

SUGGESTED ARRANGEMENT
OF
ELL, LATTICED SCREEN AND CLOSET.

CROSS SECTION OF DISTRIBUTION TILE.

A—Excavation about 3 feet in diameter.
B—Liquefying tank two 2½ or 3 foot lengths of 24 inch sewer pipe.
C—Jute or oakum gasket dipped in Portland cement grout.
D—Filler of Portland cement morter.
E—Concrete foundation and watertight seat.
F—Puddled clay refill.
G—Water surface.
H—Submerged outlet, 4 inch sewer-pipe elbow.
I—4 inch cross.
J—4 inch cast iron inspection hole and air inlet with perforated plug secured in the bell.
K—4 inch T-branch with connections for rain conductors from closet.
L—4 inch sewer laid with good grade and watertight joints.
M—Two bricks at each joint or 2 strips of furring.
N—4 inch subsurface distribution pipe, vitrified or hard burned drain tile or sewer pipe, laid with good grade and close joints, trench 1 to 2½ feet in depth.
O—Strip of tarred paper or burlap 3 inches wide and 15 inches long.
P—Screened gravel, crushed stone, broken brick, slag, coke, or cinders; top of stone kept just below plowing depth and land preferably kept in grass.
Q—Swing door hinged 4 feet above ground to facilitate cleaning out liquefying tank from rear.
R—Seat hinged to swing door and supported by cleat at each end.
S—Cover hinged to seat.
T—Hook and eye.
U—Two ⅝ inch iron rods spaced 6 inches on centers to prevent accident to small children.
V—4 inch by 4 inch screened vent flue.
W—Screened openings.

FIG. 31.—Outdoor liquefying closet. Tank is two lengths of sewer pipe connected in water-tight manner, and effluent is allowed to dribble in porous top soil or beds of coarse material. Back of house and seat may be swung up out of the way when removing solids from bottom of tank.

containing water, where fermentation and decomposition reduce a large part of the organic solids to liquid and gaseous forms. In the process of liquefaction much of the liquid evaporates and the gases diffuse so that the volume of sewage is reduced materially. More or less insoluble and undigested residue, known as sludge, gradually accumulates at the bottom of the receptacle, which, from time to time, must be cleaned out. But handling the partially clarified liquid and the sludge involves much less labor than would be needed to handle the fresh sewage.

Liquefying closets were used in Baltimore and other eastern cities for many years and gave fair satisfaction. The receptacle sometimes was a tight brick vault, but more frequently a large barrel or hogshead with one end nearly flush with the ground. Over this was mounted the seat, sometimes with iron bars beneath to prevent accident to small children, and the whole inclosed by a small frame house. The tank usually was bailed or pumped out two or three times a year.

Upon farms where there is abundant space and when slope, soil, and drainage conditions are favorable, the effluent from liquefying closets may be distributed and aerated by means of drain tile laid in top soil or in shallow beds filled with cinders, coke, gravel, or stone. This distributing tile, although receiving liquid which may appear light colored and inoffensive but still is sewage, never should be laid in the vicinity of a well or spring. Figure 31 shows a simple one-chamber liquefying closet with shallow distribution in a stone-filled trench.

OBJECTIONS TO PRIVIES.

All the methods of sewage disposal heretofore described are open to the following objections:

(1) They do not care for kitchen slops and the liquid wastes incident to a pressure water system. These, even if not as dangerous to health as human excreta, may create serious nuisance.

(2) They retain filth for a long period of time. Hence the liability of offensive odors.

(3) They require, for really satisfactory results, more personal attention and care than people generally are willing to give to such matters.

By far the most satisfactory method yet devised of caring for sewage calls for a supply of water under pressure and the flushing away of the wastes as soon as created through a water-tight sewer to an appropriate location, there to un-, dergo treatment. The importance of these two prime utilities, namely, a supply of water under pressure and an adequate system of caring for sewage, can not be impressed too strongly upon every farmer who desires to promote the health and comfort of his household.

CESSPOOLS.

Where farms have running water, an open or leaching cesspool is the most common method of disposing of the sewage. Ordinarily, cesspools are circular excavations in the ground, lined or walled with stone or brick laid without mortar. They vary from 5 to 10 feet in diameter and from 7 to 12 feet in depth. Sometimes the top is arched like a jug and is capped at the ground surface by a cover of wood or iron. At other times the walls are carried straight up, boards or planks laid across in lieu of a cover, and the entire structure hidden by means of a hedge or shrubbery.

Soil and drainage conditions vary so much that it is impossible to standardize cesspool dimensions. Eighty cubic feet may be taken as a minimum capacity. In certain arid sections, where porous material and the water table are deep, cesspools 4 feet in diameter have been dug from 20 to 60 feet in depth. Contract costs of these deep cesspools, including stone for lining, run about $1.75 per vertical foot.

Cesspools of the kinds above described are open to these serious objections:

(1) Unless located in porous, well-drained soil, stagnation is likely to occur, and failure of the liquid to seep away may result in overflow on the surface of the ground and the creation of a nuisance and a menace.

(2) They retain a mass of filth in a decomposing condition deep in the ground, where it is but slightly affected by the bacteria and air of the soil. The seepage in its movement through the ground may be strained, but there can be no assurance that the foul liquid, with little or no improvement in its condition, may not pass into the ground water and thus pollute wells and springs situated long distances away in the direction of underground flow.

For the purpose of avoiding soil and ground-water pollution, cesspools have been made water-tight like some types of tight-receptacle privy. Upon the farm, however, there is little to recommend them, for the reason that facilities for removing and disposing of the contents in a clean manner are lacking usually. Despite the objections stated above, there may be isolated farm homes so situated that some soil pollution may be permissible. In certain instances sewage may be taken in a water-tight sewer to a leaching cesspool, provided that it is located far below buildings and well, and likewise remote from neighbors' dwellings and water supplies.

Figure 32 shows a septic cesspool, which combines the principles of the liquefying closet and the leaching cesspool. With this type the solids are retained for liquefaction in the central chamber, while the partially clarified effluent escapes through the coarse, filtering medium into the subsoil. Tests of the soil water adjacent to cesspools of this type show that little reliance should be placed upon its capabilities of purifying sewage. However, since grease and other solids do not readily get into and clog the pores of the adjacent ground, this cesspool, under average soil conditions, is likely to remain free-seeping and unchoked. Still better results may be had if, instead of allowing the effluent to escape deep in the ground, it is given shallow subsurface distribution, as illustrated in figure 31. In this way not only is the area of percolation extended, but aeration and partial purification of the sewage are obtained.

PLUMBING.

Figure 32 also shows an effective, yet inexpensive, arrangement of soil and waste pipes for a two-story farmhouse, together with the connecting house sewer and the rain-water leader. Rain or other clean water conductors should be disconnected from sewers and should discharge into dry wells or a watercourse. The house sewer is 4-inch cast-iron soil pipe laid with a minimum fall of 2 feet per 100 feet and with the joints leaded and calked. Close to the cesspool an air inlet and inspection hole is provided. A 4-inch tee is turned upward and a 4-inch cast-iron riser inserted, while a 4-inch perforated plug closes the bell end of the riser. No running trap is placed on the house sewer, thus allowing free movement of air throughout the sewer and soil stack. The fixtures are located reasonably close to the soil stack, the waste pipes are ample and are fitted with drum or other nonsiphoning traps, and back vents are omitted, as experi-

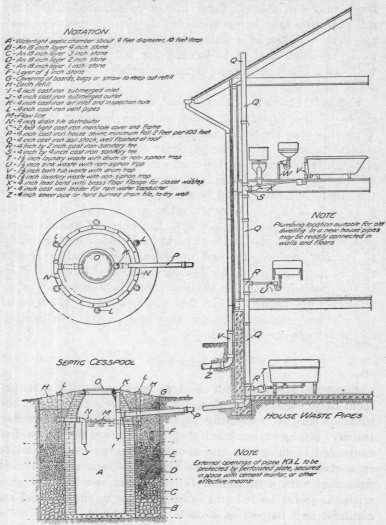

NOTATION

A - Watertight septic chamber about 4 feet diameter, 10 feet deep.
B - An 18 inch layer 4 inch stone.
C - An 18 inch layer 3 inch stone.
D - An 18 inch layer 2 inch stone.
E - An 18 inch layer 1 inch stone.
F - Layer of ½ inch stone.
G - Covering of boards, bags or straw to keep out refill.
H - Earth refill.
I - 4 inch cast iron submerged inlet.
J - 4 inch cast iron submerged outlet.
K - 4 inch cast iron air inlet and inspection hole.
L - 4 inch cast iron vent pipes.
M - Flow line.
N - 4 inch drain tile distributor.
O - 2 foot light cast iron manhole cover and frame.
P - 4 inch cast iron house sewer, minimum fall 2 feet per 100 feet.
Q - 4 inch cast iron soil stack, well flashed at roof.
R - 4 inch by 2 inch cast iron sanitary tee.
S - 4 inch by 4 inch cast iron sanitary tee.
T - 1½ inch laundry waste with drum or non-siphon trap.
U - 1½ inch sink waste with non-siphon trap.
V - 1½ inch bath tub waste with drum trap.
W - 1½ inch lavatory waste with non-siphon trap.
X - 4 inch lead bend with brass floor flange for closet wastes.
Y - 4 inch cast iron leader for rain water conductor.
Z - 4 inch sewer pipe or hard burned drain tile, to dry well.

NOTE

Plumbing location suitable for old dwelling. In a new house pipes may be readily connected in walls and floors.

SEPTIC CESSPOOL

HOUSE WASTE PIPES

NOTE

External openings of pipes K & L to be protected by perforated plate, secured in place with cement mortar, or other effective means.

FIG. 32.—House waste pipes and septic cesspool. A cesspool should be employed only when it can be located far below and far away from any well or other source of domestic water supply.

ments indicate that the **danger of transmission of disease from sewer air is slight.**

SEPTIC TANK.

There is much evidence to show that a tight, well-built, underground septic tank, so called, with shallow distribution of the effluent in porous soil, generally is the safest and least troublesome method of treating sewage upon the farm, while at the same time more or less of the irrigating and manurial value of the sewage is realized.

The antecedents of the septic tank were known in Europe more than 50 years ago. Between 1876 and 1893 a number of closed tanks with submerged inlet and outlet, and all embodying the principle of storage of sewage and liquefaction of the solids, were built in Massachusetts, New Jersey, Maryland, and Canada. In the past 20 years great advance has been made, and many plants, large and small, have been built. Much remains to be learned, but it is now certain that many of the early claims for the septic process were extravagant. There is nothing magical about a septic tank, and citizens should not trust implicitly in the name. In greater or less degree the changes described under the caption "How Sewage Decomposes," and referred to in connection with liquefying closets and cesspools, take place in septic tanks. The liquid escaping from a septic tank is assuredly not "spring water," nor is it harmless. It may contain, since the process involves intensive growths, even more bacteria than the raw sewage. As to the effects upon the growth and virulence of disease germs, little is known definitely. If disease germs be present, many of their number, along with other bacteria, may pass through with the flow or may be enmeshed in the settling solids and there survive a long time. Hence, so far as the danger of transmitting disease is concerned, septic sewage is not improved materially over crude sewage, and the farmer should safeguard wells and springs from the seepage or the discharges from a septic tank with no less certainty than from that of liquefying closets and cesspools.

In all sewage tanks a considerable portion of the solid matter, especially if the sewage contains much grease, floats on the liquid as a scum, the heavier solids settle to form sludge, while other finely divided solids and matter in a state of emulsion neither float nor subside. If the sludge is held in the bottom of the tank to be converted into liquids and gases, virtually to rot, the tank is called a septic tank and the process is known as septicization. Just how far this process may be carried to obtain the maximum sanitary benefit with the least nuisance and cost is still open to question. As previously stated, septic sewage implies offensive putrefaction. Not only is this objectionable as to odors, but numerous examples indicate that sewage reduced to the septic condition, or even highly staled, is less effectively purified, whether subjected to artificial filtration or to the natural filtration of the soil, than is moderately stale sewage. Aeration of a septic effluent seems to aid in its purification, but aeration lowers the temperature of the sewage and may result in the spread of objectionable odors or disease.

From what has preceded it is seen that the septic tank is not a complete method of sewage treatment. With the general run of small septic tanks, it probably is close to the facts to say that of all the solid matter in the crude sewage one-third is reduced to liquids and gas, one-third remains in the tank and one-third escapes with the effluent.

Every septic tank installation is a problem by itself. As a suit is fashioned to the size and needs of an individual, so should the design of a septic tank and the after disposition of the effluent be decided upon, with full consideration for the size of the family, the amount of water used, the location of property lines, buildings, wells, and drainage outlets, the slope of the land, and the character of the soil and subsoil. The designer, builder, or user of small septic tanks should bear in mind the following practical suggestions:

(1) The location should be reasonably distant from the dwelling and several hundred feet from a well or spring.

(2) The tank should be absolutely water-tight. Excellent results come from the use of concrete mixed in the proportions 1:2:4. Effective methods of waterproofing are described in United States Department of Agriculture Bulletin No. 230, entitled "Oil-Mixed Portland Cement Concrete."

(3) The tank should be 1 to 2 feet underground to secure uniformity of temperature and warmth in winter. In order to secure fall where slopes are flat, both tank and house sewer may be raised and embanked with earth.

(4) The tank should be covered tightly for the reason stated in (3), and also to guard against the spread of odors, the transmission of disease germs by flies, and accidents to children.

(5) Rain-water leaders and all surface or ground-water drains should be disconnected from sewerage systems.

(6) A plant for all-year-round use, whether discharging the effluent upon or beneath the ground surface or into an artificial filter, should have two chambers—one to secure settlement and septicization of the solids, and the other to secure periodic discharge of the effluent by the use of an automatic sewage siphon having no moving mechanical parts. The first chamber is known as the settling chamber, the second as the dosing, or siphon, chamber.

(7) The settling chamber should have a capacity below the flow line of about 24 hours' flow of sewage. Since sludge and scum accummulations soon replace the available liquid capacity, the calculated depth should be increased 25 per cent. Depth appears to be a more important dimension than either length or width. Widths may run from 2 to 4 feet inside. Length and depth may be equal and run from 5 to 7 feet inside. With liberal usage of a good, potable water under pressure, it is advisable to estimate on a basis of 40 gallons per capita for 24 hours. The inlet and outlet should be submerged about 2 feet below the surface of the liquid in the tank, though, with very little grease in the sewage, shallower submergence is permissible. Current breakers and baffle walls check velocities, diffuse the flow, and mitigate the evils of stagnation in the liquid and roiling of the sludge.

(8) The dosing chamber generally should have a dosing capacity equal to the flow of sewage for at least 8 hours. A longer dosing interval is preferable in close soils.

(9) The area for treatment of the clarified liquid should have moderate slope and deep and thorough drainage, and sunlight and air should have free access. Preferably, the soil should be sandy, gravelly, or loamy, but an impervious clay soil may be opened up and aerated by deep subsoiling, the use of dynamite, underdrainage, or the construction of trenches or beds filled with gravel, cinders, or stone. The distribution area preferably should be kept in grass, because

this is a safe crop and its water requirement is high. If properly handled, effluent discharged upon the surface may be well purified eventually, but in the vicinity of dwellings there may be annoyance from odors, and there is also the liability of the spread of disease germs through flies and other agencies. Surface discharge never should be nearer a dwelling or well than 300 feet, and there should be a properly spaced outlet for each 30 gallons of siphon dose.

Of the various methods of disposing of the liquid effluent, the subsurface discharge is preferable. Distribution should be through lines or runs composed of vitrified or hard-burned drain tile or second-quality sewer pipe. Four-inch size is preferred for this purpose, although 3 or 5 inch pipe may be used. The tile should be laid in runs of 60 feet or less in length, and in trenches 10 to 18 inches deep. To prevent flooding at the lower ends the tile should be laid upon very flat grades and short runs should be level. The tile should be laid with slightly open joints in an earthenware gutter or along a continuous track composed of two strips of furring or two bricks placed lengthwise at the low side of the pipe at each joint. The top and sides of the joint should be covered with earthenware caps or encircled with narrow strips of tarred paper or burlap to exclude dirt. The more coarse material, such as broken stone or brick, gravel, slag, coke, or cinders, placed beneath, on the sides, and immediately over the tile, the better will be the drainage and aeration. It is advantageous also to have the ends of the runs turn up and be vented above the surface of the ground. Sufficient tile should be used so that the capacity of the system will about equal the siphon discharge. In sizable installation it is preferable to have the distribution tile in two units with a switch between, so that one field may rest and become aerated while the other is in use. Where this is done it is well to alternate the switch weekly or oftener if the beds show signs of flooding. Frost usually gives little trouble in subsurface distribution, but in exposed areas where the winters are severe the tile may be laid slightly deeper or the ground may be covered with hay, straw, or leaves weighted down.

(10) Open, artificial filters of sand, coke, or stone usually have proved disappointing upon the farm. If properly de-

signed and operated, however, they are capable of splendid results. Usually they are neglected or the sewage is improperly applied, with the result that sand filters clog and the coarse-grained filters pass what is practically raw sewage. Moreover, there is likely to be annoyance from odors, and there is always the possibility of disease germs being carried by flies where sewage or sludge is exposed.

(11) If a septic tank is for use a part of the year only, as at a summer home, the siphon and siphon chamber may be omitted and the effluent may be allowed to dribble away through subsurface tile, as already explained. In such cases the joints should be very close; in fact, the tile may best be butted if good distribution is to be obtained.

(12) The siphon also may be omitted if the discharge is made into a running stream, but sewage never should be turned into any watercourse if any proper method of disposal is possible. Such practice endangers water supplies down the stream, and unless the velocity of the stream is good and its average flow at least forty times the volume of sewage discharged, serious nuisance may be created in the vicinity.

(13) There is nothing better for a house sewer, especially where the vicinity of a well must be passed, than cast-iron soil pipe with leaded, calked joints. This construction gives a permanently water-tight and root-proof sewer. Upon the farm, however, it is customary to use vitrified clay or shale pipe, and where this is used, 5-inch pipe, because of its straightness and smoothness and its lesser liability to obstruction, is preferred to the 4-inch size. In no case should the inside diameter of a sewer be less than 4 inches. The joints of a vitrified-pipe sewer may be closed with a strand of grouted oakum and good cement mortar, but as cemented joints usually are made up they leak sewage and may not keep out rootlets which by their growth frequently cause obstruction to the flow. Much better results are obtained where the joints are poured with molten sulphur and very fine sand or some flexible jointing compound. Whatever the size of the pipe and the method of closing the joints, the trouble from stoppages will be very much less if the sewer is made absolutely straight both for line and grade and the interior of the joints left clean and smooth.

(14) No chemicals should be used in a septic tank, except that occasionally, after cleaning out a tank, a deodorant may be used as necessary.

(15) Some attention must be given to every plant to insure success. Unusual or excessive foulness should be investigated. Garbage, rags, newspaper, and other solids not readily soluble in water should be kept out of sewers and sewage tanks.

Figure 33 shows, in plan and elevation, the general features of a simple septic tank installed for a small village home

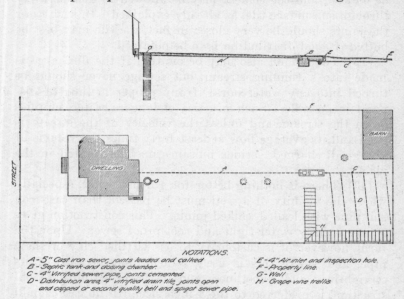

NOTATIONS:
A - 5" Cast iron sewer, joints leaded and calked
B - Septic tank and closing chamber.
C - 4" Vitrified sewer pipe, joints cemented
D - Distribution area, 4" vitrified drain tile, joints open and capped or second quality bell and spigot sewer pipe.
E - 4" Air inlet and inspection hole.
F - Property line.
G - Well
H - Grape vine trellis

FIG. 33.—Septic-tank installation for private house. Below: General plan of premises and distribution area. Above: Profile of sewer and tank. Note that house sewer past well is cast-iron pipe with leaded and calked joints.

for five or six persons. The disposal area should be farther from the well, but the location is fixed by the limits of the lot. Figure 34 shows the details of the tank. This plant was built complete in Maryland for $102.85. The cost was distributed as follows:

Excavation	$7.50
Materials and supplies, delivered	46.60
Siphon, including freight	15.75
Construction, labor	28.00
Supervision	5.00
Total	102.85

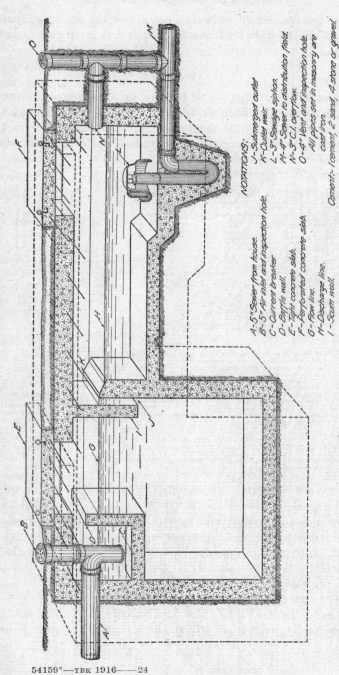

NOTATIONS:

A—5" Sewer from house.
B—5" Air inlet and inspection hole.
C—Current breaker.
D—Baffle wall.
E—Tight concrete slab.
F—Perforated concrete slab.
G—Flow line.
H—Discharge line.
I—Scum wall.
J—Submerged outlet.
K—Outlet weir.
L—3" Sewage siphon.
M—4" Sewer to distribution field.
N—3" C.I. overflow.
O—4" Vent and inspection hole.
All pipes set in masonry are cast iron.
Cement:- 1 cement, 2 sand, 4 stone or gravel. Total cost of installation, $102.85.

FIG. 34.—Details of septic tank (see also fig. 33) to accommodate five or six persons.

Figures 35 and 36 show the details of the general layout of a more elaborate septic-tank installation for a rural home housing 18 to 20 people.

CONCLUSION.

It has been the purpose of this paper to present the essential features of a number of sanitary utilities adapted to widely differing rural needs and conditions, and also to familiarize the reader with the fundamentals and the vital

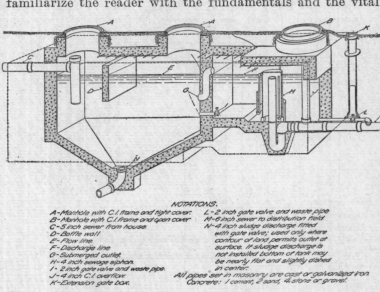

NOTATIONS.

A—Manhole with C.I. frame and tight cover.
B—Manhole with C.I. frame and open cover.
C—5 inch sewer from house.
D—Baffle wall.
E—Flow line.
F—Discharge line.
G—Submerged outlet.
H—4 inch sewage siphon.
I—2 inch gate valve and waste pipe.
J—4 inch C.I. overflow.
K—Extension gate box.

L—2 inch gate valve and waste pipe.
M—6 inch sewer to distribution field.
N—4 inch sludge discharge fitted with gate valve; used only where contour of land permits outlet at surface. If sludge discharge is not installed bottom of tank may be nearly flat and slightly dished in center.

All pipes set in masonry are cast or galvanized iron.
Concrete: 1 cement, 2 sand, 4 stone or gravel.

Fig. 35.—Details of septic tank (see also fig. 36) equipped with siphon to discharge sewage about twice a day to distribution area, and with sludge discharge pipe from bottom of tank to facilitate cleaning. Tank accommodates 18 to 20 people.

importance of sewage treatment. Each installation, no matter how small, should be based upon the best possible information and understanding, and calls for the exercise of considerable judgment to subserve the ends of health, cleanliness, convenience, permanence, and economy. Of these several factors the sanitary features unquestionably are of first importance, but every installation should be as convenient and as permanent as can be afforded.

There is general belief that the benefits of good plumbing and sewer systems cost little in the city, but are almost prohibitive in the country. That this belief is erroneous is shown clearly by a study of data upon the cost of sewerage systems in various cities, sewer assessments, and comparative values of city and farm properties. For illustration, the city of Newton, Mass., and the State of Iowa afford an interesting comparison. Newton is a well-ordered and highly improved residential city, and about 80 per cent of its population is served by a modern system of separate sewers. About one-third of the cost of this system is assessed on the lands abutting and about two-thirds borne by the issuance of bonds which are retired ultimately from the general tax levy. Iowa is a leading agricultural State and 95 per cent of its area is farm land. In the accompanying table the population of Newton is for the year 1905, while the valuation and sewer statistics include the year 1907. The statistics for Iowa are from the 1910 census and exclude all cities.

Population, valuation of private property, and sewer data, Newton, Mass., and farms of Iowa.

	Newton, Mass.	Iowa farms.
Population	36,827	1,544,717
Homes or farms, number	6,525	217,044
Valuation:		
Total	$67,743,335	$3,745,860,544
Per capita	$1,840	$2,425
Per home	$10,382	$17,259
Sewer mains:		
Length in miles	104	
Cost	$1,815,103	
Assessments	$666,142	
House connections. length in miles	69	
Houses connected, number	5,272	
Average sewer assessment, based on houses connected	$126	
Average tax levy for retirement of sewer bonds, based on total number of houses	$184	
Average cost of house connections	$45	
Average total cost for sewers and house connections	$355	

From this table it is reasonable to assume that if the average home in Newton, including personal estate, represents a valuation of $10,382 and pays $355 for sewers outside the cellar wall, then the average farm in Iowa, representing as it does a valuation of $17,259, certainly is justified in ex-

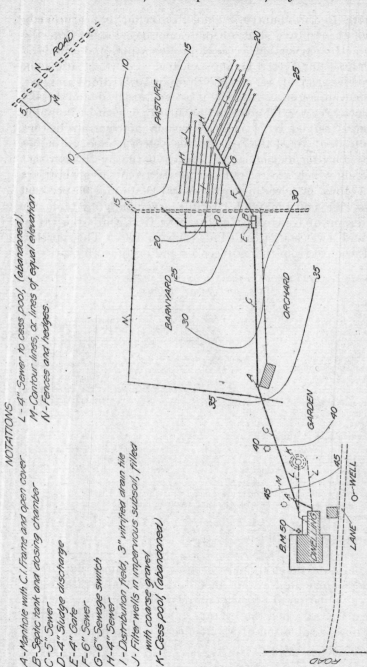

NOTATIONS

A-Manhole with C.I.Frame and open cover.
B-Septic tank and dosing chamber.
C-5" Sewer.
D-4" Sludge discharge.
E-4" Gate.
F-6" Sewer.
G-6" Sewage switch.
H-4" Sewer.
I-Distribution field, 3" vitryfied drain tile
J-Filter wells in impervious subsoil, filled
    with coarse gravel.
K-Cess pool, (abandoned)

L - 4" Sewer to cess pool, (abandoned).
M-Contour lines, or lines of equal elevation.
N-Fences and hedges.

Fig. 36.—Layout of a sewage-disposal plant for a rural house containing 18 to 20 people. Note abandonment of old cesspool near the well and garden and removal of the sewage to a lower and safer location in the pasture, where the treatment is subsurface distribution aided by a series of filter wells about 4 feet deep filled with coarse gravel.

pending the comparatively small amount that ordinarily would be required for adequate sewage disposal on the farm. It is true that because of the superior credit of a municipality, of the issuance of bonds running for long terms and bearing low rates of interest, and of the apportionment of sewer assessments over a series of years, the city dweller may have his burden distributed over a considerable period of time. On the other hand, the farmer should not lose sight of the fact that the costs in the city, as in the country, must ultimately be paid, and that deferred payments on sewer assessments seldom bear interest at a less rate than 5 per cent. Moreover, sewer work can be done more cheaply in the country than in the city.

THE STABLE-MANURE BUSINESS OF BIG CITIES.

By C. C. Fletcher,

Scientist, Investigation of Fertilizer Resources, Bureau of Soils.

FROM New York City alone more than half a million tons of stable manure are shipped to truckers and farmers each year. If for the tonnage of New York City the values of 0.5 per cent nitrogen, 0.25 per cent phosphoric acid, and 0.5 per cent potash be given, there will be available from the stables of this one city 2,500 tons of nitrogen, 1,250 tons of phosphoric acid, and 2,500 tons of potash. Translating this into other terms, the nitrogen is equal to approximately 16,000 tons of nitrate of soda, the phosphoric acid to 8,000 tons of acid phosphate, and the potash to 5,000 tons of sulphate of potash. In all the big cities of the East the collecting and shipping of stable manure is now an established business, conducted by well-organized companies, with agents in smaller places who retail to the consumer. The aggregate tonnage reaches a very large figure. Much of this business represents a clear saving, because at times quantities of manure have been thrown away, not being considered of sufficient value to justify the payment of freight charges. Now, however, stable manure is a recognized article of commerce and brings prices ranging from $1 a ton or less to as much as $3, with freight charges added. To the trucker especially the business is a benefit, as it enables him to obtain at a reasonable price a fertilizer which is of great value in the production of his crops.

SHIPMENT.

Although a great part of the manure from cities and towns is used on the truck farms in their immediate vicinity, yet from New York City some of it is shipped by rail to points in Connecticut, New Jersey, and Pennsylvania and by boat to the Norfolk trucking region. Occasional shipments have been sent even to Maine and Florida.

In many instances the zones of shipment overlap. Thus New York manure is used in the Philadelphia suburbs, and there is a region between New York and Boston where manure is used from both cities. In the trucking region between Baltimore and Washington manure is shipped from both cities, although Baltimore has more of the trade. In Norfolk dealers collect manure on their own account, act as agents for New York concerns, and, in addition, buy manure from stockyards, especially the Richmond stockyards.

As proper disposal of the manure produced in city stables is a sanitary necessity, it must be collected regularly and frequently—practically every day. Many towns, also, particularly in New England, where at times carloads of manure have been left standing on sidings in the main streets, have adopted regulations to govern the handling of such material.

In all cities some of the manure is taken directly from the stable to the farm, under private arrangements, in vehicles of all sorts, from one-horse carts to 5-ton trucks, two-horse wagons predominating. For hauls of more than 20 miles, where the roads are good, trucks are of especial service. Many interurban electric roads now are shipping manure. The manure companies, however, usually ship either by railroad or by boat. The railroad cars used hold from 20 to 50 tons each, averaging about 30 tons. On inland waterways and in protected waters, such as Long Island Sound, open barges are satisfactory, but in open water, as in the haul from New York to Norfolk, the manure is stored beneath the deck. Open barges usually carry from 200 to 500 tons and closed barges as much as 1,200 tons.

GRADING.

Manure companies sometimes divide the fresh manure into two grades, depending on the amount of bedding material included. The standard bedding is straw, but shavings, sawdust, peat moss, and peanut hulls are used sometimes. Straw is better fertilizer material than the other kinds of bedding, except perhaps peat moss, and manure containing straw brings higher prices than where other materials are used. The poorer stables often furnish the best manure, because of greater economy in the use of bedding, and be-

PLATE LXXI.

STEAM CRANES UNLOADING MANURE FROM NEW YORK CITY AT A STORAGE POINT IN NEW JERSEY.

More than 60,000 tons may be seen at one time. Steam pumps turn the leachings back upon the piles to facilitate rotting.

cause of the drying and re-use of the straw, which increases the amount of urine absorbed by it. In some of the best private stables so much straw is used that the manure is valued chiefly as mulching material.

STORING AND TREATING.

In the summer, when farmers are too busy to haul manure and the prices are low, many manure companies store their supply at points convenient to shipping facilities, but away from centers of population, and sell it later as rotted manure. One large New York company has a storage plant and private railroad yard near Monmouth Junction, N. J., where immense stacks of manure are accumulated in the slack season. More than 60,000 tons are reported on hand at one time. It is handled by steam cranes. Rotting of the stored manure is facilitated by pumping the leachings back upon the piles by means of a steam pump. Part of the manure is dried, ground, and bagged in an up-to-date manufacturing plant and is sold as pulverized stock manure, competing on the market with ordinary mixed commercial fertilizer. This is a more concentrated product than the bulky fresh manure and may be used economically by farmers at greater distances.

QUALITY.

Manure will deteriorate if not properly handled unless preservatives are added, but its low value does not warrant much expenditure for preservation. The addition of acid phosphate, for example, increases the fertilizing value of the manure and lessens the loss of nitrogen, but buyers usually are not willing to pay for the increased value. Adding water in proper quantities also will prevent loss through fermentation, but this may lead to abuses, as the product is sold by weight.

Few products have a value low enough for profitable use in adulterating manure, and although the writer has seen tannery waste, street sweepings, and sawdust used for the purpose, the practice is probably not common. New York City manure has an especially good reputation in this respect, as the street sweepings are collected separately and disposed of by the city. Where possible, however, it is advisable for the farmer himself to see his cars or barges loaded.

Street sweepings, though considered an adulterant when sold with manure, often can be obtained cheaply enough to justify their purchase. They are valuable principally for the manure they contain, but are extremely variable. When taken from highways over which there is much automobile traffic they may contain sufficient mineral oil to render their agricultural use dangerous.

SUPPLY.

The supply of manure is dependent upon the number of horses in use in cities. In some cases the number is decreasing, though the decrease appears to be slow, and in some cities horses have increased. Opinions differ greatly as to the permanence of the city manure supply, but for some time at least it probably will be an important source of fertility for the trucking districts. As it is safe to count 5 tons of manure per horse per year, the possible quantity of manure from a city may be calculated roughly if the number of horses is known.

BENEFITS.

Ordinarily it is not advisable for the general farmer to buy manure from the city if he can produce it on his farm, as his crops, owing to their lower acreage value, will not stand as high an outlay for fertilizers as will the truck crops. The railroads usually make so low a rate on manure that there is probably little direct profit in handling it. The increase in crops following its use, however, makes more tonnage of crops to be moved and also a more prosperous agricultural community with more buying power. As to truckers, there seems to be little doubt that those who are using large amounts of manure are the ones who are usually successful. While manure can be bought ordinarily at from $1 per ton or less to around $3 f. o. b., it has been known in special instances to return a profit when costing $5 spread on the truck field or in the cold frame.

The question is often asked as to whether it is advisable to use stable manure or commercial fertilizer. In most cases it is better to use both, but in case of doubt stable manure should be used, as it adds to the soil not only potash, nitrogen, and phosphoric acid, but also beneficial bacteria and humus. In cases where manure can be obtained at a reasonable price, it should find a use on a great number of farms. In estimating its agricultural value a number of factors must be considered. The chemical constituents in it may be worth only a given amount, but the effect of the manure in improving the texture of the soil often may amount to a great deal more than the value of the chemicals it contains. Also, it must be remembered that the results are more lasting than is the case with most of the other soil amendments. At the present time the cost of manure in general is below its agricultural value. In fact, one of the reasons for the increased cost of stable manure is a greater general appreciation of this fact.

Land near a big city sometimes may be bought cheaply and built up by the generous use of stable manure. If good farming is practiced, there is a fair chance of success by this method. The author has seen land appreciate in value more than 300 per cent in 5 years by the use of city stable manure, while at the same time giving a consistent profit in crops grown. And if these profits are made by the use of manure purchased in the large city markets at upward of $1 per ton, how much greater profits are to be made by the use of similar material in many places where it may be obtained for the expense of hauling.

Where sufficient manure is not obtainable, it is possible to mix the manure secured with several times its volume of peat or muck and thus secure a compost which has a value almost equal to that of manure itself. This is increased in value by the addition of acid phosphate.

DESTROYING RODENT PESTS ON THE FARM.

By David E. Lantz,
Assistant Biologist, Bureau of Biological Survey.

INTRODUCTORY.

THE tiller of the soil has enemies on all sides, eager to take toll of his crops. Frost, drought, hail, wind, rust, and mold assail him unexpectedly, while a constant warfare against him is carried on by insects and other animal pests. Rodents are among the most persistent and aggressive of his animal enemies, and against them he is often more helpless even than against insect pests, because he has had less instruction as to their habits and the means of fighting them. To assist him by giving short accounts of the more important rodents that injure farm, ranch, and orchard, together with brief practical directions for destroying the pests, is the purpose of this article.

Unfortunately, it is impossible to separate animals into two great classes, putting into one the species that are injurious on the farm or elsewhere and into the other those that are beneficial. A species may be desirable in one situation and objectionable in another or its useful and harmful activities may be so blended that it can not be placed in either class. Other species that do no actual damage to man's interests may be without beneficial habits or economic value. While these statements are true of all classes of animals, they apply with special force to rodents, an order of mammals often regarded as wholly noxious.

The rodents of North and Middle America include about 1,350 forms, that is, species and geographic races recognized by naturalists. These belong to 77 distinct groups called genera, 44 of which have representatives north of Mexico. These 44 groups include about 750 forms that inhabit the United States and Canada. Many of them live in deserts, mountains, and swamps and rarely come in contact with cultivated crops. These, therefore, can not be classed as injurious; and, indeed, many of them are beneficial to the soil, as they stir it up and fit it for future agricultural uses. A few rodents feed largely upon insects and help to keep a check upon the hordes of grasshoppers and similar pests. Certain of the rodents, too, as the beaver and the muskrat, have a decided economic value as fur bearers; while others, as the rabbits and the tree squirrels, afford sport in hunting and are useful as human food.

The noxiousness of rodents depends, therefore, largely upon the locality in which they live and upon their relation to man and his interests. All are chiefly vegetarian in diet and by reason of their rapid reproduction are capable of becoming pests; but it is only when they are actively injurious that means of control are needed. The right of animals to live when they are harmless must always be conceded.

Probably no term applied to animals has been so generally misused as the word " vermin." Originally restricted to small creeping animals, wormlike in their movements, and especially to insects, the term has been broadened by English gamekeepers to include all enemies of ground game. Usage now sometimes applies the term to all animals that are supposed to be either harmful or useless. Writers on game protection are often vehement in their condemnation of " vermin," forgetting that what may be so considered by one person may from the standpoint of another be highly useful. The interests of the sportsman or gamekeeper often run counter to those of his farmer neighbor, and they frequently clash on such matters as rabbit protection and the enforcement of trespass laws. A better understanding of the habits of birds and mammals, especially of their food and the interrelation of species that prey and are preyed upon, will greatly restrict the number of animals that may properly be called " vermin." Under natural conditions few can rightly be so designated; but man has interfered with nature until he has disturbed its balance. He has introduced artificial conditions and so changed the environments of animals that some have prospered while others have been driven out. The species that have been most favored by man's activities are, unfortunately, those that have been most harmful to his interests. As a result he must now make warfare upon foes that were once inoffensive.

HARMFUL NATIVE RODENTS.

Only four of the many forms of wild rodents found within the United States have been introduced; the others are indigenous to the country. Native rodents include among harmful kinds the short-tailed field mice, white-footed mice, cotton rats, kangaroo rats, pocket gophers, ground squirrels, prairie-dogs, woodchucks, and rabbits. A few others occasionally do slight damage to crops or other property.

SHORT-TAILED FIELD MICE.

Several groups, or genera, of short-tailed field mice occur in the United States and Canada, but only two of them have, by reason of their abundance in cultivated regions, become serious pests. These are commonly known as meadow mice [1] and pine mice.[2]

Meadow mice are widely distributed, inhabiting most parts of the Northern Hemisphere. Their invasion and ravages of crops in France, Hungary, Greece, England, Scotland, and elsewhere are matters of history. In the United States we have many species, but, fortunately, have thus far had no widespread plagues of the animals like those that have occurred abroad. However, there have been many local outbreaks, notably that of 1907–8 in the Humboldt Valley, Nevada, where much of the alfalfa crop was utterly ruined. Fortunately, few of our species come in contact with farm operations, but these few sometimes multiply enormously and inflict heavy damage by attacking and girdling fruit trees and by destroying other crops. Their presence is indicated by their many surface trails under dead grass, weeds, or other trash. The animals usually avoid open spaces, where they are exposed to such enemies as hawks and owls, birds which make these mice the chief part of their diet.

Depredations by meadow mice may be greatly lessened and serious outbreaks prevented by clean cultivation, the elimination of old fence rows, and the prompt burning of dead weeds and other trash.

Pine mice, like moles, burrow underground, where their tunnels are similar in extent and intricacy to the surface runways of meadow mice; but as their natural habitat is the woods, they come less frequently in contact with farm crops. Their most serious depredations are in orchards, although they often do serious damage in lawns and plantations ad-

---

[1] Genus *Microtus.*   [2] Genus *Pitymys.*

joining woodlands by eating bulbs and gnawing the roots of shrubbery. In such situations they frequently also destroy potatoes, peanuts, and newly planted seeds of truck crops. Their concealed operations permit them to do much harm before their presence is suspected. For this reason, also, they are less often the victims of birds of prey.

Ordinary mouse traps of the guillotine type, baited with rolled oats and set in runways of either meadow or pine mice, will free a small area of the animals; but for large areas or for operations against considerable numbers of these mice, poisons are recommended.

For poisoning meadow mice on large areas the following methods are recommended:

Dry-grain formula.—Mix thoroughly 1 ounce powdered strychnine (alkaloid), 1 ounce powdered bicarbonate of soda, and ⅛ ounce (or less) of saccharine. Put the mixture in a tin pepperbox and sift it gradually over 50 pounds of crushed wheat or 40 pounds of crushed oats in a metal tub, mixing the grain constantly so that the poison will be evenly distributed. Dry mixing has the advantage that the grain may be kept any length of time without fermentation. If it is desired to moisten the grain to facilitate thorough mixing, it will be well to use a thin starch paste (as described below, but without strychnine) before applying the poison. The starch soon hardens and fermentation is not likely to follow.

If crushed oats or wheat can not be obtained, whole oats may be used, but they should be of good quality. As mice hull the oats before eating them it is desirable to have the poison penetrate the kernels. A very thin starch paste is recommended as a medium for applying poison to the grain. Prepare as follows:

Wet-grain formula.—Dissolve 1 ounce of strychnine (sulphate) in 2 quarts of boiling water. Dissolve 2 tablespoonfuls of laundry starch in ½ pint of cold water. Add the starch to the strychnine solution and boil for a few minutes until the starch is clear. Pour the hot starch over 1 bushel of oats in a metal tub and stir thoroughly. Let the grain stand overnight to absorb the poison.

The poisoned grain prepared by either of the above formulas is to be distributed over the infested area, not more than a teaspoonful at a place, care being taken to put it in mouse runs and at the entrances of burrows. To avoid destroying birds it should whenever possible be placed under such shelters as piles of weeds, straw, brush, or other litter, or under boards. Small drain tiles 1½ inches in diameter have sometimes been used to advantage to hold poisoned grain, but old tin cans with the edges bent nearly together will serve the same purpose.

Chopped alfalfa hay poisoned with strychnine was successfully used to destroy meadow mice in Nevada during the serious outbreak of the animals in 1907–8. One ounce of strychnine (sulphate) dissolved in 2 gallons of hot water was found sufficient to poison 30 pounds of chopped alfalfa previously moistened with water. This bait, distributed in small quantities at a place, was very effective against the mice and did not endanger birds.

For poisoning mice in small areas, as lawns, gardens, seed beds, vegetable pits, and the like, a convenient bait may be prepared from ordinary rolled oats, as follows:

For small areas.—Dissolve $\frac{1}{16}$ ounce of strychnine in 1 pint of boiling water and pour it over as much oatmeal (about 2 pounds) as it will wet. Mix until all the grain is moistened. Put it out, a teaspoonful at a place, under shelter of weed and brush piles or wide boards.

The poisoned oatmeal is adapted for killing either meadow or pine mice, but for the latter, sweet potatoes, prepared as follows, have proved even more effective:

Potato formula.—Cut sweet potatoes into pieces about as large as good-sized grapes. Place in a metal pan or tub and wet with water. Drain off the water and with a tin pepperbox slowly sift over them powdered strychnine (alkaloid preferred), stirring constantly so that the poison is evenly distributed. An ounce of strychnine should poison a bushel of the cut bait.

The bait, whether of grain or pieces of potato, may be dropped into the pine mouse tunnels through the natural openings or through holes made with pieces of broom handle or other stick. Bird life will not be endangered by these baits.

WHITE-FOOTED MICE.

White-footed mice, or deer mice,[1] are of many species and are present in almost all parts of the country. They live in fields and woods, and while they feed on grain to some extent they rarely are present on cultivated lands in sufficient numbers to do serious harm. Occasionally they invade greenhouses or hotbeds and destroy seeds or sprouting

---

[1] Genus *Peromyscus*.

plants. In the seed beds of nurserymen and especially in those of the forester who tries to grow conifers they often do much injury. They are, in fact, the most serious pests known to the conifer nurseries of the Forest Service.

In ordinary places white-footed mice may be readily poisoned by the methods recommended for meadow and pine mice. Unfortunately, the seed of the pine is the favorite food of those animals and where it is planted in abundance they refuse to take grain baits. Crushed pine seeds poisoned with strychnine by the "wet-grain formula," given above, has proved effective in such places. Preliminary poisoning of these mice on areas to be seeded to pine is highly recommended. For seed beds, poisoning on surrounding areas two or three times a year will usually prevent the approach of mice and give immunity to the planted seeds.

COTTON RATS.

In parts of the Southern States a large native mouse or rat, commonly known as the cotton rat,[1] often becomes a field pest. Of some 28 known forms of this animal, 7 occur north of Mexico, in Texas, New Mexico, Arizona, Oklahoma, and southern Kansas and along the Gulf coast from Louisiana to Florida.

Cotton rats damage growing crops to some extent, but are especially destructive to grain in shocks. In many of their habits they are similar to meadow mice and they multiply fully as fast. They chiefly inhabit weedy borders and areas covered with old grass, where they are sheltered from enemies. They do not often attack the bark of trees, but, being larger than meadow mice, they are capable of destroying much more grain in a short time. They destroy melons and other truck crops and have been a serious pest to date growers in Arizona.

Cotton rats are easily poisoned by the same methods recommended for destroying meadow mice.

KANGAROO RATS.

Fifty-nine known species and races of kangaroo rats, belonging to three groups, inhabit North America, and 45 of them occur north of Mexico. Two groups[2] are widely distributed in the West; they differ in anatomical characters,

---

[1] Genus *Sigmodon*.　　　[2] *Perodipus* and *Dipodomys*.

but are much alike in general appearance and habits. The third group [1] includes three species and one race of very small animals, all of which are rather restricted in range and of slight economic importance. Kangaroo rats are gentle, easily tamed, and make sprightly and interesting pets. They live mostly in deserts, sagebrush country, and sandy places and are harmless until pioneer agriculture is pushed into these regions. They feed to some extent on green vegetation, but mainly on seeds. As they do not hibernate they lay up large stores of winter food in their burrows. They are gregarious, but being nocturnal in their activities they are seldom seen by day.

In the sand-hill and sagebrush country of the West there is much complaint of destruction of pioneer crops by kangaroo rats. The areas first cultivated are usually small, and the animals sometimes destroy an entire crop. Where corn is planted they take all the seed, securing not only temporary food, but storing in their caches large quantities for future use. They are destructive to other grains also and dig up newly planted melon and other seeds. Vegetable gardening is an impossibility where kangaroo rats are abundant. The choice is between making warfare on and destroying the animals or abandoning cultivation. Fortunately, they take poisoned grain readily and are easily trapped with baits of grain. The poison recommended for prairie-dogs is well adapted to destroy kangaroo rats. Trapping with guillotine traps, although successful, is usually too slow to be practicable.

In some instances farmers in the sandhills of the West prevent depredations by kangaroo rats and succeed in growing crops of corn by stirring the seed in hot water in which there has been mixed enough coal tar to coat the grain slightly. A large spoonful of coal tar to a gallon of boiling water is used. When the mixture has cooled somewhat the corn may be stirred in and allowed to remain several minutes without danger to germination.

POCKET GOPHERS.

Pouched rats, commonly called pocket gophers, are among the most serious of rodent pests in most of the States west of

---

[1] Genus *Microdipodops*.

the Mississippi River. They occur also in parts of Georgia, Alabama, and Florida, in the greater part of Illinois, and in southern Wisconsin. Outside the United States they are abundant southward in many parts of Mexico and Central America, and northward in northwestern Canada to Winnipeg and the Saskatchewan Valley.

Nine groups, or genera, of pocket gophers are recognized, but only three of them occur north of Mexico. Two of these[1] have a very wide distribution. They include many species and varieties, all nearly similar in habits and alike destructive. Many forms inhabit mountains and deserts, where they do not injure agriculture. Others, however, live in the richest alluvial soils, where they are destructive to all crops.

Pocket gophers do harm in many ways. They eat growing grain and cover much of it with soil. They cause loss of hay in digging burrows, by throwing up mounds which prevent close mowing. These mounds also injure much machinery. Their burrows admit surface water and aid it to wash out deep gullies on sloping land. By piercing dams and embankments the tunnels cause costly breaks. The animals ruin gardens and injure field crops. Besides all this they kill trees in orchards and forest plantings by gnawing off the roots.

Two practical methods of killing pocket gophers are always possible—trapping and poisoning. The first method is slow, but very effective on small areas or where but few pocket gophers are present; the other is the better plan on large fields and for cooperative work on adjacent farms.

While the ordinary steel trap may be used successfully for pocket gophers, much better results can be obtained with the special traps for these animals commonly on the market. In irrigated districts, where water is available, flooding the land will drive out the animals, and they may be killed by men and dogs. Fumigation of the burrows with carbon bisulphide or with sulphur smoke, while often recommended as a means of destroying pocket gophers, has been found extremely uncertain and costly.

Poison for pocket gophers.—To poison pocket gophers, cut sweet potatoes or parsnips into pieces whose largest diameter is less than an

---

[1] *Geomys* and *Thomomys.*

inch. Wash and drain 4 quarts of the cut baits. Place in a metal
pan, and from a pepperbox slowly sift over the dampened baits ⅛
ounce of powdered strychnine (alkaloid) and one-tenth as much
saccharine (well shaken together or ground together in a mortar),
stirring it to distribute the poison evenly.

Tunnels of pocket gophers, which are usually from 3 to
8 inches below the surface of the ground, may be readily
located by means of a probe. Any blacksmith can make one
by affixing a metal point to a shovel or spade handle and
attaching an iron foot rest about 15 or 16 inches
above the point. By forcing this instrument into
the soil near the pocket-gopher workings or a foot
or two back of fresh mounds, one can feel the open
tunnel as the point breaks into it. The hole may be
enlarged and its sides made firm by pressing the
soil laterally with the probe. A bait or two should
be dropped into the tunnel and the probe hole
covered. Care should be taken to place the baits in
the main tunnels rather than in the short
laterals leading to mounds. Different
forms of probes have been used successfully by the Biological Survey in its demonstration work. Two of the better kinds
are illustrated in figure 37.

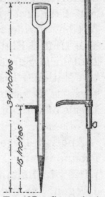

FIG. 37.—Convenient
probes for locating
pocket-gopher runs.

GROUND SQUIRRELS.

More than 50 species and races of
ground squirrels, or spermophiles,[1] inhabit the United States and Canada, and
some of them are so numerous in agricultural regions as to be a constant menace to
crops. The spermophiles comprise a group
of long, slender animals, of grayish or grayish-brown
color—sometimes mottled or striped—and with a medium or
long tail, usually less bushy than that of the larger of the
tree squirrels. These ground squirrels are often, but wrongly,
called "gophers" and are locally named "digger" squirrels
and "picket pins." They inhabit mainly open plains, mountain valleys, and borders of wet meadows, but are found also
in open places in the forests and sometimes high up the

---

[1] Genus *Citellus*.

slopes of mountains. They dig numerous deep burrows and are very destructive to nearly all crops, eating both the growing plants and the ripe or ripening grain. In irrigated districts the animals burrow in embankments and levees and are almost as troublesome as pocket gophers.

Among the largest and most destructive of these animals is the California, or "digger," ground squirrel.[1] It is gray in color and has a long, rather bushy tail. It occurs in the Southwest and West from western Texas to California and Oregon. In parts of California the race known as the Beechey ground squirrel is especially abundant and menaces not only crops and irrigation ditches, but also human life, in that it is a known carrier of bubonic plague. About a dozen cases of this disease among human beings have been traced directly to this squirrel and a large number of the animals collected by the United States Public Health Service have been found infected. The Health Service, in cooperation with State authorities, has succeeded in establishing south and east of San Francisco, in the counties that were the center of infection, a wide zone now comparatively free from squirrels. The United States Department of Agriculture, through the Biological Survey, has exterminated most of the squirrels in the National Forests that lie near the plague-infected counties. It is probable that all immediate danger of an outbreak of human plague by infection from ground squirrels has passed.

Another large and destructive species is the Columbian ground squirrel.[2] It occurs within the United States in parts of Montana, Idaho, eastern Washington, and eastern Oregon. While it inhabits chiefly the river valleys, it has been taken in Montana on mountains near timber line. Where grain is grown in the narrow valleys and in the important wheat districts of eastern Washington this species is extremely injurious. Early attempts to destroy it by poison proved unsuccessful, because the animal is able to resist much larger doses of strychnine than are needed to kill other ground squirrels.

A destructive and widely distributed species is the Richardson ground squirrel.[3] In its larger form it is found in

---

[1] *Citellus grammurus grammurus* and closely related races.
[2] *Citellus columbianus.*
[3] *Citellus richardsoni richardsoni* and *Citellus richardsoni elegans.*

much of Montana, the Dakotas, and northward far into Canada. A somewhat smaller race (*elegans*) is found in Wyoming, northern Colorado, and eastern Idaho. This spermophile is very destructive to crops, especially to grain, and within its range warfare against it is absolutely necessary to successful farming.

The striped ground squirrel,[1] the Franklin ground squirrel,[2] and some other species, which are less gregarious and seldom occur in great numbers in any locality, are less destructive than any of the three groups named. Other species are nearly as injurious as those described. The animals have been dealt with in three groups, because slightly different formulas for poisoning each of them have been worked out by field investigators of the Biological Survey. The formula for the Richardson ground squirrel is adapted for all the species except the Columbian and the California forms.

Poison for Columbian ground squirrels.—Mix 1 ounce of powdered strychnine (alkaloid), 1 ounce of powdered bicarbonate of soda, 1 teaspoonful of saccharine, and ½ pound of dry powdered laundry starch, and stir with enough cold water to make a smooth, creamy paste. Apply to 12 quarts of good, clean oats in a metal tub or other vessel and stir thoroughly to distribute the poison evenly. When the poisoned grain is dry, scatter it along squirrel trails or on hard soil on the surface near the squirrel burrows. A quart of the grain should make 40 to 50 baits, and if properly distributed stock will not be endangered by this quantity.

Poison for Richardson ground squirrels.—Mix 1 tablespoonful of laundry starch in ½ teacup of cold water, and stir it into ½ pint of boiling water to make it a thin, clear mucilage. Mix 1 ounce of powdered strychnine with 1 ounce of powdered bicarbonate of soda, and stir the mixture into the hot starch, making a smooth, creamy paste free from lumps. Stir in ¼ pint of heavy corn sirup and 1 tablespoonful of glycerine, and, finally, 1 scant teaspoonful of saccharine. Apply to 20 quarts of oats, and mix thoroughly to coat every kernel. Each quart of the poisoned grain should make 40 to 60 baits. Distribute in same manner as stated for poisoning Columbian ground squirrels.

Poison for California, or "digger," ground squirrels.—Prepare by same formula as for Richardson ground squirrel, but use 16 quarts of clean barley instead of oats. Distribute as for poisoning Columbian ground squirrels.

These poisons may be used at any time of the year when the squirrels are active. The Biological Survey has had ex-

---

[1] *Citellus tridecemlineatus.*   [2] *Citellus franklini.*

cellent results with them, even in midsummer. Trapping is too slow a process to use effectively against large colonies of ground squirrels.

PRAIRIE-DOGS.

The marmot, or prairie-dog,[1] of the Great Plains needs little description. It is widely distributed on the plains east of the Rocky Mountains, from northern Mexico almost to the Canadian border. Several other forms occupy the mountain valleys and parks westward. All live in thickly populated colonies, or " towns," and subsist on vegetation. They often take fully half the pasturage on the ranges and greatly reduce the carrying capacity for live stock. Several western States have attempted to provide for the extermination of prairie-dogs through legislative enactments; and in some of them, notably Kansas, the pest has greatly decreased. Within the National Forests settlers have complained of inability to cope with the animals, because their lands when freed from prairie-dogs are reinfested from the surrounding Government lands. For this reason and for range improvement the Department of Agriculture has undertaken systematic extermination work within the Forests and has already succeeded in freeing large areas of these animals.

Trapping is too slow a method for exterminating prairie-dogs and fumigation is too expensive. As in the case of ground squirrels, strychnine has proved to be the most satisfactory poison. Oats of the best quality obtainable should be used as bait. It has been found that prairie-dogs take this grain readily, even when green food is abundant. Wheat is well adapted for winter poisoning, and in the South, where heavy oats are rarely obtainable, milo or feterita is an excellent substitute.

Poison for prairie-dogs.—Mix thoroughly 1 ounce of powdered strychnine (alkaloid) and 1 ounce of common baking soda (bicarbonate). Dissolve 1 heaping tablespoonful of dry laundry starch in a little cold water and add it to ¾ pint of boiling water. Boil and stir until a thin, clear paste is formed. Slowly sift the mixture of strychnine and soda into the starch paste, stirring constantly to form a smooth, creamy mass. Add ¼ pint of heavy corn sirup and 1 tablespoonful of glycerine, and stir. Add ⅒ ounce of saccharine, and again stir thoroughly. Pour this mixture while still hot over 13 quarts of clean oats and mix until all the grain is coated.

---

[1] *Cynomys ludovicianus.*

B15902

FIG. I.—MOUNTAIN BEAVER (APLODONTIA).

B15917

FIG. 2.—BADGER (TAXIDEA TAXUS), USEFUL IN DESTROYING
NOXIOUS RODENTS.

B252M

FIG. 3.—KANGAROO RAT (PERODIPUS RICHARDSONI), ADULT, ONE
DAY AFTER CAPTURE.

B58M

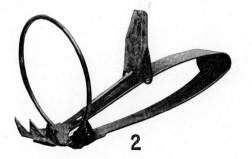

B613M

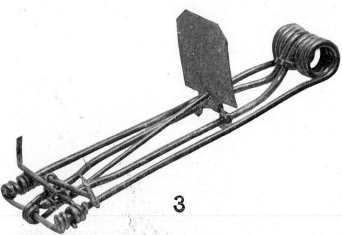

B611M

(1) MEADOW MOUSE CAUGHT IN GUILLOTINE TRAP. (2, 3) TYPES OF
SPECIAL POCKET-GOPHER TRAPS.

B11148

FIG. I.—BREAK IN IRRIGATION DITCH (LATERAL) CAUSED BY BURROWS OF CALIFORNIA GROUND SQUIRREL. SIX ACRES OF ALFALFA RUINED.

B9141

FIG. 2.—CORNFIELD RUINED BY COLUMBIAN GROUND SQUIRRELS.

B14233

FIG. I.—EROSION FOLLOWING THE DESTRUCTION OF GRASS BY PRAIRIE DOGS.

B11132

FIG. 2.—MOUND OF CALIFORNIA GROUND SQUIRREL IN OATS FIELD.

B73M

THE JACK-RABBIT DRIVE IS A WESTERN EVENT.

In some parts of the West the county agricultural agents have devoted time to organizing rabbit drives with good results. In Crook County, Oreg., for instance, organized community rabbit drives last spring netted about 6,000 rabbits at Millican, 8,000 at Hampton, and 10,000 at Rivers, and the work was continued successfully throughout the summer.

If alkaloid strychnine is not available, the sulphate may be used, either powdered or in crystals, but it is necessary to vary the formula. Dissolve the strychnine in the boiling water before adding the cold starch. After the poisoned starch paste is clear, stir in the soda very slowly. Afterwards add the sirup, glycerine, and saccharine as in the above directions and mix with the grain.

For mixing small quantities an ordinary metal washtub is convenient. For large quantities a tight, smooth box may be used, and the mixing done with a hoe or spade.

Each quart of the prepared grain is sufficient to treat about 50 prairie-dog burrows. Scatter the grain on clean, hard ground near the mounds or burrows, never on loose soil or in the holes. With reasonable care, cattle, sheep, or other live stock on the range will not be endangered.

This poison is effective at any season when prairie-dogs are active, but, on the whole, early spring or a time of drought, when green food is scarce, is preferred for poison operations. In the South, or wherever the animals do not hibernate, winter poisoning is recommended. The cost of complete extermination of the animals, including labor, need not exceed 4 or 5 cents an acre.

WOODCHUCKS.

The woodchuck, or ground hog, is the largest of our marmots. The common woodchuck[1] inhabits eastern North America from northern Georgia and middle Alabama northward, including the greater part of Canada. In the United States it ranges westward to Arkansas, eastern Kansas, and eastern Minnesota. In Canada it is found as far north as Great Slave Lake and westward to the base of the Rocky Mountains. Another species of woodchuck[2] inhabits the higher country of the Black Hills, Rocky Mountains, Sierra Nevada, Cascades, and other ranges in the West. This mountain form seldom comes in contact with agriculture, but the eastern species frequently damages garden vegetables, clover, and other crops. Also, its burrows and mounds interfere with mowing and other farm operations. In some States the animal is regarded as so obnoxious that local bounties are paid for destroying it.

Woodchucks, while somewhat gregarious, seldom occur in large colonies, and may, therefore, be kept in check by shoot-

---

[1] *Marmota monax monax* and several geographic races.
[2] *Marmota flaviventris flaviventris* and nearly a dozen races.

ing or trapping. They may be poisoned by strychnine inserted in pieces of sweet apple, carrot, or sweet potato. The animals are often destroyed in their burrows by fumigation with carbon bisulphide or by the discharge of blasting powder.

To destroy woodchucks with carbon bisulphide, saturate a wad of cotton or waste with about 1½ ounces of the liquid. Place the cotton well inside the woodchuck burrow and close the opening with a piece of sod, well stamped down. If there are two or more entrances to a burrow, all but one should be tightly closed before fumigation.

RABBITS.

The smaller forms of rabbits, known generally as cottontails,[1] are useful animals and become objectionable only when too numerous in the vicinity of orchards or nurseries. The same is true of the larger snowshoe rabbits.[2] The jack rabbits[2] of the West are of less value for human food, and, by reason of their abundance in newly settled regions, often interfere greatly with crops and the growing of orchard and other trees.

Jack rabbits are not protected in any of the States, but are everywhere regarded as a pest. They afford considerable sport in coursing with fleet greyhounds, but at times they become so abundant and destructive that entire communities unite to kill them by the organized hunt or drive. A large area is surrounded and the animals are driven toward some central point, where a wire corral has been built, into which, with the help of wing barriers, thousands of rabbits are driven and then slaughtered. When these hunts take place in cold weather the rabbits are usually shipped to large cities, where the carcasses are either sold to canning establishments or distributed to public charities.

Many of the States which have a close season for cottontail or other native rabbits permit landowners at any time to protect property from the depredations of the animals. Usually, however, close hunting and trapping in the open season afford ample protection, and only in exceptional cases is it necessary to resort to other measures for relief.

---

[1] Genus *Sylvilagus.*   [2] Genus *Lepus.*

Except where deep snows fall, orchards or other crops on small areas may be protected by the use of rabbit-proof fencing. Individual trees may be safeguarded by metal or wooden protectors attached to the trunks. In Idaho a poisoned wash of strychnine, glycerine, and starch proved effective to save trees from jack rabbits, and the method is recommended for trial in any locality where conditions warrant its use. The wash is prepared as follows:

Poison wash.—Dissolve 1 ounce of strychnine (sulphate) in 3 quarts of boiling water. Dissolve ½ pound of laundry starch in 1 pint of cold water, stirring thoroughly. Pour the starch into the vessel containing the strychnine and boil the mixture a short time until the starch is clear. Add 6 ounces of glycerine and stir. When the paste is cool enough apply to tree trunks with a paint brush.

The mixture adheres well and forms a thin coating. If rabbits attack the tree they will be killed before it is seriously injured. The wash should not be used if live stock, especially young cattle, have access to the orchard.

For poisoning jack rabbits in winter the following formula is recommended:

Poison baits.—Good oats, 12 quarts; powdered strychnine, 1 ounce; laundry starch, 1 tablespoonful; soda (bicarbonate), 1 ounce; saccharine, ⅛ ounce; water, 1 quart. Prepare as directed for mixing prairie-dog poison. Not over a tablespoonful of the poisoned grain should be used in a single bait, and this should be scattered considerably. A little alfalfa hay may be used to attract rabbits to the grain. The poison is especially effective when snow covers the ground.

Partly ripened or ripe heads of barley or wheat soaked in a sweetened solution of strychnine or coated with the starch-strychnine paste just described have also proved effective baits for rabbits, but care must be exercised in using them, as they are likely to be eaten by live stock.

OTHER NATIVE RODENTS.

Other native rodents that occasionally damage crops or other property are the muskrat, mountain beaver,[1] wood-rats,[2] tree squirrels, chipmunks, and perhaps some species of native mice not already mentioned. Muskrats are valuable fur animals and should not be destroyed unless they are doing material damage not otherwise preventable. They are

---

[1] Genus *Aplodontia*.   [2] Genus *Neotoma*.

easily trapped or may be poisoned by feeding them pieces of carrot, sweet apple, or sweet potato in which strychnine has been placed.

Mountain beavers in the United States are restricted to the coastal region of Washington, Oregon, and California, and to the Sierra Nevada in the last-named State. Their habitat does not often bring them in contact with agriculture, but in western Washington considerable complaint of their depredations on crops, particularly small fruits, has been made. The animals may readily be poisoned with apples in which strychnine has been placed.

Squirrels, chipmunks, and native mice not previously mentioned rarely do serious damage. If any become troublesome locally, shooting, trapping, or the poisons herein recommended for other rodents will prove a satisfactory means of relief.

INTRODUCED RODENTS.

The house mouse and three kinds of rats are the only rodent pests in North America not native to the country. They are our most injurious rodents, however, and probably inflict greater losses than do all the native species combined.

House mice are easily trapped or poisoned, but poison is not suited for use in occupied dwellings. Traps, however, are sufficiently effective for clearing the premises of these pests. The ordinary small guillotine traps are recommended. They should be set as lightly as possible and baited with oatmeal (rolled oats). A few grains should be placed on the trigger pan and a little more in the vicinity and close to the trap. Persistent trapping will soon clear an ordinary dwelling of mice.

Rats are much more suspicious than mice and are rather hard to trap or poison. Either method of destroying them may be made effective by making inaccessible all food other than the baits used. The importance of rat-proofing buildings in extensive operations against these pests should not be overlooked; and much loss may be prevented by rat-proofing all containers of stored grains and food products. No one kind of poison can be relied upon to be effective under every circumstance. In general, poisons can not be used in occupied dwellings without disagreeable results, for no poison will prevent decomposition of dead bodies of rats. Inside of residences, therefore, traps must be the main reliance. Simple traps of the guillotine type are recommended as best. Baits should be varied to suit local conditions—in meat markets grains are recommended, and where grain is stored meat and fish are more effective.

Some cats and some dogs are useful against rats, but the well-fed and pampered feline or canine will refuse to hunt them. Ferrets are of no use in rat catching unless handled by an experienced person helped by trained dogs. Rat viruses seldom prove satisfactory, and in occupied premises are open to the same objections that hold against poisons; besides, they are much more expensive.

Under most circumstances the best results in ridding premises of rats may be obtained by the use of a sufficient number of ordinary guillotine traps. Oatmeal is recommended for bait, but fish, bacon, sausage, and even pastry or cheese are sometimes useful as alternatives. Traps should be set lightly and all food other than baits covered or made inaccessible. Traps may be placed in runs, behind furniture or boards leaned against the walls, or at the entrances to rat holes. As they are often sprung when rats run over them, they need not always be baited. It is needless to say that in order to succeed, the trapper must take an interest in his work and attend closely to every detail.

RELATION OF CARNIVOROUS ANIMALS TO RODENTS.

Most carnivorous or flesh-eating animals feed extensively on the rodent pests of the farm. Coyotes, foxes, wildcats, badgers, skunks, minks, and other flesh-eating mammals are among the most potent agents in preventing an undue increase of mice, ground squirrels, pocket gophers, and the like; and much of the damage now done by rodents is due to the unceasing warfare that has been waged against carnivorous animals. These have been hunted, not only for their valuable pelts, but because they are considered the enemies of domestic animals and game. The fact that many of them destroy far more noxious rodents than they do useful animals has often been forgotten, and, in the name of game protection, legislatures have sometimes proscribed by bounties species that do far more good than harm. As a matter of fact many of our fur animals are an asset to the country, equally as valuable as our game, and experience has often proved that their destruction is no real help to game conservation.

Birds of prey, including eagles, hawks, and owls, may be included in the list of flesh-eating animals that on the whole are more useful than harmful, because their chief economic function is to destroy noxious rodents. A few species of hawks that feed mainly on small birds should be considered noxious, but this should not lead to warfare against hawks as a class. In almost every instance of depredations on poultry by either bird or mammal, the individual and not the species is the offender. Punishment should, therefore, be directed against the individual. It is within the law in many States for the farmer to kill an animal that destroys his property; but it is unjust to carry on an offensive campaign against all hawks or all minks because one has been a marauder on poultry. The payment of money from the public treasury in a general warfare against certain hawks or owls is especially open to danger, in that the public does not distinguish between species, and the useful ones are most likely to be destroyed.

Snakes also are extremely useful in controlling the numbers of rodents. That very few snakes are venomous is too often forgotten, and all species are wantonly destroyed. People throughout the country should acquaint themselves with the habits of snakes and learn the folly of killing them; while farmers, especially, should do all in their power to protect the harmless kinds.

COOPERATION IN CONTROLLING RODENTS.

Any farmer may by care and industry free his own premises of harmful rodents, but he is helpless to prevent an early recurrence of the trouble unless he can secure the active cooperation of his neighbors. Only by unity of effort can an entire county or township be freed of any kind of rodent that may inflict losses on crops or other property. By combining to hire labor and purchase poison the cost of treatment may be materially reduced, and when permanance of results is considered there can be no question of the economy of such cooperation. It is urged, therefore, that wherever possible the destruction of rodent pests be made a community undertaking.

THE PRESENT STATUS OF THE SUGAR-BEET SEED INDUSTRY IN THE UNITED STATES.

By C. O. Townsend,

Pathologist in Charge of Sugar-Beet Investigations, Bureau of Plant Industry.

OWING to the disturbed agricultural and trade conditions in Europe since August, 1914, the importance of developing an American beet-seed industry of sufficient magnitude to meet our requirements has become imperative. The united efforts of the Department of Agriculture and the Department of State, cooperating with the beet-sugar companies, after encountering many difficulties succeeded in securing sufficient beet seed, with the surplus then on hand, to meet the planting requirements in 1915; but the combined efforts of those agencies failed to secure sufficient seed to meet the requirements in 1916, with the result that thousands of farmers were deprived of the benefits of this crop, a number of mills were idle, and consequently the capital invested, amounting to several million dollars, was unproductive.

The present seed requirements of the beet-sugar industry in this country are annually not less than 150,000 sacks of 110 pounds each. In order to insure this quantity of seed it would be necessary to have not less than 16,000 acres devoted to seed production. Less than one-fourth of this acreage was harvested in 1916. Seven new mills were erected during 1916 and plans are under way for a still larger number in 1917. Assuming the average capacity of these mills to be 1,000 tons of roots a day, which is approximately correct, each new mill will require 10,000 acres of beets for a normal run. To plant 10,000 acres of beets, 200,000 pounds of seed, the product of approximately 200 acres of land, would be required for each mill, not considering the necessary replanting. It is apparent, therefore, that the present acreage in seed will do little more than care for the possible expansion of the beet-sugar industry and that the quantity

399

of seed which must be imported will remain approximately the same as heretofore.

The beet-sugar industry in the United States is composed of three distinct branches, namely, beet-seed production, sugar-beet growing, and beet-sugar extraction and refining. They are so linked that each is dependent upon the others, not only for its complete success but for its very existence. Without seed the sugar-beet industry, in which more than 70,000 American farmers are directly interested, could not exist, and without beets the 84 beet-sugar mills now standing, with an invested capital of more than $100,000,000, would be idle. The beet-seed industry is, of course, the foundation upon which sugar-beet growing and beet-sugar extraction rests. Because of its fundamental character, it is surprising that sugar-beet seed production in this country has not received more general and more earnest attention in the past. The two primary causes that have operated against the development of the sugar-beet seed industry in this country were (1) the fact that a sufficient quantity of seed to meet our requirements was easily obtainable from European countries at a reasonable price and (2) the prevailing idea that conditions in this country, from the standpoint either of labor cost or of climate, would not permit the successful development of the seed industry in the United States. Recent experiences, however, have shown the folly of depending upon foreign countries for our beet-seed supply, while experiments extending over many years have proved the falsity of the opinion relative to labor and climatic conditions.

PROGRESS IN AMERICAN SUGAR-BEET SEED PRODUCTION.

The earliest efforts toward sugar-beet culture in this country, in 1830, were made with seed brought from Europe. When the first permanent beet-sugar mill was established in America, in 1879, European seed was used to produce the raw material, and even at the present time, with nearly 80 mills in operation, requiring upward of 750,000 acres of beets to insure satisfactory runs, farmers are still dependent upon foreign countries for the major portion of their seed. It is true, efforts have been made in certain quarters for many years to produce sugar-beet seed in this country, but prior to 1914 they were largely experimental. The first carefully planned effort to grow sugar-beet seed in the United States was made at Schuyler, Nebr., in 1891. These experiments were continued for several years under the direction of Dr. Harvey W. Wiley, at that time chief of the Bureau of Chemistry of the United States Department of Agriculture. The results with this seed, in comparison with imported varieties, showed that the American-grown seed had a higher vitality and that the roots produced from this seed possessed a higher sugar content and gave a heavier yield than any of the imported varieties tested.[1]

For a number of years the United States Department of Agriculture conducted experiments in sugar-beet seed growing at Fairfield, Wash., with results similar to those obtained at Schuyler, Nebr., with reference to both the vitality of the seed and the quality and weight of roots produced. For many years several sugar companies have grown small quantities of commercial sugar-beet seed, and within the past year two of these beet-sugar companies have greatly increased their beet-seed acreage. In some cases the roots used for this purpose have been produced from the commercial imported seed, while in other instances special seed was used. The results of these tests have been successful from the standpoint of germination of the seed and the yield and quality of the roots produced. While there is abundant proof, therefore, that sugar-beet seed satisfactory in every particular can be grown in this country, few, if any, distinct American strains of sugar beets have been established and used for commercial beet-seed production. All experience in breeding and selection in this and in other lines would indicate that such strains when properly established and thoroughly acclimated if generally used for beet production will yield even better results than have been obtained in the experiments already carried out.

---

[1] See Farmers' Bulletin No. 52, 1897, by Dr. H. W. Wiley.

SUGAR-BEET SEED IS GROWN UNDER WIDELY VARYING CONDITIONS.

The principal areas devoted to sugar-beet seed production in the United States at present are in Michigan, Montana, Colorado, Utah, and Idaho, while several other States have smaller acreages devoted to this crop. Each of the States mentioned produced beet seed commercially last year; in several of these this crop has been grown commercially for a number of years. For the most part the seed is of good quality and the roots produced from home-grown seed have been equal in yield and quality to those grown from imported seed. It is apparent, therefore, that sugar-beet seed can be grown successfully on a commercial scale under a great variety of soil and climatic conditions. Given a good grade of seed, climate is one of the most important factors in the production of sugar beets and sugar-beet seed of good quality. It would seem, therefore, that a thoroughly acclimated strain of seed of high grade should give the best possible results in tonnage and quality of roots. In areas tested for beet-seed production, a loamy, fertile, well-drained soil is generally preferred. A study of the tillable areas in the States named indicates that there is an abundant acreage suitable for profitable beet-seed production, and a study of soil conditions in other States possessing suitable climate for beet-seed growing indicates that nature has abundantly supplied the requirements for the successful production of this crop. In the irrigated sections water should be available, so that the roots can be well supplied with moisture when planted and during the period when the seed is forming.

PRESENT PROBLEMS.

As a result of existing conditions surrounding the sugar-beet seed situation in this country two problems are confronting the beet growers and sugar producers at this time, namely, the production of a sufficient quantity of seed to meet the present planting requirements and the establishment in this country of a permanent beet-seed industry which shall meet our future needs. These requirements relate not only to the quantity of seed necessary to plant the desired acreage, but also to the quality of the seed and the quantity and quality of the roots which this seed is capable of producing.

In order to solve these problems a sugar-beet seed company, under the leadership of a capable and experienced man, has been organized, and its work is already in progress; several sugar companies and individuals are growing sugar-beet seed commercially and experimentally; and the United States Congress has made a special appropriation to enable the Federal Government to cooperate with these several agencies in solving the beet-seed problems. In the solution of the first problem it is apparent that time is an important factor, and we must therefore utilize the best available material and employ the most practical methods known, in order to accomplish the desired results in the shortest possible time. In the solution of the second problem it would seem advisable to find or to develop those strains of beets best suited to our conditions and to improve our methods of root production, selection, siloing, planting, and harvesting, in order to obtain the maximum results at the lowest cost. In the preliminary efforts to solve the first problem commercial roots for the most part have been selected, care being taken to get the best obtainable from the standpoints of yield and quality. The leaves were removed either by cutting or by twisting them off with as little injury to the crown as possible. The roots were siloed by piling them on the ground in a well-drained place and covering them with earth to keep them from freezing, care being taken not to cover them too deeply at first, in order to avoid heating. The roots were planted in the spring by hand in rows 3 feet apart and at intervals of 2 to 3 feet in the row, the distance depending upon the size of the roots. The seed was cut with sickles and thrashed by means of a grain thrasher operated at reduced speed or with a specially constructed beet-seed thrasher.

So far as this so-called emergency method of producing beet seed has been tried the results have proved satisfactory, both from the standpoint of quantity and quality of seed produced and from the standpoint of roots produced from the seed. As a rule, the germination of this seed has been superior to that of the imported seed. Just how far this work can be carried without appreciable reduction in quantity and quality of seed or roots remains to be determined. Even if this method could be employed generally for the production of commercial sugar-beet seed, it would still be desirable to solve the second problem, in order to improve the quality and yield of seed as well as the quantity and quality of the roots produced. The second general problem embraces a large number of special problems, such as types, selection, siloing, planting, and harvesting, which will be considered briefly.

TYPES OF SUGAR BEETS.

It is a startling fact that there are in this country no distinct types of commercial sugar beets. If, for example, a field of a given variety of wheat is examined it will be noted that practically every plant bears a striking resemblance to every other plant in the field, but this is not true of the sugar beet. In any commercial sugar-beet field from Michigan to California, without regard to the name of the so-called variety, can be found from 6 to 20 or more distinct types of beets. Their distinctions may be based upon shape, texture, habit of growth, color, and other characters of the leaf, as well as upon shape, texture, quality, etc., of the root. In fact, scarcely two beets growing side by side in the same field have closely related external characters of leaf or root, and the quality of the roots varies in both sugar and purity.

Equally wide variations may be found in the beet-seed fields, especially with reference to habit of growth and yield of seed. It would appear, therefore, that these so-called strains are badly mixed in the process of growth and production or that many strains or varieties are mixed before the seed is sacked. It would seem, however, from the large number of wide variations in the individual beets produced from commercial seed, that the mixed strains or varieties appearing in commercial fields are due more to the method of growth than to artificial mixing. It may be and probably is necessary to have mixed strains, or crosses, in order to combine in one plant all the desirable qualities of weight, sugar, and purity. It would seem, however, that little progress can be made in the development of desirable strains of beets until the present mixed varieties are separated into their component strains and the desirable strains recombined in their proper relation. It is no more reasonable to suppose that such a mixture of the present types of sugar beets will give the best results in yield and quality of roots than it is to assume that the highest results in livestock production can be reached with mixed breeds of animals. How quickly the Duroc-Jersey or Poland China hog is recognized! Farmers might have gone on raising " razor backs " and thought they were producing pork if these and other distinct types of hogs had not been developed.

It is true that there are some good cows in a mixed herd and not all pure breds are of equal value. Likewise, there are good sugar beets in these mixtures that are now called by distinct names and not all individuals of a pure type will be of equal value, but the average in both quality and yield is far below the limit of possibilities, and the highest plane of development of the sugar beet will not be reached until distinct strains or types are produced and fixed, so that they will come true from year to year. It will then be possible to work with the individual beet as the unit upon which the quality and yield of roots may be based, with a reasonable expectation that material and permanent improvement in quality and yield of roots may be produced by eliminating the poorer and less desirable individuals. It is not probable that in these pure strains the highest development of both size and quality will be found in any one strain, but it is necessary first to have the pure strains and to know definitely the characters they possess and are capable of transmitting before the necessary steps can be taken to produce by crossing the permanent types in which the roots shall possess the desired qualities of sugar, purity, and yield. At the same time this line of work should develop seed-producing plants of uniform type, with reference to both habit of growth of seed stalks and date of maturity of seed. The development of uniform types is of vital importance not only with reference to the yield and quality of roots and seed, but also with reference to the cost of production. The first step, therefore,

in the development of a permanent beet-seed industry in this
country lies in the direction of the development of true types
with reference to both seed beets and seed production.

SELECTION OF ROOTS.

The yield and quality of the roots and of the seed are
the all-important factors upon which the future of the
beet-sugar industry as a whole depends. After obtaining the best possible type of sugar beets, capable of coming true from year to year, the next step is to improve and
develop that type by eliminating the less desirable individuals and by perpetuating those individuals possessing in
the highest degree the desired characters. This process is
called selection. The quality of both roots and seed depends
not only upon certain inherited characters of the plant, but
also upon soil and climatic conditions. Just how far inheritance and how far soil and climate influence the quality of
roots and seed has not been determined. Observation and
experience would indicate, however, that environment has
a far greater influence upon the quality of both roots and
seed than has generally been supposed. Sugar in the beet
roots does not seem to be an inherited character, so far as
percentage or quantity of sugar is concerned. It is true
that sugar beets naturally develop and store sugar, but the
amount of sugar that a given beet will store may be greater
or less than the amount developed and stored by its parent
beet. The direction and extent of this difference will depend,
within certain limits, upon the soil and climatic conditions
under which the beet is grown. The writer has found that
wild beet seed planted under favorable conditions will produce some roots of good size containing upward of 14 per
cent of sugar the first year. Again, it has been observed that
any one of the well-known commercial strains, so called, of
sugar-beet seed, if divided and planted under widely different climatic conditions, will often show a great variation
in the quality and yield of roots produced. The importance
of inheritance of desired characters should not be under-
valued, and it should be utilized in the improvement of
sugar beets. Likewise, the influence of environment upon

the quality of the roots should not be overlooked. It is possible, furthermore, that there is a relation between certain fixed external characters of the beet and the internal qualities, sugar and purity, of the root, and the greatest advance in seed production will be made when that relation, if it exists, is definitely known. Even then it will be necessary to compare the selected roots from time to time in order to maintain the highest possible standard. In making selections, close attention must be paid not only to the yield and quality of the roots, but to the yield and quality of the seed as well. Herein the two industries, beet-seed production and sugar-beet growing, are closely related. In this connection it should be noted that many cultural problems related to sugar beets can not be solved intelligently until we have fixed and uniform types of root, leaf, and seed stalk.

SILOING THE ROOTS.

The object to be kept in mind in siloing beet roots for seed production is to get the roots through the resting period in the soundest and freshest possible condition. The steps in siloing roots consist in gathering, topping, testing, piling, and covering. As a rule, it is best to let the roots remain in the ground as late as possible without danger of freezing. The leaves will protect the crowns against some degree of frost, but in no case should the crowns or roots become frosted, either before or after harvesting. As soon as the roots are taken from the ground the leaves should be removed, either by twisting or by cutting, with as little injury as possible to the crown. In some cases the roots may be siloed without removing the leaves, but in general this practice is not recommended. If it is desired to test the roots for sugar at harvest time, this work should be arranged so that the roots will be out of the ground the least possible time before they are put into the silo, thus avoiding unnecessary drying. The simplest method of siloing is to pile the roots on a well-drained piece of ground and cover them with loose earth. The covering on the top of the pile should be light for a faw days, until the danger of heating of the roots is over, and then, as the weather gets colder, more dirt should be added, so that the roots will be cool but never frosted. Some prefer to pack the roots in sand. This is a safer but more expensive method, and is recommended for small choice lots of roots for experimental purposes. The sand should be slightly damp and may be used in the open or in a cool cellar. In no case should straw or other litter be used in contact with the beets, as this attracts mice, which frequently injure the beets by gnawing.

PLANTING.

The covering should be removed in part from the silo in the early spring, but not to the extent of injury to the roots through late freezes. If a little growth starts no harm is done; in fact, it seems to be an advantage. As soon as the soil can be prepared in the spring the roots should be planted. The importance of early planting can not be over-estimated. Several methods are used in planting the beets. It may be accomplished by means of a long spade, which should be pushed into the ground to such a depth that when it is pushed forward the root may be thrust down behind the spade, which is then withdrawn. The root should be so deep that the crown is just flush with the surface of the ground, or for very early planting a little deeper, so that a thin layer of earth covers the crown to prevent freezing. Another method employed in planting roots consists in breaking up the ground so that the roots can be thrust down into the loose soil to the desired depth. In any case, the soil should be packed firmly around the roots. Where irrigation water is available a thorough watering just after planting serves to settle the dirt around the roots, thereby preventing the formation of air spaces and at the same time supplying the roots with the necessary moisture to insure a quick and uniform growth. The roots should be planted in rows, one way at least, to admit of cultivation. The usual distance between rows is 3 feet and the distance between the beets in the row is from 18 inches to 3 feet, depending upon the size of the roots.

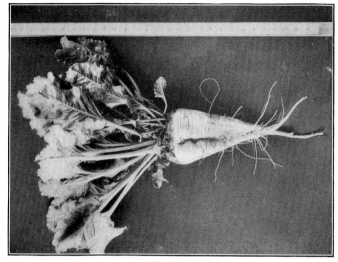

TWO OF THE MANY WIDELY VARYING TYPES OF SUGAR BEETS FOUND IN COMMERCIAL FIELDS.

TWO OF THE MANY TYPES OF SEED STALKS FOUND IN COMMERCIAL
BEET-SEED FIELDS.

HARVESTING SUGAR-BEET SEED.

FIG. I —SUGAR-BEET SEED CUT AND SHOCKED.

FIG. 2.—SUGAR-BEET SEED FIELD AFTER CUTTING AND THRASHING,
SHOWING AMOUNT OF STOCK FEED LEFT IN THE FIELD.

THRASHING THE FIRST CROP OF COMMERCIAL SUGAR-BEET SEED GROWN IN MICHIGAN.

HARVESTING THE SEED.

Under present conditions, the seed on a given plant does not all ripen at the same time. The opening of the flower buds extends over a long period, and naturally the flowers that open first form ripe seed in advance of the later flowers. If left too long before cutting, the early-maturing seed shatters, and if cut too early there is an appreciable loss due to immature seed. To avoid this condition, care must be exercised in cutting the seed at the proper time to produce the best results in yield and quality. The seed stalks upon which the seed is borne usually attain a height of 4 to 6 feet. These are cut with a sickle. In some cases the cut stalks are shocked, and sometimes they are placed on canvas to avoid the loss of the seed that falls; but if cut at the proper time and carefully handled the expense and labor in providing and using canvas are not warranted. When the seed is dry it is thrashed either by means of a specially constructed thrasher, by rolling on a smooth floor, or with an ordinary grain thrasher, which is operated at reduced speed, with a proper adjustment of sieves. The seed is then cleaned, cured, and sacked ready for shipment or planting.

A BY-PRODUCT.

The stubble and roots that remain in the field after the seed is harvested furnish feed for sheep, hogs, and other live stock.

Plans are now under way looking to the best utilization of this waste product of seed production. Heretofore these roots, which have greatly increased in size during the seeding period, have been plowed out and fed to sheep and hogs by turning the animals into the fields. In this way this by-product serves as a kind of fall pasture. If the animals are fed for market, they must be finished off with other feed before they are marketable. The rapidly increasing acreage of beet seed makes the proper utilization of these roots an important problem. The seed acreage in 1916 gave an estimated yield of not less than 24,000 tons of roots for feed. These roots contain from 6 to 10 per cent of sugar. They are much more woody than the first-year beets. Greater

On hatching, the young poults show their wild blood by making for the brush as soon as they are strong enough to travel, and considerable difficulty is experienced in preventing their return to the wild state of their parents.

By judicious breeding, turkeys have been increased markedly in size since domestication. Wild turkeys of to-day average in weight about 12 pounds for young toms and 9 pounds for young hens, while the standard weight of domestic Bronze turkeys is 25 pounds for young toms, 16 pounds for young hens, 36 pounds for mature toms, and 20 pounds for mature hens. As a matter of fact, however, in sections where little or no attempt has been made to breed turkeys up to a high standard, the majority of them average but little more than their wild ancestors in weight.

The demand for Thanksgiving and Christmas turkeys is large, and to fill this demand carloads of turkeys begin reaching the city markets shortly after the middle of November and continue well through the month of December. Should there be a surplus at Thanksgiving, those unsold are placed in cold storage until Christmas, and of those that remain unsold after Christmas, some are placed on the market from time to time throughout the year, while a part may be held over for the following Thanksgiving. By this method the market is prevented from becoming flooded at any one time to such an extent as to ruin prices, cold storage being the medium by which dealers are enabled to place on the market only that number which can be sold at a fair profit.

TURKEY RAISING AN ESTABLISHED SOURCE OF INCOME FOR THE FARM WIFE.

Next to common fowls, turkeys are one of the most widely recognized sources of income for the American farm woman. However small a business turkey raising may be considered by the farmer during the spring and summer, it frequently happens that the money obtained from the sale of turkeys plays an important part when the Christmas shopping comes around in December. On the average farm the expense of raising turkeys consists mostly of the time spent in caring for the sitting hens during the hatching season and in looking after the wants of the young poults for the first few weeks of their life; to which must be added the cost of the grain used in fattening the turkeys for market in the fall. Compared with the profit in feeding other live stock, turkeys have a marked advantage, not only because they pick up most of their food in the fields and meadows, but also because of the higher prices received when they are sold. As destroyers of weed seeds, grasshoppers, and other injurious insects, turkeys reign supreme. In many sections where grasshoppers abound farmers who have seen their crops destroyed time after time by these pests have turned their attention to turkey raising for the sole purpose of destroying them, and have not only succeeded in doing this but have made a handsome profit besides.

As with all other farm products, the price which the producer receives for turkeys varies largely with his distance from a good market, whether the birds are in good market condition, and the discretion with which he chooses a market and the time for selling. During November and December of 1915 the price per pound, live weight, received by the producer for turkeys averaged 21 cents in the State of New York, 15½ cents in Georgia, 13⅓ cents in Mississippi, 15¾ cents in Indiana, 14½ cents in Missouri, 12 cents in Texas, 20 cents in California, and 17½ cents in Washington.

WHERE TURKEYS ARE RAISED.

By far the greater number of turkeys are raised on grain and stock farms in the Middle West, which is not surprising, since here they can be fed at very little cost and cared for with the least amount of trouble. As near as can be determined, about one-tenth of the total supply of turkeys comes from Texas and almost as many from Missouri, after which come Indiana, Illinois, Kentucky, and Ohio. In New England, which formerly was famous for its well-fattened turkeys, production has decreased to small proportions, although its reputation still lives. In Texas, where there is an abundance of range suitable for turkeys, flocks of several hundred are quite common. Throughout the Middle West, however, the farms are smaller, and for this reason it is rather unusual to see more than 50 or 75 turkeys on any one farm.

PRODUCTION OF TURKEYS IS DECREASING.

That the number of turkeys in the United States is decreasing is well shown by census figures. In 1900, 6,594,695 turkeys were reported as kept for breeding purposes, while in 1910 this number had decreased to 3,688,708. No figures are available since the last census, but statements made by poultry dealers throughout the country indicate that this decrease is continuing. One reason for the falling off lies in the fact that turkeys, having inherited a wandering nature from their wild ancestors, frequently invade the grain fields of neighboring farms, thus bringing about the ill will of the owners of these farms and causing the turkey grower to give up the business. Aside from this the high mortality among young poults as ordinarily cared for on the farm, the outbreaks of disease and particularly of blackhead among turkeys in certain sections of the country, and serious losses resulting from the raids of predatory animals such as foxes, coyotes, wolves, dogs, and rats, have all tended to discourage the turkey industry.

TURKEY RANCHING.

Because of the decreasing production of turkeys on farms, the business of raising turkeys on a large scale may develop into an important and interesting form of ranching. As yet, however, it is in its infancy and has been tried only in a more or less experimental way. In the unsettled foothill regions of California and in certain sections of Arizona and other western States, a few persons have engaged in this industry to the extent of raising a thousand or more turkeys every year. Here the range is unlimited, and the natural food of the turkey, such as grasshoppers and other insects, green vegetation, and the seeds of various weeds and grasses, is abundant. Advantage also is taken of the turkey's relish for acorns, and where these are plentiful but little grain need be used for fattening in the fall. These large flocks of turkeys are managed much like herds of sheep, being taken out to the range early in the morning and brought home to roost at night. They are herded during the day by men, either on foot or on horseback, and by dogs specially trained for the work.

RAISING TURKEYS ON THE FARM.

Notwithstanding the advent of the rather spectacular enterprise of turkey ranching, the farm must still be relied upon for most of the Thanksgiving and Christmas turkeys. Here, as a side issue to her regular work, it is a common practice for the farm wife to keep half a dozen turkey hens and a tom, more commonly known as a gobbler, from which to raise annually a flock of 40 to 50 turkeys. The best hens are selected carefully from the previous year's flock and a new tom is secured from some neighboring turkey grower or, perhaps, a purebred tom is purchased from a reliable turkey breeder for the purpose of improving the size, quality, and appearance of the next crop.

Toward the latter part of winter or early in spring the turkey hens begin laying, and then comes the task of finding the nests, which are usually well hidden in a patch of weeds or bushy thicket, sometimes near home and sometimes half a mile away. The inexperienced turkey grower may spend hours in following a turkey hen before her nest is discovered, but to the initiated this is a simple task, for by confining all the hens early some morning and letting them out late in the afternoon, those that are laying will strike out on a run for their respective nests, and the secret of their hiding places can be quickly and easily learned. After the nests are found the eggs are gathered daily and kept safe from any danger of becoming chilled or from being destroyed by a dog, skunk, opossum, rat, crow, or other enemy.

As soon as each turkey hen has finished laying her litter of about 18 eggs and has become broody, a nest is carefully prepared and from 15 to 20 eggs are given her to incubate. After 28 days of sitting the poults appear, and for the next few weeks they must be fed and looked after frequently, and above all they must be protected from dampness, for if they become wet and chilled their chance of living is small indeed. Should there be no danger of rain or heavy dew the mother turkey may be allowed to range with her brood of poults and to care for them as only she can do. Late in the afternoon, however, they are driven home to be fed and also to get them into the habit of returning every night to roost.

As soon as the poults are feathered there is little danger that they will not then survive, and from this time until the turkeys are marketed in the fall the greatest difficulty with which the turkey grower has to deal is to keep the birds from ranging too far and causing trouble with the owners of neighboring farms. Aside from fencing one's farm so as to be turkey proof, which is often impracticable, the best method yet devised for keeping turkeys at home is to confine them in a pasture of an acre or more every morning, letting them out about noon. During warm weather turkeys do most of their ranging early in the morning, lying about in the shade until late in the afternoon, and then starting slowly toward their roosting place, so that by preventing them from getting an early start in the morning for the neighbors' grain fields they can be induced not to range so far and much trouble is then averted.

About the first of October the fattening season is begun by gradually increasing the amount of grain, usually corn, thrown to the turkeys just before roosting time. A week or two before marketing they receive all the grain they will clean up either two or three times a day. During the period between Thanksgiving and Christmas turkeys are found to be much more easily fattened than at any previous time, partly because they have then attained the greater part of their growth and partly because the weather is then cooler and there is less to tempt them to range so widely. Therefore many turkey growers who have plenty of grain to feed prefer to hold their turkeys for the Christmas market, while those who are short of feed, and who may experience trouble in keeping their turkeys at home, or fear that the roosts will be visited at night and the flocks reduced in numbers, which is a common occurrence, find it advisable to forego the added profit that might be obtained by further fattening, and sell their turkeys at Thanksgiving.

MARKETING.

A few turkey growers, particularly in the Middle Atlantic and New England States, dress their turkeys themselves and sell direct to the consumer or to city dealers. In some sections where turkeys are quite generally raised there is

FIG. 2.—COMMON WILD TURKEY OF THE UNITED STATES. MALE.

The Thanksgiving bird of the Pilgrim Fathers, and the foundation stock from which our common Bronze turkeys have descended.

FIG. I.—BRONZE TURKEY. MALE.

The commonest variety of turkeys in the United States, and the principal source of our Thanksgiving and Christmas table fowls.

FIG. I.—A BREEDING FLOCK OF BRONZE TURKEYS ON THE RANGE IN TEXAS.

Management of turkeys is of the highest importance in preventing losses from disease. Range is essential, but it is not necessary to let turkeys run wild. Turkeys do most of their ranging early in the morning, resting in the shade until late afternoon and then returning to the roost. If they are confined to a narrow lot during the morning they will not range far during the rest of the day.

FIG. 2.—TURKEY HENS NESTING UNDER GOOD MANAGEMENT CONDITIONS.

A profitable percentage of the poults hatched from these eggs can be raised, because careful attention can be given to the management of the young birds.

FIG. 3.—AN INEXPENSIVE BROOD COOP FOR THE MOTHER TURKEY HEN.

The poults have no opportunity to become chilled and lost by following the mother over the range.

FIG. I.—A TEXAS TURKEY DRIVE.

In many parts of the South thousands of turkeys are driven to market every fall. This flock of 700 was driven 12 miles in 9 hours.

FIG. 2.—A TURKEY-DRESSING PLANT IN TEXAS.

held twice a year, once previous to Thanksgiving and again shortly before Christmas, what is known as "Turkey Day." On this day all those who have turkeys to sell dress them and haul them to town, where they are bid on by shippers or by turkey buyers for various city produce houses and sold to the highest bidder. In these sections turkey-picking bees are often held, and as much sport is had at these as at the more common corn-husking bees. In most large turkey-growing districts, however, dressing plants have been built to handle the turkeys during November and December, the same plants being used for poultry, eggs, butter, and other farm produce throughout the remainder of the year. Some farmers haul their turkeys in wagons to these dressing plants, others drive them in if they have too many to haul, and still others, if they are too far away to bring in their turkeys themselves, sell them to the nearest country merchant, who in turn ships them or drives them along with others that he has purchased in the neighborhood.

A custom that is prevalent in Texas is for hucksters to go out from the different dressing plants for a distance of 10 or 15 or even 30 miles and stop at each farm and buy all the turkeys the farmer will sell at the price offered. A flock of 1,000 or more turkeys is often gathered up in this way, each turkey being weighed and paid for at the time of the purchase. In one case 8,000 turkeys were gathered together at one point in Texas and driven by 30 men a distance of 13 miles in two days. A flock of 700 was later driven this same distance by 5 men in a little less than 9 hours. In a drive of this kind a wagon is driven just in front of the turkeys and a little corn is thrown to the leaders to keep them moving. Should any become lame or tired, as frequently happens with old turkeys if they are fat, they are placed in the wagon and hauled the rest of the way. At nightfall, provision is made to stop under a grove of trees where the turkeys may roost, the journey being continued as soon as they fly down again in the morning. On arriving at the dressing plant, the turkeys are again weighed by driving them in flocks of about 100 at a time into a cage placed over the scales, and the huckster is then usually credited with one-half cent per pound for his work.

KILLING AND DRESSING.

As soon as possible after the arrival of the turkeys at the dressing plant they are killed and dressed to prevent the shrinkage in weight that is bound to occur if they are held for any time. Unlike chickens, turkeys confined to small quarters will eat but little and rapidly lose the flesh that has been added while on free range. The detailed operations involved in preparing turkeys for shipment vary somewhat in different dressing plants, although the general plan is the same. In one of the largest Texas turkey-dressing plants, cages for the turkeys, into which they are driven after being weighed, are built in a long row, and from them an alleyway leads into a single cage inside the dressing room. Not more than 15 or 20 turkeys are kept in the inside cage at a time, this being done to prevent the pickers from selecting all the small, easily picked hen turkeys first and then quitting their work when only the large toms are left. White turkeys are also considered harder to pick than the darker varieties, because the feathers " ripen " later, and when the pickers are allowed to choose their own birds these are invariably left until the last. The usual price paid for picking turkeys is 4 cents for hens and 5 cents for toms. In Texas most of the turkeys are picked by negroes or Mexicans.

Selecting his turkey from the inside cage, the picker hangs it by the feet with a wire fastened to an overhead track by a pulley. The turkey is then wheeled in front of the killer, who uses a narrow-bladed, sharp-pointed knife first to sever the veins on the inside of the neck to insure perfect bleeding and then to pierce the brain with an upward thrust through the roof of the mouth. The latter thrust causes the feathers to be loosened by a sudden paralysis of the muscles. A cup half filled with lead is hung to the lower jaw of the bird to catch the blood and to hold the head of the turkey down. The picker then wheels his bird over the tail and wing feather bins. The tail feathers are removed with one motion and the wing feathers with two more, after which the bird is unhooked from the overhead track and hung up by a cord at the picker's regular position along the body-feather bins. Here the body feathers are quickly removed and the bird is taken to the receiver, who pays the picker and lays the dressed turkey in a sack which, when filled, is carried into the cooling room, there to remain until thoroughly cooled, after which the turkeys are packed in boxes or barrels and shipped in refrigerator cars to New York, Chicago, San Francisco, and other distributing centers.

SHIPPING TURKEYS ALIVE.

The shipping of turkeys alive for any considerable distance always results in a heavy shrinkage, and because of this they are usually killed and dressed before shipping. One of the longest shipments of live turkeys that is ordinarily made is from Tennessee to New York City. Twice a year, once for the Thanksgiving and once for the Christmas market, a train known as the "turkey special" is made up at Morristown, Tenn., and is rushed through to New York as rapidly as possible. On the day of the shipment cars of live turkeys begin reaching Morristown from surrounding points, and these are made up into one train, a car containing about 1,200 turkeys. One man is sent with each of the cars, whose duty it is to feed and water the birds and to see that they are weighed correctly when unloaded from the car. Troughs are placed in each coop, and these are filled with a sloppy mixture of cracked corn and water. Turkeys eat very little during such a shipment, however, and their shrinkage is said by shippers to run often as high as 12 per cent for this trip, which ordinarily takes about 60 hours.

On arriving at Jersey City the cars are hauled to the poultry yard and the turkeys unloaded and weighed as soon as possible. The commission firm handling the turkeys has a man on hand, who, with the assistance of as many helpers as are needed, unloads the birds and puts them in coops large enough to hold 14 or 15 each. They are then weighed in the presence of the man who has come with the car, after which they are loaded on trucks, taken by ferry across the Hudson River to New York, and distributed by the commission firm among retailers throughout the city.

FARMERS' MUTUAL FIRE INSURANCE.

By V. N. VALGREN,

Investigator in Agricultural Insurance, Office of Markets and Rural Organization.

ONE of the most successful forms of rural cooperation in this country is that of farmers' mutual fire insurance. Up to the present time, however, it has received but little general publicity. Few men, even among the farmers themselves, are aware of its quantitative or relative importance. Many will be surprised, therefore, to learn that there are at present nearly 2,000 farmers' mutual fire insurance companies in the United States. These companies carry a total amount of insurance exceeding $5,250,000,000. The property on which this insurance is written is valued at more than $6,700,000,000, which is more than two-fifths of the value of all the insurable farm property in the 48 States. That the annual saving to the farmers through this form of cooperation is large may be seen from the cost figures to be found on succeeding pages.

ORIGIN AND GROWTH.

While mutual fire insurance in the United States dates from 1752, the first farmers' mutual fire insurance companies came into existence about 1825. New England and the Middle Atlantic States saw the first attempts at this form of cooperation by farmers. It was demonstrated soon that a considerable saving in the cost of fire insurance could be effected, and the movement spread from one community to another with a fair degree of rapidity. By the middle of the century a considerable number of farmers' companies of this kind were in existence. As insurance reports for this early period are wanting, data concerning their number or the business done by them can not be obtained. More than half a hundred of the existing companies, however, were organized before 1850.

Most of these companies were incorporated under special charters and were left to do business practically without guidance or supervision. Unfortunately, as insurance re-

421

ports issued after the creation of State insurance departments indicate, these so-called "farmers' mutuals" in some instances failed to limit themselves to the segregated risks of moderate value to which their volume of business and method of operation adapted them. Hence, the record of the farmers' mutuals of this period is by no means one of uniform success. Many of the early insurance reports are severe in their criticism of this plan of insurance. In spite of this handicap the movement continued to extend both west and south from the place of its origin. By 1875 there were about 400 farmers' mutuals, and by 1900 there were at least 1,700 such companies. Their present number exceeds 1,950.

LEGISLATION.

The rapid extension of insurance on this plan after 1850 was due, in no small measure, to favorable legislation. Such legislation did not come as a benefit bestowed upon the farmers from the outside. In the more strictly agricultural sections of the Middle West, at any rate, where farmers' mutual insurance now may be said to be most highly developed, the laws were secured by the direct efforts of the farmers themselves. In several States such laws were passed in the face of strong opposition, led in some instances by the State insurance officials.

The first farmers' mutual insurance law was passed by the State of New York in 1857. This law provided that 25 or more persons residing in any township of the State and owning a total of $50,000 worth of property which they desired to insure might form themselves into a mutual insurance company. They were allowed to insure only buildings and the goods contained therein. They could insure no city or village property, nor could they accept risks outside the borders of the home township. They could write insurance against loss or damage by fire only. This law, though evidently too strongly restrictive in its provisions regarding business territory and the risks that might be assumed, appears to have become the model for similar laws in the North Central States generally, and for some 12 other States located farther south or farther west.

The early New York law was repealed in 1862, and it was not until 1879 that a second law somewhat more liberal in its provisions was enacted. In the meantime, Wisconsin, Illinois, Michigan, Iowa, Minnesota, Ohio, and Indiana had enacted farmers' mutual fire insurance laws. These laws, as well as the second New York law, were in general reasonable and practical in their provisions, or were soon made so by proper amendments.

The business territory permitted as a rule was a number of contiguous townships or an entire county. All kinds of farm property might be insured, and the lightning hazard as well as that of fire might be assumed. With the exception of the Indiana law, they differed from the New York law of 1879, however, in that they placed the companies thus organized under the supervision of the respective State insurance departments. This step was not taken by New York until 1909.

By 1890 practically every State in the Middle West and several of those in the South had a farmers' mutual fire insurance law. A few other States in the South and in the far West have been added more recently to the list. With the exception of Vermont, which passed a farmers' mutual law in 1915, no State in New England or the Middle Atlantic group has followed the example set by New York in 1857.

The present laws upon this subject, while similar in many respects, are by no means equally complete or equally practical in all their provisions. It may be said, however, that at present 25 States have fairly satisfactory farmers' mutual fire insurance laws. Several other States have scattered provisions in their laws governing fire insurance in general, which apply particularly to farmers' mutuals. In a few States where no special reference to farmers' insurance organizations is found, such companies operate either under special charters or under laws which apply to all classes of mutual fire insurance companies. In 6 States, all located in the South or the Southwest, no record of companies of this kind has been found.

The older farmers' mutual insurance laws have seen various amendments in practically every instance. The trend of these amendments has been to enlarge the business territory permitted, and to give broader scope to the activities of the companies. In several instances these companies are allowed to operate in the entire State. As a rule, however, existing laws prescribe territorial limits varying from 1 to 5 counties. While many of the companies have availed themselves of the provisions permitting larger business territory, the great majority continue to operate in a single county, and a few still confine themselves to a single township. Similarly, there has been a growing tendency to permit the farmers' mutuals to include windstorm among the hazards assumed. This has been true especially in the Southern States.

The practice on the part of local farmers' mutuals of including windstorm with the hazards insured against can not be recommended. Each group of farm buildings, and to a considerable extent each building within the group, is a distinct and separate risk with respect to the fire and lightning hazards, but this is not true with respect to the windstorm hazard. Even in the Southern States, where the plan of giving so-called combined protection is followed most often and where severe windstorms are of less frequent occurrence, there is considerable danger of a formidable list of losses from a single storm. The practice which is rapidly gaining favor in the Middle West of operating a State-wide windstorm insurance company through the cooperative efforts of the local fire insurance companies would add much to the stability and safety of the farmers' mutual organizations in any State where combined protection is now offered by the local mutuals.

ECONOMIC IMPORTANCE AND LOCALIZATION.

The total amount of insurance carried by the 1,947 farmers' mutual fire insurance companies in existence on January 1, 1915, the latest date for which relatively complete statistics are at hand, was approximately $5,264,119,000. The total amount paid for losses during 1914 was $10,766,651, and the expenses of operation were $3,138,649, making the total cost of this insurance $13,905,300. From these figures it may be seen that the average cost per $100 of insurance in all these companies was about 26 cents.

The farmers' mutuals, almost without exception, limit the amount of the insurance written to either three-fourths or

two-thirds of the actual value of the property. A reasonable
allowance for this fact shows the total value of the farm
property insured by these companies to be approximately
$6,736,000,000.[1] The total value of all insurable farm prop-
erty in the 48 States on January 1, 1915, was, as nearly as
can be estimated, $15,886,000,000. This would indicate that
nearly 42½ per cent of all insurable farm property in the 48
States of the Union was insured in the farmers' mutual fire
insurance companies.

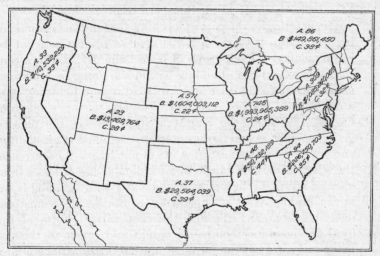

FIG. 38.—Farmers' mutual fire insurance companies, by geographic divisions.
A. Number of companies January 1, 1915.
B. Total insurance in force January 1, 1915.
C. Average cost per $100 of insurance in force during 1914.

Figure 38 is a map on which is shown, for the different
geographic divisions of the country, the number of farmers'
mutual fire insurance companies and the total amount of their

---

[1] In the New England and Middle Atlantic States, where, with the exception of New
York, the farmers' companies operate either under special charters or under laws applying to different classes of mutuals, a considerable amount of city or village property of the
less hazardous kind is also insured. In these States the urban risks carried by the companies which speak of themselves as farmers' mutuals and which are so considered by the
insurance commissioners will perhaps offset the difference between the real value of the farm
property insured and the amount of the insurance carried thereon. The total insurance in
force has therefore in these cases been taken to represent the full value of the insured farm
property. While a few detached urban risks are frequently carried by the farmers' mutuals
in other States than those above referred to, such risks would here amount to a very small
percentage of their total risks. For all such States the insurance in force has been increased
by one-third in order to allow for the fact that the companies insure only for three-fourths
or two-thirds of the actual value of the property.

insurance in force on January 1, 1915, together with the average cost per \$100 of insurance during the year 1914.

Figure 39 shows for each geographic division of the country the total value of the insurable farm property and the total value of the property insured in the farmers' mutuals. Fig-

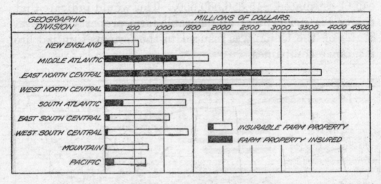

FIG. 39.—Value of insurable farm property, and value of farm property insured in farmers' mutual fire insurance companies.

ure 40 indicates for the same geographic divisions the percentage of the total farm property which was thus insured.

Figure 41 shows the average cost per \$100 of insurance in the farmers' mutuals during the year 1914 for each State having \$1,000,000 or more of such insurance in force. The

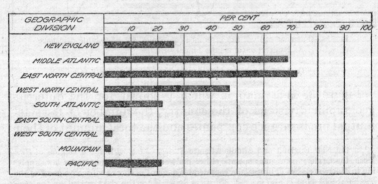

FIG. 40.—Percentage of insurable farm property insured in farmers' mutual fire insurance companies.

cost figures for States with smaller sums of insurance are likely to vary too much to be of significance when taken for a single year. Less marked yearly variations in the average cost of insurance will be found, of course, even where the total insurance in force in the State is relatively large. It

is therefore quite likely that States close together in their
cost of insurance would exchange rank from year to year.
The larger differences, however, especially where insurance

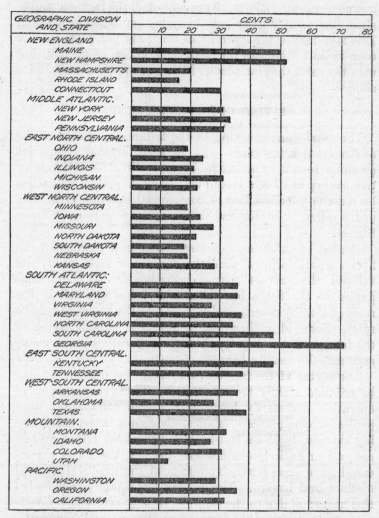

Fig. 41.—Average cost per $100 of insurance in the farmers' mutual fire insurance companies
during the year 1914 for each State in which the total insurance amounted to $1,000,000
or more.

to the amount of a score of millions or more is involved, are
undoubtedly due to more fundamental causes than mere
chance, and are likely to persist unless the causes of such
higher cost can be removed. The fact that some of these

average costs, especially for the Southern States, cover not only fire and lightning protection but also considerable amounts of windstorm protection, should be remembered in this connection. About 15 per cent of all the farmers' mutuals in the country write policies giving combined protection. This fact makes the average of 26 cents per $100 for the country as a whole all the more remarkable, when compared with the rates that farmers without mutual organizations are obliged to pay.

SAVING IN INSURANCE COST.

The total annual saving to the farmers by reason of the relatively low insurance cost in their mutual companies amounts to a very considerable sum. No close estimate of this saving has been attempted, since no special effort has been made to collect lists of commercial rates for farm risks in the different States and in the various sections of these States.

It may be safely said, however, that in a number of the States where farmers' mutual insurance is most highly developed, the average cost of insurance for all these companies in the State has fallen well below one-half of the rates quoted by commercial concerns, or the so-called bureau rates. Some idea, therefore, of the total annual saving to the farmers of the country through cooperation in fire insurance may be readily formed.

The saving of the farmers' mutuals in insurance cost may be credited mainly to two sources. First, the expenses of operation necessarily incurred by large commercial companies for commissions, salaries, dividends, taxes, rents, rating charges, legal assistance, etc., have been either greatly reduced or entirely eliminated. Second, the losses experienced have been fewer, by reason of the practical removal of the moral hazard. The more or less complete removal of this hazard is due to the careful guarding against overinsurance on the part of the farmers' companies, and frequently, even more, no doubt, to the different attitude automatically assumed by the insured toward a company consisting of friends and neighbors from that often wrongfully assumed toward a large business corporation located perhaps in a distant city.

GENERAL SIGNIFICANCE OF THE MOVEMENT.

The benefits of rural cooperation in fire insurance can not all be measured directly in money values. There is little doubt that by the reasonable cost at which protection can be secured in these local organizations many farmers have been induced to provide themselves with insurance when they would not have taken this step had it been necessary to pay the full commercial rates. Many a farmer has thus been enabled promptly to rebuild his home, or to replace lost personal property, when had it not been for cooperation in insurance he would have been severely embarrassed financially or perhaps even compelled to give up his farm.

The marked success of this form of cooperation has also been an encouragement to farmers to attempt other cooperative enterprises. It has stimulated their faith in one another and strengthened their confidence in their own ability to do things somewhat removed from their primary occupation of raising crops and producing other raw materials. If farmers could manage successfully their own insurance company and save money in so doing, why could they not make their own milk into butter and cheese, provide themselves with fresh beef by the organization of so-called meat rings, operate their own telephone company, market some of their own farm products, and even purchase cooperatively some of their needed supplies? All of these and several other forms of cooperation have been attempted, and while in many localities failures have been experienced, the percentages of success have been large.

That failures have occurred when more complex cooperative enterprises have been undertaken should not be a cause for wonder. Managers with experience and technical knowledge have been hard to find. The opposition often has been strong and well organized. The pioneer was a decided individualist, and the spirit of cooperation and of loyalty to a voluntary organization could not well be expected to develop suddenly. Yet such qualities, in generous measure, are necessary to withstand the temptation of temporary but immediate and alluring gains frequently offered to induce members to violate cooperative agreements or withdraw from the organizations. In fire insurance, however, the local cooperative company, as above indicated,

has been able to effect so large a saving, especially in the
operating expenses necessarily incurred by the more complex
commercial company, that even temporary competition on
the part of the larger concern has been exceedingly difficult.
In recent years, moreover, uniform rate laws have in many
States made local and temporary competition impossible.

It is by no means surprising that cooperation should have
been resorted to in supplying the need for insurance protection. In a broader sense all insurance may be said to be
cooperative. It implies the assumption of the loss burdens
to which the individual is subject, by a collective body of
which all the insured are in effect members, even where they
do not share in the management. The sum total of the
burdens which have been lifted from the individuals insured
rests ultimately, in all cases, not on the management but
on the membership of the body. Under the mutual plan,
however, the cooperation is more conscious and direct.
Especially is this true when the company operates in a limited territory or when the risks assumed belong, broadly
speaking, to a single class. In the farmers' mutuals both of
these conditions may be found.

POSSIBILITIES OF YET GREATER SERVICE.

The full possibilities of direct and conscious cooperation in
farmers' mutual fire insurance have not as yet been realized. At least one group of mutual companies in this country
has far outstripped the farmers' mutuals in bringing about
effective cooperation for the prevention of losses. This group
is known as the factory mutuals, and consists of 19 companies mainly located in the New England States. They
insure large factories only, and have so far limited themselves to that part of the United States east of the Mississippi
River. Not only have these companies succeeded in securing
the effective cooperation of their members in working for the
prevention of losses, but the organizations as such have freely
and generously cooperated with one another. A joint bureau
has been maintained for years in the city of Boston for the
advancement of the science of safe construction and for the
frequent and thorough inspection of their risks. Their efforts
have been highly successful. The oldest of these companies,
for example, was organized in 1835. During the first 10
years of its existence the average cost per $100 of insur-

ance was 84 cents. Such has been the reduction in the insurance cost that the average for the last 10 years has fallen below 6 cents. This means that the cost of insurance in this company has been reduced to approximately 7 per cent of what it was three-quarters of a century ago.

Besides farmers' mutuals and factory mutuals, our insurance reports reveal an increasing number of grain-dealers' mutuals, lumbermen's mutuals, implement-dealers' mutuals, hardware-dealers' mutuals, grocers' mutuals, and druggists' mutuals. All of these so-called class mutuals owe their existence to the belief that what has been done by the factory mutuals can be accomplished, in some measure at least, by other classes of mutuals. There seems no good reason why in every instance this hope should not be realized.

A group of individuals all engaged in the same business can hardly fail to elect as officers of their company men who are familiar with the particular kind of risks in question. Moreover, the members of a company of this kind know that the improvement of their risks, in response to sane requirements on the part of the company, will not merely tend to a reduction of insurance cost, but will immediately result in reduced premium charges or assessments. As a final advantage may be mentioned the fact that a class mutual is likely to have its risks widely scattered, thus reducing the danger of a conflagration loss.

While the farmers' companies, as already set forth, have much to their credit, indications are that the possibilities ahead of them far exceed, in economic and social significance, what already has been accomplished. Not only is the greater part of the field of insurable farm risks in most States still untouched, but the possibilities of further reducing the cost of insurance by the application to fire losses of what may be called the principle of stoppage at the source, are believed to be great. Hitherto the economies of the farmers' mutuals have consisted largely, as has been stated, in a reduction of the expense item and the lessening or the removal of the moral hazard. The old ratio of losses from a variety of other more or less readily removable sources has continued practically undiminished.

Many of the farmers' companies have emphasized the reduction in the expense item of their cost of insurance to the neglect of the larger possibilities in the reduction of the loss item. They have failed, in some cases at least, to take into consideration the fact that every thousand-dollar risk saved from destruction not only saves the company $1,000, but further saves the individual who owns the property from $300 to $500 on that part of the property not covered by the insurance. This important item should not be overlooked by a mutual company in a calculation of possible saving through efforts at loss prevention. One farmers' mutual insurance man recently described the situation by saying that many a director of a farmers' mutual has been holding a penny of expense so close to his eye that it has obscured a dollar that easily could have been saved in the annual fire loss. The inconveniences and privations as well as the danger to human lives that fires frequently involve, in spite of insurance, should also be considered.

It has been demonstrated that in the case of country risks as well as in that of other classes of insured property careful periodic inspection will prevent a considerable percentage of the losses that otherwise would have occurred. A group of New England companies have reduced their losses on country risks materially in the last few years by means of a system of inspection. Companies and groups of companies in other localities recently have begun activities of this kind. Most of the farmers' mutuals could well afford to double their expenses if by so doing they could reduce their losses by 25 per cent.

All risks should be thoroughly inspected at least every second or third year by a well-qualified representative of the company, and the members duly warned against any dangerous conditions or practices that may be found. When necessary, continuance as a member of the company should be made conditional upon compliance with recommendations for the removal of needless fire dangers.

The safe construction of farm buildings as well as their maintenance in a safe condition should be encouraged by a reasonable classification of risks, worked out with special reference to the particular locality. Justice as well as expediency suggests this plan. It is hardly fair to charge a man who builds carefully and guards his property against dangerous conditions the same rate as is paid by one who builds carelessly and gives little heed to the safety of his property after it is constructed. Moreover, unless the desirable features of the better risks are recognized in this way, there is danger that, in spite of the lower average cost, the very best risks in the territory occupied by a local mutual may be picked up by larger insurance concerns that do classify.

Reasonable efforts should be made by every farmers' mutual to spread information among its members not only concerning the safe construction and upkeep of their property, but also concerning devices for the checking of a fire if one should occur. Thus the value of conveniently located water supplies in tanks, barrels, or buckets, of ladders by which the roof can be reached readily, and of chemical extinguishers should be duly emphasized.

The causes of fires should be more thoroughly studied and more carefully tabulated, and the loss reports, which should be placed before every member of the company, should group the losses experienced according to these causes. By concrete and near-at-hand examples of this kind can the members be warned most effectively concerning the dangers of defective flues, of dilapidated and weather-beaten shingle roofs, of the want of lightning protection on buildings and on fences, of soot accumulations in chimneys, of the careless disposition of ashes, of rubbish accumulations in garrets or elsewhere, of the use of the so-called parlor match, and of the careless use of kerosene, gasoline, and other inflammable substances.

There is no organized private agency more directly concerned with the elimination of our needless fire waste, either in the country or in the city, than the insurance company. Where such a company is organized on the mutual plan and operates in a limited territory, or is composed of persons who have similar risks to insure, it has a special opportunity for effective service. There is then no excuse for a conflict of interests. The welfare of the company is the welfare of the insured. By more generally taking advantage of this opportunity to become vital agencies for the conservation of property, as well as for the distribution of unavoidable loss burdens, the farmers' mutuals will further promote the welfare of their members and will strengthen their position as insurance companies.

DEVELOPMENT AND LOCALIZATION OF TRUCK CROPS IN THE UNITED STATES.

By Fred J. Blair,

Truck Crop Specialist, Bureau of Crop Estimates.

TRUCK-GROWING REGIONS.

THE area devoted to the commercial production of truck crops may be divided advantageously into five sections—the Atlantic Coast States, from southern New Jersey to Florida; the Gulf States, from Alabama to Texas; the Pacific Coast States; the Southern States, including the inland territory of the Atlantic Coast and Gulf States, and Kentucky, Tennessee, Arkansas, Oklahoma, New Mexico, Arizona, and Nevada; and the northern belt of States east of the Rocky Mountains. It appears desirable to take up only that phase of the subject that relates to commercial or truck-farming areas—areas growing for shipment to more or less distant markets, leaving out market-garden communities which exist in the neighborhood of all cities and whose products are disposed of by the individual growers in the home markets. Another phase of the subject is the acreage grown for manufacture, the product of which, while it does not come upon the market as truck, is very important because of its magnitude.

The Atlantic coast, the Gulf, and the Pacific coast sections are preeminently the winter gardens of the north and from early winter to late in the spring supplies of practically every variety of green vegetables are shipped to northern markets from these sections. Florida, California, Texas, and Louisana take the lead in winter vegetables, the other States falling into line as the season advances. The Norfolk section, owing to its peculiarly favorable location, also ships certain varieties of hardy vegetables, such as spinach and kale, throughout the winter. Conditions are reversed in the late summer and the North sends its vegetables to southern markets.

Successful truck farming depends upon reasonable proximity to large centers of nonagricultural population and reasonable proximity is expressed in terms of transportation.

435

Previous to 1860 truck farming was unknown, except to a very limited extent along the steamboat and railway lines leading out 50 miles or so from a few of the larger northern cities. Long Island, New Jersey, Delaware, and southern Illinois appear to have been at that time the leading truck centers of the country. (Census of 1890, Agriculture, page 592.)

The early development of the northern Atlantic seaboard as a trucking section was due largely to the low altitude of the land and the modifying effect on climate of the presence of large bodies of water. Southern New Jersey and the Delaware, Maryland, and Virginia peninsula are protected by the Atlantic Ocean on one side and the Delaware and Chesapeake Bays on the other. This protection enables the planting of truck crops much earlier than in other localities in the same latitude. In addition to the above this region is in close proximity to several of the largest cities of the country, has the advantage of both water and rail transportation, and a soil peculiarly adapted to the production of early vegetables.

It is to be expected, therefore, that the earliest development of areas of commercial truck production will be found in southern New Jersey (Burlington, Camden, Gloucester, Salem, and Cumberland Counties) and in Delaware, these regions having had access to the markets of New York and Philadelphia from the earliest times, and that this fact will be clearly shown in the more rapid development of the trucking industry in territory lying farther south.

GROWTH OF THE TRUCKING INDUSTRY FROM 1890 TO 1915.

The census of 1900 was the first to make a detailed report on truck crops, but published by counties the acreage of potatoes and onions only. The acreage of all other vegetables was published by States. The census of 1910 collected this information, but did not publish it, and it has not been available to the general public. The census of 1890 enumerated among truck crops the acreage of Irish potatoes only, and as that crop was carried through the two succeeding census enumerations, and as it is more widely grown than any other, it seemed to be the most available for the purpose of illustrating the general growth of the trucking industry.

In considering the figures given in the following it should be borne in mind that the census of 1910 is not strictly comparable with the census of 1900, for the reason that in making the enumeration of truck-crop acreage in 1910 areas of less than 1 acre were not enumerated, while in the enumeration of 1900 all areas considered commercial areas were included. This difference would operate to decrease the percentage of increase for 1910 as compared with 1900.

Potatoes, sweet potatoes, and strawberries were not included in figures for miscellaneous vegetables.

The production of early Irish potatoes in the five counties of New Jersey mentioned above had already become large in 1890, the census of that year enumerating the area at 18,888 acres, or more than 40 per cent of the entire acreage for the State. In 1900 the area was given as 20,399 acres, or about 38 per cent of the acreage for the State, and in 1910 at 35,118 acres, or about 48 per cent of the acreage for the State. In 1915 the area for the State was estimated to be 93,000 acres by the Department of Agriculture. The average increase shown by the three census enumerations is 42 per cent, and the estimated area for the five counties in 1915 may, therefore, be stated at 39,060 acres. The increase for the 20-year period covered by the census was about 90 per cent. The area of other vegetables in 1900 in the counties under consideration was 45,951 acres, and in 1910, 52,666 acres, an increase of about 14 per cent. The census of 1890 did not report the acreage of other vegetables, and the comparison is, therefore, for the 10-year period from 1900 to 1910.

The area of early Irish potatoes in Delaware in 1890 was 4,870 acres, in 1900 the area was 5,755 acres, and in 1910 9,703 acres, or an increase for the 20-year period of about 100 per cent. The area in 1915 was estimated by the Department of Agriculture to be 11,000 acres, an increase of about 13 per cent for the 5-year period. The area of other vegetables was 23,987 acres in 1900 and 22,939 in 1910, a slight decrease.

The principal increase, it will be noted, in both New Jersey and Delaware has been in the acreage of potatoes, the increase amounting to 90 and 100 per cent for the period from 1890 to 1910, respectively. There was a small increase in the production of other vegetables in New Jersey (14 per cent), and a slight decrease in Delaware. Large quantities of all. vegetables are, however, grown for market in home cities, i. e., Philadelphia and New York, and for sale to canneries.

ATLANTIC COAST STATES.

THE EASTERN SHORE OF MARYLAND AND VIRGINIA.

The territory under consideration in Maryland is comprised in the counties of Somerset, Wicomico, and Worcester, which counties in 1890 had 1,388 acres, in 1900 3,681 acres, and in 1910 7,414 acres in early Irish potatoes, an increase of 434 per cent for the 20-year period. There appears to have been a decrease during the 5-year period ending with 1915. The acreage of all other vegetables in these three counties was 8,745 in 1900 and 11,127 in 1910, an increase of over 27 per cent.

It remains to consider the two Virginia counties—Accomac and Northampton—forming the southern end of the Maryland and Virginia peninsula, and it is in these two counties that the most remarkable development in the production of potatoes for the early spring market has taken place. In 1890 these counties had 4,262 acres in potatoes, in 1900 the acreage had grown to 11,475, in 1910 the acreage was 30,688, and in 1915 it was estimated by the Department of Agriculture to be 90,000 acres, an increase of over 2,000 per cent as compared with 1890. This remarkable growth in potato production places the Eastern Shore counties of Virginia far in the lead of all other early potato-growing sections. This district has more than double the acreage of the New Jersey district, the district next in rank, nearly four times the acreage of the Norfolk section, and more than six times the acreage of any other early-potato district.

THE NORFOLK SECTION OF VIRGINIA.

In the fifties the raising of vegetables for northern markets began at Norfolk, Va. In 1854 the steamer *Roanoke* carried the first shipment of 200 barrels of garden truck to New York. To secure proper ventilation, however, it was necessary that these should be carried on deck, so that the quantity which might be transported on any trip was not large, 400 packages being about the limit. The boats then in use required at least 36 hours to reach New York, and hence the shipment of even small quantities of highly perishable articles was attended with great risk. At the present time forced ventilation allows of loading between decks, increased tonnage enables a vessel to carry as high as 25,000 packages, and the trip is made in 19 hours. * * * The first all-rail shipment of garden truck was made from Norfolk, Va., in 1885. (Census of 1900, Vol. V, Part I, p. 304.)

The entire coast line from Norfolk south to Beaufort, S. C., is very much broken by bays, sounds, and the estuaries of many rivers and creeks, through the means of which tidewater enters far into the land area, exerting a marked influence upon climatic conditions, which is further aided by the presence of the Gulf Stream at no great distance from the coast line at any point. The climate of the Norfolk section is so modified and controlled by these influences and the low-lying altitude of the land that it enjoys a winter climate as mild and little subject to sudden changes and to the influence of destructive frosts and freezes as may be found many miles to the southward. It is, therefore, possible to grow such hardy vegetables as spinach and kale throughout the winter without protection, and to plant a cabbage crop in November to be harvested for the early spring market.

The Norfolk section in Virginia includes Isle of Wight, Nansemond, Norfolk, Princess Anne, and York Counties. In 1890 there were 8,218 acres of potatoes in these counties, in 1900, 12,875 acres, and in 1910, 16,077 acres, an increase of about 95 per cent for the 20-year period. In 1915 it is estimated there were 26,500 acres in the district, an increase of about 64 per cent for the 5-year period.

In 1900 there were 14,537 acres of other vegetables, and in 1910, 16,593 acres. In the latter year there were 4,281 acres of strawberries grown, from which 122,157 sixty-quart crates of berries were shipped. The increase in other vegetables for the 10-year period from 1900 to 1910 was about 14 per cent. The area in other vegetables is estimated for 1915 at 23,150 acres, an increase of nearly 40 per cent for the 5-year period. The area in strawberries for that year is estimated at 4,000 acres, from which 134,959 sixty-quart crates were shipped.

The census of 1900 gives the total number of pieces (barrels, boxes, and crates) shipped from the Norfolk section of Virginia in 1889 at 2,789,557. This estimate excludes small fruits, but includes potatoes and sweet potatoes. In 1910 the total number of pieces and packages of vegetables shipped from the district was 3,030,856, an increase of nearly 9 per cent. The shipments from the district in 1911 were 2,907,-848; in 1912, 3,777,282; in 1913, 3,898,159; in 1914, 3,928,384; and in 1915, 4,501,894. The increase for the 5-year period was nearly 50 per cent.

The total area in vegetables for the district in 1915, including potatoes, sweet potatoes, and strawberries, is estimated at 54,500 acres. It will be noted here that the total estimated area in all vegetables, including strawberries in 1915, is only about 2,000 acres larger than the area for the five counties in New Jersey in 1910, with potatoes, sweet potatoes, and strawberries excluded. The five counties in New Jersey increased at the rate of 14 per cent for the 10-year period 1900 to 1910, and if the increase maintained itself for the following five years, the total of all vegetables, excluding potatoes, sweet potatoes, and strawberries, would be 60,039 acres. Add to this total 39,060 acres of potatoes, about 19,000 acres of sweet potatoes, and 5,000 acres of strawberries and the grand total is 123,099 acres of all truck crops for the five counties of New Jersey, more than double the acreage of the five counties comprised in the Norfolk district.

NORTH CAROLINA.

The census of 1890 included eight northeastern counties of North Carolina in the Norfolk district. Since that time an important center of production for truck crops has developed at Wilmington, N. C., in New Hanover County, and lesser centers at Elizabeth City, Washington, Aurora, and Newbern.

The first all-rail shipment of garden vegetables was made from eastern North Carolina in 1887.

The three counties of North Carolina—Camden, Currituck, and Pasquotank—bordering on and practically a part of the Norfolk district of Virginia, are estimated to have had 4,800 acres in early potatoes in 1915, as compared with 862 acres in 1890, 1,415 acres in 1900, and 3,421 acres in 1910, an increase for the period covered of over 456 per cent. A decrease of about 29 per cent in the production of other vegetables occurred during the period from 1900 to 1910.

The counties lying to the south—Pamlico, Washington, and Beaufort—planted 4,285 acres of early potatoes in 1915, 3,585 acres of which were in Beaufort County. The same counties planted 384 acres in 1890, but with the exception of Beaufort County, have made no material increase in acreage since 1910.

SOUTH CAROLINA.

Two important trucking centers have developed in Charleston and Beaufort Counties, S. C.—at Meggetts and Beaufort, respectively—where exchanges are maintained through which a large percentage of the crops produced are marketed. The first all-rail shipment was made from Charleston in 1888, but Charleston had long been in touch with northern markets through the medium of water transportation. The Beaufort district covers all that territory tributary to the Charleston & Western Carolina Railway, from Port Royal to Yamassee, a distance of about 25 miles, and embraces practically all of Beaufort County engaged in the truck-farming industry. The trucking industry first became important with the advent of the railroad about 1889 and has steadily developed in magnitude, as is indicated below. At one time asparagus was the principal crop, but was abandoned for early Irish potatoes and cabbages. Cabbage not proving satisfactory, has been replaced by lettuce; this and Irish potatoes are now the principal crops produced. The area in tomatoes, however, is increasing steadily.

In 1890 there were 921 acres in early potatoes at Charleston and but 30 acres at Beaufort. In 1900 the area at Charleston was 2,127 acres, and 934 at Beaufort. In 1910 there were 1,238 acres at Charleston and 1,678 acres at Beaufort. In 1915 the area at Charleston was 3,000 acres and at Beaufort 2,145. The area of other vegetables in 1900 was 3,140 acres at Charleston and 1,016 at Beaufort. In 1910 the area at Charleston had increased to 3,474 acres, and at Beaufort to 1,785 acres. In 1915 the area of miscellaneous vegetables was estimated at 5,500 acres at Charleston and 2,000 acres at Beaufort.

FLORIDA.

Florida, the far-south member of the Atlantic Coast division, is perhaps the most general trucking community in the United States. A long, comparatively narrow peninsula, protected by the warm waters of the Gulf of Mexico on the west and the Atlantic Ocean on the east, with the Gulf Stream rounding its southern end and flowing northward in close proximity to its coast line, it possesses a very equable climate. Although Florida is not wholly free from frosts and freezes, such conditions are rare. Florida is not uniformly blessed with the advantage of good soil, but this defect frequently is offset by the use of fertilizers, and her nearness to the great markets of the North, and the fact that she can produce her crops without irrigation, places her in an advantageous position for the successful promotion of truck farming for the winter and spring market.

For the year 1890 the comparison is limited to the potato crop. But 1,218 acres of potatoes were enumerated for the State in 1890 and 3,752 acres in 1900. In 1910 the area had increased to 8,509 acres, or nearly 600 per cent for the 20-year period. Of the area grown in 1910, 5,089 acres, or about 60 per cent, were in the East Coast North region, and a large proportion of the area in what is known as the St. Johns district. This region had increased from 218 acres in 1890, or 2,235 per cent for the 20-year period. In 1915 the area of potatoes grown in the State is estimated at 16,000 acres, and 11,505 acres of the total was grown in the East Coast North region, of which 10,000 acres, or nearly 87 per cent, were grown in the St. Johns district.

The area of potatoes in Florida is comparatively small when compared with that devoted to the production of miscellaneous vegetables, and no figures for vegetables other than potatoes are available for the census year 1890. In 1900 the area in miscellaneous vegetables was 29,815 acres. In 1910 it had increased to 57,579 acres, or more than 93 per cent, and in 1915 the area is estimated at 79,672 acres, a further increase during the period of five years of about 38 per cent. The total area in miscellaneous vegetables in Florida in 1910, including potatoes and strawberries, was 67,452 acres, and in 1915, 99,162, an increase of 31,710 acres, or about 47 per cent for the five years.

THE GULF STATES.

The Gulf States division contains two very important truck-producing regions—southern Louisiana and southern Texas. Others of less importance exist in Alabama and Mississippi. Such a region developed early around Mobile, Ala. The census of 1890 gives the following table showing the shipment of vegetables from Mobile, Ala., in 1888, 1889, and 1890:

Vegetables shipped from Mobile, Ala., in 1888, 1889, and 1890.

Vegetable.	1890	1889	1888
Cabbage..crates..	58,309	66,950	46,592
Potatoes...barrels..	78,924	46,508	66,287
Beans...boxes..	46,178	24,949	33,487
Peas..do....	1,278	8,923	5,928
Cucumbers...barrels..	....	....	132
Tomatoes...boxes..	2,695	7,590	6,578
Watermelons......................................	10,881	3,395	4,470
Various packages.................................	785	1,409	264

The total value of the above shipments is given as follows: 1888, $393,295; 1889, $371,113; 1890, $458,065. The following statement is added: "For shipments from Mobile County 33.3 per cent should be added, not included above, making a grand total for the three years of $1,629,964 for this small section."

There were 780 acres of early potatoes in the Mobile district, including Mobile, Baldwin, and Washington Counties, in 1890; 1,966 acres in 1900; 2,265 acres in 1910; and 1,568 acres in 1915.

Shipments in car lots from Mobile in 1915, as estimated by the Bureau of Crop Estimates, were as follows: Cabbages, 556 cars; potatoes, 83 cars; snap beans, 35 cars; and miscellaneous, 21 cars; total, 695 cars. It, therefore, appears that about 80 per cent of all shipments from Mobile in 1915 were cabbages, of which there were 921 acres in 1910. The acreage for 1915 is not known.

There is an important truck-farming district around Crystal Springs, in Copiah County, Miss. The census for 1900 gives this district 3,483 acres of miscellaneous vegetables, which increased to 6,502 acres in 1910. Figures for 1915 are not available.

There were 6,325 acres of early potatoes in selected parishes in southern Louisiana in 1890; 6,546 in 1900; 11,116 in 1910; and it is estimated that there were 14,808 acres in 1915, an increase for the 25-year period from 1890 to 1915 of about 134 per cent. This is an old and well-settled trucking region and rapid development is not to be looked for in the production of miscellaneous vegetables. Lafourche Parish is perhaps the most notable for the production of potatoes, Creole onions, and garlic. This parish had 4,065 acres of potatoes in 1890; 1,817 acres in 1900; 2,318 acres in 1910; and it is estimated there were 3,000 acres in 1915. Lafourche Parish grew 762 acres of Creole onions in 1900; 2,514 acres in 1910; and it is estimated there were 2,750 acres in 1915. The parish also grew about 1,000 acres of garlic in 1915. The development of certain parishes in the production of strawberries is particularly notable and will be taken up later in connection with that crop.

The truck-farming industry has developed most rapidly in the southern districts of Texas, comprising 32 out of her 250 counties. Taking the district as a whole, there were 2,238 acres of potatoes in 1890, as compared with 4,331 acres in 1900; 10,797 acres in 1910, and 18,188 acres in 1915. The most remarkable development of the early potato industry was in Colorado and Wharton Counties, known as the Eagle Lake district, where there were 147 acres of potatoes in 1890, as compared with 2,639 acres in 1910, and 7,530 acres in 1915. The development of the Bermuda onion industry has been quite as remarkable. The census of 1900 enumerated 63 acres of onions in the 10 counties comprised in the onion district. In 1910 there were 3,514 acres, and in 1915 the area was estimated to be 9,343 acres. Similar development has taken place with other crops, such as strawberries, tomatoes, cabbages, and lettuce. The production of miscellaneous vegetables in the district under consideration in 1900 was 16,801 acres, and in 1910, 32,885 acres, an increase of nearly 100 per cent. Complete figures for 1915 are not available, but the development of practically all crops has been rapid in the last five years, as is indicated by the increase in potato and onion acreages as stated above.

PACIFIC COAST STATES.

The development of the early potato industry in southern California has been slow. In 1890 there were 7,385 acres; in 1900, 6,612 acres, and in 1910, 8,885 acres. The production of miscellaneous vegetables, however, increased rapidly. In 1900 there were 8,053 acres, and in 1910, 26,187 acres.

The area in potatoes in central California in 1890 was 22,490 acres; in 1900, 27,994, and in 1910, 50,688, an increase of about 125 per cent over 1890. With regard to southern California it may, perhaps, be taken for granted that the potato acreage is practically all for the early market, but in the central district of the State this is not the fact. It appears, however, that about 50 per cent of the total crop for the State is marketed in April, May, June, and July. The estimated crop for the State in 1915 is 78,000, which would give 39,000 acres as the total acreage in early potatoes in 1915, 33,844 acres in 1910, 21,049 acres in 1900, and 19,089 acres in 1890. The area of miscellaneous vegetables in the central district was 14,523 acres in 1900 and 41,640 in 1910.

The trucking industry in Oregon is centered in Clackamas, Marion, Multnomah, and Washington Counties. In 1890 these counties grew 8,106 acres of potatoes, 14,683 acres in 1900, and 22,113 acres in 1910. The area of miscellaneous vegetables in 1900 was 4,204 acres, and 6,778 acres in 1910. It is not known what per cent of the crop of potatoes is harvested in May, June, and July.

Clarke, King, Pierce, Spokane, Walla Walla, Whitman, and Yakima Counties of Washington grew 5,910 acres of potatoes in 1890; 11,136 acres in 1900, and 32,311 acres in 1910. There were 5,502 acres of miscellaneous vegetables in 1900 and 10,667 acres in 1910. About 20 per cent of the potato crop is harvested in May, June, and July.

THE INTERIOR SOUTHERN STATES.

Of the interior belt of southern States not already reviewed, there remain Kentucky, whose trucking center is Louisville, in Jefferson County, where onions and early potatoes are produced in large quantities. Strawberries are an important crop also, the principal center of production being at Bowling Green, where about 60 per cent of the crop of the State is produced. Tennessee is one of the most important States in strawberry production, and also produces cantaloupes and tomatoes in considerable quantities. Large quantities of cantaloupes and strawberries are grown in the western tier of counties of Arkansas, and strawberries in

White County. There is a considerable acreage in early potatoes in the Fort Smith district. Oklahoma produces a large quantity of early potatoes in the Arkansas Valley, and there is a large acreage of watermelons around Chickasha and in counties south of that point to the Texas line at Terrell. New Mexico, Arizona, and Nevada also have considerable acreages in cantaloupes.

THE NORTHERN STATES EAST OF THE ROCKY MOUNTAINS (INCLUDING COLORADO).

The two great staple truck crops produced in the northern States, potatoes, sweet potatoes, and strawberries not considered, are cabbages and onions. Other truck crops are grown in large quantities, but with the exception of tomatoes, lettuce, celery, cucumbers, watermelons, and cantaloupes, large quantities of which are grown in certain localities for shipment, it is a home-supply market. Early potatoes are produced in considerable quantities in the Orrick district of Missouri and the Kaw Valley of Kansas. Good roads, automobiles, autotrucks, and electric lines have greatly increased the territory in which the operations of the market gardener may be carried on, and the summer markets of the great northern cities are almost wholly supplied with green vegetables from tributary territory.

ONIONS.

The principal onion-producing States in the northern and western groups are: Colorado, Indiana, Iowa, Massachusetts, Michigan, Minnesota, New York, Ohio, Pennsylvania, and Wisconsin. The census of 1900 gave the area in onions for these States at 23,093 acres, in 1910 the area was 23,087 acres, and, as estimated by the Department of Agriculture, 36,161 acres in 1915.[1]

The Pacific Coast States are properly included as to onion production with the northern and western belt. In 1900 the area in onions in these States was 3,530 acres; in 1910, 5,527 acres; and in 1915, as estimated by the Department of Agriculture, 10,376 acres.

---

[1] The area planted in onions in 1915 in the principal producing States was estimated by the Department of Agriculture to be 49,573 acres. Thirteen thousand four hundred and eighty-one acres were abandoned because of blow-outs, floods, blight, thrips, etc.

CABBAGES.

The principal cabbage-producing States in the northern and western belt of States are: Colorado, Indiana, Iowa, Michigan, Minnesota, New York, Ohio, and Wisconsin. There were 52,256 acres in 1900, 66,147 acres in 1910, and 101,157 acres in 1915, in these States, an increase of over 93 per cent for the 15-year period.

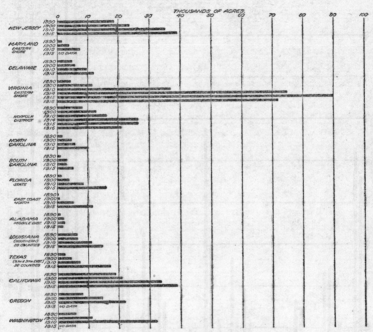

FIG. 42.—Acreage in early potatoes.

EARLY POTATOES.

Considering the Atlantic coast, Gulf coast, and Pacific coast districts together, there were 83,693 acres of early potatoes in 1890; 126,033 acres in 1900; 229,417 acres in 1910; and 324,519 in 1915, as estimated by the Department of Agriculture, an increase for the 5-year period from 1910 to 1915 of about 41 per cent.

For the districts mentioned the total area in miscellaneous vegetables in 1910 was 329,877 acres, as compared with 209,149 acres in 1900, an increase of more than 57 per cent.

STRAWBERRIES AND MISCELLANEOUS VEGETABLES.

The only important truck crop not included in miscellaneous vegetables is strawberries. This crop is produced in large quantities in the Atlantic coast, Gulf, and Pacific coast

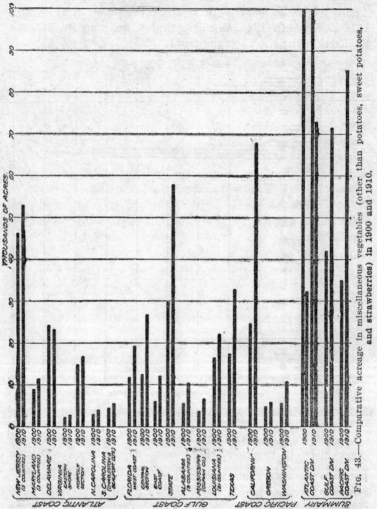

FIG. 43.—Comparative acreage in miscellaneous vegetables (other than potatoes, sweet potatoes, and strawberries) in 1900 and 1910.

groups. The territory in these groups, together with Missouri, Kentucky, Tennessee, Oklahoma, and Arkansas, grew 69,984 acres of strawberries in 1910; 93,155 acres in 1915; and 111,543 acres in 1916, an increase for 1916, as compared with 1910, of nearly 60 per cent in the territory estimated for.

Other important crops included in miscellaneous vegetables are: Asparagus in New Jersey, South Carolina, and California; cabbages in all of the States, the five leading States being New Jersey, Maryland, Virginia, Florida, and Texas; cauliflower in California and Louisiana; celery in Florida and California; cucumbers in Virginia, Florida, Texas, and California; lettuce in North Carolina, South Carolina, Florida, Louisiana, Texas, and California; onions in Louisiana, Texas, and California; peas in Delaware, Maryland, Virginia, North Carolina, South Carolina, Florida, and California; tomatoes in all of the States mentioned, but most heavily for the markets in Florida, Mississippi, New Jersey, Texas, and California; cantaloupes in California, Delaware, Georgia, North Carolina, Maryland, and Florida; watermelons, Texas, Florida, Georgia, North Carolina, South Carolina, and Alabama, these States being the principal centers of production in 1910. The total acreage for these six States was 68,059 in 1910. In 1915 the acreage of watermelons in the States named was estimated to be 81,198, an increase of over 19 per cent for the 5-year period.

SOME NOTABLE EXAMPLES OF LOCALIZATION AND RAPID DEVELOPMENT.

ASPARAGUS.

Asparagus presents an example of localization and rapid development as an industry. In 1900 but two States, California and New Jersey, grew more than 1,000 acres each. In 1910 six States grew more than 1,000 acres each. The total for the six States was 7,034 acres in 1900 and 20,755 acres in 1910, an increase of about 195 per cent. During this period the single State of California increased its area to 9,399 acres, as compared with 7,034 acres for the six States in 1910; New Jersey was second in 1910 with 5,148 acres; Illinois third with 2,241 acres; South Carolina fourth with 1,773 acres; Pennsylvania fifth with 1,191 acres; and New York sixth with 1,003 acres. The total area for the United States was 25,607 acres.

CAULIFLOWER.

Of all truck crops cauliflower is the most restricted in area. In 1910 New York grew 1,720 acres, or nearly 50 per cent of the total production for the United States. California grew 790 acres, the two States including more than 72 per cent of the total for the United States.

CELERY.

The production of celery was practically confined to six States in 1910, those States growing 12,413 acres, or more than 78 per cent of the total acreage for the United States. New York was first with 2,926 acres; California second, 2,881 acres; Michigan third, 2,850 acres; Ohio fourth, 1,473 acres; Massachusetts fifth, 1,187 acres; and Pennsylvania sixth, 1,096 acres. The same six States grew 7,148 acres of celery in 1900. The total area for the United States was 9,315 acres in 1900 and 15,852 acres in 1910.

LETTUCE.

But two States grew more than 1,000 acres of lettuce in 1910, and the total area for the United States was 5,450 acres. Florida led with 1,450 acres, and New York was second with 1,012 acres. California was third with 595 acres, and Louisiana fourth with 515 acres. The total for the four States aggregated 3,572 acres, or more than 65 per cent of the total acreage for the United States. In 1915 it is estimated that there were 4,164 acres of lettuce in Florida; 500 acres in the Beaufort district of South Carolina; 300 acres in the Wilmington district of North Carolina; and 750 acres in the Norfolk district of Virginia, aggregating 5,714 acres, or about 300 acres more than were reported for the United States in 1910. During the same period Texas with but 61 acres of lettuce in 1910 had increased its area to 2,800 acres in 1915, as estimated by the Department of Agriculture, while 1,000 acres are reported as grown in southern California in 1915.

GREEN PEPPERS.

The total area in green peppers reported by the census of 1910 was 3,483 acres. Of this area 1,882 acres, or more than 54 per cent of the total for the United States, were grown in New Jersey.

MARKET GARDEN, CANNING, AND OTHER TRUCKING CENTERS IN 1900 AND 1910.

It is not possible to secure any reliable data regarding truck grown in market-garden communities other than as furnished by the census.

The census of 1900 described the territory tributary to New York City by counties, as follows: New York—New York County, Orange, Richmond, Rockland, and Westchester; Long Island—Kings, Nassau, Queens, and Suffolk; New Jersey—Bergen, Essex, Hudson, Middlesex, Monmouth, Morris, and Warren; Connecticut—Fairfield County.

The total area in truck crops embraced in this territory in 1900 was 35,581 acres. In 1910 the area in these counties was 40,371 acres, an increase of about 13 per cent. Eighteen crops were included.

The census of 1900 (Table XXIII) reported "118 canning, pickling, and trucking or market-garden centers in the United States," and gave the counties included in each district with the total acreage for each. It was, therefore, possible to compare these districts by counties with the census of 1910. From this comparison it appears there were 456,066 acres in the 118 districts in 1900 and 765,105 acres in 1910, an increase of nearly 68 per cent.

The following table shows the area tributary to 10 of the largest cities, as shown by Table XXIII of the census of 1900, above referred to, compared with the same territory in 1910:

Area in vegetables in territory tributary to 10 cities, 1900 and 1910.

City.	Area in specified vegetables.		City.	Area in specified vegetables.	
	1900	1910		1900	1910
	Acres.	*Acres.*		*Acres.*	*Acres.*
New York	35,581	40,371	Detroit	3,086	6,050
Philadelphia	43,023	58,640	St. Louis	9,917	9,334
Baltimore	49,882	45,905	Galveston and Houston	2,317	7,267
Cleveland	1,892	3,666	San Francisco	4,819	10,474
Cincinnati	9,397	9,794			
Chicago	11,871	15,043	Total	171,785	206,544

THE CANNING INDUSTRY.

The total area in corn, peas, and tomatoes reported to the Bureau of Crop Estimates of the United States Department of Agriculture in 1913, 1914, and 1915, as contracted for by canneries, is shown on the following page.

Area in corn, peas, and tomatoes contracted for by canneries, 1913, 1914, and 1915.

Crop.	1913	1914	1915
	Acres.	*Acres.*	*Acres.*
Corn	137,561	190,178	190,106
Peas	108,066	126,177	101,698
Tomatoes	129,068	187,077	139,837
Total	374,695	503,432	431,641

The quantity bought outside of contracts reported to the Bureau of Crop Estimates of the United States Department of Agriculture in 1914 was 28,914 tons of corn, 5,864 tons of peas, and 199,081 tons of tomatoes. The total number of factories which may be engaged in canning one or more truck crops, as shown on the list of the National Canners' Association for 1915, is 2,412; of this number 735, or about 30 per cent, rendered no report and 405 of these are located in the States of Maryland and Virginia and were probably largely small canners of tomatoes. Of the 1,677 factories reporting in 1915, 365 reported idle, leaving a total of 1,312 factories reporting acreage under contract for one or more of the above crops. Eighty-four factories reported idle in 1913, 249 reported idle in 1914, and 365 reported idle in 1915. Of the factories reporting idle in 1915, 139 were located in Maryland and Virginia.

From a statement issued by the Bureau of the Census concerning the canning industry for 1914 it appears that the total value of vegetables canned in 1914 was $84,413,667, as compared with a total value in 1909 of $53,307,791, an increase of 58.4 per cent. This does not indicate an equal increase in acreage, but supports the increase in acreage indicated in the table above.

At least 14 vegetables are canned in greater or less quantities, corn (sweet), peas, and tomatoes taking the lead. A very heavy increase has occurred in the acreage of cucumbers grown for pickling, but complete figures are not available. The acreage in Michigan in 1915 may be cited as an example. The United States census of 1910 gave the total area in cucumbers for the United States as 32,310 acres, and the area for Michigan as 7,061, more than twice that of any other

State. In 1915 the area for Michigan was estimated by the State field agent of the Bureau of Crop Estimates, Department of Agriculture, after a careful canvass, at 34,260 acres, or about 6 per cent greater than the total area for the United States in 1910. It is not supposed that this ratio of increase has been maintained throughout the United States, but a heavy increase is indicated for this industry. It is estimated by the department that the product of about 16,000 acres of cabbage was manufactured into kraut in 1915.

The great extent of the area devoted to the production of truck crops would lead the uninformed to suppose the industry to be one comparatively certain to produce satisfactory results, but it is, in fact, attended with considerable risk, yielding the grower heavy returns in money one year and proving almost a total loss the next. Truck crops are generally very easily damaged by frosts, freezes, droughts, excessive moisture, and floods, and replanting at high cost is sometimes done several times before a crop is secured, or the crop is so damaged and delayed that it fails to bring a remunerative price in northern markets. A case in point is to be found in the early potato crop of 1915, which was harvested from the largest acreage ever grown in the South up to that year and was forced to compete with the largest northern crop ever produced for the early spring market. The result was that the price per barrel in many cases was below the cost of production to the southern grower. Floods in the same year completely destroyed 5,000 acres of onions in Hardin County, Ohio, and 2,000 acres of onions in Jasper County, Ind., the total abandoned acreage for that year amounting to more than 13,000 acres.

In fact, the year 1915, because of the unusually cold and backward spring, was very disastrous to truck crops in all sections of the country, with few exceptions. The exceedingly warm fall and winter of 1915–16, on the other hand, cut the production of lettuce almost one-half from North Carolina to Texas, and a number of frosts and freezes damaged all tender crops seriously.

The acreage devoted to truck crops has increased rapidly, and never so rapidly as during the last five years. This persistent increase is due largely to an urban population ever increasing in numbers and wealth, that demands green vegetables throughout the winter months. The total urban population in 1889 was 22,720,223, or 36.1 per cent of the total population of the United States. In 1909 it was 42,623,383, an increase of about 87.6 per cent, and was 46.3 per cent of the total population. This was a gain in numbers of 19,903,160 in 20 years, or nearly 1,000,000 per year. The significant fact is the gain for the urban of 10.2 points over the rural population of 1889, as compared with 1909, thus reducing the producing element proportionately while the consuming element increased heavily.

Transportation facilities have been improved to cater to this increasing demand, and the products of California and Texas are delivered in good condition in New York. Precooling plants at points of origin prepare the crops for shipment, and refrigerator cars in solid trains are rushed across the continent to deliver the green vegetables of the Pacific coast in the markets of the East. No section of the country is now too far away to market some portion of its winter and early spring crops in the great consuming centers of the East.

The maps accompanying this article were prepared by Middleton Smith, of the Bureau of Crop Estimates.

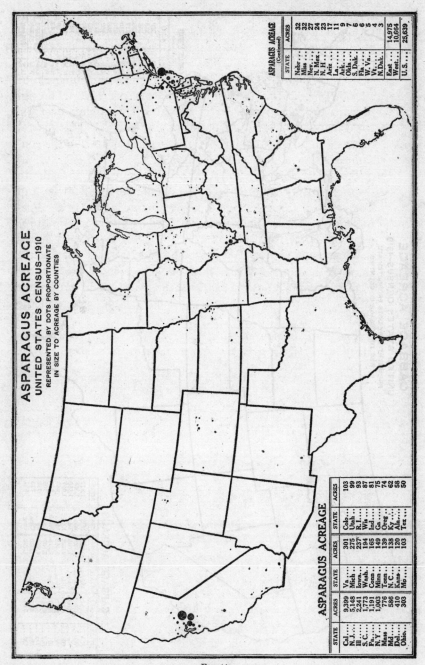

ASPARAGUS ACREAGE
UNITED STATES CENSUS—1910
REPRESENTED BY DOTS PROPORTIONATE
IN SIZE TO ACREAGE BY COUNTIES

ASPARAGUS ACREAGE

STATE	ACRES	STATE	ACRES	STATE	ACRES
Cal.	9,399	Va.	301	Colo.	103
N.J.	5,148	Mich	275	Utah	99
Ill.	2,241	Iowa.	237	R.I.	93
S.C.	1,773	Wash.	194	Wis	87
Pa.	1,191	Conn	165	Ind.	81
N.Y.	1,003	Minn	149	Ga.	75
Mass	776	Tenn	139	Oreg	74
Md.	586	N.C.	138	Ky.	62
Del.	410	Kans.	120	Ala.	58
Ohio.	303	Mo.	103	Tex.	50

ASPARAGUS ACREAGE (Continued)

STATE	ACRES
Nebr.	32
Miss	32
Nev.	27
N. Mex.	24
N.H.	23
Ariz	17
La.	11
Ark.	9
Okla.	7
S. Dak.	6
Fla.	6
W. Va.	5
Va.	4
N.Dak.	3
East	14,975
West	10,664
U.S.	25,639

Fig. 44.

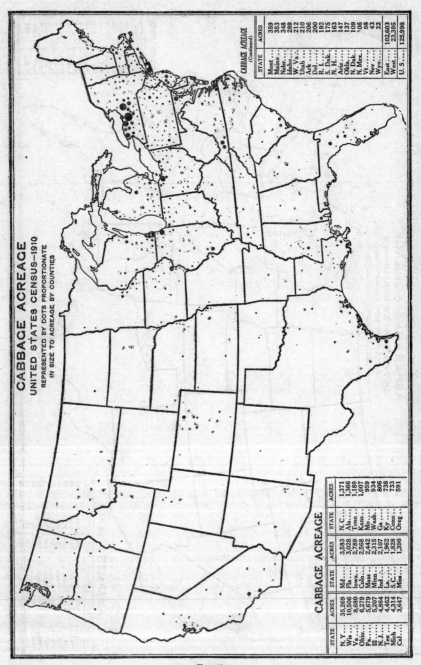

FIG. 45.

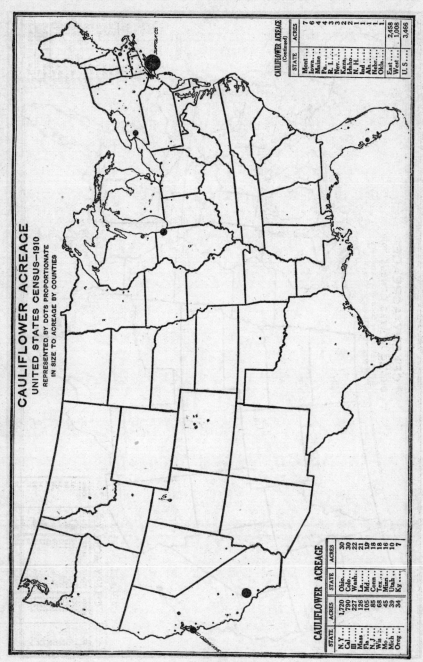

CAULIFLOWER ACREAGE

UNITED STATES CENSUS—1910

REPRESENTED BY DOTS PROPORTIONATE
IN SIZE TO ACREAGE BY COUNTIES

CAULIFLOWER ACREAGE (Continued)			
STATE	ACRES		
Mont.	7		
Iowa.	6		
Maine	4		
Pa.	4		
R. I.	3		
Nev.	2		
Kans.	2		
Idaho.	1		
N. H.	1		
Ind.	1		
Ala.	1		
Nebr.	1		
Okla.	1		
East.	2,458		
West.	1,008		
U. S.	3,466		

CAULIFLOWER ACREAGE			
STATE	ACRES	STATE	ACRES
N. Y.	1,720	Ohio.	30
Cal.	790	Colo.	22
Ill.	221	Wash.	22
Mass.	126	La.	21
Fla.	105	Md.	19
N. J.	85	Conn.	18
Wis.	68	Tex.	18
Mo.	45	Minn.	16
Mich.	39	Utah.	10
Oreg.	34	Ky.	7

Fig. 46.

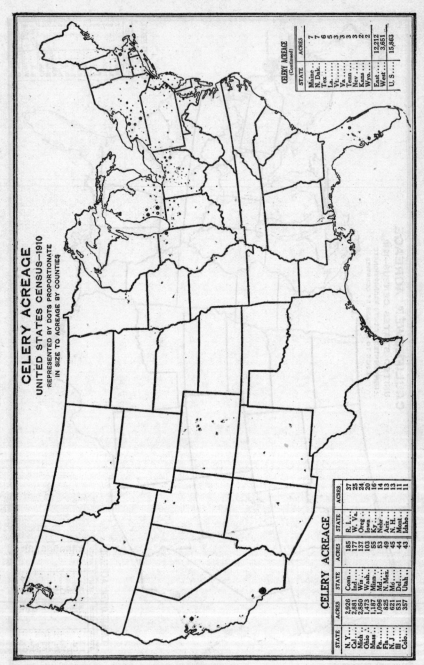

CELERY ACREAGE

UNITED STATES CENSUS—1910

REPRESENTED BY DOTS PROPORTIONATE
IN SIZE TO ACREAGE BY COUNTIES

CELERY ACREAGE (Continued)	
STATE	ACRES
Maine..	7
N. Dak.	7
Tex...	6
La...	5
Va...	3
Tenn..	3
Nev...	3
Kans..	2
Wyo...	2
East..	12,212
West..	3,651
U.S...	15,863

CELERY ACREAGE

STATE	ACRES	STATE	ACRES	STATE	ACRES
N.Y...	2,926	Conn...	185	R. I...	37
Cal...	2,881	Ind...	177	W. Va.	25
Mich..	2,850	Wis...	137	Oreg..	24
Ohio..	1,473	Wash..	103	Iowa..	20
Mass..	1,187	Minn..	55	Ky...	16
Pa...	1,096	Md...	53	Nebr..	14
Fla...	825	N. Mex.	49	Ariz..	13
N.J...	621	Mo...	45	N. H...	13
Ill...	531	Del...	44	Mont..	11
Colo..	357	Utah..	43	Idaho..	11

Fig. 47.

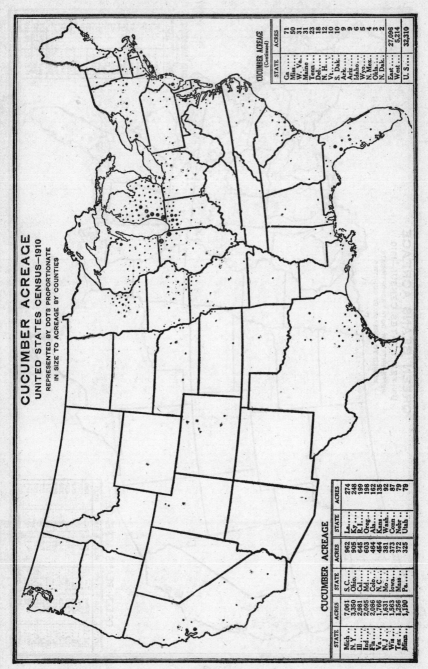

CUCUMBER ACREAGE
UNITED STATES CENSUS—1910
REPRESENTED BY DOTS PROPORTIONATE
IN SIZE TO ACREAGE BY COUNTIES

CUCUMBER ACREAGE (Continued)	
STATE	ACRES
Ga.	71
Miss.	50
W. Va.	31
Maine	31
Tenn.	23
Del.	18
N. H.	12
Vt.	10
S. Dak.	10
Ark.	9
Ariz.	6
Idaho	5
Wyo.	4
N. Mex.	3
Okla.	2
N. Dak.	
East.	27,096
West.	5,214
U. S.	32,310

CUCUMBER ACREAGE			
STATE	ACRES	STATE	ACRES
Mich.	7,061	S. C.	962	L.a.	274
N. Y.	3,350	Ohio	905	Ky.	248
Ill.	2,981	Cal.	645	R. I.	199
Ind.	2,095	Md.	603	Oreg.	198
Fla.	2,086	Colo	464	Ala.	162
Va.	1,766	N. C.	454	Kans.	135
N. J.	1,631	Mo.	381	Wash.	92
Wis.	1,563	Iowa	373	Conn.	87
Tex.	1,256	Nebr.	372	Nebr.	79
Minn.	1,190	Pa.	325	Utah.	79

FIG. 48.

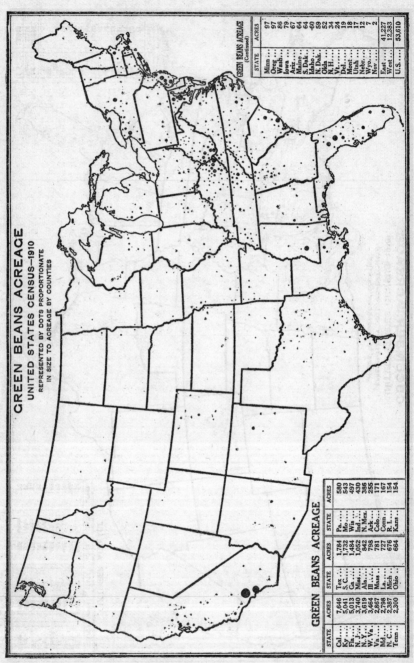

GREEN BEANS ACREAGE

UNITED STATES CENSUS—1910

REPRESENTED BY DOTS PROPORTIONATE
IN SIZE TO ACREAGE BY COUNTIES

GREEN BEANS ACREAGE (Continued)

STATE	ACRES
Minn	97
Oreg	97
Wash	86
Iowa	79
Ariz	67
Maine	64
S. Dak.	64
Idaho	60
N. Dak.	59
Okla	52
N. H.	34
Vt.	24
Del.	19
Mont.	18
Utah	17
Nebr.	12
Wyo.	7
Nev.	2
East.	41,227
West	12,383
U. S.	53,610

GREEN BEANS ACREAGE

STATE	ACRES	STATE	ACRES	STATE	ACRES
Cal.	7,646	Tex.	1,784	Pa.	580
Ky.	5,041	S. C.	1,732	Mo.	543
Fla.	5,013	Ga.	1,484	Wis.	497
N. Y.	3,740	Miss.	1,052	Ind.	430
W. Va.	3,449	Ill.	798	N. Mex.	386
Va.	2,867	Mass.	781	Ark.	255
Md.	2,798	La.	727	Colo.	171
N. C.	2,387	Mich.	676	Conn	167
Tenn.	2,300	Ohio	664	R. I.	154
				Kans.	154

FIG. 49.

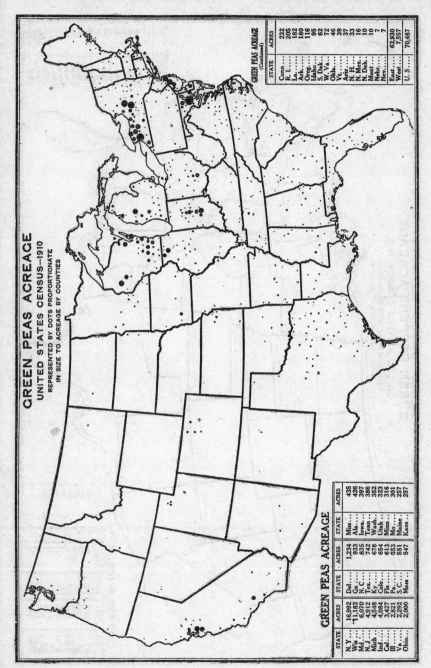

GREEN PEAS ACREAGE

UNITED STATES CENSUS—1910

REPRESENTED BY DOTS PROPORTIONATE
IN SIZE TO ACREAGE BY COUNTIES

STATE	ACRES
Conn.	232
R. I.	205
La.	182
Ark.	180
Oreg.	116
Idaho	95
S. Dak.	82
W. Va.	72
Vt.	46
Okla.	39
Ariz.	37
N. H.	33
N. Mex.	16
N. Dak.	10
Mont.	10
Nebr.	7
Nev.	7
East.	62,930
West.	7,557
U. S.	70,487

GREEN PEAS ACREAGE

STATE	ACRES	STATE	ACRES
N. Y.	16,992	Miss.	435
Wis.	11,182	Ala.	426
Md.	6,070	N. C.	397
N. J.	4,912	Iowa.	386
Mich.	4,548	Tenn.	352
Ind.	4,084	Wash.	323
Cal.	3,827	Utah	316
Ill.	2,821	Minn.	301
Pa.	2,292	Mo.	301
Va.	2,292	Maine	257
Ohio.	2,000	Kans.	257

FIG. 50.

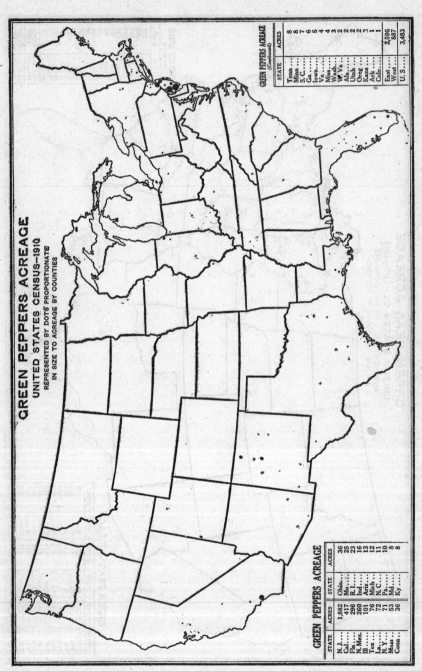

GREEN PEPPERS ACREAGE

UNITED STATES CENSUS—1910

REPRESENTED BY DOTS PROPORTIONATE
IN SIZE TO ACREAGE BY COUNTIES

GREEN PEPPERS ACREAGE		
STATE	ACRES	
N.J.	1,882	
Cal.	417	
Fla.	296	
N.Mex.	260	
Ill.	101	
Tex.	72	
La.	71	
N.Y.	53	
Mass.	36	

STATE	ACRES
Ohio	36
Mo.	25
R.I.	23
Ind.	16
Ariz.	13
Mich.	12
N.C.	11
Pa.	10
Md.	8
Ky.	8

GREEN PEPPERS ACREAGE (Continued)	
STATE	ACRES
Tenn.	8
Minn.	8
S.C.	7
Ga.	6
Iowa	5
Va.	4
Miss.	4
Utah	3
W.Va.	2
Ala.	2
Utah	2
Oreg.	2
Kans.	1
Ark.	1
Colo.	1
East.	2,596
West.	887
U.S.	3,483

FIG. 51.

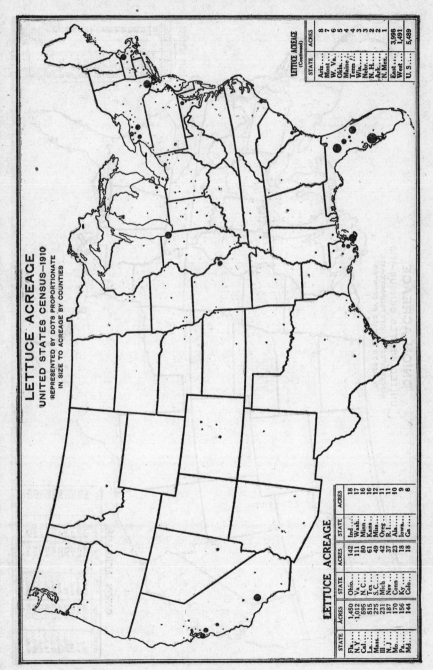

LETTUCE ACREAGE

UNITED STATES CENSUS—1910

REPRESENTED BY DOTS PROPORTIONATE
IN SIZE TO ACREAGE BY COUNTIES

LETTUCE ACREAGE				
STATE	ACRES		STATE	ACRES
Fla.	1,450		Ohio	142
N.Y.	1,212		Va.	111
Cal.	595		N.C.	80
La.	515		Kan.	61
Tex.	275		Miss.	49
Mass.	231		Oreg.	42
Ill.	187		R.I.	37
N.J.	170		Conn.	23
Mo.	156		Ky.	18
Pa.	144		Iowa.	18
Md.			Colo.	18
			Ind.	18
			Wash.	17
			Minn.	16
			S.C.	16
			Mich	12
			Nev	11
			Ala.	11
			Ga.	10
				9
				8

LETTUCE ACREAGE (Continued)	
STATE	ACRES
Ariz.	8
Mont.	7
W. Va.	6
Okla.	5
Maine	4
Tenn.	4
Wis.	3
Nebr.	3
N.H.	2
Ark.	2
N.Mex.	1
East	3,998
West	1,491
U.S.	5,489

FIG. 52.

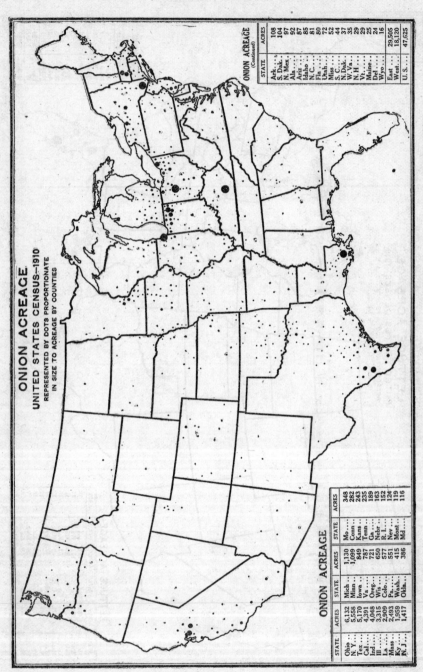

ONION ACREAGE
UNITED STATES CENSUS—1910
REPRESENTED BY DOTS PROPORTIONATE
IN SIZE TO ACREAGE BY COUNTIES

ONION ACREAGE					
STATE	ACRES	STATE	ACRES	STATE	ACRES
Ohio	6,132	Mich	1,130	Mo.	348
N. Y.	5,558	Minn	1,099	Conn	282
Tex.	5,170	Iowa	849	Kans	243
Cal.	4,391	Va.	787	Tenn	235
Ind.	4,048	Oreg	721	Ga.	189
Ill.	3,315	Wis	650	Nebr	163
La.	2,909	Colo.	577	R. I.	152
Mass	2,493	Pa.	551	Nev	124
Ky.	1,959	Wash.	415	Mont	119
N. J.	1,417	Okla.	386	Md	116

ONION ACREAGE (Continued)	
STATE	ACRES
Ark.	108
S. Dak.	104
N. Mex.	97
Ala.	92
Ariz	87
Idaho	85
N. C.	81
Fla.	80
Utah	72
Miss	52
S. C.	44
N. Dak.	37
W. Va.	35
N. H.	29
Vt.	29
Maine.	25
Del.	24
Wyo.	16
East	29,505
West.	18,120
U. S.	47,625

FIG. 53.

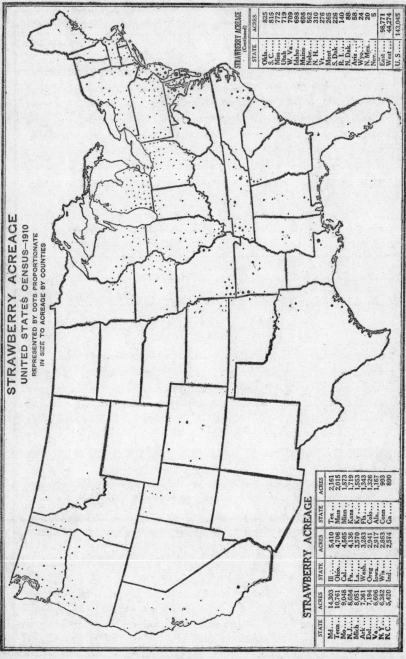

FIG. 54.

THE FUNCTION OF LIVE STOCK IN AGRICULTURE.[1]

By George M. Rommel,

Chief of the Animal Husbandry Division, Bureau of Animal Industry.

THE animal industry is the most important branch of the agriculture of the United States. With a total value so great that one can not visualize it, it has an annual production of two and three-quarters billions of dollars, which is greater than the cereal output in an ordinary year. It is three times as valuable as the annual cotton production or the hay crop, and the latter largely depends on the animal industry for its value.

All have read Ingalls's brilliant apostrophe to grass, and recall how he said that "should its harvest fail for a single year, famine would depopulate the world." Poetic and beautiful as that sentiment is, it is economically and hygienically sound.

Some form of forage is essential, fundamentally, to the maintenance of animals; the animal industry is essential to the well-being of a prosperous and permanent agriculture; and a diet in which animal products form a part is essential to human health.

The function of live stock in agriculture rests on seven main points.

THE MAINTENANCE OF SOIL FERTILITY.

The first and most important is the maintenance of soil fertility. An elaborate development of this point is not possible in this place. It may, however, be illustrated by citing the report of the Thirteenth United States Census on Agriculture. Of the 10 States which lead in the value of animals sold and slaughtered on farms, all but two, Oklahoma and Kentucky, are among the first 10 in the value of all products. The two which appear in their places are New York and Minnesota. New York, by reason of leading in dairy production and hay and forage, holds a place among the first 10 in all products and Minnesota wins her place by reason of her prominence in dairying and cereals. Of the 10 leading

---

[1] This paper was presented at a meeting of the Second Pan-American Scientific Congress, Washington, D. C.

cotton States, only 2, Oklahoma and Texas, are also among the first 10 in value of animals sold and slaughtered; Texas alone is among the first 10 in value of all products.

Taking St. Louis as the center, let a circle be described with a radius of 500 miles and it will include part or all of the 10 leading States in animal production, part or all of 9 of the 10 leading States in value of all products, and part or all of 9 of the 10 leading States in cereal production.

Surveys covering a period of years, made by the Iowa State College, show that the live-stock farms of the State produce much larger grain and hay yields per acre than the strictly grain-producing farms. To maintain soil fertility, humus is necessary. It can be obtained from two sources—green crops plowed under, or barnyard manure. In view of the fact that a large proportion of the fertilizing value of forage and feed appears in the manure, it is more economical to feed than to plow under without feeding. Therefore, the most economical and practical source of humus is stable manure. No fertilizer equals it in completeness and lasting qualities. The farmer who has an abundant supply of this fertilizer and who balances it with phosphates, and supplements it with nitrates for forcing crops, need never fear the approach of decreasing soil fertility.

THE MANUFACTURING FUNCTION.

The second function of live stock is to enable the farmer to carry out an important manufacturing process, thus completing a manufacturing cycle. He takes the lean, unfinished cattle, sheep, or hogs, and his grain and forage, all raw products, and by the application of intelligent supervision, skillful labor, and adequate equipment converts them into finished beef, mutton, pork, or dairy products. This is the process familiarly known as "marketing the farm products on four legs," and is much to be preferred to marketing on four wheels. With intelligent management the farmer thus obtains in terms of meat and dairy products a much larger profit than he could possibly derive by selling his crops in the raw state. This doubtless accounts largely for the fact that in most farming sections the most prosperous farmers are those who pay a great deal of attention to live stock. It is of the greatest importance, especially in those sections of the country which are just beginning to diversify their agriculture. In the Great Plains region and on most of the Federal reclamation projects it is, after the question of water for the crops, the most vital problem which farmers have to solve.

In the regions of settled farms, where cereal production leads all other forms of agricultural production, farmers have a difficult problem to adjust the necessity for live-stock raising with the high price of grain. We therefore see a second phase of this function in the use of live stock to convert into salable products those crops which for one reason or another have a low market value. At times the farmers of the northern part of the corn belt are at a loss to know what to do with the soft corn which early frost leaves on their hands. It is not marketable, and its only value is as a feed. Not knowing just how to dispose of it in this manner, farmers at such times send large numbers of immature pigs to market and curtail their cattle-feeding operations. The soft-corn problem, however, is an occurrence of only occasional importance. The constant problem of the farmer on high-priced land is how to keep his live stock economically. He can not afford to feed grain with a lavish hand. He must measure it by weight, not by volume. He must feed it at the time and in the manner to obtain from each bushel the maximum of gain in weight of milk produced or of work done. To the fullest extent possible he must utilize unsalable roughage. The cornstalks go into the silo or into the shock as cut fodder. The straw and coarse hay are utilized to the last calorie of energy value to supply the maintenance requirements. Crops that animals such as hogs and sheep can harvest will be utilized.

MOTIVE POWER.

The third function of live stock in agriculture is to supply most of the motive power used on the farm. This is the most important engineering problem with which the farmer has to deal. In the aggregate our farmers have to determine every year the efficient application of about 25 million horsepower, an amount equal to about half the total available water power in the entire country, excluding Alaska. The proper hitches to use, the adjustment of harness, whiffletrees, etc., are problems which for successful solution

470 Yearbook of the Department of Agriculture.

call for the correct application of some of the fundamental laws of physics. How to feed his work animals to get the maximum efficiency when at hard work, how to maintain them without serious deterioration when idle, are problems just as important and just as difficult as those of the engineer in charge of the furnaces of a manufacturing establishment.

What the effect of mechanical power on the future use of horses on the farm will be can not be predicted. Slowly but surely the auto-truck is driving dray horses from the city streets. Already the cheap automobiles have effectually put the driving horses off the country roads. The farm demand for several years has been the mainstay of the horse market, and the present tremendous exports have prevented a period of great depression of horse prices. If the farm demand hereafter is to be the chief outlet of the horse market, as no doubt it will, the question of the suitable horse for this market is highly important. The great ton drafter has been the aim of the farmer-breeder of the corn belt. That has been the horse which the city market demanded when in its prime. These horses are most valuable for moving heavy loads. With the increase in the weight and draft of farm machinery they have been also most useful for farm work, especially on heavy soils. The position of these horses on the farm is being attacked by the small tractor, and the tractor manufacturers believe that in time they will displace them. It has been observed time and again, however, that for each displacement of the horse has come an enlargement of industry which calls for further uses for horse-drawn apparatus. The question therefore is what type of horse the farmers of the future will need. This question can be answered only by speculation. Except for the heaviest farm work, such as plowing and hauling, the ton horse is not so suitable an animal as a smaller, more active one.

With the disappearance of the city demand for the heavy drafter, the farm demand will be met by breeding a lighter, more active animal. Therefore the next 25 years probably will witness, in the Percheron, for example, a return to the type of the French "diligence" horse, which was the early Percheron type, and an increase in the size and weight of the American breeds of horses, the Standardbred, the Saddle Horse, and the Morgan.

THE PRINCIPAL SOURCE OF INCOME.

In diversified farming regions live stock as the money crop of the farm is a specialty business. In dairy districts it is, of course, the main activity, and every phase of farm management is bent toward it. Where farming has been long established, however, and the principal function of live-stock feeding is to maintain soil fertility, those farms on which the live stock are the main source of income will be breeding centers for purebred animals. Only the most skilled animal husbandman can make a success of this business, and of those who engage in it successfully only the occasional man becomes really eminent, just as in any other profession. The great live-stock ranges pass with the approach of the homesteader or are limited to areas unsuitable for crop production. The large feeding stations in turn disappear with the increase in the price of land, and the Nation's supply of live stock is drawn from the production in small units, which in the aggregate make a total larger than was possible under more extensive conditions.

LIVE STOCK INCREASES THE INTEREST IN AND THE ATTRACTIVENESS OF FARM LIFE.

The fifth function of live stock is to make farm life more attractive and to increase the interest in it. The problem of how to develop agriculture by using for that purpose the best of the human life which has been developed on the farms is being attacked to-day as never before. The boys and girls who are born on the farm and have behind them the inheritance of generations of sturdy physique, clear thinking, and clean morals, and who come from life on the soil and in the fresh air, are the most valuable asset of the republic. How to encourage these young people to make farming their vocation in life transcends in importance all other problems of future agricultural development. The great Federal agricultural extension act has for its purpose bringing directly to the farmers the fruits of the last 30 years of research in agriculture, but this act will fail of its purpose if its operations stop with the training of the adult farmer. In a generation the adults are gone. Their places must be taken by their own sons and daughters. Therefore the corn clubs, canning clubs, potato clubs, poultry clubs, calf clubs,

and pig clubs have been organized among children of both
sexes of school age. This movement promises more for the
Nation than does the work with adults. Children are plastic;
they adopt suggestions; they can learn. Too often the adult
has become fixed in habits of thought and action, and try
as he may, he nearly always lacks the adaptability of his
children to grasp new ideas and methods.

The innate love of children for animals is one of the most
potent forces which an agricultural-extension worker has at
his command, and when the development of this trait is
encouraged and the child thereby taught the importance
of live stock in agriculture, something of the most fundamental importance to the agricultural development of the
Nation is accomplished.

The organization of poultry clubs and pig clubs among
boys and girls is one of the most important features of the
club movement. They are found in all sections in many
States. Probably most of the members are among the clubs
organized by the Federal Department of Agriculture, in
cooperation with the State agricultural colleges. On January
1, 1917, there were about 10,000 young people in the poultry
clubs in 8 States, and 25,000 in the pig clubs in 14 States.
This movement was started as an outgrowth of the organization of canning clubs among girls and corn clubs among
boys. It was found impossible, however, to keep the boys
out of the poultry clubs or the girls out of the pig clubs.
Therefore no discrimination is made as to sex.

The plan of the Government, briefly, is as follows: On
application from the State, the Federal department stations
at the State agricultural college a specialist whose entire time
is devoted to the direction of the club organization. At first
this agent selects certain counties in which to work, and for
the first year or two supervises most of the work himself.
His aim, however, is to train the county agents and school
teachers so that in time they can take full charge of the work,
leaving the State agent's time for new work in other sections.
The schools are a most fertile field for the organization of this
work.

Each member of a poultry or pig club is required to hatch
a setting of eggs or raise and fatten a pig, and render regular
reports of his work. At the end of the year the members

usually have an opportunity to compare the results of their efforts by exhibition at the county fairs or other places, and the winning animals at these exhibitions go to the State fair for further competition.

This work has been in progress ever since 1910, and since 1912 the Federal Department of Agriculture has been engaged in it. Already the exhibition of pigs and poultry from the clubs has become a prominent feature of some of the State fairs, especially in the South. Many of the members of the earlier years are now bona fide breeders, and many a boy is paying his way through college by the earnings from the animals in which he became interested as a club member.

METHOD, SYSTEM, AND BUSINESS ORGANIZATION.

The sixth function of live stock in agriculture is to improve the method, system, and business organization of the farm. The farm on which live stock are successfully raised must be managed in a methodical, systematic, businesslike, and sanitary manner. Farming is first of all a business operation, and no kind of farming calls for more business sense than live-stock farming. A grain farmer does not suffer seriously if his cultivating or harvesting is delayed a few hours, but the stock must be fed promptly, rain or shine. Therefore the efficiency of labor assumes great importance. If the live stock is a herd of pure-bred animals, accurate records are absolutely necessary and clerical ability of a high order is required.

The importance of sanitation on the live-stock farm is fundamental. The live-stock farmer need not be a trained veterinarian (though the more he knows of veterinary science the better), but he must be by instinct a sanitarian. He must recognize clearly the difference between things that merely appear to be clean and those which are actually, bacteriologically clean.

In the great majority of known cases human carelessness has been the most fruitful cause of the spread of contagion. In at least one county in which the Department of Agriculture has carried on work on the control of hog cholera, it was found that the most common known way in which the disease was spread was by visits to neighbors' herds. It is a prevalent custom, in some sections, to drag dead animals out to a field without burial. Birds and dogs devour the carcasses and, if death was caused by a contagious disease, spread it over a wide area. Streams and irrigation canals also are common sources of contagion. In every case of carelessness such as this the community suffers, and every member of the community sooner or later pays his share of the cost.

With the increase in population and the cost of land, and the attendant cost of raising domestic animals, sanitation assumes a constantly growing importance on the live-stock farm. It is not alone with regard to direct profit, however, that the farmer must pay strict attention to this matter. This subject may be left with the simple reference to the fact that some of the most serious human diseases have their origin in the barnyard. Their existence not only affects the health of the families that come into immediate contact with them, but they may spread with disastrous results to neighboring towns and villages.

The farmer needs education on the matter of sanitation. He needs to appreciate more fully his obligation, not only to his own family, but to the community. By realizing the fact that insanitary methods will diminish or entirely inhibit the profits from his animals he will in turn the better fulfill his obligation to safeguard the health of the community.

THE IMPROVEMENT OF THE DIET—THE REDUCTION OF LIVING EXPENSES.

The last function of live stock in agriculture to which attention is invited is to reduce the family living expenses and introduce variety into the diet. It is a remarkable fact that a large number of farms produce only a small part of the food used by the family. The annual meat bill of the farmers of some of our Southern States, for example, is enormous. Their purchases are largely carried on credit, and the year's crop goes for the most part to meet the expenses incurred during its production. Debts accrue only to be replaced by accounts newly opened. That such a practice is wasteful and depressing is apparent. With chickens and pigs, a cow, and a few sheep, but little capital is required to reduce in great measure the annual money outlay of such farmers. This production of home-grown food can be made without in the least limiting the crop output of the farm. It simply requires planning and a little more careful management.

The value of live stock in agriculture has been greatly emphasized by the announcement of the United States Public Health Service that the cause of pellagra is a dietary deficiency attributable to the excessive use of carbohydrate foods. This dreadful disease has been spreading with alarming rapidity, and the determination of its cause is a triumph of medical research. To an animal husbandman it is of especial interest to note that among the means of prevention advised are the keeping of a cow and the use of more milk, butter, and cheese; the keeping of a flock of chickens so as to have fresh poultry and eggs, and the increase of live-stock raising so that meat may form a larger part of the diet.

To recapitulate, the function of live stock in agriculture is fundamental. Soil fertility, the business success of the farmer, his happiness and contentment and that of his children, the health of the community, and the well-being of the farm family depend on the maintenance and proper management of as **much live stock** as the farm can economically support.

POSSIBILITIES OF A MARKET–TRAIN SERVICE.

By G. C. WHITE and T. F. POWELL,

Transportation Specialists, Office of Markets and Rural Organization.

IF the statement be true that more than one-half of the industrial and commercial energy of the civilized world is expended in the provision and preparation of food, it becomes all the more important, as the density of population and the economic conditions of the United States approximate those of the Old World, that the producing areas in the vicinity of large consuming centers be utilized to their full capacity, and that the products of such areas be accorded an efficient and economical transportation service.

Conditions controlling the commerce of England have developed a railway freight service characterized by light trains of high speed and frequent movement, cars of small capacity and very low minimum weights. The settlement of the greater part of the United States and its industrial development followed the advent of the railroad. The long distances separating the sources of raw material from the mills and factories utilizing it, as well as the character of the raw material, have developed high minimum weights for large cars of great weight capacity drawn in heavy trains by powerful locomotives. The development of these features of the freight service of the railroads of this country has received relatively more attention than has been given to the improvement of facilities for short-distance local traffic.

SPECIAL MARKET TRAINS.

The greater part of the trading at the principal live-stock markets of the United States is done on certain designated days each week, and special trains carrying nothing but live stock reach these markets in large numbers on those days. From a comparatively small area in the Imperial Valley of California approximately 5,000 cars of melons are shipped to market each year, the bulk of the crop being handled during four weeks in June. During the height of the shipping season special trains carrying nothing but melons move east across the desert. From certain of the Gulf ports special trains carrying only bananas run on frequent and fast schedules to northern cities. Solid trains of milk daily supply New York City with that commodity. All these may be termed "special market trains," and, for the most part, they are additional examples of the efficient handling of long-distance, high-speed traffic of large volume.

In that section of the United States lying north of the Ohio and Potomac Rivers and east of the Mississippi, known in railroad parlance as official classification territory, has taken place the greatest industrial development of the country. Here is situated much agricultural land in small units, the individual farm yielding dairy products, poultry, small live stock, and fruits and vegetables, which mature at different seasons, and producing less than a carload quantity of any commodity at one time; here are our most populous cities, daily demanding a supply of perishable foodstuffs; and here density of population and economic conditions are beginning to approximate those of the Old World. In this section are presented many opportunities for developing the possibilities of a market-train service along the lines of the service now furnished by milk trains.

Steam and electricity in passenger transportation have relieved some of the congestion of the population of large cities, but the suburban development of residential districts has withdrawn a proportionately much larger area from tillage, until most of the market gardeners have been pushed back beyond wagon range of the city markets, and many of them beyond the range of the auto-truck. Coincident with this development has come the increasing demand for greater quantities of foodstuffs, and it becomes necessary, therefore, that the commutation passenger service of the large cities find its counterpart in a similar freight service. The relatively small number of postal cars as compared with freight cars, or even with express cars, makes improbable any considerable amount of relief by the parcel post at the present time, and express service has not fully met the need.

HISTORY OF THE SERVICE.

The limited market-train service maintained by certain of the roads serving New York City, and the somewhat more extensive service of the same kind maintained by roads serving Philadelphia, were foreshadowed in some of the marketing practices which developed with the construction of the first railroads in the United States. Following the analogy of turnpike operation, the first railroad companies furnished roadway only; horses were the only motive power; farmers furnished their own motive power, paid the necessary tolls for the use of the track, and hauled their produce to market in their own vehicles. An interesting account of the methods of that period has been left in the history of the Philadelphia & Columbia Railroad, which was formally opened for traffic in 1834.

More than 50 years later, in 1888, the reports of the Interstate Commerce Commission disclose a special market-train service by four of the railroads leading to New York City, and doubtless there were other roads that offered a similar service. The service consisted in transporting on the daily milk trains, in the same cars with the milk, such commodities as fresh meat, berries, butter, and eggs, and in returning to the shippers the empty containers, such as meat baskets, berry and egg crates, and butter carriers.

The rapid increase in the milk business and other conditions peculiar to its transportation and marketing in the course of time made it necessary to restrict the milk cars almost exclusively to the transportation of milk. However, many, if not most, of the tariffs covering the transportation of milk to Boston and New York include pot cheese as a commodity which may be included in mixed carload lots of milk, cream, and buttermilk. A railroad in Vermont and another in Massachusetts permit the transportation of butter in milk cars, and a road in Maine includes eggs. One road serving sections of Pennsylvania and New York and participating in the New York City milk traffic handles in its milk cars practically every class of farm produce except fresh meat. Another road serving an extensive section of New York makes tariff provision for a similar service by its milk trains. One of the trunk lines serving New York City has had in operation since 1890 a produce train giving a carload service for farm products on one of its divisions; and on another division the same class of commodities is given a less-than-carload pick-up service by milk trains.

THE PHILADELPHIA MARKET TRAINS.

The examples given of special facilities and service, in the transportation of less-than-carload quantities of farm products, are merely some of the best-known examples and, of course, do not include all the cases throughout the country to which attention might be called. The most conspicuous examples are the market trains running to Philadelphia over the rails of two of the carriers serving that city. A brief description of the service furnished by these two roads to near-by producing sections is of interest, both as showing what is actually being done and as suggesting the lines along which it would be possible for railroads that serve other large cities to inaugurate a similar service.

The first road runs its market trains over the several divisions only once a week. The trains leave the most distant stations, some 60 miles from Philadelphia, about 7.30 a. m. and reach Philadelphia about 2 p. m. Some of the cars used are box cars fitted with adjustable ventilators in the doors and in the side walls. Some of the cars are equipped with hooks along the walls for hanging fresh meat, a fact which makes it easier to keep the meat both clean and cool. Some of them are combination stock-and-poultry cars, one end being slatted for small live stock and the other end of the solid, box type for the reception of coops of poultry. Refrigeration by means of ice bunkers built into the cars is unnecessary because of the short time of transit. Some of the cars are assigned to the more important stations and are lettered with the name of the station to which they are assigned.

The rates named are any-quantity rates, and range from 10.5 cents to 28.4 cents per 100 pounds. They apply on "marketing," which is defined as including dairy products (except milk or cream); poultry-yard products; products of the orchard, garden, or farm; fresh or dried fruits or vegetables; and such small live stock as calves, sheep, lambs, pigs, and hogs. The charges must be prepaid or guaranteed; and the rates apply only on shipments handled on designated market trains.

The railroad disclaims responsibility for loss or damage resulting from neglect on the part of marketmen to comply with its instructions, which read as follows:

All marketing must be properly packed for safe transportation and protection against loss, theft, or damage to contents of packages, plainly marked with consignee's name, and promptly and properly claimed upon arrival of market train at destination.

The suggestion is made that, for obvious reasons, shipments should be accompanied by the owners, but the freight rate does not include the transportation of the owners; they have to pay passenger fare.

The facilities are excellent for handling and taking care of the shipments on the arrival of the market trains at Philadelphia. The terminal station for the market trains is centrally located, directly adjacent to a wholesale market, and is itself equipped with a cold-storage plant. Immediately on the arrival of the trains the shipments are unloaded. They can be transferred directly from the cars to the station cold-storage rooms, or to stores of dealers in the wholesale market. If it is desirable or necessary to take them to other parts of the city, it is possible to unload them directly from the cars into wagons backed up to the cars. Apparently the one thing lacking to make the facilities complete is a retail market or a row of farmers' stands along the sidewalk in front of the station. Under the plan of this railroad, the freight is handled and delivered in the same way as general merchandise.

The second road inaugurated its market-train service more than 25 years ago. The trains are run daily, except Sundays and holidays, and the speed is that of the average passenger train. The farthest point served is not more than 75 miles distant from Philadelphia; consequently there is no need for car-lot refrigeration, although some shippers at times do ice their own packages.

The rates charged the shippers are slightly higher than the first-class freight rate, ranging from 15.8 cents to 31.5 cents per 100 pounds and applying on "marketing" "carried on market or milk trains, when accompanied by shipper holding trip or excursion ticket." The tariff naming the rates is an intrastate tariff, and does not give a list of the articles or commodities included in the general term "marketing." The charges must be prepaid, and the rates include the return of empty containers.

The principal retail market of Philadelphia occupies the street-level floor of the passenger terminal of this company, but this is not the terminal for its market trains. Freight arriving by market trains is delivered at freight stations at other points. On the whole, the facilities at these stations are not so good as those of the other road whose service has been described. Shippers or their representatives must be on hand, on the arrival of the trains, to claim and unload the consignments, as the carrier does not perform this service. The transportation is at owners' risk, the carrier disclaiming responsibility for count or condition of the packages on delivery.

A GENERAL SURVEY.

Any comprehensive discussion of a market-train service must include an account of the results and advantages of existing service, the probable advantages of a prospective service, the obstacles to be overcome to avoid failure, and the factors of cooperation necessary to success.

RESULTS AND ADVANTAGES.

It must be borne in mind that a market-train service, such as is discussed here, designed primarily for small producers and city consumers, is of equal advantage to the carriers, and is in fact an economic necessity. It is of no interest to growers whose production is sufficiently large to enable them to ship in carload lots; nor would it be of any advantage to those communities where cooperative associations have united to combine into carload shipments the output of many small farms devoted to the production of the same commodity. When the distance to market is so great as to make protection of perishable commodities by refrigeration necessary, shipping in carload lots is essential for that reason alone. Aside from the question of refrigeration, and regardless of distance, producers should combine their shipments into carload lots, whenever it is possible, for economy in transportation charges. But, for farmers living along a single operating division of some railroad, within a hundred miles of a large city, or along a branch line terminating at some large city, who can produce a variety of foodstuffs almost continuously the year round, a market-train service would be of the greatest advantage.

The fruits and vegetables on such farms mature at intervals throughout the summer; the dairy products, eggs, and poultry, to say nothing of such commodities as apples and potatoes, can be shipped throughout the year as they are ready for shipment or as the market demands. There is not enough of any one commodity on a single day along the entire division or branch line to make a carload, even if it were otherwise feasible to combine it into a carload; and there is not enough of all commodities at one station on a single day to combine into a carload, even if the great variety of products and containers did not make it impossible to load the usual minimum weight into a single car. Such are the products of farms of this kind, and the success or failure of the farmers is in proportion to their ability or inability to market their products at a profit.

Other things being equal, the market nearest to him is the best market for the small farmer who produces a great variety of commodities and does not specialize on one or two. As has been shown, distant producers can reach any market with car-lot shipments, while the small producer here described, unable to ship in carload lots, is confined to the near-by market. His nearness to the market enables him to keep in closer touch with market demands, and he can quickly adjust his supply to the demand. To a distant shipper, large quantities in transit may bring loss by reaching destination on a falling market. In comparison with the large producer, the small farmer is doing a retail business. With a retail market adjacent to or in the city terminal of the market train, he would be in a still better position to do a retail business in every sense of the word and to sell directly to consumers.

This is just what was done during a part of the summer of 1912 in the case of a market train run to East Pittsburgh, Pa., by one of the roads serving that point. The farmers shipping by the train were organized in a farmers' exchange association, and the association had a representative at East Pittsburgh, who disposed of the shipments. Some of them were sold to wholesale and retail dealers, but the greater part was sold to factory employees. While the usual facilities of a retail market were wholly lacking, the service quickly developed a retail market, as sales were made in the railroad yard directly from the car to the householder. So popular had the service become and so great a reputation had it attained at the time it was discontinued, that a more affluent class of people was beginning to take advantage of it, some of them coming long distances by automobile to do their daily marketing there.

Apparently all classes of people who bought supplies of foodstuffs here found some advantages over previous methods. It is quite evident that those who came long distances to buy got either a better quality of goods or lower prices, if not both.

This particular service was given for only 46 days during the months of April and May, when it was discontinued. The reason given for its discontinuance was that the terminal facilities were not satisfactory to the health authorities from a sanitary standpoint. The season of the year and the short period during which the train was run did not give sufficient opportunity to make a correct estimate of its probable continued success. Apparently there was no lack of patronage.

FACTORS NECESSARY TO SUCCESS.

Market-train service is not a panacea for all the ills that afflict the small farmer in the marketing of his products. Every item of labor performed by the farmer in serving the consuming public is from one point of view an element of his cooperation with others. From the standpoint of his returns for the service that he performs he alone is responsible for the efficient performance of many of the items of labor. Sometimes he fails to recognize fully his own responsibility in cooperative effort, and sometimes he is mistaken in the causes to which he attributes the failure to market his products at a profit. Again he alleges cheaper methods of production on the part of his competitor or a disadvantage against himself in the matter of freight rates.

Mention has been made of cooperative associations whose efforts are directed toward consolidating into carload shipments the output of many small farms producing the same commodity. A market-train service with adequate terminal facilities in the way of a retail market offers an ideal opportunity to the producing community served of forming a cooperative association for the sale of its products directly to city consumers. No better opportunity can be asked for restoring the custom of direct exchange between producer and consumer, as far as it is possible to restore it, in those sections where changing economic conditions coincidentally have brought about the abandonment of that custom and have developed the necessity for a market-train service. With a representative of the association at the terminal to dispose of products directly to householders, all questions of variation of price on account of quality and condition are determined at the time of the sale by an actual joint inspection of the commodities by the seller and purchaser; no vexatious correspondence is afterwards necessary in adjusting claims—correspondence which may terminate established business relations by arousing mutual suspicion of lack of good faith; and, what is by no means the least important advantage, it is a cash transaction and the purchaser avoids the annoyance of remittance by letter.

As a step toward the successful marketing of his products, the farmer must be brought to a realization of the justice of many of the criticisms against some of his methods. He must produce the commodities that the consumer wants; and only their superior quality will command prices higher than are being paid for the same commodities shipped from remote sections. If his products are not graded as carefully nor packed in containers as attractive as those of the long-distance stuff, he will not get the prices that are paid for the long-distance stuff. There is little sentiment in the daily replenishing of the family larder, and neither location of production nor short time in transit can long command a premium in the market as against quality. Home industries will be patronized in proportion as they show themselves worthy of patronage.

One of the roads furnishing a market-train service to Philadelphia states that if the service were not already established it is hardly likely that it would be established "in view of the very light yield of revenue therefrom." As the inauguration of the service in the beginning was the result of judgment based on careful estimates, no figures of actual operation being in existence, the statement would seem to indicate a desire to withdraw the service. The road that served East Pittsburgh in 1912 rendered a similar service at two other cities, Butler and Allegheny, Pa., from 1907 to the close of 1914, when the service was discontinued. The service to East Pittsburgh was inaugurated under the jurisdiction of the passenger department, as it was intended at first to handle the shipments on passenger trains. Later it became necessary to transfer it to the freight-traffic department. This road handles a large volume of heavy traffic to and from the iron and steel mills in the Pittsburgh district. Eighty-eight per cent of its entire tonnage for the fiscal year 1915 consisted of products of mines, while its total tonnage of agricultural products and products of animals was less than four-tenths of 1 per cent of its entire tonnage. Under the circumstances it readily can be seen that a market-train service would be of little interest to its freight-traffic officials from the standpoint of either tonnage or revenue, while requiring proportionately much more attention and supervision.

It is true that some producers have begun to utilize the parcel post to some extent and that the reduction in interstate express rates which became effective in the early part of 1914 has attracted some shipments by express. In some sections freight service by interurban electric lines has afforded a slight measure of relief, but the advantages of that kind of service are too frequently offset by the lack of adequate and centrally located city terminals and the restrictions imposed on the running of freight cars through city streets. In some cases the growth of intermediate towns has attracted a considerable portion of the commodities that formerly went to the large city terminal. City boards of health have imposed restrictions making it necessary to exclude other commodities from milk cars, which increases the cost of performing the transportation service on lines where one car would hold all the shipments. This competition is pointed out by roads now giving a market-train service; and roads that do not now give such a service offer these and other facts as objections to its inauguration.

The small farmer is dependent on either local freight-train service, which is too slow, or on express service, which relatively is too expensive. The slowness of local freight-train service was pointed out in the Report of the Mayor's Market Commission of New York City, submitted in December, 1913, where it was said that it took from 10 days to 2 weeks to get freight from some places distant for passengers only 2 hours from New York. The same conditions that now prevail with reference to the transportation of small quantities of miscellaneous foodstuffs formerly prevailed with reference to the transportation of milk to the large cities. The problem was solved in the case of milk, and it would seem that it can be solved as readily in the case of the other commodities. To cut off a city's supply of milk produces a crisis quickly; attention is called sharply to the situation, and a remedy is devised promptly. Lack of marketing facilities for the small farmer affects the producer more vitally than the city consumer, but the bad effects, while they make themselves felt more slowly, are none the less sure and none the less harmful to the community at large.

CONCLUSIONS.

A market-train service affords an excellent method of restoring, as far as it can be restored, where it has been abandoned, the custom of direct dealing between producer and consumer. It contemplates the shipper loading his products into the car at point of shipment and taking possession of them immediately on arrival of the train at destination. There should be a retail market, or at least a wholesale market, in or adjacent to the city terminal. The service is more valuable to the shipper than ordinary local freight-train service. The time in transit is practically that of trains carrying express matter, but collection and delivery is made by the shipper. Such a service, to be successful, depends on the organized effort of the producing community intelligently directed in sympathetic cooperation with the carrier.

B285M

FIG. 1.—FISHER.

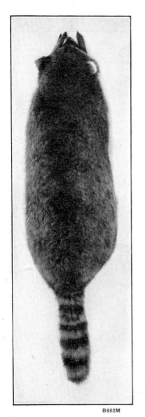

B652M

FIG. 3.—FEEDING A MINK.

B662M

FIG. 2.—A RACCOON SKIN.

B650M

FIG. 4.—A FRIENDLY FOX.

PLATE LXXXVI.

FIG. I.—MINK PENS.

B655M

FIG. 2.—PET BEAVERS.

B651M

FIG. 3.—A PAIR OF OTTERS.

B45Z

FUR FARMING AS A SIDE LINE.

By NED DEARBORN, *Assistant Biologist, Bureau of Biological Survey*

ALL domestic animals originally came under the control of man by appropriation from the wild state in time of need. As cattle, horses, sheep, and poultry have been, domesticated, distributed to the ends of the earth, and differentiated by careful breeding for specific purposes, so too will it be with our wild and valuable fur animals. The great problem now confronting the fur industry is how to obtain from a waning source the necessary stock for its permanent development. To this there is but one solution: Domesticate the fur bearers and farm them, as has been done over and over with other animals. The killing pressure on those remaining in the wild state will then be reduced, the fur trade supported, and a new farm product developed. Believers in economy and diversification will utilize the beef and chicken heads, the horse flesh, and the milk they have heretofore been wasting, in taking up fur farming as a side line, profitable as a by-product of the regular farming operations and pleasurable in the care of lively and beautiful pets.

The demand for fur has existed since primitive man first sought skins to shield his naked body from the cold. It is fundamental and will endure while man inhabits the earth and furs are to be had. Its strength can be judged by the volume of trade it supports. In 1913 the dressed and manufactured furs imported into the United States were valued at more than $15,000,000. North American furs annually marketed in the United States and England have an approximate value of $60,000,000. These figures show the commercial importance of fur, and in addition to this the fur trade furnishes a livelihood for many thousands of workers in the factories and stores of this country.

In the history of the fur trade, two facts are prominent: (1) The finer and more durable kinds of furs, as beaver, otter, mink, and marten, have become so scarce as to be largely replaced by the coarser and thinner grades which formerly were regarded as of little or no value; (2) the choicest furs are now bringing fabulous prices. Although the whims of fashion influence prices of furs, the fluctuations thus produced are compensatory. When one kind is cheap because fashion temporarily neglects it, another is dear because of her temporary favor. The dark, thick, soft, and glossy furs, however, like rare jewels, are scarcely affected by passing styles.

The demand for fine furs and their scarcity have made possible the introduction of fur farming, either as a special business or as a side line. It is open to all who love animals and have at least a back yard in which to keep them. Several species have been tested in captivity, and when rightly managed have yielded satisfactory returns. Several other species may do equally well, especially since the production of superior strains is always possible by selective breeding. The food required is mainly the same as that fed to dogs and cats, and may include table refuse, milk, butcher's waste, and horse meat. The labor of attending the animals is light. Professional men and women, as well as the mistress of the farmer's household, may take just pride in wearing furs of their own raising.

FUR ANIMALS ALREADY DOMESTICATED.

Among the score or more of different kinds of fur-bearing animals native to North America about a dozen seem to be suitable for domestication. Of these, the skunk, the mink, and the silver fox have been bred successfully in captivity in widely scattered localities.

The skunk family is peculiar to the Western Hemisphere, and those members having valuable fur belong mainly within the limits of the United States. Notwithstanding its extraordinary means of defense, which has caused it to be generally regarded with abhorrence, the skunk is coming to be recognized as a very useful animal when at large and one of the most easily domesticated when captive. Its common occurrence in settled districts and the remunerative prices offered for black skins encouraged some of the friends of the skunk to undertake its domestication about 30 years ago. To-day the number of skunk breeders in this country is greater than that of all other breeders of fur bearers combined. The animal tames quickly, is gentle, and is easily managed. The fact that it remains in its den during the severe weather of winter makes it more easily cared for than most other animals. Its fur is of medium length, erect, and possesses a brilliant sheen. These qualities make it very attractive. Unfortunately, protracted use causes it to fade from a glistening black to a dull reddish brown. The average of New York quotations for the best skunk skins during the past 12 years is $3.

Minks appear to have been the first of the wild fur bearers to be domesticated in this country. Nearly 50 years ago a resident of Oneida County, N. Y., began to breed them, and for a considerable period exhibited his tame pets at fairs and sold them for propagation. At that time the high prices incident to the Civil War made mink raising profitable. Skins were high, and live animals for breeding stock brought $30 a pair. The period of financial depression which followed made mink farming unprofitable and for many years it was abandoned and forgotten. Recently it has taken on new life, and where conditions of management and food supply are favorable, has been decidedly satisfactory to those engaged in it. Mink fur is exceedingly durable, ranking in this respect among the very best. With care it will last a lifetime. It is rather short, but very thick and soft. The guard hairs do not break readily, nor has the underfur a tendency to become matted. Although sunlight gradually gives its original dark brown color a warmer tone, its beauty is but slightly lessened. New York quotations for prime No. 1 northern mink skins during the years 1905–1916 range from $1.25 to $9 each, the average being about $6.75.

Among the progeny of a pair of red foxes it occasionally happens that one or more markedly differ in color from their parents. The underparts are black instead of white, and the upperparts also are more or less black. When the dark areas on the upperparts are concentrated in two stripes, one along the middle of the back and the other across the shoulders, and the sides are covered with a varying mixture of red and black hairs, the animal is known as a cross fox. When the red hairs of the upperparts are entirely replaced by black, the white hairs remaining as usual, it is a silver fox.

When all but a few of the white hairs are replaced by black, it is a silver-black fox. A prime silver fox skin is a rare and beautiful object, and, as such, commands a high price. Breeding silver foxes was first undertaken upward of 20 years ago on Prince Edward Island, Canada. There are now many successful fox farms in Canada and a considerable number in several of the more northern States. Foxes are naturally timid, but, if taken in hand when quite young, can be made very tame, although tameness does not seem to be an essential to success in breeding them. Fox fur is soft and rather long. Its beauty is entirely in the long guard hairs which overlie the underfur. It is not very durable, as the guard hairs break after a few seasons' wear, leaving the less attractive underfur exposed. The average of quotations for the best grade of silver fox skins during the past 12 years is about $600 each. Numbers have been sold for less than $100, while very many have brought far more than the average quotation here given.

FUR ANIMALS WHICH MAY BE DOMESTICATED.

That foxes, minks, and skunks, although presenting great differences in habits and temperament, have been brought into domestication indicates that other kinds of fur bearers also may eventually be tamed and bred in inclosures. Among the species that have been partially tested for this purpose are the marten, fisher, otter, blue fox, raccoon, and beaver, each of which is adapted to definite environmental conditions and to specific purposes.

Martens naturally inhabit the northern coniferous forests from coast to coast, extending northward to northwestern Alaska and southward along the mountain ranges to California, Colorado, and Pennsylvania. They are nervous, active creatures, but bear confinement well and are not difficult to tame. They have been bred on fur farms in Alaska and in several places in Canada. Their size is about twice that of minks. The fur, which is very soft, somewhat resembling that of foxes, is about 1½ inches long when prime. The color varies, individually, from pale gray to orange-brown and dark brown. The average of quotations for the best grade of marten-skins during the past 12 years is about $20 each.

The fisher, a member of the same family as the marten, is found over much the same range of territory, although it does not extend so far north. Its weight is about the same as that of the red fox, but its short legs give it an altogether different aspect. Although able to climb trees, it spends much of its time on the ground. Being no longer common, few efforts have been made to domesticate it. It has been tested sufficiently, however, to demonstrate its ability to thrive and increase in confinement, a sufficient reason for assuming that it will ultimately be bred regularly for its pelt. The color of fishers varies from grayish brown to nearly black. The fur when fully developed measures about 2½ inches in length. It is used mainly for muffs and neck or shoulder pieces, the large, bushy tails being particularly effective. The average of New York quotations for fisher skins during the past 12 years is about $20 each.

One of the most promising fur bearers for propagation in localities having an abundance of water is the otter. When captured young this animal tames readily and makes an engaging pet. It is said that the otter found in southern Asia is sometimes trained to catch fish for its master. A pair of otters in the National Zoological Park, Washington, D. C., have recently reared a litter of four young. Although essentially aquatic and very fond of disporting in water, they do not require a great quantity of it. Otter fur is about an inch long, erect, and very thick. It is very durable, ranking with mink fur in this respect, and is used chiefly for trimming garments. The average of prices quoted for the best grade of otter skins in the past 12 years is about $20 each.

Another animal that has attracted considerable attention in this connection is the blue fox, a dark slate or brown phase of the white or arctic fox. It is more docile than the red fox, but for some unknown reason has not been bred in inclosures with nearly the degree of success achieved with varieties of the latter species. It has, however, been propagated satisfactorily on several of the Alaskan islands, where the only limits to its movements are those set by the sea. Whatever the nature of obstacles encountered by those who have attempted to raise this animal in confinement, it is probable that eventually they will be overcome, and that persons living in the colder portions of the country will be able to wear blue fox skins of their own raising. Blue fox fur is nearly 2 inches long, and is very fine and thick. The average American quotations for the best grade of pelts for the past six years is about $44.

That the raw material for handsome and comfortable raccoon-skin coats can be produced in a spare corner of one's back yard seems to be an established fact, judging from the results attained by the few who have undertaken to raise the raccoon. This animal is distributed over the greater part of the United States, being absent only in desert and high mountain regions. It is nocturnal, and at home both on the ground and in trees. Water is essential to its welfare, but large quantities are not needful. Its nightly range is often along the shores of ponds or streams, and its food is generally washed before being eaten. In a number of instances raccoons have been bred successfully. From a strictly commercial standpoint they are not likely to become popular, however, for the reason that if their food must be purchased its cost will be prohibitive. On farms where there are milk, fruit, and corn meal in plenty raccoon raising is well worth a trial. When taken young raccoons become very tame and make quaint and interesting pets. Their fur is mottled gray in color and about $2\frac{1}{2}$ inches long on animals from northern States. In the South the fur is shorter. The average price for the best pelts is about $2.50.

Judging from the few experiments made with it, the beaver may be raised in any region containing alder, aspen, cottonwood, willow, or other trees upon which it feeds. Unlike the species hitherto considered, it subsists entirely on vegetable food. Although armed with enormous cutting teeth suitable for felling trees, beavers are tolerant among themselves and docile with their keepers. Fully grown specimens trapped wild become so gentle within a few weeks that one may handle them without danger of being bitten. Beaver fur has long been extensively used in making muffs, stoles, collars, trimmings, and the finest quality of felt hats. The average price in recent years has been about $8 a skin.

CHOICE OF SPEICES.

In making a deliberate choice of species to be propagated for fur, one should give due consideration to climate, the character of his immediate surroundings, his available space and capital, the nature and quantity of food materials at hand, and the convenience of securing breeding stock. The climate best suited to each animal is indicated by the natural distribution of that animal in the wild state. Thus, skunks, which are not found north of the temperate belt, are not likely to do well in Alaska, nor would one think seriously of attempting to breed arctic foxes in a southern climate.

The climate in the northern tier of States and southward along the mountain ranges to northern California, Colorado, and West Virginia is favorable for all of the animals that have been mentioned. Alaska is not suitable for raccoons and skunks, nor, excepting the warmer timbered part along the southern coast, for fishers. The arid Southwest and the Great Basin, between the Rocky Mountains and the Sierra Nevadas, are entirely too dry and sunny for fur raising. In the Central and Southern States one may raise minks, skunks, otters, and raccoons, although it should be clearly understood that the farther south fur is produced the thinner, shorter, and less valuable it is.

Next in importance to climatic conditions are those of capital, situation, space, and food supply. The capital necessary to build a two-pair fox ranch and stock it with four choice silver foxes will be not less than $2,000, according to prevailing prices, and it is likely that considerably more than this will be required. If stocked with cross foxes the cost will be much less, but even in this case it probably will amount to $600 or more. The cost of installing a blue-fox ranch will generally exceed that required for cross foxes. It may ultimately appear that blue foxes are not adapted to live in captivity, but this can not be determined until they have been subjected to extensive tests. Foxes can not be kept in thickly settled communities, as they have an objectionable odor and do not breed well when frequently disturbed.

The cost of installing and stocking a mink or skunk ranch is comparatively small, depending somewhat on location. Material for a single pen for either of these animals can be bought for about $2. Minks usually sell at from $8 to $12 each, and skunks at from $2 to $8, according to quality. Minks and de-scented skunks can be kept in an ordinary back yard, provided it is partially shaded. Ranch-bred minks and skunks are regularly advertised in publications devoted to fur interests.

Fishers, martens, and raccoons, although not requiring nearly so much outlay as foxes, must be confined in strong inclosures and be given room for enough activity to keep them healthy. Shade is essential to all. Most of those offered for sale have been caught wild. Prevailing prices for fishers range from $50 to $75 a pair, for martens from $35 to $65 a pair, and for raccoons from $5 to $8 a pair. The materials for a pen to accommodate one of these animals costs about $25.

One should not attempt to raise otters or beavers unless a constant supply of running water is at hand. Moreover, there should be an unfailing source of fish which can be obtained at slight expense for otters, and fresh leaves and bark of trees for beavers. The best locations for these animals are among the mountains, where brooks run swift and clear, and trees cover the slopes. There is no regular trade in either of these species. Otters are rarely offered for sale, as those caught by fur gatherers usually die in the traps. In most of the States where beavers are still found wild it is unlawful to capture them. It is generally necessary, therefore, to import beavers that are to be used for propagation. In Canada they have been sold at about $50 a pair. The cost of pens for otters or beavers can not be definitely stated, as they will vary with the location and character of the site.

INCLOSURES.

The first step in preparing to propagate fur animals is to construct suitable inclosures. In selecting a site for an inclosure it must be borne in mind that a certain amount of shade is essential to the comfort of the animals and to the development of flexible, dark-colored fur. Young deciduous trees are preferable for making shade, as mature trees are likely to be shattered by storms and in falling to demolish pens and injure or kill the animals. Evergreen trees are undesirable from the fact that they shut out sunshine in winter as well as in summer. Water is an essential, and, if possible, pens should be so located that an abundant supply can be brought by gravity to each. Materials for inclosures consist mainly of lumber and galvanized-wire netting; and in larger and more permanent structures concrete is sometimes used for foundations. Each animal requires individual quarters, particularly during the breeding season. Every complete inclosure comprises a yard or runway, usually of wire netting, although boards or galvanized sheet iron are sometimes used, and a lightproof and waterproof den, usually made of wood. Dens are often made with two compartments, the one entered from outside being designed for a shelter and feeding place, the other, opening into the first, being the sleeping compartment. A sliding door is placed at the outside entrance. Wooden dens should be raised a few inches from the ground to keep them dry. Glazed tile has been successfully employed for dens. The facility with which tile can be disinfected is a point in its favor. All dens should be made so as to be readily opened for cleaning.

The best fox yards are about 50 feet square. The walls extend well into the ground or to a concrete foundation and are from 9 to 12 feet high, depending on the snowfall. They are generally built of 1½ or 2 inch poultry netting, No. 15 or 14 wire, and provided with an overhang at the top to prevent the animals from scaling them.

Inclosures for otters, raccoons, and beavers may be built on the same general plan as for foxes, but need not be more than 5 or 6 feet high nor more than 15 or 20 feet square.

Minks can be kept in pens as small as 4 feet square, though it is better to have breeding pens about twice this size. An excellent style of pen suitable for minks and skunks can be made on the same plan as ordinary portable chicken coops, having a double-compartment den 15 or 18 inches wide and high and 3 or 4 feet long, to which is attached a runway of

1-inch mesh, No. 16 gauge, poultry netting. This runway has floor, sides, and top of netting. The top is made in a separate piece, as a door, and is hinged to the top rail of one side and hooked or locked to the top rail of the other. Such pens are inexpensive and, when the woodwork is kept painted, are very durable. The ease with which they may be moved from place to place is particularly advantageous.

Pens for martens and fishers must be constructed of the strongest wire obtainable and have the top and floor, as well as the walls, made proof against their strength. Although 1-inch mesh, No. 16 gauge, poultry netting will generally hold them, such has not invariably been the case. The style of netting known as chain netting, while more expensive, is safer and more lasting than the regular style of poultry netting. Such pens should be at least 8 feet square and 8 feet high and contain branches or the tops of trees to allow the animals to exercise their propensity for climbing.

It is always advisable to surround each group of inclosures with a high fence which can neither be scaled nor undermined, as almost inevitably, sooner or later, some of the animals escape from their pens.

FOOD.

Beavers in their native haunts eat grass, herbs, roots, foliage, and the bark of aspens, alders, birches, maples, willows, and other deciduous trees. When in captivity they readily accept bread, grain, and garden vegetables. In addition, it is thought necessary to supply them with foliage and bark of trees to the extent of perhaps a third of their food. Wild otters live mainly on birds and such aquatic creatures as fish, frogs, and crawfish. In captivity they are usually fed on fish, but when this fails they readily accept raw and cooked meat. It is not known to what extent they may be fed on other kinds of food. Minks, martens, fishers, skunks, foxes, and raccoons thrive on the diet ordinarily given to dogs and cats. While young they are fed mainly milk on bread, crackers, and graham or oatmeal mush, to the exclusion of meat, which is likely to give them rickets. Meat or fish must be included in the diet of adults, but whether extensively or sparingly depends upon its cost rather than upon any exacting requirements on the part of the animals. A variety of food is necessary, however. Fruit, boiled carrots, mashed potato, and all sorts of table refuse can be mixed with regular cooked rations to excellent advantage. The meat used may be beef, mutton, horse flesh, chicken heads, or other butchers' waste, or the flesh of rabbits, woodchucks, or ground squirrels. Food that has begun to ferment or decay should not be used. There is no economy in giving animals unwholesome food.

Surplus meat may be preserved by salting or drying. Salt meat or fish should be sliced and freshened, preferably in running water, before being used. Meat for drying is sliced and exposed to air and sunshine or the heat and smoke of a small open fire. Where conditions are unfavorable for rapid drying, the meat may be dipped in a saturated solution of hot brine before being put on the drying racks. Ice is useful in keeping food from spoiling for a few days, but should not be relied upon to preserve large quantities of meat unless used in carefully constructed refrigerating houses.

Meat suspected of being infested with parasites or disease germs should be boiled. Rabbits and other rodents should be eviscerated, as their internal organs often contain tapeworms or other parasites. Rabbits intended for young animals must be skinned to avoid the formation of stomach balls of felted hair. Adults are not likely to eat enough rabbit fur to injure them. A certain quantity of hair, feathers, and other roughage is probably beneficial. Bone is undoubtedly an essential element of food for growing animals. By passing meat containing small bones through a grinding machine such as poultrymen use, the bone is made digestible and danger of choking is avoided. Large bones bearing fragments of meat are useful for strengthening teeth, and for quieting nervous animals by giving them something to do.

Only as much food as can be eaten immediately should be given at a time; otherwise it is likely to be stored in the nest and become offensive. In regulating the diet of fur animals, it is important to remember that they must be made fat before being killed for their pelts, and kept lean when they are to be saved for breeding.

BREEDING.

As success or failure in fur farming hinges largely on the course of events during the breeding season, it is important that the instinctive habits and the temperamental characteristics of the animals, as well as the location and arrangement of pens and the manner of feeding, be carefully considered. In the wild state foxes and beavers have but one mate, while raccoons, otters, fishers, martens, and minks are polygamous. Although in rare instances male foxes in captivity have been mated with two or three females in the same year, such matings as a rule are unproductive. On the other hand, breeders of minks and skunks regularly mate a single male with from four to six females. In all cases it is well to allow the individuals proposed for mating opportunity to become acquainted by occupying adjoining yards a few days before being allowed to run together. It is not practicable to attempt to mate animals that disagree, and when first paired they should be watched in order to prevent violent quarrels which may result in serious injuries or death. Foxes and raccoons may be kept in pairs from the time the young are weaned until the succeeding litter is a month old, providing the male is good natured; if inclined to be snappish, however, the male should be removed to his own pen before the young are born. The other carnivorous species are best kept singly except for a short time in spring. An animal that has killed its mate should never be trusted again unless deprived of its canine teeth.

Breeding pens should be thoroughly cleaned and disinfected throughout shortly before the young are expected. Foxes do not care for nesting material, but the smaller animals need it. If soft dry grass or leaves be placed in the yards, the animals will carry the material into their dens and arrange it to suit themselves. Unless the dens are shaded they will become very hot in the middle of the day and the young are likely to suffer. Special care should be taken to prevent unnecessary disturbances to the young while unable to leave the den, as these may cause the mother to carry her babies about in search of another den, and thus to maltreat and expose them beyond the limit of their endurance. An important point in the care of brood animals is to avoid anything that is out of the ordinary run of their existence. If possible, they should have the same treatment and the same keeper at all times. The keeper should see how the young are getting on from day to day, and he should prepare for this long beforehand by practicing, as a part of his regular routine, whatever operations may be necessary to accomplish this. By inspecting the dens daily he can establish an habitual course of action on the part of the animals which will disarm their anxiety when he essays to examine their young.

A useful auxiliary in any fur-raising establishment is the domestic cat, which is ever ready to adopt a family of helpless young animals, regardless of pedigree or relationship. Supporting a few extra cats on a fur farm is, in reality, the premium paid for insurance against loss or damage to the crop. In general, about the time young animals first appear at the entrance of the den they are old enough to drink milk and, therefore, to be weaned if necessary. If it is desired to have them become very tame and to make pets of them, this is the time to take them away from their mothers and bring them up by hand. In no case should they be allowed to remain with the mother long enough to make her very thin in flesh. As young animals are not inclined to be quarrelsome a number of them may be allowed to run together in a large inclosure during summer and early fall if several sleeping boxes and feed pans are provided.

The principles of heredity that apply to ordinary domestic animals apply also to these. Fine animals can not be expected from poor breeding stock. In selecting breeders, size, color, temperament, and fur should be considered. There are great possibilities of improving animals by selective breeding, and the common policy of culling the poorer specimens and keeping the best, if consistently practiced, will unquestionably result in breeds of much greater value than that of the wild stock from which they originated.

DISEASES.

The more common diseases affecting fur animals are enteritis or inflamed intestines, pneumonia, diarrhea, and degenerated kidneys, all of which may largely be prevented by judicious care in housing and feeding. Pneumonia results from exposure and is likely to attack animals that have recently been trapped or shipped. It rarely occurs when they are kept in dry and well-ventilated quarters. The symptoms of pneumonia are loss of appetite, dry nose, and rubbing of throat and chest on the ground. Very little can be done for animals suffering with this disease beyond giving them clean, dustless bedding and keeping them in pens that are warm and airy but free from direct drafts. Diarrhea is caused by improper feeding. It should be the invariable duty of keepers to take note daily of the excreta of animals under their charge, and to change the diet of any showing signs of this disease. An excessive proportion of vegetable food, fats, and impure water; fermented or putrid food; and over-feeding are among the causes of this malady. A diet of milk, eggs, and fresh lean meat, given in moderate quantities, if begun promptly, is usually sufficient to correct any kind of bowel trouble. Animals that are allowed to become fat and remain so are almost certain sooner or later to die from degeneration of the kidneys. In its later stages this disease is characterized by emaciation, nervousness, and a bloodless appearance of the tongue and gums. When an animal has reached this condition there is very little chance of saving its life. This disease may be avoided by not allowing animals to become fat and by keeping those showing a tendency to do so mainly on lean meat, fish, and milk.

The peculiarities of individual animals will not be neglected by alert keepers. The moment one departs from its ordinary behavior, the reason should be sought. If a regular meal is refused or neglected, a day's fast followed by a change of food should be tried at once or sickness is likely to follow. Particular pains should be taken to give ailing animals a varied diet, clean water, and surroundings that are sanitary in every particular. Sick animals and those newly purchased should be kept in quarantine apart from the main yard for at least three weeks. There is very little use in dosing the smaller species. The tax on their vitality caused by their struggles outweighs the effects of medicine. Those the size of a fox can be treated with better prospects of success.

Injuries usually demand treatment. Shattered limbs should be amputated. Simple fractures will usually knit satisfactorily if the limb is set with splints. Wild animals taken in steel traps have survived, although maimed, after having had the injured member bathed with spirits of turpentine. An excellent antiseptic for fresh wounds is a 3 per cent solution of carbolic acid. Hydrogen peroxide is useful in cleansing sores and old wounds.

In handling animals requiring medical attention studious care and tact should be exercised. Minks, martens, skunks, and fishers, which are very strong and lithe, may be treated either in a small wire cage or in a slightly tapering funnel or cone of wire netting, into which they are driven until they reach a point where they fit so closely they can neither advance nor turn about. They can be held there by a stick thrust across the funnel behind them. Larger animals are usually picked up by the base of the tail or by means of special tongs made to clasp the neck. They are frequently rolled in a blanket or gunny sack to keep them from biting or scratching. Whatever is necessary to be done should be undertaken quietly after due preparation.

CARE OF SKINS.

The first step in the care of skins is involved in the killing. Skins of animals slaughtered by a blow are thickened and bloodshot at the spot where the blow falls. A bullet through the brain from a .22 caliber rifle kills an animal instantly, causes no swelling of the skin, and results in very little blood stain on the fur. The best results, however, are to be obtained by means of an anesthetic, as carbon bisulphide or chloroform, introduced into a clean, well-made box having a tightly fitting cover. This method of killing is humane and leaves the skin perfect. The more valuable animals, at least, ought always to be killed in this manner, as blood stains detract from the value of fur.

There are two ways of skinning fur animals, depending upon the shape in which the pelt is to be marketed. Beaver skins are always stretched flat, in a nearly circular shape, both the hair side and the flesh side being thus made available for inspection. They are cut on the underside from chin to tail and from each foot along the inner side of the leg to intersect the main opening nearly at right angles. The customary way of stretching a beaver skin is to lace the edges to a wooden hoop having a diameter somewhat larger than that of the skin. This produces what is called a flat skin. Pelts from the other animals under discussion are cut only along the underside of the tail and from heel to heel across the posterior end of the body, the skin being turned inside out as the body is withdrawn. The tail, feet, and bases of the ears are skinned out with care.

Such skins are drawn, flesh side out, over a tapering piece of board, the shape and dimensions of which permit them to dry in their natural size and proportions without wrinkles. The forward end of a stretching board should be reduced to a narrow tip that will project through the mouth of a skin half an inch or more. When a skin is dry and shrunken, a blow from a hammer on this projecting tip will loosen the board, which otherwise could be removed only with difficulty and danger to the skin. Stretching boards are sometimes cut lengthwise in three pieces, or strips, the middle one being a wedge, which makes them adjustable to skins of different size and easily removed after the skins dry. Skins thus prepared are called "cased skins." They should be dried in a cool, shady, airy place without artificial heat, unless in a climate so damp that drying without heat is impossible. Even then care should be taken to prevent overheating. Fox skins are removed from the boards and turned hair side out before they are entirely dry. Other kinds of cased skins are sold flesh side out. All skins should be divested of loose fat while they are fresh, and those impregnated with fat, as skunk skins, should be disposed of promptly. The effect of fat on skins is to harden and break down the tissue, making them brittle and worthless. Fox skins and others that are thin, firm, and not greasy may be kept safely in cold storage or in insect-proof cabinets lined with sheet metal, tarred roofing paper, or other suitable material. The cabinets should be kept in a cool place and so built that the skins may be hung by the nose, and not laid in piles, as piling has a tendency to lessen the fluffiness of fur.

If one wishes to dress his own furs the following recipe for a tanning liquor may be used, but time and patience are required to produce soft, pliable skins, as the process is largely one of manipulation: To each gallon of water add one quart of salt and a half ounce of sulphuric acid. This mixture should not be kept in a metal container. Thin skins are tanned by this liquor in one day; heavy skins must remain in it longer, and will not be harmed if left in it indefinitely. When removed they are washed several times in soapy water, wrung as dry as possible, and rubbed on the flesh side with a cake of hard soap. They are then folded in the middle, hung lengthwise over a line, hair side out, and left to dry. When both surfaces are barely dry and the interior is still moist they are laid over a smooth, rounded board and scraped on the flesh side with the edge of a worn flat file, or a similar blunt-edged tool. In this way an inner layer is removed and the skins become nearly white in color. They are then stretched, rubbed, and twisted until quite dry. If parts of a skin are still hard and stiff, the soaping, drying, and stretching process is repeated until the entire skin is soft. Fresh butter or other animal fat worked into skins while warm and then worked out again in dry hardwood sawdust, or extracted by a hasty bath in gasoline, increases their softness.

COOPERATION OF BREEDERS.

Breeders of fur animals should bear in mind that cooperation is the keynote of progress. If breeders of ordinary domestic animals find it advantageous to form associations for mutual help and encouragement, how much more will it be to the advantage of fur farmers, who are dealing with a group of animals new to domestication, to contribute their individual discoveries to the common fund of information, meet one another, discuss methods, adopt breeding standards, and unite in an effort to place their specialty in a proper light before the public, for there is considerable misapprehension regarding the character of their work.

Much of the improvement that has taken place in the various kinds of live stock has been due to the object lessons afforded by public exhibitions. The breeders of fur-bearing animals can help themselves individually and collectively by consistently preparing their finest specimens for exhibition at fairs and shows where people interested in animals assemble.

Too often the project to domesticate fur-bearing animals has been judged superficially. For example, the possibility that persons having animal pens may become poachers and capture young animals in the close season simply for the purpose of killing them for their pelts later in the year has frequently outweighed in many minds the palpable impossibility of satisfying the demand for fur by any means other than the domestication of fur bearers, and the practical certainty that as fur farming develops the present tireless pursuit of wild fur animals will decrease. As a result, fur farmers in certain States have been obliged to pay annual license fees, to give bonds, and to submit to various restrictions in the sale of breeding stock. In other States, however, the owner of a fur farm has exactly the same property rights in his animals and the same freedom in the conduct of his business as the owner of a sheep ranch or of a poultry farm. The cause of the fur farmer is intrinsically sound, and those interested in it have only to unite and fairly state it to gain popular support.

PUMPING FOR IRRIGATION ON THE FARM.

By P. E. FULLER,

Irrigation Engineer, Office of Public Roads and Rural Engineering.

THE most common method of supplying water to the irrigated lands of the United States is by gravity flow from streams. A small but increasing area is supplied by pumping plants, each of which serves a single farm from a well. A gravity supply of water has increased so much in cost that in many instances it is cheaper for a farmer to pump his own water from a well than to buy it delivered from a ditch by gravity. For this reason, principally, there will be a greater development of individual pumping. Added to it are the facts that in a great part of the Great Plains region a supply from streams is not available and pumping from the ground water is the only means of obtaining a supply, while throughout the humid section of the East both natural conditions and the laws relating to water are such as to make pumping the almost universal means of procuring water for irrigation. Many large pumping plants are lifting water which is delivered through canals to supply whole communities, but the plants supplying single farms are much more numerous, and it is this type which is discussed in this paper.

In obtaining a water supply for irrigation, cooperation has many advantages, but the individual pumping plant also has many advantages and few drawbacks. The owner of an individual plant need not wait his turn to receive water from a community source, but can obtain it when he wants it; no vexing conditions are imposed upon him by contracts or regulations, and his supply is not liable to be cut off through the negligence or cupidity of others. If a farmer has a dependable supply and a well-designed plant properly installed, he has only himself to blame if he does not get water when he wants it and when his crops need it.

In computing the costs of pumping it is necessary to include interest on first cost, depreciation, fuel, and cost of operation and maintenance. Mechanically it is possible to pump water through lifts of hundreds of feet and in almost any quantities desired, but what is commercially feasible depends upon nearness to supplies of equipment and fuel, cost of these items, the crops which can be grown, and the markets for these crops. Consequently no limits of lift and cost within which pumping is feasible can be fixed. What is feasible at one time or place may not be so at another time or place. In certain sections of California water is lifted more than 300 feet, while in other sections lifts of 25 feet can not be deemed practicable.

SIZE OF PUMPING PLANT.

The size of pumping plant needed to supply a given farm depends primarily on the area to be irrigated and the water requirements of the land, but is influenced largely by other considerations. The plant must be of sufficient capacity to supply to the land during any period of time the water needed during that time, but where areas are small it may be necessary to have a plant much larger than would be required by the above considerations, since in applying the water a very small stream can not be used to advantage. Two methods of overcoming this difficulty are used—one to install a pump of sufficient size to deliver an economical stream, and the other to use a smaller pump and provide a reservoir for storing the water until sufficient has accumulated to make such a stream. A small pump may be operated continuously, night and day, while water is used only during the day or only on occasional days. In view of fixed charges, it is the part of economy to put in a small plant and operate it for the maximum time possible, because interest on the investment, and, to a large extent, depreciation, vary with the size and are about the same whether a plant is idle or in use. In most instances it is a question of the comparative cost of larger pumping equipment and the reservoir. Where electric power is purchased on a flat rate per horsepower per year, the decrease in cost of power made possible by the use of reservoirs permitting continuous operation is a strong argument in their favor. Water stored in reservoirs is subject to loss by percolation, however, and unless reservoirs are lined to prevent such waste much of the water pumped will be lost.

It has been stated that a pumping plant must be large enough to supply to the acreage to be irrigated the quantity of water required by that acreage within a given time. In the arid region it is customary to estimate the depth of water needed during the whole irrigating season of say, 5 months, on the land to be served, and provide a pump that will deliver this quantity. If, for instance, a pump is to serve 80 acres in alfalfa, and it is estimated that the land should receive water enough in 5 months to cover it to a depth of 3 feet, it will be necessary to deliver 240 acre-feet in 153 days, or 1.57 acre-feet per day, or 356 gallons per minute, operating continuously throughout the season of 153 days. An allowance should be made for necessary shutdowns, and it is probable that a pump having a capacity of 400 to 450 gallons per minute would be recommended for such conditions. A stream of this size, however, is not large enough to use to best advantage in irrigating alfalfa and it would be necessary to install a larger pump or build a reservoir for storing water during the night. A stream of 800 to 1,000 gallons per minute could be used to much better advantage, would not require storage, and would not require continuous operation of the pump.

In the semiarid and humid regions, where irrigation water is used to supplement the rainfall and to tide over periods of drought, the quantity of water likely to be needed during some short period rather than during the whole season governs the size of plant. It should be possible to give the entire acreage one good irrigation within a period of two weeks. As a broad general average, a good irrigation requires sufficient water to cover the surface to a depth of from 4 to 6 inches. Taking 5 inches as the average and 80 acres as the acreage, again, this will require a pump discharging 540 gallons per minute if operated continuously for two weeks, or 1,080 gallons per minute if operated one-half the time.

As a rule, reservoirs are more adaptable to the semiarid sections than to the arid, since in the former a large quantity of water may be required to fill in a period of drought, in which instance, if the reservoir were of sufficient capacity, a small plant might be operated continuously during possibly several weeks, thereby holding in the reservoir a large volume to be applied when needed in a relatively short period of time.

Plate LXXXVII, figure 1, shows an alfalfa field of 150 acres at Deming, N. Mex., with plats or lands 20 by 330 feet which are irrigated from a centrifugal pump delivering 2.5 cubic feet per second (1,125 gallons per minute). Plate LXXXVII, figure 2, illustrates the exterior of this plant. It is but one of 22 similar pumps, ranging in capacity from 800 to 2,000 gallons per minute, irrigating 4,000 acres. One pump is situated at the highest point of each 160 to 200 acre tract, the largest pumps supplying more than 160 acres. The pumps are vertical centrifugal, direct-connected to 3-phase, 60-cycle, 220-volt motors ranging in size from 35 to 50 horse-power. The average depth to water level in that section is 48 feet. The total pumping head, which includes the draw-down head, is from 60 to 70 feet.

TYPES OF PUMPS.

Three types of pumping plants, distinguished by the kind of pump, are used for irrigation. The first type is that in which some form of plunger or cylinder pump and driving head is employed. In the second type some form of centrifugal pump, either horizontal or vertical, is employed. The third type is what is known as an air lift. Other types of pumps, less commonly used for irrigation, are elevators or chain pumps, rotary or cycloidal pumps, and screw pumps, the latter after a modification of the principle of the Archimedean screw.

The plunger or cylinder type of pump may include a single-acting cylinder or a double-acting cylinder, or may be a single-acting double plunger, a single-acting three plunger or even a four plunger, all operating in one cylinder, or it may be double, triplex, or quadruplex, employing two, three, or four cylinders with single plungers.

When the single-cylinder type is employed it usually is installed in a cased well, while the use of more than one cylinder requires a pit or dug well. In both cases the working head or that part of the pump operating the plungers is situated upon the surface of the ground with the cylinders and plungers below water level.

The single-cylinder pumps, whether they have one or more plungers, usually are employed for pumping against high heads—that is, where the water level occurs at 100 or more feet below the surface. As a rule the quantity pumped does not exceed 200 or 300 gallons per minute, although if a large quantity be desired such pumps may be used by employing the two or three plunger arrangement. The pumping head in such instances usually is massive and is an expensive part of the equipment. A cheaper installation, where quantities of water up to 1,000 gallons per minute or more are desired, is the vertical centrifugal pump, for which a pump pit may be dug or a 24-inch or larger casing may be installed to a depth sufficient to permit putting the pump within suction distance of the lowest point to which the water level will be drawn down by pumping, the well proper being continued from the bottom of this pit to the required depth. Where the water plane does not undergo material fluctuations and occurs at a moderate depth, a pit, either rectangular or circular, may be sunk to water level or below, and properly timbered or concreted. At the bottom thereof and connected with the well extending below may be installed a horizontal centrifugal pump, direct-connected to an electric motor or (if the depth is not excessive) belted to some form of prime mover installed upon the surface of the ground.

The air lift is utilized often for recovering water from great depths, especially where considerable sand or sediment is delivered with the water. There are two types of air lifts—the direct displacement and the expansion types. In either of these, however, the water is raised by compressed air, which requires some form of compressor.

It is impossible to recommend a particular type of pumping plant that will fit all conditions equally well, since a factor influencing the choice of one type for one section might be absent in another section. In some sections a preference is shown for the deep-well pump of the plunger type, even for large quantites of water, notwithstanding their higher first cost and the fact that the centrifugal type would be more suitable and give equal, if not better, results.

The choice of a type of pumping plant is often influenced by the fact that a pump salesman has succeeded in selling a plant which operated satisfactorily. Further installations follow without regard to whether that type is the most practical and feasible. In every case where a new installation is contemplated, the matter should be submitted for competent, impartial engineering advice before a particular type of plant is adopted.

As a general rule the plunger type of pump is well suited for lifting quantities of water from 100 to 500 gallons per minute from depths beyond 50 feet, whereas the vertical centrifugal pump is better suited for quantities of from 500 to 2,000 gallons per minute at depths beyond 50 feet. A horizontal centrifugal pump is preferable for depths of from 10 to 50 feet, where electric power is available, even for quantities as low as 100 gallons per minute; and where the depth to water is as great as 50 feet and electric power is not available, a horizontal centrifugal pump, located in a dug pit and belted to an engine upon the surface with the belt running at an incline, is to be preferred.

As a rule, the plunger pump will give a higher mechanical efficiency than the vertical centrifugal pump, often as great as 80 per cent when new, though where considerable sand and grit is encountered the wear upon the plunger leathers and valves often increases the slip or loss of water around the plungers, so that the efficiency decreases rapidly, the average operating efficiency being about 65 per cent. Under such conditions the vertical centrifugal pump, if arranged for ample lubrication of all vertical bearings by the use of inclosed line shafting, will give less trouble and a higher, more constant efficiency, and is more suitable. The ordinary stock pumps of this type seldom attain efficiencies above 50 per cent; therefore a properly designed and constructed, though more expensive, pump is to be preferred.

The horizontal centrifugal pump, if of the turbine type for high heads or of the volute type for moderate heads and correctly designed, is preferable to either of the other types of pump, and always should be used where the depth to water level is not so great as to make it impracticable. The efficiency of such pumps usually is quite high, often 70 per cent, and since there is practically no wear upon the hydraulic parts the efficiency may be maintained for a long time.

FIG. I.—ALFALFA LAND PREPARED FOR IRRIGATION BY THE BORDER METHOD.

FIG. 2.—ONE OF TWENTY-TWO PUMPS USED FOR IRRIGATING ALFALFA AT DEMING, N. MEX.

The centrifugal pump usually is compounded; that is, a stage is employed for each 50 feet in head to be contended against, though in some instances where high speeds are permissible a single-stage pump may handle water against 100 feet or more. However, the slip and short-circuit losses tend to increase with the increase in head per stage; hence it is desirable to limit that head to 50 or 75 feet.

The air lift, even under the most favorable circumstances, is not an efficient means of pumping water, for the reason that the air compressor which is a necessary part of either the expansion or the direct-displacement type is not, nor can it be, made highly efficient where air must be used at high pressures, and, since the air pressure is proportionate to the height the water is lifted in all but one form of lift, it is seldom that conditions will warrant such low pressures as will give even average high efficiencies in the compressor, and though the efficiency of the air jet be relatively high, the loss in the compressor, in combination with the loss in the jet, seldom gives a combined efficiency above 35 per cent. The direct-displacement air lift usually is more efficient in the water-expelling part than in the expansion system.

By "efficiency" is meant the ratio of the amount of work accomplished to the amount of work expended. For example, if the theoretical power required to elevate a given quantity of water in a given time were 50 horsepower, and to accomplish that work it required the expenditure of 100 horsepower, the combined efficiency of the apparatus would be 50 per cent. Evidently, then, upon the efficiency of the plant depends the cost of the water pumped. But efficiency is not the only factor to be considered, for the reliability of the equipment is of great importance and may justify a sacrifice of efficiency. Why combined reliability and high efficiency do not seem possible in the vertical centrifugal pump is not explained easily. Nevertheless, this seems to be the case, whereas in the horizontal centrifugal pump high efficiency and reliability are characteristic. Nor are efficiency and reliability jointly possible in the air lift, where efficiency is sacrificed to reliability. The plunger type of pump approaches closer to the standard of the horizontal centrifugal pump in efficiency and reliability, provided the water is relatively free from sand or grit.

The efficiency of the centrifugal pump (either vertical or horizontal), unlike that of the plunger, is influenced very greatly by fluctuations in head, and, unless the speed of the pump can be varied to meet any variation in head from that for which the pump was designed, its efficiency may be lessened considerably. For this reason it is important that a test be made upon the well to determine its capacity at a given draw-down, the exact head to be contended with thus ascertained, and its value included in the specifications of requirements submitted to the pump builders.

In ascertaining the draw-down a well need not be tested to the full capacity desired, since the draw-down is proportional to the quantity delivered, except when it affects more than one-half of the inflow area of the well. That is, if a well under test supplies 500 gallons per minute and lowers the normal water plane 10 feet, then in delivering 1,000 gallons per minute the water plane would be lowered 20 feet if the water level is not drawn down more than one-half of the total depth through which water enters the well.

FEATURES OF PROPER INSTALLATION.

Proper installation of a pumping plant is important if reliability is to be assured. Massive and well-built foundations are necessary for proper operation of the pump as well as the engine, since weak foundations permit vibration, which leads to loss of power and unnecessary wear and tear on the machinery.

Foundations should be of concrete, thoroughly mixed and comprised ordinarily of 1 part of cement to 2 parts of sand and 3 parts of gravel, and should be kept thoroughly wetted for at least seven days after completion. The machinery should be leveled by the use of iron wedges after alignment, and the bases should be grouted thoroughly into place by the use of cement grout composed of 1 part of cement to 1 part of clean, coarse sand. After this grout has become set thoroughly the foundation bolts should be tightened into place.

The matter of belt centers, that is, the distance from the center of the engine shaft to the center of the pump, is of prime importance. Short belt centers require very tight belts, resulting in loss of power and efficiency. Where vertical centrifugal pumps are used a quarter-twist belt is required, and such a belt should not require the use of idlers to provide belt tension or proper belt alignment. Therefore the belt centers in such instances should be from 30 to 35 feet, so that the weight of the belt may provide the necessary tension.

In some instances there is a tendency of the belt to climb the pump pulley when the plant is being shut down, and if the belt becomes slack there also is a tendency for the belt to run off the pulley at the lower side. To prevent this trouble it is well to provide four guide idlers close to the pump head, two at the top and two at the bottom edges of the belt, which will come into play only when needed. Where an open belt is used, as in belting from the engine to a horizontal pump located in a pit, belt centers of 25 feet will be ample, although this will be determined largely by the depth of the pit, since the pulling side of the belt should be on an incline of 45° with the horizontal. Where plunger pumps are employed an open belt is used and the centers may be 20 to 25 feet.

An effectual means of sight feed lubrication should be provided for both the engine and the pump, for, while the engine usually inherently has provision for such lubrication, the pump sometimes requires a separate oiling system.

Large internal-combustion engines, of sizes above 25 horsepower, should be arranged for starting by air. This requires a small air compressor arranged for driving from the main engine or from a small auxiliary engine. The air for starting is stored in tanks, which should withstand pressure up to 250 pounds per square inch.

Probably the most important item in connection with a pumping plant is the engine-cooling system, and great care should be exercised in supplying the feed water so as to eliminate sand or sediment. The best plan for cooling is one in which a large tank is provided and connection from the bottom of the tank is had with the lowest point upon the engine circulating jacket, the tank being placed so that its bottom is on a level with the bottom of the engine cylinder. The small circulating pump should be so connected as to deliver water into the connection at the bottom of the cylinder and permit a flow of water from the pump around the engine cylinder or into the bottom of the tank, or both. The outlet from the top of the cylinder jacket should be arranged so as to discharge into the tank or into a waste pipe discharging into the main pump discharge bay. The small pump should be piped so as to permit also connecting in series with the circulating system. In this way failure of the main pump to furnish an immediate supply, or failure of the small pump to operate, would permit circulation of cooling water by siphon action. Figure 55 shows an excellent arrangement of the circulating system. Provision should be made for draining the entire system in case of freezing temperatures.

The plant should include a galvanized-iron fuel-oil storage tank having a capacity of from 2,500 to 10,000 gallons, depending on the size of the plant. It should be installed in a curbed well so as to make possible its removal in case of needed repairs. It is important that the tank have a tight cover to prevent evaporation of the oil.

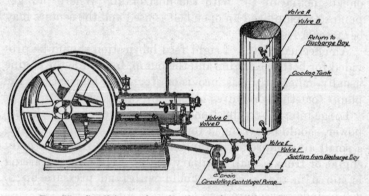

Fig. 55.—Small internal-combustion engine, with cooling system.

Careful attention should be given to housing the plant. Dust must be kept out. Concrete foundations are best, while brick, adobe, and concrete blocks are better than lumber or galvanized iron for the building materials. Galvanized iron is satisfactory for roofing if the joints and corrugations are brought to a tight fit by the use of a filler between it and the wall plate. The engine room always should have a concrete floor. The belt-race housing may be of corrugated iron. A substantial derrick should be over the well and pump and should be fitted with cable blocks and crab for lifting the heavy pump parts in case immediate repair should be necessary in the midst of an irrigation period, when delay in irrigating might prove disastrous to the crop.

Such breakdowns should be anticipated and every facility be immediately at hand so as to permit quick pulling of the pump and immediate repairs thereto, without the necessity of improvising some form of derrick or hoisting apparatus.

There are four kinds of belting which may be used for driving the pump—leather, rubber, canvas, and composition. For dry, arid climates leather is to be preferred; rubber will give excellent results under moist conditions, but is not nearly so long lived as leather; canvas is cheaper than either the leather or rubber, but is very susceptible to climatic conditions; composition costs as much, wears as well as leather, and is not affected by moisture.

WELLS.

Regarded in the proper light, the pumping plant is the heart of the farm. Upon it is dependent the value of the land as well as the successful cropping. It should be well installed, and include only the best of efficient machinery, capable of withstanding heavy and continuous strain. But without an ample and dependable water supply the best of pumping-plant equipment would be valueless, and a dependable and ample water supply could not be obtained if the proper type of well were not employed, notwithstanding the underground water-bearing material might be adequate. Two types of bored wells are in use generally—one in which the strainer is perforated before the casing is inserted, and another in which the perforations are made after the well casing is in. There are several kinds of perforated casing, such as the strainer in which rectangular slots are punched in galvanized sheet-iron which is formed into sections and riveted together as it is inserted; the shutter strainer, of heavy sheet steel with slits punched around the casing and formed at the top of the slits so as to produce a shelter, as it were, over each slit; and a strainer of steel piping liberally drilled with one-half inch holes and wrapped with a trapezoidal or triangular section wire, the width of the spaces between the wires being varied to correspond with the formation in which the strainer is to be used. Casing perforated after being inserted in the well may be either screw casing or what is known as "stovepipe" casing, the latter being employed more commonly because of the ease with which it may be perforated.

Generally, for sand or small-gravel formations, one of the perforated strainers will give the better results, whereas if the formation be of coarse bowlders and large gravel very satisfactory results will be obtained with casing perforated after it is inserted with slots 6 to 8 inches long, four each around a given section, each set from 4 to 6 inches above the other. Where stovepipe or screw casing is used it is installed as the well is drilled by the use of what is called a cable rig, or commonly a churn drill, whereas where perforated strainers are employed they usually are set in the well after it has been drilled, and a rotary drilling rig is employed for such purposes.

In drilling wells it is best to penetrate the entire depth of water-bearing material, since the greater the inflow area within the well the less will be the draw-down for a given quantity of water.

Quite as important as the well itself is the matter of developing it after it has been drilled and the casing installed. The flow of water depends upon the effective size of the soil grain comprising the water-bearing material, which may be very greatly increased by removing all of the fine sand or finer gravel. This would be justified even if the expense were one-half the initial cost of the well. There are several methods of developing wells, the more common of which is the use of a wood plunger bolted to the end of the drill stem, which is churned up and down so as to force the water outward and inward through the perforations. Special forms of water-developing jets are available which are really more effective than the wood plunger. Very frequently the flow from a well may be increased several hundred per cent by such development. In all of the 72 wells installed in connection with the Portales, N. Mex., irrigation project the flow into the wells when the wells were installed and tested seldom exceeded 300 to 400 gallons per minute, but after persistent development the flow was increased to from 1,000 to 2,000 gallons per minute. While a well will develop to some extent under ordinary pumping, it is not best to depend upon that alone.

It also is a wise provision to have chemical analyses made of the water recovered from a given section before large investment is made in a pumping plant, since the water often may contain harmful salts.

COST OF PLANT.

A first-class pumping plant, including well, may be installed, under average conditions of head and capacity, at a cost of from $5,000 to $7,000, with ample capacity to irrigate 160 acres of average forage crops. A smaller plant with a capacity of several hundred gallons a minute may be installed complete, including the well, for $2,000 or less if water-supply conditions are favorable. The cost of a reservoir may be $500 or even $1,000 if it be concrete lined. As heretofore stated, the operation of a pumping plant should extend over as great a period of time during an irrigation season as possible, so as to reduce the unit overhead cost.

COST OF OPERATION.

Efforts are being made continually to construct pumping-plant machinery with a view to operation without the necessity for constant attention, but while many plants are so operated, the only attention given being an occasional visit each day during operation, this procedure is hazardous, and if any part of the equipment were to fail during operation the engine or pump might be destroyed and the cost of repairs exceed the cost of continuous labor and attendance which might have been supplied. If, on the other hand, the distribution system is so laid out as to permit diversion of water to a given number of plats and the system be of concrete pipe or concrete-lined ditches (which, of themselves, do not require attention), the operator of the plant may set the gates for certain delivery and then return to the plant and devote the greater part of his time to its operation.

An engine that will use a low grade of fuel oil is desirable, since the cost of such oil usually is about one-fourth or one-third that of gasoline. The better type of semicrude-oil engines will deliver from 8 to 10 horsepower hours per gallon of semicrude oil known as "tops" and having a density of from 25° to 30° Baumé. This fuel may cost on an average of from 3 cents to 7 cents per gallon, delivered.

Lubricating oil is an important factor in the cost of operation of gas engines. Particularly is this true of a large engine, though if it be kept in proper repair, so that the lubricating oil does not pass by the piston rings and into combustion with the fuel oil, a much lower consumption of lubricating oil may be obtained.

Interest and depreciation always should be included as an item in the cost of the operation of a pumping plant. Further, a maintenance charge should be made so as to provide funds for repairs and maintenance of the plant up to the highest standard. Usually the depreciation on internal-combustion engines is as high as 15 per cent. The interest charges vary with the prevailing rates in the particular locality. Using 15 per cent for depreciation and 8 per cent for interest and adding the cost of fuel and lubricating oil (the former at 3 to 7 cents per gallon and the latter at 40 cents per gallon) as well as a continuous supervision labor charge, the average cost per acre-foot of water for each foot of head it is elevated may vary from 4 cents to as much as 15 to 20 cents. Thus, if the pumping head were 100 feet, the total cost would be $4 to $20 per acre-foot. This cost will be varied, depending upon the amount of time charged against plant operation.

In comparing such costs with the cost of water under a gravity project, interest and depreciation must be charged similarly against that source, as well as cost of ditch cleaning, maintenance, cultivation against weeds, etc., when the comparison between the two projects would not be so greatly to the disadvantage of the pumping plant as might appear. Where electric power is available, considering the high depreciation and possible annoying shutdowns for repairs incident to gas-engine plants, together with the fact that operative labor may be almost entirely eliminated, a cost of 2 cents or even more per kilowatt may be comparable to the cost of the same amount of power from a gas-engine plant.

OPENING UP THE NATIONAL FORESTS BY ROAD BUILDING.

By O. C. MERRILL, *Chief Engineer, Forest Service.*

SOME day in the not far distant future the farmer in Kansas, Oklahoma, Nebraska, the Dakotas, or indeed in any of the great farming States, may, when the work of harvesting is over, pack tent and camp equipment in his automobile and, with his family, seek needed rest and recreation almost anywhere in the mountain reaches of the National Forests, east or west. He will be able, if he so desires, to journey at his leisure, camping where fancy leads him and untroubled by the need for making a town or settlement each night. He may go by ways hitherto closed to all but the adventurous tourist with saddle horse and pack outfit, through the mountains of Colorado, with their snow-capped peaks and green parks, or into the beauties and health-giving air of the high Sierras of California, the coast ranges of Washington and Oregon, the northern Rockies, or the cool altitudes of the Southwest. Should the matter of distance or his own fancy turn him eastward, he will be able to penetrate the Southern Appalachians, with peaks green-clad to the summit and bathed in the soft haze which gives to the southern mountains a peculiar beauty of their own. Similarly, the farmer living within the boundaries of the National Forests may find what now is often lacking—quick and easy contact with markets for his produce and with sources of his supplies. Forest communities, now isolated through lack of good roads or even any roads at all, will be brought into touch with the outside world. All this is made possible by the section of the Federal aid road act, signed by the President on July 11, 1916, appropriating a million dollars a year for 10 years for the construction of roads within National Forests. This sum, however, represents but half, or perhaps less than half, of the amount which will

521

probably be spent for National Forest roads in the next 10 years, over and above the amount ordinarily spent each year by the Forest Service, for the law provides that an equal amount shall be contributed by the States and counties concerned. So as much as $20,000,000 ought to be available between now and the year 1927 with which to open up the National Forests for the benefit of those who live in or near them, and for the vast number of other Americans who may wish to use them as places in which to find health, rest, and recreation.

When, in 1905, the National Forests were placed under the administration of the Forest Service, they were practically without roads and lacking in trails. They were, moreover, in serious danger of burning up, because there were no means of transporting men and supplies quickly to the scene of fires. Before very much could be done, therefore, in the way of building roads primarily for the use of the public, it was necessary to give the Forests road and trail systems that would make it possible to protect them from the fire menace. In the last 10 years, with the money available from its regular appropriation, amounting in all to about $1,500,000, the Forest Service has built or repaired about 2,000 miles of road and about 25,000 miles of trail in the National Forests. These, while serving their primary object of administration and protection, have, to a certain extent, made the Forests accessible to the public. But when one considers the vastness of the Forest areas and the lack of roads at the beginning, one can see that, so far as opening up the Forests to the public is concerned, the work which it has been possible to do with the money available from the regular appropriation for the Forest Service amounts to relatively little beside the total road work that needs to be done.

The National Forests total 155,000,000 acres, an area considerably larger than the German Empire. They contain the highest altitudes and the roughest topography in the United States. The greater number of them are in the mountains of the West—the Rockies, the Sierra Nevadas, and the Coast Range—though land has been bought, and still is being bought, for National Forests in the White Mountains and in the Southern Appalachians. Within their boundaries are any number of mining camps, small agricultural communities, and individual farms. Settlement at first was on the more accessible lands along the margins of the Forests or in the river valleys. Gradually, however, as the remaining agricultural land in the Forests has been classified and opened to settlement, the less accessible areas have been taken up, making the need for roads more urgent than ever. Counties, and even individuals, have built roads when money was available, and the Forest Service has done what it could with the funds at its disposal, but in spite of all this hundreds of settlers within the National Forests still have no means of communication with the outside world better than a pack trail. As other remote areas of agricultural land in the Forests are opened to settlement, this condition will, of course, become worse instead of better. The convenience and well-being of the settlers, and the development and use of the Forests' agricultural resources, call for an adequate system of roads in the shortest practicable time.

And if there is need for giving the population within the Forests an outlet to the rest of the world, there is just as great a need for giving the people of the country in general means for getting into the Forests; for nowhere else can one find such unlimited opportunities for every kind of recreation. The most rugged and impressive of mountain scenery, forests of spruce, fir, and pine, high meadows deep in mountain wild flowers, beautiful lakes reflecting the snow-clad peaks around them, and shaded trout streams are there for the nature lover, the fisherman, or the vacationist who desires only rest and change of scene in the great outdoors. As things are at present, most of these places can be reached only after days of travel on foot or with saddle and pack horse. Roads would make them accessible, by automobile or other conveyance, to thousands of people, at a relatively small expenditure of money and time. Even to-day one of the commonest sights during the summer months on such of the National Forests as are traversed by good roads is the automobile camper with tent and other necessary equipment and with family or friends in his car, seeking pleasure and rest in the mountain country. The licenses which the cars carry show that they come from many States, near and distant—New York and Pennsylvania tags may be seen almost any day in the National Forests in

Colorado or even in California—but chiefly from the Plains States and other farming regions of the West and Middle West. The automobile has solved for many farmers the problem of a means of obtaining a vacation trip for themselves and their families. Hotel expenses there are none, and food may be obtained at reasonable prices from ranches and farms along the way. To take a family of three or four on the railroad would mean a separate ticket for each member; yet scarcely more gasoline, if any, is used when that many persons are in the car than when it carries but one. These are some of the reasons why automobile camping has increased so tremendously in the last two or three years, and why it promises to increase still more in the next two or three. And just as the motor car has met the question of how to make the vacation trip, so before very long will the National Forests answer the one of where to go.

For those who desire to spend more time on the Forest than is ordinarily consumed by a pleasure trip there are almost innumerable sites for summer homes. Such of these as are at present easily accessible have been developed and advertised by the Forest Service, and a large number of permanent camps and cottages have been erected in the Forests by those who wish to spend their summers among the beauties of the mountains. The cost of a permit for a summer-home site ranges from $10 up, according to location, size of lot, character of building which it is planned to erect, etc., but is very seldom more than $25, and usually less. New roads will, of course, make many more summer-home sites available for use. Summer communities will grow up along the shores of many of the beautiful lakes in the western mountains, now practically inaccessible, and in other places to which the view or surroundings lend a special attractiveness. Good roads, too, will undoubtedly bring hotels, as they do everywhere else, for those who wish to visit the Forests without the need of camping.

In 1912 Congress stipulated that 10 per cent of the receipts from the National Forests should be expended, under the direction of the Secretary of Agriculture, for the construction of roads and trails; and it was from this date that road building on the Forests, primarily for the benefit of the public, really began. As long ago as 1906 Congress provided that

F—19515A

A TYPE OF BRIDGE USED IN NATIONAL FOREST ROAD BUILDING. THE SYLAMORE BRIDGE, OZARK NATIONAL FOREST, ARK.

The towers are of reinforced concrete, and the roadway, which is of wood, is suspended by wire cables. A suspension bridge is cheapest and best where the span is long, or where, as over a canyon, the depth to be crossed is such that piers are impracticable.

F—25314A

FIG. I.—HOW EVEN GRADES ARE SECURED ON NATIONAL FOREST ROADS.

A switchback and fill on the Sedalia-Decker Springs road, Pike National Forest, Colo.,
with retaining wall of broken rock.

F—1405A—OCM

FIG. 2.—CROSSING A ROCK SLIDE ON THE PAYETTE NATIONAL FOREST,
IDAHO.

A retaining wall of broken rock is built on the upper side of the road to protect it from
slides, and another on the lower side to prevent washing.

F—29276A

SCENES OF BEAUTY GREET THE VISITOR IN THE NATIONAL FORESTS. A VIEW FROM THE RABBIT EARS PASS ROAD, ROUTT NATIONAL FOREST, COLO.

Some 1,500 feet above the valley, one can see to where, in the farther distance, snow-clad mountains contrast with the green of the nearer hills.

10 per cent (later increased to 25 per cent) of National Forest receipts should go to the counties in which the Forests are situated, for roads and schools; but little or none of the money thus appropriated, amounting so far to about $5,000,-000, has been spent for roads inside the Forests, the various counties preferring to use it in the more thickly settled localities outside.

What has been accomplished since 1912 is the repair of 580 miles of road in the National Forests and the construction of 860 miles of new ones—1,440 miles in all—at a total cost of $1,157,000. Of this sum $780,000 represents 10 per cent of National Forest receipts for the three years, together with certain moneys available from the regular Forest Service appropriation, while $337,000 was contributed by States, counties, and private cooperators. Here, specifically, are some of the things that have been done with a few hundred thousand dollars: Twenty-six miles of road, with a maximum grade of 6 per cent, have been built between the Big Basin, in Montana, and the Bitterroot Valley, replacing an almost impassable road, with grades as high as 25 per cent. Work is nearly complete on a road from Jacksons Hole, Wyo., over the Teton Pass to the railroad at Victor, Idaho. The closing link has been built in a road connecting the Flathead Valley, in Montana, with the Inland Empire territory. A road is under construction in California which will open for the first time the agricultural lands along the valley of the Trinity River. Another road in the same State will furnish access to summer camping grounds for residents of the Imperial Valley. A road recently completed across the Powell National Forest, in Utah, has opened communication with a settlement in the valley of the upper Colorado, hitherto practically shut off from the rest of the world. Roads across the Rabbit Ears Pass and the Cochetopa Pass, in Colorado, will open up large sections of the Routt and Cochetopa National Forests to freighting and tourist travel. These are by no means all of the roads that have been built or on which work has begun since the 10 per cent fund became available, but they serve to show how a start has been made in opening up the National Forests to general public use.

In the actual work of road building the policy is to concentrate available funds on a few projects at a time, and to complete these rapidly, rather than to scatter money among a multitude of projects and get very little in the way of an effective road system. One good road that connects up with an existing road leading to some center of population, or that gives an outlet to a railway, is worth two indifferent roads that lead nowhere in particular. Reconnaissance surveys have been made to determine the approximate location and cost of the roads most urgently needed, and the various projects arranged in the order of their relative importance. In this way it is possible to allot the money for road building, as it becomes available, with the certainty that it will be used to the best advantage. Engineers of the Department of Agriculture have kept in touch with the highway departments of the various States in which National Forests are situated, in order to insure coordination between Federal work and that of the local governments.

The character of traffic on the National Forests has seldom justified the construction of expensive surfaced roads. Medium-width earth roads, well graded and drained, are the kind which have been built. With conditions as they are on the Forests, a single-track road with a low grade has proved much better than a double-track road with a steep grade. Roads which prove to be too narrow can be widened without destroying what is already there, but to change the grade means rebuilding and complete loss of the original investment. Heavy grades on mountain roads that often have a steady upward climb of 10 or 15 miles before the crest of the divide is reached make travel by horse-drawn vehicle, or even by automobile, a slow and difficult proceeding. Six per cent has been used as the maximum grade for National Forest roads wherever practicable. All roads, moreover, are side ditched, with protection ditches as needed and good-sized culverts at frequent intervals.

In one case a road seemed to be urgently needed on a National Forest, though of a kind too costly and of too little economic utility to justify its construction by the Forest Service or by the State or county concerned. This is the so-called Pikes Peak Highway, in the Pike National Forest, completed in the summer of 1916, extending from the town of

Cascade 17 miles to the summit of Pikes Peak. The peak, which attains an altitude of 14,109 feet above sea level, is a Mecca for tourists from all over the United States. Before this year, practically the only means of reaching the top, other than on the back of a burro, was by a cog railroad. An opportunity for automobiles to reach the summit was desired by the local people, and accordingly the Secretary of Agriculture gave a permit to a private company to construct a road, after approving the amount of toll to be charged. The permit provides, among other things, that at the expiration of 15 years and at intervals of 5 years thereafter, the company may be required to transfer title and interest in the road to the United States on payment of an amount equal to its physical value, or the Secretary of Agriculture may instead impose an annual rental and have the right to fix toll charges, if necessary, to protect the public. It is not the policy of the Government to sanction the construction of toll roads in the National Forests, but since neither State nor Government funds were available for this much-needed development of the scenic resources of the Pike Forest, an exception was made in this particular case.

Once a National Forest road is built, everything possible is done to keep it in a proper state of repair. With the long dry spells and the short heavy rains and deep snow, along with alternate melting and freezing, common on most of the Forests, even the best built road would soon be ruined without some effective system of maintenance. With proper maintenance, on the other hand, the kind of material usually found on the Forests will produce excellent roads. On the more important roads patrolmen are being employed during the season of traffic to keep ditches and culverts open and to drag and crown the road whenever necessary. If the cost of maintaining National Forest roads remains as low in the future as it is at present, the system will, it is hoped, furnish an object lesson in the economy of intelligent maintenance over intermittent repairs.

Though much has been accomplished in the way of road building in a relatively short time, it would take a great many years to provide the National Forests with even the skeleton of a road system if dependence had to be placed solely on the 10 per cent of Forest receipts and such other money as the Forest Service could spare from its regular appropriation. For while it is true that the potential value of National Forest resources is exceedingly great, the money receipts from the sale of timber and from other uses are in many cases at present very small, due mainly to the very lack of roads that the 10 per cent fund was meant to remedy. A Forest that is inaccessible can not be used, and so can produce little or no revenue. Therefore, until the National Forests were given some sort of road system, relatively little increase in receipts could be expected, and correspondingly little increase in the funds available for road building. To meet this situation, the Secretary of Agriculture, in his report for 1914, made the following recommendations:

In such regions [National Forests] the Secretary of Agriculture should be authorized to make a study of the local conditions and to gather all the data necessary to formulate a plan for public-road development based on local needs. These plans should be carried into sufficient detail to provide a reasonably accurate estimate of the cost of the road construction which it is proposed that the Government shall undertake. They should be accompanied by careful and conservative appraisals of the value of the National Forest timber in each locality and a forecast of the future income which the Forests will bring in from all sources. On the basis of the showings of fact regarding the value of the Government's property, its potential income-yielding capacity, and the needs of the public, Congress should be asked to appropriate for the construction of projects recommended by the Secretary of Agriculture.

The result of this was the clause in the Federal aid road act appropriating $1,000,000 a year for 10 years for National Forest roads. The Office of Public Roads and Rural Engineering, through cooperative agreement with the Forest Service, will make surveys, prepare plans and specifications, and supervise construction. By this arrangement the administrative experience and knowledge of local conditions possessed by the Forest Service is combined with the technical equipment of the Office of Public Roads and Rural Engineering to insure the best results in the shortest time and at the least cost.

In deciding between the various projects proposed in each State, a number of things will have to be taken into account. Some of these are the relative public need for each road, to how great an extent it will help to develop resources upon which settlers or communities are dependent, and its relation to the State or county highway system. The amount of cooperation offered by the State or counties and the amount of Government money apportioned to the State will, of course, also be considered. Once these matters are settled— and the aim will be to settle them quickly—the actual work of construction can begin. The money that should be available during the next 10 years will serve to build many miles of road in the National Forests. Many of these new roads, besides serving their economic purpose, will be scenic highways unsurpassed elsewhere on the continent in the views which they will unfold to the traveler. Nearly all of them will lead to places where Nature has wrought in one medium or another—in beauties of mountain, valley, forest, or stream—her finest and most inspiring handiwork.

Viewed in its broader aspects, road building is but part, though a very important part, of the larger work of developing the resources of the National Forests in a way to insure their widest public use. The Forests were set aside, not as a domain locked up and hidden, a far country closed permanently to use and enjoyment, but as a storehouse from which the people of the United States might forever in the future draw wood and water, and where they might find pleasure, rest, and health amid scenes of beauty. In so far as the roads to be built in the next 10 years bring this plan of National Forest development nearer to completion, they will serve a broad public purpose and meet a pressing public need.

A GRAPHIC SUMMARY OF WORLD AGRICULTURE.

By V. C. Finch, *Formerly Assistant in Agricultural Geography, Office of Farm Management;* O. E. Baker, *Agriculturist, Office of Farm Management,* and R. G. Hainsworth, *Head Draftsman, Office of Farm Management.*

THE United States has a greater acreage of land in crops than any other nation, except possibly China, for which statistics are not available. The total acreage of land in crops in the United States is nearly equal to that of all Europe, excluding Russia. The other important agricultural nations, arranged in descending order of importance according to crop acreage, are Russia, India, Germany, Austria-Hungary, Argentina, France, Italy, and Canada.

The United States also has a greater crop acreage per capita of population than any other of the great nations of the world, except the sparsely settled countries of Canada and Argentina. In the United States in 1909 the number of acres of crops per person was 3.5, and of improved land, 5.2; whereas in the Old World the acres of crops per person ranged from about 0.2 acre in Japan and 0.4 acre in the United Kingdom to 1 acre in Germany, 1.5 acres in France, and 1.6 acres in the Russian Empire.

The population of eastern and southern Asia has increased comparatively· slowly in recent times, being frequently reduced by famine, but the population of Europe has increased manyfold during the past century and has now in several countries attained a density exceeding that of the Orient. According to the latest statistics, Belgium has a density of population of about 670 persons per square mile, the United Kingdom 380, Japan 370, Italy 330, Germany 320, India (British) 220, Austria-Hungary and China (proper) 200, and the United States 34.

The large amount of improved land per person in the United States and the large amount of arable but less valuable land yet unimproved, probably almost equal to the improved land in area, is in striking contrast to the great density of population across the oceans. Herein lies the basic cause of the difference in economic well-being between the Old World and the New, and of the current of westward immigration. The best statistical evidence indicates that population in the United States is now increasing somewhat more rapidly than the acreage of cropped land. The maximum acreage of improved land per capita, 5.7 acres, was attained in the census years 1880 and 1890 and dropped to 5.5 in 1900 and to 5.2 in 1910. The higher prices of farm products are in part a resultant of this pressure of population upon the food supply, and are in turn

531

an important factor in producing the increased yield per acre and the trend toward more intensive types of agriculture. Although the acreage of cropped land per capita has decreased for 20 years, more intensive methods of agriculture and higher yields per acre have prevented an appreciable decline in the per capita production of crops. Taking as a criterion the six more important food crops, corn, wheat, oats, barley, potatoes, and rye, the average production was higher in the two five-year periods, 1906–1910 and 1911–1915, than in the previous five-year periods for which figures are available.

Estimated acreage of land in crops, and food production of the principal countries.

Country.	Estimated acreage of land in crops.[1]	Estimated population.[1]	Estimated acres of crops per capita.	Estimated production of selected food crops expressed in terms of bushels of wheat (average of 1911–1913).[2]	Estimated production per capita of selected food crops in terms of bushels of wheat.
United States	318,526,000	91,972,000	3.5	4,170,690,000	45.3
Russian Empire [3]................	[4] 275,569,000	175,138,000	1.6	3,051,135,000	17.4
China (proper) [5]................	400,000,000	302,000,000	1.3	....	....
India (British)	219,192,000	244,268,000	.9	1,910,751,000	7.8
German Empire	65,445,000	67,812,000	1.0	1,442,349,000	21.3
Austria-Hungary	62,196,000	49,211,000	1.3	1,035,573,000	21.0
Argentina.......................	60,829,000	7,979,000	7.6	[6] 449,086,000	56.3
France..........................	59,128,000	39,602,000	1.5	707,815,000	17.9
Italy............................	51,309,000	36,120,000	1.4	346,757,000	9.6
Canada.........................	36,939,000	7,180,000	5.1	505,219,000	70.4
United Kingdom	19,413,000	45,371,000	.4	251,892,000	5.6
Australia.......................	14,683,000	4,951,000	3.0	122,258,000	24.7

[1] Statesman's Yearbook, 1916, except for United States and China.
[2] The relative value, without reference to protein ratio, of the different food crops per bushel used in compiling this table is based principally on Danish experiments in feeding and is as follows: Wheat, 60; corn, 56; rye, 56; oats, 32; barley, 48; potatoes, 10; clean rice, 60; millet, 48; sugar, equivalent to wheat.
[3] Exclusive of Finland.
[4] Exclusive of 95,756,000 acres of meadows.
[5] Rough estimate.
[6] Average of 1912–1914.

The following maps of the world's agriculture are designed to furnish a convenient means of comparing the geographic distribution and density of production of the more important crops and farm animals in the United States with the distribution and density in foreign countries, while the graphs at the bottom of the maps visualize the relative importance of the United States in the world's production and markets. The system of uniform-sized dots employed to show distribution does not permit of an easy computation of totals, but the value of the dot is shown for each map, and from the graphs the acreage or production of the important countries can be approximately determined. Since acreage is less subject to fluctuation than crop production, and since it affords better comparison of the importance of one crop with another, statistics of area have been mapped so far as figures were available. In the maps of rice, cotton, tobacco, sugar, and coffee, however, it was found necessary to use statistics of production. All the maps represent an average of the years 1911, 1912, and 1913, compiled from official reports, except in the case of the United States, for which the statistics collected in the census of 1910 were used, and in that for the provinces of Russian Asia, which refer to the two years 1912 and 1914.

Because of the distortion resulting from any attempt to represent the curved surface of the earth on a flat map, the ratio of dot area to land area is not the same in all portions of the map, which is a Mercator projection. The density of dots in any section of the map is strictly comparable only with that of other places in the same latitude.

Data are lacking for some countries or provinces, particularly for China and the native states of India, and in such cases hachuring has been employed to show the probable distribution and density.

The following table provides a summary of the more important statistics graphically portrayed in the maps and graphs:

Production of principal crops in the principal countries: Average for 1911–1913.

Country.	Corn.	Wheat.	Oats.	Rye.
	Bushels.	*Bushels.*	*Bushels.*	*Bushels.*
United States	2,701,074,000	704,995,000	1,154,134,300	36,721,300
Russian Empire	78,110,000	727,133,300	1,050,574,700	935,010,300
India	87,526,700	369,612,300		
German Empire		160,236,700	595,660,700	455,181,700
France	20,557,000	324,136,700	309,380,300	48,078,700
Austria-Hungary	210,855,300	247,141,000	245,937,700	163,640,000
Italy	100,245,300	190,840,000	37,582,700	5,390,300
United Kingdom		61,297,300	179,359,000	1,666,700
Argentina[1]	251,875,300	155,828,300	65,311,000	1,748,300
Canada	17,636,000	228,933,300	387,159,000	2,406,700
Australia	10,432,000	88,961,000	14,134,000	95,700

Country.	Barley.	Potatoes.	Rice.	Sugar.
	Bushels.	*Bushels.*	*Bushels.*[2]	*Long tons.*
United States	187,417,700	348,303,000	11,808,700	1,639,000
Russian Empire	484,848,000	1,287,880,700	6,151,900	1,630,700
India	38,097,700		1,087,002,300	2,407,000
German Empire	157,921,700	1,698,826,000		2,227,000
France	47,608,700	506,884,700	39,100	643,000
Austria-Hungary	153,437,000	642,149,000		1,496,700
Italy	10,029,300	61,410,300	11,052,600	186,300
United Kingdom	62,528,300	259,482,700		
Argentina[1]	5,096,700	38,029,000	410,300	242,900
Canada	47,370,700	78,222,300		
Australia	2,816,700	13,842,700		253,700

[1] Average of 1912-1914.   [2] 60 pounds clean rice.

LIST OF MAPS.

534

FIG. 56. *Identification map.*—The maps of the world showing the geographic distribution of the crops and live stock should be compared with this map to ascertain the name of a country. In Europe the boundaries shown are those existing in 1913, after the Balkan Wars. The Japanese name Chosen is recognized for the peninsula formerly known as Korea, and Taiwan for the island formerly known as Formosa. The Republic of China is considered as including not only China proper but also Manchuria, Mongolia, Chinese Turkestan, and Tibet, a situation more nominal than real. India is recognized as including Burma and Beluchistan. There is serious exaggeration in area in the northern and southern portions of the map, due to the Mercator projection.

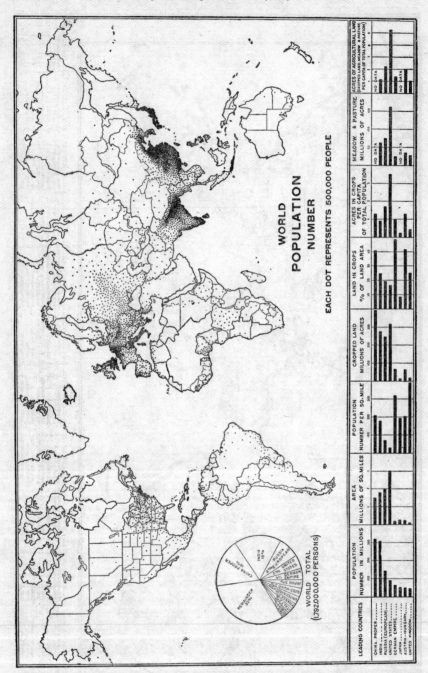

Fig. 57. *Population.*—Seven centers of dense population may be noted on the map—Japan, China, Java, India, Italy, northwestern Europe, and the coast of the United States from Boston to Baltimore. Among the nations of the world the greatest density is in Belgium, where there were at the last census nearly 700 people per square mile. The density in Massachusetts is about 420, in the United Kingdom about 400, in Germany and in Italy over 300, in China and in India about 200, while the average for the United States is 34. Of more significance is the acres of crops per person, which ranges from about ¼ of an acre in Japan, about 1 acre in India and Germany, 1½ acres in China, and 3½ acres in the United States, to 7 acres in Argentina.

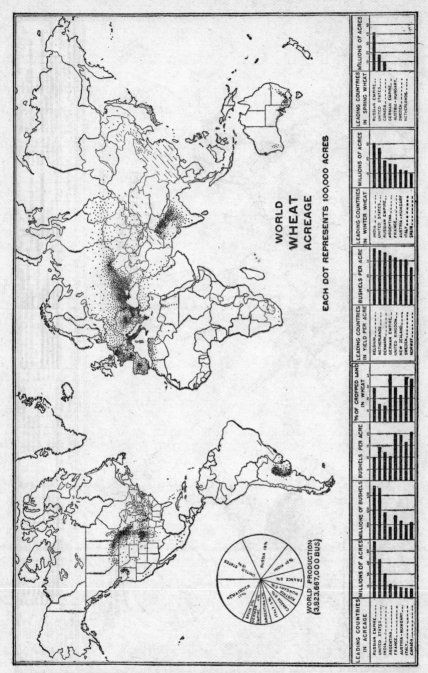

FIG. 58. *Wheat.*—Four widely separated wheat regions of world importance will be noted—southern Europe, central North America, India, and Argentina. Of these, southern Europe is most important, the combined acreage of all European countries being more than twice that of all North America, which ranks next. The surplus crop is grown principally in subhumid, temperate climates, where the population is sparse, the type of agriculture is extensive, the land is yet cheap, and where wheat is free in large measure from the competition of more productive crops. Most of the important wheat regions of the world have an average annual rainfall of less than 30 inches.

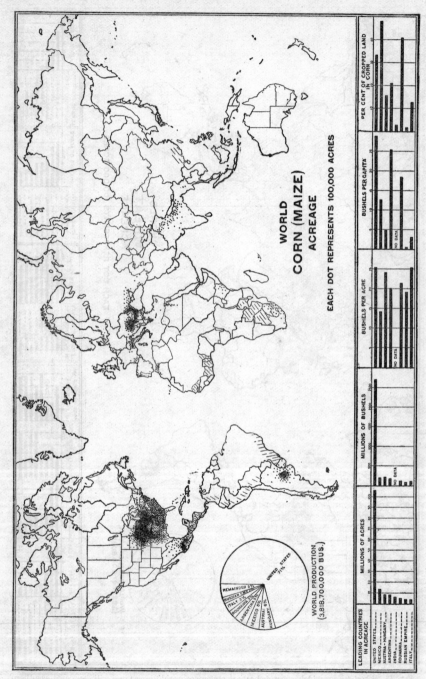

FIG. 59. *Corn.*—The corn (maize) acreage of the United States is nearly double that of the rest of the world. The other important producing regions are southern Europe, particularly Roumania and Hungary, Mexico, Argentina, and India. Relative to the population, corn is a more important crop in the United States than in any other country. Relative to the acreage of other crops, it reaches its highest importance in Mexico, where it is the staple food of the poorer classes. The highest yield per acre is found in Canada, a country of inconspicuous acreage. The corn acreage of all European countries is about equal to that of Illinois, Iowa, and Missouri.

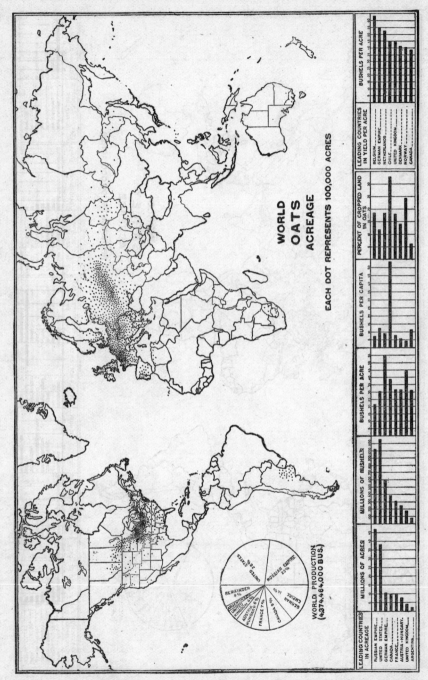

FIG. 60. *Oats.*—Oats are grown mostly in cooler and moister climates than is either wheat or barley. The three principal regions of production are in the northeastern United States and adjoining provinces of Canada, in northwestern Europe, and in Russia. The United States leads in production, Russia has the largest acreage, while the local importance of the crop, as measured by the proportion of cropped land it occupies, and the per capita production, is greatest in Canada. In yield per acre Belgium leads, as it does in wheat, rye, and barley. Most of the world's oat crop is spring sown, but in regions of mild winters it is sown in the autumn.

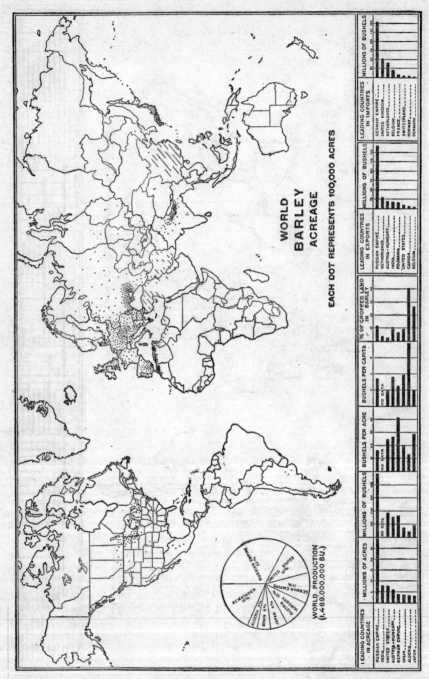

FIG. 61. *Barley.*—Barley is a less important world crop than wheat or oats. The important centers of production are southern Russia, northern Africa, southern Spain, Austria, Germany, eastern England, the north central United States, California, Japan, China, and India. The geographic distribution of barley is more widespread than that of oats and is similar to that of wheat, though extending somewhat farther north in Europe and slightly farther into the arid regions of northern Africa and America. The wide distribution of the crop results from its ability to mature in a short, warm season in high latitudes and in a short, moist season on the borders of the deserts.

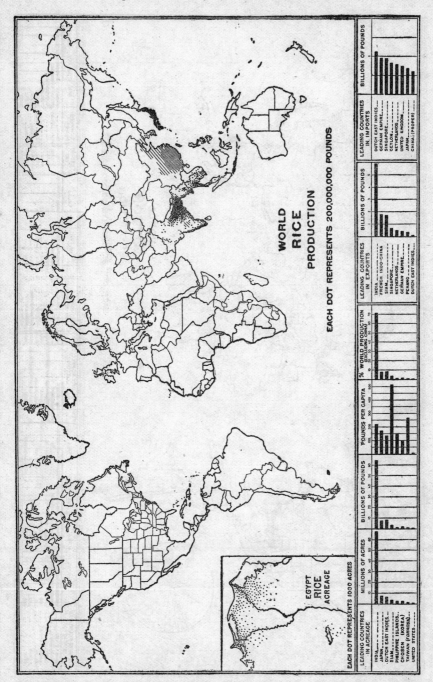

FIG. 62. *Rice.*—Rice is produced in many countries, but it is primarily the food crop of the Orient, 97 per cent of the world's production being grown in southern and eastern Asia and adjoining islands. There are many varieties of rice, most of which require irrigation. In general, rice is grown on level, wet lands, particularly river deltas such as those of the Yangtze, Ganges, Nile, Po, and Mississippi. In some regions the level land is artificially produced by terracing. For this type of agriculture the dense population and cheap labor of the Orient are necessary. The rice production of Africa and the American continents is so small that it barely shows on this map.

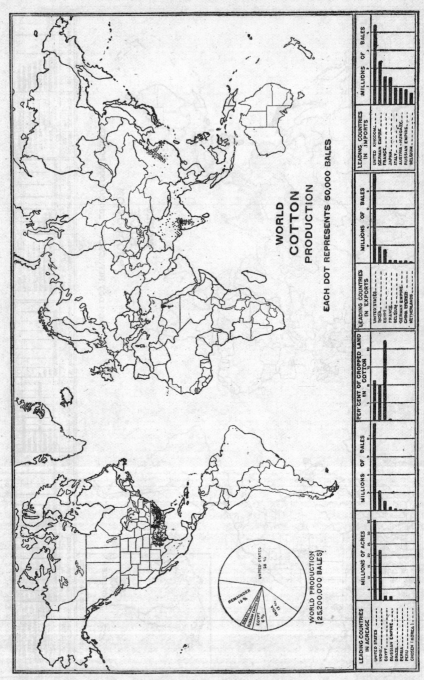

FIG. 63. *Cotton.*—The United States produces about three-fifths of the world's cotton, India and Egypt being the only other countries whose crop is of much commercial importance. China and Russian Turkestan produce considerable cotton, but the crop is consumed almost entirely within the country of production. A little cotton is grown in eastern Brazil, in Peru, in Mexico, and in Asiatic Turkey. The extensive production of cotton is restricted to regions having an average frostless season of 200 days or more, and 95 per cent of the world's crop is grown south of the 37th parallel of latitude.

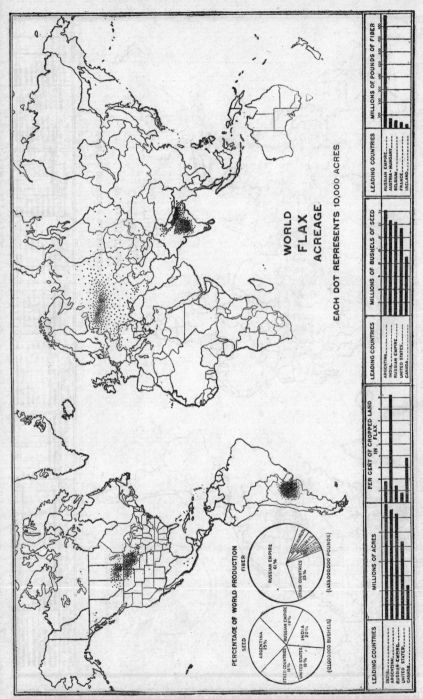

FIG. 64. *Flax.*—Flax is grown both for its fiber and its seed, but it seldom attains high quality in both at the same time. Four centers of flax culture are to be noted—India, Argentina, Russia, and United States. Of these only Russia is important in the commercial production of flax fiber. Smaller centers of fiber production are located in northern France, Belgium, and northern Ireland. In the American continents the scarcity of labor makes it difficult to produce flax fiber at a profit under existing prices. From these western centers comes the bulk of the linseed oil and flaxseed by-products of the world. In India flax is grown for its seed.

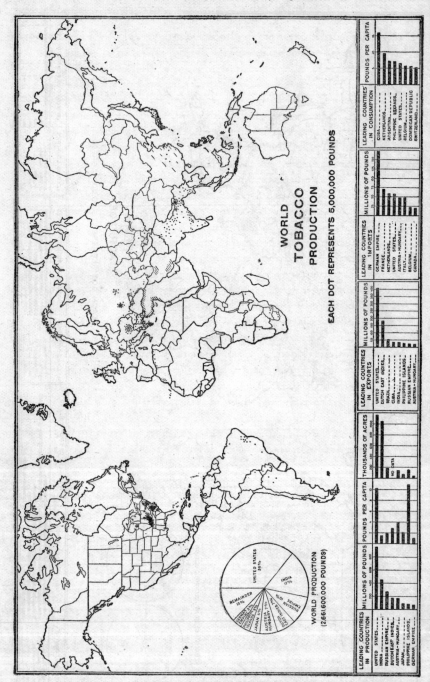

FIG. 65. *Tobacco.*—Although few crops are cultivated under a wider range of climatic conditions, tobacco is produced on a commercial scale in only a few areas situated so favorably as to yield a leaf of superior quality. In the United States, the Connecticut Valley and Florida produce excellent wrapper and binder leaf for cigars, Pennsylvania and Ohio chiefly filler, and Wisconsin binder leaf. Kentucky produces the well-known Burley, Virginia and the Carolinas flue-cured tobacco. Outside the United States, Sumatra and Java produce a famed cigar wrapper type and Turkey the finest cigarette leaf, while Cuba, especially the noted Vuelta Abajo district, leads the world in the excellence of its cigar leaf.

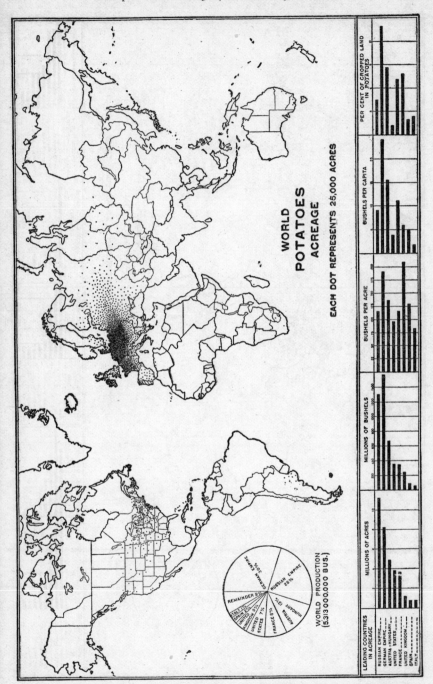

FIG. 66. *Potatoes.*—Although the potato was in origin an American plant, over 90 per cent of the world's potato crop is now grown in Europe, the production of that continent vastly exceeding in volume and almost equaling in value the wheat crop of the world. Germany has an average potato acreage twice as great and a production four times as great as that of the United States. Nearly 14 per cent of the cropped land in Germany is in potatoes as compared with 1.2 per cent in the United States. Russia and Austria-Hungary also each have a greater acreage and yield of potatoes than the United States. The Southern Hemisphere has no important potato-raising centers.

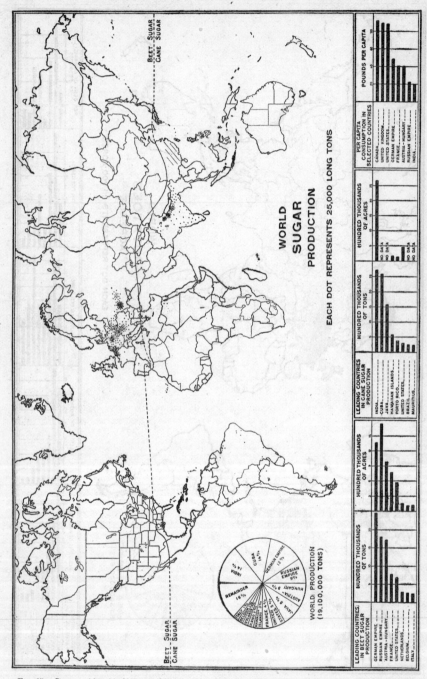

FIG. 67. *Sugar.*—About half the world's sugar comes from the beet and half from cane. The areas occupied by these two sugar crops are, in general, very distinct. The centers of beet-sugar production are southwestern Russia, Austria, central Germany, northern France, southern Belgium, Michigan, Colorado, and California. The centers of cane-sugar production are the Ganges Valley of India, Java, Hawaii, Cuba, Porto Rico, and Louisiana. The course of the dividing line on the map through Asia is merely conventional, since there is no beet-sugar production to the north of the line. The sugar crops of Argentina, South Africa, and Australia are entirely cane.

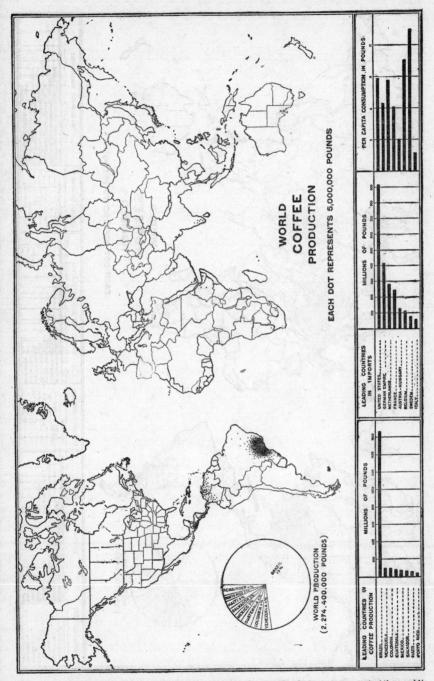

FIG. 68. *Coffee.*—Although the coffee tree is native to the Eastern Hemisphere, 95 per cent of the world's crop is now grown in South and Central America and the West Indies. The outstanding importance of the Brazilian area on the map distracts attention from other important areas, namely, Venezuela, Colombia, Central America, Mexico, and the West India Islands, Abyssinia, southern Arabia, India, and Java. The large production of Brazil (over 70 per cent of the world crop) makes it impossible to restrict properly the dotted area in Brazil and still show less important producing regions.

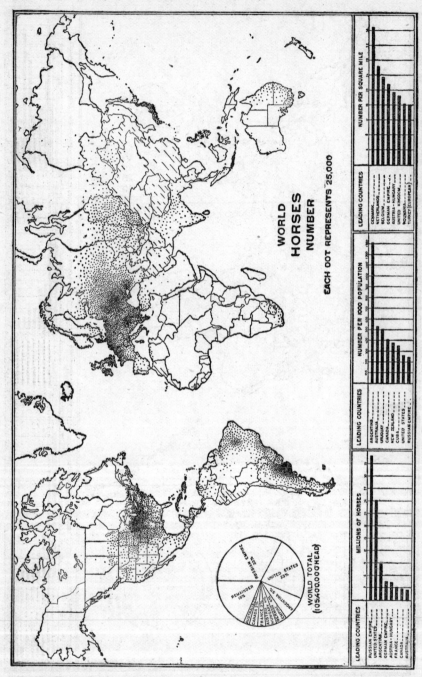

FIG. 69. *Horses.*—In Europe and in countries settled by Europeans, the distribution of horses corresponds in general to the distribution of the human population. Russia and the United States, the largest agricultural nations, lead in actual number of horses. Relative to the population horses are most numerous in those countries which have extensive agricultural and grazing industries and sparse populations. The number of horses relative to area, however, is greatest in northwestern Europe, where agriculture is highly developed and intensive. In the Orient, where human labor is plentiful and cheap, and cattle are used both in agricultural labor and in transportation, horses are few.

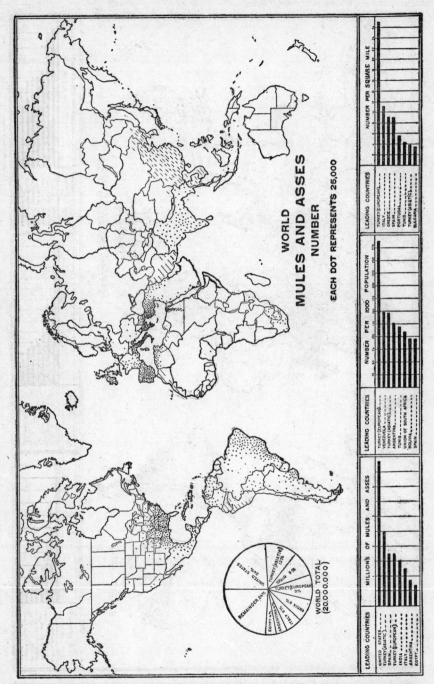

FIG. 70. *Mules.*—The geographic distribution of mules and asses when compared with that of horses shows striking dissimilarity. Owing to their hardihood, their stolidity, their sureness of foot, and ability to subsist on meager forage, the mule and the ass are the beasts of burden of the dry and rough lands or of poor peoples. Their importance is greatest in southern Europe, in the mountains of South America, in Ireland, and among the negro farmers of southern United States. Asses are more common than horses in China, but their number is not known. The number of mules and asses shown in Brazil is an estimate and is not included in the graphs.

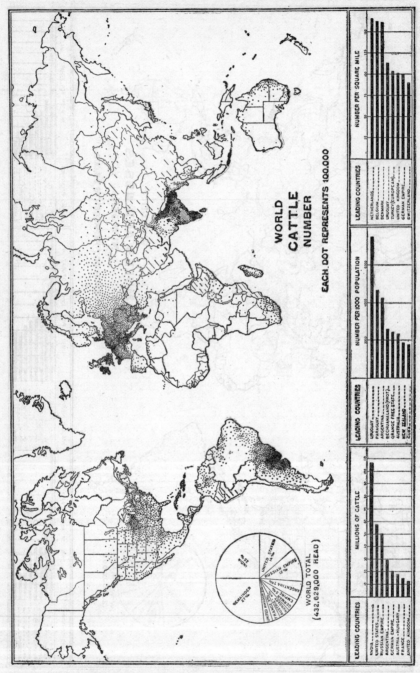

FIG. 71. *Cattle.*—The four important cattle-producing regions of the world are Europe, particularly the northwestern portion, India, the United States, eastern Argentina, Uruguay, and southern Brazil. Of these countries India ranks first in number, although the cattle are used very little for meat or milk but mostly for beasts of burden. It should be observed, however, that owing to the character of the projection the greater density of cattle in India than in Europe is only apparent. Relative to the population the number of cattle is highest in those new countries of the Southern Hemisphere where the population is sparse and the grazing industry extensive.

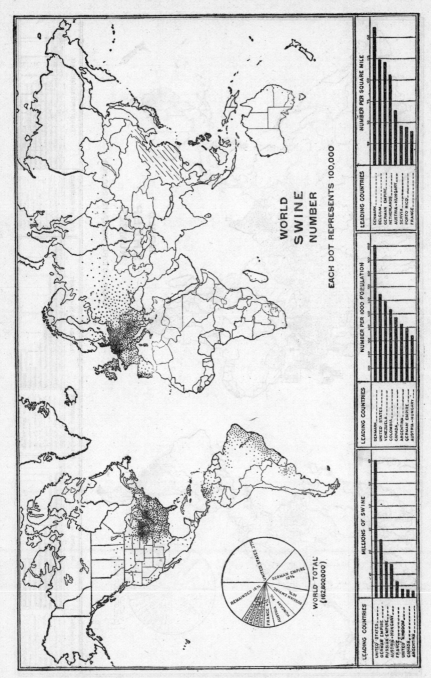

FIG. 72. *Swine.*—The United States has more swine (hogs) than any other three nations of the world, but in number per square mile it falls far behind many European countries. Swine are most numerous in countries having relatively intensive agriculture and an abundance of certain food products, particularly corn, barley, potatoes, and dairy by-products. In the United States the geographic distribution of swine corresponds closely with that of corn, but in Europe it follows rather the distribution of potatoes and dairy cows. Swine are barred from countries under Moslem influence. They are known to be numerous in China, but their number or distribution can not even be approximated.

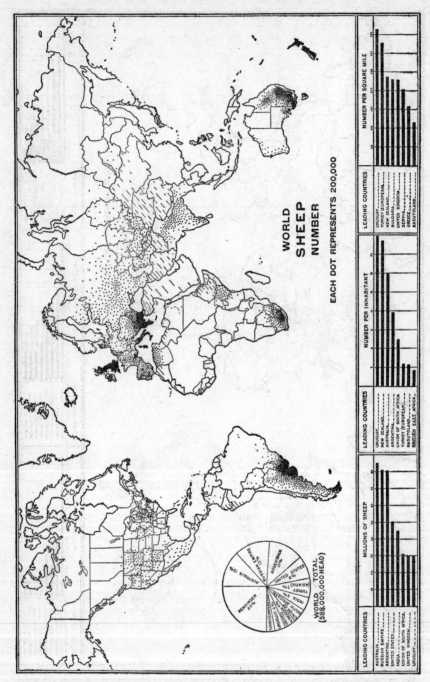

FIG. 73. *Sheep.*—There are six world centers of sheep raising, of which four—the South American countries, South Africa, Australia, and New Zealand—are new lands with sparse population and are all located in the Southern Hemisphere. In Asia Minor and in the Balkan States conditions of topography, climate, and the nomadic habits of the people in the recent past cause sheep to be important farm animals. In Great Britain many factors combine to make sheep raising a prominent industry in spite of apparently unfavorable climatic conditions. The Russian Empire and the United States are, owing to large area, far down the list in number per square mile.

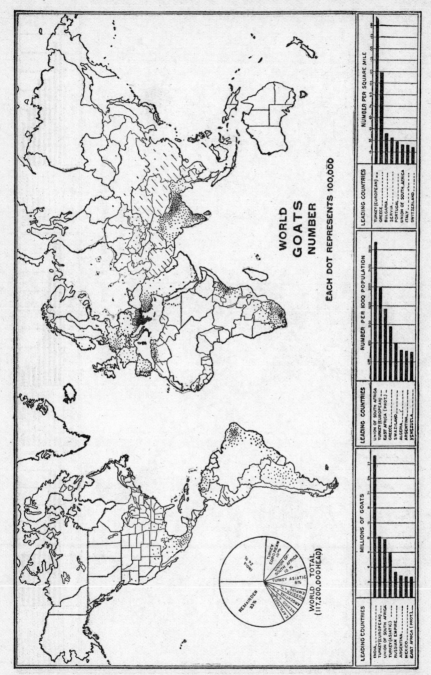

FIG. 74. *Goats.*—Goats are found in practically all the countries of the world, but their distribution is much the densest in the Balkan States of southeastern Europe. The other principal centers are in Asia Minor, northern Africa, India, East and South Africa, Argentina, Brazil, Venezuela, Mexico, the southwestern United States, and the countries of western Europe. The goat is even hardier than the sheep in its ability to subsist on scant forage and in regions of rough topography. It has the added advantage of a relatively large milk production. The goat is therefore found principally in rough or dry lands or among poor peoples.

APPENDIX.

AGRICULTURAL COLLEGES IN THE UNITED STATES.[1]

College instruction in agriculture is given in the colleges and universities receiving the benefits of the acts of Congress of July 2, 1862, August 30, 1890, and March 4, 1907, which are now in operation in all the States and Territories except Alaska. The total number of these institutions is 69, of which 67 maintain courses of instruction in agriculture. In 23 States and Porto Rico the agricultural colleges are departments of the State universities. In 17 States separate institutions having courses in agriculture are maintained for the colored race. All of the agricultural colleges for white persons and several of those for negroes offer four-year courses in agriculture and its related sciences leading to bachelors' degrees, and many provide for graduate study. About 60 of these institutions also provide special, short, or correspondence courses in the different branches of agriculture, including agronomy, horticulture, animal husbandry, poultry raising, cheese making, dairying, sugar making, rural engineering, farm mechanics, and other technical subjects. The agricultural experiment stations, with very few exceptions, are departments of the agricultural colleges. The total number of persons engaged in the work of education and research in the land-grant colleges and the experiment stations in 1916 was 7,066, the number of students (white) in interior courses in the colleges of agriculture and mechanic arts, 69,075; the total number of students (white) in the whole institutions, 119,628;[2] the number of students (white) in the four-year college courses in agriculture, 18,525; the total number of students in the institutions for negroes, 10,510, of whom 2,055 were enrolled in agricultural courses. With a few exceptions, each of these colleges offers free tuition to residents of the State in which it is located. In the excepted cases scholarships are open to promising and energetic students, and in all opportunities are found for some to earn part of their expenses by their own labor. The expenses are from $125 to $300 for the school year.

Agricultural colleges in the United States.

State or Territory.	Name of institution.	Location.	President.
Alabama........	Alabama Polytechnic Institute..........	Auburn.............	C. C. Thach.
	Agricultural School of the Tuskegee Normal and Industrial Institute.	Tuskegee Institute..	R. R. Moton.[3]
	Agricultural and Mechanical College for Negroes.	Normal.............	W. S. Buchanan.
Arizona.........	College of Agriculture of the University of Arizona.	Tucson.............	R. H. Forbes.[4]
Arkansas........	College of Agriculture of the University of Arkansas.	Fayetteville.........	Martin Nelson.[4]
	Branch Normal College...................	Pine Bluff..........	J. G. Ish, jr.
California.......	College of Agriculture of the University of California.	Berkeley............	T. F. Hunt.[4]
Colorado........	The State Agricultural College of Colorado.	Fort Collins.........	C. A. Lory.
Connecticut.....	Connecticut Agricultural College..........	Storrs..............	C. L. Beach.
Delaware........	Delaware College........................	Newark.............	S. C. Mitchell.
	State College for Colored Students........	Dover..............	W. C. Jason.

[1] Including only institutions established under the land-grant act of July 2, 1862.
[2] Not including students in correspondence courses and extension schools.
[3] Principal.
[4] Dean.

555

Agricultural colleges in the United States—Continued.

State or Territory.	Name of institution.	Location.	President.
Florida.........	College of Agriculture of the University of Florida.	Gainesville..........	P. H. Rolfs.[1]
	Florida Agricultural and Mechanical College for Negroes.	Tallahassee..........	N. B. Young.
Georgia.........	Georgia State College of Agriculture.......	Athens.............	A. M. Soule.
	Georgia State Industrial College..........	Savannah...........	R. R. Wright.
Hawaii.........	College of Hawaii......................	Honolulu...........	A. L. Dean.
Idaho...........	College of Agriculture of the University of Idaho.	Moscow.............	E. J. Iddings.[1]
Illinois.........	College of Agriculture of the University of Illinois.	Urbana.............	E. Davenport.[1]
Indiana.........	School of Agriculture of Purdue University.	La Fayette..........	J. H. Skinner.[1]
Iowa............	Iowa State College of Agriculture and Mechanic Arts.	Ames...............	R. A. Pearson.
Kansas.........	Kansas State Agricultural College.........	Manhattan..........	H. J. Waters.
Kentucky.......	The College of Agriculture of the State University.	Lexington	George Roberts.[2]
	The Kentucky Normal and Industrial Institute for Colored Persons.	Frankfort...........	G. P. Russell.
Louisiana.......	Louisiana State University and Agricultural and Mechanical College.	Baton Rouge........	T. D. Boyd.
	Southern University and Agricultural and Mechanical College of the State of Louisiana.	Scotland Heights, Baton Rouge.	J. S. Clark.
Maine..........	College of Agriculture of the University of Maine.	Orono..............	L. S. Merrill.[1]
Maryland.......	Maryland State College of Agriculture....	College Park.......	H. J. Patterson.
	Princess Anne Academy, Eastern Branch of the Maryland State College of Agriculture.	Princess Anne.......	T. H. Kiah.[3]
Massachusetts...	Massachusetts Agricultural College........	Amherst...........	K. L. Butterfield.
	Massachusetts Institute of Technology [4]...	Boston.............	R. C. Maclaurin.
Michigan........	Michigan Agricultural College.............	East Lansing.......	F. S. Kedzie.
Minnesota.......	College of Agriculture of the University of Minnesota.	University Farm, St. Paul.	A. F. Woods.[1]
Mississippi......	Mississippi Agricultural and Mechanical College.	Agricultural College.	W. H. Smith.
	Alcorn Agricultural and Mechanical College.	Alcorn.............	L. J. Rowan.
Missouri........	College of Agriculture of the University of Missouri.	Columbia..........	F. B. Mumford.[1]
	School of Mines and Metallurgy of the University of Missouri.[4]	Rolla..............	—— ——
	Lincoln Institute......................	Jefferson City......	B. F. Allen.
Montana........	Montana State College of Agriculture and Mechanic Arts.	Bozeman...........	Jas. M. Hamilton.
Nebraska.......	College of Agriculture of the University of Nebraska.	Lincoln	E. A. Burnett.[1]
Nevada.........	College of Agriculture of the University of Nevada.	Reno...............	C. S. Knight.[1]
New Hampshire	New Hampshire College of Agriculture and the Mechanic Arts.	Durham...........	C. H. Pettee.[5]
New Jersey.....	Rutgers College (the New Jersey State College for the Benefit of Agriculture and the Mechanic Arts).	New Brunswick.....	W. H. S. Demarest.
New Mexico.....	New Mexico College of Agriculture and Mechanic Arts.	State College........	George E. Ladd.
New York......	New York State College of Agriculture....	Ithaca.............	A. R. Mann.[2]
North Carolina..	The North Carolina College of Agriculture and Mechanic Arts.	West Raleigh.......	W. C. Riddick.
	Negro Agricultural and Technical College.	Greensboro........	J. B. Dudley.
North Dakota ..	North Dakota Agricultural College........	Agricultural College.	E. F. Ladd.
Ohio............	College of Agriculture of Ohio State University.	Columbus..........	Alfred Vivian.[1]
Oklahoma.......	Oklahoma Agricultural and Mechanical College.	Stillwater.........	J. M. Cantwell.
	Agricultural and Normal University......	Langston...........	I. E. Page.
Oregon.........	Oregon State Agricultural College.........	Corvallis..........	W. J. Kerr.
Pennsylvania...	The School of Agriculture of the Pennsylvania State College.	State College........	R. L. Watts.[1]
Porto Rico.....	College of Agriculture and Mechanic Arts of the University of Porto Rico.	Mayaguez	R. S. Garwood.[1]
Rhode Island...	Rhode Island State College..............	Kingston...........	Howard Edwards.
South Carolina..	The Clemson Agricultural College of South Carolina.	Clemson College.....	W. M. Riggs.
	State Agricultural and Mechanical College of South Carolina.	Orangeburg........	R. S. Wilkinson.
South Dakota...	South Dakota State College of Agriculture and Mechanic Arts.	Brookings..........	E. C. Perisho.

[1] Dean.
[2] Acting dean.
[3] Principal.
[4] Does not maintain courses in agriculture.
[5] Acting president.

Agricultural colleges in the United States—Continued.

State or Territory.	Name of institution.	Location.	President.
Tennessee.......	College of Agriculture, University of Tennessee.	Knoxville...........	H. A. Morgan.
	Tennessee Agricultural and Industrial State Normal School.	Nashville...........	W. J. Hale.
Texas.........	Agricultural and Mechanical College of Texas.	College Station......	W. B. Bizzell.
	Prairie View State Normal and Industrial College.	Prairie View........	E. L. Blackshear.[2]
Utah.........	The Agricultural College of Utah.........	Logan..............	E. G. Peterson.
Vermont........	College of Agriculture of the University of Vermont.	Burlington...........	J. L. Hills.[1]
Virginia.........	The Virginia Agricultural and Mechanical College and Polytechnic Institute.	Blacksburg..........	J. D. Eggleston.
	The Hampton Normal and Agricultural Institute.	Hampton...........	H. B. Frissell.[2]
Washington.....	State College of Washington.............	Pullman...........	E. O. Holland.
West Virginia...	College of Agriculture of West Virginia University.	Morgantown........	J. L. Coulter.[1]
	The West Virginia Collegiate Institute....	Institute............	Byrd Prillerman.
Wisconsin.......	College of Agriculture of the University of Wisconsin.	Madison..............	H. L. Russell.[1]
Wyoming.......	College of Agriculture, University of Wyoming.	Laramie.............	H. G. Knight.[1]

[1] Dean.   [2] Principal.

AGRICULTURAL EXPERIMENT STATIONS OF THE UNITED STATES, THEIR LOCATIONS AND DIRECTORS.

Alabama (College), Auburn: J. F. Duggar.
Alabama (Canebrake), Uniontown: L. H. Moore.
Alabama (Tuskegee), Tuskegee Institute: G. W. Carver.
Alaska, Sitka (Rampart, Kodiak, and Fairbanks): C. C. Georgeson.[1]
Arizona, Tucson: R. H. Forbes.
Arkansas, Fayetteville: Martin Nelson.
California, Berkeley: T. F. Hunt.
Colorado, Fort Collins: C. P. Gillette.
Connecticut (State), New Haven⎫
Connecticut (Storrs), Storrs.....⎬ E. H. Jenkins.
Delaware, Newark: Harry Hayward.
Florida, Gainesville: P. H. Rolfs.
Georgia, Experiment: H. P. Stuckey.[2]
Guam:[3] C. W. Edwards.[4]
Hawaii (Federal), Honolulu: J. M. Westgate.[1]
Hawaii (Sugar Planters'), Honolulu: H. P. Agee.
Idaho, Moscow: J. S. Jones.
Illinois, Urbana: E. Davenport.
Indiana, La Fayette: Arthur Goss.
Iowa, Ames: C. F. Curtiss.
Kansas, Manhattan: W. M. Jardine.
Kentucky, Lexington: A. M. Peter.[2]
Louisiana (Sugar), New Orleans⎫
Louisiana (State), Baton Rouge⎪
Louisiana (North), Calhoun.....⎬ W. R. Dodson.
Louisiana (Rice), Crowley.......⎭
Maine, Orono: C. D. Woods.
Maryland, College Park: H. J. Patterson.
Massachusetts, Amherst: W. P. Brooks.
Michigan, East Lansing: R. S. Shaw.
Minnesota, University Farm, St. Paul: A. F. Woods.
Mississippi, Agricultural College: E. R. Lloyd.

Missouri (College), Columbia: F. B. Mumford.
Missouri (Fruit), Mountain Grove: Paul Evans.
Montana, Bozeman: F. B. Linfield.
Nebraska, Lincoln: E. A. Burnett.
Nevada, Reno: S. B. Doten.
New Hampshire, Durham: J. C. Kendall.
New Jersey (College), New Brunswick⎫
New Jersey (State), New Brunswick⎬ J. G. Lipman.
New Mexico, State College: Fabian Garcia.
New York (State), Geneva: W. H. Jordan.
New York (Cornell), Ithaca: A. R. Mann.[2]
North Carolina, Raleigh and West Raleigh: B. W. Kilgore.
North Dakota, Agricultural College: T. P. Cooper.
Ohio, Wooster: C. E. Thorne.
Oklahoma, Stillwater: W. L. Carlyle.
Oregon, Corvallis: A. B. Cordley.
Pennsylvania, State College: R. L. Watts.
Pennsylvania (Institute of Animal Nutrition), State College: H. P. Armsby.
Porto Rico (Federal), Mayaguez: D. W. May.[1]
Porto Rico (Insular), Rio Piedras: W. V. Tower.
Rhode Island, Kingston: B. L. Hartwell.
South Carolina, Clemson College: ——— ———
South Dakota, Brookings: J. W. Wilson.
Tennessee, Knoxville: H. A. Morgan.
Texas, College Station: B. Youngblood.
Utah, Logan: F. S. Harris.
Vermont, Burlington: J. L. Hills.
Virginia (College), Blacksburg: A. W. Drinkard, jr.
Virginia (Truck), Norfolk: T. C. Johnson.
Washington, Pullman: I. D. Cardiff.
West Virginia, Morgantown: J. L. Coulter.
Wisconsin, Madison: H. L. Russell.
Wyoming, Laramie: H. G. Knight.

[1] Agronomist in charge.
[2] Acting director.
[3] Address: Island of Guam, via San Francisco.
[4] Animal husbandman in charge.

STATE OFFICIALS IN CHARGE OF AGRICULTURE.

Alabama: Commissioner of Agriculture, Montgomery.

Alaska: Agronomist in charge of Experiment Stations, Sitka.

Arizona: Director of Experiment Station, Tucson.

Arkansas: Commissioner of Agriculture, Little Rock.

California: Secretary of State Board of Agriculture, Sacramento.

Colorado: Secretary of State Board of Agriculture, Fort Collins.

Connecticut: Secretary of State Board of Agriculture, Hartford.

Delaware: Secretary of State Board of Agriculture, Dover.

Florida: Commissioner of Agriculture, Tallahassee.

Georgia: Commissioner of Agriculture, Atlanta.

Guam: Agronomist in charge of Experiment Station, Guam.

Hawaii: Secretary of Territorial Board of Agriculture, Honolulu.

Idaho: Commissioner of Immigration, Labor, and Statistics, Boise.

Illinois: Secretary of State Board of Agriculture, Springfield.

Indiana: Secretary of State Board of Agriculture, Indianapolis.

Iowa: Secretary of State Board of Agriculture, Des Moines.

Kansas: Secretary of State Board of Agriculture, Topeka.

Kentucky: Commissioner of Agriculture, Frankfort.

Louisiana: Commissioner of Agriculture, Baton Rouge.

Maine: Commissioner of Agriculture, Augusta.

Maryland: State Board of Agriculture, College Park.

Massachusetts: Secretary of State Board of Agriculture, Boston.

Michigan: Secretary of State Board of Agriculture, East Lansing.

Minnesota: Secretary of State Agricultural Society, St. Paul.

Mississippi: Commissioner of Agriculture, Jackson.

Missouri: Secretary of State Board of Agriculture, Columbia.

Montana: Commissioner of Agriculture and Publicity, Helena.

Nebraska: Secretary of State Board of Agriculture, Lincoln.

Nevada: Secretary of State Board of Agriculture, Carson City.

New Hampshire: Secretary of State Board of Agriculture, Concord.

New Jersey: Secretary of State Department of Agriculture, Trenton.

New Mexico: Director of Experiment Station, State College.

New York: Commissioner of Agriculture, Albany.

North Carolina: Commissioner of Agriculture, Raleigh.

North Dakota: Commissioner of Agriculture, Bismarck.

Ohio: Secretary of State Board of Agriculture, Columbus.

Oklahoma: Commissioner of Agriculture, Oklahoma.

Oregon: Secretary of State Board of Agriculture, Salem.

Pennsylvania: Commissioner of Agriculture, Harrisburg.

Philippine Islands: Director of Agriculture, Manila.

Porto Rico: President Board of Commissioners of Agriculture, Rio Piedras.

Rhode Island: Secretary of State Board of Agriculture, Providence.

South Carolina: Commissioner of Agriculture, Columbia.

South Dakota: Secretary of State Board of Agriculture, Huron.

Tennessee: Commissioner of Agriculture, Nashville.

Texas: Commissioner of Agriculture, Austin.

Utah: Director of Experiment Station, Logan.

Vermont: Commissioner of Agriculture, Montpelier.

Virginia: Commissioner of Agriculture, Richmond.

Washington: Commissioner of Agriculture, Olympia.

West Virginia: Commissioner of Agriculture, Charleston.

Wisconsin: Commissioner of Agriculture, Madison.

Wyoming: Director of Experiment Station, Laramie.

STATE OFFICERS IN CHARGE OF COOPERATIVE AGRICULTURAL EXTENSION WORK.

Alabama: J. F. Duggar, Alabama Polytechnic Institute, Auburn.

Arizona: E. P. Taylor, College of Agriculture, University of Arizona, Tucson.

Arkansas: W. C. Lassetter,[1] Little Rock.

California: W. T. Clarke, College of Agriculture, University of California, Berkeley.

Colorado: H. T. French, State Agricultural College of Colorado, Fort Collins.

Connecticut: H. J. Baker, Connecticut Agricultural College, Storrs.

Delaware: H. Hayward, Delaware College, Newark.

Florida: P. H. Rolfs, College of Agriculture, University of Florida, Gainesville.

Georgia: J. Phil Campbell, Georgia State College of Agriculture, Athens.

Idaho: O. D. Center, The Statehouse, Boise.

Illinois: W. F. Handschin, College of Agriculture, University of Illinois, Urbana.

Indiana: G. I. Christie, Purdue University, La Fayette.

Iowa: R. K. Bliss, Iowa State College, Ames.

Kansas: E. C. Johnson, Kansas State Agricultural College, Manhattan.

[1] Acting director.

Kentucky: Fred Mutchler, College of Agriculture, State University, Lexington.

Louisiana: W. R. Dodson, Louisiana State University and Agricultural and Mechanical College, Baton Rouge.

Maine: L. S. Merrill, College of Agriculture, University of Maine, Orono.

Maryland: T. B. Symons, Maryland State College of Agriculture, College Park.

Massachusetts: W. D. Hurd, Massachusetts Agricultural College, Amherst.

Michigan: R. J. Baldwin, Michigan Agricultural College, East Lansing.

Minnesota: A. D. Wilson, College of Agriculture, University of Minnesota, University Farm, St. Paul.

Mississippi: E. R. Lloyd, Mississippi Agricultural and Mechanical College, Agricultural College.

Missouri: A. J. Meyer, College of Agriculture, University of Missouri, Columbia.

Montana: F. S. Cooley, Montana State College of Agriculture and Mechanic Arts, Bozeman.

Nebraska: C. W. Pugsley, College of Agriculture, University of Nebraska, Lincoln.

Nevada: C. A. Norcross, College of Agriculture, University of Nevada, Reno.

New Hampshire: J. C. Kendall, New Hampshire College of Agriculture and the Mechanic Arts, Durham.

New Jersey: Alva Agee, Rutgers College, New Brunswick.

New Mexico: A. C. Cooley, New Mexico College of Agriculture and Mechanic Arts, State College.

New York: A. R. Mann,[1] New York State College of Agriculture, Ithaca.

North Carolina: B. W. Kilgore, North Carolina College of Agriculture and Mechanic Arts, West Raleigh.

North Dakota: T. P. Cooper, North Dakota Agricultural College, Agricultural College.

Ohio: C. S. Wheeler, College of Agriculture, Ohio State University, Columbus.

Oklahoma: J. A. Wilson, Oklahoma Agricultural and Mechanical College, Stillwater.

Oregon: R. D. Hetzel, Oregon State Agricultural College, Corvallis.

Pennsylvania: M. S. McDowell, Pennsylvania State College, State College.

Rhode Island: A. E. Stene, Rhode Island State College, Kingston.

South Carolina: W. W. Long, Clemson Agricultural College of South Carolina, Clemson College.

South Dakota: G. W. Randlett, South Dakota State College, Brookings.

Tennessee: C. A. Keffer, College of Agriculture, University of Tennessee, Knoxville.

Texas: Clarence Ousley, Agricultural and Mechanical College of Texas, College Station.

Utah: J. T. Caine, 3d, Agricultural College of Utah, Logan.

Vermont: Thos. Bradlee, University of Vermont and State Agricultural College, Burlington.

Virginia: J. M. Jones, Virginia Polytechnic Institute, Blacksburg.

Washington: W. S. Thornber, State College of Washington, Pullman.

West Virginia: C. R. Titlow, College of Agriculture, West Virginia University, Morgantown.

Wisconsin: K. L. Hatch, College of Agriculture, University of Wisconsin, Madison.

Wyoming: A. E. Bowman, College of Agriculture, University of Wyoming, Laramie.

[1] Acting director.

STATISTICS OF GRAIN CROPS, 1916.

CORN.

Table 1.—*Corn: Area and production in undermentioned countries, 1914–1916.*

Country.	Area.			Production.		
	1914	1915	1916	1914	1915	1916
NORTH AMERICA.	*Acres.*	*Acres.*	*Acres.*	*Bushels.*	*Bushels.*	*Bushels.*
United States............	103,435,000	106,197,000	105,954,000	2,672,804,000	2,994,793,000	2,583,241,000
Canada:						
Ontario...............	239,000	237,000	160,000	13,410,000	13,860,000	5,976,000
Quebec..............	17,000	16,000	13,000	514,000	508 000	295,000
Other................	(1)	(2)	(2)	(2)	(2)	(2)
Total, Canada......	256,000	253,000	173,000	13,924,000	14,368,000	6,271,000
Mexico.................	4,748,000	(3)	(3)	78,443,000	60,000,000	(3)
Total............				2,765,171,000	3,069,161,000	
SOUTH AMERICA.						
Argentina...............	10,260,000	10,386,000	9,930,000	263,135,000	338,235,000	161,133,060
Chile....................	59,000	(3)	(3)	1,505,000	1,822,000	(3)
Uruguay................	692,000	852,000	588,000	7,142,000	11,382,000	(3)
Total..............	11,011,000			271,782,000	351,439,000	
EUROPE.						
Austria-Hungary:						
Austria.............	[4] 465,000	(3)	(3)	[4] 10,771,000	[4] 10,000,000	(3)
Hungary proper......	6,129,000	6,194,000	(3)	172,308,000	180,550,000	(3)
Croatia-Slavonia.....	(3)	(3)	(3)	25,000,000	25,000,000	(3)
Bosnia-Herzegovina..	(3)	(3)	(3)	7,000,000	7,000,000	(3)
Total, Austria-Hungary.........	(3)	(3)		215,079,000	222,550,000	
Bulgaria...............	1,571,000	(3)	(3)	30,901,000	35,000,000	(3)
France.................	1,128,000	766,000	812,000	22,530,000	14,000,000	(3)
Italy...................	3,680,000	3,886,000	3,830,000	104,966,000	121,824,000	78,736,000
Portugal...............	(3)	(3)	(3)	15,000,000	9,275,000	(3)
Roumania..............	5,104,000	5,207,000	5,056,000	102,552,000	86,412,000	(3)
Russia:						
Russia proper........	3,186,000	3,119,000	3,666,000	61,670,000	44,655,000	71,989,000
Northern Caucasia...	834,000	930,000	(3)	19,241,000	18,743,000	(3)
Total, Russia......	4,020,000	4,049,000		80,911,000	63,398,000	
Serbia..................	(3)	(3)	(3)	20,000,000	12,000,000	(3)
Spain..................	1,137,000	1,152.000	(3)	30,325,000	29,096,000	(3)
Total............				622,264,000	593,555,000	
ASIA.						
India:						
British.............	6,079,000	6,073,000	(3)	82,400,000	82,200,000	(3)
Native States........	(3)	(3)	(3)	(3)	(3)	(3)
Total............				82,400,000	82,200,000	
Japan...................	141,000	144,000	157,000	3,753,000	3 570,000	4,102,000
Philippine Islands.......	1,041,000	1,095,000	(3)	13,336,000	14,753,000	(3)
Total............				99,489,000	100,523,000	
AFRICA.						
Algeria..................	(3)	(3)	(3)	350,000	9,350,000	(3)
Egypt...................	1,763,000	1,907,000	1,850,000	78,253 000	39,803,000	(3)
Union of South Africa....	(3)	(3)	(3)	[5] 30,830,000	30,750,000	31,168,000
Total............				109,433,000	70,903,000	

[1] Less than 500 acres.
[2] No crop.
[3] No official statistics.
[4] Galicia and Bukowina not included.
[5] Census of 1911.

CORN—Continued.

TABLE 1.—*Corn: Area and production in undermentioned countries, 1914–1916*—Contd.

Country.	Area.			Production.		
	1914	1915	1916	1914	1915	1916
AUSTRALASIA.						
Australia:	*Acres.*	*Acres.*	*Acres.*	*Bushels.*	*Bushels.*	*Bushels.*
Queensland..........	157,000	176,000	146,000	4,039,000	4,394,000	2,067,000
New South Wales [1]...	157,000	(2)	(2)	4,593,000	(2)	(2)
Victoria..............	18,000	(2)	(2)	826,000	(2)	(2)
Western Australia....	(3)	(2)	(2)	1,000	(2)	(2)
South Australia [4].....	(3)	(2)	(2)	3,000	(2)	(2)
Total, Australia....	332,000	340,000	....	9,462,000	8,721,000	8,769,000
New Zealand............	6,000	5,000	7,000	312,000	284,000	350,000
Total, Australasia..	338,000	345,000	....	9,774,000	9,005,000	9,119,000
Grand total........	....	....	....	3,877,913,000	4,194,586,000	....

[1] Includes Federal territory.　　　　[3] Less than 500 acres.
[2] No official statistics.　　　　[4] Includes northern territory.

TABLE 2.—*Corn: Total production of countries named in Table 1, 1895–1916.*

Year.	Production.	Year.	Production.	Year.	Production.	Year.	Production.
	Bushels.		*Bushels.*		*Bushels.*		*Bushels.*
1895....	2,834,750,000	1901.....	2,366,883,000	1906.....	3,963,645,000	1911.....	3,481,007,000
1896....	2,964,435,000	1902.....	3,187,311,000	1907.....	3,420,321,000	1912.....	4,371,888,000
1897....	2,587,206,000	1903.....	3,066,506,000	1908.....	3,606,931,000	1913.....	3,587,429,000
1898....	2,682,619,000	1904.....	3,109,252,000	1909.....	3,563,226,000	1914.....	3,877,913,000
1899....	2,724,100,000	1905.....	3,461,181,000	1910.....	4,031,630,000	1915.....	4,194,586,000
1900....	2,792,561,000					1916.....	....

TABLE 3.—*Corn: Acreage, production, value, exports, etc., in the United States, 1849–1916.*

NOTE.—Figures in *italics* are census returns; figures in roman are estimates of the Department of Agriculture. Estimates of acres are obtained by applying estimated percentages of increase or decrease to the published numbers of the preceding year, except that a revised base is used for applying percentage estimates whenever new census data are available.

Year.	Acreage.	Average yield per acre.	Production.	Average farm price per bushel Dec. 1.	Farm value Dec. 1.	Chicago cash price per bushel, contract.[1]				Domestic exports, including corn meal, fiscal year beginning July 1.	Per cent of crop exported.
						December.		Following May.			
						Low.	High.	Low.	High.		
	Acres.	*Bush.*	*Bushels.*	*Cents.*	*Dollars.*	*Cts.*	*Cts.*	*Cts.*	*Cts.*	*Bushels.*	*P.ct.*
1849 . .	....	......	*592,071,000*	......	....	....	....	....	....	7,632,860	1.3
1859 . .	....	......	*838,793,000*	......	....	....	....	....	....	4,248,991	.5
1866. .	34,307,000	25.3	867,946,000	47.4	411,451,000	53	62	64	79	16,026,947	1.8
1867. .	32,520,000	23.6	768,320,000	57.0	437,770,000	61	65	61	71	12,493,522	1.6
1868. .	34,887,000	26.0	906,527,000	46.8	424,057,000	38	58	44	51	8,286,665	.9
1869. .	37,103,000	23.6	874,320,000	59.8	522,551,000	56	67	73	85	2,140,487	.2
1869 . .	....	......	*760,945,000*	......	....	....	....	....	....	....	......
1870. .	38,647,000	28.3	1,094,255,000	49.4	540,520,000	41	59	46	52	10,673,553	1.0
1871. .	34,091,000	29.1	991,898,000	43.4	430,356,000	36	39	38	43	35,727,010	3.6
1872. .	35,527,000	30.8	1,092,719,000	35.3	385,736,000	27	28	34	39	40,154,374	3.7
1873. .	39,197,000	23.8	932,274,000	44.2	411,961,000	40	49	49	59	35,985,834	3.9
1874. .	41,037,000	20.7	850,148,000	58.4	496,271,000	64	76	53	67	30,025,036	3.5
1875. .	44,841,000	29.5	1,321,069,000	36.7	484,675,000	40	47	41	45	50,910,532	3.9
1876. .	49,033,000	26.2	1,283,828,000	34.0	436,109,000	40	43	43	56	72,652,611	5.7
1877. .	50,369,000	26.7	1,342,558,000	34.8	467,635,000	41	49	35	41	87,192,110	6.5
1878. .	51,585,000	26.9	1,388,219,000	31.7	440,281,000	30	32	33	36	87,884,892	6.3
1879. .	53,085,000	29.2	1,547,902,000	37.5	580,486,000	39	43½	32⅜	36½	99,572,329	6.4
1879 . .	*62,369,000*	*28.1*	*1,754,592,000*	......	....	....	....	....	....	....	......

No. 2 to 1908.

CORN—Continued.

TABLE 3.—*Corn: Acreage, production, value, exports, etc., in the United States, 1849–1916—Continued.*

Year.	Acreage.	Average yield per acre.	Production.	Average farm price per bushel Dec. 1.	Farm value Dec. 1.	Chicago cash price per bushel, contract. December. Low.	December. High.	Following May 1. Low.	Following May 1. High.	Domestic exports, including corn meal, fiscal year beginning July 1.	Per cent of crop exported.
	Acres.	*Bush.*	*Bushels.*	*Cents.*	*Dollars.*	*Cts.*	*Cts.*	*Cts.*	*Cts.*	*Bushels.*	*P. ct.*
1880..	62,318,000	27.6	1,717,435,000	39.6	679,714,000	35⅝	42	41⅛	45	93,648,147	5.5
1881..	64,262,000	18.6	1,194,916,000	63.6	759,482,000	58½	63½	69	76⅞	44,340,683	3.7
1882..	65,660,000	24.6	1,617,025,000	48.5	783,867,000	49¼	61	53½	56¼	41,655,653	2.6
1883..	68,302,000	22.7	1,551,067,000	42.4	658,051,000	54¼	63½	52½	57	46,258,606	3.0
1884..	69,684,000	25.8	1,795,528,000	35.7	640,736,000	34½	40½	44½	49	52,876,456	2.9
1885..	73,130,000	26.5	1,936,176,000	32.8	635,675,000	36	42¾	34½	36⅜	64,829,617	3.3
1886..	75,694,000	22.0	1,665,441,000	36.6	610,311,000	35¼	38	36½	39⅜	41,368,584	2.5
1887..	72,393,000	20.1	1,456,161,000	44.4	646,107,000	47	51½	54	60	25,360,869	1.7
1888..	75,673,000	26.3	1,987,790,000	34.1	677,562,000	33½	35½	33½	35⅜	70,841,673	3.6
1889..	78,320,000	27.0	2,112,892,000	28.3	597,919,000	29¼	35	32¾	35	103,418,709	4.9
1889..	*72,088,000*	*29.4*	*2,122,328,000*	.....	.....	.....	.....	.....	.....	.....	.....
1890..	71,971,000	20.7	1,489,970,000	50.6	754,433,000	47½	53	55	69½	32,041,529	2.2
1891..	76,205,000	27.0	2,060,154,000	40.6	836,439,000	39⅜	59	40⅞	¹100	76,602,285	3.7
1892..	70,627,000	23.1	1,628,464,000	39.4	642,147,000	40	42⅛	39¼	44½	47,121,894	2.9
1893..	72,036,000	22.5	1,619,496,000	36.5	591,626,000	34½	36½	36¾	38½	66,489,529	4.1
1894..	62,582,000	19.4	1,212,770,000	45.7	554,719,000	44⅜	47½	47¾	55½	28,585,405	2.4
1895..	82,076,000	26.2	2,151,139,000	25.3	544,986,000	25	26⅛	27⅛	29½	101,100,375	4.7
1896..	81,027,000	28.2	2,283,875,000	21.5	491,007,000	22½	23⅜	23	25½	178,817,417	7.8
1897..	80,095,000	23.8	1,902,968,000	26.3	501,073,000	25	27½	32⅜	37	212,055,543	11.1
1898..	77,722,000	24.8	1,924,185,000	28.7	552,023,000	33½	38	32½	34⅛	177,255,046	9.2
1899..	82,109,000	25.3	2,078,144,000	30.3	629,210,000	30	31½	36	40½	213,123,412	10.3
1899..	*94,914,000*	*28.1*	*2,666,324,000*	.....	.....	.....	.....	.....	.....	.....	.....
1900..	83,321,000	25.3	2,105,103,000	35.7	751,220,000	35¼	40½	42⅜	58½	181,405,473	8.6
1901..	91,350,000	16.7	1,522,520,000	60.5	921,556,000	62½	67½	59⅛	64⅜	28,028,688	1.8
1902..	94,044,000	26.8	2,523,648,000	40.3	1,017,017,000	43⅞	57¼	44	46	76,639,261	3.0
1903..	88,092,000	25.5	2,244,177,000	42.5	952,869,000	41	43¾	47¼	50	58,222,061	2.6
1904..	92,232,000	26.8	2,467,481,000	44.1	1,087,461,000	43½	49	48	64½	90,293,483	3.7
1905..	94,011,000	28.8	2,707,994,000	41.2	1,116,697,000	42	50½	47½	50	119,893,833	4.4
1906..	96,738,000	30.3	2,927,416,000	39.9	1,166,626,000	40	46	49¼	56	86,368,228	3.0
1907..	99,931,000	25.9	2,592,320,000	51.6	1,336,901,000	57½	61½	67¾	82	55,063,860	2.1
1908..	101,788,000	26.2	2,668,651,000	60.6	1,616,145,000	56¼	62¼	72¼	76	37,665,040	1.4
1909..	108,771,000	25.5	2,772,376,000	.....	.....	.....	.....	.....	.....	.....	.....
1909..	*98,383,000*	*25.9*	*2,552,190,000*	57.9	1,477,222,000	62½	66	56	63	38,128,498	1.5
1910²	104,035,000	27.7	2,886,260,000	48.0	1,384,817,000	45½	50	52½	55½	65,614,522	2.3
1911..	105,825,000	23.9	2,531,488,000	61.8	1,565,258,000	68	70	76½	82½	41,797,291	1.7
1912..	107,083,000	29.2	3,124,746,000	48.7	1,520,454,000	47½	54	55½	60	50,780,143	1.6
1913..	105,820,000	23.1	2,446,988,000	69.1	1,692,092,000	64	73½	67	72½	10,725,819	.4
1914..	103,435,000	25.8	2,672,804,000	64.4	1,722,070,000	62¼	68¼	50½	56	50,668,303	1.9
1915..	106,197,000	28.2	2,994,793,000	57.5	1,722,680,000	69½	75	69	78½	39,896,928	1.3
1916..	105,954,000	24.4	2,583,241,000	88.9	2,295,783,000	88	96				

¹ Coincident with "corner."   ² Figures adjusted to census basis.

TABLE 4.—*Corn: Acreage, production, ana total farm value, by States, 1915 and 1916.*

State.	Thousands of acres. 1916	Thousands of acres. 1915	Production (thousands of bushels). 1916	Production (thousands of bushels). 1915	Total value, basis Dec. 1 price (thousands of dollars). 1916	Total value, basis Dec. 1 price (thousands of dollars). 1915
Maine	15	16	645	656	768	558
New Hampshire	19	22	874	990	1,005	752
Vermont	45	47	1,935	2,256	2,128	1,895
Massachusetts	42	48	1,764	2,304	2,117	1,843
Rhode Island	11	12	341	516	471	516
Connecticut	63	65	2,709	3,250	3,251	2,762
New York	540	605	16,200	24,200	17,820	18,876
New Jersey	270	285	10,800	10,830	10,800	8,122
Pennsylvania	1,450	1,520	56,550	58,520	54,854	40,964
Delaware	205	210	6,970	6,615	6,203	4,101
Maryland	700	710	27,300	24,850	24,297	15,158
Virginia	2,140	2,125	60,990	60,562	56,721	42,999
West Virginia	725	800	22,112	25,200	22,333	18,648
North Carolina	2,900	2,900	53,650	60,900	59,015	46,893
South Carolina	2,065	2,130	32,008	35,145	36,169	30,576

CORN—Continued.

TABLE 4.—*Corn: Acreage, production, and total farm value, by States, 1915 and 1916*—Continued.

State.	Thousands of acres.		Production (thousands of bushels).		Total value, basis Dec. 1 price (thousands of dollars).	
	1916	1915	1916	1915	1916	1915
Georgia	4,000	4,330	62,000	64,950	62,000	50,661
Florida	840	800	12,600	12,000	11,340	8,760
Ohio	3,675	3,700	115,762	153,550	104,186	85,988
Indiana	5,137	5,025	174,658	190,950	146,713	97,384
Illinois	10,400	10,400	306,800	374,400	257,712	202,176
Michigan	1,650	1,750	45,375	56,000	43,106	38,080
Wisconsin	1,690	1,775	60,840	40,825	55,973	27,761
Minnesota	2,520	2,800	84,420	64,400	67,536	39,928
Iowa	10,050	9,950	366,825	298,500	293,460	152,235
Missouri	6,775	6,500	132,112	191,750	118,901	109,298
North Dakota	510	700	13,515	9,800	11,353	6,566
South Dakota	2,950	3,250	84,075	94,250	64,738	46,182
Nebraska	7,400	7,100	192,400	213,000	150,072	100,110
Kansas	6,950	5,550	69,500	172,050	62,550	87,746
Kentucky	3,400	3,500	95,200	105,000	82,824	58,800
Tennessee	3,250	3,450	84,500	93.150	79,430	54,027
Alabama	3,735	3,900	46,688	66,300	47,622	45,747
Mississippi	3,400	3,550	47,600	67,450	46.648	43,842
Louisiana	2,134	2,200	44,814	45,100	42,125	28,864
Texas	6,900	7,100	131,100	166,850	136,344	96,773
Oklahoma	3,950	3,800	53,325	112,100	49,592	51,566
Arkansas	2,550	2,700	45,135	62,100	44,232	39,744
Montana	74	70	1,850	1,960	1,720	1,352
Wyoming	25	35	550	875	495	586
Colorado	475	470	7,362	11,280	6,626	6,204
New Mexico	125	105	2,625	2,730	2,966	1,993
Arizona	22	20	770	600	1,078	690
Utah	13	13	429	442	493	354
Nevada	1	1	34	35	42	33
Idaho	21	22	735	770	735	500
Washington	38	39	1,406	1,053	1,406	811
Oregon	40	33	1,340	1,155	1,273	947
California	64	64	2,048	2,624	2,540	2,309
United States	105,954	106,197	2,583,241	2,994,793	2,295,783	1,722,680

TABLE 5.—*Corn: Production and distribution in the United States, 1897–1916.*

[000 omitted.]

Year.	Old stock on farms Nov. 1.	Crop.	Total supplies.	Stock on farms Mar. 1 following.	Shipped out of county where grown.
	Bushels.	*Bushels.*	*Bushels.*	*Bushels.*	*Bushels.*
1897	290,934	1,902,968	2,193,902	782,871	411,617
1898	137,894	1,924,185	2,062,079	800,533	396,005
1899	113,644	2,078,144	2,191,788	773,730	348,098
1900	92,328	2,105,103	2,197,431	776,166	478,417
1901	95,825	1,522,520	1,618,345	441,132	153,213
1902	29,267	2,523,648	2,552,915	1,050,653	557,296
1903	131,210	2,244,177	2,375,387	839,053	419,877
1904	80,246	2,467,481	2,547,727	954,268	551,635
1905	82,285	2,707,994	2,790,279	1,108,364	681,539
1906	119,633	2,927,416	3,047,049	1,297,979	679,544
1907	130,995	2,592,320	2,723,315	962,429	467,675
1908	71,124	2,668,651	2,739,775	1,047,763	568,129
1909	79,779	2,552,190	2,631,969	977,561	635,248
1910	115,696	2,886,260	3,001,956	1,165,378	661,777
1911	123,824	2,531,488	2,655,312	884,069	517,704
1912	64,764	3,124,746	3,189,510	1,289,655	680,796
1913	137,972	2,446,988	2,584,960	866,392	422,091
1914	80,046	2,672,804	2,752,850	910,894	498,285
1915	96,009	2,994,793	3,090,802	1,116,559	560,824
1916	87,908	2,583,241	2,671,149	....	....

CORN—Continued.

TABLE 6.—*Corn: Yield per acre, price per bushel Dec. 1, and value per acre, by States.*

State	Yield per acre (bushels).											Farm price per bushel (cents).						Value per acre (dollars).[1]	
	10-year average, 1907-1916.	1907	1908	1909	1910	1911	1912	1913	1914	1915	1916	10-year average, 1907-1916.	1912	1913	1914	1915	1916	5-year average, 1911-1915.	1916
Me	41.4	37.0	40.5	38.0	46.0	44.0	40.0	38.0	46.0	41.0	43.0	85	75	87	88	85	119	35.60	51.17
N. H	42.0	35.0	39.0	35.1	45.0	25.0	46.0	37.0	46.0	45.0	46.0	81	75	81	82	76	115	34.66	52.90
Vt	41.0	36.0	40.3	37.0	43.0	41.0	40.0	37.0	47.0	46.0	43.0	80	72	81	81	84	110	33.66	47.30
Mass	42.5	36.0	40.4	38.0	45.5	44.0	45.0	40.5	47.0	47.0	42.0	84	77	85	85	80	120	36.63	50.40
R. I	38.6	31.2	42.8	33.2	40.0	45.0	41.5	36.5	42.0	43.0	31.0	97	88	99	98	100	138	39.91	42.78
Conn	44.4	33.0	41.3	41.0	53.2	48.5	50.0	38.5	46.0	50.0	43.0	84	77	85	89	85	110	38.98	51.60
N. Y	35.7	27.0	38.8	36.0	38.3	38.5	38.6	28.5	41.0	40.0	30.0	79	70	81	83	78	110	28.99	33.00
N. J	36.9	31.5	38.0	32.7	36.0	36.8	38.0	39.5	38.5	38.0	40.0	73	68	75	76	75	100	27.87	40.00
Pa	39.1	32.5	39.5	32.0	41.0	44.5	42.5	39.0	42.5	38.5	39.0	71	63	72	73	70	97	28.62	37.83
Del	32.3	27.5	32.0	31.0	31.8	34.0	34.0	31.5	36.0	31.5	34.0	60	51	59	62	62	89	19.70	30.26
Md	35.3	34.2	36.6	31.4	33.5	36.5	36.5	33.0	37.0	35.0	39.0	64	55	65	68	61	89	22.21	34.71
Va	25.1	25.0	26.0	23.2	25.5	24.0	24.0	26.0	20.5	28.5	28.5	74	71	76	81	71	93	18.23	26.50
W. Va	30.0	28.0	31.2	31.4	26.0	25.7	33.8	31.0	31.0	31.5	30.5	77	65	80	83	74	101	23.12	30.80
N. C	18.6	16.5	18.0	16.8	18.6	18.4	18.2	19.5	20.3	21.0	18.5	84	83	88	86	77	110	16.20	20.35
S. C	17.0	15.1	14.1	16.7	18.5	18.2	17.9	19.5	18.5	16.5	15.5	91	85	97	92	87	113	16.42	17.52
Ga	14.4	13.0	12.5	13.9	14.5	16.0	13.8	15.5	14.0	15.0	15.5	84	85	91	85	78	100	12.54	15.50
Fla	13.6	11.3	10.5	12.6	13.0	14.6	13.0	15.0	16.0	15.0	15.0	81	79	82	80	73	90	11.60	13.50
Ohio	38.0	34.6	38.5	39.5	36.5	38.6	42.8	37.5	39.1	41.5	31.5	59	45	63	61	56	90	22.47	28.35
Ind	36.3	36.0	30.3	40.0	39.3	36.0	40.3	36.0	33.0	38.0	34.0	54	42	60	58	51	84	19.30	28.56
Ill	33.7	36.0	31.6	35.9	39.1	33.0	40.0	27.0	29.0	36.0	29.5	55	41	63	61	54	84	17.74	24.78
Mich	32.6	30.1	31.8	35.4	32.4	33.0	34.0	33.5	36.0	32.0	27.5	65	57	67	67	68	95	21.83	26.12
Wis	34.3	32.0	33.7	33.0	32.5	36.3	35.7	40.5	40.5	23.0	36.0	62	51	60	65	68	92	21.25	33.12
Minn	32.3	27.0	29.0	34.8	32.7	33.7	34.5	40.0	35.0	23.0	33.5	54	37	53	52	62	80	16.86	26.80
Iowa	34.2	29.5	31.7	31.5	36.3	31.0	43.0	34.0	38.0	30.0	36.5	51	35	60	55	51	80	17.62	29.20
Mo	26.4	31.0	27.0	26.4	33.0	26.0	32.0	17.5	22.0	29.5	19.5	60	46	74	68	57	90	15.01	17.55
N. Dak	23.8	20.0	23.8	31.0	14.0	25.0	26.7	28.8	28.0	14.0	26.5	60	43	52	58	67	84	13.42	22.26
S. Dak	27.4	25.5	29.7	31.7	25.0	22.0	30.6	25.5	26.0	29.0	28.5	51	37	56	50	49	77	12.89	21.94
Nebr	24.2	24.0	27.0	24.8	25.8	21.0	24.0	15.0	24.5	30.0	26.0	51	37	65	53	47	78	11.45	20.28
Kans	18.3	22.1	22.0	19.9	19.0	14.5	23.0	3.2	18.5	31.0	10.0	58	40	78	63	51	90	9.66	9.00
Ky	27.1	28.2	25.2	29.0	29.0	26.0	30.4	20.5	25.0	30.0	28.0	63	55	76	64	56	87	16.30	24.36
Tenn	25.0	26.0	24.8	22.0	25.9	26.8	26.5	20.5	24.0	27.0	26.0	67	61	77	68	58	94	16.05	24.44
Ala	16.1	15.5	14.7	13.5	18.0	18.0	17.2	17.3	17.0	17.0	12.5	81	79	89	80	69	102	13.67	12.75
Miss	17.8	17.0	17.3	14.5	20.5	19.0	18.3	20.0	18.5	19.0	14.0	76	71	77	73	65	98	13.58	13.72
La	20.3	17.5	19.8	23.0	23.6	18.5	18.0	22.0	19.3	20.5	21.0	71	68	77	75	64	94	13.95	19.74
Tex	19.9	21.0	25.7	15.0	20.6	9.5	21.0	24.0	19.5	23.5	19.0	72	64	82	74	58	104	13.76	19.76
Okla	17.4	24.4	24.8	17.0	16.0	6.5	18.7	11.0	12.5	29.5	13.5	59	41	72	64	46	93	8.34	12.56
Ark	19.8	17.2	20.2	18.0	24.0	20.8	20.4	19.7	17.5	23.0	17.7	72	67	78	80	64	98	14.44	17.35
Mont	26.8	22.5	23.4	35.0	23.0	26.5	25.5	31.5	28.0	28.0	25.0	80	70	77	76	69	93	20.78	23.25
Wyo	23.0	25.0	28.0	21.0	10.0	15.0	20.8	15.0	23.0	24.0	25.0	74	64	80	70	67	90	16.71	19.80
Colo	20.0	23.5	20.2	24.2	19.9	14.0	20.8	15.0	23.0	24.0	15.5	67	50	73	60	55	90	11.85	13.95
N. Mex	25.1	29.0	27.0	31.3	23.0	24.7	22.4	18.5	28.0	26.0	21.0	83	75	75	80	73	113	18.56	23.73
Ariz	32.6	37.5	33.2	32.1	32.5	33.0	33.0	28.0	32.0	30.0	35.0	109	100	110	120	115	140	33.74	49.00
Utah	31.8	25.5	29.4	31.4	30.3	35.0	30.0	34.0	35.0	34.0	33.0	81	75	70	75	80	115	25.62	37.95
Nev	32.8				30.0	30.5	30.0	34.0	36.0	35.0	34.0	103	98	118	110	93	125	33.82	42.50
Idaho	31.7	30.0	29.0	30.6	32.0	30.0	32.8	32.0	31.0	35.0	35.0	75	70	68	72	65	100	23.06	35.00
Wash	28.3	27.0	25.5	27.8	28.0	28.5	27.3	28.0	27.0	27.0	37.0	79	77	80	73	77	100	21.29	37.00
Oreg	29.8	27.5	27.8	30.7	25.5	28.5	31.5	28.5	30.0	35.0	33.5	80	75	70	82	82	95	23.93	31.82
Cal	35.3	34.0	32.0	34.8	37.5	36.0	37.0	33.0	36.0	41.0	32.0	91	85	88	87	88	124	32.06	39.68
U. S	26.0	25.9	26.2	25.5	27.7	23.9	29.2	23.1	25.8	28.2	24.4	61.0	48.7	69.1	64.4	57.5	88.9	15.57	21.67

[1] Based upon farm price Dec. 1.

CORN—Continued.

TABLE 7.—*Corn: Wholesale price per bushel, 1912–1916.*

Date.	New York.		Baltimore.		Cincinnati.		Chicago.		Detroit.		St. Louis.		San Francisco.	
	No. 2 yellow.		Mixed.		No. 2 mixed.		Contract.		No. 3.		No. 2.		White (per 100 lbs.).	
	Low.	High.	Low.	High.	Low.	High.	Low.	High.	Low.	High.	Low.	High.	Low.	High.
1912.	*Cts.*	*Cts.*	*Cts.*	*Cts.*	*Cts.*	*Cts.*	*Cts.*	*Cts.*	*Cts.*	*Cts.*	*Cts.*	*Cts.*	*Cts.*	*Cts.*
Jan.-June	67½	87½	67	85	64	87	63½	82½	62½	83½	63	85	155	197½
July-Dec	54½	84	52	87	47	84	47½	83	48	81½	45	80½	150	195
1913.														
Jan.-June	57¼	71¼	52⅜	65½	48	65	46½	63	48	62	45	64	145	155
July-Dec	67	87¼	64½	68	63½	81	60	78¼	60¾	78½	61¾	82	151½	187
1914.														
Jan.-June	60	82½	66¼	77	64	75	60	73½	62	74	63	73½	161	178
July-Dec	71¾	93¾	67½	89	63½	88½	62¼	86	63½	88	62⅜	87	167½	193
1915.														
January	77½	86⅛	74	81¾	70	78½	68½	77	70	77½	69	77	182½	185
February	80¼	88⅝	72	83½	70	81	68½	78	70½	79	68½	78	182½	190
March	82	89½	73	77½	71	77	70	75	70½	75	70	75½	185	187½
April	83½	90¼	75⅛	84¾	75	81	72	79	74	80	74½	78½	178	187½
May	82¼	88¾	76½	83½	77	80	50½	56	75½	80	73½	77⅛	176	180
June	78¼	86¾	76½	81	74½	79½	71¼	76½	73	78½	71½	76	172	177
Jan.-June	77½	90¼	72	84¾	70	81	50½	79	70	80	68½	78½	172	190
July	86½	92¾	79	87	77	84	75¾	82	78	83½	73⅞	80⅝	173	177
August	86	92¾	86	86	77½	82	75¼	82¼	82	84	72½	81	174	178
September	75	88⅝	......	......	67	79	65¼	78	71	81½	68½	78	174	175
October	72⅜	78¼	......	......	63½	69	59¾	67	65	69	58¾	66	146	167
November	74½	80½	67½	71	62	69	61½	68½	64	69½	60	65	153	164
December	80	85½	70⅝	78	64½	69½	69½	75	66½	75	65	75½	162	180
July-Dec	72⅜	92¾	67½	87	62	84	59¾	82¼	64	84	58¾	81	146	180
1916.														
January	85½	89½	70	82½	70½	77½	72½	79½	72½	78	70	77	170	175
February	83½	88½	74¾	80½	71	78	71½	79½	72	77½	71½	77	172	172
March	80½	86¼	75¾	81	72½	76½	70	77	72	76	71	74½	170	172
April	85¼	91¾	80¼	82¼	76	79	74¾	79	76	79	73½	76	170	180
May	79⅜	92¾	73⅝	82⅜	75½	78	69	78½	71½	79	69½	76½	176	180
June	79⅛	88⅞	75⅝	84⅞	72½	78½	69¼	78¼	72½	79½	70	76½	170	177
Jan.-June	79⅛	92¾	70	84⅞	70½	79	69	79½	71½	79½	69½	77	170	180
July	88⅜	93¾	85¼	90	79	83½	78	84¼	79½	85	75½	82½	175	190
August	92⅞	100⅛	88¼	94	83	89	82	88½	84½	91	80½	87½	188	205
September	96¼	101¾	92	95	86½	88½	84¾	90	88	92	83½	89	196	205
October	98¾	120	92	107	88	103	88¼	111	91	115	86½	111	196	215
November	104	119⅓	105	105	97	107	90	110	98	117	91	107½	215	245
December	102¼	108⅜	95	104½	85	91	88	96	94½	102	88½	94½	205	245
July—Dec.	88⅜	120	85¼	107	79	107	78	111	79½	117	75½	111	175	245

TABLE 8.—*Corn: Condition of crop, United States, on first of months named, 1896–1916.*

Year.	July.	Aug.	Sept.	Oct.	Year.	July.	Aug.	Sept.	Oct.	Year.	July.	Aug.	Sept.	Oct.
	P. ct.	*P. ct.*	*P. ct.*	*P. ct.*		*P. ct.*	*P. ct.*	*P. ct.*	*P. ct.*		*P. ct.*	*P. ct.*	*P. ct.*	*P. ct.*
1896	92.4	96.0	91.0	90.5	1903	79.4	78.7	80.1	80.8	1910	85.4	79.3	78.2	80.3
1897	82.9	84.2	79.3	77.1	1904	86.4	87.3	84.6	83.9	1911	80.1	69.6	70.3	70.4
1898	90.5	87.0	84.1	82.0	1905	87.3	89.0	89.5	89.2	1912	81.5	80.0	82.1	82.2
1899	86.5	89.9	85.2	82.7	1906	87.5	88.0	90.2	90.1	1913	86.9	75.8	65.1	65.3
1900	89.5	87.5	80.6	78.2	1907	80.2	82.8	80.2	78.0	1914	85.8	74.8	71.7	72.9
1901	81.3	54.0	51.7	52.1	1908	82.8	82.5	79.4	77.8	1915	81.2	79.5	78.8	79.7
1902	87.5	86.5	84.3	79.6	1909	89.3	84.4	74.6	73.8	1916	82.0	75.3	71.3	71.5

CORN—Continued.

TABLE 9.—*Corn: Farm price per bushel on first of each month, by geographical divisions, 1915 and 1916.*

Month.	United States.		North Atlantic States.		South Atlantic States.		N. Central States east of Miss. R.		N. Central States west of Miss. R.		South Central States.		Far Western States.	
	1916	1915	1916	1915	1916	1915	1916	1915	1916	1915	1916	1915	1916	1915
	Cts.	*Cts.*	*Cts.*	*Cts.*	*Cts.*	*Cts.*	*Cts.*	*Cts.*	*Cts.*	*Cts.*	*Cts.*	*Cts.*	*Cts.*	*Cts.*
January.......	62.1	66.2	76.5	76.6	77.3	81.5	62.2	63.3	56.2	58.5	62.1	75.1	70.2	74.1
February.....	66.7	72.8	79.5	81.2	81.8	85.8	66.6	69.9	61.1	67.1	66.9	79.4	71.5	78.1
March........	68.2	75.1	81.6	84.6	85.4	92.4	66.4	70.1	60.2	67.0	72.4	86.9	78.7	82.2
April.........	70.3	75.1	82.6	84.5	87.3	92.2	66.9	70.3	63.1	66.1	75.8	88.2	75.9	87.1
May..........	72.3	77.7	83.0	85.3	89.1	94.3	70.2	73.7	65.3	68.8	76.2	90.0	79.3	82.9
June..........	74.1	77.9	84.1	85.8	92.1	95.8	70.6	73.5	66.6	68.6	79.9	91.0	77.0	82.3
July.........	75.4	77.7	84.3	84.8	92.7	96.4	71.6	73.2	68.7	68.8	81.0	90.3	79.3	77.9
August........	79.4	78.9	87.4	86.9	95.0	96.8	76.8	76.0	73.3	71.5	83.6	86.5	85.4	80.5
September....	83.6	77.3	93.8	87.6	98.4	95.5	81.7	75.3	77.9	70.9	86.4	81.8	88.7	75.1
October.......	82.3	70.5	94.3	84.5	96.9	89.2	81.5	70.3	76.9	64.9	83.4	69.6	87.2	71.2
November....	85.0	61.9	97.2	76.5	95.0	79.4	82.8	61.7	81.6	57.8	86.6	58.9	88.7	65.7
December.....	88.9	57.5	101.5	73.7	100.2	75.0	86.4	55.3	81.5	51.9	96.4	58.4	101.2	67.1
Average...	74.3	71.5	86.9	82.4	91.1	89.1	71.1	69.1	67.4	64.3	80.0	74.9	80.9	76.9

TABLE 10.—*Corn (including meal): International trade, calendar years 1913–1915.*

[The item *maicena* or *maizena* is included as "Corn and corn meal."]

GENERAL NOTE.—Substantially the international trade of the world. It should not be expected that the world export and import totals for any year will agree. Among sources of disagreement are these: (1) Different periods of time covered in the "year" of the various countries; (2) imports received in year subsequent to year of export; (3) want of uniformity in classification of goods among countries; (4) different practices and varying degrees of failure in recording countries of origin and ultimate destination; (5) different practices of recording reexported goods; (6) opposite methods of treating free ports; (7) clerical errors, which, it may be assumed, are not infrequent.

The exports given are domestic exports, and the imports given are imports for consumption as far as it is feasible and consistent so to express the facts. While there are some inevitable omissions, on the other hand there are some duplications because of reshipments that do not appear as such in official reports. For the United Kingdom, import figures refer to imports for consumption, when available, otherwise total imports, less exports, of "foreign and colonial merchandise." Figures for the United States include Alaska, Porto Rico, and Hawaii.

EXPORTS.

[000 omitted.]

Country.	1913	1914 (prelim.).	1915 (prelim.).	Country.	1913	1914 (prelim.).	1915 (prelim.).
	Bushels.	*Bushels.*	*Bushels.*		*Bushels.*	*Bushels.*	*Bushels.*
Argentina..........	189,240	139,461	170,490	Russia	22,900	11,275	26
Austria-Hungary...	30	....	....	United States......	46,923	17,022	50,337
Belgium...........	6,134	....	....	Uruguay...........	3	3	....
British South Africa	741	4,778	6,860	Other countries....	7,225	6,713	....
Bulgaria	11,362	....	....				
Netherlands........	11,846	4,345	804	Total........	334,767	225,401	....
Roumania	38,363	41,804	....				

IMPORTS.

Country.	1913	1914 (prelim.).	1915 (prelim.).	Country.	1913	1914 (prelim.).	1915 (prelim.).
Austria-Hungary ..	25,844	....	....	Netherlands........	39,467	25,674	43,308
Belgium...........	25,036	....	....	Norway...........	1,149	1,672	1,769
British South Africa	818	6	25	Portugal...........	4,114	3,105	....
Canada............	9,041	8,347	10,980	Russia	662	576	....
Cuba..............	3,198	2,890	3,242	Spain..............	22,403	7,960	8,134
Denmark..........	15,938	10,346	26,019	Sweden............	2,395	2,195	8,292
Egypt.............	1,184	687	2	Switzerland........	4,785	3,068	4,461
France............	23,279	16,331	17,582	United Kingdom...	97,721	75,499	92,226
Germany..........	36,165	....	....	Other countries....	9,422	24,368	....
Italy..............	13,847	331	786				
Mexico............	1,347	....	....	Total........	337,815	183,055	....

WHEAT.

TABLE 11.—*Wheat: Area and production of undermentioned countries, 1914–1916.*

Country.	Area.			Production.		
	1914	1915	1916	1914	1915	1916
NORTH AMERICA.	*Acres.*	*Acres.*	*Acres.*	*Bushels.*	*Bushels.*	*Bushels.*
United States...........	53,541,000	60,469,000	52,785,000	891,017,000	1,025,801,000	639,886,000
Canada:						
New Brunswick.....	13,000	14,000	14,000	234,000	267,000	(1)
Ontario.............	834,000	1,093,000	872,000	17,658,000	30,252,000	(1)
Manitoba...........	2,616,000	3,343,000	2,342,000	38,605,000	96,425,000	(1)
Saskatchewan.......	5,348,000	6,838,000	5,252,000	73,494,000	195,168,000	(1)
Alberta.............	1,371,000	1,564,000	1,474,000	28,859,000	51,355,000	(1)
Other..............	111,000	134,000	131,000	2,430,000	2,837,000	(1)
Total Canada.....	10,293,000	12,986,000	10,085,000	161,280,000	376,304,000	220,367,000
Mexico.................	1,478,000	(1)	(1)	4,389,000	4,000,000	(1)
Total...........	....	....	....	1,056,686,000	1,406,105,000	....
SOUTH AMERICA.						
Argentina...............	16,243,000	15,471,000	16,420,000	113,904,000	168,468,000	172,620,000
Chile	1,018,000	1,278,000	(1)	16,403,000	19,002,000	21,145,000
Uruguay................	911,000	783,000	950,000	5,887,000	3,596,000	8,167,000
Total.............	18,172,000	17,532,000	....	136,194,000	191,066,000	201,932,000
EUROPE.						
Austria-Hungary:						
Austria.............	[2] 1,660,000	(1)	(1)	[2] 38,024,000	[2] 38,000,000	(1)
Hungary proper.....	8,016,000	8,288,000	(1)	105,237,000	152,934,000	(1)
Croatia-Slavonia....	741,000	(1)	(1)	7,716,000	15,000,000	(1)
Bosnia-Herzegovina.	(1)	(1)	(1)	2,500,000	3,000,000	(1)
Total Austria-Hungary........	....	....	....	153,477,000	208,934,000	....
Belgium.................	400,000	(1)	(1)	13,973,000	8,000,000	(1)
Bulgaria................	2,638,000	(1)	(1)	25,979,000	46,212,000	38,241,000
Denmark................	[3] 134,000	164,000	152,000	5,785,000	7,979,000	6,040,000
Finland.................	(1)	(1)	(1)	130,000	130,000	(1)
France.................	14,975,000	13,564,000	12,855,000	282,689,000	225,132,000	213,214,000
Germany................	4,932,000	4,950,000	(1)	145,944,000	141,676,000	(1)
Greece.................	(1)	(1)	(1)	7,000,000	6,000,000	(1)
Italy...................	11,783,000	12,502,000	11,678,000	169,581,000	170,541,000	176,529,000
Montenegro.............	(1)	(1)	(1)	200,000	200,000	(1)
Netherlands............	148,000	160,000	136,000	5,779,000	6,143,000	4,034,000
Norway.................	(1)	(1)	14,000	269,000	269,000	305,000
Portugal...............	(1)	(1)	(1)	10,000,000	6,571,000	7,343,000
Roumania..............	5,218,000	4,705,000	4,843,000	49,270,000	89,241,000	78,520,000
Russia:						
Russia proper.......	50,986,000	49,052,000	48,525,000	463,748,000	525,450,000	595,419,000
Poland [4]..........	343,000	(1)	(1)	5,883,000	(1)	(1)
Northern Caucasia..	10,597,000	10,031,000	(1)	109,636,000	[5] 127,756,000	(1)
Total Russia, European..........	61,926,000	59,083,000	....	579,267,000	653,206,000	....
Serbia.................	(1)	(1)	(1)	9,000,000	10,000,000	(1)
Spain..................	9,681,000	10,037,000	10,070,000	116,089,000	139,298,000	152,329,000
Sweden................	269,000	(1)	(1)	8,472,000	9,170,000	(1)
Switzerland............	113,000	111,000	124,000	3,277,000	3,957,000	3,821,000
United Kingdom:						
England.............	1,770,000	2,122,000	1,862,000	59,217,000	68,437,000	55,825,000
Wales...............	37,000	49,000	50,000	1,082,000	1,415,000	1,383,000
Scotland............	61,000	77,000	63,000	2,642,000	3,053,000	2,336,000
Ireland..............	37,000	87,000	76,000	1,415,000	3,238,000	2,827,000
Total United Kingdom........	1,905,000	2,335,000	2,051,000	64,356,000	76,143,000	62,371,000
Total.............	....	....	....	1,650,537,000	1,808,802,000	....

[1] No official statistics.
[2] Galicia and Bukowina not included in 1914 and 1915.
[3] Census of 1910.
[4] Winter wheat in 1914 in 5 governments only
[5] Includes 1 government of Transcaucasia.

WHEAT—Continued.

TABLE 11.—*Wheat: Area and production in undermentioned countries, 1914–1916*—Con.

Country.	Area.			Production.		
	1914	1915	1916	1914	1915	1916
ASIA. India: British [1] .... Native States.......	*Acres.* 28,475,000 ([2])	*Acres.* 32,475,000 ([2])	*Acres.* 30,143,000 ([2])	*Bushels.* 312,032,000 ([2])	*Bushels.* 376,731,000 ([2])	*Bushels.* 318,005,000 ([2])
Total............	....	....	....	312,032,000	376,731,000	318,005,000
Cyprus.................	([2])	([2])	([2])	2,500,000	2,000,000	([2])
Japanese Empire: Japan................ Formosa............	1,174,000 16,000	1,250,000 ([2])	1,280,000 ([2])	22,975,000 195,000	25,798,000 200,000	24,444,000 ([2])
Total..............	1,190,000	....	....	23,170,000	25,998,000	....
Persia..................	([2])	([2])	([2])	14,000,000	16,000,000	([2])
Russia: Central Asia (4 governments of)...... Siberia (4 governments of).......... Transcaucasia (1 government)......	5,501,000 7,931,000 11,000	6,518,000 7,727,000 ([3])	([2]) ([2]) ([2])	68,448,000 104,038,000 82,000	58,025,000 50,321,000 ([3])	([2]) ([2]) ([2])
Total..............	13,443,000	14,245,000	....	172,568,000	108,346,000	....
Turkey (Asia Minor only)..............	([2])	([2])	([2])	35,000,000	35,000,000	([2])
Total.............	....	....	....	559,270,000	564,075,000	....
AFRICA. Algeria................ Egypt................. Tunis................. Union of South Africa...	3,368,000 1,301,000 1,010,000 ([2])	3,209,000 1,582,000 1,112,000 ([2])	([2]) 1,447,000 1,482,000 557,000	30,000,000 32,831,000 2,205,000 [4] 6,034,000	34,654,000 39,148,000 11,023,000 7,076,000	([2]) 36,543,000 7,165,000 4,857,000
Total.............	....	....	....	71,070,000	91,901,000	....
AUSTRALASIA. Australia: Queensland......... New South Wales... Victoria............ South Australia..... Western Australia.. Tasmania...........	132,000 3,205,000 2,566,000 2,268,000 1,097,000 18,000	127,000 2,758,000 2,864,000 2,502,000 1,376,000 24,000	94,000 4,235,000 3,680,000 2,739,000 1,733,000 49,000	1,825,000 39,219,000 33,974,000 17,470,000 13,751,000 361,000	1,635,000 13,235,000 4,065,000 3,639,000 2,707,000 396,000	427,000 69,445,000 60,366,000 35,210,000 18,811,000 1,025,000
Total Australia... New Zealand...........	9,286,000 167,000	9,651,000 230,000	12,530,000 328,000	106,600,000 5,559,000	25,677,000 6,854,000	185,284,000 7,294,000
Total Australasia..	9,453,000	9,881,000	12,858,000	112,159,000	32,531,000	192,579,000
Grand total......	....	....	....	3,585,916,000	4,094,480,000	....

[1] Including certain Feudatory States.   [3] Included in Northern Caucasia.
[2] No official statistics.   [4] Yield of 1911 census.

TABLE 12.—*Wheat: Total production of countries named in Table 11, 1891–1916.*

Year.	Production.	Year.	Production.	Year.	Production.	Year.	Production.
	Bushels.		*Bushels.*		*Bushels.*		*Bushels.*
1891....	2,432,322,000	1898.....	2,948,305,000	1905.....	3,327,084,000	1912.....	3,791,951,000
1892....	2,481,805,000	1899.....	2,783,885,000	1906.....	3,434,354,000	1913.....	4,127,437,000
1893....	2,559,174,000	1900.....	2,610,751,000	1907.....	3,133,965,000	1914.....	3,585,916,000
1894....	2,660,557,000	1901.....	2,955,975,000	1908.....	3,182,105,000	1915.....	4,094,480,000
1895....	2,593,312,000	1902.....	3,090,116,000	1909.....	3,581,519,000	1916.....	....
1896....	2,506,320,000	1903.....	3,189,813,000	1910.....	3,575,055,000		
1897....	2,236,268,000	1904.....	3,163,542,000	1911.....	3,551,795,000		

WHEAT—Continued.

TABLE 13.—*Wheat: Average yield per acre in undermentioned countries, 1890–1915.*

Year.	United States.	Russia (European).[1]	Germany.[1]	Austria.[1]	Hungary proper.[1]	France.[2]	United Kingdom.[2]
Average:	*Bushels.*	*Bushels.*	*Bushels.*	*Bushels.*	*Bushels.*	*Bushels.*	*Bushels.*
1890–1899	13.2	8.9	24.5	16.2	....	18.6	31.2
1900–1909	14.1	9.7	28.9	18.0	17.5	20.5	33.1
1906	15.5	7.7	30.3	20.3	22.5	20.2	34.8
1907	14.0	8.0	29.6	18.0	14.9	23.2	35.1
1908	14.0	8.8	29.7	21.0	17.5	19.6	33.4
1909	15.4	12.5	30.5	19.9	14.1	22.0	35.0
1910	13.9	11.2	29.6	19.2	19.8	15.9	31.4
1911	12.5	7.0	30.6	19.6	20.9	19.8	34.0
1912	15.9	10.3	33.6	22.3	19.8	21.0	30.0
1913	15.2	13.5	35.1	19.9	19.6	19.9	32.7
1914	16.6	9.4	29.6	[3] 22.4	13.1	18.9	33.8
1915	17.0	....	28.6	....	....	16.6	32.7
Average (1906–1915)	15.0	....	....	....	....	....	33.3

[1] Bushels of 60 pounds. [2] Winchester bushels. [3] Galicia and Bukowina not included.

TABLE 14.—*Wheat: Acreage, production, value, exports, etc., in the United States, 1849–1916.*

NOTE.—Figures in *italics* are census returns; figures in roman are estimates of the Department of Agriculture. Estimates of acres are obtained by applying estimated percentages of increase or decrease to the published numbers of the preceding year, except that a revised base is used for applying percentage estimates whenever new census data are available.

Year.	Acreage harvested.	Average yield per acre.	Production.	Average farm price per bushel Dec. 1.	Farm value Dec. 1.	Chicago cash price per bushel, No. 1 northern spring. December. Low.	December. High.	Following May. Low.	Following May. High.	Domestic exports, including flour, fiscal year beginning July 1.	Per cent of crop exported.
	Acres.	*Bush.*	*Bushels.*	*Cents.*	*Dollars.*	*Cts.*	*Cts.*	*Cts.*	*Cts.*	*Bushels.*	*P. ct.*
1849			*100,486,000*							7,535,901	7.5
1859			*173,105,000*							17,213,133	9.9
1866	15,424,000	9.9	152,000,000	152.7	232,110,000	129	145	185	211	12,646,941	8.3
1867	18,322,000	11.6	212,441,000	145.2	308,387,000	126	140	134	161	26,323,014	12.4
1868	18,460,000	12.1	224,037,000	108.5	243,033,000	80	88	87	96	29,717,201	13.3
1869	19,181,000	13.6	260,147,000	76.5	199,025,000	63	76	79	92	53,900,780	20.7
1869			*287,746,000*								
1870	18,993,000	12.4	235,885,000	94.4	222,767,000	91	98	113	120	52,574,111	22.3
1871	19,944,000	11.6	230,722,000	114.5	264,076,000	107	111	120	143	38,995,755	16.9
1872	20,858,000	12.0	249,997,000	111.4	278,522,000	97	108	112	122	52,014,715	20.8
1873	22,172,000	12.7	281,255,000	106.9	300,670,000	96	106	105	114	91,510,398	32.5
1874	24,967,000	12.3	308,103,000	86.3	265,881,000	78	83	78	94	72,912,817	23.7
1875	26,382,000	11.1	292,136,000	89.5	261,397,000	82	91	89	100	74,750,682	25.6
1876	27,627,000	10.5	289,356,000	97.0	280,743,000	104	117	130	172	57,043,936	19.7
1877	26,278,000	13.9	364,194,000	105.7	385,089,000	103	108	98	113	92,141,626	25.3
1878	32,109,000	13.1	420,122,000	77.6	325,814,000	81	84	91	102	150,502,506	35.8
1879	32,546,000	13.8	448,757,000	110.8	497,030,000	122	133½	112½	119	180,304,181	40.2
1879	*35,430,000*	*13.0*	*459,483,000*								
1880	37,987,000	13.1	498,550,000	95.1	474,202,000	93½	109¾	101	112⅝	186,321,514	37.4
1881	37,709,000	10.2	383,280,000	119.2	456,880,000	124¾	129	123	140	121,892,389	31.8
1882	37,067,000	13.6	504,185,000	88.4	445,602,000	91⅛	94¾	108	113⅜	147,811,316	29.3
1883	36,456,000	11.6	421,086,000	91.1	383,649,000	94⅝	99¼	85	94¾	111,534,182	26.5
1884	39,476,000	13.0	512,765,000	64.5	330,862,000	69½	76⅜	85⅜	90¾	132,570,366	25.9
1885	34,189,000	10.4	357,112,000	77.1	275,320,000	82⅞	89	72⅛	79	94,565,793	26.5
1886	36,806,000	12.4	457,218,000	68.7	314,226,000	75⅛	79½	80¾	88¾	153,804,969	33.6
1887	37,642,000	12.1	456,329,000	68.1	310,613,000	75⅛	79¼	81¼	89⅞	119,625,344	26.2
1888	37,336,000	11.1	415,868,000	92.6	385,248,000	96⅝	105½	77¼	95½	88,600,743	21.3
1889	38,124,000	12.9	490,560,000	69.8	342,492,000	76¾	80½	89¾	100	109,430,467	22.3
1889	*33,580,000*	*13.9*	*468,374,000*								
1890	36,087,000	11.1	399,262,000	83.8	334,774,000	87½	92¾	98⅞	108¼	106,181,316	26.6
1891	39,917,000	15.3	611,781,000	83.9	513,473,000	89⅜	93¼	80	85¾	225,665,811	36.9
1892	38,554,000	13.4	515,947,000	62.4	322,112,000	69½	73	68¼	76¼	191,912,635	37.2

WHEAT—Continued.

TABLE 14.—*Wheat: Acreage, production, value, exports, etc., in the United States, 1849–1916*—Continued.

Year.	Acreage harvested.	Average yield per acre.	Production.	Average farm price per bushel Dec. 1.	Farm value Dec. 1.	Chicago cash price per bushel, No. 1 northern spring. December. Low.	December. High.	Following May. Low.	Following May. High.	Domestic exports, including flour, fiscal year beginning July 1.	Per cent of crop exported.
	Acres.	*Bush.*	*Bushels.*	*Cents.*	*Dollars.*	*Cts.*	*Cts.*	*Cts.*	*Cts.*	*Bushels.*	*P. ct.*
1893..	34,629,000	11.4	396,132,000	53.8	213,171,000	59⅛	64½	52⅛	60½	164,283,129	41.5
1894..	34,882,000	13.2	460,267,000	49.1	225,902,000	52¾	63⅝	60¾	85⅜	144,812,718	31.5
1895..	34,047,000	13.7	467,103,000	50.9	237,939,000	53¾	64¾	57⅛	67⅝	126,443,968	27.1
1896..	34,619,000	12.4	427,684,000	72.6	310,598,000	74⅝	93⅛	68¾	97⅞	145,124,972	33.9
1897..	39,465,000	13.4	530,149,000	80.8	428,547,000	92	109	117	185	217,306,005	41.0
1898..	44,055,000	15.3	675,149,000	58.2	392,770,000	62¾	70	68⅜	79½	222,618,420	33.0
1899..	44,593,000	12.3	547,304,000	58.4	319,545,000	64	69½	63⅝	67½	186,096,762	34.0
1899..	*52,589,000*	*12.5*	*658,534,000*	......	......	......	......	......	......	......	.....
1900..	42,495,000	12.3	522,230,000	61.9	323,515,000	69¼	74⅝	70	75⅛	215,990,073	41.4
1901..	49,896,000	15.0	748,460,000	62.4	467,360,000	73	79½	72⅜	76¼	234,772,516	31.4
1902..	46,202,000	14.5	670,063,000	63.0	422,224,000	71⅞	77¾	74¾	80⅝	202,905,598	30.3
1903..	49,465,000	12.9	637,822,000	69.5	443,025,000	77¾	87	87¾	101½	120,727,613	18.9
1904..	44,075,000	12.5	552,400,000	92.4	510,490,000	115	122	89½	113¾	44,112,910	8.0
1905..	47,854,000	14.5	692,979,000	74.8	518,373,000	82½	90	80¼	87¼	97,609,007	14.1
1906..	47,306,000	15.5	735,261,000	66.7	490,333,000	......	......	84	106	146,700,425	20.0
1907..	45,211,000	14.0	634,087,000	87.4	554,437,000	......	......	......	......	163,043,669	25.7
1908..	47,557,000	14.0	664,602,000	92.8	616,826,000	106½	112	126½	137	114,268,468	17.2
1909..	46,723,000	15.8	737,189,000	......	......	......	......	......	......	......	.....
1909..	*44,262,000*	*15.4*	*683,379,000*	98.6	668,680,000	106	119¾	100	119¼	87,364,318	12.8
1910[1]	45,681,000	13.9	635,121,000	88.3	561,051,000	104	110	98	106	69,311,760	10.9
1911..	49,543,000	12.5	621,338,000	87.4	543,063,000	105	110	115	122	79,689,404	12.8
1912..	45,814,000	15.9	730,267,000	76.0	555,280,000	85	90¾	90½	96	142,879,596	19.6
1913..	50,184,000	15.2	763,380,000	79.9	610,122,000	89½	93	96	100	145,590,349	19.1
1914..	53,541,000	16.6	891,017,000	98.6	878,680,000	115	131	141	164½	332,464,975	37.3
1915..	60,469,000	17.0	1,025,801,000	91.9	942,303,000	106	128½	116	126	243,117,026	23.7
1916..	52,785,000	12.1	639,886,000	160.3	1,025,765,000	155½	190	......	......	......	.....

[1] Figures adjusted to census basis.

TABLE 15.—*Winter and spring wheat: Acreage, production, and farm value Dec. 1, by States in 1916, and United States totals, 1890–1916.*

State.	Winter wheat. Acreage.	Average yield per acre.	Production.	Average farm price Dec. 1.	Farm value Dec. 1.	Spring wheat. Acreage.	Average yield per acre.	Production.	Average farm price Dec. 1.	Farm value Dec. 1.
	Acres.	*Bu.*	*Bushels.*	*Cts.*	*Dollars.*	*Acres.*	*Bu.*	*Bushels.*	*Cts.*	*Dollars.*
Me........	....	......	....	......	....	5,000	27.0	135,000	187	252,000
Vt........	....	......	....	......	....	1,000	25.0	25,000	165	41,000
N. Y.......	430,000	21.0	9,030,000	168	15,170,000	....	......	....	......	....
N. J.......	90,000	20.0	1,800,000	164	2,952,000	....	......	....	......	....
Pa........	1,375,000	19.0	26,125,000	162	42,322,000	....	......	....	......	....
Del.......	124,000	15.0	1,860,000	162	3,013,000	....	......	....	......	....
Md........	640,000	16.0	10,240,000	171	17,510,000	....	......	....	......	....
Va........	1,300,000	12.5	16,250,000	165	26,812,000	....	......	....	......	....
W. Va......	320,000	14.5	4,640,000	160	7,424,000	....	......	....	......	....
N. C.......	950,000	10.5	9,975,000	176	17,556,000	....	......	....	......	....
S. C.......	210,000	10.6	2,226,000	189	4,207,000	....	......	....	......	....
Ga........	334,000	11.4	3,808,000	186	7,083,000	....	......	....	......	....
Ohio......	1,500,000	13.5	20,250,000	169	34,222,000	....	......	....	......	....
Ind.......	1,620,000	12.0	19,440,000	169	32,854,000	....	......	....	......	....
Ill........	1,475,000	11.0	16,225,000	165	26,771,000	....	......	....	......	....

WHEAT—Continued.

TABLE 15.—*Winter and spring wheat: Acreage, production, and farm value Dec. 1, by States in 1916, and United States totals, 1890–1916*—Continued.

State and year.	Winter wheat.					Spring wheat.				
	Acreage.	Average yield per acre.	Production.	Average farm price Dec.1.	Farm value Dec. 1.	Acreage.	Average yield per acre.	Production.	Average farm price Dec.1.	Farm value Dec. 1.
	Acres.	*Bu.*	*Bushels.*	*Cts.*	*Dollars.*	*Acres.*	*Bu.*	*Bushels.*	*Cts.*	*Dollars.*
Mich........	800,000	17.0	13,600,000	167	22,712,000	....	....	....	....	....
Wis........	81,000	19.0	1,539,000	160	2,462,000	107,000	16.6	1,776,000	160	2,842,000
Minn.......	65,000	14.0	910,000	162	1,474,000	3,650,000	7.3	26,645,000	162	43,165,000
Iowa.......	340,000	18.5	6,290,000	156	9,812,000	320,000	13.0	4,160,000	156	6,490,000
Mo.........	1,950,000	8.5	16,575,000	165	27,349,000	....	....	....	....	....
N. Dak....	....	....	....	....	....	7,150,000	5.5	39,325,000	152	59,774,000
S. Dak.....	150,000	18.5	2,775,000	150	4,162,000	3,500,000	6.3	22,050,000	150	33,075,000
Nebr......	3,240,000	20.0	64,800,000	160	103,680,000	300,000	12.5	3,750,000	160	6,000,000
Kans......	8,130,000	12.0	97,560,000	164	159,998,000	44,000	10.5	462,000	164	758,000
Ky.........	890,000	9.0	8,010,000	166	13,297,000	....	....	....	....	....
Tenn......	865,000	9.2	7,958,000	169	13,449,000	....	....	....	....	....
Ala........	110,000	9.5	1,045,000	185	1,933,000	....	....	....	....	....
Miss.......	6,000	15.0	90,000	175	158,000	....	....	....	....	....
Tex........	1,200,000	11.0	13,200,000	173	22,836,000	....	....	....	....	....
Okla.......	3,050,000	9.7	29,585,000	167	49,407,000	....	....	....	....	....
Ark........	255,000	8.0	2,040,000	163	3,325,000	....	....	....	....	....
Mont......	550,000	21.5	11,825,000	161	19,038,000	935,000	18.0	16,830,000	161	27,096,000
Wyo.......	70,000	21.0	1,470,000	145	2,132,000	95,000	22.0	2,090,000	145	3,030,000
Colo.......	370,000	20.0	7,400,000	150	11,100,000	230,000	19.5	4,485,000	150	6,728,000
N. Mex.....	65,000	16.5	1,072,000	150	1,608,000	48,000	21.5	1,032,000	150	1,548,000
Ariz.......	40,000	29.0	1,160,000	150	1,740,000	....	....	....	....	....
Utah.......	250,000	20.0	5,000,000	152	7,600,000	76,000	25.0	1,900,000	152	2,888,000
Nev........	20,000	24.5	490,000	140	686,000	35,000	31.5	1,102,000	140	1,543,000
Idaho......	344,000	24.0	8,256,000	146	12,054,000	290,000	23.5	6,815,000	146	9,950,000
Wash......	690,000	26.5	18,285,000	143	26,148,000	900,000	21.5	19,350,000	143	27,670,000
Oreg.......	580,000	23.0	13,340,000	145	19,343,000	270,000	23.0	6,210,000	145	9,004,000
Cal.........	350,000	16.0	5,600,000	152	8,512,000	....	....	....	....	....
U. S. ...	34,829,000	13.8	481,744,000	162.7	783,911,000	17,956,000	8.8	158,142,000	152.9	241,854,000
1915........	41,308,000	16.3	673,947,000	94.7	638,149,000	19,161,000	18.4	351,854,000	86.4	304,154,000
1914........	36,008,000	19.0	684,990,000	98.6	675,623,000	17,533,000	11.8	206,027,000	98.6	203,057,000
1913........	31,699,000	16.5	523,561,000	82.9	433,995,000	18,485,000	13.0	239,819,000	73.4	176,127,000
1912........	26,571,000	15.1	399,919,000	80.9	323,572,000	19,243,000	17.2	330,348,000	70.1	231,708,000
1911........	29,162,000	14.8	430,656,000	88.0	379,151,000	20,381,000	9.4	190,682,000	86.0	163,912,000
1910........	27,329,000	15.9	434,142,000	88.1	382,318,000	18,352,000	11.0	200,979,000	88.9	178,733,000
1909 [1]......	27,151,000	15.5	419,733,000	102.4	426,184,000	17,111,000	15.4	263,646,000	92.5	242,496,000
1908........	30,349,000	14.4	437,908,000	93.7	410,330,000	17,208,000	13.2	226,694,000	91.1	206,496,000
1907........	28,132,000	14.6	409,442,000	88.2	361,217,000	17,079,000	13.2	224,645,000	86.0	193,220,000
1906........	29,600,000	16.7	492,888,000	68.3	336,435,000	17,706,000	13.2	242,373,000	63.5	153,898,000
1905........	29,864,000	14.3	428,463,000	78.2	334,987,000	17,990,000	14.7	264,517,000	69.3	183,386,000
1904........	26,866,000	12.4	332,935,000	97.8	325,611,000	17,209,000	12.8	219,464,000	84.2	184,879,000
1903........	32,511,000	12.3	399,867,000	71.6	286,243,000	16,954,000	14.0	237,955,000	65.9	156,782,000
1902........	28,581,000	14.4	411,789,000	64.8	266,727,000	17,621,000	14.7	258,274,000	60.2	155,497,000
1901........	30,240,000	15.2	458,835,000	66.1	303,227,000	19,656,000	14.7	289,626,000	56.7	164,133,000
1900........	26,236,000	13.3	350,025,000	63.3	221,668,000	16,259,000	10.6	172,204,000	59.1	101,847,000
1899........	25,358,000	11.5	291,706,000	63.0	183,767,000	19,235,000	13.3	255,598,000	53.1	135,778,000
1898........	25,745,000	14.9	382,492,000	62.2	237,736,000	18,310,000	16.0	292,657,000	53.0	155,034,000
1897........	22,926,000	14.1	323,616,000	85.1	275,323,000	16,539,000	12.5	206,533,000	74.2	153,224,000
1896........	22,794,000	11.8	267,934,000	77.0	206,270,000	11,825,000	13.5	159,750,000	65.3	104,328,000
1895........	22,609,000	11.6	261,242,000	57.8	150,944,000	11,438,000	18.0	205,861,000	42.3	86,995,000
1894........	23,519,000	14.0	329,290,000	49.8	164,022,000	11,364,000	11.5	130,977,000	47.2	61,880,000
1893........	23,118,000	12.0	278,469,000	56.3	156,720,000	11,511,000	10.2	117,662,000	48.0	56,451,000
1892........	26,209,000	13.7	359,416,000	65.1	234,037,000	12,345,000	12.7	156,531,000	56.3	88,075,000
1891........	27,524,000	14.7	405,116,000	88.0	356,415,000	12,393,000	16.7	206,665,000	76.0	157,058,000
1890........	23,520,000	10.9	255,374,000	87.5	223,362,000	12,567,000	11.4	143,890,000	77.4	111,411,000

[1] Census acreage and production.

WHEAT—Continued.

TABLE 16.—*Winter and spring wheat: Yield per acre in States producing both, for 10 years.*

WINTER WHEAT.

State.	10-year aver., 1907–1916.	1907	1908	1909	1910	1911	1912	1913	1914	1915	1916
Wisconsin	19.6	15.5	19.5	20.4	20.0	17.5	19.5	20.1	21.5	23.0	19.0
Minnesota	17.3							16.2	19.5	19.5	14.0
Iowa	21.0	18.5	21.0	21.6	21.2	19.7	23.0	23.4	21.6	21.5	18.5
South Dakota	15.5							9.0	14.0	20.5	18.5
Nebraska	18.1	19.0	17.8	19.4	16.5	13.8	18.0	18.6	19.3	18.5	20.0
Kansas	13.7	11.3	12.8	14.5	14.2	10.8	15.5	13.0	20.5	12.5	12.0
Montana	26.0			32.5	22.0	31.7	24.5	25.6	23.0	27.0	21.5
Wyoming	25.8		25.0	32.5	25.0	26.0	28.0	25.0	24.0	26.0	21.0
Colorado	23.4			29.7	23.0	18.0	24.5	21.1	25.0	26.0	20.0
New Mexico	21.0				20.0	25.0	20.0	18.6	25.0	22.0	16.5
Arizona	28.6				22.3	30.0	31.0	32.0	28.0	28.0	29.0
Utah	22.7		23.0	24.0	20.5	20.0	24.0	23.0	25.0	25.0	20.0
Nevada	25.1			24.0	24.0	23.0	27.5	23.0	29.0	26.0	24.5
Idaho	27.7	26.0	30.0	29.0	23.7	31.5	28.7	27.4	27.5	29.0	24.0
Washington	26.3	29.5	24.5	25.8	20.5	27.3	27.6	27.0	26.5	27.6	26.5
Oregon	23.3	25.5	23.2	21.0	23.7	22.2	26.8	21.4	22.0	24.0	23.0
United States	15.6	14.6	14.4	15.8	15.9	14.8	15.1	16.5	19.0	16.3	13.8

SPRING WHEAT.

State.	10-year aver., 1907–1916.	1907	1908	1909	1910	1911	1912	1913	1914	1915	1916
Wisconsin	17.6	13.5	17.5	19.0	18.7	14.5	18.5	18.6	17.0	22.5	16.6
Minnesota	13.5	13.0	12.8	16.8	16.0	10.1	15.5	16.2	15.0	17.0	7.3
Iowa	15.5	12.8	15.5	14.7	20.9	13.8	17.0	17.0	13.5	16.7	13.0
South Dakota	11.0	11.2	12.8	14.1	12.8	4.0	14.2	9.0	9.0	17.0	6.3
Nebraska	12.9	12.0	13.0	14.0	13.9	10.0	14.1	12.0	11.5	16.0	12.5
Kansas	9.6	5.8	5.5	11.5	8.4	4.2	15.0	8.5	15.0	12.0	10.5
Montana	23.5	28.8	24.2	28.8	22.0	25.2	23.5	21.5	17.0	26.0	18.0
Wyoming	25.7	28.5	25.5	27.0	25.0	26.0	29.2	25.0	22.0	27.0	22.0
Colorado	22.9	29.0	21.0	29.4	21.9	19.5	24.0	21.0	22.5	21.0	19.5
New Mexico	22.2	24.0	25.0	24.5	20.0	20.5	22.0	19.0	23.0	22.5	21.5
Arizona	24.9	25.9	26.7	25.0	22.3	25.0	28.0	24.5	23.0	24.0	24.5
Utah	27.2	28.8	27.5	28.5	25.3	27.0	29.2	28.0	25.0	28.0	25.0
Nevada	30.7	32.0	30.0	28.7	29.0	32.5	30.2	31.0	30.0	32.0	31.5
Idaho	25.6	24.5	25.4	26.0	20.4	29.0	28.3	28.0	24.0	26.5	23.5
Washington	19.7	24.5	15.0	20.6	14.5	19.5	20.4	19.0	20.0	22.2	21.5
Oregon	18.8	21.5	16.5	18.7	18.0	17.7	19.5	19.5	16.5	17.0	23.0
United States	13.2	13.2	13.2	15.8	11.0	9.4	17.2	13.0	11.8	18.4	8.8

TABLE 17.—*All wheat: Acreage, production, and total farm value, by States, 1915 and 1916.*

State.	Thousands of acres.		Production (thousands of bushels).		Total value, basis Dec. 1 price (thousands of dollars).	
	1916	1915	1916	1915	1916	1915
Maine	5	4	135	112	252	125
Vermont	1	1	25	30	41	32
New York	430	475	9,030	11,875	15,170	11,994
New Jersey	90	78	1,800	1,560	2,952	1,654
Pennsylvania	1,375	1,330	26,125	24,605	42,322	25,589
Delaware	124	125	1,860	1,875	3,013	2,044
Maryland	640	638	10,240	10,272	17,510	10,786
Virginia	1,300	1,230	16,250	16,974	26,812	18,332
West Virginia	320	300	4,640	4,500	7,424	4,860
North Carolina	950	900	9,975	9,810	17,556	11,772
South Carolina	210	225	2,226	2,430	4,207	3,353
Georgia	334	325	3,808	3,575	7,083	4,612
Ohio	1,500	1,980	20,250	40,194	34,222	41,802
Indiana	1,620	2,650	19,440	45,580	32,854	46,492
Illinois	1,475	2,800	16,225	53,200	26,771	53,200

WHEAT—Continued.

TABLE 17.—*All wheat: Acreage, production, and total farm value, by States, 1915 and 1916*—Continued.

State.	Thousands of acres.		Production (thousands of bushels).		Total value, basis Dec. 1 price (thousands of dollars).	
	1916	1915	1916	1915	1916	1915
Michigan	800	960	13,600	20,448	22,712	20,652
Wisconsin	188	205	3,315	4,662	5,304	4,429
Minnesota	3,715	4,160	27,555	70,870	44,639	63,783
Iowa	660	950	10,450	18,985	16,302	16,517
Missouri	1,950	2,773	16,575	34,108	27,349	33,426
North Dakota	7,150	8,350	39,325	151,970	59,774	132,214
South Dakota	3,650	3,725	24,825	63,762	37,237	54,835
Nebraska	3,540	3,876	68,550	71,018	109,680	59,655
Kansas	8,174	8,525	98,022	106,538	160,756	94,819
Kentucky	890	900	8,010	9,900	13,297	10,395
Tennessee	865	860	7,958	9,030	13,449	9,752
Alabama	110	100	1,045	1,200	1,933	1,500
Mississippi	6	5	90	100	158	105
Texas	1,200	1,650	13,200	25,575	22,836	27,365
Oklahoma	3,050	3,350	29,585	38,860	49,407	34,585
Arkansas	255	220	2,040	2,750	3,325	2,778
Montana	1,485	1,590	28,655	42,180	46,134	32,900
Wyoming	165	125	3,560	3,315	5,162	2,586
Colorado	600	570	11,885	13,770	17,828	11,016
New Mexico	113	89	2,104	1,976	3,156	1,779
Arizona	40	39	1,160	1,092	1,740	1,256
Utah	326	320	6,900	8,225	10,488	7,074
Nevada	55	56	1,592	1,660	2,229	1,577
Idaho	634	670	15,071	18,730	22,004	14,984
Washington	1,590	2,000	37,635	51,420	53,818	42,165
Oregon	850	900	19,550	20,025	28,347	16,821
California	350	440	5,600	7,040	8,512	6,688
United States	52,785	60,469	639,886	1,025,801	1,025,765	942,303

TABLE 18.—*Wheat: Production and distribution in the United States, 1897–1916.*

[000 omitted.]

Year.	Old stock on farms July 1.	Crop.	Total supplies.	Stock on farms Mar. 1 following.	Shipped out of county where grown.
	Bushels.	*Bushels.*	*Bushels.*	*Bushels.*	*Bushels.*
1897	23,347	530,149	553,496	121,320	269,126
1898	17,839	675,149	692,988	198,056	398,882
1899	64,061	547,304	611,365	158,746	305,020
1900	50,900	522,230	573,130	128,098	281,372
1901	30,552	748,460	779,012	173,353	372,717
1902	52,437	670,063	722,500	164,047	388,554
1903	42,540	637,822	680,362	132,608	369,582
1904	36,634	552,400	589,034	111,055	302,771
1905	24,257	692,979	717,236	158,403	404,092
1906	46,053	735,261	781,314	206,642	427,253
1907	54,853	634,087	688,940	148,721	367,607
1908	33,797	664,602	698,399	143,692	393,435
1909	15,062	683,379	698,441	159,100	414,165
1910	35,680	635,121	670,801	162,705	352,906
1911	34,071	621,338	655,409	122,025	348,821
1912	23,876	730,267	754,143	156,483	449,906
1913	35,515	763,380	798,895	151,809	411,753
1914	32,236	891,017	923,253	152,903	541,198
1915	28,972	1,025,801	1,054,773	244,448	633,380
1916	74,731	639,886	714,617		

WHEAT—Continued.

TABLE 19.—*Wheat: Yield per acre, price per bushel Dec. 1, and value per acre, by States.*

State.	Yield per acre (bushels).											Farm price per bushel (cents).						Value per acre (dollars).[1]	
	10-year average,1907-1916.	1907	1908	1909	1910	1911	1912	1913	1914	1915	1916	10-year average, 1907-1916.	1912	1913	1914	1915	1916	5-year average, 1911-1915.	1916
Me	25.7	26.2	23.5	25.5	29.7	21.0	23.5	25.5	27.0	28.0	27.0	114	103	101	109	112	187	26.77	50.49
Vt	26.2	23.0	23.0	25.0	29.3	27.8	25.0	24.5	29.0	30.0	25.0	109	98	100	100	107	165	27.52	41.25
N. Y	20.4	17.3	17.5	21.0	23.7	19.5	16.0	20.0	22.5	25.0	21.0	107	99	93	108	101	168	20.50	35.28
N. J	18.4	18.5	17.3	17.9	18.5	17.4	18.5	17.6	18.0	20.0	20.0	108	98	96	109	106	164	18.51	32.80
Pa	17.6	18.6	18.5	17.0	17.8	13.5	18.0	17.0	18.1	18.5	19.0	104	95	91	104	104	162	16.61	30.78
Del	16.6	20.5	15.0	14.0	17.0	16.7	17.5	14.5	20.5	15.0	15.0	104	96	88	109	109	162	16.66	24.30
Md	16.5	19.0	16.4	14.5	17.4	15.5	15.0	13.3	21.5	16.1	16.0	105	95	89	106	105	171	15.98	27.36
Va	12.6	12.5	11.4	11.2	12.8	12.0	11.6	13.6	14.5	13.8	12.5	108	101	96	108	108	165	13.37	20.62
W. Va	13.4	12.2	13.0	13.0	12.5	11.5	14.5	13.0	15.0	15.0	14.5	110	101	100	108	108	160	14.35	23.20
N. C	10.5	9.5	10.0	9.5	11.4	10.6	8.9	11.7	12.0	10.9	10.5	118	111	106	117	120	176	12.04	18.48
S. C	10.4	8.5	9.0	10.0	11.0	11.4	9.2	12.3	11.5	10.8	10.6	137	119	130	145	138	189	14.51	20.03
Ga	10.7	9.0	9.2	10.0	10.5	12.0	9.3	12.2	12.1	11.0	11.4	132	122	120	134	129	186	14.01	21.20
Ohio	15.9	16.3	16.0	15.9	16.2	16.0	8.0	18.0	18.5	20.3	13.5	105	98	90	105	104	169	15.83	22.82
Ind	15.0	14.4	16.6	15.3	15.6	14.7	8.0	18.5	17.4	17.2	12.0	103	93	88	103	102	169	14.45	20.28
Ill	15.5	18.0	13.0	17.4	15.0	16.0	8.3	18.7	18.5	19.0	11.0	100	88	86	101	100	165	15.06	18.15
Mich	17.1	14.5	18.0	18.8	18.0	18.0	10.0	15.3	19.7	21.3	17.0	103	96	89	103	101	167	16.17	28.39
Wis	18.5	14.1	18.2	19.5	19.3	15.9	19.0	19.3	19.1	22.7	17.6	98	83	82	100	95	160	17.31	28.16
Minn	13.5	13.0	12.8	16.8	16.0	10.1	15.5	16.2	10.6	17.0	7.4	97	73	76	102	90	162	11.81	11.99
Iowa	18.0	13.4	17.2	17.0	21.0	16.4	19.8	20.6	18.6	20.0	15.8	93	78	76	96	87	156	16.16	24.65
Mo	13.5	13.2	10.0	14.7	13.8	15.7	12.5	17.1	17.0	12.3	8.5	99	90	84	98	98	165	13.63	14.02
N. Dak	11.2	10.0	11.6	13.7	5.0	8.0	18.0	10.5	11.2	18.2	5.5	93	69	73	101	87	152	10.87	8.36
S. Dak	11.1	11.2	12.8	14.1	12.8	4.0	14.2	9.0	9.1	17.1	6.8	92	69	71	94	86	150	8.62	10.20
Nebr	17.6	18.1	17.2	18.8	16.2	13.4	17.6	17.9	18.6	18.3	19.4	90	69	71	95	84	160	13.91	31.04
Kans	13.6	11.0	12.6	14.4	14.1	10.7	15.5	13.0	20.5	12.5	12.0	94	74	79	95	89	164	12.42	19.68
Ky	12.1	12.0	11.6	11.8	12.8	12.7	10.0	13.6	15.5	11.0	9.0	106	99	96	103	105	166	12.64	14.94
Tenn	11.1	9.5	10.0	10.4	11.7	11.5	10.5	12.0	15.5	10.5	9.2	108	100	98	105	108	169	12.18	15.55
Ala	11.2	10.0	11.5	10.5	12.0	11.5	10.6	11.7	13.0	12.0	9.5	124	113	115	126	125	185	14.12	17.58
Miss	13.6	11.0	14.5	11.0	14.0	12.0	12.0	14.3	20.0	15.0	11.0	112	97	95	125	105	175	14.84	26.25
Tex	12.4	7.4	11.0	9.1	15.0	9.4	15.0	17.5	13.0	15.5	11.0	108	93	94	99	107	173	13.85	19.03
Okla	12.1	9.0	11.6	12.8	16.3	8.0	12.8	10.0	19.0	11.6	9.7	96	75	82	92	89	167	10.59	16.20
Ark	11.2	9.5	10.0	11.4	13.9	10.5	10.0	13.0	13.0	12.5	8.0	103	94	90	99	101	163	11.21	13.04
Mont	24.8	28.8	24.2	30.8	22.0	28.7	24.1	23.8	20.2	26.5	19.3	88	64	66	91	78	161	18.46	31.07
Wyo	25.8	28.5	25.4	28.7	25.0	26.0	28.7	25.0	22.9	26.5	21.6	91	80	72	89	78	145	21.29	31.32
Colo	23.4	29.0	21.0	29.5	22.3	18.9	24.2	21.0	23.8	24.2	19.8	89	73	78	87	80	150	18.00	29.70
N. Mex	22.1	24.0	25.0	24.5	20.0	22.9	20.9	18.8	24.2	22.2	18.6	102	90	97	90	90	150	20.34	27.90
Ariz	27.7	25.9	26.7	25.0	22.3	29.6	30.7	32.0	28.0	28.0	29.0	119	110	110	125	115	150	32.86	43.50
Utah	24.7	28.8	26.5	25.9	22.1	25.3	24.2	25.0	25.7	21.2	18.9	88	75	73	86	86	152	19.23	32.22
Nev	29.0	32.0	30.0	28.7	26.5	28.3	29.2	27.7	29.6	29.6	28.9	104	100	82	95	95	140	27.01	40.46
Idaho	26.9	25.3	28.2	27.8	22.6	30.7	28.6	27.6	26.2	28.0	23.8	81	66	63	87	80	146	20.34	34.75
Wash	22.7	26.0	18.8	23.2	16.9	22.7	23.5	23.2	23.5	25.7	23.7	86	68	73	100	82	143	18.72	33.89
Oreg	22.0	23.4	20.8	20.2	22.1	21.0	20.5	20.8	22.3	20.0	23.8	89	72	75	102	84	140	17.87	33.35
Cal	16.0	15.0	14.6	14.0	18.0	18.0	17.0	14.0	17.0	16.0	16.0	103	93	95	104	95	152	15.57	24.32
U. S	14.7	14.0	14.0	15.8	13.9	12.5	15.9	15.2	16.6	17.0	12.1	96.2	76.0	79.9	98.6	91.9	160.3	13.45	19.43

[1] Based upon farm price Dec. 1.

WHEAT—Continued.

TABLE 20.—*Winter and spring wheat: Condition of crop, United States, on first of months named, 1890–1917.*

Year.	Winter wheat.					Spring wheat.			
	December of previous year.	April.	May.	June.	When harvested.	June.	July.	August.	When harvested.
	P. ct.	*P. ct.*	*P. ct.*	*P. ct.*	*P. ct.*	*P. ct.*	*P. ct.*	*P. ct.*	*P. ct.*
1890	95.3	81.0	80.0	78.1	76.2	91.3	94.4	83.2	79.7
1891	98.4	96.9	97.9	96.6	96.2	92.6	94.1	95.5	97.2
1892	85.3	81.2	84.0	88.3	89.6	92.3	90.9	87.3	81.2
1893	87.4	77.4	75.4	75.5	77.7	86.4	74.1	67.0	68.9
1894	91.5	86.7	81.4	83.2	83.9	88.0	68.4	67.1	69.9
1895	89.0	81.4	82.9	71.1	65.8	97.8	102.2	95.9	94.9
1896	81.4	77.1	82.7	77.9	75.6	99.9	93.3	78.9	73.8
1897	99.5	81.4	80.2	78.5	81.2	89.6	91.2	86.7	80.8
1898	....	86.7	86.5	90.8	85.7	100.9	95.0	96.5	91.7
1899	92.6	77.9	76.2	67.3	65.6	91.4	91.7	83.6	77.2
1900	97.1	82.1	88.9	82.7	80.8	87.3	55.2	56.4	56.1
1901	97.1	91.7	94.1	87.8	88.3	92.0	95.6	80.3	78.4
1902	86.7	78.7	76.4	76.1	77.0	95.4	92.4	89.7	87.2
1903	99.7	97.3	92.6	82.2	78.8	95.9	82.5	77.1	78.1
1904	86.6	76.5	76.5	77.7	78.7	93.4	93.7	87.5	66.2
1905	82.9	91.6	92.5	85.5	82.7	93.7	91.0	89.2	87.3
1906	94.1	89.1	90.9	82.7	85.6	93.4	91.4	86.9	83.4
1907	94.1	89.9	82.9	77.4	78.3	88.7	87.2	79.4	77.1
1908	91.1	91.3	89.0	86.0	80.6	95.0	89.4	80.7	77.6
1909	85.3	82.2	83.5	80.7	82.4	95.2	92.7	91.6	88.6
1910	95.8	80.8	82.1	80.0	81.5	92.8	61.6	61.0	63.1
1911	82.5	83.3	86.1	80.4	76.8	94.6	73.8	59.8	56.7
1912	86.6	80.6	79.7	74.3	73.3	95.8	89.3	90.4	90.8
1913	93.2	91.6	91.9	83.5	81.6	93.5	73.8	74.1	75.3
1914	97.2	95.6	95.9	92.7	94.1	95.5	92.1	75.5	68.0
1915	88.3	88.8	92.9	85.8	84.4	94.9	93.3	93.4	94.6
1916	87.7	78.3	82.4	73.2	75.7	88.2	89.0	63.4	48.6
1917	85.7	....	....	....	....	....	....	....	....

TABLE 21.—*Winter wheat: Per cent of area sown which was abandoned (not harvested).*

Year.	Per cent.	Year.	Per cent.	Year.	Per cent.
1902	15.2	1907	11.2	1912	20.1
1903	2.8	1908	4.2	1913	4.7
1904	15.4	1909	7.5	1914	3.1
1905	4.6	1910	13.7	1915	2.7
1906	5.5	1911	10.7	1916	11.4

TABLE 22.—*Wheat: Farm price per bushel on first of each month, by geographical divisions, 1915 and 1916.*

Month.	United States.		North Atlantic States.		South Atlantic States.		N. Central States east of Miss. R.		N. Central States west of Miss. R.		South Central States.		Far Western States.	
	1916	1915	1916	1915	1916	1915	1916	1915	1916	1915	1916	1915	1916	1915
	Cts.	*Cts.*	*Cts.*	*Cts.*	*Cts.*	*Cts.*	*Cts.*	*Cts.*	*Cts.*	*Cts.*	*Cts.*	*Cts.*	*Cts.*	*Cts.*
January	102.8	107.8	110.0	112.1	119.0	117.2	111.2	113.4	101.9	106.5	106.0	107.9	88.1	101.4
February	113.9	129.9	121.7	135.5	129.0	139.3	121.0	135.7	114.6	129.5	110.6	129.0	99.3	120.8
March	102.9	133.6	113.6	142.8	123.1	146.0	109.6	138.6	99.6	132.4	109.4	134.9	94.3	124.8
April	98.6	131.7	109.7	138.2	117.9	144.9	104.7	137.7	97.0	130.5	103.4	133.9	86.6	121.3
May	102.5	139.6	111.6	145.2	117.7	148.5	109.0	142.9	102.1	142.0	104.9	138.9	88.9	122.5
June	100.0	131.5	105.8	140.2	115.6	141.5	104.9	135.9	99.1	133.1	103.4	131.9	89.0	114.5
July	93.0	102.8	99.5	112.6	109.5	115.7	99.4	105.0	92.0	104.9	92.0	96.6	83.7	89.5
August	107.1	106.5	108.9	107.6	115.0	110.2	114.4	101.7	108.5	112.2	109.4	104.1	91.0	90.9
September	131.2	95.0	131.3	102.8	133.7	108.8	135.8	96.7	132.5	93.8	137.3	101.5	118.4	86.1
October	136.3	90.9	138.4	100.4	140.8	107.5	143.5	98.6	136.0	88.1	142.4	98.8	124.5	78.1
November	158.4	93.1	166.0	101.3	164.5	111.4	166.6	102.1	159.5	89.4	167.1	100.0	138.2	83.3
December	160.3	91.9	163.6	103.2	170.6	112.8	167.3	101.5	159.7	88.0	168.6	98.9	149.1	81.9
Average	126.7	105.0	132.6	112.0	132.4	118.4	128.3	109.9	126.6	104.7	123.3	106.7	119.8	89.4

WHEAT—Continued.

TABLE 23.—*Wheat: Wholesale price per bushel, 1912–1916.*

Date.	New York.		Baltimore.		Chicago.		Detroit.		St. Louis.		Minneapolis.		San Francisco.	
	No. 2 red winter.[1]		No. 2 red.		No. 1 northern spring.		No. 2 red.		No. 2 red winter.		No. 1 northern.		No. 1 California (per 100 lbs.).[2]	
	Low.	High.	Low.	High.	Low.	High.	Low.	High.	Low.	High.	Low.	High.	Low.	High.
1912.	*Cts.*	*Cts.*	*Cts.*	*Cts.*	*Cts.*	*Cts.*	*Cts.*	*Cts.*	*Cts.*	*Cts.*	*Cts.*	*Cts.*	*Cts.*	*Cts.*
Jan.–June	98¼	127	95¼	116½	107	122	95¾	120	92½	125½	103½	118⅞	150	190
July–Dec	103½	118¼	94½	106	85	116	101¾	112	94	115½	80½	112¼	140	165
1913.														
Jan.–June	107	114½	105¾	109½	87¼	96	102½	116¼	93	115	82⅛	89⅝	155	182½
July–Dec	94	107	89¼	96½	85	95¼	87½	102½	83	97¾	80¾	93½	155	172½
1914.														
Jan.–June	87½	111¾	83	103	89	100	86¼	99¼	75¾	99½	84⅝	98¼	151¼	165
July–Dec	86¼	136½	82¾	127	88½	133	80	127¾	76	127½	85½	129⅛	152	200
1915.														
January	138	162	132¼	151	128	154	128½	152	127½	152	125	149⅛	(3)	(3)
February	157	178	148½	164	146	167	148	165	145	164	140½	157½	225	240
March	149½	172¼	140¼	162¾	138	162½	136½	159½	136½	157¾	133⅜	156¾	225	230
April	159	169¾	155¼	168½	152½	165½	152½	161	149	160	138¾	165⅝	215	230
May	147	170	141½	163½	141	164½	139	160½	137	159½	146	165	195	220
June	126	141	111	140	123	149	114½	138	110	132	114⅞	144¾	165	200
Jan.–June	126	178	111	168½	123	167	114½	165	110	164	114⅞	165⅝	165	240
July	118¾	144½	105½	114¼	132	153¾	110	132	108	128	127½	151½	165	185
August	110½	128¼	102	121½	108	131	106½	117½	107	120¾	96⅜	155	160	185
September	108¼	128	100¾	110½	99½	119½	106	114	106	122	89	104⅞	140	165
October	118	130	106	116	99	115½	107	115	109	129	92¾	109½	140	175
November	(3)	(3)	110½	114¼	102½	111	111	114	111	125	98⅜	105¾	150	170
December	(3)	(3)	113¼	128⅞	106	128½	113½	126	115	129	103⅜	123⅜	150	170
July–Dec	108¼	144½	100¾	128⅞	99	153¾	106	132	106	129	89	155	140	185
1916.														
January	138½	156¼	123	141¼	119¾	139½	122	137	122	143	118⅞	138¾	150	190
February	130¾	154	116	137½	112	138	111½	135½	116	142	108⅛	136¼	160	185
March	130¾	139	112½	119½	109⅜	123	110½	118¼	112	122	108⅞	120⅞	160	175
April	129¾	143	114¾	123	118¾	128	117	124	116	130½	117⅞	126⅛	160	170
May	124½	136	104	119⅛	116	126	108¾	123½	106	125	113¼	128⅜	160	170
June	113¼	132½	100¼	105¾	106½	118	103	113¼	106	114	106½	116¼	160	170
Jan.–June	113¼	156¼	100¼	141¼	106½	139½	103	137	106	143	106½	138¾	150	190
July	123½	143	102½	126	110	131⅞	104	129½	109	136½	107⅞	132½	160	185
August	144	179	125½	157	126⅛	164¼	130	154¾	129	165	127⅜	165⅞	160	210
September	168½	184⅝	148¼	157	150	171½	144½	156	147	172	152	167⅝	185	225
October	185¾	209½	156¼	192¼	164	202	157½	188	158	195	169⅛	199⅛	185	275
November	198	215	174	193¼	165	200	173	189½	177	196	177	200	240	290
December	183	206	159	183	155½	190	157	183½	168	187	159⅞	188⅝	250	290
July–Dec	123½	215	102½	193¼	110	202	104	189½	109	196	107⅞	200	160	290

[1] No. 1 northern spring in 1916.
[2] Northern club, in 1913. White, subsequent to 1913.
[3] Nominal.

WHEAT—Continued.

TABLE 24.—*Wheat flour: Wholesale price per barrel, 1912–1916.*

Date.	Chicago.				Cincinnati.		New York.		St. Louis.	
	Winter patents.		Spring patents.		Winter family.		Spring patents.		Winter patents.	
	Low.	High.	Low.	High.	Low.	High.	Low.	High.	Low.	High.
1912.	*Dolls.*	*Dolls.*	*Dolls.*	*Dolls.*	*Dolls.*	*Dolls.*	*Dolls.*	*Dolls.*	*Dolls.*	*Dolls.*
Jan.-June............	3.75	5.45	4.50	5.60	3.40	4.50	4.25	5.50	4 40	5.85
July-Dec............	4.50	5.30	4.00	5.30	4.00	4.50	4.50	5.20	4.20	5.60
1913.										
Jan.-June............	4.30	5.10	4.10	5.60	3.25	4.15	4.40	5.00	4.30	5.15
July-Dec............	3.90	4.35	4.00	5.50	2.90	3.50	4.40	5.00	3.70	4.55
1914.										
Jan.-June............	3.50	4.40	4.00	5.50	3.20	3.50	4.50	5.10	3.35	4.35
July-Dec............	3.45	5.50	4.00	6.90	3.05	4.90	4.35	7.00	3.35	5.70
1915.										
January............	6.10	7.10	6.60	7.60	4.75	6.15	6.25	7.40	5.50	6.75
February............	7.10	7.80	7.20	8.00	6.25	6.65	7.25	8.25	6.60	7.50
March..............	6.60	7.25	6.65	8.00	6.00	6.55	6.85	7.85	6.30	6.85
April...............	6.80	7.60	7.10	8.30	6.15	6.55	7.25	8.10	6.40	6.90
May................	6.70	7.50	7.30	8.30	6.00	6.55	7.35	8.10	6.35	6.90
June................	5.10	6.65	5.50	8.10	5.25	5.90	5.50	7.90	5.10	6.30
Jan.-June.....	5.10	7.80	5.50	8.30	4.75	6.65	5.50	8.25	5.10	7.50
July................	4.60	5.75	5.75	7.50	5.25	5.65	5.50	7.25	4.90	5.90
August..............	4.75	5.75	6.00	7.50	5.50	5.65	5.15	7.25	4.60	5.10
September..........	4.50	5.50	4.50	6.30	5.00	5.65	4.90	6.85	4.60	5.00
October............	5.00	5.50	4.80	6.30	4.65	5.15	5.05	6.10	4.80	5.40
November..........	5.00	5.50	5.00	6.30	4.65	4.75	5.40	5.90	5.00	5.25
December..........	5.25	5.75	5.15	6.90	4.65	5.25	5.60	6.70	5.10	5.60
July-Dec.....	4.50	5.75	4.50	7.50	4.65	5.65	4.90	7.25	4.60	5.90
1916.										
January............	5.50	6.80	5.60	7.50	5.15	5.40	6.25	7.25	5.25	6.10
February............	5.60	6.60	5.60	7.50	5.40	5.50	5.45	7.25	5.25	6.10
March..............	5.15	6.25	5.10	6.90	5.15	5.35	5.70	6.40	5.10	5.40
April...............	5.50	6.25	5.65	6.70	5.15	5.25	6.05	6.60	5.20	5.50
May................	5.30	5.75	5.40	6.70	5.10	5.35	5.80	6.50	4.90	5.35
June................	5.00	5.60	5.20	6.70	4.50	5.35	5.50	6.15	4.75	5.05
Jan.-June.....	5.00	6.80	5.10	7.50	4.50	5.50	5.45	7.25	4.75	6.10
July................	5.00	5.50	5.00	7.30	4.50	5.00	5.50	6.85	4.75	6.00
August..............	5.50	7.00	6.50	8.75	4.75	7.00	6.50	8.55	5.85	7.30
September..........	6.90	7.60	7.20	8.90	6.75	7.00	7.90	8.75	7.10	7.50
October............	7.20	8.50	7.80	10.20	6.75	7.75	8.34	9.90	7.25	8.75
November..........	8.35	9.30	9.20	10.30	7.50	8.75	9.30	10.00	8.25	9.00
December..........	7.80	8.50	7.50	9.60	7.00	8.25	8.35	9.45	7.85	8.60
July-Dec.....	5.00	9.30	5.00	10.30	4.50	8.75	5.50	10.00	4.75	9.00

WHEAT—Continued.

TABLE 25.—*Wheat and flour: International trade, calendar years 1913–1915.*

["Temporary" imports into Italy of wheat, to be used for manufacturing products for export, are included in the total imports as given in the official Italian returns. In the trade returns of Chile the item *trigo mote* (prepared corn) which might easily be confused with *trigo* (wheat) is omitted. See "General note," Table 10.]

EXPORTS.

[000 omitted.]

Country.	Wheat.			Flour.			Wheat and flour.[1]		
	1913	1914 (prelim.)	1915 (prelim.)	1913	1914 (prelim.)	1915 (prelim.)	1913	1914 (prelim.)	1915 (prelim.)
	Bushels.	*Bushels.*	*Bushels.*	*Barrels.*	*Barrels.*	*Barrels.*	*Bushels.*	*Bushels.*	*Bushels.*
Argentina	103,328	36,028	92,281	1,402	757	1,305	109,637	39,435	98,155
Australia	42,923	52,878	1,113	2,285	1,778	81	53,207	60,878	1,476
Austria-Hungary	71			369			1,730		
Belgium	12,991			646			15,898		
British India	50,558	26,130	26,505	923	683	600	54,711	29,204	29,207
Bulgaria	[2]9,238			[3]493			[3]11,456		
Canada	129,950	70,302	151,900	4,894	4,671	5,569	151,975	91,322	176,959
Chile	1,922	149	12	69	34	5	2,235	301	34
Germany	19,781			2,191			29,638		
Netherlands	63,598	37,063	1,807	201	115	5	64,501	37,583	1,830
Roumania	42,362	19,744		1,385	842		48,594	23,535	
Russia	122,336	88,609	6,681	1,836	1,274	932	130,596	94,342	10,875
United States	99,509	173,862	205,830	12,278	12,768	15,681	154,760	231,318	276,393
Other countries	7,499	13,358		2,813	2,858		20,160	26,216	
Total	706,066	518,123		31,785	25,780		849,098	634,134	

IMPORTS.

Country.	1913	1914 (prelim.)	1915 (prelim.)	1913	1914 (prelim.)	1915 (prelim.)	1913	1914 (prelim.)	1915 (prelim.)
Belgium	69,628			36			69,790		
Brazil	16,109	14,047	13,622	1,914	1,503	1,449	24,722	20,808	20,142
British South Africa	5,359	3,782	3,611	890	706	384	9,366	6,957	5,338
Denmark	5,176	2,942	2,334	670	552	421	8,190	5,424	4,230
France	57,160	60,882	61,417	113	1,048	3,413	57,669	65,598	76,776
Germany	93,547			201			94,451		
Greece	6,882	6,671		15	7		6,950	6,704	
Italy	66,532	3,732	8,268	23	17	88	66,635	3,810	8,665
Japan	6,255	4,360	817	195	137	21	7,131	4,976	910
Netherlands	79,369	50,770	23,782	2,259	1,596	1,050	89,534	57,951	28,507
Portugal	6,399	5,429					6,399	5,439	
Spain	6,405	15,528	13,647	1	10	10	6,409	15,575	13,691
Sweden	7,355	4,895	8,784	97	107	257	7,793	5,378	9,939
Switzerland	19,446	16,714	17,771	429			21,376	16,714	17,771
United Kingdom	196,809	192,725	165,179	6,704	5,622	5,752	226,978	218,025	191,064
Other countries	13,073	20,094		13,060	38,496		71,843	193,325	
Total	655,504	402,581		26,607	49,801		775,236	626,684	

[1] Flour is reduced to terms of grain, where included in these 3 columns, by assuming 1 barrel of flour to be the product of 4½ bushels of wheat.
[2] Data for 1912.

OATS.

TABLE 26.—*Oats: Area and production in undermentioned countries, 1914–1916.*

Country.	Area.			Production.		
	1914	1915	1916	1914	1915	1916
NORTH AMERICA.	*Acres.*	*Acres.*	*Acres.*	*Bushels.*	*Bushels.*	*Bushels.*
United States..........	38,442,000	40,996,000	41,539,000	1,141,060,000	1,549,030,000	1,251,992,000
Canada:						
New Brunswick.....	200,000	201,000	198,000	6,488,000	5,560,000	
Quebec..............	1,327,000	1,400,000	1,138,000	42,119,000	42,182,000	
Ontario.............	2,840,000	3,095,000	2,410,000	99,400,000	122,810,000	
Manitoba............	1,331,000	1,441,000	1,363,000	31,951,000	69,471,000	(¹)
Saskatchewan.......	2,520,000	2,937,000	2,657,000	61,816,000	157,629,000	
Alberta.............	1,502,000	1,912,000	1,653,000	57,076,000	107,741,000	
Other...............	341,000	379,000	376,000	14,228,000	14,710,000	
Total Canada......	10,061,000	11,365,000	9,795,000	313,078,000	520,103,000	351,174,000
Mexico..................	(¹)	(¹)	(¹)	17,000	17,000	(¹)
Total..............	....	....	....	1,454,155,000	2,069,150,000	....
SOUTH AMERICA.						
Argentina...............	3,087,000	2,869,000	2,565,000	50,981,000	57,251,000	75,280,000
Chile..................	122,000	151,000	(¹)	4,437,000	7,105,000	(¹)
Uruguay...............	97,000	82,000	106,000	1,850,000	933,000	2,283,000
Total..............	....	....	....	57,268,000	65,289,000	....
EUROPE.						
Austria-Hungary:						
Austria...............	²2,835,000	(¹)	(¹)	²132,114,000	²132,000,000	(¹)
Hungary proper.....	2,603,000	2,664,000	(¹)	86,537,000	80,925,000	(¹)
Croatia-Slavonia.....	(¹)	(¹)	(¹)	4,000,000	5,000,000	(¹)
Bosnia-Herzegovina.	(¹)	(¹)	(¹)	3,000,000	4,000,000	(¹)
Total Austria-Hungary........	....	....	....	225,651,000	221,925,000	....
Belgium...............	686,000	(¹)	(¹)	49,742,000	40,000,000	(¹)
Bulgaria..............	379,000	(¹)	(¹)	8,080,000	9,545,000	7,372,000
Denmark..............	³1,059,000	1,024,000	1,040,000	38,653,000	42,834,000	42,282,000
Finland...............	(¹)	(¹)	(¹)	18,678,000	22,000,000	(¹)
France................	8,877,000	8,062,000	7,796,000	274,458,000	206,795,000	246,158,000
Germany..............	10,843,000	11,404,000	(¹)	622,674,000	412,400,000	(¹)
Italy..................	1,213,000	1,208,000	1,102,000	26,827,000	31,443,000	26,189,000
Netherlands...........	346,000	381,000	343,000	19,957,000	19,644,000	22,239,000
Norway...............	³270,000	(¹)	296,000	9,325,000	9,325,000	10,919,000
Roumania.............	1,056,000	1,065,000	1,068,000	25,015,000	29,054,000	28,935,000
Russia:						
Russia proper.......	39,195,000	37,302,000	35,491,000	692,197,000	745,150,000	869,960,000
Poland...............	(¹)	(¹)	(¹)	(¹)	(¹)	(¹)
Northern Caucasia..	1,099,000	⁴987,000	(¹)	30,291,000	⁴25,303,000	(¹)
Total..............	40,294,000	38,289,000	....	722,488,000	770,453,000	....
Serbia.................	(¹)		(¹)	5,000,000	4,000,000	(¹)
Spain..................	1,304,000	1,403,000	1,391,000	31,227,000	36,949,000	34,948,000
Sweden................	1,960,000	(¹)	(¹)	52,557,000	91,311,000	(¹)
United Kingdom:						
England..............	1,730,000	1,889,000	1,862,000	71,408,000	78,409,000	78,090,000
Wales...............	200,000	199,000	222,000	7,431,000	7,305,000	8,237,000
Scotland............	920,000	972,000	990,000	38,115,000	40,313,000	37,362,000
Ireland..............	1,029,000	1,089,000	1,072,000	63,287,000	68,604,000	62,354,000
Total United Kingdom........	3,879,000	4,139,000	4,146,000	180,241,000	194,631,000	186,043,000
Total..........	....	....	....	2,310,573,000	2,142,309,000	....

[1] No official statistics. [3] Census of 1910.
[2] Galicia and Bukowina not included. [4] Includes 1 government of Transcaucasia.

OATS—Continued.

TABLE 26.—*Oats: Area and production in undermentioned countries, 1914–1916*—Contd.

Country.	Area.			Production.		
	1914	1915	1916	1914	1915	1916
ASIA.	*Acres.*	*Acres.*	*Acres.*	*Bushels.*	*Bushels.*	*Bushels.*
Cyprus..................	(1)	(1)	(1)	400,000	400,000	(1)
Russia:						
Central Asia (4 Governments of)......	1,127,000	1,337,000	(1)	27,887,000	26,586,000	(1)
Siberia (4 governments of)..........	5,148,000	5,161,000	(1)	133,275,000	68,381,000	(1)
Transcausia (1 government of).......	2,000	(2)	(1)	31,000	(2)	(1)
Total Russia (Asiatic)........	6,277,000	....	....	161,193,000	94,967,000	....
Total..............	....	....	....	161,593,000	95,367,000	....
AFRICA.						
Algeria...................	573,000	590,000	(1)	10,000,000	15,082,000	(1)
Tunis...................	99,000	148,000	(1)	689,000	3,445,000	2,067,000
Union of South Africa...	(1)	(1)	(1)	[3]9,661,000	[3]9,661,000	(1)
Total............	....	....	....	20,350,000	28,188,000	....
AUSTRALASIA.						
Australia:						
Queensland.........	4,000	3,000	(1)	58,000	46,000	(1)
New South Wales...	103,000	43,000	61,000	1,893,000	530,000	1,454,000
Victoria.............	442,000	435,000	(1)	9,170,000	1,659,000	(1)
South Australia.....	117,000	141,000	(1)	1,239,000	380,000	(1)
Western Australia..	134,000	96,000	103,000	1,708,000	479,000	1,843,000
Tasmania...........	59,000	57,000	(1)	1,644,000	1,384,000	(1)
Total Australia....	859,000	775,000	725,000	15,712,000	4,478,000	17,127,000
New Zealand...........	362,000	288,000	213,000	15,206,000	11,797,000	7,894,000
Total Australasia..	1,221,000	1,063,000	938,000	30,918,000	16,275,000	25,021,000
Grand total......	....	....	....	4,034,857,000	4,416,578,000	....

[1] No official statistics.   [2] Included in Northern Caucasia.   [3] Census of 1911.

TABLE 27.—*Oats: Total production in countries named in Table 26, 1895–1916.*

Year.	Production.	Year.	Production.	Year.	Production.	Year.	Production.
	Bushels.		*Bushels.*		*Bushels.*		*Bushels.*
1895....	3,008,154,000	1901.....	2,862,615,000	1907.....	3,603,896,000	1913.....	4,697,437,000
1896....	2,847,115,000	1902.....	3,626,303,000	1908.....	3,591,012,000	1914.....	4,034,857,000
1897....	2,633,971,000	1903.....	3,378,034,000	1909.....	4,312,882,000	1915.....	4,416,578,000
1898....	2,903,974,000	1904.....	3,611,302,000	1910.....	4,182,410,000	1916.....	....
1899....	3,256,256,000	1905.....	3,510,167,000	1911.....	3,808,561,000		
1900....	3,166,002,000	1906.....	3,544,961,000	1912.....	4,617,394,000		

TABLE 28.—*Oats: Average yield per acre in undermentioned countries, 1890–1915.*

Year.	United States.	Russia (European).[1]	Germany.[1]	Austria.[1]	Hungary proper.[1]	France.[2]	United Kingdom.[2]
	Bushels.	*Bushels.*	*Bushels.*	*Bushels.*	*Bushels.*	*Bushels.*	*Bushels.*
Average:							
1890–1899.................	26.1	17.8	40.0	25.3	....	29.8	43.6
1900–1909.................	29.3	20.0	50.7	29.8	30.7	31.6	44.3
1906..........................	31.2	15.1	55.7	34.1	34.2	27.0	43.8
1907..........................	23.7	19.7	58.3	35.7	30.0	31.8	45.1
1908..........................	25.0	20.1	50.2	32.0	26.8	29.6	43.5
1909..........................	28.6	25.7	59.0	37.4	33.8	34.1	45.9
1910..........................	31.6	22.5	51.3	31.5	26.8	29.8	44.3
1911..........................	24.4	18.6	49.6	33.7	33.8	30.8	41.5
1912..........................	37.4	23.6	54.1	36.2	31.1	31.9	41.7
1913..........................	29.2	26.3	61.1	39.3	34.6	31.6	43.0
1914..........................	29.7	17.9	57.4	[3]46.6	33.2	30.9	44.0
1915..........................	37.8		36.2	....	....	25.7	44.3
Average (1906–1915).......	29.9	....	....	....	....	....	43.7

[1] Bushels of 32 pounds.   [2] Winchester bushels.   [3] Galicia and Bukowina not included.

OATS—Continued.

TABLE 29.—*Oats: Acreage, production, value, exports, etc., in the United States, 1849–1916.*

NOTE.—Figures in *italics* are census returns; figures in roman are estimates of the Department of Agriculture. Estimates of acres are obtained by applying estimated percentages of increase or decrease to the published numbers of the preceding year, except that a revised base is used for applying percentage estimates whenever new census data are available.

Year.	Acreage.	Average yield per acre.	Production.	Average farm price per bushel Dec. 1.	Farm value, Dec. 1.	Chicago cash price per bushel, contract.[1] December. Low.	December. High.	Following May. Low.	Following May. High.	Domestic exports, including oatmeal, fiscal year beginning July 1.[2]	Imports during fiscal year beginning July 1.[3]
	Acres.	*Bush.*	*Bushels.*	*Cts.*	*Dollars.*	*Cts.*	*Cts.*	*Cts.*	*Cts.*	*Bushels.*	*Bushels.*
1849			*146,584,000*								
1859			*172,643,000*								
1866	8,864,000	30.2	268,141,000	35.1	94,058,000	36	43	59	78	825,895	778,198
1867	10,082,000	27.6	278,698,000	44.5	123,903,000	52	57¼			122,554	780,798
1868	9,666,000	26.4	254,961,000	41.7	106,356,000	43	49½	56¾	62½	481,871	326,659
1869	9,461,000	30.5	288,334,000	38.0	109,522,000	40	44¾	46½	53½	121,517	2,266,785
1869			*282,107,000*								
1870	8,792,000	28.1	247,277,000	39.0	96,444,000	37¾	41	47¼	51	147,572	599,514
1871	8,366,000	30.6	255,743,000	36.2	92,591,000	30¾	33	34¾	42½	262,975	535,250
1872	9,001,000	30.2	271,747,000	29.9	81,304,000	23½	25¾	30	34	714,072	225,555
1873	9,752,000	27.7	270,340,000	34.6	93,474,000	34	40⅝	44	48½	812,873	191,802
1874	10,897,000	22.1	240,369,000	47.1	113,134,000	51¾	54½	57¼	64½	504,770	1,500,040
1875	11,915,000	29.7	354,318,000	32.0	113,441,000	29½	30½	28⅝	31½	1,466,228	121,547
1876	13,359,000	24.0	320,884,000	32.4	103,845,000	31¾	34½	37¼	45¾	2,854,128	41,597
1877	12,826,000	31.7	406,394,000	28.4	115,546,000	24⅛	27	23	27	3,715,479	21,391
1878	13,176,000	31.4	413,579,000	24.6	101,752,000	19⅝	20⅜	24⅜	30½	5,452,136	13,395
1879	12,684,000	28.7	363,761,000	33.1	120,533,000	32¾	36¾	29½	34⅞	766,366	489,576
1879	*16,145,000*	*25.3*	*407,859,000*								
1880	16,188,000	25.8	417,885,000	36.0	150,244,000	29⅛	33½	36¼	39½	402,904	64,412
1881	16,832,000	24.7	416,481,000	46.4	193,199,000	43½	46¾	48¾	56⅜	625,690	1,850,983
1882	18,495,000	26.4	488,251,000	37.5	182,978,000	34¾	41½	38¾	42¾	461,496	815,017
1883	20,325,000	28.1	571,302,000	32.7	187,040,000	29⅜	36⅛	30¾	34¼	3,274,622	121,069
1884	21,301,000	27.4	583,628,000	27.7	161,528,000	22½	25¼	34½	37	6,203,104	94,310
1885	22,784,000	27.6	629,409,000	28.5	179,632,000	27	29	26¼	29⅝	7,311,306	149,480
1886	23,658,000	26.4	624,134,000	29.8	186,138,000	25¾	27¼	25⅛	27½	1,374,635	139,575
1887	25,921,000	25.4	659,618,000	30.4	200,700,000	28⅝	30⅞	32½	38	573,080	123,817
1888	26,998,000	26.0	701,735,000	27.8	195,424,000	25	26⅞	21⅜	23⅝	1,191,471	131,501
1889	27,462,000	27.4	751,515,000	22.9	171,781,000	20	21	24¾	30	15,107,238	153,232
1889	*28,321,000*	*28.6*	*809,251,000*								
1890	26,431,000	19.8	523,621,000	42.4	222,048,000	39⅞	43⅞	45¼	54	1,382,836	41,848
1891	25,582,000	28.9	738,394,000	31.5	232,312,000	31⅛	33⅝	28⅛	33½	10,586,644	47,782
1892	27,064,000	24.4	661,035,000	31.7	209,254,000	25⅝	31¼	28¾	32¼	2,700,793	49,433
1893	27,273,000	23.4	638,855,000	29.4	187,576,000	27½	29⅛	32½	36	6,290,229	31,759
1894	27,024,000	24.5	662,037,000	32.4	214,817,000	28¾	29⅜	27½	30¾	1,708,824	330,318
1895	27,878,000	29.6	824,444,000	19.9	163,655,000	16⅝	17½	18	19⅜	15,156,618	66,602
1896	27,566,000	25.7	707,346,000	18.7	132,485,000	16½	18¾	16⅞	18¾	37,725,083	131,204
1897	25,730,000	27.2	698,768,000	21.2	147,975,000	21	23⅞	26	32	73,880,307	25,093
1898	25,777,000	28.4	730,907,000	25.5	186,405,000	26	27¾	24	27¾	33,534,362	28,098
1899	26,341,000	30.2	796,178,000	24.9	198,168,000	22¼	23	21¼	23¾	45,048,857	54,576
1899	*29,540,000*	*31.9*	*943,389,000*								
1900	27,365,000	29.6	809,126,000	25.8	208,669,000	21¾	22¾	27⅞	31	42,268,931	32,107
1901	28,541,000	25.8	736,809,000	39.9	293,659,000	42	48¼	41	49½	13,277,612	38,978
1902	28,653,000	34.5	987,843,000	30.7	303,585,000	29¼	32	33⅜	38¼	8,381,805	150,065
1903	27,638,000	28.4	784,094,000	34.1	267,662,000	34¼	38	39⅝	44¾	1,960,740	183,983
1904	27,843,000	32.1	894,596,000	31.3	279,900,000	28¼	32	28⅝	32	8,394,692	55,699
1905	28,047,000	34.0	953,216,000	29.1	277,048,000	29½	32¾	32⅛	34¾	48,434,541	40,025
1906	30,959,000	31.2	964,905,000	31.7	306,293,000	33	35¾	44½	48½	6,386,334	91,289
1907	31,837,000	23.7	754,443,000	44.3	334,568,000	46½	50⅞	52¾	56½	2,518,855	383,418
1908	32,344,000	25.0	807,156,000	47.2	381,171,000	48⅜	50½	56¼	62½	2,333,817	6,691,700
1909	33,204,000	30.3	1,007,353,000								
1909	*35,159,000*	*28.6*	*1,007,143,000*	40.2	405,121,000	40	45	36½	43¼	2,548,726	1,034,511
1910[4]	37,548,000	31.6	1,186,341,000	34.4	408,388,000	31	32½	31⅞	36	3,845,850	107,318
1911	37,763,000	24.4	922,298,000	45.0	414,663,000	46¼	47⅜	50½	58	2,677,749	2,622,357
1912	37,917,000	37.4	1,418,337,000	31.9	452,469,000	31	31¾	35⅛	43	36,455,474	723,899
1913	38,399,000	29.2	1,121,768,000	39.2	439,596,000	37⅝	40⅛	37	42½	2,748,743	22,273,624
1914	38,442,000	29.7	1,141,060,000	43.8	499,431,000	46⅞	49¾	50½	56	100,609,272	630,722
1915	40,996,000	37.8	1,549,030,000	36.1	559,506,000	40⅞	44	39½	49½	98,963,217	665,314
1916	41,539,000	30.1	1,251,992,000	52.4	656,179,000	46¾	54				

[1] Quotations are for No. 2 to 1906.
[2] Oatmeal not included 1866 to 1882, inclusive.
[3] Oatmeal not included 1867 to 1882, inclusive, and 1909.
[4] Figures adjusted to census basis.

OATS—Continued.

TABLE 30.—*Oats: Acreage, production, and total farm value, by States, 1915 and 1916.*

State.	Thousands of acres.		Production (thousands of bushels).		Total value, basis Dec. 1 price (thousands of dollars).	
	1916	1915	1916	1915	1916	1915
Maine	170	175	6,120	7,000	4,100	3,150
New Hampshire	12	12	444	456	306	246
Vermont	80	81	2,560	3,483	1,664	1,846
Massachusetts	15	12	480	432	317	220
Rhode Island	2	2	54	66	37	33
Connecticut	15	13	450	422	310	232
New York	1,206	1,340	31,356	54,270	19,441	24,422
New Jersey	69	70	2,070	2,275	1,263	1,092
Pennsylvania	1,130	1,140	35,030	43,320	19,967	19,061
Delaware	4	4	120	134	74	68
Maryland	46	45	1,357	1,530	828	750
Virginia	250	225	5,750	5,625	3,622	3,094
West Virginia	140	120	3,220	3,480	2,061	1,775
North Carolina	375	350	6,562	8,050	4,856	4,991
South Carolina	500	525	9,000	9,975	7,200	6,683
Georgia	860	905	16,770	17,648	13,248	11,648
Florida	60	61	900	1,220	639	854
Ohio	1,717	1,683	48,076	69,003	25,480	24,841
Indiana	1,750	1,638	52,500	65,520	26,775	22,277
Illinois	4,470	4,343	172,095	195,435	87,768	68,402
Michigan	1,423	1,530	42,690	64,260	22,626	22,491
Wisconsin	2,200	2,100	81,400	97,650	41,514	35,154
Minnesota	3,325	3,225	88,112	138,675	41,413	44,376
Iowa	5,050	4,950	186,850	198,000	89,688	63,360
Missouri	1,290	1,225	32,250	31,850	17,092	12,103
North Dakota	2,500	2,450	53,750	98,000	23,650	26,460
South Dakota	1,850	1,725	56,425	72,450	25,956	20,286
Nebraska	2,250	2,200	79,875	70,400	37,541	21,824
Kansas	1,550	1,500	36,425	39,750	20,034	14,708
Kentucky	300	250	6,300	6,500	3,780	3,120
Tennessee	360	357	7,560	8,746	4,687	4,373
Alabama	600	600	10,500	11,400	7,875	7,182
Mississippi	320	300	5,760	6,450	4,262	3,870
Louisiana	110	120	2,090	3,000	1,421	1,650
Texas	1,500	1,500	42,750	53,250	26,078	22,365
Oklahoma	1,160	1,350	15,080	36,450	8,596	12,758
Arkansas	350	375	7,350	10,125	4,998	5,265
Montana	660	600	25,080	31,200	11,788	9,984
Wyoming	245	227	8,575	9,534	5,145	4,100
Colorado	290	300	9,570	11,700	5,742	4,797
New Mexico	64	60	1,856	2,160	1,244	1,080
Arizona	9	9	338	333	270	213
Utah	103	100	4,480	4,700	2,733	2,115
Nevada	14	13	602	585	452	322
Idaho	310	335	13,330	15,745	7,198	5,353
Washington	275	275	14,300	13,750	7,293	5,088
Oregon	360	365	17,280	16,060	8,467	5,942
California	200	211	6,500	6,963	4,680	3,482
United States	41,539	40,996	1,251,992	1,549,030	656,179	559,506

OATS—Continued.

TABLE 31.—*Oats: Production and distribution in the United States, 1897–1916.*

[000 omitted.]

Year.	Old stock on farms Aug. 1.	Crop.	Total supplies.	Stock on farms Mar. 1 following.	Shipped out of county where grown.
	Bushels.	*Bushels.*	*Bushels.*	*Bushels.*	*Bushels.*
1897	71,139	698,768	769,907	271,729	204,147
1898	44,554	730,907	775,461	283,209	193,527
1899	50,537	796,178	846,715	290,937	223,014
1900	54,214	809,126	863,340	292,803	242,850
1901	47,713	736,809	784,522	226,393	143,398
1902	30,570	987,843	1,018,413	364,926	258,438
1903	73,352	784.094	857,446	273,708	223,959
1904	42,194	894,596	936,790	347,166	261,989
1905	55,836	953,216	1,009,052	379,805	277,133
1906	67,688	964,905	1,032,593	384,461	266,182
1907	68,258	754,443	822,701	267,476	210,923
1908	37,797	807,156	844,953	278,847	244,444
1909	26,323	1,007,143	1,033,466	365,438	329,255
1910	61,420	1,186,341	1,247,761	442,665	363,103
1911	67,793	922,298	990,091	289,988	265,958
1912	34,872	1,418,337	1,453,209	604,216	438,084
1913	103,900	1,121,768	1,225,668	419,476	297,326
1914	62,467	1,141,060	1,203,527	379,369	335,539
1915	55,607	1,549,030	1,604,637	598,148	465,823
1916	113,728	1,251,992	1,365,720	....	......

TABLE 32.—*Oats: Yield per acre, price per bushel Dec. 1, and value per acre, by States.*

State.	Yield per acre (bushels).											Farm price per bushel (cents).						Value per acre (dollars).[1]	
	10-year average, 1907-1916.	1907	1908	1909	1910	1911	1912	1913	1914	1915	1916	10-year average, 1907-1916.	1912	1913	1914	1915	1916	5-year average, 1911-1915.	1916
Me	38.1	37.1	34.0	37.0	42.4	38.5	34.6	40.0	41.0	40.0	36.0	56	51	55	57	45	67	20.36	24.12
N. H	35.8	32.5	30.6	31.5	42.8	33.8	39.0	35.0	38.0	38.0	37.0	58	48	56	58	54	69	20.30	25.53
Vt	37.6	34.0	33.3	32.2	41.5	35.0	43.0	39.0	42.5	43.0	32.0	56	48	52	55	53	65	21.55	20.80
Mass	34.4	35.0	33.0	31.0	35.5	35.0	34.0	35.0	37.0	36.0	32.0	56	47	54	56	51	66	18.85	21.12
R. I	29.2	29.5	31.0	25.0	35.0	29.0	28.6	26.0	27.5	33.0	27.0	56	45	50	58	50	68	15.03	18.36
Conn	31.4	31.5	32.6	27.5	36.8	35.1	30.7	28.0	29.0	32.5	30.0	55	49	55	55	55	69	16.79	20.70
N. Y	31.5	30.7	30.1	28.2	34.5	29.5	30.8	33.5	31.5	40.5	26.0	50	42	47	51	45	62	15.60	16.12
N. J	29.9	29.5	30.7	25.5	37.1	28.5	27.6	29.0	29.0	32.5	30.0	51	44	47	54	48	61	14.26	18.30
Pa	31.0	29.6	27.3	26.0	35.2	28.3	33.1	31.0	30.0	38.0	31.0	49	41	46	51	44	57	14.80	17.67
Del	30.1	30.0	29.8	25.5	33.8	30.0	30.5	30.5	27.0	33.5	30.0	50	45	51	50	51	62	14.79	18.60
Md	28.4	27.5	25.5	25.4	30.0	27.0	30.0	28.0	27.0	34.0	29.5	50	45	48	52	49	61	14.17	16.00
Va	20.7	19.6	19.1	19.0	22.0	20.2	22.2	21.5	15.5	25.0	23.0	54	52	52	58	55	63	11.25	14.49
W. Va	23.2	19.3	19.0	22.0	25.2	22.0	28.0	24.0	20.0	29.0	23.0	54	47	51	55	51	64	12.70	14.72
N. C	17.9	15.6	16.5	16.5	18.2	16.5	18.6	19.5	17.5	23.0	17.5	64	62	61	65	62	74	11.89	12.95
S. C	20.4	20.0	20.0	21.0	21.0	20.4	21.5	23.5	20.0	19.0	18.0	71	66	71	71	67	80	14.50	14.40
Ga	19.4	16.7	17.2	19.0	18.2	21.5	20.8	22.0	20.0	19.5	19.5	70	65	68	70	66	79	14.08	15.40
Fla	16.3	13.7	14.5	17.0	16.2	13.5	17.2	18.0	18.0	20.0	15.0	71	70	70	70	70	71	12.27	10.65
Ohio	32.5	22.8	26.4	32.5	37.2	32.1	44.0	30.2	30.5	41.0	28.0	42	33	40	45	36	53	13.90	14.84
Ind	29.6	20.2	21.2	30.5	35.4	28.7	40.1	21.4	28.5	40.0	30.0	40	30	38	43	34	51	11.67	15.30
Ill	33.1	24.5	23.0	36.6	38.0	28.8	43.3	23.8	29.3	45.0	38.5	40	30	38	44	35	51	12.55	19.64
Mich	31.4	20.8	29.7	30.5	34.0	28.6	34.9	30.0	33.5	42.0	30.0	42	33	39	45	35	53	13.23	15.90
Wis	33.2	22.0	31.1	35.0	29.8	29.8	37.3	36.5	27.0	46.5	27.0	41	32	37	43	36	51	13.44	18.87
Minn	30.8	24.5	22.0	33.0	28.7	22.8	41.7	37.8	28.0	43.0	26.5	37	26	32	40	32	47	11.40	12.46
Iowa	32.8	24.2	24.3	27.0	37.8	25.4	44.8	33.0	21.2	21.5	26.0	42	27	34	41	32	48	12.09	17.76
Mo	24.3	21.5	19.3	27.0	33.6	14.8	33.0	21.2	21.5	26.0	25.0	42	35	45	44	38	53	9.42	13.25

[1] Based upon farm price Dec. 1.

OATS—Continued.

TABLE 32.—*Oats: Yield per acre, price per bushel Dec. 1, and value per acre, by States—* Continued.

State.	Yield per acre (bushels).											Farm price per bushel (cents).						Value per acre (dollars).[1]	
	10-year average, 1907–1916.	1907	1908	1909	1910	1911	1912	1913	1914	1915	1916	10-year average, 1907–1916.	1912	1913	1914	1915	1916	5-year average, 1911–1915.	1916
N. Dak	26.7	24.5	23.4	32.0	7.0	23.5	41.4	25.7	28.0	40.0	21.5	35	22	30	37	27	44	9.52	9.46
S. Dak	26.8	24.7	23.0	30.0	23.0	7.4	33.8	26.5	27.5	42.0	30.5	36	25	34	38	28	46	10.57	14.03
Nebr	26.0	20.4	22.0	25.0	28.0	13.9	24.4	26.5	32.0	32.0	35.5	37	30	38	40	31	47	9.22	16.68
Kans	24.8	15.0	22.0	28.2	33.3	15.0	32.0	19.5	33.5	26.5	23.5	42	35	45	42	37	55	10.12	12.92
Ky	21.4	17.6	16.2	22.3	25.0	18.4	26.9	19.8	21.0	26.0	21.0	51	44	52	53	48	60	10.99	12.60
Tenn	21.6	20.8	21.0	20.0	23.0	19.5	21.7	21.0	23.0	24.5	21.0	52	47	53	53	50	62	11.10	13.02
Ala	18.9	17.5	18.0	16.5	18.5	19.2	20.0	20.5	22.0	19.0	17.5	67	62	69	69	63	75	13.27	13.12
Miss	18.9	17.9	17.5	16.0	19.2	18.4	17.4	20.0	23.0	21.5	18.0	64	60	63	65	60	74	12.57	13.32
La	20.7	14.5	20.0	20.0	21.5	21.0	20.8	22.0	23.0	25.0	19.0	59	51	57	63	55	68	13.01	12.92
Tex	28.4	19.0	28.9	18.7	35.0	25.1	36.0	32.5	25.0	35.5	28.5	52	43	51	48	42	61	14.50	17.38
Okla	22.5	15.0	25.0	29.0	36.5	9.0	25.1	18.0	27.5	27.0	13.0	44	34	45	41	35	57	8.34	7.41
Ark	23.0	19.5	21.4	22.8	27.5	20.0	19.9	26.5	24.0	27.0	21.0	54	50	53	53	52	68	12.27	14.28
Mont	44.6	49.0	41.6	51.3	38.0	49.8	48.0	43.5	35.0	52.0	38.0	41	35	32	39	32	47	16.19	17.86
Wyo	36.7	37.0	36.4	35.0	32.0	34.5	41.8	38.0	35.0	42.0	35.0	48	37	40	48	43	60	16.56	21.00
Colo	37.9	38.0	39.5	38.1	39.1	35.0	42.8	35.0	40.0	39.0	33.0	48	38	44	45	41	60	16.49	19.80
N. Mex	34.6	38.5	33.5	40.0	27.4	38.8	34.7	30.0	38.0	36.0	29.0	57	45	60	45	50	67	18.17	19.43
Ariz	38.8	29.0	36.0	37.0	40.1	42.0	44.7	43.0	42.0	37.0	37.5	70	70	50	70	64	80	26.21	30.00
Utah	46.1	45.0	49.5	46.1	43.0	44.7	46.4	46.0	50.0	47.0	43.5	48	49	40	43	45	61	20.96	26.54
Nev	44.1	43.0	45.0	40.0	44.7	45.0	40.0	43.0	52.0	45.0	43.0	62	52	65	55	55	75	26.00	32.25
Idaho	45.1	50.5	44.0	44.5	38.5	44.0	48.9	46.5	44.0	47.0	43.0	41	35	32	38	34	54	16.46	23.22
Wash	48.8	55.5	44.5	49.0	42.8	51.7	48.2	47.5	47.0	50.0	52.0	44	40	40	42	37	51	19.96	26.52
Oreg	38.3	35.0	33.4	37.8	34.5	34.7	38.2	42.3	35.0	44.0	48.0	44	41	38	45	37	49	15.81	23.52
Cal	34.0	33.5	33.5	31.4	37.0	34.0	39.0	31.6	35.0	33.0	32.5	60	55	60	53	50	72	19.10	23.40
U. S.	29.9	23.7	25.0	30.3	31.6	24.4	37.4	29.2	29.7	37.8	30.1	41.5	31.9	39.2	43.8	36.1	52.4	12.20	15.80

[1] Based upon farm price Dec. 1.

TABLE 33.—*Oats: Farm price per bushel on first of each month, by geographical divisions, 1915 and 1916.*

Month.	United States.		North Atlantic States.		South Atlantic States.		N. Central States east of Miss. R.		N. Central States west of Miss. R.		South Central States.		Far Western States.	
	1916	1915	1916	1915	1916	1915	1916	1915	1916	1915	1916	1915	1916	1915
	Cts.	Cts.	Cts.	Cts.	Cts.	Cts.	Cts.	Cts.	Cts.	Cts.	Cts.	Cts.	Cts.	Cts.
January	39.1	45.0	45.9	52.5	63.4	65.7	38.4	45.1	35.4	41.9	45.4	51.5	39.3	43.4
February	44.6	50.1	50.6	57.0	64.3	67.4	45.5	51.1	41.5	47.1	47.5	56.1	40.8	46.1
March	42.7	52.1	50.7	61.2	64.6	70.2	41.7	52.0	38.2	48.8	51.0	59.6	46.1	50.2
April	42.0	53.4	51.5	61.5	65.8	71.8	40.9	54.1	37.6	50.1	50.1	60.9	43.7	49.8
May	42.6	53.4	52.6	64.3	65.6	70.9	41.9	54.0	38.2	49.6	49.4	58.9	44.0	52.1
June	42.1	51.3	53.9	62.2	66.0	70.4	40.8	51.4	37.3	47.9	50.3	56.6	44.8	49.9
July	40.4	46.7	51.3	61.5	63.9	66.3	38.4	46.2	36.1	43.0	47.2	49.1	45.9	47.9
August	40.1	45.4	50.5	59.3	64.2	63.6	38.6	44.0	35.8	42.9	44.6	45.6	46.1	46.6
September	43.1	38.5	52.2	54.9	66.2	62.9	41.5	36.1	39.0	34.2	51.6	44.5	45.2	42.9
October	44.5	34.5	52.8	46.6	68.9	63.6	42.9	32.1	40.6	30.4	53.7	44.6	46.6	37.2
November	49.0	34.9	58.1	45.5	72.6	62.3	48.1	33.5	44.6	30.7	57.7	44.4	49.4	37.1
December	52.4	36.1	60.3	45.0	74.5	62.7	51.5	35.2	47.9	31.3	63.4	44.6	54.0	37.7
Average	43.9	42.7	52.9	54.2	66.7	66.1	42.8	42.1	40.0	38.4	50.3	48.0	46.2	42.3

OATS—Continued.

TABLE 34.—*Oats: Condition of crop, United States, on first of months named, 1896–1916.*

Year	June.	July.	August.	When harvested.	Year.	June.	July.	August.	When harvested.	Year.	June.	July	August.	When harvested.
	P. ct.	*P. ct.*	*P. ct.*	*P. ct.*		*P. ct.*	*P. ct.*	*P. ct.*	*P. ct.*		*P. ct.*	*P. ct.*	*P. ct.*	*P. ct.*
1896....	98.8	96.3	77.3	74.0	1903....	85.5	84.3	79.5	75.7	1910....	91.0	82.2	81.5	83.3
1897....	89.0	87.5	86.0	84.6	1904....	89.2	89.8	86.6	85.6	1911....	85.7	68.8	65.7	64.5
1898....	98.0	92.8	84.2	79.0	1905....	92.9	92.1	90.8	90.3	1912....	91.1	89.2	90.3	92.3
1899....	88.7	90.0	90.8	87.2	1906....	85.9	84.0	82.8	81.9	1913....	87.0	76.3	73.8	74.0
1900....	91.7	85.5	85.0	82.9	1907....	81.6	81.0	75.6	65.5	1914....	89.5	84.7	79.4	75.8
1901....	85.3	83.7	73.6	72.1	1908....	92.9	85.7	76.8	69.7	1915....	92.2	93.9	91.6	91.1
1902....	90.6	92.1	89.4	87.2	1909....	88.7	88.3	85.5	83.8	1916....	86.9	86.3	81.5	78.0

TABLE 35.—*Oats: Wholesale price per bushel, 1912–1916.*

Date.	New York.		Baltimore.		Cincinnati.		Chicago.		Milwaukee.		Duluth.		Detroit.		San Francisco.	
	No. 2 white.[1]		No. 3 white.		No. 2 mixed.		Contract.		No. 3 white.		No. 3 white.		Standard.		White (per 100 lbs.).	
	Low.	High.	Low.	High.	Low.	Hi h.	Low.	High.	Low.	High.	Low.	High.	Low.	High.	Low.	High.
1912.	*Cts.*	*Cts.*	*Cts.*	*Cts.*	*Cts.*	*Cts.*	*Cts.*	*Cts.*	*Cts.*	*Cts.*	*Cts.*	*Cts.*	*Cts.*	*Cts.*	*Dolls*	*Dolls.*
Jan.-June	53½	64	52¾	65	50	61	46⅞	58½	47	59¾	44⅞	56⅛	50½	63½	1.70	2.12½
July-Dec.	38½	62½	37½	66½	32	55	30¼	57	30¾	57	28⅜	51	33½	61	1.47½	1.95
1913.																
Jan.-June	36½	48	38½	47	33½	43½	31⅝	43⅛	31¼	42½	27⅛	41⅜	34½	44½	1.43½	1.67½
July-Dec.	44	50	45	47½	39	47	36⅜	43⅜	37½	44	33⅞	42⅛	41	45½	1.37½	1.57½
1914.																
Jan.-June	43½	48½	42½	46¾	39¼	43	36⅝	42½	36½	43	33⅝	40	39½	45	1.22½	1.46¼
July-Dec.	43½	58½	41½	54½	35	52½	33½	51⅛	34¼	52	33⅛	50⅝	37¾	53	1.20	1.60
1915.																
Jan......	55½	64	52	60½	51	58½	49	58⅝	50	58¾	49¼	56⅞	52½	59¼	1.50	1.85
Feb......	61½	66	61	62½	57	59½	53	60	53¾	61	52⅛	58⅜	56½	62	1.77½	1.85
Mar......	61	66½	59¼	64	56	61½	53⅝	60⅛	53	61½	51⅜	58⅞	56½	62	1.72½	1.80
Apr......	61½	64	62	62¾	56½	59½	53⅞	57½	54¾	58	52	56⅜	58½	61½	1.75	1.80
May......	59	63½	56	62	51½	57	50½	56	51½	56¾	50⅛	54½	54½	58½	1.65	1.80
June.....	53¾	57½	50	56½	46	52	46⅜	49¾	47¼	51½	44⅛	48⅜	50	54	1.40	1.70
Jan.-June	53¾	66½	50	64	46	61½	46⅜	60⅛	47¼	61½	44⅛	58⅞	50	62	1.40	1.85
July......	56½	65½	50½	63½	48	58	48¾	59½	49	57	47	58	51	59	1.42½	1.50
Aug......	55	70½	41	66	36½	54	46	60	33¼	63	33¼	54½	41	65	1.37½	1.50
Sept.....	Nominal..		38	40	33	38	35½	39	34	38	32	33⅝	36½	40	1.30	1.40
Oct......	...do......		38	42	35	39	35¾	39⅜	34½	38½	31⅝	35⅜	39	42	1.30	1.40
Nov......	...do......		41	43	37	39	37¼	41½	35½	40½	32¼	37⅞	38	41	1.35	1.40
Dec......	...do......		42½	48	39	45	40⅞	44	40½	45½	37⅜	42⅞	42	45	1.32½	1.40
July-Dec.	55	70½	38	66	33	58	35½	60	33¼	63	31⅝	58	36½	65	1.30	1.50
1916.																
Jan......	48½	57½	48	55¼	44	55½	43¼	51	43½	55	42¼	49½	46	55½	1.32½	1.55
Feb......	48½	56½	47	55	42	53	41¾	50	40¾	52½	38⅞	47⅞	44½	53½	1.42½	1.55
Mar......	44½	56	45½	47	42	46	42	47	41	46½	39¼	42½	44½	48	1.40	1.45
Apr......	49¾	51	47	49½	43	46	44½	47	43¾	46¾	41⅛	42⅜	46½	48½	1.40	1.42½
May.....	44½	52	43	50½	38	45	39½	49¼	38¾	46½	37⅜	43¾	41	48½	1.40	1.57½
June.....	44½	46	43	44½	38	40½	37⅜	41½	38¼	41½	36⅛	38⅜	41	43	1.50	1.55
Jan.-June	44½	57½	43	55¼	38	53½	37⅜	51	38¼	55	36⅛	49½	41	55½	1.32½	1.57½
July.....	44½	47½	43¾	46	39	42½	38⅝	42	38½	43¼	36⅝	40	43	46	1.50	1.60
Aug......	45¾	54	45	51½	41	47½	41	47	40½	49	38⅜	47¼	42½	49	1.57½	1.72½
Sept.....	45	55	50½	52½	46½	48½	44⅛	47⅛	44	48½	42¾	45¾	48	51½	1.62½	1.72½
Oct......	51½	59½	51	58	47½	55	45½	53¾	46	54¼	43¾	51¼	49½	57	1.62½	2.00
Nov......	58½	64	57½	61½	53½	58½	51½	57	51½	58½	50⅛	57⅛	55	60½	1.95	2.07½
Dec......	55½	61½	57½	60½	84	91	46¾	54	48½	55	44¼	52⅜	54	59	2.00	2.07½
July-Dec.	44½	64	43¾	61½	39	91	38⅝	54	38½	58½	36⅝	57⅛	42½	60½	1.50	2.07½

[1] No. 3 white in 1916.

OATS—Continued.

TABLE 36.—*Oats: International trade, calendar years 1913–1915.*

[See "General note," Table 10.]

EXPORTS.

[000 omitted.]

Country.	1913	1914 (prelim.)	1915 (prelim.)	Country.	1913	1914 (prelim.)	1915 (prelim.)
	Bushels.	*Bushels.*	*Bushels.*		*Bushels.*	*Bushels.*	*Bushels.*
Algeria	3,888	5,291	4,011	Netherlands	31,131	14,411	34
Argentina	61,298	24,368	40,840	Roumania	11,963	7,030	....
Bulgaria	173	....	....	Russia	41,309	19,235	117
Canada	31,732	20,174	18,496	Sweden	4,730	2,651	....
China	285	324	324	United Kingdom	1,655	1,321	717
Chile	3,687	3,372	7,313	United States	5,275	35,067	104,549
Denmark	194	168	2	Other countries	4,221	3,768	....
Finland	456	350	237				
Germany	45,584	....	....	Total	247,581	137,560	....

IMPORTS.

Austria-Hungary	1,047	....	....	Philippine Islands	537	74	441
Belgium	9,555	....	....	Russia	2,608	1,899	276
Denmark	4,224	3,739	217	Sweden	4,431	5,008	2,072
Cuba	1,503	1,534	1,004	Switzerland	12,205	10,235	6,913
Finland	1,002	1,393	157	United Kingdom	64,470	55,905	59,165
France	39,992	35,473	56,610	United States	13,309	9,429	264
Germany	34,793	....	....	Other countries	2,461	4,830	....
Italy	7,331	455	2,765				
Netherlands	38,711	20,006	4,332	Total	238,572	151,021	....
Norway	393	1,041	1,093				

BARLEY.

TABLE 37.—*Barley: Area and production in undermentioned countries, 1914–1916.*

Country.	Area.			Production.		
	1914	1915	1916	1914	1915	1916
NORTH AMERICA.	*Acres.*	*Acres.*	*Acres.*	*Bushels.*	*Bushels.*	*Bushels.*
United States	7,565,000	7,148,000	7,674,000	194,953,000	228,851,000	180,927,000
Canada:						
New Brunswick	2,000	2,000	2,000	64,000	48,000	
Quebec	85,000	85,000	77,000	2,261,000	2,255,000	
Ontario	461,000	449,000	340,000	13,987,000	15,369,000	
Manitoba	468,000	490,000	475,000	9,828,000	17,763,000	(¹)
Saskatchewan	290,000	287,000	262,000	4,901,000	10,570,000	
Alberta	178,000	185,000	161,000	4,806,000	6,984,000	
Other	12,000	11,000	12,000	354,000	342,000	
Total Canada	1,496,000	1,509,000	1,329,000	36,201,000	53,331,000	41,318,000
Mexico	292,000	(¹)	(¹)	10,839,000	10,000,000	(¹)
Total	....	....	....	241,993,000	292,182,000	....
SOUTH AMERICA.						
Argentina	418,000	375,000	431,000	8,037,000	5,144,000	(¹)
Chile	153,000	224,000	(¹)	5,567,000	3,750,000	(¹)
Uruguay	14,000	5,000	10,000	165,000	40,000	115,000
Total	....	....	....	13,769,000	8,934,000	....

[1] No official statistics.

BARLEY—Continued.

TABLE 37.—*Barley: Area and production in undermentioned countries, 1914–1916*—Con.

Country.	Area.			Production.		
	1914	1915	1916	1914	1915	· 1916
EUROPE.						
	Acres.	*Acres.*	*Acres.*	*Bushels.*	*Bushels.*	*Bushels.*
Austria-Hungary:						
Austria.............	¹ 1,729,000	(²)	(²)	¹ 58,458,000	¹ 58,000,000	(²)
Hungary proper.....	2,705,000	2,830,000	(²)	65,265,000	56,186,000	(²)
Croatia-Slavonia....	(²)	(²)	(²)	1,940,000	1,938,000	(²)
Bosnia-Herzegovina.	(²)	(²)	(²)	3,000,000	3,000,000	(²)
Total Austria-Hungary........				128,663,000	119,124,000	
Belgium................	84,000	(²)	(²)	4,232,000	4,000,000	(²)
Bulgaria...............	554,000	(²)	(²)	9,217,000	14,697,000	14,739,000
Denmark...............	(²)	644,000	633,000	20,780,000	25,898,000	22,306,000
Finland................	(²)	(²)	(²)	4,047,000	5,000,000	(²)
France.................	1,780,000	1,575,000	1,547,000	42,719,000	30,963,000	37,778,000
Germany...............	3,909,000	4,002,000	(²)	144,125,000	114,077,000	(²)
Italy...................	610,000	608,000	596,000	6,917,000	11,050,000	10,104,000
Netherlands............	67,000	63,000	60,000	3,019,000	3,233,000	2,499,000
Norway.................	(²)	(²)	98,000	2,591,000	2,821,000	3,026,000
Roumania..............	1,405,000	1,371,000	1,454,000	25,505,000	28,688,000	30,038,000
Russia:						
Russia proper.......	25,260,000	24,094,000	25,105,000	310,249,000	311,246,000	442,381,000
Poland.............	(²)	(²)	(²)	(²)	(²)	(²)
Northern Caucasia..	4,495,000	4,404,000	(²)	73,323,000	³ 69,575,000	(²)
Total Russia (European).........	29,755,000	28,498,000		383,572,000	380,821,000	
Serbia.................	(²)	(²)	(²)	3,000,000	2,250,000	(²)
Spain..................	3,404,000	3,786,000	4,035,000	72,272,000	82,763,000	84,372,000
Sweden................	436,000	(²)	(²)	12,195,000	14,252,000	(²)
United Kingdom:						
England.............	1,420,000	1,152,000	1,245,000	48,205,000	34,898,000	40,324,000
Wales...............	84,000	80,000	87,000	2,743,000	2,467,000	2,732,000
Scotland.............	194,000	150,000	170,000	7,616,000	5,183,000	5,341,000
Ireland..............	172,000	142,000	150,000	8,073,000	5,828,000	6,537,000
Total United Kingdom.......	1,870,000	1,524,000	1,652,000	66,637,000	48,376,000	54,934,000
Total............				929,491,000	888,013,000	
ASIA.						
India:						
British.............	7,098,000	7,758,000	(²)	125,113,000	142,846,000	(²)
Native States.......	981,000	(²)	(²)	(²)	(²)	(²)
Total.............	8,079,000	7,758,000		125,113,000	142,846,000	
Cyprus.................	(²)	(²)	(²)	2,000,000	2,000,000	(²)
Japanese Empire:						
Japan...............	3,294,000	3,239,000	3,109,000	85,775,000	100,891,000	99,822,000
Formosa.............	(²)	(²)	(²)	60,000	75,000	(²)
Total Japanese Empire.........				85,835,000	100,966,000	
Russia:						
Central Asia (4 governments of)......	485,000	⁴ 600,000	(²)	7,929,000	⁴ 7,946,000	(²)
Siberia (4 governments of).........	630,000	652,000	(²)	11,498,000	5,707,000	(²)
Transcaucasia (1 government of)..	2,000	(⁵)	(²)	24,000	(⁵)	(²)
Total Russia (Asiatic)........	1,117,000			19,451,000	13,653,000	
Total............				232,399,000	259,465,000	

¹ Galicia and Bukowina not included.
² No official statistics.
³ Includes 1 government of Transcaucasia.
⁴ Includes Oural.
⁵ Included in Northern Caucasia.

BARLEY—Continued.

TABLE 37.—*Barley: Area and production in undermentioned countries, 1914–1916*—Con.

Country.	Area.			Production.		
	1914	1915	1916	1914	1915	1916
AFRICA.	*Acres.*	*Acres.*	*Acres.*	*Bushels.*	*Bushels.*	*Bushels.*
Algeria..................	3,131,000	2,703,000	(1)	35,785,000	39,866,000	(1)
Tunis..................	795,000	1,608,000	(1)	3,215,000	11,482,000	6,889,000
Union of South Africa...	(1)	(1)	64,000	2 1,359,000	2 1,359,000	(1)
Total..............	....	....	....	40,359,000	52,707,000	....
AUSTRALASIA.						
Australia:						
Queensland.........	9,000	7,000	(1)	120,000	109,000	(1)
New South Wales...	21,000	(1)	6,000	313,000	48,000	100,000
Victoria.............	83,000	62,000	(1)	1,870,000	620,000	(1)
South Australia.....	91,000	66,000	(1)	1,375,000	461,000	(1)
Western Australia..	11,000	4,000	(1)	173,000	17,000	(1)
Tasmania...........	8,000	(1)	(1)	193,000	100,000	(1)
Total Australia....	223,000	....	....	4,044,000	1,355,000	....
New Zealand............	32,000	18,000	30,000	1,234,000	616,000	843,000
Total Australasia..	255,000	....	....	5,278,000	1,971,000	....
Grand total.......	....	....	....	1,463,289,000	1,503,272,000	....

[1] No official statistics.   [2] Census of 1911.

TABLE 38.—*Barley: Total production of countries named in Table 37, 1895–1916.*

Year.	Production.	Year.	Production.	Year.	Production.	Year.	Production.
	Bushels.		*Bushels.*		*Bushels.*		*Bushels.*
1895....	915,504,000	1901.....	1,072,195,000	1907.....	1,271,237,000	1913.....	1,650,265,000
1896....	932,100,000	1902.....	1,229,132,000	1908.....	1,274,897,000	1914.....	1,463,289,000
1897....	864,605,000	1903.....	1,235,786,000	1909.....	1,458,263,000	1915.....	1,503,272,000
1898....	1,030,581,000	1904.....	1,175,784,000	1910.....	1,388,734,000	1916.....	....
1899....	965,720,000	1905.....	1,180,053,000	1911.....	1,373,286,000		
1900....	959,622,000	1906.....	1,296,579,000	1912.....	1,466,977,000		

TABLE 39.—*Barley: Average yield per acre in undermentioned countries, 1890–1915.*

Year.	United States.	Russia (European).[1]	Germany.[1]	Austria.[1]	Hungary proper.[1]	France.[2]	United Kingdom.[2]
	Bushels.	*Bushels.*	*Bushels.*	*Bushels.*	*Bushels.*	*Bushels.*	*Bushels.*
Average:							
1890–1899..................	23.4	13.3	29.4	21.1	....	22.6	39.8
1900–1909..................	25.5	14.3	35.3	26.3	23.4	23.6	35.0
1906........................	28.3	13.0	35.2	26.1	26.8	20.8	36.1
1907........................	23.8	14.2	38.2	27.3	23.1	24.4	36.8
1908........................	25.1	14.2	34.9	25.2	21.3	22.6	34.9
1909........................	22.5	17.9	39.5	28.4	25.1	25.4	38.9
1910........................	22.5	16.3	34.4	24.9	19.7	23.5	34.3
1911........................	21.0	14.4	37.0	27.5	26.9	25.0	34.0
1912........................	29.7	16.2	40.7	29.7	26.9	26.1	33.1
1913........................	23.8	18.5	41.3	29.7	27.0	24.5	35.1
1914........................	25.8	12.9	36.8	3 33.8	24.1	24.0	35.6
1915........................	32.0	....	28.5	....	....	19.7	31.8
Average (1906–1915).......	25.4	....	....	....	....	....	35.1

[1] Bushels of 48 pounds.   [2] Winchester bushels.   [3] Galicia and Bukowina not included.

BARLEY—Continued.

TABLE 40.—*Barley: Acreage, production, value, exports, etc., in the United States, 1849–1916.*

NOTE.—Figures in *italics* are census returns; figures in roman are estimates of the Department of Agriculture. Estimates of acres are obtained by applying estimated percentages of increase or decrease to the published numbers of the preceding year, except that a revised base is used for applying percentage estimates whenever new census data are available.

Year.	Acreage.	Average yield per acre.	Production.	Average farm price per bushel Dec. 1.	Farm value Dec. 1.	Chicago cash price per bushel, low malting to fancy.[1] December.		Following May.		Domestic exports, fiscal year beginning July 1.	Imports, fiscal year beginning July 1.
						Low.	High.	Low.	High.		
	Acres.	*Bush.*	*Bushels.*	*Cents.*	*Dollars.*	*Cents.*	*Cents.*	*Cents.*	*Cents.*	*Bushels.*	*Bushels.*
1849	......	......	*5,167,000*	......	......	......	......	......	......	......	......
1859	......	......	*15,826,000*	......	......	......	......	......	......	......	......
1866	493,000	22.9	11,284,000	70.2	7,916,000	59	70	85	100	......	3,247,250
1867	1,131,000	22.7	25,727,000	70.1	18,028,000	150	180	227	250	9,810	3,783,966
1868	937,000	24.4	22,896,000	109.0	24,948,000	140	170	149	175	59,077	5,069,880
1869	1,026,000	27.9	28,652.000	70.8	20,298,000	74	85	50	62	255,490	6,727,597
1869	......	......	*29,761,000*	......	......	......	......	......	......	......	......
1870	1,109,000	23.7	26,295,000	79.1	20,792,000	68	80	72	95	340,093	4,866,700
1871	1,114,000	24.0	26,718,000	75.8	20,264,000	55½	64	55	71	86,891	5,565,591
1872	1,397,000	19.2	26,846,000	68.6	18,416,000	60	70	71	85	482,410	4,244,751
1873	1,387,000	23.1	32,044,000	86.7	27,794,000	132	158	130	155	320,399	4,891,189
1874	1,581,000	20.6	32,552,000	86.0	27,998,000	120	129½	115	137	91,118	6,255,063
1875	1,790,000	20.6	36,909,000	74.1	27,368,000	81	88	62½	72½	317,781	10,285,957
1876	1,767,000	21.9	38,710,000	63.0	24,403,000	63¾	68½	80	85	1,186,129	6,702,965
1877	1,669,000	21.4	35,638,000	62.5	22,287,000	56¼	64	46½	52½	3,921,501	6,764,228
1878	1,790,000	23.6	42,246.000	57.9	24,454,000	91	100	64	73	715,536	5,720,979
1879	1,681,000	24.0	40,283,000	58.9	23,714,000	86	92	75	80	1,128,923	7,135,258
1879	*1,998,000*	*22.0*	*43,997,000*	......	......	......	......	......	......	......	......
1880	1,843,000	24.5	45,165,000	66.6	30,091,000	100	120	95	105	885,246	9,528,616
1881	1,968,000	20.9	41,161,000	82.3	33,863,000	101	107	100	100	205,930	12,182,722
1882	2,272,000	21.5	48,954,000	62.9	30,768,000	79	82	80	80	433,005	10,050,687
1883	2,379,000	21.1	50,136,000	58.7	29,420,000	62	67	65	74	724,955	8,596,122
1884	2,609,000	23.5	61,203,000	48.7	29,779,000	53	58	65	65	629,130	9,986,507
1885	2,729,000	21.4	58,360,000	56.3	32,868,000	62	65	58	60	252,183	10,197,115
1886	2,653,000	22.4	59,428,000	53.6	31,841,000	51	54	57	57	1,305,300	10,355,594
1887	2,902,000	19.6	56,812,000	51.9	29,464,000	80	80	69	77	550,884	10,831,461
1888	2,996,000	21.3	63,884,000	59.0	37,672,000	......	......	......	......	1,440,321	11,368.414
1889	3,221,000	24.3	78,333,000	41.6	32,614,000	58	58	......	......	1,408,311	11,332,545
1889	*3,221,000*	*24.3*	*78,333,000*	......	......	......	......	......	......	......	......
1890	3,135,000	21.4	67,168,000	62.7	42,141,000	......	......	......	......	973,062	5,078,733
1891	3,353,000	25.9	86,839,000	52.4	45,470,000	......	......	......	......	2,800,075	3,146,328
1892	3,400,000	23.6	80,097,000	47.5	38,026,000	65	67	65	65	3,035,267	1,970,129
1893	3,220,000	21.7	69,869,000	41.1	28,729,000	52	54	55	60	5,219,405	791,061
1894	3,171,000	19.4	61,400,000	44.2	27,134,000	53½	55½	51	52	1,563,754	2,116,816
1895	3,300,000	26.4	87,073.000	33.7	29,312,000	33	40	25	36	7,680,331	837,384
1896	2,951,000	23.6	69,695,000	32.3	22,491,000	22	37	24½	35	20,030,301	1,271,787
1897	2,719,000	24.5	66,685,000	37.7	25,142,000	25½	42	36	53	11,237,077	124,804
1898	2,583,000	21.6	55,792,000	41.3	23,064,000	40	50½	36	42	2,267,403	110,475
1899	2,878,000	25.5	73,382,000	40.3	29,594,000	35	45	36	44	23,661,662	189,757
1899	*4,470,000*	*26.8*	*119,635,000*	......	......	......	......	......	......	......	......
1900	2,894,000	20.4	58,926,000	40.9	24,075,000	37	61	37	57	6,293,207	171,004
1901	4,296,000	25.6	109,933,000	45.2	49,705,000	56	63	64	72	8,714,268	57,406
1902	4,661,000	29.0	134,954,000	45.9	61,899,000	36	70	48	56	8,429,141	56,462
1903	4,993,000	26.4	131,861,000	45.6	60,166,000	42	61½	38	59	10,881,627	90,708
1904	5,146,000	27.2	139,749,000	42.0	58,652,000	38	52	40	50	10,661,655	81,020
1905	5,096,000	26.8	136,551,000	40.5	54,993,000	37	53	42	55½	17,729,360	18,049
1906	6,324,000	28.3	178,916,000	41.5	74,236,000	44	56	66	85	8,238,842	38,319
1907	6,448,000	23.8	153,597,000	66.6	102,290,000	78	102	60	75	4,349,078	199,741
1908	6,646,000	25.1	166,756,000	55.4	92,442,000	57	64½	66	75	6,580,393	2,644
1909	7,011,000	24.3	170,284,000	......	......	......	......	......	......	......	......
1909	*7,699,000*	*22.5*	*173,344,000*	54.0	93,539,000	55	72	50	68	4,311,566	......
1910[2]	7.743,000	22.5	173,832,000	57.8	100,426,000	72	90	75	115	9,399,346	......
1911	7,627,000	21.0	160,240,000	86.9	139,182,000	102	130	68	132	1,585,242	......
1912	7,530,000	29.7	223,824,000	50.5	112,957,000	43	77	45	68	17,536,703	......
1913	7,499,000	23.8	178,189,000	53.7	95,731,000	50	79	51	66	6,644,747	......
1914	7,565,000	25.8	194,953.000	54.3	105,903,000	60	75	74½	82	26,754,522	......
1915	7,148,000	32.0	228,851,000	51.6	118,172,000	62	77	70	83	27,473,160	......
1916	7,674,000	23.6	180,927,000	88.2	159,534,000	95	125	......	......	......	......

[1] Prices 1895 to 1908 for No. 3 grade.

[2] Figures adjusted to census basis.

BARLEY—Continued.

TABLE 41.—*Barley: Acreage, production, and total farm value, by States, 1916.*

[000 omitted.]

State.	Acreage.	Production.	Farm value Dec. 1.	State.	Acreage.	Production.	Farm value Dec. 1.
	Acres.	*Bushels.*	*Dollars.*		*Acres.*	*Bushels.*	*Dollars.*
Maine............	6	156	162	Kansas............	300	4,800	3,696
New Hampshire...	1	28	25	Kentucky.........	6	156	140
Vermont..........	15	412	412	Tennessee........	10	237	237
New York........	81	1,887	1,906	Texas............	9	153	122
Pennsylvania.....	12	300	225	Oklahoma........	8	100	100
Maryland.........	6	192	140	Montana..........	95	2,660	2,022
Virginia.........	13	358	304	Wyoming.........	25	825	718
Ohio.............	33	917	734	Colorado.........	160	5,120	4,198
Indiana..........	15	405	304	New Mexico......	11	308	308
Illinois..........	60	1,920	1,978	Arizona..........	32	1,120	1,210
Michigan.........	100	2,450	2,230	Utah.............	34	1,224	930
Wisconsin........	610	18,300	19,215	Nevada...........	12	492	467
Minnesota........	1,375	26,125	22,729	Idaho............	190	7,410	6,076
Iowa............	295	8,702	7,919	Washington.......	165	6,814	5,724
Missouri.........	5	100	93	Oregon...........	140	5,390	4,312
North Dakota.....	1,725	26,738	21,390	California........	1,190	33,320	31,654
South Dakota.....	825	18,728	15,544				
Nebraska.........	110	3,080	2,310	United States.	7,674	180,927	159,534

TABLE 42.—*Barley: Yield per acre, price per bushel Dec. 1, and value per acre, by States.*

State.	Yield per acre (bushels).											Farm price per bushel (cents).						Value per acre (dollars).[1]	
	10-year aver. 1907–1916.	1907	1908	1909	1910	1911	1912	1913	1914	1915	1916	10-year aver. 1907–1916.	1912	1913	1914	1915	1916	5-year average, 1911–1915.	1916
Me.........	28.0	28.0	28.0	28.5	31.0	28.0	26.2	28.0	30.0	26.5	26.0	82	77	80	81	75	104	22.39	27.04
N. H.......	26.9	24.0	24.0	25.0	26.0	24.0	28.0	32.0	30.0	28.0	28.0	82	84	80	82	79	90	23.30	25.20
Vt.........	31.7	28.5	33.0	30.0	31.0	30.5	35.0	32.0	34.5	35.0	27.5	78	80	80	75	75	100	26.15	27.50
N. Y.......	26.5	25.0	26.0	24.8	28.3	25.0	26.0	27.8	28.0	32.0	23.3	77	68	69	71	75	101	20.85	23.53
Pa.........	26.1	25.5	26.0	21.8	26.5	25.0	27.5	26.0	28.0	29.5	25.0	69	68	71	70	75	75	19.03	18.75
Md.........	30.4	33.0	30.0	32.0	31.0	23.0	27.0	29.0	33.0	34.0	32.0	65	68	64	66	70	73	19.26	23.36
Va.........	27.1	29.0	28.0	25.0	29.3	23.0	25.0	26.0	29.0	27.5	27.5	72	55	70	80	75	85	19.12	23.38
Ohio.......	27.6	28.0	27.5	25.9	28.5	27.2	31.0	24.0	25.0	31.0	27.8	64	55	58	59	54	80	17.06	22.24
Ind........	25.5	20.5	23.0	23.5	27.0	26.5	29.5	25.0	25.0	28.0	27.0	64	60	50	67	65	75	17.01	20.25
Ill........	29.6	28.0	28.5	28.0	30.2	8.0	31.5	26.0	29.5	34.0	32.0	66	53	57	61	57	103	18.93	32.96
Mich.......	25.3	22.0	25.5	24.7	26.0	24.0	26.0	24.8	26.5	27.3	24.5	68	65	60	65	62	91	17.52	22.30
Wis........	28.0	23.0	30.0	28.0	25.9	25.5	29.4	25.0	27.3	35.5	30.0	69	55	60	62	56	105	19.64	31.50
Minn.......	23.6	22.5	25.0	23.6	21.0	19.0	28.2	24.0	23.3	30.5	19.0	60	41	48	53	49	87	13.69	16.53
Iowa.......	26.8	25.5	27.0	22.0	29.5	21.9	31.0	25.0	26.0	31.0	29.5	61	52	55	55	49	91	15.95	26.84
Mo.........	23.4	23.0	23.0	25.0	27.0	20.0	24.8	22.0	24.0	25.0	20.0	67	66	60	65	63	93	15.18	18.60
N. Dak.....	20.1	18.3	19.5	21.0	5.5	19.5	29.9	20.0	19.5	32.0	15.5	53	35	40	44	44	80	11.58	12.40
S. Dak.....	21.4	23.0	26.5	19.5	18.2	5.4	26.0	17.5	23.0	32.0	22.7	56	42	46	50	46	83	8.99	18.84
Nebr.......	21.6	20.8	23.5	22.0	18.5	11.0	22.0	16.0	23.5	31.0	16.0	50	42	49	47	42	75	9.55	21.00
Kans.......	17.4	12.0	16.0	18.0	18.0	6.5	23.5	8.1	24.5	31.0	16.0	53	40	55	47	42	77	8.46	12.32
Ky.........	26.4	25.0	25.0	24.0	24.0	28.7	26.0	26.6	28.5	30.0	26.0	76	75	78	77	77	90	21.59	23.40
Tenn.......	24.6	20.0	25.0	24.0	23.0	28.0	26.0	25.0	27.0	24.0	23.7	80	80	70	82	75	100	20.73	23.70
Tex........	23.2	17.0	24.0	19.4	30.0	18.0	29.3	24.0	25.0	28.0	17.0	81	78	81	70	68	80	19.11	13.60
Okla.......	19.8	18.7	23.0	23.0	30.0	10.0	20.0	9.0	25.0	26.5	12.5	62	50	80	53	50	100	9.96	12.50
Mont.......	33.4	38.0	35.0	38.0	28.0	34.5	36.5	31.0	30.5	34.0	28.0	59	53	48	53	48	76	18.03	21.28
Wyo........	32.8	32.0	35.0	31.0	30.0	34.0	34.0	30.5	33.0	36.0	33.0	68	62	61	64	55	87	21.22	28.71
Colo.......	34.8	40.0	38.0	36.0	32.0	29.0	32.5	38.5	36.0	32.0	33.0	61	50	56	55	48	82	19.23	26.24
N. Mex.....	32.0	26.0	42.0	40.0	25.0	33.0	35.0	24.0	34.0	33.0	28.0	79	71	72	75	70	100	22.77	28.00
Ariz.......	37.3	35.5	38.0	40.0	36.0	36.5	40.0	39.0	36.0	37.0	35.0	81	87	73	60	56	108	27.47	37.80
Utah.......	41.0	39.0	45.0	40.0	36.0	43.0	45.0	38.5	45.0	42.5	32.0	60	59	55	50	52	76	24.14	27.36
Nev........	40.6	40.0	30.0	38.0	40.0	40.0	41.0	41.0	47.0	48.0	41.0	79	87	90	57	70	95	33.82	38.95
Idaho......	40.4	44.5	41.0	40.0	33.0	42.0	43.5	42.0	38.0	40.5	39.0	57	51	48	50	52	82	22.36	31.98
Wash.......	38.2	40.5	30.5	39.5	29.0	37.0	43.0	40.5	39.0	41.5	41.3	60	53	52	52	56	84	22.51	34.69
Oreg.......	34.4	42.0	29.0	31.5	31.5	34.0	36.0	35.0	36.0	36.0	38.5	62	55	55	61	62	80	20.35	30.80
Cal........	28.1	28.9	23.5	26.5	31.0	28.0	30.0	26.0	30.0	29.0	28.0	72	70	68	59	62	95	19.63	26.60
U. S.......	25.2	23.8	25.1	24.3	22.5	21.0	29.7	23.8	25.8	32.0	23.6	62.0	50.5	53.7	54.3	51.6	88.2	15.31	20.79

[1] Based upon farm price Dec. 1.

BARLEY—Continued.

TABLE 43.—*Barley: Condition of crop, United States, on first of months named, 1895–1916.*

Year.	June.	July.	August.	When harvested.	Year.	June.	July.	August.	When harvested.
	P. ct.	P. ct.	P. ct.	P. ct.		P. ct.	P. ct.	P. ct.	P. ct.
1895	90.3	91.9	87.2	87.6	1906	93.5	92.5	90.3	89.4
1896	98.0	88.1	82.9	83.1	1907	84.9	84.4	84.5	78.5
1897	87.4	88.5	87.5	86.4	1908	89.7	86.2	83.1	81.2
1898	78.8	85.7	79.3	79.2	1909	90.6	90.2	85.4	80.5
1899	91.4	92.0	93.6	86.7	1910	89.6	73.7	70.0	69.8
1900	86.2	76.3	71.6	70.7	1911	90.2	72.1	66.2	65.5
1901	91.0	91.3	86.9	83.8	1912	91.1	88.3	89.1	88.9
1902	93.6	93.7	90.2	89.7	1913	87.1	76.6	74.9	73.4
1903	91.5	86.8	83.4	82.1	1914	95.5	92.6	85.3	82.4
1904	90.5	88.5	88.1	87.4	1915	94.6	94.1	93.8	94.2
1905	93.7	91.5	89.5	87.8	1916	86.3	87.9	80.0	74.6

TABLE 44.—*Barley: Farm price per bushel on first of each month, by geographical divisions, 1915 and 1916.*

Month.	United States.		North Atlantic States.		South Atlantic States.		N. Central States east of Miss. R.		N. Central States west of Miss. R.		South Central States.		Far Western States.	
	1916	1915	1916	1915	1916	1915	1916	1915	1916	1915	1916	1915	1916	1915
	Cts.	Cts.	Cts.	Cts.	Cts.	Cts.	Cts.	Cts.	Cts.	Cts.	Cts.	Cts.	Cts.	Cts.
January	54.9	54.3	75.4	77.2	74.0	73.0	60.7	62.1	50.5	49.8	61.4	62.5	59.6	56.9
February	61.7	62.9	74.9	80.6	72.0	76.0	67.3	67.0	60.5	59.4	59.4	76.5	61.7	65.4
March	59.6	67.7	78.6	84.9	76.0	81.0	67.5	72.6	53.0	61.9	64.4	80.2	67.8	73.2
April	57.2	64.7	79.2	81.0	72.0	73.4	64.9	72.3	53.0	59.9	63.2	70.8	60.6	68.1
May	59.6	63.8	79.6	87.7	74.0	78.0	65.4	69.5	55.9	60.3	63.8	71.3	62.9	65.6
June	59.6	62.0	81.5	83.0	73.3	78.2	66.6	68.6	56.0	60.1	59.4	85.2	62.2	61.2
July	59.3	55.8	80.8	85.6	74.0	76.0	67.1	66.4	56.0	56.0	55.5	78.0	61.3	50.4
August	59.3	56.7	74.6	81.6	85.0	78.0	66.9	66.8	55.3	56.8	57.4	57.0	63.0	51.8
September	72.9	51.9	82.0	80.2	60.0	74.0	89.9	58.8	70.8	46.7	64.8	56.5	69.4	55.6
October	76.5	46.8	93.4	72.5	80.0	69.2	90.7	52.6	72.8	40.1	99.6	60.0	77.0	52.9
November	83.2	50.1	94.0	73.5	70.0	78.0	98.6	55.3	80.4	43.0	78.1	53.7	81.7	57.3
December	88.2	51.6	98.1	75.0	80.7	73.4	102.0	56.7	83.5	46.0	92.7	67.0	89.1	58.6
Average	71.6	53.7	86.0	77.7	73.4	74.7	83.0	60.5	70.0	47.3	72.1	62.5	72.5	57.5

TABLE 45.—*Barley: Wholesale price per bushel, 1912–1916.*

Date.	Cincinnati.		Chicago.		Milwaukee.		Minneapolis.		San Francisco.	
	Spring malt.		Low malting to fancy.		No. 3.		All grades.		Feed (per 100 lbs.)	
	Low.	High.	Low.	High.	Low.	High.	Low.	High.	Low.	High.
1912.	Cents.	Cents.	Cents.	Cents.	Cents.	Cents.	Cents.	Cents.	Cents.	Cents.
Jan.–June	110	132	60	140	95	138	50	130	152½	195
July–Dec	55	78	40	110	64	110	34	95	115	152½
1913.										
Jan.–June	54½	70	42	71	60	73	39	63	130	150
July–Dec	57	80	43	85	60	82	42	73	122½	140
1914.										
Jan.–June	60	70	49	79	53	68	41	65	90	132½
July–Dec	70	80	50	82	51½	82	40	76	95	130
1915.										
January	72	90	66	88	70½	88	58	83	125	160
February	86	90	73	91	78	93	64	86	142½	162½
March	79	90	71	89	74½	86	62	81	125	147½
April	76	82	71	84	76	80½	64	76	125	147½
May	76	102	74½	82	75½	78½	67	75	111½	130
June	86	98	68	79	71	77½	62	71	100	112½
Jan.–June	72	102	66	91	70½	93	58	86	100	162½

BARLEY—Continued.

TABLE 45.—*Barley: Wholesale price per bushel, 1912–1916*—Continued.

Date.	Cincinnati. Spring malt.		Chicago. Low malting to fancy.		Milwaukee. No. 3.		Minneapolis. All grades.		San Francisco. Feed (per 100 lbs.)	
	Low.	High.	Low.	High.	Low.	High.	Low.	High.	Low.	High.
	Cents.	*Cents.*	*Cents.*	*Cents.*	*Cents.*	*Cents.*	*Cents.*	*Cents.*	*Cents.*	*Cents.*
July	86	98	69	79	72½	79	63	73	100	120
August	88	98	54	85	61	81	45	78	115	130
September	76	102	51	65	54	60	42	57	112½	120
October	70	86	53	65	56	62	47	57	115	130
November	70	76	56	73	59	68	50	62	122½	132½
December	76	79	62	77	67	73½	56	67½	125	132½
July–Dec	70	102	51	85	54	81	42	78	100	132½
1916.										
January	83	88	68	84	71	82	61	76½	127½	132½
February	89	98	64	83	68	79½	59	75½	130	135
March	83	98	64	78	70½	77	59	72½	130	135
April	89	98	64	83	68	79½	59	75½	130	135
May	91	102	70	83	74½	80	60	75½	130	136¼
June	93	102	70	86	73	78	60	73½	127½	132½
Jan.–June	83	102	64	86	68	82	59	76½	127½	136¼
July	93	102	68	80	70	80	57	74½	127½	145
August	93	136	68	115	75	113	57	108	140	170
September	123	136	84	117	97	115	63	101	165	170
October	123	132	85	123	105	123	60	106	167½	202½
November	136	145	98	128	112	128	72	112	200	225
December	136	145	95	125	112	124	70	110	215	225
July–Dec	93	145	68	128	70	128	57	112	127½	225

TABLE 46.—*Barley and malt: International trade, calendar years 1913–1915.*

[See "General note," Table 10.]

EXPORTS.

[000 omitted.]

Country.	Barley. 1913	1914 (prelim.)	1915 (prelim.)	Malt. 1913	1914 (prelim.)	1915 (prelim.)	Barley and malt in terms of barley. 1913	1914 (prelim.)	1915 (prelim.)
	Bushels.	*Bushels.*	*Bushels.*	*Bushels.*	*Bushels.*	*Bushels.*	*Bushels.*	*Bushels.*	*Bushels.*
Algeria	4,342	3,903	1,690	......	......	......	4,342	3,903	1,690
Argentina	1,871	1,152	440	......	......	......	1,871	1,152	3,440
Austria-Hungary	8,190	......	......	12,189	......	......	19,271	......	......
Belgium	2,612	......	......	218	......	......	2,811	......	......
British India	10,069	1,290	7,441	......	......	......	10,069	1,290	7,441
Bulgaria	819	......	......	......	......	......	819	......	......
Canada	13,906	6,838	4,665	3	5	12	13,909	6,843	4,677
Chile	427	2,839	1,287	23	233	298	449	3,051	1,557
China	738	524	191	......	......	......	738	524	191
Denmark	3,566	3,379	3	117	......	......	3,673	3,379	2
France	438	167	536	19	210	702	455	357	1,174
Germany	280	......	......	1,198	......	......	1,369	......	......
Netherlands	31,993	13,385	1	449	439	......	32,402	13,784	1
Roumania	17,319	9,284	......	4	......	......	17,322	9,284	......
Russia	180,344	90,783	305	197	161	......	180,523	90,930	305
United Kingdom	48	85	79	806	898	3,982	781	902	3,699
United States	12,782	17,208	26,491	487	728	2,253	13,225	17,870	28,539
Other countries	15,957	1,278	......	11	6	......	15,967	1,282	......
Total	305,701	152,115	......	15,721	2,680	......	319,996	154,551	......

BARLEY—Continued.

TABLE 46.—*Barley and malt: International trade, calendar years 1913–1915*—Continued·

IMPORTS.

[000 omitted.]

Country.	Barley.			Malt.			Barley and malt in terms of barley.		
	1913	1914 (prelim.)	1915 (prelim.)	1913	1914 (prelim.)	1915 (prelim.)	1913	1914 (prelim.)	1915 (prelim.)
	Bushels.	*Bushels.*	*Bushels.*	*Bushels.*	*Bushels.*	*Bushels.*	*Bushels.*	*Bushels.*	*Bushels.*
Argentina	4	1	1	1,597	1,134	720	1,456	1,032	656
Austria-Hungary	351			2			353		
Belgium	17,336			734			18,004		
Brazil	1	1	7	1,364	702	944	1,241	639	865
British South Africa	2	1	5	348	289	232	319	265	216
Canada	38	39	39	358	107	47	363	136	82
Cuba	273	285	343				273	285	343
Denmark	1,933	2,390	4,414	58			1,986	2,390	4,414
Egypt	1,338	475	365	534	42	95	1,824	512	452
France	5,330	4,761	4,242	108	194	145	5,428	4,938	4,374
Finland	392	167	242	278	230	354	645	376	564
Germany	148,728			3,532			151,939		
Italy	728	8	20		106	47	728	105	63
Netherlands	40,783	21,047	5,033	4,183	3,242	5	44,585	23,994	5,038
Norway	3,851	3,845	1,134	157	242	259	3,994	4,064	1,369
Russia	1,106	756		58	28		1,158	781	
Switzerland	1,190	769	1,057	3,302	3,066	1,743	4,192	3,556	2,641
United Kingdom	52,331	36,422	27,969	146	137	7	52,464	36,547	27,976
Other countries	1,216	1,594		661	673		1,815	2,207	
Total	276,931	72,561		17,420	10,192		292,767	81,827	

RYE.

TABLE 47.—*Rye: Area and production in undermentioned countries, 1914–1916.*

Country.	Area.			Production.		
	1914	1915	1916	1914	1915	1916
NORTH AMERICA.						
United States	*Acres.* 2,541,000	*Acres.* 3,129,000	*Acres.* 3,096,000	*Bushels.* 42,779,000	*Bushels.* 54,050,000	*Bushels.* 47,383,000
Canada:						
Quebec	9,000	9,000	8,000	156,000	145,000	(2)
Ontario	78,000	78,000	69,000	1,341,000	1,551,000	(2)
Manitoba	5,000	6,000	6,000	100,000	155,000	(2)
Saskatchewan	3,000	3,000	3,000	54,000	76,000	(2)
Alberta	16,000	17,000	15,000	360,000	463,000	(2)
Other	(1)	(1)	(1)	6,000	4,000	(2)
Total Canada	111,000	113,000	101,000	2,017,000	2,394,000	2,896,000
Mexico	(2)	(2)	(2)	70,000	70,000	(2)
Total				44,866,000	56,514,000	
SOUTH AMERICA.						
Argentina	228,000	229,000	212,000	3,346,000	1,811,000	2,008,000
Chile	6,000	(2)	(2)	151,000	150,000	(2)
Uruguay	(1)	(1)	(1)	5,000	1,000	1,000
Total				3,502,000	1,962,000	
EUROPE.						
Austria-Hungary:						
Austria	[3] 3,138,000	(2)	(2)	[3] 74,555,000	[3] 75,000,000	(2)
Hungary	2,638,000	2,625,000	(2)	42,410,000	45,975,000	(2)
Croatia-Slavonia	163,000	(2)	(2)	2,082,000	2,500,000	(2)
Bosnia-Herzegovina	(2)	(2)	(2)	500,000	600,000	(2)
Total Austria-Hungary				119,547,000	124,075,000	

[1] Less than 500 acres.   [2] No official statistics.   [3] Galicia and Bukowina not included.

RYE—Continued.

TABLE 47.—*Rye: Area and production in undermentioned countries, 1914–1916*—Contd.

Country.	Area.			Production.		
	1914	1915	1916	1914	1915	1916
EUROPE—contd.	*Acres.*	*Acres.*	*Acres.*	*Bushels.*	*Bushels.*	*Bushels.*
Belgium	645,000	(1)	(1)	23,137,000	18,000,000	(1)
Bulgaria	527,000	(1)	(1)	7,255,000	7,622,000	8,490,000
Denmark	(1)	521,000	479,000	10,905,000	12,989,000	10,580,000
Finland	(1)	(1)	(1)	10,806,000	10,000,000	(1)
France	2,614,000	2,309,000	2,275,000	32,002,000	33,072,000	35,524,000
Germany	15,565,000	15,843,000	(1)	410,478,000	360,310,000	(1)
Italy	304,000	294,000	284,000	5,260,000	4,362,000	5,342,000
Netherlands	563,000	546,000	499,000	13,471,000	13,727,000	12,391,000
Norway	[2] 37,000	(1)	48,000	1,046,000	829,000	729,000
Roumania	208,000	187,000	200,000	1,959,000	2,911,000	(1)
Russia:						
Russia proper	65,967,000	65,866,000	58,407,000	787,625,000	877,522,000	840,722,000
Poland	[3] 1,676,000	(1)	(1)	[3] 27,984,000	(1)	(1)
Northern Caucasia	439,000	[4] 329,000	(1)	5,469,000	[4] 4,633,000	(1)
Total Russia (European)	68,082,000	66,195,000	....	821,078,000	882,155,000	....
Serbia	74,000	(1)	(1)	1,000,000	800,000	(1)
Spain	1,887,000	1,820,000	1,856,000	23,950,000	26,102,000	31,436,000
Sweden	981,000	(1)	921,000	27,599,000	23,133,000	26,000,000
United Kingdom	67,000	62,000	60,000	1,800,000	1,700,000	(1)
Total	....	....	....	1,511,293,000	1,521,787,000	....
ASIA.						
Russia:						
Central Asia (4 governments of)	133,000	378,000	(1)	1,206,000	3,070,000	(1)
Siberia (4 governments of)	2,676,000	2,452,000	(1)	35,887,000	20,143,000	(1)
Transcaucasia (1 government of)	1,000	(5)	(1)	11,000	(5)	(1)
Total Russia (Asiatic)	2,810,000	....	....	37,104,000	23,213,000	....
AUSTRALASIA.						
Australia:						
Queensland	(6)	(1)	(1)	1,000	(1)	(1)
New South Wales	5,000	3,000	2,000	70,000	37,000	22,000
Victoria	2,000	2,000	(1)	20,000	(1)	(1)
South Australia	1,000	(1)	(1)	13,000	6,000	(1)
Western Australia	1,000	(1)	(1)	4,000	(1)	(1)
Tasmania	1,000	(1)	(1)	9,000	(1)	(1)
Total Australia	10,000	....	....	117,000	....	....
New Zealand	(1)	(1)	(1)	(1)	(1)	(1)
Total Australasia	....	....	....	117,000	....	....
Grand total	....	....	....	1,596,882,000	....	....

[1] No official statistics.
[2] 1910 figures (census).
[3] Winter rye in 1914 in 5 governments only.

[4] Includes 1 government of Transcaucasia.
[5] Included in Northern Caucasia.
[6] Less than 500 acres.

TABLE 48.—*Rye: Total production of countries named in Table 47, 1895–1916.*

Year.	Production.	Year.	Production.	Year.	Production.	Year.	Production.
	Bushels.		*Bushels.*		*Bushels.*		*Bushels.*
1895	1,468,212,000	1901	1,416,022,000	1907	1,538,778,000	1913	1,880,387,000
1896	1,499,250,000	1902	1,647,845,000	1908	1,590,057,000	1914	1,596,882,000
1897	1,300,645,000	1903	1,659,961,000	1909	1,747,123,000	1915	....
1898	1,461,171,000	1904	1,742,112,000	1910	1,673,473,000	1916	....
1899	1,583,179,000	1905	1,495,751,000	1911	1,753,933,000		
1900	1,557,634,000	1906	1,433,395,000	1912	1,886,517,000		

RYE—Continued.

TABLE 49.—*Rye: Average yield per acre in undermentioned countries, 1890–1915.*

Year.	United States.	Russia (European).[1]	Germany.[1]	Austria.[1]	Hungary proper.[1]	France.[2]	Ireland.[1]
	Bushels.	*Bushels.*	*Bushels.*	*Bushels.*	*Bushels.*	*Bushels.*	*Bushels.*
Average:							
1890–1899	13.9	10.4	20.9	16.1	....	17.6	25.2
1900–1909	15.7	11.5	25.6	19.0	17.6	17.1	27.5
1906	16.7	8.8	25.1	19.9	19.8	16.3	27.6
1907	16.4	10.8	25.8	18.9	16.0	18.2	27.0
1908	16.4	11.0	28.0	22.0	17.5	16.8	29.2
1909	13.4	12.6	28.8	22.3	17.8	18.1	30.8
1910	16.0	12.3	27.1	21.3	18.9	14.7	30.3
1911	15.6	10.5	28.2	20.9	18.7	15.8	29.0
1912	16.8	14.3	29.5	23.3	19.4	16.5	30.6
1913	16.2	13.5	30.4	22.0	19.6	17.0	30.0
1914	16.8	12.1	26.4	[3] 23.7	16.1	12.2	29.4
1915	17.3	....	22.7	....	....	14.3	29.2
Average (1906–1915)	16.2	....	....	....	....	....	29.3

[1] Bushels of 56 pounds. [2] Winchester bushels. [3] Galicia and Bukowina not included

TABLE 50.—*Rye: Acreage, production, value, exports, etc., in the United States, 1849–1916.*

NOTE.—Figures in *italics* are census returns; figures in roman are estimates of the Department of Agriculture. Estimates of acres are obtained by applying estimated percentages of increase or decrease to the published numbers of the preceding year, except that a revised base is used for applying percentage estimates whenever new census data are available.

Year.	Acreage harvested.	Average yield per acre.	Production.	Average farm price per bushel Dec. 1.	Farm value Dec. 1.	Chicago cash price per bushel, No. 2.				Domestic exports, including rye flour, fiscal year beginning July 1.
						December.		Following May.		
						Low.	High.	Low.	High.	
	Acres.	*Bush.*	*Bushels.*	*Cents.*	*Dollars.*	*Cts.*	*Cts.*	*Cts.*	*Cts.*	*Bushels.*
1849	....	......	*14,189,000*	......	....	......	......	......	......	....
1859	....	......	*21,101,000*	......	....	......	......	......	......	....
1866	1,548,000	13.5	20,865,000	82.2	17,150,000	......	......	142	150	234,971
1867	1,689,000	13.7	23,184,000	100.4	23,281,000	132	157	173	185	564,901
1868	1,651,000	13.6	22,505,000	94.9	21,349,000	106½	118	100	115½	92,869
1869	1,658,000	13.6	22,528,000	77.0	17,342,000	66	77½	78	83½	199,450
1869	....	......	*16,919,000*	......	....	......	......	......	......	....
1870	1,176,000	13.2	15,474,000	73.2	11,327,000	67	74	81	91	87,174
1871	1,070,000	14.4	15,366,000	71.1	10,928,000	62	63¾	75	93	832,689
1872	1,049,000	14.2	14,889,000	67.6	10,071,000	57½	70	68½	70	611,749
1873	1,150,000	13.2	15,142,000	70.3	10,638,000	70	81	91	102	1,923,404
1874	1,117,000	13.4	14,991,000	77.4	11,610,000	93	99½	103	107½	267,058
1875	1,360,000	13.0	17,722,000	67.1	11,894,000	67	68¾	61½	70½	589,159
1876	1,468,000	13.9	20,375,000	61.4	12,505,000	65½	73	70	92½	2,234,856
1877	1,413,000	15.0	21,170,000	57.6	12,202,000	55½	56½	54	60	4,249,684
1878	1,623,000	15.9	25,843,000	52.5	13,566,000	44	44½	47	52	4,877,821
1879	1,625,000	14.5	23,639,000	65.6	15,507,000	73½	81	73½	85	2,943,894
1879	*1,842,000*	*10.8*	*19,832,000*	......	....	......	......	......	......	....
1880	1,768,000	13.9	24,541,000	75.6	18,565,000	82	91½	115	118	1,955,155
1881	1,789,000	11.6	20,705,000	93.3	19,327,000	96½	98	77	83	1,003,609
1882	2,228,000	13.4	29,960,000	61.5	18,439,000	57	58½	62	67	2,206,212
1883	2,315,000	12.1	28,059,000	58.1	16,301,000	56½	60	60½	62½	6,247,590
1884	2,344,000	12.2	28,640,000	51.9	14,857,000	51	52	68	73	2,974,390
1885	2,129,000	10.2	21,756,000	57.9	12,595,000	58½	61	58	61	216,699
1886	2,130,000	11.5	24,489,000	53.8	13,181,000	53	54½	54½	56½	377,302
1887	2,053,000	10.1	20,693,000	54.5	11,283,000	55½	61½	63	68	94,827
1888	2,365,000	12.0	28,415,000	58.8	16,722,000	50	52	39	41½	309,266
1889	2,171,000	13.1	28,420,000	42.3	12,010,000	44	45½	49½	54	2,280,975
1889	*2,172,000*	*13.1*	*28,421,000*	......	....	......	......	......	......	....
1890	2,142,000	12.0	25,807,000	62.9	16,230,000	64½	68½	83	92	358,263
1891	2,176,000	14.6	31,752,000	77.4	24,589,000	86	92	70¼	79	12,068,628
1892	2,164,000	12.9	27,979,000	54.2	15,160,000	46	51	50½	62	1,493,924
1893	2,038,000	13.0	26,555,000	51.3	13,612,000	45	47½	44½	48	249,152
1894	1,945,000	13.7	26,728,000	50.1	13,395,000	47½	49	62½	67	32,045

RYE—Continued.

TABLE 50.—*Rye: Acreage, production, value, exports, etc., in the United States, 1849–1916*—Continued.

Year.	Acreage harvested.	Average yield per acre.	Production.	Average farm price per bushel Dec. 1.	Farm value Dec. 1.	Chicago cash price per bushel, No. 2. December. Low.	December. High.	Following May. Low.	Following May. High.	Domestic exports, including rye flour, fiscal year beginning July 1.
	Acres.	*Bush.*	*Bushels.*	*Cents.*	*Dollars.*	*Cts.*	*Cts.*	*Cts.*	*Cts.*	*Bushels.*
1895	1,890,000	14.4	27,210,000	44.0	11,965,000	32	35¾	33	36½	1,011,128
1896	1,831,000	13.3	24,369,000	40.9	9,961,000	37	42½	32¾	35½	8,575,663
1897	1,704,000	16.1	27,363,000	44.7	12,240,000	45¾	47	48	75	15,562,035
1898	1,643,000	15.6	25,658,000	46.3	11,875,000	52½	55½	56½	62	10,169,822
1899	1,659,000	14.4	23,962,000	51.0	12,214,000	49	52	53	56¼	2,382,012
1899	*2,054,000*	*12.4*	*25,569,000*							
1900	1,591,000	15.1	23,996,000	51.2	12,295,000	45¾	49¾	51½	54	2,345,512
1901	1,988,000	15.3	30,345,000	55.7	16,910,000	59	65¾	54½	58	2,712,077
1902	1,979,000	17.0	33,631,000	50.8	17,081,000	48	49¾	48	50½	5,445,273
1903	1,907,000	15.4	29,363,000	54.5	15,994,000	50½	52½	69¾	78	784,068
1904	1,793,000	15.2	27,242,000	68.8	18,748,000	73	75	70	84	29,749
1905	1,730,000	16.5	28,486,000	61.1	17,414,000	64	68	58	62	1,387,826
1906	2,002,000	16.7	33,375,000	58.9	19,671,000	61	65	69	87½	769,717
1907	1,926,000	16.4	31,566,000	73.1	23,068,000	75	82	79	86	2,444,588
1908	1,948,000	16.4	31,851,000	73.6	23,455,000	75	77¼	83	90	1,295,701
1909	2,006,000	16.1	32,239,000							
1909	*2,196,000*	*13.4*	*29,520,000*	71.8	21,163,000	72	80	74	80	242,262
1910 [1]	2,185,000	16.0	34,897,000	71.5	24,953,000	80	82	90	113	40,123
1911	2,127,000	15.6	33,119,000	83.2	27,557,000	91	94	90	95½	31,384
1912	2,117,000	16.8	35,664,000	66.3	23,636,000	58	64	60	64	1,854,738
1913	2,557,000	16.2	41,381,000	63.4	26,220,000	61	65	62	67	2,272,492
1914	2,541,000	16.8	42,779,000	86.5	37,018,000	107½	112½	115	122	13,026,778
1915	3,129,000	17.3	54,050,000	83.4	45,083,000	94½	98½	96½	99½	15,250,151
1916	3,096,000	15.3	47,383,000	122.1	57,857,000	130	151			

[1] Figures adjusted to census basis.

TABLE 51.—*Rye: Acreage, production, and total farm value, by States, 1916.*

[000 omitted.]

State.	Acreage.	Production.	Farm value Dec. 1.	State.	Acreage.	Production.	Farm value Dec. 1.
	Acres.	*Bushels.*	*Dollars.*		*Acres.*	*Bushels.*	*Dollars.*
Vermont	1	20	24	North Dakota	350	4,655	5,819
Massachusetts	3	56	71	South Dakota	250	4,500	5,310
Connecticut	7	137	171	Nebraska	192	3,072	3,564
New York	151	2,718	3,479	Kansas	46	667	734
New Jersey	70	1,330	1,556	Kentucky	22	246	317
Pennsylvania	260	4,420	4,818	Tennessee	15	150	202
Delaware	1	15	18	Alabama	4	52	91
Maryland	23	356	392	Texas	2	20	24
Virginia	75	938	1,004	Oklahoma	9	90	112
West Virginia	20	320	381	Arkansas	1	10	12
North Carolina	55	534	694	Montana	10	205	197
South Carolina	5	49	91	Wyoming	10	155	167
Georgia	13	124	198	Colorado	28	392	412
Ohio	75	1,088	1,306	Utah	12	144	144
Indiana	185	2,590	3,082				
Illinois	43	666	813	Idaho	2	34	32
Michigan	325	4,648	6,042	Washington	7	102	113
Wisconsin	375	6,075	8,019	Oregon	30	510	586
Minnesota	335	5,025	6,382	California	8	104	121
Iowa	55	935	1,075	United States	3,096	47,383	57,857
Missouri	21	231	284				

RYE—Continued.

TABLE 52.—*Rye: Condition of crop, United States, on first of months named, 1891–1917.*

Year.	December of previous year.	April.	May.	June.	When harvested.	Year.	December of previous year.	April.	May.	June.	When harvested.
	P. ct.	P. ct.	P. ct.	P. ct.	P. ct.		P. ct.	P. ct.	P. ct.	P. ct.	P. ct.
1891	99.0	95.4	97.2	95.4	93.9	1905	90.5	92.1	93.5	94.0	93.2
1892	88.8	87.0	88.9	91.0	92.8	1906	95.4	90.9	92.9	89.9	91.3
1893	89.4	85.7	82.7	84.6	85.3	1907	96.2	92.0	88.0	88.1	89.7
1894	94.6	94.4	90.7	93.2	87.0	1908	91.4	89.1	90.3	91.3	91.2
1895	96.2	87.0	88.7	85.7	80.7	1909	87.6	87.2	88.1	89.6	91.4
1896	94.9	82.9	87.7	85.2	88.4	1910	94.1	92.3	91.3	90.6	87.5
1897	99.8	88.9	88.0	89.9	93.4	1911	92.6	89.3	90.0	88.6	85.0
1898	91.0	92.1	94.5	97.1	94.6	1912	93.3	87.9	87.5	87.7	88.2
1899	98.9	84.9	85.2	84.5	85.6	1913	93.5	89.3	91.0	90.9	88.6
1900	98.2	84.8	88.5	87.6	80.4	1914	95.3	91.3	93.4	93.6	92.9
1901	99.1	93.1	94.6	93.9	93.0	1915	93.6	89.5	93.3	92.0	92.0
1902	89.9	85.4	83.4	88.1	90.2	1916	91.5	87.8	88.7	86.9	87.0
1903	98.1	97.9	93.3	90.6	89.5	1917	88.8				
1904	92.7	82.3	81.2	86.3	88.9						

TABLE 53.—*Rye: Yield per acre, price per bushel Dec. 1, and value per acre, by States.*

State.	Yield per acre (bushels).											Farm price per bushel (cents).						Value per acre (dollars).[1]	
	10-year average, 1907–1916.	1907	1908	1909	1910	1911	1912	1913	1914	1915	1916	10-year average, 1907–1916.	1912	1913	1914	1915	1916	5-year average, 1911–1915.	1916
Vt	18.2	17.0	15.0	15.5	17.5	22.5	20.0	18.0	20.0	17.0	20.0	91	90	90	80	85	120	17.21	24.00
Mass	17.7	16.5	16.5	16.2	17.0	16.0	18.5	18.5	19.0	20.0	18.5	101	100	98	101	102	127	18.28	23.50
Conn	19.0	17.0	18.5	18.7	20.0	18.5	17.5	19.3	19.0	21.5	19.6	95	92	92	98	102	125	18.32	24.50
N. Y	17.3	16.5	16.5	17.0	18.3	16.7	16.5	17.2	17.7	18.7	18.0	87	76	75	89	93	128	14.69	23.04
N. J	17.7	17.5	16.2	16.3	18.0	16.4	17.5	18.0	18.5	20.0	19.0	85	79	80	82	92	117	15.08	22.23
Pa	16.9	16.7	16.5	15.3	17.0	15.1	17.5	17.5	18.0	18.0	17.0	81	77	74	83	84	109	13.71	18.53
Del	15.2	16.5	15.5	14.0	15.5	15.0	14.0	14.0	17.5	15.5	15.0	88	81	79	92	99	123	13.62	18.45
Md	15.5	16.0	15.0	14.1	16.1	14.5	15.5	14.4	17.0	16.5	15.5	83	80	76	86	88	110	12.98	17.05
Va	12.9	14.0	12.3	12.3	13.5	11.5	12.5	12.3	13.0	14.5	12.5	87	85	81	90	93	107	11.20	13.38
W. Va	13.3	12.0	13.0	13.5	12.9	11.0	13.0	13.5	14.5	14.0	16.0	91	84	87	90	93	119	11.73	19.04
N. C	10.0	10.5	8.9	9.4	10.0	10.0	9.3	10.3	10.0	11.5	9.7	104	105	98	105	105	130	10.49	12.61
S. C	10.1	10.0	9.6	9.8	10.0	10.0	9.5	10.5	11.5	10.0	9.8	148	145	150	150	151	185	15.28	18.13
Ga	9.3	9.0	8.7	9.0	10.4	9.5	9.2	9.5	9.3	9.2	9.5	140	140	135	150	140	160	13.13	15.20
Ohio	16.4	17.2	16.7	15.7	16.5	15.5	15.5	16.5	17.0	17.5	14.5	81	75	69	81	83	120	12.89	17.40
Ind	15.4	17.0	15.0	16.5	15.8	13.7	14.5	15.2	16.3	16.0	14.0	78	68	62	85	82	119	11.44	16.66
Ill	17.0	18.5	17.1	17.8	17.4	16.8	16.0	16.0	16.5	18.5	15.5	80	70	65	85	83	122	12.90	18.91
Mich	14.9	14.5	15.5	15.5	15.3	14.6	13.4	13.6	16.0	15.5	14.3	80	65	62	91	85	130	11.53	18.59
Wis	17.3	18.0	19.0	16.3	16.0	17.0	18.3	17.5	18.5	18.5	16.2	79	61	57	91	87	132	13.31	21.38
Minn	18.7	18.5	18.5	19.0	17.0	18.7	23.0	19.0	18.8	19.5	15.0	73	50	48	89	81	127	13.55	19.05
Iowa	18.4	17.8	20.0	17.8	18.5	18.0	19.0	18.2	19.0	18.5	17.0	73	62	60	77	80	115	13.20	19.55
Mo	14.1	15.4	12.8	15.0	15.0	14.1	14.8	15.0	14.0	13.5	11.0	84	80	75	87	86	123	11.74	13.53
N. Dak	15.5	16.0	18.0	18.4	8.5	16.6	18.0	14.4	17.1	15.0	13.3	70	47	45	84	79	125	10.75	16.62
S. Dak	16.6	17.0	17.5	17.5	17.0	10.0	19.5	13.2	17.0	19.5	18.0	69	52	50	78	76	118	10.48	21.24
Nebr	15.8	17.0	16.0	16.5	16.0	13.0	16.5	14.0	16.0	17.5	16.0	69	56	60	74	73	116	10.41	18.56
Kans	14.5	12.0	13.3	14.2	14.0	11.0	15.9	14.0	20.0	16.0	14.5	78	68	75	80	76	110	11.68	15.95
Ky	12.7	13.7	13.5	12.7	13.0	12.0	13.0	12.4	13.7	12.0	11.2	93	88	87	95	94	129	11.56	14.45
Tenn	11.3	10.0	12.5	10.7	11.0	11.9	11.5	12.0	13.0	10.5	10.0	100	98	99	98	103	135	11.70	13.50
Ala	11.2	10.5	10.0	11.3	12.0	10.0	11.5	11.0	13.0	10.0	13.0	132	134	140	110	135	175	14.22	22.75
Tex	13.2	10.0	15.5	11.2	11.5	10.5	6.5	14.8	17.0	10.0	10.0	106	110	101	99	103	120	15.25	12.00
Okla	12.1	10.0	13.5	13.5	13.7	9.5	12.0	9.5	16.0	13.5	10.0	90	87	86	95	77	125	10.82	12.50
Ark	10.5	9.9	10.0	10.5	12.0	10.0	10.5	11.5	10.5	10.5	10.0	100	105	95	105	100	115	10.49	11.50
Mont	22.2	22.0	20.0	29.0	20.0	23.0	23.5	21.0	21.0	22.5	20.5	70	60	55	70	65	96	14.31	19.68
Wyo	19.8	21.5	22.0	26.0	18.5	20.0	19.0	19.0	17.0	20.0	15.5	81	65	64	81	90	108	14.86	16.74
Colo	17.0	20.5	15.5	22.0	14.0	12.0	19.5	17.0	17.5	17.5	14.0	70	55	60	65	70	105	10.59	14.70
Utah	16.8	20.0	15.5	22.0	18.5	15.5	15.0	17.0	17.5	15.5	12.0	69	68	60	60	65	100	10.37	12.00
Idaho	21.0	24.7	20.0	21.5	20.0	22.5	22.0	22.0	20.0	20.0	17.0	68	60	58	67	68	95	13.61	16.15
Wash	19.8	21.5	19.5	21.0	20.5	20.0	20.0	21.0	19.7	18.2	14.5	83	60	60	85	75	111	14.72	16.10
Oreg	17.0	16.0	18.0	17.0	15.1	19.5	16.0	17.5	16.0	18.0	17.0	91	70	75	100	90	115	14.81	19.55
Cal	15.5	19.0	12.0	13.8	17.0	17.0	17.6	15.0	17.0	14.0	13.0	90	90	75	85	90	116	13.72	15.08
U. S	16.3	16.4	16.4	16.1	16.0	15.6	16.8	16.2	16.8	17.3	15.3	79.7	66.3	63.4	86.5	83.4	122.1	12.67	18.69

[1] Based upon farm price Dec. 1.

RYE—Continued.

TABLE 54.—*Rye: Farm price per bushel on first of each month, by geographical divisions, 1915 and 1916.*

Month.	United States.		North Atlantic States.		South Atlantic States.		N. Central States east of Miss. R.		N. Central States west of Miss. R.		South Central States.		Far Western States.	
	1916	1915	1916	1915	1916	1915	1916	1915	1916	1915	1916	1915	1916	1915
	Cts.	*Cts.*	*Cts.*	*Cts.*	*Cts.*	*Cts.*	*Cts.*	*Cts.*	*Cts.*	*Cts.*	*Cts.*	*Cts.*	*Cts.*	*Cts.*
January......	85.3	90.2	88.8	88.9	90.9	92.7	86.5	93.5	81.4	87.7	97.2	97.1	77.8	76.1
February.....	88.3	100.6	92.7	96.8	92.6	96.0	89.8	105.7	84.6	99.3	89.8	101.7	78.9	84.7
March........	85.6	105.4	88.2	106.7	96.8	102.5	86.8	108.3	81.2	102.8	91.7	108.6	80.7	89.6
April........	83.6	100.4	90.4	101.3	96.0	95.4	84.6	101.9	76.7	99.2	92.3	105.4	81.7	93.9
May..........	83.7	101.9	88.7	102.6	93.7	95.4	84.4	103.0	78.8	101.0	92.2	103.1	78.3	100.9
June.........	83.8	98.1	90.2	99.5	91.8	98.1	84.9	98.6	78.1	96.6	91.3	100.9	73.6	95.2
July.........	83.3	93.7	89.4	95.1	87.9	95.3	83.3	93.3	79.4	94.6	84.0	92.4	81.8	82.1
August.......	83.4	89.0	88.6	92.8	90.5	92.5	84.6	88.5	77.9	87.0	96.3	94.9	80.0	81.4
September....	99.7	85.5	96.9	87.9	95.7	92.2	102.0	85.5	100.1	83.2	109.3	90.1	90.2	78.5
October......	104.1	81.7	99.6	86.0	103.2	90.4	108.9	83.0	102.0	76.0	119.5	94.3	91.8	71.4
November....	115.3	85.7	115.8	86.5	103.7	95.1	117.3	86.8	114.8	83.2	129.5	98.7	105.9	71.4
December.....	122.1	83.4	116.6	88.3	118.9	98.2	127.8	85.0	121.4	78.1	133.5	97.7	107.7	77.2
Average.....	97.8	90.0	98.9	91.8	97.6	94.3	99.8	91.1	98.6	85.6	106.4	96.8	89.6	79.8

TABLE 55.—*Rye: Wholesale price per bushel, 1912–1916.*

Date.	Philadelphia.		Cincinnati.		Chicago.		Duluth.		San Francisco (per 100 lbs.).	
			No. 2.		No. 2.					
	Low.	High.	Low.	High.	Low.	High.	Low.	High.	Low.	High.
1912.	*Cents.*	*Cents.*	*Cents.*	*Cents.*	*Cents.*	*Cents.*	*Cents.*	*Cents.*	*Cents.*	*Cents.*
January–June..............	82	105	78	100	75	96½	66	91½	147½	172½
July–December.............	68	85	62	81	58	76	53	70	140	172½
1913.										
January–June..............	65	70	60	70	58	65½	52	59	132½	147½
July–December.............	65	77	60	72	61	70½	50	65	135	165
1914.										
January–June..............	65	75	62	71	58	67	50	62	152½	165
July–December.............	65	125	60	115	55	112½	57	107	130	165
1915.										
January....................	115	125	113½	130	111½	126½	106	123½	160	225
February..................	125	130	118	133	115	131	113	128	200	225
March.....................	125	130	108	120	112	121	106	119	200	225
April.....................	110	120	110	116	115½	118	106	116	200	225
May.......................	110	115	112	120	115	122	110	118	200	225
June......................	105	110	107	113	114	119	110	114	(1)	(1)
January–June...........	105	130	107	133	111½	131	106	128	160	225
July......................	92	99	98	112	96	119	95	111	(1)	(1)
August...................	90	95	98	105	96	119	91	107	·155	165
September................	91	105	92	102	91	100½	89	96	145	160
October..................	95	112	98	107	95	107	90	99	145	160
November.................	100	110	98	107	94	103	87	96	155	160
December.................	105	112	95	104	94½	98½	87	93	155	160
July–December.........	90	112	92	112	91	119	87	111	145	165
1916.										
January...................	106	112	99	104	97	104¾	93	98	155	160
February..................	110	115	90	106	90	103	87	97	150	160
March.....................	115	118	90	100	90½	96	87	91	152½	160
April.....................	105	110	98	104	94	98½	91	96	152½	155
May.......................	95	105	92	101	96½	99½	91	95	152½	155
June......................	90	95	92	100	97	99½	91	95	152½	155
January–June...........	90	115	92	104	90	104¾	87	98	150	160
July......................	90	100	96	105	94	101	89	95	152½	155
August...................	100	110	103	127½	100	126½	94	120	152½	180
September................	110	125	123	128	115	125½	115	122	175	200
October..................	125	150	125	141	124	141	120	138	195	225
November.................	143	155	139	155	140	153	137	149	215	235
December.................	135	155	138	153	130	151	138	150	225	265
July–December.........	90	155	96	155	94	153	89	150	152½	265

[1] Nominal

RYE—Continued.

TABLE 56.—*Rye (including flour): International trade, calendar years 1913–1915.*

[See "General note," Table 10.]

EXPORTS.

[000 omitted.]

Country.	1913	1914 (prelim.)	1915 (prelim.)	Country.	1913	1914 (prelim.)	1915 (prelim.)
	Bushels.	*Bushels.*	*Bushels.*		*Bushels.*	*Bushels.*	*Bushels.*
Argentina	861	451	194	Roumania	2,604	1,241	
Belgium	673			Russia	33,170	20,298	13,273
Bulgaria	¹2,029			United States	2,034	8,164	13,655
Canada	127	146	501	Other countries	480	100	
Denmark	319	5					
Germany	51,979			Total	114,567	40,823	
Netherlands	20,291	10,418	197				

IMPORTS.

Country.	1913	1914	1915	Country.	1913	1914	1915
Austria-Hungary	268			Norway	11,088	8,128	7,884
Belgium	6,372			Russia	7,769	5,453	
Denmark	9,846	5,082	2,707	Sweden	4,446	2,586	1,770
Finland	15,813	9,898	13,425	Switzerland	661	267	16
France	3,712	1,441	36	United Kingdom	2,276	2,073	1,436
Germany	13,946			Other countries	886	537	
Italy	1,245	233					
Netherlands	32,273	17,539	2,232	Total	110,601	53,237	

¹ Data for 1912.

BUCKWHEAT.

TABLE 57.—*Buckwheat: Acreage, production, and value in the United States, 1849–1916.*

NOTE.—Figures in *italics* are census returns; figures in roman are estimates of the Department of Agriculture. Estimates of acres are obtained by applying estimated percentages of increase or decrease to the published numbers of the preceding year, except that a revised base is used for applying percentage estimates whenever new census data are available.

Year.	Acreage (thousands of acres).	Average yield per acre (bushels).	Production (thousands of bushels).	Average farm price Dec. 1 (cents per bushel).	Farm value Dec. 1 (thousands of dollars).	Year.	Acreage (thousands of acres).	Average yield per acre (bushels).	Production (thousands of bushels).	Average farm price Dec. 1 (cents per bushel).	Farm value Dec. 1 (thousands of dollars).
1849			*8,957*			1890	845	14.7	12,433	57.4	7,133
1859			*17,572*			1891	849	15.0	12,761	57.0	7,272
1866	1,046	21.8	22,792	67.6	15,413	1892	861	14.1	12,143	51.8	6,296
1867	1,228	17.4	21,359	78.7	16,812	1893	816	14.9	12,132	58.3	7,074
1868	1,114	17.8	19,864	78.0	15,490	1894	789	16.1	12,668	55.6	7,040
1869	1,029	16.9	17,431	71.9	12,535	1895	763	20.1	15,341	45.2	6,936
1869			*9,822*			1896	755	18.7	14,090	39.2	5,522
1870	537	18.3	9,842	70.5	6,937	1897	718	20.9	14,997	42.1	6,319
1871	414	20.1	8,329	74.5	6,208	1898	678	17.3	11,722	45.0	5,271
1872	448	18.1	8,134	73.5	5,979	1899	670	16.6	11,094	55.7	6,184
1873	454	17.3	7,838	75.0	5,879	*1899*	*807*	*13.9*	*11,234*		
1874	453	17.7	8,017	72.9	5,844	1900	638	15.0	9,567	55.8	5,341
1875	576	17.5	10,082	62.0	6,255	1901	811	18.6	15,126	56.3	8,523
1876	666	14.5	9,669	66.6	6,436	1902	805	18.1	14,530	59.6	8,655
1877	650	15.7	10,177	66.9	6,808	1903	804	17.7	14,244	60.7	8,651
1878	673	18.2	12,247	52.6	6,441	1904	794	18.9	15,008	62.2	9,331
1879	640	20.5	13,140	59.8	7,856	1905	760	19.2	14,585	58.7	8,565
1879	*848*	*13.9*	*11,817*			1906	789	18.6	14,642	59.6	8,727
1880	823	17.8	14,618	59.4	8,682	1907	800	17.9	14,290	69.8	9,975
1881	829	11.4	9,486	86.5	8,206	1908	803	19.8	15,874	75.6	12,004
1882	847	13.0	11,019	73.0	8,039	1909	834	20.9	17,438		
1883	857	8.9	7,669	82.2	6,304	*1909*	*878*	*16.9*	*14,849*	*70.1*	*10,346*
1884	879	12.6	11,116	58.9	6,549	1910 ¹	860	20.5	17,598	66.1	11,636
1885	914	13.8	12,626	55.9	7,057	1911	833	21.1	17,549	72.6	12,735
1886	918	12.9	11,869	54.5	6,465	1912	841	22.9	19,249	66.1	12,720
1887	911	11.9	10,844	56.5	6,122	1913	805	17.2	13,833	75.5	10,445
1888	913	13.2	12,050	63.3	7,628	1914	792	21.3	16,881	76.4	12,892
1889	837	14.5	12,110	50.5	6,113	1915	769	19.6	15,056	78.7	11,843
1889	*837*	*14.5*	*12,110*			1916	845	14.0	11,840	112.9	13,364

Figures adjusted to census basis.

BUCKWHEAT—Continued.

TABLE 58.—*Buckwheat: Acreage, production, and total farm value, by States, 1916.*

[000 omitted.]

State	Acreage	Production	Farm value Dec. 1.	State	Acreage	Production	Farm value Dec. 1.
	Acres.	*Bush.*	*Dolls.*		*Acres.*	*Bush.*	*Dolls.*
Maine	14	336	319	Ohio	19	336	370
New Hampshire	1	20	20	Indiana	8	144	161
Vermont	12	210	220	Illinois	4	68	88
Massachusetts	2	32	45	Michigan	75	825	949
Connecticut	3	57	68	Wisconsin	20	280	325
New York	290	3,480	4,246	Minnesota	10	150	168
New Jersey	15	285	308	Iowa	10	150	188
Pennsylvania	270	3,780	4,196	Missouri	4	56	74
Delaware	3	57	67	Nebraska	1	17	19
Maryland	10	189	208	Tennessee	3	54	54
Virginia	25	480	456				
West Virginia	36	659	666	United States	845	11,840	13,364
North Carolina	10	175	149				

TABLE 59.—*Buckwheat: Condition of crop, United States, on first of months named, 1896–1916.*

Year.	Aug.	Sept.	When harvested.
	P. ct.	*P. ct.*	*P. ct.*
1896	96.0	93.2	86.0
1897	94.9	95.1	90.8
1898	87.2	88.8	76.2
1899	93.2	75.2	70.2
1900	87.9	80.5	72.8
1901	91.1	90.9	90.5
1902	91.4	86.4	80.5
1903	93.9	91.0	83.0
1904	92.8	91.5	88.7
1905	92.6	91.8	91.6
1906	93.2	91.2	84.9
1907	91.9	77.4	80.1
1908	89.4	87.8	81.6
1909	86.4	81.0	79.5
1910	87.9	82.3	81.7
1911	82.9	83.8	81.4
1912	88.4	91.6	89.2
1913	85.5	75.4	65.9
1914	88.8	87.1	83.3
1915	92.6	88.6	81.9
1916	87.8	78.5	66.9

TABLE 60.—*Buckwheat: Yield per acre, price per bushel Dec. 1, and value per acre, by States.*

State	Yield per acre (bushels).											Farm price per bushel (cents).						Value per acre (dollars).[1]	
	10-year aver. 1907–1916	1907	1908	1909	1910	1911	1912	1913	1914	1915	1916	10-year aver. 1907–1916	1912	1913	1914	1915	1916	5-year average, 1911–1915	1916
Me	28.9	28.0	30.0	28.0	32.5	30.0	29.4	32.0	29.0	26.0	24.0	70	70	56	60	70	95	19.02	22.80
N. H	26.1	22.0	21.5	22.0	31.0	27.3	31.0	31.0	25.0	30.0	20.0	76	72	66	70	81	100	21.34	20.00
Vt	24.2	22.0	22.0	22.0	24.4	24.3	30.0	25.0	28.0	27.0	17.5	79	72	80	82	82	105	21.47	18.38
Mass	19.0	21.0	18.0	19.3	22.0	21.0	21.0	17.0	18.5	16.0	16.0	88	85	80	84	95	140	16.18	22.40
Conn	18.7	16.0	18.2	19.5	19.5	19.0	20.5	17.0	18.5	20.0	19.0	93	88	95	95	96	120	17.80	22.80
N. Y	19.9	17.5	21.4	24.0	23.0	21.3	23.8	14.3	23.0	19.0	12.0	78	64	81	76	80	122	15.01	14.64
N. J	20.5	16.5	20.0	21.8	21.5	20.0	22.0	22.0	21.0	21.0	19.0	79	72	76	83	83	108	16.48	20.52
Pa	19.6	18.0	19.2	19.5	19.5	21.9	24.2	18.5	20.5	21.0	14.0	74	64	73	76	78	111	15.21	15.54
Del	20.3	24.0	30.0	19.8	20.5	19.0	16.0	17.0	19.0	18.5	19.0	74	66	69	76	75	118	12.59	22.42
Md	18.4	19.0	18.5	16.8	18.5	20.0	17.5	16.5	18.5	20.0	18.9	76	71	75	81	72	110	13.52	20.79
Va	19.2	19.0	18.0	18.0	18.0	16.0	21.5	23.1	19.4	20.0	19.2	78	75	80	84	80	95	15.62	18.24
W. Va	21.3	18.5	18.0	22.7	23.0	24.0	21.0	21.5	22.0		18.3	81	75	78	83	80	101	18.04	18.48
N. C	18.0	15.5	16.4	19.8	19.0	19.0	17.5	19.3	19.0	17.5	17.5	80	85	78	83	82	85	15.05	14.88
Ohio	20.0	19.5	18.5	21.2	18.0	21.0	19.0	18.5	18.0	24.0	17.7	80	70	76	76	77	110	15.93	19.47
Ind	17.3	15.5	17.0	17.3	17.7	18.3	19.0	18.5	17.5	14.0	18.0	79	73	75	78	80	112	13.23	20.16
Ill	18.2	17.0	18.2	18.2	20.0	18.1	22.0	17.0	17.7	17.0	17.0	91	80	80	95	90	130	16.10	22.10
Mich	15.3	15.5	13.5	14.3	15.3	18.0	17.0	15.0	18.5	14.5	11.0	73	65	70	71	72	115	11.58	12.65
Wis	15.3	16.0	15.2	12.3	14.0	17.5	17.0	16.5	17.5	13.0	14.0	79	66	69	76	83	116	11.96	16.24
Minn	16.9	14.7	18.2	15.2	16.0	18.0	21.0	16.5	17.0	17.5	15.0	75	65	64	70	75	112	12.58	16.80
Iowa	15.7	15.0	15.5	14.9	17.5	19.0	14.0	18.3	13.0		15.0	85	75	81	77	80	125	13.17	18.75
Mo	15.4	16.0	20.1	21.0	16.5	10.0	15.0	11.0	15.5	15.0	14.0	95	85	85	93	90	133	12.40	18.62
Nebr	17.8	14.5	18.0	16.0	20.0	16.0	18.0	20.0	18.5	20.0	17.0	90	90	79	84	95	110	16.35	18.70
Kans	14.2	12.0	18.7	14.0	15.0	12.0	16.0	10.0	16.0	14.0		90	78	80	90	99		12.10	
Tenn	16.8	15.0	15.3	15.0	15.0	16.0	18.0	15.0	22.3	18.0	18.0	81	78	75	78	76	100	13.80	18.00
U. S.	19.5	17.9	19.8	20.9	20.5	21.1	22.9	17.2	21.3	19.6	14.0	76.4	66.1	75.5	76.4	78.7	112.9	15.01	15.82

[1] Based upon farm price Dec. 1.

BUCKWHEAT—Continued.

TABLE 61.—*Buckwheat: Farm price per bushel on first of each month, by geographical divisions, 1915 and 1916.*

Month.	United States.		North Atlantic States.		South Atlantic States.		N. Central States east of Miss. R.		N. Central States west of Miss. R.		South Central States.	
	1916	1915	1916	1915	1916	1915	1916	1915	1916	1915	1916	1915
	Cts.	Cts.	Cts.	Cts.	Cts.	Cts.	Cts.	Cts.	Cts.	Cts.	Cts.	Cts.
January	81.5	77.9	81.6	77.6	82.5	81.2	78.1	76.5	87.7	87.5	80.0	74.0
February	80.7	83.7	81.1	84.0	81.3	85.0	75.6	80.8	93.0	79.0	76.0	76.0
March	83.2	85.5	83.0	87.0	84.9	85.1	79.6	77.0	102.7	82.5	74.0	80.0
April	83.1	85.3	83.5	84.8	81.9	89.2	79.0	85.1	101.0	90.0	76.0	78.0
May	84.9	84.6	85.2	84.7	83.1	89.0	84.4	79.6	93.5	90.5	74.0	77.0
June	87.0	86.9	88.7	87.6	81.2	86.7	80.0	82.7	100.0	91.0	74.0	76.0
July	93.1	92.1	94.8	93.3	85.6	87.1	90.6	86.2	87.0	117.5	77.0	77.0
August	89.0	89.2	90.8	91.3	83.9	83.2	76.9	78.9	91.7	102.0	75.0	77.0
September	86.4	81.4	87.1	81.6	84.4	82.0	82.4	78.3	98.5	97.5	76.0	75.0
October	90.4	73.7	90.8	73.9	84.6	77.0	94.4	68.0	87.5	88.0	80.0	70.0
November	102.9	78.5	104.6	79.0	88.8	75.2	105.9	76.3	115.0	97.5	77.0	71.0
December	112.9	78.7	114.9	79.0	99.1	79.1	114.5	75.7	120.4	81.5	100.0	76.0

FLAX.

TABLE 62.—*Flax: Area and production in undermentioned countries, 1913–1915.*

[000 omitted.]

Country.	Area.			Production.					
				Seed.			Fiber.		
	1913	1914	1915	1913	1914	1915	1913	1914	1915
NORTH AMERICA.	Acres.	Acres.	Acres.	Bushels.	Bushels.	Bushels.	Pounds.	Pounds.	Pounds.
United States	2,291	1,645	1,387	17,853	13,749	14,030			
Canada:									
Quebec	1	1	1	9	8	7			
Ontario	7	5	4	164	84	62			
Manitoba	54	40	34	632	338	374			
Saskatchewan	1,386	958	697	15,579	6,131	9,061			
Alberta	105	80	70	1,155	614	1,124			
Total Canada	1,553	1,084	806	17,539	7,175	10,628			
Mexico	(1)	(1)	(1)	150	150	150			
Total	(1)	(1)	(1)	35,542	21,074	24,808			
SOUTH AMERICA.									
Argentina	4,283	4,397	4,258	44,486	39,171	44,309			
Uruguay	141	128	101	1,302	963	588			
Total	4,424	4,525	4,359	45,788	40,134	44,897			
EUROPE.									
Austria-Hungary:									
Austria	90	[2] 57	(1)	608	[2] 455	(1)	48,976	[2] 37,046	(1)
Hungary proper	32	(1)	(1)	255	(1)	(1)	29,999	(1)	(1)
Croatia-Slavonia	16	(1)	(1)	18	(1)	(1)	8,640	(1)	(1)
Bosnia-Herzegovina	(1)	(1)	(1)	4	(1)	(1)	1,000	(1)	(1)
Total Austria-Hungary				885			88,615		
Belgium	57	32	(1)	387	(1)	(1)	39,437	(1)	(1)
Bulgaria	1	2	(1)	8	(1)	(1)	(1)	(1)	(1)
France [3]	75	2	47	24	740	336	(1)	48,437	23,370	43,497

[1] No official statistics.   [3] Excluding the invaded zone in 1914 and 1915.
[2] Galicia and Bukowina not included.

FLAX—Continued.

TABLE 62.—*Flax: Area and production in undermentioned countries, 1913–1915*—Contd.

[000 omitted.]

Country.	Area.			Production.					
				Seed.			Fiber.		
	1913	1914	1915	1913	1914	1915	1913	1914	1915
EUROPE—contd.	*Acres.*	*Acres.*	*Acres.*	*Bushels.*	*Bushels.*	*Bushels.*	*Pounds.*	*Pounds.*	*Pounds.*
Ireland............	59	49	53	(1)	(1)	(1)	28,341	18,202	21,648
Italy............	22	22	21	405	323	323	5,732	5,070	5,511
Netherlands.......	36	19	22	326	212	(1)	16,606	10,811	10,818
Roumania.........	67	21	14	569	165	134	4,759	2,137	1,187
Russia:									
Russia proper....	3,443	3,401	3,060	22,898	14,222	(1)	....	....	....
Poland...........	88	(1)	(1)	878	(1)	(1)	....	....	....
Northern Caucasia...........	144	182	48	680	1,391	(1)	....	....	....
Total........	3,675	....	....	24,456	....	....	1,152,349	868,613	....
Serbia............	(1)	(1)	(1)	(1)	(1)	(1)	(1)	(1)	(1)
Sweden [2].........	3	3	(1)	3	3	(1)	481	401	(1)
Total........	....	....	....	....	....	....	....	....	....
ASIA.									
India:									
British..........	4,125	3,031	3,325	21,684	15,448	15,880	....	....	....
Native States....	433	(1)	(1)	(1)	(1)	(1)	....	....	....
Total........	4,558	3,031	3,325	21,684	15,448	15,880	....	....	....
Russia:									
Central Asia (4 Governments of)............	117	105	94	575	836	(1)	....	....	....
Siberia (4 Governments of)..	176	191	153	1,094	1,584	(1)	....	....	....
Transcaucasia (1 Government of)	(1)	(1)	(1)	(1)	(1)	(1)	....	....	....
Total........	....	....	....	....	....	....	....	....	....
AFRICA.									
Algeria............	(1)	(1)	(1)	15	(1)	(1)	(1)	(1)	(1)
Grand total..	....	....	....	132,477	....	....	1,384,757	....	....

[1] No official statistics.   [2] Includes hemp.

TABLE 63.—*Flax (seed and fiber): Total production of countries named in Table 62, 1896–1915.*

Year.	Production.		Year.	Production.	
	Seed.	Fiber.		Seed.	Fiber.
	Bushels.	*Pounds.*		*Bushels.*	*Pounds.*
1896..............	82,684,000	1,714,205,000	1906..............	88,165,000	1,871,723,000
1897..............	57,596,000	1,498,054,000	1907..............	102,960,000	2,042,390,000
1898..............	72,938,000	1,780,693,000	1908..............	100,850,000	1,907,591,000
1899..............	66,348,000	1,138,763,000	1909..............	100,820,000	1,384,524,000
1900..............	62,432,000	1,315,931,000	1910..............	85,253,000	913,112,000
1901..............	72,314,000	1,050,260,000	1911..............	101,339,000	1,011,350,000
1902..............	83,891,000	1,564,840,000	1912..............	130,291,000	1,429,967,000
1903..............	110,455,000	1,492,383,000	1913..............	132,477,000	1,384,757,000
1904..............	107,743,000	1,517,922,000	1914..............	....	....
1905..............	100,458,000	1,494,229,000	1915..............	....	....

FLAX—Continued.

TABLE 64.—*Flaxseed: Acreage, production, value, and condition in the United States, 1849–1916.*

NOTE.—Figures in *italics* are census returns; figures in roman are estimates of the Department of Agriculture. Estimates of acres are obtained by applying estimated percentages of increase or decrease to the published numbers of the preceding year, except that a revised base is used for applying percentage estimates whenever new census data are available.

Year.	Acreage.	Average yield per acre.	Production.	Average farm price per bushel Dec. 1.	Farm value Dec. 1.	Condition of growing crop.			
						July 1.	Aug. 1.	Sept. 1.	When harvested.
	Acres.	*Bushels.*	*Bushels.*	*Cents.*	*Dollars.*	*P. ct.*	*P. ct.*	*P. ct.*	*P. ct.*
1849			*562,000*						
1859			*567,000*						
1869			*1,730,000*						
1879			*7,170,000*						
1889	*1,319,000*	*7.8*	*10,250,000*						
1899	*2,111,000*	*9.5*	*19,979,000*						
1902	3,740,000	7.8	29,285 000	105.2	30,815,000				
1903	3,233,000	8.4	27,301,000	81.7	22,292,000	86.2	80.3	80.5	74.0
1904	2,264,000	10.3	23,401,000	99.3	23,229,000	86.6	78.9	85.8	87.0
1905	2,535,000	11.2	28,478,000	84.4	24,049,000	92.7	96.7	94.2	91.5
1906	2,506,000	10.2	25,576,000	101.3	25,899,000	93.2	92.2	89.0	87.4
1907	2,864,000	9.0	25,851,000	95.6	24,713,000	91.2	91.9	85.4	78.0
1908	2,679,000	9.6	25,805,000	118.4	30,577,000	92.5	86.1	82.5	81.2
1909	2,742,000	9.4	25,856,000						
1909	*2,083,000*	*9.4*	*19,513,000*	*153.0*	*29,796,000*	*95.1*	*92.7*	*88.9*	*84.9*
1910 [1]	2,467,000	5.2	12,718,000	231.7	29,472,000	65.0	51.7	48.3	47.2
1911	2,757,000	7.0	19,370,000	182.1	35,272,000	80.9	71.0	68.4	69.6
1912	2,851,000	9.8	28,073,000	114.7	32,202,000	88.9	87.5	86.3	83.8
1913	2,291,000	7.8	17,853,000	119.9	21,399,000	82.0	77.4	74.9	74.7
1914	1,645,000	8.4	13,749,000	126.0	17,318,000	90.5	82.1	72.9	77.4
1915	1,387,000	10.1	14,030,000	174.0	24,410,000	88.5	91.2	87.6	84.5
1916	1,605,000	9.6	15,459,000	248.1	38,350,000	90.3	84.0	84.8	86.2

[1] Figures adjusted to census basis.

TABLE 65.—*Flaxseed: Acreage, production, and total farm value, by States, 1916.*

State.	Acreage.	Average yield per acre.	Production.	Average farm price per bushel Dec. 1.	Farm value Dec. 1.
	Acres.	*Bushels.*	*Bushels.*	*Dollars.*	*Dollars.*
Wisconsin	5,000	12.0	60,000	2.40	144,000
Minnesota	275,000	8.5	2,338,000	2.40	5,611,000
Iowa	18,000	10.0	180,000	2.15	387,000
Missouri	5,000	7.0	35,000	2.12	74,000
North Dakota	790,000	10.3	8,137,000	2.52	20,505,000
South Dakota	150,000	9.3	1,395,000	2.47	3,446,000
Nebraska	4,000	8.0	32,000	2.30	74,000
Kansas	30,000	5.8	174,000	2.34	407,000
Montana	325,000	9.5	3,088,000	2.48	7,658,000
Wyoming	2,000	7.0	14,000	2.25	32,000
Colorado	1,000	6.0	6,000	1.95	12,000
United States	1,605,000	9.6	15,459,000	2.48	38,350,000

FLAX—Continued.

TABLE 66.—*Flaxseed: Yield per acre, price per bushel Dec. 1, and value per acre, by States.*

State.	Yield per acre (bushels).											Farm price per bushel (cents).						Value per acre (dollars).[1]	
	10-year average, 1907–1916.	1907	1908	1909	1910	1911	1912	1913	1914	1915	1916	10-year average, 1907–1916.	1912	1913	1914	1915	1916	5-year average, 1911–1915.	1916.
Wis	13.2	14.2	16.0	14.5	10.0	12.0	12.5	14.0	13.5	13.5	12.0	155	127	123	125	180	240	19.30	28.80
Minn	9.4	10.5	10.6	10.0	7.5	8.0	10.2	9.0	9.3	10.5	8.5	157	120	123	128	176	240	13.65	20.40
Iowa	10.2	11.5	10.9	9.8	12.2	8.0	11.5	9.4	9.5	9.0	10.0	147	124	123	120	150	215	13.10	21.50
Mo	7.0	10.0	7.0	8.1	8.4	3.0	6.0	5.0	8.0	8.0	7.0	138	110	115	104	135	212	7.43	14.84
N. Dak	8.3	8.0	9.0	9.3	3.6	7.6	9.7	7.2	8.3	9.9	10.3	158	114	121	128	178	252	12.40	25.96
S. Dak	8.4	10.0	10.7	9.4	5.0	5.3	8.6	7.2	7.5	11.0	9.3	154	113	120	123	167	247	11.08	22.97
Nebr	8.5	11.0	11.0	8.5	8.0	5.0	9.5	6.0	7.0	11.0	8.0	147	128	110	119	147	230	10.50	18.40
Kans	6.4	10.0	6.5	7.0	8.2	3.0	6.0	6.0	6.0	5.7	5.8	145	130	116	125	145	234	7.24	13.57
Mont	10.0	13.0	11.5	12.0	7.0	7.7	12.0	9.0	8.0	10.5	9.5	153	112	115	120	170	248	13.02	23.56
Wyo	9.8	....	....	....	10.0	....	12.0	9.9	7.0	13.0	7.0	....	....	....	....	145	225	....	15.75
Colo	7.2	....	....	....	7.0	7.0	8.0	5.0	8.0	9.4	6.0	151	125	115	100	120	195	9.53	11.70
U. S.	8.6	9.0	9.6	9.4	5.2	7.0	9.8	7.8	8.4	10.1	9.6	156.3	114.7	119.9	126.0	174.0	248.1	12.31	23.89

[1] Based upon farm price Dec. 1.

TABLE 67.—*Flaxseed: Farm price per bushel, on first of each month, by geographical divisions, 1915 and 1916.*

Month.	United States.		North Central States east of Mississippi River.		North Central States west of Mississippi River.		Far Western States.	
	1916	1915	1916	1915	1916	1915	1916	1915
	Cents.	*Cents.*	*Cents.*	*Cents.*	*Cents.*	*Cents.*	*Cents.*	*Cents.*
January	185.9	134.8	....	135.0	184.7	136.8	193.0	125.0
February	210.9	163.7	200.0	140.0	211.2	161.6	210.0	175.0
March	202.5	157.9	150.0	130.0	204.6	160.0	192.0	148.0
April	202.1	167.7	192.0	....	201.8	167.3	205.0	170.0
May	191.8	169.6	198.0	150.0	190.9	169.7	197.0	170.0
June	176.5	169.5	180.0	130.0	174.1	168.7	191.0	175.0
July	163.2	152.5	160.0	155.0	164.1	153.8	158.0	146.0
August	178.1	144.6	161.0	....	176.3	145.1	190.0	142.0
September	190.2	143.5	200.0	100.0	188.6	145.6	200.0	135.0
October	199.2	148.1	200.0	125.0	199.1	148.3	200.0	148.0
November	234.7	162.9	218.0	....	234.0	163.9	240.0	158.0
December	248.1	174.0	240.0	180.0	248.2	175.0	247.8	169.6

FLAX—Continued.

TABLE 68.—*Flaxseed: Wholesale price per bushel, 1912–1916.*

Date.	Cincinnati.		Minneapolis.		Milwaukee. No. 1 Northwestern.		Duluth.	
	Low.	High.	Low.	High.	Low.	High.	Low.	High.
1912.								
January–June	$2.50	$2.56	$2.01	$2.36	$2.01¼	$2.39	$2.00	$2.53
July–December	1.50	2.80	1.22	2.10	1.24½	2.18½	1.22	2.20¾
1913.								
January–June	1.50	1.50	1.23⅛	1.40	1.25½	1.42¾	1.22⅝	1.39
July–December	1.50	1.50	1.31¼	1.53¼	1.30¾	1.54½	1.34⅜	1.53⅛
1914.								
January	1.50	1.50	1.47¼	1.61¼	1.45¼	1.75	1.48	1.63¼
June	1.40	1.50	1.28	1.88	1.30	1.93	1.28¾	1.93
1915.								
January	....	....	1.59½	1.94¼	1.51½	1.98	1.61½	1.93
February	....	....	1.80⅞	1.92½	1.81	1.87¾	1.83⅞	1.91½
March	1.80	1.80	1.80	2.08½	1.81	2.05	1.84¼	2.09
April	1.75	1.80	1.85	1.97¼	1.85	1.95	1.86½	1.98¼
May	1.70	1.75	1.87	2.00¼	1.87	1.98¼	1.91	2.02¼
June	1.70	1.70	1.68½	1.86	1.68½	1.84	1.70½	1.85½
January–June	1.70	1.80	1.59½	2.08½	1.51½	2.05	1.61½	2.09
July	1.70	1.70	1.52½	1.75¼	1.52½	1.73¼	1.53	1.76¼
August	....	....	1.60	1.74½	1.60	1.72½	1.58½	1.69
September	....	....	1.61½	1.87½	1.61½	1.84½	1.62	1.82½
October	....	....	1.77	1.91½	1.77	1.87½	1.76	1.90¼
November	....	....	1.82½	2.09½	1.82½	2.07½	1.87½	2.12¼
December	....	....	1.98⅛	2.21	1.97	2.18	2.00¼	2.20½
July–December	1.70	1.70	1.52½	2.21	1.52½	2.18	1.53	2.20½
1916.								
January	....	....	2.15¾	2.41¼	2.15¾	2.38	2.17¾	2.42¾
February	....	....	2.25	2.39	2.25	2.35	2.23	2.43⅜
March	2.85	2.85	2.15¾	2.35½	2.15¾	2.32½	2.15¾	2.32½
April	2.85	2.85	2.00	2.22¼	2.00	2.19¼	2.01	2.19¼
May	2.85	2.85	1.83½	2.09¼	1.83½	2.05¼	1.84½	2.05¾
June	2.85	2.85	1.73½	1.89	1.73½	1.84½	1.76	1.97¾
January–June	2.85	2.85	1.73½	2.35½	1.73½	2.38	1.76	2.43⅜
July	2.85	2.85	1.77	2.12½	1.77	2.08	1.80	2.11½
August	1.50	1.50	1.60	2.28	2.04	2.24	2.05	2.26½
September	1.50	1.50	2.00¾	2.31	2.00¾	2.28	2.02½	2.31
October	1.50	1.80	2.40	2.70	2.40	2.67	2.43	2.72
November	1.80	2.25	2.59¾	2.93½	2.59¾	2.89	2.65¾	2.94½
December	2.25	2.25	2.75	2.94	2.76½	2.88¾	2.79½	2.93¼
July–December	1.50	2.85	1.60	2.94	1.77	2.89	1.80	2.94½

RICE.

TABLE 69.—*Rice: Area and production in undermentioned countries, 1913–1915.*

[Expressed in terms of cleaned rice.]

Country.	Area.			Production.		
	1913	1914	1915	1913	1914	1915
NORTH AMERICA.	*Acres.*	*Acres.*	*Acres.*	*Pounds.*	*Pounds.*	*Pounds.*
United States..........	827,000	694,000	803,000	715,111,000	656,917,000	804,083,000
Hawaii [1]..............	9,000	(2)	(2)	25,820,000	(2)	(2)
Porto Rico [1].........	16,000	(2)	(2)	4,298,000	(2)	(2)
Central America:						
Guatemala.........	(2)	(2)	(2)	3,501,000	24,085,000	24,015,000
Salvador..........	(2)	27,000	(2)	(2)	12,344,000	(2)
Costa Rica.........	(2)	7,000	(2)	(2)	(2)	(2)
Honduras...........	(2)	(2)	(2)	(2)	(2)	3,252,000
Mexico.................	(2)	41,000	(2)	(2)	33,921,000	(2)
SOUTH AMERICA.						
Argentina..............	[3] 20,000	(2)	(2)	(2)	(2)	(2)
Brazil: São Paulo......	231,000	(2)	(2)	109,625,000	116,416,000	79,380,000
British Guiana..........	42,000	34,000	47,000	61,185,000	51,160,000	91,630,000
Dutch Guiana..........	(2)	(2)	(2)	4,918,000	6,913,000	(2)
Peru...................	138,000	(2)	(2)	108,869,000	(2)	85,500,000
EUROPE.						
Bulgaria................	7,000	(2)	(2)	5,656,000	(2)	(2)
France.................	1,000	(2)	(2)	980,000	(2)	(2)
Italy..................	362,000	361,000	356,000	739,221,000	741,263,000	762,900,000
Russia (Northern Caucasia)...............	1,000	1,000	(2)	564,000	729,000	(2)
Spain..................	96,000	97,000	102,000	303,310,000	336,925,000	320,022,000
ASIA.						
India:						
British [4]...........	75,425,000	76,625,000	76,792,000	64,490,272,000	61,022,080,000	73,644,480,000
Native States......	2,518,000	(2)	(2)	(2)	(2)	(2)
Ceylon [5].............	672,000	685,000	(2)	356,191,000	290,819,000	(2)
Federated Malay States	124,000	(2)	(2)	87,321,000	(2)	(2)
Japanese Empire:						
Japan..............	7,425,000	7,434,000	7,563,000	15,787,969,000	17,908,918,000	17,569,018,000
Chosen............	2,560,000	(2)	(2)	3,167,719,000	3,678,878,000	3,518,928,000
Formosa...........	1,222,000	1,235,000	(2)	1,610,461,000	1,447,709,000	(2)
Java and Madura [6]....	6,310,000	6,346,000	(2)	7,951,044,000	7,826,026,000	(2)
Philippine Islands.....	2,820,000	3,076,000	2,794,000	1,512,285,000	1,403,516,000	1,099,914,000
Russia: Transcaucasia and Turkestan [7]...	668,000	636,000	(2)	512,947,000	380,546,000	(2)
Straits Settlements.....	[8] 92,000	(2)	(2)	(2)	(2)	(2)
Siam...................	5,286,000	5,096,000	5,181,000	5,884,956,000	5,711,133,000	5,517,167,000
AFRICA.						
Egypt..................	252,000	37,000	331,000	505,118,000	81,229,000	806,610,000
Nyasaland..............	(2)	(2)	(2)	3,385,000	2,695,000	1,606,000
OCEANIA.						
Australia..............	(9)	(9)	(2)	75,000	7,000	(2)
Fiji...................	14,000	12,000	(2)	(2)	(2)	(2)

[1] Census of 1909.
[2] No official statistics.
[3] Census of 1908.
[4] Excluding a large area the production of which is not officially reported.
[5] Excluding production for Matara, which in 1913 was 55,483,000 pounds.
[6] Excluding Soerakarta, Djokjakarta and private lands.
[7] Excluding Khiva and Bokhara.
[8] Data for 1912.
[9] Less than 500 acres.

RICE—Continued.

TABLE 70.—*Rice (cleaned): Total production in principal countries for which estimates are available, 1900–1913.*

[The figures below include the principal countries for which estimates are available. The totals shown are merely approximate. China and French Indo-China are not included below. Three Provinces of China in 1910 produced 47,204,000,000 pounds of rice. The totals below may represent at least two-thirds of the total world production of rice.]

Year.	Production.	Year.	Production.	Year.	Production.
	Pounds.		*Pounds.*		*Pounds.*
1900	100,400,000,000	1905	102,400,000,000	1910	126,100,000,000
1901	94,400,000,000	1906	105,800,000,000	1911	102,100,000,000
1902	101,600,000,000	1907	100,300,000,000	1912	97,300,000,000
1903	101,800,000,000	1908	102,900,000,000	1913	100,700,000,000
1904	110,700,000,000	1909	127,700,000,000		

TABLE 71.—*Rice: Acreage, production, value, and condition, in the United States, 1904–1916.*

Year.	Acreage.	Average yield per acre.	Production.	Average farm price per bushel Dec. 1.	Farm value Dec. 1.	Condition of growing crop.			
						July 1.	Aug. 1.	Sept. 1.	When harvested.
	Acres.	*Bushels.*	*Bushels.*	*Cents.*	*Dollars.*	*Per ct.*	*Per ct.*	*Per ct.*	*Per ct.*
1904...	662,000	31.9	21,096,000	65.8	13,802,000	88.2	90.2	89.7	87.3
1905...	482,000	28.2	13,607,000	95.2	12,956,000	88.0	92.9	92.2	89.3
1906...	575,000	31.1	17,855,000	90.3	16,121,000	82.9	83.1	86.8	87.2
1907...	627,000	29.9	18,738.000	85.8	16,081,000	88.7	88.6	87.0	88.7
1908...	655,000	33.4	21,890,000	81.2	17,771,000	92.9	94.1	93.5	87.7
1909...	720,000	33.8	24,368,000						
1909...	*610,000*	*35.8*	*21,839,000*	79.6	17,383,000	90.7	84.5	84.7	81.2
1910...	723,000	33.9	24,510,000	67.8	16,624,000	86.3	87.6	88.8	88.1
1911...	696,000	32.9	22,934,000	79.7	18,274,000	87.7	88.3	87.2	85.4
1912...	723,000	34.7	25,054,000	93.5	23,423,000	86.3	86.3	88.8	89.2
1913...	827,000	31.1	25,744,000	85.8	22,090,000	88.4	88.7	88.0	80.3
1914...	694,000	34.1	23,649,000	92.4	21,849,000	86.5	87.6	88.9	88.0
1915...	803,000	36.1	28,947,000	90.6	26,212,000	90.5	90.0	82.3	80.9
1916...	866,000	47.0	40,702,000	88.9	36,187,000	92.7	92.2	91.2	91.5

TABLE 72.—*Rice: Acreage, production, and farm value, by States, 1916.*

State.	Acreage.	Average yield per acre.	Production.	Average farm price per bushel Dec. 1.	Farm value Dec. 1.
	Acres.	*Bushels.*	*Bushels.*	*Cents.*	*Dollars.*
North Carolina	300	21.0	6,000	85	5,000
South Carolina	3,500	14.0	49,000	90	44,000
Georgia	800	20.0	16,000	87	14,000
Florida	700	25.0	18,000	75	14,000
Missouri	200	51.0	10,000	100	10,000
Alabama	300	25.0	8,000	75	6,000
Mississippi	1,900	28.0	53,000	80	42,000
Louisiana	443,300	46.0	20,392,000	90	18,353,000
Texas	235,000	45.0	10,575,000	86	9,094,000
Arkansas	125,000	50.5	6,312,000	96	6,060,000
California	55,300	59.0	3,263,000	78	2,545,000
United States	866,300	47.0	40,702,000	88.9	36,187,000

RICE—Continued.

TABLE 73.—*Rice: Yield per acre, price per bushel Dec. 1, and value per acre, by States.*

State.	Yield per acre (bushels).											Farm price per bushel (cents).						Value per acre (dollars).[1]	
	10-year average, 1907–1916.	1907	1908	1909	1910	1911	1912	1913	1914	1915	1916	10-year average, 1907–1916.	1912	1913	1914	1915	1916	5-year average, 1911–1915.	1916
N. C.	24.8	23.0	25.2	30.2	26.5	25.6	25.0	24.0	26.3	21.0	21.0	84	90	80	75	85	85	19.75	17.85
S. C.	22.9	27.0	24.0	25.6	21.0	11.7	25.0	30.0	26.0	24.3	14.0	91	93	90	92	90	90	20.96	12.60
Ga.	27.1	34.0	25.0	23.9	22.0	26.8	30.0	32.0	28.0	29.3	20.0	89	90	83	89	88	87	24.98	17.40
Fla.	25.1	30.0	25.0	25.0	21.0	25.0	25.0	25.0	25.0	25.0	25.0	80	90	60	70	75	75	18.50	18.75
Mo.	....	....	....	....	....	....	....	....	....	50.0	51.0	....	....	....	....	100	100	.....	51.00
Ala.	28.0	25.0	45.0	35.0	25.0	20.0	30.0	22.0	28.0	25.0	25.0	76	90	60	70	75	75	18.51	18.75
Miss.	29.5	22.0	31.0	30.0	30.0	36.0	35.0	28.0	30.0	25.0	28.0	81	90	70	85	88	80	25.26	22.40
La.	33.6	28.0	33.0	33.8	34.4	31.5	33.5	29.0	32.1	34.2	46.0	84	93	84	93	90	90	28.21	41.40
Tex.	34.5	32.0	34.5	34.0	33.0	34.3	35.5	32.0	33.8	30.5	45.0	84	94	86	92	89	86	29.31	38.70
Ark.	40.9	37.0	41.0	40.0	40.0	39.0	37.5	36.0	39.8	48.4	50.5	88	94	90	90	95	96	36.29	48.48
Cal.	50.0	....	....	....	33.0	40.0	50.0	48.0	53.3	66.7	59.0	86	91	100	100	90	78	47.37	46.02
U. S.	34.7	29.9	33.4	33.8	33.9	32.9	34.7	31.1	34.1	36.1	47.0	84.5	93.5	85.8	92.4	90.6	88.9	29.90	41.77

[1] Based upon farm price Dec. 1.

TABLE 74.—*Rice: Wholesale price per pound, 1912–1916.*

Date.	New York.		Cincinnati.		Lake Charles.		New Orleans.		Houston.	
	Domestic (good).		Prime.		Rough.[1]		Honduras, cleaned.		Head rice, cleaned.	
	Low.	High.	Low.	High.	Low.	High.	Low.	High.	Low.	High.
1912.	*Cts.*	*Cts.*	*Cts.*	*Cts.*	*Dolls.*	*Dolls.*	*Cts.*	*Cts.*	*Cts.*	*Cts.*
Jan.-June	4¼	5¼	6	7	....	....	2¼	5¾	4⅛	5¼
July-Dec	4¾	5¼	6	7	....	....	2	6	4	5⅝
1913.										
Jan.-June	4¾	5	5¼	6¼	2.50	3.82	2⅜	5⅝	4	5½
July-Dec	4¾	5¼	5¾	6¼	2.00	3.76	1.15	7	4¼	6
1914.										
Jan.-June	4¾	5	5¾	6¼	1.40	3.76	1¼	6¼	3⅜	5¾
July-Dec	4¾	5⅞	5¾	6¼	2.00	4.55	1½	6⅝	3	5½
1915.										
January	5	5½	5¾	6¼	2.85	4.10	2¼	5½	4½	4¾
February	5¼	5½	5¾	6½	3.00	4.50	2½	5¾	4½	4¾
March	[2] 5¼	5½	6	6½	3.00	4.61½	2½	5¾	4½	4¾
April	5¼	5½	6	6½	....	....	2½	5½	4½	4⅞
May	5¼	5½	6	6½	....	....	2⅞	5⅜	4⅝	4⅞
June	5¼	5½	6	6½	....	....	3	5⅜	4¾	5
Jan.-June	5	5½	5¾	6½	2.85	4.61½	2¼	5¾	4½	5
July	5¼	5½	6	6½	....	....	3	5⅜	4⅞	5⅛
August	5	5½	5½	6½	3.05	3.47	2¼	5	4¾	5⅜
September	4½	5¼	5	6	2.90	3.63	2	4⅝	4¾	5¼
October	4½	5¼	5	6	2.80	3.35	2	5½	4¾	5⅛
November	5	5¼	5	5¾	3.17	3.65	2	5½	4¾	5⅛
December	5	5¼	5¼	5¾	3.00	3.65	2	5½	4¾	5
July-Dec	4½	5½	5	6½	2.80	3.65	2	5½	4¾	5⅜

[1] Per barrel of 162 pounds.

[2] Mar. 15, the grade was changed to fancy head.

RICE—Continued.

TABLE 74.—*Rice: Wholesale price per pound, 1912–1916*—Continued.

Date.	New York.		Cincinnati.		Lake Charles.		New Orleans.		Houston.	
	Domestic (good.)		Prime.		Rough.[1]		Honduras, cleaned.		Head rice, cleaned.	
	Low.	High.	Low.	High.	Low.	High.	Low.	High.	Low.	High.
1916.	*Cts.*	*Cts.*	*Cts.*	*Cts.*	*Dolls.*	*Dolls.*	*Cts.*	*Cts.*	*Cts.*	*Cts.*
January	5	5¼	5¼	5¾	2.65	3.35	2	5	4	4½
February	5	5¼	5¼	5¾	3.00	3.55	2	5¼	4	4¾
March	5	5¼	5¼	5¾	2.85	3.80	2½	5¼	4	4¾
April	5	5¼	5¼	5¾	3.00	4.02	2⅜	5⅛	4	4½
May	5	5¼	5¼	5¾	3.25	4.02	2⅞	5⅛	3¾	4¼
June	5	5¼	5¼	5¾	3.75	4.25	2⅞	5½	3¾	4¼
Jan.-June	5	5¼	5¼	5¾	2.65	4.25	2	5½	3¾	4¾
July	5	5¼	5¼	5¾	....	....	2¾	5⅛	3¾	4¼
August	5	5⅜	5¼	5¾	....	....	2½	5	3¾	4¼
September	5	5⅜	5¼	5¾	2.60	3.38	2¼	4¾	4	4¼
October	5	5⅜	5¼	5¾	2.65	3.40	2½	5	4¼	4¾
November	5	5½	5¼	5¾	3.35	3.65	2½	5¼	4½	4¾
December	5¼	5½	5¼	5¾	3.25	3.60	2½	5¼	4½	4¾
July-Dec	5	5½	5¼	5¾	2.60	3.65	2½	5¼	3¾	4¾

[1] Per barrel of 162 pounds.

TABLE 75.—*Rice: International trade, calendar years 1913–1915.*

[Mostly cleaned rice. Under rice is included paddy, unhulled, rough, cleaned, polished, broken, and cargo rice, in addition to rice flour and meal. Rice bran is not included. Rough rice or paddy, where specifically reported, has been reduced to terms of cleaned rice at ratio of 162 pounds rough, or unhulled, to 100 pounds cleaned. "Rice, other than whole or cleaned rice," in the returns of United Kingdom is not considered paddy, since the chief sources of supply indicate that it is practically all hulled rice. Cargo rice, a mixture of hulled and unhulled, is included without being reduced to terms of cleaned. Broken rice and rice flour and meal are taken without being reduced to terms of whole cleaned rice. See "General note," Table 10.]

EXPORTS.

[000 omitted.]

Country.	1913	1914 (prelim.)	1915 (prelim.)	Country.	1913	1914 (prelim.)	1915 (prelim.)
	Pounds.	*Pounds.*	*Pounds.*		*Pounds.*	*Pounds.*	*Pounds.*
Belgium	91,066	....	....	Penang	[1] 378,754	354,835	....
British India	5,761,625	4,520,152	329,591	Siam	2,531,795	2,605,150	2,421,283
Dutch East Indies	144,609	108,792	....	Singapore	[1] 683,897	908,438	....
France	65,044	123,021	113,153	Other countries	900,209	970,899	....
French Indo-China	2,831,962	3,060,373	....				
Germany	406,414	....	....	Total	14,339,692	13,185,081	....
Netherlands	544,317	533,421	7,211				

IMPORTS.

Country.	1913	1914 (prelim.)	1915 (prelim.)	Country.	1913	1914 (prelim.)	1915 (prelim.)
Austria-Hungary	166,011	....	....	Netherlands	903,971	776,891	133,511
Belgium	161,240	....	....	Penang	[1] 621,161	537,749	....
Brazil	17,146	14,407	15,317	Perak	202,904	207,764	186,268
British India	286,154	331,065	391,607	Philippine Islands	191,799	213,673	481,576
Ceylon	880,136	866,892	842,331	Russia	269,727	268,513	199,700
China	721,986	908,534	1,130,141	Selangor	[1] 192,304	190,084	178,438
Cuba	283,872	254,150	319,894	Singapore	[1] 965,390	1,279,688	....
Dutch East Indies	1,117,271	1,058,978	....	United Kingdom	771,512	756,144	1,305,701
Egypt	119,735	110,933	54,809	United States	229,812	255,064	254,568
France	537,935	761,106	525,279	Other countries	1,397,593	1,070,098	....
Germany	1,052,917	....	....				
Japan	1,212,423	416,182	94,158	Total	12,443,283	10,416,327	....
Mauritius	140,284	138,412	....				

[1] Data for 1912.

STATISTICS OF CROPS OTHER THAN GRAIN CROPS, 1916.

POTATOES.

TABLE 76.—*Potatoes: Area and production of undermentioned countries, 1913-1915.*

Country.	Area. 1913	1914	1915	Production. 1913	1914	1915
NORTH AMERICA.	*Acres.*	*Acres.*	*Acres.*	*Bushels.*	*Bushels.*	*Bushels.*
United States	3,668,000	3,711,000	3,734,000	331,525,000	409,921,000	359,721,000
Canada:						
Prince Edward Island	32,000	32,000	31,000	6,219,000	6,806,000	3,558,000
Nova Scotia	32,000	32,000	34,000	5,369,000	7,165,000	4,759,000
New Brunswick	44,000	44,000	40,000	10,629,000	10,534,000	5,772,000
Quebec	116,000	115,000	117,000	20,504,000	21,811,000	17,510,000
Ontario	152,000	154,000	155,000	18,105,000	25,772,000	14,362,000
Manitoba	26,000	27,000	28,000	5,120,000	3,172,000	3,104,000
Saskatchewan	31,000	31,000	30,000	5,138,000	4,085,000	4,428,000
Alberta	26,000	26,000	27,000	4,350,000	3,652,000	5,155,000
British Columbia	15,000	15,000	16,000	3,110,000	2,675,000	3,956,000
Total Canada	474,000	476,000	478,000	78,544,000	85,672,000	62,604,000
Mexico	(3)	(3)	(3)	[1] 924,000	(3)	(3)
Newfoundland	(3)	(3)	(3)	[2] 1,524,000	(3)	(2)
Total				412,517,000		
SOUTH AMERICA.						
Argentina	278,000	293,000	306,000	38,029,000	(3)	(3)
Chile	78,000	81,000	(3)	8,753,000	9,169,000	9,482,000
Total	371,000	387,000		46,782,000		
EUROPE.						
Austria-Hungary:						
Austria	3,152,000	[4] 1,774,000	(1)	424,457,000	[4] 285,070,000	(3)
Hungary proper	1,513,000	1,513,000	(3)	179,133,000	195,266,000	(3)
Croatia-Slavonia	194,000	(3)	(3)	21,140,000	(3)	(3)
Bosnia-Herzegovina	67,000	(3)	(3)	2,998,000	(3)	(2)
Total Austria-Hungary	4,926,000			627,728,000		
Belgium	395,000	411,000	(3)	117,613,000	(2)	(3)
Bulgaria	[5] 8,000	(3)	(3)	[2] 503,000	(3)	(3)
Denmark	[5] 151,000	[5] 151,000	164,000	42,231,000	37,335,000	42,350,000
Finland	(3)	(3)	(3)	23,424,000	37,344,000	(5)
France	3,825,000	3,676,000	3,225,000	499,194,000	440,652,000	332,788,000
Germany	8,432,000	8,367,000	8,827,000	1,988,591,000	1,675,370,000	1,983,161,000
Italy	722,000	727,000	725,000	65,741,000	61,104,000	56,768,000
Luxemburg	(3)	(3)	(3)	7,637,000	5,288,000	(3)
Malta	[5] 4,000	(3)	(3)	[2] 750,000	(3)	(3)
Netherlands	420,000	424,000	438,000	109,260,000	120,780,000	126,741,000
Norway	102,000	(3)	(2)	27,780,000	27,548,000	18,589,000
Roumania [6]	25,000	26,000	28,000	2,523,000	2,654,000	3,765,000
Do.[7]	60,000	56,000	52,000	1,066,000	1,083,000	865,000
Russia, European:						
Russia proper	8,664,000	8,652,000	8,210,000	873,999,000	891,579,000	713,908,000
Poland	2,662,000	(3)	(3)	383,736,000	(3)	(3)
Northern Caucasia	194,000	204,000	[8] 167,000	16,720,000	17,907,000	[8] 15,897,000
Total Russia, European	11,520,000			1,274,455,000		

[1] Data for 1906.
[2] Production for 1912.
[3] No official statistics.
[4] Galicia and Bukowina not included.
[5] Area for 1912.
[6] Grown alone.
[7] Grown with corn.
[8] Includes one government of Transcaucasia.

POTATOES—Continued.

TABLE 76.—*Potatoes: Area and production of undermentioned countries, 1913–1915—*
Continued.

Country.	Area.			Production.		
	1913	1914	1915	1913	1914	1915
EUROPE—continued.	*Acres.*	*Acres.*	*Acres.*	*Bushels.*	*Bushels.*	*Bushels.*
Serbia..................	[1] 31,000	([2])	([2])	[3] 2,173,000	([2])	([2])
Spain..................	[1] 632,000	688,000	([2])	[3] 93,089,000	76,657,000	([2])
Sweden.................	383,000	376,000	382,000	58,206,000	48,817,000	78,806,000
Switzerland............	137,000	137,000	159,000	31,783,000	22,046,000	38,672,000
United Kingdom:						
England...........	417,000	436,000	437,000	102,834,000	104,804,000	100,881,000
Scotland..........	149,000	152,000	144,000	36,243,000	40,230,000	36,291,000
Wales.............	25,000	25,000	26,000	5,233,000	5,445,000	5,821,000
Ireland...........	582,000	583,000	594,000	139,602,000	128,642,000	138,509,000
Total United Kingdom.......	1,173,000	1,196,000	1,201,000	283,912,000	279,121,000	281,502,000
Total.............	....	....	....	5,257,659,000	....	....
ASIA.						
Japan..................	186,000	204,000	194,000	26,139,000	32,312,000	25,077,000
Russia, Asiatic:						
Central Asia (4 governments of)......	99,000	110,000	[4] 109,000	5,230,000	8,111,000	[4] 9,076,000
Siberia (4 governments of).........	298,000	441,000	296,000	27,773,000	47,075,000	24,308,000
Transcaucasia (1 government of)....	2,000	2,000	([5])	148,000	90,000	([5])
Total Russia, Asiatic.............	399,000	553,000	....	33,151,000	55,276,000	....
Total.............	585,000	757,000	....	59,290,000	87,588,000	....
AFRICA.						
Algeria.................	48,000	([2])	([2])	2,119,000	([2])	([2])
Union of South Africa...	[6] 62,000	([2])	([2])	[6] 3,685,000	([2])	([2])
Total.............	110,000	....	....	5,804,000	....	....
AUSTRALASIA.						
Australia:						
Queensland........	9,000	10,000	8,000	612,000	618,000	598,000
New South Wales...	34,000	39,000	39,000	3,145,000	3,573,000	3,989,000
Victoria..........	48,000	75,000	65,000	7,135,000	6,593,000	7,056,000
South Australia....	9,000	11,000	8,000	1,235,000	1,230,000	673,000
Western Australia..	5,000	5,000	5,000	506,000	665,000	550,000
Tasmania..........	[7] 25,000	31,000	32,000	[7] 2,711,000	3,001,000	2,946,000
Total Australia...	130,000	171,000	157,000	15,344,000	15,680,000	15,812,000
New Zealand...........	23,000	29,000	22,000	5,514,000	5,869,000	4,952,000
Total Australasia..	153,000	200,000	179,000	20,858,000	21,549,000	20,764,000
Grand total......	....	....	....	5,802,910,000	....	....

[1] Area for 1912.
[2] No official statistics.
[3] Production for 1912.
[4] Includes Province of Oural.
[5] Included in Northern Caucasia.
[6] Census of 1911.
[7] Includes Federal territory.

TABLE 77.—*Potatoes: Total production of countries mentioned in Table 76, 1900–1915.*

Year.	Production.	Year.	Production.	Year.	Production.	Year.	Production.
	Bushels.		*Bushels.*		*Bushels.*		*Bushels.*
1900....	4,382,031,000	1904.....	4,298,049,000	1908.....	5,295,043,000	1912.....	5,872,953,000
1901....	4,669,958,000	1905.....	5,254,598,000	1909.....	5,595,567,000	1913.....	5,802,910,000
1902....	4,674,000,000	1906.....	4,789,112,000	1910.....	5,242,278,000	1914......	....
1903....	4,409,793,000	1907.....	5,122,078,000	1911......	4,842,109,000	1915......	....

POTATOES—Continued.

TABLE 78.—*Potatoes: Average yield, per acre, of undermentioned countries in 1900–1915.*

Year.	United States.	Russia (European).[1]	Germany.[1]	Austria.[1]	Hungary proper.[1]	France.[1]	United Kingdom.[1]
	Bushels.	*Bushels.*	*Bushels.*	*Bushels.*	*Bushels.*	*Bushels.*	*Bushels.*
Average (1900–1909)	91. 4	99. 9	200. 0	151. 1	118. 7	133. 8	193. 8
1906	102. 2	94. 9	193. 3	158. 4	128. 7	99. 5	192. 2
1907	95. 4	102. 4	205. 3	173. 2	126. 6	136. 2	171. 0
1908	85. 7	102. 9	209. 2	154. 0	96. 6	163. 7	231. 1
1909	106. 8	111. 5	208. 9	157. 3	125. 2	160. 3	222. 1
1910	93. 8	121. 1	196. 1	160. 0	117. 4	81. 9	209. 1
1911	80. 9	104. 2	153. 9	137. 2	106. 3	121. 8	241. 5
1912	113. 4	121. 5	223. 5	149. 0	129. 2	142. 9	177. 0
1913	90. 4	110. 6	235. 8	134. 7	118. 4	127. 3	242. 0
1914	110. 5	102. 8	200. 1	160. 7	129. 0		233. 3
1915	96. 3						234. 1
Average (1906–1915)	97. 5						215. 3

[1] Bushels of 60 pounds.

TABLE 79.—*Potatoes: Acreage, production, value, exports, etc., in the United States, 1849–1916.*

NOTE.—Figures in *italics* are census returns; figures in roman are estimates of the Department of Agriculture. Estimates of acres are obtained by applying estimated percentages of increase or decrease to the published numbers of the preceding year, except that a revised base is used for applying percentage estimates whenever new census data are available.

Year.	Acreage.	Average yield per acre.	Production.	Average farm price per bushel Dec. 1.	Farm value Dec. 1.	Chicago cash price per bushel, fair to fancy.[1] December. Low.	December. High.	Following May. Low.	Following May. High.	Domestic exports, fiscal year beginning July 1.	Imports during fiscal year beginning July 1.
	Acres.	*Bush.*	*Bushels.*	*Cts.*	*Dollars.*	*Cts.*	*Cts.*	*Cts.*	*Cts.*	*Bushels.*	*Bushels.*
1849			*65,798,000*							155,595	
1859			*111,149,000*							380,372	
1866	1,069,000	100. 2	107,201,000	47. 3	50,723,000					512,380	198,265
1867	1,192,000	82. 0	97,783,000	65. 9	64,462,000					378,605	209,555
1868	1,132,000	93. 8	106,090,000	59. 3	62,919,000					508,249	138,470
1869	1,222,000	109. 5	133,886,000	42. 9	57,481,000					596,968	75,336
1869			*143,337,000*								
1870	1,325,000	86. 6	114,775,000	65. 0	74,621,000					553,070	458,758
1871	1,221,000	98. 7	120,462,000	53. 9	64,905,000					621,537	96,259
1872	1,331,000	85. 3	113,516,000	53. 5	60,692,000					515,306	346,840
1873	1,295,000	81. 9	106,089,000	65. 2	69,154,000					497,413	549,073
1874	1,310,000	80. 9	105,981,000	61. 5	65,223,000					609,642	188,757
1875	1,510,000	110. 5	166,877,000	34. 4	57,358,000					704,379	92,148
1876	1,742,000	71. 7	124,827,000	61. 9	77,320,000					529,650	3,205,555
1877	1,792,000	94. 9	170,092,000	43. 7	74,272,000					744,409	528,584
1878	1,777,000	69. 9	124,127,000	58. 7	72,924,000					625,342	2,624,149
1879	1,837,000	98. 9	181,626,000	43. 6	79,154,000					696,080	721,863
1879			*169,459,000*								
1880	1,843,000	91. 0	167,660,000	48. 3	81,062,000					638,840	2,170,372
1881	2,042,000	53. 5	109,145,000	91. 0	99,291,000					408,286	8,789,860
1882	2,172,000	78. 7	170,973,000	55. 7	95,305,000					439,443	2,362,362
1883	2,289,000	90. 9	208,164,000	42. 2	87,849,000					554,613	425,408
1884	2,221,000	85. 8	190,642,000	39. 6	75,524,000					380,868	658,633
1885	2,266,000	77. 2	175,029,000	44. 7	78,153,000			33	50	494,948	1,937,416
1886	2,287,000	73. 5	168,051,000	46. 7	78,442,000	44	47	65	90	434,864	1,432,490
1887	2,357,000	56. 9	134,103,000	68. 2	91,507,000	70	83	65	85	403,880	8,259,538
1888	2,533,000	79. 9	202,365,000	40. 2	81,414,000	30	37	24	45	471,955	883,380
1889	2,648,000	77. 4	204,881,000	35. 4	72,611,090	33	45	30	60	406,618	3,415,578
1889			*217,546,000*								
1890	2,652,000	55. 9	148,290,000	75. 8	112,342,000	82	93	95	110	341,189	5,401,912
1891	2,715,000	93. 7	254,424,000	35. 8	91,013,000	30	40	30	50	557,022	186,871
1892	2,548,000	61. 5	156,655,000	66. 1	103,568,000	60	72	70	98	845,720	4,317,021
1893	2,605,000	70. 3	183,034,000	59. 4	108,662,000	51	60	64	88	803,111	3,002,578
1894	2,738,000	62. 4	170,787,000	53. 6	91,527,000	43	58	40	70	572,957	1,341,533
1895	2,955,000	100. 6	297,237,000	26. 6	78,985,000	18	24	10	23	680,049	175,240

[1] Burbank to 1910.

POTATOES—Continued.

TABLE 79.—*Potatoes: Acreage, production, value, exports, etc., in the United States, 1849–1916—Continued.*

Year.	Acreage.	Average yield per acre.	Production.	Average farm price per bushel Dec. 1.	Farm value Dec. 1.	Chicago cash price per bushel, fair to fancy.[1]				Domestic exports, fiscal year beginning July 1.	Imports during fiscal year beginning July 1.
						December.		Following May.			
						Low.	High.	Low.	High.		
	Acres.	*Bush.*	*Bushels.*	*Cts.*	*Dollars.*	*Cts.*	*Cts.*	*Cts.*	*Cts.*	*Bushels.*	*Bushels.*
1896...	2,767,000	91.1	252,235,000	28.6	72,182,000	18	26	19	26	926,646	246,178
1897...	2,535,000	64.7	164,016,000	54.7	89,643,000	50	62	60	87	605,187	1,171,378
1898...	2,558,000	75.2	192,306,000	41.4	79,575,000	30	36	33	52	579,833	530,420
1899...	2,581,000	88.6	228,783,000	39.0	89,329,000	35	46	27	39	809,472	155,861
1899...	*2,939,000*	*93.0*	*273,318,000*								
1900...	2,611,000	80.8	210,927,000	43.1	90,811,000	40	48	35	60	741,483	371,911
1901...	2,864,000	65.5	187,598,000	76.7	143,979,000	75	82	58	100	528,484	7,656,162
1902...	2,966,000	96.0	284,633,000	47.1	134,111,000	42	48	42	60	843,075	358,505
1903...	2,917,000	84.7	247,128,000	61.4	151,638,000	60	66	95	116	484,042	3,166,581
1904...	3,016,000	110.4	332,830,000	45.3	150,673,000	32	38	20	25	1,163,270	181,199
1905...	2,997,000	87.0	260,741,000	61.7	160,821,000	55	66	48	73	1,000,326	1,948,160
1906...	3,013,000	102.2	308,038,000	51.1	157,547,000	40	43	55	75	1,530,461	176,917
1907...	3,128,000	95.4	298,262,000	61.8	184,184,000	46	58	50	80	1,203,894	403,952
1908...	3,257,000	85.7	278,985,000	70.6	197,039,000	60	77	70	150	763,651	8,383,966
1909...	3,525,000	106.8	376,537,000								
1909...	*3,669,000*	*106.1*	*389,195,000*	54.1	210,662,000	20	58	16	34	999,476	353,208
1910[2]..	3,720,000	93.8	349,032,000	55.7	194,566,000	30	48	35	75	2,383,887	218,984
1911...	3,619,000	80.9	292,737,000	79.9	233,778,000	70	100	90	200	1,237,276	13,734,695
1912...	3,711,000	113.4	420,647,000	50.5	212,550,000	40	65	33	70	2,028,261	337,230
1913...	3,668,000	90.4	331,525,000	68.7	227,903,000	50	70	60	90	1,794,073	3,645,993
1914...	3,711,000	110.5	409,921,000	48.7	199,460,000	30	66	34	150	3,135,474	270,942
1915...	3,734,000	96.3	359,721,000	61.7	221,992,000	53	95	80	110	4,017,760	209,542
1916...	3,550,000	80.4	285,437,000	146.1	417,063,000	125	190				

[1] Burbank to 1910.   [2] Figures adjusted to census basis.

TABLE 80.—*Potatoes: Acreage, production, and total farm value, by States, 1916.*

[000 omitted.]

State.	Acreage.	Production.	Farm value Dec. 1.	State.	Acreage.	Production.	Farm value Dec. 1.
	Acres.	*Bushels.*	*Dollars.*		*Acres.*	*Bushels.*	*Dollars.*
Maine..............	125	25,500	36,210	North Dakota......	75	6,975	8,021
New Hampshire...	15	1,800	2,988	South Dakota......	65	4,290	5,877
Vermont..........	23	2,576	3,581	Nebraska..........	105	7,665	11,498
Massachusetts.....	25	2,275	3,981	Kansas............	70	4,970	8,200
Rhode Island......	5	370	684	Kentucky..........	49	4,116	5,845
Connecticut........	22	2,090	3,658	Tennessee.........	36	2,952	4,398
New York.........	320	22,400	35,392	Alabama..........	20	1,800	3,042
New Jersey........	85	10,370	16,074	Mississippi........	12	780	1,248
Pennsylvania......	272	19,040	28,179	Louisiana.........	25	1,625	2,714
Delaware..........	10	900	1,125	Texas............	40	2,000	3,800
Maryland.........	43	4,085	5,433	Oklahoma........	34	1,802	3,514
Virginia...........	125	16,250	22,262	Arkansas.........	25	1,625	3,088
West Virginia.....	48	4,224	6,674	Montana..........	39	4,875	5,850
North Carolina....	34	3,230	4,522	Wyoming.........	18	2,340	2,995
South Carolina.....	10	750	1,312	Colorado..........	50	6,900	9,315
Georgia...........	15	900	1,575	New Mexico.......	8	816	1,428
Florida...........	15	1,110	2,220	Arizona..........	1	115	207
Ohio..............	140	6,300	11,466	Utah.............	20	3,600	4,680
Indiana...........	74	3,256	5,763	Nevada...........	14	2,660	3,458
Illinois............	125	7,250	12,978	Idaho............	27	4,050	5,144
Michigan..........	320	15,360	24,576	Washington........	60	9,900	9,702
Wisconsin.........	290	13,630	20,036	Oregon...........	55	8,250	7,425
Minnesota........	280	16,800	21,840	California..........	75	10,575	14,805
Iowa.............	115	4,830	8,452				
Missouri..........	91	5,460	9,828	United States..	3,550	285,437	417,063

POTATOES—Continued.

TABLE 81.—*Potatoes: Condition of crop, United States, on first of months named, 1895–1916.*

Year.	July.	Aug.	Sept.	Oct.	Year.	July.	Aug.	Sept.	Oct.
	P. ct.	*P. ct.*	*P. ct.*	*P. ct.*		*P. ct.*	*P. ct.*	*P. ct.*	*P. ct.*
1895	91.5	89.7	90.8	87.4	1906	91.5	89.0	85.3	82.2
1896	99.0	94.8	83.2	81.7	1907	90.2	88.5	80.2	77.0
1897	87.8	77.9	66.7	61.6	1908	89.6	82.9	73.7	68.7
1898	95.5	83.9	77.7	72.5	1909	93.0	85.8	80.9	78.8
1899	93.8	93.0	86.3	81.7	1910	86.3	75.8	70.5	71.8
1900	91.3	88.2	80.0	74.4	1911	76.0	62.3	59.8	62.3
1901	87.4	62.3	52.2	54.0	1912	88.9	87.8	87.2	85.1
1902	92.9	94.8	89.1	82.5	1913	86.2	78.0	69.9	67.7
1903	88.1	87.2	84.3	74.6	1914	83.6	79.0	75.8	78.3
1904	93.9	94.1	91.6	89.5	1915	91.2	92.0	82.7	74.2
1905	91.2	87.2	80.9	74.3	1916	87.8	80.8	67.4	62.6

TABLE 82.—*Potatoes: Yield per acre, price per bushel Dec. 1, and value per acre, by States.*

State.	Yield per acre (bushels). 10-year average, 1907–1916.	1907	1908	1909	1910	1911	1912	1913	1914	1915	1916	Farm price per bushel (cents). 10-year average, 1907–1916.	1912	1913	1914	1915	1916	Value per acre (dollars).[1] 5-year average, 1911–1915.	1916
Me	206	145	225	225	220	180	198	220	260	179	204	64	55	53	33	70	142	115.04	289.68
N. H	126	120	100	130	150	125	140	122	159	95	120	81	61	83	60	95	166	96.21	199.20
Vt	124	120	73	155	130	105	140	127	168	108	112	68	55	72	47	81	139	83.57	155.68
Mass	116	120	95	125	125	93	130	105	155	120	91	91	75	85	71	94	175	99.78	159.25
R. I	122	110	150	125	136	110	113	130	165	110	74	95	77	90	70	92	185	107.46	136.90
Conn	104	100	80	120	125	85	107	92	140	95	95	93	78	87	65	96	175	86.99	166.25
N. Y	94	98	82	120	102	74	106	74	145	62	70	74	58	80	44	82	158	60.38	110.60
N. J	102	120	72	90	105	73	108	95	108	130	122	85	66	82	61	75	155	77.84	189.10
Pa	83	88	72	78	88	56	109	88	105	72	70	78	57	80	58	75	148	59.90	103.60
Del	89	99	82	96	103	60	100	87	80	95	90	79	70	75	70	75	125	64.02	112.50
Md	86	95	77	80	95	45	112	87	78	97	95	72	58	67	60	62	133	54.23	126.35
Va	90	80	88	92	98	45	87	94	65	125	130	78	65	80	77	61	137	60.25	178.10
W. Va	86	83	84	98	92	45	112	83	54	117	88	86	62	90	81	65	158	62.15	139.04
N. C	78	88	79	74	89	48	85	80	52	90	95	88	76	82	92	73	140	59.12	133.00
S. C	79	70	81	85	90	70	90	80	70	80	75	122	112	130	125	115	175	93.94	131.25
Ga	74	83	78	81	82	72	78	81	60	65	60	110	87	105	105	99	175	71.89	105.00
Fla	84	80	83	95	90	90	93	76	80	80	74	125	110	117	113	115	200	100.82	148.00
Ohio	79	76	77	93	82	65	112	64	95	82	45	78	53	85	53	70	182	55.22	81.90
Ind	77	87	57	95	84	58	114	53	80	95	44	76	50	84	56	56	177	50.00	77.88
Ill	75	87	71	91	75	50	101	46	60	110	58	81	60	89	61	59	179	49.61	103.82
Mich	90	90	72	105	105	94	105	96	121	59	48	58	41	53	30	56	160	45.99	76.80
Wis	97	91	80	102	95	116	120	109	124	87	47	55	34	54	30	45	147	49.59	69.09
Minn	99	101	76	115	61	115	135	110	114	106	60	54	28	52	32	39	130	47.90	78.00
Iowa	79	85	80	89	72	74	109	48	86	105	42	72	46	82	59	54	175	50.19	73.50
Mo	68	82	80	85	86	27	84	38	45	98	60	86	69	93	73	60	180	42.50	108.00
N. Dak	95	89	85	110	41	120	128	85	109	90	93	59	28	56	42	41	115	46.42	106.95
S. Dak	82	84	90	80	44	72	105	78	90	115	66	64	36	63	47	35	137	43.98	90.42
Nebr	73	73	78	78	60	52	80	48	80	105	73	74	51	78	54	42	150	42.68	109.50
Kans	64	65	80	79	57	22	82	40	62	83	71	93	73	91	77	74	165	45.75	117.15
Ky	77	80	62	92	92	39	101	49	45	126	84	84	67	102	84	55	142	53.30	119.28
Tenn	73	85	80	75	80	41	88	64	43	88	82	86	70	97	91	63	149	52.51	122.18
Ala	83	95	85	80	80	78	81	84	79	80	90	106	90	105	101	90	169	80.99	152.10
Miss	84	90	91	87	85	83	89	80	80	90	65	102	90	100	95	84	160	81.43	104.00
La	68	67	82	75	55	69	73	70	70	51	65	100	83	96	97	95	167	62.63	108.55
Tex	59	73	71	50	51	57	63	52	61	65	50	116	105	112	104	105	190	65.58	95.00
Okla	62	70	78	70	60	18	60	60	70	85	53	108	93	105	90	84	195	55.10	103.35
Ark	72	70	82	70	84	55	70	72	60	90	65	102	92	100	97	76	190	65.25	123.50
Mont	146	150	138	180	120	150	165	140	140	155	125	67	40	67	64	50	120	87.58	150.00
Wyo	133	200	158	160	100	42	140	140	108	150	130	81	60	65	70	60	128	79.88	166.40
Colo	127	150	125	160	100	35	95	115	120	135	138	68	41	65	50	55	135	56.52	186.30
N. Mex	88	100	100	85	47	80	100	68	100	100	102	106	65	140	95	95	175	86.04	178.50
Ariz	105	140	110	90	92	95	125	75	110	95	115	133	125	135	120	100	180	123.50	207.00
Utah	153	100	160	180	142	140	185	180	140	125	180	67	49	58	60	63	130	95.36	234.00
Nev	164	200	120	180	150	160	178	160	130	172	190	82	60	68	70	70	130	115.16	247.00
Idaho	158	145	130	200	142	180	185	170	155	125	150	60	29	50	48	56	127	80.01	190.50
Wash	145	150	120	170	131	160	167	123	128	135	165	61	36	60	55	53	98	76.93	161.70
Oreg	127	125	99	160	105	130	155	135	97	115	150	62	31	58	60	60	90	68.13	135.00
Cal	130	145	107	130	130	135	130	119	138	130	141	84	65	70	70	75	140	96.68	197.40
U. S	95.4	95.4	85.7	106.8	93.8	80.9	113.4	90.4	110.5	96.3	80.4	69.9	50.5	68.7	48.7	61.7	146.1	59.44	117.48

[1] Based upon farm price Dec. 1.

POTATOES—Continued.

TABLE 83.—*Potatoes: Farm price per bushel on first of each month, by geographical divisions, 1915 and 1916.*

Month.	United States.		North Atlantic States.		South Atlantic States.		N. Central States east of Miss. R.		N. Central States west of Miss. R.		South Central States.		Far Western States.	
	1916	1915	1916	1915	1916	1915	1916	1915	1916	1915	1916	1915	1916	1915
	Cts.	Cts.	Cts.	Cts.	Cts.	Cts.	Cts.	Cts.	Cts.	Cts.	Cts.	Cts.	Cts.	Cts.
January	70.6	49.7	85.1	48.4	77.4	81.1	67.5	37.2	57.9	49.5	81.7	97.3	63.0	56.7
February	88.0	50.4	106.4	45.6	88.4	79.3	87.4	37.4	73.4	52.3	100.5	98.4	76.1	66.0
March	94.4	50.4	109.2	44.7	94.1	81.4	88.7	36.1	82.4	54.4	119.6	104.3	87.8	65.7
April	97.6	47.8	113.6	38.4	100.2	80.5	90.5	35.9	85.1	51.7	121.9	104.4	90.4	66.9
May	94.8	50.5	109.8	40.2	102.6	80.3	87.7	36.5	81.1	54.5	112.3	102.3	91.1	79.0
June	98.8	50.8	114.8	38.8	108.0	78.1	91.9	35.3	84.3	54.0	107.9	103.5	97.1	89.2
July	102.3	52.1	121.2	39.3	101.3	68.2	96.6	36.6	90.2	58.8	109.9	89.4	96.6	95.8
August	95.4	56.3	101.5	44.1	85.3	56.2	96.0	50.4	83.0	64.0	88.3	74.5	116.9	87.3
September	109.3	50.5	106.8	49.3	91.9	57.8	128.1	42.8	105.0	45.7	105.6	77.8	104.0	67.7
October	112.0	48.8	110.7	54.7	93.8	62.0	132.3	38.7	112.0	39.9	126.4	79.5	85.8	54.9
November	135.7	60.8	146.5	78.9	127.4	66.7	149.0	50.7	133.9	40.1	148.5	84.0	102.0	54.8
December	146.1	61.7	151.3	77.1	143.5	67.3	163.4	55.2	144.6	46.1	165.6	75.4	120.2	60.9

TABLE 84.—*Potatoes: Wholesale price, 1912–1916.*

Date.	New York. State and western, per 180 pounds.		Chicago. Fair to fancy, per bushel.		Minneapolis. Per bushel.		St. Louis. Burbank, per bushel.		Cincinnati. Per bushel.		Denver. Per 100 pounds.		San Francisco. Burbank, Rivers, per 100 pounds.	
	Low.	High.	Low.	High.	Low.	High.	Low.	High.	Low.	High.	Low.	High.	Low.	High.
1912.														
Jan.-June			$0.50	$2.00			$0.90	$1.52	$0.88	$1.50				
July-Dec.			.32	1.15			.35	1.20	.50	1.15				
1913.														
Jan.-June	$1.70	$2.87	.15	.70	$0.33	$0.60	.30	.87	.30	1.00	$0.50	$4.00	$0.20	1.65
July-Dec.	1.75	2.37	.50	.82	.50	1.00	.45	.93	.65	1.00	.60	2.50	.50	1.25
1914.														
Jan.-June	2.00	3.00	.56	1.75	.55	1.35	.65	1.60	.65	1.15	1.00	2.50	.80	1.65
July-Dec.	1.25	2.12	.28	1.65	.28	1.50	.33	1.50	.45	1.70	.90	2.75	.60	1.30
1915.														
January	1.25	1.65	.30	.50	.33	.48	.42	.54	.45	.50	.90	1.25	1.10	1.25
February	1.00	1.50	.35	.50	.33	.65	.38	.54	.45	.50	.90	1.25	1.20	1.35
March	1.25	1.50	.30	.50	.30	.50	.40	.53	.45	.50	1.00	1.75	1.20	1.30
April	1.25	1.75	.30	.47	.37	.45	.48	.55	.45	.50	1.25	1.75	1.30	1.30
May	1.25	1.45	.34	1.50	.32	.55	.44	.48	.42	.50	1.50	1.75	2.25	3.50
June			.18	1.50	.32	.55	.52	.52	.30	.45	1.50	2.25	1.00	1.75
Jan.-June	1.00	1.75	.18	1.50	.30	.65	.38	.55	.30	.50	.90	2.25	1.00	3.50
July			.17	.85	.40	1.00	.22	.55	.30	.35	1.50	2.25	.90	1.00
August			.45	.63	.27	.50	.27	.56	.35	.45	1.00	2.00	.95	1.15
September		2.00	.32	.60	.25	.36	.32	.55	.35	.50	.85	1.35	.85	1.00
October	1.75	2.50	.37	.70	.35	.65	.40	.60	.50	.75	.85	1.25	.90	1.15
November	2.00	2.50	.38	.68	.40	.60	.43	.70	.55	.70	.90	1.40	1.00	1.25
December	2.40	3.00	.53	.95	.40	.90	.65	.96	.65	.90	1.10	1.60	1.25	1.50
July-Dec.	1.75	3.00	.17	.95	.25	1.00	.22	.96	.30	.90	.85	2.25	.85	1.50
1916.														
January	2.85	3.85	.80	1.30	.75	1.35	.94	1.13	.65	1.18	1.40	2.15	.90	1.60
February	3.00	3.60	.80	1.30	.87	1.25	.88	1.03	1.05	1.10	1.50	2.15	1.00	1.60
March	3.30	3.75	.80	1.05	.77	1.20	.73	1.09	1.00	1.12	1.50	2.00	1.00	1.75
April	3.00	3.85	.60	1.00	.62	1.10	.78	1.06	.85	1.12	1.50	2.00	1.25	1.75
May	3.00	3.90	.80	1.10	.75	1.25	.92	1.28	.85	1.30	1.65	5.00	1.00	1.60
June	3.00	3.90	.85	1.30	.85	1.20	1.03	1.35	1.15	1.30	1.65	3.25	1.35	2.25
Jan.-June	2.85	3.90	.60	1.30	.62	1.35	.73	1.35	.65	1.30	1.40	5.00	.90	2.25
July			.65	1.05	.75	1.10	[1]1.50	.83	.80	1.25	1.65	3.25	1.30	1.90
August			.65	1.90	.90	1.05	[1]1.55	2.00	.80	1.15	1.65	3.00	1.15	2.25
September			.95	2.00	1.05	1.50	[1]1.90	2.10	.90	1.30	1.75	2.50	1.00	2.00
October	3.40	5.00	1.00	1.90	1.00	1.50	[1]1.10	1.73	1.25	1.70	1.75	3.00	1.25	2.50
November	4.50	5.25	1.35	1.85	1.50	1.75	1.53	1.80	1.50	1.75	2.50	3.00	1.85	2.40
December	4.25	5.25	1.25	1.90	1.40	1.70	1.38	1.85	1.65	1.90	2.25	3.00	1.96	2.27
July-Dec.	3.40	5.25	.65	2.00	.75	1.75	.50	2.10	.80	1.90	1.65	3.25	1.00	2.50

[1] Bulk home grown Early Ohio.

POTATOES—Continued.

TABLE 85.—*Potatoes: International trade, calendar years 1913–1915.*

[See "General note," Table 10.]

EXPORTS.

[000 omitted.]

Country.	1913	1914 (prelim.).	1915 (prelim.).	Country.	1913	1914 (prelim.).	1915 (prelim.).
	Bushels.	*Bushels.*	*Bushels.*		*Bushels.*	*Bushels.*	*Bushels.*
Argentina	794	544	224	Netherlands	15,279	15,234	
Austria-Hungary	1,179			Portugal	556	672	
Belgium	9,067			Russia	3,007	1,007	311
Canada	2,012	1,116	885	Spain	2,502	1,743	2,102
China	346	272	375	United Kingdom	911	1,893	1,231
Denmark	510	769		United States	1,817	2,715	3,900
France	6,654	3,976	3,865	Other countries	1,745	995	
Germany	12,216						
Italy	5,177	630	39	Total	64,175	31,962	
Japan	403	396	383				

IMPORTS.

Algeria	1,181	1.079	979	Norway	176	174	64
Argentina	314	421	1,533	Philippine Islands	330	311	317
Austria-Hungary	4,506			Portugal	686	1,291	
Belgium	4,683			Russia	395	493	3
Brazil	1,095	697	322	Sweden	735	452	
Canada	400	664	348	Switzerland	3,443	4,873	1,117
Cuba	2,225	2,298	2,751	United Kingdom	17,444	6,184	4,011
Egypt	549	540	400	United States	3,171	800	236
Finland	385	409	412	Other countries	2,508	1,298	
France	8,490	8,745	1,330				
Germany	14,038			Total	68,795	32,041	
Netherlands	2,041	1,312					

SWEET POTATOES.

TABLE 86.—*Sweet potatoes: Acreage, production, and value, in the United States, 1849–1916.*

NOTE.—Figures in *italics* are census returns; figures in roman are estimates of the Department of Agriculture. Estimates of acres are obtained by applying estimated percentages of increase or decrease to the published numbers of the preceding year, except that a revised base is used for applying percentage estimates whenever new census data are available.

Year.	Acreage.	Average yield per acre.	Production.	Average farm price per bushel Dec. 1.	Farm value Dec. 1.
	Acres.	*Bushels.*	*Bushels.*	*Cents.*	*Dollars.*
1849			*38,268,000*		
1859			*42,095,000*		
1869			*21,710,000*		
1879			*33,379,000*		
1889			*43,950,000*		
1899	*537,000*	*79.1*	*42,517,000*	*46.7*	*19,870,000*
1900	544,000	88.9	48,346,000	50.6	24,478,000
1901	547,000	81.7	44,697,000	57.5	25,720,000
1902	532,000	85.2	45,344,000	58.1	26,358,000
1903	548,000	89.2	48,870,000	58.3	28,478,000
1904	548,000	88.9	48,705,000	60.4	29,424,000
1905	551,000	92.6	51,034,000	58.3	29,734,000
1906	554,000	90.2	49,948,000	62.2	31,003,000
1907	565,000	88.2	49,813,000	70.0	34,858,000
1908	599,000	92.4	55,352,000	66.1	36,564,000
1909	*641,000*	*92.4*	*59,232,000*	*69.4*	*41,052,000*
1910	641,000	93.5	59,938,000	67.1	40,216,000
1911	605,000	90.1	54,538,000	75.5	41,202,000
1912	583,000	95.2	55,479,000	72.6	40,264,000
1913	625,000	94.5	59,057,000	72.6	42,884,000
1914	603,000	93.8	56,574,000	73.0	41,294,000
1915	731,000	103.5	75,639,000	62.1	46,980,000
1916	774,000	91.7	70,955,000	84.8	60,141,000

SWEET POTATOES—Continued.

TABLE 87.—*Sweet potatoes: Acreage, production, and total farm value, by States, 1916.*

[000 omitted.]

State.	Acreage.	Production.	Farm value Dec. 1.	State.	Acreage.	Production.	Farm value Dec. 1.
	Acres.	*Bushels.*	*Dollars.*		*Acres.*	*Bushels.*	*Dollars.*
New Jersey	23	2,300	2,760	Missouri	7	490	735
Pennsylvania	1	100	135	Kansas	4	368	552
Delaware	5	625	506	Kentucky	10	900	900
Maryland	9	1,134	998	Tennessee	27	2,700	2,349
Virginia	39	5,070	4,563	Alabama	85	6,290	4,655
West Virginia	2	280	353	Mississippi	77	6,314	4,230
North Carolina	87	9,309	6,982	Louisiana	64	5,760	3,802
South Carolina	66	5,676	4,825	Texas	80	7,120	6,408
Georgia	94	7,520	6,091	Oklahoma	13	962	1,299
Florida	25	2,500	2,150	Arkansas	35	3,185	2,866
Ohio	1	99	148	California	6	960	960
Indiana	3	300	450				
Illinois	8	720	900	United States	774	70,955	60,141
Iowa	3	273	524				

TABLE 88.—*Sweet potatoes: Condition of crop, United States, on first of months named, 1896–1916.*

Year.	July.	Aug.	Sept.	Oct.	Year.	July.	Aug.	Sept.	Oct.	Year.	July.	Aug.	Sept.	Oct.
	P. ct.	*P. ct.*	*P. ct.*	*P. ct.*		*P. ct.*	*P. ct.*	*P. ct.*	*P. ct.*		*P. ct.*	*P. ct.*	*P. ct.*	*P. ct.*
1896	89.3	87.1	71.7	71.1	1903	90.2	88.7	91.1	83.7	1910	87.3	85.7	83.9	80.2
1897	86.5	86.4	85.4		1904	87.3	88.5	89.9	86.1	1911	78.4	77.7	79.1	78.1
1898		92.0	90.6	89.9	1905	90.6	90.1	89.5	88.6	1912	86.9	85.0	84.1	82.0
1899	85.1	84.1	80.7	74.9	1906	90.9	91.2	88.7	86.0	1913	86.5	85.8	81.4	80.1
1900	93.7	92.2	83.6	80.0	1907	85.9	85.7	85.7	82.7	1914	77.1	75.5	81.8	80.7
1901	93.1	80.7	78.7	79.0	1908	89.8	88.8	88.7	85.5	1915	88.7	85.5	87.5	85.0
1902	83.6	78.3	77.2	79.7	1909	89.7	86.9	81.3	77.8	1916	90.4	85.9	82.7	79.2

TABLE 89.—*Sweet potatoes: Yield per acre, price per bushel Dec. 1, and value per acre, by States.*

State.	Yield per acre (bushels).											Farm price per bushel (cents).						Value per acre (dollars).[1]	
	10-year average, 1907–1916	1907	1908	1909	1910	1911	1912	1913	1914	1915	1916	10-year average, 1907–1916	1912	1913	1914	1915	1916	5-year average, 1911–1915	1916
N. J	124	105	133	123	140	130	120	138	100	155	100	86	84	78	95	70	120	108.39	120.00
Pa	106	100	102	88	105	121	120	110	105	100	100	91	75	90	86	75	135	97.02	135.00
Del	123	93	125	125	115	140	120	135	120	135	125	68	68	60	70	62	81	85.66	101.25
Md	120	100	110	115	110	115	125	141	125	130	126	70	63	60	70	70	88	85.62	110.88
Va	100	86	95	100	100	90	90	108	92	110	130	72	75	70	76	65	90	70.22	117.00
W. Va	102	86	72	100	101	110	115	91	92	110	140	97	90	100	98	92	126	99.17	176.40
N. C	96	90	93	99	105	86	90	100	90	105	107	61	62	61	65	56	75	57.66	80.25
S. C	91	83	88	95	91	84	105	92	85	105	86	69	68	75	70	65	85	65.73	73.10
Ga	86	95	86	93	83	81	90	87	85	85	80	67	66	68	69	61	81	57.64	64.80
Fla	110	105	115	105	108	108	112	110	120	112	100	75	73	75	80	68	86	85.21	86.00
Ohio	100	85	83	110	98	113	118	90	110	95	99	100	87	106	96	98	150	101.95	148.50
Ind	98	90	71	101	104	114	116	78	100	104	100	98	89	103	90	90	150	95.32	150.00
Ill	93	90	80	110	110	89	98	70	84	110	90	98	95	106	95	82	125	87.04	112.50
Iowa	94	75	93	110	98	105	90	80	100	95	91	122	108	150	127	108	192	112.46	174.72
Mo	85	82	91	90	102	91	88	56	84	100	70	99	95	105	96	82	150	80.12	105.00
Kans	93	95	105	96	101	75	99	50	110	110	92	111	103	110	106	100	150	96.21	138.00
Ky	90	85	84	88	85	96	90	75	105	105	90	82	85	94	77	70	100	77.17	90.00
Tenn	90	82	89	87	85	85	90	80	100	105	100	71	72	80	69	59	87	64.70	87.00
Ala	88	80	85	80	85	97	100	95	93	90	74	66	71	67	65	57	74	62.47	54.76
Miss	92	92	92	82	94	85	97	98	90	110	82	63	62	63	55	67		58.16	54.94
La	88	86	86	90	93	90	84	85	87	92	90	63	65	70	64	50	66	53.96	59.40
Tex	78	75	88	50	56	71	75	80	101	98	89	92	104	95	87	70	90	76.86	80.10
Okla	84	85	88	70	70	75	92	64	102	115	74	104	109	104	89	73	135	87.06	99.90
Ark	92	75	100	58	98	92	88	90	95	130	91	80	90	80	77	61	90	75.82	81.90
Cal	148	130	105	160	160	140	156	170	161	135	160	93	94	100	87	80	100	143.74	160.00
U. S	93.3	88.2	92.4	90.1	93.5	90.1	95.2	94.5	93.8	103.5	91.7	71.5	72.6	72.6	73.0	62.1	84.8	67.70	77.70

[1] Based upon farm price Dec. 1.

SWEET POTATOES—Continued.

TABLE 90.—*Sweet potatoes: Wholesale price per barrel, 1912–1916.*

Date.	Baltimore.		St. Louis.		New Orleans.[1]		New York.			
							Jersey.		Southern.	
	Low.	High.	Low.	High.	Low.	High.	Low.	High.	Low.	High.
1912.										
Jan.-June............	$2.00	$4.50	$1.50	$3.50	$1.75	$2.00	$2.50	$3.50	$2.00	$3.00
July-Dec.............	1.00	6.00	.75	5.00	2.00	2.00	1.50	3.50	.50	6.00
1913.										
Jan.-June............	2.00	3.50	1.63	3.75	2.00	2.00	2.00	3.00	1.75	2.50
July-Dec.............	.75	7.00	.88	6.25	2.00	2.00	1.25	3.50	.40	5.50
1914.										
Jan.-June............	1.00	2.50	1.50	2.50	1.00	3.20	1.50	2.00	.75	1.50
July-Dec.............	1.00	5.50	1.75	4.50	.80	3.50	2.00	3.50	.75	5.00
1915.										
January.............	1.50	3.25	2.50	3.25	1.00	1.20	2.50	3.00	....	....
February...........	1.50	3.50	2.50	3.00	1.00	1.60	....	....	....	....
March..............	1.50	4.00	2.50	4.50	1.00	2.00	....	....	2.00	3.50
April...............	1.50	5.50	....	....	1.50	2.00	....	....	2.50	3.50
May................	4.00	5.00	....	....	1.80	2.50	....	....	....	....
June................	....	....	....	....	2.50	3.00	....	....	....	....
Jan.-June.......	1.50	5.50	2.50	4.50	1.00	3.00	2.50	3.00	2.00	3.50
July................	3.50	6.50	....	....	2.50	3.00	....	....	....	....
August.............	2.25	4.00	....	....	2.00	3.00	....	....	2.00	5.00
September..........	1.25	2.50	1.50	3.40	1.00	1.80	....	....	1.00	3.50
October.............	1.00	2.00	1.90	2.40	.70	2.10	1.25	2.25	1.00	2.37
November...........	1.25	2.00	1.90	2.25	.70	1.20	.50	2.25	1.00	2.00
December...........	.75	2.25	2.00	2.75	1.00	1.60	1.75	2.50	.50	2.25
July-Dec.......	.75	6.50	1.50	3.40	.70	3.00	.50	2.50	.50	5.00
1916.										
January.............	1.00	2.25	1.75	2.65	1.00	1.70	1.75	2.50	1.00	2.00
February...........	1.50	2.25	1.85	2.25	.50	1.70	1.75	2.50	....	....
March..............	1.50	2.50	1.50	2.10	.80	1.50	....	....	....	....
April...............	1.50	2.75	1.50	1.75	.80	1.30	....	....	1.50	2.00
May................	1.75	3.00	1.50	1.50	.70	1.30	....	....	1.50	2.00
June................	1.50	2.25	2.25	2.25	.50	1.20	....	....	....	....
Jan.-June.......	1.00	3.00	1.50	2.65	.50	1.70	1.75	2.50	1.00	2.00
July................	4.00	5.50	....	....	.80	1.20	....	....	3.50	5.50
August.............	1.75	4.25	2.50	3.25	1.00	2.00	....	....	1.00	5.00
September..........	1.25	2.35	2.35	2.80	1.00	2.50	....	....	1.25	3.50
October.............	1.50	2.25	2.25	2.90	1.00	1.50	2.00	3.50	1.25	3.00
November...........	1.75	3.00	2.85	2.85	1.00	1.50	2.50	3.25	1.75	3.50
December...........	2.50	4.00	2.00	3.00	1.00	1.70	....	....	2.00	4.25
July-Dec.......	1.25	5.50	2.00	3.25	.80	2.50	2.00	3.25	1.00	5.50

[1] Prices as quoted were per half-barrel sack of 80 pounds; barrel prices obtained by doubling same.

HAY.

TABLE 91.—*Hay: Acreage, production, value, exports, etc., in the United States,1849–1916.*

NOTE.—Figures in *italics* are census returns; figures in roman are estimates of the Department of Agriculture. Estimates of acres are obtained by applying estimated percentages of increase or decrease to the published numbers of the preceding year, except that a revised base is used for applying percentage estimates whenever new census data are available.

Year.	Acreage.	Average yield per acre.	Production.	Average farm price per ton Dec. 1.	Farm value Dec. 1.	Chicago prices No.1 timothy per ton, by carload lots.				Domestic exports, fiscal year beginning July 1.
---	---	---	---	---	---	December.		Following May.		
						Low.	High.	Low.	High.	
	Acres.	*Tons.[1]*	*Tons.[1]*	*Dolls.*	*Dollars.*	*Dolls.*	*Dolls.*	*Dolls.*	*Dolls.*	*Tons.[2]*
1849			*13,839,000*							
1859			*19,084,000*							
1866	17,669,000	1.23	21,779,000	10.14	220,836,000					5,028
1867	20,021,000	1.31	26,277,000	10.21	268,301,000					5,645
1868	21,542,000	1.21	26,142,000	10.08	263,589,000					
1869	18,591,000	1.42	26,420,000	10.18	268 933,000					
1869			*27,316,000*							6,723
1870	19,862,000	1.23	24,525,000	12.47	305,743,000					4,581
1871	19,009,000	1.17	22,239,000	14.30	317,940,000					5,266
1872	20,319,000	1.17	23,813,000	12.94	308,025,000					4,557
1873	21,894,000	1.15	25,085,000	12.53	314,241,000					4,889
1874	21,770,000	1.15	25,134,000	11.94	300,222,000					7,183
1875	23,508,000	1.19	27,874,000	10.78	300,378,000					7,528
1876	25,283,000	1.22	30,867,000	8.97	276,991,000			9.00	10.00	7,287
1877	25,368,000	1.25	31,629,000	8.37	264,880,000	9.50	10.50	9.75	10.75	9,514
1878	26,931,000	1.47	39,608,000	7.20	285,016,000	8.00	8.50	9.00	11.50	8,127
1879	27,485,000	1.29	35,493,000	9.32	330,804,000	14.00	14.50	14.00	15.00	13,739
1879	*30,631,000*	*1.15*	*35,151,000*							
1880	25,864,000	1.23	31,925,000	11.65	371,811,000	15.00	15.50	17.00	19.00	12,662
1881	30,889,000	1.14	35,135,000	11.82	415,131,000	16.00	16.50	15.00	16.50	10,570
1882	32,340,000	1.18	38,138,000	9.73	371,170,000	11.50	12.25	12.00	13.00	13,309
1883	35,516,000	1.32	46,864,000	8.19	383,834,000	9.00	10.00	12.50	17.00	16,908
1884	38,572,000	1.26	48,470,000	8.17	396,139,000	10.00	11.50	15.50	17.50	11,142
1885	39,850,000	1.12	44,732,000	8.71	389,753,000	11.00	12.00	10.00	12.00	13,390
1886	36,502,000	1.15	41,796,000	8.46	353,438,000	9.50	10.50	11.00	12.50	13,873
1887	37,665,000	1.10	41,454,000	9.97	413,440,000	13.50	14.50	17.00	21.00	18,198
1888	38,592,000	1.21	46,643,000	8.76	408,500,000	11.00	11.50	10.50	21.00	21,928
1889	52,949,000	1.26	66,831,000	7.04	470,394,000	9.00	10.00	9.00	14.00	36,274
1889	*52,949,000*	*1.26*	*66,831,000*							
1890	50,713,000	1.19	60,198,000	7.87	473,570,000	9.00	10.50	12.50	15.50	28,066
1891	51,044,000	1.19	60,818,000	8.12	494,114,000	12.50	15.00	13.50	14.00	35,201
1892	50,853,000	1.18	59,824,000	8.20	490,428,000	11.00	11.50	12.00	13.50	33,084
1893	49,613,000	1.33	65,766,000	8.68	570,883,000	10.00	10.50	10.00	10.50	54,446
1894	48,321,000	1.14	54,874,000	8.54	468,578,000	10.00	11.00	10.00	10.25	47,117
1895	44,206,000	1.06	47,079,000	8.35	393,186,000	12.00	12.50	11.50	12.00	59,052
1896	43,260,000	1.37	59,282,000	6.55	388,146,000	8.00	8.50	8.50	9.00	61,658
1897	42,427,000	1.43	60,665,000	6.62	401,391,000	8.00	8.50	9.50	10.50	81,827
1898	42,781,000	1.55	66,377,000	6.00	398,061,000	8.00	8.25	9.50	10.50	64,916
1899	41,328,000	1.37	56,656,000	7.27	411,926,000	10.50	11.50	10.50	12.50	72,716
1899	*43,127,000*	*1.25*	*53,828,000*							
1900	39,133,000	1.28	50,111,000	8.89	445,539,000	11.50	14.00	12.50	13.50	89,364
1901	39,391,000	1.28	50,591,000	10.01	506,192,000	13.00	13.50	12.50	13.50	153,431
1902	39,825,000	1.50	59,858,000	9.06	542,036,000	12.00	12.50	13.50	15.00	50,974
1903	39,934,000	1.54	61,306,000	9.07	556,276,000	12.00	12.00	12.00	15.00	60,730
1904	39,999,000	1.52	60,696,000	8.72	529,108,000	10.50	11.50	11.00	12.00	66,557
1905	39,362,000	1.54	60,532,000	8.52	515,960,000	10.00	12.00	11.50	12.50	70,172
1906	42,476,000	1.35	57,146,000	10.37	592,540,000	15.50	18.00	15.50	20.50	58,602
1907	44,028,000	1.45	63,677,000	11.68	743,507,000	13.00	17.50	13.00	14.00	77,281
1908	45,970,000	1.52	70,050,000	9.02	631,683,000	11.50	12.00	12.00	13.00	64,641
1909	45,744,000	1.42	64,938,000							
1909	*51,041,000*	*1.35*	*68,883,000*	10.49	722,385,000	16.00	17.00	12.50	16.00	55,007
1910[3]	51,015,000	1.36	69,378,000	12.14	842,252,000	16.00	19.00	18.50	23.50	55,223
1911	48,240,000	1.14	54,916,000	14.29	784,926,000	20.00	22.00	24.00	28.00	59,730
1912	49,530,000	1.47	72,691,000	11.79	856,695,000	13.00	18.00	14.00	16.50	60,720
1913	48,954,000	1.31	64,116,000	12.43	797,077,000	14.50	18.00	15.00	17.50	50,151
1914	49,145,000	1.43	70,071,000	11.12	779,068,000	15.00	16.00	16.50	17.50	105,508
1915	51,108,000	1.68	85,920,000	10.63	913,644,000	14.50	16.50	17.50	20.00	178,336
1916	54,965,000	1.64	89,991,000	11.21	1,008,894,000	15.00	17.50			

[1] 2,000 pounds.   [2] 2,240 pounds.   [3] Figures adjusted to census basis.

HAY—Continued.

TABLE 92.—*Hay: Acreage, production, and total farm value, by States, 1916.*

[000 omitted.]

State	Acreage (Acres.)	Production (Bushels.)	Farm value Dec. 1 (Dollars.)
Maine	1,200	1,740	21,576
New Hampshire	529	767	11,122
Vermont	980	1,666	20,992
Massachusetts	480	749	14,231
Rhode Island	60	81	1,620
Connecticut	370	574	10,619
New York	4,500	7,290	86,751
New Jersey	375	585	10,296
Pennsylvania	3,255	5,208	71,870
Delaware	80	116	1,844
Maryland	465	688	9,632
Virginia	790	1,066	15,990
West Virginia	825	1,270	18,415
North Carolina	390	507	8,872
South Carolina	250	325	5,428
Georgia	300	375	6,075
Florida	56	70	1,120
Ohio	3,100	4,867	51,590
Indiana	2,300	3,312	36,101
Illinois	3,100	4,495	50,794
Michigan	2,750	4,372	43,720
Wisconsin	2,600	4,420	51,272
Minnesota	1,890	3,496	24,472
Iowa	3,600	5,796	52,164
Missouri	3,350	4,355	40,502
North Dakota	520	884	5,304
South Dakota	730	1,387	7,490
Nebraska	1,850	4,070	28,897
Kansas	1,680	2,604	19,790
Kentucky	1,080	1,415	17,829
Tennessee	1,050	1,449	21,735
Alabama	275	358	4,654
Mississippi	275	371	4,081
Louisiana	260	429	4,719
Texas	480	576	6,048
Oklahoma	550	825	7,425
Arkansas	375	469	5,862
Montana	825	1,402	15,422
Wyoming	580	1,044	12,528
Colorado	970	1,988	21,868
New Mexico	185	370	5,180
Arizona	165	627	9,092
Utah	384	845	12,675
Nevada	225	540	5,184
Idaho	725	1,812	21,925
Washington	836	2,006	27,683
Oregon	850	1,955	21,310
California	2,500	4,375	55,125
United States	54,965	89,991	1,008,894

TABLE 93.—*Hay: Yield per acre, price per ton Dec. 1, and value per acre, by States.*

State	Average yield per acre (tons).											Farm price per ton (dollars).						Value per acre (dollars).[1]	
	10-year average, 1907–1916	1907	1908	1909	1910	1911	1912	1913	1914	1915	1916	10-year average, 1907–1916	1912	1913	1914	1915	1916	5-year average, 1911–1915	1916
Me	1.16	1.50	0.90	0.95	1.25	1.10	1.16	1.00	1.15	1.15	1.45	13.64	13.70	13.90	13.10	14.90	12.40	15.57	17.98
N.H	1.13	1.35	.92	.97	1.20	1.05	1.25	1.00	1.15	1.00	1.45	16.38	15.00	17.20	17.00	17.40	14.50	18.19	21.02
Vt	1.36	1.60	1.11	1.25	1.35	1.30	1.50	1.25	1.21	1.20	1.35	13.86	14.00	14.50	14.60	15.50	12.60	19.24	21.42
Mass	1.28	1.30	1.20	1.15	1.28	1.08	1.25	1.21	1.32	1.50	1.56	20.21	21.50	21.10	21.50	22.00	19.00	27.73	29.64
R.I	1.22	1.35	1.50	1.10	1.18	1.00	1.13	1.17	1.17	1.24	1.35	20.46	22.20	21.20	20.20	22.50	20.00	25.10	27.00
Conn	1.25	1.30	1.20	1.15	1.35	1.10	1.15	1.14	1.25	1.35	1.55	19.52	22.50	20.10	19.50	20.00	18.50	25.20	28.68
N.Y	1.24	1.25	1.20	1.05	1.32	1.02	1.25	1.14	1.20	1.30	1.62	14.60	14.90	15.30	14.60	15.70	11.90	18.45	19.28
N.J	1.40	1.45	1.60	1.25	1.50	1.05	1.44	1.30	1.35	1.45	1.56	18.28	20.00	19.10	19.50	19.10	17.60	26.09	27.46
Pa	1.36	1.45	1.50	1.20	1.38	1.00	1.43	1.32	1.28	1.40	1.60	15.18	15.60	14.90	14.50	15.60	13.80	20.48	22.08
Del	1.31	1.40	1.60	1.40	1.43	.88	1.33	1.30	1.10	1.20	1.45	16.29	15.00	15.70	17.00	17.00	15.90	19.85	23.06
Md	1.29	1.40	1.60	1.20	1.35	.72	1.51	1.26	1.15	1.20	1.48	15.53	14.40	15.20	15.30	16.20	14.00	18.81	20.72
Va	1.17	1.40	1.30	1.30	1.19	.64	1.20	1.27	.72	1.35	1.35	15.49	15.20	15.50	17.20	15.70	15.00	16.92	20.25
W.Va	1.26	1.45	1.45	1.25	1.20	.66	1.38	1.25	.92	1.50	1.54	15.14	14.90	17.20	15.60	14.90	17.20	18.17	22.33
N.C	1.38	1.50	1.50	1.38	1.50	1.05	1.30	1.31	1.15	1.35	1.30	16.03	16.70	16.50	17.10	16.50	17.50	22.25	22.75
S.C	1.24	1.50	1.25	1.23	1.25	1.08	1.15	1.16	1.15	1.30	1.30	16.58	18.00	18.70	17.00	15.60	16.70	20.12	21.71
Ga	1.41	1.75	1.75	1.35	1.40	1.35	1.35	1.40	1.35	1.15	1.25	16.40	17.00	17.90	16.20	15.10	16.20	22.04	20.25
Fla	1.31	1.35	1.35	1.38	1.33	1.30	1.25	1.35	1.35	1.20	1.25	16.98	18.10	18.20	17.20	16.00	16.00	22.73	20.00
Ohio	1.36	1.45	1.53	1.43	1.39	.98	1.36	1.30	1.13	1.44	1.57	12.52	13.00	12.80	13.40	12.70	10.60	17.25	16.64
Ind	1.28	1.35	1.50	1.40	1.30	.94	1.37	1.00	1.01	1.44	1.54	12.15	11.40	14.10	14.10	11.00	10.90	15.22	15.70
Ill	1.26	1.40	1.53	1.45	1.33	.98	1.30	.85	1.54	1.45	1.12	12.60	14.10	14.40	10.80	11.30	14.60	14.60	16.33
Mich	1.31	1.25	1.45	1.30	1.30	1.16	1.33	1.05	1.28	1.40	1.59	12.32	12.70	13.10	12.00	12.20	10.00	16.56	15.90
Wis	1.52	1.35	1.70	1.53	1.00	1.20	1.60	1.62	1.75	1.75	1.70	11.38	12.10	11.10	9.30	9.90	11.60	17.93	19.72
Minn	1.58	1.70	1.68	1.75	1.00	1.00	1.53	1.50	1.89	1.91	1.85	7.24	6.40	6.60	6.10	6.40	7.00	11.07	12.95
Iowa	1.43	1.40	1.70	1.64	1.05	.80	1.40	1.48	1.38	1.80	1.61	8.98	9.50	9.60	10.10	8.70	9.00	13.42	14.49
Mo	1.16	1.40	1.50	1.35	1.30	.60	1.30	.60	.70	1.52	1.30	10.28	9.80	14.50	13.60	8.50	9.30	10.37	12.09

[1] Based upon farm price Dec. 1.

HAY—Continued.

TABLE 93.—*Hay: Yield per acre, price per ton Dec. 1, and value per acre, by States—*
Continued.

State.	10-year average, 1907-1916.	1907	1908	1909	1910	1911	1912	1913	1914	1915	1916	10-year average, 1907-1916.	1912	1913	1914	1915	1916	5-year average, 1911-1915.	1916
	Average yield per acre (tons).											Farm price per ton (dollars).						Value per acre (dollars).[1]	
N. Dak	1.28	1.30	1.30	1.37	.55	1.10	1.40	1.14	1.45	1.50	1.70	5.91	5.50	5.80	5.20	5.70	6.00	7.62	10.20
S. Dak	1.40	1.40	1.50	1.50	.80	.55	1.46	1.20	1.70	2.00	1.90	5.93	6.10	6.50	5.70	5.30	5.40	8.34	10.26
Nebr	1.56	1.50	1.55	1.50	1.00	.85	1.35	1.34	1.69	2.60	2.20	7.26	8.40	8.70	6.90	5.80	7.10	11.60	15.62
Kans	1.39	1.15	1.50	1.45	1.15	.85	1.50	.90	1.51	2.30	1.55	7.74	7.60	12.50	7.40	5.60	7.60	11.02	11.78
Ky	1.21	1.35	1.35	1.36	1.29	.95	1.23	.87	.95	1.40	1.31	13.81	13.70	16.50	16.00	12.50	12.60	16.07	16.51
Tenn	1.35	1.50	1.50	1.50	1.40	1.00	1.30	1.21	1.20	1.47	1.38	14.76	15.80	16.20	17.00	13.90	15.00	19.53	20.70
Ala	1.44	1.80	1.60	1.50	1.43	1.40	1.25	1.36	1.31	1.45	1.30	13.52	14.60	14.20	13.80	12.40	13.00	18.31	16.90
Miss	1.45	1.60	1.50	1.47	1.42	1.50	1.48	1.33	1.45	1.40	1.35	11.87	12.50	13.50	12.00	11.00	11.00	17.15	14.85
La	1.64	2.00	1.40	1.50	1.75	1.30	1.65	1.50	1.90	1.75	1.75	11.87	12.70	12.50	12.00	10.30	11.00	19.23	18.15
Tex	1.33	1.30	1.65	.95	1.15	1.00	1.40	1.16	1.75	1.70	1.20	10.52	10.40	11.80	9.80	7.90	10.50	14.15	12.60
Okla	1.24	1.20	1.45	.90	1.05	.80	1.25	.85	1.13	2.30	1.50	7.55	7.40	10.40	7.90	5.60	9.00	9.26	13.50
Ark	1.28	1.25	1.50	1.25	1.35	1.15	1.23	1.20	1.05	1.60	1.25	11.75	12.00	13.50	12.90	10.30	12.50	15.19	15.62
Mont	1.88	1.70	2.00	1.79	1.40	2.00	1.90	1.80	2.50	2.00	1.70	9.54	8.30	9.60	8.70	7.50	11.00	17.96	18.70
Wyo	2.11	2.10	2.00	2.40	2.40	2.10	1.90	1.90	2.30	2.20	1.80	8.92	8.60	6.70	7.50	7.80	12.00	17.02	21.60
Colo	2.26	2.70	2.50	2.50	2.00	2.00	2.19	2.05	2.40	2.20	2.05	9.30	8.70	10.00	7.40	7.60	11.00	18.53	22.55
N. Mex	2.25	2.05	2.00	2.60	2.10	2.60	2.33	2.08	2.50	2.20	2.00	10.96	8.50	12.10	9.30	8.80	14.00	24.28	28.00
Ariz	3.30	2.90	3.20	3.30	2.10	3.86	3.40	4.00	3.20	3.30	3.80	11.99	12.00	11.00	8.80	9.60	14.50	38.00	55.10
Utah	2.56	2.10	2.50	2.90	3.00	2.50	2.78	2.33	2.75	2.50	2.20	8.92	8.00	9.10	7.70	8.00	15.00	21.42	33.00
Nev	2.73	1.75	2.00	2.35	3.40	3.40	3.00	2.75	3.25	3.00	2.40	9.47	8.70	11.00	8.30	7.50	9.60	27.63	23.04
Idaho	2.82	2.40	3.25	2.85	3.00	3.10	2.80	2.90	2.65	2.70	2.50	8.19	6.30	7.20	7.30	7.70	12.10	20.44	30.25
Wash	2.24	2.10	2.25	2.10	2.10	2.40	2.20	2.30	2.20	2.30	2.40	12.43	10.10	10.90	11.00	10.80	13.80	25.03	33.12
Oreg	2.10	2.00	2.00	2.05	2.10	2.10	2.20	2.10	2.00	2.20	2.30	9.98	8.30	9.00	9.20	9.50	10.90	19.32	25.07
Cal	1.69	1.75	1.35	1.70	1.83	1.75	1.53	1.50	1.95	1.80	1.75	11.70	13.70	13.50	8.20	11.20	12.60	19.29	22.05
U. S.	1.44	1.45	1.52	1.42	1.36	1.14	1.47	1.31	1.43	1.68	1.64	11.49	11.79	12.43	11.12	10.63	11.21	16.72	18.36

[1] Based upon farm price Dec. 1.

TABLE 94.—*Hay: Farm price per ton on first of each month, by geographical divisions,*
1915 and 1916.

Month.	United States.		North Atlantic States.		South Atlantic States.		N. Central States east of Miss. R.		N. Central States west of Miss. R.		South Central States.		Far Western States.	
	1916	1915	1916	1915	1916	1915	1916	1915	1916	1915	1916	1915	1916	1915
	Dolls.	*Dolls.*	*Dolls.*	*Dolls.*	*Dolls.*	*Dolls.*	*Dolls.*	*Dolls.*	*Dolls.*	*Dolls.*	*Dolls.*	*Dolls.*	*Dolls.*	*Dolls.*
January	10.94	11.29	16.26	15.39	15.86	16.97	11.43	12.17	7.17	8.80	10.74	13.06	9.93	8.30
February	11.40	11.69	16.64	15.94	16.66	17.15	11.82	12.43	7.63	9.09	11.15	13.50	10.47	8.84
March	11.62	11.71	16.48	15.79	16.25	17.69	11.91	12.57	7.42	9.38	11.36	13.72	11.86	8.53
April	11.78	11.74	17.19	15.41	16.54	17.79	12.20	12.39	7.51	9.72	11.61	13.95	11.48	8.74
May	12.22	11.82	17.91	15.59	16.87	18.35	12.70	12.62	7.76	9.66	11.89	13.97	11.89	8.70
June	12.46	11.96	18.33	15.74	17.13	18.38	13.07	12.73	7.63	9.57	12.11	13.90	12.36	9.08
July	12.09	11.70	17.74	16.40	16.31	17.90	12.74	12.66	7.69	8.74	11.60	13.34	11.69	8.55
August	10.68	11.02	15.43	16.64	15.03	16.57	10.29	11.31	6.94	7.59	10.94	11.98	10.98	8.32
September	10.42	10.80	13.66	16.64	15.11	16.20	10.47	11.04	7.23	7.19	10.89	11.41	10.69	8.19
October	10.36	10.69	13.47	16.22	15.10	15.85	10.39	11.00	7.08	7.07	10.85	11.00	10.86	8.46
November	10.68	10.83	13.33	16.16	15.04	15.85	10.41	11.00	7.58	7.11	11.62	10.73	11.59	9.00
December	11.21	10.63	13.35	16.23	15.25	15.67	10.88	11.28	7.91	7.07	12.28	10.46	12.26	9.15

HAY—Continued.

TABLE 95.—*Hay: Wholesale price (baled) per ton, 1912–1916.*

Date.	Chicago. No. 1 timothy.		Cincinnati. No. 1 timothy.		St. Louis. No. 1 timothy.		New York. No. 1 timothy.[1]		San Francisco. No. 1 wheat, light bales.	
	Low.	High.	Low.	High.	Low.	High.	Low.	High.	Low.	High.
1912.										
Jan.-June............	$17.50	$28.00	$21.50	$31.00	$19.50	$31.00	$25.00	$32.00	....	....
July–Dec............	13.00	22.00	15.50	27.00	13.00	24.50	21.50	29.00	....	....
1913.										
Jan.-June............	13.00	18.50	14.00	19.00	12.00	18.50	19.50	23.00	....	....
July–Dec............	13.50	19.50	15.25	21.00	13.50	24.00	20.00	22.00	....	....
1914.										
Jan.-June............	13.50	17.50	17.50	21.00	15.00	23.00	19.50	23.00	$13.00	$21.00
July–Dec............	13.00	18.50	17.50	21.50	14.50	22.50	18.50	25.00	{[2]7.50 / 11.00	} 14.00
1915.										
January............	15.00	17.50	18.00	19.25	17.00	19.50	21.00	22.50	11.00	12.00
February............	15.00	16.00	18.00	19.00	16.00	21.00	20.50	21.50	11.00	12.00
March...............	14.50	16.00	18.00	19.50	17.50	22.00	18.00	22.00	11.00	12.00
April...............	14.50	18.00	18.00	20.00	18.00	21.00	20.50	22.50	11.00	12.50
May................	16.50	17.50	19.00	21.00	18.00	22.00	22.00	25.00	11.50	12.50
June................	17.00	18.00	19.00	22.00	17.00	20.50	23.50	25.00	11.50	14.00
Jan.-June.......	14.50	18.00	18.00	22.00	16.00	22.00	18.00	25.00	11.00	14.00
July................	17.50	21.00	18.00	22.50	12.50	24.00	24.00	29.00	13.00	14.50
August.............	12.00	21.00	16.00	23.00	12.00	23.00	26.00	31.50	13.50	14.50
September..........	14.00	17.00	16.00	19.00	12.00	18.00	24.50	26.00	13.50	16.00
October............	14.00	18.00	13.00	21.00	13.00	18.00	24.00	26.00	14.50	18.00
November..........	14.50	16.50	18.50	19.50	13.00	18.00	25.00	26.00	17.00	18.00
December..........	14.50	16.50	18.00	20.00	14.00	19.00	24.00	26.00	17.00	18.00
July–Dec.......	12.00	21.00	13.00	23.00	12.00	24.00	24.00	31.50	13.00	18.00
1916.										
January............	15.50	17.00	18.00	21.00	15.00	20.00	24.00	26.00	16.00	18.00
February............	14.50	16.50	19.00	21.00	15.00	19.00	25.00	26.00	16.00	19.00
March...............	15.00	18.50	19.50	20.50	15.00	20.00	26.00	28.00	17.00	18.00
April...............	17.50	20.00	20.00	22.00	14.00	20.50	26.00	28.00	17.00	18.00
May................	17.50	20.00	21.00	24.00	16.50	21.00	26.50	30.00	17.00	18.00
June................	17.00	19.00	18.00	22.00	15.00	20.00	27.00	31.00	14.50	18.00
Jan.-June.......	14.50	20.00	18.00	24.00	14.00	21.00	24.00	31.00	14.50	19.00
July................	14.00	18.00	18.00	18.50	11.00	19.50	24.00	28.00	14.50	16.50
August.............	9.50	18.00	15.00	18.00	11.50	18.00	24.00	25.00	15.00	17.00
September..........	12.50	18.00	16.00	16.50	13.00	17.25	20.00	26.00	16.00	18.50
October............	14.50	17.00	14.25	16.50	14.00	17.00	18.00	20.00	17.50	18.50
November..........	13.00	17.00	15.00	16.50	14.50	17.50	18.50	23.00	17.50	19.00
December..........	15.00	17.50	15.50	16.50	15.50	18.50	19.00	22.00	18.00	20.00
July–Dec.......	9.50	18.00	14.25	18.50	11.00	19.50	18.00	28.00	14.50	20.00

[1] Per hundred pounds, 1900, 1901, and 1907.   [2] New hay.

CLOVER AND TIMOTHY SEED.

TABLE 96.—*Clover and timothy seed: Wholesale price, 1912–1916.*

Date.	Clover (bushels of 60 pounds).								Timothy.							
	Cincinnati. Prime.		Chicago. Poor to prime.		Toledo. Poor to choice.		Detroit.		Cincinnati. Per bushel (of 45 pounds).		Chicago. Poor to choice (per 100 pounds).		Milwaukee. Per 100 pounds.		St. Louis. Poor to prime (per 100 pounds).	
	Low.	High.	Low.	High.	Low.	High.	Low.	High.	Low.	High.	Low.	High.	Low.	High.	Low.	High.
1912.	Dols.	Dols.	Dols.	Dols.	Dols.	Dols.	Dols.	Dols.	Dols.	Dols.	Dols.	Dols.	Dols.	Dols.	Dols.	Dols.
Jan.–June	10.00	13.00	5.40	13.80	4.00	14.20	12.00	14.00	4.00	6.50	11.50	16.25	5.00	15.50	2.50	15.50
July–Dec	9.00	11.00	4.80	10.80	3.00	11.72½	10.25	12.50	1.50	5.00	3.80	12.00	2.50	10.00	2.75	10.00
1913.																
Jan.–June	8.00	11.50	4.20	13.20	3.00	13.85	11.15	13.40	1.50	1.80	2.50	5.40	2.50	4.60	2.00	4.00
July–Dec	5.00	9.00	4.20	9.60	1.60	12.75	7.50	9.45	2.50	5.40	3.50	5.90	3.75	5.50	2.25	5.50
1914.																
Jan.–June	5.00	9.00	7.00	15.00	2.00	9.45	7.40	9.40	1.40	2.25	3.00	5.75	3.00	5.50	2.00	5.35
July–Dec	5.00	9.25	9.00	18.50	2.40	11.40	8.20	11.25	1.40	2.70	3.50	7.85	3.50	7.00	3.25	7.00
1915.																
January	7.40	9.65	10.00	14.75	8.80	9.55	9.30	9.60	2.60	3.60	5.50	7.00	5.50	6.50	5.00	7.00
February	7.40	9.65	9.00	14.75	8.40	9.25	8.90	9.35	2.60	3.60	4.50	7.00	4.50	7.00	3.50	6.50
March	7.00	9.65	7.50	14.25	7.80	8.90	8.15	9.15	2.00	3.60	4.00	6.75	4.50	5.50	3.50	5.88
April	6.90	8.50	7.00	13.00	7.45	8.25	7.90	8.40	2.00	3.25	4.00	6.50	4.50	6.00	3.00	6.00
May	6.50	8.40	7.00	13.00	7.25	7.75	7.85	8.00	2.00	3.25	4.75	6.75	4.75	6.00	3.00	6.25
June	6.50	8.25	7.00	12.75	7.25	7.90	7.85	8.20	2.00	3.20	5.00	6.50	4.75	7.00	3.00	7.00
Jan.–June.	6.50	9.65	7.00	14.75	7.25	9.55	7.85	9.60	2.00	3.60	4.00	7.00	4.50	7.00	3.00	7.00
July	6.50	8.35	7.00	13.50	7.40	8.15	7.70	8.25	1.90	3.20	4.50	6.35	4.50	6.50	5.25	7.00
August	6.50	8.50	9.00	16.25	7.85	9.55	8.20	9.60	1.90	3.30	4.50	7.25	4.50	7.00	4.75	7.00
September	6.75	8.50	9.50	19.25	8.85	12.60	9.35	11.65	1.90	3.30	4.50	7.75	5.00	7.50	5.00	7.45
October	9.20	11.00	9.00	20.50	11.20	13.10	11.75	12.40	2.20	3.60	4.50	7.50	4.75	7.75	3.75	7.42½
November	8.60	12.20	9.00	19.25	11.00	12.00	11.90	12.25	2.10	3.75	5.00	7.75	4.75	7.75	3.00	7.40
December	8.50	12.15	9.00	19.75	9.35	12.30	12.00	12.55	2.20	3.75	5.00	8.00	4.75	8.00	4.00	7.50
July–Dec.	6.50	12.20	7.00	20.50	7.40	13.10	7.70	12.55	1.90	3.75	4.50	8.00	4.50	8.00	3.00	7.50
1916.																
January	8.40	10.50	8.00	19.00	11.65	12.10	11.85	12.10	2.30	3.30	5.00	8.00	4.75	8.00	6.00	7.50
February	8.75	11.50	9.00	22.00	11.95	13.70	12.00	13.25	2.30	3.30	4.50	8.50	4.75	8.50	5.75	7.15
March	7.75	11.25	10.00	20.50	10.65	12.75	10.75	12.75	2.00	3.20	4.00	8.00	4.00	7.75	3.75	6.50
April	7.00	9.00	7.00	17.00	8.30	10.70	8.75	10.75	1.85	3.00	4.00	8.00	4.00	7.75	5.00	6.25
May	6.50	8.40	8.00	14.00	8.45	8.85	8.75	8.85	1.80	2.80	4.50	8.50	4.50	8.50	4.00	7.25
June	6.50	8.40	6.00	14.00	8.70	9.00	8.85	9.00	1.80	2.80	5.00	8.50	5.00	8.50	4.00	7.50
Jan.–June.	6.50	11.50	6.00	22.00	8.30	13.70	8.75	13.25	1.80	3.30	4.00	8.50	4.00	8.50	3.75	7.50
July	6.50	9.00	7.00	14.00	8.72½	9.35	8.90	9.30	1.50	2.80	4.00	7.50	4.50	8.00	4.00	6.80
August	8.00	9.50	7.00	16.00	8.40	11.10	8.60	10.75	1.20	2.50	3.00	5.50	4.50	5.00	3.00	5.40
September	7.00	9.00	6.00	14.75	8.80	10.05	8.75	9.70	1.20	1.90	3.00	5.00	4.35	5.25	3.25	4.65
October	7.00	9.25	8.00	17.00	9.62½	10.85	9.50	10.60	1.20	2.00	3.00	5.50	3.50	5.50	3.00	4.75
November	8.50	10.00	12.00	18.00	10.45	11.15	10.60	11.00	1.30	2.15	3.00	5.50	3.75	5.50	3.50	4.90
December	8.75	10.00	12.00	17.50	10.35	10.80	10.25	10.85	1.30	2.15	3.00	5.75	4.00	5.75	3.00	5.05
July–Dec.	6.50	10.00	6.00	18.00	8.40	11.15	8.60	11.00	1.20	2.80	3.00	7.50	3.50	8.00	3.00	6.80

COTTON.

TABLE 97.—*Cotton: Area and production of undermentioned countries, 1913–1915.*

[Bales of 478 pounds, net.]

Country.	Area.			Production.		
	1913	1914	1915	1913	1914	1915
NORTH AMERICA.	*Acres.*	*Acres.*	*Acres.*	*Bales.*	*Bales.*	*Bales.*
United States[1]	37,089,000	36,832,000	31,412,000	14,156,000	16,135,000	11,192,000
Porto Rico	(2)	(2)	(2)	3 569	3 693	3 739
Total						
West Indies:						
British—						
Bahamas	(2)	(2)	(2)	4 28	....	4 43
Barbados	3,970	2,985	(2)	888	598	4 648
Grenada	(2)	(2)	(2)	4 839	4 749	4 772
Jamaica	(2)	(2)	(2)	4 145	4 67	4 88
Leeward Islands	(2)	(2)	(2)	4 2,574	4 2,637	4 2,413
St. Lucia	(2)	(2)	(2)	4 8	4 11	4 7
St. Vincent	5,444	5,006	(2)	1,018	958	4 791
Trinidad and Tobago	(2)	(2)	(2)	4 15	....	....
Danish (St. Croix)	(2)	(2)	(2)	4 745	4 290	(2)
Dominican Republic	(2)	(2)	(2)	4 1,140	4 771	(2)
Haiti	(2)	(2)	(2)	4 8,970	(2)	(2)
SOUTH AMERICA.						
Argentina	6,919	5,478	8,154	(2)	(2)	(2)
Brazil	(2)	(2)	(2)	320,000	385,000	440,000
Chile	334	(2)	(2)	740	....	(2)
Ecuador	(2)	(2)	(2)	4 757	4 165	(2)
Peru	(2)	(2)	(2)	4 110,314	4 105,617	(2)
EUROPE.						
Bulgaria	1,730	1,730	(2)	(2)	(2)	(2)
Malta	1,042	1,006	(2)	473	411	384
ASIA.						
India:						
British [6]	22,023,000	25,023,000	24,595,000	3,858,000	4,239,000	4,359,000
Native States	1,472,609	1,787,407	(2)	(2)	(2)	(2)
Total	23,500,609	26,810,407				
Ceylon	(2)	(2)	(2)	4 28	4 47	....
Cyprus	(2)	(2)	(2)	9,655	9,498	5,619
Dutch East Indies	(2)	(2)	(2)	18,966	(2)	(2)
Indo-China	(2)	(2)	(2)	(2)	(2)	(2)
Japanese Empire:						
Japan	6,178	5,887	(2)	4,462	4,582	(2)
Chosen (Korea)	141,844	(2)	(2)	32,787	(2)	(2)
Philippine Islands	5 7,544	5 7,544	5 7,544	5 6,098	5 6,098	5 6,098
Russia, Asiatic:						
Turkestan	1,382,743	1,442,757	1,516,980	953,281	1,176,477	1,424,114
Transcaucasia	310,466	364,460	269,970	119,821	132,198	132,649
Total	1,693,209	1,807,217	1,786,950	1,073,102	1,308,675	1,556,763
Siam	(2)	(2)	(2)	4 6,411	(2)	(2)
AFRICA.						
British Africa:						
Northern Rhodesia	(2)	(2)	(2)	4 483	4 475	4 264
Nyasaland Protectorate	(2)	(2)	(2)	4 5,023	5,541	4 6,413
East Africa	(2)	(2)	(2)	4 282	37	(2)
Gold Coast	(2)	(2)	(2)	4 19	4 16	4 8
Nigeria	(2)	(2)	(2)	13,308	11,820	5,642
Uganda	(2)	(2)	(2)	23,733	27,461	20,837
Union of South Africa	(2)	(2)	(2)	4 68	4 87	243

[1] Linters not included. Quantity of linters produced: 638,881 bales in 1913, 856,900 in 1914, and 880,780, in 1915.
[2] No official estimates.
[3] Exports to foreign countries plus shipments to the United States.
[4] Exports.
[5] Census of 1902.
[6] Includes Feudatory States.

COTTON—Continued.

TABLE 97.—*Cotton: Area and production of undermentioned countries, 1913–1915—*
Continued.

Country.	Area.			Production.		
	1913	1914	1915	1913	1914	1915
	Acres.	*Acres.*	*Acres.*	*Bales.*	*Bales.*	*Bales.*
Egypt..........................	1,788,000	1,822,000	1,231,072	1,588,000	1,425,000	1,349,242
French Africa:						
Dahomey.................	(1)	(1)	(1)	[2] 790	[2] 621	(1)
Guinea....................	(1)	(1)	(1)	[2] 230	[2] 168	(1)
Ivory Coast...............	(1)	(1)	(1)	[2] 84	[2] 339	(1)
German Africa:						
East Africa...............	(1)	(1)	(1)	[2] 10,109	(1)	(1)
Togo.....................	(1)	(1)	(1)	[2] 2,322	(1)	(1)
Italian Africa—Eritrea........	(1)	(1)	(1)	[2] 751	[2] 378	(1)
Sudan (Anglo-Egyptian)......	(1)	(1)	(1)	[2] 10,737	7,901	(1)
OCEANIA.						
British:						
Queensland...............	(1)	(1)	(1)	25	14	13
Solomon Islands..........	(1)	(1)	(1)	[2] 24	(1)	(1)
French:						
New Caledonia............	(1)	(1)	(1)	[2] 1,109	[2] 1,596	[2] 2,124
Tahiti....................	(1)	(1)	(1)	73	(1)	(1)

[1] No official estimates.   [2] Exports.

TABLE 98.—*Cotton: Total production of countries for which estimates were available,*
1900–1910.

Year.	Production.	Year.	Production.	Year.	Production.	Year.	Production.
	Bales.[1]		*Bales.*[1]		*Bales.*[1]		*Bales.*[1]
1900....	15,893,591	1904.....	21,005,175	1908.....	23,688,292	1912......	
1901....	15,926,048	1905.....	18,342,075	1909.....	20,679,334	1913......	
1902....	17,331,503	1906.....	22,183,148	1910.....	22,433,269	1914......	
1903....	17,278,881	1907.....	18,328,613	1911.....			

[1] Bales of 478 pounds, net.

TABLE 99.—*Cotton: Acreage harvested, by States, 1907–1916.*

[Thousands of acres.]

State.	1907	1908	1909	1910	1911	1912	1913	1914	1915	1916 [1]
Virginia..............	23	28	25	33	43	47	47	45	34	44
North Carolina......	1,408	1,458	1,359	1,478	1,624	1,545	1,576	1,527	1,282	1,432
South Carolina......	2,485	2,545	2,492	2,534	2,800	2,695	2,790	2,861	2,516	2,834
Georgia..............	4,566	4,848	4,674	4,873	5,504	5,335	5,318	5,433	4,825	5,344
Florida...............	209	265	237	257	308	224	188	221	193	197
Alabama.............	3,148	3,591	3,471	3,560	4,017	3,730	3,760	4,007	3,340	3,219
Mississippi..........	3,081	3,395	3,291	3,317	3,340	2,889	3,067	3,054	2,735	3,114
Louisiana...........	1,540	1,550	930	975	1,075	929	1,244	1,299	990	1,203
Texas...............	8,478	9,316	9,660	10,060	10,943	11,338	12,597	11,931	10,510	11,517
Arkansas............	1,902	2,296	2,218	2,238	2,363	1,991	2,502	2,480	2,170	2,635
Tennessee...........	693	754	735	765	837	783	865	915	772	878
Missouri.............	63	87	79	100	129	103	112	145	96	132
Oklahoma...........	2,064	2,311	1,767	2,204	3,050	2,665	3,009	2,847	1,895	2,593
California............				9	12	9	14	47	39	72
All other............								20	15	25
United States.	29,660	32,444	30,938	32,403	36,045	34,283	37,089	36,832	31,412	35,239

[1] Preliminary estimate.

COTTON—Continued.

TABLE 100.—*Cotton: Production of lint (excluding linters) in 500-pound gross weight bales, by States, and total value of crop, 1907 to 1916.*

[Thousands of bales and dollars. As finally reported by U. S. Bureau of the Census.]

State.	1907	1908	1909	1910	1911	1912	1913	1914	1915	1916[1]
Virginia	9	12	10	15	30	24	23	25	16	29
North Carolina	605	647	601	706	1,076	866	793	931	699	646
South Carolina	1,119	1,171	1,100	1,164	1,649	1,182	1,378	1,534	1,134	920
Georgia	1,816	1,931	1,804	1,767	2,769	1,777	2,317	2,718	1,909	1,845
Florida	50	62	54	59	83	53	59	81	48	43
Alabama	1,113	1,346	1,024	1,194	1,716	1,342	1,495	1,751	1,021	525
Mississippi	1,468	1,656	1,083	1,263	1,204	1,046	1,311	1,246	954	800
Louisiana	676	470	253	246	385	376	444	449	341	440
Texas	2,300	3,815	2,523	3,049	4,256	4,880	3,945	4,592	3,227	3,775
Arkansas	775	1,033	714	821	939	792	1,073	1,016	816	1,145
Tennessee	275	344	247	332	450	277	379	384	303	378
Missouri	36	62	45	60	97	56	67	82	48	62
Oklahoma	862	691	545	923	1,022	1,021	840	1,262	640	835
All other	3	2	2	10	17	11	32	64	36	68
United States	11,107	13,242	10,005	11,609	15,693	13,703	14,156	16,135	11,192	11,511
Total value of crop	$613,630	$588,810	$688,350	$809,710	$749,890	$786,800	$885,350	$591,130	$627,940	....

[1] Preliminary estimate.

TABLE 101.—*Cotton: Condition of crop, United States, monthly, 1895–1916.*

[Prior to 1901 figures of condition relate to first of month following dates indicated.]

Year.	May 25.	June 25.	July 25.	Aug. 25.	Sept. 25.	Year.	May 25.	June 25.	July 25.	Aug. 25.	Sept. 25.
	P. ct.	*P. ct.*	*P. ct.*	*P. ct.*	*P. ct.*		*P. ct.*	*P. ct.*	*P. ct.*	*P. ct.*	*P. ct.*
1895	81.0	82.3	77.9	70.8	65.1	1906	84.6	83.3	82.9	77.3	71.6
1896	97.2	92.5	80.1	64.2	60.7	1907	70.5	72.0	75.0	72.7	67.7
1897	83.5	86.0	86.9	78.3	70.0	1908	79.7	81.2	83.0	76.1	69.7
1898	89.0	91.2	91.2	79.8	75.4	1909	81.1	74.6	71.9	63.7	58.5
1899	85.7	87.8	84.0	68.5	62.4	1910	82.0	80.7	75.5	72.1	65.9
1900	82.5	75.8	76.0	68.2	67.0	1911	87.8	88.2	89.1	73.2	71.1
1901	81.5	81.1	77.2	71.4	61.4	1912	78.9	80.4	76.5	74.8	69.6
1902	95.1	84.7	81.9	64.0	58.3	1913	79.1	81.8	79.6	68.2	64.1
1903	74.1	77.1	79.7	81.2	65.1	1914	74.3	79.6	76.4	78.0	73.5
1904	83.0	88.0	91.6	84.1	75.8	1915	80.0	80.3	75.3	69.2	60.8
1905	77.2	77.0	74.9	72.1	71.2	1916	77.5	81.1	72.3	61.2	56.3

TABLE 102.—*Cotton: Yield per acre, price per pound Dec. 1, and value per acre, by States.*

State.	Yield per acre (pounds of lint).											Farm price per pound (cents).						Value per acre (dollars).[1]	
	10-year average, 1907–1916.	1907	1908	1909	1910	1911	1912	1913	1914	1915	1916[2]	10-year average, 1907–1916.	1912	1913	1914	1915	1916	5-year average, 1911–1915.	1916
Va	243	190	210	190	212	330	250	240	265	225	315	11.8	12.0	13.1	7.3	11.4	19.4	27.23	61.11
N.C.	244	205	211	210	227	315	267	239	290	260	215	11.8	12.2	12.6	6.9	11.2	19.4	27.91	41.71
S.C.	221	215	219	210	216	280	209	235	255	215	155	11.9	12.4	12.7	6.9	11.3	19.6	24.46	30.38
Ga.	194	190	190	184	173	240	159	208	239	189	165	12.0	12.4	12.8	6.9	11.4	19.9	21.15	32.84
Fla.	124	115	112	110	110	130	113	150	175	120	105	17.2	15.7	17.0	12.2	14.8	31.0	19.59	32.55
Ala.	165	169	179	142	160	204	172	190	209	146	78	11.8	12.1	12.7	6.7	11.1	19.5	18.62	15.21
Miss.	183	228	233	157	182	172	173	204	195	167	123	12.1	12.3	12.6	6.8	11.5	20.5	20.53	26.24
La.	164	210	145	130	120	170	193	170	165	165	175	11.6	11.5	11.7	6.9	11.2	19.1	17.42	33.42
Tex.	163	130	196	125	145	186	206	150	184	147	157	11.5	11.5	11.5	6.8	11.1	19.4	17.15	30.46
Ark.	191	195	215	153	175	190	190	205	196	180	208	11.8	12.3	11.6	6.6	11.6	19.6	19.58	40.77
Tenn.	200	190	218	158	207	257	169	210	200	188	206	11.8	12.4	12.7	6.4	11.3	19.5	20.86	40.17
Mo.	281	275	340	271	285	360	260	286	270	240	225	11.4	11.3	11.5	6.5	11.0	19.0	27.58	42.75
Okla.	169	200	143	147	200	160	183	132	212	162	154	11.2	11.3	11.4	6.5	11.3	19.0	16.12	29.28
Cal.	422				335	390	450	500	500	380	400	12.1	12.5	13.0	7.0	11.2	20.0	45.61	80.00
U.S.	181.5	178.3	194.9	154.3	170.7	207.7	190.9	182.0	209.2	170.3	156.3	11.8	11.9	12.2	6.8	11.3	19.6	19.36	30.64

[1] Based upon farm price Dec. 1.   [2] Preliminary.

COTTON—Continued.

TABLE 103.—*Cotton: Farm price per pound on first of each month, by geographical divisions, 1915 and 1916.*

Month.	United States.		South Atlantic States.		N. Cent. States west of Miss. R.		South Central States.		Far Western States.	
	1916	1915	1916	1915	1916	1915	1916	1915	1916	1915
	Cts.	*Cts.*	*Cts.*	*Cts.*	*Cts.*	*Cts.*	*Cts.*	*Cts.*	*Cts.*	*Cts.*
January	11.4	6.6	11.5	6.7	10.7	6.2	11.4	6.5	....	....
February	11.5	7.4	11.5	7.6	11.2	6.9	11.5	7.3	....	10.0
March	11.1	7.4	11.1	7.5	9.0	7.1	11.1	7.4	12.0	8.6
April	11.5	8.1	11.6	8.3	10.6	7.0	11.5	8.0	....	7.0
May	11.5	9.1	11.6	9.4	11.2	8.0	11.4	9.0	....	9.1
June	12.2	8.6	12.3	8.9	11.0	8.0	12.2	8.5	....	....
July	12.5	8.6	12.6	8.7	11.1	8.0	12.4	8.5	....	....
August	12.6	8.1	12.8	8.2	12.2	8.2	12.5	8.0	....	7.0
September	14.6	8.5	14.8	8.6	12.0	8.5	14.6	8.5	....	....
October	15.5	11.2	15.6	11.5	....	10.8	15.5	11.1	....	11.0
November	18.0	11.6	18.4	11.9	18.0	11.8	17.8	11.7	....	....
December	19.6	11.3	19.9	11.4	19.0	11.0	19.5	11.2	20.0	11.2

TABLE 104.—*Cotton: Closing price of middling upland per pound, 1912–1916.*

Date.	New York.		New Orleans.		Memphis.		Galveston.		Savannah.		Charleston.	
	Low.	High.	Low.	High.	Low.	High.	Low.	High.	Low.	High.	Low.	High.
1912.												
Jan.–June	9.35	12.00	$9\frac{3}{16}$	$12\frac{1}{4}$	$9\frac{7}{16}$	$12\frac{1}{8}$	$9\frac{3}{8}$	$12\frac{1}{8}$	$8\frac{5}{8}$	12	$8\frac{3}{4}$	$11\frac{9}{16}$
July–Dec	10.75	13.40	$10\frac{11}{16}$	$13\frac{1}{4}$	11	$13\frac{1}{4}$	$10\frac{7}{8}$	$13\frac{5}{16}$	$10\frac{9}{16}$	$12\frac{3}{4}$	11	$12\frac{3}{4}$
1913.												
Jan.–June	11.70	13.40	$12\frac{1}{8}$	13	12	$13\frac{1}{8}$	12	13	$11\frac{7}{8}$	$12\frac{3}{4}$	$11\frac{3}{4}$	$12\frac{5}{8}$
July–Dec	11.90	14.50	$11\frac{7}{8}$	14	$11\frac{3}{4}$	$13\frac{3}{4}$	$11\frac{3}{4}$	$14\frac{3}{8}$	$11\frac{1}{4}$	$14\frac{1}{8}$	$12\frac{3}{8}$	$13\frac{7}{8}$
1914.												
Jan.–June	12.30	14.50	$12\frac{5}{8}$	$13\frac{15}{16}$	13	$13\frac{3}{4}$	$12\frac{1}{2}$	14	$12\frac{3}{8}$	$13\frac{7}{8}$	$12\frac{1}{4}$	$13\frac{1}{2}$
July–Dec	7.25	13.25	$6\frac{1}{2}$	$13\frac{9}{16}$	$6\frac{1}{2}$	$13\frac{3}{4}$	$6\frac{5}{8}$	$13\frac{5}{8}$	$6\frac{1}{2}$	$13\frac{7}{8}$	$6\frac{1}{2}$	$8\frac{1}{2}$
1915.												
January	7.90	8.70	$7\frac{3}{8}$	$8\frac{1}{8}$	$7\frac{1}{8}$	$8\frac{1}{2}$	$7\frac{3}{4}$	$8\frac{7}{16}$	$7\frac{3}{8}$	$8\frac{1}{4}$	$7\frac{1}{4}$	$8\frac{1}{8}$
February	8.35	8.70	7.75	$8\frac{3}{16}$	7.76	8	8.30	$8\frac{1}{2}$	8	$8\frac{3}{8}$	$7\frac{3}{4}$	$8\frac{1}{8}$
March	8.25	9.65	7.75	9.06	7.88	8.87	8.25	9.35	8	$8\frac{7}{8}$	$7\frac{3}{4}$	$8\frac{3}{4}$
April	9.80	10.60	9.06	9.68	8.87	9.50	9.35	10.10	$8\frac{7}{8}$	$9\frac{5}{8}$	$8\frac{3}{4}$	$9\frac{5}{8}$
May	9.50	10.40	9.00	9.43	9.12	9.50	9.00	10.00	$9\frac{1}{4}$	$9\frac{3}{4}$	9	$9\frac{5}{8}$
June	9.45	9.85	9.00	9.38	8.75	9.12	8.95	9.35	$8\frac{15}{16}$	$9\frac{1}{8}$	......	9
Jan.–June	7.90	10.60	$7\frac{3}{8}$	9.68	$7\frac{1}{8}$	9.50	$7\frac{3}{8}$	10.10	$7\frac{3}{8}$	$9\frac{3}{4}$	$7\frac{1}{4}$	$9\frac{5}{8}$
July	8.90	9.60	8.50	9.00	8.62	8.82	8.50	9.00	$8\frac{1}{2}$	$8\frac{15}{16}$	......	$8\frac{1}{2}$
August	9.20	9.85	8.69	9.38	8.75	9.25	8.75	9.50	$8\frac{5}{8}$	9	......	......
September	9.75	12.40	9.31	11.75	9.25	11.75	9.50	11.90	$9\frac{1}{8}$	$11\frac{5}{8}$	9	$11\frac{5}{8}$
October	11.85	12.75	11.75	12.13	11.75	12.25	11.75	12.45	$11\frac{1}{2}$	$12\frac{1}{2}$	$11\frac{1}{2}$	12
November	11.60	12.50	11.25	12.00	11.38	11.88	11.50	12.40	$11\frac{1}{2}$	$12\frac{1}{2}$	$11\frac{1}{2}$	12
December	11.95	12.75	11.69	12.13	11.75	12.25	12.00	12.60	12	$12\frac{1}{8}$	$11\frac{3}{4}$	12
July–Dec	8.90	12.75	8.50	12.13	8.62	12.25	8.50	12.60	$8\frac{3}{8}$	$12\frac{1}{2}$	9	12
1916.												
January	11.80	12.60	11.75	12.19	12.00	12.38	12.05	12.50	12	$12\frac{1}{4}$	$11\frac{5}{8}$	12
February	11.20	12.15	11.13	11.62	11.38	12.00	11.45	12.10	$11\frac{1}{2}$	12	11	$11\frac{5}{8}$
March	11.45	12.15	11.13	12.00	11.38	12.00	11.60	12.35	$11\frac{1}{2}$	$12\frac{1}{8}$	11	$11\frac{3}{4}$
April	11.95	12.20	11.88	11.88	12.00	12.00	12.20	12.35	$11\frac{7}{8}$	12	$11\frac{5}{8}$	$11\frac{5}{8}$
May	12.30	13.35	12.00	12.94	12.12	13.00	12.40	13.30	12	$12\frac{3}{4}$	$11\frac{3}{4}$	$12\frac{3}{4}$
June	12.65	13.45	12.63	13.06	13.00	13.25	12.95	13.75	$12\frac{5}{8}$	13	$12\frac{3}{8}$	$12\frac{3}{4}$
Jan.–June	11.20	13.45	11.13	13.06	11.38	13.25	11.45	13.75	$11\frac{1}{2}$	13	11	$12\frac{3}{4}$
July	12.90	13.30	13.00	13.13	13.12	13.25	13.65	13.75	13	13	$12\frac{5}{8}$	$12\frac{3}{4}$
August	13.35	16.40	13.13	15.63	13.37	15.75	13.75	16.00	13	$15\frac{3}{4}$	13	$15\frac{1}{2}$
September	15.15	16.30	14.69	15.63	15.15	15.75	15.05	16.00	$14\frac{3}{4}$	$15\frac{7}{8}$	$14\frac{1}{2}$	$15\frac{1}{2}$
October	16.60	19.30	16.00	18.75	16.00	18.75	16.25	18.90	$16\frac{1}{8}$	19	16	$18\frac{3}{4}$
November	18.75	20.95	18.13	20.38	18.75	20.50	18.60	20.85	$18\frac{3}{4}$	$20\frac{5}{8}$	$18\frac{1}{2}$	$20\frac{1}{2}$
December	16.20	20.30	17.25	20.25	18.00	20.50	17.00	20.40	$18\frac{1}{4}$	$20\frac{1}{2}$	$19\frac{1}{2}$	$20\frac{1}{8}$
July–Dec	12.90	20.95	13.00	20.38	13.12	20.50	13.65	20.85	13	$20\frac{5}{8}$	$12\frac{5}{8}$	$20\frac{1}{2}$

COTTON—Continued.

TABLE 105.—*Cotton: International trade, calendar years 1913–1915.*

[Expressed in bales of 500 pounds gross weight, or 478 pounds net. The figures for cotton refer to ginned and unginned cotton and linters, but not to mill waste, cotton batting, *scarto* (Egypt and Sudan). Wherever unginned cotton has been separately stated in the original reports it has been reduced to ginned cotton in this statement at the ratio of 3 pounds unginned to 1 pound ginned. See "General note," Table 10.]

EXPORTS.

[000 omitted.]

Country.	1913	1914 (prelim.).	1915 (prelim.).	Country.	1913	1914 (prelim.).	1915 (prelim.).
	Bales.	*Bales.*	*Bales.*		*Bales.*	*Bales.*	*Bales.*
Belgium	298	....	....	Netherlands	150	111	190
Brazil	173	140	24	Persia [1]	117	105	....
British India	2,223	2,791	2,103	Peru	110	106	....
China	206	188	202	United States	9,376	6,873	9,126
Egypt	1,445	1,225	1,430	Other countries	234	111	....
France	267	209	41				
Germany	243	....	....	Total	14,842	11,859	....

IMPORTS.

Country.	1913	1914 (prelim.).	1915 (prelim.).	Country.	1913	1914 (prelim.).	1915 (prelim.).
Austria-Hungary	953	....	....	Russia	908	801	244
Belgium	647	....	....	Spain	407	389	660
Canada	166	152	197	Sweden	99	107	580
France	1,518	949	1,055	Switzerland	126	101	147
Germany	2,404	....	....	United Kingdom	4,010	3,447	4,820
Italy	931	879	1,343	United States	220	332	424
Japan	1,821	1,705	2,015	Other countries	339	287	....
Mexico	20	....	....				
Netherlands	317	245	365	Total	14,886	9,394	....

[1] Year beginning Mar. 21.

COTTONSEED OIL.

TABLE 106.—*Cottonseed oil: International trade, calendar years 1913–1915.*

[See "General note," Table 10.]

EXPORTS.

[000 omitted.]

Country.	1913	1914 (prelim.).	1915 (prelim.).	Country.	1913	1914 (prelim.).	1915 (prelim.).
	Gallons.	*Gallons.*	*Gallons.*		*Gallons.*	*Gallons.*	*Gallons.*
Belgium	1,014	....	....	United Kingdom	7,626	8,213	7,827
China	1,182	2,261	2,303	United States	35,304	28,841	47,016
Egypt	619	491	1,253	Other countries	59	31b	....
France	271	135	160				
Netherlands	31	143	4,265	Total	46,106	40,399	....

IMPORTS.

Country.	1913	1914 (prelim.).	1915 (prelim.).	Country.	1913	1914 (prelim.).	1915 (prelim.).
Algeria	[1]118	....	....	Mexico	3,869	....	....
Australia	175	189	....	Netherlands	7,765	6,438	19,040
Austria-Hungary	16	....	....	Norway	1,542	1,912	3,520
Belgium	2,005	....	....	Roumania	481	....	....
Brazil	440	383	377	Senegal	451	....	....
Canada	4,104	4,079	4,083	Serbia [3]	396	....	....
Egypt	118	74	3	Sweden	702	940	....
France	2,604	1,410	3,547	United Kingdom	4,990	6,193	8,337
Germany	4,786	....	....	Other countries	6,466	5,410	....
Italy	3,957	702	472				
Malta [2]	278	....	....	Total	45,539	28,015	....
Martinique	276	285	320				

[1] Data for 1912   [2] Year beginning Apr. 1.   [3] Data for 1911.

TOBACCO.

TABLE 107.—*Tobacco: Area and production of undermentioned countries, 1913–1915.*

Country.	Area.			Production.		
	1913	1914	1915	1913	1914	1915
NORTH AMERICA.	*Acres.*	*Acres.*	*Acres.*	*Pounds.*	*Pounds.*	*Pounds.*
United States	1,216,100	1,223,500	1,369,900	958,734,000	[3]1,034,679,000	1,062,237,000
Porto Rico	17,808	18,040	(1)	[3]9,244,490	[3]9,285,333	(1)
Canada:						
Ontario	6,000	5,000	4,500	8,000,000	6,000,000	4,950,000
Quebec	5,000	4,750	4,500	4,500,000	5,000,000	4,050,000
Total	11,000	9,750	9,000	12,500,000	11,000,000	9,000,000
Costa Rica	(1)	2,734	(1)	(1)	(1)	(1)
Cuba	(1)	(1)	(1)	73,087,800	80,770,080	50,077,920
Dominican Republic	(1)	(1)	(1)	28,000,000	[2]8,169,253	8,050,000
Guatemala	(1)	1,236	(1)	(1)	(1)	(1)
Jamaica	1,144	(1)	(1)	(1)	(1)	(1)
Mexico	(1)	(1)		(1)	(1)	(1)
SOUTH AMERICA.						
Argentina	23,860	36,744	37,955	(1)	(1)	(1)
Brazil	(1)	(1)	(1)	[2]64,788,421	[2]59,481,096	[2]59,734,874
Chile	3,430	(1)	(1)	8,523,645	6,282,228	(1)
Uruguay	4,159	2,503	(1)	3,062,062	1,737,805	(1)
EUROPE.						
Austria-Hungary:						
Austria	8,263	[4]4,262	(1)	13,692,771	[4]6,908,555	(1)
Hungary	117,429	(1)	(1)	105,489,669	(1)	(1)
Croatia-Slavonia	190	(1)	(1)	106,703	(1)	(1)
Bosnia-Herzegovina	(1)	(1)	(1)	13,227,600	(1)	(1)
Total				132,516,743		
Belgium	9,941	10,309	(1)	19,702,290	(1)	(1)
Bulgaria	17,297	(1)	(1)	13,227,600	33,069,000	(1)
Denmark	(1)	(1)	(1)	(1)	(1)	(1)
France	38,906	38,135	(1)	57,324,891	53,291,796	(1)
Germany	34,996	25,587	22,313	56,953,423	50,191,866	(1)
Italy	18,060	18,038	18,532	18,739,100	20,943,700	(1)
Netherlands	1,149	929	860	(1)	(1)	(1)
Roumania	27,122	27,070	32,232	20,941,275	16,970,129	18,566,921
Russia:						
Russia proper	95,588	95,324	(1)	180,877,567	147,744,290	(1)
Poland			(1)			(1)
Northern Caucasia	20,731	31,254	(1)	21,111,362	33,978,353	(1)
Serbia	(1)	(1)	(1)	(1)	(1)	(1)
Sweden	(1)	(1)	(1)	1,746,043	1,444,013	
Switzerland	791	618	618	1,327,169	815,702	947,978
ASIA.						
India:						
British	964,726	1,001,710	(1)	(1)	(1)	(1)
Native States	68,717	36,546	(1)	(1)	(1)	(1)
Total	1,033,443	1,038,256				
British North Borneo	(1)	(1)	(1)	3,621,754	(1)	(1)
Ceylon	12,968	(1)	(1)	[2]4,273,136	(1)	(1)
Dutch East Indies:						
Java and Madura	413,185	394,636	(1)	[2]134,017,760	[2]108,979,540	(1)
Sumatra, East Coast of	(1)	(1)	(1)	43,944,757	46,632,068	(1)
Japanese Empire:						
Japan	77,176	88,670	75,479	111,955,049	126,206,328	105,820,800
Formosa	839	(1)	(1)	959,477	(1)	(1)
Chosen	48,135	(1)	(1)	31,357,538	(1)	(1)
Philippine Islands	170,477	150,459	131,808	101,544,736	103,024,183	84,442,714
Russia, Asiatic	37,993	57,960	(1)	31,462,230	42,950,903	(1)
AFRICA.						
Algeria	(1)	(1)	(1)	(1)	(1)	(1)
Tunis	(1)	297	314		376,325	(1)
Nyasland	10,499	(1)	(1)	[2]3,763,014	(1)	(1)
Rhodesia	5,000	(1)	(1)	3,000,000	(1)	(1)
Union of South Africa	[5]19,364	[5]19,364	[5]19,364		(1)	(1)
OCEANIA.						
Australia	2,745	3,007	(1)	1,869,392	2,599,408	(1)
Fiji	144	(1)	(1)	81,312	(1)	(1)

[1] No official statistics.   [3] Exports year beginning July 1.   [5] Census of 1911.
[2] Exports.   [4] Excluding Galicia and Bukowina.

TOBACCO—Continued.

TABLE 108.—*Tobacco: Total production of countries for which estimates were available, 1900–1911.*[1]

Year.	Production.	Year.	Production.	Year.	Production.	Year.	Production.
	Pounds.		*Pounds.*		*Pounds.*		*Pounds.*
1900....	2,201,193,000	1904.....	2,146,641,000	1908.....	2,382,601,000	1912.....	....
1901....	2,270,213,000	1905.....	2,279,728,000	1909.....	2,742,500,000	1913.....	....
1902....	2,376,054,000	1906.....	2,270,298,000	1910.....	2,833,729,000	1914.....	....
1903....	2,401,268,000	1907.....	2,391,061,000	1911.....	2,566,202,000	1915.....	....

[1] Data for 1911 not strictly comparable with earlier years.

TABLE 109.—*Tobacco: Acreage, production, value, condition, etc., in the United States, 1849–1916.*

NOTE.—Figures in *italics* are census returns; figures in roman are estimates of the Department of Agriculture. Estimates of acres are obtained by applying estimated percentages of increase or decrease to the published numbers of the preceding year, except that a revised base is used for applying percentage estimates whenever new census data are available.

Year.	Acreage (000 omitted).	Average yield per acre.	Production (000 omitted).	Average farm price per pound Dec. 1.	Farm value Dec. 1 (000 omitted).	Domestic exports of unmanufactured, fiscal year beginning July 1.	Imports of unmanufactured, fiscal year beginning July 1.	Condition of growing crop.			
								July 1.	Aug. 1.	Sept. 1.	When harvested.
	Acres.	*Lbs.*	*Lbs.*	*Cts.*	*Dolls.*	*Pounds.*	*Pounds.*	*P. ct.*	*P. ct.*	*P. ct.*	*P. ct.*
1849	....	....	*199,753*	......	......	....	....	......	......	......	......
1859	....	....	*434,209*	......	......	....	....	......	......	......	......
1869	....	....	*262,735*	......	......	....	....	......	......	......	......
1879	*639*	*789.7*	*472,661*	......	......	....	....	......	......	......	......
1889	*695*	*702.5*	*488,257*	......	......	....	....	......	......	......	......
1899	*1,101*	*788.5*	*868,113*	......	......	....	....	......	......	......	......
1900	1,046	778.0	814,345	6.6	53,661	315,787,782	26,851,253	88.5	82.9	77.5	76.1
1901	1,039	788.0	818,953	7.1	58,283	301,007,365	29,428,837	86.5	72.1	78.2	81.5
1902	1,031	797.3	821,824	7.0	57,564	368,184,084	34,016,956	85.6	81.2	81.5	84.1
1903	1,038	786.3	815,972	6.8	55,515	311,971,831	31,162,636	85.1	82.9	83.4	82.3
1904	806	819.0	660,461	8.1	53,383	334,302,091	33,288,378	85.3	83.9	83.7	85.6
1905	776	815.6	633,034	8.5	53,519	312,227,202	41,125,970	87.4	84.1	85.1	85.8
1906	796	857.2	682,429	10.0	68,233	340,742,864	40,898,807	86.7	87.2	86.2	84.6
1907	821	850.5	698,126	10.2	71,411	330,812,658	35,005,131	81.3	82.8	82.5	84.8
1908	875	820.2	718,061	10.3	74,130	287,900,946	43,123,196	86.6	85.8	84.3	84.1
1909	1,180	804.3	949,357								
1909	*1,295*	*815.3*	*1,055,765*	10.1	106,599	357,196,074	46,853,389	89.8	83.4	80.2	81.3
1910[1]	1,366	807.7	1,103,415	9.3	102,142	355,327,072	48,203,288	85.3	78.5	77.7	80.2
1911	1,013	893.7	905,109	9.4	85,210	379,845,320	54,740,380	72.6	68.0	71.1	80.5
1912	1,226	785.5	962,855	10.8	104,063	418,796,906	67,977,118	87.7	82.8	81.1	81.8
1913	1,216	784.3	953,734	12.8	122,481	449,749,982	61,174,751	82.8	78.3	74.5	76.6
1914	1,224	845.7	1,034,679	9.8	101,411	348,346,091	45,764,728	66.0	66.5	71.4	81.8
1915	1,370	775.4	1,062,237	9.1	96,281	441,569,581	48,013,335	85.5	79.7	80.7	81.9
1916	1,412	815.0	1,150,622	14.7	169,008	....	....	87.6	84.4	85.5	85.6

[1] Figures adjusted to census basis.

TABLE 110.—*Tobacco: Acreage, production, and total farm value, by States, 1916.*

State.	Acreage.	Production.	Farm value Dec. 1	State.	Acreage.	Production.	Farm value Dec. 1
	Acres.	*Pounds.*	*Dollars.*		*Acres.*	*Pounds.*	*Dollars.*
New Hamp..	100	165,000	28,000	Ohio..........	100,000	95,000,000	12,350,000
Vermont.....	100	160,000	30,000	Indiana......	14,800	13,764,000	1,789,000
Mass........	7,300	12,118,000	3,030,000	Illinois........	700	525,000	52,000
Connecticut..	22,200	36,186,000	9,770,000	Wisconsin....	43,900	55,753,000	6,969,000
New York...	3,700	4,551,000	592,000	Missouri.....	3,200	3,040,000	456,000
Pennsylvania	36,100	49,096,000	6,972,000	Kentucky....	484,000	435,600,000	55,321,000
Maryland....	25,500	19,635,000	3,142,000	Tennessee....	102,200	81,760,000	8,258,000
Virginia......	190,000	129,200,000	18,863,000	Alabama.....	200	60,000	18,000
West Virginia	14,100	12,690,000	1,904,000	Louisiana.....	200	90,000	25,000
N. Carolina..	320,000	176,000,000	35,200,000	Texas.........	200	140,000	28,000
S. Carolina..	39,000	20,280,000	2,839,000	Arkansas.....	500	250,000	50,000
Georgia......	1,300	1,534,000	414,000				
Florida.......	2,500	3,025,000	908,000	U. S....	1,411,800	1,150,622,000	169,008,000

TOBACCO—Continued.

TABLE 111.—*Tobacco: Yield per acre, price per pound December 1, and value per acre, by States.*

State.	Yield per acre (pounds).											Farm price per pound (cents).						Value per acre (dollars).[1]	
	10-year average 1907–1916.	1907	1908	1909	1910	1911	1912	1913	1914	1915	1916	10-year average 1907–1916.	1912	1913	1914	1915	1916	5-year average 1911–1915.	1916
New Hampshire	1,674	1,650	1,800	1,700	1,720	1,700	1,700	1,650	1,770	1,400	1,650	15.6	18.5	18.0	18.0	12.0	17.0	274.02	280.50
Vermont	1,618	1,625	1,735	1,675	1,600	1,700	1,700	1,550	1,700	1,300	1,600	15.5	18.5	18.0	18.0	11.0	19.0	262.90	304.00
Massachusetts	1,592	1,525	1,650	1,650	1,730	1,650	1,700	1,550	1,750	1,100	1,600	17.8	23.9	18.0	17.7	14.5	25.0	306.21	415.00
Connecticut	1,620	1,510	1,680	1,650	1,730	1,625	1,700	1,550	1,770	1,350	1,630	19.0	24.1	21.0	18.5	17.0	27.0	325.05	440.10
New York	1,213	1,150	1,175	1,250	1,250	1,175	1,300	1,020	1,300	1,200	1,230	10.2	12.2	12.2	12.0	9.5	13.0	139.31	159.90
Pennsylvania	1,330	1,260	1,325	985	1,500	1,420	1,450	1,200	1,450	1,350	1,360	9.4	8.5	7.5	8.0	9.2	14.2	119.12	193.12
Maryland	720	660	700	710	690	735	660	740	800	740	770	8.7	8.0	9.3	8.0	8.5	16.0	60.73	123.20
Virginia	738	760	815	775	780	800	600	770	650	870	680	10.6	11.0	13.9	11.0	9.4	14.6	76.97	99.28
West Virginia	776	720	750	875	640	750	760	680	820	870	900	11.4	11.0	12.0	11.5	10.0	15.0	80.48	135.00
North Carolina	632	625	670	600	600	710	620	670	650	620	550	13.0	16.0	18.5	11.5	11.2	20.0	89.94	110.00
South Carolina	730	900	865	800	630	810	700	760	730	580	520	10.5	10.9	13.8	9.7	7.0	14.0	78.93	72.80
Georgia	900	880	975	680	680	900	830	1,000	1,000	910	1,180	29.3	30.0	31.0	25.0	23.0	27.0	252.68	318.60
Florida	920	925	990	710	680	940	840	1,000	1,000	910	1,210	30.9	30.0	31.0	30.0	23.0	30.0	266.90	363.00
Ohio	865	900	670	925	810	925	920	750	900	810	950	9.7	9.0	11.4	8.8	9.0	13.0	79.94	123.50
Indiana	860	940	700	950	880	910	800	750	900	840	930	9.9	9.0	11.0	9.0	7.3	13.0	73.56	120.90
Illinois	788	800	755	750	790	750	760	1,180	780	830	750	9.8	9.0	11.5	12.0	9.0	10.0	75.50	75.00
Wisconsin	1,153	1,100	1,130	1,180	1,050	1,250	1,290	1,180	1,180	900	1,270	9.6	11.0	12.7	11.0	6.0	12.5	118.46	158.75
Missouri	914	825	875	885	1,050	800	1,000	650	1,200	900	900	12.5	12.0	12.7	13.0	12.0	15.0	112.51	142.50
Kentucky	839	890	815	835	810	880	780	760	910	810	900	9.4	8.7	10.0	8.4	7.8	12.7	70.25	114.30
Tennessee	765	800	800	730	760	810	660	720	820	750	800	8.3	7.1	8.4	7.5	6.3	10.1	56.99	80.80
Alabama	565	450	450	600	500	700	750	700	700	500	300	26.4	35.0	25.0	28.0	22.0	30.0	183.70	90.00
Louisiana	477	350	850	550	550	450	300	450	400	420	450	30.1	30.0	25.0	35.0	30.0	28.0	121.60	126.00
Texas	648	700	800	650	600	650	700	600	580	500	650	23.4	17.5	22.0	21.0	27.0	20.0	128.26	140.00
Arkansas	604	570	610	600	650	600	650	650	610	600	500	16.1	18.0	16.4	18.0	17.0	20.0	101.48	100.00
United States	818.2	850.5	820.2	804.3	807.7	893.7	785.5	784.3	845.7	775.4	815.0	10.6	10.8	12.8	9.8	9.1	14.7	84.58	119.71

[1] Based upon farm price Dec. 1.

TOBACCO—Continued.

TABLE 112.—*Tobacco: Acreage, production, and farm value, by types and districts, 1915 and 1916.*

Type and district.	Acreage (thousands of acres).		Yield per acre (pounds).		Production (thousands of pounds).		Average farm price per pound Dec. 1 (cents).		Total farm value (thousands of dollars).[1]	
	1916	1915	1916	1915	1916	1915	1916	1915	1916	1915
I. CIGAR TYPES.										
New England	29.7	29.7	1,640	1,285	48,629	38,270	26.2	16.4	12,858	6,290
New York	3.7	4.4	1,230	1,200	4,551	5,280	13.0	9.5	592	502
Pennsylvania	36.1	31.4	1,360	1,350	49,096	42,390	14.2	9.2	6,972	3,900
Ohio—Miami Valley	60.0	60.3	970	900	58,200	54,270	12.0	9.0	6,984	4,884
Wisconsin	43.9	41.0	1,270	900	55,753	36,900	12.5	6.0	6,969	2,214
Georgia and Florida	3.8	5.6	1,199	900	4,559	5,045	29.0	23.0	1,322	1,160
II. CHEWING, SMOKING, SNUFF, AND EXPORT TYPES.										
Burley district	265.0	244.2	970	890	257,050	217,338	15.5	9.5	39,843	20,647
Dark districts of Kentucky and Tennessee:										
Paducah district	100.0	93.1	780	730	78,000	67,963	9.8	6.0	7,644	4,078
Henderson or stemming district...	107.0	93.0	890	760	95,230	70,680	10.0	6.0	9,523	4,240
One-Sucker district	48.0	38.4	870	780	41,760	29,952	10.0	5.5	4,176	1,647
Clarksville and Hopkinsville district.	125.0	118.7	790	750	98,750	89,025	10.8	6.5	10,665	5,787
Virginia sun-cured district	12.0	12.0	690	850	8,280	10,200	14.0	8.0	1,159	816
Virginia dark district	65.6	65.0	820	840	53,792	54,600	10.4	8.0	5,594	4,368
Bright yellow district:										
Old belt—Virginia and North Carolina	240.0	255.0	570	640	136,800	163,200	18.9	10.5	25,855	17,136
New belt—Eastern North Carolina and South Carolina	230.0	240.0	550	620	126,500	148,800	19.2	10.6	24,288	15,773
Maryland and eastern Ohio export....	30.0	23.9	780	760	23,400	18,164	15.6	8.5	3,650	1,544
Perique-Louisiana	.2	.3	450	420	90	126	28.0	30.0	25	38
Scattering	11.8	12.7	......	......	10,182	8,384	......	......	889	1,017

[1] Based upon farm price Dec. 1.

TABLE 113.—*Tobacco: Wholesale price per pound, 1912–1916.*

Date.	Cincinnati, leaf, plug, stock, common to good red.		Hopkinsville, leaf, common to fine.		Louisville, leaf (Burley, dark red), common to good.		Clarksville, leaf, common to fine.		Richmond, leaf, smokers, common to good.[3]		Baltimore, leaf (Maryland), medium to fine red.	
	Low.	High.	Low.	High.	Low.	High.	Low.	High.	Low.	High.	Low.	High.
	Cents.	*Cents.*	*Cents.*	*Cents.*	*Cents.*	*Cents.*	*Cents.*	*Cents.*	*Cents.*	*Cents.*	*Cents.*	*Cents.*
1912.												
Jan.–June	6.00	13.00	8.00	16.00	7.50	12.00	9.50	15.00	6.00	12.00	8.50	13.00
July–Dec	5.00	14.00	9.00	16.00	7.00	13.00	9.50	15.00	6.00	12.00	8.50	15.00
1913.												
Jan.–June	5.50	13.75	[1] 7.00	14.00	7.00	14.00	9.00	14.00	6.00	16.00	8.50	15.00
July–Dec	5.50	13.75	[1] 8.75	14.00	9.00	16.00	8.50	15.00	7.00	16.00	8.50	15.00
1914.												
Jan.–June	5.50	14.00	[1] 8.00	14.00	9.00	16.00	9.50	16.00	7.00	20.00	8.50	15.00
July–Dec	5.50	13.00	[1] 7.50	14.00	9.00	16.00	7.50	16.00	7.00	20.00	8.00	15.00
1915.												
January	6.00	13.00	[2] 4.00	12.50	9.00	14.00	6.00	13.00	7.00	20.00	8.00	13.00
February	6.00	13.00	5.00	12.50	9.00	14.00	6.00	13.00	7.00	20.00	8.00	13.00
March	6.00	13.00	5.00	12.00	9.00	14.00	6.00	13.00	7.00	20.00	8.00	13.00
April	6.00	13.00	5.50	12.25	8.00	14.00	6.00	12.00	7.00	20.00	8.00	13.00
May	6.00	13.00	5.50	11.50	8.00	14.00	6.00	12.00	7.00	20.00	8.00	13.00
June	6.00	13.00	5.50	10.50	8.00	14.00	6.00	12.00	7.00	20.00	8.00	13.00
Jan.–June..	6.00	13.00	4.00	12.50	8.00	14.00	6.00	13.00	7.00	20.00	8.00	13.00

[1] Common to good, February to November, inclusive.
[2] All grades, January to November, inclusive.
[3] Brights, smokers, common to fine 1913 to 1916, inclusive.

TOBACCO—Continued.

TABLE 113.—*Tobacco: Wholesale price per pound, 1912–1916*—Continued.

Date.	Cincinnati, leaf, plug, stock, common to good red.		Hopkinsville, leaf, common to fine.		Louisville, leaf (Burley, dark red), common to good.		Clarksville, leaf, common to fine.		Richmond, leaf, smokers, common to good.[2]		Baltimore, leaf (Maryland), medium to fine red.	
	Low.	High.	Low.	High.	Low.	High.	Low.	High.	Low.	High.	Low.	High.
1915.	*Cents.*	*Cents.*	*Cents.*	*Cents.*	*Cents.*	*Cents.*	*Cents.*	*Cents.*	*Cents.*	*Cents.*	*Cents.*	*Cents.*
July	6.00	13.00			10.00	15.00	6.00	12.00	7.00	20.00	8.00	14.00
August	6.00	13.00			10.00	15.00	6.00	12.00	7.00	20.00	8.00	14.00
September	5.00	13.00			10.00	15.00			7.00	20.00	8.00	14.00
October	5.00	13.00			10.00	15.00			7.00	20.00	8.00	14.00
November	5.00	13.00	6.00	6.00	10.00	15.00	[1] 7.00	13.00	7.00	20.00	9.00	14.00
December	5.00	13.00	[1] 5.50	10.00	10.00	15.00	[1] 7.50	13.00	7.00	20.00	9.00	14.00
July–Dec	5.00	13.00	5.50	10.00	10.00	15.00	6.00	13.00	7.00	20.00	8.00	14.00
1916.												
January	5.00	14.00	5.00	10.25	10.00	15.00	[1] 7.50	13.00	7.00	20.00	9.00	14.00
February	5.00	14.00	5.50	10.50	10.00	15.00	4.50	13.00	7.00	20.00	9.00	14.00
March	5.00	14.00	5.00	11.75	10.00	15.00	4.50	10.00	7.00	20.00	9.00	14.00
April	5.00	14.00	6.00	11.75	10.00	16.00	4.50	10.00	9.00	18.00	9.00	14.00
May	5.00	16.00	7.00	14.00	11.00	16.00	4.50	12.00	9.00	18.00	9.00	15.00
June	7.50	16.00			11.00	16.00	4.50	12.00	9.00	18.00	9.50	16.00
Jan.–June	5.00	16.00	5.00	14.00	10.00	16.00	4.50	13.00	7.00	20.00	9.00	16.00
July	7.50	17.00	7.50	14.00	11.00	16.00	4.50	12.00	9.00	18.00	11.00	17.00
August	9.00	17.00			11.00	16.00	4.50	10.00	9.00	18.00	13.00	19.00
September	9.00	17.00			11.00	16.00	4.50	10.00	9.00	18.00	16.00	21.00
October	9.00	17.00			11.00	16.00			9.00	18.00	17.00	21.00
November	9.00	17.00			11.00	16.00			9.00	18.00	17.00	21.00
December	9.00	17.00	9.50	14.50	11.00	19.00			9.00	18.00	17.00	21.00
July–Dec	7.50	17.00	7.50	14.50	11.00	19.00	4.50	12.00	9.00	18.00	11.00	21.00

[1] Common to good throughout 1916.
[2] Brights, smokers, common to fine, 1913 to 1916, inclusive.

TABLE 114.—*Tobacco (unmanufactured): International trade, calendar years 1913–1915.*

[Tobacco comprises leaf, stems, strippings, and *tombac*, but not snuff. See "General note," Table 10.]

EXPORTS.

[000 omitted.]

Country.	1913	1914 (prelim.).	1915 (prelim.).	Country.	1913	1914 (prelim.).	1915 (prelim.)
	Pounds.	*Pounds.*	*Pounds.*		*Pounds.*	*Pounds.*	*Pounds.*
Aden [1]	9,440	7,047		Greece	21,876	21,876	20,347
Algeria	8,366	10,356	14,282	Mexico	1,783		
Austria-Hungary	19,247			Netherlands	3,454	3,663	7,053
Brazil	64,788	59,481	59,735	Paraguay	11,962	9,993	15,782
British India	35,843	23,349	32,877	Persia [3]	3,593	1,493	
Bulgaria	[2] 3,578			Philippine Islands	28,585	29,533	24,663
Ceylon	4,273	4,821	3,118	Russia	28,291	9,955	6,139
Cuba	30,669	36,868	38,799	United States	444,372	347,295	435,895
Dominican Republic	21,584	8,169	13,747	Other countries	57,910	46,462	
Dutch East Indies	193,632	145,268		Total	993,246	765,629	

IMPORTS.

Country.	1913	1914	1915	Country.	1913	1914	1915
Aden [1]	14,595	9,822		Italy	56,160	41,425	36,693
Argentina	17,917	17,040	17,644	Netherlands	65,913	59,708	58,592
Australia	15,805	10,688		Norway	4,044	4,645	4,591
Austria-Hungary	48,174			Portugal	7,013	7,662	
Belgium	21,597			Nigeria	[2] 6,602		
British India	7,048	5,914	5,315	Spain	60,279	35,677	40,780
Canada	21,958	16,934	18,245	Sweden	10,319	9,383	
China	21,545	15,781	10,230	Switzerland	18,470	22,300	17,630
Denmark	10,407			United Kingdom	158,668	154,437	190,608
Egypt	19,613	17,077	15,472	United States	66,899	57,407	41,304
Finland	9,450	10,674	13,719	Other countries	53,529	41,245	
France	81,781	61,349	51,425				
Germany	182,775			Total	980,561	599,168	

Year beginning Apr. 1.   [2] Data for 1912.   [3] Year beginning Mar. 21.

APPLES.

Table 115.—*Apples: Production, and prices Dec. 1, by States, 1910–1916.*

State.	Production, barrels of 3 bushels (000 omitted).							Farm price per bushel (cents).						
	1910	1911	1912	1913	1914	1915	1916	1910	1911	1912	1913	1914	1915	1916
Maine	1,183	2,267	1,800	1,000	2,467	720	1,680	80	55	50	100	53	89	75
New Hampshire	600	533	733	267	667	353	532	80	79	55	113	53	90	90
Vermont	900	750	867	233	1,067	324	1,104	92	78	79	123	57	94	90
Massachusetts	967	1,000	1,100	767	1,467	885	1,150	90	89	76	134	65	90	99
Rhode Island	100	133	100	100	133	59	87	89	62	82	116	65	108	107
Connecticut	600	800	567	700	833	511	610	80	70	75	94	65	97	100
New York	5,667	13,000	14,667	6,500	16,533	8,528	12,600	100	59	50	95	45	78	75
New Jersey	567	1,033	567	700	1,133	777	750	78	60	72	85	55	80	100
Pennsylvania	3,867	6,833	4,233	3,400	7,700	5,085	6,207	75	54	70	89	50	71	80
Delaware	117	100	140	60	167	122	83	....	85	82	117	58	70	100
Maryland	900	867	883	433	1,167	800	848	65	52	60	100	41	63	80
Virginia	4,033	2,400	5,000	1,733	5,100	4,392	4,433	80	74	60	86	46	63	78
West Virginia	2,367	2,600	3,433	333	4,133	2,513	3,344	78	71	55	130	49	64	76
North Carolina	2,400	1,200	1,200	1,000	3,000	1,972	2,358	98	88	75	95	49	75	80
South Carolina	247	157	200	87	267	221	196	100	126	100	145	85	117	125
Georgia	467	267	467	300	667	625	541	105	118	101	108	80	90	117
Ohio	1,967	6,233	3,533	1,600	4,433	5,984	2,867	93	54	67	110	63	55	100
Indiana	1,633	2,967	1,400	2,200	1,433	3,883	1,307	90	68	84	88	70	53	120
Illinois	267	3,533	1,933	2,733	1,233	4,716	1,616	115	68	79	94	84	47	115
Michigan	1,400	4,100	5,733	2,967	5,733	3,150	4,160	102	70	50	82	49	74	87
Wisconsin	133	1,000	667	1,333	733	1,473	878	112	93	88	95	90	75	110
Minnesota	50	433	233	600	233	412	422	162	102	98	105	90	102	145
Iowa	67	3,167	500	2,367	533	3,220	1,575	130	81	101	112	97	70	145
Missouri	2,533	3,867	6,400	2,633	4,167	6,287	2,700	85	70	53	93	71	51	105
South Dakota	10	80	67	107	67	100	116	150	114	104	145	117	115	150
Nebraska	467	1,200	933	767	400	1,267	567	98	83	88	108	96	66	140
Kansas	2,200	800	2,233	900	1,033	2,125	1,040	78	100	71	110	95	76	130
Kentucky	1,767	2,033	3,200	2,300	3,000	4,170	2,147	100	92	85	92	78	69	113
Tennessee	1,733	967	2,967	1,300	2,867	2,025	1,772	92	104	81	106	75	81	107
Alabama	333	233	400	300	533	532	380	90	130	100	115	94	95	140
Mississippi	110	80	150	123	167	141	116	125	122	106	112	95	105	120
Texas	133	67	167	100	167	187	156	130	128	115	130	108	100	135
Oklahoma	400	350	567	367	500	780	275	107	120	92	122	90	94	145
Arkansas	900	1,000	1,700	1,333	1,667	1,183	1,018	105	115	92	102	83	70	100
Montana	140	300	300	280	300	347	256	120	115	103	142	76	70	110
Wyoming	3	7	10	10	....	....	....	....	....	....	150	138	145	180
Colorado	500	900	1,033	1,100	1,500	693	735	115	122	80	108	70	70	94
New Mexico	113	227	250	217	300	273	119	140	119	120	128	98	87	160
Arizona	33	37	43	30	32	40	46	191	195	204	217	186	170	182
Utah	137	153	227	203	267	142	33	130	110	89	96	63	95	160
Nevada	53	33	87	53	67	40	16	145	151	124	132	125	135	175
Idaho	417	400	550	467	567	573	147	99	112	85	98	78	85	114
Washington	1,933	1,167	2,567	2,300	2,767	2,433	3,225	80	118	70	93	64	80	80
Oregon	1,267	500	1,367	1,167	1,200	1,043	1,285	100	111	69	85	81	75	85
California	1,533	1,567	1,900	1,000	2,000	1,563	1,918	82	92	90	117	76	-85	98
United States	47,213	71,340	78,407	48,470	84,400	76,670	67,415	89.6	72.1	66.3	98.1	59.4	69.0	91.8

APPLES—Continued.

TABLE 116.—*Approximate relative production of principal varieties of apples, expressed as percentages of a normal crop of all apples.*

Variety.	United States.	Maine.	New York.	Pennsylvania.	Virginia.	West Virginia.	Ohio.	Michigan.	Illinois.	Missouri.	Kentucky.	Arkansas.	Washington.	Oregon.	California.
	P.ct.	P.ct.	P.ct.	P.ct.	P.ct.	P.ct.	P.ct.	P.ct.	P.ct.	P.ct.	P.ct.	P.ct.	P.ct.	P.ct.	P.ct.
Arkansas (Mammoth Black Twig)	0.7	0.2	....	0.3	3.1	0.7	0.6	0.0	0.6	1.1	0.9	2.3	0.3	....	0.3
Arkansas Black	.9	....	....	.2	.7	.8	.1	....	.9	1.5	3.0	3.0	2.3	1.1	1.0
Baldwin	13.4	34.5	31.3	17.8	2.8	5.8	15.1	17.0	2.7	1.5	2.9	.4	7.8	12.6	3.2
Ben Davis	13.3	9.8	5.0	6.0	11.4	15.7	13.9	8.5	37.8	34.2	16.8	44.1	7.4	4.9	3.9
Early Harvest (Prince's Harvest)	2.8	.9	.9	3.1	4.7	3.9	3.7	1.8	2.2	2.8	6.4	2.0	.8	.7	.7
Fall Pippin	1.7	.7	1.7	3.1	1.8	1.5	1.8	1.6	1.1	.4	2.4	.7	.8	.8	.6
Fameuse (Snow)	1.3	3.5	2.4	.6	.1	.0	.6	3.0	1.5	.4	.0	.1	.3	.2	.0
Gano	1.6	.3	.2	.8	.6	1.6	1.3	.3	3.8	6.5	.2	6.6	.8	1.0	.2
Golden Russet	1.4	1.7	2.0	2.5	.3	1.6	.9	3.7	.7	.3	1.0	.1	.3	.6	.1
Gravenstein	1.1	2.3	.9	1.0	.1	.1	.3	.1	.1	.1	.0	....	4.1	7.3	8.9
Grimes (Grimes Golden)	2.2	.2	.1	2.6	2.6	4.6	5.0	1.2	4.9	3.6	2.6	2.1	1.6	.4	.1
Horse (Yellow Horse)	.9	....	....	....	1.0	.0	.0	.0	.2	.5	2.1	1.5	....	.1	....
Jonathan	3.6	.8	.4	1.4	1.0	1.7	1.8	2.2	9.3	10.4	2.5	3.7	13.8	4.4	1.7
Limbertwig (Red Limbertwig)	1.6	.0	.0	....	2.5	.8	.3	0	.6	1.5	4.0	5.8	....	.2	.3
McIntosh (McIntosh Red)	.9	3.7	1.6	.7	.1	.1	.1	.3	.4	.1	.1	....	.3	.1	.1
Maiden Blush	2.0	.3	1.0	3.0	1.5	2.5	4.5	2.6	2.3	2.8	4.5	1.0	.3	.2	.4
Missouri (Missouri Pippin)	.8	.0	.0	.0	.2	.1	.1	.1	1.2	3.0	.5	1.4	.5	.1	.8
Northern Spy	6.1	7.1	13.1	11.4	.8	4.2	7.7	17.9	1.4	1.1	1.4	.5	3.8	7.4	.6
Northwestern Greening	.9	.3	.9	.4	.0	.4	.6	1.9	.3	.3	.4	....	1.0	.1	.2
Oldenburg (Duchess of Oldenburg)	1.9	2.9	2.2	1.1	.1	.5	1.0	5.0	1.7	.5	.1	....	1.1	.3	.1
Red Astrachan	1.9	3.9	2.1	3.5	.8	2.1	2.7	2.8	.8	.8	.3	.5	1.7	2.2	3.3
Red June (Carolina Red June)	1.6	....	.7	.3	1.8	1.3	.2	.0	1.2	1.9	4.3	2.7	1.3	1.3	1.4
Rhode Island Greening (Greening)	4.7	4.1	14.8	5.5	.3	1.4	5.7	5.4	.8	.3	.2	.6	2.2	2.6	2.7
Rome Beauty	3.1	.1	.3	2.1	1.2	18.7	10.8	.2	3.8	1.7	9.6	1.8	12.2	5.6	2.4
Stayman Winesap	1.5	.6	.1	1.8	5.3	1.9	1.3	.1	.5	1.8	1.9	1.7	2.7	1.8	.9
Tolman (Talman Sweet)	1.0	2.6	2.1	1.1	.1	.4	.5	2.4	.3	.2	.3	....	.9	....	.0
Tompkins King (King of Tompkins Co.)	1.4	2.4	4.1	1.5	.0	.5	.6	2.1	.1	.1	.0	....	2.7	5.1	1.1
Wealthy	2.2	5.4	1.8	1.2	.0	1.1	1.2	3.7	1.6	1.3	.4	.1	1.5	1.1	.1
White Pearmain (White Winter Pearmain)	.5	....	.1	.0	.2	.2	.1	.0	.2	.3	.3	.1	.6	.5	7.5
Winesap	5.1	.5	.1	1.8	20.7	1.8	1.8	.4	5.6	6.8	14.0	8.4	7.1	2.9	1.4
Wolf River	.9	1.4	.3	.3	.2	.6	.5	1.5	.4	.7	.3	....	.8	1.7	.1
Yellow Bellflower	1.4	1.7	.3	2.3	.2	1.5	1.3	1.2	.5	1.0	.6	.1	1.9	3.4	18.6
Yellow Newtown (Albemarle; Newtown Pippin)	1.6	.0	.2	.6	7.0	.3	.4	.3	.2	.1	.2	....	2.9	11.3	28.7
Yellow Transparent	1.5	1.1	.3	1.7	1.5	3.2	2.1	1.4	2.1	1.1	3.2	.4	1.5	1.6	.2
York Imperial (Johnson Fine Winter)	2.1	....	.1	7.5	15.1	5.0	1.3	.3	.8	1.1	.1	.1	.2	.9	.1
Other varieties	10.4	7.0	8.9	12.8	10.2	13.4	10.1	11.0	7.4	8.2	12.5	8.2	12.5	15.5	8.2
Total	100.0	100.0	100.0	100.0	100.0	100.0	100.0	100.0	100.0	100.0	100.0	100.0	100.0	100.0	100.0

NOTE.—In important apple-producing States not included in table, the principal varieties and their respective percentages of all apples in a normal crop are:

Indiana.—Ben Davis 22.8, Baldwin 7.2, Grimes Golden 6.7, Winesap 6.7, Maiden Blush 5.8, Rome Beauty 4.4, Northern Spy 4.2. *North Carolina.*—Limbertwig 14.3, Winesap 12.2, Ben Davis 7.5, Early Harvest 7.2, Horse 7.2, Red June 5.9. *Tennessee.*—Winesap 14.1, Ben Davis 12.2, Limbertwig 12.1, Early Harvest 8.4, Horse 6.3, Red June 5.4. *Iowa.*—Ben Davis 15.2, Wealthy 12.4, Jonathan 10.3, Oldenburg 8.9, Grimes Golden 4.9, Northwestern Greening 4.3. *Kansas.*—Ben Davis 19.4, Winesap 15.3, Jonathan 13.8, Missouri Pippin 8.6, Gano 6.0, Maiden Blush 4.3. *Colorado.*—Ben Davis 26.3, Jonathan 18.3, Gano 7.8, Rome Beauty 4.8, Winesap 4.1. *Massachusetts.*—Baldwin 48.4, Rhode Island Greening 9.3, Gravenstein 5.7, McIntosh Red 5.7, Northern Spy 5.1. *Nebraska.*—Ben Davis 21.3, Winesap 13.6, Jonathan 9.4, Wealthy 6.2, Oldenburg 5.8, Grimes Golden 4.8, Missouri Pippin 4.2, Gano 4.0. *Wisconsin.*—Oldenburg 14.7, Wealthy 13.7, Northwestern Greening 11.1, Fameuse (Snow) 8.0, Wolf River 7.5, Ben Davis 5.1, Golden Russet 4.2. *Maryland.*—Ben Davis 17.0, York Imperial 16.2, Baldwin 8.8, Winesap 7.6, Stayman Winesap 7.0, Arkansas 4.4, Early Harvest 4.2. *New Jersey.*—Baldwin 25.2, Ben Davis 14.5, Rome Beauty 5.0, Early Harvest 4.7, Rhode Island Greening 4.3, Northern Spy 4.2. *Vermont.*—Baldwin 15.1, Rhode Island Greening 12.8, Northern Spy 12.0, Fameuse (Snow) 8.1, McIntosh 6.1, Ben Davis 5.6, Yellow Bellflower 4.2. *Connecticut.*—Baldwin 42.2, Rhode Island Greening 16.9, Golden Russet 5.2. *New Hampshire.*—Baldwin 51.9, Rhode Island Greening 5.9, Northern Spy 5.2, McIntosh 4.4. *Idaho.*—Jonathan 21.3, Rome Beauty 16.6, Ben Davis 13.1, Gano 7.8, Winesap 4.6. *Oklahoma.*—Ben Davis 25.8, Missouri Pippin 12.1, Jonathan 8.2, Winesap 8.1, Arkansas Black 5.6, Gano 4.0. *Georgia.*—Horse 14.3 ,Ben Davis 12.2, Red June 10.0, Limbertwig 8.8, Winesap 7.6, Early Harvest 6.1, Arkansas Black 4.6.

PEACHES.

TABLE 117.—*Peaches: Production, and prices Sept. 15, by States, 1910–1916.*

State.	Production, bushels (000 omitted).							Farm price per bushel (cents).						
	1910	1911	1912	1913	1914	1915	1916	1910	1911	1912	1913	1914	1915	1916
New Hampshire	56	.....	.....	44	3	58	24	.....	.....	.....	190	.....	150	200
Massachusetts	68	97	51	105	31	152	66	.....	275	220	180	180	130	226
Rhode Island	18	22	16	29	14	29	14	.....	.....	.....	175	170	103	148
Connecticut	291	249	128	263	142	335	134	.....	200	221	147	175	96	190
New York	1,762	1,536	1,400	1,742	530	2,106	1,238	137	142	160	140	160	90	140
New Jersey	810	440	638	483	1,140	1,275	689	128	175	135	150	98	70	160
Pennsylvania	1,533	1,006	660	922	1,541	2,044	1,069	137	180	186	180	125	80	150
Delaware	810	249	521	312	608	842	346	.....	.....	150	125	95	39	150
Maryland	1,080	492	672	480	1,032	1,248	600	91	138	140	105	98	35	150
Virginia	1,075	318	1,058	312	911	1,358	660	99	138	96	150	100	80	128
West Virginia	598	230	788	132	886	1,164	520	112	154	112	210	105	75	150
North Carolina	1,955	437	2,093	598	1,863	1,955	897	85	124	93	120	95	90	138
South Carolina	1,204	649	1,020	405	1,166	864	545	102	128	105	125	110	100	105
Georgia	5,395	2,145	6,175	1,950	5,785	5,330	3,510	102	140	101	130	100	100	155
Florida	178	126	190	112	188	177	119	100	150	100	.....	100	75	200
Ohio	1,239	1,735	1,055	931	1,653	2,448	1,350	160	140	144	200	140	97	155
Indiana	703	1,147	185	1,276	1,128	648	888	137	118	169	130	110	120	135
Illinois	140	2,310	82	1,998	1,755	874	780	165	84	146	115	105	110	150
Michigan	1,215	2,228	700	1,539	1,247	2,360	2,010	139	111	165	150	140	97	124
Iowa	16	240	24	632	472	112	64	217	152	133	135	135	150	200
Missouri	1,440	2,700	900	4,320	3,780	3,300	1,080	108	98	107	93	90	85	105
Nebraska	150	36	240	210	192	120	30	133	125	156	150	150	140	225
Kansas	2,432	851	2,016	875	1,760	2,442	150	105	124	100	150	120	100	180
Kentucky	770	770	1,210	1,430	1,980	1,320	880	121	109	94	90	75	95	110
Tennessee	1,440	360	2,820	1,140	2,640	2,460	1,080	92	125	77	110	78	80	95
Alabama	1,980	840	2,760	1,140	2,310	2,640	1,110	85	100	100	100	100	90	100
Mississippi	1,340	460	1,800	1,020	1,440	1,540	975	98	121	96	98	85	83	88
Louisiana	488	190	693	460	356	456	567	100	83	150	110	100	88	75
Texas	3,400	1,204	4,140	2,107	1,196	4,081	2,860	106	148	97	120	140	87	100
Oklahoma	1,460	656	2,121	860	220	2,408	230	95	128	68	120	130	57	120
Arkansas	2,000	2,346	4,524	3,120	3,180	5,940	2,340	100	107	78	90	87	63	87
Colorado	346	363	1,035	360	1,025	650	405	180	175	100	124	60	125	125
New Mexico	50	86	84	52	106	154	40	128	85	137	150	130	65	170
Arizona	42	51	54	57	60	60	60	.....	225	215	200	175	.....	200
Utah	195	208	323	284	380	212	84	140	183	106	115	71	95	125
Nevada	2	10	10	8	9	7	1	.....	.....	.....	.....	.....	120	.....
Idaho	60	81	112	92	120	162	25	.....	154	134	120	100	70	165
Washington	348	320	445	446	486	566	415	90	106	76	110	96	80	96
Oregon	317	190	292	311	387	432	276	137	174	133	130	110	84	100
California	9,765	7,412	9,308	7,150	10,387	9,768	8,808	103	111	94	182	80	55	80
United States	48,171	34,880	52,343	39,707	54,109	64,097	36,939	107.9	122.1	102.0	131.6	97.7	80.0	114.0

HOPS.

TABLE 118.—*Hops: Area and production of undermentioned countries, 1913–1915.*

Country.	Area.			Production.		
	1913	1914	1915	1913	1914	1915
NORTH AMERICA.	*Acres.*	*Acres.*	*Acres.*	*Pounds.*	*Pounds.*	*Pounds.*
United States [1]	(2)	(2)	(2)	62,898,718	43,415,352	59,320,295
Canada	[3] 1,164	(2)	(2)	[3] 1,208,450	(2)	(2)
Total				64,107,168		

[1] Commercial movement for years beginning July 1.   [2] No official statistics.   [3] Census of 1910.

HOPS—Continued.

TABLE 118.—*Hops: Area and production of undermentioned countries, 1913–1915*—Con.

Country.	Area.			Production.		
	1913	1914	1915	1913	1914	1915
EUROPE.						
Austria-Hungary:	*Acres.*	*Acres.*	*Acres.*	*Pounds.*	*Pounds.*	*Pounds.*
Austria....................	50,149	[1] 45,664	([2])	19,102,859	[1] 36,252,442	17,857,260
Hungary...................	5,444	([2])	([2])	4,623,928	([2])	2,755,750
Croatia-Slavonia..........	751	([2])	....	292,991	([2])	([2])
Total....................	56,344	....	([2])	24,019,778	....	....
Belgium....................	5,943	6,140	([2])	7,395,331	7,560,000	([2])
France.....................	7,292	6,748	6,511	8,028,492	7,034,438	5,363,130
Germany...................	66,836	68,410	58,654	23,408,222	51,227,408	32,106,251
Russia.....................	([2])	([2])	([2])	16,973,016	14,083,992	([2])
United Kingdom: England....	35,676	36,661	34,744	28,631,792	56,812,896	28,516,208
Total....................	....	....	....	108,456,631	172,971,176	....
AUSTRALASIA.						
Australia:						
Victoria................	131	117	([2])	155,344	107,632	([2])
South Australia...........	5	3	([2])	2,240	4,480	([2])
Tasmania.................	1,247	1,353	([2])	1,920,576	1,554,560	([2])
Total....................	1,383	1,473	([2])	2,078,160	1,666,672	....
Grand total............	....	....	....	174,641,959	....	....

[1] Galicia and Bukowina not included.   [2] No official statistics.

TABLE 119.—*Hops: Total production of countries named in Table 118, 1895–1915.*

Year.	Production.	Year.	Production.	Year.	Production.
	Pounds.		*Pounds.*		*Pounds.*
1895...............	204,894,000	1902..............	170,063,000	1909..............	128,173,000
1896...............	168,509,000	1903..............	174,457,000	1910..............	188,951,000
1897...............	189,219,000	1904..............	178,802,000	1911..............	163,810,000
1898...............	166,100,000	1905..............	277,260,000	1912..............	224,493,000
1899...............	231,563,000	1906..............	180,998,000	1913..............	174,642,000
1900...............	174,683,000	1907..............	215,923,000	1914..............	....
1901...............	201,902,000	1908..............	230,220,000	1915..............	....

TABLE 120.—*Hops: Wholesale price per pound, 1912–1916.*

Date.	New York.		Cincinnati.		Chicago.		San Francisco.					
	Choice State.		Prime.[1]		Pacific coast, good to choice.		Sacramento Valley, choice.		Willamette Valley, choice.[2]		Eastern Washington,[3] choice.	
	Low.	High.	Low.	High.	Low.	High.	Low.	High.	Low.	High.	Low.	High.
	Cts.	*Cts.*	*Cts.*	*Cts.*	*Cts.*	*Cts.*	*Cts.*	*Cts.*	*Cts.*	*Cts.*	*Cts.*	*Cts.*
1912.												
Jan.-June...............	37	56	41	49	40	50	40	50	38	50	36	50
July-Dec................	22	42	22½	34	20	30	17	20½	18½	21	18½	21
1913.												
Jan.-June...............	17	32	18	23	15	24	18	20	19	21	19	21
July-Dec................	17	48	18	32	17	31	18	28	18	30	19	30
1914.												
Jan.-June...............	36	48	21	27½	18	27	16	28	16	30	16	30
July-Dec................	23	50	13½	22	13	22	10	19	11	20	10	20

[1] Choice 1912–1913.
[2] 1912 quotations are for all grades.   Called "Oregon" hops in 1916.
[3] Called "Washington" hops in 1916.

HOPS—Continued.

TABLE 120.—*Hops: Wholesale price per pound, 1912–1916*—Continued.

Date.	New York.		Cincinnati.		Chicago.		San Francisco.					
	Choice State.		Prime.		Pacific coast, good to choice.		Sacramento Valley, choice.		Willamette Valley, choice.[1]		Eastern Washington,[2] choice.	
	Low.	High.	Low.	High.	Low.	High.	Low.	High.	Low.	High.	Low.	High.
1915.	*Cts.*	*Cts.*	*Cts.*	*Cts.*	*Cts.*	*Cts.*	*Cts.*	*Cts.*	*Cts.*	*Cts.*	*Cts.*	*Cts.*
January	21	25	17	17	12	15	11½	12½	12	13	11	12
February	16	23	16½	16½	12	16	11½	14	12	15	11	14
March	16	17	17	17	12	16	13	15	14	16	13	15
April	15	17	17	17	12	18	9	15	10	16	10	15
May	13	15	17	17	11	15	9	10	10	11	10	11
June	13	14	16	16	10	13	9	10	10	11	10	11
Jan.-June	13	25	16	17	10	18	9	15	10	16	10	15
July	13	14	16	16	10	14	9	[3] 12	10	[3] 12½	10	[3] 12
August	13	14	16	16	12	16	11½	14	11½	16	11	15
September	13	[3] 30	16	16	12	16	13	14	15	16	14	15
October	28	30	15½	15½	12	15	9	14	11	16	10	15
November	28	30	15½	15½	12	16	8	11	11	13	10	13
December	26	30	16	16	12	16	7½	11	10	13	10	13
July-Dec	13	30	15½	16	10	16	7½	14	10	16	10	15
1916.												
January	24	27	......	......	14	16	7½	11	9	12½	9	12½
February	24	25	......	......	14	16	8	11	10	12½	10	12½
March	22	23	......	......	15	17	8	11	10	12½	10	12½
April	19	23	......	......	15	17	8	11	10	12½	10	12½
May	18	20	......	......	14	16	8	11	10	12½	10	12½
June	20	22	......	......	14	16	8	11	10	12½	10	12½
Jan.-June	18	27	......	......	14	17	7½	11	9	12½	9	12½
July	16	21	......	......	14	16	8	11	10	12½	10	12½
August	15	18	......	......	13	15	8	11	10	12½	10	12½
September	[3] 28	55	......	......	12	14	8	14	7	14	8	13
October	[3] 53	55	......	......	14	18	13	14	13	14	12	13
November	49	53	......	......	11	17	10	14	9	11	8	14
December	47	50	......	......	10	16	10	14	9	11	7	14
July-Dec	15	55	......	......	10	18	8	14	7	14	8	13

[1] Called "Oregon" hops in 1916. [2] Called "Washington" hops in 1916. [3] New crop.

TABLE 121.—*Hops: International trade, calendar years 1913–1915.*

[Lupulin and *hopfenmehl* (hop meal) are not included with hops in the data shown. See "General note," Table 10.]

EXPORTS.

[000 omitted.]

Country.	1913	1914 (prelim.).	1915 (prelim.).	Country.	1913	1914 (prelim.).	1915 (prelim.).
	Pounds.	*Pounds.*	*Pounds.*		*Pounds.*	*Pounds.*	*Pounds.*
Austria-Hungary	15,306	....	....	Russia	3,873	254	289
Belgium	5,908	....	....	United Kingdom	1,263	1,117	928
France	340	212	1,259	United States	25,701	11,056	20,865
Germany	14,299	....	....	Other countries	306	44	....
Netherlands	2,704	1,301	....				
New Zealand	498	389	486	Total	70,198	14,373	....

IMPORTS.

Country.	1913	1914 (prelim.).	1915 (prelim.).	Country.	1913	1914 (prelim.).	1915 (prelim.).
Australia	1,511	1,058	....	Netherlands	4,085	3,287	....
Austria-Hungary	1,150	....	....	Russia	1,165	235	....
Belgium	6,975	....	....	Sweden	1,018	1,428	....
British India	162	118	141	Switzerland	1,125	1,420	967
British South Africa	484	442	458	United Kingdom	27,562	9,362	22,327
Canada	1,723	1,613	955	United States	7,313	7,483	6,767
Denmark	751	....	....	Other countries	4,929	3,147	....
France	4,655	2,358	102				
Germany	5,541	....	....	Total	70,149	31,951	....

BEANS.

TABLE 122.—*Beans: Area and production of undermentioned countries, 1913–1915.*

Country.	Area.			Production.		
	1913	1914	1915	1913	1914	1915
NORTH AMERICA.	*Acres.*	*Acres.*	*Acres.*	*Bushels.*	*Bushels.*	*Bushels.*
United States..............	[1] 80?,000	(²)	(²)	[1]11,251,000	(²)	(²)
Canada:						
Nova Scotia............	1,000	1,000	1,000	22,000	18,000	15,000
New Brunswick.........	(³)	(³)	(³)	4,000	6,000	6,000
Quebec...............	5,000	5,000	5,000	97,000	89,000	103,000
Ontario...............	40,000	28,000	37,000	670,000	684,000	600,000
British Columbia........	(³)	(³)	....	8,000	....	....
Total Canada..........	47,000	44,000	43,000	801,000	797,000	703,000
SOUTH AMERICA.						
Argentina....................	65,000	72,000	(²)	(²)	(²)	(²)
Chile......................	85,000	76,000	(²)	1,551,000	1,377,000	1,876,000
EUROPE.						
Austria-Hungary:						
Austria [4]...............	664,000	[5] 265,000	(²)	8,725,000	[5] 4,989,000	(²)
Hungary [6]..............	28,000	(²)	(²)	393,000	(²)	(²)
Do. [7].................	1,471,000	(²)	(²)	7,865,000	(²)	(²)
Croatia-Slavonia [6]........	24,000	(²)	(²)	337,000	(²)	(²)
Do [7].................	411,000	(²)	(²)	1,760,000	(²)	(²)
Total Austria-Hungary..	2,598,000	....	....	19,080,000	....	....
Belgium [8]...................	20,000	(²)	(²)	514,000	(²)	(²)
Bulgaria [8].................	212,000	(²)	(²)	2,482,000	(²)	(²)
Denmark [4]...............	[8] 10,000	(²)	7,000	255,000	211,000	192,000
France...................	583,000	547,000	(²)	10,235,000	9,354,000	....
Italy.....................	2,838,000	2,705,000	2,702,000	23,159,000	16,997,000	24,629,000
Luxemburg...............	3,000	(²)	(²)	61,000	(²)	(²)
Netherlands..............	60,000	59,000	58,000	1,821,000	1,946,000	(²)
Roumania [6]	108,000	161,000	186,000	1,303,000	2,122,000	1,793,000
Do. [7].................	1,366,000	1,409,000	1,455,000	4,454,000	3,666,000	3,573,000
Russia: [9]						
Russia proper.............	1,111,000	1,175,000	1,157,000	12,199,000	8,482,000	8,304,000
Poland..................	25,000	(²)	(²)	439,000	(²)	(²)
Northern Caucasia........	6,000	9,000	(²)	79,000	94,000	(²)
Total European Russia..	1,142,000	....	....	12,717,000	....	....
Serbia....................	(²)	(²)	(²)	(²)	(²)	(²)
Spain....................	1,139,000	1,149,000	1,194,000	11,737,000	12,527,000	13,217,000
Sweden..................	5,000	6,000	(²)	164,000	75,000	148,000
United Kingdom:						
England.................	258,000	283,000	257,000	7,517,000	8,907,000	7,353,000
Wales..................	1,000	1,000	1,000	31,000	36,000	29,000
Scotland...............	6,000	6,000	5,000	230,000	243,000	201,000
Ireland................	1,000	1,000	1,000	64,000	57,000	42,000
Total United Kingdom..	266,000	291,000	264,000	7,842,000	9,243,000	7,625,000
ASIA.						
India:						
British [4]..................	11,707,000	8,950,000	13,757,000	[10]124,096,000	[10]69,888,000	[10]141,755,000
Native States............	3,522,000	(²)	(²)	(²)	(²)	(²)
Total India.............	15,229,000	....	....	....	....	....
Japan....................	1,618,000	1,570,000	(²)	20,906,000	25,927,000	(²)
Formosa [4]................	86,000	92,000	(²)	703,000	681,000	(²)
Russia (9 governments).......	3,000	3,000	(²)	18,000	36,000	(²)
AFRICA.						
Algeria...................	(²)	(²)	(²)	(²)	(²)	(²)
Egypt....................	496,000	445,000	647,000	(²)	(²)	(²)

[1] Census for 1909.
[2] No official statistics.
[3] Less than 500 acres.
[4] Includes other pulse.
[5] Galicia and Bukowina not included.
[6] Grown alone.
[7] Grown with corn.
[8] 1912 figures.
[9] Includes lentils.
[10] Incomplete.

BEANS—Continued.

TABLE 122.—*Beans: Area and production of undermentioned countries, 1913–1915*—Con.

Country.	Area.			Production.		
	1913	1914	1915	1913	1914	1915
AUSTRALASIA.						
Australia:[1]	*Acres.*	*Acres.*	*Acres.*	*Pounds.*	*Pounds.*	*Pounds.*
Queensland	([2])	([2])	([2])	2,000	1,000	([3])
New South Wales	([2])	([2])	([2])	16,000	10,000	([3])
Victoria	12,000	13,000		240,000	234,000	([3])
South Australia	9,000	9,000	10,000	134,000	112,000	17,000
Western Australia	1,000	2,000	2,000	8,000	7,000	6,000
Tasmania	17,000	15,000	([3])	476,000	304,000	([3])
Total Australia	40,000	39,000		876,000	668,000	

[1] Includes peas.   [2] Less than 500 acres.   [3] No official statistics.

TABLE 123.—*Beans: Wholesale price per bushel, 1912–1916.*

Date.	Boston. Pea.		Chicago. Pea.		Detroit. Pea.		San Francisco. Small white (per 100 lbs.).	
	Low.	High.	Low.	High.	Low.	High.	Low.	High.
1912.	*Dolls.*	*Dolls.*	*Dolls.*	*Dolls.*	*Dolls.*	*Dolls.*	*Dolls.*	*Dolls.*
Jan.–June	2.55	3.05	2.35	2.98	2.32	2.70	4.00	4.75
July–Dec	2.55	3.10	1.90	3.20	2.15	2.70	4.00	4.80
1913.								
Jan.–June	2.35	2.60	1.25	2.50	1.80	2.20	4.50	5.85
July–Dec	2.15	2.40	1.15	2.25	1.75	2.05	4.50	5.85
1914.								
Jan.–June	2.10	2.35	1.60	2.30	1.80	2.10	4.75	5.50
July–Dec	2.15	3.10	1.95	3.10	1.85	2.90	4.00	6.00
1915.								
January	2.95	3.25	2.40	3.25	2.70	3.05	4.50	5.50
February	3.30	3.50	3.00	3.50	3.00	3.20	5.50	5.70
March	3.15	3.40	3.00	3.50	2.85	3.05	5.50	5.70
April	3.10	3.30	2.80	3.25	2.15	3.00	5.50	5.70
May	3.20	3.30	2.90	3.25	3.00	3.05	5.50	5.70
June	3.15	3.30	2.95	3.25	2.90	3.10	4.85	5.70
Jan.–June	2.95	3.50	2.40	3.50	2.70	3.10	4.50	5.70
July	3.00	3.15	2.62	3.25	2.65	2.90	4.85	4.85
August	2.85	3.15	2.62	3.00	2.60	3.00	4.50	4.85
September	3.20	3.30	2.62	3.25	2.95	3.10	4.50	4.60
October	3.10	3.90	2.75	4.00	3.15	3.50	4.60	5.50
November	3.75	4.10	3.25	4.10	3.30	3.60	5.50	6.15
December	3.95	4.10	3.70	4.10	3.55	3.60	6.10	6.40
July–Dec	2.85	4.10	2.62	4.10	2.60	3.60	4.50	6.40
1916.								
January	3.95	4.10	3.85	4.15	3.55	3.70	6.35	6.40
February	3.90	4.10	3.55	4.15	3.60	3.70	6.35	6.40
March	3.80	4.00	3.45	4.60	3.50	3.65	6.35	6.40
April	3.80	4.10	3.00	4.60	3.65	3.75	6.25	6.65
May	3.80	4.35	3.50	4.25	3.80	4.10	6.65	7.25
June	4.00	5.85	3.75	8.00	4.10	6.00	7.25	11.50
Jan.–June	3.80	5.85	3.00	8.00	3.50	6.00	6.25	11.50
July	5.00	6.50	5.00	8.00	5.50	7.00	10.00	11.00
August	4.50	6.00	5.00	7.00	5.50	5.75	7.50	10.00
September	4.50	5.75	5.00	6.25	4.90	5.75	8.00	8.50
October	4.50	6.75	5.40	6.25	4.90	6.50	7.50	9.50
November	6.75	7.25	6.50	7.50	6.00	6.75	9.50	10.50
December	6.50	7.25	6.40	7.50	5.75	6.40	10.50	10.50
July–Dec	4.50	7.25	5.00	8.00	4.90	7.00	7.50	11.00

PEAS.

TABLE 124.—*Peas: Area and production of undermentioned countries, 1913–1915.*

Country.	Area.			Production.		
	1913	1914	1915	1913	1914	1915
NORTH AMERICA.	*Acres.*	*Acres.*	*Acres.*	*Bushels.*	*Bushels.*	*Bushels.*
United States...............	[1] 1,305,000	(2)	(2)	[1] 7,129,000	(2)	(2)
Canada:						
Prince Edward Island.....	(3)	(3)	(3)	2,000	3,000	1,000
Nova Scotia...............	(3)	(3)	(3)	7,000	4,000	3,000
New Brunswick...........	1,000	(3)	(3)	11,000	10,000	7,000
Quebec...................	26,000	24,000	24,000	451,000	432,000	404,000
Ontario..................	190,000	179,000	169,000	3,431,000	2,864,000	3,007,000
Manitoba.................	(3)	(3)	(3)			
Saskatchewan.............	(3)	(3)	(3)	7,000	....	9,000
Alberta..................	(3)	(3)	(3)	8,000	8,000	9,000
British Columbia..........	1,000	1,000	1,000	35,000	41,000	39,000
Total Canada..........	219,000	206,000	196,000	3,952,000	3,362,000	3,479,000
SOUTH AMERICA.						
Chile [4]......................	35,000	27,000	(2)	501,000	373,000	(2)
EUROPE.						
Austria.....................	(5)	(5)	(5)	(5)	(5)	(5)
Hungary [6].................	30,000	(2)	(2)	426,000	(2)	(2)
Croatia-Slavonia [6].........	10,000	(2)	(2)	147,000	(2)	(2)
Belgium...................	[7] 12,000	(2)	(2)	[7] 400,000	(2)	(2)
France [6]...................	66,000	61,000	(2)	1,178,000	1,116,000	(2)
Italy [4]....................	(2)	(2)	(2)	4,167,000	3,698,000	3,020,000
Luxemburg [6]...............	2,000	(2)	(2)	28,000	(2)	(2)
Netherlands...............	68,000	65,000	61,000	1,488,000	1,871,000	(2)
Roumania [6]...............	61,000	56,000	45,000	1,076,000	869,000	755,000
Russia:						
Russia proper.............	2,265,000	2,183,000	1,792,000	26,930,000	17,329,000	12,744,000
Poland...................	367,000	(2)	(2)	5,776,000	(2)	(2)
Northern Caucasia........	5,000	5,000	3,000	82,000	72,000	72,000
Total Russia, European.	2,637,000	....	....	32,788,000	....	....
Serbia.....................	(2)	(2)	(2)	70,000	(2)	(2)
Spain [4]....................	1,244,000	1,268,000	1,346,000	9,298,000	11,016,000	11,382,000
Sweden....................	56,000	57,000	(2)	1,317,000	717,000	1,150,000
United Kingdom:						
England.................	127,000	129,000	98,000	3,470,000	3,063,000	2,461,000
Wales...................	(3)	(3)	(3)	10,000	10,000	8,000
Scotland................	(3)	(3)	(3)	5,000	5,000	3,000
Ireland.................	(3)	(3)	(3)	7,000	9,000	6,000
Total United Kingdom .	128,000	130,000	98,000	3,492,000	3,087,000	2,478,000
ASIA.						
Japan......................	106,000	121,000	(2)	1,935,000	2,168,000	(2)
Russia (9 Governments).......	75,000	82,000	(2)	775,000	995,000	(2)
AFRICA.						
Algeria.....................	[7] 26,000	(2)	(2)	[7] 277,000	....	....
AUSTRALASIA.						
Australia...................	(5)	(5)	(5)	(5)	(5)	(5)
New Zealand................	20,000	14,000	13,000	524,000	453,000	367,000

[1] Census for 1909.
[2] No official statistics.
[3] Less than 500 acres.
[4] Includes chick-peas, lentils, and vetches.
[5] Included under beans.
[6] Includes lentils.
[7] 1912 figures.

SUGAR.

TABLE 125.—*Sugar: Production in the United States and its possessions, 1856–57 to 1916–17.*[1]

[Data for 1912–13 and subsequently beet sugar, also Louisiana and Hawaii cane sugar, estimated by United States Department of Agriculture; Porto Rico, by Treasury Department of Porto Rico; Philippine Islands, exports for years ending June 30. For sources of data for earlier years, see Yearbook for 1912, p. 650. A short ton is 2,000 pounds.]

Year.	Beet sugar (chiefly refined).	Cane sugar (chiefly raw).					Total.
		Louisiana.	Other States.[2]	Porto Rico.	Hawaii.	Philippine Islands.[3]	
	Short tons.	*Short tons.*	*Short tons.*	*Short tons.*	*Short tons.*	*Short tons.*	*Short tons.*
Average:							
1856–7 to 1860–61	....	132,402	5,978	75,364	....	46,446	260,190
1861–62 to 1865–66	269	74,036	1,945	71,765	....	54,488	202,503
1866–67 to 1870–71	448	44,768	3,818	96,114	....	81,485	226,633
1871–72 to 1875–76	403	67,341	4,113	87,606	(4)	119,557	279,020
1876–77 to 1880–81	470	104,920	5,327	76,579	27,040	169,067	383,403
1881–82 to 1885–86	692	124,868	7,280	87,441	76,075	189,277	485,633
1886–87 to 1890–91	1,922	163,049	8,439	70,112	125,440	186,129	555,091
1891–92 to 1895–96	19,406	268,655	6,634	63,280	162,538	286,629	807,142
1896–97 to 1900–1901	58,287	282,399	4,405	61,292	282,585	134,722	823,690
1901–2 to 1905–6	239,730	352,053	12,126	141,478	403,308	108,978	1,257,673
1906–7 to 1910–11	479,153	348,544	13,664	282,136	516,041	145,832	1,785,370
1901–2	184,606	360,277	4,048	103,152	355,611	75,011	1,082,705
1902–3	218,406	368,734	4,169	100,576	437,991	123,108	1,252,984
1903–4	240,604	255,894	22,176	138,096	367,475	82,855	1,107,100
1904–5	242,113	398,195	16,800	151,188	426,248	125,271	1,359,715
1905–6	312,921	377,162	13,440	214,480	429,213	138,645	1,485,861
1906–7	483,612	257,600	14,560	206,864	440,017	132,602	1,535,255
1907–8	463,628	380,800	13,440	230,095	521,123	167,242	1,776,328
1908–9	425,884	397,600	16,800	277,093	535,156	123,876	1,776,409
1909–10	512,469	364,000	11,200	346,786	517,090	140,783	1,892,328
1910–11	510,172	342,720	12,320	349,840	566,821	164,658	1,946,531
1911–12	599,500	352,874	8,000	371,076	595,038	205,046	2,131,534
1912–13	692,556	153,573	9,000	398,004	546,524	234,000	2,033,657
1913–14	733,401	292,698	7,800	351,666	612,000	235,000	2,232,565
1914–15	722,054	242,700	3,920	346,490	646,000	206,000	2,167,164
1915–16	874,220	137,500	1,120	483,590	592.763	344,000	2,433,193
1916–17 (preliminary)	918,800	304,700	7,000	....	....	....	....

[1] Census returns give production of beet sugar for 1899 as 81,729 short tons; for 1904, 253,921; 1909, 501,682; production of cane sugar in Louisiana for 1839, 59,974 short tons; 1849, 226,001 hogsheads; 1859, 221,726 hogsheads; 1869, 80,706 hogsheads; 1879, 171,706 hogsheads; 1889, 146,062 short tons; 1898, 278,497 short tons; 1899, 159,583; and 1909, 325,516 short tons; cane sugar in other States, 1839, 491 short tons; in 1849, 21,576 hogsheads; in 1859, 9,256 hogsheads; in 1869, 6,337 hogsheads; in 1879, 7,166 hogsheads; in 1889, 4,580 short tons; in 1899, 1,691 and in 1909, 8,687 short tons.
[2] Includes Texas only, subsequent to 1902–3. Unofficial returns.
[3] Exports, for years ending June 30.
[4] Complete data not available for this period. Production in 1878–79, 1,254 short tons; in 1879–80, 1,304 short tons.

SUGAR—Continued.

TABLE 126.—*Sugar beets and beet sugar: Production in the United States, 1911–1916.*

[Figures for 1916 are based upon returns made before the end of the season, and are subject to revision.]

State and year.[1]	Number of factories.	Average length of campaign.	Sugar made (chiefly refined).	Sugar beets used.				Analysis of beets.		Recovery of sucrose.[4]		Loss.[5]
				Area harvested.	Average yield per acre.	Quantity worked.	Average price per ton.	Percentage of sucrose.[2]	Purity coefficient.[3]	Percentage of weight of beets.	Percentage of total sucrose in beets.	
	Number.	*Days.*	*Short tons.*	*Acres.*	*Short tons.*	*Short tons.*	*Dolls.*	*Per cent.*	*Per cent.*	*Per cent.*	*Per cent.*	*Per cent.*
California:												
1916............	11	.....	243,800	144,200	10.0	1,439,000	6.44	......	......	16.9	......	......
1915............	11	97	195,343	122,737	10.2	1,249,111	5.86	17.82	82.65	15.64	87.77	2.18
1914............	10	97	169,004	104,000	10.4	1,082,000	5.68	18.46	82.70	15.62	84.62	2.84
Colorado:												
1916............	14	.....	261,200	189,600	10.6	2,015,000	6.36	......	......	13.0	......	......
1915............	14	104	273,780	171,222	11.0	1,888,860	5.88	16.53	84.84	14.49	87.66	2.04
1914............	13	96	220,799	135,400	12.6	1,706,300	5.68	15.35	84.22	12.94	84.30	2.41
Idaho:												
1916............	5	.....	54,100	45,100	9.5	427,000	5.78	......	......	12.7	......	......
1915............	4	100	51,225	35,068	9.7	339,859	5.08	17.85	87.14	15.07	84.43	2.78
1914............	4	78	39,613	25,300	10.5	264,400	4.96	17.78	87.74	14.98	84.25	2.80
Michigan:												
1916............	15	.....	81,600	99,300	6.1	604,000	6.06	......	......	13.5	......	......
1915............	15	78	129,997	122,000	8.2	997,972	5.91	15.45	84.08	13.03	84.34	2.42
1914............	15	68	110,630	101,300	8.5	857,100	5.23	15.78	82.85	12.91	81.81	2.87
Ohio:												
1916............	4	.....	22,500	24,600	7.5	183,000	6.50	......	......	12.3	......	......
1915............	4	80	33,472	25,684	10.9	279,427	5.29	14.19	81.99	11.98	84.43	2.21
1914............	3	56	21,425	17,800	10.4	184,700	5.04	14.50	83.82	11.60	80.00	2.90
Utah:												
1916............	11	.....	116,400	72,700	13.0	941,000	5.67	......	......	12.4	......	......
1915............	8	96	85,014	56,226	11.2	629,204	4.91	16.43	85.06	13.51	82.23	2.92
1914............	7	100	78,619	41,300	13.7	564,600	4.79	17.03	85.60	13.92	81.74	3.11
Other States:												
1916[6].........	14	.....	139,200	104,500	10.2	1,062,000	6.07	......	......	13.1	......	......
1915............	11	84	105,389	78,364	9.8	765,860	5.67	16.38	84.24	13.76	84.00	2.62
1914............	8	76	81,964	58,300	10.8	629,500	5.67	15.80	83.35	13.02	82.40	2.78
United States:												
1916............	74	.....	918,800	680,000	9.81	6,671,000	6.17	......	......	13.8	......	......
1915............	67	92	874,220	611,301	10.1	6,150,293	5.67	16.49	84.38	14.21	86.17	2.28
1914............	60	85	722,054	483,400	10.9	5,288,500	5.45	16.38	83.89	13.65	83.33	2.73
1913............	71	85	733,401	580,006	9.76	5,659,462	5.69	15.78	83.22	12.96	82.13	2.82
1912............	73	86	692,556	555,300	9.41	5,224,377	5.82	16.31	84.49	13.26	81.12	3.05
1911............	66	94	599,500	473,877	10.68	5,062,333	5.50	15.89	82.21	11.84	74.51	4.05

[1] Acreage and production of beets are credited, as in former reports, to the State in which the beets were made into sugar.
[2] Based upon weight of beets.
[3] Percentage of sucrose (pure sugar) in the total soluble solids of the beets.
[4] Percentage of sucrose actually extracted by factories.
[5] Percentage of sucrose (based upon weight of beets) remaining in molasses and pulp.
[6] Includes 3 factories in Nebraska, 3 in Wisconsin, 2 in Wyoming, and 1 each in Indiana, Illinois, Minnesota, Kansas, Montana, and Oregon.

TABLE 127.—*Cane-sugar production of Louisiana, 1911–1916.*

[Figures for 1916 are from returns made before the end of the season, and are subject to revision.]

Year of cane harvest.	Factories in operation.	Sugar made.	Average sugar made, per ton of cane.	Cane used for sugar.			Molasses made.[1]	
				Area.	Average per acre.	Production.	Total.	Per ton of sugar.
	Number.	*Short tons.*	*Pounds.*	*Acres.*	*Short tons.*	*Short tons.*	*Gallons.*	*Gallons.*
1911............	188	352,874	120	310,000	19	5,887,292	35,062,525	99
1912............	126	153,573	142	197,000	11	2,162,574	14,302,169	93
1913............	153	292,698	139	248,000	17	4,214,000	24,046,320	82
1914............	149	242,700	152	213,000	15	3,199,000	17,177,443	71
1915............	136	137,500	135	183,000	11	2,018,000	12,743,000	93
1916............	148	304,700	146	......	......	4,172,000	......	......

[1] Figures for molasses, 1911–1914, are as reported by the Louisiana Sugar Planters' Association; figures for 1915 as reported by Bureau of Crop Estimates, U. S. Department of Agriculture.

SUGAR—Continued.

TABLE 128.—*Cane-sugar production of Hawaii, 1913–1916.*

Island, and year ending Sept. 30.	Factories in operation.	Average length of campaign.	Sugar made.	Cane used for sugar.			Total area in cane.	Average extraction of sugar.	
				Area harvested.	Average yield per acre.	Production.		Per cent of cane.	Per short ton of cane.
	Number.	*Days.*	*Short tons.*	*Acres.*	*Short tons.*	*Short tons.*	*Acres.*	*Per cent.*	*Pounds.*
Hawaii:									
1916	....	179	197,130	52,627	33	1,713,759	98,787	11.50	230
1915	....	196	240,300	50,800	41	2,099,000	100.200	11.45	229
1914	23	174	213,000	51,000	36	1,854,000	....	11.49	230
1913	24	170	197,212	53,600	32	1,703,000	....	11.58	232
Kauai:									
1916	....	191	108,632	21,392	43	927.970	51,712	11.71	234
1915	....	203	115,700	21,000	45	941,000	49,200	12.30	246
1914	9	214	121,000	21,600	50	1,089,000	....	11.11	222
1913	9	198	100,340	20,800	42	841,000	....	11.93	239
Maui:									
1916	....	168	150,311	19,911	55	1,098,247	51,897	13.69	274
1915	....	174	160,300	19,800	57	1,126,000	44,400	14.24	285
1914	7	167	145,000	19,400	54	1,054,000	....	13.76	275
1913	7	152	124,820	19,700	47	929,000	....	13.44	269
Oahu:									
1916	....	179	136,690	21,489	52	1,119,448	43,936	12.21	244
1915	....	205	129,700	21,600	47	1,019,000	46,000	12.73	255
1914	7	188	133,000	20,700	44	903,000	....	14.73	295
1913	10	157	124,152	20,500	49	1,003,000	....	12.38	248
Territory of Hawaii:									
1916	....	180	592,763	115,489	42	4,859.424	246,332	12.20	244
1915	....	195	646,000	113,200	46	5,185.000	239,800	12.46	249
1914	46	183	612,000	112,700	43	4,900,000	....	12.49	250
1913	50	169	546,524	114,600	39	4,476,000	....	12.21	244

TABLE 129.—*Sugar: Wholesale price per pound, on New York market, 1912–1916.*

Date.	Raw.				Refined.											
	Molasses. 89° polarization.		Centrifugal, 96° polarization.		Cut loaf.		Powdered.		Granulated, fine or standard.		Soft sugar No. 1.		Soft sugar No. 15.			
	Low.	High.	Low.	High.	Low.	High.	Low.	High.	Low.	High.	Low.	High.	Low.	High.		
	Cts.	*Cts.*	*Cts.*	*Cts.*	*Cts.*	*Cts.*	*Cts.*	*Cts.*	*Cts.*	*Cts.*	*Cts.*	*Cts.*	*Cts.*	*Cts.*		
1912.																
Jan.-June	3.33	4.30	3.83	4.80	5.80	6.65	5.10	5.90	5.00	5.85	4.85	5.65	4.25	5.05		
July-Dec	3.23	3.86	3.73	4.36	5.70	5.90	5.00	5.20	4.90	5.15	4.65	4.95	4.05	4.35		
1913.																
Jan.-June	2.75	3.23	3.25	3.73	5.05	5.70	4.35	5.00	4.25	4.95	4.00	4.65	3.40	4.05		
July-Dec	2.62	3.30	3.12	3.80	5.05	5.60	4.25	4.90	4.15	4.85	4.05	4.55	3.45	3.95		
1914.																
Jan.-June	2.27	2.98	2.92	3.48	5.05	5.25	3.95	4.40	3.85	4.35	3.60	4.10	3.00	3.50		
July-Dec	2.61	5.87	3.26	6.52	5.25	8.40	4.40	7.60	3.85	7.55	4.10	7.30	3.50	6.70		
1915.																
January	3.20	3.46	3.95	4.20	5.85	5.95	5.05	5.15	5.95	5.10	4.70	4.80	4.10	4.20		
February	3.45	4.27	4.20	5.02	5.95	6.65	5.15	5.85	5.05	5.80	4.80	5.50	4.20	4.90		
March	3.81	4.18	4.58	4.95	6.65	6.80	5.85	6.00	5.75	5.95	5.50	5.65	4.90	5.05		
April	3.84	4.12	4.61	4.89	6.80	6.90	6.00	6.10	5.90	6.05	5.65	5.75	5.05	5.15		
May	3.87	4.12	4.64	4.89	......	6.90	......	6.10	6.00	6.05	......	5.75	......	5.15		
June	4.12	4.18	4.89	4.95	6.90	7.00	6.10	6.20	6.00	6.15	5.75	5.85	5.15	5.25		
Jan.-June	3.20	4.27	3.95	5.02	5.85	7.00	5.05	6.20	5.05	6.15	4.70	5.85	4.10	5.25		
July	3.87	4.27	4.64	4.95	6.70	7.00	5.90	6.20	5.80	6.15	5.55	5.85	4.95	5.25		
August	3.62	4.18	4.39	4.95	6.50	6.70	5.70	5.90	5.60	5.85	5.35	5.55	4.75	4.95		
September	2.98	4.00	3.75	4.77	5.80	6.50	5.00	5.70	4.90	5.65	4.65	5.35	4.05	4.75		
October	2.73	3.68	3.50	4.45	5.80	6.15	5.00	5.35	4.90	5.30	4.65	5.00	4.05	4.40		
November	3.62	4.37	4.39	5.14	6.25	6.90	5.45	6.10	5.35	6.05	5.10	5.75	4.50	5.15		
December	3.68	4.43	4.45	5.20	6.85	7.05	6.05	6.25	5.95	6.20	5.70	5.90	5.10	5.30		
July-Dec	2.73	4.43	3.50	5.20	5.80	7.05	5.00	6.25	4.90	6.20	4.65	5.90	4.05	5.30		

SUGAR—Continued.

TABLE 129.—*Sugar: Wholesale price per pound, on New York market, 1912–1916*—Con.

Date.	Raw.				Refined.									
	Molasses. 89° polarization.		Centrifugal, 96° polarization.		Cut loaf.		Powdered.		Granulated, fine or standard.		Soft sugar No. 1.		Soft sugar No. 15.	
	Low.	High.	Low.	High.	Low.	High.	Low.	High.	Low.	High.	Low.	High.	Low.	High.
1916.	*Cts.*	*Cts.*	*Cts.*	*Cts.*	*Cts.*	*Cts.*	*Cts.*	*Cts.*	*Cts.*	*Cts.*	*Cts.*	*Cts.*	*Cts.*	*Cts.*
January	3.56	4.00	4.33	4.77	6.65	6.85	5.85	6.05	5.75	6.00	5.50	5.70	4.90	5.10
February	3.93	4.31	4.70	5.08	6.90	7.40	6.10	6.35	6.00	6.30	5.75	6.10	5.15	5.50
March	4.12	5.25	4.83	6.02	7.40	8.15	6.35	7.10	6.25	7.05	6.10	6.85	5.50	6.25
April	5.06	5.69	5.83	6.46	8.15	8.55	7.10	7.50	7.00	7.45	6.85	7.25	6.25	6.65
May	5.25	5.75	6.02	6.52	8.55	8.80	7.50	7.75	7.40	7.70	7.25	7.50	6.65	6.90
June	5.25	5.63	6.02	6.40	8.80	8.80	7.75	7.75	7.65	7.70	7.50	7.50	6.90	6.90
Jan.–June.	3.56	5.75	4.33	6.52	6.65	8.80	5.85	7.75	5.75	7.70	5.50	7.50	4.90	6.90
July	5.31	5.63	6.08	6.40	8.80	8.80	7.75	7.75	7.65	7.70	7.50	7.50	6.90	6.90
August	4.09	5.50	4.89	6.27	8.15	8.80	7.10	7.75	7.00	7.70	6.85	7.50	6.25	6.90
September	4.09	5.25	4.89	6.02	7.40	8.15	6.35	7.10	6.25	7.05	6.10	6.85	5.50	6.25
October	5.00	5.88	5.77	6.65	7.90	8.65	6.85	7.60	6.75	7.55	6.60	7.35	6.00	6.75
November	4.87	5.75	5.64	6.52	8.65	8.65	7.60	7.60	7.50	7.55	7.35	7.35	6.75	6.75
December	4.25	4.87	5.02	5.64	8.00	8.65	6.95	7.60	6.85	7.55	6.70	7.35	6.10	6.75
July–Dec.	4.09	5.88	4.89	6.65	7.40	8.80	6.35	7.75	6.25	7.70	6.10	7.50	5.50	6.90

TABLE 130.—*Sugar: International trade, calendar years 1913–1915.*

[The following kinds and grades have been included under the head of sugar: Brown, white, candied, caramel, *chancaca* (Peru), crystal cube, maple, muscovado, *panela*. The following have been excluded: "Candy" (meaning confectionery), confectionery, glucose, grape sugar, jaggery, molasses, and sirup. See "General note," Table 10.]

EXPORTS.

[000 omitted.]

Country.	1913	1914 (prelim.)	1915 (prelim.)	Country.	1913	1914 (prelim.)	1915 (prelim.)
	Pounds.	*Pounds.*	*Pounds.*		*Pounds.*	*Pounds.*	*Pounds.*
Argentina	131	142,616	118,658	Germany	2,462,020		
Austria-Hungary	2,368,765			Guadeloupe	58,722	87,340	
Barbados	22,375	66,006		Martinique	88,542	39,000	85,814
Belgium	251,935			Mauritius	414,372	638,200	
Brazil	11,832	70,239	130,235	Netherlands	440,817	333,000	327,449
British Guiana	195,807	239,988		Peru	315,041	389,488	
British India	53,181	43,207	34,474	Philippine Islands	346,858	521,383	465,199
China	14,555	19,040	32,950	Reunion	85,918	72,941	77,710
Cuba	5,476,901	5,574,683	5,731,998	Russia	324,837	281,218	206,240
Dominican Republic	173,832	223,610	226,634	Trinidad and Tobago	73,147	107,718	
Dutch East Indies	2,823,310	2,912,062		United Kingdom	52,492	33,975	11,292
Egypt	11,316	29,398	58,939	Other countries	784,382	1,296,815	
Fiji	212,150	206,331					
France	442,554	242,848	222,660	Total	17,505,792	13,571,106	

IMPORTS.

Country.	1913	1914 (prelim.)	1915 (prelim.)	Country.	1913	1914 (prelim.)	1915 (prelim.)
Argentina	166,578	14,068	79	Japan	725,067	441,451	276,909
Australia	167,690	29,400		Netherlands	147,002	226,266	37,136
British India	1,922,009	1,211,769	1,091,344	New Zealand	137,790	108,975	141,692
British South Africa	60,480	48,883	17,379	Norway	118,049	130,787	130,347
Canada	670,234	691,166	599,701	Persia	234,308	286,120	194,564
Chile	197,073	185,425	156,612	Portugal	85,631	83,927	
China	948,230	835,467	636,877	Singapore	[1] 224,529	153,361	
Denmark	26,888			Switzerland	258,513	296,645	267,724
Egypt	72,609	27,964	45,226	United Kingdom	3,872,309	3,761,740	3,675,612
Finland	105,106	97,524	101,774	United States [2]	4,762,014	5,417,995	5,286,218
France	253,435	359,947	1,116,760	Other countries	792,360	450,551	
Italy	15,345	10,774	6,776	Total	15,963,249	14,870,205	

[1] Data for 1912.

[2] Not including receipts from Hawaii, amounting in 1913 to 1,075,591,712; in 1914 to 1,210,862,124, and in 1915 to 1,212,360,888 pounds; and from Porto Rico, in 1913 to 750,428,443; in 1914 to 641,754,932 and in 1915 to 638,101,561 pounds.

SUGAR—Continued.

TABLE 131.—*Sugar production of undermentioned countries, campaigns of 1913–14 to 1915–16.*

BEET SUGAR (RAW).

Country.	1913–14	1914–15	1915–16	Country.	1913–14	1914–15	1915–16
NORTH AMERICA.				**EUROPE—cont'd.**			
	Short tons.	*Short tons.*	*Short tons.*		*Short tons.*	*Short tons.*	*Short tons.*
United States[1]	733,401	722,054	874,220	Germany	2,993,704	2,755,750	1,895,956
Canada [1]	11,982	13,773	18,419	Italy	336,823	184,084	198,414
				Netherlands [1]	231,073	316,455	262,125
Total	745,383	735,827	892,639	Roumania	41,240	33,259	
				Russia	1,681,247	1,947,486	1,699,485
EUROPE.				Serbia	7,165	2,000	
				Spain	186,680	116,197	118,712
Austria-Hungary:				Sweden	150,760	169,836	140,340
Austria	1,287,787 }	}1,766,215	1,212,530	Switzerland	4,861	4,134	2,646
Hungary	566,382						
Belgium	251,023	225,064	124,501	Total	8,688,400	8,027,651	5,956,269
Denmark	158,865	167,803	138,008				
France [1]	790,790	339,368	163,552	Grand total	9,433,783	8,763,478	6,848,908

CANE SUGAR.

Country.	1913–14	1914–15	1915–16	Country.	1913–14	1914–15	1915–16
NORTH AMERICA.				**EUROPE.**			
United States:				Spain	8,000	8,000	
Louisiana	293,000	243,000	138,000				
Texas [2]	8,000	4,000	1,000	**ASIA.**			
Hawaii	612,000	646,000	646,000	British India	2,566,000	2,757,440	2,952,320
Porto Rica	364,000	346,000	484,000	Formosa	213,000	222,000	406,822
Central America:				Japan	73,000	60,000	
Costa Rica		2,926		Java	1,502,852	1,436,818	
Guatemala		43,108		Philippine Islands	408,000	421,192	
Nicaragua	5,000						
Salvador				Total	4,762,852	4,897,450	
Mexico [2]	143,000	121,000					
West Indies:				**AFRICA.**			
British—							
Antigua	[3] 12,000	10,248	9,397	Egypt	76,000	83,000	
Barbados	11,000	32,932	72,800	Mauritius	275,000	275,250	243,262
Jamaica	15,000	25,852	16·960	Natal	97,000	115,000	
St. Christopher–				Portuguese East			
Nevis	13,000	10,080		Africa	38,000	45,000	
St. Lucia [3]	5,000			Reunion	41,000	44,000	
Trinidad and							
Tobago	62,147	65,881	71,931	Total	527,000	562,250	
Cuba	2,891,000	2,967,427	3,368,865				
Danish [3]	6,000	5,833	4,497	**OCEANIA.**			
Dominican Re-							
public [3]	117,000	119,000		Australia	297,000	235,200	
French—				Fiji	110,000	106,794	95,831
Guadaloupe [3]	44,000	44,000					
Martinique [3]	43,000	44,000		Total	407,000	341,994	
Total	4,644,147	4,731,287		Total cane sugar	11,270,200	11,621,619	
SOUTH AMERICA.							
Argentina	304,000	370,324	137,788	Total beet and cane sugar	20,703,983	20,385,097	
Brazil	[2] 228,000	[2] 269,000					
Guiana:							
British [3]	119,995	136,891	130,171				
Dutch [3]	15,000	13,000					
Paraguay	2,821	1,694					
Peru	251,385	289,729	277,780				
Total	921,201	1,080,638					

[1] Refined sugar. [2] Unofficial figures. [3] Exports.

SUGAR—Continued.

TABLE 132.—*Sugar: Total production of countries mentioned in Table 131, 1895–96 to 1914–15.*

Year.	Production.			Year.	Production.		
	Cane.[1]	Beet.	Total.		Cane.[1]	Beet.	Total.
	Short tons.	*Short tons.*	*Short tons.*		*Short tons.*	*Short tons.*	*Short tons.*
1895–96.......	3,259,000	4,832,000	8,091,000	1905–6........	7,551,000	8,090,000	15,641,000
1896–97.......	3,171,000	5,549,000	8,720,000	1906–7........	8,365,000	7,587,000	15,952,000
1897–98.......	3,206,000	5,457,000	8,663,000	1907–8........	7,926,000	7,390,000	15,316,000
1898–99.......	3,355,000	5,616,000	8,971,000	1908–9........	8,654,000	7,350,000	16,004,000
1899–1900.....	3,389,000	6,262,000	9,651,000	1909–10.......	9,423,000	6,991,000	16,414,000
1900–1901.....	4,084,000	6,795,000	10,879,000	1910–11.......	9,540,000	9,042,000	18,582,000
1901–2........	6,818,000	7,743,000	14,561,000	1911–12.......	10,275,000	7,072,000	17,347,000
1902–3........	6,782,000	6,454,000	13,236,000	1912–13.......	10,908,000	9,509,769	20,518,000
1903–4........	6,909,000	6,835,000	13,744,000	1913–14.......	[2]11,270,200	9,433,783	20,703,983
1904–5........	7,662,000	5,525,000	13,187,000	1914–15.......	[3]11,621,619	8,763,478	20,385,097

[1] Prior to 1901–2 these figures include exports instead of production for British India.
[2] Excluding Costa Rica, Guatemala, and Salvador.
[3] Excluding Nicaragua, Salvador, and St. Lucia.

TABLE 133.—*Beet and sugar production of undermentioned countries.*

Country and year.	Factories in operation.	Sugar made, raw.	Beets used for sugar.			Average extraction of sugar.	
			Area harvested.	Average yield per acre.	Quantity worked.	Percentage of weight of beets used.	Per short ton of beets used.
Austria-Hungary:	*Number.*	*Short tons.*	*Acres.*	*Short tons.*	*Short tons.*	*Per cent.*	*Pounds.*
1910–11	214	1,549,102	918,201	11.95	11,038,503	17.5	281
1911–12	210	1,180,605	968,771	8.18	8,623,578	16.6	274
1912–13	218	2,093,439	1,088,088	13.00	13,911,305	14.8	301
			Area cultivated.			*P.c. of wt. of beets produced.*	*Per ton of beets produced.*
Belgium:					*Produced.*		
1910–11	92	299,035	148,858	13.41	1,996,977	14.97	299
1911–12	89	258,780	145,119	11.45	1,660,872	15.58	312
1912–13	88	309,308	152,913	12.47	1,907,358	16.22	324
1913–14	84	249,395	129,527	11.85	1,534,311	16.25	325
Denmark:							
1910–11	8	110,792	....	....	817,381	13.56	271
1911–12	8	128,032	....	....	809,616	15.81	316
1912–13	9	148,447	79,986	14.49	1,159,369	12.80	256
1913–14	9	179,002	....	....	1,025,140	17.46	349
			Area harvested.			*P.c. of wt. of beets used.*	*Per ton of beets used.*
France:		*Refined.*			*Worked.*		
1910–11	239	717,033	549,969	10.76	6,426,226	11.80	236
1911–12	220	512,986	555,575	8.09	4,669,083	11.41	228
1912–13	213	967,440	566,539	12.99	7,960,926	13.15	263
1913–14	206	790,790	534,230	12.24	6,539,725	12.09	242
1914–15	69	333,953	242,781	11.92	2,892,878	11.54	231
1915–16	64	149,801	146,305	8.65	1,265,518	11.84	237
Germany:[1]		*Raw.*					
1910–11	354	2,770,001	1,180,913	11.72	17,360,003	15.96	319
1911–12	342	1,551,797	1,247,213	8.03	9,987,473	15.54	311
1912–13	342	2,901,564	1,353,181	13.56	18,344,738	15.82	316
1913–14	341	2,885,572	1,316,655	14.19	18,672,939	15.45	309
			Area cultivated.				
Italy:							
1910–11	35	190,901	124,044	14.92	1,698,551	11.24	225
1911–12	37	174,894	131,260	13.30	1,621,760	10.78	216
1912–13	37	218,628	133,434	14.40	1,879,328	11.63	233
1913–14	37	336,823	152,700	19.70	2,994,816	11.25	225

[1] The production of sugar in Germany, including refined from imported raw sugar, was 2,983,085 short tons in 1912–13 and 2,993,704 in 1913–14.

SUGAR—Continued.

TABLE 133.—*Beet and sugar production of undermentioned countries*—Continued.

Country and year.	Factories in operation.	Sugar made, raw.	Beets used for sugar.			Average extraction of sugar.	
			Area harvested.	Average yield per acre.	Quantity worked.	Percentage of weight of beets used.	Per short ton of beets used.
	Number.	*Short tons refined.*	*Acres cultivated.*	*Short tons.*	*Short tons.*	*Per cent.*	*Pounds.*
Netherlands:							
1910–11	27	219,947	138,554	12.94	1,678,803	13.10	262
1911–12	27	265,401	137,388	16.06	1,896,187	14.00	280
1912–13	27	315,775	160,180	14.99	2,228,851	14.17	283
1913–14	27	231,073	149,001	12.27	1,705,878	13.55	271
1914–15	27	316,346	156,251	14.06	2,193,577	14.42	288
1915–16 (prelim.)	23	240,828	139,644	13.52	1,755,964	13.71	274
Russia:		*Raw.*					
1910–11	276	2,074,410	1,631,188	8.9	14,437,305	14.61	292
1911–12	281	2,036,990	1,923,539	7.8	14,754,312	13.84	277
1912–13	287	1,361,842	1,847,313	6.4	11,538,078	11.73	235
1913–14	293	1,680,893	1,756,160	7.7	13,436,058	12.51	250
1914–15	265	1,958,975	1,941,122	7.4	13,979,662	14.01	280
1915–16	235	1,697,356	1,748,466	7.0	12,324,612	13.77	275
Spain:							
1910–11	33	68,743	(1)		532,882	12.90	258
1911–12	32	102,859	90,787	(1)	872,834	11.78	236
1912–13	33	171,839	105,213		1,302,871	11.33	264
1913–14	31	186,680	146,745		1,478,114	12.62	252
Sweden:							
1910–11	24	191,713	86,816	13.56	1,218,166	15.53	315
1911–12	24	140,409	71,790	14.83	908,372	15.27	309
1912–13	24	145,462	66,900	13.95	922,083	15.59	316
		Refined.	*Area harvested.*				
United States:							
1910–11	61	510,172	398,029	10.17	4,047,292	12.61	252
1911–12	66	599,500	473,877	10.68	5,062,333	11.84	237
1912–13	73	692,556	555,300	9.41	5,224,377	13.26	265
1913–14	71	733,401	580,006	9.76	5,659,462	12.96	259
1914–15	60	722,054	483,400	10.9	5,288,500	13.65	273
1915–16	67	862,800	624,000	10.4	6,462,000	13.4	267
1916–17 (prelim.)	74	918,800	680,000	9.81	6,671,000	13.8	276

[1] No data.

TABLE 134.—*Cane and sugar production of undermentioned countries.*

Country and year.	Factories in operation.	Sugar made.	Cane used for sugar.			Average extraction of sugar.
			Area harvested.	Average per acre.	Quantity worked.	Per ton[1] of cane used.
	Number.	*Short tons.*	*Acres cultivated.*	*Short tons.*	*Short tons.*	*Pounds.*
Argentina:						
1910–11	(1)	163,701	178,060	(1)	(1)	(1)
1911–12	(1)	198,515	230,866	(1)	(1)	(1)
1912–13	39	162,313	232,830	(1)	2,338,594	139
1913–14	38	304,389	263,656	(1)	3,451,321	176
1914–15	37	370,324	269,833	(1)	4,027,067	184
Australia:			*Harvested.*		*Produced.*	
1910–11	53	253,131	100,237	22.36	2,240,849	226
1911–12	53	210,292	101,010	18.65	1,884,120	223
1912–13	50	144,776	84,279	15.09	1,271,358	228
Cuba:			*Cultivated.*			
1910–11	171	1,670,151	(2)	(2)	14,736,981	227
1911–12	172	2,142,420	(2)	(2)	20,679,593	207
1912–13	171	2,737,264	1,340,139	(2)	25,137,684	218
1913–14	170	2,891,281	1,334,070	(2)	25,644,949	226

[1] No data.

SUGAR—Continued.

TABLE 134.—*Cane and sugar production of undermentioned countries*—Continued.

Country and year.	Factories in operation.	Sugar made.	Cane used for sugar.			Average extraction of sugar.
			Area harvested.	Average per acre.	Quantity worked.	Per ton of cane used.
	Number.	*Short tons.*	*Acres cultivated.*	*Short tons.*	*Short tons.*	*Pounds.*
Hawaii:						
1911–12	(1)	595,038	113,000	42.0	4,774,000	249
1912–13	(1)	546,524	114,600	39.0	4,476,000	244
1913–14	46	612,000	112,700	45.0	5,094,000	240
1914–15	45	646,000	113,200	46.0	5,185,000	249
Japan:			*Cultivated.*			
1910–11	13	72,454	49,166	18.49	892,662	162
1911–12	14	75,797	52,153	18.16	941,550	161
1912–13	17	68,867	51,293	17.15	879,624	157
1913–14	16	72,613	53,300	17.91	954,758	152
Java (factory plantations):			*Harvested.*			
1910–11	189	1,583,178	321,720	46.43	14,936,035	212
1911–12	193	1,424,657	336,021	40.71	13,679,962	208
1912–13	191	1,527,584	340,739	45.11	15,370,765	199
Spain:			*Cultivated.*			
1910–11	27	22,371	11,666	21.9	258,138	173
1911–12	23	17,831	9,983	16.5	167,092	213
1912–13	21	14,585	9,844	15.6	153,707	190
1913–14	22	8,131	4,581	17.4	79,719	204
United States (Louisiana):			*Harvested for sugar.*			
1911–12	188	352,874	310,000	19.0	5,887,292	120
1912–13	126	153,573	197,000	11.0	2,162,574	142
1913–14	153	292,698	248,000	17.0	4,214,000	139
1914–15	149	242,700	213,000	15.0	3,199,000	152
1915–16	136	137,500	183,000	11.0	2,018,000	138
1916–17 (preliminary)	148	304,700	....		4,172,000	146

[1] No data.

TABLE 135.—*Sugar beets: Area and production of undermentioned countries, 1913–1915.*

Country.	Area.			Production.		
	1913	1914	1915	1913	1914	1915
NORTH AMERICA.	*Acres.*	*Acres.*	*Acres.*	*Short tons.*	*Short tons.*	*Short tons.*
United States	580,000	483,000	611,000	5,886,000	5,585,000	6,511,000
Canada	17,000	12,000	18,000	148,000	109,000	141,000
Total	597,000	495,000	629,000	6,034,000	5,694,000	6,652,000
EUROPE.						
Austria-Hungary:						
Austria	629,000	[1] 600,000	[1] 435,000	7,674,000	[1] 7,468,000	(2)
Hungary	439,000	439,000	266,000	5,264,000	4,425,000	2,743,000
Croatia-Slavonia	11,000	(2)	(2)	98,000	(2)	(2)
Bosnia-Herzegovina	3,000	(2)	(2)	13,000	(2)	(2)
Total Austria-Hungary	1,082,000	....	....	13,049,000	....	....
Belgium	130,000	130,000	109,000	1,534,000	(2)	(2)
Bulgaria	9,000	(2)	(2)	94,000	(2)	(2)
Denmark	[3] 80,000	(2)	79,000	1,025,000	1,066,000	910,000
England	4,000	2,000	(2)	(2)	(2)	(2)
France	616,000	[4] 331,000	[4] 208,000	6,547,000	[4] 4,135,000	[4] 1,663,000
Germany	1,317,000	1,406,000	917,000	18,673,000	18,650,000	(2)
Italy	153,000	101,000	123,000	3,009,000	1,488,000	1,639,000
Netherlands	149,000	156,000	140,000	1,835,000	2,198,000	1,889,000
Roumania	32,000	37,000	34,000	311,000	248,000	204,000

[1] Galicia and Bukowina not included.
[2] No official statistics.
[3] Census of 1912.
[4] Exclusive of invaded area, in which 115,900 acres were under sugar beets in 1914.

SUGAR—Continued.

TABLE 135.—*Sugar beets: Area and production of undermentioned countries, 1913–1915—* Continued.

Country.	Area.			Production.		
	1913	1914	1915	1913	1914	1915
EUROPE—continued.						
Russia:	*Acres.*	*Acres.*	*Acres.*	*Short tons.*	*Short tons.*	*Short tons.*
Russia proper.............	1,578,000	1,873,000	1,871,000	12,119,000	13,716,000	(1)
Poland....................	170,000	(1)	(1)	1,399,000	(1)	(1)
Northern Caucasia (Kuban)...................	8,000	10,000	11,000	84,000	72,000	(1)
Total Russia, European.	1,756,000	1,883,000	1,882,000	13,602,000	13,788,000	(1)
Serbia.....................	7,000	(1)	(1)	7,000	(1)	(1)
Spain.....................	147,000	79,000	(1)	2 2,956,000	3 709,000	(1)
Sweden...................	71,000	80,000	79,000	946,000	967,000	856,000
Switzerland..............	2,000	2,000	2,000	21,000	30,000	28,000
Total.................	5,555,000	....	....	63,609,000	....	....
Grand total.............	6,152,000	....	....	69,643,000	....	....

1 No official statistics.
2 Beets entered in factories during sugar campaign of 1913–14.
3 Beets entered in factories up to December 31, 1914 for sugar campaign of 1914–15.

TEA.

TABLE 136.—*Tea: International trade, calendar years, 1913–1915.*

["Tea" includes tea leaves only and excludes dust, sweepings, and *yerba maté.* See "General note," Table 10.]

EXPORTS.

[000 omitted.]

Country.	1913	1914 (prelim.).	1915 (prelim.).	Country.	1913	1914 (prelim.).	1915 (prelim.).
	Pounds.	*Pounds.*	*Pounds.*		*Pounds.*	*Pounds.*	*Pounds.*
British India.......	291,583	292,607	319,864	Japan..............	30,128	35,077	41,441
Ceylon..............	191,511	193,584		Singapore...........	1 2,913	2,717	....
China..............	192,122	197,785	233,474	Other countries....	6,997	7,787	....
Dutch East Indies..	58,527	70,344	....				
Formosa............	23,931	22,936	....	Total.........	797,712	822,837	....

IMPORTS.

Country.	1913	1914 (prelim.).	1915 (prelim.).	Country.	1913	1914 (prelim.).	1915 (prelim.).
Argentina..........	4,148	3,103	3,012	Germany.........	9,458	....	....
Australia...........	37,349	41,622		Netherlands........	12,052	14,244	15,556
Austria-Hungary...	3,575	....	....	New Zealand.......	7,069	9,952	9,150
British India.......	8,653	8,816	12,101	Persia.............	10,414	6,302	
British South Africa	6,567	6,374	6,664	Russia.............	167,140	172,558	169,667
Canada.............	35,927	39,035	42,885	Singapore..........	1 6,692	6,290	
Chile..............	3,849	2,787	3,017	United Kingdom...	305,690	317,664	317,429
China..............	25,898	22,778	24,337	United States......	89,018	97,810	106,106
Dutch East Indies..	7,889	9,127	....	Other countries....	36,685	20,925	....
France.............	2,660	4,366	6,260				
French Indo-China.	5,320	2,634	....	Total........	786,053	786,387	....

1 Data for 1912.

TEA—Continued.

TABLE 137.—*Tea: Wholesale price per pound, on New York market, 1912–1916.*

Date.	Foochow, fair to fine.		Formosa, fine to choice.		Japans, pan-fired.		India orange pekoe.		Ceylon orange pekoe.	
	Low.	High.	Low.	High.	Low.	High.	Low.	High.	Low.	High.
1912.	*Cts.*	*Cts.*	*Cts.*	*Cts.*	*Cts.*	*Cts.*	*Cts.*	*Cts.*	*Cts.*	*Cts.*
Jan.-June	11½	22¾	20	39	15	21	18	25	20	26
July-Dec	11	21	23	39	15	18	18	25	20	26
1913.										
Jan.-June	12	22	24	39	13½	35	18½	24	18½	24
July-Dec	12	22	24	39	13½	28	18½	21	18½	24
1914.										
Jan.-June	12	22	24	39	12½	30	18½	21	18½	24
July-Dec	12½	22	23	39	12½	38	18½	27	18½	26
1915.										
January	15	22	23	39	18	28	(1)	(1)	21	22
February	15	22	23	39	18	28	(1)	(1)	21	27
March	15½	22	23	39	18	33	(1)	(1)	25	30
April	15½	22	23	39	19	33	....	....	27	30
May	15½	22	23	39	19	35	....	....	27	30
June	16½	22	23	39	23	35	....	....	27	30
Jan.-June	15	22	23	39	18	35	....	....	21	30
July	17	22	23	39	23	35	31	32	29	31
August	18	21	23	39	20	40	28	32	27	31
September	18	21	23	39	20	40	24	29	24	28
October	18	21	23	39	19	40	24	26	24	26
November	18	21	23	39	19	40	24	26	24	26
December	18	21	23	39	18	40	24	26	24	26
July-Dec	17	22	23	39	18	40	24	32	24	31
1916.										
January	18	21	23	39	18	18	24	26	24	26
February	18	21	23	39	18	18	26	28	26	28
March	18	21	23	39	16½	35½	26	30	27	30
April	18	21	23	39	16	35	27	30	27	30
May	18½	21	23	39	16	35	27	30	27	30
June	17½	21	23	39	16	35	28	30	28	30
Jan.-June	17½	21	23	39	16	35½	24	30	24	30
July	17½	21	23	39	16	35	28	30	28	30
August	17½	21	23	39	16	35	28	30	28	30
September	17½	21	23	39	16	35	28	30	28	30
October	17½	21	23	39	16	35	28	30	28	30
November	17½	21	23	39	16	35	28	30	28	30
December	17½	21	23	39	16	35	28	30	28	30
July-Dec	17½	21	23	39	16	35	28	30	28	30

[1] Nominal.

COFFEE.

TABLE 138.—*Coffee: International trade, calendar years 1913–1915.*

[The item of coffee comprises unhulled and hulled, roasted, ground, or otherwise prepared, but imitation or "surrogate" coffee and chicory are excluded. See "General note," Table 10.]

EXPORTS.

[000 omitted.]

Country.	1913	1914 (prelim.).	1915 (prelim.).	Country.	1913	1914 (prelim.).	1915 (prelim.).
	Pounds.	*Pounds.*	*Pounds.*		*Pounds.*	*Pounds.*	*Pounds.*
Belgium	24,945	....	....	Netherlands	202,823	244,270	372,359
Brazil	1,754,973	1,490,715	2,256,818	Nicaragua	26,440	22,817	20,134
British India	22,073	39,973	22,441	Salvador	63,471	76,425	....
Colombia	134,993	136,500	149,423	Singapore	[2] 4,842	3,256	....
Costa Rica	28,702	39,064	....	United States[1]	52,905	48,179	47,226
Dutch East Indies	63,799	71,238	....	Venezuela	142,016	121,350	137,967
Guatemala	93,014	84,298	....	Other countries	61,603	45,351	....
Haiti	57,594	....	....				
Jamaica	6,518	8,932	....	Total	2,787,180	2,432,368	....
Mexico	46,469	....	....				

[1] Chiefly from Porto Rico.　　　　[2] Data for 1912.

COFFEE—Continued.

TABLE 138.—*Coffee: International trade, calendar years 1913–1915*—Continued.

IMPORTS.

[000 omitted.]

Country.	19r3	1914 (prelim.).	1915 (prelim.).	Country.	1913	1914 (prelim.).	1159 (prelim.).
	Pounds.	*Pounds.*	*Pounds.*		*Pounds.*	*Pounds.*	*Pouuds.*
Argentina	32,602	30,925	36,142	Norway	30,193	26,231	53,246
Austria-Hungary	130,960	....	....	Russia	27,862	18,309	20,729
Belgium	118,195	....	....	Singapore	[1] 6,527	5,051	....
British SouthAfrica	26,910	25,820	32,275	Spain	33,365	30,280	35,219
Cuba	25,108	17,672	21,215	Sweden	75,484	64,724	....
Denmark	36,091	....	....	Switzerland	25,470	23,864	29,092
Egypt	13,975	13,116	18,701	United Kingdom	28,100	28,846	32,723
Finland	28,371	22,438	28,820	United States	852,529	1,011,072	1,228,762
France	254,157	256,658	304,874	Other countries	115,296	84,696	....
Germany	371,131	....	....				
Italy	63,194	62,176	88,119	Total	2,615,092	1,997,344	....
Netherlands	319,572	275,466	458,314				

[1] Data for 1912.

TABLE 139.—*Coffee: Wholesale price per pound, on the New York and New Orleans markets, 1912–1916.*

Date.	New York.												New Orleans.			
	Rio No. 7.		Santos No. 7.		Mocha.		Padang.		Cucuta, washed.		Mexican Cordoba, washed.[1]		Rio No. 7.		Santos No. 7.	
	Low.	High.	Low.	High.	Low.	High.	Low.	High.	Low.	High.	Low.	High.	Low.	High.	Low.	High.
	Cts.	*Cts.*	*Cts.*	*Cts.*	*Cts.*	*Cts.*	*Cts.*	*Cts.*	*Cts.*	*Cts.*	*Cts.*	*Cts.*	*Cts.*	*Cts.*	*Cts.*	*Cts.*
1912.																
Jan.-June	13⅞	15	14¼	15½	18½	19½	20	22	15½	18½	17½	18½	13⅞	15	14¼	15⅝
July-Dec	14	15¼	14½	16¼	18½	21	19½	22	15⅛	18½	15¾	18½	13⅞	15¼	14¾	16⅜
1913.																
Jan.-June	9½	14	10⅞	15⅝	18	21	19	22	12	17¾	15	18	9⅝	14	11⅛	15
July-Dec	8⅞	11⅛	10⅜	13¼	18	20	21	23	11¾	17¾	15	16½	9	11½	10½	12⅞
1914.																
Jan.-June	8½	9⅝	10¼	11¾	17½	21	21	23	14¼	18	15¼	16½	8⅝	9¾	10½	11¾
July-Dec	6¼	9⅞	8¼	12¾	19½	30	21	24	11	18¼	12	17¼	6⅜	10⅜	8¾	13½
1915.																
January	7¼	8¼	8½	9	21½	30	21	23½	12¼	15¾	12	14½	7½	8⅝	9	9¼
February	7⅝	8¼	8⅜	9	23	30	21	23	12¾	15¾	12	14½	7¾	8⅝	8¾	9¼
March	7⅝	8	8½	9¼	23	30	21	23	12¾	15½	12	14	7¾	8½	8¾	9⅝
April	7¾	8⅛	9	9¼	23	30	21	23	13	15¼	12	14	7¾	8⅜	9⅜	9½
May	7⅛	7¾	8¾	9¼	23	30	21	23	11½	15½	11½	14	7	7⅞	8¾	9½
June	7	7⅜	8½	9	23	30	21	22	11¼	14½	11	13½	7⅛	7½	8¾	9
Jan.-June	7	8¼	8⅜	9¼	21½	30	21	23½	11¼	15¾	11	14½	7	8⅝	8¾	9⅝
July	7⅜	7¾	8¾	9	23	30	21	22	11¼	14½	11	13	7⅜	7½	8¾	9
August	7	7⅜	8⅜	9	25	27	21	22	11	14½	11	13	7	7⅜	7¾	8¾
September	6⅝	7	7¾	8½	25	27	21	22	11	14	10½	13	6⅞	7¼	7⅝	8½
October	6¾	7½	7¾	8	25	27	21	23	11	15	10½	13	7	7¾	7⅞	8½
November	7½	7⅞	7¾	8½	25	27	22½	23	11½	15¼	11½	13½	7½	8	8⅛	8¾
December	7⅝	7⅝	7⅞	8⅜	25	27	22½	23	11½	15¼	11	13½	7⅝	7⅞	8⅛	8⅜
July-Dec	6⅝	7⅞	7¾	9	23	30	21	23	11	15¼	10½	13½	6⅞	8	7⅝	9
1916.																
January	7⅝	8¼	7⅞	8½	25	27	22½	23	11½	15½	11½	13¾	7⅝	8½	8⅛	8⅞
February	8¼	9⅜	8⅜	9⅜	19	27	22½	23	12	16	12	14	8⅜	9½	8⅜	9½
March	9¼	9⅝	9	9⅜	19	22½	22¾	26	12½	16½	12¼	14½	9⅛	9¾	9⅛	9⅝
April	9½	9¾	9	9⅝	19½	22½	25	26½	13	16¼	13	14½	9½	9⅞	9⅜	9⅞
May	9¾	9⅞	9½	9⅞	19½	22	26	26½	13	16¼	12½	14½	9¾	10⅛	9¾	10
June	9	9⅞	9½	9⅞	19	22	26	26½	12	16¼	12	14	8⅛	9⅞	9⅛	9⅞
Jan.-June	7⅝	9⅞	7⅞	9⅞	19	27	22½	26½	11½	16½	11½	14½	7⅝	10⅛	8⅛	10
July	9	9½	9½	9¾	19	20½	25	26½	12	14¾	11¾	13½	8⅞	9⅝	9¼	10
August	9⅜	9⅞	9½	10⅜	18¾	20½	25	26	12	14½	11¾	13¼	9½	10⅛	9⅝	10½
September	9½	10⅛	10¼	11	18¾	20	25	26	12	14½	11¾	13¼	9⅝	10½	10¼	10⅞
October	9⅜	9⅝	9⅞	10½	18¾	20	25	26	12¼	14½	11½	13¼	9⅝	10	10⅛	10⅝
November	9¼	9½	9¾	10½	18¾	20	25	26	12¼	14½	11½	13	9⅜	9¾	9⅞	10½
December	9¼	9¾	9¾	10¼	18¾	20	25	26	12¼	14¾	11½	13	9¼	9⅞	9¾	10⅜
July-Dec	9	10⅛	9½	11	18¾	20½	25	26½	12	14¾	11½	13½	8⅞	10½	9¼	10⅞

[1] Prices nominal because of small arrivals (January to September, inclusive).

OIL CAKE AND OIL-CAKE MEAL.

TABLE 140.—*Oil cake and oil-cake meal: International trade, calendar years 1913–1915.*

[The class called here "oil cake and oil-cake meal" includes the edible cake and meal remaining after making oil from such products as cotton seed, flaxseed, peanuts, corn, etc. See "General note," Table 10.]

EXPORTS.

[000 omitted.]

Country.	1913	1914 (prelim.).	1915 (prelim.).	Country.	1913	1914 (prelim.).	1915 (prelim.).
	Pounds.	*Pounds.*	*Pounds.*		*Pounds.*	*Pounds.*	*Pounds.*
Argentina	46,191	38,367	46,215	Italy	43,401	120,695	12,659
Austria-Hungary	111,252	....	....	Mexico	27,848	....	....
Belgium	125,241	....	....	Netherlands	228,492	110,882	....
British India	400,818	334,141	335,901	Russia	1,620,106	948,526	160,666
Canada	65,530	30,567	32,730	United Kingdom	52,741	73,295	25,829
China	175,073	183,581	164,212	United States	1,952,184	1,579,171	1,458,452
Denmark	21,061	....	....	Other countries	97,345	53,484	....
Egypt	138,839	176,339	246,183				
France	473,550	396,644	244,884	Total	6,228,208	4,045,692	....
Germany	648,536	....	....				

IMPORTS.

Country.	1913	1914	1915	Country.	1913	1914	1915
Austria-Hungary	79,860	....	....	Japan	284,310	256,968	197,822
Belgium	567,391	....	....	Netherlands	766,498	564,275	538,478
Canada	11,090	15,625	22,215	Norway	66,407	83,716	71,156
Denmark	1,250,972	....	....	Sweden	351,106	284,538	....
Dutch East Indies	465	1,560	....	Switzerland	54,955	38,818	38,226
Finland	25,533	23,698	88,810	United Kingdom	904,606	731,264	936,681
France	223,928	160,299	8,344	Other countries	21,776	32,506	....
Germany	1,826,618	....	....				
Italy	6,520	2,471	5,997	Total	6,442,035	2,195,738	....

ROSIN.

TABLE 141.—*Rosin: International trade, calendar years 1913–1915.*

[For rosin, only the resinous substance known as "rosin" in the exports of the United States, is taken. See "General note," Table 10.]

EXPORTS.

[000 omitted.]

Country.	1913	1914 (prelim.).	1915 (prelim.).	Country.	1913	1914 (prelim.).	1915 (prelim.).
	Pounds.	*Pounds.*	*Pounds.*		*Pounds.*	*Pounds.*	*Pounds.*
Austria-Hungary	2,327	....	....	Russia [1]	18,328	19,148	29,423
Belgium	57,491	....	....	Spain	729,419	489,580	387,194
France	90,159	101,487	118,667	United States	729,419	489,580	387,194
Germany	56,884	....	....	Other countries	3,394	5,917	....
Greece	3,982	9,174	....				
Netherlands	59,713	62,583	....	Total	1,021,697	687,889	....

IMPORTS.

Country.	1913	1914 (prelim.).	1915 (prelim.).	Country.	1913	1914 (prelim.).	1915 (prelim.).
Argentina	43,906	35,463	45,487	Italy	39,918	32,978	54,541
Australia	16,924	8,450	....	Japan	15,649	10,669	17,809
Austria-Hungary	74,208	....	....	Netherlands	79,452	77,809	....
Belgium	82,426	....	....	Norway	8,104	6,602	13,256
Brazil	41,730	29,340	40,682	Roumania	4,811	....	....
British India	5,705	3,535	3,914	Russia [2]	81,373	64,030	21,238
Canada	28,462	22,883	27,314	Serbia [2]	586	....	....
Chile	7,832	4,515	4,200	Spain	683	645	431
Cuba	4,771	4,239	5,391	Switzerland	5,209	4,236	7,723
Denmark	3,513	....	....	United Kingdom	187,934	154,655	173,360
Dutch East Indies	17,287	15,448	....	Other countries	17,928	10,170	....
Finland	7,594	4,923	5,103				
France	1,966	1,256	569	Total	990,197	491,846	....
Germany	212,226	....	....				

[1] In former editions of the Yearbook exports from Russia of *smola drevyesnaya* (tar) were erroneously included in this table as "rosin."
[2] Data for 1911.

TURPENTINE.

TABLE 142.—*Turpentine (spirits): International trade, calendar years 1913–1915.*

[*"Spirits of turpentine" includes only "spirits" or "oil" of turpentine and, for Russia, *skipidar;* it excludes crude turpentine, pitch, and, for Russia, *terpentin.* See "General note," Table 10.]

EXPORTS.

[000 omitted.]

Country.	1913	1914 (prelim.)	1915 (prelim.)	Country.	1913	1914 (prelim.)	1915 (prelim.)
	Gallons.	Gallons.	Gallons.		Gallons.	Gallons.	Gallons.
Belgium	1,693	....	....	Spain	1,329	1,052	922
France	2,990	2,004	1,475	United States	20,018	11,118	10,624
Germany	578	....	....	Other countries	741	617	....
Netherlands	4,112	2,883	7				
Russia	2,269	1,337	113	Total	33,730	19,011	....

IMPORTS.

Country.	1913	1914	1915	Country.	1913	1914	1915
Argentina	698	489	524	New Zealand	200	81	130
Australia	524	471	....	Russia	363	243	180
Austria-Hungary	2,668	....	....	Sweden	158	110	....
Belgium	2,994	....	....	Switzerland	592	375	395
Canada	1,253	1,152	1,113	United Kingdom	8,356	5,031	7,446
Chile	180	140	114	Other countries	1,161	783	....
Germany	10,726	....	....				
Italy	1,061	874	968	Total	36,998	13,381	....
Netherlands	6,064	3,632	27				

INDIA RUBBER.

TABLE 143.—*India rubber: International trade, calendar years 1913–1915.*

[Figures for india rubber include "india rubber," so called, and *caoutchouc, caucho, jebe* (Peru), *hule* (Mexico), *borracha, massaranduba, mangabeira, maniçoba, sorva* and *seringa* (Brazil), *gomelastiek* (Dutch East Indies), *caura, sernambi* (Venezuela). See "General note," Table 10.]

EXPORTS.

[000 omitted.]

Country.	1913	1914 (prelim.).	1915 (prelim.).	Country.	1913	1914 (prelim.).	1915 (prelim.).
	Pounds.	Pounds.	Pounds.		Pounds.	Pounds.	Pounds.
Angola	4,458	4,066	....	Kamerun	2,608	....	....
Belgian Kongo	[1] 7,737	....	....	Mexico	8,549	....	....
Belgium	24,456	....	....	Netherlands	12,368	11,665	....
Bolivia	11,339	13,415	....	Peru	6,131	5,009	....
Brazil	79,876	73,924	77,525	Senegal	193	4	....
Ceylon	27,518	37,344	48,804	Singapore	[1] 8,472	28,474	....
Dutch East Indies	15,910	22,908	....	Nigeria	7,505	373	....
Ecuador	428	325	....	Negri Sembilan	8,951	11,881	18,316
France	20,733	14,358	5,148	Perak	17,160	24,732	37,325
French Guinea	3,209	2,037	....	Selangor	26,618	32,041	43,053
French Kongo	3,866	397	....	Venezuela	527	252	380
Germany	8,756	....	....	Other countries	2,161	26,164	....
Gold Coast	1,317	654	....				
Ivory Coast	2,121	301	....	Total	312,967	310,324	....

IMPORTS.

Country.	1913	1914	1915	Country.	1913	1914	1915
Austria-Hungary	7,975	....	....	Russia	28,135	25,086	23,040
Belgium	32,492	....	....	United Kingdom	56,617	41,596	33,760
Canada	4,802	5,108	9,731	United States	115,881	143,065	221,482
France	33,836	25,499	29,317	Other countries	17,240	30,925	....
Germany	45,188	....	....				
Italy	6,271	6,733	11,833	Total	366,160	293,707	....
Netherlands	17,723	15,695	....				

[1] Data for 1912.

SILK.

TABLE 144.—*Production of raw silk in undermentioned countries, 1911–1915.*

[Estimates of the Silk Merchants' Union of Lyons, France.]

Country.	1911	1912	1913	1914	1915 (preliminary).
Western Europe:	*Pounds.*	*Pounds.*	*Pounds.*	*Pounds.*	*Pounds.*
Italy	7,694,000	9,050,000	7,804,000	8,950,000	6,345,000
France	886,000	1,113,000	772,000	893,000	287,000
Spain	194,000	172,000	181,000	161,000	110,000
Austria	} 772,000	{ 410,000	331,000	388,000	225,000
Hungary		238,000	271,000	278,000	143,000
Total	9,546,000	10,983,000	9,359,000	10,670,000	7,110,000
Levant and Central Asia:					
Broussa and Anatolia	1,290,000	844,000	1,025,000	761,000	386,000
Syria and Cyprus	1,157,000	882,000	1,080,000	948,000	772,000
Other Provinces of Asiatic Turkey	353,000	254,000	298,000	242,000	143,000
Turkey in Europe [1]			187,000	132,000	66,000
Saloniki and Adrianople	827,000	573,000			
Balkan States (Bulgaria, Serbia, and Roumania)	375,000	320,000	298,000	386,000	220,000
Greece, Saloniki,[1] and Crete	137,000	110,000	408,000	309,000	176,000
Caucasus	1,058,000	871,000	849,000	794,000	276,000
Persia (exports)	} 1,329,000	{ 500,000	463,000	176,000	88,000
Turkestan (exports)[2]		569,000	496,000	187,000	110,000
Total	6,526,000	4,923,000	5,104,000	3,935,000	2,237,000
Far East:					
China—					
Exports from Shanghai	13,095,000	14,198,000	12,709,000	9,116,000	12,213,000
Exports from Canton	3,814,000	4,983,000	6,063,000	4,233,000	4,321,000
Japan—					
Exports from Yokohama	20,657,000	23,957,000	26,720,000	20,922,000	24,802,000
British India—					
Exports from Bengal and Cashmere	494,000	370,000	249,000	75,000	179,000
Indo-China—					
Exports from Saigon, Haiphong, etc	35,000	33,000	26,000	35,000	31,000
Total	38,095,000	43,541,000	45,767,000	34,381,000	41,546,000
Grand total	54,167,000	59,447,000	60,230,000	48,986,000	50,893,000

[1] Prior to 1913 Turkey in Europe included the Vilayet of Saloniki, which now belongs to Greece.
[2] Including "Central Asia" subsequent to 1911.

TABLE 145.—*Total production of raw silk in countries mentioned in Table 144, 1900–1915.*

Year.	Production.	Year.	Production.	Year.	Production.
	Pounds.		*Pounds.*		*Pounds.*
1900	40,724,000	1906	46,106,000	1911	54,167,000
1901	42,393,000	1907	48,634,000	1912	59,447,000
1902	41,368,000	1908	53,087,000	1913	60,230,000
1903	39,981,000	1909	54,035,000	1914	48,986,000
1904	45,195,000	1910	54,002,000	1915 (preliminary)	50,893,000
1905	41,513,000				

WOOD PULP.

TABLE 146.—*Wood pulp: International trade, calendar years 1913–1915.*

[All kinds of pulp from wood have been taken for this item, but no pulp made from other fibrous substances. See "General note," Table 10.]

EXPORTS.

[000 omitted.]

Country.	1913	1914 (prelim.).	1915 (prelim.).	Country.	1913	1914 (prelim.).	1915 (prelim.).
	Pounds.	*Pounds.*	*Pounds.*		*Pounds.*	*Pounds.*	*Pounds.*
Austria-Hungary...	225,489	....	....	Sweden............	2,225,232	2,054,813	....
Belgium............	74,351	....	....	Switzerland........	14,659	15,573	22,877
Canada.............	596,339	849,766	728,341	United States......	39,552	24,674	40,575
Finland............	278,907	221,420	213,843	Other countries....	136,540	121,167	....
Germany...........	412,195	....	....				
Norway............	1,558,473	1,407,299	1,614,870	Total........	5,591,098	4,701,227	....
Russia.............	29,361	6,515	....				

IMPORTS.

Country.	1913	1914 (prelim.).	1915 (prelim.).	Country.	1913	1914 (prelim.).	1915 (prelim.).
Argentina..........	70,531	51,441	33,679	Russia.............	58,770	62,880	176,700
Austria-Hungary...	13,377	....	....	Spain.............	134,352	87,233	111,302
Belgium............	291,900	....	....	Sweden............	10,601	10,616	....
Denmark...........	130,654	....	....	Switzerland........	26,602	16,115	21,839
France.............	1,025,025	702,640	627,499	United Kingdom...	2,153,077	2,201,302	2,131,945
Germany...........	121,124	....	....	United States......	1,082,914	1,351,130	1,145,717
Italy..............	212,241	193,943	135,084	Other countries....	197,245	205,803	....
Japan..............	105,509	100,764	119,307				
Portugal...........	21,192	17,129	....	Total........	5,655,114	5,000,996	....

LIVE STOCK, 1916, AND MISCELLANEOUS DATA.

FARM ANIMALS AND THEIR PRODUCTS.

TABLE 147.—*Live stock in principal and other countries.*

[Latest census or other official figures available, with comparison for earlier years. Census returns are in italics; other official figures are in Roman type.]

PRINCIPAL COUNTRIES.

Country.	Date.	Cattle.	Buffaloes.	Swine.	Sheep.	Goats.	Horses.	Mules.	Asses.
		Thousand.	*Thousand.*	*Thousand.*	*Thousand.*	*Thousand.*	*Thousand.*	*Thousand.*	*Thousand,*
United States:									
On farms.........	Jan. 1, 1917	63,617	....	67,453	48,483	(1)	21,126	4,639	(1)
	Jan. 1, 1916	61,920	....	67,766	48,625	(1)	21,159	4,593	(1)
	Jan. 1, 1915	58,329	....	64,618	49,956	(1)	21,195	4,479	(1)
	Apr. 15, 1910	*61,804*	....	*58,186*	*52,448*	*2,915*	*19,833*	*4,210*	*106*
Not on farms.....	*Apr. 15, 1910*	*1,879*	....	*1,288*	*391*	*115*	*3,183*	*270*	*17*
Alaska (on farms and not on farms)......	*Jan. 1, 1910*	*1*	*2 22*	(3)	(3)	(3)	*2*	(3)	(3)
Hawaii (on farms and not on farms)......	*Apr. 15, 1910*	*149*	....	*31*	*77*	*5*	*28*	*9*	*3*
Porto Rico (on farms and not on farms)..	*Apr. 15, 1910*	*316*	....	*106*	*6*	*49*	*58*	*5*	*1*
Algeria.............	Dec. 31, 1912	1,107	....	114	8,338	3,772	221	192	271
	Sept., 1910	1,128	....	109	9,042	3,990	230	192	276
	Sept., 1905	1,067	....	91	9,063	4,030	221	174	278
	Sept., 1900	993	....	82	6,724	3,563	202	147	263
	Sept., 1895	1,121	....	84	7,892	3,545	217	142	287
Argentina.............	Dec. 31, 1913	30,796	....	3,197	81,485	4,564	9,366	584	345
	May 1, 1908	*29,124*	....	*1,404*	*67,384*	*3,947*	*7,538*	*465*	*285*
	May, 1895	*21,702*	....	*653*	*74,380*	*2,749*	*4,447*	*285*	*198*
	1888	*21,962*	....	*394*	*66,706*	*1,894*	*4,234*	*417*	
Australia.............	Dec. 31, 1915	9,924	....	760	69,706	4 262	2,395	4 8	
	Dec. 31, 1914	11,051	....	862	78,600	....	2,521	(1)	(1)
	Dec. 31, 1910	11,745	....	1,026	92,047	314	2,166	5	
	Dec. 31, 1905	8,528	....	1,015	74,541	(1)	1,675	(1)	(1)
	Dec. 31, 1900	8,640	....	950	70,603	(1)	1,610	(1)	(1)
	Dec. 31, 1895	11,767	....	823	90,690	(1)	1,680	(1)	(1)
	1890	10,300	....	891	97,881	(1)	1,522	(1)	(1)
Austria-Hungary:									
Austria.............	*Dec. 31, 1910*	*9,159*	*1*	*6,432*	*2,428*	*1 257*	*1,803*	*21*	*58*
	Dec. 31, 1900	*9,511*	(1)	*4,683*	*2,621*	*1,020*	*1,716*	*20*	*46*
	Dec. 31, 1890	*8,644*	(1)	*3,550*	*3,187*	*1,056*	*1,548*	*17*	*41*
	Dec. 31, 1880	*8,584*	(1)	*2,722*	*3,841*	*1,007*	*1,463*	*50*	
Hungary.........	Apr., 1913	6,045	162	6,825	6,560	269	2,005	1	16
	Feb. 28, 1911	*6,184*		*6,416*	*7,698*	*331*	*2,001*	*1*	*18*
	Nov. 20, 1895	*5,830*		*6,447*	*7,527*	*237*	*1,997*	*22*	
	1884	*4,879*		*4,804*	*10,595*	*270*	*1,749*	*23*	
Croatia-Slavonia..	*Mar. 24, 1911*	*1,135*		*1,164*	*850*	*96*	*350*	*3*	
	Dec. 31, 1895	*909*		*883*	*596*	*22*	*311*	*1*	*1*
Bosnia - Herzegovina	{Oct. 10} 1910 {Nov. 10}	*1,309*	*1*	*527*	*2,499*	*1,393*	*222*	(3)	*6*
	{Apr. 22} 1895 {May 22}	*1,416*	*1*	*662*	*3,231*	*1,447*	*231*	*1*	*5*
Belgium...........	Dec. 31, 1913	1,849	....	1,412	(1)	(1)	267	(1)	....
	Dec. 31, 1910	*1,880*	....	*1,494*	*185*	*218*	*317*	*11*	
	Dec. 31, 1895	*1,421*	....	*1,163*	*236*	*241*	*272*	*7*	
	Dec. 31, 1880	*1,383*	....	*646*	*365*	(1)	*272*	(1)	(1)
Brazil.............	1913	30,705	....	18,399	10,653	10,049	7,289	3,208	
Bulgaria.............	Dec. 31, 1910	1,603	415	527	8,632	1,459	478	12	118
	Dec. 31, 1905	1,696	477	465	8,131	1,384	538	12	124
	Dec. 31, 1900	1,596	431	368	7,015	1,405	495	9	107
	Dec. 31, 1892	1,426	342	462	6,868	1,264	344	8	82
Canada.............	June 30, 1916	5,917	....	2,815	1,965	(1)	2,991	(1)	(1)
	June 30, 1915	6,066	....	3,112	2,039	(1)	2,996	(1)	(1)
	June 1, 1911	*6,533*	....	*3,610*	*2,175*	(1)	*2,596*	(1)	(1)
	June 31, 1901	*5,576*	....	*2,354*	*2,510*	(1)	*1,577*	(1)	(1)
	1891	*4,121*	....	*1,734*	*2,564*	(1)	*1,471*	(1)	(1)
	1881	*3,515*	....	*1,208*	*3,049*	(1)	*1,059*	(1)	(1)

[1] No official statistics.　　　　[2] Reindeer.　　　　[3] Less than 500.　　　　[4] Dec. 31, 1913.

Table 147.—*Live stock in principal and other countries*—Continued.

PRINCIPAL COUNTRIES—Continued.

Country	Date	Cattle	Buffaloes	Swine	Sheep	Goats	Horses	Mules	Asses
		Thousand.	*Thousand.*	*Thousand.*	*Thousand.*	*Thousand.*	*Thousand.*	*Thousand.*	*Thousand.*
Denmark	Feb. 29, 1916	2,290	....	1,983	255	([1])	515	([1])	([1])
	May 15, 1915	2,417	....	1,919	533	([1])	526	([1])	([1])
	July 15, 1914	2,463	....	2,497	515	41	568	([1])	([1])
	July 15, 1909	2,254	....	1,468	727	40	535	([1])	([1])
	July 15, 1903	1,840	....	1,457	877	39	487	([1])	([1])
	July 15, 1898	1,745	....	1,168	1,074	32	449	([1])	([1])
Finland	1910	1,573	[2]120	418	1,309	13	361	([1])	([1])
	1905	1,481	[2]142	220	938	6	324	([1])	([1])
	1900	1,428	[2]119	211	985	8	311	([1])	([1])
	1890	1,305	[2]86	194	1,054	15	293	([1])	([1])
France	[3]July 1, 1916	12,724	....	4,448	12,079	([1])	2,317	163	317
	[3]Dec. 31, 1915	12,514	....	4,916	12,379	1,230	2,156	144	324
	[3]Dec. 31, 1914	12,668	....	5,926	14,038	1,317	2,105	152	337
	Dec. 31, 1913	14,807	....	7,048	16,213	1,453	3,231	193	360
	Dec. 31, 1910	14,533	....	6,900	17,111	1,418	3,198	193	361
	Dec. 31, 1900	14,521	....	6,740	20,180	1,558	2,903	205	356
	Nov. 30, 1892	13,709	....	7,421	21,116	1,845	2,795	217	369
	1882	12,997	....	7,147	23,809	1,851	2,838	251	296
	1862	12,812	....	6,038	29,530	1,726	2,914	([1])	([1])
Germany	Dec. 1, 1915	20,317	....	17,287	5,073	3,438	[4]3,342	([1])	([1])
	Dec. 1, 1914	21,829	....	25,341	5,471	3,538	[4]3,435	([1])	([1])
	Dec. 1, 1913	20,994	....	25,659	5,521	3,548	3,227	([1])	([1])
	Dec. 2, 1912	20,182	....	21,924	5,803	3,410	4,523	13	
	Dec. 2, 1907	20,631	....	22,147	7,704	3,534	4,345	11	
	Dec. 1, 1904	19,332	....	18,921	7,907	3,330	4,267	([1])	([1])
	Dec. 1, 1900	18,940	....	16,807	9,693	3,267	4,195	8	
	Dec. 1, 1897	18,491	....	14,275	10,867	([1])	4,038	([1])	([1])
	Dec. 1, 1892	17,556	....	12,174	13,590	3,092	3,836	7	
	Jan. 10, 1883	15,787	....	9,206	19,190	3,641	3,523	10	([1])
Greece	1914	300	([1])	227	3,547	2,638	149	80	133
India:									
British	1913-14	[5]125,042	[6]18,235	([1])	23,092	30,673	1,643	86	1,501
	1910-11	[5]94,664	[6]16,628	([1])	22,922	28,518	1,524	110	1,342
	1904-5	[5]77,111	[6]12,871	([1])	17,562	24,803	1,278	54	1,177
	1899-1900	[5]72,666	[6]12,120	([1])	17,805	19,005	1,308	1,227	
	1894-95	[5]67,045	[6]11,826	([1])	17,260	15,272	1,134	1,102	
Native states [7]	1913-14	[5]12,236	[6]1,765	([1])	8,306		175	181	
	1909-10	[5]10,391	[6]1,559	([1])	7,129		141	155	
	1904-5	[5]8,178	[6]1,347	([1])	6,318		92	129	
	1900-1	[5]7,397	[6]1,228	([1])	4,538		85	115	
Italy	1914	6,646		2,722	13,824		2,235		
	Mar. 10, 1908	6,199	19	2,508	11,163	2,715	956	388	860
	Feb. 13, 1881	4,772	11	1,164	8,596	2,016	658	294	674
Japanese Empire:									
Japan	Dec. 31, 1914	1,387	([1])	332	3	95	1,579	([1])	([1])
	Dec. 31, 1913	1,389	([1])	310	3	89	1,582	([1])	([1])
	Dec. 31, 1910	1,384	([1])	279	3	92	1,565	([1])	([1])
	Dec. 31, 1905	1,168	([1])	228	4	72	1,368	([1])	([1])
	Dec. 31, 1900	1,261	([1])	181	2	60	1,542	([1])	([1])
Chosen (Korea)	Dec. 31, 1913	1,211	([1])	761	....	10	51	14	
	Dec. 31, 1910	704	([1])	566	....	7	40	([1])	([1])
Formosa (Taiwan)	Dec. 31, 1914	2	398	1,313	([8])	125	([8])		
	Dec. 31, 1905	([8])	341	1,018	([8])	108	([8])		
Mexico	June 30, 1902	5,142	....	616	3,424	4,206	859	334	288
Netherlands	May, 1915	2,390	....	1,487	([1])	([1])	([1])	([1])	([1])
	June, 1913	2,097	....	1,350	842	232	334	([1])	([1])
	May 20/June 20 1910	2,027	....	1,260	889	224	227	([1])	([1])
	Dec. 31, 1904	1,691	....	862	607	166	295	([1])	([1])
	Dec. 31, 1900	1,656	....	747	771	180	295	([1])	([1])
	Dec. 31, 1890	1,533	....	579	819	165	273	([1])	([1])
New Zealand	Apr. 30, 1916				24,608				
	Apr. 1, 1911	2,020		349		6	404	([8])	([8])
	Apr. 30, 1911				23,996				
	Apr. 30, 1905				19,131				
	Oct., 1905	1,811		250			327	([8])	([8])
	Apr. 30, 1900				19,355	([1])			
	Oct., 1900	1,257		251		([1])	266	([8])	([8])
	Apr., 1895				19,827	([1])			
	1895	1,048		240		([1])	237	([8])	([8])
	1891	832		309	18,128	9	211	([8])	([8])

[1] No official statistics.
[2] Reindeer.
[3] Excludes invaded area.
[4] Excluding Army horses.
[5] Including calves and young buffaloes.
[6] Not including young buffaloes.
[7] Figures incomplete.
[8] Less than 500.

TABLE 147.—*Live stock in principal and other countries*—Continued.

PRINCIPAL COUNTRIES—Continued.

Country.	Date.	Cattle.	Buffaloes.	Swine.	Sheep.	Goats.	Horses.	Mules.	Asses.
		Thousand.	*Thousand.*	*Thousand.*	*Thousand.*	*Thousand.*	*Thousand.*	*Thousand.*	*Thousand.*
Norway...............	Sept. 30, 1915	1,121	(1)	209	1,330	240	186	(1)	(1)
	Sept. 30, 1914	1,146	(1)	228	1,327	237	182	(1)	(1)
	Sept. 30, 1910	1,134	(1)	334	1,398	288	168	(1)	(1)
	Sept. 30, 1907	*1,089*	*2 143*	*307*	*1,391*	*296*	*164*	*(1)*	*(1)*
	1900	950	2 109	165	999	215	173	(1)	(1)
	1890	1,006	2 170	121	1,418	272	151	(1)	(1)
Philippine Islands....	Dec. 31, 1915	534	1,222	2,521	129	644	223	(1)	(1)
	Dec. 31, 1910	270	757	1,682	94	441	143	(1)	(1)
	Dec. 31, 1902	*128*	*641*	*1,179*	*30*	*124*	*144*	*(1)*	*(1)*
Portugal.............	*Oct.,*	*1906*	*703*	*(1)*	*1,111*	*3,073*	*1,034*	*88*	*58*	*144*
	1870	*625*	*(1)*	*971*	*2,977*	*937*	*87*	*51*	*138*
Roumania...........	Apr.,	1916	2,938		1,382	7,811	301	1,219	(3)	12
		1911	2,667		1,021	5,269	187	825	4	
		1907	2,585		1,124	5,105	191	808	5	
	Dec.,	*1900*	*2,545*	*44*	*1,709*	*5,655*	*233*	*864*	*1*	*7*
		1890	2,520		926	5,002	210	595	6	
		1884	2,376		886	4,655	245	533	2	
Russian Empire: Russia, European		1913	31,974	2 605	13,458	41,426	873	22,771	6	7
		1910	31,315	2 462	12,049	40,734	857	21,868	5	2
		1900	31,661	2 350	11,761	47,628	1,017	19,744	1	2
		1890	25,528	(1)	9,554	46,052	(1)	19,779	(3)	(3)
		1881	22,122	(1)	9,265	45,522	1,157	15,534	(3)	(3)
Poland...........		1913	2,011	(3)	491	683	9	1,116	(3)	(3)
		1910	2,301	(3)	612	1,050	9	1,222	(3)	(3)
		1900	2,823	(3)	1,402	2,823	11	1,392	(3)	1
		1890	3,013	(3)	1,499	3,755	(1)	1,207	(3)	(1)
	In summer.	4 1881	5,055	(3)	706	3,375	10	1,037	(1)	(1)
Russia, Asiatic (33 governments of the Caucusus, Central Asia, and Siberia)........		1913	18,404	(1)	2,895	38,696	4,791	11,959	)	(1)
Serbia................	Dec. 31, 1910	*957*	*7*	*866*	*3,819*	*631*	*153*	*1*	*1*
	Dec. 31, 1905	*963*	*7*	*908*	*3,160*	*510*	*174*	*1*	*1*
Spain................		1914	2,743	....	2,810	16,128	3,265	525	984	841
		1913	*2,879*	....	*2,710*	*16,441*	*3,394*	*542*	*948*	*849*
	Dec. 31, 1910	2,369	....	2,424	15,117	3,216	520	886	868
	Dec. 31, 1906	2,497	....	2,080	13,481	2,440	440	802	744
		1891	2,218	....	1,928	13,359	2,534	397	768	754
Sweden..........	Dec. 31, 1914	2,761	....	1,015	993	77	603	(1)	(1)
	Dec. 31, 1913	2,721	....	968	988	71	596	(1)	(1)
	Dec. 31, 1910	2,748	2 273	957	1,004	69	587	(1)	(1)
	Dec. 31, 1905	2,550	2 226	830	1,074	67	555	(1)	(1)
		1900	2,583	2 232	806	1,261	80	533	(1)	(1)
		1890	2,399	2 288	645	1,351	87	487	(1)	(1)
Switzerland..........	Apr. 19, 1916	*1,616*	....	*544*	*172*	*358*	*137*	*3*	*1*
	Apr. 21, 1911	*1,443*	....	*570*	*161*	*341*	*144*	*3*	*2*
	Apr. 20, 1906	*1,498*	....	*549*	*210*	*362*	*135*	*3*	*2*
	Apr. 19, 1901	*1,340*	....	*555*	*219*	*355*	*125*	*3*	*2*
Turkey. European and Asiatic.		1912	(1)	(1)	73	27,095	20,269	(1)	(1)	(1)
		1910	(1)	(1)	175	27,662	21,283	(1)	(1)	(1)
		1905	(1)	(1)	196	23,614	16,411	(1)	(1)	(1)
Union of South Africa.	Dec. 31, 1913	(1)	(1)	(1)	35,711	11,521	(1)	(1)	(1)
	May 7, 1911	*5,797*	*(1)*	*1,082*	*30,657*	*11,763*	*719*	*94*	*337*
	1904	*3,500*	*(1)*	*679*	*16,323*	*9,771*	*450*	*135*	*142*
United Kingdom: Great Britain.....	June 5, 1916	7,442	....	2,315	24,990	(1)	1,567	(1)	(1)
	June 4, 1915	7,288	....	2,579	24,598	(1)	1,213	(1)	(1)
	June 4, 1914	7,093	....	2,634	24,286	(1)	1,296	(1)	(1)
	June 4, 1913	6,964	....	2,234	23,931	(1)	1,324	(1)	(1)
	June 4, 1910	7,037	....	2,350	27,103	(1)	1,545	(1)	(1)
	June 4, 1900	6,805	....	2,382	26,592	(1)	1,500	(1)	(1)
	June 4, 1890	6,509	....	2,744	27,272	(1)	1,432	(1)	(1)
	June 4, 1880	5,912	....	2,001	26,619	(1)	1,421	(1)	(1)
Ireland...........	June 1, 1916	4,970	....	1,290	3,764	293	599	28	230
	June 1, 1915	4,844	....	1,205	3,600	243	561	29	227
	June 1, 1914	5,052	....	1,306	3,601	242	619	31	245
	June 1, 1913	4,933	....	1,060	3,621	246	614	30	243
	June 1, 1910	4,689	....	1,200	3,980	243	613	31	241
	June 1, 1900	4,609	....	1,269	4,387	306	567	31	242
	June 1, 1890	4,241	....	1,570	4,324	327	585	30	213
	June 1, 1880	3,921	....	850	3,561	266	557	25	186

1 No official statistics.   3 Less than 500.
2 Reindeer.   4 Exclusive of the Government of Radom.

TABLE 147.—*Live stock in principal and other countries*—Continued.

PRINCIPAL COUNTRIES—Continued.

Country.	Date.	Cattle.	Buffa-loes.	Swine.	Sheep.	Goats.	Horses.	Mules.	Asses.
United Kingdom—Continued.		*Thou-sand.*	*Thou-sand.*	*Thou-sand.*	*Thou-sand.*	*Thou-sand.*	*Thou-sand.*	*Thou-sand.*	*Thou-sand.*
Isle of Man and Channel Islands	June 5, 1916	40	....	11	78	[1]	10	[1]	[1]
Uruguay.............	1908	8,193	....	180	26,286	20	556	18	
	1900	6,827	....	94	18,609	20	561	23	
	1860	3,632	....	6	1,990	5	518	8	

OTHER COUNTRIES.

Country.	Date.	Cattle.	Buffa-loes.	Swine.	Sheep.	Goats.	Horses.	Mules.	Asses.
Azores and Madeira Islands...........	1900	89.	....	93	87	38	2	3	9
Basutoland...........	1911	437		[1]	1,369	[1]	88	[1]	[1]
Bechuanaland Pro-tectorate.........	1911	324		[1]	358		4		
Bolivia.............	1910	735	....	114	1,455	473	97	45	174
British East Africa [2]..	Mar. 31, 1915	900	(1)	4	6,555	4,020	2	[1]	[1]
British Guiana......	1915	90	(3)	11	20	15	1	2	6
Ceylon.............	1914	1,484		84	64	190	4	[1]	[1]
Chile..............	Dec. 31, 1913	1,969	....	221	4,602	299	458	38	33
Costa Rica..........	1914	336	....	64	(3)	1	52	2	(3)
Cuba..............	Dec. 31, 1914	3,395	....	[1]	[1]	[1]	673	50	3
Cyprus............	Mar. 31, 1915	61	....	39	263	244	68		
Dutch East Indies:									
Java and Madura.	1913	4,786		[1]	[1]	[1]	274	[1]	[1]
Other possessions.	1905	449	447	[1]	[1]	[1]	119	[1]	[1]
Dutch Guiana......	Dec. 13, 1914	8	(1)	4	(3)	3	(3)	(3)	1
Egypt..............	{Aug.-Sept.,}1914	601	568	[1]	[1]	[1]	40	22	632
Falkland Islands.....	1914	8	....	(3)	701	[1]	3	[1]	[1]
Faroe Islands.......	1914	4	....	(3)	112	(3)	[1]	[1]	[1]
Fiji...............	1914	53	....	[1]	3	16	7	[1]	[1]
French Guiana......	1914	400	....	[1]	150	140	3	(1)	[1]
French Indo-China:									
Annam...........	1914	215	(1)	[1]	[1]	[1]	[1]	[1]	[1]
Cochin-China.....	1914	109	242	709	3		[1]	[1]	[1]
Guam..............	1913	6	....	[1]	[1]	[1]	[1]	[1]	[1]
Gambia............	1907	83	....	[1]	[1]	[1]	4	[1]	[1]
Guatemala.........	Dec. 31, 1914	655	....	177	402	59		114	
German East Africa.	1913	3,994	....	6	6,440	25	(3)	(3)	25
German S. W. Africa..	1913	206	....	8	555	517	16	14	
Honduras...........	1914	489	....	180	6	23	68	25	
Iceland............	1912	26	....		601	1	46	[1]	[1]
Jamaica...........	1914	115	....	31	11	18	55	[1]	[1]
Luxemburg.........	Dec. 1, 1913	102	....	137	5	10	19	[1]	[1]
Madagascar........	Dec. 31, 1914	....	[4] 6,784	643	247	168	2	(3)	(3)
Malta.............	Mar. 31, 1915	5	....	4	21	21	9		
Mauritius..........	1913	41	....	17	2	37	2	1	[1]
Morocco (western)....	1915	675	....	16	3,175	1,052	123		226
Newfoundland......	1911	39	....	27	93	17	14	[1]	[1]
Nicaragua'.........	1908	252	....	12	(3)	1	28	6	1
Nyasaland Protecto-rate..............	1915	82	....	22	28	137	(3)	(3)	(3)
Panama...........	1905	65	....	28	[1]	3	17	2	[1]
Rhodesia...........	1911	500		2	300	602		20	
Salvador...........	1906	284	....	423	21	[1]	74	[1]	[1]
Siam.............	January, 1915	2,398	1,999	[1]	....		92	[1]	[1]
Straits Settlements...	1914	40	....	113	35	18	2	[1]	[1]
Swaziland.........	1915	90	....	9	200		1	[1]	[1]
Togo [2]............	1913	65	(1)	[1]	[1]	[1]	[1]	[1]	[1]
Trinidad and Tobago.	1914	13	....	9	2	6	5	5	[1]
Tunis.............	July 31, 1915	269	....	12	1,119	499	38	30	86
Uganda Protectorate [2]	1914	845	....	1	678		(3)	(3)	(3)
Venezuela..........	1912	2,004	....	1,618	177	1,667	191	89	313

[1] No official statistics. [2] Figures incomplete. [3] Less than 500. [4] Zebus.

TABLE 148.—*Hides and skins: International trade, calendar years 1913–1915.*

[This table gives the classification as found in the original returns, and the summary statements for "All countries" represent the total for each class only so far as it is disclosed in the original returns. The following kinds are included: Alligator, buffalo, calf, camel, cattle, deer, goat and kid, horse and colt, kangaroo, mule and ass, sheep and lamb, and all other kinds except furs, bird skins, sheepskins with wool on, skins of rabbits and hares, and tanned or partly tanned hides and skins. Number of pounds computed from stated number of hides and skins. See "General note," Table 10.]

EXPORTS.

[000 omitted.]

Country and classification.	1913	1914 (prelim.)	1915 (prelim.)	Country and classification.	1913	1914 (prelim.)	1915 (prelim.)
Argentina:	*Pounds.*	*Pounds.*	*Pounds.*	Germany:	*Pounds.*	*Pounds.*	*Pounds.*
Cattle, dried....	46,779	31,984	56,391	Calf............	19,158	....	....
Cattle, salted.....	144,963	140,118	141,641	Cattle.........	104,653	....	....
Deer.............	1	1	6	Goat............	2,912	....	....
Goat...........	4,387	3,193	5,203	Horse..........	14,594	....	....
Horse, dried.....	2,297	2,464	4,782	Sheep..........	947	....	....
Horse, salted.....	310	610	835	Unclassified.....	1,296	....	....
Kid..............	995	406	342	Italy:			
Sheep and lamb..	47,920	33,329	50,705	Cattle.........	48,094	33,443	16,576
Austria-Hungary:				Calf............	7,446	5,379	423
Calf, dried......	3,177	....	....	Goat............	1,191	598	192
Calf, green.....	22,004	....	....	Kid.............	989	644	62
Cattle, dried.....	7,795	....	....	Lamb..........	2,207	2,043	9
Cattle, green.....	27,371	....	....	Sheep..........	782	517	1
Goat...........	2,014	....	....	Unclassified.....	1,316	1,067	1,324
Horse, dried.....	1,230	....	....	Mexico:			
Horse, green.....	3,810	....	....	Alligator........	34	....	....
Kid.............	1,355	....	....	Cattle.........	34,773	....	....
Lamb..........	3,138	....	....	Deer...........	606	....	....
Sheep..........	5,884	....	....	Goat............	4,641	....	....
Unclassified.....	1,351	....	....	Netherlands:			
Belgium:				Hides, dried.....	24,161	16,701	1,464
Unclassified.....	116,608	....	....	Hides, fresh.....	162	79	....
Brazil:				Hides, salted.....	42,399	28,435	10,265
Cattle, dried.....	20,460	19,569	34,595	Sheep..........	993	1,243	....
Cattle, green.....	56,866	49,730	47,153	New Zealand:			
Deer...........	387	284	305	Sheep..........	20,671	21,923	24,974
Goat...........	5,062	3,786	6,873	Unclassified.....	7,004	5,130	6,010
Sheep..........	1,594	1,337	2,796	Peru:			
Unclassified.....	82	76	109	Cattle.........	6,930	4,826	.
British India:				Goat............	872	944	....
Cattle...........	124,525	97,586	89,443	Sheep..........	172	151	....
Goat...........	52,438	46,906	42,477	Unclassified.....	....	1	....
Unclassified.....	7,160	5,755	5,496	Russia:			
British South Africa:				Hides, large.....	54,411	34,097	12,278
Cattle...........	21,515	14,765	15,415	Hides, small.....	36,676	12,723	....
Goat...........	9,105	7,944	8,324	Sheep and goat...	23,471	15,614	144
Sheep..........	32,319	30,403	37,282	Singapore:			
Canada:				Unclassified.....	[2] 7,163	5,184	....
Sheep..........	36	....	....	Spain:			
Unclassified [1].....	60,000	53,000	42,000	Goat............	1,923	1,019	2,472
China:				Sheep..........	9,203	8,597	5,092
Buffalo..........	66,405	58,259	58,319	Unclassified.....	6,470	2,678	611
Horse..........	1,518	1,542	1,851	Sweden:			
Goat...........	22,176	17,646	22,652	Cattle, wet.......	21,359	24,703	....
Sheep..........	1,105	825	1,325	Cattle, dry.......	366	166	....
Chosen (Korea):				Horse, wet.......	813	1,331	....
Cattle...........	4,649	5,628	....	Horse, dry.......	1	2	....
Cuba:				Goat, kid, lamb,			
Cattle..........	14,207	14,458	16,539	and sheep, wet.	688	854	....
Unclassified.....	322	264		Goat, lamb, and			
Denmark:				sheep, dry......	157	132	....
Unclassified.....	20,814	....	....	Unclassified, dry.	8	2	....
Dutch East Indies:				Unclassified, wet.	175	166	....
Unclassified.....	16,011	11,609	....	Switzerland:			
Egypt:				Unclassified.....	23,851	24,138	14,671
Cattle and camel.	7,029	6,883	5,100	United Kingdom:			
Sheep and goat..	2,946	2,211	2,573	Cattle.........	2,175	589	....
France:				Sheepskins.....	17,837	14,055	9,566
Calf.............	34,164	21,150	10,050	Unclassified.....	22,213	17,583	11,034
Goat...........	5,411	3,964	900	United States:			
Kid.............	2,601	1,045	166	Calf............	583	798	830
Lamb..........	1,983	1,144	1,284	Cattle.........	14,454	15,310	19,404
Sheep..........	13,030	6,943	1,437	Unclassified.....	7,119	5,476	2,196
Unclassified......	82,304	61,493	30,180				

[1] Unofficial estimate.   [2] Data for 1912.

TABLE 148.—*Hides and skins: International trade, calendar years 1913–1915*—Contd.

EXPORTS—Continued.

[000 omitted]

Country and classification.	1913	1914 (prelim.)	1915 (prelim.)	Country and classification.	1913	1914 (prelim.)	1915 (prelim.)
Uruguay:	*Pounds.*	*Pounds.*	*Pounds.*	Othercountries-Con.			
Calf..............	188	228	....	Skins—Contd.	*Pounds.*	*Pounds.*	*Pounds.*
Cattle, dried	6,836	5,831	....	Sheep and lamb	17,864	17,977	....
Cattle, salted.....	27,402	24,930	....	Sheep and goat,			
Horse, dried.....	80	41	....	mixed........	11,687	1,035	....
Horse, salted.....	1	....	....	Unclassified....	54,370	24,637	....
Lamb..........	678	48	....				
Sheep..........	23,674	9,563	....	Total.........	2,015,873	1,268,346	....
Yearling, dried...	1,116	1,195	....				
Yearling, salted..	489	272	....	All countries:			
Venezuela:				Hides—			
Cattle..........	7,013	6,587	7,644	Cattle and buffalo..........	924,854	649,850	....
Deer..........	354	362	200	Horse..........	25,015	6,148	....
Goat..........	1,606	2,041	1,612	Skins—			
Unclassified....	....	....	260	Alligator.......	106	55	....
Other countries:				Calf.............	90,753	31,862	....
Hides—				Deer..........	2,789	1,942	....
Cattle and buffalo..........	106,630	93,018	....	Goat and kid...	137,924	98,251	....
Horse..........	361	158	....	Sheep and lamb	202,037	150,098	....
Skins—				Sheep and goat,			
Alligator.......	72	55	....	mixed........	38,949	19,846	....
Calf..........	4,033	4,307	....	Unclassified....	593,446	310,294	....
Deer..........	1,441	1,295	....				
Goat and kid...	18,246	8,115	....	Total.........	2,015,873	1,268,346	....

IMPORTS.

Country and classification.	1913	1914 (prelim.)	1915 (prelim.)	Country and classification.	1913	1914 (prelim.)	1915 (prelim.)
Austria-Hungary:				Greece:			
Calf, dried	1,071			Unclassified......	5,219	4,086	....
Calf, green...	1,581			Italy:			
Cattle, dried.....	42,309			Calf.............	1,211	726	2,144
Cattle, green.....	37,440			Cattle..........	47,615	35,965	72,687
Goat..........	1,500			Sheep..........	4,270	2,502	4,185
Horse, dried.....	245			Goat..........	104	90	288
Horse, green.....	243			Kid..........	61	20	17
Kid..........	586			Lamb..........	537	363	2,139
Lamb..........	10,124			Unclassified....	184	162	871
Sheep..........	3,770			Japan:			
Unclassified......	608			Cattle..........	7,171	5,949	15,053
Belgium:				Deer..........	509	571	483
Hides, green....	197,072			Netherlands:			
British India:				Hides, dried......	41,384	26,450	13,695
Cattle..........	14,401	15,301	8,477	Hides, fresh......	25	32	....
Unclassified......	5,737	5,255	5,544	Hides, salted.....	34,189	25,369	6,453
Canada:				Sheep..........	4,812	2,894	....
Unclassified......	44,667	50,782	60,297	Norway:			
Denmark:				Hides, dry......	3,507	2,011	2,933
Unclassified......	10,766			Hides, green.....	9,336	8,504	8,221
Finland:				Hides, salted.....	608	560	....
Hides, dried	6,200	2,563	646	Unclassified......	29	32	....
Hides, green.....	6,374	2,945	11,063	Portugal:			
Sheep..........	310	109	91	Hides, dried......	5,895	4,404	....
France:				Hides, green......	339	104	....
Calf..............	5,123	3,205	1,022	Roumania:			
Goat..........	19,131	16,699	5,095	Buffalo and cattle	6,326	....	
Kid..........	4,151	3,092	1,094	Horse and swine..	7	....	
Lamb..........	334	257	79	Sheep, lamb, and			
Sheep..........	3,139	3,729	398	goat..........	514		
Unclassified......	131,148	86,609	43,348	Russia:			
Germany:				Hides, dry......	14,110	11,006	61
Calf, dried......	10,641			Hides, green.....	102,700	59,212	506
Calf, green	75,846			Goat and kid.....	3,399	2,244	4
Cattle, dried.....	120,063			Sheep..........	10,078	12,162	867
Cattle, green....	249,518			Singapore:			
Goat, with hair on.	24,426			Unclassified......	[1] 10,965	8,942	....
Horse, dried.....	4,333			Spain:			
Horse, green.....	25,096			Unclassified......	18,236	11,977	28,194
Sheep and lamb..	2,582			Sweden:			
Unclassified......	2,239			Cattle, wet......	19,159	17,187	....

[1] Data for 1912.

TABLE 148.—*Hides and skins: International trade, calendar years 1913–1915*—Contd.

IMPORTS—Continued.

[000 omitted.]

Country and classification.	1913	1914 (prelim.)	1915 (prelim.)	Country and classification.	1913	1914 (prelim.)	1915 (prelim.)
Sweden—Contd.	*Pounds.*	*Pounds.*	*Pounds.*	Other countries:			
Cattle, dry	7,000	3,206	....	Hides—			
Horse, wet	26	196	....	Cattle and buffalo	*Pounds.*	*Pounds.*	*Pounds.*
Goat, kid, lamb, and sheep, wet	343	374	....		14,684	5,230	....
				Horse	54	18	....
Goat, lamb, and sheep, dry	365	363	....	Skins—			
Unclassified	65	32	....	Deer	12	14	....
United Kingdom:				Goat and kid	556	3	....
Calf, dry	24	167	....	Sheep and lamb	906	1,175	....
Calf, wet	666	1,046	1,094	Sheep and goat, mixed	235	87	....
Goat	7,203	7,541	13,287	Unclassified	48,221	20,895	....
Hides, dry and wet	105,165	117,535	164,881	Total	2,100,395	1,149,429	....
Sheep	1,717	1,283	2,426				
United States:				All countries:			
Calf, dry	26,302	13,899	22,703	Hides—			
Calf, green or pickled	50,152	53,016	26,211	Cattle and buffalo	801,966	403,341	....
				Horse	47,155	10,830	....
Cattle and buffalo, dry	77,625	83,730	140,944	Skins—			
Cattle and buffalo, green or pickled	158,655	236,773	281,141	Calf	172,617	72,059	....
				Deer	521	585	....
Goat, dry	64,509	57,983	62,721	Goat and kid	150,794	105,544	....
Goat, green or pickled	25,168	17,872	16,566	Kangaroo	1,309	1,008	....
Horse, dry	9,726	5,810	5,452	Sheep and lamb	110,785	90,418	....
Horse, green or pickled	7,425	4,806	4,475	Sheep and goat, mixed	1,457	824	....
Kangaroo	1,309	1,008	963	Unclassified	813,791	464,820	....
Sheep, dry	27,552	24,999	36,801	Total	2,100,395	1,149,429	....
Sheep, green or pickled	40,654	40,945	38,286				
Unclassified	8,803	15,353	9,991				

HORSES AND MULES.

TABLE 149.—*Horses and mules: Number and value on farms in the United States, 1867–1917.*

NOTE.—Figures in *italics* are census returns; figures in roman are estimates of the Department of Agriculture. Estimates of numbers are obtained by applying estimated percentages of increase or decrease to the published numbers of the preceding year, except that a revised base is used for applying percentage estimates whenever new census data are available. It should also be observed that the census of 1910, giving numbers as of Apr. 15, is not strictly comparable with former censuses, which related to numbers June 1.

Jan. 1—	Horses.			Mules.		
	Number.	Price per head Jan. 1.	Farm value Jan. 1.	Number.	Price per head Jan. 1.	Farm value Jan. 1.
1867	5,401,000	$59.05	$318,924,000	822,000	$66.94	$55,048,000
1868	5,757,000	54.27	312,416,000	856,000	56.04	47,954,000
1869	6,333,000	62.57	396,222,000	922,000	79.23	73,027,000
1870	8,249,000	67.43	556,251,000	1,180,000	90.42	106,654,000
1870, census, June 1	*7,145,370*			*1,125,415*		
1871	8,702,000	71.14	619,039,000	1,242,000	91.98	114,272,000
1872	8,991,000	67.41	606,111,000	1,276,000	87.14	111,222,000
1873	9,222,000	66.39	612,273,000	1,310,000	85.15	111,546,000
1874	9,334,000	65.15	608,073,000	1,339,000	81.35	108,953,000
1875	9,504,000	61.10	580,708,000	1,394,000	71.89	100,197,000
1876	9,735,000	57.29	557,747,000	1,414,000	66.46	94,001,000
1877	10,155,000	55.83	567,017,000	1,444,000	64.07	92,482,000
1878	10,330,000	56.63	584,999,000	1,638,000	62.03	101,579,000
1879	10,939,000	52.36	572,712,000	1,713,000	56.00	95,942,000
1880	11,202,000	54.75	613,297,000	1,730,000	61.26	105,948,000
1880, census, June 1	*10,357,488*			*1,812,808*		
1881	11,430,000	58.44	667,954,000	1,721,000	69.79	120,096,000
1882	10,522,000	58.53	615,825,000	1,835,000	71.35	130,945,000
1883	10,838,000	70.59	765,041,000	1,871,000	79.49	148,732,000
1884	11,170,000	74.64	833,734,000	1,914,000	84.22	161,215,000
1885	11,565,000	73.70	852,283,000	1,973,000	82.38	162,497,000
1886	12,078,000	71.27	860,823,000	2,053,000	79.60	163,381,000
1887	12,497,000	72.15	901,686,000	2,117,000	78.91	167,058,000
1888	13,173,000	71.82	946,096,000	2,192,000	79.78	174,854,000
1889	13,663,000	71.89	982,195,000	2,258,000	79.49	179,444,000
1890	14,214,000	68.84	978,517,000	2,331,000	78.25	182,394,000
1890, census, June 1	*14,969,467*			*2,295,532*		
1891	14,057,000	67.00	941,823,000	2,297,000	77.88	178,847,000
1892	15,498,000	65.01	1,007,594,000	2,315,000	75.55	174,882,000
1893	16,207,000	61.22	992,225,000	2,331,000	70.68	164,764,000
1894	16,081,000	47.83	769,225,000	2,352,000	62.17	146,233,000
1895	15,893,000	36.29	576,731,000	2,333,000	47.55	110,928,000
1896	15,124,000	33.07	500,140,000	2,279,000	45.29	103,204,000
1897	14,365,000	31.51	452,649,000	2,216,000	41.66	92,302,000
1898	13,961,000	34.26	478,362,000	2,190,000	43.88	96,110,000
1899	13,665,000	37.40	511,075,000	2,134,000	44.96	95,963,000
1900	13,538,000	44.61	603,969,000	2,086,000	53.55	111,717,000
1900, census, June 1	*18,267,020*			*3,264,615*		
1901 [1]	16,745,000	52.86	885,200,000	2,864,000	63.97	183,232,000
1902	16,531,000	58.61	968,935,000	2,757,000	67.61	186,412,000
1903	16,557,000	62.25	1,030,706,000	2,728,000	72.49	197,753,000
1904	16,736,000	67.93	1,136,940,000	2,758,000	78.88	217,533,000
1905	17,058,000	70.37	1,200,310,000	2,889,000	87.18	251,840,000
1906	18,719,000	80.72	1,510,890,000	3,404,000	98.31	334,681,000
1907	19,747,000	93.51	1,846,578,000	3,817,000	112.16	428,064,000
1908	19,992,000	93.41	1,867,530,000	3,869,000	107.76	416,939,000
1909	20,640,000	95.64	1,974,052,000	4,053,000	107.84	437,082,000
1910	21,040,000			4,123,000		
1910, census, Apr. 15	*19,833,113*	108.03	2,142,524,000	*4,209,769*	120.20	506,049,000
1911 [1]	20,277,000	111.46	2,259,981,000	4,323,000	125.92	544,359,000
1912	20,509,000	105.94	2,172,694,000	4,362,000	120.51	525,657,000
1913	20,567,000	110.77	2,278,222,000	4,386,000	124.31	545,245,000
1914	20,962,000	109.32	2,291,638,000	4,449,000	123.85	551,017,000
1915	21,195,000	103.33	2,190,102,000	4,479,000	112.36	503,271,000
1916	21,159,000	101.60	2,149,786,000	4,593,000	113.83	522,834,000
1917	21,126,000	102.94	2,174,629,000	4,639,000	118.32	548,864,000

[1] Estimates of numbers revised, based on census data.

HORSES AND MULES—Continued.

TABLE 150.—*Horses and mules: Number and value on farms Jan. 1, 1916 and 1917, by States.*

State.	Horses.						Mules.					
	Number (thousands) Jan. 1—		Average price per head, Jan. 1—		Farm value (thousands of dollars) Jan. 1—		Number (thousands) Jan. 1—		Average price per head, Jan. 1—		Farm value (thousands of dollars) Jan. 1—	
	1917	1916	1917	1916	1917	1916	1917	1916	1917	1916	1917	1916
Me....	109	109	$152.00	$142.00	$16,568	$15,478						
N. H..	44	44	135.00	132.00	5,940	5,808						
Vt....	89	89	134.00	130.00	11,926	11,570						
Mass..	59	60	156.00	146.00	9,204	8,760						
R. I...	8	9	155.00	151.00	1,240	1,359						
Conn..	46	46	147.00	146.00	6,762	6,716						
N. Y..	609	609	139.00	139.00	84,651	84,651	4	4	$155.00	$148.00	$620	$592
N. J..	92	92	149.00	144.00	13,708	13,248	4	4	169.00	164.00	676	656
Pa....	596	602	126.00	124.00	75,096	74,648	48	47	137.00	137.00	6,576	6,439
Del...	36	36	90.00	95.00	3,240	3,420	6	6	116.00	114.00	696	684
Md....	169	169	105.00	105.00	17,745	17,745	25	25	127.00	121.00	3,175	3,025
Va....	361	361	100.00	99.00	36,100	35,739	64	64	122.00	120.00	7,808	7,680
W.Va.	196	194	107.00	108.00	20,972	20,952	12	12	117.00	116.00	1,404	1,392
N. C..	185	185	125.00	122.00	23,125	22,570	200	200	150.00	140.00	30,000	28,000
S. C...	85	84	136.00	135.00	11,560	11,340	174	171	162.00	161.00	28,188	27,531
Ga....	127	125	129.00	126.00	16,383	15,750	324	315	163.00	156.00	52,812	49,140
Fla....	60	59	120.00	112.00	7,200	6,608	31	29	166.00	154.00	5,146	4,466
Ohio..	892	901	119.00	116.00	106,148	104,516	26	26	120.00	119.00	3,120	3,094
Ind....	845	854	108.00	104.00	91,260	88,816	95	95	114.00	111.00	10,830	10,545
Ill.....	1,452	1,452	106.00	103.00	153.912	149,556	150	152	115.00	111.00	17,250	16,872
Mich..	680	680	121.00	128.00	82,280	87,040	4	4	122.00	133.00	488	532
Wis...	715	712	120.00	124.00	85,800	88,288	3	3	117.00	120.00	351	360
Minn .	900	890	109.00	109.00	98,100	97,010	6	6	110.00	116.00	660	696
Iowa..	1,552	1,584	107.00	105.00	166,064	166,320	62	61	116.00	110.00	7,192	6,710
Mo....	1,040	1,060	92.00	90.00	95,680	95,400	350	340	104.00	99.00	36,400	33,660
N.Dak	825	801	106.00	110.00	87,450	88,110	9	9	122.00	124.00	1,098	1,116
S. Dak	774	759	93.00	93.00	71,982	70,587	15	15	108.00	109.00	1,620	1,635
Nebr..	1,018	1,028	95.00	94.00	96,710	96,632	112	98	106.00	104.00	11,872	10,192
Kans..	1,120	1,109	99.00	97.00	110,880	107,573	265	255	108.00	105.00	28,620	26,775
Ky....	434	434	93.00	90.00	40,362	39,060	224	229	112.00	102.00	25,088	23,358
Tenn..	350	349	105.00	101.00	36,750	35,249	270	272	120.00	113.00	32,400	30,736
Ala....	150	150	99.00	101.00	14,850	15,150	278	281	118.00	121.00	32,804	34,001
Miss..	243	243	87.00	88.00	21,141	21,384	292	292	109.00	110.00	31,828	32,120
La....	195	193	86.00	82.00	16,770	15,826	139	132	125.00	121.00	17,375	15,972
Tex...	1,156	1,180	78.00	78.00	90,168	92,040	760	768	103.00	100.00	78,280	76,800
Okla..	743	743	86.00	85.00	63,898	63,155	276	282	104.00	98.00	28,704	27,636
Ark...	275	270	87.00	82.00	23,925	22,140	250	240	114.00	102.00	28,500	24,480
Mont..	452	430	92.00	86.00	41,584	36,980	4	4	107.00	98.00	428	392
Wyo..	191	185	80.00	82.00	15,280	15,170	3	3	97.00	99.00	291	297
Colo...	365	361	93.00	90.00	33,945	32,490	20	19	104.00	101.00	2,080	1,919
N.Mex	250	234	62.00	58.00	15,500	13,572	19	17	89.00	85.00	1,691	1,445
Ariz...	129	124	75.00	71.00	9,675	8,804	8	7	104.00	99.00	832	693
Utah..	138	146	87.00	86.00	12,006	12,556	2	2	79.00	78.00	158	156
Nev...	73	77	76.00	75.00	5,548	5,775	3	3	85.00	75.00	255	225
Idaho.	239	241	93.00	90.00	22,227	21,690	4	4	100.00	95.00	400	380
Wash..	305	308	98.00	94.00	29,890	28,952	18	17	111.00	106.00	1,998	1,802
Oreg..	286	295	98.00	89.00	28,028	26,255	10	10	103.00	93.00	1,030	903
Cal....	468	493	97.00	96.00	45,396	47,328	70	70	116.00	110.00	8,120	7,700
U.S.	21,126	21,159	102.94	101.60	2,174,629	2,149,786	4,639	4,593	118.32	113.83	548,864	522.834

HORSES AND MULES.

TABLE 151.—*Prices of horses and mules at St. Louis, 1900–1916.*

Year and month.	Range of prices.				Year and month.	Range of prices.				Year and month.	Range of prices.			
	Horses, grade, good to choice draft.		Mules, grade, 16 to 16½ hands.			Horses, grade, good to choice draft.		Mules, grade, 16 to 16½ hands.			Horses, grade, good to choice draft.		Mules, grade, 16 to 16½ hands.	
	L.	H.	L.	H.		L.	H.	L.	H.		L.	H.	L.	H.
1900	$140	$190	$90	$150	1915.					1916.				
1901	150	175	110	165	Jan	$185	$220	$125	$250	Jan	$150	$185	$135	$270
1902	160	185	120	160	Feb	185	220	125	250	Feb	150	185	135	275
1903	160	185	120	175	Mar	185	225	125	250	Mar	150	185	150	275
1904	175	200	135	200	Apr	185	225	120	265	Apr	150	190	150	275
1905	175	225	120	210	May	175	220	120	265	May	160	200	150	275
1906	175	225	125	215	June	175	220	125	265	June	160	200	150	275
1907	175	225	125	250	July	175	220	125	265	July	175	225	150	270
1908	175	250	125	200	Aug	180	220	135	265	Aug	175	225	140	250
1909	140	225	130	225	Sept	185	225	135	265	Sept	175	225	150	250
1910	165	240	150	275	Oct	185	225	135	275	Oct	160	220	140	235
1911	165	235	150	275	Nov	185	225	135	275	Nov	150	220	140	235
1912	165	240	160	285	Dec	160	185	135	275	Dec	150	220	150	275
1913	200	250	160	280										
1914	175	220	120	250	Year, 1915.	160	225	120	275	Year, 1916.	150	225	135	275

TABLE 152.—*Average price per head for horses on the Chicago horse market, 1901–1916.*

Date.	Drafters.	Carriage teams.	Drivers.	General.	Bussers, trammers.	Saddlers.[1]	Southern chunks.
1901	$157.00	$400.00	$137.00	$102.00	$121.00	$147.00	$52.00
1902	166.00	450.00	145.00	117.00	135.00	151.00	57.00
1903	171.00	455.00	150.00	122.00	140.00	156.00	62.00
1904	177.00	475.00	150.00	140.00	140.00	160.00	64.00
1905	186.00	486.00	156.00	132.00	145.00	172.00	70.00
1906	188.00	486.00	158.00	154.00	147.00	174.00	72.50
1907	194.00	482.00	165.00	137.00	152.00	172.00	77.50
1908	180.00	450.00	156.00	129.00	138.00	164.00	69.00
1909	194.00	482.00	165.00	137.00	152.00	172.00	77.00
1910	200.00	473.00	172.00	144.00	161.00	177.00	87.00
1911	205.00	483.00	182.00	155.00	170.00	190.00	92.00
1912	210.00	473.00	177.00	160.00	175.00	195.00	97.00
1913	213.00	493.00	174.00	165.00	176.00	189.00	98.00
1914	208.00	483.00	169.00	160.00	171.00	184.00	93.00
1915.							
January	205.00	440.00	165.00	150.00	160.00	180.00	90.00
February	215.00	490.00	170.00	155.00	170.00	190.00	95.00
March	220.00	510.00	175.00	160.00	175.00	195.00	100.00
April	220.00	510.00	175.00	160.00	175.00	195.00	100.00
May	215.00	510.00	170.00	155.00	170.00	190.00	95.00
June	210.00	510.00	165.00	150.00	165.00	185.00	90.00
July	205.00	480.00	165.00	145.00	165.00	180.00	85.00
August	195.00	470.00	160.00	140.00	160.00	175.00	80.00
September	190.00	455.00	155.00	145.00	170.00	170.00	75.00
October	190.00	440.00	155.00	145.00	165.00	165.00	75.00
November	195.00	440.00	155.00	140.00	160.00	165.00	80.00
December	190.00	440.00	155.00	140.00	160.00	165.00	90.00
Year	205.00	473.00	164.00	155.00	166.00	179.00	88.00
1916.							
January	225.00		150.00	160.00	165.00	125.00	110.00
February	250.00		200.00	160.00	165.00	125.00	110.00
March	275.00		150.00	160.00	165.00	125.00	110.00
April	275.00		150.00	160.00	165.00	125.00	110.00
May	250.00		200.00	160.00	165.00	125.00	110.00
June	225.00		150.00	160.00	165.00	125.00	110.00
July	225.00	No sales.	150.00	160.00	165.00	115.00	110.00
August	250.00		175.00	160.00	165.00	115.00	110.00
September	250.00		175.00	160.00	165.00	115.00	110.00
October	275.00		200.00	160.00	165.00	115.00	110.00
November[2]	263.00		145.00	162.00	175.00	142.00	102.00
December[2]	263.00		145.00	162.00	175.00	142.00	102.00
Year	252.00		166.00	160.00	167.00	124.00	109.00

[1] Cavalry horses, 1916.　　　　[2] Mean of low and high quotations.

HORSES AND MULES—Continued.

TABLE 153.—*Number of horses and mules received at principal live-stock markets.*

[From reports of stockyards companies.]

Year and month.	Horses.	Horses and mules.		
	Chicago.	St. Louis (National Stock Yards, Ill.)	Kansas City.	Omaha.
1900	99,010	144,921	103,308	59,645
1901	109,353	128,880	96,657	36,391
1902	102,100	109,295	76,844	42,079
1903	100,603	128,615	67,274	52,829
1904	105,949	181,341	67,562	46,845
1905	127,250	178,257	65,582	45,422
1906	126,979	166,393	69,629	42,269
1907	102,055	117,379	62,341	44,020
1908	92,138	109,393	56,335	39,998
1909	91,411	122,471	67,796	31,711
1910	83,439	130,271	69,628	29,734
1911	104,545	170,379	84,861	31,771
1912	92,977	163,973	73,445	32,520
1913	90,615	156,825	82,110	31,580
1914	106,282	148,128	87,155	30,688
1915.				
January	11,213	25,554	16,671	4,981
February	12,616	29,979	11,800	4,233
March	14,930	25,794	12,820	4,420
April	10,895	23,849	13,748	3,001
May	13,831	25,944	11,425	2,355
June	14,978	25,627	4,917	3,498
July	11,726	21,400	4,425	3,758
August	14,931	16,543	3,030	2,655
September	18,004	14,426	3,990	4,081
October	17,742	27,458	7,424	4,557
November	14,339	17,066	6,714	3,518
December	10,048	16,972	5,189	622
Total, 1915	165,253	270,612	102,153	41,679
1916.				
January	12,986	25,809	7,886	1,443
February	15,913	20,114	4,735	2,135
March	17,469	17,599	5,012	2,952
April	14,882	14,881	7,073	1,695
May	18,240	20,695	8,171	3,036
June	17,557	15,785	7,156	2,338
July	18,990	26,574	11,027	2,177
August	23,896	23,292	13,414	3,152
September	21,132	26,655	13,349	3,332
October	18,952	31,147	17,145	2,042
November	14,342	22,244	13,093	1,731
December	11,090	22,023	15,080	1,453
Total, 1916	205,449	266,818	123,141	27,486

HORSES AND MULES—Continued.

TABLE 154.—*Horses and mules: Imports, exports, and prices, 1893–1916.*

Year ending June 30—	Imports of horses.			Exports of horses.			Exports of mules.		
	Number.	Value.	Average import price.	Number.	Value.	Average export price.	Number.	Value.	Average export price.
1893	15,451	$2,388,267	$154.57	2,967	$718,607	$242.20	1,634	$210,278	$128.69
1894	6,166	1,319,572	214.01	5,246	1,108,995	211.40	2,063	240,961	116.80
1895	13,098	1,055,191	80.56	13,984	2,209,298	157.99	2,515	186,452	74.14
1896	9,991	662,591	66.32	25,126	3,530,703	140.52	5,918	406,161	68.63
1897	6,998	464,808	66.42	39,532	4,769,265	120.64	7,473	545,331	72.97
1898	3,085	414,899	134.49	51,150	6,176,569	120.75	8,098	664,789	82.09
1899	3,042	551,050	181.15	45,778	5,444,342	118.93	6,755	516,908	76.52
1900	3,102	596,592	192.32	64,722	7,612,616	117.62	43,369	3,919,478	90.38
1901	3,785	985,738	260.43	82,250	8,873,845	107.89	34,405	3,210,267	93.31
1902	4,832	1,577,234	326.41	103,020	10,048,046	97.53	27,586	2,692,298	97.60
1903	4,999	1,536,296	307.32	34,007	3,152,159	92.69	4,294	521,725	121.47
1904	4,726	1,460,287	308.99	42,001	3,189,100	75.93	3,658	412,971	112.90
1905	5,180	1,591,083	307.16	34,822	3,175,259	91.19	5,826	645,464	110.79
1906	6,021	1,716,675	285.11	40,087	4,365,981	108.91	7,167	989,639	138.08
1907	6,080	1,978,105	325.35	33,882	4,359,957	131.99	6,781	850,901	125.48
1908	5,487	1,604,392	292.40	19,000	2,612,587	137.50	6,609	990,667	149.90
1909	7,084	2,007,276	283.35	21,616	3,386,617	156.67	3,432	472,017	137.53
1910	11,620	3,296,022	283.65	28,910	4,081,157	141.17	4,512	614.094	136.18
1911	9,593	2,692,074	280.63	25,145	3,845,253	152.92	6,585	1,070,051	162.50
1912	6,607	1,923,025	291.06	34,828	4,764,815	136.81	4,901	732,005	149.30
1913	10,008	2,125,875	212.42	28,707	3,960,102	137.95	4,744	733,795	154.68
1914	33,019	2,605,029	78.89	22,776	3,388,819	148.79	4,883	690,974	141.51
1915	12,652	977,380	77.25	289,340	64,046,534	221.35	65,788	12,726,143	193.44
1916	15,556	1,618,245	104.03	357,553	73,531,146	205.65	111,915	22,946,312	205.03

CATTLE.

TABLE 155.—*Cattle (live): Imports, exports, and prices, 1893–1916.*

Year ending June 30—	Imports.			Exports.		
	Number.	Value.	Average import price.	Number.	Value.	Average export price.
1893	3,293	$45,682	$13.87	287,094	$26,032,428	$90.68
1894	1,592	18,704	11.75	359,278	33,461,922	93.14
1895	149,781	765,853	5.11	331,722	30,603,796	92.26
1896	217,826	1,509,856	6.93	372,461	34,560,672	92.79
1897	328,977	2,589,857	7.87	392,190	36,357,451	92.70
1898	291,589	2,913,223	9.99	439,255	37,827,500	86.12
1899	199,752	2,320,362	11.62	389,490	30,516,833	78.35
1900	181,006	2,257,694	12.47	397,286	30,635,153	77.11
1901	146,022	1,931,433	13.23	459,218	37,566,980	81.81
1902	96,027	1,608,722	16.75	392,884	29,902,212	76.11
1903	66,175	1,161,548	17.55	402,178	29,848,936	74.22
1904	16,056	310,737	19.35	593,409	42,256,291	71.21
1905	27,855	458,572	16.46	567,806	40,598,048	71.50
1906	29,019	548,430	18.90	584,239	42,081,170	72.03
1907	32,402	565,122	17.44	423,051	34,577,392	81.73
1908	92,356	1,507,310	16.32	349,210	29,339,134	84.02
1909	139,184	1,999,422	14.37	207,542	18,046,976	86.96
1910	195,938	2,999,824	15.37	139,430	12,200,154	87.50
1911	182,923	2,953,077	16.14	150,100	13,163,920	87.70
1912	318,372	4,805,574	15.09	105,506	8,870,075	84.07
1913	421,649	6,640,668	15.75	24,714	1,177,199	47.63
1914	868,368	18,696,718	21.53	18,376	647,288	35.22
1915	538,167	17,513,175	32.54	5,484	702,847	128.16
1916	439,185	15,187,593	34.58	21,666	2,383,765	110.02

CATTLE—Continued.

TABLE 156.—*Cattle: Number and value on farms in the United States, 1867–1917.*

NOTE.—Figures in *italics* are census returns; figures in roman are estimates of the Department of Agriculture. Estimates of numbers are obtained by applying estimated percentages of increase or decrease to the published numbers of the preceding year, except that a revised base is used for applying percentage estimates whenever new census data are available. It should also be observed that the census of 1910, giving numbers as of Apr. 15, is not strictly comparable with former censuses, which related to numbers June 1.

Jan. 1—	Milch cows.			Other cattle.		
	Number.	Price per head Jan. 1.	Farm value Jan. 1.	Number.	Price per head Jan. 1.	Farm value Jan. 1.
1867	8,349,000	$28.74	$239,947,000	11,731,000	$15.79	$185,254,000
1868	8,692,000	26.56	230,817,000	11,942,000	15.06	179,888,000
1869	9,248,000	29.15	269,610,000	12,185,000	18.73	228,183,000
1870	10,096,000	32.70	330,175,000	15,388,000	18.87	290,401,000
1870, census June 1	*8,935,332*			*13,566,005*		
1871	10,023,000	33.89	339,701,000	16,212,000	20.78	336,860,000
1872	10,304,000	29.45	303,438,000	16,390,000	18.12	296,932,000
1873	10,576,000	26.72	282,559,000	16,414,000	18.06	296,448,000
1874	10,705,000	25.63	274,326,000	16,218,000	17.55	284,706,000
1875	10,907,000	25.74	280,701,000	16,313,000	16.91	275,872,000
1876	11,085,000	25.61	283,879,000	16,785,000	17.00	285,387,000
1877	11,261,000	25.47	286,778,000	17,956,000	15.99	287,156,000
1878	11,300,000	25.74	290,898,000	19,223,000	16.72	321,346,000
1879	11,826,000	21.71	256,721,000	21,408,000	15.38	329,254,000
1880	12,027,000	23.27	279,899,000	21,231,000	16.10	341,761,000
1880, census June 1	*12,443,120*			*22,488,550*		
1881	12,369,000	23.95	296,277,000	20,939,000	17.33	362,862,000
1882	12,612,000	25.89	326,489,000	23,280,000	19.89	463,070,000
1883	13,126,000	30.21	396,575,000	28,046,000	21.81	611,549,000
1884	13,501,000	31.37	423,487,000	29,046,000	23.52	683,229,000
1885	13,905,000	29.70	412,903,000	29,867,000	23.25	694,383,000
1886	14,235,000	27.40	389,986,000	31,275,000	21.17	661,956,000
1887	14,522,000	26.08	378,790,000	33,512,000	19.79	663,138,000
1888	14,856,000	24.65	366,252,000	34,378,000	17.79	611,751,000
1889	15,299,000	23.94	366,226,000	35,032,000	17.05	597,237,000
1890	15,953,000	22.14	353,152,000	36,849,000	15.21	560,625,000
1890, census June 1	*16,511,950*			*33,734,128*		
1891	16,020,000	21.62	346,398,000	36,876,000	14.76	544,128,000
1892	16,416,000	21.40	351,378,000	37,651,000	15.16	570,749,000
1893	16,424,000	21.75	357,300,000	35,954,000	15.24	547,882,000
1894	16,487,000	21.77	358,999,000	36,608,000	14.66	536,790,000
1895	16,505,000	21.97	362,602,000	34,364,000	14.06	482,999,000
1896	16,138,000	22.55	363,956,000	32,085,000	15.86	508,928,000
1897	15,942,000	23.16	369,240,000	30,508,000	16.65	507,929,000
1898	15,841,000	27.45	434,814,000	29,264,000	20.92	612,297,000
1899	15,990,000	29.66	474,234,000	27,994,000	22.79	637,931,000
1900	16,292,000	31.60	514,812,000	27,610,000	24.97	689,486,000
1900, census June 1	*17,135,633*			*50,585,777*		
1901 [1]	16,834,000	30.00	505,093,000	45,500,000	19.93	906,644,000
1902	16,697,000	29.23	488,130,000	44,728,000	18.76	839,126,000
1903	17,105,000	30.21	516,712,000	44,659,000	18.45	824,055,000
1904	17,420,000	29.21	508,841,000	43,629,000	16.32	712,178,000
1905	17,572,000	27.44	482,272,000	43,669,000	15.15	661,571,000
1906	19,794,000	29.44	582,789,000	47,068,000	15.85	746,172,000
1907	20,968,000	31.00	645,497,000	51,566,000	17.10	881,557,000
1908	21,194,000	30.67	650,057,000	50,073,000	16.89	845,938,000
1909	21,720,000	32.36	702,945,000	49,379,000	17.49	863,754,000
1910	21,801,000			47,279,000		
1910, census Apr. 15	*20,625,432*	35.29	727,802,000	*41,178,434*	19.07	785,261,000
1911 [1]	20,823,000	39.97	832,209,000	39,679,000	20.54	815,184,000
1912	20,699,000	39.39	815,414,000	37,260,000	21.20	790,064,000
1913	20,497,000	45.02	922,783,000	36,030,000	26.36	949,645,000
1914	20,737,000	53.94	1,118,487,000	35,855,000	31.13	1,116,333,000
1915	21,262,000	55.33	1,176,338,000	37,067,000	33.38	1,237,376,000
1916	22,108,000	53.92	1,191,955,000	39,812,000	33.53	1,334,928,000
1917	22,768,000	59.66	1,358,435,000	40,849,000	35.88	1,465,786,000

[1] Estimates of numbers revised, based on census data.

CATTLE—Continued.

TABLE 157.—*Cattle: Number and value on farms Jan. 1, 1916 and 1917, by States.*

State.	Milch cows.						Other cattle.					
	Number (thousands) Jan. 1—		Average price per head Jan. 1—		Farm value (thousands of dollars) Jan. 1—		Number (thousands) Jan. 1—		Average price per head Jan. 1—		Farm value (thousands of dollars) Jan. 1—	
	1917	1916	1917	1916	1917	1916	1917	1916	1917	1916	1917	1916
Maine............	162	159	$58.00	$50.00	$9,396	$7,950	110	105	$27.90	$24.60	$3,069	$2,583
New Hampshire.	97	97	66.50	60.00	6,450	5,820	63	63	31.60	28.50	1,991	1,796
Vermont........	281	273	62.50	54.00	17,562	14,742	172	170	25.70	23.30	4,420	3,961
Massachusetts...	160	158	75.00	68.00	12,000	10,744	88	85	29.60	25.40	2,605	2,159
Rhode Island...	22	22	77.00	77.00	1,694	1,694	11	11	31.30	28.30	344	311
Connecticut.....	121	119	73.50	68.30	8,894	8,128	73	72	30.80	29.70	2,248	2,138
New York......	1,539	1,539	66.00	57.20	101,574	88,031	939	939	31.00	26.90	29,109	25,259
New Jersey.....	155	152	76.00	71.00	11,780	10,792	74	73	34.00	32.50	2,516	2,372
Pennsylvania...	980	971	62.50	56.50	61,250	54,862	664	657	30.80	27.10	20,451	17,805
Delaware........	43	42	56.00	53.00	2,408	2,226	21	21	31.90	28.00	670	588
Maryland.......	183	181	58.00	52.00	10,614	9,412	125	125	32.20	28.80	4,025	3,600
Virginia........	373	359	46.50	41.50	17,344	14,898	486	472	31.80	28.20	15,455	13,310
West Virginia...	245	241	53.50	50.00	13,108	12,050	369	362	38.70	36.30	14,280	13,141
North Carolina..	315	321	39.00	34.00	12,285	10,914	364	375	19.40	16.80	7,062	6,300
South Carolina..	189	189	40.00	34.50	7,560	6,520	215	215	18.30	15.40	3,934	3,311
Georgia.........	418	414	37.00	31.50	15,466	13,041	686	686	16.20	13.50	11,113	9,261
Florida.........	141	136	43.00	40.00	6,053	5,440	865	800	16.50	14.90	14,272	11,920
Ohio............	950	922	60.00	56.00	57,000	51,632	863	872	36.40	33.80	31,413	29,474
Indiana.........	706	672	58.50	54.50	41,301	36,624	735	728	39.00	36.80	28,665	26,790
Illinois..........	1,057	1,047	68.00	60.20	71,876	63,029	1,251	1,239	43.30	38.50	54,168	47,702
Michigan........	865	847	61.50	56.20	53,198	47,601	720	735	30.20	27.30	21,744	20,066
Wisconsin.......	1,750	1,675	65.00	55.00	113,750	92,125	1,340	1,313	29.80	25.20	39,932	33,088
Minnesota.......	1,302	1,240	58.00	51.00	75,516	63,240	1,340	1,275	26.50	22.40	35,510	28,560
Iowa............	1,405	1,391	66.50	58.50	93,432	81,374	2,754	2,737	43.20	38.30	118,973	104,827
Missouri........	845	837	58.50	54.40	49,432	45,533	1,600	1,555	40.90	38.90	65,440	60,490
North Dakota...	410	373	61.50	57.00	25,215	21,261	629	577	38.20	35.00	24,028	20,195
South Dakota...	524	485	67.00	59.00	35,108	28,615	1,181	1,064	43.70	38.40	51,610	40,858
Nebraska.......	676	650	68.00	60.00	45,968	39,000	2,349	2,237	44.30	40.50	104,061	90,598
Kansas.........	900	835	64.50	60.60	58,050	50,601	2,115	2,160	43.10	41.70	91,156	90,072
Kentucky.......	418	406	49.50	44.80	20,691	18,189	570	570	33.70	30.80	19,209	17,556
Tennessee.......	366	366	43.00	39.50	15,738	14,457	528	518	25.50	22.60	13,464	11,707
Alabama........	405	405	36.50	32.00	14,782	12,960	534	534	14.70	13.00	7,850	6,942
Mississippi......	450	447	38.00	33.50	17,100	14,974	535	535	16.40	14.10	8,774	7,544
Louisiana.......	274	271	42.00	37.00	11,508	10,027	475	475	20.00	16.80	9,500	7,980
Texas...........	1,175	1,119	54.50	51.00	64,038	57,069	5,482	5,428	32.60	33.10	178,713	179,667
Oklahoma.......	535	519	60.00	55.00	32,100	28,545	1,222	1,186	38.90	37.90	47,536	44,949
Arkansas.......	402	402	44.00	38.00	17,688	15,276	550	523	19.20	17.00	10,560	8,891
Montana........	148	129	79.00	77.50	11,692	9,998	983	894	53.10	50.40	52,197	45,058
Wyoming.......	55	50	81.50	80.50	4,482	4,025	825	750	52.70	52.70	43,478	39,525
Colorado........	237	219	73.50	72.00	17,420	15,768	1,150	1,096	44.70	44.80	51,405	49,101
New Mexico.....	85	76	68.00	67.00	5,780	5,092	1,145	1,090	39.70	40.10	45,456	43,709
Arizona.........	81	58	85.00	78.00	6,885	4,524	864	838	37.30	34.20	32,227	28,660
Utah...........	91	96	61.00	62.00	5,551	5,952	408	408	34.90	35.80	14,239	14,606
Nevada.........	26	25	76.00	76.00	1,976	1,900	470	472	39.50	39.70	18,565	18,738
Idaho...........	130	126	63.50	66.00	8,255	8,316	418	406	38.60	38.60	16,135	15,672
Washington.....	263	263	59.50	60.50	15,648	15,912	275	255	30.40	30.30	8,360	7,726
Oregon.........	222	216	55.00	55.00	12,210	11,880	577	553	37.30	32.20	21,522	17,807
California.......	591	568	67.00	69.00	39,597	39,192	1,636	1,558	38.10	36.30	62,332	56,555
United States.	22,768	22,108	59.66	53.92	1,358,435	1,191,955	40,849	39,812	35.88	33.53	1,465,786	1,334,928

CATTLE—Continued.

TABLE 158.—*Cattle: Wholesale price per 100 pounds, 1912–1916.*

Date.	Chicago. Inferior to prime.		Cincinnati. Fair to medium.		St. Louis. Good to choice native steers.		Kansas City. Common to prime.		Omaha. Native beeves.	
	Low.	High.	Low.	High.	Low.	High.	Low.	High.	Low.	High.
1912.										
January–June.....	$1.75	$9.60	$4.10	$6.25	$7.35	$9.50	$4.60	$9.50	....	....
July–December...	2.25	11.25	4.05	6.75	8.30	11.00	5.50	12.40	....	....
1913.										
January–June.....	3.00	9.50	4.65	7.65	8.00	9.25	4.75	9.00	$3.25	$8.80
July–December...	3.00	10.25	4.50	7.00	8.50	10.00	4.50	10.00	3.00	9.60
1914.										
January–June.....	6.60	9.75	5.35	7.25	8.00	9.00	5.20	9.40	6.50	9.25
July–December...	4.85	11.25	4.65	7.25	8.00	9.50	4.50	11.35	6.00	10.75
1915.										
January............	4.60	9.65	4.85	6.25	8.50	9.25	6.00	9.75	8.50	8.50
February..........	4.25	9.25	5.00	6.65	7.40	8.85	6.00	8.85	8.30	8.30
March.............	4.50	9.15	5.10	6.50	8.50	9.00	6.00	8.65	8.45	8.45
April..............	4.65	8.90	5.00	6.50	7.35	8.85	6.00	9.00	8.50	8.50
May...............	4.90	9.65	5.25	7.00	8.50	9.30	6.00	9.25	9.00	9.00
June...............	4.75	9.95	5.35	7.00	9.00	9.40	6.00	9.35	9.35	9.35
Jan.–June...	4.25	9.95	4.85	7.00	7.35	9.40	6.00	9.75	8.30	9.35
July..............	4.50	10.40	5.25	7.00	9.60	10.35	6.60	10.10	10.10	10.10
August...........	4.50	10.50	4.60	6.65	9.25	10.00	6.80	10.00	9.85	9.85
September.......	4.25	10.50	4.15	6.00	10.00	10.00	6.60	10.10	9.85	9.85
October..........	4.00	10.60	4.00	5.80	10.00	10.35	6.60	10.25	9.90	9.90
November........	4.50	10.55	4.50	5.75	9.75	10.30	6.00	10.25	10.00	10.00
December........	4.50	13.60	4.50	6.00	8.80	10.40	5.50	10.35	10.00	10.00
July–Dec....	4.00	13.60	4.15	7.00	8.80	10.40	5.50	10.35	9.85	10.10
1916.										
January...........	5.50	9.85	5.00	6.25	8.40	9.60	7.15	9.75	6.00	8.75
February.........	5.70	9.75	5.00	6.40	8.50	9.00	6.90	9.75	6.25	8.65
March.............	6.75	10.05	5.50	7.40	9.00	10.00	7.10	10.05	7.00	9.40
April.............	7.25	10.00	6.00	7.75	9.25	10.00	7.50	10.00	7.25	9.50
May..............	7.50	10.90	6.25	9.25	9.55	10.35	7.50	11.05	7.65	10.65
June...............	7.15	11.50	6.25	8.50	10.60	11.35	8.00	11.50	7.25	11.00
Jan.–June...	5.50	11.50	5.00	9.25	8.40	11.35	6.90	11.50	6.00	11.00
July..............	6.00	11.30	6.00	8.00	9.60	11.00	7.75	11.30	6.75	10.40
August...........	6.00	11.50	6.00	7.50	9.20	10.50	7.75	11.35	6.50	10.60
September.......	5.60	11.50	5.75	7.25	10.35	10.85	9.50	11.25	6.50	10.85
October..........	5.50	11.65	5.50	7.00	10.60	11.15	7.75	10.50	6.50	11.10
November........	5.65	12.40	5.50	7.35	9.00	9.85	6.00	11.75	6.50	11.10
December........	6.25	13.00	6.00	7.75	8.00	11.50	6.00	12.00	7.00	11.50
July–Dec....	5.50	13.00	5.50	8.00	8.00	11.50	6.00	12.00	6.50	11.50

BUTTER AND EGGS.

TABLE 159.—*Butter: Wholesale price per pound, 1912–1916.*

Date.	Elgin.		Chicago.				Cincinnati.		Milwaukee.		New York.	
	Creamery, extra.		Creamery, extra.		Dairies, firsts to extras.		Creamery, extra.		Creamery, fancy.		Creamery, extra.	
	Low.	High.	Low.	High.	Low.	High.	Low.	High.	Low.	High.	Low.	High.
	Cts.	*Cts.*	*Cts.*	*Cts.*	*Cts.*	*Cts.*	*Cts.*	*Cts.*	*Cts.*	*Cts.*	*Cts.*	*Cts.*
1912.												
January–June	25	40	25	40	22	34	27½	42½	25	40	26	41
July–December	25	35½	24	37	22	33	27½	39	25	35½	26	38
1913.												
January–June	26½	35	25	36	24	33	31	40	27	35	26½	42
July–December	26	35½	24	36	24	33	30	39½	26	35½	26	37½
1914.												
January–June	23½	35½	24	35½	20	33	27½	39½	23½	35½	24½	50
July–December	26	34	26	34	22	33½	30	38	26	34	26¾	36½
1915.												
January	30	34	30	34	27½	32	34	38	30	34	32	36
February	29	32	29	32	26	30	34	36	30½	32	24	30
March	28½	29	28	29½	22	28	32	34½	28	30	28½	32
April	28	31½	27½	31	22	30	32	35½	28	31½	29	32
May	25½	28	26	28½	21	27	29½	32½	25½	28	27½	31
June	26½	28	27	27½	23	27	30½	32	26½	28½	28	28½
January–June	25½	34	26	34	21	32	29½	38	25½	34	24	36
July	24½	27	25	27	22	26	28½	31	25	26½	26	28½
August	24	25	24	25	21	25	28	29	24	24½	25	26¾
September	24½	26	24	26½	21	24	28	30	24	26	25½	28¼
October	26	28	26½	28	22	27	30	32	26	28	28	29
November	28	33	28	32	23	30	32	37	28	33	28¾	34
December	33	34	32	34	25	30	37	38	33	34	33	36½
July–December	24	34	24	34	21	30	28	38	24	34	25	36½
1916.												
January	30	31½	30	32	25	30	35	35½	30	31½	31	33½
February	30	34	30	33½	25	31½	34	37	30	34	30½	36
March	34	36	34	36½	28	35	38	40	34	36	36	38
April	32	36	32½	36	31	35	37	40	33	36	33½	37¾
May	28	32	28½	32	27	32	32	37	28	32	30	34
June	28	29	27½	29	25	29	32	33	28	29	29	30½
January–June	28	36	27½	36½	25	35	32	40	28	36	29	38
July	27½	28	27½	28	25	27½	31½	32	27½	28	28½	30
August	28	31	28½	31½	......	......	32	35	28	31	30	33½
September	31½	34	31½	34	......	......	35	37	31	33	33	34
October	34	35	34	35	......	......	37	39	34	35	35½	36½
November	35	42	35	42	......	......	39	46	35	42	36	42½
December	37	42	37	40	......	......	41	46	37	42	37	41½
July–December	27½	42	27½	42	25	27½	31½	46	27½	42	28½	42½

BUTTER AND EGGS—Continued.

TABLE 160.—*Butter: International trade, calendar years 1913–1915.*

[Butter includes all butter made from milk, melted and renovated butter, but does not include margarine cocoa butter, or ghee. See "General note," Table 10.]

EXPORTS.

[000 omitted.]

Country.	1913	1914	1915 (prelim.)	Country.	1913	1914	1915 (prelim.)
	Pounds.	*Pounds.*	*Pounds.*		*Pounds.*	*Pounds.*	*Pounds.*
Argentina	8,342	7,676	10,192	Netherlands	81,702	84,407	93,113
Australia	76,334	56,163		New Zealand	41,693	48,616	47,056
Austria-Hungary	3,039			Norway	2,346	1,575	3,607
Belgium	2,147			Russia	172,903	118,997	111,950
Canada	1,220	2,500	3,593	Sweden	43,330	41,941	
Denmark	200,670			United States	3,115	3,688	17,941
Finland	27,867	24,567	20,015	Other countries	4,033	2,649	
France	38,360	44,619	50,337				
Germany	602			Total	712,837	446,708	
Italy	6,034	9,310	7,689				

IMPORTS.

Country.	1913	1914	1915 (prelim.)	Country.	1913	1914	1915 (prelim.)
Austria-Hungary	14,616			Germany	119,576		
Belgium	14,522			Netherlands	5,529	3,880	904
Brazil	4,336	2,364	732	Russia	3,382	2,969	1,517
British South Africa	3,910	3,924	2,030	Sweden	432	189	
Canada	7,886	7,250	5,661	Switzerland	11,155	8,900	5,700
Denmark	6,242			United Kingdom	451,736	436,019	426,355
Dutch East Indies	4,550	4,965		Other countries	29,737	29,019	
Egypt	1,958	1,945	1,194				
Finland	3,333	2,959	4,916	Total	695,934	518,038	
France	13,034	13,655	1,710				

BUTTER AND EGGS—Continued.

TABLE 161.—*Butter: Average price received by farmers on first of each month, by States, 1916.*

State and division.	Butter, cents per pound.											
	January.	February.	March.	April.	May.	June.	July.	August.	September.	October.	November.	December.
Maine	32	31	31	32	32	32	31	33	31	34	35	37
New Hampshire	34	34	33	30	32	34	32	33	34	36	39	39
Vermont	33	34	34	35	36	34	32	32	34	34	37	39
Massachusetts	35	35	36	36	38	36	34	36	37	37	41	41
Rhode Island	36	34	34	37	35	34	32	36	37	40	40	40
Connecticut	35	34	34	34	35	35	35	34	36	38	37	40
New York	33	32	32	32	34	32	30	30	32	34	36	39
New Jersey	36	34	36	34	36	35	34	34	35	37	39	41
Pennsylvania	34	32	32	33	32	29	28	29	31	34	36	39
Delaware	36	30	32		30	32	38	36	32			38
Maryland	29	30	28	29	28	26	24	26	28	29	32	35
Virginia	26	26	26	26	26	25	23	23	26	26	28	30
West Virginia	28	27	26	27	28	24	23	25	26	27	30	32
North Carolina	25	24	24	23	24	24	24	24	25	26	26	29
South Carolina	26	25	26	26	28	27	28	28	27	28	32	31
Georgia	25	25	25	26	25	25	25	25	26	28	29	30
Florida	35	34	36	34	34	35	34	36	35	37	36	39
Ohio	29	27	27	28	28	26	26	26	27	29	31	35
Indiana	25	24	24	25	25	24	24	24	25	26	29	32
Illinois	28	27	27	28	27	26	26	26	28	29	30	34
Michigan	28	28	27	28	28	26	25	26	28	30	32	36
Wisconsin	33	31	31	33	32	30	28	28	30	32	35	40
Minnesota	30	30	29	29	31	29	28	27	29	30	33	37
Iowa	28	29	27	29	29	27	26	27	28	30	32	36
Missouri	24	24	23	24	25	24	23	23	24	26	28	31
North Dakota	29	28	26	24	25	26	24	24	25	28	30	35
South Dakota	29	27	26	26	28	27	26	25	26	29	32	36
Nebraska	26	25	25	25	26	25	24	24	25	27	29	33
Kansas	27	26	25	25	26	25	25	25	26	28	30	33
Kentucky	22	21	22	21	22	21	21	21	22	23	24	27
Tennessee	21	21	20	20	20	19	18	19	19	21	23	26
Alabama	22	22	21	23	22	22	22	22	24	24	25	27
Mississippi	24	24	24	24	23	23	23	24	24	24	25	27
Louisiana	30	28	28	29	28	29	29	29	29	28	33	32
Texas	25	24	23	23	23	23	22	23	24	24	27	31
Oklahoma	26	25	24	24	25	25	24	24	25	28	29	32
Arkansas	25	24	23	23	24	23	23	24	25	25	27	29
Montana	35	35	35	32	33	31	28	31	29	32	39	39
Wyoming	33	32	31	29	30	27	28	30	29	31	35	38
Colorado	30	29	28	28	29	27	27	27	29	30	33	36
New Mexico	35	34	33	34	33	31	34	33	32	33	34	37
Arizona	38	38	35	36	35	37	39	38	37	38	38	42
Utah	28	28	28	28	28	25	26	28	30	29	36	37
Nevada	33	34	32	37	36	32	34	32	34	36	41	39
Idaho	31	32	30	29	30	28	27	27	29	31	35	38
Washington	34	33	33	32	32	29	29	29	31	32	37	39
Oregon	32	33	32	33	32	29	28	29	31	32	34	38
California	32	32	32	29	27	29	27	28	29	31	32	37
United States	**28.3**	**27.6**	**27.1**	**27.6**	**27.9**	**26.5**	**25.7**	**26.1**	**27.4**	**29.0**	**31.1**	**34.4**
North Atlantic	33.5	32.3	32.4	32.8	33.4	31.4	29.9	30.5	32.1	34.3	36.3	39.0
South Atlantic	26.5	26.1	25.8	26.0	26.4	25.1	24.4	25.0	26.3	27.2	29.0	31.0
N. Central E. Miss. R	28.5	27.3	27.1	28.2	27.9	26.3	25.7	26.0	27.5	29.1	31.3	35.3
N. Central W. Miss. R	27.3	27.0	25.9	26.5	27.5	26.1	25.3	25.3	26.4	28.4	30.6	34.3
South Central	23.7	23.0	22.5	22.6	22.7	22.2	21.8	22.4	23.2	23.9	25.8	28.6
Far Western	32.0	31.9	31.5	30.2	29.5	28.6	27.6	28.4	29.8	31.2	34.1	37.5

BUTTER AND EGGS—Continued.

TABLE 162.—*Butter: Receipts at seven leading markets in the United States, 1891–1916.*

[From Board of Trade, Chamber of Commerce, and Merchants' Exchange reports.]

[000 omitted.]

Year.	Boston.	Chicago.	Mil-waukee.	St. Louis	San Fran-cisco.	Total 5 cities.	Cincin-nati.	New York.
Averages:	*Pounds.*	*Pounds.*	*Pounds.*	*Pounds.*	*Pounds.*	*Pounds.*	*Packages.*	*Packages.*
1891–1895.........	40,955	145,225	3,996	13,944	15,240	219,360	88	1,741
1896–1900.........	50,790	232,289	5,096	14,582	14,476	317,233	157	2,010
1901–1905.........	57,716	245,203	7,164	14,685	15,026	339,794	177	2,122
1906–1910.........	66,612	286,518	8,001	17,903	13,581	392,615	169	2,207
1901.................	57,500	253,809	5,590	13,477	14,972	345,348	238	2,040
1902.................	54,574	219,233	7,290	14,573	14,801	310,471	223	1,933
1903.................	54,347	232,032	6,857	14,080	13,570	320,886	121	2,113
1904.................	55,435	249,024	7,993	15,727	14,336	342,515	147	2,170
1905.................	66,725	271,915	8,091	15,566	17,450	379,747	155	2,355
1906.................	65,152	248,648	8,209	13,198	9,282	344,489	205	2,242
1907.................	63,589	263,715	8,219	13,453	16,725	365,701	187	2,113
1908.................	69,843	316,695	8,798	18,614	13,528	427,478	166	2,175
1909.................	65,054	284,547	7,458	21,086	14,449	392,594	150	2,250
1910.................	69,421	318,986	7,319	23,163	13,922	432,811	135	2,257
1911.................	63,874	334,932	8,632	24,839	17,606	449,883	162	2,405
1912.................	72,109	286,213	7,007	20,521	28,172	414,022	109	2,436
1913.................	70,737	277,651	9,068	24,726	23,122	405,304	103	2,517
1914.................	73,028	307,899	9,496	24,614	22,421	437,458	82	2,513
1915.................	82,396	341,202	8,624	21,334	28,349	481,905	130	2,734
1916.................	79,305	344,381	7,705	16,435	28,029	475,855	256	2,929
1916.								
January.............	2,849	18,499	453	1,080	1,791	24,672	129	150
February............	3,769	17,549	453	1,016	1,766	24,553	5	152
March...............	2,912	20,884	542	1,306	2,469	28,113	11	207
April................	4,052	20,652	444	1,270	3,404	29,822	6	185
May.................	8,864	29,918	644	1,176	3,259	43,861	10	264
June.................	16,361	49,795	1,252	1,781	3,066	72,255	16	443
July.................	13,375	49,244	1,016	1,688	2,212	67,535	13	371
August..............	9,681	35,309	811	1,225	2,284	49,310	16	319
September...........	6,629	31,123	672	1,752	2,141	42,317	6	269
October.............	5,188	30,571	692	1,457	1,881	39,789	11	254
November...........	3,149	22,223	342	1,393	1,856	28,963	15	163
December...........	2,476	18,614	384	1,291	1,900	24,065	18	153

BUTTER AND EGGS—Continued.

TABLE 163.—*Eggs: Average price received by farmers on first of each month, by States, 1916.*

State and division.	Eggs, cents per dozen.											
	January.	February.	March.	April.	May.	June.	July.	August.	September.	October.	November.	December.
Maine	37	31	27	23	21	24	26	29	35	39	42	50
New Hampshire	41	35	28	22	23	25	29	31	37	41	46	51
Vermont	39	33	29	26	21	22	24	26	33	37	41	50
Massachusetts	44	36	35	28	26	28	34	34	44	52	49	60
Rhode Island	47	36	30	27	26	27	31	35	43	44	50	63
Connecticut	44	37	28	28	22	25	29	33	40	44	52	61
New York	41	34	27	24	22	23	25	28	33	39	44	50
New Jersey	45	37	33	28	25	26	28	31	35	42	50	55
Pennsylvania	37	29	25	22	20	21	24	26	29	33	38	44
Delaware	34	24	22	......	21	24	27	29	30	......	......	46
Maryland	31	26	21	19	19	20	21	22	26	31	33	42
Virginia	29	23	20	18	18	19	19	20	24	28	30	36
West Virginia	31	27	22	19	18	18	20	21	24	27	33	36
North Carolina	26	21	17	16	16	17	18	18	22	26	27	31
South Carolina	26	22	18	18	18	19	19	19	22	25	29	34
Georgia	28	21	17	17	16	17	17	19	23	26	29	34
Florida	33	26	24	20	22	22	23	24	27	30	32	37
Ohio	32	25	20	18	18	20	21	23	26	30	34	40
Indiana	30	26	19	17	19	19	19	21	22	28	32	38
Illinois	31	29	22	18	18	19	20	20	23	27	31	38
Michigan	31	28	23	19	19	20	20	23	25	27	32	38
Wisconsin	31	29	25	18	19	20	20	21	24	26	31	36
Minnesota	31	28	24	17	18	19	19	20	22	26	31	36
Iowa	28	27	22	17	18	19	19	20	21	26	30	34
Missouri	26	25	18	17	18	18	18	17	18	25	28	34
North Dakota	31	30	28	17	15	16	16	16	19	23	28	36
South Dakota	29	26	23	16	16	17	18	18	20	25	29	35
Nebraska	27	25	19	15	16	17	17	17	18	24	28	34
Kansas	26	25	17	16	17	17	17	17	18	25	29	35
Kentucky	26	23	17	16	17	17	17	18	20	25	28	34
Tennessee	24	22	17	15	15	16	16	16	19	24	27	33
Alabama	23	20	16	14	14	15	16	15	19	24	25	30
Mississippi	26	21	17	15	16	16	16	16	20	23	25	31
Louisiana	27	22	18	16	17	18	17	18	22	24	29	31
Texas	27	22	16	14	15	15	14	16	18	23	27	35
Oklahoma	25	24	16	15	16	16	15	15	15	22	28	35
Arkansas	26	23	16	14	15	15	16	16	18	23	26	32
Montana	46	41	36	22	19	21	23	25	26	30	41	46
Wyoming	39	38	32	21	20	22	22	25	28	29	37	42
Colorado	36	31	25	18	19	21	21	22	25	30	36	42
New Mexico	37	29	27	23	20	24	24	25	26	28	31	39
Arizona	45	38	28	23	27	28	29	35	34	40	38	48
Utah	35	31	25	18	17	20	20	22	24	27	35	42
Nevada	55	37	30	26	25	28	27	30	35	38	45	51
Idaho	39	37	32	20	19	21	22	24	24	30	36	44
Washington	40	35	30	20	20	22	23	26	30	32	42	47
Oregon	36	35	27	20	20	22	23	24	28	31	37	45
California	40	33	25	19	20	23	25	26	31	35	46	49
United States	30.6	26.8	21.2	17.9	18.1	19.0	19.7	20.7	23.3	28.1	32.2	38.1
North Atlantic	39.9	32.5	27.4	23.9	21.7	23.1	25.9	28.3	33.1	38.2	42.8	49.5
South Atlantic	29.0	23.4	19.5	17.9	17.7	18.6	19.4	20.3	23.9	27.4	30.2	35.8
N. Central E. Miss. R	31.1	27.2	21.4	18.0	18.5	19.5	20.1	21.6	24.0	27.9	32.1	38.3
N. Central W. Miss. R	27.5	26.0	20.1	16.5	17.4	18.0	18.0	18.2	19.4	25.2	29.1	34.5
South Central	25.7	22.2	16.5	14.8	15.5	15.8	15.6	16.2	18.7	23.5	26.9	33.2
Far Western	39.1	33.9	27.0	19.5	19.8	22.3	23.6	25.2	28.8	32.5	41.4	46.4

BUTTER AND EGGS—Continued.

TABLE 164.—*Eggs: Receipts at seven leading markets in the United States, 1891–1916.*

[From Board of Trade, Chamber of Commerce, and Merchants' Exchange reports.]

Year.	Boston.	Chicago.	Cincinnati.	Milwaukee.	New York.	St. Louis.	San Francisco.	Total.
	Cases.	*Cases.*	*Cases.*	*Cases.*	*Cases.*	*Cases.*	*Cases.*	*Cases.*
Averages:								
1891–1895.........	722,363	1,879,065	288,548	90,943	2,113,946	557,320	166,059	5,818,244
1896–1900.........	912,807	2,196,631	362,262	113,327	2,664,074	852,457	194,087	7,295,645
1901–1905.........	1,155,340	2,990,675	418,842	139,718	3,057,298	1,000,935	304,933	9,067,741
1906–1910.........	1,517,995	4,467,040	509,017	180,362	4,046,360	1,304,719	334,766	12,360,259
1901...............	1,040,555	2,783,709	493,218	128,179	2,909,194	1,022,646	277,500	8,655,001
1902...............	1,053,165	2,659,340	464,799	114,732	2,743,642	825,999	285,058	8,146,735
1903...............	1,164,777	3,279,248	338,327	129,278	2,940,091	959,648	335,228	9,146,597
1904...............	1,122,819	3,113,858	377,263	166,409	3,215,924	1,216,124	319,637	9,532,034
1905...............	1,395,385	3,117,221	420,604	159,990	3,477,638	980,257	307,243	9,858,338
1906...............	1,709,531	3,583,878	484,208	187,561	3,981,013	1,023,125	137,074	11,106,390
1907...............	1,594,576	4,780,356	588,636	176,826	4,262,153	1,288,977	379,439	13,070,963
1908...............	1,436,786	4,569,014	441,072	207,558	3,703,990	1,439,868	347,436	12,145,724
1909...............	1,417,397	4,557,906	519,652	160,418	3,903,867	1,395,987	340,185	12,295,412
1910...............	1,431,686	4,844,045	511,519	169,448	4,380,777	1,375,638	469,698	13,182,811
1911...............	1,441,748	4,707,335	605,131	175,270	5,021,757	1,736,915	587,115	14,275,271
1912...............	1,580,106	4,556,643	668,942	136,621	4,723,558	1,391,611	638,920	13,696,401
1913...............	1,589,399	4,593,800	594,954	187,931	4,666,117	1,397,962	574,222	13,604,385
1914...............	1,531,329	4,083,163	461,783	221,345	4,762,174	1,470,716	619,508	13,150,018
1915...............	1,766,185	4,896,246	806,834	199,521	4,582,218	1,452,856	629,571	14,333,431
1916...............	1,649,828	5,452,737	1,534,622	221,808	4,864,343	1,521,855	575,014	15,820,207
1916.								
January...............	73,414	158,955	812,371	4,280	179,639	64,476	31,996	1,325,131
February.............	73,422	109,848	8,922	5,710	212,250	82,606	58,400	551,158
March...............	179,855	604,538	92,332	12,414	537,975	289,879	85,474	1,802,467
April................	304,205	1,144,454	166,351	47,305	786,620	314,177	80,870	2,844,042
May.................	296,241	1,034,105	100,003	47,365	785,132	216,134	70,974	2,549,954
June.................	199,615	717,803	83,337	32,848	601,601	165,267	36,836	1,837,307
July.................	132,195	495,437	91,841	16,295	432,170	110,304	39,143	1,317,385
August...............	120,476	354,444	52,310	18,783	407,619	74,630	42,373	1,070,635
September............	94,509	297,417	7,363	12,670	299,902	66,236	36,436	814,533
October..............	84,632	262,791	37,378	10,153	296,315	55,388	31,297	777,954
November............	49,573	177,343	35,266	7,350	188,686	45,448	27,689	531,355
December............	41,691	95,602	47,148	6,575	136,434	37,310	33,526	398,286

BUTTER AND EGGS—Continued.

TABLE 165.—*Eggs: Wholesale price per dozen, 1912–1916.*

Date.	Chicago. Fresh.		Cincinnati.		St. Louis. Average best fresh.		Milwaukee. Fresh.		New York. Average best fresh.	
	Low.	High.	Low.	High.	Low.	High.	Low.	High.	Low.	High.
1912.	*Cents.*	*Cents.*	*Cents.*	*Cents.*	*Cents.*	*Cents.*	*Cents.*	*Cents.*	*Cents.*	*Cents.*
Jan.-June	17	40	17	40	16	39	15	38	20½	48
July-Dec	17½	27½	18	36	14½	27	16	30	23	60
1913.										
Jan.-June	16½	27½	15½	27½	14¼	25	14	25	20	40
July-Dec	16	37	18½	42	12	35	13	35	25	65
1914.										
Jan.-June	17	32½	16½	36	14	31	15	30	20	50
July-Dec	18	36	18½	38½	18	35	16	32	24	62
1915.										
January	29	38	20	40½	28¼	37½	25	34	30	44
February	21	28	16	27	20	28	20	29	33	40
March	17	19½	14	20	17	18¾	16	20½	18¼	20¾
April	18¼	19¾	14½	19½	17¾	19	16½	18½	19½	22
May	16½	18¾	12½	18	16	18	16	18	18	21½
June	16	18	12½	18½	15¼	16¾	15½	16½	18½	21
Jan.-June	16	38	12½	40½	15¼	37½	15½	34	18	44
July	16	17½	11	19	14½	15½	15½	16	18	21
August	16	21½	10	24	15½	20	15½	21	18	24½
September	21	24	17	27	20	22	19½	22½	24	29
October	23	27½	17½	30	21½	25½	20½	26	27	34
November	27	30½	17	36	26	30	24	30	30	40
December	26½	30½	19	34½	24½	29½	26	32	31	37
July-Dec	16	30½	10	36	14½	30	15½	32	18	40
1916.										
January	27	32¼	18	34½	24½	31	25	31	26	35
February	20¾	29½	18½	28½	19	30	20½	28	22	30½
March	18½	22	17½	23	17	20½	17	21	21¾	28½
April	19¼	21	17	21	18½	20	17½	19	20½	22½
May	20½	21¾	17½	21½	19	20½	18½	20	21¼	23¾
June	20½	22¼	18	22½	19	20	19	20	22	24½
Jan.-June	18½	32¼	17	34½	17	31	17	31	20½	35
July	21¾	23	17½	24	....	....	19	22	23¾	27½
August	23	26	18½	30	22	26	19	25	26½	34
September	25½	30½	21	31½	24	28	21	27	31	35
October	30	32½	25½	35½	28	31	22	30	32½	37
November	31½	39½	28	43	31	39	27	38	35½	46
December	37	41	31	47	36	38	33	38	41½	47
July-Dec	21¾	41	17½	47	22	39	19	38	23½	47

CHEESE.

TABLE 166.—*Cheese: International trade, calendar years 1913–1915.*

[Cheese includes all cheese made from milk; "cottage cheese," of course, is included.   See "General note,"
Table 10.]

EXPORTS.

[000 omitted.]

Country.	1913	1914 (prelim.)	1915 (prelim.)	Country.	1913	1914 (prelim.)	1915 (prelim.)
	Pounds.	*Pounds.*	*Pounds.*		*Pounds.*	*Pounds.*	*Pounds.*
Bulgaria	[1] 4,030			Russia	8,373	3,827	
Canada	148,849	138,265	160,660	Switzerland	78,739	77,573	74,775
France	31,405	26,576	16,242	United States	2,654	3,797	63,227
Germany	1,603			Other countries	13,903	12,206	
Italy	72,321	66,004	65,781				
Netherlands	145,337	149,574	190,107	Total	575,720	574,565	
New Zealand	68,506	96,743	91,533				

IMPORTS.

Country.	1913	1914 (prelim.)	1915 (prelim.)	Country.	1913	1914 (prelim.)	1915 (prelim.)
Algeria	7,084	6,719	4,614	Germany	57,903		
Argentina	11,122	8,453	7,306	Italy	12,355	9,838	3,472
Australia	365	230		Russia	4,545	4,190	3,716
Austria-Hungary	13,200			Spain	5,749	5,150	3,202
Belgium	35,845			Switzerland	7,763	4,717	3,410
Brazil	4,196	3,288	2,300	United Kingdom	249,972	266,591	299,920
British South Africa	5,694	5,300	4,012	United States	55,590	55,477	38,919
Cuba	5,200	4,229	2,839	Other countries	22,262	11,343	
Denmark	1,475						
Egypt	6,378	5,953	5,785	Total	558,563	436,999	
France	51,865	45,521	46,743				

[1] Data for 1912.

CHICKENS.

TABLE 167.—*Chickens: Average price received by farmers on first of each month, by States,*
1916.

State and division.	Chickens, cents per pound.											
	Jan.	Feb.	Mar.	Apr.	May.	June.	July.	Aug.	Sept.	Oct.	Nov.	Dec.
Me	13.5	14.8	14.6	14.5	15.5	16.0	15.6	17.0	17.2	16.4	17.2	16.9
N. H	15.1	14.8	15.3	13.5	16.5	16.0	18.0	19.7	17.8	17.0	17.0	19.4
Vt	15.0	14.3	14.2	15.4	15.3	15.9	14.8	16.6	15.7	16.5	16.3	17.0
Mass	16.7	17.0	16.8	16.6	17.6	17.4	20.1	21.0	18.2	19.5	18.9	20.9
R. I	17.5	16.0	15.5	18.3	18.3	19.0	18.5	23.5	23.0	23.0	20.0	20.0
Conn	18.6	16.5	17.2	18.2	18.3	18.5	18.6	20.0	19.2	20.8	20.2	21.0
N. Y	15.2	15.5	15.7	15.8	16.9	16.9	17.1	16.8	17.4	17.8	17.2	16.8
N. J	17.3	18.2	17.3	17.9	18.2	19.6	18.9	18.3	18.9	19.4	21.0	21.0
Pa	13.7	14.2	14.5	15.3	15.4	15.8	15.8	16.1	16.4	16.3	16.0	15.7
Del	14.0	14.0	13.5		15.0	16.0	18.0	*18.0	19.0			17.0
Md	14.4	14.7	15.9	16.1	17.0	18.7	19.0	19.6	17.5	18.5	17.4	17.1
Va	13.5	13.8	14.5	14.8	15.0	16.4	16.7	16.6	16.2	16.6	16.2	16.3
W. Va	12.5	12.8	12.9	13.1	13.5	14.0	13.7	14.9	14.8	14.7	14.7	15.0
N. C	11.6	12.0	12.1	12.2	13.1	13.6	14.2	13.7	13.6	13.7	14.2	14.1
S. C	14.3	13.0	12.6	13.3	14.0	14.9	14.6	14.2	13.8	15.0	14.7	14.5
Ga	13.2	13.3	13.0	13.3	12.6	13.3	13.9	13.5	14.0	14.4	14.9	14.7
Fla	17.1	15.6	17.3	15.8	16.3	17.3	15.5	17.2	17.1	16.6	16.8	19.8
Ohio	11.6	12.3	13.2	13.6	14.5	14.3	14.4	15.0	14.9	15.8	14.8	14.0
Ind	11.0	11.6	12.3	12.8	13.1	14.0	14.0	14.1	14.2	14.5	14.4	14.0
Ill	11.1	11.8	11.8	12.6	13.3	13.5	14.0	13.9	14.0	14.5	14.6	14.2
Mich	11.0	12.1	12.5	13.1	13.5	13.8	13.4	14.0	14.4	14.2	14.1	13.8
Wis	10.9	11.4	12.0	12.7	13.4	13.4	12.8	13.9	13.7	13.1	13.7	13.5
Minn	9.7	10.0	10.1	10.8	11.0	11.3	11.6	11.5	12.3	12.1	12.1	12.2
Iowa	10.0	10.7	10.7	11.4	11.9	11.8	12.2	12.4	13.1	13.7	13.6	13.6
Mo	10.2	11.0	11.0	12.2	12.8	13.2	14.0	13.1	13.0	13.9	13.8	13.3
N. Dak	9.4	10.3	9.5	9.8	10.3	10.2	10.2	15.5	11.1	10.7	11.4	11.1
S. Dak	8.6	9.4	8.9	9.8	9.9	9.6	11.0	10.6	10.5	11.6	11.6	11.9
Nebr	9.1	10.2	10.4	10.8	11.5	11.5	11.6	11.9	12.3	12.2	12.7	12.2
Kans	9.7	10.2	10.3	10.7	11.3	11.6	12.1	12.1	12.2	12.9	12.8	12.4
Ky	10.3	11.1	11.4	11.9	12.8	13.3	14.4	14.3	13.4	14.1	14.0	13.0
Tenn	9.9	11.2	11.5	12.0	12.8	13.5	13.7	13.2	13.1	12.9	13.4	13.0
Ala	11.2	11.6	11.5	11.4	11.9	12.6	13.2	12.7	12.8	13.4	13.7	13.8
Miss	11.0	11.6	11.7	11.8	12.8	12.7	12.9	12.4	12.5	13.5	13.7	14.1
La	12.9	14.5	13.9	13.9	14.3	15.9	14.8	15.4	15.2	16.0	18.1	16.0
Tex	10.3	10.0	10.6	10.8	10.8	11.1	11.4	11.3	11.4	12.3	12.2	13.9
Okla	9.4	10.1	9.9	10.5	11.3	11.6	12.3	11.6	11.6	11.8	12.7	12.4
Ark	10.3	10.2	9.5	10.0	11.7	11.9	12.7	11.4	11.9	11.9	12.3	12.6
Mont	15.5	13.5	14.8	14.8	13.7	15.2	14.1	14.9	15.2	16.0	15.6	14.6
Wyo	12.9	13.0	13.0	11.9	13.3	14.4	15.5	15.1	15.7	16.5	15.9	15.0
Colo	12.2	11.5	13.0	12.3	13.2	13.1	13.5	13.7	13.3	13.7	13.6	13.0
N. Mex	13.0	14.0	14.4	12.0	12.6	13.4	12.6	14.0	13.3	13.0	13.1	14.1
Ariz	18.5	17.6	16.7	17.7	17.6	18.1	17.9	17.8	19.3	17.4	16.3	19.0
Utah	12.9	12.9	12.5	13.0	12.2	13.0	13.0	13.9	14.2	14.7	13.7	13.5
Nevada	22.0	19.3	18.7	21.3	21.1	20.4	21.2	20.0	24.0	22.0	18.0	21.0
Idaho	10.8	11.2	10.6	10.6	12.1	12.0	10.9	11.3	11.9	11.8	12.2	11.9
Wash	12.2	13.0	12.7	13.0	15.0	14.4	14.4	15.2	15.0	15.0	14.0	13.5
Oreg	11.9	13.1	12.7	13.0	12.7	13.8	13.2	13.0	13.0	12.5	12.9	13.5
Cal	16.3	16.2	15.6	15.4	16.9	16.0	15.9	15.5	15.9	15.7	16.6	17.0
U. S	11.4	11.9	12.2	12.6	13.2	13.5	13.8	13.8	13.9	14.3	14.3	14.2
North Atlantic	15.0	15.2	16.0	15.8	16.4	16.7	16.9	17.2	17.3	17.5	17.3	17.3
South Atlantic	13.4	13.3	13.6	13.8	14.1	15.1	15.3	15.3	15.1	15.4	15.3	15.5
N. Central E. Miss. R	11.2	11.9	12.4	13.0	13.6	13.8	13.8	14.2	14.3	14.6	14.4	14.0
N. Central W. Miss. R	9.8	10.5	10.5	11.2	11.7	11.9	12.4	12.3	12.6	13.1	13.1	12.9
South Central	10.5	11.0	11.1	11.4	12.0	12.5	12.9	12.5	12.5	13.0	13.4	13.6
Far Western	14.2	14.3	14.1	14.0	14.9	14.8	14.6	14.6	14.8	14.7	14.9	15.1

SHEEP AND WOOL.

TABLE 168.—*Sheep: Number and value on farms in the United States, 1867–1917.*

NOTE.—Figures in *italics* are census returns; figures in roman are estimates of the Department of Agriculture. Estimates of numbers are obtained by applying estimated percentages of increase or decrease to the published numbers of the preceding year, except that a revised base is used for applying percentage estimates whenever new census data are available. It should also be observed that the census of 1910 giving numbers as of Apr. 15, is not strictly comparable with former censuses, which related to numbers June 1.

Year.	Number.	Price per head Jan. 1.	Farm value Jan. 1.	Year.	Number.	Price per head Jan. 1.	Farm value Jan. 1.
1867	39,385,000	$2.50	$98,644,000	1892	44,938,000	$2.58	$116,121,000
1868	38,992,000	1.82	71,053,000	1893	47,274,000	2.66	125,909,000
1869	37,724,000	1.64	62,037,000	1894	45,048,000	1.98	89,186,000
1870	40,853,000	1.96	79,876,000	1895	42,294,000	1.58	66,686,000
1870, census, June 1	*28,477,951*			1896	38,299,000	1.70	65,168,000
1871	31,851,000	2.14	68,310,000	1897	36,819,000	1.82	67,021,000
1872	31,679,000	2.61	82,768,000	1898	37,657,000	2.46	92,721,000
1873	33,002,000	2.71	89,427,000	1899	39,114,000	2.75	107,698,000
1874	33,938,000	2.43	82,353,000	1900	41,883,000	2.93	122,666,000
1875	33,784,000	2.55	86,278,000	*1900, census, June 1*	*61,503,713*		
1876	35,935,000	2.37	85,121,000	1901 [1]	59,757,000	2.98	178,072,000
1877	35,804,000	2.13	76,362,000	1902	62,039,000	2.65	164,446,000
1878	35,740,000	2.21	78,898,000	1903	63,965,000	2.63	168,316,000
1879	38,124,000	2.07	78,965,000	1904	51,630,000	2.59	133,530,000
1880	40,766,000	2.21	90,231,000	1905	45,170,000	2.82	127,332,000
1880, census, June 1	*35,192,074*			1906	50,632,000	3.54	179,056,000
1881	43,570,000	2.39	104,071,000	1907	53,240,000	3.84	204,210,000
1882	45,016,000	2.37	106,596,000	1908	54,631,000	3.88	211,736,000
1883	49,237,000	2.53	124,366,000	1909	56,084,000	3.43	192,632,000
1884	50,627,000	2.37	119,903,000	1910	57,216,000		
1885	50,360,000	2.14	107,961,000	*1910, census, Apr. 15*	*52,447,861*	4.12	216,030,000
1886	48,322,000	1.91	92,444,000	1911 [1]	53,633,000	3.91	209,535,000
1887	44,759,000	2.01	89,873,000	1912	52,362,000	3.46	181,170,000
1888	43,545,000	2.05	89,280,000	1913	51,482,000	3.94	202,779,000
1889	42,599,000	2.13	90,640,000	1914	49,719,000	4.02	200,045,000
1890	44,336,000	2.27	100,660,000	1915	49,956,000	4.50	224,687,000
1890, census, June 1	*35,935,364*			1916	48,625,000	5.17	251,594,000
1891	43,431,000	2.50	108,397,000	1917	48,483,000	7.14	346,064,000

[1] Estimates of numbers revised based on census data.

SHEEP AND WOOL—Continued.

Table 169.—*Sheep: Number and value on farms Jan. 1, 1916 and 1917, by States.*

State.	Number (thousands) Jan. 1—		Average price per head, Jan. 1—		Farm value (thousands of dollars) Jan. 1—	
	1917	1916	1917	1916	1917	1916
Maine	157	160	$6.30	$4.80	$989	$768
New Hampshire	35	35	6.70	5.50	234	192
Vermont	100	100	7.30	5.90	730	590
Massachusetts	25	26	6.70	5.50	168	143
Rhode Island	5	6	7.20	5.90	36	35
Connecticut	18	18	7.60	5.80	137	104
New York	840	849	8.40	6.20	7,056	5,264
New Jersey	29	29	7.20	6.40	209	186
Pennsylvania	835	835	7.10	5.60	5,928	4,676
Delaware	8	8	5.90	5.30	47	42
Maryland	223	223	6.60	5.40	1,472	1,204
Virginia	686	700	6.50	4.90	4,459	3,430
West Virginia	715	720	6.60	5.10	4,719	3,672
North Carolina	140	155	3.90	3.20	546	496
South Carolina	30	30	3.20	2.70	96	81
Georgia	150	161	2.80	2.40	420	386
Florida	119	119	2.70	2.30	321	274
Ohio	2,944	3,067	7.20	5.40	21,197	16,562
Indiana	1,005	1,005	8.20	6.10	8,241	6,130
Illinois	898	907	8.20	5.90	7,364	5,351
Michigan	1,834	1,931	7.80	5.70	14,305	11,007
Wisconsin	645	664	7.50	5.30	4,838	3,519
Minnesota	541	536	7.60	4.80	4,112	2,573
Iowa	1,240	1,240	8.80	6.30	10,912	7,812
Missouri	1,370	1,416	7.70	5.80	10,549	8,213
North Dakota	250	240	7.40	5.10	1,850	1,224
South Dakota	658	604	7.40	5.20	4,869	3,141
Nebraska	381	374	7.50	5.40	2,858	2,020
Kansas	348	341	7.60	5.60	2,645	1,910
Kentucky	1,155	1,155	7.10	4.90	8,200	5,660
Tennessee	650	650	5.80	4.10	3,770	2,665
Alabama	121	119	3.20	2.60	387	309
Mississippi	193	208	3.00	2.50	579	520
Louisiana	240	185	2.90	2.30	696	426
Texas	2,328	2,156	4.40	3.70	10,243	7,977
Oklahoma	104	95	6.30	5.00	655	475
Arkansas	124	124	3.90	2.90	484	360
Montana	3,744	3,941	7.10	5.10	26,582	20,099
Wyoming	4,381	4,338	7.60	5.60	33,296	24,293
Colorado	1,950	1,839	7.50	5.20	14,625	9,563
New Mexico	3,300	3,440	5.80	4.30	19,140	14,792
Arizona	1,632	1,700	6.30	4.70	10,282	7,990
Utah	2,089	2,089	7.90	5.40	16,503	11,281
Nevada	1,455	1,532	8.20	5.80	11,931	8,886
Idaho	3,195	3,102	8.20	5.60	26,199	17,371
Washington	585	568	7.10	5.30	4,154	3,010
Oregon	2,484	2,435	8.10	5.20	20,120	12,662
California	2,524	2,450	6.70	5.00	16,911	12,250
United States	48,483	48,625	7.14	5.17	346,064	251,594

SHEEP AND WOOL—Continued.

TABLE 170.—*Sheep: Imports, exports, and prices, 1893–1916.*

Year ending June 30—	Imports.			Exports.		
	Number.	Value.	Average import price.	Number.	Value.	Average export price.
1893	459,484	$1,682,977	$3.66	37,260	$126,394	$3.39
1894	242,568	788,181	3.25	132,370	832,763	6.29
1895	291,461	682,618	2.34	405,748	2,630,686	6.48
1896	322,692	853,530	2.65	491,565	3,076,384	6.26
1897	405,633	1,019,668	2.51	244,120	1,531,645	6.27
1898	392,314	1,106,322	2.82	199,690	1,213,886	6.08
1899	345,911	1,200,081	3.47	143,286	853,555	5.96
1900	381,792	1,365,026	3.58	125,772	733,477	5.83
1901	331,488	1,236,277	3.73	297,925	1,933,000	6.49
1902	266,953	956,710	3.58	358,720	1,940,060	5.41
1903	301,623	1,036,934	3.44	176,961	1,067,860	6.03
1904	238,094	815,289	3.42	301,313	1,954,604	6.49
1905	186,942	704,721	3.77	268,365	1,687,321	6.29
1906	240,747	1,020,359	4.24	142,690	804,090	5.64
1907	224,798	1,120,425	4.98	135,344	750,242	5.54
1908	224,765	1,082,606	4.82	101,000	589,285	5.83
1909	102,663	502,640	4.90	67,656	365,155	5.40
1910	126,152	696,879	5.52	44,517	209,000	4.69
1911	53,455	377,625	7.06	121,491	636,272	5.24
1912	23,588	157,257	6.67	157,263	626,985	3.99
1913	15,428	90,021	5.83	187,132	605,725	3.24
1914	223,719	532,404	2.38	152,600	534,543	3.50
1915	153,317	533,967	3.48	47,213	182,278	3.86
1916	235,659	917,502	3.89	52,278	231,535	4.43

SHEEP AND WOOL—Continued.

TABLE 171.—*Sheep: Wholesale price per 100 pounds, 1912–1916.*

Date.	Chicago. Native.		Cincinnati. Good to extra.		St. Louis. Good to choice natives.		Kansas City. Native.[1]		Omaha. Western.	
	Low.	High.	Low.	High.	Low.	High.	Low.	High.	Low.	High.
1912.										
Jan.–June	$2.50	$7.50	$3.00	$5.50	$4.00	$7.00	$3.30	$8.00		
July–Dec	2.00	5.65	2.85	4.00	3.75	5.00	3.35	7.35		
1913.										
Jan.–June	2.50	7.90	3.60	7.00	4.75	7.25	2.75	7.50	$3.75	$8.15
July–Dec	2.00	6.00	3.25	4.50	4.00	5.00	2.00	7.00	2.75	6.75
1914.										
Jan.–June	2.00	7.00	4.10	6.15	5.00	6.50	2.50	7.25	5.00	7.50
July–Dec	2.00	6.50	4.00	5.35	4.50	5.75	2.25	7.50	4.80	8.00
1915.										
January	3.00	8.00	4.10	5.00	5.50	6.00	4.50	7.80	4.75	4.75
February	3.75	8.65	4.50	5.75	6.50	6.50	5.00	8.00	4.75	4.75
March	4.00	9.25	5.50	8.75	7.40	7.90	5.50	8.75	7.00	7.00
April	4.00	8.50	6.10	7.00	7.75	8.50	6.50	10.00	7.00	7.00
May	3.50	10.65	5.00	8.75	7.00	7.50	5.50	9.75	6.75	6.75
June	2.50	9.25	4.25	5.50	5.25	5.50	4.50	9.00	4.00	4.00
Jan.–June	2.50	10.65	4.10	8.75	5.25	8.50	4.50	10.00	4.00	7.00
July	2.00	8.75	4.50	5.75	5.25	5.50	4.50	8.00	4.25	4.25
August	2.50	7.75	4.75	8.75	5.50	5.75	4.00	8.00	4.50	4.50
September	2.00	7.50	4.60	5.50	5.25	5.25	4.00	8.00	4.50	4.50
October	3.00	7.65	4.75	8.15	5.50	5.85	4.00	8.00	4.50	4.50
November	2.75	7.75	4.75	6.00	5.25	5.50	5.00	7.25	4.50	4.50
December	3.00	8.50	4.75	6.25	5.75	6.00	5.00	8.25	4.00	4.00
July–Dec	2.00	8.75	4.50	8.75	5.25	6.00	4.00	8.25	4.00	4.50
1916.										
January	3.00	8.25	5.50	6.85	6.50	7.50	5.00	9.50	6.25	9.15
February	4.00	8.75	5.75	7.75	7.50	8.00	6.50	10.00	7.00	9.85
March	4.00	9.00	6.50	8.00	8.00	8.50	6.50	10.90	7.50	10.50
April	3.50	9.25	6.50	8.00	8.50	8.85	7.00	11.00	8.00	10.25
May	2.50	10.00	6.50	8.50	8.35	8.75	7.00	11.50	6.50	11.00
June	2.50	9.00	6.00	7.25	7.25	7.75	6.35	10.50	6.75	8.75
Jan.–June	2.50	10.00	3.75	8.75	7.25	8.85	5.00	11.50	6.25	11.00
July	3.00	8.50	5.50	7.00	7.25	7.25	6.75	10.00	6.50	8.25
August	2.50	8.25	5.00	7.00	7.25	7.25	6.50	10.35	6.25	8.25
September	3.00	8.50	5.00	6.75	7.00	7.25	6.00	8.75	6.25	8.50
October	3.00	8.50	5.50	6.75	7.00	7.25	6.00	8.75	6.50	8.50
November	3.25	9.00	5.50	7.00	5.50	9.00	6.00	9.75	6.25	10.00
December	3.50	10.25	6.00	8.50	6.75	9.25	7.25	11.75	6.75	11.75
July–Dec	2.50	10.25	5.00	8.50	5.50	9.25	6.00	11.75	6.25	11.75

[1] Not including lambs for 1912 and 1914.

SHEEP AND WOOL—Continued.

TABLE 172.—*Wool: Product, by States, 1915 and 1916.*

[Estimate of U.·S. Department of Agriculture.]

States.	Fleeces (000 omitted).		Weight per fleece.		Wool production (000 omitted).		Price per pound (monthly mean).	
	1916	1915	1916	1915	1916	1915	1916	1915
	Number.	*Number.*	*Pounds.*	*Pounds.*	*Pounds.*	*Pounds.*	*Cents.*	*Cents.*
Maine...................	130	135	6.5	6.3	850	850	35.0	28.1
New Hampshire.........	28	29	6.6	6.4	185	185	31.5	25.5
Vermont................	78	83	7.4	7.1	580	590	33.9	27.3
Massachusetts...........	18	18	6.9	6.4	125	115	29.0	25.0
Rhode Island...........	5	5	5.0	5.0	25	25	32.3	25.8
Connecticut.............	14	15	5.4	5.3	75	80	31.0	24.3
New York..............	530	535	6.7	6.5	3,550	3,480	33.1	27.3
New Jersey.............	16	17	5.0	5.6	80	95	31.7	25.0
Pennsylvania............	650	650	6.5	6.2	4,225	4,030	32.0	25.6
Delaware................	5	5	6.0	6.0	30	30	31.5	24.0
Maryland...............	129	127	5.8	5.9	750	750	33.2	25.5
West Virginia...........	550	550	5.0	5.0	2,750	2,750	32.9	27.2
Kentucky...............	625	650	5.0	4.9	3,125	3,185	32.3	25.7
Ohio....................	1,950	2,000	7.0	6.8	13,650	13,600	32.5	27.1
Michigan................	1,165	1,170	7.1	6.9	8,275	8,075	33.4	27.5
Indiana.................	650	690	6.8	6.8	4,420	4,690	32.8	26.4
Illinois.................	515	530	7.5	7.5	3,855	3,975	30.1	25.0
Wisconsin...............	335	350	7.5	7.2	2,510	2,520	30.4	25.4
Minnesota...............	385	380	7.0	7.0	2,695	2,660	27.5	21.8
Iowa....................	650	700	7.5	7.6	4,875	5,325	29.1	23.8
Missouri................	680	730	6.8	6.7	4,625	4,890	29.9	24.6
Total.............	9,108	9,369	6.73	6.61	61,255	61,900	31.7	25.6
Virginia................	378	390	5.0	4.7	1,900	1,835	32.6	25.8
North Carolina..........	135	140	4.2	3.9	570	545	27.9	22.6
South Carolina..........	24	25	4.0	4.0	95	100	24.5	19.4
Georgia.................	165	175	3.0	2.6	495	460	26.5	22.0
Florida.................	111	107	3.1	3.1	345	330	28.2	23.9
Alabama................	100	100	3.5	3.8	350	380	21.6	19.0
Mississippi.............	150	150	3.6	3.5	540	520	22.3	18.4
Louisiana...............	170	145	3.5	3.7	590	536	19.4	15.4
Arkansas...............	85	85	4.1	4.5	350	385	22.8	19.4
Tennessee...............	425	425	4.4	4.4	1,870	1,870	27.7	21.4
Total.............	1,743	1,742	4.08	4.00	7,105	6,961	25.4	20.7
Kansas..................	185	175	7.2	7.1	1,330	1,240	25.0	20.0
Nebraska...............	230	225	8.0	7.4	1,830	1,665	27.2	22.9
South Dakota...........	475	450	7.5	7.0	3,560	3,150	27.0	21.4
North Dakota...........	180	175	7.5	7.2	1,350	1,260	25.7	19.4
Montana................	3,150	3,500	7.8	7.7	24,570	26,950	29.4	25.2
Wyoming...............	3,675	3,650	8.4	8.0	31,000	29,200	26.0	22.6
Idaho..................	1,980	1,935	7.6	7.9	15,000	15,285	27.7	22.8
Washington............	555	525	8.6	8.7	4,750	4,560	25.9	19.4
Oregon.................	1,760	1,850	7.5	8.0	13,200	14,820	27.2	22.8
California..............	1,850	1,900	6.3	6.1	11,600	11,590	22.0	18.6
Nevada.................	1,340	1,210	7.5	7.9	10,000	9,500	21.7	20.0
Utah...................	2,080	2,000	7.2	7.5	15,000	15,000	24.8	20.8
Colorado...............	1,400	1,300	6.0	6.0	8,400	7,800	25.2	21.2
Arizona................	915	950	6.5	6.3	5,950	5,985	26.2	20.0
New Mexico............	3,200	3,325	5.7	5.6	18,240	18,620	22.8	18.5
Texas..................	1,800	1,800	5.7	5.4	10,250	9,750	23.0	17.4
Oklahoma..............	74	70	6.8	7.0	500	490	23.7	19.7
Total.............	24,849	25,040	7.10	7.06	176,530	176,865	25.3	20.7
United States......	35,700	36,151	6.86	6.80	244,890	245,726	27.6	22.8
Pulled wool........					43,600	40,000		
Total product......					288,490	285,726		

SHEEP AND WOOL—Continued.

TABLE 173.—*Wool: Wholesale price per pound in Boston, 1912–1916.*

Date.	Ohio fine, unwashed.		Kentucky, quarter blood, unwashed.[1]		Ohio XX, washed.		Ohio half blood combing, washed.		Ohio Delaine, washed.		Michigan fine, unwashed.[1]	
	Low.	High.	Low.	High.	Low.	High.	Low.	High.	Low.	High.	Low.	High.
1912.	*Cts.*	*Cts.*	*Cts.*	*Cts.*	*Cts.*	*Cts.*	*Cts.*	*Cts.*	*Cts.*	*Cts.*	*Cts.*	*Cts.*
January–June	21	23	22½	29	28	30	26	30	30	35	19	22
July–December	22	25	27½	33	30	33	28½	31	33	35	21	23
1913.												
January–June	20	24	24	32	27	32	23	29	27	34	19	23
July–December	20	21	23½	26	25	30	23	25	26	28	19	20
1914.												
January–June	20	25	23½	27	25½	29	23	28	26	32	19	23
July–December	23	25	26	29	27	31½	27	30	28	32	22	23
1915.												
January	23	25	29	32	29	31	29	32	30	32	22	23
February	25	29	33	37	30	33	31	36	32	36	23	26
March	28	29	37	38	33	34	35	38	35½	37	26	26
April	26	29	31	38	32	33	34	38	34	36	22	26
May	26	27	36	37	32	32	33	36	32	35	22	23
June	26	27	36	39	32	32	34	35	32	34	22	23
January–June	23	29	29	39	29	34	29	38	30	37	22	26
July	26	27½	38	39½	32	32	35	36	33½	35	23	23
August	26	27½	38½	39½	32	32	35	36	34	35	23	24
September	26	27½	37	39½	32	32	33	36	34	35	23	27½
October	25	27	36	37	32	32½	32½	34	34	35	23	24
November	25	27	36	38	32	32½	32½	34	34	25	23	24
December	26	27	38	38	32½	32½	34	35	35	36	25	25
July–December	25	27½	36	39½	32	32½	32½	36	33½	36	23	27½
1916.												
January	26	29	38	39	32½	33	32	35	35½	36	25	26½
February	28	30	39	40	33	33	34	36	36	36	26	27
March	29	31	39	40	33	33	36	37	36	40	26	28
April	30	31	39	40	34	35	36	37	37	40	27	28
May	30	31	39	40	34	35	36	37	37	38	27	28
June	30	31	39	41	34	35	36	38	37	38	27	28
January–June	26	31	38	41	32½	35	32	38	35½	40	25	28
July	30	31	41	44	35	36	37	39	38	40	27	28
August	30	31	44	44	35	37	39	39	39	40	27	28
September	30	31	43	44	36	37	39	40	39	41	27	28
October	31	34	43	44	36	36	39½	42	40	42	29	31
November	34	35	44	46	37	40	42	44	40	45	31	33
December	35	38	45	50	40	47	43	46	45	52	32	37
July–December	30	38	41	50	35	47	37	46	38	52	27	37

[1] Indiana quarter blood unwashed, 1912 and 1913.

SHEEP AND WOOL—Continued.

TABLE 173.—*Wool: Wholesale price per pound in Boston, 1912–1916*—Continued.

Date.	Fine Territory, staple scoured.		Fine medium Territory, clothing scoured.		Texas, 12 months, scoured.		Fine fall, Texas scoured.		Pulled, A super, scoured.		Pulled, B super, scoured.	
	Low.	High.	Low.	High.	Low.	High.	Low.	High.	Low.	High.	Low.	High.
1912.	*Cts.*	*Cts.*	*Cts.*	*Cts.*	*Cts.*	*Cts.*	*Cts.*	*Cts.*	*Cts.*	*Cts.*	*Cts.*	*Cts.*
Jan.-June	60	65	48	55	52	56	42	45	45	53	41	54
July-Dec	63	67	53	59	54	63	43	48	52	58	48	54
1913.												
Jan.-June	55	67	49	59	52	65	45	50	48	58	43	54
July-Dec	51	56	46	50	50	53	41	46	42	52	36	45
1914.												
Jan.-June	51	63	46	55	50	62	41	50	43	53	36	43
July-Dec	60	65	55	57	55	62	42	50	50	55	40	56
1915.												
January	62	66	55	59	56	60	42	52	56	59	57	63
February	67	75	60	68	64	73	53	58	57	62	58	72
March	72	75	65	68	71	75	58	60	60	68	65	74
April	70	73	65	68	70	73	58	60	61	65	58	65
May	68	70	63	68	65	70	54	60	60	63	57	63
June	68	70	63	65	65	68	54	55	63	65	60	65
Jan.-June	62	75	55	68	56	75	42	60	56	68	57	74
July	70	73	63	65	66	70	54	57	63	65	60	65
August	71	74	65	65	68	70	55	57	63	65	60	65
September	72	74	65	65	68	70	55	57	60	65	58	65
October	70	73	65	65	66	68	55	57	60	65	55	63
November	70	73	62	65	65	67	55	57	60	66	55	64
December	73	75	65	68	65	70	54	56	62	66	59	64
July-Dec	70	75	63	68	65	70	54	57	60	66	55	65
1916.												
January	73	77	65	69	67	70	53	55	63	66	59	65
February	77	80	70	71	68	75	53	55	65	68	60	65
March	80	80	70	71	72	75	54	55	65	68	60	65
April	80	80	70	71	72	75	54	55	65	68	60	65
May	80	82	72	75	72	75	54	55	65	68	60	65
June	82	85	73	75	72	77	54	55	65	68	60	66
Jan.-June	73	85	65	75	67	77	53	55	63	68	59	66
July	82	88	75	77	77	83	55	58	65	72	60	68
August	82	88	75	77	80	83	57	58	66	72	63	63
September	85	92	75	78	80	85	57	58	66	72	63	68
October	88	95	75	80	80	85	57	58	66	72	63	71
November	95	105	77	87	85	90	63	65	66	73	60	73
December	100	112	85	87	87	100	63	78	72	85	70	80
July-Dec	82	112	75	87	77	100	55	78	65	85	60	80

SHEEP AND WOOL—Continued.

TABLE 174.—*Wool: Wholesale price per pound, 1912-1916.*

Date.	Boston. Ohio XX, washed.		Philadelphia. Ohio XX, washed.[1]		St. Louis. Best tub, washed.	
	Low.	High.	Low.	High.	Low.	High.
1912.	*Cents.*	*Cents.*	*Cents.*	*Cents.*	*Cents.*	*Cents.*
January–June	28	30	25	30	27	35
July–December	30	33	28	31	35	38
1913.						
January–June	27	32	24	31	28	37
July–December	25	30	22	25	28	35
1914.						
January–June	25½	29	22	28	28	33
July–December	27	31½	25	29	31	33
1915.						
January	29	31	29	31	31	34
February	30	33	30	33	33	40
March	33	34	33	34	40	40
April	32	33	31	33½	37	40
May	32	32	31	32	38	41
June	32	32	31	32½	40	41
January–June	29	34	29	34	31	41
July	32	32	28	32½	40	42
August	32	32	29	32	40	42
September	32	32	31	32	40	42
October	32	32	31	32	40	42
November	32	32½	31½	32½	40	42
December	32½	32½	32	33½	40	44
July–December	32	32½	28	33½	40	44
1916.						
January	32½	33	32½	33½	42	44
February	33	33	32½	33	42	44
March	33	33	32½	33	43	44
April	34	35	32½	35	43	44
May	34	35	34	37	43	47
June	34	35	34	35	46	48
January–June	32½	35	32½	37	42	48
July	35	36	34	36	47	48
August	35	37	35	39	47	48
September	36	37	35	37	47	48
October	36	36	35	36	47	49
November	34	35	35	40	48	49
December	40	47	39	44	48	49
July–December	34	47	34	44	47	49

[1] One-fourth to three-eighths unwashed, 1912-1914.

SHEEP AND WOOL—Continued.

TABLE 175.—*Wool: International trade, calendar years 1913–1915.*

["Wool" in this table includes: Washed, unwashed, scoured, and pulled wool; slipe, sheep's wool on skins (total weight of wool and skins taken); and all other animal fibers included in United States classification of wool. The following items have been considered as not within this classification: Corded, combed, and dyed wool; flocks, goatskins with hair on, mill waste, noils, and tops. See "General note," Table 10.]

EXPORTS.

[000 omitted.]

Country.	1913	1914 (prelim.)	1915 (prelim.)	Country.	1913	1914 (prelim.)	1915 (prelim.)
	Pounds.	*Pounds.*	*Pounds.*		*Pounds.*	*Pounds.*	*Pounds.*
Algeria	21,410	15,992	24,828	New Zealand	193,338	227,148	200,102
Argentina	264,728	258,533	259,415	Persia	9,934	9,447	
Australia	603,271	414,286		Peru	9,770	10,665	
Belgium	218,193			Russia	38 200	16,482	2,347
British India	51,031	44,705	59,694	Spain	31,937	27,810	12,658
British South Africa	194,343	152,851	186,331	United Kingdom	29,079	38,848	32,151
Chile	28,418	27,043		Uruguay	150,883	98,298	
China	43,327	45,072	55,868	Other countries	33,343	26,622	
France	79,600	68,077	11,755				
Germany	47,774			Total	2,078,752	1,492,686	
Netherlands	30,173	10,807	97				

IMPORTS.

Country	1913	1914	1915	Country	1913	1914	1915
Austria-Hungary	58,650			Russia	121,691	97,763	8,631
Belgium	329,074			Sweden	6,022	4,669	
British India	29,116	22,749	39,286	Switzerland	10,444	9,152	17,414
Canada	8,587	9,518	16,611	United Kingdom	582,618	502,927	889,133
France	593,781	457,112	144,625	United States	130,183	260,193	412,721
Germany	481,571			Other countries	64,843	42,016	
Japan	11,741	12,736	52,771				
Netherlands	38,419	17,323	15,805	Total	2,466,740	1,436,158	

SWINE.

TABLE 176.—*Swine: Number and value on farms in the United States, 1867–1917.*

NOTE.—Figures in *italics* are census returns; figures in roman are estimates of the department of Agriculture. Estimates of numbers are obtained by applying estimated percentages of increase or decrease to the published numbers of the preceding year, except that a revised base is used for applying percentage estimates whenever new census data are available. It should also be observed that the census of 1910, giving numbers as of Apr. 15, is not strictly comparable with former censuses, which related to numbers June 1.

Jan. 1—	Number.	Price per head.	Farm value.	Jan. 1—	Number.	Price per head.	Farm value.
1867	24,694,000	$4.03	$99,637,000	1891	50,625,000	$4.15	$210,194,000
1868	24,317,000	3.29	79,976,000	1892	52,398,000	4.60	241,031,000
1869	23,316,000	4.65	108,431,000	1893	46,095,000	6.41	295,426,000
1870	26,751,000	5.80	155,108,000	1864	45,206,000	5.98	270,385,000
1870, census, June 1	*25,134,569*			1895	44,166,000	4.97	219,501,000
				1896	42,843,000	4.35	186,530,000
1871	29,458,000	5.61	165,312,000	1897	40,600,000	4.10	166,273,000
1872	31,796,000	4.01	127,453,000	1898	39,760,000	4.39	174,351,000
1873	32,632,000	3.67	119,632,000	1899	38,652,000	4.40	170,110,000
1874	30,861,000	3.98	122,695,000	1900	37,079,000	5.00	185,472,000
1875	28,062,000	4.80	134,581,000	*1900, census, June 1*	*62,868,041*		
1876	25,727,000	6.00	154,251,000				
1877	28,077,000	5.66	158,873,000	1901 [1]	56,982,000	6.20	353,012,000
1878	32,262,000	4.85	156,577,000	1902	48,699,000	7.03	342,121,000
1879	34,766,000	3.18	110,508,000	1903	46,923,000	7.78	364,974,000
1880	34,034,000	4.28	145,782,000	1904	47,009,000	6.15	289,225,000
1880, census, June 1	*47,681,700*			1905	47,321,000	5.99	283,255,000
				1906	52,103,000	6.18	321,803,000
1881	36,248,000	4.70	170,535,000	1907	54,794,000	7.62	417,791,000
1882	44,122,000	5.97	263,543,000	1908	56,084,000	6.05	339,030,000
1883	43,270,000	6.75	291,951,000	1909	54,147,000	6.55	354,794,000
1884	44,201,000	5.57	246,301,000	1910	47,782,000		
1885	45,143,000	5.02	226,402,000	*1910, census, Apr. 15*	*58,185,676*	9.17	533,309,000
1886	46,092,000	4.26	196,570,000				
1887	44,613,000	4.48	200,043,000	1911 [1]	65,620,000	9.37	615,170,000
1888	44,347,000	4.98	220,811,000	1912	65,410,000	8.00	523,328,000
1889	50,302,000	5.79	291,307,000	1913	61,178,000	9.86	603,109,000
1890	51,603,000	4.72	243,418,000	1914	58,933,000	10.40	612,951,000
1890, census, June 1	*57,409,583*			1915	64,618,000	9.87	637,479,000
				1916	67,766,000	8.40	569,573,000
				1917	67,453,000	11.73	791,242,000

[1] Estimates of numbers revised, based on census data.

SWINE—Continued.

TABLE 177.—*Swine: Number and value on farms Jan. 1, 1916 and 1917, by States.*

State.	Number (thousands) Jan. 1—		Average price per head Jan. 1—		Farm value (thousands of dollars) Jan. 1—	
	1917	1916	1917	1916	1917	1916
Maine	100	102	$16.60	$12.00	$1,660	$1,224
New Hampshire	53	55	15.60	12.50	827	688
Vermont	113	113	13.00	10.30	1,469	1,164
Massachusetts	112	112	15.00	13.20	1,680	1,478
Rhode Island	14	15	14.50	11.00	203	165
Connecticut	58	59	17.50	13.60	1,015	802
New York	759	799	14.70	11.80	11,157	9,428
New Jersey	163	161	17.00	12.80	2,771	2,061
Pennsylvania	1,174	1,210	13.90	10.40	16,319	12,584
Delaware	60	61	11.60	9.00	696	549
Maryland	359	359	11.50	8.50	4,128	3,052
Virginia	1,023	1,023	9.20	7.00	9,412	7,161
West Virginia	380	378	10.00	9.00	3,800	3,402
North Carolina	1,550	1,550	9.70	7.80	15,035	12,090
South Carolina	920	870	9.50	8.50	8,740	7,395
Georgia	2,585	2,348	9.00	7.70	23,265	18,080
Florida	1,100	996	6.50	6.00	7,150	5,976
Ohio	3,527	3,713	12.20	9.00	43,029	33,417
Indiana	3,970	4,010	11.50	8.50	45,655	34,085
Illinois	4,444	4,489	13.70	9.00	60,883	40,401
Michigan	1,345	1,462	12.40	9.00	16,678	13,158
Wisconsin	2,060	2,142	14.30	9.00	29,458	19,278
Minnesota	1,733	1,716	14.50	9.50	25,128	16,302
Iowa	9,370	9,069	14.70	9.30	137,739	84,342
Missouri	4,280	4,505	10.00	7.10	42,800	31,986
North Dakota	650	706	13.00	9.00	8,450	6,354
South Dakota	1,432	1,314	15.50	10.10	22,196	13,271
Nebraska	4,309	4,266	14.00	9.40	60,326	40,100
Kansas	2,535	2,815	12.30	9.10	31,180	25,616
Kentucky	1,589	1,709	8.90	6.50	14,142	11,108
Tennessee	1,485	1,531	8.40	6.80	12,474	10,411
Alabama	1,850	1,715	8.50	7.60	15,725	13,034
Mississippi	1,698	1,617	7.50	6.20	12,735	10,025
Louisiana	1,584	1,553	9.20	7.30	14,573	11,337
Texas	3,229	3,197	9.50	7.70	30,676	24,617
Oklahoma	1,372	1,491	10.20	7.20	13,994	10,735
Arkansas	1,575	1,589	8.20	5.40	12,915	8,581
Montana	269	298	12.00	9.00	3,228	2,682
Wyoming	69	70	11.20	9.40	773	658
Colorado	352	320	12.00	8.20	4,224	2,624
New Mexico	101	91	10.50	9.00	1,060	819
Arizona	80	40	13.00	11.00	1,040	440
Utah	101	112	10.50	7.80	1,060	874
Nevada	37	40	11.00	9.00	407	360
Idaho	292	344	10.40	7.00	3,037	2,408
Washington	283	314	11.10	8.50	3,141	2,669
Oregon	315	370	10.00	7.10	3,150	2,627
California	994	947	10.10	8.40	10,039	7,955
United States	67,453	67,766	11.73	8.40	791,242	569,573

SWINE—Continued.

TABLE 178.—*Hogs (live): Wholesale price per 100 pounds, 1912–1916.*

Date.	Cincinnati. Packing, fair to good.		St. Louis. Mixed packers.		Chicago. Mixed and packers.		Kansas City.		Omaha.	
	Low.	High.	Low.	High.	Low.	High.	Low.	High.	Low.	High.
1912.										
Jan.-June.........	$6.10	$8.25	$5.75	$8.05	$5.55	$8.17½	$5.65	$8.05	....	....
July-Dec..........	7.10	9.35	7.15	9.25	6.80	9.40	6.90	9.05	....	....
1913.										
Jan.-June.........	7.35	10.00	7.20	9.50	6.85	9.70	6.95	9.25	$7.02	$9.05
July-Dec..........	7.40	9.60	7.25	9.50	7.00	9.65	7.20	9.25	7.34	9.15
1914.										
Jan.-June.........	8.00	9.15	7.65	9.00	7.60	9.00	7.55	8.80	7.50	8.72
July-Dec..........	6.40	9.90	6.80	10.00	6.00	10.20	6.65	9.75	6.50	9.35
1915.										
January..........	6.65	7.35	6.65	7.35	6.15	7.40	6.50	7.40	6.00	7.95
February.........	6.70	7.15	6.55	7.15	6.30	7.25	6.35	7.02½	6.25	6.95
March............	6.50	7.50	6.65	7.25	6.35	7.05	6.50	7.05	6.35	6.82
April............	7.25	8.00	6.90	7.80	6.60	7.85	6.60	7.65	6.40	7.50
May..............	7.55	7.95	7.40	7.95	7.10	7.95	7.20	7.90	7.00	7.60
June.............	7.45	7.95	7.40	7.97½	7.05	7.92½	7.20	7.85	6.75	7.60
Jan.-June...	6.50	8.00	6.55	7.97½	6.15	7.95	6.35	7.90	6.00	7.95
July.............	7.35	8.00	6.75	8.10	6.15	8.10	7.00	7.80	5.90	7.65
August...........	7.10	7.75	6.50	7.85	5.90	8.00	6.30	7.70	5.90	7.60
September........	7.35	8.45	7.50	8.30	6.15	8.45	7.10	8.25	6.00	8.95
October..........	7.00	8.70	6.85	8.75	6.25	8.95	6.90	8.65	6.75	8.90
November........	6.35	7.70	6.40	7.10	5.80	7.75	6.20	7.50	6.00	7.35
December.........	6.25	7.25	6.15	6.85	5.80	7.05	6.00	6.75	4.00	8.00
June-Dec....	6.25	8.40	6.15	8.75	5.80	8.95	6.00	8.65	4.00	8.95
1916.										
January..........	6.75	8.10	6.00	8.25	6.50	8.10	6.25	8.00	6.00	7.80
February.........	8.00	8.95	7.50	8.92½	7.50	8.90	7.40	8.50	7.20	8.55
March............	8.70	10.20	7.90	10.10	8.65	10.10	8.40	9 80	8.00	9.65
April............	9.45	9.95	9.15	10.00	9.10	10.10	9.05	9.90	8.90	9.85
May..............	9.15	10.15	9.00	10.25	9.30	10.30	9.15	10.05	9.00	9.90
June.............	9.00	9.80	9.00	10.10	8.70	10.15	8.90	10.00	8.80	9.80
Jan.-June...	6.75	10.20	6.00	10.25	6.50	10.30	6.25	10.05	6.00	9.90
July.............	9.55	9.95	9.35	10.25	9.00	10.25	9.10	10.10	9.00	10.00
August...........	9.85	11.30	9.25	11.50	8.85	11.55	9.30	11.00	8.50	10.85
September........	10.15	11.50	9.50	11.50	9.25	11.60	7.75	10.50	9.25	11.10
October..........	9.00	10.35	8.90	10.50	8.50	10.55	8.75	10.40	8.50	10.15
November........	9.25	10.05	9.35	10.95	8.75	10.25	9.00	10.15	9.00	10.15
December.........	9.50	10.75	9.35	10.80	8.90	10.80	9.35	10.60	9.00	10.35
June-Dec....	9.00	11.50	8.90	11.50	8.50	11.60	7.75	11 00	8.50	11.10

THE FEDERAL MEAT INSPECTION.

Some of the principal facts connected with the Federal meat inspection as administered by the Bureau of Animal Industry are shown in the following tables. The figures cover the annual totals for the fiscal years 1907 to 1914, inclusive, the former being the first year of operations under the meat-inspection law now in force. The data given comprise the number of establishments at which inspection is conducted; the number of animals of each species inspected at slaughter; the number of each species condemned, both wholly and in part, and the percentage condemned of each species and of all animals; the quantity of meat products prepared or processed under Federal supervision, and the quantity and percentage of the latter condemned.

Further details of the Federal meat inspection are published each year in the Annual Report of the Chief of the Bureau of Animal Industry.

FEDERAL MEAT INSPECTION—Continued.

TABLE 179.—*Number of establishments and total number of animals inspected at slaughter under Federal inspection annually, 1907 to 1916.*

Fiscal year.	Establishments.	Cattle.	Calves.	Swine.	Sheep.	Goats.	All animals.
1907	708	7,621,717	1,763,574	31,815,900	9,681,876	52,149	50,935,216
1908	787	7,116,275	1,995,487	35,113,077	9,702,545	45,953	53,973,337
1909	876	7,325,337	2,046,711	35,427,931	10,802,903	69,193	55,672,075
1910	919	7,962,189	2,295,099	27,656,021	11,149,937	115,811	49,179,057
1911	936	7,781,030	2,219,908	29,916,363	13,005,502	54,145	52,976,948
1912	940	7,532,005	2,242,929	34,966,378	14,208,724	63,983	59,014,019
1913	910	7,155,816	2,098,484	32,287,538	14,724,465	56,556	56,322,859
1914	893	6,724,117	1,814,904	33,289,705	14,958,834	121,827	56,909,387
1915	896	6,964,402	1,735,902	36,247,958	12,909,089	165,523	58,022,884
1916	875	7,346,709	2,041,341	40,287,692	11,970,869	179,693	61,826,304

TABLE 180.—*Condemnations of animals at slaughter, 1907–1916.*

Fiscal year.	Cattle.			Calves.			Swine.		
	Whole.	Part.	Per cent.[1]	Whole.	Part.	Per cent.[1]	Whole.	Part.	Per cent.[1]
1907	27,933	93,174	1.58	6,414	245	0.38	105,879	436,161	1.70
1908	33,216	67,482	1.41	5,854	396	.31	127,933	636,589	2.18
1909	35,103	99,739	1.84	8,213	409	.42	86,912	799,300	2.50
1910	42,426	122,167	2.07	7,524	500	.35	52,439	726,829	2.82
1911	39,402	123,969	2.10	7,654	781	.38	59,477	877,528	3.13
1912	50,363	134,783	2.46	8,927	1,212	.45	129,002	323,992	1.30
1913	50,775	130,139	2.53	9,216	1,377	.50	173,937	373,993	1.70
1914	48,356	138,085	2.77	6,696	1,234	.44	204,942	422,275	1.88
1915	52,496	178,409	3.32	5,941	1,750	.44	213,905	464,217	1.87
1916	57,579	188,915	3.35	6,681	1,988	.42	195,107	546,290	1.84

Fiscal year.	Sheep.			Goats.			All animals.		
	Whole.	Part.	Per cent.[1]	Whole.	Part.	Per cent.[1]	Whole.	Part.	Per cent.[1]
1907	9,524	296	0.10	42	....	0.08	149,792	529,876	1.33
1908	8,090	198	.09	33	1	.07	175,126	704,666	1.63
1909	10,747	179	.10	82	1	.12	141,057	899,628	1.87
1910	11,127	24,714	.32	226	1	.19	113,742	874,211	2.01
1911	10,789	7,394	.14	61	....	.11	117,383	1,009,672	2.13
1912	15,402	3,871	.13	84	1	.13	203,778	463,859	1.13
1913	16,657	939	.12	76	1	.14	250,661	506,449	1.34
1914	20,563	1,564	.15	746	8	.62	281,303	563,166	1.48
1915	17,611	298	.14	653	14	.40	290,606	644,688	1.61
1916	15,057	1,007	.13	663	161	.46	275,087	738,361	1.64

[1] Includes both whole and parts. It should be understood that the parts here recorded are primal parts; a much larger number of less important parts, especially in swine, are condemned in addition.

TABLE 181.—*Quantity of meat and meat food products prepared, and quantity and percentage condemned, under Federal supervision annually, 1907 to 1916.*

Fiscal year.	Prepared or processed.	Condemned.	Percentage condemned.	Fiscal year.	Prepared or processed.	Condemned.	Percentage condemned.
	Pounds.	*Pounds.*			*Pounds.*	*Pounds.*	
1907	4,464,213,208	14,874,587	0.33	1912	7,279,558,956	18,096,587	0.25
1908	5,958,298,364	43,344,206	.73	1913	7,094,809,809	18,851,930	.27
1909	6,791,437,032	24,679,754	.36	1914	7,033,295,975	19,135,469	.27
1910	6,223,964,593	19,031,808	.31	1915	7,533,070,002	18,780,122	.25
1911	6,934,233,214	21,073,577	.31	1916	7,474,242,192	17,897,367	.24

The principal items in the above table, in the order of magnitude, are: Cured pork, lard, lard substitute, sausage, and oleo products. The list includes a large number of less important items.

It should be understood that the above products are entirely separate and additional to the carcass inspection at time of slaughter. They are, in fact, reinspections of such portions of the carcass as have subsequently undergone some process of manufacture.

TABLE 182.—*Quantity of meat and meat food products imported, and quantity and percentage condemned or refused entry, 1914 to 1916.*

Fiscal year.	Total imported.	Condemned.	Refused entry.	Percentage condemned or refused entry.
	Pounds.	*Pounds.*	*Pounds.*	*Per cent.*
1914 (9 months)	197,389,348	551,859	....	0.28
1915	245,023,437	2,020,291	70,454	.85
1916	110,514,476	298,276	113,907	.37

MISCELLANEOUS DATA.

TABLE 183.—*Estimated value of farm products, 1879–1916.*

[Based on prices at the farm.]

Year.	Total, gross.	Crops.		Animals and animal products.	
		Value.	Percentage of total.	Value.	Percentage of total.
1879 (census)	*$2,212,540,927*	....	....	....	....
1889 (census)	*2,460,107,454*				
1897	3,960,821,685	$2,519,082,592	63.6	$1,441,739,093	36.4
1898	4,338,945,829	2,759,569,547	63.6	1,579,376,282	36.4
1899 (census)	*4,717,069,973*	*2,998,704,412*	*63.6*	*1,718,365,561*	*36.4*
1900	5,009,595,006	3,191,941,763	63.7	1,817,653,243	36.3
1901	5,302,120,039	3,385,179,114	63.8	1,916,940,925	36.2
1902	5,594,645,072	3,578,416,465	64.0	2,016,228,607	36.0
1903	5,887,170,104	3,771,653,816	64.1	2,115,516,288	35.9
1904	6,121,778,001	3,981,675,866	65.0	2,140,102,135	35.0
1905	6,273,997,362	4,012,652,758	64.0	2,261,344,604	36.0
1906	6,764,210,423	4,263,134,353	63.0	2,501,076,070	37.0
1907	7,487,988,622	4,761,111,839	63.6	2,726,876,783	36.4
1908	7,890,625,522	5,098,292,549	64.6	2,792,332,973	35.4
1909 (census)	*8,558,161,223*	*5,487,161,223*	*64.1*	*3,071,000,000*	*35.9*
1910	9,037,390,744	5,486,373,550	60.7	3,551,017,194	39.3
1911	8,819,174,959	5,562,058,150	63.1	3,257,116,809	36.9
1912	9,342,790,149	5,842,220,449	62.5	3,500,569,700	37.5
1913	9,849,512,511	6,132,758,962	62.3	3,716,753,549	37.7
1914	9,894,960,531	6,111,684,020	61.8	3,783,276,511	38.2
1915	10,775,490,412	6,907,186,742	64.1	3,868,303,670	35.9
1916, preliminary	13,448,310,509	9,109,868,650	67.7	4,338,441,859	32.3

TABLE 184.—*Tonnage carried on railways in the United States, 1913–1915.*[1]

Product.	Year ending June 30—		
	1913	1914	1915
FARM PRODUCTS.	*Short tons.*	*Short tons.*	*Short tons.*
Animal matter:			
Animals, live....................................	15,042,000	14,811,000	15,021,432
Packing-house products—			
Dressed meats...........................	2,407,000	2,283,000	2,503,317
Hides (including leather).................	1,121,000	1,081,000	1,149,930
Other packing-house products............	2,345,000	2,375,000	2,540,376
Total packing-house products...........	5,873,000	5,739,000	6,193,623
Poultry (including game and fish)............	847,000	915,000	861,670
Wool.......................................	398,000	409,000	370,426
Other animal matter.........................	4,286,000	5,264,000	4,212,584
Total animal matter......................	26,446,000	27,138,000	26,659,735
Vegetable matter:			
Cotton....................................	3,942,000	4,141,000	5,012,705
Fruit and vegetables.......................	16,099,000	16,795,000	17,898,288
Grain and grain products—			
Grain..................................	50,945,000	46,015,000	53,446,686
Grain products—			
Flour...............................	9,523,000	9,697,000	9,596,703
Other grain products.................	7,830,000	7,824,000	8,036,745
Total grain and grain products.............	68,298,000	63,536,000	71,080,194
Hay..	7,145,000	7,319,000	7,649,093
Sugar......................................	3,599,000	3,926,000	3,727,194
Tobacco....................................	1,091,000	1,071,000	1,051,648
Other vegetable matter......................	9,493,000	9,338,000	10,347,913
Total vegetable matter...................	109,667,000	106,126,000	116,767,035
Total farm products.....................	136,113,000	133,264,000	143,426,770
OTHER FREIGHT.			
Products of mines...............................	650,940,000	626,076,000	556,581,950
Products of forests.............................	112,079,000	110,878,000	93,971,282
Manufactures...................................	161,933,000	145,257,000	132,410,447
All other (including all freight in less than carload lots).......	83,775,000	78,649,000	76,013,494
Total tonnage...........................	1,144,840,000	1,094,124,000	1,002,403,943

[1] Compiled from reports of the Interstate Commerce Commission. Original shipments only, excluding freight received by each railway from connecting railways and other carriers. Figures exclude the relatively small tonnage originating on railroads of Class III (roads having operating revenues of less than $100,000 a year).

TABLE 185.—*Rural and agricultural population in various countries.*

Country.	Rural population.			Population dependent upon agriculture.		
	Year	Number.	Per cent of total population.	Year.	Number.	Per cent of total population.
United States...............	1910	49,348,883	53.7	....	....	......
Austria-Hungary:						
Austria.............				1900	13,447,362	51.4
Hungary.............				1900	13,061,118	67.8
Total Austria-Hungary.............				1900	26,508,480	58.4
Belgium.....	1910	1,654,277	22.3			
British India.............				1901	191,691,731	65.1
Bulgaria.............				1905	3,089,301	76.6
Denmark.............	1911	1,647,350	59.7	1911	1,023,962	37.1
Finland.............				1900	1,555,357	57.3
France.............	1906	22,715,011	57.9	1891	17,435,888	45.7
Germany.............				1907	17,089,496	27.7
Norway.............				1900	854,787	38.5
Portugal.............	1890	3,458,996	68.5	1900	3,367,199	62.1
Roumania.............	1900	4,836,904	81.2			
Russia:						
Caucasus.............				1897	7,266,428	78.2
Central Asia.............				1897	6,361,466	82.1
Poland.............				1897	5,302,850	56.4
Russia proper.............				1897	69,470,360	74.3
Siberia.............				1897	4,448,456	77.2
Total Russia.............				1897	92,849,560	73.9
Serbia.............				1900	2,097,988	84.2
Sweden.............				1900	2,344,612	45.6
Switzerland.............	1900	1,047,795	31.6	1900	1,067,905	32.2
United Kingdom:						
England and Wales.............	1911	7,907,556	21.9	....	....	......

TABLE 186.—*Number of persons engaged in agriculture in various countries.*

Country.	Year.	Males.		Females.		Total persons engaged in agriculture.	
		Number.	Per cent of males in all occupations.	Number.	Per cent of females in all occupations.	Number.	Per cent of persons in all occupations.
United States...............	1910	10,582,039	35.2	1,806,584	22.4	12,388,623	32.5
Algeria.....................	1881	636,078	74.8	91,602	53.7	727,680	71.3
Argentina..................	1895	318,149	28.0	67,174	13.4	385,323	23.6
Australia...................	1901	377,626	29.5	39,029	11.1	416,655	25.6
Austria-Hungary...........	1900	8,185,250	58.5	5,935,805	70.3	14,121,055	63.0
Belgium....................	1900	533,665	23.6	163,707	17.6	697,372	21.9
Bolivia....................	1900	....	.....	....	.....	564,009	43.5
British India..............	1901	63,026,365	67.3	27,867,210	66.5	90,893,575	67.1
British North Borneo.......	1901	....	.....	....	.....	32,892	64.2
Bulgaria...................	1905	895,206	73.3	837,406	94.9	1,732,612	82.4
Canada....................	1901	707,997	45.4	8,940	3.7	716,937	39.9
Ceylon....................	1901	745,074	65.0	318,551	65.4	1,063,625	65.1
Chile.....................	1907	448,546	50.3	21,877	6.2	470,423	37.7
Cuba.....................	1907	364,821	52.2	3,110	4.2	367,921	47.6
Cyprus...................	1901	33,611	62.8	2,757	20.8	36,368	54.5
Denmark..................	1911	386,016	45.7	110,169	28.5	496,185	40.3
Egypt.....................	1907	2,258,005	67.2	57,144	33.3	2,315,149	65.6
Federated Malay States.....	1901	115,027	28.2	52,324	82.7	167,351	35.5
Finland...................	1900	321,538	51.4	102,008	39.6	423,546	48.0
Formosa..................	1905	763,456	70.6	263,664	82.4	1,027,120	73.3
France....................	1906	5,452,392	41.9	3,324,661	43.2	8,777,053	42.4
Germany..................	1907	5,146,723	27.7	4,585,749	48.3	9,732,472	34.6
Greece....................	1907	321,120	47.3	6,972	12.2	328,092	44.6
Grenada..................	1901	8,816	57.1	7,722	49.7	16,538	53.4
Italy.....................	1901	6,370,277	57.9	3,196,063	60.5	9,566,340	58.3
Jamaica...................	1911	....	.....	....	.....	271,493	66.1
Malta and Gozo...........	1901	10,235	13.3	3,613	15.8	13,848	13.9
Mauritius.................	1901	72,493	57.1	5,989	38.0	78,482	55.0
Netherlands...............	1899	490,694	32.9	79,584	18.4	570,278	29.6
New Zealand..............	1911	103,644	28.5	7,472	8.3	111,116	24.5
Norway...................	1910	....	.....	....	.....	307,528	33.4
Philippine Islands..........	1903	1,163,777	57.8	90,286	8.8	1,254,063	41.3
Porto Rico................	1899	196,893	73.3	1,868	3.9	198,761	62.8
Portugal..................	1900	1,127,268	65.3	380,293	52.0	1,507,561	61.4
Russia:							
In Europe..............	1897	13,808,505	59.6	1,974,164	38.0	15,782,669	55.6
In Asia.................	1897	2,092,965	69.2	105,137	30.5	2,198,102	65.3
Total.................	1897	15,901,470	60.7	2,079,301	37.5	17,980,771	56.7
St. Lucia..................	1901	....	.....	....	.....	15,796	54.1
Serbia....................	1900	311,700	65.5	13,524	50.5	325,224	64.7
Sierra Leone..............	1901	8,705	28.7	4,544	21.7	13,249	25.9
Spain.....................	1900	3,741,730	58.1	775,270	51.8	4,517,000	56.9
Sweden...................	1900	761,016	52.4	333,264	53.8	1,094,280	52.8
Switzerland...............	1900	392,971	37.1	80,326	16.1	473,297	30.4
Trinidad and Tobago.......	1901	51,744	54.7	25,765	39.3	77,509	48.4
Union of South Africa......	1904	863,223	56.3	847,057	77.5	1,710,280	65.1
United Kingdom...........	1901	2,109,812	16.3	152,642	2.9	2,262,454	12.4

TABLE 187.—*Total area and agricultural land in various countries.*

[As classified and reported by the International Institute of Agriculture.]

Country.	Year.	Total area.	Productive land.[1]		Cultivated land.[2]	
			Amount.	Per cent of total area.	Amount.	Per cent of total area.
NORTH AMERICA.		*Acres.*	*Acres.*	*Per cent.*	*Acres.*	*Per cent.*
United States...............	1910	1,903,269,000	878,789,000	46.2	293,794,000	15.4
Canada......................	1901	2,397,082,000	63,420,000	2.6	19,880,000	.8
Costa Rica..................	1909–10	13,343,000	3,090,000	23.2	442,000	3.3
Cuba.......................	1899	28,299,000	8,717,000	30.8	778,000	2.7
SOUTH AMERICA.						
Argentina...................	1909–10	729,575,000	537,805,000	73.7	44,446,000	6.1
Chile[3]......................	1910–11	187,145,000	15,144,000	8.1	2,557,000	1.4
Uruguay....................	1908	46,189,000	40,875,000	88.5	1,962,000	4.2
EUROPE.						
Austria-Hungary:						
Austria..................	1911	74,132,000	69,939,000	94.3	26,272,000	35.4
Hungary.................	1910	80,272,000	77,225,000	96.2	35,178,000	43.8
Total Austria-Hungary	....	154,404,000	147,164,000	95.3	61,450,000	39.8
Belgium.....................	1895	7,278,000	6,443,000	88.5	3,582,000	49.2
Bulgaria....................	1910	23,807,000	18,959,000	79.6	8,574,000	36.9
Denmark....................	1907	9,629,000	9,078,000	94.3	6,376,000	66.2
Finland.....................	1901	82,113,000	....	....	3,875,000	4.7
France......................	1910	130,854,000	123,642,000	94.5	59,124,000	45.2
Germany....................	1900	133,594,000	126,401,000	94.6	63,689,000	47.7
Italy.......................	1911	70,839,000	65,164,000	92	33,815,000	47.7
Luxemburg..................	1911	639,000	616,000	96.4	300,000	46.9
Netherlands.................	1911	8,057,000	7,258,000	90.1	2,210,000	27.4
Norway.....................	1907	79,810,000	22,942,000	28.7	1,830,000	2.3
Portugal....................	1912	22,018,000	17,281,000	78.5	5,777,000	26.2
Roumania...................	1905	32,167,000	24,645,000	76.6	14,829,000	46.1
Russia, European...........	1911	1,278,203,000	698,902,000	51.7	245,755,000	19.2
Serbia......................	1897	11,936,000	6,246,000	52.3	2,534,000	21.2
Spain......................	1908–11	124,666,000	112,665,000	90.4	41,264,000	33.1
Sweden.....................	1911	110,667,000	65,196,000	58.9	9,144,000	8.3
Switzerland[4]................	1905	10,211,000	7,635,000	74.8	605,000	5.9
United Kingdom:						
Great Britain...........	1911	56,802,000	47,737,000	84	14,587,000	25.7
Ireland.................	1911	20,350,000	18,789,000	92.3	3,275,000	16.1
Total United Kingdom	....	77,152,000	66,526,000	86.2	17,862,000	23.2
ASIA.						
British India...............	1910–11	615,695,000	465,706,000	75.6	264,858,000	43.0
Formosa....................	1911	8,858,000	1,972,000	22.3	1,884,000	21.3
Japan......................	1911	94,495,000	74,180,000	78.5	17,639,000	18.7
Russia, Asiatic.............	1911	4,028,001,000	715,838,000	17.8	33,860,000	.8
AFRICA.						
Algeria.....................	1910	124,976,000	50,846,000	40.7	11,434,000	9.1
Egypt......................	1912	222,390,000	5,486,000	2.5	5,457,000	2.5
Tunis......................	1912	30,888,000	22,239,000	72.0	6,919,000	22.4
Union of South Africa.......	1909–10	302,827,000	3,569,000	1.2	3,385,000	1.1
OCEANIA.						
Australia...................	1910–11	1,903,664,000	119,942,000	6.3	14,987,000	.8
New Zealand................	1910	66,469,000	57,310,000	86.2	6,955,000	10.5
Total, 36 countries.....	....	15,071,209,000	4,591,691,000	30.5	1,313,832,000	8.7

[1] Includes besides cultivated land, also natural meadows and pastures, forests, woodlots, and lands devoted to cultivated trees and shrubs.
[2] Includes fallow lands; also artificial grass lands.
[3] The figure for "productive land" in Chile excludes marshes, heaths, and productive but uncared-for lands.
[4] The figure for "cultivated land" in Switzerland excludes artificial meadows and pastures.

NATIONAL FORESTS.

TABLE 188.—*National forests: Timber disposed of, quantity, price, and number of users, revenue under specified heads, and details of grazing privileges, years ended June 30, 1911 to 1916.*

[Reported by the Forest Service.]

Item.	Year ended June 30—					
	1911	1912	1913	1914	1915	1916
Free timber given:						
Number of users..........	40,660	38,749	38,264	39,466	40,040	42,055
Timber cut..........M ft..	123,488	123,233	121,750	120,575	123,259	119,483
Value..............dolls..	196,930	196,335	191,825	183,223	206,597	184,715
Timber sales:						
Number..................	5,653	5,772	6,182	8,303	10,905	10,840
Quantity...........M ft..	830,304	799,417	2,137,311	1,540,084	1,093,589	906,906
Price per thousand board feet (average).....dolls..	2.56	2.00	2.01	2.30	2.44	1.98
Grazing:						
Number of permits........	25,604	26,501	27,466	28,945	30,610	33,328
Kinds of stock—						
Cattle............No..	1,351,922	1,403,025	1,455,922	1,508,639	1,627,321	1,758,764
Goats............No..	77,668	83,849	76,898	58,616	51,409	43,268
Hogs.............No..	4,500	4,330	3,277	3,381	2,792	2,968
Horses...........No..	91,516	95,343	97,919	108,241	96,933	98,903
Sheep............No..	7,371,747	7,467,890	7,790,953	7,560,186	7,232,276	7,843,205
Total..........No..	8,897,353	9,054,437	9,424,969	9,239,063	9,010,731	9,747,108
Special use and water-power permits.................No..	5,145	4,967	5,245	5,089	5,657	5,251
Revenue:						
From—						
Timber sales...dolls..	935,128	994,314	1,282,647	1,243,195	1,211,985	1,367,111
Timber settlements,[1] dollars..............	22,035	33,287	36,105	39,927	3,181	2,299
Penalties for timber trespass......dolls..	43,236	40,291	17,558	12,981	7,284	37,712
Turpentine sales,[2] dollars.............	....	....	....	15,372	8,915	14,402
Fire trespass....dolls..	14,371	21,810	5,028	7,950	661	5,471
Special uses[3]...dolls..	76,646	48,249	67,278	68,773	78,691	85,235
Grazing fees....dolls..	930,966	962,175	1,001,156	997,583	1,130,175	1,202,405
Grazing trespass, dollars..............	4,524	6,667	6,583	4,765	5,818	7,810
Water power...dolls..	....	50,563	51,235	47,164	89,104	101,096
Total revenue.dolls..	2,026,906	2,157,356	2,467,590	2,437,710	[4]2,535,814	2,823,541

[1] Includes timber taken in the exercise of permits for rights of way, development of power, etc.
[2] Prior to 1914 receipts from sale of turpentine were included with timber sales.
[3] Included under "Special use" prior to 1912.
[4] Refunds during year, $54,575.

NATIONAL FORESTS—Continued.

TABLE 189.—*Area of national forest lands, June 30, 1916.*

[Reported by Forest Service.]

State and forest.	Net area.	State and forest.	Net area.
Alaska:	*Acres.*	**Idaho:**	*Acres.*
Chugach	5,430,018	Boise	1,054,302
Tongass	15,454,110	Cache [1]	514,317
		Caribou [1]	686,349
Total	20,884,128	Challis	1,260,600
		Clearwater	785,179
Arizona:		Coeur d'Alene	650,336
Apache	1,184,582	Idaho	1,193,513
Chiricahua [1]	348,160	Kaniksu [1]	199,190
Coconino	1,599,677	Lemhi	1,067,741
Coronado	959,961	Minidoka [1]	510,003
Crook	867,102	Nez Perce	1,703,168
Dixie [1]	17,680	Palisade [1]	297,020
Kaibab	1,072,170	Payette	832,109
Manzano [1]	27,708	Pend Oreille	678,054
Prescott	1,434,122	St. Joe	577,135
Sitgreaves	667,168	Salmon	1,621,477
Tonto	1,996,280	Sawtooth	1,203,554
Tusayan	1,605,823	Selway	1,694,171
		Targhee [1]	694,372
Total	11,780,433	Weiser	562,743
Arkansas:		Total	17,785,333
Arkansas	622,003		
Ozark	294,916	**Michigan:**	
		Michigan	89,466
Total	916,919		
		Minnesota:	
California:		Minnesota	197,832
Angeles	885,216	Superior	857,330
California	822,364		
Cleveland	591,750	Total	1,055,162
Crater [1]	46,980		
Eldorado [1]	549,950	**Montana:**	
Inyo [1]	1,268,604	Absaroka	843,443
Klamath [1]	1,470,848	Beartooth	662,855
Lassen	992,804	Beaverhead	1,338,197
Modoc	1,182,298	Bitterroot	1,047,805
Mono [1]	801,485	Blackfeet	873,414
Monterey	401,492	Cabinet	831,494
Plumas	1,146,645	Custer	430,142
Santa Barbara	1,695,175	Deerlodge	834,709
Sequoia	2,196,199	Flathead	1,812,019
Shasta	828,367	Gallatin	565,575
Sierra	1,493,474	Helena	688,346
Siskiyou [1]	349,650	Jefferson	1,042,912
Stanislaus	809,679	Kootenai	1,337,991
Tahoe [1]	546,326	Lewis and Clark	811,727
Trinity	1,428,168	Lolo	850,505
		Madison	960,120
Total	19,507,474	Missoula	1,028,127
		Sioux [1]	98,805
Colorado:			
Arapahoe	636,899	Total	16,058,186
Battlement	651,227		
Cochetopa	907,532	**Nebraska:**	
Colorado	494,656	Nebraska	206,074
Durango	614,275		
Gunnison	908,109	**Nevada:**	
Hayden [1]	66,718	Dixie [1]	282,543
Holy Cross	576,945	Eldorado [1]	400
La Sal [1]	27,444	Humboldt	691,758
Leadville	935,229	Inyo [1]	72,817
Montezuma	700,571	Mono [1]	465,012
Pike	1,137,659	Nevada	1,237,943
Rio Grande	1,137,067	Ruby	343,185
Routt	847,882	Santa Rosa	270,072
San Isabel	598,912	Tahoe [1]	14,687
San Juan	618,075	Toiyabe	1,907,643
Sopris	596,852		
Uncompahgre	790,589	Total	5,286,060
White River	848,337		
		New Mexico:	
Total	13,094,978	Alamo	610,529
		Carson	854,562
Florida:		Chiricahua [1]	126,478
Florida	309,546	Datil	2,671,925
		Gila	1,437,147

[1] For total area, see "National Forests extending into two States."

NATIONAL FORESTS—Continued.

TABLE 189.—*Area of national forest lands, June 30, 1916*—Continued.

State and forest.	Net area.	State and forest.	Net area.
New Mexico—Continued.	*Acres.*	**Utah—Continued**	*Acres.*
Lincoln	551,760	Fillmore	700,626
Manzano [1]	755,894	Fishlake	661,699
Santa Fe	1,355,034	La Sal [1]	519,644
		Manti	781,800
Total	8,363,329	Minidoka [1]	69,402
		Powell	689,685
North Dakota:		Sevier	729,614
Dakota	6,054	Uinta	1,005,252
		Wasatch	607,732
Oklahoma:			
Wichita	61,480	Total	7,447,797
Oregon:		**Washington:**	
Cascade	1,016,569	Chelan	677,389
Crater [1]	787,454	Columbia	776,480
Deschutes	1,287,486	Colville	756,395
Fremont	888,887	Kaniksu [1]	258,776
Klamath [1]	3,998	Okanogan	1,487,136
Malheur	1,057,682	Olympic	1,534,680
Minam	398,086	Rainier	1,316,057
Ochoco	716,482	Snoqualmie	695,332
Oregon	1,031,902	Washington	1,454,356
Santiam	606,776	Wenaha [1]	313,434
Siskiyou [1]	997,139	Wenatchee	657,644
Siuslaw	541,280		
Umatilla	486,183	Total	9,927,679
Umpqua	1,011,417		
Wallowa	993,181	**Wyoming:**	
Wenaha [1]	425,504	Ashley [1]	5,987
Whitman	877,564	Bighorn	1,123,430
		Black Hills [1]	144,759
Total	13,127,590	Bonneville	607,013
		Bridger	572,083
Porto Rico:		Caribou [1]	6,707
Luquillo	32,975	Hayden [1]	322,222
		Medicine Bow	469,786
South Dakota:		Palisade [1]	254,964
Black Hills [1]	483,782	Shoshone	1,576,349
Harney	556,220	Targhee [1]	84,970
Sioux [1]	75,844	Teton	1,908,074
		Washakie	387,447
Total	1,115,846	Wyoming	899,980
Utah:			
Ashley [1]	982,493	Total	8,363,771
Cache [1]	267,066		
Dixie [1]	432,784	Grand total, National Forests	155,420,280

[1] For total area, see "National Forests extending into two States."

NATIONAL FORESTS EXTENDING INTO TWO STATES.

Forest.	States.	Net area.
		Acres.
Chiricahua	Arizona–New Mexico	474,638
Dixie	Arizona–Nevada–Utah	733,007
Manzano	Arizona–New Mexico	783,602
Crater	California–Oregon	834,434
Eldorado	California–Nevada	550,350
Inyo	California–Nevada	1,341,421
Klamath	California–Oregon	1,474,846
Mono	California–Nevada	1,266,497
Siskiyou	California–Oregon	1,346,789
Tahoe	California–Nevada	561,013
Hayden	Colorado–Wyoming	388,940
La Sal	Colorado–Utah	547,088
Cache	Idaho–Utah	781,383
Caribou	Idaho–Wyoming	693,056
Kaniksu	Idaho–Washington	457,966
Minidoka	Idaho–Utah	579,405
Palisade	Idaho–Wyoming	551,984
Targhee	Idaho–Wyoming	779,342
Sioux	Montana–South Dakota	174,649
Wenaha	Oregon–Washington	738,938
Black Hills	South Dakota–Wyoming	628,541
Ashley	Utah–Wyoming	988,480

NATIONAL FORESTS—Continued.

TABLE 190.—*Grazing allowances for national forests, 1916.*

Forest.	Number of stock authorized:			Yearlong rates (cents).			
	Cattle and horses.	Swine.	Sheep and goats.	Cattle.	Horses.	Swine.	Sheep and goats.
District 1:							
Absaroka	+ 6,835	....	102,000	54	67	....	13.5
Beartooth	+ 4,500	300	− 48,800	54	67	32	13.5
Beaverhead	− 24,500	....	− 114,000	54	67	....	13.5
Bitterroot	+ 3,800	....	+ 40,000	54	67	....	13.5
Blackfeet	2,000	....	10,000	48	60	....	12
Cabinet	+ 3,000	....	22,250	54	67	....	13.5
Clearwater	− 2,350	....	− 52,900	48	60	....	12
Coeur d'Alene	500	....	25,000	54	67	....	13.5
Custer	+ 19,250	....	− 6,250	54	67	....	13.5
Dakota	− 380	....	....	54	67	....	....
Deerlodge	− 15,200	....	− 60,000	54	67	....	13.5
Flathead	− 3,150	....	5,000	48	60	....	12
Gallatin	+ 8,500	....	+ 63,000	54	67	....	13.5
Helena	+ 18,900	....	− 98,500	54	67	....	13.5
Jefferson	+ 17,600	....	+ 129,000	54	67	....	13.5
Kaniksu	1,000	....	11,500	48	60	....	12
Kootenai	+ 2,100	....	− 43,500	48	60	....	12
Lewis and Clark	7,900	....	40,000	54	67	....	13.5
Lolo	− 1,000	....	− 20,000	54	67	....	13.5
Madison [1]	+ 27,000	....	+ 135,000	60	75	....	15
Missoula	7,800	....	− 14,500	54	67	....	13.5
Nezperce	10,000	....	50,000	54	67	....	13.5
Pend Oreille	+ 1,100	....	− 33,500	48	60	....	12
Selway	− 5,250	....	+ 10,000	48	60	....	12
Sioux	− 6,500	....	− 3,000	54	67	....	13.5
St. Joe	1,000	....	78,000	48	60	....	12
	+201,115	300	−1,215,700	....	....	....	....
District 2:							
Arapaho	+ 12,600	....	− 21,000	54	67	....	13.5
Battlement [1]	+ 43,700	....	....	54	67	....	....
Bighorn	+ 36,450	....	− 106,500	60	75	....	15
Black Hills [2]	+ 18,000	2,500	....	54	67	32	....
Bridger [1][3]	+ 16,600	....	− 62,800	54	67	....	13.5
Cochetopa	+ 18,000	....	− 62,000	54	67	....	13.5
Colorado	− 9,000	....	....	54	67	....	....
Durango	− 11,760	....	+ 93,850	54	67	....	13.5
Gunnison	+ 31,000	....	+ 10,000	54	67	....	13.5
Harney	− 9,765	....	....	54	67	....	....
Hayden	+ 7,400	....	120,000	54	67	....	13.5
Holy Cross [4]	+ 11,000	....	− 31,500	54	67	....	13.5
Leadville	12,200	....	+ 80,000	54	67	....	13.5
Medicine Bow	+ 9,800	....	62,000	54	67	....	13.5
Michigan	+ 900	....	+ 900	54	67	....	13.5
Minnesota	2,000	....	....	54	67	....	....
Montezuma	− 28,850	....	+ 45,700	54	67	....	13.5
Nebraska [1]	13,000	....	....	72	90	....	....
Pike	− 15,900	....	− 16,500	54	67	....	13.5
Rio Grande	+ 23,400	....	+ 266,500	54	67	....	13.5
Routt	− 32,500	....	− 91,400	54	67	....	13.5
San Isabel	13,700	....	15,500	54	67	....	13.5
San Juan [4]	+ 12,585	....	+ 97,250	54	67	....	13.5
Shoshone [1]	+ 12,300	....	+ 71,300	54	67	....	13.5
Sopris	− 15,250	....	− 61,000	54	67	....	13.5
Uncompahgre	− 28,440	....	+ 57,744	54	67	....	13.5
Washakie [1][5]	+ 12,350	....	+ 44,100	54	67	....	13.5
White River	− 40,000	....	+ 22,000	54	67	....	13.5
	−498,450	2,500	+1,439,044	....	....	....	....
District 3:							
Alamo	+ 14,250	75	− 11,000	48	60	29	12
Apache	31,500	100	+ 62,000	48	60	29	12
Carson	+ 8,100	+ 50	+ 161,300	48	60	29	12
Chiricahua	12,000	300	2,000	48	60	29	12
Coconino [1]	44,000	+ 250	92,000	48	60	29	12
Coronado	23,200	....	17,000	48	60	....	12
Crook	+ 18,300	100	− 1,350	48	60	29	12

[1] Term applications authorized.
[2] Includes Sundance Forest.
[3] Sheep increased by adding part of Washakie; total shows decrease in sheep for 1916.
[4] Term applications previously approved effective till expiration of period.
[5] Increased by adding Bonneville.

NATIONAL FORESTS—Continued.

TABLE 190.—*Grazing allowances for national forests, 1916*—Continued.

Forest.	Number of stock authorized.			Yearlong rates (cents).			
	Cattle and horses.	Swine.	Sheep and goats.	Cattle.	Horses.	Swine.	Sheep and goats.
District 3—Continued.							
Datil	+ 43,700	+ 800	− 125,300	48	60	29	12
Gila	+ 41,500	350	− 17,800	48	60	29	12
Lincoln	9,400	500	13,000	48	60	29	12
Manzano	9,300		95,000	48	60		12
Prescott	+ 53,550	50	− 71,000	48	60	29	12
Santa Fe	17,100	+ 550	100,900	48	60	29	12
Sitgreaves	10,800		77,000	48	60		12
Tonto	− 68,000	650	100	48	60	29	12
Tusayan	− 22,200	50	+ 72,400	48	60	29	12
	+426,900	+3,825	+ 919,150				
District 4:							
Ashley	+ 10,100		97,000	60	75		15
Boise [1]	4,000	100	140,000	54	67	32	13.5
Cache	+ 31,700		− 143,400	54	67		13.5
Caribou	+ 14,400		− 288,000	54	67		13.5
Challis [1]	+ 7,700		+ 91,000	54	67		13.5
Dixie	− 9,650	400	− 1,000	48	60	29	12
Fillmore	+ 20,000	+ 500	− 47,500	60	75	36	15
Fishlake	+ 18,900		− 70,000	60	76		15
Humboldt	+ 28,600		− 295,000	54	67		13.5
Idaho [1]	− 2,400		− 100,000	54	67		13.5
Kaibab [2]	− 9,700		− 5,000	48	60		12
La Sal	27,000	100	35,500	54	67	32	13.5
Lemhi	+ 10,000		77,500	54	67		13.5
Manti	+ 27,300		150,400	60	75		15
Minidoka	+ 25,650		+ 75,750	54	67		13.5
Nevada [2]	− 6,000		− 58,000	54	67		13.5
Palisade	+ 6,900		97,000	54	67		13.5
Payette [2]	+ 7,300		− 91,500	54	67		13.5
Powell	+ 13,500		72,000	54	67		13.5
Ruby	+ 16,400		+ 35,500	54	67		13.5
Salmon	14,700		+ 110,000	54	67		13.5
Santa Rosa	14,500		− 50,000	54	67		13.5
Sawtooth [1]	+ 7,000		− 310,000	54	67		13.5
Sevier	+ 11,400	− 50	− 115,000	54	67	32	13.5
Targhee [1]	+ 10,300		+ 129,000	54	67		13.5
Teton	+ 14,000			54	67		
Toiyabe	+ 18,000		− 22,000	54	67		13.5
Uinta [1][3]	+ 31,700		− 199,300	60	75		15
Wasatch	− 12,700		− 61,100	60	75		15
Weiser	+ 11,700	+ 600	− 73,000	54	67	32	13.5
Wyoming	+ 11,000		216,500	54	57		13.5
	+454,200	+1,750	−3,256,950				
District 5:							
Angeles [2]	4,100			60	75		
California	+ 6,700	1,000	− 58,000	60	75	36	15
Cleveland	− 2,000		− 1,500	60	75		15
Eldorado [1]	+ 10,100	50	+ 19,000	72	90	43	18
Inyo [4]	5,700		30,500	72	90		18
Klamath [2]	+ 8,350	600	− 5,600	56	70	34	14
Lassen	+ 12,750	+ 500	+ 36,250	64	80	38	16
Modoc	41,300		+ 63,000	60	75		15
Mono	+ 4,650		67,700	72	90		18
Monterey	2,250	900	2,000	64	80	38	16
Plumas [2]	− 13,100		+ 76,000	68	85		17
Santa Barbara [2]	− 7,650	300	+ 3,200	64	80	38	16
Sequoia [2]	+ 30,550	−2,300	− 9,900	72	90	43	18
Shasta	+ 9,900	500	24,700	60	75	36	15
Sierra [4]	15,000	500	21,000	72	90	43	18
Stanislaus [2]	+ 18,500	300	+ 15,350	72	90	43	18
Tahoe [2]	7,800	100	59,500	72	90	43	18
Trinity	+ 12,900	+ 415	+ 20,000	56	70	34	14
	+213,300	+7,465	+ 513,200				

[1] Term applications authorized.
[2] Term applications previously approved effective till expiration of period.
[3] Sheep increased by adding part of Washakie; total shows decrease in sheep for 1916.

NATIONAL FORESTS—Continued.

TABLE 190 —*Grazing allowances for national forests, 1916*—Continued.

Forest.	Number of stock authorized.			Yearlong rates (cents).			
	Cattle and horses.	Swine.	Sheep and goats.	Cattle.	Horses.	Swine.	Sheep and goats.
District 6:							
Cascade [1]	+ 1,000	....	− 27,600	64	80	....	16
Chelan	500	....	+ 31,600	60	75	....	15
Columbia	+ 1,300	....	+ 29,000	64	80	....	16
Colville	6,000	....	60,000	60	75	....	15
Crater	7,800	500	8,700	60	75	36	15
Deschutes	+ 5,000	....	+ 52,000	60	75	....	15
Fremont	+ 15,000	....	− 100,000	60	75	....	15
Malheur	+ 30,000	50	128,000	60	75	36	15
Minam	+ 11,900	....	+ 64,500	60	75	....	15
Ochoco	+ 13,700	....	− 86,000	60	75	....	15
Okanogan	+ 10,000	....	+ 90,000	60	75	....	15
Olympic	2,500	....	....	60	75	....	...
Oregon	+ 3,500	....	− 29,800	64	80	....	16
Rainier	+ 6,400	....	− 47,000	64	80	....	16
Santiam	+ 320	....	− 19,700	64	80	....	16
Siskiyou	+ 4,100	+1,000	+ 4,200	56	70	34	14
Siuslaw	1,200	....	4,000	56	70	....	14
Snoqualmie	....	....	6,000	....	....	....	16
Umatilla	10,300	....	− 59,400	60	75	....	15
Umpqua	1,200	....	12,000	64	80	....	16
Wallowa	− 19,000	100	− 105,000	60	75	36	15
Washington	+ 250	....	5,000	64	80	....	16
Wenaha	+ 11,650	....	− 102,000	60	75	....	15
Wenatchee	700	....	− 59,300	64	80	....	16
Whitman	+ 9,700	10	− 110,300	60	75	36	15
	+173,020	+1,660	−1,241,100	....	....	....	....
District 7:							
Arkansas	15,000	22,000	2,000	48	60	29	12
Florida	6,000	3,000	7,000	48	60	29	12
Ozark	− 8,500	−12,800	− 1,400	48	60	29	12
Wichita	4,630	....	....	1.00	1.25	....	...
	− 34,130	−37,800	− 10,400	....	....	....	....
Purchase areas:							
Cherokee	1,500	400	200	1.50	2.00	90	45
Georgia	860	430	500	.85	1.10	50	25
Massanutten	+ 300	....	100	1.50	....	....	45
Mount Mitchell	600	100	50	1.50	2.00	90	45
Nantahala	+ 500	2,100	150	1.50	2.00	90	45
Natural Bridge	+ 400	....	....	1.50	2.00	....	...
Potomac	− 240	....	− 490	1.50	2.00	....	45
Savannah (N)	− 150	+ 200	200	1.50	2.00	90	45
Savannah (S)	+ 160	+ 160	+ 80	1.50	2.00	90	45
Shenandoah	2,000	....	150	1.50	2.00	....	45
Unaka	500	150	75	1.50	2.00	90	45
White Mountain	100	....	....	1.50	2.00	....	...
White Top	− 250	− 150	150	1.50	2.00	90	45
	+ 7,560	− 3,690	− 2,145	....	....	....	....
Totals, 1913	1,852,999	59,535	8,521,308	....	....	....	....
Totals, 1914	1,891,119	65,645	8,867,906	....	....	....	....
Totals, 1915	1,983,775	64,040	8,747,025	....	....	....	....
Totals, 1916	2,008,675	58,990	8,597,689	....	....	....	....
Increase or decrease in 1916 over 1915	+ 24,900	− 5,030	− 149,336	....	....	....	....

[1] Term applications previously approved effective till expiration of period.

NOTE.—The symbols (+) or (−) indicate respectively that there was an increase or decrease in 1916 compared with 1915. The figures themselves refer to actual numbers of stock authorized in 1916.

IMPORTS AND EXPORTS OF AGRICULTURAL PRODUCTS.[1]

TABLE 191.—*Agricultural imports of the United States during the 3 years ending June 30, 1916.*

[Compiled from reports of the foreign commerce and navigation of the United States, U. S. Department of Commerce.]

Article imported.	Year ending June 30—					
	1914		1915		1916 (preliminary).	
	Quantity.	Value.	Quantity.	Value.	Quantity.	Value.
ANIMAL MATTER.						
Animals, live:						
Cattle—						
For breeding purposes, ...number..	718,352	$16,328,819	538,167	$17,513,175	439,185	$15,187,593
Other ....do....	150,016	2,367,899	....	....	....	....
Total cattle.......do....	868,368	18,696,718	538,167	17,513,175	439,185	15,187,593
Horses—						
For breeding purposes, ...number..	4,406	1,476,905	1,849	473,138	1,536	659,022
Other ....do....	28,613	1,128,124	10,803	504,242	14,020	959,223
Total horses......do....	33,019	2,605,029	12,652	977,380	15,556	1,618,245
Sheep—						
For breeding purposes, ...number..	221,836	516,912	153,317	533,967	235,659	917,502
Other ....do....	1,883	15,492	....	....	....	....
Total sheep.......do....	223,719	532,404	153,317	533,967	235,659	917,502
Swine.............do....	(2)	(2)	(2)	(2)	4,626	42,615
All other, including fowls...	....	2,877,960	....	3,254,559	....	883,124
Total live animals.......	....	24,712,111	....	22,279,081	....	18,649,079
Beeswax............pounds..	1,412,200	476,364	1,564,506	439,541	....	....
Dairy products:						
Butter...............do....	7,842,022	1,753,461	3,828,227	977,262	712,998	212,370
Cheese...............do....	63,784,313	11,010,693	50,138,520	9,370,048	30,087,999	7,058,420
Cream............gallons..	1,773,152	1,549,549	2,077,384	1,800,180	1,193,745	1,042,775
Milk.....................		1,089,440		2,556,787		1,515,354
Total dairy products....	....	15,403,143	....	14,704,277	....	9,828,919
Eggs.................dozens..	6,014,955	1,089,164	3,046,631	438,760	732,566	110,638
Egg yolks or frozen eggs, ...pounds..	3,420,412	504,619	8,571,758	798,129	....	....
Feathers and downs, crude:						
Ostrich...................	....	3,944,928	....	2,183,171	....	2,195,497
Other.....................		926,735		319,452		525,654
Fibers, animal:						
Silk—						
Cocoons.........pounds..	1,413	1,118	51,495	35,114	197,073	142,743
Raw, or as reeled from the cocoon.......pounds..	28,594,672	97,828,243	26,030,925	80,531,785	33,070,902	119,484,223
Waste..............do....	5,949,744	3,100,664	4,970,254	2,563,658	8,657,322	4,706,689
Total silk.........do....	34,545,829	100,930,025	31,052,674	83,130,557	41,925,297	124,333,655
Wool, and hair of the camel, goat, alpaca, and like animals—						
Class 1, clothing..pounds..	125,088,761	30,681,759	222,017,420	52,008,509	403,121,585	112,145,657
Class 2, combing....do....	18,839,698	4,906,967	15,054,694	3,735,158	13,292,160	3,916,708
Class 3, carpet......do....	102,003,313	17,029,611	65,709,752	10,865,475	109,268,999	23,955,236
Hair of the Angora goat, alpaca, etc...pounds..	1,717,097	572,430	5,301,563	1,633,426	9,145,278	2,403,133
Total wool.......do....	247,648,869	53,190,767	308,083,429	68,242,568	534,828,022	142,420,734
Total animal fibers, ...pounds..	282,194,698	154,120,792	339,136,103	151,373,125	576,753,319	266,754,389

[1] Forest products come within the scope of the Department of Agriculture and are therefore included in alphabetical order in these tables.
[2] Included in "All other, including fowls."

TABLE 191.—*Agricultural imports of the United States during the 3 years ending June 30, 1916*—Continued.

Article imported.	Year ending June 30—					
	1914		1915		1916 (preliminary).	
	Quantity.	Value.	Quantity.	Value.	Quantity.	Value.
ANIMAL MATTER—continued.						
Gelatin..............pounds..	2,441,317	$738,731	2,714,229	$816,521	1,600,235	$501,509
Glue..................do....	22,714,877	1,805,543	8,705,147	824,136	3,008,485	217,033
Honey..............gallons..	75,079	38,665	303,965	124,843	....	....
Packing-house products:						
Bladders, other than fish....	....	52,336	....	....	....	....
Blood, dried...............	....	391,816	....	227,198	....	....
Bones, cleaned.............	....	5,023	....	69	....	....
Bones, hoofs, and horns.....	....	1,061,466	....	911,473	....	867,242
Bristles—						
Crude, unsorted..pounds..	28,359	25,495	45,466	3,336	86,374	14,990
Sorted, bunched, or prepared..........pounds..	3,408,796	3,170,974	4,016,594	3,609,748	3,850,087	3,612,052
Total bristles.....do....	3,437,155	3,196,469	4,062,060	3,613,084	3,936,461	3,627,042
Grease.....................	....	1,028,595	....	1,146,721	....	490,470
Gut........................	....	122,733	....	....	....	....
Hair—						
Horse............pounds..	3,738,836	1,663,448	3,541,903	1,500,666	6,198,938	2,071,429
Other animal.......do....	10,507,680	1,051,698	8,148,570	744,187	9,692,037	988,342
Hide cuttings and other glue stock........................	....	2,158,514	....	1,510,608	....	972,106
Hides and skins, other than furs—						
Buffalo hides, dry ....pounds..	14,492,943	3,073,717	12,422,803	2,325,243	13,003,888	2,463,270
Calfskins—						
Dry..............do....	27,767,882	11,582,807	15,678,046	4,166,617	26,913,217	7,835,605
Green or pickled..do....	54,635,708	11,799,146	30,288,655	6,552,157	37,222,276	9,071,349
Cattle hides—						
Dry..............do....	71,485,650	18,083,314	93,001,127	21,424,552	153,339,079	37,453,897
Green or pickled .do....	208,477,838	34,098,628	241,340,290	39,753,213	280,838,692	50,596,221
Goatskins—						
Dry..............do....	63,374,054	19,037,307	50,713,062	13,925,565	85,505,514	25,198,246
Green or pickled..do....	21,385,374	3,153,956	15,834,101	2,263,984	15,151,507	2,207,658
Horse and ass skins—						
Dry..............do....	7,619,625	1,619,178	5,425,173	1,253,001	6,779,725	1,236,440
Green or pickled..do....	4,645,213	514,833	3,800,451	399,682	11,346,910	1,079,284
Kangaroo..........do....	1,328,668	898,087	769,125	427,127	1,219,129	722,300
Sheepskins—[1]						
Dry..............do....	29,338,146	6,165,947	20,886,018	3,963,438	54,599,884	11,330,341
Green or pickled..do....	40,738,679	6,427,270	37,833,520	6,021,432	46,859,397	7,509,009
Other..............do....	15,780,906	3,835,591	10,225,362	1,701,095	10,890,642	2,157,756
Total hides and skins, ...pounds..	561,070,686	120,289,781	538,217,733	104,177,106	743,669,860	158,861,376
Meat—						
Cured—						
Bacon and hams, ... pounds..	2,008,960	383,669	7,542,446	1,161,090	667,667	111,486
Meat prepared or preserved..................	....	1,676,360	....	1,193,268	....	325,381
Sausage, bologna, ...pounds..	730,326	186,824	209,484	53,660	47,287	12,322
Fresh—						
Beef and veal..pounds..	180,137,183	15,423,911	184,490,759	16,942,661	71,101,756	7,107,949
Mutton and lamb.do....	12,710,905	1,114,730	15,528,855	1,474,422	20,257,999	1,784,310
Pork.............do....	4,624,799	540,801	16,250,514	2,011,065	2,169,084	234,873
Other, including meat extracts..................	....	1,075,849	....	2,561,906	....	1,486,395
Total meat............	....	20,402,144	....	25,398,072	....	11,062,716
Oleo stearin........pounds..	5,243,553	459,989	2,424,009	209,545	910,478	81,280
Rennets....................	....	129,720	....	101,017	....	....
Sausage casings....pounds..	....	2,955,657	....	2,944,501	....	3,865,877
Total packing-house products..	....	154,969,389	....	142,484,247	....	182,887,880
Total animal matter.....	....	358,730,184	....	336,785,283	....	481,670,598

[1] Except sheepskins with the wool on.

TABLE 191.—*Agricultural imports of the United States during the 3 years ending June 30, 1916*—Continued.

Article imported.	Year ending June 30—					
	1914		1915		1916 (preliminary).	
	Quantity.	Value.	Quantity.	Value.	Quantity.	Value.
VEGETABLE MATTER.						
Argols, or wine lees...pounds..	29,793,011	$3,228,674	28,624,554	$3,094,380	34,721,043	$5,306,246
Breadstuffs. (*See* Grain and grain products.)						
Broom corn........long tons..	1,272	141,730	129	15,912	158	24,643
Cocoa and chocolate:						
Cocoa—						
Crude, and leaves and shells of........pounds..	176,267,646	20,797,790	192,306,634	22,893,241	243,231,939	35,143,865
Chocolate.............do....	3,096,445	706,193	2,427,561	584,915	2,347,162	660,377
Total cocoa and chocolate..........pounds..	179,364,091	21,503,983	194,734,195	23,478,156	245,579,101	35,804,242
Coffee....................do....	1,001,528,317	110,725,392	1,118,690,524	106,765,644	1,201,104,485	115,485,970
Coffee substitutes:						
Chicory root—						
Roasted, ground, or otherwise prepared, pounds...............	2,292,430	47,882	755,680	17,389		
Other............pounds..	188,446	21,498				
Total coffee substitutes, pounds................	2,480,876	69,380	755,680	17,389		
Curry and curry powder.......		11,861				
Fibers, vegetable:						
Cotton.............pounds..	123,346,899	19,456,588	185,204,579	23,208.960	232,801.062	40,150,342
Flax.............long tons..	9,885	2,870,274	4,694	1,875,701	6,939	3,508,295
Hemp.................do....	8,822	1,564,483	5,310	1,156,129	6,506	1,642,418
Istle, or Tampico fiber.do....	10,660	1,036,431	12,300	1,216,466	30,812	2,905,494
Jute and jute butts...do....	106,033	11,174,028	83,140	4,677,334	108,322	7,914,782
Kapoc.................do....	1,827	441,109	3,860	767,509	5,642	1,139,648
Manila.................do....	49,688	9,779,539	51,081	9,200,793	78,892	14,066,838
New Zealand flax.....do....	6,171	716,953	2,944	319,936	7,180	1,130,995
Sisal grass.............do....	215,547	25,860,729	185,764	20,572,347	228,610	25,803,433
Other.................do....	9,799	906,449	6,697	633,802	9,313	1,348,159
Total vegetable fibers...		73,806,583		63,628,977		99,610,404
Flowers, natural...............		24,540				
Forest products:						
Charcoal...............		60,634				
Cinchona bark.....pounds..	3,648,868	464,412	3,944,549	561,106	3,947,320	777,637
Cork wood or cork bark....		3,851,794		2,762,895		3,134,884
Dyewoods, and extracts of—						
Dyewoods—						
Logwood.....long tons..	30,062	378,064	55,059	742,234	134,629	3,437,698
Other.............do....	7,663	108,928	13,361	197,122	24,592	468,669
Total dyewoods.do....	37,725	486,992	68,420	939,356	159,221	3,906,367
Extracts and decoctions of............pounds..	8,810,040	306,934	6,191,232	202,675	5,471,251	382,880
Total dyewoods, and extracts of.............		793,926		1,142,031		4,289,247
Gums—						
Camphor—						
Crude..........pounds..	3,476,908	929,715	3,729,207	1,003,261	4,574,430	1,236,172
Refined.........do....	566,106	182,790	1,170,666	417,861	1,866,154	619,320
Chicle... ....do....	8,040,891	3,012,458	6,499,664	2,459,810	7,346,969	2,828,184
Copal, kauri, and damar, pounds................	32,693,412	3,354,679	27,450,545	2,821,346	44,528,856	3,587,020
Gambier, or terra japonica, pounds................	14,936,129	571,067	14,169,490	542,200	12,819,859	928,924

TABLE 191.—*Agricultural imports of the United States during the 3 years ending June 30, 1916—Continued.*

Article imported.	Year ending June 30—					
	1914		1915		1916 (preliminary).	
	Quantity.	Value.	Quantity.	Value.	Quantity.	Value.
VEGETABLE MATTER—contd.						
Forest products—Continued.						
Gums—Continued.						
India rubber, gutta percha, etc.—						
Balata..........pounds..	1,533,024	$793,126	2,472,224	$963,384	2,544,405	$996,102
Guayule gum.....do....	1,475,804	607,076	5,111,849	1,441,367	2,816,068	880,813
Gutta-joolatong, or East Indian gum..pounds..	24,926,571	1,155,402	14,851,264	731,995	27,858,335	1,322,262
Gutta-percha.....do....	1,846,109	323,567	1,618,214	230,750	3,188,449	342,226
India rubber......do....	131,995,742	71,219,851	172,068,428	83,030,269	267,775,557	155,044,790
Total India rubber, etc.......pounds..	161,777,250	74,099,022	196,121,979	86,397,765	304,182,814	158,586,193
Shellac...........do....	16,719,756	2,689,269	24,153,363	3,016,472	25,817,509	3,302,825
Other....................	....	2,001,631	....	1,581,704	....	2,324,092
Total gums..........	....	86,840,631	....	98,240,419	....	173,412,730
Ivory, vegetable...pounds..	27,135,406	881,354	21,059,746	510,677	32,942,115	840,464
Naval stores:						
Tar and pitch (of wood), barrels..................	561	7,946	....	....	....	....
Turpentine, spirits of, gallons..................	68,966	28,818	13,750	5,102	....	....
Total naval stores.....	....	36,764	13,750	5,102	....	....
Palm leaf, natural.........	....	14,044	....	....	....	....
Tanning materials:						
Mangrove bark..long tons..	7,689	196,891	8,096	218,952	21,186	582,929
Quebracho, extract of, pounds.................	93,329,087	2,543,302	120,450,283	3,676,749	81,501,952	5,432,468
Quebracho wood..l. tons..	73,956	900,880	54,955	753,981	106,864	1,598,465
Sumac, ground..pounds..	10,770,400	258,738	13,165,182	323,448	21,542,390	555,276
Other....................	....	468,230	....	370,133	....	668,159
Total tanning materials..............	....	4,368,041	....	5,343,263	....	8,837,297
Wood, not elsewhere specified—						
Brier root or brierwood and ivy or laurel root...	....	241,493	....	334,552	....	457,537
Chair cane or reed.........	....	451,099	....	169,181	....	265,305
Cabinet woods, unsawed—						
Cedar...........M feet..	17,285	982,152	15,875	947,313	14,369	740,488
Mahogany........do....	70,470	4,925,126	42,325	2,640,705	39,855	2,781,372
Other....................	....	1,217,410	....	683,757	....	489,247
Total cabinet woods...	....	7,124,688	....	4,271,775	....	4,011,107
Logs and round timber, M feet..................	148,938	1,657,605	131,544	1,263,641	150,401	1,417,859
Lumber—						
Boards, deals, planks, and other sawed lumber.......M feet..	931,408	17,817,550	940,687	17,865,582	1,218,068	23,113,664
Laths.................M..	564,778	1,613,586	672,023	1,916,214	771,823	2,207,223
Shingles.............M..	895,038	2,190,170	1,487,116	3,104,698	1,769,333	3,593,696
Other....................	....	815,279	....	621,097	....	709,696
Total lumber.........	....	22,436,585	....	23,507,591	....	29,624,279
Pulp wood—						
Peeled...........cords..	630,863	4,062,835	551,239	3,516,460	627,290	3,959,732
Rossed...........do....	255,844	2,118,910	187,047	1,597,750	164,714	1,282,658
Rough............do....	186,316	1,063,721	247,400	1,458,629	187,006	1,131,359
Rattan and reeds.........	....	1,210,390	....	771,628	....	1,720,816
All other.................	....	559,036	....	511,682	....	793,692
Total wood, n. e. s.....	....	40,926,362	....	37,402,889	....	44,664,344

TABLE 191.—*Agricultural imports of the United States during the 3 years ending June 30, 1916*—Continued.

Article imported.	Year ending June 30—					
	1914		1915		1916 (preliminary).	
	Quantity.	Value.	Quantity.	Value.	Quantity.	Value.
VEGETABLE MATTER—contd.						
Forest products—Continued.						
Wood, not elswhere specified—Continued.						
Wood pulp—						
Chemical—						
Bleached.....pounds..	177,833,052	$4,153,036	[1]100,555	$5,256,724	[1]55,757	$3,025,941
Unbleached.....do....	605,926,470	10,136,707	[1]300,114	11,483,268	[1]264,882	10,693,736
Mechanical.......do....	354,967,673	2,733,595	[1]187,253	3,141,119	[1]186,406	3,148,173
Total wood pulp..do..	1,138,727,195	17,023,338	[1]587,922	19,881,111	[1]507,045	16,867,850
Total forest products..	....	155,261,300	....	165,849,493	....	252,824,453
Fruits:						
Fresh or dried—						
Bananas.......bunches..	48,683,592	16,397,884	41,091,585	13,512,960	36,754,704	12,106,158
Currants.........pounds..	32,083,177	1,233,228	30,350,527	1,209,273	25,373,029	1,382,839
Dates.................do....	34,073,608	679,527	24,949,374	420,203	31,075,424	547,433
Figs.................do....	19,284,868	941,207	20,779,730	1,024,495	7,153,250	315,831
Grapes........cubic feet..	1,334,163	1,599,969	1,323,928	1,523,547	623,856	703,274
Lemons..........pounds..	(²)	5,981,635		3,730,075		2,062,030
Olives............gallons..	5,316,364	2,292,837	3,622,275	1,607,903	5,938,446	2,433,304
Oranges.........pounds..	(²)	93,472		50,022		89,464
Pineapples.................		1,287,862		1,309,750		964,623
Raisins..........pounds..	4,554,549	309,511	2,808,806	238,958	1,024,296	143,750
Other.....................		1,710,009		1,431,242		1,582,692
Total fresh or dried.....	....	32,527,141	....	26,058,428	....	22,331,398
Prepared or preserved.......	....	1,111,193	....	1,022,971	....	954,418
Total fruits.............	....	33,638,334	....	27,081,399	....	23,285,816
Ginger, preserved or pickled, pounds.....................	478,058	36,434	....	....	....	....
Grain and grain products:						
Grain—						
Corn.............bushels..	12,367,369	7,917,243	9,897,939	6,083,385	5,208,497	2,865,003
Oats.................do....	22,273,624	7,885,837	630,722	290,180	665,314	302,547
Wheat...............do....	1,978,937	1,761,995	426,469	469,847	5,703,078	5,789,321
Total grain........do....	36,619,930	17,565,075	10,955,130	6,843,412	11,576,889	8,956,871
Grain products—						
Bread and biscuit........	....	415,318	....	266,079	....	213,400
Macaroni, vermicelli, etc., pounds..................	126,128,621	5,698,783	56,542,480	3,061,337	21,789,602	1,525,695
Malt............bushels..	13,472	16,367	....	....	....	....
Meal and flour—						
Wheat flour....barrels..	89,911	363,855	64,200	309,742	329,905	1,689,418
Other.....................	....	3,382,879	....	2,037,786	....	3,251,976
Total grain products..	....	9,877,202	....	5,674,944	....	6,680,489
Total grain and grain products..............	....	27,442,277	....	12,518,356	....	15,637,360
Hay...............long tons..	170,786	1,634,390	20,187	228,906	43,184	679,412
Hops.................pounds..	5,382,025	2,790,516	11,651,332	2,778,735	675,704	144,627
Indigo.................do....	8,125,211	1,093,226	7,975,709	1,596,978	6,599,583	8,235,670
Licorice root..............do....	115,636,131	2,047,192	65,958,501	1,252,989	41,003,295	1,609,571
Liquors, alcoholic:						
Distilled spirits—						
Brandy........proof galls..	602,563	1,617,483	400,203	1,035,562	536,342	1,576,481
Cordials, liqueurs, etc., proof galls..............	515,575	1,063,267	408,090	858,599	330,452	794,553
Gin............proof galls..	1,055,885	1,017,569	742,439	717,131	805,749	749,775
Whisky.............do....	1,571,870	3,186,627	1,327,759	2,641,617	1,742,197	3,677,662
Other...............do....	414,950	378,902	411,236	317,413	538,759	433,098
Total distilled spirits, proof galls.............	4,160,843	7,263,848	3,289,727	5,570,322	3,953,499	7,231,569

[1] Long tons (2,240 pounds).   [2] Not stated.

TABLE 191.—*Agricultural imports of the United States during the 3 years ending June 30, 1916*—Continued.

Article imported.	Year ending June 30—					
	1914		1915		1916 (preliminary).	
	Quantity.	Value.	Quantity.	Value.	Quantity.	Value.
VEGETABLE MATTER—contd.						
Liquors, alcholic—Continued.						
Malt liquors—						
Bottled..........gallons..	1,213,320	$1,152,598	799,946	$768,893	872,402	$850,913
Unbottled..........do....	5,963,913	1,814,431	2,551,158	818,505	1,740,333	605,980
Total malt liquors..do....	7,177,233	2,967,029	3,351,104	1,587,398	2,612,735	1,456,893
Wines—						
Champagne and other sparkling...doz. quarts..	270,002	4,418,958	114,630	2,004,680	206,210	3,532,022
Still wines—						
Bottled....doz. quarts..	728,303	2,940,277	626,865	2,273,916	547,119	2,197,311
Unbottled......gallons..	5,220,380	2,757,434	3,860,273	1,968,587	3,455,756	2,267,561
Total still wines......	....	5,697,711	....	4,242,503	....	4,464,872
Total wines..........	....	10,116,669	....	6,247,183	....	7,996,894
Total alcoholic liquors.	....	20,347,546	....	13,404,903	....	16,685,356
Malt, barley. (*See* Grain and grain products.)						
Malt extract, fluid and solid...	....	16,566	....	....	....	....
Malt liquors. (*See* Liquors, alcoholic.)						
Nursery stock:						
Plants, trees, shrubs, and vines—						
Bulbs, bulbous roots or corns, cultivated for their flowers or foliage M....................	216,138	2,092,139	255,700	2,375,316	231,733	2,180,687
Other.................	....	1,514,669	....	1,376,234	....	1,505,661
Total nursery stock.....	....	3,606,808	....	3,751,550	....	3,686,348
Nuts:						
Almonds—						
Shelled..........pounds..	13,307,631	4,040,785	12,208,551	3,100,428	13,667,766	3,700,298
Unshelled..........do....	5,730,774	638,504	4,902,713	499,151	2,929,155	272,815
Coconuts, unshelled..........	....	2,133,416	....	1,593,517	....	1,876,966
Coconut meat, broken, or copra—						
Not shredded, desiccated, or prepared....pounds..	45,437,155	2,395,013	90,548,715	3,397,657	110,077,844	4,551,427
Shredded, desiccated, or prepared......pounds..	10,297,554	807,198	5,936,212	432,993	8,490,069	693,765
Cream and Brazil..pounds..	20,423,497	1,075,907	16,172,581	878,272	14,798,912	917,613
Filberts—						
Shelled..........pounds..	1,643,507	261,785	1,973,192	275,026	1,133,915	230,854
Unshelled..........do....	10,992,972	834,078	11,717,370	949,099	9,785,545	819,508
Peanuts—						
Shelled..........do....	27,077,158	1,239,227	9,643,691	333,980	19,392,832	722,939
Unshelled..........do....	17,472,631	660,010	14,540,982	490,779	9,020,848	328,099
Walnuts—						
Shelled..........do....	8,928,029	2,042,680	11,107,490	2,322,754	14,228,714	3,157,933
Unshelled..........do....	28,267,699	2,296,801	22,338,348	1,661,473	22,630,220	1,899,012
Other......................	....	1,463,197	....	895,803	....	1,989,262
Total nuts............	....	19,888,601	....	16,830,932	....	21,160,491
Oil cake..............pounds..	11,656,803	120,078	21,188,658	219,635	....	....
Oils, vegetable:						
Fixed or expressed—						
Cocoa butter or butterine, ...pounds..	2,838,761	793,451	150,378	42,185	400,371	129,654
Coconut oil......pounds..	74,386,213	6,703,942	63,135,428	5,430,581	66,007,560	6,047,183
Cottonseed..........do....	17,293,201	1,044,834	15,162,361	728,961	17,180,542	915,972
Flaxseed or linseed, ...gallons..	192,282	91,555	535,291	248,403	50,148	33,295

TABLE 191.—*Agricultural imports of the United States during the 3 years ending June 30, 1916*—Continued.

Article imported.	1914 Quantity.	1914 Value.	1915 Quantity.	1915 Value.	1916 (preliminary). Quantity.	1916 (preliminary). Value.
VEGETABLE MATTER—contd.						
Oils, vegetable—Continued.						
Fixed or expressed—Contd.						
Nut oil, or oil of nuts.						
n. e. s.—						
Chinese nut....gallons..	4,932,444	$1,962,389	4,940,330	$1,733,264	4,968,262	$1,977.823
Peanut...........do....	1,337,136	918,614	852,905	581,150	1,475,123	818,283
Olive for mechanical purposes...........gallons..	763,924	477,210	653,064	450,001	884,944	684,896
Olive, salad........do....	6,217.560	7,916,980	6,710,967	8,225,485	7,224,431	9,746,672
Palm oil.........pounds..	58,040,202	3,858,001	31,485,661	2,025,060	40,496,731	2,885,595
Palm kernel........do....	34,327,600	3,087,343	4,905,852	446,763	6,760,928	512,666
Rapeseed.......gallons..	1,464,265	704,655	1,498,642	786,485	2,561,244	1,426,659
Soya bean........pounds..	16,360,452	830,790	19,206,521	899,819	98,119,695	5,128,200
Other............		439,009		212,116		502,613
Total fixed or expressed.		28,828,773		21,810,273		30,809,511
Volatile or essential—						
Birch and cajeput........		(1)		(1)		22,175
Lemon...........pounds..	385,959	858,220	577,595	600,642	543,857	441,910
Other............		2,633,789		2,370,364		2,645,571
Total volatile or essential		3,492,009		2,971,006		3,109,656
Total vegetable oils.....		32,320,782		24,781,279		33,919,167
Opium, crude........pounds..	455,200	1,810,429	484,027	2,445,005	146,658	879,699
Rice, rice meal, etc.:						
Rice—						
Cleaned.........pounds..	95,503,998	3,017,108	112,118,326	2,655,739	121,023,906	2,867,453
Uncleaned, including paddy...........pounds..	54,784,051	1,917,658	90,241,834	2,340,968	87,671,332	2,215,273
Rice flour, rice meal, and broken rice..pounds..	139,906,868	2,538,941	74,831,312	1,307,509	55,628,767	1,010,885
Total rice, etc.....do....	290,194,917	7,473,707	277,191,472	6,304,216	264,324,005	6,093,611
Sago, tapioca, etc.............		1,641,540		1,434,219		2,226,697
Seeds:						
Castor beans or seeds bushels...................	1,030,543	1,139,311	924,604	993,577	1,071,963	1,555,899
Clover—						
Red.............pounds..	6,764,218	835,691	8,749,757	1,072,468	33,476,401	4,918,171
Other............do....	23,343,431	2,047,941	15,406,954	1,162,810	8,363,360	822,572
Flaxseed or linseed..bushels..	8,653,235	10,571,410	10,666,215	13,374,536	14,679,233	20,220,921
Grass seed, n. e. s..pounds..	31,937,701	1,634,627	34,690,259	1,384,372	8,790,920	698,630
Sugar beet.........do..	10,293,898	799,525	15,882,661	1,409,973	9,042,490	1,030,788
Other............		3,055,679		3,657,084		4,324,716
Total seeds.............		20,084,184		23,054,820		33,571,697
Spices:						
Unground—						
Cassia, or cassia vera, pounds.............	6,771,901	404,853	5,786,324	357,071	9,707,982	623,478
Ginger root, not preserved, pounds................	3,771,086	171,250	3,127,722	150,515	7,322,399	540,007
Pepper, black or white, pounds................	24,173,621	2,427,927	30,267,384	3,086,782	37,777,324	4,505,380
Other............pounds..	2,806,823	309,184	6,438	387		
Total unground, pounds................	37,613,431	3,313,214	39,187,868	3,594,755	54,807,705	5,668,865
Ground...........pounds..	18,961,068	2,282,295	20,902,214	2,332,604	28,072,632	3,277,757
Total spices.......do....	56,574,499	5,595,509	60,090,082	5,927,359	82,880,337	8,946,622
Spirits, distilled. (*See* Liquors, alcoholic.)						
Starch..............pounds..	15,518,434	408,922	13,233,383	343,805	2,467.038	123,838
Straw and grass....long tons..	6,060	33,499				

[1] Not stated.

TABLE 191.—*Agricultural imports of the United States during the 3 years ending June 30, 1916*—Continued.

Article imported.	Year ending June 30—					
	1914		1915		1916 (preliminary).	
	Quantity.	Value.	Quantity.	Value.	Quantity.	Value.
VEGETABLE MATTER—contd.						
Sugar and molasses:						
Molasses...........gallons..	51,410,271	$1,744,719	70,839,623	$1,963,505	85,716,673	$3,775,894
Sugar—						
Raw—						
Beet..........pounds..	2,367,708	70,829	877,623	29,386	2,050	174
Cane............do....	5,061,564,621	101,365,561	5,418,630,482	173,837,646	5,631,272,766	208,572,890
Maple sugar and sirup, pounds..............	2,095,983	163,047	1,473,762	125,571	1,886,933	196,335
Total raw....pounds..	5,066,028,312	101,599,437	5,420,981,867	173,992,603	5,633,161,749	208,769,399
Refined...........do....	793,561	49,938	....	....	....	....
Total sugar.....do....	5,066,821,873	101,649,375	5,420,981,867	173,992,603	5,633,161,749	208,769,399
Total sugar and molasses...............	....	103,394,094	....	175,956,108	....	212,545,293
Tea................pounds..	91,130,815	16,735,302	96,987,942	17,512,619	109,865,935	20,599,857
Tea, waste, etc., for manufacturing..............pounds..	5,874,308	194,293	4,230,456	137,155	....	....
Teazels.................		24,310				
Tobacco:						
Leaf—						
Wrapper.........pounds..	6,092,787	7,785,387	7,241,178	9,267,044	5,070,308	7,246,942
Filler and other leaf.do....	54,047,436	27,247,259	38,568,035	17,893,526	42,943,027	17,372,126
Stems.............do....	1,034,528	5,874	....	....	....	....
Total tobacco.....do....	61,174,751	35,038,520	45,809,213	27,160,570	48,013,335	24,619,068
Vanilla beans...........do....	898,100	2,277,675	888,569	1,863,515	914,386	1,697,543
Vegetables:						
Fresh and dried—						
Beans...........bushels..	1,634,070	2,955,663	905,647	1,461,917	659,259	1,288,034
Onions...........do....	1,114,811	909,204	829,177	657,374	815,872	749,150
Peas, dried........do....	866,488	1,849,274	546,903	1,305,633	943,821	2,868,683
Potatoes...........do....	3,645,993	1,763,782	270,942	274,915	209,542	331,814
Other......................	....	1,630,113	....	1,350,101	....	1,907,879
Total fresh and dried....	....	9,108,036	....	5,049,940	....	7,145,560
Prepared or preserved—						
Mushrooms......pounds..	9,188,177	1,306,818	6,195,819	885,653	4,313,095	985,408
Pickles and sauces........	....	1,246,249	....	839,916	....	515,048
Other......................	....	3,472,432	....	2,554,223	....	2,165,377
Total prepared or preserved.................	....	6,025,499	....	4,279,792	....	3,665,833
Total vegetables.......	....	15,133,535	....	9,329,732	....	10,811,393
Vinegar..............gallons..	311,643	94,597	249,645	73,361	....	....
Wafers, unmedicated..........		32,797				
Wax, vegetable......pounds..	4,255,686	1,049,126	5,634,809	1,012,402	9,727,312	1,580,530
Wines. (*See* Liquors, alcoholic.)						
Total vegetable matter, including forest products..................		720,778,232	....	739,850,499	....	957,795,624
Total vegetable matter, excluding forest products..................	....	565,516,932	....	574,001,006	....	704,971,171
Total agricultural imports, including forest products.............	....	1,079,508,416	....	1,076,635,782	....	1,439,466,222
Total agricultural imports, excluding forest products.............	....	924,247,116	....	910,786,289	....	1,186,641,769

TABLE 192.—*Agricultural exports (domestic) of the United States during the 3 years ending June 3, 1916.*

Article exported.	Year ending June 30—					
	1914		1915		1916 (preliminary).	
	Quantity.	Value.	Quantity.	Value.	Quantity.	Value.
ANIMAL MATTER.						
Animals, live:						
Cattle..............number..	18,376	$647,288	5,484	$702,847	21,666	$2,383,765
Horses.............do....	22,776	3,388,819	289,340	64,046,534	357,553	73,531,146
Mules..............do....	4,883	690,974	65,788	12,726,143	111,915	22,946,312
Sheep..............do....	152,600	534,543	47,213	182,278	52,278	231,535
Swine..............do....	10,122	133,751	7,799	93,067	22,048	238,713
Others (including fowls)....	....	408,284	....	202,817	....	331,337
Total live animals......	....	5,803,659	....	77,953,686	....	99,662,813
Beeswax.............pounds..	96,215	27,292	181,328	57,971	....	....
Dairy products:						
Butter.............do....	3,693,597	877,453	9,850,704	2,392,480	13,503,279	3,592,415
Cheese.............do....	2,427,577	414,124	55,362,917	8,463,174	44,394,251	7,430,089
Milk—						
Condensed.........do....	16,209,082	1,341,140	37,235,627	3,066,642	155,734,322	12,404,384
Other, including cream....	....	333,217	....	343,583	....	835,106
Total dairy products, pounds.............	....	2,965,934	....	14,265,879	....	24,261,994
Eggs............dozens...	16,148,849	3,734,087	20,784,424	5,003,764	26,396,206	6,134,441
Egg yolks.............	....	47,968	....	88,865	....	....
Feathers.............	....	640,020	....	281,806	....	312,113
Fibers, animal:						
Silk waste.........pounds..	27,597	8,178	32,285	8,403	....	....
Wool..............do....	335,348	124,127	8,158,300	2,216,187	....	....
Total animal fibers......	362,945	132,305	8,190,585	2,224,590	....	....
Glue.................pounds..	2,351,773	258,611	2,874,225	298,136	4,946,298	531,329
Honey........................	....	135,669	....	114,038	....	....
Packing-house products:						
Beef—						
Canned..........pounds..	3,464,733	461,901	75,243,261	11,973,530	50,416,690	9,353,450
Cured or pickled....do....	23,265,974	2,289,516	31,874,743	3,382,670	38,060,682	4,034,195
Fresh.............do....	6,394,404	788,793	170,440,934	21,731,633	231,215,075	28,886,115
Oils—oleo oil......do....	97,017,065	10,156,665	80,481,946	9,341,188	102,645,914	12,519,115
Oleomargarine......do....	2,532,821	263,453	5,252,183	617,035	5,426,221	640,480
Tallow.............do....	15,812,831	1,002,011	20,239,988	1,386,445	16,288,743	1,326,472
Total beef........do....	148,487,828	14,962,339	383,533,055	48,432,501	444,053,325	56,759,827
Bones, and manufactures of..	....	47,651	....	34,796	....	....
Grease, grease scraps, and all soap stock—						
Lubricating............	....	2,394,918	....	2,384,395	....	3,994,436
Soap stock.............	....	5,046,959	....	4,266,097	....	3,156,568
Hair........................	....	1,085,038	....	1,402,189	....	2,038,833
Hides and skins, other than furs—						
Calfskins.........pounds..	323,417	69,515	1,074,529	248,547	1,574,369	469,637
Cattle hides.........do....	12,524,901	1,933,705	21,135,730	4,013,172	3,284,190	2,938,925
Horse.............do....	5,742,855	610,456	605,054	67,798	266,743	34,481
Other.............do....	1,275,962	193,577	2,117,867	356,207	1,996,717	432,208
Total.............do....	19,867,135	2,807,253	24,933,180	4,685,724	7,122,019	3,875,251
Hoofs, horns, and horn tips, strips, and waste..........	....	61,180	....	16,182	....	37,558
Lard compounds...pounds..	58,303,564	5,489,139	69,980,614	6,045,752	52,843,311	5,147,434
Meat, canned, n. e. s........	....	1,350,218	....	2,192,464	....	2,835,005
Mutton............pounds..	4,685,496	523,023	3,877,413	448,221	5,552,918	696,882
Oils, animal, n. e. s.gallons..	891,035	609,294	559,197	405,635	655,587	492,964
Pork—						
Canned..........pounds..	3,074,303	492,822	4,644,418	745,928	9,610,732	1,815,586

TABLE 192.—*Agricultural exports (domestic) of the United States during the 3 years ending June 30, 1916*—Continued.

Article exported.	Year ending June 30—					
	1914		1915		1916 (preliminary).	
	Quantity.	Value.	Quantity.	Value.	Quantity.	Value.
ANIMAL MATTER—continued.						
Packing-house products—Con.						
Pork—Continued.						
Cured—						
Bacon..........pounds..	193,964,252	$25,879,056	346,718,227	$47,326,129	579,808,786	$78,615,616
Hams and shoulders, pounds...............	165,881,791	23,767,447	203,701,114	29,049,931	282,208,611	40,803,022
Salted or pickled, pounds...............	45,543,085	4,896,574	45,655,574	4,911,307	63,460,713	6,752,356
Total cured.pounds.	405,389,128	54,543,077	596,074,915	81,287,367	925,478,110	126,170,994
Fresh...............do....	2,668,020	359,181	3,908,193	473,801	63,005,524	7,523,408
Lard...............do....	481,457,792	54,402,911	475,531,908	52,440,133	427,011,338	47,634,376
Lard, neutral.......do....	29,323,786	3,270,236	26,021,054	3,022,321	34,426,590	4,050,397
Oils—lard oil....gallons..	111,199	87,364	184,019	111,637	419,969	308,642
Total pork.........	....	113,155,591	....	138,081,187	....	187,503,403
Sausage and sausage meats—						
Canned..........pounds..	1,446,582	202,120	1,821,958	307,726	6,823,085	1,269,866
Other...............do....	4,562,983	755,794	5,183,525	845,661	8,590,236	1,732,231
Sausage casings......do....	30,092,206	4,077,882	30,818,551	4,859,815	14,708,893	2,867,681
Stearin...........do....	2,724,181	234,121	11,457,907	1,083,665	13,062,247	1,461,661
All other.................	....	1,685,351	....	2,412,842	....	5,268,862
Total packing-house products.............	....	154,487,871	....	217,904,852	....	279,138,467
Poultry and game..........	....	913,632	....	1,187,771	....	1,561,398
Silk waste. (*See* Fibers, animal.)						
Wool. (*See* Fibers, animal.)						
Total animal matter.....	....	169,147,048	....	319,381,358	....	411,602,555
VEGETABLE MATTER.						
Breadstuffs. (*See* Grain and grain products.)						
Broom corn........long tons..	2,959	327,426	3,764	368,051	3,698	454,749
Cocoa, ground or prepared, and chocolate..............	....	336,940	....	1,934,166	....	1,668,657
Coffee:						
Green or raw......pounds..	52,649,233	8,550,642	49,177,146	6,841,575	35,421,530	5,369,753
Roasted or prepared..do....	1,815,835	427,009	2,421,664	461,030	1,851,100	378,268
Total coffee.......do....	54,465,068	8,977,651	51,598,810	7,302,605	37,272,630	5,748,021
Cotton:						
Sea island.........{bales.... {pounds..	19,186 7,420,455	} 1,619,847	6,158 2,437,602	} 484,465	4,247 1,731,796	} 483,184
Upland...........{bales.... {pounds..	9,146,114 4,753,520,083	} 608,855,454	8,201,189 4,288,295,926	} 372,068,490	5,698,960 2,956,810,277	} 364,710,378
Linters..........{bales.... {pounds..	} (1)	(1)	218,950 112,844,971	} 3,665,017	252,627 125,528,052	} 8,992,685
Total cotton......do....	4,760,940,538	610,475,301	4,403,578,499	376,217,972	3,084,070,125	374,186,247
Flavoring extracts and fruit juices....	....	106,892	....	136,742	....	....
Flowers, cut.............	....	121,287	....	56,698	....	....
Forest products:						
Bark, and extract of, for tanning—						
Bark.........long tons..	1,212	26,939	825	21,424	....	....
Bark, extracts of..........	....	639,941	....	2,226,457	....	5,902,799
Total bark, etc..........	....	666,880	....	2,247,881	....	5,902,799
Charcoal.............	....	81,997	....	105,009	....	....
Moss.................	....	51,006	....	36,738	....	....

[1] Included in "Upland."

TABLE 192.—*Agricultural exports (domestic) of the United States during the 3 years ending June 30, 1916*—Continued.

Article exported.	Year ending June 30—					
	1914		1915		1916 (preliminary).	
	Quantity.	Value.	Quantity.	Value.	Quantity.	Value.
VEGETABLE MATTER—contd.						
Forest products—Continued.						
Naval stores—						
Rosin..............barrels.	2,417,950	$11,217,316	1,372,316	$6,220,321	1,571,279	$8,874,313
Tar, turpentine, and pitch............barrels..	351,353	568,891	239,661	430,612	67,616	291,939
Turpentine, spirits of, gallons..................	18,900,704	8,095,958	9,464,120	4,476,306	9,309,968	4,337,355
Total naval stores.....	....	19,882,165	....	11,127,239	....	13,503,607
Wood—						
Logs—						
Hickory........M feet..	8.425	297,613	2,020	73,786	2,302	75,888
Oak..............do....	1,872	63,850	226	10,563	2,019	53,668
Walnut..........do....	6,951	382,059	1,090	78,338	1,114	88,965
Other............do....	120,819	2,512,501	41,175	720,836	38,921	755,527
Total............do....	138,067	3.256,023	44,511	883,523	44,356	.974,048
Lumber—						
Boards, deals, and planks—						
Cyprus.......M feet..	14,098	420,982	10,078	319,065	10,521	366,510
Fir..............do....	680,380	8,709,140	368,886	4,251,620	268,455	2,964,948
Gum............do....	70,714	2,164,017	24,588	715,756	32,155	969.338
Oak.............do....	231,308	10,644,310	97,397	4,870,864	98,990	4,665,527
Pine—						
White........do....	43,878	1,606,864	18,398	662,786	34,206	1,139,537
Yellow—						
Pitch pine..do....	911,223	19,521,719	403,254	7,565,272	504,952	9,150,115
Short-leaf pine, M feet..........	22,453	634,103	5,261	160,219	2,185	79,147
Other pine, M feet..........	127,289	3,001,399	49,716	1,123,212	47,236	1,156,090
Poplar........M feet..	30,860	1,448,622	19,891	962,248	23,356	1,044,883
Redwood.......do....	67,155	1,917,315	36,419	1,102,532	38,739	1,169,975
Spruce.........do....	18,105	557,838	15,610	462,087	37,332	1,611,892
Other...........do....	187,833	6,948,239	79,707	2,925,984	78,638	3,594,338
Total.........do....	2,405,296	57,574,548	1,129,205	25,121,645	1,176,765	27,912,300
Joists and scantling, M feet.................	12,143	206,919	6,007	103,456	....	....
Railroad ties..number..	5,123,004	2,564,543	3,874,298	2,036,200	4,086,721	2,435,094
Shingles.............M..	46,964	112,463	11,291	30,578	20,590	55,604
Shooks—						
Box........number..	11,149,532	1,270,477	11,682,495	1,303,127	....	1,908,643
Other..........do....	867,805	1,542,272	620,043	1,024,093	583,724	1,024,348
Total shooks..do....	12,017,337	2,812,749	12,302,538	2,327,220	....	2,932,991
Staves and heading—						
Heading..............	....	332,662	....	258,670	....	288,587
Staves......number..	77,150,535	5,852,230	39,297,268	2,481,592	57,820,610	3,533,181
Total staves and heading...........	....	6,184,892	....	2,740,262	....	3,821,768
Other....................	....	3,028,642	....	1,650,760	....	3,497,217
Total lumber.......	....	72,484,756	....	34,010,121	....	40,654,974
Timber—						
Hewn..........M feet..	29,859	788,327	6,118	163,106	9,628	252,576
Sawed—						
Pitch pine......do....	390,149	7,821,364	159,064	2,785,379	175,763	3,473,686
Other..........do....	21,158	562,720	8,607	229,491	15,814	340,345
Total timber..do....	441,166	9,172,411	173,789	3,177,976	201,205	4,066,607
All other, including firewood..................	....	201,089	....	156,234	....	164,532
Total wood........	....	85,114,279	....	38,227,854	....	45,860,161

TABLE 192.—*Agricultural exports (domestic) of the United States during the 3 years ending June 30, 1916*—Continued.

Article exported.	Year ending June 30—					
	1914		1915		1916 (preliminary).	
	Quantity.	Value.	Quantity.	Value.	Quantity.	Value.
VEGETABLE MATTER—contd.						
Forest products—Continued.						
Wood alcohol......gallons..	1,598,776	$652,486	944,374	$438,846	1,472,258	$857,161
Wood pulp........pounds..	26,961,254	529,741	18,838,400	369,969	[1]35,994	1,703,374
Total forest products....	....	106,978,554	....	52,553,536	....	67,827,102
Fruits:						
Fresh or dried—						
Apples, dried....pounds..	33,566,160	2,628,445	42,589,169	3,270,658	16,219,174	1,304,224
Apples, fresh.....barrels..	1,506,569	6,089,701	2,351,501	8,087,466	1,466,321	5,518,772
Apricots, dried...pounds..	17,401,692	1,937,771	23,764,342	2,241,061	23,939,790	2,168,808
Berries.................	....	717,079	....	535,479	....	639,501
Lemons............boxes..	70,075	308,707	122,914	372,781	175,070	494,019
Oranges............do....	1,558,921	3,824,889	1,759,405	3,851,013	1,575,042	3,690,080
Peaches, dried...pounds..	6,712,296	449,549	14,464,655	834,813	13,739,342	893,587
Pears, fresh.............	....	1,402,924	....	992,497	....	691,732
Prunes...........pounds..	69,813,711	4,662,546	43,478,892	3,274,197	57,422,827	3,975,396
Raisins............do....	14,766,416	997,575	24,845,414	1,718,547	75,014,753	5,407,219
Other..................	....	2,922,740	....	2,717,449	....	3,261,109
Total fresh or dried......	....	25,941,926	....	27,895,961	....	28,044,447
Preserved—						
Canned.................	....	4,863,946	....	6,064,765	....	7,050,036
Other..................	....	224,841	....	269,180	....	978,568
Total preserved.........	....	5,088,787	....	6,333,945	....	8,028,604
Total fruits...........	....	31,030,713	....	34,229,906	....	36,073,051
Ginseng.............pounds..	224,605	1,832,686	103,184	919,931	256,082	1,597,508
Glucose and grape sugar:						
Glucose.........pounds..	162,680,378	3,766,284	125,434,878	3,103,561	148,523,098	3,772,860
Grape sugar..........do..	36,850,496	799,635	33,027,630	781,672	37,863,084	962,101
Grain and grain products:						
Grain—						
Barley..........bushels..	6,644,747	4,253,129	26,754,522	18,184,079	27,473,160	20,663,533
Buckwheat........do....	580	695	413,643	396,987	515,304	481,014
Corn.............do....	9,380,855	7,008,028	48,786,291	39,339,064	38,217,012	30,780,887
Oats.............do....	1,859,949	757,527	96,809,551	57,469,964	95,921,620	47,993,096
Rye.............do....	2,222,934	1,555,012	12,544,888	14,733,409	14,532,437	15,374,499
Wheat...........do....	92,393,775	87,953,456	259,642,533	333,552,226	173,274,015	215,532,681
Total grain.......do....	112,502,840	101,527,847	444,951,428	463,675,729	349,933,548	330,825,710
Grain products—						
Bran and middlings, long tons...............	2,570	71,043	11,426	329,425	14,613	432,288
Breadstuff preparations—						
Bread and biscuit, pounds...............	12,645,551	728,447	11,687,452	702,509	11,433,410	787,567
Other.................	....	2,323,412	....	4,306,899	....	5,074,983
Total breadstuff preparations...........	....	3,051,859	....	5,009,408	....	5,862,550
Distillers' and brewers' grains and malt sprouts, long tons...............	59,788	1,467,028	7,590	177,987	1,633	47,448
Malt...........bushels..	330,608	270,059	2,153,060	2,301,535	....	....
Meal and flour—						
Corn meal......barrels..	336,241	1,185,891	470,503	1,923,214	419,979	1,601,258
Oatmeal........pounds..	15,998,286	569,204	68,394,979	2,416,068	54,748,747	1,885,622
Rye flour.......barrels..	8,293	31,119	80,315	416,182	119,619	646,941
Wheat flour......do....	11,821,461	54,454,175	16,182,765	94,869,343	15,520,669	87,347,805
Total meal and flour..	....	56,240,389	....	99,624,807	....	91,481,626

[1] Long tons (2,240 pounds).

TABLE 192.—*Agricultural exports (domestic) of the United States during the 3 years ending June 30, 1916*—Continued.

Article exported.	Year ending June 30—					
	1914		1915		1916 (preliminary).	
	Quantity.	Value.	Quantity.	Value.	Quantity.	Value.
VEGETABLE MATTER—contd.						
Grain and grain products—Continued.						
Grain products—Continued.						
Mill feed.......long tons..	67,690	$1,840,011	25,459	$787,048	25,652	$801,054
All other................	....	346,888	....	1,045,396	....	1,293,091
Total grain products....	....	63,287,277	....	109,275,606	....	99,918,057
Total grain and grain products....	....	164,815,124	....	572,951,335	....	430,743,767
Hay................long tons..	50,151	827,205	105,508	1,980,297	178,336	3,267,028
Hops................pounds..	24,262,896	6,953,529	16,210,443	3,948,020	22,409,818	4,383,929
Lard compounds. (*See* Meat and meat products.)						
Liquors, alcoholic:						
Distilled spirits—						
Alcohol, including cologne spirits....proof gallons..	187,845	67,728	200,455	108,985	24,433,243	8,784,742
Rum................do....	1,388,738	1,815,121	1,240,804	1,588,552	1,586,900	1,887,307
Whisky—						
Bourbon..........do....	47,775	92,331	34,823	69,497	88,802	113,863
Rye.............do....	134,152	259,523	86,564	168,386	124,700	208,879
Total whisky...do....	181,927	351,854	121,387	237,883	213,502	322,742
Other.............do....	25,408	41,129	30,152	46,599	50,259	67,595
Total distilled spirits, proof gallons..........	1,783,918	2,275,832	1,592,798	1,982,019	26,283,904	11,062,386
Malt liquors—						
Bottled....dozen quarts..	962,627	1,405,581	696,690	1,010,222	668,228	961,582
Unbottled........gallons..	326,946	79,595	245,494	71,890	340,064	103,045
Total malt liquors......	....	1,485,176	....	1,082,112	....	1,064,627
Wines.............gallons..	941,357	373,412	819,310	332,369	1,133,274	450,598
Total alcoholic liquors...	....	4,134,420	....	3,396,500	....	12,577,611
Malt. (*See* Grain and grain products.)						
Malt liquors. (*See* Liquors, alcoholic.)						
Malt sprouts. (*See* Grain and grain products.)						
Nursery stock................	....	315,065	....	170,218	....	203,671
Nuts:						
Peanuts............pounds..	8,054,817	421,367	5,875,076	325,725	8,669,430	450,765
Other.....................	....	398,312	....	377,486	....	441,512
Total nuts.............	....	819,679	....	703,211	....	892,277
Oil cake and oil-cake meal:						
Corn...........pounds..	59,030,623	909,407	45,026,125	798,206	18,996,490	297,041
Cottonseed:						
Cake................do...⎱	799,974,252	11,007,441⎰	1,222,699,889	15,432,126	980,664,572	14,749,489
Meal ....do...⎰		⎱	256,365,126	3,474,244	77,256,997	1,149,478
Flaxseed or linseed...do....	662,868,639	9,650,379	524,794,434	9,048,061	640,916,204	11,935,130
Other................do....	8,484,936	100,445	9,900,878	126,414	28,876,367	410,166
Total.............do....	1,530,358,450	21,667,672	2,058,786,452	28,879,051	1,746,710,630	28,541,304
Oils, vegetable:						
Fixed or expressed—						
Corn.........pounds..	18,281,576	1,307,204	17,789,635	1,302,159	8,967,826	770,076
Cottonseed.........do....	192,963,079	13,843,179	318,366,525	21,872,948	266,529,960	22,659,804
Linseed..........gallons..	239,188	134,540	1,212,133	660,089	714,120	479,231
Other.....................	....	338,956	....	1,198,852	....	2,230,002
Total fixed or expressed.	....	15,623,879	....	25,034,048	....	26,139,113

TABLE 192.—*Agricultural exports (domestic) of the United States during the 3 years ending June 30, 1916*—Continued.

Article exported.	Year ending June 30—					
	1914		1915		1916 (preliminary.	
	Quantity.	Value.	Quantity.	Value.	Quantity.	Value.
VEGETABLE MATTER—contd.						
Oils, vegetable—Continued.						
Volatile, or essential—						
Peppermint.....pounds..	117,809	$397,050	184,981	$384,593	154,096	$323,070
Other...................	....	230,557	....	413,104	....	705,037
Total volatile, or essential	....	627,607	....	797,697	....	1,028,107
Total vegetable oils......	....	16,251,486	....	25,831,745	....	27,167,220
Rice, rice meal, etc.:						
Rice.............pounds..	18,223,264	721,046	75,448,635	3,158,335	120,695,213	4,942,373
Rice bran, meal, and polish, pounds...................	4,191,062	36,274	2,031,430	15,541	1,273,921	10,489
Rice hulls................	....	126,888	....	5,122	....	....
Total..................	....	884,208	....	3,178,998	....	4,952,862
Roots, herbs, and barks, n. e. s.	....	513,071	....	470,090	....	768,977
Seeds:						
Cotton seed........pounds..	16,342,384	215,115	6,314,439	94,237	2,475,907	37,811
Flaxseed, or linseed, bushels.................	305,546	436,874	4,145	9,748	2,614	6,501
Grass and clover seed—						
Clover...........pounds..	4,640,852	691,437	9,750,064	1,563,304	7,116,220	1,294,944
Timothy.............do....	12,480,294	688,118	17,333,144	1,153,066	13,610,257	1,038,301
Other...............do....	5,156,801	600,368	4,342,926	451,595	3,613,026	401,925
Total grass and clover seed........:pounds..	22,277,947	1,979,923	31,426,134	3,167,965	24,339,503	2,735,170
All other seeds.............	....	558,833	....	589,114	....	759,026
Total seeds.............	....	3,190,745	....	3,861,064	....	3,538,508
Spices......................	....	84,427	....	76,297	....	....
Spirits, distilled. (*See* Liquors, alcoholic.)						
Starch...............pounds..	76,713,779	1,825,230	107,036,638	2,939,453	210,185,192	5,576,914
Stearin, vegetable...........	....	....	....	144,850	....	....
Straw.............long tons..	288	4,714	260	4,911	....	....
Sugar, molasses, and sirup:						
Molasses...........gallons..	1,002,441	175,498	1,148,741	145,274	4,387,369	524,861
Sirup.................do....	11,630,528	1,491,639	11,439,133	1,653,495	10,031,693	2,107,068
Sugar—						
Refined..........pounds..	50,895,726	1,839,983	549,007,411	25,615,016	1,630,150,863	79,390,147
Total sugar, molasses, and sirup....	....	3,507,120	....	27,413,785	....	82,022,076
Tobacco:						
Leaf...............pounds..	446,944,435	53,903,336	347,997,276	44,479,890	434,742,937	52,813,252
Stems and trimmings.do....	2,805,547	60,334	348,815	13,939	6,826,644	350,343
Total.............do....	449,749,982	53,963,670	348,346,091	44,493,829	441,569,581	53,163,595
Vegetables:						
Fresh or dried—						
Beans and peas..bushels..	314,655	875,493	1,214,281	3,638,526	1,760,383	5,914,198
Onions.............do....	386,322	435,953	727,983	602,585	563,739	578,792
Potatoes............do....	1,794,073	1,463,514	3,135,474	2,345,731	4,017,760	3,485,740
Total fresh or dried, bushels...............	2,495,050	2,774,960	5,077,738	6,586,842	6,341,882	9,978,730
Prepared or preserved—						
Canned..............	....	1,520,879	....	1,898,840	....	2,529,694
Pickles and sauces........	....	928,611	....	959,016	....	1,166,811
Other................:	....	1,711,950	....	1,368,453	....	2,277,177
Total prepared or preserved.................	....	4,161,440	....	4,226,309	....	5,973,682
Total vegetables........	....	6,936,400	....	10,813,151	....	15,952,412

TABLE 192.—*Agricultural exports (domestic) of the United States during the 3 years ending June 30, 1916*—Continued.

Article exported.	Year ending June 30—					
	1914		1915		1916 (preliminary).	
	Quantity.	Value.	Quantity.	Value.	Quantity.	Value.
VEGETABLE MATTER—contd.						
Vinegar..............gallons..	125,666	$25,112	106,708	$17,731	....	....
Wines. (*See* Liquors, alcoholic.)						
Yeast..............	....	332,895	....	230,409	....	....
Total vegetable matter, including forest products......	....	1,051,805,141	....	1,209,109,785	....	$1,166,042,447
Total vegetable matter, excluding forest products......	....	944,826,587	....	1,156,556,249	....	1,098,215,345
Total agricultural exports, including forest products......	....	1,220,952,189	....	1,528,491,143	....	1,577,645,002
Total agricultural exports, excluding forest products......	....	1,113,973,635	....	1,475,937,607	....	1,509,817,900

TABLE 193.—*Foreign trade of the United States in agricultural products, 1852–1916.*

[Compiled from reports of Foreign Commerce and Navigation of the United States. All values are gold.]

Year ending June 30—	Agricultural exports.[1]			Agricultural imports.[1]		Excess of agricultural exports (+) or of imports (−).
	Domestic.		Foreign.	Total.	Percentage of all imports.	
	Total.	Percentage of all domestic exports.				
Average:						
1852–1856..............	$164,895,146	80.9	$8,059,875	$77,847,158	29.1	+$95,107,863
1857–1861..............	215,708,845	81.1	10,173,833	121,018,143	38.2	+104,864,535
1862–1866..............	148,865,540	75.7	9,287,669	122,221,547	43.0	+ 35,931,662
1867–1871..............	250,713,058	76.9	8,538,101	179,774,000	42.3	+ 79,477,159
1872–1876..............	396,666,397	78.5	8,853,247	263,155,573	46.5	+142,364,071
1877–1881..............	591,350,518	80.4	8,631,780	266,383,702	50.4	+333,598,596
1882–1886..............	557,472,922	76.3	9,340,463	311,707,564	46.8	+255,105,821
1887–1891..............	573,286,616	74.7	6,982,328	366,950,109	43.3	+213,318,835
1892–1896..............	638,748,318	73.0	8,446,491	398,332,043	51.6	+248,862,766
1897–1901..............	827,566,147	65.9	10,961,539	376,549,697	50.2	+461,977,989
1902–1906..............	879,541,247	59.5	11,922,292	487,881,038	46.3	+403,582,501
1907–1911..............	975,398,554	53.9	12,126,228	634,570,734	45.2	+352,954,048
1901..................	951,628,331	65.2	11,293,045	391,931,051	47.6	+570,990,325
1902..................	857,113,533	63.2	10,308,306	413,744,557	45.8	+453,677,282
1903..................	878,480,557	63.1	13,505,343	456,199,325	44.5	+435,786,575
1904..................	859,160,264	59.9	12,625,026	461,434,851	46.6	+410,350,439
1905..................	826,904,777	55.4	12,316,525	553,851,214	49.6	+285,370,088
1906..................	976,047,104	56.8	10,856,259	554,175,242	45.2	+432,728,121
1907..................	1,054,405,416	56.9	11,613,519	626,836,808	43.7	+439,182,127
1908..................	1,017,396,404	55.5	10,298,514	539,690,121	45.2	+488,004,797
1909..................	906,238,122	55.1	9,584,934	638,612,602	48.7	+274,210,364
1910..................	871,158,425	50.9	14,469,627	687,509,115	44.2	+198,118,937
1911..................	1,030,794,402	51.2	14,664,548	680,204,932	44.5	+365,254,018
1912..................	1,050,627,131	48.4	12,107,656	783,457,471	47.4	+279,277,316
1913..................	1,123,651,985	46.3	15,029,444	815,300,510	45.0	+323,380,919
1914..................	1,113,973,635	47.8	17,729,462	924,247,116	48.8	+207,456,481
1915..................	1,475,937,607	54.3	34,420,077	910,786,289	54.4	+599,571,395
1916..................	1,509,817,900	35.3	41,647,502	1,186,641,769	54.0	+364,823,633

[1] Not including forest products.

TABLE 194.—*Value of principal groups of farm and forest products exported from and imported into the United States, 1914–1916.*

[Compiled from reports on the Foreign Commerce of the United States.]

Article.	Exports (domestic merchandise).			Imports.		
	Year ending June 30—					
	1914	1915	1916 (prel.).	1914	1915	1916 (prel.).
FARM PRODUCTS.						
ANIMAL MATTER.						
Animals, live	$5,803,659	$77,953,686	$99,662,813	$24,712,111	$22,279,081	$18,649,079
Dairy products	2,965,934	14,265,879	24,261,994	15,403,143	14,704,277	9,828,919
Eggs	3,734,087	5,003,764	6,134,441	1,089,164	438,760	110,638
Feathers and downs, crude	640,020	281,806	312,113	4,871,663	2,502,623	2,721,151
Fibers, animal:						
Silk	8,178	8,403		100,930,025	83,130,557	124,333,655
Wool	124,127	2,216,187		53,190,267	68,242,568	142,420,734
Packing-house products	154,487,871	217,904,852	279,138,467	154,969,389	142,484,247	182,887,880
Other animal matter	1,383,172	1,746,781	2,092,727	3,563,922	3,003,170	718,542
Total animal matter	169,147,048	319,381,358	411,602,555	358,729,684	336,785,283	481,670,598
VEGETABLE MATTER.						
Argols or wine lees				3,228,674	3,094,380	5,306,246
Cocoa and chocolate	336,940	1,934,166	1,668,657	21,503,983	23,478,156	35,804,242
Coffee	8,977,651	7,302,605	5,748,021	110,725,392	106,765,644	115,485,970
Cotton	610,475,301	376,217,972	374,186,247	19,456,588	23,208,960	40,150,342
Fibers, vegetable, other				54,349,995	40,420,017	59,460,062
Fruits	31,030,713	34,229,906	36,073,051	33,638,334	27,081,399	23,285,816
Ginseng	1,832,686	919,931	1,597,508			
Glucose and grape sugar	4,565,919	3,885,233	4,734,961			
Grain and grain products	164,815,124	572,951,335	430,743,767	27,442,277	12,518,356	15,637,360
Hay	827,205	1,980,297	3,267,028	1,634,390	228,906	679,412
Hops	6,953,529	3,948,020	4,383,929	2,790,516	2,778,735	144,627
Indigo				1,093,226	1,596,978	8,235,670
Licorice root				2,047,192	1,252,989	1,609,571
Liquors, alcoholic	4,134,420	3,396,500	12,577,611	20,347,546	13,404,903	16,685,356
Nursery stock (plants, trees, etc.)	315,065	170,218	203,671	3,606,808	3,751,550	3,686,348
Nuts	819,679	703,211	892,277	19,888,601	16,830,932	21,160,491
Oil cake and oil cake meal	21,667,672	28,879,051	28,541,304	120,078	219,635	
Oil, vegetable	16,251,486	25,831,745	27,167,220	32,320,782	24,781,279	33,919,167
Opium, crude				1,810,429	2,445,005	879,699
Rice, rice flour, meal, and broken rice	884,208	3,178,998	4,952,862	7,473,707	6,304,216	6,093,611
Sago, tapioca, etc				1,641,540	1,434,219	2,226,697
Seeds	3,190,745	3,861,064	3,538,508	20,084,184	23,054,820	33,571,697
Spices	84,427	76,297		5,595,509	5,927,359	8,946,622
Starch	1,825,230	2,939,453	5,576,914	408,922	343,805	123,838
Sugar, molasses, and sirup	3,507,120	27,413,785	82,022,076	103,394,094	175,956,108	212,545,293
Tea				16,735,302	17,512,619	20,599,857
Tobacco	53,963,670	44,493,829	53,163,595	35,038,520	27,160,570	24,619,068
Vanilla beans				2,277,675	1,863,515	1,697,543
Vegetables	6,936,400	10,813,151	15,952,412	15,133,535	9,329,732	10,811,393
Wax, vegetable				1,049,126	1,012,402	1,580,530
Other vegetable matter	1,431,397	1,429,482	1,223,726	680,007	243,817	24,643
Total vegetable matter	944,826,587	1,156,556,249	1,098,215,345	565,516,932	574,001,006	704,971,171
Total farm products	1,113,973,635	1,475,937,607	1,409,817,900	924,246,616	910,786,289	1,186,641,769
FOREST PRODUCTS.						
Cork wood or cork bark				3,851,794	2,762,895	3,134,884
Dyewoods, and extracts of				793,926	1,142,031	4,289,247
India rubber				71,219,851	83,030,269	155,044,790
Gums, other than india rubber				15,620,780	15,210,150	18,367,940
Naval stores	19,882,165	11,127,239	13,503,607	36,764	5,102	

TABLE 194.—*Value of principal groups of farm and forest products exported from and imported into the United States, 1914–1916*—Continued.

Article.	Exports (domestic merchandise).			Imports.		
	Year ending June 30—					
	1914	1915	1916 (prel.).	1914	1915	1916 (prel.).
FARM PRODUCTS— Continued.						
FOREST PRODUCTS— continued.						
Tanning materials, n. e. s.	$666,880	$2,247,881	$5,902,799	$4,368,041	$5,343,263	$8,837,297
Wood:						
Cabinet, unsawed...				7,124,688	4,271,775	4,011,107
Lumber...	72,484,756	34,010,121	40,654,974	22,436,585	23,507,591	29,624,279
Pulp wood...				7,245,466	6,572,839	6,373,749
Timber and logs...	12,428,434	4,061,499	5,040,655	1,657,605	1,263,641	1,417,859
Rattan and reeds...				1,210,390	771,628	1,720,816
Wood pulp...	529,741	369,969	1,703,374	17,023,338	19,881,111	16,867,850
Other forest products..	986,578	736,827	1,021,693	2,672,072	2,087,198	3,134,635
Total forest products	106,978,554	52,553,536	67,827,102	155,261,300	165,849,493	252,824,453
Total farm and forest products...	1,220,952,189	1,528,491,143	1,577,645,002	1,079,507,916	1,076,635,782	1,439,466,222

TABLE 195.—*Exports of selected domestic agricultural products, 1852–1916.*

[Compiled from reports of Foreign Commerce and Navigation of the United States. Where figures are lacking, either there were no exports or they were not separately classified for publication. "Beef salted or pickled," and "Pork, salted or pickled," barrels, 1851–1865, were reduced to pounds at the rate of 200 pounds per barrel, and tierces, 1855–1865, at the rate of 300 pounds per tierce; cottonseed oil, 1910, pounds reduced to gallons at the rate of 7.5 pounds per gallon. It is assumed that 1 barrel of corn meal is the product of 4 bushels of corn, and 1 barrel of wheat flour the product of 5 bushels of wheat prior to 1880 and of 4½ bushels of wheat in 1880 and subsequently.]

Year ending June 30—	Cattle.	Cheese.	Packing-house products.				
			Beef, cured— salted or pickled.	Beef, fresh.	Beef oils— oleo oil.	Beef tallow.	Beef and its products— total, as far as ascertainable.[1]
	Number.	*Pounds.*	*Pounds.*	*Pounds.*	*Pounds.*	*Pounds.*	*Pounds.*
Average:							
1852–1856 .	1,431	6,200,385	25,980,520	....	....	7,468,910	33,449,430
1857–1861 .	20,294	13,906,430	26,985,880	....	....	13,214,614	40,200,494
1862–1866 .	6,531	42,683,073	27,662,720	....	....	43,202,724	70,865,444
1867–1871 .		52,880,978	26,954,656	....	....	27,577,269	54,531,925
1872–1876 .	45,672	87,173,752	35,826,646	....	....	78,994,360	114,821,006
1877–1881 .	127,045	129,670,479	40,174,643	69,601,120	....	96,822,695	218,709,987
1882–1886 .	131,605	108,790,010	47,401,470	97,327,819	30,276,133	48,745,416	225,625,631
1887–1891 .	244,394	86,354,842	65,613,851	136,447,554	50,482,249	91,608,126	411,797,859
1892–1896 .	349,032	66,905,798	64,898,780	207,372,575	102,038,519	56,976,840	507,177,430
1897–1901 .	415,488	46,108,704	52,242,288	305,626,184	139,373,402	86,082,497	637,268,235
1902–1906 .	508,103	19,244,482	59,208,292	272,148,180	156,925,317	59,892,601	622,843,230
1907–1911 .	253,867	9,152,083	46,187,175	144,799,735	170,530,432	66,356,232	448,024,017
1901...	459,218	39,813,517	55,312,632	351,748,333	161,651,413	77,166,889	705,104,772
1902...	392,884	27,203,184	48,632,727	301,824,473	138,546,088	34,065,758	596,254,520
1903...	402,178	18,987,178	52,801,220	254,795,963	126,010,339	27,368,924	546,055,244
1904...	593,409	23,335,172	57,584,710	299,579,671	165,183,839	76,924,174	663,147,095
1905..	567,806	10,134,424	55,934,705	236,486,568	145,228,245	63,536,992	575,874,718
1906...	584,239	16,562,451	81,088,098	268,054,227	209,658,075	97,567,156	732,884,572
1907...	423,051	17,285,230	62,645,281	281,651,502	195,337,176	127,857,739	689,752,420
1908...	349,210	8,439,031	46,958,367	201,154,105	212,541,157	91,397,507	579,303,478
1909...	207,542	6,822,842	44,494,210	122,952,671	179,985,246	53,332,767	418,844,332
1910...	139,430	2,846,709	36,554,266	75,729,666	126,091,675	29,379,992	286,295,874
1911...	150,100	10,366,605	40,283,749	42,510,731	138,696,906	29,813,154	265,923,983
1912...	105,506	6,337,559	38,087,907	15,264,320	126,467,124	39,451,419	233,924,626
1913...	24,714	2,599,058	25,856,919	7,362,388	92,849,757	30,586,350	166,463,344
1914...	18,376	2,427,577	23,265,974	6,394,404	97,017,065	15,812,831	148,487,828
1915...	5,484	55,362,917	31,874,743	170,440,934	80,481,946	20,239,988	383,533,055
1916...	21,666	44,394,251	38,060,682	231,215,075	102,645,914	16,288,743	444,053,325

[1] Includes canned, cured, and fresh beef, oleo oil, oleomargarine, and tallow.

TABLE 195.—*Exports of selected domestic agricultural products, 1852–1916*—Continued.

Year ending June 30—	Packing-house products.					Apples, fresh.	Corn and corn meal (in terms of grain).
	Pork, cured— bacon.	Pork, cured— hams and shoulders.	Pork, cured— salted or pickled.	Pork— lard.	Pork and its products— total, as far as ascertain-able.[1]		
Average:	*Pounds.*	*Pounds.*	*Pounds.*	*Pounds.*	*Pounds.*	*Barrels.*	*Bushels.*
1852–1856 .	30,005,479	....	40,542,600	33,354,976	103,903,056	37,412	7,123,286
1857–1861 .	30,583,297	....	34,854,400	37,965,993	103,403,690	57,045	6,557,610
1862–1866 .	10,796,961	....	52,550,758	89,138,251	252,485,970	119,433	12,059,794
1867–1871 .	45,790,113	....	28,879,085	53,579,373	128,248,571	....	9,924,235
1872–1876 .	313,402,401	....	60,429,361	194,197,714	568,029,477	132,756	38,560,557
1877–1881 .	643,633,709	....	85,968,138	331,457,591	1,075,793,475	509,735	88,190,030
1882–1886 .	355,905,444	47,634,675	72,354,682	263,425,058	739,455,913	401,886	49,992,203
1887–1891 .	419,935,416	60,697,365	73,984,682	381,388,854	936,247,966	522,511	54,606,273
1892–1896 .	438,847,549	96,107,152	64,827,470	451,547,135	1,052,133,760	520,810	63,979,898
1897–1901 .	536,287,266	200,853,226	112,788,498	652,418,143	1,528,138,779	779,980	192,531,378
1902–1906 .	292,721,953	206,902,427	116,823,284	592,130,894	1,242,136,649	1,368,608	74,615,465
1907–1911 .	209,005,144	189,603,211	90,809,879	519,746,378	1,028,996,659	1,225,655	56,568,030
1901........	456,122,741	216,571,803	138,643,611	611,357,514	1,462,369,849	883,673	181,405,473
1902........	383,150,624	227,653,232	115,896,275	556,840,222	1,337,315,909	459,719	28,028,688
1903........	207,336,000	214,183,365	95,287,374	490,755,821	1,042,119,570	1,656,129	76,639,261
1904........	249,665,941	194,948,864	112,224,861	561,302,643	1,146,255,441	2,018,262	58,222,061
1905........	262,246,635	203,458,724	118,887,189	610,238,899	1,220,031,970	1,499,942	90,293,483
1906........	361,210,563	194,267,949	141,820,720	741,516,886	1,464,960,356	1,208,989	119,893,833
1907........	250,418,699	209,481,496	166,427,409	627,559,660	1,268,065,412	1,539,267	86,368,228
1908........	241,189,929	221,769,634	149,505,937	603,413,770	1,237,210,760	1,049,545	55,063,860
1909........	244,578,674	212,170,224	52,354,980	528,722,933	1,053,142,056	896,279	37,665,040
1910........	152,163,107	146,885,385	40,031,599	362,927,671	707,110,062	922,078	38,128,498
1911........	156,675,310	157,709,316	45,729,471	476,107,857	879,455,006	1,721,106	65,614,522
1912........	208,574,208	204,044,491	56,321,469	532,255,865	1,071,951,724	1,456,381	41,797,291
1913........	200,993,584	159,544,687	53,749,023	519,025,384	984,696,710	2,150,132	50,780,143
1914........	193,964,252	165,881,791	45,543,085	481,457,792	921,913,029	1,506,569	10,725,819
1915........	346,718,227	203,701,114	45,655,574	475,531,908	1,106,180,488	2,351,501	50,668,303
1916........	579,808,786	282,208,611	63,460,713	427,011,338	1,459,532,294	1,466,321	39,896,928

Year ending June 30—	Lard com-pounds.	Cotton.	Glucose and grape sugar.	Corn-oil cake and oil-cake meal.	Cottonseed-oil cake and oil-cake meal.	Prunes.	Tobacco.
Average:	*Pounds.*	*Pounds.*	*Pounds.*	*Pounds.*	*Pounds.*	*Pounds.*	*Pounds.*
1852–1856...	....	1,110,498,083	....	....	....	....	140,183,800
1857–1861...	....	1,125,715,497	....	....	....	....	167,710,800
1862–1866...	....	137,582,133	....	....	....	....	140,207,850
1867–1871...	....	902,410,338	....	....	....	....	194,753,537
1872–1876...	....	1,248,805,497	....	....	....	....	241,848,410
1877–1881...	....	1,738,892,268	....	....	....	....	266,315,190
1882–1886...	....	1,968,178,266	4,473,550	....	....	....	237,941,913
1887–1891...	....	2,439,650,456	27,686,298	....	....	....	259,248,361
1892–1896...	....	2,736,655,351	125,574,007	....	....	....	281,746,279
1897–1901...	21,792,477	3,447,909,578	209,279,772	....	1,005,099,895	....	304,401,701
1902–1906...	52,954,358	3,632,267,952	154,866,980	21,888,135	1,066,790,196	48,550,774	325,538,515
1907–1911...	75,765,254	4,004,770,051	145,064,783	61,732,807	989,738,130	47,039,287	334,395,923
1901.........	23,359,966	3,359,062,360	204,209,974	12,703,209	1,258,687,317	10,021,564	315,787,782
1902.........	36,201,744	3,528,974,636	130,419,611	14,740,498	1,050,466,246	23,358,849	301,007,365
1903.........	46,130,004	3,569,141,969	126,239,981	8,093,222	1,100,392,988	66,385,215	368,184,084
1904.........	53,603,545	3,089,855,906	152,768,716	14,014,885	820,349,073	73,146,214	311,971,831
1905.........	61,215,187	4,339,322,077	175,250,580	24,171,127	1,251,907,996	54,993,849	334,302,091
1906.........	67,621,310	3,634,045,170	189,656,011	48,420,942	1,110,834,678	24,869,744	312,227,202
1907.........	80,148,861	4,518,217,220	151,629,441	56,808,972	1,340,967,136	44,400,104	340,742,864
1908.........	75,183,210	3,816,998,693	129,686,834	66,127,704	929,287,467	28,148,450	330,812,658
1909.........	75,183,196	4,447,985,202	112,224,504	53,233,890	1,233,750,327	22,602,288	287,900,946
1910.........	74,556,603	3,206,708,226	149,820,088	49,108,598	640,088,766	89,014,880	357,196,074
1911.........	73,754,400	4,033,940,915	181,963,046	83,384,870	804,596,955	51,030,711	355,327,072
1912.........	62,522,888	5,535,125,429	171,156,259	72,490,021	1,293,690,138	74,328,074	379,845,320
1913.........	67,456,832	4,562,295,675	200,149,246	76,262,845	1,128,092,367	117,950,875	418,796,906
1914.........	58,303,564	4,760,940,538	199,530,874	59,030,623	799,974,252	69,813,711	449,749,982
1915.........	69,980,614	4,403,578,499	158,462,508	45,026,125	1,479,065,015	43,478,892	348,346,091
1916.........	52,843,311	3,084,070,125	186,386,182	18,996,490	1,057,921,569	57,422,827	441,569,581

[1] Includes canned, fresh, salted or pickled pork, lard, neutral lard, bacon, and hams.

TABLE 195.—*Exports of selected domestic agricultural products, 1852–1916*—Continued.

Year ending June 30—	Hops.	Oils, vegetable—cottonseed oil.	Rice and rice bran, meal, and polish.	Sugar, raw and refined.	Wheat.	Wheat flour.	Wheat and wheat flour (in terms of grain).
	Pounds.	*Gallons.*	*Pounds.*	*Pounds.*	*Bushels.*	*Barrels.*	*Bushels.*
Average:							
1852–1856	1,162,802	....	56,514,840	7,730,322	4,715,021	2,891,562	19,172,830
1857–1861	2,216,095	....	65,732,080	6,015,058	12,378,351	3,318,280	28,969,749
1862–1866	4,719,330	....	2,257,860	3,007,777	22,529,735	3,530,757	40,183,518
1867–1871	6,486,616	....	1,856,948	4,356,900	22,106,833	2,585,115	35,032,409
1872–1876	3,446,466	547,450	391,344	20,142,169	48,957,518	3,415,871	66,036,873
1877–1881	10,445,654	4,498,436	602,442	41,718,443	107,780,556	5,375,583	133,262,753
1882–1886	9,584,437	3,467,905	561,406	107,129,770	82,883,913	8,620,199	121,674,809
1887–1891	7,184,147	7,120,796	3,209,653	75,073,838	64,739,011	11,286,568	115,528,568
1892–1896	14,546,667	15,782,647	10,277,947	13,999,349	99,913,895	15,713,279	170,623,652
1897–1901	15,467,314	42,863,203	18,407,139	11,213,664	120,247,430	17,151,070	197,427,246
1902–1906	11,476,272	38,605,737	45,977,670	14,807,014	70,527,077	15,444,100	140,025,529
1907–1911	14,774,185	38,783,550	27,194,549	61,429,802	62,854,580	11,840,699	116,137,728
1901	14,963,676	49,356,741	25,527,846	8,874,860	132,060,667	18,650,979	215,990,073
1902	10,715,151	33,042,848	29,591,274	7,572,452	154,856,102	17,759,203	234,772,516
1903	7,794,705	35,642,994	19,750,448	10,520,156	114,181,420	19,716,484	202,905,598
1904	10,985,988	29,013,743	29,121,763	15,418,537	44,230,169	16,999,432	120,727,613
1905	14,858,612	51,535,580	113,282,760	18,348,077	4,394,402	8,826,335	44,112,910
1906	13,026,904	43,793,519	38,142,103	22,175,846	34,973,291	13,919,048	97,609,000
1907	16,809,534	41,880,304	30,174,371	21,237,603	76,569,423	15,584,667	146,700,425
1908	22,920,480	41,019,991	28,444,415	25,510,643	100,371,057	13,927,247	163,043,669
1909	10,446,884	51,087,329	20,511,429	79,946,297	66,923,244	10,521,161	114,268,468
1910	10,589,254	29,860,667	26,779,188	125,507,022	46,679,876	9,040,987	87,364,318
1911	13,104,774	30,069,459	30,063,341	54,947,444	23,729,302	10,129,435	69,311,760
1912	12,190,663	53,262,796	39,446,571	79,594,034	30,160,212	11,006,487	79,689,404
1913	17,591,195	42,031,052	38,908,057	43,994,761	91,602,974	11,394,805	141,132,166
1914	24,262,896	25,728,411	22,414,326	50,895,726	92,393,775	11,821,461	145,590,349
1915	16,210,443	42,448,870	77,480,065	549,007,411	259,642,533	16,182,765	332,464,975
1916	22,409,818	35,537,328	121,969,134	1,630,150,863	173,274,015	15,520,669	243,117,025

TABLE 196.—*Imports of selected agricultural products, 1852–1916.*

[Compiled from reports of Foreign Commerce and Navigation of the United States. Where figures are lacking, either there were no imports or they were not separately classified for publication. "Silk" includes, prior to 1881, only "Silk, raw or as reeled from the cocoon;" in 1881 and 1882 are included this item and "Silk waste;" after 1882, both these items and "Silk cocoons." From "Cocoa and chocolate" are omitted in 1860, 1861, and in 1872 to 1881, small quantities of chocolate, the official returns for which were given only in value. "Jute and jute butts" includes in 1858 and 1859 an unknown quantity of "Sisal grass, coir, etc.," and in 1865–1868 an unknown quantity of "Hemp." Cattle hides are included in "Hides and skins other than cattle and goat" in 1895–1897. Olive oil for table use includes in 1862–1864 and 1885–1905 all olive oil. Sisal grass includes in 1884–1890 "Other vegetable substances." Hemp includes in 1885–1888 all substitutes for hemp.]

Year ending June 30—	Cheese.	Silk.	Wool.	Almonds.	Argols or wine lees.	Cocoa and chocolate, total.	Coffee.
	Pounds.	*Pounds.*	*Pounds.*	*Pounds.*	*Pounds.*	*Pounds.*	*Pounds.*
Average:							
1852–1856	1,053,983	....	19,067,447	3,460,807	....	2,486,572	196,582,863
1857–1861	1,378,147	....	....	3,251,091	....	3,063,893	216,235,090
1862–1866	....	....	....	2,482,063	1,354,947	2,453,141	124,551,992
1867–1871	....	681,669	....	....	2,360,529	3,502,614	248,726,019
1872–1876	....	1,094,948	....	....	4,951,473	4,857,364	307,006,928
1877–1881	....	1,922,269	62,744,282	....	12,403,256	6,315,488	384,282,199
1882–1886	....	4,672,846	83,293,800	....	17,551,967	11,568,173	529,578,782
1887–1891	8,335,323	6,564,121	117,763,889	5,860,728	21,433,570	18,322,049	509,367,994
1892–1896	9,649,752	8,382,892	162,640,491	7,487,676	26,469,990	25,475,234	597,484,217
1897–1901	12,588,515	10,962,210	163,979,079	7,361,198	24,379,847	38,209,423	816,570,082
1902–1906	22,165,754	17,187,544	193,656,402	10,920,881	27,647,440	70,901,254	980,119,167
1907–1911	37,662,812	22,143,461	199,562,649	15,297,414	29,350,692	113,673,368	934,533,322
1901	15,329,099	10,405,555	103,583,505	5,140,232	28,598,781	47,620,204	854,871,310
1902	17,067,714	14,234,826	166,576,966	9,868,982	29,276,148	52,878,587	1,091,004,252
1903	20,671,384	15,270,859	177,137,796	8,142,164	29,966,557	65,046,884	915,086,380
1904	22,707,103	16,722,709	173,742,834	9,838,852	24,571,730	75,070,746	995,043,284
1905	23,095,705	22,357,307	249,135,746	11,745,081	26,281,931	77,383,024	1,047,792,984
1906	27,286,866	17,352,021	201,688,668	15,009,326	28,140,835	84,127,027	851,668,933
1907	33,848,766	18,743,904	203,847,545	14,233,613	30,540,893	97,059,513	985,321,473
1908	32,530,830	16,662,132	125,980,524	17,144,968	26,738,834	86,604,684	890,640,057
1909	35,548,143	25,187,957	266,409,304	11,029,421	32,115,646	132,660,931	1,049,868,768
1910	40,817,524	23,457,223	263,928,232	18,556,356	28,182,956	111,070,834	871,469,516
1911	45,568,797	26,666,091	137,647,641	15,522,712	29,175,133	140,970,877	875,366,797
1912	46,542,007	26,584,962	193,400,713	17,231,458	23,661,078	148,785,846	885,201,247
1913	49,387,944	32,101,555	195,293,255	15,670,558	29,473,011	143,509,852	863,130,757
1914	63,784,313	34,545,829	247,648,869	19,038,405	29,793,011	179,364,091	1,001,528,317
1915	50,138,520	31,052,674	308,083,429	17,111,264	28,624,554	194,734,195	1,118,690,524
1916	30,087,999	41,925,297	534,828,022	16,596,921	34,721,043	245,579,101	1,201,104,485

TABLE 196.—*Imports of selected agricultural products, 1852–1916*—Continued.

Year ending June 30—	Flax.	Hemp.	Hops.	Jute and jute butts.	Licorice root.	Manila.	Molasses.
Average:	*Long tons.*	*Long tons.*	*Pounds.*	*Long tons.*	*Pounds.*	*Long tons.*	*Gallons.*
1852–1856.....	1,143	1,574	....	3,244	....	12,084	28,488,888
1857–1861.....	....	2,652	....	17,239	1,372,573	....	30,190,875
1862–1866.....	....	....	....	3,213	1,887,892	15,566	34,262,933
1867–1871.....	....	....	....	14,909	....	....	53,322,088
1872–1876.....	4,170	22,711	....	49,188	....	....	44,815,321
1877–1881.....	4,260	22,458	....	62,496	....	....	32,638,963
1882–1886.....	5,678	30,557	1,618,879	91,058	....	....	35,019,689
1887–1891.....	7,021	36,919	7,771,672	104,887	59,275,373	....	30,543,299
1892–1896.....	6,785	5,409	2,386,240	84,111	86,444,974	47,354	15,474,619
1897–1901.....	7,008	4,107	2,381,899	93,970	87,475,620	47,217	6,321,160
1902–1906.....	8,574	5,230	5,205,867	101,512	99,543,395	60,813	17,191,821
1907–1911.....	9,721	6,368	6,769,965	100,420	96,111,469	67,289	24,147,348
1901..........	6,878	4,057	2,606,708	103,140	100,105,654	43,735	11,453,156
1902..........	7,772	6,054	2,805,293	128,963	109,077,323	56,453	14,391,215
1903..........	8,155	4,919	6,012,510	79,703	88,580,611	61,648	17,240,399
1904..........	10,123	5,871	2,758,163	96,735	89,463,182	65,666	18,828,530
1905..........	8,089	3,987	4,339,379	98,215	108,443,892	61,562	19,477,885
1906..........	8,729	5,317	10,113,989	103,945	102,151,969	58,738	16,021,076
1907..........	8,656	8,718	6,211,893	104,489	66,115,863	54,513	24,630,935
1908..........	9,528	6,213	8,493,265	107,533	109,355,720	52,467	18,882,756
1909..........	9,870	5,208	7,386,574	156,685	97,742,776	61,902	22,092,696
1910..........	12,761	6,423	3,200,560	68,155	82,207,496	93,253	31,292,165
1911..........	7,792	5,278	8,557,531	65,238	125,135,490	74,308	23,838,190
1912..........	10,900	5,007	2,991,125	101,001	74,582,225	68,536	28,828,213
1913..........	12,421	7,663	8,494,144	125,389	105,116,227	73,823	33,926,521
1914..........	9,885	8,822	5,382,025	106,033	115,636,131	49,688	51,410,271
1915..........	4,694	5,310	11,651,332	83,140	65,958,501	51,081	70,839,623
1916..........	6,939	6,506	675,704	108,322	41,003,295	78,892	85,716,673

Year ending June 30—	Olive oil, for table use.	Opium, crude.	Potatoes.	Rice, and rice flour, rice meal, and broken rice.	Sisal grass.	Sugar, raw and refined.	Tea.
Average:	*Gallons.*	*Pounds.*	*Bushels.*	*Pounds.*	*Long tons.*	*Pounds.*	*Pounds.*
1852–1856.......	....	110,143	406,611	....	....	479,373,648	24,959,922
1857–1861.......	....	113,594	....	....	....	691,323,833	28,149,643
1862–1866.......	177,947	128,590	251,637	70,893,331	615	672,637,141	30,869,450
1867–1871.......	152,827	209,096	216,077	52,953,577	....	1,138,464,815	44,052,805
1872–1876.......	174,555	365,071	254,615	72,536,435	....	1,614,055,119	62,436,359
1877–1881.......	218,507	407,656	1,850,106	62,614,706	....	1,760,508,290	67,583,083
1882–1886.......	....	391,946	2,834,736	99,870,675	....	2,458,490,409	74,781,418
1887–1891.......	758,352	475,299	3,878,580	156,868,635	40,274	3,003,283,854	84,275,049
1892–1896.......	773,692	528,785	1,804,649	160,807,652	50,129	3,827,799,481	92,782,175
1897–1901.......	909,249	567,681	495,150	165,231,669	70,297	3,916,433,945	86,809,270
1902–1906.......	1,783,425	537,576	2,662,121	150,913,684	96,832	3,721,782,404	98,677,584
1907–1911.......	3,897,224	489,513	1,907,405	215,892,467	102,440	3,997,156,461	96,742,977
1901..........	983,059	583,208	371,911	117,199,710	70,076	3,975,005,840	89,806,453
1902..........	1,339,097	534,189	7,656,162	157,658,894	89,583	3,031,915,875	75,579,125
1903..........	1,494,132	516,570	358,505	169,656,284	87,025	4,216,108,106	108,574,905
1904..........	1,713,590	573,055	3,166,581	154,221,772	109,214	3,700,623,613	112,905,541
1905..........	1,923,174	594,680	181,199	106,483,515	100,301	3,680,932,998	102,706,599
1906..........	2,447,131	469,387	1,948,160	166,547,957	98,037	3,979,331,430	93,621,750
1907..........	3,449,517	565,252	176,917	209,603,180	99,061	4,391,839,975	86,368,490
1908..........	3,799,112	285,845	403,952	212,783,392	103,994	3,371,997,112	94,149,564
1909..........	4,129,454	517,388	8,383,966	222,900,422	91,451	4,189,421,018	114,916,520
1910..........	3,702,210	449,239	353,208	225,400,545	99,966	4,094,545,936	85,626,370
1911..........	4,405,827	629,842	218,984	208,774,795	117,727	3,937,978,265	102,563,942
1912..........	4,836,515	399,837	13,734,695	190,063,331	114,467	4,104,618,393	101,406,816
1913..........	5,221,001	508,433	327,230	222,103,547	153,869	4,740,041,488	94,812,800
1914..........	6,217,560	455,200	3,645,993	300,194,917	215,547	5,066,821,873	91,130,815
1915..........	6,710,967	484,027	270,942	277,191,472	185,764	5,420,981,867	96,987,942
1916..........	7,224,431	146,658	209,542	264,324,005	228,610	5,633,161,749	109,865,935

TABLE 196.—*Imports of selected agricultural products, 1852–1916*—Continued.

Year ending June 30—	Beeswax.	Onions.	Plums and prunes.	Raisins.	Currants.	Dates.	Figs.
	Pounds.	*Bushels.*	*Pounds.*	*Pounds.*	*Pounds.*	*Pounds.*	*Pounds.*
Average:							
1887–1891	128,790	....	60,237,642	38,545,635	....	14,914,349	9,783,650
1892–1896	279,839	....	12,405,549	17,745,925	34,397,754	14,914,349	10,117,049
1897–1901	265,143	628,358	560,762	7,669,593	27,520,440	15,653,642	8,919,921
1902–1906	456,727	924,418	563,900	7,344,676	35,457,213	25,649,432	14,334,760
1907–1911	845,720	1,103,034	....	5,283,145	35,258,628	26,059,353	19,848,037
1901	213,773	774,042	745,974	3,860,836	16,049,198	20,013,681	9,933,871
1902	408,706	796,316	522,478	6,683,545	36,238,976	21,681,159	11,087,131
1903	488,576	925,599	633,819	6,715,675	33,878,209	43,814,917	16,482,142
1904	425,168	1,171,242	494,105	6,867,617	38,347,649	21,058,164	13,178,061
1905	373,569	856,366	671,604	4,041,689	31,742,919	19,257,250	13,364,107
1906	587,617	872,566	497,494	12,414,855	37,078,311	22,435,672	17,562,358
1907	917,088	1,126,114	323,377	3,967,151	38,392,779	31,270,899	24,346,173
1908	671,526	1,275,333	335,089	9,132,353	38,652,656	24,958,343	18,836,574
1909	764,937	574,530	296,123	5,794,320	32,482,111	21,869,218	15,235,513
1910	972,145	1,024,226	....	5,042,683	33,326,030	22,693,713	17,362,197
1911	902,904	1,514,967	....	2,479,220	33,489,565	29,504,592	23,459,728
1912	1,076,741	1,436,037	....	3,255,861	33,151,396	25,208,248	18,765,408
1913	828,793	789,458	....	2,579,705	30,843,735	34,304,951	16,837,819
1914	1,412,200	1,114,811	....	4,554,549	32,033,177	34,073,608	19,284,868
1915	1,564,506	829,177	....	2,808,806	30,350,527	24,949,374	20,779,730
1916	....	815,872	....	1,024,296	25,373,029	31,075,424	7,153,250

Year ending June 30—	Hides and skins, other than furs.			Macaroni, vermicelli, and all similar preparations.	Lemons.	Oranges.	Walnuts.
	Cattle.	Goat.	Other than cattle and goat.				
	Pounds.	*Pounds.*	*Pounds.*	*Pounds.*	*Pounds.*	*Pounds.*	*Pounds.*
Average:							
1897–1901	....	68,052,973	91,173,311	....	153,160,863	41,104,544	....
1902–1906	126,995,011	93,674,819	115,952,418	....	153,160,863	41,104,544	....
1907–1911	178,681,537	94,329,840	143,351,321	99,724,072	153,343,434	12,089,790	30,980,661
1901	129,174,624	73,745,596	77,989,617	....	148,514,614	50,332,914	....
1902	148,627,907	88,038,516	89,457,680	....	164,075,309	52,742,476	....
1903	131,644,325	85,114,070	102,340,303	28,787,821	152,004,213	56,872,070	12,362,567
1904	85,370,168	86,338,547	103,024,752	40,224,202	171,923,221	35,893,260	23,670,761
1905	113,177,357	97,803,571	126,893,934	53,441,080	139,084,321	28,880,575	21,684,104
1906	156,155,300	111,079,391	158,045,419	77,926,029	138,717,252	31,134,341	24,917,028
1907	134,671,020	101,201,596	135,111,199	87,720,730	157,859,906	21,267,346	32,597,592
1908	98,353,249	63,640,758	120,770,918	97,233,708	178,490,003	18,397,429	28,887,110
1909	192,252,083	104,048,244	148,253,998	85,114,003	135,183,550	8,435,873	26,157,703
1910	318,003,538	115,844,758	174,770,732	113,772,801	160,214,785	4,676,118	33,641,466
1911	150,127,796	86,913,842	137,849,757	114,779,116	134,968,924	7,672,186	33,619,434
1912	251,012,513	95,340,703	191,414,882	108,231,028	145,639,396	7,628,662	37,213,674
1913	268,042,390	96,250,305	207,903,995	106,500,752	151,416,412	12,252,960	26,662,441
1914	279,963,488	84,759,428	196,347,770	126,128,621	....	....	37,195,728
1915	334,341,417	66,547,163	137,439,153	56,542,480	....	....	33,445,838
1916	434,177,771	100,657,021	208,835,068	21,789,602	....	....	36,858,934

TABLE 197.—*Foreign trade of the United States in forest products, 1852–1916.*

[Compiled from reports of Foreign Commerce and Navigation of the United States. All values are gold.]

Year ending June 30—	Exports.		Imports.	Excess of exports (+) or of imports (−).
	Domestic.	Foreign.		
Average:				
1852–1856	$6,819,079	$694,037	$3,256,302	+ $4,256,814
1857–1861	9,994,808	962,142	6,942,211	+ 4,014,739
1862–1866	7,366,103	798,076	8,511,370	− 347,191
1867–1871	11,775,297	690,748	14,812,576	− 2,346,531
1872–1876	17,906,771	959,862	19,728,458	− 861,825
1877–1881	17,579,313	552,514	22,006,227	− 3,874,400
1882–1886	24,704,992	1,417,226	34,252,753	− 8,130,535
1887–1891	26,060,729	1,442,760	39,647,287	− 12,143,798
1892–1896	29,276,428	1,707,307	45,091,081	− 14,107,346
1897–1901	45,960,863	3,283,274	52,326,879	− 3,082,742
1902–1906	63,584,670	3,850,221	79,885,457	− 12,450,566
1907–1911	88,764,471	6,488,455	137,051,471	− 41,798,545
1901	55,369,161	3,599,192	57,143,650	+ 1,824,703
1902	48,928,764	3,609,071	59,187,049	− 6,649,214
1903	58,734,016	2,865,325	71,478,022	− 9,878,681
1904	70,085,789	4,177,352	79,619,296	− 5,356,155
1905	63,199,348	3,790,097	92,680,555	− 25,691,110
1906	76,975,431	4,809,261	96,462,364	− 14,677,672
1907	92,948,705	5,500,331	122,420,776	− 23,971,740
1908	90,362,073	4,570,397	97,733,092	− 2,800,622
1909	72,442,454	4,982,810	123,920,126	− 46,494,862
1910	85,030,230	9,801,881	178,871,797	− 84,039,686
1911	103,038,892	7,586,854	162,311,565	− 51,685,819
1912	108,122,254	6,413,343	172,523,465	− 57,987,868
1913	124,835,784	7,431,851	180,502,444	− 48,234,809
1914	106,978,554	4,517,766	155,261,300	− 43,764,980
1915	52,553,536	5,089,299	165,849,493	−108,206,658
1916	67,827,102	4,334,335	252,824,453	−180,663,016

TABLE 198.—*Exports of selected domestic forest products, 1852–1916.*

[Compiled from reports of Foreign Commerce and Navigation of the United States. Where figures are lacking, either there were no exports or they were not separately classified for publication.]

Year ending June 30—	Lumber.			Rosin.	Spirits of turpentine.	Timber.	
	Boards, deals, and planks.[1]	Shooks, other than box.	Staves.			Hewn.	Sawed.
	M feet.	*Number.*	*Number.*	*Barrels.*	*Gallons.*	*Cubic feet.*	*M feet.*
Average:							
1852–1856	129,499			552,210	1,369,250		
1857–1861	205,476			664,206	2,735,104		
1862–1866	138,020			69,314	107,162		
1867–1871	138,720			491,774	2,693,412		
1872–1876	221,658			845,803		17,459,632	
1877–1881	303,114				7,138,556	18,316,876	
1882–1886	433,963			1,289,869	9,301,894	13,701,663	
1887–1891	531,755	593,054		1,533,834	10,794,025	6,401,543	218,796
1892–1896	616,090	435,581		2,006,427	14,258,928	6,062,418	263,641
1897–1901	957,218	668,797		2,477,696	18,349,386	5,146,927	428,755
1902–1906	212,476	765,215	51,234,056	2,453,280	16,927,090	3,968,469	508,212
1907–1911	1,649,203	925,828	56,181,900	2,355,560	16,658,955	3,406,245	479,776
1901	1,101,815	714,651	47,363,262	2,820,815	20,240,851	4,624,698	533,920
1902	942,814	788,241	46,998,512	2,535,962	19,177,788	5,388,439	412,750
1903	1,065,771	566,205	55,879,010	2,396,498	16,378,787	3,291,498	530,659
1904	1,426,784	533,182	47,420,095	2,585,108	17,202,808	3,788,740	558,690
1905	1,283,406	872,192	48,286,285	2,310,275	15,894,813	3,856,623	486,411
1906	1,343,607	1,066,253	57,586,378	2,438,556	15,981,253	3,517,046	552,548
1907	1,623,964	803,346	51,120,171	2,560,966	15,854,676	3,278,110	600,865
1908	1,548,130	900,812	61,696,949	2,712,732	19,532,583	4,883,506	463,440
1909	1,357,822	977,376	52,583,016	2,170,177	17,502,028	2,950,528	383,309
1910	1,684,489	928,197	49,783,771	2,144,318	15,587,737	3,245,196	451,721
1911	2,031,608	1,019,411	65,725,595	2,189,607	14,817,751	2,673,887	499,547
						M feet.	
1912	2,306,680	1,161,591	64,162,599	2,474,460	19,599,241	31,067	406,954
1913	2,550,308	1,710,095	89,005,624	2,806,046	21,039,597	34,502	477,135
1914	2,405,296	867,805	77,150,535	2,417,950	18,900,704	29,859	411,307
1915	1,129,205	620,043	39,297,268	1,372,316	9,464,120	6,118	167,671
1916	1,176,765	583,724	57,820,610	1,571,279	9,309,968	9,628	191,577

[1] Including "Joists and scantling" prior to 1884.

TABLE 199.—*Imports of selected forest products, 1852–1916.*

| Year ending June 30— | Camphor, crude. | India rubber. | Rubber gums, total. | Lumber. | | Shellac. | Wood pulp. |
				Boards, deals, planks, and other sawed.	Shingles.		
	Pounds.	*Pounds.*	*Pounds.*	*M feet.*	*M.*	*Pounds.*	*Long tons.*
Average:							
1852–1856........	213,720	....	....	....	....	....	....
1857–1861........	360,522	....	....	....	....	....	....
1862–1866........	386,731	....	....	....	....	634,276	....
1867–1871........	....	....	¹ 7,389,890	....	....	....	....
1872–1876........	....	....	12,631,388	564,642	88,197	....	....
1877–1881........	1,515,614	....	15,610,634	417,907	55,394	....	....
1882–1886........	1,958,608	....	24,480,997	577,728	87,760	....	....
1887–1891........	2,273,883	....	33,226,520	646,745	184,050	5,086,421	37,251
1892–1896........	1,491,902	38,359,547	39,671,553	661,495	....	5,848,339	42,771
1897–1901........	1,858,018	47,469,136	52,974,744	566,394	....	8,839,232	46,827
1902–1906........	2,139,183	57,903,641	75,908,633	727,205	772,340	11,613,967	130,764
1907–1911........	2,939,167	80,129,167	121,504,098	899,659	866,565	19,046,030	319,007
1901............	2,175,784	55,275,529	64,927,176	490,820	555,853	9,608,745	46,757
1902............	1,831,058	50,413,481	67,790,069	665,603	707,614	9,064,789	67,416
1903............	2,472,440	55,010,571	69,311,678	720,937	724,131	11,590,725	116,881
1904............	2,819,673	59,015,551	74,327,584	589,232	770,373	10,933,413	144,796
1905............	1,904,002	67,234,256	87,004,384	710,538	758,725	10,700,817	167,504
1906............	1,668,744	¹57,844,345	81,109,451	949,717	900,856	15,780,090	157,224
1907............	3,138,070	¹76,963,838	106,747,589	934,195	881,003	17,785,960	213,110
1908............	2,814,299	¹62,233,160	85,809,625	791,288	988,081	13,361,932	237,514
1909............	1,990,499	¹88,359,895	114,598,768	846,024	1,058,363	19,185,137	274,217
1910............	3,026,648	¹101,044,681	154,620,629	1,054,416	762,798	29,402,182	378,322
1911............	3,726,319	72,046,260	145,743,880	872,374	642,582	15,494,940	491,873
1912............	2,154,646	110,210,173	175,965,538	905,275	514,657	18,745,771	477,508
1913............	3,709,264	113,384,359	170,747,339	1,090,628	560,297	21,912,015	502,913
1914............	3,476,908	131,995,742	161,777,250	928,873	895,038	16,719,756	508,360
1915............	3,729,207	172,068,428	196,121,979	939,322	1,487,116	24,153,363	587,922
1916............	4,574,430	267,775,557	304,182,814	1,218,068	1,769,333	25,817,509	507,045

¹ Includes "Gutta-percha" only for 1867.

TABLE 200.—*Principal farm products imported from specified countries into the United States, 1914–1916.*

| Country from which consigned, and article. | Year ending June 30— | | | | | |
| | 1914 | | 1915 | | 1916 | |
	Quantity.	Value.	Quantity.	Value.	Quantity.	Value.
Brazil:						
Cocoa (crude)...pounds.	25,870,186	$2,764,766	19,708,616	$2,017,224	45,657,401	$6,086,847
Coffee..............do....	743,113,500	76,016,463	773,400,315	65,492,280	849,405,925	73,541,315
British West Indies:						
Bananas.......bunches..	15,677,191	4,849,037	11,957,935	3,483,373	4,691,518	1,365,705
Cocoa..........pounds..	44,062,426	5,372,327	40,728,851	5,407,262	39,933,405	6,038,665
Canada: Tea....do....	3,112,383	864,814	3,446,615	981,933	2,600,705	861,236
China: Tea........do....	20,139,342	2,755,512	23,100,548	3,149,308	20,422,700	2,990,751
Colombia: Coffee....do....	91,830,513	11,556,038	111,077,449	13,710,164	109,363,456	13,519,545
Cuba:						
Bananas.......bunches..	2,354,395	853,536	2,708,624	929,761	2,859,021	1,072,035
Sugar (raw).....pounds..	4,926,606,243	98,394,782	4,784,888,157	156,181,349	5,150,852,007	192,558,595
Dominican Republic:						
Cocoa..........pounds..	26,782,966	3,187,006	46,620,464	5,499,510	48,990,707	6,946,412
Ecuador: Cocoa......do....	26,319,735	2,693,674	33,418,752	3,351,797	31,878,350	4,198,249
France:						
Cheese...........do....	5,418,904	1,032,817	3,554,297	737,212	2,321,543	783,323
Olive oil (salad).gallons..	949,858	1,512,324	802,092	1,215,632	895,369	1,402,972
Italy:						
Cheese...........pounds..	26,453,626	5,024,270	25,662,362	5,108,850	16,084,059	3,855,856
Macaroni..........do....	121,924,372	5,481,187	54,591,991	2,944,398	20,221,908	1,426,730
Olive oil (salad).gallons..	4,319,567	5,552,098	4,864,388	6,089,646	4,696,812	6,725,524
Japan: Tea....pounds..	41,913,273	7,171,202	43,869,012	7,683,356	52,359,526	8,975,993
Mexico: Coffee.......do....	49,385,504	8,028,186	52,706,120	6,898,161	49,832,801	6,222,326
Netherlands:						
Cheese...........do....	3,656,763	455,159	2,210,861	287,620	578,201	121,588
Coffee...........do....	5,905,654	636,763	1,583,672	253,731	50,896	10,884
Philippine Islands: Sugar, pounds..	116,749,211	2,553,601	326,842,296	7,511,126	217,190,825	6,389,017
Portugal: Cocoa...pounds..	17,738,638	2,292,959	3,516,655	512,270	7,531,924	1,368,032
Switzerland: Cheese, pounds..	22,489,706	3,617,651	14,766,682	2,677,249	9,514,008	2,031,590
United Kingdom:						
Cocoa...........pounds..	12,903,640	1,633,424	21,062,767	2,578,996	13,408,058	2,186,624
Tea.................do..	14,077,601	3,858,970	12,869,968	3,386,476	19,066,241	4,670,251

TABLE 201.—*Principal farm products exported to specified countries from the United States, 1914–1916.*

Country to which consigned, and article.	Year ending June 30—					
	1914		1915		1916	
	Quantity.	Value.	Quantity.	Value.	Quantity.	Value.
Belgium:						
Corn..............bushels..	60,227	$38,198	103,927	$82,324	4,550	$4,191
Wheat..............do....	12,873,372	12,479,315	5,320,685	6,392,090	2,682,920	3,342,519
Bacon..........pounds..	5,110,170	743,371	5,737,181	603,344	60,160,749	6,251,526
Hams and shoulders..do....	4,080,669	563,140	6,596,068	801,837	2,792,605	367,070
Lard..............do....	15,915,380	1,833,325	5,128,630	528,764	70,132,156	7,327,075
Brazil: Wheat flour..barrels..	748,612	3,752,105	707,705	3,972,690	734,726	1,216,205
Canada:						
Corn..............bushels..	4,641,737	3,328,785	8,283,156	6,154,904	6,562,323	4,964,555
Wheat..............do....	4,113,701	3,821,159	19,664,674	19,941,388	6,244,732	7,430,824
Wheat flour.......barrels..	122,752	539,942	110,938	592,011	50,424	254,717
Bacon..........pounds..	11,082,930	1,644,388	10,025,242	1,363,621	39,590,591	5,342,490
Hams and shoulders..do....	4,006,649	672,855	1,514,602	219,257	2,673,658	370,783
Lard..............do....	15,995,669	1,847,515	7,721,616	887,910	6,330,140	635,024
Pork, pickled........do....	12,825,741	1,373,501	8,500,049	870,937	17,835,273	1,701,324
China: Wheat flour..barrels..	136,374	540,154	13,273	57,066	10,762	54,631
Cuba:						
Corn..............bushels..	2,410,156	1,878,664	2,267,305	1,896,907	3,231,323	2,587,501
Wheat flour.......barrels..	892,705	4,057,806	924,989	5,379,266	1,124,562	6,468,442
Bacon..........pounds..	13,733,773	1,634,755	13,360,139	1,616,045	13,543,082	1,685,946
Hams and shoulders..do....	5,637,829	940,720	6,842,425	1,127,283	11,493,464	1,875,091
Lard..............do....	49,609,751	5,582,074	45,349,283	5,011,657	53,811,784	5,930,069
Pork, pickled........do....	4,090,780	447,374	3,874,892	428,050	7,846,918	888,699
Denmark: Corn......bushels..	118	95	11,169,550	9,052,044	9,826,259	7,997,250
Finland: Wheat flour. barrels..	429,354	2,085,441	35,588	165,057	....	....
France:						
Wheat..............bushels..	5,536,731	5,384,663	49,878,655	66,352,832	21,802,818	27,898,645
Bacon..........pounds..	197,353	25,416	44,712,253	5,766,832	52,501,448	6,442,595
Lard..............do....	5,307,986	573,493	32,172,876	3,503,946	42,282,883	5,075,237
Germany:						
Corn..............bushels..	303,303	225,209	15,785	16,500	....	....
Wheat..............do....	10,983,060	10,604,692	2,652,128	2,487,115	....	....
Wheat flour.......barrels..	176,485	891,171	8,240	42,841	....	....
Lard..........pounds..	146,208,598	16,593,043	3,878,433	412,751	....	....
Lard, neutral........do....	6,309,792	709,101	312,933	44,176	....	....
Oleo oil..........do....	16,180,268	1,631,254	1,001,252	98,081	....	....
Hongkong: Wheat flour, barrels......................	1,141,095	4,501,672	626,978	2,840,779	356,263	1,620,227
Italy:						
Wheat..............bushels..	1,839,830	1,789,400	47,122,740	66,538,785	31,441,667	38,191,428
Lard..........pounds..	5,958,983	616,948	4,123,209	451,326	3,487,719	390,806
Japan: Wheat flour...barrels..	793,269	3,045,532	68,542	279,315	54,475	269,609
Mexico:						
Corn..............bushels..	467,424	379,675	1,587,420	1,388,902	3,678,934	3,083,408
Wheat..............do....	306,376	313,910	296,581	380,697	17,624	22,982
Lard..........pounds..	3,294,437	392,580	3,191,515	365,024	8,736,712	966,395
Netherlands:						
Corn..............bushels..	373,770	287,417	15,875,674	12,969,747	5,705,625	4,699,487
Wheat..............do....	19,949,519	19,380,347	31,551,992	42,070,210	21,070,335	26,224,787
Wheat flour.......barrels..	958,063	4,669,565	1,725,807	10,553,446	219,644	1,318,349
Bacon..........pounds..	1,718,481	204,260	8,284,647	1,199,393	12,846,176	1,632,440
Lard..............do....	43,469,536	4,859,367	22,245,433	2,589,995	13,281,671	1,467,341
Lard, neutral........do....	13,174,294	1,438,696	9,847,645	1,142,321	9,059,503	1,152,883
Oleo oil..........do....	47,414,421	4,944,474	32,767,906	3,637,839	29,762,451	3,558,189
Norway: Oleo oil......do....	7,285,043	764,333	9,954,544	1,160,460	14,062,716	1,796,590
Philippine Islands: Wheat flour...........barrels..	236,902	944,747	303,792	1,647,098	385,371	1,989,941
United Kingdom:						
Corn..............bushels..	540,515	388,620	2,850,252	2,297,878	5,627,128	4,438,126
Wheat..............do....	27,961,348	26,015,351	65,911,501	80,039,502	53,550,376	67,388,601
Wheat flour.......barrels..	2,809,800	13,805,674	4,156,097	23,668,245	3,145,030	17,532,505
Bacon..........pounds..	132,819,680	18,103,518	201,042,923	28,388,432	339,341,069	48,740,987
Hams and shoulders..do....	146,007,141	20,558,228	179,376,833	25,440,034	251,025,795	35,899,072
Lard..............do....	164,632,676	18,412,791	189,349,874	20,650,513	192,075,591	21,640,498
Oleo oil..........do....	9,243,952	1,010,834	14,361,603	1,734,445	30,657,569	3,684,779
Pork, pickled.........do....	5,571,720	624,462	6,534,240	700,078	13,124,077	1,644,441

TABLE 202.—*Shipments of principal domestic farm and forest products from the United States to Hawaii and Porto Rico, 1914–1916.*

[These shipments are not included in the domestic exports from or imports into the United States.]

Possession and article.	Year ending June 30—					
	1914		1915		1916	
	Quantity.	Value.	Quantity.	Value.	Quantity.	Value.
HAWAII.						
Dairy products......pounds..	4,275,534	$562,516	4,930,995	$584,141	4,819,844	$629,825
Meat products..............	....	528,960	....	542,924	....	883,174
Grain and grain products.....	....	2,221,197	....	2,493,054	....	2,322,166
Rice.................pounds..	5,031,515	216,252	974,272	39,755	191,840	7,307
Lumber......................	....	876,544	....	1,139,434	....	1,002,976
PORTO RICO.						
Dairy products......pounds..	2,210,881	207,817	2,496,076	267,491	3,861,569	496,177
Meat products..............	....	3,678,741	....	3,382,875	....	3,551,176
Beans and dried peas.bushels..	163,843	469,661	190,793	672,163	216,747	795,276
Grain and grain products.....	....	2,248,045	....	2,756,391	....	2,994,388
Rice.................pounds..	139,836,581	5,306,364	127,310,116	4,851,533	143,171,261	5,596,068
Sugar...................do....	16,855,067	727,966	12,329,041	648,414	10,265,579	612,041
Tobacco................do....	1,627,405	327,790	1,106,120	178,924	1,764,344	285,041
Lumber......................	....	969,124	....	633,747	....	756,434

TABLE 203.—*Shipments of principal domestic farm products from Hawaii and Porto Rico to the United States, 1914–1916.*

Possession and article.	Year ending June 30—					
	1914		1915		1916	
	Quantity.	Value.	Quantity.	Value.	Quantity.	Value.
HAWAII.						
Coffee.................pounds..	4,430,722	$657,853	3,191,274	$486,054	2,252,364	$343,829
Pineapples, canned..........	....	4,536,919	....	5,986,190	....	6,547,055
Sugar.................pounds..	1,114,750,702	33,187,920	1,280,863,812	52,949,697	1,137,159,828	54,418,095
PORTO RICO.						
Grapefruit.............boxes..	206,200	751,769	276,550	834,356	296,613	836,932
Oranges................do....	348,870	752,088	200,268	378,092	404,367	790,667
Pineapples..................	....	1,245,215	....	1,723,694	....	1,176,319
Molasses and sirup...gallons..	15,577,832	927,227	18,004,811	658,661	16,279,073	1,073,786
Sugar.................pounds..	641,252,527	20,239,831	588,922,493	27,277,839	849,763,491	45,799,299
Tobacco, leaf...........do....	6,308,227	2,961,614	7,035,777	2,954,804	6,705,823	2,857,036

TABLE 204.—*Destination of principal farm products exported from the United States, 1913–1916.*

Article, and country to which consigned.	Quantity.				Per cent of total.			
	Year ending June 30—							
	1913	1914	1915	1916 (prel.).	1913	1914	1915	1916 (prel.).
ANIMAL MATTER.								
Cattle:	*Number.*	*Number.*	*Number.*	*Number.*	*Per ct.*	*Per ct.*	*Per ct.*	*Per ct.*
Canada	11,691	8,957	751	4,511	47.3	48.7	13.7	20.8
United Kingdom	1,773			815	7.2			3.8
Other countries	11,250	9,419	4,733	16,340	45.5	51.3	86.3	75.4
Total	24,714	18,376	5,484	21,666	100.0	100.0	100.0	100.0
Horses:								
Canada	26,560	17,700	42,036	82,311	92.5	77.7	14.5	23.0
United Kingdom	430	609	92,737	49,412	1.5	2.7	32.1	13.8
Other countries	1,717	4,467	154,567	225,830	6.0	19.6	53.4	63.2
Total	28,707	22,776	289,340	357,553	100.0	100.0	100.0	100.0
Butter:								
Central American States and British Honduras	*Pounds.* 775,246	*Pounds.* 810,254	*Pounds.* 726,552	*Pounds.* 931,774	21.6	21.9	7.4	6.9
West Indies and Bermuda	1,392,508	1,158,111	1,143,822	1,517,306	38.8	31.4	11.6	11.2
Other countries	1,417,846	1,725,232	7,980,330	11,054,199	39.6	46.7	81.0	81.9
Total	3,585,600	3,693,597	9,850,704	13,503,279	100.0	100.0	100.0	100.0
Meat products: Beef products— Beef, canned—								
United Kingdom	3,117,149	1,157,104	64,700,738	37,819,212	45.6	33.4	86.0	75.0
Other countries	3,723,199	2,307,629	10,542,523	12,597,478	54.4	66.6	14.0	25.0
Total	6,840,348	3,464,733	75,243,261	50,416,690	100.0	100.0	100.0	100.0
Beef, fresh—								
Panama	5,935,198	5,534,391	3,706,596	1,504,403	80.6	86.6	2.2	.7
United Kingdom	126,885		54,497,192	117,305,639	1.7		32.0	50.7
Other countries	1,300,305	860,013	112,237,146	112,405,033	17.7	13.4	65.8	48.6
Total	7,362,388	6,394,404	170,440,934	231,215,075	100.0	100.0	100.0	100.0
Beef, pickled, and other cured—								
Canada	712,086	1,331,150	1,659,165	5,047,349	2.8	5.7	5.2	13.3
Germany	3,080,823	1,757,786	378,548	400	11.9	7.6	1.2	0.0
Newfoundland and Labrador	3,807,237	4,935,657	4,331,261	5,027,163	14.7	21.2	13.6	13.2
West Indies and Bermuda	4,274,549	3,900,281	2,697,974	3,089,623	16.5	16.8	8.5	8.1
United Kingdom	5,929,949	4,113,347	10,994,101	12,003,390	22.9	17.7	34.5	31.5
Other countries	8,052,275	7,227,753	11,813,694	12,892,757	31.2	31.0	37.0	33.9
Total	25,856,919	23,265,974	31,874,743	38,060,682	100.0	100.0	100.0	100.0
Oleo oil—								
Germany	17,480,760	16,180,268	1,001,252		18.8	16.7	1.2	
Netherlands	46,337,137	47,414,421	32,767,906	29,762,451	49.9	48.9	40.7	29.0
Norway	6,607,526	7,285,043	9,954,544	14,062,716	7.1	7.5	12.4	13.7
United Kingdom	8,008,915	9,243,952	14,361,603	30,657,569	8.6	9.5	17.8	29.9
Other countries	14,415,419	16,893,381	22,396,641	28,163,178	15.6	17.4	27.9	27.4
Total	92,849,757	97,017,065	80,481,946	102,645,914	100.0	100.0	100.0	100.0

TABLE 204.—*Destination of principal farm products exported from the United States, 1913–1916*—Continued.

Article, and country to which consigned.	Quantity.				Per cent of total.			
	Year ending June 30—							
	1913	1914	1915	1916 (prel.).	1913	1914	1915	1916 (prel.).
ANIMAL MATTER—con.								
Meat products—Con.								
Lard compounds—	*Pounds.*	*Pounds.*	*Pounds.*	*Pounds.*	*Per ct.*	*Per ct.*	*Per ct.*	*Per ct.*
Cuba............	17,525,703	14,673,201	19,046,472	11,895,200	26.0	25.2	27.2	22.5
Mexico..........	4,127,593	3,119,285	3,772,943	4,597,585	6.1	5.4	5.4	8.7
United Kingdom.	21,115,679	19,929,949	26,357,467	18,486,477	31.3	34.2	37.7	35.0
Other countries..	24,687,857	20,581,129	20,803,732	17,864,049	36.6	35.2	29.7	33.8
Total..........	67,456,832	58,303,564	69,980,614	52,843,311	100.0	100.0	100.0	100.0
Pork products—								
Bacon—								
Belgium.......	9,140,688	5,110,170	5,737,181	60,160,749	4.5	2.6	1.7	10.4
Canada.........	6,868,480	11,082,930	10,025,242	39,590,591	3.4	5.7	2.9	6.8
Cuba..........	6,658,202	13,733,773	13,360,139	13,543,082	3.3	7.1	3.9	2.3
France........	2,096,868	197,353	44,712,253	52,501,448	1.0	.1	12.9	9.1
Netherlands....	7,639,281	1,718,481	8,284,647	12,846,176	3.8	.9	2.4	2.2
United Kingdom...	138,133,416	132,819,680	201,042,923	339,341,069	68.7	68.5	58.0	58.5
Other countries	30,456,649	29,301,865	63,555,842	61,825,671	15.3	15.1	18.2	10.7
Total........	200,993,584	193,964,252	346,718,227	579,808,786	100.0	100.0	100.0	100.0
Hams and shoulders, cured—								
Belgium.......	5,821,638	4,080,669	6,596,068	2,792,605	3.6	2.5	3.2	1.0
Canada.........	6,785,477	4,006,649	1,514,602	2,673,658	4.3	2.4	.7	.9
Cuba..........	6,002,471	5,637,829	6,842,425	11,493,464	3.8	3.4	3.4	4.1
United Kingdom...	134,016,686	146,007,141	179,376,833	251,025,795	84.0	88.0	88.1	89.0
Other countries	6,918,415	6,149,503	9,371,186	14,223,089	4.3	3.7	4.6	5.0
Total........	159,544,687	165,881,791	203,701,114	282,208,611	100.0	100.0	100.0	100.0
Lard—								
Belgium.......	18,761,624	15,915,380	5,128,630	70,132,156	3.6	3.3	1.1	16.4
Canada.........	11,079,696	15,995,669	7,721,616	6,330,140	2.1	3.3	1.6	1.5
Cuba..........	46,526,427	49,609,751	45,349,283	53,811,784	9.0	10.3	9.5	12.6
France........	17,428,157	5,307,986	32,172,876	42,282,883	3.4	1.1	6.8	9.9
Germany.......	160,862,204	146,208,598	3,878,433	....	31.0	30.4	.8	......
Italy.........	6,106,153	5,958,983	4,123,209	3,487,719	1.2	1.2	.9	.8
Mexico........	8,468,353	3,294,437	3,191,515	8,736,712	1.6	.7	.7	2.0
Netherlands....	43,383,774	43,469,536	22,245,433	13,281,671	8.4	9.0	4.7	3.1
United Kingdom...	168,379,790	164,632,676	189,349,874	192,075,591	32.4	34.2	39.8	45.0
Other countries	38,029,206	31,064,776	162,371,039	36,872,682	7.3	6.5	34.1	8.7
Total........	519,025,384	481,457,792	475,531,908	427,011,338	100.0	100.0	100.0	100.0
Lard, neutral—								
Germany.......	9,368,924	6,309,792	312,933	....	20.9	21.5	1.2	......
Netherlands....	27,123,927	13,174,294	9,847,645	9,059,503	60.6	44.9	37.8	26.3
Other countries	8,284,841	9,839,700	15,860,476	25,367,087	18.5	33.6	61.0	73.7
Total........	44,777,692	29,323,786	26,021,054	34,426,590	100.0	100.0	100.0	100.0
Pork, pickled—								
Canada.........	9,436,506	12,825,741	8,500,049	17,835,273	17.6	28.2	18.6	28.1
Cuba..........	9,141,098	4,090,780	3,874,892	7,846,918	17.0	9.0	8.5	12.4
Newfoundland and Labrador.	5,672,961	7,911,743	5,244,462	7,070,090	10.6	17.4	11.5	11.1
United Kingdom...	14,619,714	5,571,720	6,354,240	13,124,077	27.2	12.2	14.3	20.7
Other countries	14,878,744	15,143,101	21,501,931	17,584,355	27.6	33.2	47.1	27.7
Total........	53,749,023	45,543,085	45,655,574	63,460,713	100.0	100.0	100.0	100.0

TABLE 204.—*Destination of principal farm products exported from the United States,* 1913–1916—Continued.

Article, and country to which consigned.	Quantity.				Per cent of total.			
	Year ending June 30—							
	1913	1914	1915	1916 (prel.).	1913	1914	1915	1916 (prel.).
VEGETABLE MATTER.								
Cotton:	*Pounds.*	*Pounds.*	*Pounds.*	*Pounds.*	*Per ct.*	*Per ct.*	*Per ct.*	*Per ct.*
Austria-Hungary...	56,591,125	53,255,407	227,373	....	1.2	1.1	0.0	....
Belgium............	113,483,414	113,736,761	2,528,388	....	2.5	2.4	.1	....
Canada............	76,007,216	75,496,339	91,395,082	98,816,838	1.7	1.6	2.1	3.2
France............	537,493,608	569,699,520	346,349,629	445,187,759	11.8	12.0	7.9	14.4
Germany..........	1,221,943,252	1,442,161,777	147,096,823	....	26.8	30.3	3.3	....
Italy..............	250,411,639	268,678,515	563,700,142	418,457,552	5.5	5.6	12.8	13.6
Japan.............	198,389,341	176,720,027	214,403,032	251,538,465	4.3	3.7	4.9	8.2
Mexico...........	10,488,465	17,335,397	19,863,621	11,847,741	.2	.4	.5	.4
Russia, European....	37,453,772	49,538,075	41,062,654	86,724,722	.8	1.0	.9	2.8
Spain.............	158,976,935	148,669,641	232,251,950	170,122,980	3.5	3.1	5.3	5.5
United Kingdom....	1,858,449,027	1,790,750,498	1,959,874,664	1,380,444,961	40.7	37.6	44.5	44.8
Other countries....	42,607,881	54,898,581	784,825,141	220,929,107	1.0	1.2	17.7	7.1
Total..........	4,562,295,675	4,760,940,538	4,403,578,499	3,084,070,125	100.0	100.0	100.0	100.0
Fruits:								
Apples, dried—								
Germany.........	17,970,592	17,645,697	108,434	....	43.2	52.6	.3	....
Netherlands......	12,846,054	9,147,104	5,200,178	1,878,251	30.9	27.3	12.2	11.6
Other countries..	10,757,916	6,773,359	37,280,557	14,340,923	25.9	20.1	87.5	88.4
Total..........	41,574,562	33,566,160	42,589,169	16,219,174	100.0	100.0	100.0	100.0
Apples, fresh—	*Barrels.*	*Barrels.*	*Barrels.*	*Barrels.*				
Germany.........	272,382	168,792	....	....	12.7	11.2	....	....
United Kingdom.	1,318,426	827,028	1,747,396	874,587	61.3	54.9	74.3	59.6
Other countries..	559,324	510,749	604,105	591,734	26.0	33.9	25.7	40.4
Total..........	2,150,132	1,506,569	2,351,501	1,466,321	100.0	100.0	100.0	100.0
Apricots, dried—	*Pounds.*	*Pounds.*	*Pounds.*	*Pounds.*				
France............	4,214,153	3,074,146	1,911,296	2,570,491	12.0	17.7	8.0	10.6
Germany.........	7,806,944	3,841,032	289,850	....	22.3	22.1	1.2	....
Netherlands......	3,625,314	2,064,471	1,285,632	2,526,953	10.4	11.9	5.4	10.6
United Kingdom.	13,174,672	4,473,534	9,017,358	5,783,717	37.6	25.7	37.9	24.2
Other countries..	6,195,647	3,948,509	11,260,206	13,058,629	17.7	22.6	47.5	54.6
Total..........	35,016,730	17,401,692	23,764,342	23,939,790	100.0	100.0	100.0	100.0
Oranges—	*Boxes.*	*Boxes.*	*Boxes.*	*Boxes.*				
Canada..........	1,017,545	1,491,539	1,682,824	1,489,746	95.7	95.7	95.6	94.6
Other countries..	45,688	67,382	76,581	85,296	4.3	4.3	4.4	5.4
Total..........	1,063,233	1,558,921	1,759,405	1,575,042	100.0	100.0	100.0	100.0
Prunes—	*Pounds.*	*Pounds.*	*Pounds.*	*Pounds.*				
Canada..........	10,956,827	12,757,585	9,321,355	11,857,965	9.3	18.3	21.4	20.7
France...........	11,962,280	13,514,086	1,129,323	4,869,201	10.1	19.4	2.6	8.5
Germany.........	49,084,901	17,417,865	1,100	....	41.6	24.9	0.0	....
United Kingdom.	8,492,618	11,175,968	10,368,576	14,967,084	7.2	16.0	23.8	26.1
Other countries..	37,454,249	14,948,207	22,658,538	25,728,577	31.8	21.4	52.2	44.7
Total..........	117,950,875	69,813,711	43,478,892	57,422,827	100.0	100.0	100.0	100.0
Fruits, canned—	*Dollars.*	*Dollars.*	*Dollars.*	*Dollars.*				
United Kingdom.	3,892,646	3,182,051	4,924,824	5,284,344	69.5	65.4	81.2	75.0
Other countries..	1,706,727	1,681,895	1,139,941	1,765,692	30.5	34.6	18.8	25.0
Total..........	5,599,373	4,863,946	6,064,765	7,050,036	100.0	100.0	100.0	100.0
Glucose and grape sugar:	*Pounds.*	*Pounds.*	*Pounds.*	*Pounds.*				
United Kingdom...	155,597,018	162,715,262	131,751,252	134,636,730	77.7	81.5	83.1	72.2
Other countries....	44,552,228	36,815,612	26,711,256	51,749,452	22.3	18.5	16.9	27.8
Total..........	200,149,246	199,530,874	158,462,508	186,386,182	100.0	100.0	100.0	100.0

TABLE 204.—*Destination of principal farm products exported from the United States,
1913–1916*—Continued.

Article, and country to which consigned.	Quantity.				Per cent of total.			
	Year ending June 30—							
	1913	1914	1915	1916 (prel.).	1913	1914	1915	1916 (prel.).
VEGETABLE MATTER— continued.								
Grain and grain products:								
Corn—	*Bushels.*	*Bushels.*	*Bushels.*	*Bushels.*	*Per ct.*	*Per ct.*	*Per ct.*	*Per ct.*
Belgium.........	1,648,089	60,227	103,927	4,550	3.4	0.6	0.2	0.0
Canada..........	8,097,882	4,641,737	8,283,156	6,562,323	16.5	49.5	17.0	17.2
Cuba............	2,372,678	2,410,156	2,267,305	3,231,323	4.8	25.7	4.6	8.5
Denmark........	5,389,897	118	11,169,550	9,826,259	11.0	....	22.9	25.7
Germany........	6,545,521	303,303	15,785	....	13.3	3.2	0.0	....
Mexico..........	543,340	467,424	1,587,420	3,678,934	1.1	5.0	3.3	9.6
Netherlands......	7,192,420	373,770	15,875,674	5,705,625	14.7	4.0	32.5	14.9
United Kingdom.	14,982,604	540,515	2,850,252	5,627,128	30.5	5.8	5.8	14.7
Other countries..	2,292,536	583,605	6,633,222	3,580,870	4.7	6.2	13.7	9.4
Total..........	49,064,967	9,380,855	48,786,291	38,217,012	100.0	100.0	100.0	100.0
Wheat—								
Belgium.........	10,601,248	12,873,372	5,320,685	2,682,920	11.6	13.9	2.0	1.5
Canada..........	851,139	4,113,701	19,664,674	6,244,732	.9	4.5	7.6	3.6
France..........	4,931,708	5,536,731	49,878,655	21,802,818	5.4	6.0	19.2	12.6
Germany........	12,112,223	10,983,060	2,652,128	....	13.2	11.9	1.0	....
Italy...........	7,217,479	1,839,830	47,122,740	31,441,667	7.9	2.0	18.1	18.1
Mexico..........	644,377	306,376	296,581	17,624	.7	.3	.1	0.0
Netherlands......	14,832,000	19,949,519	31,551,992	21,070,335	16.2	21.6	12.2	12.2
United Kingdom.	31,548,507	27,961,348	65,911,501	53,550,376	34.4	30.3	25.4	30.9
Other countries..	8,864,293	8,829,838	37,243,577	36,463,543	9.7	9.5	14.4	21.1
Total..........	91,602,974	92,393,775	259,642,533	173,274,015	100.0	100.0	100.0	100.0
Wheat flour—	*Barrels.*	*Barrels.*	*Barrels.*	*Barrels.*				
Brazil	538,418	748,612	707,705	734,726	5.1	6.3	4.3	4.7
Canada..........	98,665	122,752	110,938	50,424	.9	1.0	.7	.3
China...........	127,814	136,374	13,273	10,762	1.1	1.2	.1	.1
Cuba...........	907,786	892,705	924,989	1,124,562	8.0	7.6	5.7	7.2
Finland.........	405,832	429,354	35,588	....	3.6	3.6	.2	....
Germany........	170,345	176,485	8,240	....	1.5	1.5	.1	....
Haiti...........	288,495	208,266	112,620	221,455	2.5	1.8	.7	1.4
Hongkong.......	1,301,306	1,141,095	626,978	356,263	11.4	9.7	3.9	2.3
Japan..........	878,623	793,269	68,542	54,475	7.7	6.7	.4	.4
Netherlands......	859,987	958,063	1,725,807	219,644	7.5	8.1	10.7	1.4
Philippine Islands...........	370,939	236,902	303,792	385,371	3.3	2.0	1.9	2.5
United Kingdom.	2,428,167	2,809,800	4,156,097	3,145,030	21.3	23.8	25.7	20.3
Other countries..	2,973,428	3,167,784	7,388,196	9,217,957	26.1	26.7	45.6	59.4
Total..........	11,394,805	11,821,461	16,182,765	15,520,669	100.0	100.0	100.0	100.0
Hops:	*Pounds.*	*Pounds.*	*Pounds.*	*Pounds.*				
Canada..........	1,035,729	1,214,028	1,071,601	626,126	5.9	5.0	6.6	2.8
United Kingdom...	15,409,093	22,219,620	13,823,889	19,703,283	87.6	91.6	85.3	87.9
Other countries....	1,146,373	829,248	1,314,953	2,080,409	6.5	3.4	8.1	9.3
Total..........	17,591,195	24,262,896	16,210,443	22,409,818	100.0	100.0	100.0	100.0
Oil cake and oil-cake meal:								
Cottonseed—								
Belgium.........	38,953,330	19,685,564	223,100	....	3.5	2.5	0.0	....
Denmark........	429,490,872	347,584,172	1,067,161,664	812,720,685	38.1	43.4	72.2	76.8
Germany........	364,266,905	240,348,664	6,819,250	....	32.3	30.0	.5	....
Netherlands......	62,479,858	22,310,420	15,469,040	4,818,400	5.5	2.8	1.0	.5
United Kingdom.	163,960,512	131,292,496	173,948,786	105,360,887	14.5	16.4	11.8	10.0
Other countries..	68,940,890	38,752,936	215,443,175	135,021,597	6.1	4.9	14.5	12.7
Total..........	1,128,092,367	799,974,252	1,479,065,015	1,057,921,569	100.0	100.0	100.0	100.0

TABLE 204.—*Destination of principal farm products exported from the United States, 1913–1916*—Continued.

Article, and country to which consigned.	Quantity. Year ending June 30—				Per cent of total. Year ending June 30—			
	1913	1914	1915	1916 (prel.).	1913	1914	1915	1916 (prel.).
VEGETABLE MATTER— continued.								
Oil cake and oil-cake meal—Continued.								
Linseed or flax-seed—	*Pounds.*	*Pounds.*	*Pounds.*	*Pounds.*	*Per ct.*	*Per ct.*	*Per ct.*	*Per ct.*
Belgium	330,952,259	332,697,680	26,931,718	....	39.5	50.2	5.1	......
France	49,700,150	20,671,619	1,375,773	13,100	5.9	3.1	.3	0.0
Netherlands	391,513,427	266,792,954	431,248,843	445,707,867	46.7	40.2	82.2	69.5
United Kingdom	53,796,998	29,084,892	22,829,656	25,532,292	6.4	4.4	4.4	4.0
Other countries	12,156,820	13,621,494	42,408,444	169,662,945	1.5	2.1	8.0	26.5
Total	838,119,654	662,868,639	524,794,434	640,916,204	100.0	100.0	100.0	100.0
Oils, vegetable:								
Cottonseed—								
Argentina	14,708,379	14,989,927	17,314,259	9,275,577	4.7	7.8	5.4	3.5
Austria-Hungary	8,475,683	4,211,198	70,394	....	2.7	2.2	0.0	......
Belgium	1,970,255	3,452,229	11,646	....	.6	1.8	0.0	......
Canada	25,227,397	25,493,039	20,578,973	35,438,474	8.0	13.2	6.5	13.3
France	17,924,337	8,268,808	8,425,210	33,500,328	5.7	4.3	2.6	12.6
Germany	13,440,312	7,682,622	62,871	....	4.3	4.0	0.0	......
Italy	39,516,645	14,015,326	15,782,234	9,424,790	12.5	7.3	5.0	3.5
Mexico	23,743,576	6,219,064	4,821,390	2,674,740	7.5	3.2	1.5	1.0
Netherlands	75,349,314	26,994,772	90,979,466	56,981,676	23.9	14.0	28.6	21.4
Norway	8,986,253	6,985,490	26,442,259	31,055,628	2.9	3.6	8.3	11.7
Turkey, European	12,556,417	4,947,994	354,910	....	4.0	2.6	.1	......
United Kingdom	31,845,444	31,071,865	84,378,878	32,112,143	10.1	16.1	26.5	12.0
Other countries	41,488,880	38,630,745	49,144,035	56,066,604	13.1	19.9	15.5	21.0
Total	315,232,892	192,963,079	318,366,525	266,529,960	100.0	100.0	100.0	100.0
Tobacco, leaf, stems, and trimmings:								
Belgium	10,235,594	11,677,604	1,131,439	....	2.4	2.6	.3	......
British Africa	8,377,246	6,600,312	4,655,691	7,820,355	2.0	1.5	1.3	1.8
British Oceania	17,516,283	13,186,680	9,042,967	[1] 9,784,653	4.2	2.9	2.6	2.2
Canada	16,309,480	17,688,562	16,156,268	18,621,186	3.9	3.9	4.6	4.2
China	6,641,628	11,445,697	3,478,641	8,908,844	1.6	2.5	1.0	2.0
France	49,131,788	54,915,178	37,710,975	82,977,894	11.7	12.2	10.8	18.7
Germany	30,054,681	32,057,051	10,018,503	....	7.2	7.1	2.9	......
Italy	44,779,059	45,190,995	24,279,246	39,276,163	10.7	10.0	7.0	8.9
Japan	5,266,034	3,696,273	3,110,555	1,158,083	1.3	.8	.9	.3
Netherlands	26,688,355	28,233,746	21,223,143	56,928,306	6.4	6.3	6.1	12.9
Spain	23,081,022	16,822,696	7,030	8,647,232	5.5	3.7	0.0	2.0
United Kingdom	150,110,570	174,779,326	189,345,349	150,639,054	35.8	38.9	54.4	34.1
Other countries	30,605,166	33,455,862	28,186,284	56,807,811	7.3	7.6	8.1	12.9
Total	418,796,906	449,749,982	348,346,091	441,569,581	100.0	100.0	100.0	100.0
FOREST PRODUCTS.								
Naval stores:								
Rosin—	*Barrels.*	*Barrels.*	*Barrels.*	*Barrels.*				
Argentina	131,286	102,028	143,407	97,306	4.7	4.2	10.4	6.2
Austria-Hungary	84,070	66,257	....	....	3.0	2.7	......	......
Belgium	141,013	111,735	80,267	....	5.0	4.6	5.8	......
Brazil	180,701	99,632	105,529	132,545	6.4	4.1	7.7	8.4
Canada	86,702	77,064	74,113	120,146	3.1	3.2	5.4	7.6
Germany	809,745	796,757	53,331	....	28.9	33.0	3.9	......
Italy	116,019	109,380	94,217	117,740	4.1	4.5	6.9	7.5
Netherlands	228,360	247,339	48,883	18,175	8.1	10.2	3.6	1.2
Russia, European	143,336	144,653	5,447	70,537	5.1	6.0	.4	4.5
United Kingdom	632,515	504,400	500,545	557,611	22.5	20.9	36.5	35.5
Other countries	252,299	158,705	266,577	457,219	9.1	6.6	19.4	29.1
Total	2,806,046	2,417,950	1,372,316	1,571,279	100.0	100.0	100.0	100.0

[1] Australia only, for the six months, Jan. 1 to June 30, 1916.

TABLE 204.—*Destination of principal farm products exported from the United States,*
1913–1916—Continued.

Article, and country to which consigned.	Quantity.				Per cent of total.			
	Year ending June 30—							
	1913	1914	1915	1916 (prel.).	1913	1914	1915	1916 (prel.).
FOREST PRODUCTS—continued.								
Naval stores—Contd. Turpentine, spirits of—	*Gallons.*	*Gallons.*	*Gallons.*	*Gallons.*	*Per ct.*	*Per ct.*	*Per ct.*	*Per ct.*
Belgium	1,872,893	1,027,355	113,672		8.9	5.4	1.2	
British Oceania	686,989	499,248	708,843	[1] 586,780	3.3	2.7	7.5	6.3
Canada	1,039,768	1,114,863	917,912	1,026,511	4.9	5.9	9.7	11.0
Germany	3,849,191	3,275,929	196,622		18.3	17.3	2.1	
Netherlands	4,242,340	4,393,902	625,736	442,682	20.2	23.2	6.6	4.8
United Kingdom	7,432,271	7,109,851	5,338,724	5,561,957	35.3	37.6	56.4	59.7
Other countries	1,916,145	1,479,556	1,562,611	1,692,038	9.1	7.9	16.5	18.2
Total	21,039,597	18,900,704	9,464,120	9,309,968	100.0	100.0	100.0	100.0
Wood: Lumber— Boards, deals, planks, joists, and scantling—	*M ft.*	*M ft.*	*M ft.*	*M ft.*				
Argentina	248,363	208,177	66,754	86,884	9.6	8.6	5.9	7.4
Belgium	78,662	62,772	8,793		3.1	2.6	.8	
Brazil	69,823	38,125	10,370	8,107	2.7	1.6	.9	.7
British Oceania	260,473	293,009	187,439	[1] 148,858	10.1	12.1	16.5	12.6
Canada	545,257	434,399	182,734	140,650	21.2	18.0	16.1	12.0
Central American States and British Honduras	56,509	81,251	45,777	49,351	2.2	3.4	4.0	4.2
China	88,749	107,115	56,238	30,746	3.4	4.4	5.0	2.6
Cuba	137,982	122,938	88,000	174,676	5.4	5.1	7.8	14.8
France	30,202	39,563	6,145	12,722	1.2	1.6	.5	1.1
Germany	83,752	69,852	7,983		3.3	2.9	.7	
Italy	44,319	53,623	20,662	40,831	1.7	2.2	1.8	3.5
Mexico	121,657	69,111	31,296	45,616	4.7	2.9	2.8	3.9
Netherlands	125,201	120,661	17,218	2,789	4.9	5.0	1.5	.2
Philippine Islands	15,747	22,485	6,623	4,833	.6	.9	.6	.4
United Kingdom	333,390	332,457	260,098	275,726	12.9	13.8	22.9	23.4
Other countries	336,147	361,901	139,082	154,976	13.0	14.9	12.2	13.2
Total	2,576,233	2,417,439	1,135,212	1,176,765	100.0	100.0	100.0	100.0
Timber, hewn and sawed—								
Canada	39,705	37,846	15,382	12,812	7.8	8.6	8.9	6.4
France	39,950	32,047	6,192	2,859	7.8	7.3	3.6	1.4
Germany	32,023	17,506	2,337		6.3	4.0	1.3	
Italy	44,726	65,314	25,763	29,946	8.7	14.8	14.8	14.9
Netherlands	60,692	57,776	6,733	9,098	11.9	13.1	3.9	4.5
United Kingdom	213,016	186,906	99,318	117,221	41.6	42.4	57.1	58.3
Other countries	81,525	43,771	18,064	29,269	15.9	9.8	10.4	14.5
Total	511,637	441,166	173,789	201,205	100.0	100.0	100.0	100.0

[1] Australia only for the six months, Jan. 1 to June 30, 1916.

TABLE 205.—*Origin of principal farm products imported into the United States, 1913–1916.*

Article, and country to which consigned.	Quantity.				Per cent of total.			
	Year ending June 30—							
	1913	1914	1915	1916 (prel.).	1913	1914	1915	1916 (prel.).
ANIMAL MATTER.								
Cattle:	*Number.*	*Number.*	*Number.*	*Number.*	*Per ct.*	*Per ct.*	*Per ct.*	*Per ct.*
Mexico	391,477	625,253	343,809	197,788	92.8	72.0	64.2	45.0
Other countries	30,172	243,115	194,358	241,397	7.2	28.0	35.8	55.0
Total	421,649	868,368	538,167	439,185	100.0	100.0	100.0	100.0
Horses:								
Canada	2,063	4,435	3,515	6,244	20.6	13.4	27.8	40.1
France	1,925	1,171	235	113	19.2	3.5	1.8	.7
Other countries	6,020	27,413	8,902	9,199	60.2	83.1	70.4	59.2
Total	10,008	33,019	12,652	15,556	100.0	100.0	100.0	100.0
Dairy products: Cheese, including substitutes—	*Pounds.*	*Pounds.*	*Pounds.*	*Pounds.*				
France	3,982,513	5,418,904	3,554,297	2,321,543	8.1	8.5	7.1	7.7
Italy	21,326,445	26,453,826	25,662,362	16,084,059	43.2	41.5	51.2	53.5
Switzerland	17,371,616	22,490,006	14,766,682	9,514,008	35.2	35.3	29.5	31.6
Other countries	6,707,370	9,421,577	6,155,179	2,168,389	13.5	14.7	12.2	7.2
Total	49,387,944	63,784,313	50,138,520	30,087,999	100.0	100.0	100.0	100.0
Fibers, animal: Silk, raw—								
China	5,510,607	5,926,745	5,097,169	7,419,616	21.2	20.7	19.6	22.4
Italy	2,811,606	1,997,428	2,610,570	2,545,845	10.8	7.0	10.0	7.7
Japan	17,425,353	20,196,212	18,217,083	22,914,898	66.9	70.6	70.0	69.3
Other countries	301,906	474,287	106,103	190,543	1.1	1.7	.4	.6
Total	26,049,472	28,594,672	26,030,925	33,070,902	100.0	100.0	100.0	100.0
Wool, class 1—								
Argentina	22,603,402	30,959,660	65,373,017	110,085,992	33.6	24.8	29.4	27.3
Australia, Commonwealth of	5,619,342	23,757,714	66,063,841	157,433,859	8.4	19.0	29.8	39.1
Belgium	266,930	4,581,419	3,002,967		.4	3.7	1.4	
New Zealand	6,306,874	4,710,748	413,679	16,697,578	9.4	3.8	.2	4.1
United Kingdom	29,368,707	45,223,714	38,897,503	30,188,711	43.7	36.2	17.5	7.4
Uruguay	2,657,620	7,972,159	14,612,703	8,941,506	4.0	6.4	6.6	2.2
Other countries	415,840	7,883,347	33,653,710	79,773,939	.5	6.1	15.1	19.9
Total	67,238,715	125,088,761	222,017,420	403,121,585	100.0	100.0	100.0	100.0
Wool, class 2—								
Canada	243,908	4,542,139	5,094,660	4,930,170	1.4	24.1	33.8	37.1
United Kingdom	13,505,151	12,301,661	8,607,638	4,135,963	80.0	65.3	57.2	31.1
Other countries	3,137,387	1,995,898	1,352,396	4,226,027	18.6	10.6	9.0	31.8
Total	16,886,446	18,839,698	15,054,694	13,292,160	100.0	100.0	100.0	100.0
Wool, class 3—								
Argentina	2,337,196	5,452,526	10,509,249	14,670,272	2.1	5.3	16.0	13.4
British East Indies	3,962,811	2,788,130	859,121	3,025,191	3.6	2.7	1.3	2.8
China	35,926,815	29,884,054	35,455,392	44,192,310	32.3	29.3	54.0	40.4
Russia (Asiatic and European)	25,645,077	22,627,514	2,273,360	2,562,854	23.1	22.2	3.5	2.3
Turkey (Asiatic)	7,394,257	5,350,091	2,486,957	42,560	6.7	5.2	3.8	0.0
United Kingdom	20,900,746	22,105,267	10,233,744	25,969,190	18.8	21.7	15.6	23.8
Other countries	15,001,192	13,795,731	3,891,929	18,806,622	13.4	13.6	5.8	17.3
Total	111,168,094	102,003,313	65,709,752	109,268,999	100.0	100.0	100.0	100.0

TABLE 205.—*Origin of principal farm products imported into the United States, 1913–1916*—Continued.

Article, and country to which consigned.	Quantity.				Per cent of total.			
	Year ending June 30—							
	1913	1914	1915	1916 (prel.).	1913	1914	1915	1916 (prel.).
ANIMAL MATTER—continued.								
Packing-house products:								
Hides and skins, other than furs—								
Calf skins—	*Pounds.*	*Pounds.*	*Pounds.*	*Pounds.*	*Per ct.*	*Per ct.*	*Per ct.*	*Per ct.*
Belgium........	4,724,643	5,157,640	978,751	....	5.0	6.3	2.1	......
Canada........	5,930,010	5,734,207	4,441,310	4,612,406	6.3	7.0	9.7	7.2
France.........	4,991,299	5,800,673	7,406,904	7,994,908	5.3	7.0	16.1	12.5
Germany......	16,916,203	16,560,316	2,613,289	....	17.9	20.1	5.7	......
Netherlands....	8,142,510	12,006,926	4,152,980	8,750,387	8.6	14.6	9.0	13.6
Russia (European)	30,247,647	19,747,462	1,471,713	....	32.0	24.0	3.2	......
Other countries	23,606,823	17,396,366	24,901,754	42,777,792	24.9	21.0	54.2	66.7
Total........	94,559,135	82,403,590	45,966,701	64,135,493	100.0	100.0	100.0	100.0
Cattle hides—								
Argentina......	67,041,938	79,787,332	113,366,344	149,537,519	25.0	28.5	33.9	34.4
Belgium........	7,106,337	7,313,906	3,416,605	....	2.7	2.6	1.0	......
Brazil..........	1,743,956	3,259,873	23,223,310	59,362,639	.7	1.2	6.9	13.7
Canada........	41,608,176	46,588,543	33,394,505	27,217,476	15.5	16.6	10.0	6.3
Colombia......	5,461,505	5,098,244	8,394,503	10,736,678	2.0	1.8	2.5	2.5
Cuba..........	2,840,141	5,528,502	15,260,111	16,068,265	1.1	2.0	4.6	3.7
East Indies....	6,929,176	4,474,768	5,705,638	19,388,264	2.6	1.6	1.7	4.5
France........	20,102,370	19,036,552	7,951,693	2,885,199	7.5	6.8	2.4	.7
Germany......	9,787,312	4,989,795	811,463	654	3.7	1.8	.2	0.0
Italy..........	2,411,973	1,967,552	3,125,932	....	.9	.7	1.3	......
Mexico........	29,500,427	33,194,289	43,384,173	42,873,741	11.0	11.9	13.0	9.9
Netherlands....	7,270,864	4,099,899	2,870,004	4,214,621	2.7	1.5	.9	1.0
Russia (European)........	22,906,231	9,043,103	693,102	....	8.5	3.2	.2	......
United Kingdom.	8,588,600	11,204,957	6,514,409	6,578,567	3.2	4.0	1.9	1.5
Uruguay........	7,244,806	13,403,443	21,809,611	43,497,431	2.7	4.8	6.5	10.0
Venezuela......	4,470,501	5,149,398	7,033,582	7,530,524	1.7	1.8	2.1	1.7
Other countries	23,028,077	25,823,332	37,386,432	44,286,193	8.5	9.2	10.9	10.1
Total........	268,042,390	279,963,488	334,341,417	434,177,771	100.0	100.0	100.0	100.0
Goatskins—								
Aden..........	3,129,594	3,595,909	2,291,012	4,151,509	3.3	4.2	3.4	4.1
Africa..........	2,625,746	2,817,948	1,440,984	6,901,232	2.7	3.3	2.2	6.9
Argentina......	4,276,365	3,470,013	3,738,020	6,337,138	4.4	4.1	5.6	6.3
Brazil..........	3,357,781	4,191,124	4,260,495	6,919,497	3.5	4.9	6.4	6.9
China..........	9,827,646	7,304,761	7,897,387	15,084,600	10.2	8.6	11.9	15.0
East Indies....	41,594,938	35,831,857	28,651,497	40,877,117	43.2	42.3	43.1	40.6
France.........	2,406,371	2,171,224	1,891,445	971,848	2.5	2.6	2.8	1.0
Mexico........	4,815,304	4,010,150	3,507,940	3,833,616	5.0	4.7	5.3	3.8
Russia (European)........	7,183,542	5,131,075	1,556,154	....	7.5	6.1	2.3	......
United Kingdom.	5,436,922	5,281,468	4,089,212	5,936,107	5.6	6.2	6.1	5.9
Other countries	11,596,096	10,953,899	7,223,017	9,644,357	12.1	13.0	10.9	9.5
Total........	96,250,305	84,759,428	66,547,163	100,657,021	100.0	100.0	100.0	100.0
Sheepskins—								
Argentina......	6,848,065	3,874,944	8,689,826	13,308,025	9.5	5.5	14.8	13.1
Brazil..........	993,321	1,582,333	1,384,888	3,257,445	1.4	2.3	2.4	3.2
British Oceania	8,179,576	9,848,498	11,007,719	8,838,626	11.4	14.1	18.7	8.7
Canada........	1,860,948	3,678,117	4,102,461	3,105,651	2.6	5.2	7.0	3.2
France.........	2,999,829	2,221,769	823,209	2,089,161	4.2	3.2	1.4	2.1
Russia (European)........	8,484,377	9,158,287	826,898	22,840	11.8	13.1	1.4	0.0
United Kingdom.	28,885,579	26,384,892	22,616,881	33,287,127	40.2	37.7	38.5	32.8
Other countries	13,533,024	13,327,985	9,267,656	37,550,406	18.9	18.9	15.8	36.9
Total........	71,784,719	70,076,825	58,719,538	101,459,281	100.0	100.0	100.0	100.0

TABLE 205.—*Origin of principal farm products imported into the United States, 1913–1916*—Continued.

Article, and country to which consigned.	Quantity.				Per cent of total.			
	Year ending June 30—							
	1913	1914	1915	1916 (prel.).	1913	1914	1915	1916 (prel.).
VEGETABLE MATTER.								
Cocoa, crude:	*Pounds.*	*Pounds.*	*Pounds.*	*Pounds.*	*Per ct.*	*Per ct.*	*Per ct.*	*Per ct.*
Brazil	14,354,460	25,870,186	19,708,616	45,657,401	10.3	14.7	10.2	18.8
British West Indies	29,588,055	44,062,426	40,728,851	39,933,405	21.1	25.0	21.2	16.4
Dominican Republic	27,241,763	26,782,966	46,620,464	48,990,707	19.5	15.2	24.2	20.1
Ecuador	15,229,159	26,319,735	33,418,752	31,878,350	10.9	14.9	17.4	13.1
Portugal	23,040,617	17,738,638	3,516,655	7,531,924	16.5	10.1	1.8	3.1
United Kingdom	11,660,464	12,903,640	21,062,767	13,408,058	8.3	7.3	11.0	5.5
Other countries	18,924,654	22,590,055	27,250,529	55,832,094	13.4	12.8	14.2	23.0
Total	140,039,172	176,267,646	192,306,634	243,231,939	100.0	100.0	100.0	100.0
Coffee:								
Brazil	639,262,011	743,113,500	773,400,315	849,405,925	74.1	74.2	69.1	70.7
Central American States and British Honduras	32,172,524	40,202,480	75,350,258	95,573,010	3.7	4.0	6.7	8.0
Colombia	89,684,514	91,830,513	111,077,449	109,363,456	10.4	9.2	9.9	9.1
East Indies	7,559,765	8,673,941	11,354,631	6,274,413	.9	.7	1.0	.5
Mexico	26,121,439	49,385,504	52,706,120	49,832,801	3.0	4.9	4.7	4.1
Netherlands	1,956,676	5,811,934	1,583,672	50,896	.2	.6	.1	0.0
Venezuela	49,671,060	49,953,478	72,463,140	73,405,301	5.8	5.0	6.5	6.1
West Indies and Bermuda	4,110,032	4,711,269	16,230,552	10,072,668	.5	.5	1.4	.8
Other countries	12,592,736	7,845,698	4,524,387	7,126,015	1.4	.9	.6	.7
Total	863,130,757	1,001,528,317	1,118,690,524	1,201,104,485	100.0	100.0	100.0	100.0
Fibers, vegetable: Cotton—								
Egypt	94,333,483	63,668,055	117,596,646	171,528,669	77.4	51.6	63.5	73.7
Peru	4,871,835	6,455,946	5,262,394	4,934,448	4.0	5.2	2.8	2.1
United Kingdom	8,354,253	2,557,041	3,417,851	14,227,785	6.9	2.1	1.8	6.1
Other countries	14,292,445	50,665,857	58,927,688	42,110,160	11.7	41.1	31.9	18.1
Total	121,852,016	123,346,899	185,204,579	232,801,062	100.0	100.0	100.0	100.0
Flax—	*Long tons.*	*Long tons.*	*Long tons.*	*Long tons.*				
Belgium	1,919	1,266	122	20	15.4	12.8	2.6	.3
Russia, European	4,450	2,735	336	2,521	35.8	27.7	7.2	36.3
United Kingdom	4,464	5,076	3,767	3,209	35.9	51.4	80.3	46.2
Other countries	1,588	808	469	1,189	12.9	8.1	9.9	17.2
Total	12,421	9,885	4,694	6,939	100.0	100.0	100.0	100.0
Jute and jute butts—								
British East Indies	120,511	100,755	80,444	99,780	96.1	95.0	96.8	92.1
Other countries	4,878	5,278	2,696	8,542	3.9	5.0	3.2	7.9
Total	125,389	106,033	83,140	108,322	100.0	100.0	100.0	100.0
Manila fiber—								
Philippine Islands	69,629	49,285	50,587	78,809	94.3	99.2	99.0	99.9
Other countries	4,194	403	494	83	5.7	.8	1.0	.1
Total	73,823	49,688	51,081	78,892	100.0	100.0	100.0	100.0
Sisal grass—								
Mexico	136,559	195,086	175,884	220,994	88.8	90.5	94.7	96.7
Other countries	17,310	20,461	9,880	7,616	11.2	9.5	5.3	3.3
Total	153,869	215,547	185,764	228,610	100.0	100.0	100.0	100.0

TABLE 205.—*Origin of principal farm products imported into the United States, 1913-1916*—Continued.

Article, and country to which consigned.	Quantity.				Per cent of total.			
	Year ending June 30—							
	1913	1914	1915	1916 (prel.).	1913	1914	1915	1916 (prel.).
VEGETABLE MATTER— continued.								
Fruits:								
Bananas—	*Bunches.*	*Bunches.*	*Bunches.*	*Bunches.*	*Per ct.*	*Per ct.*	*Per ct.*	*Per ct.*
British West Indies...........	11,164,894	15,677,191	11,957,935	4,691,518	26.4	32.2	29.1	12.8
Central American States and British Honduras..	25,108,590	25,432,760	22,470,600	24,694,566	59.3	52.1	54.7	67.2
Cuba...........	2,213,733	2,354,395	2,708,624	2,859,021	5.2	4.8	6.6	7.8
South America...	2,869,247	2,271,866	1,567,461	2,710,047	6.8	4.7	3.8	7.4
Other countries..	1,000,645	2,947,380	2,386,965	1,799,552	2.3	6.2	5.8	4.8
Total..........	42,357,109	48,683,592	41,091,585	36,754,704	100.0	100.0	100.0	100.0
Nuts:								
Walnuts—	*Pounds.*	*Pounds.*	*Pounds.*	*Pounds.*				
Austria-Hungary	4,409	514,455	....	....	.0	1.4		
France...........	20,379,294	19,020,143	18,716,938	22,443,477	76.4	51.1	56.0	60.9
Italy...........	3,315,483	6,275,717	6,440,934	8,489,385	12.4	16.9	19.3	23.0
Turkey (Asiatic).	424,418	1,712,209	16,135	....	1.6	4.6	.0	....
Other countries..	2,538,837	9,673,204	8,271,831	5,926,072	9.6	26.0	24.7	16.1
Total..........	26,662,441	37,195,728	33,445,838	36,858,934	100.0	100.0	100.0	100.0
Oil, vegetable:								
Olive, salad—	*Gallons.*	*Gallons.*	*Gallons.*	*Gallons.*				
France...........	932,536	949,858	802,092	895,369	17.9	15.3	12.0	12.4
Italy.............	3,584,945	4,319,567	4,864,388	4,696,812	68.7	69.5	72.5	65.0
Other countries..	703,520	948,135	1,044,487	1,632,250	13.4	15.2	15.5	22.6
Total..........	5,221,001	6,217,560	6,710,967	7,224,431	100.0	100.0	100.0	100.0
Soya-bean oil—	*Pounds.*	*Pounds.*	*Pounds.*	*Pounds.*				
Japan.............	7,979,144	6,425,306	5,471,911	70,384,049	64.7	39.3	28.5	71.7
United Kingdom.	2,523,321	1,453,932	906,134	187,722	20.4	8.9	4.7	.2
Other countries..	1,837,720	8,481,214	12,828,476	27,547,924	14.9	51.8	66.8	28.1
Total..........	12,340,185	16,360,452	19,206,521	98,119,695	100.0	100.0	100.0	100.0
Opium:								
Turkey (Asiatic and European)...	420,406	383,489	440,529	27,883	82.7	83.2	91.0	19.0
United Kingdom...	61,782	39,372	38,258	62,665	12.2	8.6	7.9	42.7
Other countries....	26,245	32,339	5,240	56,110	5.1	8.2	1.1	38.3
Total..........	508,433	455,200	484,027	146,658	100.0	100.0	100.0	100.0
Seeds:								
Flaxseed or linseed—	*Bushels.*	*Bushels,*	*Bushels.*	*Bushels.*				
Argentina.........	429,254	....	3,927,542	11,468,039	8.1	....	36.8	78.1
Belgium.........	157	3	....	....	.0	.0	....	....
British India.....	128,981	50	39,990	....	2.4	.0	.4	....
Canada...........	4,732,316	8,647,168	6,629,860	3,094,735	89.4	99.9	62.2	21.1
United Kingdom.	2,453	6,010	....	....	.0	.1	....	....
Other countries..	1,135	4	68,823	116,459	.1	.0	.6	.8
Total..........	5,294,296	8,653,235	10,666,215	14,679,233	100.0	100.0	100.0	100.0
Grass seed—								
Clover—	*Pounds.*	*Pounds.*	*Pounds.*	*Pounds.*				
Canada.........	2,887,143	5,741,516	1,525,080	1,620,609	13.6	19.1	6.3	3.9
France.........	6,857,096	15,402,710	18,879,326	26,964,867	32.3	51.2	78.2	64.4
Germany......	5,655,553	4,200,141	336,575	....	26.6	14.0	1.4	....
Italy.........	2,816,795	44,000	343,546	10,300,153	13.3	.1	1.4	24.6
Other countries	3,007,965	4,719,282	3,072,184	2,954,132	14.2	15.6	12.7	7.1
Total........	21,224,557	30,107,649	24,156,711	41,839,761	100.0	100.0	100.0	100.0

TABLE 205.—*Origin of principal farm products imported into the United States, 1913–1916*—Continued.

Article, and country to which consigned.	Quantity. Year ending June 30—				Per cent of total.			
	1913	1914	1915	1916 (prel.).	1913	1914	1915	1916 (prel.).
VEGETABLE MATTER—continued.								
Sugar, raw cane:	*Pounds.*	*Pounds.*	*Pounds.*	*Pounds.*	*Perct.*	*Perct.*	*Per ct.*	*Perct.*
Cuba	4,311,744,043	4,926,606,243	4,784,888,157	5,150,852,007	94.7	97.3	88.3	91.5
Dutch East Indies	12,759,756	....	22,235	32,941	.3	......	.0	0.0
Philippine Islands	203,160,972	116,749,211	326,842,296	217,190,825	4.5	2.3	6.0	3.9
Santo Domingo	2,670,630	4,316,282	86,188,211	107,503,110	.1	.1	1.6	1.9
South America	20,047,828	9,386,732	120,869,986	118,709,613	.4	.2	2.2	2.1
Other countries	3,666,643	4,506,153	99,819,597	36,984,270	.0	.1	1.9	.6
Total	4,554,049,872	5,061,564,621	5,418,630,482	5,631,272,766	100.0	100.0	100.0	100.0
Tea:								
Canada	3,024,508	3,112,383	3,446,615	2,600,705	3.2	3.4	3.6	2.4
China	23,728,418	20,139,342	23,100,548	20,422,700	25.0	22.1	23.8	18.6
East Indies	10,411,288	10,551,735	12,645,303	14,855,825	11.0	11.6	13.0	13.5
Japan	44,381,278	41,913,273	43,869,012	52,359,526	46.8	46.0	45.2	47.7
United Kingdom	12,238,114	14,077,601	12,869,968	19,066,241	12.9	15.4	13.3	17.3
Other countries	1,029,194	1,336,481	1,056,496	560,938	1.1	1.5	1.1	.5
Total	94,812,800	91,130,815	96,987,942	109,865,935	100.0	100.0	100.0	100.0
Tobacco, leaf: Wrapper—								
Netherlands	6,193,042	5,846,504	7,061,943	4,963,761	96.8	96.0	97.5	97.9
Other countries	205,740	246,283	179,235	106,547	3.2	4.0	2.5	2.1
Total	6,398,782	6,092,787	7,241,178	5,070,308	100.0	100.0	100.0	100.0
Other leaf—								
Cuba	27,553,759	26,617,545	21,987,848	23,920,259	45.1	49.3	57.1	55.7
Germany	1,659,390	456,445	91,578	....	2.7	.8	.2	......
Turkey (Asiatic)	18,955,295	15,616,543	6,714,654	....	31.0	28.9	17.4	......
Turkey (European)	10,816,048	8,502,742	5,950,915	19,890	17.7	15.7	15.4	.0
Other countries	2,071,471	2,821,450	3,778,555	19,002,878	3.5	5.3	9.9	44.3
Total	61,055,963	54,014,725	38,523,550	42,943,027	100.0	100.0	100.0	100.0
FOREST PRODUCTS.								
India rubber, crude:								
Belgium	5,917,440	11,005,246	1,902,370	....	5.2	8.3	1.1	......
Brazil	43,518,861	40,641,305	48,753,670	54,968,227	38.4	30.8	28.3	20.5
Central American States and British Honduras	989,772	565,487	790,368	1,313,454	.9	.4	.5	.5
East Indies	12,255,500	16,597,105	27,898,683	125,532,067	10.8	12.6	16.2	46.9
France	2,968,232	2,629,287	685,699	509,675	2.6	2.0	.4	.2
Germany	7,790,742	7,079,260	739,105	....	6.9	5.4	.4	......
Mexico	2,033,791	641,029	1,827,912	3,261,507	1.8	.5	1.1	1.2
Portugal	873,249	556,560	4,130,624	2,773,656	.8	.4	2.4	1.0
United Kingdom	34,164,908	48,279,674	75,168,236	72,459,408	30.1	36.6	43.7	27.1
Other countries	2,871,864	4,000,780	10,171,761	6,957,563	2.5	3.0	5.9	2.6
Total	113,384,359	131,995,742	172,068,428	267,775,557	100.0	100.0	100.0	100.0
Wood: Cabinet woods, mahogany—	*M feet.*	*M feet.*	*M feet.*	*M feet.*				
British Africa	7,655	12,888	6,941	6,888	11.5	18.3	16.4	17.3
Central American States and British Honduras	13,526	23,356	17,955	10,450	20.4	33.1	42.4	26.2
Mexico	10,866	10,381	8,119	8,453	16.4	14.7	19.2	21.2
United Kingdom	20,866	18,289	5,918	7,248	31.5	26.0	14.0	18.2
Other countries	13,405	5,556	3,392	6,816	20.2	7.9	8.0	17.1
Total	66,318	70,470	42,325	39,855	100.0	100.0	100.0	100.0

TABLE 205.—*Origin of principal farm products imported into the United States, 1913–1916*—Continued.

Article, and country to which consigned.	Quantity.				Per cent of total.			
	Year ending June 30—							
	1913	1914	1915	1916 (prel.).	1913	1914	1915	1916 (prel.),
FOREST PRODUCTS—continued.								
Wood—Continued.								
Boards, planks, deals, and other sawed lumber—	*M feet.*	*M feet.*	*M feet.*	*M feet.*	*Per ct.*	*Per ct.*	*Per ct.*	*Per ct.*
Canada...........	1,021,810	892,833	908,663	1,180,018	93.7	96.1	96.7	96.9
Other countries..	68,818	36,040	30,659	38,050	6.3	3.9	3.3	3.1
Total...........	1,090,628	928,873	939,322	1,218,068	100.0	100.0	100.0	100.0
Wood pulp:	*Pounds.*	*Pounds.*	*Pounds.*	*Pounds.*				
Canada.............	463,877,981	524,251,441	660,656,640	790,997,760	41.2	46.0	50.2	69.6
Germany............	151,481,033	149,171,214	83,119,680	237,440	13.4	13.1	6.3	.0
Norway.............	189,951,459	181,255,024	200,934,720	115,978,240	16.9	15.9	15.3	10.2
Sweden.............	283,916,347	265,457,874	350,183,680	225,955,520	25.2	23.3	26.6	19.9
Other countries....	37,298,387	18,591,642	22,050,560	2,611,840	3.3	1.7	1.6	.3
Total...........	1,126,525,207	1,138,727,195	1,316,945,280	1,135,780,800	100.0	100.0	100.0	100.0

INDEX.

Page.